abled. Plaintiffs primarily used the Rehabilitation Act of 1973 (29 U.S.C.A. § 701 et seq.), the earliest law of this type. But the Rehabilitation Act has a limited scope: it applies only to federally funded workplaces and institutions, and says nothing about those that do not receive government money.

With passage of the ADA in 1990, Congress gave broad protection to people with AIDS who work in the private sector. In general, the ADA is designed to increase access for disabled persons, and it also forbids discrimination in hiring or promotion in companies with fifteen or more employees. Specifically, employers may not discriminate if the person in question is otherwise qualified for the job. Moreover, they cannot use tests to screen out disabled persons, and they must provide reasonable accommodation for disabled workers. The ADA, which took effect in 1992, has quickly emerged as the primary means for bringing AIDS-related discrimination lawsuits.

AIDS and Health Care Closely related to work is the issue of health care. In some cases, the two overlap: health insurance, Social Security, and disability benefits for AIDS victims were often hard to obtain during the 1980s. Insurance was particularly difficult because employers feared rising costs and insurance companies did not want to pay claims. To avoid the costs of AIDS, insurance companies used two traditional industry techniques: they attempted to exclude AIDS coverage from general policies, and they placed caps (limits on benefits payments) on AIDS-related coverage.

In January 1995, the settlement in a lawsuit brought by a Philadelphia construction worker with AIDS illustrated that the ADA can be used to fight caps on coverage. In 1992, the joint union-management fund for the Laborers' District Council placed a $10,000 limit on AIDS benefits, in stark contrast to the $100,000 allowed for other catastrophic illnesses. At that time, the fund said the cap on AIDS benefits was designed to curb all health costs. In 1993, the EEOC ruled that it violated the ADA, and, backed by the AIDS Law Project of Philadelphia, the worker sued. Rather than fight an expensive lawsuit, the insurance fund settled.

AIDS and Education Issues in the field of education include the rights of HIV-positive students to attend class and of HIV-positive teachers to teach, the confidentiality of HIV records, and how best to teach young people about AIDS. A few areas have been settled in court: for instance, the right of students to attend classes was of greater concern in the early years of the epidemic, and no longer remains in dispute.

Certain students with AIDS may assert their right to public education under the Education for All Handicapped Children Act of 1975 (EAHCA), but the law is only relevant in cases involving special education programs. More commonly, students' rights are protected by the Rehabilitation Act.

Schools play a major role in the effort to educate the public on AIDS. Several states have mandated AIDS prevention instruction in their schools. But the subject is controversial: it evokes personal, political, and moral reactions to sexuality. During the 1980s, those who often criticized liberal approaches to sex education argued that AIDS materials should not be explicit, encourage sexuality, promote the use of contraceptives, or favorably portray gays and lesbians.

Civil Litigation TORT law has seen an explosion of AIDS-related suits. This area of law is used to discourage individuals from subjecting others to unreasonable risks, and to compensate those who have been injured by unreasonably risky behavior. The greatest number of AIDS-related LIABILITY lawsuits has involved the receipt of HIV-infected blood and blood products. A second group has concerned the sexual transmission of HIV. A third group involves AIDS-related psychic distress. In these cases, plaintiffs have successfully sued and recovered damages for their fear of having contracted HIV.

CROSS-REFERENCES
Disabled Persons; Discrimination; Food and Drug Administration; Gay and Lesbian Rights; Health Care; Patients' Rights; Physicians and Surgeons; Privacy.

ALLRED, GLORIA Gloria Allred, born July 3, 1941, in Philadelphia, is a flamboyant, widely recognized lawyer, feminist, activist, and radio talk show host. Though her critics dismiss her as a publicity monger and a dilettante, Allred has received praise from others who believe that she is a master at using the power of the news media to draw attention to the day-to-day struggles of ordinary people.

Born Gloria Rachel Bloom, Allred grew up in Philadelphia with her parents, Morris Bloom, a door-to-door salesman, and Stella Davidson Bloom, a homemaker. Her conventional middle-class childhood gave no hint of the outspoken activist to come. Allred graduated with honors from the University of Pennsylvania in 1963 with a bachelor's degree in English. She moved to New York to pursue a master's degree in teaching at New York University. Wh[ile she was] interested in the CIVIL RIGHT[S movement, which] was beginning to gain mom[entum, she received] her master's degree in 19[...]

BIOGRAPHY

Gloria Allred

Cross-references at end of article

Timeline for subject of biography, including general historical events and life events

Biography of contributor to American law

GLORIA ALLRED 1941–

1973 U.S. Supreme Court upheld Roe v. Wade, legalizing abortion
1966 Received master's in teaching from NYU; moved to Los Angeles to teach in Watts
1969 Watts riots in Los Angeles
Graduated from Univ. Pennsylvania, with honors
1941 Born Philadelphia, Pa.
1955–68 Martin Luther King active in civil rights movement
1974 Received J.D. from UCLA; Formed law partnership with Nathan Goldberg and Michael Maroko
1990 Sued L.A. County to stop shackling of pregnant inmates during labor and delivery
Lawsuit v. Rochest. 1990
1988 Sued Frank Club, L.A. for sex discrimination
Wrote "Protection of Prevention" for L.A. Times advocating legalization of prostitution

1925   1950   1975   2000

Philadelphia to teach at a high school with a predominantly black enrollment.

Allred says her interest in the struggle for equal rights arose from personal experiences. While she was in college, she married, gave birth to a daughter, and divorced. Unable to collect CHILD SUPPORT from her former husband, she was forced to return to her parents' home. She also recalls being paid less than a man for what she considered equal work. The reason given was that the man had a family to support, but at the time, Allred was the single mother of an infant.

After moving to California, Allred taught in the turbulent Watts section of Los Angeles and became the first full-time female staff member in United Teachers of Los Angeles, the union representing Los Angeles teachers. The experience stirred her interest in CIVIL RIGHTS and collective bargaining and prompted her to go to law school. She received her law degree, with honors, from Loyola Marymount University, Los Angeles, Law School in 1974. Soon after, she entered a law firm partnership with her classmates Nathan Goldberg and Michael Maroko.

Allred is probably the most flamboyant and well known member of her firm. She has achieved notoriety and name recognition through staged press conferences and demonstrations publicizing and dramatizing the cause she is championing at the time. She also accepts controversial cases that naturally attract media attention. During her years in practice, she has successfully sued Los Angeles County to stop the practice of shackling and chaining pregnant inmates during labor and delivery; put a halt on the city of El Segundo's quizzing job applicants about their sexual histories (*Thorne v. City of El Segundo*, 802 F.2d 1131 [9th Cir. 1986]); represented a client who was turned down for a job as a police officer after a six-hour lie detector exam that included questions about her sex life; and sued a dry cleaning establishment for discrimination because it charged more to launder women's shirts than men's.

Allred relishes confrontation, and her showy tactics have earned her both praise and criticism.

"THERE ARE ENOUGH HIGH HURDLES TO CLIMB, AS ONE TRAVELS THROUGH LIFE, WITHOUT HAVING TO SCALE ARTIFICIAL BARRIERS CREATED BY LAW OR SILLY REGULATIONS."

Defending what many have called self-promoting publicity stunts, Allred says she tries to use the few moments she is in the spotlight to make her point as forcefully as possible. Her detractors say that she wastes her time and energy on trivial issues that do not advance any worthwhile cause and deflect attention away from serious issues. Yet, she points out, she is often stopped on the street by people who recognize her and want to thank her for taking on the small fights that no one else wants.

Some critics say she is all show and no substance. But Allred has many supporters as well. Among them is Justice Joan Dempsey Klein, of the California Court of Appeal, who credits Allred with moving women's issues forward. Klein also points out that Allred saves her dramatics for outside the courtroom and always observes proper decorum when before the bench. According to Klein, Allred is always well-prepared and, for that reason, is quite successful.

Dressed in her trademark reds and electric blues, her striking black hair set off by deep red lipstick, Allred is a potent combination of scholarship and theatrics. Her keen intelligence and shrewd understanding of the power of the media have made her a contemporary success story in the world of law and politics.

ARBITER [*Latin, One who attends something to view it as a spectator or witness.*] Any person who is given an absolute power to judge and rule on a matter in a dispute.

Internal cross references

Quotation from subject of biography

Full cite for case

Definition enclosed in book logos with Latin translation provided

WEST'S
ENCYCLOPEDIA
of
AMERICAN
LAW

WEST'S ENCYCLOPEDIA *of* AMERICAN LAW

Volume 9

WEST GROUP

This encyclopedia is the result of efforts by numerous individuals and entities from the Twin Cities and around the United States. West Group wishes to thank all who made this publication, its quality and content, a priority in their lives.

In addition to the individuals who worked on *West's Encyclopedia of American Law*, West Group recognizes Harold W. Chase (1922–1982) for his contributions to *The Guide to American Law: Everyone's Legal Encyclopedia*.

COPYRIGHT ©1998 By
   WEST GROUP
   610 Opperman Drive
   P.O. Box 64526
   St. Paul, MN 55164-0526
All rights reserved
Printed in the United States of America
05 04 03 02 01 00 99 98   8 7 6 5 4 3 2 1 0
Library of Congress Cataloging in
   Publication Data
ISBN: 0-314-20166-1 (Hard)

West's encyclopedia of American law.
      p.   cm.
      Includes bibliographical references and
      indexes.
      ISBN 0-314-20166-1 (hard   :
      alk. paper)
      1. Law—United States—Encyclopedias.
      2. Law—United States—Popular works.
      I. West Publishing Company.
KF154.W47   1997
348.73'03—dc20
[347.30803]   96-34350
                            CIP

PRODUCTION CREDITS
Cover, interior design, and page layout:
   David J. Farr, ImageSmythe
Composition: Carlisle Communications
Proofreading: Wiest International
Photo research: Elsa Peterson Ltd.
Art research: Nanette E. Bertaut
Editorial research: Pat Lewis
Artwork: Patricia Isaacs, Parrot Graphics
Indexing: Schroeder Indexing Services

WEST'S COMMITMENT TO THE ENVIRONMENT

In 1906, West Publishing Company began recycling materials left over from the production of books. This began a tradition of efficient and responsible use of resources. Today, 100 percent of our legal bound volumes are printed on acid-free, recycled paper consisting of 50 percent new paper pulp and 50 percent paper that has undergone a de-inking process. We also use vegetable-based inks to print all of our books. West recycles nearly 27,700,000 pounds of scrap paper annually—the equivalent of 229,300 trees. Since the 1960s, West has devised ways to capture and recycle waste inks, solvents, oils, and vapors created in the printing process. We also recycle plastics of all kinds, wood, glass, corrugated cardboard, and batteries, and have eliminated the use of polystyrene book packaging. We at West are proud of the longevity and the scope of our commitment to the environment.

West pocket parts and advance sheets are printed on recyclable paper and can be collected and recycled with newspapers. Staples do not have to be removed. Bound volumes can be recycled after removing the cover.

Production, printing, and binding by West Group.

PREFACE

The legal system of the United States is admired around the world for the freedoms it allows the individual and the fairness with which it attempts to treat all persons. On the surface, it may seem simple. Yet, those who have delved into it know that this system of federal and state constitutions, statutes, regulations, and common-law decisions is elaborate and complex. It derives from the English common law, but includes principles older than England, and from other lands. Many concepts are still phrased in Latin. The U.S. legal system, like many others, has a language all its own. Too often it is an unfamiliar language.

In 1983, West published *The Guide to American Law: Everyone's Legal Encyclopedia*, in response to a dearth of reference sources weaving the language of the law into the language of everyday life. *West's Encyclopedia of American Law (WEAL)*, developed with generous feedback from users of *The Guide*, replaces that set as an improved and updated legal encyclopedia. *WEAL* is a reference source devoted to the terms and concepts of U.S. law. It also covers a wide variety of persons, entities, and events that have shaped the U.S. legal system. *WEAL* contains thousands of entries, and a number of unique features and visual aids. It is the most complete reference source of its kind.

Main Features of This Set

Entries This encyclopedia contains over 4,000 entries devoted to terms, concepts, events, movements, cases, and persons significant to U.S. law. Entries on legal terms contain a definition of the term, followed by explanatory text if necessary. Entries are arranged alphabetically in standard encyclopedia format for ease of use. A wide variety of additional features, listed later in this preface, provide interesting background and supplemental information.

Definitions Every entry on a legal term is followed by a definition, which begins and ends with the symbol of an open book (📖). The appendix volume includes a glossary containing all the definitions from the *WEAL*.

Cross-References To facilitate research, *WEAL* provides two types of cross-references, within and following entries. Within the entries, terms are set in small capital letters—for example, LIEN—to indicate that they have their own entry in the encyclopedia. At the end of the entries, related entries the reader may wish to explore are listed alphabetically by title.

In Focus Pieces In Focus pieces accompany related entries and provide additional facts, details, and arguments on particularly interesting, important, or controversial issues raised by those entries. The subjects covered include hotly contested issues, such as abortion, capital punishment, and gay rights; detailed processes, such as the Food and Drug Administration's approval process for new drugs; and important historical or social issues, such as debates over the formation of the U.S. Constitution. In Focus pieces are marked by the symbol that appears in the margin.

Sidebars Sidebars provide brief highlights of some interesting facet of accompanying entries. They complement regular entries and In Focus pieces by adding informative details. Sidebar topics include the Million Man March, in Washington, D.C., and the branches of the

IN FOCUS

U.S. armed services. Sidebars appear at the top of a text page and are set in a blue box.

Biographies WEAL profiles a wide variety of interesting and influential people—including lawyers, judges, government and civic leaders, and historical and modern figures—who have played a part in creating or shaping U.S. law. Each biography includes a time line, which shows important moments in the subject's life as well as important historical events of the period. Biographies appear alphabetically by the subject's last name.

Additional Features of This Set

Milestones in the Law A special section, Milestones in the Law, appearing at the end of selected volumes, allows readers to take a close look at landmark cases in U.S. law. Readers can explore the reasoning of the judges and the arguments of the attorneys that produced major decisions on important legal and social issues. Included in the Milestones section are the opinions of the lower courts; the briefs presented by the parties to the U.S. Supreme Court; and the decision of the Supreme Court, including the majority opinion and all concurring and dissenting opinions for each case.

Enhancements Throughout WEAL, readers will find a broad array of photographs, charts, graphs, manuscripts, legal forms, and other visual aids enhancing the ideas presented in the text.

Tables and Indexes WEAL features several detailed tables and indexes at the back of each volume, as well as a cumulative index contained in a separate volume.

Appendixes An appendix volume included with WEAL contains hundreds of pages of documents, laws, manuscripts, and forms fundamental to and characteristic of U.S. law.

Citations Wherever possible, WEAL entries include citations for cases and statutes mentioned in the text. These allow readers wishing to do additional research to find the opinions and statutes cited. Two sample citations, with explanations of common citation terms, can be seen below and opposite.

Bibliography A bibliography is included at the end of each book and in the index volume.

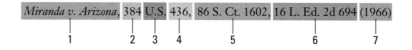

1. *Case title.* The title of the case is set in italics and indicates the names of the parties. The suit in this sample citation was between Ernesto A. Miranda and the state of Arizona.
2. *Reporter volume number.* The number preceding the reporter name indicates the reporter volume containing the case. (The volume number appears on the spine of the reporter, along with the reporter name.)
3. *Reporter name.* The reporter name is abbreviated. The suit in the sample citation is from the reporter, or series of books, called *U.S. Reports,* which contains cases from the U.S. Supreme Court. (Numerous reporters publish cases from the federal and state courts.)
4. *Reporter page.* The number following the reporter name indicates the reporter page on which the case begins.
5. *Additional reporter citation.* Many cases may be found in more than one reporter. The suit in the sample citation also appears in volume 86 of the *Supreme Court Reporter,* beginning on page 1602.
6. *Additional reporter citation.* The suit in the sample citation is also reported in volume 16 of the *Lawyer's Edition,* second series, beginning on page 694.
7. *Year of decision.* The year the court issued its decision in the case appears in parentheses at the end of the cite.

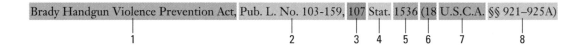

Brady Handgun Violence Prevention Act, Pub. L. No. 103-159, 107 Stat. 1536 (18 U.S.C.A. §§ 921–925A)

1.   2   3 4 5 6 7   8

1. *Statute title.*
2. *Public law number.* In the sample citation, the number 103 indicates that this law was passed by the 103d Congress, and the number 159 indicates that it was the 159th law passed by that Congress.
3. *Reporter volume number.* The number preceding the reporter name indicates the reporter volume containing the statute.
4. *Reporter name.* The reporter name is abbreviated. The statute in the sample citation is from *Statutes at Large.*
5. *Reporter page.* The number following the reporter name indicates the reporter page on which the statute begins.

6. *Title number.* Federal laws are divided into major sections with specific titles. The number preceding a reference to the *U.S. Code Annotated* is the title number. Title 18 of the U.S. Code is Crimes and Criminal Procedure.
7. *Additional reporter.* The statute in the sample citation may also be found in the *U.S. Code Annotated.*
8. *Section numbers.* The section numbers following a reference to the *U.S. Code Annotated* indicate where the statute appears in that reporter.

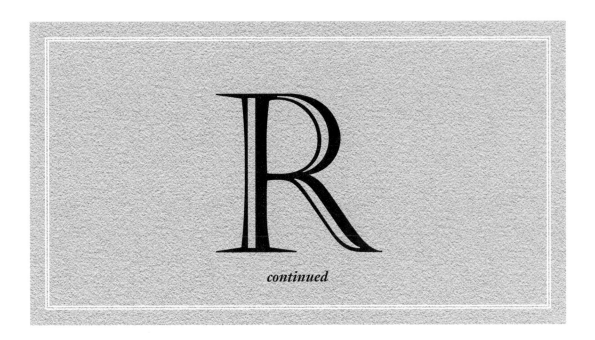

continued

REPUBLICAN PARTY The Republican party was founded in 1854 by a group of renegade Democrats, Whigs, and political independents who opposed the expansion of SLAVERY into new U.S. territories and states. What began as a single-issue, independent party became a major political force in the United States. Six years after the new party was formed, Republican nominee ABRAHAM LINCOLN won the U.S. presidential election. The Republican party and its counterpart, the DEMOCRATIC PARTY, became the mainstays of the nation's de facto two-party system.

Lincoln's victory in 1860 signaled the demise of the Whig party and the ascendance of Republican politics. From 1860 to 1931, the Republicans dominated U.S. presidential ELECTIONS. Only two Democrats were elected to the White House during the seventy-year period of Republican preeminence.

The early Republican party was shaped by political conscience and regionalism. Throughout the early and mid-nineteenth century, states in the North and South were bitterly divided over the issues of slavery and state sovereignty. In 1854 the enactment of the KANSAS-NEBRASKA ACT inflamed political passions. Under the act residents of the new territories of Kansas and Nebraska could decide whether to permit slavery in their regions. In effect, the act invalidated the MISSOURI COMPROMISE of 1820, which prohibited the extension of slavery in new areas of the United States. Opponents of slavery condemned the measure, and violence erupted in Kansas.

Antislavery parties had already sprung up in the United States. The abolitionist Liberty party began in 1840, and the Free Soil party was formed in 1848. In much the same spirit, the Republican party arose to protest the Nebraska-Kansas Act. The new group drew support from third parties and disaffected Democrats and Whigs. After organizational meetings in 1854 in Ripon, Wisconsin, and Jackson, Michigan, the Republican party was born.

In 1856 the Republicans nominated their first presidential candidate, John C. Frémont, a former explorer who opposed the expansion of slavery in new U.S. territories and states. Although defeated in the national election by Democrat JAMES BUCHANAN, Frémont received one-third of the popular vote.

In 1860 Abraham Lincoln from Illinois was the Republican presidential nominee. Lincoln appealed not only to antislavery voters but to business owners in the East and farmers in the Midwest. The Democratic party was in turmoil over slavery. The northern Democrats nominated STEPHEN A. DOUGLAS, who tried to sidestep the issue, and the southern Democrats backed John C. Breckinridge, who denounced government efforts to prohibit slavery. Lincoln defeated both candidates.

Although Lincoln's election was a triumph for the Republicans, his support was concentrated primarily in the North. Shortly after Lincoln's victory, several southern states seceded from the Union, and the bloody U.S. Civil War began.

Throughout the war Lincoln and his policies took a drubbing from the press and public. When Lincoln ran for reelection, the Republican party temporarily switched its name to the

THE GRANGER COLLECTION, NEW YORK

HON. ABRAHAM LINCOLN, OF ILLINOIS. HON. HANNIBAL HAMLIN, OF MAINE,

FOR PRESIDENT. FOR VICE PRESIDENT.

The Republican Party nominated Abraham Lincoln and Hannibal Hamlin as candidates for president and vice president in the 1860 elections.

Union party. Lincoln sought a second term with Democrat ANDREW JOHNSON as his running mate in order to deflect criticism of the Republican party. Johnson, from Tennessee, was one of the few southerners to support the preservation of the Union. Despite his critics Lincoln defeated the Democratic nominee, George B. McClellan, who ran on a peace platform.

After the North's victory in 1865, the Republicans oversaw Reconstruction, a period of rebuilding for the vanquished South. Lincoln favored a more conciliatory attitude toward the defeated Confederacy. Radical Republicans, however, sought a complete overhaul of the South's economic and social system. After Lincoln's ASSASSINATION in 1865, the Republicans' Reconstruction policies—such as conferring citizenship and VOTING RIGHTS to former slaves—created long-lasting resentment among many southern whites.

Republicans depended upon the support of northern voters and courted the vote of emancipated slaves. The party fanned hostility by reminding northern voters of the South's disloyalty during the war. The Republicans were the dominant party in the United States from 1860 to 1931, and the party's base among southern whites began to grow in the 1950s, when political loyalties began to shift.

During their long period of political dominance, Republicans sent the following candidates to the White House: ULYSSES S. GRANT, RUTHERFORD B. HAYES, JAMES GARFIELD (died in office), CHESTER A. ARTHUR (vice president who succeeded Garfield), BENJAMIN HARRISON, WILLIAM McKINLEY (died in office), THEODORE ROOSEVELT (vice president who succeeded McKinley and was later elected on his own), WILLIAM HOWARD TAFT, WARREN G. HARDING, CALVIN COOLIDGE, and HERBERT HOOVER.

During the 1880s and 1890s, there was an important shift in party affiliation. Struggling Republican farmers throughout the Midwest, South, and West switched their political allegiance to the Democrats who promised them government assistance. The financially strapped farmers were concerned about the depressed national economy. Many turned to the populist movement headed by Democrat WILLIAM JENNINGS BRYAN. A brilliant orator, Bryan called for the free coinage of silver currency, whereas the Republicans favored the gold standard.

Despite his popularity Bryan was defeated by Republican William McKinley in the 1896 presidential election. The Democrats appealed to farmers, but the Republicans had captured the business and urban vote. After the U.S. economy improved during the McKinley administration, supporters dubbed the Republican party "the Grand Old Party," or the GOP, a nickname that endured.

After President McKinley was assassinated in 1901, Vice President Theodore Roosevelt assumed the presidency. He pursued ambitious social reforms such as stricter ANTITRUST LAWS, tougher meat and drug regulations, and new environmental measures. In 1912 Roosevelt and his followers broke off from the Republicans to form the Bull Moose party. The third party split helped Democrat WOODROW WILSON defeat Republican candidate William Howard Taft.

After eight years of Democratic power, during which the U.S. fought in World War I, the Republicans returned to the White House in 1920 with Warren G. Harding. Unable to stave off or reverse the Great Depression, the Republicans lost control of the Oval Office in 1932.

During the Great Depression, the public became impatient with the ineffectual economic policies of Republican President Herbert Hoover. Democrat FRANKLIN D. ROOSEVELT swept into the White House with a promise of a NEW DEAL for all Americans. From 1932 to 1945, Roosevelt lifted the nation from its economic collapse and guided it through World War II. During Roosevelt's administration the Republican party lost its traditional constituency of African Americans and urban workers. HARRY S. TRUMAN followed Roosevelt in office and in 1948 withstood a strong challenge from Republican THOMAS E. DEWEY.

Republican DWIGHT D. EISENHOWER won the presidency in 1952 and 1956. A popular World War II hero, Eisenhower oversaw a good economy and a swift end to the Korean War. Eisenhower was succeeded in 1960 by Democrat JOHN F. KENNEDY who defeated Eisenhower's vice president, Republican nominee RICHARD M. NIXON. In 1964 Republicans nominated ultraconservative BARRY M. GOLDWATER who was trounced at the polls by Democrat LYNDON B. JOHNSON, the incumbent. Johnson, Kennedy's vice president, had assumed the presidency after Kennedy's assassination in 1963.

When Republican Richard M. Nixon was elected president in 1968, he began the reduction of U.S. military troops in Southeast Asia. Nixon opened trade with China and improved foreign relations through a policy of detente with the former Soviet Union. During his term the shift of southern Democrats to the Republican party accelerated. (In fact, from 1972 to 1988, the South was the most Republican region of the United States.)

The nadir for the Republican party occurred in 1974 when Nixon left office in the midst of the WATERGATE scandal, a botched attempt to burglarize and wiretap the Democratic National Committee headquarters. Implicated in the scandal's cover-up, Nixon became the only president in U.S. history to resign from office. He was succeeded by Vice President GERALD R. FORD of Michigan who served the remainder of Nixon's term and pardoned the disgraced president.

Ford lost the 1976 presidential election to Democrat JIMMY CARTER of Georgia. A sour economy and the bungling of foreign affairs (most notably the Iran hostage crisis) led to Carter's defeat in 1980 by Republican challenger RONALD REAGAN and his running mate, GEORGE BUSH.

The Republicans controlled the White House for twelve years, with Reagan serving two terms and Bush one. During Reagan's tenure, southern Democrats turned in droves to the Republican party, embracing Reagan's politically conservative message. Pointing to widespread ticket-splitting, many analysts believe

Political Party Identification of Adult Population, 1972 and 1994

Covers citizens of voting age living in private housing units in the contiguous United States. Data are from the National Election Studies and are based on a sample and subject to sampling variability.

Year

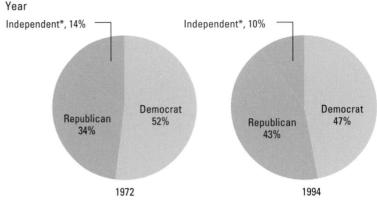

1972   1994

Sex, 1994

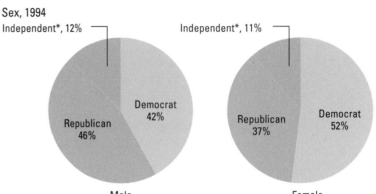

Male   Female

Race, 1994

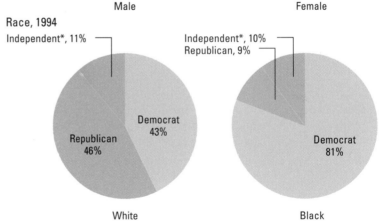

White   Black

*Includes those who self-designate as "apolitical."

Source: Center for Political Studies, University of Michigan, Ann Arbor, MI, unpublished data.

voters embraced the charismatic Reagan, not the party. Bush became president in 1988 but was defeated in 1992, by Democrat BILL CLINTON of Arkansas.

Although considered the party of business and the suburbs, the GOP has made significant inroads in traditionally Democratic areas such as labor and the South. An extremely conservative element dominated the Republican party in the 1980s, but a more moderate wing began to

Republican National Political Convention Sites, 1856 to 1996			
Year	Site	Year	Site
1856	Philadelphia	1928	Kansas City, KS
1860	Chicago	1932	Chicago
1864	Baltimore	1936	Cleveland
1868	Chicago	1940	Philadelphia
1872	Philadelphia	1944	Chicago
1876	Cincinnati	1948	Philadelphia
1880	Chicago	1952	Chicago
1884	Chicago	1956	San Francisco
1888	Chicago	1960	Chicago
1892	Minneapolis	1964	San Francisco
1896	St. Louis	1968	Miami Beach
1900	Philadelphia	1972	Miami Beach
1904	Chicago	1976	Kansas City, MO
1908	Chicago	1980	Detroit
1912	Chicago	1984	Dallas
1916	Chicago	1988	New Orleans
1920	Chicago	1992	Houston
1924	Cleveland	1996	San Diego

SOURCE: *The World Almanac,* 1997 (copyright).

exert influence in the late 1990s. Many of these moderates were elected to Congress in 1994, giving the Republicans control of both houses for the first time in more than 40 years.

See also ELECTION CAMPAIGN FINANCING; INDEPENDENT PARTIES.

REPUBLICATION 📖 The reexecution or reestablishment by a TESTATOR of a WILL that he or she had once revoked. 📖

REPUDIATION 📖 The rejection or refusal of a duty, relation, right, or privilege. 📖

Repudiation of a CONTRACT means a refusal to perform the duty or obligation owed to the other party.

ANTICIPATORY REPUDIATION is an act or declaration before performance is due under a contract that indicates that the party will not perform his or her obligation on the future date specified in the contract.

REPUGNANCY 📖 An inconsistency or opposition between two or more clauses of the same DEED, CONTRACT, or STATUTE, between two or more material ALLEGATIONS of the same PLEADING or between any two writings. 📖

Inconsistent DEFENSES or CLAIMS are permitted under the Federal Rules of Civil Procedure.

See also CIVIL PROCEDURE.

REQUIREMENTS CONTRACT 📖 A written agreement whereby a buyer assents to purchase for a sufficient CONSIDERATION (the inducement to enter into an agreement) all the merchandise of a designated type that he or she might require for use in his or her own established business. 📖

The UNIFORM COMMERCIAL CODE (UCC), a body of law adopted by the states that governs commercial transactions, provides that the parties must act in GOOD FAITH where quantity is to be measured by the requirements of the purchaser or, in the case of OUTPUT CONTRACTS, the output of the seller. No quantity that is unreasonably disproportionate to any stated estimate or to any normal or otherwise comparable previous output or requirements can be tendered or demanded.

Although the UCC does not explicitly make output and requirements agreements enforceable as CONTRACTS, the implication of validity is clear. The theoretical difficulty with these agreements has been that they border on being illusory. An agreement by a buyer to purchase from the seller all the particular GOODS that he or she requires can be interpreted to leave the buyer with a choice as to whether he or she wishes to require any goods at all. Similarly an agreement by which a seller assents to sell all of his or her output to a buyer can be interpreted as leaving the seller free to control his or her output. If read in such manner, these agreements appear to leave one of the parties free to perform or not to perform as he or she sees fit. Valid commercial reasons exist, however, for these contracts, and the courts have discovered means of upholding both output and requirements agreements if the only objection to their enforceability is that they are too indefinite. The UCC does not attempt to dictate contract terms, but it contains two rules of CONSTRUCTION that further remove these agreements from the contention that they are too indefinite to enforce and that provide guidance to courts in regard to their enforcement.

First, the measure of the quantity entailed must be determined in good faith. The buyer in a requirements agreement or the seller in an output agreement is not free, with an uncontrolled discretion, to determine the quantity of goods that can be demanded or tendered under the agreement. An illustration of a type of agreement in which one of the parties has an uncontrolled discretion would be one in which the buyer can order as much of a specified quantity of goods "as he or she wants." Such an agreement, unless there are unusual circumstances that require a different construction of these words, leaves the buyer free to buy or not to buy at his or her discretion. It does not entail mutual duties and constitutes no more than an OFFER, a proposal by the seller that would become a contract with each order from the buyer, but that could be revoked by the seller at any time prior to ACCEPTANCE. The buyer is not free to order or not to order at his or her discretion, if an agreement calls for the seller to sell and the buyer to buy all or a stated portion of the buyer's requirements. When the buyer has requirements, he or she must purchase them from the seller and exercise good faith in ascertaining them. The nonmerchant must act with honesty in fact; the merchant must meet this same test but must also conduct business in accordance with commercial standards of fair dealing in the trade, so that his or her requirements approximate a reasonably foreseeable figure. A seller under an output agreement must meet the same test.

Second, the UCC furnishes a center around which the quantity is to be determined. The buyer cannot demand and, therefore, the seller is not obligated to deliver, and the seller cannot tender and, therefore, the buyer is not required to accept any quantity that is unreasonably disproportionate to any estimate that the parties have stated or if no estimate was stated, to any comparable previous requirements or output. If, for example, a seller has agreed to deliver all of the buyer's requirements of a certain product, and if the buyer has been ordering approximately 500 units each month, the seller would not be obligated to deliver 1,500 units in one month, even though the buyer could prove that 1,500 units were required for his or her business. The determination of which prior period is "comparable" depends upon the nature of the business involved. The UCC does not require that the chosen comparable period be one in which the parties were dealing with each other. If this is the first output or requirements contract between the parties and no estimate is stated, the UCC permits any normal or comparable period involving the seller's output or the buyer's requirements to be employed in measuring the obligations under such an agreement.

Even though output and requirements contracts are sufficiently defined for enforcement, difficult problems of determining the obligations under these agreements arise whenever there is an unexpected shift in the demand for, or the price of, the goods involved. In these instances, a merchant might search for methods of altering production schedules or modifying output (if a seller) or requirements (if a buyer).

Attempts to increase or decrease requirements often result in disputes between the parties that require judicial intervention. In order to resolve these situations, the "unreasonably disproportionate" test of the UCC supplies a tool that, when combined with the requirement of good faith, permits the courts to resolve these disputes. The UCC also provides that a lawful agreement that results in an exclusive dealing in goods imposes, unless otherwise agreed, an obligation by the seller to make his

or her best effort to supply the goods and an obligation by the buyer to make his or her best effort to promote their sale. This requirement is a specific application of the general doctrine of good faith.

The legality of output, requirements, or other exclusive dealing contracts depends upon the application of federal or state ANTITRUST ACTS, laws that protect commerce and trade from unlawful restraints, price discriminations, and PRICE FIXING. The UCC provides that only "lawful" agreements may be enforced.

REQUISITION 📖 A written demand; a formal request or requirement. The formal demand by one government upon another, or by the governor of one state upon the governor of another state, of the surrender of a FUGITIVE FROM JUSTICE. The taking or seizure of property by government. 📖

Requisition refers to the seizure of PERSONAL PROPERTY, whereas CONDEMNATION entails the taking of REAL PROPERTY.

RES 📖 [*Latin, A thing.*] An object, a subject matter, or a status against which legal proceedings have been instituted. 📖

For example, in a suit involving a captured ship, the seized vessel is the *res*, and proceedings of this nature are said to be IN REM. *Res*, however, does not always refer to tangible PERSONAL PROPERTY. In matrimonial actions, for example, the *res* is the marital status of the parties.

RES ADJUDICATA See RES JUDICATA.

RESCIND 📖 To declare a contract VOID—of no legal force or binding effect—from its inception and thereby restore the parties to the positions they would have occupied had no CONTRACT ever been made. 📖

RESCISSION 📖 The cancellation of a prison inmate's tentative PAROLE date. The ABROGATION of a CONTRACT, effective from its inception,

The owner of a gas station may enter into a requirements contract with the supplier of gasoline, agreeing to purchase from the supplier all of the gasoline required for the station.

thereby restoring the parties to the positions they would have occupied if no contract had ever been formed. 📖

By Agreement Mutual rescission, or rescission by agreement, is a discharge of both parties from the obligations of a contract by a new agreement made after the execution of the original contract but prior to its performance. Rescission by mutual assent is separate from the right of one of the parties to RESCIND or cancel the contract for cause, or pursuant to a provision in the contract.

The parties to an EXECUTORY or incomplete contract can rescind it at any time by mutual agreement, even if the contract itself contains a contrary provision. A rescission by mutual assent can properly include a promise by either or both parties to make RESTITUTION as part of the contract of rescission.

The right to rescind is limited to the parties to the contract or those legally authorized to act for them. As with other contracts, the parties to the rescission agreement must be mentally COMPETENT.

Form The rescission agreement can be either written or oral. An IMPLIED agreement is also effective, provided the assent of the parties can be shown by their acts and the surrounding circumstances. An EXPRESS rescission of a contract as a whole is adequate and effective, without specifically designating each and every clause to be rescinded.

Unless a statute provides otherwise, an oral rescission agreement is valid, even though the contract being rescinded contains a provision that it can be altered only in writing.

Assent All the parties to the contract must assent to its rescission because mutual rescission involves the formation of a new contract. A MEETING OF MINDS can be reached by an offer to rescind and an acceptance by the other party. One party to a contract cannot rescind it simply by giving notice to the other party that he or she intends to do so.

Although a breach of contract by one party is not an offer to rescind, the other party can treat the REPUDIATION as an offer to rescind that he or she can accept, leading to rescission of the contract by mutual assent. Rescission must be clearly expressed, however, and the conduct of the parties must be inconsistent with the existence of the contract. The fact that some of the materials that form part of the subject matter of the contract have been returned is not conclusive as to whether rescission has occurred.

Consideration An agreement to rescind a prior contract must be based on a sufficient CONSIDERATION, an inducement. When a contract remains executory on both sides, an agreement to rescind by one side is sufficient consideration for the agreement to cancel on the other, and vice versa. If the contract has been executed on one side, an agreement to rescind that is made without any new consideration is void—of no legal force or binding effect.

Operation and Effect The mutual rights of the parties are controlled by the terms of their rescission agreement. The parties are generally

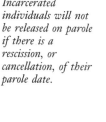

Incarcerated individuals will not be released on parole if there is a rescission, or cancellation, of their parole date.

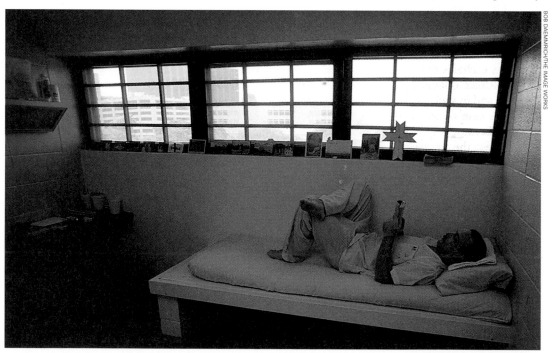

BOB DAEMMRICH/THE IMAGE WORKS

restored to their original rights in regard to the subject matter. They no longer have any rights or obligations under the rescinded contract, and no CLAIM or ACTION for subsequent breach can be maintained.

Whether rights or obligations already accrued are abandoned when the contract is rescinded in the COURSE OF PERFORMANCE depends on the intention of the parties, as deduced from all attending facts and circumstances, and on whether the parties have reserved such rights. Recovery can be allowed, however, for partial performance.

Wrong or Default of Adverse Party
No arbitrary right exists to rescind a contract. An executory contract that is VOIDABLE can be rescinded on the grounds of FRAUD, MISTAKE, or INCAPACITY.

A contract, whether oral or written, can be rescinded on the ground of fraud. The right to rescind for fraud is not barred because the defrauded party has failed to perform. Generally, false statements of value, or the failure to perform a promise to do something in the future without fraudulent intent, will not provide a basis for rescission for fraud or misrepresentation. A party proves sufficient grounds for rescission by showing that he or she was induced to part with some legal right or to assume some legal LIABILITY that he or she otherwise would not have done but for the fraudulent representations.

On discovering the fraud, the victimized party can affirm the contract and sue for DAMAGES. He or she might instead repudiate the contract, tender back what he or she has received, and recover what he or she has parted with, or its value; the adoption of one remedy, however, excludes the other.

A contract obtained by DURESS can be rescinded, and in such a case, the same rules apply as in the case of fraud. A contract cannot be avoided because of duress or COERCION, however, unless the duress was sufficient to overcome completely the will of the party who is seeking to avoid the contract.

A MUTUAL MISTAKE concerning a material fact entitles the party affected by the mistake to rescind the contract, unless the contract has already been completed and rescission would be an injustice to the other party. Rescission can also be allowed even for a unilateral, or one-sided, mistake in order to prevent an UNJUST ENRICHMENT of the other party. On rescission, the aggrieved party can recover the money he or she has paid or the property he or she has delivered under the contract.

A contract made by a person of unsound mind can be rescinded when the parties can be restored to the status quo. This rule applies even if the opposite party was unaware of the mental condition, and the contract was fair, reasonable, and made in GOOD FAITH for adequate consideration. When one party knows of the other's incapacity, the contract can be rescinded on the ground of fraud. When both parties are sane and the contract is valid, subsequent insanity of one of the parties is not a ground for rescission, unless it affects the substance or purpose of the contract, as in the case of a personal services contract.

As a general rule, a contract cannot be rescinded because one of the parties was intoxicated at the time it was made. If, however, unfair advantage was taken of a person's intoxicated condition, or if the intoxication was induced by the party seeking to take advantage of the contract, the contract can be set aside on the ground of fraud. Similarly, habitual drunkenness that impairs a party's mental abilities can constitute a ground for rescission.

Inadequate Consideration Mere inadequacy of consideration is not a sufficient reason to justify rescission. When the consideration is so inadequate that it shocks the conscience of the court or is so closely connected with suspicious circumstances or misrepresentations as to provide substantial evidence of fraud, it can furnish a basis for relief.

Nonperformance or Breach One party to a contract can rescind it because of substantial nonperformance or breach by the other party. The party who knowingly and willfully fails to perform cannot complain that the other party to the contract has injured him or her by terminating the contract. The right to rescind does not arise from every breach but is permitted only when the breach is so substantial and fundamental that it defeats the objective of the parties in making the agreement. The breach must pertain to the essence of the contract. The act must be an unqualified refusal by the other party to perform and should amount to a decision not to be bound by the contract in the future. A party to a contract who is in DEFAULT cannot, however, rescind because of a breach by the other party.

When TIME IS OF THE ESSENCE in a contract, failure to perform within the time stipulated is a ground for rescission. Otherwise a delay in the time of performance is not considered a material breach justifying rescission. When performance is intended within a reasonable time, one party cannot suddenly and without reasonable notice terminate the contract while the other party is attempting in good faith to perform it.

An unconditional notice by one party that he does not intend to perform a contract is a ground for rescission by the other party. In order to justify rescission, the refusal must be absolute and unconditional.

When one party to a contract abandons it and refuses further performance, or her conduct shows that she is repudiating the contract, the other party is entitled to rescission. A disagreement over the terms of the contract and a subsequent refusal to perform in a particular manner by one of the parties do not constitute an abandonment of the contract justifying rescission.

Time A right to rescind must be exercised promptly or within a reasonable time after the discovery of the facts that authorize the right. A reasonable time is defined by the circumstances of the particular case. The rule that rescission must be prompt does not operate where an excuse or justification for a delay is shown.

RESCUE 📖 The crime of forcibly and knowingly freeing another from arrest, imprisonment, or legal CUSTODY.

In ADMIRALTY AND MARITIME LAW, the taking back of property seized as PRIZE from the possession of the captors by the party who originally lost it. 📖

At COMMON LAW, the crime of rescue involved illegally freeing a prisoner. From the nineteenth century onward, such crimes became romanticized in the popular entertainment of Westerns and crime dramas, where prisoners were freed from jail by their criminal associates. Today, this form of rescue is an offense under federal law. Some states treat it as a common-law offense, whereas others define it under statute. In a different legal sense, rescue under admiralty and maritime law means the taking back of goods that have been captured at sea.

The crime of rescue has four elements. First, the arrest of a prisoner must be lawful. Second, the prisoner must be in actual custody, that is, in the personal custody of an officer or in a prison or jail. Third, at common law and under some statutes, the rescue must be forcibly made. Fourth, the prisoner must actually escape. At common law, the person guilty of rescue is guilty of the same grade of offense, whether FELONY or MISDEMEANOR, as the person who is rescued.

Under federal law, rescue of a prisoner held in federal custody is a felony. As defined by 18 U.S.C.A. § 752 (1994), rescue is the crime of instigating or assisting ESCAPE from lawful cus-

tody. The law takes its punishment provisions from the federal statute (18 U.S.C.A. § 751 [1994]) that makes it unlawful for a prisoner to escape from a place of confinement: conviction carries fines of up to $5,000 and imprisonment of up to five years for the rescue of an adult, and equivalent fines and imprisonment of up to a year for the rescue of a MINOR. Thus, like the common-law definition, the same punishment applies to a person aiding an escape as that given to the person escaping.

Criminal cases involving rescue can be dramatic. In the 1933 case of *Merrill v. State*, 42 Ariz. 341, 26 P.2d 110, Herbert Merrill appealed his conviction for attempting to rescue Albert De Raey from the Maricopa County, Arizona, jail. On January 10, 1933, Merrill brought acid to the jail at De Raey's request so that De Raey could use it to cut through the bars on his jail cell. Merrill was subsequently convicted of attempting to rescue under section 4537 of Arizona's Revised Code of 1928. On appeal, however, the APPELLATE COURT reversed the conviction: it found that although Merrill had apparently assisted in an escape attempt, he had not forcibly attempted to effect a rescue. Thus he had been improperly charged, the conviction could not stand, and the case was sent back to the lower court.

In 1989 a California case raised the issue of when rescue is defensible. On November 5, 1986, Ronald J. McIntosh landed a helicopter on the grounds of the Federal Correctional Institution at Pleasanton, California, and then flew off with his girlfriend, Samantha D. Lopez, who was being held as a prisoner there. McIntosh was later convicted of aiding Lopez's escape and two other felonies; Lopez was convicted of escape. In a joint appeal, they alleged that their offenses were necessary to save Lopez's life because she had been threatened by prison officials and was in immediate danger (*United States v. Lopez*, 885 F.2d 1428 [9th C.C.A. 1989]). In fact, such a defense—called a NECESSITY defense—can excuse the otherwise criminal act of escape. The appeal alleged that the trial court had improperly instructed the jury as to the availability of this defense to both defendants. However, in upholding their convictions, the appellate court found that the trial judge committed no error in the instructions with respect to Lopez, and only a HARMLESS ERROR where McIntosh was concerned.

Under admiralty and maritime law, rescue has another definition entirely. It means recovering goods that have been forcibly taken by one vessel from another. The property in ques-

DAVID WEINTRAUB/STOCK BOSTON

Under the rescue doctrine, if one of these rescuers suffered injury while trying to help this fallen hiker, the injured rescuer would have a claim against the party whose negligence put the hiker in danger.

tion is referred to as a prize, and its rescue may be effected by reclaiming the property with force or by escaping. Generally, such actions occur when two belligerent powers clash, either in a limited dispute or at war.

RESCUE DOCTRINE 📖 The principle that one who has, through her NEGLIGENCE, endangered the safety of another can be held liable for injuries sustained by a third person who attempts to save the imperiled person from injury. 📖

This doctrine is based on the idea that danger invites rescue. It also provides that one who sees a person in imminent and serious peril as the result of the negligence of another cannot be charged with contributory negligence, as a MATTER OF LAW, in risking his own life or serious injury in attempting a rescue, provided the attempt is not recklessly made.

See also GOOD SAMARITAN DOCTRINE.

RESERVATION 📖 A clause in a DEED of REAL PROPERTY whereby the GRANTOR, one who transfers property, creates and retains for the grantor some right or interest in the ESTATE granted, such as rent or an EASEMENT, a right of use over the land of another. A large tract of land that is withdrawn by public authority from sale or settlement and appropriated to specific public uses, such as parks or military posts. A tract of land under the control of the Bureau of Indian Affairs to which an American Indian tribe retains its original TITLE to ownership, or that has been set aside from the PUBLIC DOMAIN for use by a tribe. 📖

See also NATIVE AMERICAN RIGHTS.

RESERVE 📖 Funds set aside to cover future expenses, losses, or claims. To retain; to keep in store for future or special use; to postpone to a future time. 📖

A legal reserve is a monetary account required by law to be established by insurance companies and banks as protection against losses.

A trial court reserves a point of law by setting it aside for future consideration and allowing the trial to proceed as if the question had been resolved, subject to alteration of the JUDGMENT in the event the court EN BANC decides the question differently.

RES GESTAE 📖 [*Latin, Things done.*] Secondhand statements considered trustworthy for the purpose of admission as EVIDENCE in a lawsuit when repeated by a WITNESS because they were made spontaneously and concurrently with an event. 📖

Res gestae describes a COMMON-LAW doctrine governing TESTIMONY. Under the HEARSAY rule, a court normally refuses to admit as evidence statements that a witness says he or she heard another person say. The doctrine of res gestae provided an exception to this rule. During the nineteenth century and much of the twentieth century, courts applied the exception by following an assortment of common-law rules. With the introduction of the Federal Rules of Evidence, FEDERAL COURTS abolished res gestae as a common-law doctrine and replaced it with explicit exceptions to the ban on hearsay. To varying degrees, state rules of evidence are modeled on the federal rules. Although the term is now infrequently used, the legacy of res gestae is an integral part of the modern framework of hearsay evidence.

Traditionally, two reasons have made hearsay inadmissible: unfairness and possible inaccuracy. Allowing a witness to repeat hearsay does not provide the accused with an opportunity to question the speaker of the original statement, and the witness may have misunderstood or misinterpreted the statement. Thus, in a trial, counsel can object to a witness's testimony as hearsay. But in the nineteenth century, the borrowing of the concept of res gestae from English law offered an exception to this rule. Res gestae is based on the belief that because certain statements are made naturally, spontaneously, and without deliberation during the course of an event, they carry a high degree of credibility and leave little room for misunderstanding or misinterpretation. The doctrine held that such statements are more trustworthy than other secondhand statements and therefore should be ADMISSIBLE as evidence.

As the common-law rule developed, it acquired a number of tests for determining admissibility. To be admissible, the statements must relate, explain, or characterize an event or transaction. They must be natural statements growing out of the event, as opposed to a narrative of a past, completed affair. Additionally, the statements must be spontaneous, evoked by the event itself, and not the result of premeditation. Finally, the original speaker must have participated in the transaction or witnessed the event in question. Thus, for example, a witness might testify that during a bank robbery, she or he heard another person shout, "That person is robbing the bank!" and the statement could be admitted as an exception to the ban on hearsay.

In practice, cases involving res gestae were usually decided by applying some variation of these tests. In the 1959 case of *Carroll v. Guffey*, 20 Ill. App. 2d 470, 156 N.E.2d 267, an Illinois APPELLATE COURT heard the APPEAL of a defendant who was held liable for injuries sustained by another motorist in a car crash. The trial court had admitted the testimony of the plaintiff concerning unidentified eyewitnesses who allegedly saw the accident, over the objection of defense counsel who argued that the statements were hearsay. The appellate court ruled that the declarations of the eyewitnesses were not res gestae exceptions: they were not made concurrently with the collision, but afterward, and were only a narrative of what the eyewitnesses said had taken place. Thus the appellate court reversed the trial court's decision.

The process of refining the concept began in the 1920s, when the influential lawyer and educator Edmund M. Morgan attacked its pliability and vagueness: "[T]his troublesome expression owes its existence and persistence in our law of evidence to an inclination of judges and lawyers to avoid the toilsome exertion of exact analysis and precise thinking." In an attempt at clarification, Morgan developed seven categories for the exception. In the 1940s the Model Code of Evidence made further refinements, and by the 1970s the Federal Rules of Evidence had included elements of res gestae in Rule 803 as one of its many exceptions to the hearsay rule.

RESIDENCE 📖 Personal presence at some place of abode. 📖

Although the domicile and residence of a person are usually in the same place, and the two terms are frequently used as if they had the same meaning, they are not synonymous. A

Your home may be your residence, but it is not your domicile unless you have an intent to make it your permanent home.

person can have two places of residence, such as one in the city and one in the country, but only one domicile. Residence means living in a particular locality, but domicile means living in that locality with the intent to make it a fixed and permanent home. Residence merely requires bodily presence as an inhabitant in a given place, whereas domicile requires bodily presence in that place and also an intention to make it one's permanent home.

RESIDENCY 📖 A duration of stay required by state and local laws that entitles a person to the legal protection and benefits provided by applicable statutes. 📖

States have required state residency for a variety of rights, including the right to vote, the right to run for public office, the ability to practice a profession, and the ability to receive public assistance. The courts have invalidated some residency requirements because they violate the Equal Protection Clause of the FOURTEENTH AMENDMENT, while allowing others to stand because there is a COMPELLING STATE INTEREST.

There are two types of residency requirements. A bona fide residency requirement asks a person to establish that she actually lives at a certain location and usually is demonstrated by the address listed on a driver's license, a voter registration card, a lease, an income tax return, property tax bills, or utilities bills. If a person has conducted a substantial amount of business in a state, some states will recognize that person as an actual resident and grant her certain advantages of residency. Courts have recognized the validity of imposing bona fide requirements in order for a person to receive certain rights from the states.

A durational residency requirement obligates a person to show that, in addition to being a bona fide resident of the state or its subdivision (county, city, town, school district), she has resided in the location for an additional period of time. Attempts by states to make certain fundamental rights conditional upon the durational residency of the person applying for such benefits have been challenged in court.

Fundamental Rights The U.S. Supreme Court has made clear that a state can impose residency requirements as a condition of eligibility for fundamental rights only under certain circumstances. A fundamental right is any right that is guaranteed by the U.S. Constitution. A state must have a compelling state interest to justify the restriction of basic rights by the imposition of residency requirements. The courts ultimately determine whether the state has a significant interest by examining and balancing the interests of the state against the rights of the person. Where a residency requirement does not serve compelling state interests, it will be held unconstitutional as a denial of EQUAL PROTECTION of the laws guaranteed by the Constitution. The courts have addressed residency requirements involving welfare and public housing benefits, basic medical care, and voting that are based on fundamental rights.

Welfare In *Shapiro v. Thompson*, 394 U.S. 618, 89 S. Ct. 1322, 22 L. Ed. 2d 600 (1969), the Supreme Court reviewed two state laws that imposed durational residency requirements on persons applying for WELFARE. Both states required a person to be a resident for one year before becoming eligible for benefits. The states claimed that this discriminatory treatment of new arrivals within their borders maintained the fiscal integrity of state public assistance programs, provided an objective method of determining residency, and encouraged new residents to seek employment.

The Court rejected these arguments, concluding that the constitutional guarantee of personal liberty gave each citizen the right to travel throughout the United States without unreasonable restrictions. This implied fundamental right of travel was restricted by the residency requirements, which were based on unsubstantiated claims of administrative convenience. Therefore the Court struck down the durational residency requirements as a violation of equal protection of the laws. The Court noted that a case-by-case examination was necessary to determine whether other types of durational requirements promoted compelling state interests or violated the constitutional right of interstate travel.

Public Housing Durational residency requirements were imposed as conditions for admission to low- and moderate-income public housing projects in various cities during the 1960s. The city of New Rochelle, New York, imposed a five-year residency period before a person could apply for public housing. Because the waiting list of applicants was long, a person could wait between eight and fifteen years before obtaining public housing. When the law was challenged, a federal APPELLATE COURT ruled that it was an unconstitutional deprivation of equal protection (*King v. New Rochelle Municipal Housing Authority*, 442 F.2d 646 [2d Cir. 1971], *cert. denied*, 404 U.S. 863, 92 S. Ct. 113, 30 L. Ed. 2d 107 [1971]). The appeals court rejected the city's contention that it had a compelling state interest to restrict public housing to long-time residents because each community has a responsibility to take care of its own citizens first. The court disagreed, finding that the city's plan created discriminatory classifications among its citizens without justification.

Medical Services A person who is a bona fide resident cannot be deprived of the right to receive basic medical services merely because he has not fulfilled durational residency requirements. The Supreme Court in *Memorial Hospital v. Maricopa County*, 415 U.S. 250, 94 S. Ct. 1076, 39 L. Ed. 2d 306 (1974), overturned an Arizona law that stated that an indigent person must be a resident of one year in the county before receiving nonemergency hospitalization or medical care at the expense of the county. The Court ruled that medical care is a basic necessity of life to an indigent person, comparable to welfare assistance. As in the *Shapiro* case, the Court held that the residency requirement restricted the right to travel. The fact that public services would be depleted by allowing new residents the same treatment as other residents did not justify the residency requirement because a state cannot apportion its services among its citizens.

Voting Rights A state has the right to require bona fide residency as a prerequisite to the exercise of the right to vote in its ELECTIONS. The courts have also upheld durational residency requirements for voting. Beginning in the mid-1970s, however, many states began to abandon durational requirements, making it possible for a new resident to register to vote when he applied for a state driver's license. This "motor-voter" statute was first enacted in Minnesota (Minn. Stat. Ann. § 201.161 [West 1992]), and by 1992 twenty-seven states had some form of motor-voter law. Congress eliminated durational residency requirements for voting with the passage of the National Voter Registration Act of 1993 (42 U.S.C.A. § 1973gg et seq.). The act allows anyone over the age of eighteen to register to vote while obtaining a driver's license. See also VOTING RIGHTS.

Other Rights Courts have upheld residency requirements involving rights that are not fundamental rights under the Constitution. These requirements govern the right to run for public office, the right to start a lawsuit in a state court, the right to attend particular public schools, the right to practice a profession, and the right to work for a government agency. The state needs to provide a rational basis for the residency requirement, which is a lesser standard of constitutional review. Generally, most statutes can be upheld on a rational basis standard because it requires the state only to offer a reasonable justification for the law. See also RATIONAL BASIS TEST.

Candidate for Public Office The right to become a candidate for public office is not a fundamental right. A state has the right to impose certain requirements on persons who decide to run for public office within its borders. A bona fide resident of the state or local government subdivision may run for state or local public office. A durational requirement specifying more than a short period of time will likely be struck down as a violation of equal protection.

Jurisdiction When a person's legal rights have been violated, he is entitled to bring a lawsuit in the courts of his state against those who have committed the violation. A state or its subdivision will not allow a person to resort to its courts unless that person can establish that he has some relationship with it that justifies the exercise of JURISDICTION of the court. States typically impose residency requirements as a prerequisite to bringing a DIVORCE action. The Supreme Court, in *Sosna v. Iowa*, 419 U.S. 393, 95 S. Ct. 553, 42 L. Ed. 2d 532 (1975), upheld an Iowa durational residency requirement that prohibited the filing of a divorce ACTION until a person had resided for one year in the state. The Court concluded that the one-year residency requirement merely delayed obtaining judicial relief and was not a permanent barrier. In addition, the state had a compelling interest to justify the one-year requirement. The Court noted that a divorce case affects both spouses, the children of the marriage, and various property rights. Iowa had a compelling interest in making sure that it, rather than another state, was the appropriate place for the lawsuit.

Schools Depending upon state law, the residency of a child and her parents or guardians in a particular school district determines which public elementary and secondary schools that child will attend. States can also validly establish residency requirements to help determine which students are entitled to lower tuition costs at state-operated COLLEGES AND UNIVERSITIES. Federal courts have upheld the right of a state to impose more stringent admission standards and higher tuition costs on out-of-state residents seeking to attend its institutions of higher learning. There is a reasonable basis for this residency requirement because a state university is created for the citizens of the state and is substantially supported by state taxes. See also SCHOOLS AND SCHOOL DISTRICTS.

Professional Requirements A state has the right to establish qualifications that must be satisfied by persons seeking to practice their professions within its borders. Doctors, lawyers, optometrists, dentists, and architects must comply with state regulations that are designed to protect the public from the work of unqualified individuals. Various courts have upheld the requirement that a professional be a resident in the state in which she is seeking to practice, on the basis that the applicant's residency prior to, or during, the time she is seeking a LICENSE gives the state examining body a sufficient opportunity to investigate her character and fitness. A residency requirement, however, must accomplish this purpose or it is invalid.

Employment Residency requirements have been consistently upheld as valid prerequisites to municipal or CIVIL SERVICE employment. Because there is no constitutional right to be employed by a public agency, any residency requirements must be examined to determine if they have some rational basis. Public bodies base residency requirements for their workers on a number of state interests, including the promotion of ethnic and racial balance in the community, the reduction of high unemployment rates of inner-city minority groups, the ready availability of workers in emergency situations, and the general economic benefits ensuing from local expenditures of employees' salaries. As long as a municipal employee residency requirement is rationally related to one or more of these legitimate government purposes, it does not violate the equal protection of the laws.

Commercial Licenses A state can require that applicants for various types of commercial licenses, such as barbers, bar owners, restaurant owners, or taxi drivers, meet certain residency requirements. This exercise of the state POLICE POWER to protect the public health and safety is valid as long as the residency requirements constitute a reasonable way of enabling the state to accomplish its legitimate goals.

RESIDUARY CLAUSE ◫ A provision in a WILL that disposes of property not expressly disposed of by other provisions of the will. ◫

RESIDUUM ◫ That which remains after any process of separation or deduction; a balance; that which remains of a decedent's estate after debts have been paid and gifts deducted. ◫

RES IPSA LOQUITUR ◫ [*Latin, The thing speaks for itself.*] A REBUTTABLE PRESUMPTION or INFERENCE that the defendant was negligent, which arises upon proof that the instrumentality or condition causing the injury was in the defendant's exclusive control and that the accident was one that ordinarily does not occur in the absence of NEGLIGENCE. ◫

Res ipsa loquitur, or *res ipsa*, as it is commonly called, is really a rule of EVIDENCE, not a rule of substantive law.

Negligence is conduct that falls below the standard established by law for the protection of others against an unreasonable risk of harm. In order to prevail in a negligence ACTION, a plaintiff must establish by a PREPONDERANCE OF EVIDENCE that the defendant's conduct was unreasonable in light of the particular situation and that such conduct caused the plaintiff's injury. The mere fact that an accident or an injury has occurred, with nothing more, is not evidence of negligence. There must be evidence that negligence has caused the event. Such

evidence can consist of direct TESTIMONY by EYEWITNESSES who observed the defendant's unreasonable conduct and its injurious result.

Negligence can also be established by CIRCUMSTANTIAL EVIDENCE when no DIRECT EVIDENCE exists. *Circumstantial evidence* is evidence of one recognized fact or set of facts from which the fact to be determined can be reasonably inferred, because it is the logical conclusion that can be drawn from all the known facts. For example, skid marks at the scene of an accident are circumstantial evidence that a car was driven at an excessive speed. The reasoning process must be based upon the facts offered as evidence, together with a sufficient background of human experience, to justify the conclusion. Evidence that merely suggests the possibility of negligence is insufficient, since negligence must appear more likely than not to have occurred. This inference must cover all the necessary elements of negligence: that the defendant owed the plaintiff a duty, which the defendant violated by failing to act according to the required standard of conduct, and that such negligent conduct injured the plaintiff.

Res ipsa loquitur is one form of circumstantial evidence that permits a REASONABLE PERSON to surmise that the most PROBABLE CAUSE of an accident was the defendant's negligence. This concept was first advanced in 1863 in a case in which a barrel of flour rolled out of a warehouse window and fell upon a passing pedestrian. *Res ipsa loquitur* was the reasonable conclusion because, under the circumstances, the defendant was probably culpable since no other explanation was likely. The concept was rapidly applied to cases involving injuries to passengers caused by CARRIERS, such as railroads, which were required to prove they had not been negligent. *Res ipsa loquitur*, as it is currently applied by nearly all of the fifty states, deals with the sufficiency of circumstantial evidence and, as in some states, affects the burden of proof in negligence cases.

Elements Three basic requirements must be satisfied before a court can submit the question of negligence to the jury under *res ipsa loquitur*.

Inference of Negligence The plaintiff's injury must be of a type that does not ordinarily occur unless someone has been negligent. This requirement, which is the inference of negligence, allows *res ipsa* to be applied to a wide variety of situations, such as the falling of elevators, the presence of a dead mouse in a bottle of soda, a human toe found in a wad of chewing tobacco, or a streetcar careening through a restaurant. Although many of the cases involve freakish and improbable situations, ordinary events, such as where a passenger is injured when a vehicle stops abruptly, will also warrant the application of *res ipsa*. Commercial air travel has become so safe in recent years that planes engaged in regularly scheduled commercial flights generally do not crash unless someone has been negligent. Vehicular accidents caused by a sudden loss of control, such as a car suddenly swerving off the road or a truck skidding on a slippery road and crossing into the wrong lane of traffic, justify the conclusion that such an event would not normally occur except for someone's negligence.

This inference of negligence does not mean that all other possible causes of the injurious event must be eliminated. A plaintiff using *res ipsa* to enable her case to go to the jury must prove that the defendant's negligence is the most probable cause of her injuries. The particular nature of the defendant's negligence need not be pinpointed. For instance, where a bottle of soda explodes in a supermarket immediately after its delivery by the bottler, the injured person does not have to prove that the bottler failed to notice a defect in the bottle or that the soda was overcarbonated. It is sufficient to establish that the explosion would not have occurred unless the bottler had been negligent.

Where the inference of negligence depends upon facts beyond the common knowledge of jurors, expert testimony is necessary to furnish this information. Such testimony is usually presented in cases of professional negligence, such as medical MALPRACTICE. An expert WITNESS can testify directly in regard to the inferred fact itself, such as when the expert testifies that the plaintiff's injury would not have occurred if the doctor had not been negligent.

Exclusive Control by the Defendant The plaintiff's injury or damage must have been caused by an instrumentality or condition that was within the exclusive control of the defendant. Some courts interpret this requirement to mean that exclusive control or management must have existed at the time of the injury. This interpretation has led to harsh results. In one case, a customer sat down in a chair in a store while waiting for a salesperson. The chair collapsed and the customer was injured. The court denied recovery to the customer in her negligence action against the store because it found that the chair was not within the exclusive control of the store, but rather was under the exclusive control of the customer at the time of injury.

This application of the rule has been regarded as inflexible by many courts, since it severely restricts the type of case to which *res ipsa* can be applied. In response, many states prescribe that the negligence must occur while the defendant has control over the instrumentality. In the example of the exploding soda bottle, the negligence of the bottler occurred somewhere in the bottling process. The fact that the bottle was sitting on a supermarket shelf and was no longer in the immediate possession of the bottler does not prevent the reasonable conclusion that the injury resulted from the negligence of the bottler. The injured plaintiff must first show that the bottle was not cracked by mishandling after it left the plant of the bottler. This does not mean, however, that the plaintiff must account for every minute of the existence of the bottle from the time it left the plant. If the plaintiff can substantiate the fact of careful handling in general and the absence of unusual incidents, such as the deliberate tampering of the bottled goods by an unknown person, such facts would permit reasonable persons to conclude that the injury was more likely than not to have been caused by the defendant's negligence while he had exclusive control of the bottle.

Since there must be exclusive control by the defendant, *res ipsa* cannot be used against multiple defendants in a negligence case where the plaintiff claims he has been injured by the negligence of another. For example, a pedestrian is injured when he is struck by a car that had just collided with another vehicle. The pedestrian institutes a negligence action against one driver, and seeks to have *res ipsa* applied to his case. An inference of negligence does not arise from the mere fact of the collision, since neither driver is in exclusive control of the situation. If, however, one driver is cleared of fault by some specific evidence, the jury is justified in inferring that the injury was the result of the other driver's negligence.

The requirement of exclusive control by the defendant is not applied in cases involving VICARIOUS LIABILITY or shared responsibility for the same instrumentality or condition. In one case, a person was injured when an elevator in which she was riding fell very rapidly. She brought a negligence action against both the owner of the building and the elevator company that manufactured the elevator and had the maintenance service contract for the building. The plaintiff relied completely on *res ipsa*. The jury found for the plaintiff since a falling elevator is not the type of accident that usually occurs without negligence, so that the negligence of those in control can be inferred. The service contract between the elevator company and the building owner established the fact that they exerted joint control over the elevator. The requirement of exclusive control by a defendant of the instrumentality causing injury does not mean that only a single entity has control. Where two or more defendants are acting jointly, the doctrine of *res ipsa* can be applied to establish their negligence.

Some state courts have departed from the requirement of exclusive control and applied *res ipsa loquitur* against multiple defendants. In one case, while an anesthetized patient was undergoing an operation for appendicitis, he suffered a traumatic injury to his shoulder. *Res ipsa* was applied against all of the doctors and hospital employees connected with the operation, although not all of them were negligent. The court based its decision on the special responsibility for the plaintiff's safety undertaken by everyone concerned.

Freedom from Contributory Negligence The event in question must not have been attributable to any cause for which the plaintiff is responsible. The plaintiff must not have done anything that significantly contributed to the accident that caused the injury. In one case, a water skier was injured when the propeller of the boat that had been towing him struck his arm as the boat was attempting to pick him up. He sued the driver and the owner of the boat for negligence, which could be found if *res ipsa* was applied. The plaintiff attempted to dive underwater when he saw the boat approaching him, but he was unsuccessful in escaping injury. The defendants claimed that the attempted dive caused the accident and, therefore, *res ipsa* was inapplicable.

The trial court accepted this argument, which was later rejected by the APPELLATE COURT. The appellate court decided that the question of whether the attempted dive caused the accident should have been presented to the jury under *res ipsa*. It stated that a plaintiff may rely upon *res ipsa loquitur* even though he has participated in the events leading to the accident if the evidence excludes his conduct as the responsible cause. In light of the skier's testimony that he was about to be struck by the boat, as well as the testimony of other eyewitnesses, the jury could logically conclude that the attempted dive was not a cause of the accident.

Accessibility of Evidence In addition to the three basic requirements, a few states apply *res ipsa* in negligence cases where the evidence of the facts of the event is more accessible to the defendant than to the plaintiff. In one state, for example, a plaintiff was injured

when the bleacher section in which she was sitting collapsed during a basketball game under the management and supervision of the defendant high school athletic association. She sued the association for negligence under the doctrine of *res ipsa*. The appellate court, reviewing a VERDICT for the plaintiff, affirmed it because "the underlying reason for the *res ipsa* rule is that the chief evidence of the true cause of the injury is practically accessible to the defendant but inaccessible to the injured person."

The Effect of Res Ipsa *Res ipsa loquitur* is usually used when there is no direct evidence of the defendant's negligence. The facts presented to the court must meet the three basic requirements. Once the court decides that the facts of a particular case warrant the application of *res ipsa*, it instructs the jury on the basic principles, but it is the function of the jury to decide the credibility and weight of the inference to be drawn from the known facts. The jury can conclude that the defendant was negligent, but the jury is not compelled to do so. Everything depends upon the particular facts of each case. An inference of negligence might be so clear that no reasonable person could fail to accept it. If the defendant offers no explanation, the court can direct a verdict for the plaintiff if the inference is so strong that reasonable jurors could not reach any other conclusion. Where the jury considers the question of negligence, it can decide that the facts do not logically lead to an inference of the defendant's negligence, even if the defendant did not offer any evidence in her defense. If the defendant presents evidence that makes it unlikely that she has acted negligently, the plaintiff will lose his case unless he can rebut the evidence, since such evidence destroys the inference of negligence created by *res ipsa*.

A minority of courts hold that *res ipsa* creates a rebuttable presumption of negligence. Unless the defendant offers sufficient evidence to contradict it, the court must direct a verdict for the plaintiff. Some states have gone as far as to shift the burden of proof to the defendant, requiring her to introduce evidence of greater weight than that of the plaintiff.

RES JUDICATA 📖 [*Latin, A thing adjudged.*] A rule that a final JUDGMENT on the MERITS by a court having JURISDICTION is conclusive between the parties to a suit as to all matters that were litigated or that could have been litigated in that suit. 📖

The U.S. legal system places a high value on allowing a party to litigate a civil lawsuit for money DAMAGES only once. U.S. courts employ the rule of res judicata to prevent a dissatisfied party from trying to litigate the issue a second time.

Res judicata will be applied to a pending lawsuit if several facts can be established by the party asserting the res judicata defense. First, the party must show that a final judgment on the merits of the case had been entered by a court having jurisdiction over the matter. This means that a FINAL DECISION in the first lawsuit was based on the factual and legal disputes between the parties rather than a procedural defect, such as the failure to serve the defendant with legal process.

Once a court makes a final decision, it enters a final judgment in the case. The judgment recites pertinent data about the case, such as the names of the PARTIES, the fact that a jury VERDICT was rendered, and the disposition made. The judgment is filed with the COURT ADMINISTRATOR for that judicial jurisdiction.

The party asserting res judicata, having introduced a final judgment on the merits, must then show that the decision in the first lawsuit was conclusive as to the matters in the second suit. For example, assume that the plaintiff in the first lawsuit asserted that she was injured in an auto accident. She sues the driver of the other auto under a theory of NEGLIGENCE. A jury returns a verdict that finds that the defendant was not negligent. The injured driver then files a second lawsuit alleging additional facts that would help her prove that the other driver was negligent. A court would dismiss the second lawsuit under res judicata because the second lawsuit is based on the same CAUSE OF ACTION (negligence) and the same injury claim.

Under the companion rule of COLLATERAL ESTOPPEL, the plaintiff will not be allowed to file a second lawsuit for money damages using a different cause of action or claim. Under collateral estoppel, the parties are precluded from litigating a second lawsuit using a different cause of action based on any issue of fact common to both suits that had been litigated and determined in the first suit. For example, the plaintiff who lost her auto accident case based on a theory of negligence cannot proceed with a second lawsuit based on an allegation that the driver intentionally struck her auto, thus making it an intentional tort cause of action. A court would assert collateral estoppel because the plaintiff could have alleged an intentional tort cause of action in the original COMPLAINT.

The application of res judicata and collateral estoppel produces finality for the parties and promotes judicial economy. Parties know that when final judgment is entered and all APPEALS are exhausted, the case is over and the decision will be binding on all issues determined in the lawsuit.

RESOLUTION 📖 The official expression of the opinion or will of a LEGISLATIVE body. 📖

The practice of submitting and voting on resolutions is a typical part of business in Congress, state legislatures, and other public assemblies. These bodies use resolutions for two purposes. First, resolutions express their consensus on matters of PUBLIC POLICY: lawmakers routinely deliver criticism or support on a broad range of social issues, legal rights, court opinions, and even decisions by the EXECUTIVE BRANCH. Second, they pass resolutions for internal, administrative purposes. Resolutions are not laws; they differ fundamentally in their purpose. However, under certain circumstances resolutions can have the effect of LAW.

In all legislative bodies, the process leading to a resolution begins with a lawmaker making a formal proposal called a *motion*. The rules of the legislative body determine how much support must be given to the MOTION before it can be put to a general vote. The rules also specify what number of votes the resolution must attract to be passed. If successful it becomes the official position of the legislative body.

As a spontaneous expression of opinion, a resolution is intended to be timely and to have a temporary effect. Typically resolutions are used when passage of a law is unnecessary or unfeasible. In many cases relevant laws already exist. The resolution merely asserts an opinion that lawmakers want to emphasize. Thus, for example, state and federal laws already criminalize illicit drugs, but lawmakers have frequently passed resolutions decrying illegal drug use. Political frustration sometimes leads lawmakers to declare their opposition to laws that they cannot change. Additionally, resolutions are common in times of emergency. War commonly brings resolutions in support of the nation's armed forces and the president (who, at other times, can be the subject of critical resolutions).

When resolutions are mere expressions of opinion, they differ fundamentally from laws. In essence, laws are intended to permanently direct and control matters applying to persons or issues in general; moreover, they are enforceable. By contrast, resolutions expressing the views of lawmakers are limited to a specific issue or event. They are neither intended to be permanent nor to be enforceable. Nor do they carry the weight of COURT OPINIONS. In a certain respect, they resemble the opinions expressed by a newspaper on its editorial page, but they are nonetheless indicative of the ideas and values of elected representatives and, as such, commonly mirror the outlook of voters.

In addition to delivering statements for public consumption, resolutions also play an important role in the administration of legislatures. Lawmakers pass resolutions to control internal rules on matters such as voting and conduct. Typically legislatures also use them to conduct housekeeping: resolutions can thank a member for service to the LEGISLATURE or criticize him or her for disservice. The latter form of resolution is known as *censure*, a rarely used formal process by which the legislature as a whole votes on whether to denounce a member for misdeeds.

Either house of a legislature can issue its own resolutions. When both houses adopt the same motion, it is called a *joint resolution*. Besides carrying the greater force of unanimity, the JOINT RESOLUTION also has a specific legal value in state and federal government. When such a resolution has been approved by the president or a chief executive—or passed with the president's approval—it has the effect of law. In some states a joint resolution is treated as a BILL. It can become a law if it is properly passed and signed by the chief executive officer. In Congress a related form of action is the *concurrent resolution*: it is passed in the form of a resolution of one house with the other house in agreement. Unlike a joint resolution, a CONCURRENT RESOLUTION does not require the approval of the president.

See also CONGRESS OF THE UNITED STATES; LEGISLATION.

RESPONDEAT SUPERIOR 📖 [*Latin, Let the master answer.*] A COMMON-LAW doctrine that makes an employer liable for the actions of an employee when the actions take place within the SCOPE OF EMPLOYMENT. 📖

The common-law doctrine of *respondeat superior* was established in seventeenth-century England to define the legal LIABILITY of an employer for the actions of an employee. The doctrine was adopted in the United States and has been a fixture of AGENCY law. It provides a better chance for an injured party to actually recover DAMAGES, because under *respondeat superior* the employer is liable for the injuries caused by an employee who is working within the scope of his employment relationship.

The legal relationship between an employer and an employee is called agency. The employer is called the PRINCIPAL when engaging someone to act for him. The person who does the work for the employer is called the AGENT. The theory behind *respondeat superior* is that the principal controls the agent's behavior and must then assume some responsibility for the agent's actions.

An employee is an agent for her employer to the extent that the employee is authorized to act for the employer and is partially entrusted with the employer's business. The employer controls, or has a right to control, the time, place, and method of doing work. When the facts show that an employer-employee (principal-agent) relationship exists, the employer can be held responsible for the injuries caused by the employee in the course of employment.

In general, employee conduct that bears some relationship to the work will usually be considered within the scope of employment. The question whether an employee was acting within the scope of employment at the time of the event depends on the particular facts of the case. A court may consider the employee's job description or assigned duties, the time, place, and purpose of the employee's act, the extent to which the employee's actions conformed to what she was hired to do, and whether such an occurrence could reasonably have been expected.

An employee is not necessarily acting outside the scope of employment merely because she does something that she should not do. An employer cannot disclaim liability simply by showing that the employee had been directed not to do what she did. A forbidden act is within the scope of employment for purposes of *respondeat superior* if it is necessary to accomplish an assigned task or if it might reasonably be expected that an employee would perform it.

Relatively minor deviations from the acts necessary to do assigned work usually will not be outside the scope of employment. Personal acts such as visiting the bathroom, smoking, or getting a cup of coffee are ordinarily within the scope of employment, even though they do not directly entail work. When an employee substantially departs from the work routine by engaging in a FROLIC—an activity solely for the employee's benefit—the employee is not acting within the scope of her employment.

An employer is liable for harm done by the employee within the scope of employment, whether the act was accidental or reckless. The employer is even responsible for intentional wrongs if they are committed, at least in part, on the employer's behalf. For example, a bill collector who commits ASSAULT AND BATTERY to extract an overdue payment subjects the employer to legal liability.

Where the employer is someone who legally owes a duty of special care and protection, such as a COMMON CARRIER (airplane, bus, passenger train), motel owner, or a hospital, the employer

When Is an Employee on the Job?

The crucial question in a respondeat superior claim is whether the employee was acting within the *scope of employment:* Was the employee involved in some activity related to the job? In 1991 the Supreme Court of Virginia decided a case, *Sayles v. Piccadilly Cafeterias, Inc.,* 242 Va. 328, 410 S.E.2d 632, that illustrates how difficult answering this question can sometimes be.

The case began with a Christmas Eve accident in 1987. Charles Sayles was a passenger in an automobile hit by another car, driven by Stephen Belcastro. Both men were leaving the Christmas party held on the premises of their company, Piccadilly Cafeterias, Inc, of Richmond, Virginia. Belcastro had become intoxicated at the party and, later, explained that he was "fooling around" when he drove his car into the left-hand lane of the road, lost control, and struck the other car, injuring Sayles.

Because Belcastro was intoxicated as a result of having drinks provided by their employer at a company-sponsored event, Sayles sued Piccadilly under the doctrine of respondeat superior. The jury returned a verdict in Sayles's favor and awarded him damages of $11.5 million. The trial court set aside the judgment, however, ruling that Belcastro had been acting outside the scope of his employment when the accident occurred.

On appeal, Sayles cited a Virginia appellate case, *Kim v. Sportswear,* 10 Va. App. 460, 393 S.E.2d (1990), from the previous year. *Kim* was a workers' compensation case whose facts were similar: it involved an employee fatally injured while attending a Korean New Year's party sponsored and hosted by the employer. The appellate court had allowed recovery of damages against the employer.

The Supreme Court of Virginia declined to follow *Kim,* however. The court noted first that *Kim* was a workers' compensation case, governed by a statute that is to be "liberally construed in favor of the claimant." The court also made several factual distinctions: employees were expected to attend the party in the *Kim* case, whereas the party in *Sayles* did not carry such expectations. Further, the injury in *Kim* took place on the employer's premises, in contrast to *Sayles,* where the collision did not occur until five minutes after the drivers had left the party. Based on these facts, the *Sayles* court held that Belcastro was not engaged in the business of serving his employer at the time of the accident and therefore the employer could not be held liable.

---

is usually liable to the customer or patient even if the employee acts for purely personal reasons. The theory underlying such liability is that employers should not hire dangerous people and expose the public to a risk while the employee is under the employer's supervision.

The employer may also be liable for her own actions, such as in hiring a diagnosed psychopath to be an armed guard. An employer, therefore, can be liable for her own carelessness and as a principal whose employee is an agent.

These rules do not allow the employee to evade responsibility for harm she has caused. Injured parties generally sue both the employee and employer, but because the employee usually is unable to afford to pay the amount of damages awarded in a lawsuit, the employer is the party who is more likely to pay.

See also EMPLOYMENT LAW.

RESPONDENT 📖 In EQUITY practice, the party who answers a BILL or other proceeding in equity. The party against whom an APPEAL or MOTION, an application for a court order, is instituted and who is required to answer in order to protect his or her interests. 📖

RESPONSIVE PLEADING 📖 A formal declaration by a party in reply to a prior declaration by an opponent. 📖

Before a lawsuit goes to trial, each party makes a series of formal written declarations to the court. These declarations are called *pleadings.* Generally, they consist of factual CLAIMS, ALLEGATIONS, and legal DEFENSES; the parties assert their respective versions of what happened and how they want the court to rule. Typically, this involves the plaintiff filing a COMPLAINT and the defendant responding with an ANSWER. This process can occur several times, depending on the complexity of the case. For example, a party may amend its pleadings, which in turn allows the opposing party to answer the amended pleading. When the answers respond to the factual assertions of an opponent's prior PLEADING, for example, by denying them, they are called *responsive pleadings.* This process is also known as *joining issue.*

The distinguishing feature of a responsive pleading is that it replies to the MERITS of the allegations raised by an opposing party. By contrast, parties may choose to ignore the substance of an opponent's pleading and ask the court to dismiss the lawsuit on some other grounds, such as the court's lack of JURISDICTION over the suit.

REST To cease motion, exertion, or labor.

In a lawsuit, a party is said to "rest," or "rest her case," when that party indicates that she has produced all the EVIDENCE that she intends to offer at that stage and submits the case either finally, or subject to the right to offer rebutting evidence after her opponent has introduced her evidence.

RESTATEMENT OF LAW A series of volumes regarded as an authoritative work of legal scholarship prepared by the authors, scholars, and members of the judiciary who comprise the American Law Institute (ALI), which presents a survey of a general area of the law and the changes that have occurred therein.

Restatements are published in the areas of CONTRACTS, TORTS, AGENCY, TRUSTS, conflict of laws, JUDGMENTS, PROPERTY, SECURITY, and RESTITUTION. They set out the general COMMON LAW, including not only that developed by judicial decisions but also that which has grown from the judicial application of statutes that have been in force for many years. A restatement titled *Foreign Relations Law of the United States* summarizes U.S. law and practice in international relations.

Restatements are sources of SECONDARY AUTHORITY to be cited in the support or defense of a particular claim made in a lawsuit. Although not legally binding upon the courts, restatements are effective in persuading a court to accept an argument advanced in an ACTION. They are divided into sections, each beginning with a general statement of a legal principle accompanied by explanatory text. The discussion is illustrated with particular cases and variations used as examples of the operation of the principle. When new developments occur in a particular area, a subsequent edition of the restatement is prepared and published. The restatements have their own individual indexes, and a single general index for all the volumes also exists. A glossary contains definitions of significant words appearing in the text.

See also SHEPARD'S CITATIONS.

RESTITUTION In the context of CRIMINAL LAW, state programs under which an offender is required, as a condition of his or her sentence, to repay money or donate services to the victim or society; with respect to maritime law, the restoration of articles lost by jettison, done when the remainder of the cargo has been saved, at the general charge of the owners of the

cargo; in the law of torts, or civil wrongs, a measure of DAMAGES; in regard to CONTRACT law, the restoration of a party injured by a breach of contract to the position that party occupied before she or he entered the contract.

The general term *restitution* describes the act of restoration. The term is used in different areas of the law but carries the same meaning throughout.

The basic purpose of restitution is to achieve fairness and prevent the UNJUST ENRICHMENT of a party. Restitution is used in contractual situations where one party has conferred a benefit on another party but cannot collect payment because the contract is defective or no contract exists. For instance, assume that a person builds a barn on the property of another person. Assume further that the structure is not erected pursuant to a contract or agreement and that the owner of the property on which the barn sits refuses to pay the builder for the barn. Despite the absence of a contract, a court can order the owner to pay the builder the cost of the labor and materials under the doctrine of restitution.

Courts in seventeenth century England first developed the doctrine of restitution as a contractual REMEDY. The concept migrated to courts in the United States, and it has since expanded beyond its original contractual roots. Courts now apply restitution in the areas of maritime or admiralty law, criminal law, and torts. In admiralty law restitution may be ordered when a shipping crew must throw goods overboard to keep the ship afloat. In such a case the owner of the jettisoned goods may gain some recovery for the goods from the owners of the other cargo under the doctrine of restitution.

Convicted criminals and juvenile offenders ordered to provide restitution, a payback to those victimized by their crimes, may work to earn money through various state programs designed for this purpose.

AP/WIDE WORLD PHOTOS

In criminal law restitution is a regular feature in the sentences of criminal defendants. Restitution in the criminal arena refers to an affirmative performance by the defendant that benefits either the victim of the crime or the general public. If a victim can be identified, a judge will order the defendant to make restitution to the victim. For example, if a defendant is convicted of stealing a person's stereo, the defendant may be sentenced to reimburse the victim for the value of the stereo, in addition to punishment such as jail time and monetary fines.

Courts try to fashion the restitution of a criminal defendant according to the crime committed. For example, a defendant convicted of solicitation of PROSTITUTION may be ordered to perform work for a local shelter for battered women as a form of restitution to the general public.

In TORT LAW restitution applies to the measure of damages required to restore the plaintiff to the position he or she held prior to the commission of the tort. For example, if a person is injured by another person, the injured party may collect medical expenses and lost wages as restitutionary damages. Other civil damages are distinct from restitutionary damages because they are not based on the amount required to restore the injured party to his or her former status. PUNITIVE DAMAGES, for example, are damages assessed against a civil defendant for the purpose of punishing the defendant's conduct, not to provide restitution.

See also ADMIRALTY AND MARITIME LAW; SENTENCING.

RESTORATIVE JUSTICE ▣ A philosophical framework and a series of programs for the criminal justice system that emphasize the need to repair the harm done to crime victims through a process of negotiation, MEDIATION, victim empowerment, and REPARATION. ▣

The U.S. criminal justice system historically has employed two models for dealing with crime and criminals. The retribution model emphasizes deterrence and punishment through the adversarial criminal justice process, and the REHABILITATION model emphasizes the need for society to assist criminals in changing their attitudes and behavior. Since the 1970s, however, a third model, called restorative justice, has begun to find acceptance in many U.S. communities. Restorative justice emphasizes an equal concern for crime victims and offenders, while de-emphasizing the importance of coercion. It also seeks to focus on the harm done to persons and relationships rather than on the violation of a law. Beyond its philosophical framework, the restorative justice model includes a number of programs for addressing the needs of crime victims, the community, and offenders.

Restorative justice began in Canada in the mid-1970s as an idea for victim-offender reconciliation. Offenders were brought to their victims' homes to see and hear how their crimes had affected the victims and the victims' families and communities. The Mennonite Church was at the forefront of the restorative justice movement, emphasizing Christian principles of personal salvation and peacemaking. Though restorative justice became more secularized in the 1980s and 1990s, many of its core principles are based on Christianity's belief in forgiveness and healing.

Originally viewed as a fringe idea, restorative justice developed respectability in the 1990s, in part because the retribution model had proved to be an expensive and seemingly ineffective way of dealing with crime in the United States. Proponents of restorative justice argue that it is a clear alternative to retribution, emphasizing the need for community involvement in addressing criminal behavior.

There are many programs and ideas associated with restorative justice. Several hundred communities have adopted the Victim Offender Reconciliation Program (VORP), which brings the victim and the offender together to talk about the crime and its impact on the victim and to mediate a solution acceptable to both parties. In a VORP mediation, the offender recognizes the injustice he has committed and negotiates a plan to restore the victim and repair the damage. In addition to seeking financial RESTITUTION for the victim, VORP attempts to heal the victim's emotional wounds and to impress upon the offender the consequences of the crime and the need to change behavior.

Ideally, restorative justice programs such as VORP rely on cooperation rather than coercion to make the offender feel accountable for his actions. However, coercion may be used if the goal is to encourage the offender to cooperate.

Other restorative justice programs include community service options for offenders, often with the input of crime victims; comprehensive victim services; and community advisory boards on crimes that address situations that promote crime.

A prime component of restorative justice is restitution to crime victims. For example, if an offender vandalizes a car, she must pay for the repairs. Restitution has also become part of the retribution model of justice as well, with courts making restitution to the victim along with sentencing the offender to jail or imposing a fine. In restorative justice, restitution is part of a larger goal to restore the crime victim's loss and to impress upon the offender the destructive aspects of crime.

See also SENTENCING; VICTIMS OF CRIME.

RESTRAINING ORDER 📖 A command of the court issued upon the filing of an application for an INJUNCTION, prohibiting the defendant from performing a threatened act until a HEARING on the application can be held. 📖

A restraining order is an official command issued by a court to refrain from certain activity. Restraining orders are sought by plaintiffs in a wide variety of instances for the same reason: the plaintiff wishes to prevent the defendant from doing something that he or she has threatened. Restraining orders are used in a variety of contexts, including employment disputes, COPYRIGHT infringement, and cases of harassment, domestic abuse, and STALKING. All restraining orders begin with an application to the court, which decides the merits of the request by using a traditional test. Limited in their duration and effect, restraining orders are distinguished from the more lasting form of court intervention called an injunction. Generally they are sought as a form of immediate relief while a plaintiff pursues a permanent injunction.

A court submits a request for a restraining order to one of several tests. These tests vary slightly across different JURISDICTIONS, but generally they involve the analysis of four separate factors: (1) whether the moving party will suffer IRREPARABLE INJURY if the relief is not granted; (2) whether the moving party is likely to succeed on the MERITS of the case; (3) whether the opposing party will be harmed more than the moving party is helped; and (4) whether granting the relief is in the PUBLIC INTEREST.

Usually, restraining orders are not permanent. They exist because of the need for immediate relief: the plaintiff requires fast action from the court to prevent injury. Seeking a permanent injunction can take months or years because it involves a full hearing, but the process of obtaining a restraining order can take a matter of days or weeks. For even faster relief, moving parties can seek a TEMPORARY RESTRAINING ORDER (TRO). These are often issued EX PARTE, meaning that only the moving party is

A sample temporary restraining order

[*Title of Court and Cause*]

Upon the Complaint of _____ and the affidavit of _____ , it is ORDERED that the defendants show cause before this Court at _____ , _____ on _____ , 19 ____ , at _____ o'clock ____ .M. or as soon thereafter as counsel can be heard, why a preliminary injunction should not issue herein; and

It appearing to the court that defendants will take action which would prevent plaintiff from and interfere with her carrying out her duties as a teacher at _____ Junior High School by discharging plaintiff from such employment and that immediate and irreparable injury, loss, and damage will result to plaintiff before notice can be served and the hearing had on plaintiff's Motion for Preliminary Injunction defendants should be required by reason of the likelihood of immediate action being taken by the defendants which would disturb the present situation of the parties; it is further

ORDERED that the defendants, their agents, employees, servants, or any person acting in their behalf, be restrained from taking any action which would prevent plaintiff or interfere with her carrying out her duties as a teacher at _____ Junior High School or from discharging plaintiff from employment.

ORDERED that service of this order to show cause and temporary restraining order together with the Motion for Preliminary Injunction and Affidavit, as well as the Complaint, on defendants on or before _____ , 19 ____ , at _____ o'clock ____ .M., be deemed sufficient service.

Issued at _____ , ____ .M., this _____ day of _____ , 19 ____ .

_____
United States District Judge.

present in court. The TRO usually lasts only until an injunctive hearing involving both parties can be held.

Harassment of an individual can result in a permanent restraining order. This command of the court is also called a PROTECTIVE ORDER. All states permit individuals to seek a restraining order when they are subjected to harassment by another individual or organization, typically involving behavior such as repeated, intrusive, and unwanted acts. Application for such an order usually is made to the district court. If granted, it prohibits the party named from initiating any contact with the protected party. In the 1990s most states passed anti-stalking laws designed to protect women from criminal harassment by men. These laws generally require that a plaintiff first secure a restraining order before criminal charges can be filed.

RESTRAINT OF TRADE 📖 CONTRACTS or combinations that tend, or are designed, to eliminate or stifle competition, create a MONOPOLY, artificially maintain prices, or otherwise hamper or obstruct the course of trade as it would be carried on if it were left to the control of natural economic forces. 📖

As used in the SHERMAN ANTI-TRUST ACT (15 U.S.C.A. § 1 et seq.), unreasonable restraints of trade are illegal PER SE and interfere with free competition in business and commercial transactions. Such restraint tends to restrict production, affect prices, or otherwise control the market to the detriment of purchasers or consumers of goods and services. A restraint of trade that is ordinarily reasonable can be rendered unreasonable if it is accompanied by a specific intent to achieve the equivalent of a forbidden restraint.

See also ANTITRUST LAW; COMBINATION IN RESTRAINT OF TRADE.

RESTRICTIVE COVENANT 📖 A provision in a DEED limiting the use of the PROPERTY and prohibiting certain uses. A clause in CONTRACTS of PARTNERSHIP and employment prohibiting a contracting party from engaging in similar employment for a specified period of time within a certain geographical area. 📖

A COVENANT is a type of contractual arrangement. A restrictive covenant is a clause in a deed or LEASE to REAL PROPERTY that limits what the owner of the land or lease can do with the property. Restrictive covenants allow surrounding property owners, who have similar covenants in their deeds, to enforce the terms of the covenants in a court of law. They are intended to enhance property values by controlling development.

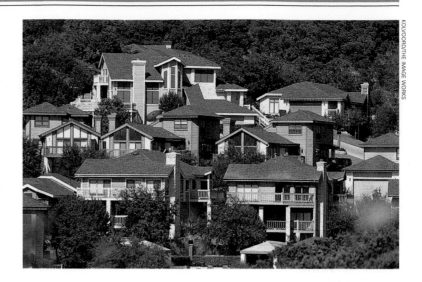

KOLVOORD/THE IMAGE WORKS

Restrictive covenants, provisions in land deeds that limit the use of the property, are common in residential areas, such as a limitation that the land may only be used for a single family dwelling.

Land developers typically use restrictive covenants when they subdivide property for residential developments. A land developer, after platting the subdivision into lots, blocks, and streets, will impose certain limitations on the use of the lots in the development. These may include a provision restricting construction to single-family dwellings with no detached outbuildings, as well as specifying that the dwellings are to be built at least a specified distance from the street and from the side and back lot lines, commonly called a "set back" requirement. Another common restrictive covenant specifies a minimum square footage for dwellings. There may be a variety of other restrictive covenants that seek to control the way the development looks and is maintained. These covenants are filed with the approved PLAT.

A person who purchases a lot in a development with restrictive covenants must honor the limitations. When the purchaser resells the lot to a buyer, the new owner will take the property subject to the restrictive covenants, because the covenants are said to "run with the land."

If a person violates or attempts to violate one or more of the covenants, a person who is benefited by the covenants, usually an adjacent property owner, may sue to enforce the restrictions. Courts generally strictly construe restrictive covenants to allow a landowner to use her land for any purpose that is not specifically prohibited by the restrictive covenants or by the local government. Therefore, if a developer wants to restrict a subdivision to single-family residences, the developer must state "single family residential" rather than "residential" in the covenant.

Restrictive covenants at one time were used

to prevent minorities from moving into residential neighborhoods. A group of homeowners would agree not to sell or rent their homes to African Americans, Jews, and other minorities by including this restriction in their REAL ESTATE deeds. Until 1948 it was thought that this form of private discrimination was legal because the state was not involved. However, in *Shelley v. Kraemer*, 334 U.S. 1, 68 S. Ct. 836, 92 L. Ed. 1161 (1948), the U.S. Supreme Court held such covenants to be unenforceable in state courts because any such enforcement would amount to state action in contravention of the FOURTEENTH AMENDMENT to the U.S. Constitution. For a state court to enforce such an agreement would foster a perception that the state approved of racially restrictive covenants. Although this kind of restrictive covenant is no longer judicially enforceable, racial restrictions are still contained in some deeds.

Apart from real estate law, restrictive covenants may be used in partnership agreements or employment contracts to protect a business if a partner or employee leaves. For example, a life insurance company may require a prospective employee to sign an employment contract in which the employee agrees not to sell life insurance in that geographical area for a specified period of time after leaving the company. If the time and geographical restrictions are reasonable, a court may enforce the restrictions. Some restrictive covenants may be so unfair, however, that a court will declare them contrary to PUBLIC POLICY and make them legally unenforceable.

CROSS-REFERENCES

Employment Law; Land-Use Control; Running with the Land; Zoning.

RESTRICTIVE INDORSEMENT 📖 The act of a PAYEE or other holder of an instrument, such as a CHECK, that consists of signing his or her name upon the back of the instrument in order to transfer it to another and wording the SIGNATURE in such a manner as to bar the further negotiability of the instrument. 📖

For example, the phrases *Pay the contents to A only*, or *to A for my use*, are restrictive indorsements and terminate the transferability of the document.

An indorsement is restrictive if it (1) is conditional; (2) purports to proscribe further transfer of the instrument; (3) includes the terms *for collection, for deposit, pay any bank*, or similar terms denoting a purpose of deposit or collection; or (4) states that it is for the benefit or use of the indorser—the one who signs the back of the instrument in order to transfer it—or of another person.

RESULTING TRUST 📖 An arrangement whereby one person holds property for the benefit of another, which is implied by a court in certain cases where a person transfers property to another and gives him or her legal TITLE to it but does not intend him or her to have an equitable or BENEFICIAL INTEREST in the property. 📖

Since this beneficial interest is not given to anyone else, it is said to "result" to the person who transferred the property.

A resulting trust arises when an express trust fails. A SETTLOR, one who creates a TRUST, transfers his property to a TRUSTEE, one appointed, or required by law, to execute a trust, to hold in trust for a BENEFICIARY, one who profits from the act of another. If, without the settlor's knowledge, the beneficiary died before the trust was created, the express trust would fail for want of a beneficiary. The trustee holds the property in resulting trust for the settlor.

When an express trust does not use or exhaust all the trust property, a resulting trust arises. For example, the settlor transfers $200,000 in trust to pay the beneficiary during her lifetime $2,000 a month from PRINCIPAL, trust property, as opposed to income generated by investment of the principal. No other disposition is specified. The beneficiary dies after having received $20,000. The trustee holds the unexpended funds in a resulting trust for the settlor.

A purchase money resulting trust arises when one person purchases and pays for property and the name of another person is on the title. For example, a person purchases a farm for $100,000 and directs the seller to make the DEED out to a third person. Nothing further appears concerning the purchaser's intention, and no relationship exists between the purchaser and the third person. In this situation, a resulting trust is created. The purchaser's intention is inferred from the absence of expressed intention that she intends the third person to have an interest in the farm. This occurs because a person usually does not intend to dispose of property without receiving something in return for it, unless she makes an express statement to the contrary, such as announcing an intention to make a GIFT or loan. If the purchaser is the spouse or parent of the third person, which is not the case here, it is presumed that a gift is intended. In this case, the third person holds a purchase money resulting trust for the purchaser.

A purchase money resulting trust does not arise, however, if the person who pays the purchase price manifests an intention that no resulting trust should arise. Purchase money resulting trusts have been abolished or restricted in a number of states.

The resulting trust attempts to dispose of the property in the manner the person who transferred it would have wanted if he had anticipated the situation. The court will order that the person with legal title to the trust property hold it in a resulting trust for the person who transferred it. When a CHARITABLE TRUST—a trust designed for the benefit of a class or the public generally—fails, a resulting trust will be invoked only if the doctrine of CY PRES is deemed not to apply. This doctrine implements the intention of a person as nearly as possible when giving the intent literal effect would be illegal or impossible.

RETAINER 📖 A contract between ATTORNEY and CLIENT specifying the nature of the services to be rendered and the cost of the services. 📖

Retainer also denotes the fee that the client pays when employing an attorney to act on her behalf. When a client retains an attorney to act for her, the client thereby prevents the attorney from acting for an adversary.

A *right to retainer* refers to the authority by which the executor or administrator of the estate of a deceased person reserves out of the ASSETS an amount sufficient to pay any DEBT due to him from the deceased in priority to the other CREDITORS whose debts are of equal degree.

See also EXECUTORS AND ADMINISTRATORS.

RETALIATORY EVICTION 📖 The act of a LANDLORD in ejecting or attempting to eject a TENANT from the rented premises, or in refusing to renew a LEASE, because of the tenant's complaints or participation in a tenant's union or in similar activities with which the landlord is not in accord. 📖

In some states, such retaliation will bar the landlord from enforcing normal eviction REMEDIES against the tenant.

See also LANDLORD AND TENANT.

RETORSION 📖 A phrase used in INTERNATIONAL LAW to describe retaliatory action taken by one foreign government against another for the stringent or harsh regulation or treatment of its citizens who are within the geographical boundaries of the foreign country. 📖

The typical methods of retorsion are the use of comparably severe measures against citizens of the foreign nation found within the borders of the retaliating nation.

RETRACTION 📖 In the law of DEFAMATION, a formal recanting of the libelous or slanderous material. 📖

Retraction is not a DEFENSE to defamation, but under certain circumstances, it is admissible in mitigation of DAMAGES.

See also LIBEL AND SLANDER.

RETRO 📖 [*Latin, Back; backward; behind.*] A prefix used to designate a prior condition or time. 📖

RETROACTIVE 📖 Having reference to things that happened in the past, prior to the occurrence of the act in question. 📖

A retroactive or retrospective law is one that takes away or impairs vested rights acquired under existing laws, creates new obligations, imposes new duties, or attaches a new and different legal effect to transactions or considerations already past. COMMON-LAW principles do not favor the retroactive effect of laws in the majority of cases, and canons of legislative CONSTRUCTION presume that legislation is not intended as retroactive unless its language expressly makes it retroactive.

Retroactive criminal laws that increase punishment for acts committed prior to their enactments are deemed EX POST FACTO laws and are unenforceable because they violate Article I, Section 9, Clause 3, and Section 10, Clause 1, of the U.S. Constitution and comparable provisions of state constitutions.

RETURN 📖 To bring, carry, or send back; to restore, redeliver, or replace in the custody of someone. Merchandise brought back to a seller for credit or a refund. The profit made on a sale; the income from an investment. A schedule of information required by some governmental agencies, such as the TAX RETURN that must be submitted to the INTERNAL REVENUE SERVICE.

The official report made by a court, body of magistrates, or other official board charged with counting votes cast in an election. The redelivery of a WRIT, notice, or other form of legal process to the court after its proper service on the defendant or after it cannot be served. 📖

For example, the Federal Rules of Civil Procedure require a plaintiff to begin an ACTION in FEDERAL COURT by preparing a COMPLAINT and giving it to the court. Then the clerk of the court issues a SUMMONS and delivers the summons and complaint to a U.S. MARSHAL or a DEPUTY, unless the court designates someone else. That person must take the papers, called legal process, and serve them on the named defendant. The PROCESS SERVER must promptly report back to the court the circumstances of the service or the failure to serve the papers.

This report with the process server's signature on it is called the return of service. It recites facts to demonstrate that the defendant has actually been given notice that she is required to appear in court. The failure to make a proper return does not make the service invalid or defeat its effectiveness for starting the lawsuit, but it can be grounds for disciplining the process server. The return is important to the court because it is proof that service was properly made on the correct person and that the action has been legally commenced.

See also SERVICE OF PROCESS.

RETURN DAY 📖 The day on which votes are counted and the election results announced. The day named in a WRIT or other form of legal process as the date when the response to that paper must be made.

The day on which an officer, such as a U.S. MARSHAL, must file proof with the court that he or she has served legal process on a defendant or that he or she cannot serve the papers. The statement is made under OATH and is called the RETURN or return of process. 📖

For example, a defendant may make a motion in separate papers challenging some action taken by the plaintiff during pretrial DISCOVERY. In the motion papers, the defendant must specify the day when the plaintiff must deliver papers if he objects to the relief sought by the defendant. That date is called the return day, or return date.

REVENUE 📖 Return or profit such as the annual or periodic rents, profits, interest, or income from any type of real or personal PROPERTY, received by an individual, a CORPORATION, or a government. 📖

Public revenues are the sources of income that a government collects and receives into its treasury and appropriates for the payment of its expenses.

REVERSE 📖 To overthrow, invalidate, repeal, or revoke. 📖

For example, an appeals court reverses the JUDGMENT, decree, or sentence of a lower court either by substituting its own decision or by returning the case to the lower court with instructions for a new trial.

REVERSION 📖 Any future interest kept by a person who transfers property to another. 📖

A reversion occurs when a PROPERTY owner makes an effective transfer of property to another but retains some future right to the property. For example, if Sara transfers a piece of property to Shane for life, Shane has the use of the property for the rest of his life. Upon his death, the property reverts, or goes back, to Sara, or if Sara has died, it goes to her HEIRS. Shane's interest in the property, in this example, is a LIFE ESTATE. Sara's ownership interest during Shane's life, and her right or the right of her heirs to take back the property upon Shane's death, are called reversionary interests.

A reversion differs from a REMAINDER because a reversion arises through the OPERATION OF LAW rather than by act of the parties. A remainder is a future interest that is created in some person other than the GRANTOR or transferor, whereas a reversion creates a future interest in the grantor or his or her heirs. If Sara's transfer had been "to Shane for life, then to Lily," Lily's interest would be a remainder.

See also ESTATE.

REVERTER, POSSIBILITY OF 📖 A CONTINGENT future interest in REAL PROPERTY that a GRANTOR of a determinable fee possesses after he or she has conveyed property. 📖

The *possibility of reverter* arises when the grantor of real property has conveyed land subject to the possibility that the ESTATE will return to her or to her heirs if a certain specified limitation occurs. For example, if A, owner of BLACKACRE in FEE SIMPLE, makes the CONVEYANCE, "To B and B's heirs as long as the land is used for church purposes," then A has a possibility of reverter. A is entitled to the return of the land if B and B's heirs do not use the land for the designated purpose.

REVIEW 📖 To reexamine judicially or administratively; a judicial reconsideration for purposes of correction, for example, the examination of a case by an APPELLATE COURT. 📖

A BILL OF REVIEW is a proceeding in EQUITY instituted for the purpose of reversing or correcting the prior JUDGMENT of the trial court after the judgment has become final.

REVISED STATUTES 📖 A body of statutes that have been revised, collected, arranged in order, and reenacted as a whole. The legal title of the collection of compiled laws of the United States, as well as some of the individual states. 📖

REVIVAL OF AN ACTION 📖 A mechanism of legal PROCEDURE that operates at the PLEADING stage of litigation to subsequently renew an action that has been abated, terminated, or suspended for reasons other than the MERITS of the CLAIM. 📖

Lawsuits abate primarily because of the death of a party. In the past, under COMMON LAW, a lawsuit terminated automatically whenever a party died. This rule was part of the substance of the law involved and was not merely a matter of procedure. Whether the CAUSE OF ACTION abated depended on whether the lawsuit was considered personal to the parties. CONTRACT and PROPERTY cases were thought to involve issues separate from the parties themselves. They were not personal and did not necessarily end on the death of a party. PERSONAL INJURY cases, including claims not only for physical assault or negligent injuries inflicted on the body but also other injuries to the person, such as libel, slander, and MALICIOUS PROSECUTION, were considered personal and abated when one of the parties died.

Today most lawsuits do not abate. Statutes permit the revival of a lawsuit that was pending when a party died. PERSONAL REPRESENTATIVES, such as EXECUTORS AND ADMINISTRATORS, may be substituted for the deceased party, and the lawsuit may continue. These are not the same as survival statutes, which permit the maintenance of a lawsuit on behalf of a person who has died, whether it began before the deceased's death or not. A lawsuit can be revived only if the underlying cause of action, the ground for the suit, continues to have a legal existence after the party's death. Revival statutes vary from state to state.

Matrimonial actions do not usually fall within the scope of revival statutes. An action for DIVORCE or separation is considered entirely personal and generally cannot be maintained after the death of a spouse. Different states sometimes make exceptions to settle certain questions of property ownership. The ANNULMENT of a marriage after the death of an innocent spouse may be permitted if it is clear that the marriage resulted from FRAUD and the perpetrator of the fraud would inherit property she would otherwise not be allowed to take.

See also ABATEMENT OF AN ACTION.

REVIVE 📖 To renew. 📖

For example, revival is the act of renewing the legal force of a CONTRACT or DEBT, either by acknowledging it or by giving a new promise, when the contract or debt is no longer a sufficient foundation for a lawsuit because it is barred by the running of the STATUTE OF LIMITATIONS.

REVOCATION 📖 The recall of some power or authority that has been granted. 📖

Revocation by the act of a party is intentional and voluntary, such as when a person cancels a power of attorney that he has given or a WILL that he has written. The revocation of a will takes place when a TESTATOR makes a later will containing terms that are inconsistent with the terms of an earlier will, or when the testator destroys the former will.

A revocation by OPERATION OF LAW or CONSTRUCTIVE revocation occurs without regard to the intention of the parties. A power of attorney, therefore, is ordinarily revoked automatically by operation of law upon the death of the PRINCIPAL.

REVOKE 📖 To annul or make VOID by recalling or taking back; to cancel, RESCIND, REPEAL, or REVERSE. 📖

REVOLUTION 📖 A sudden, tumultuous, and radical transformation of an entire system of government, including its legal and political components. 📖

In many instances, revolutions encompass society as a whole, bringing fundamental change to a culture's economic, religious, and institutional framework. Fundamental change that is incrementally wrought over time is more properly considered evolutionary rather than revolutionary. A revolution also should be contrasted with a *coup d'etat*, which generally involves the violent ousting of a particular regime or its leaders, but which otherwise leaves intact the culture's political, legal, and economic infrastructure.

In many ways law and revolution occupy polar extremes in a political system. Law serves as one of the principal edifices upon which social order is built. Revolutions, on the other hand, seek to dismantle the existing social order. Legal systems are established in part to replace private forms of justice, such as self-help and vigilantism, which can lead to endless cycles of revenge. Revolutions, conversely, depend on persons who are willing to take law into their own hands.

At the same time, law can serve as the motivating force behind revolutionary activity. In writing the DECLARATION OF INDEPENDENCE, THOMAS JEFFERSON explained that it had become necessary for the colonies to dissolve their formal ties with Great Britain because the king of England had abused his autocratic power by denying Americans their inalienable rights to life, liberty, and the pursuit of happiness. These rights, Jefferson said, are guaranteed by an unwritten NATURAL LAW. The American Revolution, then, was fought to restore the RULE OF LAW in the United States, which was not fully accomplished until the power of government was subordinated to the will of the people in the state and federal constitutions.

Along these same lines, JOHN LOCKE, in his *Second Treatise of Government* (1690), postulated the right of all citizens to revolt against tyrants who subvert the law and oppress the populace through the wanton use of force and terror.

In a revolution, a sudden and radical transformation of a government, the revolting forces may take control through violence.

Such tyrannical ABUSE OF POWER, Locke said, may be resisted because every person is born with the rights to self-defense and self-preservation, which supersede the laws of a despotic sovereign. However, neither Jefferson nor Locke prescribed a formula to determine when governmental behavior becomes sufficiently despotic to justify revolution.

The traditional meaning of the term *revolution* has been watered down by popular culture. Every day Americans are inundated with talk of revolution. The fitness revolution, the technology revolution, the computer revolution, and the information revolution are just a few examples of the everyday usage of this term. Such common usage has diluted the meaning of revolution to such an extent that it is now virtually synonymous with benign terms such as *change*, *development*, and *progress*.

Yet traditional revolutions are rarely benign. The French Revolution of 1789 is historically associated with the unfettered bloodletting at the guillotine. The twentieth-century revolutions in Russia, Southeast Asia, and Central America were marked by the mass extermination and persecution of political opponents.

These revolutions demonstrate the tension separating power from the rule of law. Following a revolution, members of new regimes are inevitably tempted to "get even" with the leaders of the ousted regime to whom they attribute the commission of horrible acts while in office. Now holding the reins of sovereignty, the new regime has acquired the power to impose an expedient form of justice upon members of the old regime. This form of justice has many faces, including the confiscation of property without a hearing, forcible detention without trial, and the implementation of summary executions.

However, the rule of law requires governments to act in strict accordance with clearly defined and well-established legal procedures and principles. The rule of law disfavors arbitrary and capricious governmental action. Thus, every revolutionary regime faces a similar dilemma: how to make a deposed regime pay for its tyrannical behavior without committing acts of tyranny itself. The identity and ideological direction of a revolutionary regime is often determined by the manner in which this dilemma is resolved.

CROSS-REFERENCES

Anarchism; Communism; Lenin, Vladimir Ilich; Marx, Karl.

REVOLUTIONARY WAR See WAR OF INDEPENDENCE.

REVOLVING CHARGE A type of CREDIT arrangement that permits a buyer or a borrower to purchase merchandise or obtain loans on a continuing basis as long as the outstanding balance of the account does not exceed a certain limit.

Revolving charge agreements are usually made in connection with the use of a bank or a department store credit card. The term *revolving charge* is used interchangeably with the term *revolving credit*.

When all outstanding charges are paid before or on the payment due date, which is usually immediately before the date of the second billing, no interest charge is assessed against the account, although this policy might change in the future. For example, a customer charges $200 in merchandise during the first week in January and receives the statement of her outstanding balance on February 2. If the customer pays the $200 balance in full before March 2, the payment due date, no service charge is added to the account.

When the customer does not wish to pay the outstanding balance in full, she may make monthly installment payments, if the credit agreement so provides. The amount of each payment is determined according to a schedule based on a percentage of the outstanding balance of the account. A monthly interest charge is also added to the unpaid balance, usually at the rate of 1½ percent per month.

Ordinarily each customer has his own LINE OF CREDIT, the maximum amount that the customer is permitted to charge. Once this limit is reached, no additional merchandise can be charged to that account until some payment has been made to reduce the outstanding DEBT.

REWARD 📖 A sum of money or other compensation offered to the public in general, or to a class of persons, for the PERFORMANCE of a special service. 📖

It is commonplace for the police to offer a reward for information leading to the arrest and conviction of an offender, or for a pet owner to post notices in a neighborhood offering a reward for the return of a lost dog or cat. In legal terms, the person promising a reward is offering to enter into a contract with the person who performs the requested action, that is, turning in a criminal or returning a lost pet. Performance will be rewarded with money or some other compensation. Therefore, the legal concepts involving rewards are derived from the law of CONTRACTS.

An actual, valid OFFER must be made to create a contract of reward. The offer is merely a proposal or a conditional PROMISE by the person offering the reward, known legally as the offerer. It is not a consummated contract until the requested action is performed.

The person offering the reward can do so on any terms she wishes, and the terms must be met before the reward can be recovered. The subject matter of the offer can entail the discovery of information leading to the arrest and conviction of a person, the discovery of stolen property and the apprehension of the thief, the return of lost property, or the recovery or rescue of a person.

A PRIZE or PREMIUM can be a valid offer of a reward for exhibits, architectural plans, paintings, the best performance in a tournament, the suggestion of a name, or the achievement of the best time in a race.

Any person, including CORPORATIONS, legally capable of making a contract can bind herself by an offer of reward. Legislatures have the power to offer rewards for acts that will be of public benefit. Legislatures, however, typically empower officers, such as the governor, the U.S. attorney general, or a federal MARSHAL, to offer rewards for certain purposes, such as the apprehension of criminals.

Unless a statute requires the offer to be in writing, the offer of reward can be made orally. An offer can be made by a private contract with a particular person or by an advertisement or public statement on television or radio, or in a newspaper, handbill, or circular.

A contract of reward, like any contract, must be supported by CONSIDERATION, something of value. The consideration that supports the promise of reward is the trouble or inconvenience resulting to the person who has acted on the faith of the promise.

Because an unaccepted offer of reward grants no contractual rights, the offer can be revoked or canceled at any time prior to its acceptance by performance. Once a person has performed or partially performed the requested action, an offer of reward cannot be revoked to deprive a person of compensation. An offer must be revoked either in the way in which it was made or in a manner that gives the REVOCATION the same publicity as the offer. A later offer, in different terms from the first, does not revoke the first offer.

Generally an offer of reward that has no time limit is considered to have been withdrawn after a REASONABLE time. What constitutes a reasonable period of time depends largely on the circumstances under which the offer was made. In some JURISDICTIONS a reward for the discovery of criminal offenders only lapses when the STATUTE OF LIMITATIONS has expired against the crime.

A reward can be claimed only by a person who has complied with the conditions of the offer before it expires or is revoked. Performance can be completed by a third person, such as an AGENT or servant, who is acting on behalf of the claimant's interest.

When the reward is offered for information leading to an arrest and conviction, the return

Reward: Prominent Villain

Rewards have ended countless criminal careers. On occasion, the lure of money has even been enough to entice criminals to turn in their associates. Such was the downfall of the famous nineteenth-century outlaw Jesse James (1847–82).

After the Civil War, James quickly became one of the most notorious bandits on the U.S. frontier. With his older brother Frank, Jesse led the so-called James Gang through several robberies and murders during the 1860s and 1870s. Their daring holdups of banks, stage coaches, and trains made them figures of romantic myth for readers and prime targets for law enforcement posses, which they long managed to evade.

A reward brought James to his end. Having barely escaped with his life after a thwarted bank robbery in Northfield, Minnesota, in 1876 that left two of his gang dead, James hired new outlaws and lived under an alias in Missouri. In 1881 Thomas T. Crittenden, the state's governor, offered a reward of $10,000 for James's capture—dead or alive. One of the new gang members, Robert Ford, contacted the governor, then bided his time. On April 3, 1882, Ford saw his chance in James's house. When the gunslinger laid down his pistols and climbed on a chair to adjust a picture frame, Ford shot him in the head and instantly killed him. What the law had been unable to do, one of the lawless accomplished.

---

of property, the location of a missing person, or for other purposes, the person who furnishes the information is entitled to the reward. This rule applies even if, in the case of arrest, the person does nothing more than disclose the information and others make the physical capture. The informant need not become involved in the prosecution or appear as a WITNESS at the offender's trial to collect the reward.

The information must be adequate and timely for a person to collect a reward. If a criminal has surrendered or the information was already known when the informant provided it, no reward will be given. Likewise, if the information does not lead to the desired end included in the initial offer, such as an arrest and conviction, or the recovery of property, the reward will be denied. However, when the reward is for the detection or discovery of an offender, a conviction is not necessary as long as the discovery or arrest occurs.

When a reward is offered for the apprehension or arrest of a criminal, a personal arrest by the claimant is usually not necessary. The arrest of the wanted person must be lawful, no matter who makes it. Those making an unlawful arrest cannot recover the reward because an agreement for an unlawful arrest is against PUBLIC POLICY and unenforceable. If the offender voluntarily surrenders or is en route to surrender, the captors have not earned the reward.

Generally when a reward is offered for the arrest and conviction of an offender, the person claiming the reward must have caused both the arrest and subsequent conviction because both are conditions of recovery under the contract. The reward in such a case cannot be apportioned between what is due for the arrest and what is due for the conviction.

When lost property is involved, some states have statutes that provide for a reward for the finder or for compensation for the expense of recovering and preserving the property. If only a proportionate share is returned, the finder is entitled to a proportionate part of the reward. When such a statute does not exist, however, a finder has no right to a reward for the return of property to its owner if none has been offered.

If the offered reward is definite and certain, the finder has a LIEN on the property in the amount of the reward until it is paid. A lien is a charge against property to secure the payment of a DEBT or the performance of an obligation. For example, if John offers a reward of $100 for the return of his missing motorcycle and Bob goes looking and finds it, Bob can file a lien for $100 against the motorcycle with the local court if John does not pay him the reward. If the offer is indefinite, such as one that states "liberal reward" for the return of the motorcycle, there is no lien on the property.

Except in the case of statutory rewards, the general rule is that the person who claims the reward must have performed the services knowing of the offer and for the purpose of collecting the reward. For example, if Bob happens to find John's motorcycle in a ditch and returns it to John not knowing that he had offered a $100 reward, Bob cannot claim the $100. This rule is based on the theory that without such knowledge there can be no meeting of the minds, which is essential to the formation of a contract. Knowledge of a statutory remedy is not necessary to entitle the claimant to recover it.

When a reward is offered to the public, anyone who performs the required service can claim and accept the reward, except persons who are under a DUTY to perform such services. A law enforcement officer, therefore, cannot claim a reward if the service performed is within the line and scope of the officer's duty. This prohibition will apply even if the officer performed the service at a time when he was not on duty or was outside his territorial jurisdiction. When, however, an officer acts beyond the scope and line of duty, there is no prohibition in claiming the reward.

A person who aids and abets the commission of a crime has no right to a reward for the arrest of the perpetrator. Similarly a person who purchases stolen property with reasonable grounds for believing it has been stolen cannot receive a reward offered for its return.

See also FINDING LOST GOODS.

REX 📖 [*Latin, The king.*] The phrase used to designate the king as the party prosecuting an accused in a criminal ACTION, such as an action entitled *Rex v. Doe.* 📖

REYNOLDS v. SIMS *Reynolds v. Sims* is a landmark case, 377 U.S. 533, 84 S. Ct. 1362, 12 L. Ed. 2d 506 (1964), in which the U.S. Supreme Court established the principle of ONE PERSON, ONE VOTE based on the Equal Protection Clause of the FOURTEENTH AMENDMENT. As a result of the decision, almost every state had to redraw its legislative districts, and power shifted from rural to urban areas. All subsequent constitutional law on APPORTIONMENT has relied on the principles established in *Reynolds v. Sims.*

Reynolds completed a change in direction by the Supreme Court concerning the apportionment of voting districts. Until 1962 the Court had refused to hear lawsuits that challenged legislative districting, concluding that such issues were POLITICAL QUESTIONS that were not JUSTICIABLE. In 1962 the Court, in *Baker v. Carr,* 369 U.S. 186, 82 S. Ct. 691, 7 L. Ed. 2d 663, reversed course and ruled that state legislative apportionment cases could be reviewed by the FEDERAL COURTS. As a result, lawsuits challenging the constitutionality of the apportionment of legislative districts were filed in many states.

Reynolds involved the apportionment of the Alabama state LEGISLATURE. The facts in the case were common to many states also undergoing court challenges. When the Alabama Constitution of 1901 was ratified, it provided that the legislature should periodically reapportion itself. The legislature ignored this mandate, however, and the legislative districts remained unchanged for sixty years. During that period Alabama, like other states, had seen a dramatic population shift from rural to urban areas. Thus, the Alabama legislature in 1960 was dominated by rural legislators, who were unwilling to reapportion and lose power. The disparities between population and voting strength were staggering. The 1960 census revealed that only about 25 percent of the total population of the state lived in districts represented by a majority of state senators, and counties with only 27.5 percent of the total population elected a majority of state representatives. Population variance ratios of up to 41 to 1 existed in the Senate and up to 16 to 1 in the House. For example, Bullock County with a population of approximately 13,500 was allocated two seats in the Alabama House, while Mobile County with a population of 314,000 was given only three seats.

Faced with these disparities and the unwillingness of the Alabama legislature to reapportion the legislative districts based upon population, a group of citizens filed a lawsuit in federal court. The three-judge panel of federal district judges at first tried to defer to the legislature for a solution. When that failed, the judges implemented a temporary redistricting plan based on population. Alabama challenged the judges' redistricting order in the U.S. Supreme Court.

The Court ignored the claims of Alabama and other states that they should be allowed to apportion their legislative districts as they wished under the concept of FEDERALISM. This concept calls for the federal courts to abstain from making decisions that are the proper province of the states.

Chief Justice EARL WARREN, in his majority opinion, made clear that the Court had no choice but to step in. The Alabama legislature had refused to reapportion itself, leaving the citizens with few viable options to effect the change. Alabama law did not provide for an INITIATIVE procedure that would have permitted voters to decide on reapportionment. A constitutional amendment was also unlikely, as a three-fifths majority in both houses of the legislature would have to approve any proposals. With no effective political remedy, the Court was obligated to examine the issue to determine if Alabama had violated the Fourteenth Amendment's Equal Protection Clause.

The Court recognized that U.S. democracy is based on a representative form of government. The right to vote for a candidate "is the essence of a democratic society, and any restrictions on that right strike at the heart of representative government." The "debasement or dilution" of a person's vote can be just as effective as prohibiting that person from voting.

Warren concluded that minority control over the majority of state legislators could not be sanctioned. He emphasized that "[l]egislators represent people, not trees or acres. Legislators are elected by voters, not farms or cities or economic interests." To permit the minority to have power over the majority would be a violation of the Equal Protection Clause. Diluting the weight of a person's vote because of where that person lived was as invidious a form of DISCRIMINATION as if the dilution had been based on that person's race or financial status. Therefore, the Court would require that "each citizen have an equally effective voice in the election of members of his state legislature."

The Court also rejected Alabama's contention that it should be allowed to apportion its Senate based on the equal representation of units of government, in this case counties, rather than of people. Alabama's argument was based on the so-called federal analogy, a reference to the U.S. Senate, where each state has two seats regardless of population. Warren dismissed this analogy, calling it "irrelevant to state legislative redistricting schemes." He pointed out that the original constitutions of thirty-six states provided that representation in both legislative houses would be based completely, or predominantly, on population. In addition, there was no evidence that the Framers of the U.S. Constitution intended to establish this model for the states. The arrangements for representation in the U.S. House of Representatives and Senate were devised at the Constitutional Convention as a solution to a particular political dilemma.

Having dismissed the federal analogy, Warren stated that the Equal Protection Clause requires that both houses of a state legislature be apportioned on the basis of population. To aid the states, the Court provided guidelines that recognized that standards of state legisla-

tive apportionment cannot be hard and fast but must be fair and made in good faith. The primary objective to be reached was "substantial equality of population." Warren made clear, however, that the Court was not mandating perfect proportionality, for "mathematical exactness or precision is hardly a workable constitutional requirement." A state could constitutionally consider many factors other than population in devising an apportionment plan, but history, economics, and group interests were impermissible factors. Population was to be the starting point in all apportionment discussions, and if a plan debased a citizen's right to vote, it would be unconstitutional.

Warren also directed the states to reapportion their legislatures, at minimum, every ten years, based on the population figures derived from the federal decennial CENSUS. A state need not readjust its legislative districts constantly as the population changed, but the Court made clear that inaction such as that of the Alabama legislature would no longer be tolerated. If a state did not reapportion every ten years, any new redistricting plan submitted by the state would be "constitutionally suspect."

The *Reynolds* decision produced sweeping changes in state legislatures. Within two years at least one house in nearly all state legislatures had been held invalid; in most states both houses had to be reapportioned. Rural domination declined as urban areas gained a substantial number of legislative seats. The one-person, one-vote requirement soon moved to the municipal level, where city councils and county boards also adjusted voting districts to reflect population.

CROSS-REFERENCES
Baker v. Carr; Equal Protection; Voting Rights.

RICHARDSON, ELLIOT LEE
Elliot Lee Richardson has had a distinguished career in government service, including holding four different cabinet positions—the first person in U.S. history to do so. He is best known, however, for his brief tenure as U.S. attorney general under President RICHARD M. NIXON. Rich-

BIOGRAPHY

Elliot Lee Richardson

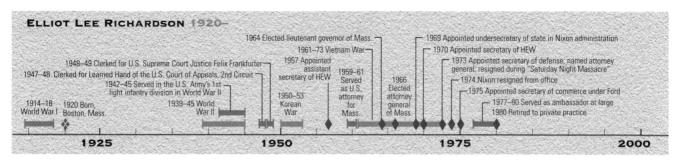

ELLIOT LEE RICHARDSON 1920–

1914–18 World War I

1920 Born, Boston, Mass.

1939–45 World War II

1942–45 Served in the U.S. Army's 1st light infantry division in World War II

1947–48 Clerked for Learned Hand of the U.S. Court of Appeals, 2nd Circuit

1948–49 Clerked for U.S. Supreme Court Justice Felix Frankfurter

1950–53 Korean War

1957 Appointed assistant secretary of HEW

1959–61 Served as U.S. attorney for Mass.

1961–73 Vietnam War

1964 Elected lieutenant governor of Mass.

1966 Elected attorney general of Mass.

1969 Appointed undersecretary of state in Nixon administration

1970 Appointed secretary of HEW

1973 Appointed secretary of defense; named attorney general; resigned during "Saturday Night Massacre"

1974 Nixon resigned from office

1975 Appointed secretary of commerce under Ford

1977–80 Served as ambassador at large

1980 Retired to private practice

1925   1950   1975   2000

ardson served from May 25, 1973, to October 20, 1973, during the unfolding of the WATERGATE scandal. He resigned the office during the "Saturday Night Massacre" rather than fire the special Watergate prosecutor as Nixon had directed.

Richardson was born on July 20, 1920, in Boston, Massachusetts. He graduated from Harvard University in 1941 and then served in the U.S. Army during World War II. Following the war he attended Harvard Law School, where he was the president of the *Harvard Law Review*. After graduation in 1947, he was law clerk for Judge LEARNED HAND of the U.S. Court of Appeals for the Second Circuit. In 1948 he went to Washington, D.C., to clerk for Justice FELIX FRANKFURTER at the U.S. Supreme Court.

Richardson returned to Boston in 1949 to practice law, but by 1953 he was back in Washington, serving as an assistant to Senator Leverett Saltonstall of Massachusetts. He left for Boston and private practice again in 1954 but was summoned by President DWIGHT D. EISENHOWER in 1957 to be assistant secretary of health, education, and welfare. In 1958 Richardson served as acting secretary of the department for four months. He was appointed U.S. attorney for Massachusetts in 1959, serving until 1961. In 1961 he served as special assistant attorney general.

In 1964 Richardson turned to the political arena. He was elected lieutenant governor of Massachusetts. In 1966 he was elected attorney general of the state. He left state government in 1969 when President Nixon appointed him under secretary of state. In June 1970 Nixon named Richardson secretary of health, education, and welfare, a position he held until the end of Nixon's first term. Following a cabinet reshuffle, Nixon made Richardson secretary of defense in January 1973. Less than four months later, however, Nixon named Richardson attorney general.

Richardson's appointment came at a time of growing concern about the credibility of Nixon's assertions that the White House was not involved in the 1972 burglary of the Democratic National Committee's headquarters in the Watergate office complex in Washington, D.C. Richardson succeeded RICHARD KLEINDIENST, who left under a cloud of scandal for his involvement with Watergate and other politically charged issues.

Richardson's personal and professional integrity gave the Nixon administration new credibility. He appointed ARCHIBALD COX, a professor at Harvard Law School, as special Watergate prosecutor to investigate whether federal laws were broken in connection with the break-in and the attempted cover-up. Richardson assured Cox, who was a personal friend, that he would have complete independence in his work.

In July 1973 it was revealed that Nixon had secretly recorded conversations in his White House offices. Cox immediately subpoenaed the tapes of the conversations. When Nixon refused to honor the SUBPOENA, Judge John Sirica ordered that the tapes be turned over. After the federal court of appeals upheld the order, Nixon offered Cox written summaries of the conversations in return for an agreement that no more presidential documents would be sought.

Cox refused the proposal. On Saturday, October 20, Nixon ordered Richardson to fire Cox. Richardson and his deputy attorney general, William D. Ruckelshaus, resigned rather than carry out the order. Cox was fired that night by Solicitor General ROBERT H. BORK. The two resignations and the firing of Cox became known as the Saturday Night Massacre. Though Nixon would not resign until August 9, 1974, the events of October 20 signaled the beginning of the end for his administration. Richardson, on the other hand, was celebrated for his courage and integrity.

GERALD R. FORD became president upon Nixon's resignation. He named Richardson U.S. ambassador to Great Britain in 1975. In 1976 Ford appointed Richardson secretary of commerce and in 1977 named him ambassador at large, a post he held until 1980. Richardson was a senior partner at a Washington, D.C., law firm from 1980 to 1992.

See also SPECIAL PROSECUTOR.

RICO See RACKETEERING INFLUENCED AND CORRUPT ORGANIZATIONS ACT.

RIDER 📖 A schedule or writing annexed to a document such as a legislative BILL or insurance POLICY. 📖

A rider is an ATTACHMENT, schedule, AMENDMENT, or other writing that is annexed (added) to a document in order to modify it. The changes may be small or large, but in either case the primary purpose of the rider is to avoid rewriting or redrafting the document entirely. The language of the rider is understood to be incorporated into the document. Riders are commonly used in CONTRACTS and records and also have complex uses in LEGISLATION and INSURANCE. As part of the lawmaking process in both state legislatures and Congress, riders are typically added to bills at a late stage in their evolution. In the insurance industry, riders are

"CERTAINTY IS THE STRAIGHTJACKET OF LIBERTY; TO DRESS A TRUTH IN AUTHORITY IS TO STULTIFY FREEDOM OF THOUGHT."

added to insurance policies to modify both benefits and the conditions of coverage.

The use of riders in the legislative process is a time-honored tradition. Lawmakers do not add riders immediately but instead wait for the appropriate stage in the evolution of a bill. Traditionally legislative bills start out as proposals that are sent to committees for approval or disapproval. Once a bill successfully passes out of committee, lawmakers frequently amend it with a rider. The rider may simply add a new clause to the law that is the main subject of the bill, or it may go further and add an entirely new, unrelated law.

The addition of riders reveals much about the political agendas of lawmakers. Riders make ideal opportunities to introduce controversial or unpopular fiscal changes. Often these are attached to appropriations bills, which must be passed annually to fund the operation of state and federal government. Some lawmakers have traditionally seen such bills as the place to add extra appropriations for projects they and their constituents favor—a kind of funding known pejoratively as *pork*. Conversely, legislators may add riders that cut spending in areas that would attract public protest if the changes were the single subject of a bill and thus more noticeable.

Lawmakers' attempts to add new laws to bills through riders are sometimes controversial. Since a rider need not be related to the subject matter of the bill, legislators sometimes seize the opportunity to further their political agendas. A rider may be attached to a bill in an attempt to sneak through a measure that would not attract majority support if proposed by itself. Sometimes, too, a bill's opponents may attempt to defeat it by adding a controversial rider.

In insurance, riders change the contract, or policy, between the purchaser and the insurance company. Also known as *endorsements*, they can either expand or restrict the benefits provided by the policy. Thus, for example, personal automobile insurance policies generally cover only typical use of the vehicle. A rider specifies that commercial use of the car will make the policy null and void. This form of insurance rider is called an *exclusion*.

Riders in HEALTH INSURANCE policies have other effects. They increase the cost of the policy or even exclude coverage altogether when the purchaser has certain preexisting health conditions. For example, someone suffering from high blood pressure may pay higher costs for insurance. In certain cases the insurer may choose to issue a policy with the stipulation that it will cover certain health-related costs but not those costs associated with the preexisting condition.

RIGHT 📖 In an abstract sense, justice, ethical correctness, or harmony with the rules of law or the principles of morals. In a concrete legal sense, a power, privilege, demand, or claim possessed by a particular person by virtue of law. 📖

Each LEGAL RIGHT that an individual possesses relates to a corresponding legal duty imposed on another. For example, when a person owns a home and property, he has the right to possess and enjoy it free from the interference of others, who are under a corresponding duty not to interfere with the owner's rights by trespassing on the property or breaking into the home.

In constitutional law, rights are classified as natural, civil, and political. Natural rights are those that are believed to grow out of the nature of the individual human being and depend on her personality, such as the rights to life, liberty, PRIVACY, and the pursuit of happiness.

CIVIL RIGHTS are those that belong to every citizen of the state, and are not connected with the organization or administration of government. They include the rights of property, marriage, protection by law, freedom to contract, trial by jury, and the like. These rights are capable of being enforced or redressed in a CIVIL ACTION in a court.

Political rights entail the power to participate directly or indirectly in the establishment or administration of government, such as the right of citizenship, the right to vote, and the right to hold public office.

Opponents of gun control rally together to affirm their right, or privilege, to own firearms.

APWIDE WORLD PHOTOS

RIGHT OF ACTION 📖 The privilege of instituting a lawsuit arising from a particular transaction or state of facts, such as a suit that is based on a CONTRACT or a TORT, a civil wrong. 📖

RIGHT OF ELECTION 📖 The prerogative of a surviving spouse to accept the provision the dead spouse made in the WILL or to disregard the will and claim the share specified by statute. 📖

At death spouses commonly leave money and property to their surviving husband or wife. This ESTATE is granted in a formal legal document known as a *will*, established by the deceased person (the DECEDENT). But a will is not the final word on what happens to the decedent's estate. The surviving spouse may either accept the provisions of the will or choose an alternative called the *right of election*. In most states statutes specify a portion of the estate that the surviving spouse can elect to take instead of receiving the amount specified in the will. The right of election ensures that the spouse receives a fair share of the estate. The option sometimes provides a more favorable outcome for the spouse than accepting the property distribution in the will.

Historically, a surviving spouse has enjoyed protection under the law of wills. This protection is an exception to the freedom a person generally has to decide the disposition of her estate after death. By custom the maker of a will, or the *testator*, decides how her estate is to be divided. This freedom includes the right to DISINHERIT even close relatives by leaving them nothing. Traditionally, however, the law has prevented a TESTATOR from disinheriting a spouse. The reasons for this intervention lie in the law's philosophical view of MARRIAGE as an economic union that entitles both parties to share in each other's material wealth, even after one spouse's death.

At COMMON LAW the surviving spouse was granted specific rights in the estate of the deceased spouse through the legal doctrines of *dower* and *curtesy*. These doctrines protected the spouse against total disinheritance. DOWER entitled a widow to claim a share of her husband's lands upon his death in order to support herself and her children. CURTESY functioned similarly for men. Most states have abolished these doctrines. In the few JURISDICTIONS where they remain in effect, they are used primarily to solve problems arising when a spouse has died INTESTATE, that is, without a will.

The right of election is available under most contemporary state laws. The surviving spouse may choose between accepting the terms of the will or receiving a share of the estate as defined by statute. This share is called a minimum or "elective" share. It varies in amount from state to state; generally, however, it is one-third of the estate if the decedent has children and one-half of the estate otherwise. Statutes may also specify minimum dollar amounts. Under a 1992 New York state law, for instance, the elective share is the greater of $50,000 or one-third of the net estate.

For some spouses, choosing the right of election is more advantageous than accepting the terms of the will. Besides protecting a spouse against total disinheritance, the right of election can be useful when the testator has left little to the spouse, when the testator has left the spouse's share in TRUST, or when other parties assert competing claims to the estate. Statutes establish different conditions and qualifications under which a spouse may claim the right to elect against the will; these range from ESTATE AND GIFT TAX issues to marital status at the time of the other spouse's death.

CROSS-REFERENCES

Descent and Distribution; Elective Share; Husband and Wife.

RIGHT OF REENTRY 📖 A right, retained by the GRANTOR at the time land is conveyed, to reenter and take POSSESSION of the land if a certain condition occurs or fails to occur. 📖

The right of reentry, also known as the POWER OF TERMINATION, applies to a type of interest in land known as a FEE SIMPLE subject to condition subsequent. The right of reentry means that the GRANTEE must abide by the specified condition or the grantor, or the grantor's HEIRS, may reenter and take back the PROPERTY. For example, a grantor conveys land "to Hennepin County, but if the land is not used for a fire station, then the grantor has the right to reenter and repossess the property." Once a grantor has exercised the right of reentry, the grantee has no further right to the property.

Sometimes a right of reentry is discussed with respect to a grant in the form, "to Hennepin County as long as the land is used for a fire station." However, this grant is known as a fee simple determinable, which means that upon the county's failure to use the land for a fire station, the property reverts back to the grantor by OPERATION OF LAW. Technically, then, this grant requires no right of reentry because a failure to abide by its terms automatically reinstates possession in the grantor. With a true right of reentry, the transfer is not automatic, and the grantor must affirmatively reenter the land or, if that is not feasible, bring a court ACTION to recover the property.

Leases also frequently include a right of reentry allowing the LESSOR to reclaim the property if the LESSEE fails to abide by the terms of the LEASE. When the lessor exercises the right of reentry and reclaims the property, the lessee has no further right to the premises. However, the lessor may have to take reasonable care to prevent damage to any PERSONAL PROPERTY left on the premises by the lessee.

RIGHT OF SURVIVORSHIP The power of the successor or successors of a deceased individual to acquire the PROPERTY of that individual upon his or her death; a distinguishing feature of JOINT TENANCY.

The right of survivorship determines what happens to a certain type of co-owned property after one of its owners dies. Under law there are many kinds of co-ownership, but the right of survivorship is found only in *joint tenancy*, a CONTRACT between two or more parties specifying their simultaneous ownership of some form of *real or personal property* such as a house, land, or money. In all joint tenancies, at the death of one of the joint tenants, ownership of the remaining property passes to the surviving TENANTS, or successors, who assert the right of survivorship. This is a powerful legal right because it takes precedence over other claims upon the property. Originally a right at COMMON LAW, it is recognized by statute in all states.

In order for co-owners of property to realize the right of survivorship, the property must be owned in joint tenancy. Joint tenancy describes an ownership interest in property held by two or more people called *tenants*. The tenants acquire their ownership interest in the property in the same way and at the same time, and each holds an equal share. Joint tenancies are created by DEED, WILL, or other transfer of property. Property that is held under a different form of co-ownership can be converted into a joint tenancy by amending the TITLE to the property.

When one of the joint tenants dies, the right of survivorship takes effect, passing the deceased tenant's interest in the property to the other joint tenant or tenants. Husbands and wives often create joint tenancies for co-ownership of their REAL PROPERTY; under the common law this form of joint tenancy is called a TENANCY BY THE ENTIRETY. It is an attractive legal option because of the right of survivorship. Upon one spouse's death, the right of survivorship takes precedence over claims on the property by the deceased person's HEIRS, BENEFICIARIES, and CREDITORS. The right passes outside *probate*—the procedure by which a deceased person's will is approved—so legal professionals sometimes call joint tenancy a PROBATE avoidance device. The dissolution of a MARRIAGE usually ends any subsequent claim of right of survivorship.

A joint tenancy continues as long as more than one joint tenant survives. Upon the death of one tenant, the shares of the other tenants increase equally; in a sense they absorb the ownership interest of the deceased person. This automatic process continues until only one surviving joint tenant is left; this survivor becomes the sole owner of the property.

Courts frequently hear claims based on the right of survivorship. The surviving joint tenant furnishes proof of the death of the other joint tenant as well as valid LEGAL TITLES indicating that the relevant real property was held in a joint tenancy. Documentary evidence establishing the existence of a joint tenancy is generally required to overcome a challenge to the right of survivorship.

RIGHT OF WAY An EASEMENT, a privilege to pass over the land of another, whereby the holder of the easement acquires only a reasonable and usual enjoyment of the property, and the owner of the land retains the benefits and privileges of ownership consistent with the easement.

Right of way is also used to describe that strip of land upon which railroad companies construct their roadbed; in this context, the term refers to the land itself, not the right of passage over it.

Railroads generally own the strip of land that their tracks cover, called a right of way.

ROY GUMPEL/LIAISON INTERNATIONAL

The term *right of way* also refers to a preference of one of two vehicles or vessels, or between a motor vehicle and a pedestrian, asserting the right of passage at the same place and time. It is not an absolute right, however, since the possessor of the right of way is not relieved from the duty of exercising due CARE for her own safety and that of others.

RIGHT TO COUNSEL The SIXTH AMENDMENT to the U.S. Constitution holds, in part, that "[i]n all criminal prosecutions, the accused shall enjoy the right . . . to have the Assistance of Counsel for his defence." This clause grants to all defendants the right to an ATTORNEY from the moment they are taken into police custody.

The decisions of the U.S. Supreme Court have also construed this Right to Counsel Clause to mean that an impoverished, or indigent, defendant has the constitutional right to the presence of a court-appointed attorney at critical stages in the criminal proceedings. These critical stages include CUSTODIAL INTERROGATION, postindictment LINEUPS, preliminary hearings, arraignment, trial, SENTENCING, and the first APPEAL of conviction.

The Right to Counsel Clause was a reaction against the English practice of denying the assistance of an attorney in serious criminal cases and requiring defendants to appear before the court and defend themselves in their own words. The 1586 trial of Mary Stuart, Queen of Scots, illustrates the harshness of denying the assistance of counsel in a criminal case. Queen Mary was charged with TREASON for allegedly conspiring to assassinate Queen Elizabeth I. Mary asked for the assistance of counsel, pleading that "the laws and statutes of England are to me most unknown; I am destitute of counsellors . . . and no man dareth step forth to be my advocate" (Winick 1989, 787). Her requests were denied, and Mary was summarily convicted and executed by decapitation.

The Framers of the U.S. Constitution considered the deprivation of counsel repugnant to basic principles of criminal justice. According to the Framers, the assistance of counsel was a critical element in maintaining an accusatorial system of justice. (An accusatorial system places the burden on the prosecution to establish the guilt of the defendant. This is opposed to an INQUISITORIAL SYSTEM, wherein guilt or innocence is determined through interrogation of the defendant.)

For 150 years, the Right to Counsel Clause was construed as simply granting to a defendant the right to retain a private attorney. This did not mean that an impoverished criminal defendant had the right to a court-appointed attorney without cost. In 1932, the U.S. Supreme Court began to reverse this interpretation in *Powell v. Alabama*, 287 U.S. 45, 53 S. Ct. 55, 77 L. Ed. 158. In *Powell*, nine black youths were accused of raping a white girl in a train going through Alabama on March 25, 1931. A sheriff's posse rounded up the youths and held them in custody. None of the youths were from Alabama, and none were given the opportunity to contact their family.

The youths were indicted on March 31. On April 6, they were tried with the assistance of unprepared counsel and convicted, and subsequently sentenced to death. The youths thereafter received the assistance of counsel for their appeals. The Supreme Court of Alabama affirmed the convictions. The U.S. Supreme Court reversed the convictions and returned the case to the Alabama state court. According to the Court, the trial court's appointment of an unprepared attorney in a capital case is a violation of the defendant's due process rights.

The *Powell* decision did not mandate the appointment of an attorney for all impoverished defendants. The Court in *Powell* merely held that due process requires the appointment of prepared counsel to indigent defendants in a case that involves the death penalty. *Powell* did, however, provide the basis for the requirement of free counsel for defendants faced with serious federal charges.

In *Johnson v. Zerbst*, 304 U.S. 458, 58 S. Ct. 1019, 82 L. Ed. 1461 (1938), the U.S. Supreme Court held that an indigent federal criminal defendant who faces a serious criminal charge, such as a FELONY, is entitled to an attorney at the expense of the government. According to the Court, the right to counsel is "one of the safeguards . . . deemed necessary to insure fundamental human rights of life and liberty." In making this decision, the Court noted "the obvious truth that the average defendant does not have the professional legal skill to protect himself."

Significantly, the *Johnson* opinion did not force states to provide the right to counsel for all indigent criminal defendants in state court; this right to counsel applied only to indigent defendants facing serious charges in FEDERAL COURT. In state court, by virtue of the *Powell* opinion, only indigent defendants accused of capital crimes had the right to a court-appointed attorney. Many states did provide for the right to an attorney for accused felons through statutes; other states did not. In 1963, the Supreme Court corrected these inequalities in *Gideon v. Wainwright*, 372 U.S. 335, 83 S. Ct. 792, 9 L. Ed. 2d 799.

In *Gideon*, defendant Clarence Gideon was charged in a Florida state court with breaking and entering a poolroom with the intent to commit a MISDEMEANOR. Under Florida law, this was a felony. Gideon valiantly represented himself, but he was found guilty and sentenced to five years in prison.

On appeal to the U.S. Supreme Court, Gideon was represented by ABE FORTAS, who had been appointed by the Court. Through Fortas, Gideon argued that the right to counsel was a fundamental right and essential to a fair trial. The Court agreed, stating that the "noble ideal" of a fair trial cannot be achieved "if the poor man charged with a crime has to face his accusers without a lawyer to assist him." The Court reversed Gideon's conviction, holding that all states must provide counsel to indigent defendants who face serious criminal charges. The legal basis for the decision was the Due Process Clause of the FOURTEENTH AMENDMENT to the U.S. Constitution. This clause forbids states to enact laws denying DUE PROCESS OF LAW to citizens of the United States. On retrial, represented by appointed counsel, Gideon was acquitted.

In a companion case decided the same day as *Gideon*, the U.S. Supreme Court created the right to counsel for indigent defendants on appeal. In *Douglas v. California*, 372 U.S. 353, 82 S. Ct. 814, 9 L. Ed. 2d 811 (1963), defendants William Douglas and Bennie Will Meyes, represented by a single PUBLIC DEFENDER, were tried jointly in a California state court and convicted of various felonies. Both defendants appealed to the California District Court of Appeal. This first appeal was granted as a matter of right to all criminal defendants. Under California law, however, indigent defendants did not have the right to an appointed attorney for the first appeal.

Douglas and Meyes, both indigent, prepared and filed their own appeal briefs. The District Court of Appeal affirmed the convictions. Meyes petitioned to the California Supreme Court for himself and on behalf of Douglas. That court denied the petition without a hearing.

On appeal to the U.S. Supreme Court, Douglas and Meyes, this time represented by Supreme Court–appointed counsel, argued that they deserved the right to an attorney on their appeal. The Court agreed, lecturing that "there can be no equal justice where the kind of an appeal a man enjoys 'depends on the amount of money he has' " (quoting *Griffin v. Illinois*, 351 U.S. 12, 76 S. Ct. 585, 100 L. Ed. 891 [1956]). According to the Court in *Douglas*, the Equal Protection and Due Process Clauses of the Fourteenth Amendment prevent states from granting criminal appeals in such a way as to discriminate against poor people.

Thus, under the *Douglas* decision, a state must provide free counsel to indigent defendants on appeal, if the state offers an appeal as a matter of right. All states do allow one appeal as a matter of right. For discretionary appeals, or appeals that are not granted as a matter of right—such as appeals to the state's highest court in states with a lower reviewing court, and appeals to the U.S. Supreme Court—there is no

right to counsel. However, many states maintain laws that provide free counsel to indigent defendants even for these discretionary appeals.

A year after *Gideon* and *Douglas*, the Supreme Court decided two more cases that further extended a defendant's right to counsel. In *Massiah v. United States*, 377 U.S. 201, 84 S. Ct. 1199, 12 L. Ed. 2d 246 (1964), defendant Winston Massiah was indicted by a federal GRAND JURY on narcotics charges. Massiah retained a lawyer and pleaded not guilty. While free on bail, Massiah was contacted by a codefendant, Jesse Colson. Unbeknownst to Massiah, Colson was cooperating with federal law enforcement authorities. Massiah and Colson met and spoke in an automobile for several hours about the case, and Massiah made incriminating statements that were transmitted by radio to a federal agent located a few blocks away. The statements were used as EVIDENCE in Massiah's trial. Massiah was convicted and sentenced to nine years in prison.

On appeal to the Supreme Court, Massiah argued that he had the right to counsel while being interrogated by law enforcement, even when the interrogation was not conducted in person by an officer. The Court agreed and reversed Massiah's conviction. The Court in *Massiah* established that the police may not interrogate someone who has been indicted unless the person's attorney is present or the person has knowingly waived the right to have counsel present.

Approximately one month later, the Supreme Court extended *Massiah* in *Escobedo v. Illinois*, 378 U.S. 478, 84 S. Ct. 1758, 12 L. Ed. 2d 977 (1964). In *Escobedo*, defendant Danny Escobedo was arrested and taken to police headquarters for questioning regarding the recent MURDER of his brother-in-law. Escobedo was not indicted for the crime. However, he was held in police custody and was not free to leave. Escobedo's retained attorney arrived at police headquarters while Escobedo was being questioned, but the police prevented the two from speaking to each other. Under interrogation, Escobedo admitted to some knowledge of the murder. Eventually, Escobedo confessed to having participated in the crime.

At trial, Escobedo's statements were admitted as evidence, and Escobedo was convicted of murder. On appeal, the Supreme Court overturned Escobedo's conviction. The Court specifically held that where an investigation is "no longer a general inquiry into an unsolved crime but has begun to focus on a particular suspect," the suspect is effectively in custody and has the right to consult a lawyer. Citing the prolific legal theorist Dean JOHN HENRY WIGMORE, the Court warned that any criminal justice system that relies on " 'compulsory self-disclosure as a source of proof must itself suffer morally thereby.' " The *Escobedo* opinion established that when a suspect asks to speak with an attorney, the police must comply with the request, even before formal charges have been filed against the suspect.

After this slew of right-to-counsel cases, it remained for the Supreme Court to decide what criminal charges required the availability of free counsel. Under *Johnson* and *Gideon*, a defendant had the right to counsel for all "serious" cases, but this standard proved difficult to apply. To clarify this aspect of the right to counsel, the Court seized on *Argersinger v. Hamlin*, 407 U.S. 25, 92 S. Ct. 2006, 32 L. Ed. 2d 530 (1972).

In *Argersinger*, the defendant, Jon Richard Argersinger, an indigent person, was charged in a Florida state court with carrying a concealed weapon. The offense carried a punishment of up to six months in prison and a $1,000 fine. Proceeding without counsel, Argersinger was convicted and sentenced to ninety days in jail.

On appeal, the Supreme Court vacated Argersinger's conviction. The Court concluded that "the problems associated with misdemeanor and petty offenses often require the presence of counsel to insure the accused a fair trial." Under the rule formulated in *Argersinger*, an indigent defendant who is not offered the services of a court-appointed attorney at trial may not be sentenced to prison, even if the defendant is convicted of a crime for which INCARCERATION is an authorized punishment.

The apparent fairness of the rule established in *Argersinger* can be deceiving. In *Nichols v. United States*, 511 U.S. 738, 114 S. Ct. 1921, 128 L. Ed. 2d 745 (1994), defendant Kenneth O. Nichols pleaded guilty in federal court to CONSPIRACY to distribute cocaine. Nichols was sentenced to nineteen years and seven months' imprisonment. To justify this lengthy term, the sentencing court relied on a previous misdemeanor conviction that resulted from a trial in which Nichols was not represented by counsel. When Nichols appealed the sentence, the Supreme Court held that it is not a violation of the Sixth and Fourteenth Amendments to enhance punishment based on a prior conviction in which an indigent defendant was not afforded an attorney.

The Supreme Court has, at times, displayed considerable latitude in deciding various right-to-counsel issues. The Court has held that an indigent defendant has the right to counsel in deciding whether to submit to a psychiatric examination when statements made during that examination may be used at trial (*Estelle v. Smith*, 451 U.S. 454, 101 S. Ct. 1866, 68 L. Ed. 2d 359 [1981]). Under *United States v. Wade*, 388 U.S. 218, 87 S. Ct. 1926, 18 L. Ed. 2d 1149 (1967), an indigent defendant has the right to have appointed counsel present during postindictment identification lineups. Under the Sixth Amendment, juveniles have the right to an attorney when their liberty is at stake (*Application of Gault*, 387 U.S. 1, 87 S. Ct. 1428, 18 L. Ed. 2d 527 [1967]).

The Court has also construed the Sixth Amendment to mean that a criminal defendant is entitled to "effective assistance" of counsel. This means that a defendant has the right to conscientious, meaningful representation. If a defendant does not receive effective assistance of counsel at trial, the conviction will be reversed. However, the standard of proof for the defendant is high. A defense attorney's assistance is considered ineffective only if it undermined the adversarial process and made the result of the trial unreliable (*Strickland v. Washington*, 466 U.S. 668, 104 S. Ct. 2052, 80 L. Ed. 2d 674 [1984]).

The Supreme Court has been less generous on other issues. Generally, an indigent defendant has no right to counsel in a proceeding after conviction (*Pennsylvania v. Finley*, 481 U.S. 551, 107 S. Ct. 1990, 95 L. Ed. 2d 539 [1987]). An indigent defendant does not have an *absolute* right to counsel for revocation of PAROLE or probation hearings (*Gagnon v. Scarpelli*, 411 U.S. 778, 93 S. Ct. 1756, 36 L. Ed. 2d 656 [1973]). If the parolee or probationer denies committing the offense or if there are mitigating circumstances that may limit the parolee or probationer's guilt, the court may appoint an attorney. An indigent defendant has no constitutional right to an attorney for a HABEAS CORPUS petition (*Finley*) unless the defendant faces death, in which case he or she is entitled to an attorney for a habeas corpus petition (*McFarland v. Scott*, 512 U.S. 849, 114 S. Ct. 2568, 129 L. Ed. 2d 666 [1994]).

An indigent defendant has the right to appointed counsel during preindictment identification lineups conducted by the police (*Kirby v. Illinois*, 406 U.S. 682, 92 S. Ct. 1877, 32 L. Ed. 2d 411 [1972]). *Kirby* would seem to contradict *Escobedo*, where the defendant was entitled to counsel after arrest but before INDICTMENT. However, *Escobedo* has been limited to its facts, and has been construed as upholding the defendant's right against self-incrimination more than the right to counsel.

The Supreme Court has carved out other exceptions to the right to counsel after an arrest. It has allowed law enforcement officials to have EX PARTE contacts with defendants to determine whether the defendant is in fact represented by counsel. It has also allowed ex parte communications that are made with the consent of defendant's counsel; those made pursuant to DISCOVERY procedures, such as SUB-POENAS; communications in the course of a criminal investigation; communications necessary to protect the life or safety of another person; and those made by a represented person, so long as the person has knowingly, intelligently, and voluntarily waived the right to have counsel present. These exceptions apply to all persons, regardless of whether they can afford their own attorney.

Finally, law enforcement officials need not advise criminal suspects of their right to an attorney until those suspects are actually taken into custody or are not free to leave the presence of the officers. This rule gives law enforcement the freedom necessary to conduct reasonable investigations for the safety of the general public.

CROSS-REFERENCES

Criminal Law; Criminal Procedure; *Gideon v. Wainwright*; *In re Gault*; Juvenile Law; *Miranda v. Arizona*; *Powell v. Alabama*.

RIGHT-TO-WORK LAWS 📖 State laws permitted by section 14(b) of the TAFT-HARTLEY ACT that provide in general that employees are not required to join a union as a condition of getting or retaining a job. 📖

Right-to-work laws forbid unions and employers to enter into agreements requiring employees to join a union and pay dues and fees to it in order to get or keep a job. Twenty-one states, mostly in the South and West, have right-to-work laws.

The ability of states to pass right-to-work laws was authorized by the Taft-Hartley Act of 1947, also known as the Labor Management Relations Act (29 U.S.C.A. § 141 et seq.). Taft-Hartley, which sought to curtail union power in the workplace, amended the NATIONAL LABOR RELATIONS ACT (NLRA) of 1935 (29 U.S.C.A. § 151 et seq.). The NLRA as first passed preempted state regulation of labor relations in interstate commerce, with the goal of developing a national labor law. Taft-Hartley departed from this goal in section 14(b) (29 U.S.C.A. § 164[b]), expressly authorizing the states to adopt right-to-work measures. Organized labor has tried repeatedly, without success, to secure the repeal of section 14(b). The Federal Railway Labor Act (45 U.S.C.A. § 151 et seq.) prevents the application of state right-to-work laws to the RAILROAD and AIRLINE industries.

Section 14(b) works with other provisions of Taft-Hartley to limit the ability of unions to mandate compulsory union membership. Sections 8(a)(3) and 8(b)(2) prohibit a type of union security clause (a provision that describes the obligations of employees to support the union) from being inserted into a COLLECTIVE BARGAIN-

Right-to-work laws mandate that employees, such as this construction worker, cannot be required to join a labor union as a condition of obtaining or retaining a job.

ING AGREEMENT. A *closed shop* clause obligates the employer to hire only union members and to discharge any employee who drops union membership. The CLOSED SHOP is forbidden under Taft-Hartley.

Although the act permits the *union shop*, section 14(b) allows the states to prohibit it. A UNION SHOP clause requires an employee to become a member of the union in order to retain a job, although no one needs to be a member in order to be hired; every newly hired person has a prescribed period of time to become a member.

Section 14(b) also allows states to prohibit the *agency shop*. An agency shop clause requires every company employee to pay to the union an amount equal to the union's customary initiation fees and monthly dues. It does not require the employee to become a formal member of the union, be a member before being hired, take an oath of obligation, or observe any internal rules and regulations of the union except with regard to dues. The U.S. Supreme Court, in *National Labor Relations Board v. General Motors Corp.*, 373 U.S. 734, 83 S. Ct. 1453, 10 L. Ed. 2d 670 (1963), held that an employer does not violate the NLRA by agreeing to include an agency shop clause in a bargaining agreement.

Therefore, when a state passes a right-to-work law, it prohibits both mandatory union membership and initiation fees and dues obligations of agency shops, and permits employees who do not voluntarily pay dues and initiation fees to receive the benefits the union provides. Unions call such people "free riders."

Right-to-work advocates argue that no person should be forced to become a union member or to provide financial support for a labor organization as a condition of employment. Such compulsion is said to be contrary to the U.S. concept of individual rights and freedom of association. It is also alleged that compulsory unionism enables large labor organizations to exert excessive power in the workplace and in the political arena.

Organized labor believes that right-to-work laws allow free riders at the expense of their fellow workers. Opponents of these laws argue that everyone should pay a proportionate share of the costs of the union in negotiating contract benefits that will go to all. Unions also maintain that the real objective of right-to-work laws is to sow dissension among workers and thus weaken the labor movement.

The bitter controversy over right-to-work laws peaked in the 1950s, when almost every state legislature considered the issue. Some scholars suggest the importance of the issue has been exaggerated. Studies have indicated that where unions are well established, employees tend to enroll without regard to right-to-work statutes. Such laws may be more a symptom than a cause of union weakness in certain industries and geographical areas.

CROSS-REFERENCES

Collective Bargaining; Labor Law; Labor Union.

RIOT A DISTURBANCE OF THE PEACE by several persons, assembled and acting with a common intent in executing a lawful or unlawful enterprise in a violent and turbulent manner.

Riot, rout, and UNLAWFUL ASSEMBLY are related offenses, yet they are separate and distinct. A rout differs from a riot in that the persons involved do not actually execute their purpose but merely move toward it. The degree of execution that converts a rout into a riot is often difficult to determine.

An unlawful assembly transpires when persons convene for a purpose that, if executed, would make them rioters, but who separate without performing any act in furtherance of their purpose. For example, when a restaurant owner refused to serve a certain four customers and barred them from entering the establishment, the four men remained in front of the doors of the restaurant and blocked the entrance to all other customers. Although a riot did not result from their actions, the men were arrested and convicted of unlawful assembly.

Inciting to riot is another distinct crime, the gist of which is that it instigates a BREACH OF THE PEACE, even though the parties might have initially assembled for an innocent purpose. It means using language, signs, or conduct to lead or cause others to engage in conduct that, if completed, becomes a riot.

CONSPIRACY to riot is also a separate offense. In one case, the leader of a small Marxist group took to the streets preaching REVOLUTION and organized resistance to lawful authority. Cursing the police, he spoke about how to fight and kill them and generally advocated violent means to gain political ends. The court ruled that a person who agrees with others to organize a future riot and who commits an OVERT act in conformity with the agreement is guilty, not of riot, but of conspiracy to riot.

In legal usage, the term *mob* is practically synonymous with riot or with riotous assembly. A federal court held that night riders were a mob and that their act of burning a building constituted the crime of riot.

Nature and Elements Riot is an offense against the public peace and good order, rather

In 1992, following the verdict in the Rodney King trial, a riot broke out in Los Angeles.

than a violation of the rights of any particular person. It is not commonly applied to brief disturbances, even if MALICIOUS MISCHIEF and violence are involved in the commotion. For example, a lock company was picketed in a labor dispute. When the police attempted to escort some people through the picket line, a brief general commotion, some scuffling, and an exchange of blows took place. The police testified that the entire fracas lasted about "two or three minutes." The court held that the crime of riot does not apply to brief disturbances, even those involving violence, nor to disturbances that occur during the PICKETING accompanying a labor dispute.

The elements that comprise the offense are determined either by the COMMON LAW or by the statute defining it. In some JURISDICTIONS, the necessary elements are an unlawful assembly, the intent to provide mutual assistance against lawful authority, and acts of violence. Under some statutes, the elements are the use of FORCE or violence, or threats to use force and violence, along with the immediate power of execution.

Other statutes provide that the essential elements are an assembly of persons for any unlawful purpose; the use of force or violence against persons or property; an attempt or threat to use force or violence or to do any unlawful act, coupled with the power of immediate execution; and a resulting disturbance of the peace.

Force or Violence The element of force or violence required under the common law means a defiance of lawful authority and the rights of other persons. Similarly the force or violence contemplated by the statutes is the united force of the participants acting in concert with the increased capacity to overcome resistance. The statutes further specify that the type of force and violence, not mere physical exertion, must threaten law-abiding nonparticipants.

Order to Disperse Under some statutes, the crime of riot is committed, even though no order to disperse has been given. The statutory offense of remaining at a place of riot cannot occur, however, until a command to disperse has been given.

Unlawful Conduct Riots can arise from any violent and turbulent activity of a group, such as bands of people creating an uproar and displaying weapons; wildly marching on a public street; violently disrupting a public meeting; threatening bystanders with displays of force; or forcibly destroying property along the way. In one case, striking orange pickers armed with clubs, metal cables, sticks, and other weapons rushed into an orange grove and assaulted non-striking pickers. After the nonstrikers were driven out of the grove, the strikers overturned the boxes full of picked oranges and threw oranges and boxes at the nonstrikers. The court held this to be riotous conduct. When one city was wracked by racial disturbances, the court ruled that racial disorders constituted a general "riot," or a series of "riots," and that whether there was a single, identifiable group or a number of riotous groups was not significant when their one common purpose was to injure and destroy.

Number of Persons Necessary The common law rule, and most of the statutes that define riot, require three or more persons to be involved. Some statutes fix the minimum number at two.

Purpose of Original Assembly The jurisdictions differ on whether the original assembly must be an unlawful one. Some require premeditation by the rioters, but others prescribe that riots can arise from assemblies that were originally lawful or as a result of groups of persons who had inadvertently assembled.

Common Intent A previous agreement or conspiracy to riot is not usually an element of a riot. A common intent, however, to engage in an act of violence, combined with a concert of action, is sometimes necessary. In one case, following a high school football game, a group of boys staged a "violent, brutal and indecent" ASSAULT on the color guard and band members of the visiting team. When the visitors attempted to leave, the attacks continued. On trial, the attackers claimed that the charge of riot did not apply to them because they had had no "common intent." The court held that "an intent is a mental state which can be inferred from conduct." They were found guilty of riot and the decision was affirmed on appeal.

Terror When a riot arises from an unlawful act, such as an assault, terror need not be shown because in every riotous situation there are elements of force and violence that are by their very nature terrifying. When a riot arises from lawful conduct, terror must be shown. For example, if a group of neighbors decides to remove a NUISANCE, such as a pile of malodorous garbage, which would be a lawful activity, but does so in a violent and tumultuous manner, terror would have to be shown before the conduct would constitute a riot. Only one person need be alarmed to fulfill the terror requirement.

Persons Liable Principal rioters are those who are present and actively participate in the riot. All persons present who are not actually assisting in the suppression of the riot can be regarded as participants when their presence is intentional and tends to encourage the rioters.

Municipal Liability In the absence of a statute, a MUNICIPAL CORPORATION, such as a city, town, or village, is not liable for injuries caused by mobs or riotous assemblages. Where statutes do impose LIABILITY, the particular statute determines the type of action one can institute against a city, town, or village.

Defenses There is never any justification for a riot. The only DEFENSE that can be claimed is that an element of the offense is absent. Participation is an essential element. Establishing that an accused's presence at the scene of a riot was accidental can remove any PRESUMPTION of guilt arising from his or her presence at a riotous assemblage.

Suppression of Riot Private persons can, on their own authority, lawfully try to suppress a riot, and courts have ruled that they can arm themselves for such a purpose if they comply with appropriate statutory provisions concerning the possession of firearms or other weapons. Execution of this objective will be supported and justified by law. Generally every citizen capable of bearing arms must help to suppress a riot if called upon to do so by an authorized peace officer.

The state is primarily responsible for protecting lives and property from the unlawful violence of mobs. If the MILITIA reports to civil authorities to help quash a riot, it has the same powers as civil officers and must render only such assistance as is required by civil authorities.

In an emergency, and in the absence of constitutional restrictions, a governor can order the intervention of the militia to suppress a riot without complying with statutory formalities. When troops are ordered to quell a riot, they are not subject to local authorities but are in the service of the state.

RIPARIAN RIGHTS 📖 The rights, which belong to landowners through whose PROPERTY a natural watercourse runs, to the benefit of such stream for all purposes to which it can be applied. 📖

Riparian water, as distinguished from *flood water*, is the water that is below the highest line of normal flow of the river or stream.

See also WATER RIGHTS.

RIPENESS 📖 The mandate contained in Article III of the Constitution that requires an APPELLATE COURT to consider whether a case has matured into a CONTROVERSY worthy of ADJUDICATION before it can hear the case. 📖

An actual, current controversy worthy of adjudication must exist before a FEDERAL COURT may hear a case. The court determines if a controversy between parties with adverse legal interests is of sufficient immediacy and reality to warrant judicial intervention (*Lake Carriers' Ass'n v. MacMullan*, 406 U.S. 498, 92 S. Ct. 1749, 32 L. Ed. 2d 257 [1972]).

The rationale behind the ripeness limitation is to prevent the courts from entering a controversy before it has solidified or before other available remedies have been exhausted. In disputes involving regulations or decisions promulgated by ADMINISTRATIVE AGENCIES, a controversy is not considered ripe until the agency's decision has been formalized and the challenging parties have felt its effects. Similarly, if a state court REMEDY is available, a controversy is not ripe for federal court review until all state court remedies have been exhausted.

The courts generally apply a two-part test to determine if a controversy is ripe for judicial intervention. The first criterion is whether the controversy is fit for judicial decision, that is, whether it presents a QUESTION OF LAW rather than a QUESTION OF FACT. Secondly, the courts determine the impact on the parties of withholding judicial consideration. In *Abbott Laboratories v. Gardner*, 387 U.S. 136, 87 S. Ct. 1507, 18 L. Ed. 2d 681 (1967), the Supreme Court examined whether a regulation that required drug manufacturers to use labels showing both the generic and the proprietary drug names was ripe for review before it was actually enforced. The Court held that the controversy was ripe because the regulation had an immediate and expensive impact on the plaintiffs' day-to-day operations and the plaintiffs risked a substantial sanction if they did not comply with the regulation.

Ripeness is a major consideration when parties seek injunctive or declarative relief before a statute or regulation has been applied. Courts are reluctant to enter an abstract disagreement over administrative policies (*Ruckelshaus v. Monsanto*, 467 U.S. 986, 104 S. Ct. 2862, 81 L. Ed. 2d 815 [1984]). However, in some cases, the courts will hear a request for an INJUNCTION or DECLARATORY JUDGMENT if the question presented is entirely or substantially legal and if postponing a decision until after a statute or regulation is applied would work a substantial hardship on the challenging party (*Pacific Gas and Electric Co. v. State Energy Resources Conservation & Development Commission*, 461 U.S. 190, 103 S. Ct. 1713, 75 L. Ed. 2d 752 [1983]).

See also CASE OR CONTROVERSY.

RISK 📖 The potential danger that threatens to harm or destroy an object, event, or person. 📖

A risk that is specified in an INSURANCE policy is a contingency which might or might not occur. The policy promises to reimburse the person who suffers a loss resulting from the risk for the amount of damage done up to the financial limits of the policy.

In SALES transactions, the CONTRACT and the UNIFORM COMMERCIAL CODE (UCC) determine who bears responsibility for the risk of loss of the merchandise until the buyer takes possession of the goods.

RISK ARBITRAGE 📖 The purchase of STOCK in a CORPORATION that appears to be the target of an imminent TAKEOVER in the hope of making large profits if the takeover occurs. 📖

Risk arbitrage is practiced by investors called risk arbitrageurs. The strategy can return large profits if a takeover occurs but can also result in large losses if the transaction does not take place. Obviously, then, the more information an arbitrageur has about a possible takeover, the less risk the strategy involves. Buying SECURITIES of takeover candidates on the basis of rumors is legal, but it is illegal for an arbitrageur to purchase securities based on inside, or nonpublic, information. INSIDER trading violates rule 10(b)-5 of the Securities Exchange Act of 1934, 15 U.S.C.A. § 78a et seq., which is a federal law that governs the operation of the stock exchanges and over-the-counter trading.

To obtain information, arbitrageurs often develop relationships with investment banking firms and corporations, as well as with other sources of information and financial backing. These activities alone do not constitute a violation of the Securities Exchange Act, but if the risk arbitrageur uses these relationships or resources to gather information that is not available to the general public, the resulting purchase of securities is illegal.

In the late 1980s, the SECURITIES AND EXCHANGE COMMISSION (SEC) began to investigate several prominent risk arbitrageurs for their roles in insider trading. This action, combined with the increasing number of corporate takeovers, brought the issue of risk arbitrage to the headlines of Wall Street and the world. Between 1980 and 1988 in the U.S. District Court for the Southern District of New York alone, fifty-seven arbitrageurs were criminally prosecuted for insider trading. One of the best-known cases involved risk arbitrageur Ivan Boesky, who allegedly realized a $9.075 million net profit through stock trades he made based on nonpublic information about three different mergers and takeovers. As part of the settlement with the SEC and the FEDERAL COURTS, Boesky was barred from any future securities trading.

Because risk arbitrage can involve significant blocks of shares worth hundreds of thousands, even millions, of dollars, this practice can have a large impact on both the market and the value of the company's stock. Professionals in the securities field generally agree that risk arbitrage based on inside information has a negative effect on the market, as well as on the reputation of arbitrageurs in general. Many of these commentators, however, are concerned that existing securities laws do not reach risk arbitrageurs who do not owe a FIDUCIARY duty to the people who are harmed by the arbitrageur's use of nonpublic information. The Securities and Exchange Act specifies that a violation of rule 10(b)-5 requires the accused violator to have breached a fiduciary duty to the injured party.

Chiarella v. United States, 445 U.S. 222, 100 S. Ct. 1108, 63 L. Ed. 2d 348 (1980), is one of the leading cases on rule 10(b)-5 liability. Vincent F. Chiarella was employed at a financial printer and, as part of his duties, handled a series of documents that detailed an upcoming takeover bid; although the names were left blank or falsified, Chiarella was able to figure out the companies involved. Then, without disclosing that he had inside information, he bought stock in the companies that were targeted in the takeover; when the takeover was made public, he sold the shares and made a profit of approximately $30,000. Shortly thereafter, Chiarella was indicted on seventeen counts of violating rule 10(b)-5. The U.S. Supreme Court reversed the conviction, however, on the grounds that Chiarella had not violated the rule because he was not a fiduciary and therefore did not have a duty to disclose.

See also MERGERS AND ACQUISITIONS.

RIVERS See BOUNDARIES; INTERNATIONAL WATERWAYS; WATER RIGHTS.

ROBBERY ▥ The taking of money or goods in the possession of another, from his or her person or immediate presence, by FORCE or intimidation. ▥

Robbery is a crime of THEFT and can be classified as LARCENY by force or by threat of force. The elements of the crime of robbery include the use of force or intimidation and all the elements of the crime of larceny. The penalty for robbery is always more severe than for larceny.

The general elements of robbery are the taking of PERSONAL PROPERTY or money from the person or presence of another, the use of actual or constructive force, the lack of consent on the part of the victim, and the intent to steal on the part of the offender. Neither deliberation nor premeditation is necessary, nor is an express demand for the property.

Robbery requires a taking of property from the person or presence of the victim. This means that the taking must be from the victim's POSSESSION, whether actual or constructive. Property is on the victim's person if it is in his hand, in the pocket of the clothing he wears, or otherwise attached to his body or clothing. The phrase "from the presence" or "in the presence" has been construed to mean proximity or control rather than within eyesight of the victim. For example, a robber takes property from the victim's presence if the robber locks the victim in one room and then takes the valuable from another room. There is sufficient proximity even though the victim cannot see through the walls into the room where the valuables are stored.

The property taken must be close enough to the victim and sufficiently under his control that had the robber not used violence or intimidation, the victim could have prevented the taking. As an example, if a robber uses force to immobilize a property owner at one place while an accomplice takes the owner's property from a place several miles away, the distance between the owner and the owner's property is such that the owner could not have prevented the taking even if he had been free to try to interfere.

A robbery must also include a taking or ASPORTATION, a carrying away by which the goods are taken from the victim's possession and transferred to the possession of the robber. The crime is complete when the robber acquires possession of the property, even for a short time. The robber does not have to transport the property away from the physical presence of the person who has lawful possession of it, or even escape with it. The slightest change of location is sufficient to establish asportation. Once the robber takes possession of the property, the offense is complete, even if the robber later abandons the property.

The personal property that is taken must have some value, but the amount of its value is immaterial. The crime of robbery can be committed even if the property taken is of slight value. Actual monetary value is not essential as long as it appears that the property had some value to the person robbed.

The property does not have to be taken from the owner or holder of LEGAL TITLE. The robber may rob someone who has possession or CUSTODY of property, though that person is not the owner of it. The person from whom the property was taken must have exerted control over it.

The taking must be accomplished either by force or by intimidation. This element is the essence and distinguishing characteristic of the offense. Taking by force without intimidation is robbery. Taking by intimidation without the use of actual force is also robbery. Force and intimidation are alternate requirements, and either is sufficient without the other.

Types of Weapons Used in Robberies, 1995

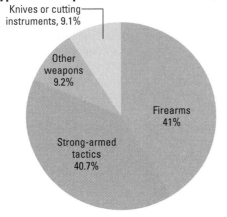

Source: U.S. Federal Bureau of Investigation, *Crime in the United States*, annual.

The force must be sufficient to effect the transfer of the property from the victim to the robber. It must amount to actual personal violence. The line between robbery and larceny from the person is not always easy to draw. For example, when a thief snatches a purse from the owner's grasp so suddenly that the owner cannot offer any resistance to the taking, the force involved is not sufficient to constitute robbery. Hence that crime would be larceny. If a struggle for the purse ensues before the thief can gain possession of it, however, there is enough force to make the taking robbery. The same is true of pickpocketing. If the victim is unaware of the taking, no robbery has occurred and the crime is larceny. But if the victim catches the pickpocket in the act and struggles unsuccessfully to keep possession, the pickpocket's crime becomes robbery.

The particular degree of force becomes important only when considered in connection with the grade of the offense or the punishment to be imposed. Evidence establishing a personal injury or a blow, or force sufficient to overcome any resistance the victim was capable of offering, is not required.

A robber may also render the victim helpless by more subtle means. Constructive force includes demonstrations of force, menace, and other means that prevent a victim from exercising free will or resisting the taking of property. Administering intoxicating liquors or drugs in order to produce a state of unconsciousness or stupefaction is using force for purposes of robbery. Constructive force will support a robbery charge.

Intimidation means putting in fear. The accused must intentionally cause the fear and induce a reasonable apprehension of danger, but not necessarily a great terror, panic, or hysteria in the victim. The fear must be strong enough to overcome the victim's resistance and cause the victim to part with the property. The victim who is not fearful of harm from the robber so long as she does what the robber says, but who expects harm if she refuses, is nevertheless "put in fear" for the purposes of robbery.

Putting the victim in fear of bodily injury is sufficient. The fear can be aroused by words or gestures, such as threatening the victim with a weapon. The threat of immediate bodily injury or death does not have to be directed at the owner of the property. It may be made to a member of the owner's family, other relatives, or even someone in the owner's company.

The force or intimidation must either precede or be contemporaneous with the taking to constitute a robbery. Violence or intimidation after the taking is not robbery. If, however, the force occurs so soon after the taking that it forms part of the same transaction, the violence is legally concurrent with the taking. Force or intimidation employed after the taking and merely as a means of escape is not a sufficient basis for a robbery charge.

Unless a statute provides otherwise, a robbery cannot be committed without criminal intent. The robber must have a specific intent to rob the owner of the property. The element of force or intimidation is not a substitute for the intent to steal.

The offender's INTENT must be determined from her words and actions. A person who forcibly takes property by mistake or merely as a joke, without an intent to deprive the owner of the property permanently, is not guilty of robbery. The intent to steal must be present at the time the property is taken, but premeditation is not part of the criminal intent necessary for the commission of robbery.

Most robbery statutes distinguish between simple robbery and aggravated robbery. The most common aggravating factors are that the robber was armed with a deadly weapon or represented that she had a gun, that the robber actually inflicted serious bodily injury, or that the robber had an accomplice.

There are three important federal robbery statutes. The Federal Bank Robbery Act (18 U.S.C.A. § 2113) punishes robbery of property in the custody or possession of any national bank or of any bank that is insured by the federal government. Two provisions (18 U.S.C.A. §§ 2112, 2114) punish robbery where the property taken is from the U.S. mail or is property belonging to the federal government. The Hobbs Act (18 U.S.C.A. § 1951) punishes the obstruction of interstate commerce by robbery.

ROBERTS, OWEN JOSEPHUS

Owen Josephus Roberts served as an associate justice of the U.S. Supreme Court for fifteen years. His years on the Court included the NEW DEAL era when the federal government, under the leadership of President FRANKLIN D. ROOSEVELT, expanded its regulation of the economy in an effort to address the effects of the Great Depression. Roberts cast the deciding vote in a major case that marked a shift in the Court's approach to such regulation.

Roberts was born on May 2, 1875, in Germantown, Pennsylvania, where he spent much of his childhood. He graduated from the University of Pennsylvania, receiving a bachelor of arts degree in 1895 and a bachelor of laws degree in 1898. In 1898 Roberts established a law practice in Philadelphia, becoming the first district attorney for Philadelphia County. Roberts also taught for twenty years at the University of Pennsylvania, serving as a law professor from 1898 to 1918. In 1924 President CALVIN COOLIDGE named Roberts special attorney for the prosecution in the TEAPOT DOME scandal, which involved unethical behavior in the oil industry. In 1930 President HERBERT HOOVER appointed Roberts to the U.S. Supreme Court.

Roberts's tenure on the Supreme Court is largely remembered for the decisive fifth vote he cast in *West Coast Hotel v. Parrish*, 300 U.S. 379, 57 S. Ct. 578, 81 L. Ed. 703 (1937), which upheld the constitutionality of a Washington state MINIMUM WAGE law. The Court's decision in *West Coast Hotel* brought an end to the *Lochner* Era in constitutional law, named after the case *Lochner v. New York*, 198 U.S. 45, 25 S. Ct. 539, 49 L. Ed. 937 (1905). In *Lochner* the Court struck down a New York law regulating the number of hours that employees could work each week in the baking industry because it violated the free market principles embodied in the doctrine of substantive due process, a doctrine derived from the Due Process Clause of the Fifth and Fourteenth Amendments to the U.S. Constitution.

For three decades after *Lochner,* the Court invalidated numerous state and federal laws

Owen Josephus Roberts

"THE JUDICIAL BRANCH . . . HAS ONLY ONE DUTY—TO LAY THE ARTICLE OF THE CONSTITUTION WHICH IS INVOKED BESIDE THE STATUTE WHICH IS CHALLENGED AND TO DECIDE WHETHER THE LATTER SQUARES WITH THE FORMER."

PORTRAIT BY ALFRED JONNIAUX COLLECTION OF THE SUPREME COURT OF THE UNITED STATES.

regulating businesses, including laws that prescribed certain terms and conditions of employment. After *West Coast Hotel,* the Court adopted a more permissive stance toward such laws, permitting both the state and federal governments to pass reasonable business regulations that benefit society. Roberts's vote to uphold the state minimum wage law in *West Coast Hotel* is memorable not only because it was the decisive vote in a landmark case but also because he had previously voted to strike down similar regulations on a number of occasions.

Roberts's change of heart has been characterized as "the switch in time that saved nine," suggesting that Roberts cast his vote to defeat President Roosevelt's court-packing plan. To dilute the voting power of the existing nine justices on the Supreme Court, who had been striking down much New Deal legislation, Roosevelt had proposed to expand the number of justices, a move that would enable him to add justices more favorable to his New Deal objectives. Historians disagree, however, over whether Roberts had knowledge of Roosevelt's plan at the time he cast his vote. Additionally, Roberts had previously voted in favor of state legislation that had been enacted to address the worst effects of the Great Depression, much like some of the New Deal legislation Congress had passed at the federal level. For example, in *Home Building & Loan Association v. Blaisdell*, 290 U.S. 398, 54 S. Ct. 231, 78 L. Ed. 413 (1934), Roberts joined four other justices in upholding a Minnesota law that placed a moratorium on the FORECLOSURE of MORTGAGES.

Roberts's constitutional JURISPRUDENCE is difficult to categorize and was somewhat unpredictable. In *Grovey v. Townsend*, 295 U.S. 45, 55 S. Ct. 622, 79 L. Ed. 1292 (1935), for example, Roberts wrote for a unanimous Court in upholding the constitutionality of white primaries, which denied African Americans the right to elect party delegates for the national convention. Three years later, in *Missouri ex rel. Gaines v. Canada*, 305 U.S. 337, 59 S. Ct. 232, 83 L. Ed. 208 (1938), Roberts concurred with a majority of justices who relied on the Equal Pro-

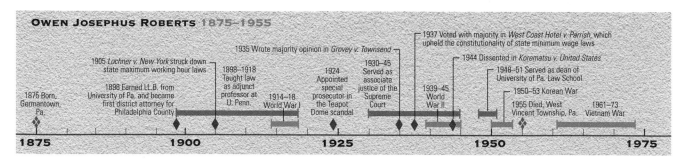

OWEN JOSEPHUS ROBERTS 1875-1955

1875 Born, Germantown, Pa.

1898 Earned LL.B. from University of Pa. and became first district attorney for Philadelphia County

1898-1918 Taught law as adjunct professor at U. Penn.

1905 *Lochner v. New York* struck down state maximum working hour laws

1914-18 World War I

1924 Appointed special prosecutor in the Teapot Dome scandal

1930-45 Served as associate justice of the Supreme Court

1935 Wrote majority opinion in *Grovey v. Townsend*

1937 Voted with majority in *West Coast Hotel v. Parrish*, which upheld the constitutionality of state minimum wage laws

1939-45 World War II

1944 Dissented in *Korematsu v. United States*

1948-51 Served as dean of University of Pa. Law School

1950-53 Korean War

1955 Died, West Vincent Township, Pa.

1961-73 Vietnam War

1875   1900   1925   1950   1975

tection Clause to invalidate a state statute authorizing the University of Missouri to exclude blacks from its law school.

Although Roberts upheld white primaries in *Grovey*, he supported racial minorities in *Korematsu v. United States*, 323 U.S. 214, 65 S. Ct. 193, 89 L. Ed. 194 (1944). In *Korematsu* the Supreme Court upheld the constitutionality of an EXECUTIVE ORDER authorizing the forcible detention of more than a hundred thousand Americans of Japanese descent during World War II. Roberts dissented, attacking the rationale underlying the executive order, which ostensibly had been promulgated for the purpose of protecting the United States from risks of sabotage. Roberts argued that forcible detention was really just a euphemism for imprisonment and that Japanese Americans were being punished solely on the grounds of their ancestry "without evidence or inquiry concerning [their] loyalty and good disposition towards the United States." In this light Roberts concluded that the record revealed a clear constitutional violation.

Roberts retired from the Supreme Court in 1945. He then returned to the University of Pennsylvania where he served as dean of the law school from 1948 to 1951. Three years later, on May 17, 1955, Roberts suffered a heart attack and died at his Pennsylvania farm in West Vincent Township.

CROSS-REFERENCES

Japanese American Evacuation Cases; *Korematsu v. United States*; *West Coast Hotel v. Parrish*.

ROBERTS v. UNITED STATES JAYCEES

Roberts v. United States Jaycees was a 1984 Supreme Court decision, 468 U.S. 609, 104 S. Ct. 3244, 82 L. Ed. 2d 462, that held that the right to FREEDOM OF ASSOCIATION guaranteed under the First and Fourteenth Amendments to the Constitution did not include the right of a commercial association to deny women admission to the organization because of their gender. In a unanimous vote, the Court emphasized that the state had a compelling interest to eliminate SEX DISCRIMINATION and assure its citizens equal access to publicly available goods and services.

The U.S. Jaycees (Jaycees) was founded as the Junior Chamber of Commerce in 1920. It is a national organization, which at the time of the litigation had more than 235,000 members. The national organization set membership requirements for local chapters, one of which limited membership to men between the ages of eighteen and thirty-five. When the Minneapolis and St. Paul chapters of the Jaycees admitted women in the mid-1970s, the U.S. Jaycees imposed a number of sanctions on those chapters for violating the BYLAWS. For example, it denied their members eligibility for state or national office or awards programs and refused to count their membership in computing votes at national conventions.

In December 1978 the president of the Jaycees advised both chapters that a motion to revoke their charters would be considered at a forthcoming meeting of the national board of directors. Members of both chapters filed charges of sex discrimination with the Minnesota Department of Human Rights, alleging that the exclusion of women from full membership required by the national organization's bylaws violated the Minnesota Human Rights Act (Minn. Stat. § 363.03, subd. 3 [1982]). The members argued that the Jaycees organization was a public accommodation within the meaning of the act and was therefore bound not to discriminate on the basis of gender.

The Minnesota Human Rights Department ruled that the membership policy violated the act. The Jaycees then filed suit in federal court alleging that a requirement that would force the organization to accept women as regular members would violate the male members' constitutional rights of free speech and association. The federal court certified a question to the Minnesota Supreme Court, asking whether the Jaycees organization was a "place of public accommodation" within the meaning of the state's Human Rights Act.

The supreme court answered affirmatively, concluding that the Jaycees organization is a "business" in that it sells goods and extends privileges in exchange for annual membership dues, it is a "public" business in that it solicits and recruits dues-paying members based on unselective criteria, and it is a public business "facility" in that it conducts its activities at fixed and mobile sites within the state of Minnesota.

The federal district court ruled in the state's favor, and the Jaycees appealed. The Eighth Circuit Court of Appeals reversed the decision, finding that in requiring the admission of women, the act violated the First and Fourteenth Amendment rights of the organization's members.

The U.S. Supreme Court disagreed. In a unanimous ruling, the Court admitted that the Jaycees' freedom of association rights were infringed by the Minnesota Human Rights Act. Justice WILLIAM J. BRENNAN, JR., noted that the Jaycees' freedom of association related to the expression of collective views and interests. The right of association was not absolute, however.

If the state could demonstrate a COMPELLING STATE INTEREST and show that the remedy was narrowly tailored, the prohibition on gender discrimination would be permitted.

Brennan found that the act reflected Minnesota's "strong historical commitment to eliminating discrimination and assuring its citizens equal access to publicly available goods and services." This goal "plainly serves compelling state interests of the highest order."

Having found a compelling state interest, Brennan concluded that in applying the act to the Jaycees, the state had advanced its interests in the least restrictive way. The Jaycees could not demonstrate any "serious burdens on the male members' freedom of expressive association." The Court dismissed the contention by the Jaycees that women members might have a different view or agenda than men. This contention was based on "unsupported generalizations about the relative interests and perspectives of men and women." The Court would not, stated Brennan, "indulge in the sexual stereotyping that underlies" the Jaycees' argument.

In a concurring opinion, Justice Sandra Day O'Connor stated that the Jaycees was a nonexpressive commercial association and that these associations have long been the subject of greater government regulatory control.

CROSS-REFERENCES

Equal Protection; First Amendment; Fourteenth Amendment; Women's Rights.

ROBINSON, SPOTTSWOOD WILLIAM, III

Spottswood William Robinson III is a federal appeals court judge, who before his appointment was a law professor and an attorney actively involved in the CIVIL RIGHTS MOVEMENT. Robinson worked with THURGOOD MARSHALL and the NATIONAL ASSOCIATION FOR THE ADVANCEMENT OF COLORED PEOPLE (NAACP) Legal Defense and Educational Fund during the 1940s and 1950s to desegregate racially segregated schools.

Robinson was born on July 26, 1916, in Richmond, Virginia. He attended Virginia

BIOGRAPHY

Spottswood William Robinson III

APWIDE WORLD PHOTOS

Union University and received his LL.B. degree from Howard University School of Law in 1939. He joined the Howard Law School faculty immediately after graduation and served as a professor of law until 1948. Robinson was admitted to the Virginia bar in 1943.

During his years at Howard, Robinson worked with the dean of the law school, CHARLES HAMILTON HOUSTON, and other professors and Howard Law graduates, in a concerted effort to end racial SEGREGATION in public schools. As counsel to the Virginia branch of the NAACP Legal Defense and Educational Fund from 1948 to 1950, Robinson pursued legal action against Virginia's segregated education system. He continued this legal attack on the "SEPARATE-BUT-EQUAL doctrine" as the NAACP Southeast Regional counsel in 1951, a position he retained until 1960. The NAACP's litigation ultimately led to the momentous decision of *Brown v. Board of Education of Topeka, Kansas,* 347 U.S. 483, 74 S. Ct. 686, 98 L. Ed. 873 (1954), which overturned the separate-but-equal doctrine and struck down state-mandated segregation of public schools.

Robinson established a private law practice in 1955 but returned to Howard University Law School in 1960 to become its dean. During this period he also served as a member of the U.S. Commission on Civil Rights. In 1963 Robinson became vice president and general counsel of Consolidated Bank and Trust Company, where he served until he was appointed to the U.S. District Court for the District of Columbia in 1964.

Robinson was appointed to the U.S. Court of Appeals for the District of Columbia Circuit in November 1966, serving as chief judge from May 1981 to July 1986. He took senior status on September 1, 1989.

See also SCHOOL DESEGREGATION.

ROBINSON-PATMAN ACT

The Robinson-Patman Act is a 1936 statute (15 U.S.C.A. §§ 13(a–f) that amended Section 2 of the Clayton Act (Oct. 15, 1914, ch. 323, 38 Stat. 730), which was the first antitrust statute aimed at price discrimination. The Robinson-Patman

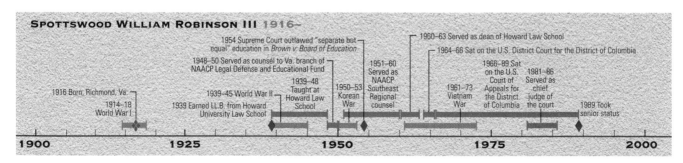

SPOTTSWOOD WILLIAM ROBINSON III 1916–

1916 Born, Richmond, Va.

1914–18 World War I

1939 Earned LL.B. from Howard University Law School

1939–45 World War II

1939–48 Taught at Howard Law School

1948–50 Served as counsel to Va. branch of NAACP Legal Defense and Educational Fund

1950–53 Korean War

1951–60 Served as NAACP Southeast Regional counsel

1954 Supreme Court outlawed "separate but equal" education in *Brown v. Board of Education*

1960–63 Served as dean of Howard Law School

1961–73 Vietnam War

1964–66 Sat on the U.S. District Court for the District of Columbia

1966–89 Sat on the U.S. Court of Appeals for the District of Columbia

1981–86 Served as chief judge of the court

1989 Took senior status

1900   1925   1950   1975   2000

Act prohibits a seller of commodities from selling comparable GOODS to different buyers at different prices, except in certain circumstances.

The Robinson-Patman Act seeks to limit the ability of large, powerful buyers to gain price discounts through the use of their buying power. Although the act remains an important antitrust statute, private parties do not use it nearly as often as they use the Sherman Act, in part due to the Robinson-Patman Act's convoluted and complicated language. The government, which may bring an action under the Robinson-Patman Act through the Federal Trade Commission (FTC), rarely initiates actions under the statute.

In fact, the Robinson-Patman Act has been severely criticized throughout its history, both for its poor drafting and the economic theory behind it. Even the Supreme Court has criticized the act on more than one occasion, stating in 1952 that it is "complicated and vague in itself and even more so in its context. Indeed, the Court of Appeals seems to have thought it almost beyond understanding" (*FTC v. Ruberoid Co.*, 343 U.S. 470, 72 S. Ct. 800, 96 L. Ed. 1081 [1952]). Nevertheless, the Robinson-Patman Act remains an important deterrent and remedy to market power abuses by large and powerful buyers.

The Robinson-Patman Act was passed during the Great Depression following the emergence of large, successful grocery-store chains. Small, independent grocery stores and their suppliers lobbied Congress to do something about the large chains, which were alleged to have exercised their superior buying power to achieve price discounts, driving small grocers out of business. The United States Wholesale Grocers Association drafted the original bill of what was to become the Robinson-Patman Act. Many critics of the act point out that Congress passed the act with the protection of small grocers and their wholesalers in mind, rather than the welfare of competition or the consumer.

The Robinson-Patman Act was intended to remedy perceived shortcomings in the CLAYTON ACT. The federal courts had determined that the Clayton Act did not apply to price discrimination based on quantity, which was precisely what the small, independent businesses were worried about. The Robinson-Patman Act considerably expanded the scope of the Clayton Act. The Robinson-Patman Act specifically prohibits discounts based solely on quantity, except in certain situations. The act's provisions apply both to sellers who offer discriminatory prices and buyers who knowingly receive them.

The act is also intended to remedy secondary line injury, which is injury to competitors of a buyer who receives a discriminatory price, in addition to primary line injury, which refers to injury to competitors of a seller who offers a discriminatory price. Both private parties and the FTC may use the statute. A private party can obtain, in appropriate circumstances, TREBLE DAMAGES from a price discriminator—in other words, three times the party's actual damages.

To invoke the provisions of the Robinson-Patman Act, certain jurisdictional elements must be established. The act applies only (1) to sales (2) in commerce (3) of commodities (4) of like grade and quality. The sales requirement excludes transfers, LEASES, or CONSIGNMENT sales from the act's provisions. Other transfers that do not meet the legal definition of a *sale*, such as an offer or bid, are not covered by the act. Finally, the plural *sales* is important. The act applies only where there are two completed sales to different purchasers at different prices. The commerce specification requires at least one of the sales to be in interstate commerce, meaning that the goods must have physically crossed a state line.

The Robinson-Patman Act applies only to sales of commodities or TANGIBLE goods. The courts have determined that the act is not available to remedy discriminatory pricing of services, money (e.g., loans), INSURANCE, electricity, advertising, or photo processing (primarily a service). In a case such as photo processing, where the product is really both a commodity and a service, the courts look to the "dominant feature" of the transaction. If the dominant feature is not a COMMODITY, the act will not apply. Finally, the act applies only to goods of "like grade or quality." Obviously the determination of whether two goods are of like grade and quality is somewhat subjective. The courts have applied several evidentiary standards to this determination. For the act to apply, the goods must be at least reasonably interchangeable. For example, a generic and brand-name food product are of "like grade and quality" if the only real difference between them is the brand name or label itself.

After the jurisdictional elements of the Robinson-Patman Act have been satisfied, a plaintiff must establish price discrimination by the defendant and injury to competition to prove a violation of the main provisions of the act. The price discrimination element is actually easy to establish; only a difference in price in two different sales is required. The price refers to the actual price paid, net of discounts

The Robinson-Patman Act, designed to stop price discrimination, forbids a seller of commodities, such as the owner of this general store, from charging different prices to different people buying comparable goods.

and allowances. Conversely, there is no price discrimination under the act where the same price is charged to two buyers, even if the seller's costs in serving one buyer are much higher than the costs of serving the other.

The injury to competition element is more difficult to establish. Harm to only the individual plaintiff is not enough to prove injury to competition. Although the plaintiff need not prove actual harm to competition, due to the difficulty of proving it in court, there must be at least a "reasonable possibility" that the price discrimination affected competition in the overall market for the product. As noted earlier, there are two types of injury to competition due to price discrimination: primary line injury and secondary line injury. Primary line injury refers to injury to the competitors of the seller, who lose the business of the buyers who take advantage of the seller's discriminatory price. Secondary line injury refers to injury to the competitors of the buyer, who are unable to take advantage of the discriminatory prices obtained by the buyer.

A primary line injury may be proved in two ways. A plaintiff may present EVIDENCE of the seller's intent to destroy a competitor, either by DIRECT EVIDENCE or INDIRECT EVIDENCE such as

business tactics and unexplained price moves. Otherwise, the plaintiff must prove that the seller's discriminatory price caused a substantial change in market shares in the product. The latter is nearly impossible to prove, because courts, commentators, and economists have frequently rejected the idea that discriminatory pricing poses a long-term threat to competition. It is also difficult to prove a seller's INTENT to destroy a competitor, because a seller isn't likely to leave evidence of such an intent and it is difficult to infer such an intent. One way to prove intent to injure competition is to show that the seller made sales at prices below the seller's average cost of producing the product long enough to force equally efficient competitors out of business. Because of the difficulties in proving a primary line injury under the Robinson-Patman Act, plaintiffs alleging a primary line injury from a discriminatory price are more likely to seek a remedy under other antitrust statutes.

A plaintiff claiming a secondary line injury must also meet several requirements to prove injury to competition. The plaintiff must show that it competed in fact, not potentially, with a buyer who received a discriminatory price, that the price difference was substantial, and that the price difference existed over time. Once these factors are established, a PRESUMPTION is created that the price discrimination injured competition. This presumption can be overcome only by evidence proving there was no causal connection between the discriminatory price received by the buyer and lost sales or profits of the buyer's competitors.

Even if a plaintiff establishes the jurisdictional elements of a claim under the Robinson-Patman Act and proves a discriminatory price and injury to competition, the defendant may still raise defenses that will defeat the plaintiff's claim. Three main defenses exist: "meeting competition," "cost justification," and "functional availability."

Under the meeting competition defense, a discriminatory price is lawful when the seller is acting in GOOD FAITH to meet an equally low price of a competitor. This defense is absolute and will bar a claim under the Robinson-Patman Act regardless of injury to competitors or competition.

Under the cost justification defense, a seller who offered a discriminatory price may defeat a Robinson-Patman Act claim by establishing that the difference in price was justified by "differences in the cost of manufacture, sale, or delivery resulting from the differing methods or quantities" in which the goods are sold. Proving cost justification is difficult because of the complicated accounting analysis required to establish the defense, and therefore it is rarely used.

Although it is not mentioned in the act itself, the functional availability defense allows a seller who offered a discriminatory price to avoid LIABILITY under the Robinson-Patman Act if the seller can prove that the discriminatory price the disfavored buyer did not receive was functionally or realistically available to that buyer. Usually this defense involves proof that the disfavored buyer was able to qualify for some discount offered by the seller but failed to take advantage of it.

The basic prohibitions and defenses are contained in sections 2(a) and 2(b) of the Robinson-Patman Act. The act contains some special provisions as well. Sections 2(d) and 2(e) of the act deal with services and promotional payments that might be provided in connection with a sale of goods. Section 2(d) allows a seller to give discounts to buyers who perform certain services, such as promotions, that the seller would otherwise provide. Substantially similar discounts must be offered to all buyers of like goods, or else the act is violated. Section 2(e) prohibits a seller from discriminating in the furnishing of facilities and services for the processing, handling, or sale of goods.

Section 2(c) of the act prohibits bogus brokerage arrangements whereby large buyers attempt to obtain illegal discounts disguised as brokerage commissions. This provision is usually invoked where the "broker" does not actually render any service to the seller but is merely a large-volume buyer. This section also applies to certain illegal brokerage payments and commercial BRIBERY. Section 2(f) of the act specifically provides that it is unlawful for a buyer to knowingly solicit or receive an unlawfully discriminatory price.

The Robinson-Patman Act has been widely criticized throughout its history, although Congress has retained the act in its original form. The complicated and convoluted language of the act makes it difficult to understand and interpret. The courts have applied its provisions inconsistently over the years and have often confused the proof required for a violation of the Robinson-Patman Act with the standards used in cases brought under the Sherman Act (July 2, 1890, ch. 647, 26 Stat. 209, 15 U.S.C.A. §§ 1 et seq.). Also, many critics suggest that the act is designed merely to protect small business and that it protects competitors rather than competition.

The act has been attacked on economic grounds as well. Most economists believe that discriminatory pricing cannot lead to MONOPOLY power and injury to competition, because the seller offering the discriminatory price cannot profitably sustain the discriminatory price long enough to drive out competitors and, more importantly, keep them out. In fact, the act may discourage competition. For example, the Supreme Court held in the widely criticized *Utah Pie* case that under the Robinson-Patman Act, a national frozen pie seller that sought to enter a new geographical market could not charge a lower price in the new market than it charged in its existing markets (*Utah Pie Co. v. Continental Baking Co.*, 386 U.S. 685, 87 S. Ct. 1326, 18 L. Ed. 2d 406 [1967]). Critics suggest that this interpretation of the act may discourage large, national sellers from entering a new market, even though the consumer and competition in the new market would benefit.

Over the last several decades, fewer and fewer enforcement agencies and private litigants have used the Robinson-Patman Act, for several reasons. First, the nation's attitude toward large, commercial businesses has changed since the act was passed during the Depression, partly because these large businesses have often increased competition, resulting in lower prices for consumers. Also, the legal precedents and theories behind the act have become so complex that plaintiffs usually resort to the more basic antitrust statutes, such as the Sherman Act. Finally, the defenses to actions under the Robinson-Patman Act, such as the meeting competition defense, have become substantially more available and effective as the markets for most products have expanded and increased in sophistication.

Despite the decline in its use, the Robinson-Patman Act is still an important antitrust statute. It acts as both a deterrent and a remedy to abuses to market power by large and powerful businesses and reflects the nation's desire to offer some protection to small, family businesses against the predatory acts of powerful competitors.

CROSS-REFERENCES

Antitrust Law; Sales Law; Sherman Antitrust Act.

ROBINSON v. CALIFORNIA The U.S. Supreme Court, in *Robinson v. California*, 370 U.S. 660, 82 S. Ct. 1417, 8 L. Ed. 2d 758 (1962), made two landmark rulings on the scope and meaning of the Cruel and Unusual Punishments Clause of the EIGHTH AMENDMENT to the U.S. Constitution.

The Eighth Amendment guarantees that "Excessive bail shall not be required, nor excessive fines imposed, nor cruel and unusual punishments inflicted." At issue in *Robinson v. California* was the constitutionality of a California criminal law that made being a narcotics addict a crime. To reach this issue, however, the Court first broke new ground and ruled that the Eighth Amendment applied to the states through the Due Process Clause of the FOURTEENTH AMENDMENT.

Lawrence Robinson was stopped on a city street by a Los Angeles police officer, who had noticed that Robinson's arms were scabbed, discolored, and filled with needle marks. The officer arrested Robinson, who was sent to the Los Angeles central jail. The next day his arms were again examined, this time by a member of the narcotics division of the police department. Based on his examination, the officer concluded the marks and discoloration were the result of the injection of unsterilized hypodermic needles into Robinson's arms. Both police officers claimed that Robinson admitted he had occasionally used narcotics.

Robinson was charged with violating a California criminal law that made it illegal to "be addicted to the use of narcotics." At his trial Robinson denied that he had told police he used narcotics and asserted that the marks on his arm were the result of an allergic condition contracted while he was in military service. Two witnesses corroborated his testimony. The jury was instructed that it could convict Robinson if it believed he was addicted to the use of narcotics. Unlike most criminal laws, which require that a person be convicted for a criminal act, in this case Robinson could be convicted for his condition, or status, as a drug addict. The jury convicted Robinson of the MISDEMEANOR, and the California APPELLATE COURTS upheld the conviction.

The U.S. Supreme Court accepted Robinson's APPEAL and reversed the conviction. Justice POTTER STEWART, in his majority opinion, had to cross a major constitutional barrier before ruling on the Eighth Amendment issue. Until the 1960s the Court had abided by PRECEDENT that held that the rights guaranteed to criminal defendants by the Fourth, Fifth, Sixth, and Eighth Amendments applied only to the FEDERAL COURTS. During the 1940s Justice HUGO L. BLACK had advocated the incorporation of these amendments into the Due Process Clause of the Fourteenth Amendment, thus making the amendments applicable to the states.

The Court eventually came around to Black's position and in 1961 started to selectively apply these rights to the states. In *Mapp v. Ohio*, 367 U.S. 643, 81 S. Ct. 1684, 6 L. Ed. 2d 1081 (1961), the Court used the Fourteenth Amendment to apply the FOURTH AMENDMENT'S EXCLUSIONARY RULE to the states; this rule prevents illegally obtained evidence from being introduced at trial. Stewart reflected this shift in position when he announced in *Robinson* that the California statute "is repugnant to the Fourteenth Amendment of the Constitution." This meant that the rights guaranteed under the Eighth Amendment now applied to the states.

Having established the right of the Court to examine state criminal law for Eighth Amendment violations, Stewart reviewed the California statute. He acknowledged that the state had a right to regulate the sale and use of illegal narcotics, establish drug treatment programs, and seek ways of improving the economic and social conditions under which drug addiction flourishes. But he also observed that the state could choose among many options in addressing the problem without violating a person's constitutional rights.

The major defect of the law was making the "status" of narcotic addiction a criminal offense, for which the offender might be prosecuted at any time before reforming his ways. Stewart was troubled that "a person can be continuously guilty of this offense, whether or not he has ever used or possessed any narcotics within the State, and whether or not he has been guilty of any antisocial behavior there."

Establishing the criminal status of "narcotics addict" violated the ban on CRUEL AND UNUSUAL PUNISHMENT because a person addicted to drugs suffers from an illness. Stewart pointed out that government no longer makes it a criminal offense to be a person suffering from a contagious physical disease or mental illness. Those persons may legally be subject to compulsory treatment, such as quarantine or confinement, but they are not charged with a crime. An attempt by a state to do so, "in the light of contemporary human knowledge," would be a violation of the Eighth and Fourteenth Amendments.

The Court noted that even California admitted narcotic addiction was an illness that may be contracted innocently or involuntarily. In light of this admission, Stewart held that a "state law which imprisons a person thus afflicted as a criminal" inflicts cruel and unusual punishment in violation of the Fourteenth Amendment. Though Robinson would have been confined for only ninety days, "[e]ven one day in prison would be a cruel and unusual punishment for the 'crime' of having a common cold."

In dissenting opinions, Justices TOM CLARK and BYRON WHITE argued that the Court had unfairly disturbed a "comprehensive and enlightened program for the control of narcotism based on the overriding policy of prevention and cure." Clark stated that the criminal statute was intended for persons still in the early stages of addiction who retained self-control and required short-term confinement and PAROLE with frequent drug tests. Though the law appeared penal, its provisions were very similar to those for civil commitment and treatment of addicts "who have lost the power of self-control." The civil and criminal laws shared the common purpose of rehabilitating narcotic addicts and preventing continued addiction. In light of this common purpose, opined Clark, that one law "might be labeled 'criminal' seems irrelevant." It was within the power of California to design its course of treatment.

The elimination of drug addiction as a status offense meant that the criminal justice system could only address specific actions of traffickers and users. Possession of narcotics is a crime, but the physical condition of addiction cannot be. The state may address addiction through civil commitment for drug treatment.

Despite the Court's holding that narcotics addiction is an illness, it later proved unwilling to draw the same conclusion concerning ALCOHOL abuse. In *Powell v. Texas*, 392 U.S. 514, 88 S. Ct. 2145, 20 L. Ed. 2d 1254 (1968), the Court, by a 5–4 vote, upheld a Texas law that made it a crime to be publicly intoxicated. The Court reasoned that the Texas law was constitutional because it did not make the status of being an alcoholic an offense but prohibited the specific offense of public intoxication. Rather than following the *Robinson* approach, the Court said that knowledge about alcoholism and the record in the case were inadequate to make the punishment of alcohol-related offenses cruel and unusual. Justice ABE FORTAS, in a dissenting opinion, argued that the *Robinson* rule should be followed and that "criminal penalties may not be inflicted upon a person for being in a condition he is powerless to change."

CROSS-REFERENCES

Drugs and Narcotics; Due Process of Law; Incorporation Doctrine.

ROCHIN v. CALIFORNIA In *Rochin v. California*, 342 U.S. 165, 72 S. Ct. 205, 96 L. Ed. 183 (1952), the U.S. Supreme Court ruled that it was unconstitutional for police to pump a criminal suspect's stomach and use the resulting EVIDENCE at trial. The Court held that such conduct was "shocking to the conscience" and that the evidence must be suppressed under the Due Process Clause of the FOURTEENTH AMENDMENT.

On the morning of July 1, 1949, three Los Angeles County deputy sheriffs went to the home of Antonio Rochin. The police did not have a search warrant but had some information that Rochin was selling narcotics. Finding the outside door open, they entered the dwelling. They went to the second floor, where they forced open the door to Rochin's room. They found Rochin sitting partly dressed on the side of the bed, where his wife was lying. One of the deputies noticed two capsules on a nightstand and asked, "Whose stuff is this?" Rochin grabbed the capsules and put them in his mouth. The three deputies then wrestled with Rochin and sought to open his mouth so they could extract the pills. When this failed, the deputies handcuffed Rochin and took him to a hospital, where at their direction a doctor forced an emetic solution through a tube into Rochin's stomach. The solution induced vomiting, and in the vomited matter the deputies found two morphine capsules.

Rochin was tried and convicted of narcotics possession. The conviction was based solely on the morphine capsules, though Rochin unsuccessfully challenged their admission. After the

California APPELLATE COURTS upheld the conviction, Rochin filed an APPEAL with the U.S. Supreme Court.

At the time of *Rochin v. California*, the U.S. Supreme Court rarely intruded into the police procedures of the states. Not until the 1960s would the Court apply the Bill of Rights amendments dealing with CRIMINAL PROCEDURE to the states (despite the consistent efforts of Justices HUGO L. BLACK and WILLIAM O. DOUGLAS to incorporate these rights through the Due Process Clause of the Fourteenth Amendment).

Because of this situation, Rochin could not rely on the FOURTH AMENDMENT, which protects the people against unreasonable searches and seizures, or the FIFTH AMENDMENT, which protects a person from being a witness against himself. At that time the Fourth and Fifth Amendments applied only against the federal government. If they had applied to the states, the searches of Rochin's home and stomach would have been unconstitutional and the evidence suppressed under the Fourth Amendment's EXCLUSIONARY RULE.

A majority of the Court in *Rochin* refused to apply the Fifth Amendment to the states despite the arguments of Justices Black and Douglas in their concurring opinions. Instead, the Court relied solely on the Fourteenth Amendment's Due Process Clause as the basis for striking down the search. Justice FELIX FRANKFURTER wrote for the majority that the Due Process Clause contains a general standard of conduct by which states must abide. A state cannot offend "those canons of decency and fairness which express the notions of justice of English-speaking peoples." DUE PROCESS OF LAW requires the state to observe those principles that are "so rooted in the traditions and conscience of our people as to be ranked as fundamental."

The police conduct here did more than offend "private sentimentalism about combating crime too energetically." This conduct "shock[ed] the conscience," offending even those with hardened sensibilities. The treatment of Rochin was "too close to the rack and screw to permit of constitutional differentiation."

Frankfurter defended the "SHOCK THE CONSCIENCE" TEST as a responsible means of forcing states in their criminal prosecutions to "respect certain decencies of civilized conduct." Due process of law cannot be precisely defined, as it is a "historic and generative principle." It was clear to the Court that a coercive search of Rochin's stomach contents offended "the community's sense of fair play and decency" as much as a coerced verbal CONFESSION would.

At the time of *Rochin*, coerced confessions were inadmissible in state courts. The Supreme Court, in *Adamson v. California*, 332 U.S. 46, 67 S. Ct. 1672, 91 L. Ed. 1903 (1947), had applied the Due Process Clause to reach this result. It would have been unfair to admit the morphine capsules obtained by physical abuse while suppressing a confession obtained by physical abuse. Characterizing the police action as "brutal conduct," Frankfurter concluded that allowing admission of the morphine capsules would discredit the law and "brutalize the temper of a society."

Justice Black, in his concurring opinion, agreed that the police conduct was unconstitutional but argued that the Court did not have to resort to its vague and subjective shock the conscience test. Black, noting the precise language of the Fifth Amendment, believed the Court could easily ground its authority in that amendment by incorporating it into the Fourteenth Amendment. This was preferable to the "nebulous standards" articulated by Frankfurter.

Justice Douglas, in his concurring opinion, attacked the shock the conscience test for its conclusion that California's state law that admitted evidence such as Rochin's violated "decencies of civilized conduct." He pointed out that only three states would probably exclude the *Rochin* evidence. The remaining states were served by "responsible courts with judges as sensitive as we are to the proper standards for law administration." He also noted that even the Fifth Amendment's provision against SELF-INCRIMINATION was not recognized by "all civilized legal procedures." The fact that the Framers required the Fifth Amendment to be used in federal courts made it "impossible for me to say it is not a requirement of due process for a trial in the state courthouse."

Whether *Rochin* retains any legal relevance has been much debated over the years. The Supreme Court incorporated the Fifth Amendment privilege against self-incrimination into the Fourteenth Amendment in 1964 (*Malloy v. Hogan*, 378 U.S. 1, 84 S. Ct. 1489, 12 L. Ed. 2d 653) and the Fourth Amendment's exclusionary rule in 1961 (*Mapp v. Ohio*, 367 U.S. 643, 81 S. Ct. 1684, 6 L. Ed. 2d 1081). As a result, state and federal criminal constitutional rights are identical.

Some commentators believe *Rochin* is important because it stands for the proposition that the Due Process Clause provides a protection for citizens separate from, and independent of, the BILL OF RIGHTS provisions like the Fourth Amendment that have now been applied to the states. The case also shows that even if the Supreme Court were to abandon the Fourth Amendment exclusionary rule, the Due Process Clause will sometimes require exclusion of evidence in cases where police conduct is egregious enough to shock the conscience.

Other commentators and judges have expressed misgivings about the shock the conscience test. In their view, the test is too vague and gives federal judges too much power over state law enforcement. These critics argue that no clear line separates conduct that is merely offensive from conduct that shocks the conscience.

CROSS-REFERENCES
Criminal Law; Criminal Procedure; Incorporation Doctrine; Search and Seizure.

RODNEY, CAESAR AUGUSTUS Caesar Augustus Rodney served as U.S. attorney general from 1807 to 1811. His term as attorney general was unusual in that he served in both the Jefferson and Madison administrations. A member of a prominent Delaware family, Rodney held many positions in state government as well as in the federal government.

Rodney was born on January 4, 1772, in Dover, Delaware. His father was Thomas Rodney, an attorney, politician, and member of the Delaware Supreme Court. Rodney was named after his uncle, who was a delegate to the CONTINENTAL CONGRESS, president (governor) of Delaware, and a key signer of the DECLARATION OF INDEPENDENCE.

Rodney graduated from the University of Pennsylvania in 1789. He then studied law under Joseph B. McKean in Philadelphia and was admitted to the Delaware bar in 1793. He practiced law in Wilmington and New Castle for the next few years.

Rodney, like his father and uncle, was attracted to politics. He was elected to the Delaware House of Representatives in 1796. He served in the U.S. House of Representatives from 1803 to 1805. He was a staunch supporter of President THOMAS JEFFERSON and sided with the Republicans in their political battles with

BIOGRAPHY

CULVER PICTURES

Caesar Augustus Rodney

the Federalist party. Rodney served as one of the House managers in the IMPEACHMENT trials of Judge John J. Pickering of the U.S. District Court for New Hampshire and Associate Justice SAMUEL CHASE, the only Supreme Court justice ever tried on a bill of impeachment. Both judges were Federalists and the impeachment trials were politically motivated. Pickering was found guilty, but Chase was acquitted when moderate Republicans abandoned their party on the issue of political rather than criminal impeachments.

Jefferson appointed Rodney attorney general on January 20, 1807, midway through his second term. The last two years of the Jefferson administration were relatively tranquil in the domestic sphere. President JAMES MADISON, who was a close friend and political ally of Jefferson, took office in 1809 and asked Rodney to continue in his post. Rodney resigned his position on December 5, 1811.

During the War of 1812, Rodney commanded a company of volunteers in defense of the city of Baltimore. He returned to the U.S. House of Representatives in 1821 and was elected to the U.S. Senate in 1822. He resigned from the Senate in 1823 to accept an appointment as U.S. minister to the Argentine Republic. He died in Buenos Aires on June 10, 1824.

ROE 🕮 A fictitious surname used for an unknown or anonymous person or for a hypothetical person in an illustration. 🕮

A lawsuit is generally named for the persons who are parties to it. When the name of a PARTY is unknown, the court CLERK may direct that the person be called a fictitious name in the papers of the lawsuit. This also may be done to hide the identity of a person who would needlessly suffer if his name were known—for example, the name of a parent who is giving up a child for adoption or the name of a juvenile charged with a crime.

Frequently used fictitious party names include Richard Roe, Mary Roe, and John Doe.

ROE v. WADE *Roe v. Wade* was a landmark decision by the U.S. Supreme Court, 410 U.S. 113, 93 S. Ct. 705, 35 L. Ed. 2d 147 (1973), that

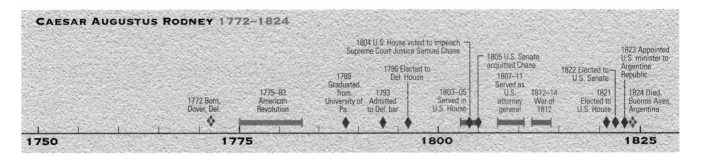

CAESAR AUGUSTUS RODNEY 1772–1824

1772 Born, Dover, Del.

1775–83 American Revolution

1789 Graduated from University of Pa.

1793 Admitted to Del. bar

1796 Elected to Del. House

1803–05 Served in U.S. House

1804 U.S. House voted to impeach Supreme Court Justice Samuel Chase

1805 U.S. Senate acquitted Chase

1807–11 Served as U.S. attorney general

1812–14 War of 1812

1821 Elected to U.S. House

1822 Elected to U.S. Senate

1823 Appointed U.S. minister to Argentine Republic

1824 Died, Buenos Aires, Argentina

1750   1775   1800   1825

declared a pregnant woman is entitled to have an ABORTION until the end of the first trimester of pregnancy without any interference by the state.

In a 7–2 decision on January 22, 1973, the Supreme Court struck down an 1857 Texas statute that made abortion illegal except where the life of the mother was in danger. The Court's opinion, as written by Justice HARRY A. BLACKMUN, set forth guidelines for the drafting of future state legislation on the issue. In a long and detailed opinion, the Court specified the points during a woman's pregnancy when the interests of the state in the health of the mother and of the fetus emerge. *Roe* established the parameters of the abortion debate for decades to come.

The case involved an unmarried pregnant woman who was at the time identified only as Jane Roe in order to maintain her anonymity but who has since publicly identified herself as Norma McCorvey. McCorvey, a resident of Texas, wanted to have an abortion, but the existing state law prevented her from doing so. She filed a lawsuit in federal district court on behalf of herself and all other pregnant women. The suit sought to have the Texas abortion law declared unconstitutional as an invasion of her right to PRIVACY as guaranteed by the First, Fourth, Fifth, Ninth, and Fourteenth Amendments. She also sought to have an INJUNCTION, or court order, issued against the statute's enforcement so that she might go forward with

the abortion. A physician, James Hubert Hallford, who was being prosecuted under the statute for two abortions he had performed, also filed suit against the law, as did a childless couple, the Does (Mary Doe and John Doe). A three-judge district court combined the cases of McCorvey and Hallford, and dismissed the suit brought by the Does on the grounds that neither of them had violated the law and Mary Doe was not pregnant.

The district court agreed with McCorvey that the law was unconstitutionally vague and violated her right to privacy under the NINTH AMENDMENT—which allows for the existence of rights, like that of privacy, not explicitly named in the Constitution's BILL OF RIGHTS—and the FOURTEENTH AMENDMENT. It refused, however to grant the injunction allowing her to go ahead with the abortion. McCorvey appealed the denial of the injunction to the U.S. Supreme Court. The Supreme Court agreed to hear the case along with another, *Doe v. Bolton*, 410 U.S. 179, 93 S. Ct. 739, 35 L. Ed. 2d 201 (1973), relating to a 1968 Georgia abortion statute. The Court dismissed Hallford's case because of the pending prosecutions against him. Hallford made no allegation of any substantial and immediate threat to any federal protected right that could not be asserted in his defense against the state prosecution. Nor did he allege harassment or bad-faith prosecution by the state. Hallford's case fell clearly within the ambit of the rule announced in prior Supreme Court cases that a defendant in a pending state criminal case cannot affirmatively challenge in federal court the statutes under which the state is prosecuting him or her (*Samuels v. Mackell*, 401 U.S. 66, 91 S. Ct. 764, 27 L. Ed. 2d 688 [1971]; *Younger v. Harris*, 401 U.S. 37, 91 S. Ct. 746, 27 L. Ed. 2d 669 [1971]; *Boyle v. Landry*, 401 U.S. 77, 91 S. Ct. 758, 27 L. Ed. 2d 696 [1971]).

After hearing many months of expert TESTIMONY, the Court found the Texas abortion law to be unconstitutional. It declared that such laws "violate the Due Process Clause of the Fourteenth Amendment, which protects against state action the right to privacy, including [a] woman's qualified right to terminate her pregnancy." Chief Justice WARREN E. BURGER chose Justice Blackmun—who had served for many years as legal counsel to the Mayo Clinic, in Rochester, Minnesota—to write the Court's opinion. Justice WILLIAM H. REHNQUIST wrote a dissenting opinion.

In its opinion, the Court ruled that the right to terminate a pregnancy is part of a woman's right to privacy. At the same time, however, it declared that "[t]his right is not unqualified and

Norma McCorvey, known as Jane Roe in the abortion case of Roe v. Wade, *withdrew her support from pro-abortion groups and is now an antiabortion activist in Texas.*

Norma McCorvey: The Real Jane Roe

In a 1984 television interview, Norma McCorvey revealed that she is Jane Roe, the plaintiff in the most famous abortion case in U.S. history, *Roe v. Wade.* In 1994, she published an autobiography, *I Am Roe: My Life, Roe v. Wade, and Freedom of Choice,* that puts a human face on the story of Roe. In her book, McCorvey candidly recounts the difficulties of her life, including growing up with an abusive mother, spending time in reform school as an adolescent, struggling with addictions to drugs and alcohol, and coming out as a lesbian.

McCorvey was born Norma Leah Nelson on September 22, 1947, in the bayou country of Lettesworth, Louisiana. Half Cajun and part Native American, she eventually moved with her poor, working-class family to Dallas, where she has since lived most of her life. After an unsuccessful marriage to an abusive husband, she divorced and gave up a daughter to relatives. Wrestling with drug and alcohol addictions amid the counterculture swirl of the 1960s, she later gave up two more children to adoption, including the child she carried when she brought *Roe* to court.

In September 1969, while working as a carnival freak show barker, McCorvey learned that she was pregnant for the third time and returned to Dallas. Out of work, severely depressed, with no money, she decided to seek an abortion. After being told that abortion was legal in cases of rape or incest, friends advised her to lie and say that she had been raped. However, since no police report of the fictitious rape existed, the ruse did not work. She then went to an illegal abortion clinic but found that it had been closed by the police; all that was left was an abandoned building where "dirty instruments were scattered around the room, and there was dried blood on the floor."

Eventually, McCorvey was referred to Sarah Weddington and Linda Coffee, young attorneys who were looking for a plaintiff to challenge the Texas abortion law. Weddington herself had been forced to go to Mexico in order to obtain an abortion during the 1960s. McCorvey agreed to participate in a lawsuit against Henry Wade, the Dallas district attorney. Although she still hoped to finish the suit in time to have an abortion, McCorvey told her attorneys, "Let's do it for other women." McCorvey chose to remain anonymous for several reasons: she feared publicity would hurt her five-year-old daughter, her parents were against abortion, and she had lied about being raped. She did not participate in court hearings in order to maintain her anonymity.

On March 3, 1970, when *Roe* was filed in court, McCorvey was six months pregnant. In June, at twenty-three years of age, she gave birth, and her child went up for adoption. On January 22, 1973, over two years too late to alter the course of her pregnancy, McCorvey learned that she had won her case: the Supreme Court had ruled that the Texas abortion law was unconstitutional.

In 1989, McCorvey decided to ally herself publicly with the abortion rights movement. Shortly before she participated in a large pro-choice rally in Washington, D.C., someone fired gunshots at her house and car, in one of many incidents of harassment she has had to endure since making her identity known. Frightened but undaunted, she joined the April 9 rally and made a speech on Capitol Hill before hundreds of thousands of people. McCorvey worked for a time at a family planning clinic and traveled around the United States giving speeches promoting the reproductive rights of women.

In August 1995, McCorvey announced that she had switched sides on the abortion debate. "I'm pro-life," McCorvey stated. "I think I have always been pro-life, I just didn't know it." McCorvey's reversal was attributed to her new friendship with the Reverend Philip ("Flip") Benham, national director of the militant antiabortion group Operation Rescue. The group had moved its national headquarters into an office next to the clinic where McCorvey worked. After being baptized by Benham, McCorvey declared that she would work on behalf of Operation Rescue.

must be considered against important state interests in regulation." The state, the Court argued, "has legitimate interests in protecting both the pregnant woman's health and the potentiality of human life," interests that change in importance as the pregnancy progresses. In the first trimester, the Court said, the state has no interest in regulating the right of a woman to obtain an abortion. In making this decision, the Court pointed to evidence showing that the health of the mother is not endangered by an abortion during the first twelve weeks of pregnancy. According to that evidence, women are less likely to die from complications of an abortion conducted in the first trimester than from carrying their pregnancy to term. The Court also found that the state may require that all abortions be performed only by licensed physicians under medically safe conditions.

The Court found that the state's interest in regulating abortion and protecting a pregnant woman's health emerges in the second trimester. "[I]n promoting its interest in the health of the mother," the Court declared, "the state may regulate the abortion procedure in ways that are reasonably related to maternal health." It may, for example, impose requirements regarding the qualifications and licensing of those performing abortions; it may also regulate where abortions can be performed. Beyond these rules, the woman, in consultation with her physician, is free to decide whether to end her pregnancy.

In the third trimester, the interest of the state in "the potentiality of human life"—that is, the life of the fetus before birth—makes it possible to regulate and even prohibit abortions except when necessary to save the life or health of the mother. By this period, the fetus is determined to be viable—that is, capable of living outside the womb—and therefore entitled to protection by the state.

The Court did not accept arguments that the fetus be regarded as a person within the meaning of the Due Process Clause of the Fourteenth Amendment, which declares that no state shall "deprive any person of life, liberty, or property, without due process of law" (§ 1). "There is no medical or scientific proof that life is present from conception," wrote the Court.

> [W]e need not resolve the difficult question of when life begins, when those trained in the respective fields of medicine, philosophy and theology are unable to arrive at any consensus. The judiciary at this point in the development of man's knowledge is not in a position to speculate as to the answer.

As author of the Court's opinion, Justice Blackmun made it clear that abortion was an extraordinarily difficult issue:

> We forthwith acknowledge our awareness of the sensitive and emotional nature of the abortion controversy, of the vigorous opposing views, even among physicians, and of the deep and seemingly absolute convictions that the subject inspires. One's philosophy, one's experiences, one's exposure to the raw edges of human existence, one's religious training, one's attitudes toward life and family and their values, and the moral standards one establishes and seeks to observe, are all likely to influence and to color one's thinking and conclusions about abortion.
>
> In addition, population growth, pollution, poverty, and racial overtones tend to complicate and not to simplify the problem.
>
> Our task, of course, is to resolve the issue by constitutional measurement free of emotion and predilection.

Although the opinion went into the "medical and medical-legal" history of the issue and quoted medical authorities frequently, the Court chose to decide the case on constitutional rather than medical or philosophical grounds. In this case, the crucial constitutional consideration was the right to privacy, which some would argue is as old as the Constitution. The most important PRECEDENT for the *Roe* decision on this issue was the 1965 Supreme Court case *Griswold v. Connecticut*, 381 U.S. 479, 85 S. Ct. 1678, 14 L. Ed. 2d 510, which clearly set forth a constitutional right to privacy—in this instance, a married couple's right to privacy when

U.S. Abortion Patients, by Age and Marital Status, 1994–1995

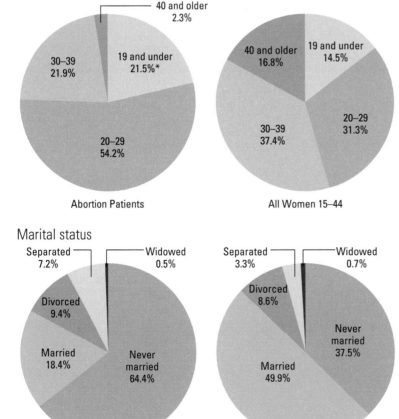

Age group

40 and older 2.3%
30–39 21.9%
19 and under 21.5%*
20–29 54.2%

Abortion Patients

40 and older 16.8%
19 and under 14.5%
30–39 37.4%
20–29 31.3%

All Women 15–44

Marital status

Separated 7.2%
Widowed 0.5%
Divorced 9.4%
Married 18.4%
Never married 64.4%

Abortion Patients

Separated 3.3%
Widowed 0.7%
Divorced 8.6%
Married 49.9%
Never married 37.5%

All Women 15–44

Source: Alan Guttmacher Institute, New York, NY.

deciding whether or not to use contraceptives. *Roe* was in fact part of a gradual expansion of the right to privacy during the 1960s and 1970s, to include not only a right to freedom from physical SEARCHES AND SEIZURES, for example, but also a right to make individual decisions free of coercion, whether physical or psychological, especially in matters regarding the family and reproduction.

In his dissent in *Roe*, Justice Rehnquist differed with the majority on a number of points. For one thing, McCorvey had given birth in 1970 and had given her child up for ADOPTION. He argued that because McCorvey was no longer in the first term of her pregnancy, indeed was no longer pregnant, when her case came before the Supreme Court, the case had become hypothetical rather than actual and therefore outside the JURISDICTION of the Court. Rehnquist also argued that the regulation of abortion should be left to the states and that the right of privacy had nothing to do with the case. "I have difficulty in concluding, as the Court does, that the right of 'privacy' is involved in this case," he wrote. "The decision here to break pregnancy into three distinct terms and to outline the permissible restrictions the State may impose in each one, for example, partakes more of judicial legislation than it does of a determination of the intent of the drafters of the Fourteenth Amendment." Moreover, in Rehnquist's view, the Texas abortion law met the test of having "a rational relation to a valid state objective." Rehnquist's fellow dissenter in *Roe*, Justice BYRON R. WHITE, called the decisions in *Doe* and *Roe* "an example of raw judicial power" and "an improvident and extravagant exercise of the power of judicial review" (*Doe*, 410 U.S. 179 at 221, 93 S. Ct. 762).

The *Roe* decision has largely been perceived as a victory for the abortion reform and WOMEN'S RIGHTS movements and a defeat for antiabortion forces, but in many ways it was a compromise between the two sides. While antiabortion forces were unhappy with the establishment of a right to abortion for women in the first trimester of pregnancy, pro-abortion groups were displeased with the limits on abortion allowed in the last two trimesters of pregnancy. The Court also compromised in its decision as to when life begins and who is to be defined as a person with full rights under the Constitution. It did not agree with the pro-abortion movement, which declared that life does not begin until birth, or with the antiabortion movement, which maintained that life begins at conception. Instead, it chose to define the rights of the fetus as emerging when it reaches the stage of viability, when it can survive independently outside of the womb. In making this decision, some have argued, the Court made personhood subject to change, particularly as science has moved the time of viability further back.

Feminists and women's rights advocates saw *Roe* as a vindication of women's reproductive rights and a step toward greater equality between the sexes. Such equality, they argued, can happen only when women have the ability to control reproduction. Others, opposed to the decision in *Roe*, believed that the Supreme Court had overstepped its bounds by effectively making new social policy, a task they felt was better left to elected members of state legislatures. Still others felt that the Court had violated the sanctity of human life by permitting abortion. In any case, *Roe* has been a far-reaching decision, affecting many spheres of U.S. life, including medicine, religion, and the family.

In the decades following *Roe*, antiabortion groups have mounted continual campaigns to repeal the decision. Despite these challenges, the Supreme Court has repeatedly supported the essential elements of that decision, particularly as regards the right to privacy.

CROSS-REFERENCES
Due Process of Law; Fetal Rights; Fetal Tissue Research; *Griswold v. Connecticut*; Penumbra; Wattleton, Faye.

ROGATORY LETTERS A commission from one judge to another judge requesting the latter to examine a witness.

Rogatory letters can be sent to a court in a sister state or to a court or judge in a foreign country. Granting the request is a matter of COMITY—courtesy and respect—between courts.

ROGERS, WILLIAM PIERCE William Pierce Rogers served as U.S. attorney general from 1957 to 1961. Rogers, who would later serve as secretary of state in the Nixon administration, distinguished himself as attorney general by vigorously enforcing CIVIL RIGHTS law and seeking ways of ending racially segregated public schools.

Rogers was born on June 23, 1913, in Norfolk, New York. He graduated from Colgate University in 1934 and received his law degree from Cornell Law School in 1937. He was admitted to the New York bar in 1937 and entered private practice. Rogers was assistant district attorney for New York County from 1938 until 1942, when he joined the U.S. Navy, serving as a lieutenant commander in World War II. In 1946, after the war, he returned to his district attorney position.

BIOGRAPHY

William Pierce Rogers

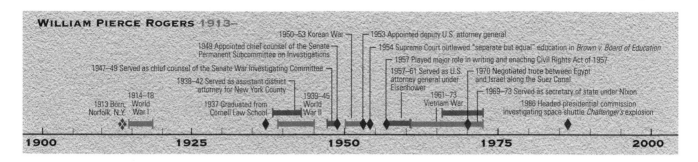

WILLIAM PIERCE ROGERS 1913–

- 1913 Born, Norfolk, N.Y.
- 1914–18 World War I
- 1937 Graduated from Cornell Law School
- 1938–42 Served as assistant district attorney for New York County
- 1939–45 World War II
- 1947–49 Served as chief counsel of the Senate War Investigating Committee
- 1949 Appointed chief counsel of the Senate Permanent Subcommittee on Investigations
- 1950–53 Korean War
- 1953 Appointed deputy U.S. attorney general
- 1954 Supreme Court outlawed "separate but equal" education in *Brown v. Board of Education*
- 1957 Played major role in writing and enacting Civil Rights Act of 1957
- 1957–61 Served as U.S. attorney general under Eisenhower
- 1961–73 Vietnam War
- 1969–73 Served as secretary of state under Nixon
- 1970 Negotiated truce between Egypt and Israel along the Suez Canal
- 1986 Headed presidential commission investigating space shuttle *Challenger's* explosion

1900   1925   1950   1975   2000

Rogers's career shifted from state to federal government in the late 1940s. In 1947 and 1948 he was chief counsel of the Senate War Investigating Committee, becoming chief counsel of the Senate Permanent Subcommittee on Investigations in 1949.

In 1950 Rogers returned to private practice in New York. With the election of President DWIGHT D. EISENHOWER, Rogers was soon back in Washington, becoming deputy attorney general in 1953. He assisted Attorney General Herbert Brownell in the administration of the Justice Department and became a key figure in the emerging debate over civil rights. In the wake of *Brown v. Board of Education of Topeka, Kansas*, 347 U.S. 483, 74 S. Ct. 686, 98 L. Ed. 873 (1954), which prohibited state-imposed racial SEGREGATION in public schools, many southern communities pledged to defy or evade the Supreme Court decision. Some school boards closed the schools and encouraged attendance at white-only private schools, while others refused to integrate. Rogers was an advocate for federal leadership to end segregation and promote INTEGRATION. He played a major role in the writing and enactment of the Civil Rights Act of 1957, 42 U.S.C.A. § 1975 et seq., the first federal civil rights legislation since the 1870s.

In November 1957 Rogers was appointed attorney general by President Eisenhower. He continued to enforce civil rights laws and promote a vision of an integrated society. During his tenure he also prosecuted several high-level Justice Department officials for corruption. Rogers remained attorney general until the end of the Eisenhower administration in January 1961.

During the 1960s Rogers resumed his law practice. In 1969 President RICHARD M. NIXON appointed Rogers secretary of state, a position he held for the president's entire first term. Rogers played a diminished role in foreign policy, however, because Nixon and National Security adviser HENRY KISSINGER assumed most of the responsibility for charting relations with other nations. Rogers's most notable accomplishment as secretary was negotiating a truce

"THERE CAN BE NO LASTING PEACE WITHOUT A JUST SETTLEMENT OF THE PROBLEMS OF T[HE] PALESTINIANS . . . [WHICH] MUST TAKE INTO ACCOUNT THE DESIRES AND ASPIRATIONS OF [BOTH] THE REFUGEES AND THE LEGITIMATE CONCERNS OF THE GOVERNMENTS IN THE AREA."

between Egypt and Israel along the Suez Canal in 1970. He loyally defended the administration's VIETNAM WAR policies, but left all major policy decisions to Kissinger.

Rogers returned to private practice in 1973. In 1986 he was asked to head a presidential commission to investigate the explosion of the space shuttle *Challenger.* The commission issued a report that was critical of the performance of the National Aeronautics and Space Administration.

ROLL To commit a ROBBERY by force. A record of the proceedings of a court or public office.

In some states, a *judgment roll* is required to be filed by the CLERK of the court when he or she enters JUDGMENT. It normally contains the SUMMONS, PLEADINGS, ADMISSIONS, and each judgment and order involving the MERITS of the case or affecting the final judgment. In the FEDERAL COURTS and most state courts, judgments are recorded in the civil DOCKET or criminal docket.

In old English practice, a judgment roll was a roll of parchment containing the entries of the proceedings in an ACTION at law including the entry of judgment. It was filed in the treasury of the court.

A *tax roll* is a list of the persons and property subject to the payment of a particular tax, with the amounts due; it is compiled and verified in proper form to enable the collecting officers to enforce the tax.

ROMAN LAW Between 753 B.C. and A.D. 1453, the legal principles, procedures, and institutions of Roman law dominated Western, and parts of Eastern, civilization. The legal systems of western Europe, with the exception of Great Britain, are based on Roman law and are called civil-law systems. Even the common-law tradition found in the English-speaking world has been influenced by it. In the United States, the COMMON LAW has been paramount, but Roman law has influenced the law of the state of Louisiana, a former French territory that adopted a French civil-law CODE.

Roman law began as an attempt to codify a set of legal principles for all citizens. In 450 B.C.

the Twelve Tables were erected in the Roman Forum. Set forth in tablets of wood or bronze, the law was put on public display, where it could be invoked by persons seeking remedies for their problems. Though the texts of the tablets have not survived, historians believe they dealt with legal procedures, torts, and family law issues.

From 753 to 31 B.C., the Roman republic developed the *jus civile*, or CIVIL LAW. This law was based on both custom and legislation and applied only to Roman citizens. By the third century B.C., the Romans developed the *jus gentium*, rules of INTERNATIONAL LAW that were applied to interactions between Romans and foreigners. Over time the *jus gentium* became a massive compendium of law produced by magistrates and governors.

Romans divided the law into *jus scriptum*, written law, and *jus non scriptum*, unwritten law. The unwritten law was based on custom and usage, while the written law came from legislation and many types of written sources, including edicts and proclamations issued by magistrates, resolutions of the Roman Senate, laws issued by the emperor, and legal disquisitions of prominent lawyers. Roman law concerned itself with every type of legal issue, including contracts, inheritance of property, family law, business organizations, and criminal acts.

Roman law steadily accumulated during the course of the empire, and over time it became contradictory and confusing. In the early sixth century A.D., the Byzantine emperor JUSTINIAN I, appointed a commission to examine the body of law and determine what should be kept and what should be discarded. From this effort came the *Corpus Juris Civilis*, a codification of Roman law that became the chief lawbook of what remained of the Roman Empire.

The decline of the Roman Empire also led to the diminution of interest in Roman law in western Europe. The *Corpus* was unknown to western scholars for centuries. During the twelfth century, however, Roman law studies revived in western Europe. In the late eleventh century, a manuscript containing part of the *Corpus* was discovered in Pisa, Italy. The remainder of the compilation was soon recovered, and schools where Roman law could be studied were established in Bologna, Italy, and then elsewhere in Europe. By the twelfth century, commentaries on the *Corpus Juris Civilis* appeared, and in time men trained in Roman law found posts in secular and ecclesiastical bureaucracies throughout Europe.

As a result, the legal systems of the Catholic Church and of almost every country in Europe were influenced by Roman law. Around the year 1140, the scholar Gratian prepared the *Concordance of Discordant Canons*, or *Decretum*. The *Decretum* was the largest and best-organized compendium of canon (church) law up to that time. Gratian used the *Corpus Juris Civilis* as his model, and later canonists studying the *Decretum* used the same methods that Roman lawyers applied to the *Corpus Juris Civilis*. Many scholars became masters of both Roman and CANON LAW.

Among the nations of western Europe, England, which had already established a viable common-law tradition and a system of royal courts by the time that Roman law became accessible, felt the impact of the revival of Roman law the least. Nevertheless, English law drew upon Roman admiralty law, and the crimes of FORGERY and LIBEL were based on Roman models. English ECCLESIASTICAL COURTS applied canon law, which was based on Roman law, and the universities of Oxford and Cambridge taught canon and Roman law. Scholars have noted the similarities between the Roman and English actions of TRESPASS, and the equi-

The Roman empire developed an extensive set of codified laws and legal customs that greatly influenced the legal systems of many European nations.

table method of INJUNCTION may have been derived from canon law. Much of western European commercial law, which contained Roman law, became part of English law without much change.

The legal systems of most continental European nations owe their basic structures and categories to Roman law. Scholars point to several reasons for this "reception" of Roman law. In some areas such as southern France where remnants of Roman law had survived the collapse of the Roman Empire, the *Corpus Juris Civilis* helped to explain the institutions that were already in existence. More important in ensuring the reception of Roman law were the political principles that it contained. Law that had been produced in a centralized state under a sovereign emperor could be used to buttress the arguments of the European rulers as they struggled to assert their SOVEREIGNTY over the feudal nobility.

At the same time that many of these rulers were consolidating their power, they were also expanding royal administration. This created new positions in government that often were filled by men with training in Roman law. Such men compiled collections of unwritten customs, drafted statutes, and presided over the courts, all of which provided opportunities for the penetration of Roman law.

Roman law did not displace local customs. Instead, its influence was subtle and selective. A compiler of unwritten German customs might arrange the collection according to Roman principles of organization. A royal judge confronted with an issue on which customs of different regions in the kingdom disagreed might turn to Roman law, the only law in many cases that was common to the entire kingdom. Similarly, Roman law could be used when local customs offered no solutions. For example, the Roman law of contracts was particularly influential because European customary law had developed in an agrarian economy and was often inadequate for an economy in which commerce played an increasingly larger role.

After 1600 the reception of Roman law slowed in most countries but did not entirely disappear. In nineteenth-century Europe, the *Corpus Juris Civilis* provided inspiration for several CODIFICATIONS of law, notably the French Code Napoléon of 1804, the Austrian code of 1811, the German code of 1889, and the Swiss codes of 1889 and 1907. Through these codes, elements of Roman law spread beyond Europe. The Code Napoléon served as a model for codes in Louisiana, Québec, Canada, and most of the countries of Latin America. German law influenced Hungarian, Brazilian, Japanese, and Greek law, and Turkey borrowed from Swiss law. In addition, the law of both Scotland and the Republic of South Africa derives from Roman law.

Commentators, while noting the differences between common law and civil law, which is based on Roman law, also point out that these differences can be overemphasized. Common-law countries, like the United States, enact statutes and even comprehensive codes, such as the UNIFORM COMMERCIAL CODE, while civil-law countries have laws that have been developed by the courts and not enacted through legislation. Roman law itself contained these conflicting impulses of codification and judicial interpretation.

See also CORPUS JURIS CIVILIS; NAPOLEONIC CODE.

ROMER v. EVANS *Romer v. Evans*, __U.S. __, 116 S. Ct. 1620, 134 L. Ed. 2d 855 (1996), is a landmark and controversial decision, in which the U.S. Supreme Court declared unconstitutional an amendment to the Colorado state constitution that prohibited state and local governments from enacting any law, regulation, or policy that would, in effect, protect the CIVIL RIGHTS of gays, lesbians and bisexuals.

The amendment at issue in *Romer v. Evans*, known as Amendment 2, was placed on the November 1992 ballot following a petition drive. The amendment provided in part that neither the state nor any of its political subdivisions "shall enact, adopt or enforce any statute, regulation, ordinance or policy whereby homosexual, lesbian, or bisexual orientation, conduct, practices or relationships shall constitute or otherwise be the basis or entitle any person or class of persons to have or claim any minority status, quota preferences, protected status or claim of discrimination."

The amendment was immediately challenged in state court by eight individuals and the cities of Denver, Boulder, and Aspen, which had gay rights ORDINANCES in effect. They sued Governor Roy Romer, Attorney General Gale Norton, and the State of Colorado. The plaintiffs argued that the amendment violated their FIRST AMENDMENT right to free expression and their FOURTEENTH AMENDMENT right to EQUAL PROTECTION of the laws. They obtained a permanent injunction in state court that prevented the amendment from going into effect.

In 1994 the Colorado Supreme Court affirmed the trial court (*Evans v. Romer*, 882 P.2d. 1335). The court applied the STRICT SCRUTINY standard in analyzing the amendment. This standard, which is the most exacting under the

Equal Protection Clause, is reserved for laws or amendments that discriminate against members of traditionally suspect classes (race, alien status, national ancestry, and ethnic origin). Laws will be upheld under strict scrutiny if they are supported by a COMPELLING STATE INTEREST and are narrowly drawn to achieve that interest in the least restrictive manner possible.

Reviewing a series of U.S. Supreme Court decisions involving voter registration, legislative APPORTIONMENT, and attempts to limit the ability of certain groups to have legislation implemented through the normal political processes, the court found a common thread. The Equal Protection Clause guarantees the fundamental right to participate equally in the political process. Therefore, any attempt to infringe on that right "must be subject to strict scrutiny and can be held constitutionally valid only if supported by a compelling state interest." Where the effect of a law is to exclude a class of voters, strict scrutiny must be used.

The Colorado Supreme Court found that the ultimate result of Amendment 2 was to prohibit any legislation dealing with sexual orientation unless the state constitution was first amended to permit such measures. Unlike all other citizens, who could seek legislative redress, gays and lesbians would have to first amend the state constitution by a majority vote. Thus, the amendment singled out one form of DISCRIMINATION and prevented one class of persons from using normal political processes to overturn the discrimination. This discrimination, coupled with the state's failure to offer any compelling state interests that would justify the enactment of Amendment 2, led the court to invalidate the amendment.

On appeal to the U.S. Supreme Court, Colorado argued that the amendment put gays and lesbians in the same position as all other persons and merely denied homosexuals special rights. Justice ANTHONY KENNEDY, in his majority opinion, rejected this interpretation as implausible. Relying on the Colorado Supreme Court's reading of the amendment, Kennedy quoted a passage that noted that Amendment 2 would have forced the "repeal of existing statutes, regulations, ordinances, and policies of state and local entities that barred discrimination based on sexual orientation." The enforcement of the amendment would lead to sweeping and comprehensive changes that, in Kennedy's view, put homosexuals "in a solitary class with respect to transactions and relations in both the private and governmental spheres."

These modifications would produce far-reaching changes in the legal status of gays and

lesbians and the structure and operation of modern anti-discrimination laws. Kennedy pointed out that the Boulder and Denver anti-discrimination ordinances prohibited discrimination on account of sexual orientation in places of public accommodation, which include hotels, restaurants, hospitals, dental clinics, theaters, banks, common carriers, travel and insurance agencies, and shops and stores that deal with goods and services. In addition, Amendment 2 would remove anti-discrimination protections for all transactions involving housing, the sale of real estate, insurance, health and welfare services, private education, and employment.

Based on this analysis of the potential reach of Amendment 2, Kennedy concluded that the amendment went well beyond merely depriving gays and lesbians of special rights. The amendment imposed a "special disability upon those persons alone." The only way homosexuals could obtain civil rights protection under Colorado law would be to convince enough citizens to vote to amend the state constitution. The kinds of protections that Amendment 2 would take away were those "against exclusion from an almost limitless number of transactions and endeavors that constitute civic life in a free society."

The key question for the Court was whether the amendment violated the Fourteenth Amendment's Equal Protection Clause, which promises that no person shall be denied the

Gays and lesbians celebrate the 1996 decision in Romer v. Evans *that declared unconstitutional laws that forbid state and local governments from protecting the civil rights of homosexuals through legislation.*

equal protection of the laws. In equal protection cases, the Court will uphold a legislative classification if it neither burdens a fundamental right nor targets a suspect class, and if it bears a rational relation to some legitimate end. In *Romer* this type of inquiry broke down, because the amendment was both too narrow and too broad. It imposed "a broad and undifferentiated disability on a single named group," and the "sheer breadth is so discontinuous with the reasons offered for it that the amendment seems inexplicable by anything but animus toward the class it affects; it lacks a rational relationship to legitimate state interests."

Justice Kennedy viewed the disqualification of gays and lesbians from the right to obtain specific protection from the law as unprecedented and a denial of equal protection "in the most literal sense." Reflecting on the constitutional tradition, he concluded that the idea of the rule of law and the guarantee of equal protection were based on "the principle that government and each of its parts remain open on impartial terms to all who seek its assistance."

The Court drew from Amendment 2 "the inevitable inference that the disadvantage imposed is born of animosity toward the class of persons affected." The desire to harm a politically unpopular group can never be a legitimate government interest. Colorado's primary justification for the amendment was respect for other citizens' FREEDOM OF ASSOCIATION, especially landlords or employers who have personal or religious objections to homosexuality. Kennedy concluded that the amendment's breadth was too far removed from this justification. Amendment 2 was a "status-based enactment divorced from any factual context from which we [the Court] could discern a relationship to legitimate interests." In light of the serious deficiencies in the amendment's scope and the failure of the state to articulate a legitimate state interest, the Court ruled that Amendment 2 violated the Equal Protection Clause.

Justice ANTONIN SCALIA, in a dissenting opinion joined by Chief Justice WILLIAM REHNQUIST and Justice CLARENCE THOMAS, characterized Amendment 2 as "rather a modest attempt by seemingly tolerant Coloradans to preserve traditional sexual mores against the efforts of a politically powerful minority to revise those mores through use of the laws." He criticized the majority for "imposing upon all Americans the resolution favored by the elite class from which the Members of this institution are selected." Noting that the U.S. Constitution does not deal with sexual orientation, Scalia concluded that states should be permitted to resolve these kinds of issues through "normal democratic means, including the democratic adoption of provisions in state constitutions."

See also GAY AND LESBIAN RIGHTS.

BIOGRAPHY

Anna Eleanor Roosevelt

ROOSEVELT, ANNA ELEANOR Eleanor Roosevelt, wife of U.S. President FRANKLIN D. ROOSEVELT (FDR), transformed the role of first lady and influenced the course and content of twentieth-century U.S. politics. During FDR's nearly four terms in office (1933–1945), Roosevelt was an acknowledged political adviser with her own progressive agenda.

Roosevelt was a committed reformer. Born into wealth and privilege, she lent early and conspicuous support to child welfare laws, equal pay and employment legislation, CIVIL RIGHTS, and WOMEN'S RIGHTS. Her ideals helped define FDR's NEW DEAL and modern Democratic liberalism. Although Roosevelt was admired by many, her high political profile was harshly criticized by people who believed she was too opinionated and influential.

After FDR's death in 1945, Roosevelt continued to support social and benevolent causes throughout the United States and the world. Although no longer first lady, she secured her reputation as a tireless activist and humanitarian.

Roosevelt was born on October 11, 1884, in New York City. Her parents, Elliott and Anna Hall Roosevelt, were socially and politically prominent. Her father was the younger brother of U.S. President THEODORE ROOSEVELT.

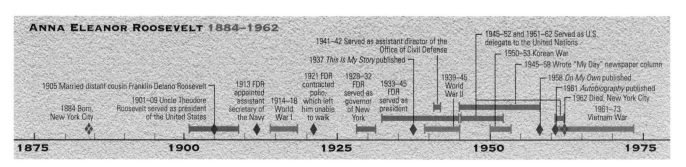

ANNA ELEANOR ROOSEVELT 1884–1962

1905 Married distant cousin Franklin Delano Roosevelt

1901–09 Uncle Theodore Roosevelt served as president of the United States

1884 Born, New York City

1913 FDR appointed assistant secretary of the Navy

1914–18 World War I

1921 FDR contracted polio, which left him unable to walk

1928–32 FDR served as governor of New York

1933–45 FDR served as president

1937 *This Is My Story* published

1941–42 Served as assistant director of the Office of Civil Defense

1939–45 World War II

1945–52 and 1961–62 Served as U.S. delegate to the United Nations

1950–53 Korean War

1945–58 Wrote "My Day" newspaper column

1958 *On My Own* published

1961 *Autobiography* published

1962 Died, New York City

1961–73 Vietnam War

1875   1900   1925   1950   1975

Roosevelt's childhood was lonely; she had an emotionally detached mother and a loving but alcoholic father. Both parents died by the time Eleanor was ten years old. A serious, timid child, Roosevelt was sent by her grandmother in 1899 to Allenswood, a private girls' school near London. There she overcame her shyness and became an active, well-liked student. When Roosevelt returned to New York, she entered high society. At the same time, she taught at a settlement house in a New York slum.

Roosevelt married FDR, her distant cousin, on March 17, 1905. Her domineering mother-in-law, Sara Roosevelt, disapproved of Roosevelt and put an immediate strain on the marriage. The couple had six children, five of whom survived to adulthood.

Roosevelt was not fulfilled by running a large household and attending social functions. When FDR was elected to the New York State Senate in 1910, she turned her attention to politics. In time, she discovered her talent for political organization and strategy.

FDR became the assistant secretary to the Navy in 1913. After the United States entered World War I, Roosevelt found an outlet for her tremendous energy, organizing Red Cross efforts and working in military canteens.

In 1918 Roosevelt discovered that FDR was having an affair with her social secretary Lucy Page Mercer. The marriage survived but became a union based primarily on politics, not love.

Roosevelt was determined to carve out her own niche in public service and national affairs. She became active in the League of Women Voters (although she had opposed female suffrage at one time) and the Women's Trade Union League. She assumed an increasingly active role in Democratic politics. In 1926 Roosevelt opened a furniture company in Hyde Park, New York, to provide jobs for unemployed workers. In 1927 Roosevelt and some colleagues founded the Todhunter School, where she was vice principal and taught government and history.

FDR was the unsuccessful Democratic candidate for vice president in the 1920 U.S. presidential election. In 1921 he contracted poliomyelitis, which left him permanently disabled. Because FDR could no longer walk independently, Roosevelt became his surrogate, filling in for him at meetings, state inspections, and public appearances. Her political skills and confidence grew in her role as FDR's emissary.

FDR was elected governor of New York in 1928. Four years later he became the thirty-second president of the United States, defeating incumbent Republican President HERBERT HOOVER. FDR's mandate was to pull the country out of the Great Depression. His economic recovery plan, popularly known as the New Deal, included sweeping, government-sponsored programs that were supported by Roosevelt.

From the outset Roosevelt was a different kind of first lady. Visible and outspoken, she wrote her own newspaper column, "My Day," and held regular press conferences with female reporters. She insisted on hard news coverage, not society-page trivia. Roosevelt lectured extensively throughout the United States, donating her fees to charity. Most importantly, she was FDR's legs and eyes, describing to him the actual, on-site progress of his social and economic programs.

Roosevelt wielded considerable influence over the development of the New Deal. She openly supported legislation to create the National Youth Administration, a program that provided jobs for young people. Roosevelt worked hard for measures to improve the lives of children, women, unemployed workers, minority groups, and poor people. She also encouraged the appointment of women to key positions within FDR's administration, such as the appointment of FRANCES PERKINS to secretary of labor.

Roosevelt demonstrated the courage of her convictions. In 1939 she publicly resigned her membership to the elite Daughters of the American Revolution (DAR). The DAR had denied permission to African American singer Marian Anderson to perform in Constitution Hall. Outraged at the group's racism, Roosevelt helped organize an alternate concert for Anderson at the Lincoln Memorial.

Roosevelt served in an official public capacity for a short time. From 1941 to 1942, she was assistant director of the Office of Civil Defense. When some of her appointments were criticized, however, Roosevelt stepped down from the position.

The United States' involvement in World War II meant increased travel for Roosevelt. As a fact finder and a morale booster, she visited U.S. armed forces throughout the world. After the war Roosevelt supported the resettlement of European Jews in newly established Israel.

FDR died of a cerebral hemorrhage on April 12, 1945. After his death Roosevelt remained in the public eye. She was one of the first U.S. delegates to the UNITED NATIONS, appointed by President HARRY S. TRUMAN in December 1945.

"IT IS NOT FAIR TO ASK OF OTHERS WHAT YOU ARE NOT WILLING TO DO YOURSELF."

She served as chair of the Commission on Human Rights and helped draft the U.N. Declaration of Human Rights.

Roosevelt also remained active in Democratic politics and organized Americans for Democratic Action, a liberal unit within the party. She backed ADLAI STEVENSON in his unsuccessful quest for the U.S. presidency in 1952 and 1956 and was a player in the 1952, 1958, and 1960 Democratic conventions. In 1952, with Republican DWIGHT D. EISENHOWER in the White House, she resigned from the U.N. Democratic President JOHN F. KENNEDY reappointed her to the post in 1961.

Roosevelt published several books, including *This Is My Story* (1937), *This I Remember* (1949), *On My Own* (1958), and *You Learn By Living* (1960).

Roosevelt died in New York City on November 7, 1962.

ROOSEVELT, FRANKLIN DELANO

Franklin Delano Roosevelt served as the thirty-second president of the United States from 1933 to 1945. During his unprecedented four terms in office, Roosevelt established himself as a towering national leader, leading the United States out of the Great Depression through the active involvement of the federal government in the national economy. The federal government grew dramatically in size and power as Congress enacted Roosevelt's NEW DEAL program. As president, Roosevelt was responsible for the creation of SOCIAL SECURITY, federal labor laws, rural electrification programs, and myriad projects that assisted farmers, business, and labor. During World War II Roosevelt's leadership was vital to rallying the spirits of the citizenry and mobilizing a wartime economy. Nevertheless, Roosevelt was a controversial figure. Many economic conservatives believed his programs owed more to state socialism than to free enterprise.

Roosevelt was born on January 30, 1882, in Hyde Park, New York, the only son of James and Sara Delano Roosevelt. The young Roosevelt was taught to be a gentleman and to exercise Christian stewardship through public

BIOGRAPHY

Franklin Delano Roosevelt

service. He graduated from Harvard University in 1904 and in 1905 wed ELEANOR ROOSEVELT, the niece of his fifth cousin, President THEODORE ROOSEVELT. Roosevelt attended Columbia University Law School but left without receiving a degree when he passed the New York bar exam in 1907.

In 1910 Roosevelt was elected to the New York Senate as a member of the Democratic party. Reelected in 1912, he resigned in 1913 to accept an appointment from President WOODROW WILSON as assistant secretary of the navy. For the next seven years, Roosevelt proved an effective administrator and an advocate of reform in the navy.

Roosevelt was nominated for vice president on the 1920 Democratic party ticket. He waged a vigorous campaign in support of the presidential nominee, James M. Cox, but the Republican ticket headed by WARREN G. HARDING soundly defeated Cox and Roosevelt. After the election Roosevelt joined a Maryland bonding company and began investing in various business schemes.

Roosevelt's life changed in August 1921, when he was stricken with poliomyelitis while vacationing at Campobello Island, New Brunswick. Initially, Roosevelt was completely paralyzed, but over several years of intense therapy, he made gradual improvement. His legs, however, suffered permanent paralysis. For the rest of his life, he used a wheelchair and could walk only a few steps with the help of leg braces.

Eleanor Roosevelt believed her husband's recovery depended on his reentry into New York politics. She attended meetings, made speeches, and reported back to him on the political events of the day. By 1924 Roosevelt was at the Democratic National Convention nominating Governor Alfred E. Smith of New York for president. Smith, who lost the presidential elections in 1924 and 1928, showed Roosevelt the ways of New York state politics and pushed him to run for governor in 1928. A reluctant Roosevelt won by a narrow margin, but soon was governing as if he had won by a landslide. With the stock market crash of Oc-

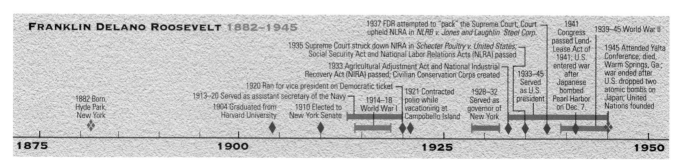

FRANKLIN DELANO ROOSEVELT 1882–1945

1937 FDR attempted to "pack" the Supreme Court; Court upheld NLRA in *NLRB v. Jones and Laughlin Steel Corp.*

1935 Supreme Court struck down NIRA in *Schecter Poultry v. United States*; Social Security Act and National Labor Relations Acts (NLRA) passed

1933 Agricultural Adjustment Act and National Industrial Recovery Act (NIRA) passed; Civilian Conservation Corps created

1920 Ran for vice president on Democratic ticket

1913–20 Served as assistant secretary of the Navy

1882 Born, Hyde Park, New York

1904 Graduated from Harvard University

1910 Elected to New York Senate

1914–18 World War I

1921 Contracted polio while vacationing at Campobello Island

1928–32 Served as governor of New York

1933–45 Served as U.S. president

1941 Congress passed Lend-Lease Act of 1941; U.S. entered war after Japanese bombed Pearl Harbor on Dec. 7.

1939–45 World War II

1945 Attended Yalta Conference; died, Warm Springs, Ga.; war ended after U.S. dropped two atomic bombs on Japan; United Nations founded

1875   1900   1925   1950

tober 25, 1929, the United States was thrown into a national economic depression of unprecedented severity. As governor, Roosevelt set up the first state public relief agency and tried to find ways to spark an economic recovery. His landslide reelection in 1930 made him the logical candidate to face the Republican president HERBERT HOOVER in the next presidential election.

Roosevelt was nominated for president on the third ballot of the 1932 Democratic National Convention. During the campaign Roosevelt called for the federal government to take action to revive the economy and end the suffering of the thirteen million unemployed people. Hoover advocated a more limited role for the federal government in the national economy. Roosevelt easily defeated Hoover and brought with him large Democratic majorities in both houses of Congress.

Roosevelt took office on March 4, 1933, at a time when the economy appeared hopeless. In his inaugural address he reassured the nation that "the only thing we have to fear is fear itself." He proposed a New Deal for the people of the United States and promised to use the power of the EXECUTIVE BRANCH to address the economic crisis.

During his first hundred days in office, Roosevelt sent Congress many pieces of legislation that sought to boost economic activity and restore the circulation of money through federally funded work programs. The Civilian Conservation Corps (CCC) provided unemployment relief and an opportunity for national service to young workers, while promoting conservation through reforestation and flood control work. Federal funds were given to state relief agencies for direct relief, and the Reconstruction Finance Company was given the authority to make loans to small and large businesses.

The centerpieces of Roosevelt's New Deal legislation were the Agricultural Adjustment Act (AAA) of 1933 (7 U.S.C.A. § 601 et seq.) and the NATIONAL INDUSTRIAL RECOVERY ACT (NIRA) of 1933 (48 Stat. 195). The AAA sought to raise farm prices by giving farmers federal subsidies if they reduced their agricultural production.

The NIRA was a comprehensive attempt to manage all phases of U.S. business. It established the National Recovery Administration (NRA) to administer codes of fair practice within each industry. Under these codes labor and management negotiated MINIMUM WAGES, maximum hours, and fair-trade practices for each industry. The Roosevelt administration sought to use these codes to stabilize production, raise prices, and protect labor and consumers. By early 1934 there were 557 basic codes and 208 supplementary ones. In 1935, however, the Supreme Court struck down the NIRA in *A.L.A. Schechter Poultry Corp. v. United States*, 295 U.S. 495, 55 S. Ct. 837, 79 L. Ed. 1570.

In 1935 Roosevelt and the Congress passed the SOCIAL SECURITY ACT (42 U.S.C.A. § 301 et seq.), a fundamental piece of social welfare legislation that provided unemployment compensation and pensions for those over the age of sixty-five. More groundbreaking legislation came with the passage of the Wagner Act, also known as the NATIONAL LABOR RELATIONS ACT (NLRA) of 1935 (29 U.S.C.A. § 151 et seq.), which recognized for the first time the right of workers to organize unions and engage in COLLECTIVE BARGAINING with employers.

Roosevelt handily defeated Republican Alfred M. Landon, the governor of Kansas, in the 1936 presidential election. In his second term, however, Roosevelt met more resistance to his legislative initiatives. Between 1935 and 1937, the Supreme Court struck down as unconstitutional eight New Deal programs that attempted to regulate the national economy. Most of the conservative justices who voted against the New Deal statutes were over the age of seventy. Roosevelt responded by proposing that justices be allowed to retire at age seventy at full pay. Any justice who declined this offer would be forced to have an assistant with full voting rights. The assistant, of course, as a Roosevelt appointee, would be more likely to be sympathetic to the president's political ideals. This plan to "pack" the Court was met with hostility by Democrats and Republicans and rejected as an act of political interference. Despite the rejection of his plan, Roosevelt ultimately prevailed. In 1937 the Supreme Court upheld the Wagner Act in *NLRB v. Jones and Laughlin Steel Corp.*, 301 U.S. 1, 57 S. Ct. 615, 81 L. Ed. 893, signaling an end to the invalidation of New Deal laws that sought to reshape the national economy. From *Jones* onward the Court permitted the federal government to take a dominant role in matters of commerce.

By 1937 the national economy appeared to be recovering. In the fall of 1937, however, the economy went into a recession, accompanied by a dramatic increase in unemployment. Roosevelt responded by instituting massive government spending, and by June 1938 the economy had stabilized.

During the later 1930s, Roosevelt became preoccupied with foreign policy. The rise of

"THE TEST OF OUR PROGRESS IS NOT WHETHER WE ADD MORE TO THE ABUNDANCE OF THOSE WHO HAVE MUCH; IT IS WHETHER WE PROVIDE ENOUGH FOR THOSE WHO HAVE TOO LITTLE."

ADOLF HITLER and Nazism in Germany, coupled with a militaristic Japanese government that had invaded Manchuria in 1933, created international tensions that Roosevelt realized might come to involve the United States. U.S. foreign policy had traditionally counseled against entanglements with other nations, and the 1930s had seen a resurgence of isolationist thought. Roosevelt, while publicly agreeing with isolationist legislators, quietly moved to enhance U.S. military strength.

With the outbreak of World War II in Europe in August 1939, Roosevelt sought to aid Great Britain and France against Germany and Italy. The Neutrality Act of 1939 (22 U.S.C.A. § 441), however, prohibited the export of arms to any belligerent. With some difficulty Roosevelt secured the repeal of this provision so that military equipment could be sold to Great Britain and France.

In 1940 Roosevelt took the unprecedented step of seeking a third term. Although there was no constitutional prohibition against a third term, President GEORGE WASHINGTON had established the tradition of serving only two terms. Nevertheless, Roosevelt was concerned about the approach of war and decided a third term was necessary to continue his plans. He defeated the Republican nominee, Wendell L. Willkie, pledging that he would keep the United States out of war. Roosevelt's margin of victory in the popular vote was closer than in 1936, but he still won the electoral college vote easily.

Following his reelection, Roosevelt became more public in his support of the Allies. At his urging, Congress moved further away from neutrality by passing the LEND-LEASE ACT of 1941 (55 Stat. 31). Lend-Lease provided munitions, food, machinery, and services to Great Britain and other Allies without immediate cost.

The United States entered World War II following the Japanese attack on the U.S. naval base at Pearl Harbor, Hawaii, on December 7, 1941. Roosevelt rallied a stunned citizenry and began the mobilization of a wartime economy. In his public speeches and "fireside chats" on the radio, Roosevelt imparted the strong determination that the United States would prevail in the conflict. He met with Winston Churchill, the prime minister of Great Britain, and JOSEPH STALIN, the leader of the Soviet Union, several times during the war to discuss military strategy and to plan power-sharing in the postwar world. Roosevelt, who needed the Soviet Union's cooperation in defeating Germany, sought to minimize conflicts with Stalin over postwar boundaries in Europe.

In 1944 Roosevelt decided to run for a fourth term. Though his health had seriously declined, he wished to remain commander in chief for the remainder of the war. The Republican party nominated Governor THOMAS E. DEWEY of New York for president, but again Roosevelt turned back the challenge, winning 432 electoral votes to Dewey's 99.

In February 1945 Roosevelt traveled to Yalta in the Crimea to meet with Churchill and Stalin. Germany was on the edge of defeat, but Japan's defeat did not appear imminent. Stalin accepted Roosevelt and Churchill's offer of territorial concessions in Asia in return for his promise that the Soviet Union would enter the war against Japan once Germany was defeated. At Yalta the leaders reaffirmed earlier agreements and made plans for the establishment of democratic governments in eastern Europe. The Yalta agreements were not clearly written, however, and therefore were open to differing interpretations by the Allies. Within a month after Yalta, Roosevelt sent a sharp message to Stalin concerning Soviet accusations that Great Britain and the United States were trying to rob the Soviets of their legitimate territorial interests.

Early in the war, Roosevelt decided that an effective international organization should be established after the war to replace the LEAGUE OF NATIONS. At Yalta, Roosevelt pressed for the creation of the UNITED NATIONS as a mechanism to preserve world peace. A conference attended by fifty nations was scheduled to begin on April 25, 1945, in San Francisco, California, to draft a United Nations charter. Roosevelt had planned to attend, but his health had steadily declined since the 1944 election.

Instead, Roosevelt went to his retreat in Warm Springs, Georgia, where he had begun his rehabilitation from polio in the 1920s. He died there on April 12, 1945. Vice President HARRY S. TRUMAN succeeded Roosevelt. On May 7 the war in Europe ended with Germany's surrender; four months later, on September 2, Japan also surrendered, ending the war in the Pacific.

BIOGRAPHY

Theodore Roosevelt

LIBRARY OF CONGRESS

ROOSEVELT, THEODORE   Theodore ("Teddy") Roosevelt served as the twenty-sixth president of the United States from 1901 to 1909. A writer, explorer, and soldier, as well as a politician, Roosevelt distinguished himself as president by advocating conservation of natural resources, waging legal battles against economic monopolies and trusts, and exercising leadership in foreign affairs. An energetic man with a colorful personality, Roosevelt later sought to reclaim the presidency in 1912 as the head of the Progressive party.

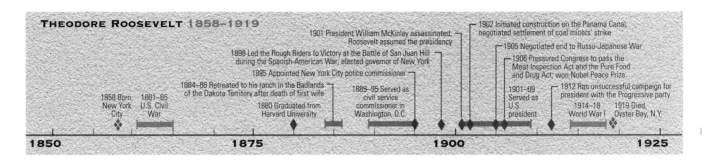

THEODORE ROOSEVELT 1858–1919

1858 Born, New York City

1861–65 U.S. Civil War

1880 Graduated from Harvard University

1884–86 Retreated to his ranch in the Badlands of the Dakota Territory after death of first wife

1889–95 Served as civil service commissioner in Washington, D.C.

1895 Appointed New York City police commissioner

1898 Led the Rough Riders to Victory at the Battle of San Juan Hill during the Spanish-American War; elected governor of New York

1901 President William McKinley assassinated; Roosevelt assumed the presidency

1901–09 Served as U.S. president

1902 Initiated construction on the Panama Canal; negotiated settlement of coal miners' strike

1905 Negotiated end to Russo-Japanese War

1906 Pressured Congress to pass the Meat Inspection Act and the Pure Food and Drug Act; won Nobel Peace Prize

1912 Ran unsuccessful campaign for president with the Progressive party

1914–18 World War I

1919 Died, Oyster Bay, N.Y.

1850   1875   1900   1925

Roosevelt was born on October 27, 1858, in New York City, a descendant of a wealthy and aristocratic family that first settled in New York in the 1600s. A sickly boy, Roosevelt developed a regimen of diet and exercise that transformed him into a vigorous young man. He graduated from Harvard University in 1880 and was elected to the New York State Assembly in 1881.

Roosevelt resigned in 1884, following the death of his wife, and spent two years at his ranch in the Badlands of the Dakota Territory. During this period he developed both his association with the Wild West world of cowboys and his appreciation of the wilderness. He returned to New York City in 1886 and ran unsuccessfully for mayor. From 1889 to 1895, Roosevelt served as a civil service commissioner in Washington, D.C. In 1895 he was appointed as a reform-minded New York City police commissioner. His main occupation, however, was that of writer: he wrote many magazine articles and twelve books between 1880 and 1900.

Roosevelt's rise to national prominence came during the Spanish-American War of 1898. Anxious to be a part of the forces that would go to Cuba, he organized a group of cowboys and New York aristocrats into a cavalry regiment nicknamed the Rough Riders. As a lieutenant colonel, Roosevelt became a national hero and darling of the national news media when he led his Rough Riders to victory at the Battle of San Juan Hill in July 1898.

The New York Republican party, under the leadership of Senator Thomas C. Platt, nominated Roosevelt for governor in 1898, in the hope that his popularity could rescue a party plagued by scandal. Roosevelt was easily elected but soon offended party leaders by asserting his political independence. Platt became so frustrated with Roosevelt's reform agenda that he persuaded President WILLIAM MCKINLEY to make Roosevelt his vice presidential running mate in 1900. Reluctantly, Roosevelt accepted the nomination. His popularity helped McKinley win a second term. On September 6, 1901, an anarchist named Leon F. Czolgosz shot

"NO MAN IS ABOVE THE LAW AND NO MAN IS BELOW IT; NOR DO WE ASK ANY MAN'S PERMISSION WHEN WE ASK HIM TO OBEY IT."

McKinley when he visited the Pan-American Exposition in Buffalo, New York. Eight days later McKinley died and Roosevelt assumed the presidency.

As president, Roosevelt sought to attack corruption and to promote economic and political reform. He insisted that government should be the arbiter of economic conflicts between capital and labor. He demonstrated his convictions by negotiating a settlement of a STRIKE between coal miners and mine operators in 1902, the first time a president had intervened in a labor dispute. Roosevelt referred to his platform for business and labor as the Square Deal.

Roosevelt won public acclaim for being a "trust buster." By the early twentieth century, a few large companies in key industries, including RAILROADS, oil, and steel, had stifled competition and created monopolies. In one of his first major acts, Roosevelt filed suit to dissolve the Northern Securities Company, a trust controlled by the three major railroads in the Northwest. Using the SHERMAN ANTI-TRUST ACT of 1890 (15 U.S.C.A. § 1 et seq.), the Roosevelt administration successfully broke up Northern Securities; antitrust lawsuits against forty-three other major corporations soon followed.

In 1904 the Republican party nominated Roosevelt for a second term. He easily defeated the Democratic candidate Alton B. Parker of New York. In his second term Roosevelt helped enact several groundbreaking pieces of federal legislation. Spurred in part by public concern over the unsanitary food packing methods revealed by Upton Sinclair's 1906 novel *The Jungle*, Roosevelt pressured Congress and the meat packing industry to support the Meat Inspection Act of 1906 (21 U.S.C.A. § 601 et seq.). In 1906 Congress also passed the Pure Food and Drug Act (21 U.S.C.A. § 301 et seq.), which criminalized the misleading and harmful sale of patent medicines that made false claims about their medicinal effects. The act also established the FOOD AND DRUG ADMINISTRATION, putting in place a federal agency dedicated to CONSUMER PROTECTION. Roosevelt also was instrumental in the passage of the Hepburn Act of

1906 (34 Stat. 584), which increased the powers of the INTERSTATE COMMERCE COMMISSION (ICC), allowing the ICC to inspect the business records of railroads.

Roosevelt became the first president to play a major international role in foreign policy. His favorite motto, based on an African proverb, was "speak softly and carry a big stick." The motto epitomized Roosevelt's foreign policy, as he increased the size of the U.S. Navy and sent the fleet around the world in 1908 to demonstrate both U.S. military strength and U.S. involvement in world affairs.

Roosevelt initiated the construction of the Panama Canal in 1902, reduced domestic discord by making an agreement with Japan on limiting the number of Japanese immigrants to the United States, and negotiated the end of the Russo-Japanese War of 1904–1905 at a peace conference held in Portsmouth, Maine. He earned the Nobel Peace Prize in 1906 for mediating the peace agreement.

Perhaps the most innovative aspect of Roosevelt's presidency was his commitment to the conservation of natural resources. He lobbied successfully for funds to convert large portions of federal land into national forests. In seven years 194 million additional acres of federal land were closed to commercial development, five times more than his three predecessors had reserved for conservation purposes. Roosevelt also approved the Newlands Act of 1903 (32 Stat. 388), which called for part of the receipts from the sale of public lands in the western states and territories to be reserved for dams and reclamation projects. The legislation saved much western wildlife from extinction.

Despite his relative youth and energy, Roosevelt declined to run for another term. His progressive reforms had angered many conservative Republicans in Congress. In addition, his public comments on "race suicide," in which he lamented the declining birthrate of U.S. citizens of northern European ancestry and the accelerating birthrate of Russian and southern European immigrants, troubled many people. He approved the Republican presidential nomination of his secretary of war, WILLIAM HOWARD TAFT, in the belief that Taft was a progressive Republican. Taft won the presidency in November 1908.

After leaving office in March 1909, Roosevelt spent ten months in Africa on a hunting trip and then visited Europe. Upon his return to the United States in 1910, he was shocked at Taft's capitulation to the conservative Republicans in Congress. His animosity toward Taft grew, and in 1912 Roosevelt declared his candidacy for the Republican presidential nomination. Although he won most of the primaries, the Republican party leaders controlled enough votes to give the nomination to Taft. Undaunted, Roosevelt formed a third party, called the Progressive party. Following a failed assassination attempt against him in Milwaukee, Wisconsin, in October 1912, he said that it would take more than that to kill a bull moose. Thereafter, the Progressives were nicknamed the Bull Moose party.

Roosevelt won more votes than Taft, but the division of Republican strength allowed Democrat WOODROW WILSON to be elected president. Roosevelt grew to despise Wilson and his policies, leveling harsh criticism against Wilson's foreign policy. Incensed when Wilson denied him the opportunity to form a regiment and fight in World War I, Roosevelt denounced Wilson's proposal for the LEAGUE OF NATIONS, even though Roosevelt himself had once advocated such an organization.

Roosevelt's health deteriorated rapidly in his last years. He died on January 6, 1919, at his home in Oyster Bay, New York.

See also ANTITRUST LAW; MONOPOLY.

ROSENBERG, JULIUS AND ETHEL In

1951 Julius and Ethel Rosenberg were convicted of CONSPIRACY to commit ESPIONAGE for helping the Soviet Union steal the secrets to the atomic bomb from the United States during World War II. Judge Irving R. Kaufman, who presided at the trial, sentenced the Rosenbergs to death after concluding that their "betrayal . . . undoubtedly . . . altered the course of history to the disadvantage of [the United States]." The Rosenbergs maintained their innocence from the time of their arrest until they were executed. The Rosenbergs' two sons, Michael and Robert Meeropol, have spent much of their adult lives attempting to clear their parents' names.

Morton Sobell (born April 11, 1917), a former employee for the Naval Bureau of Ordnance, was also indicted for conspiracy to commit espionage with the Rosenbergs and named as a codefendant. During June 1950 Sobell fled to Mexico with his wife under an assumed name. After being apprehended and extradited back to the United States, Sobell was convicted of the conspiracy charge and sentenced to thirty years in prison. He was paroled in January 1969.

Both of the Rosenbergs were members of the American Communist party. Julius, who had been born on May 12, 1918, came from an impoverished background. He had received a degree in electrical engineering from City College of New York but had trouble obtaining and keeping employment. At the time of his arrest, he was struggling to run a small machine shop with David Greenglass, Ethel's brother. Like her husband, Ethel, who had been born on September 28, 1915, came from a poor family.

The Rosenbergs' trial has been the subject of legal, political, and historical controversy for nearly half a century. Some view the Rosenbergs as martyred victims of the Communist hysteria that menaced the political landscape in the United States during the 1950s. Others see the Rosenbergs as criminals who were singularly responsible for ending the United States' nuclear monopoly and compromising the security of millions of people. The picture painted by historians has always been incomplete because many materials concerning the Rosenbergs remain classified.

The U.S. government did not indict the Rosenbergs for TREASON and might have encountered constitutional difficulties if it had pursued such an INDICTMENT. Article III, Section 3, of the Constitution defines treason as giving "aid and comfort" to the enemies of the United States. During World War II, the Soviet Union was an ally, not an enemy, of the United States. Further, the Constitution requires that every "overt act of treason" be witnessed by two persons. Yet, as the trial revealed, many of the conspiratorial acts committed by the Rosenbergs were witnessed by only one person.

The Rosenbergs' trial began on March 6, 1951, at the federal courthouse in New York City. Spectators and members of the press packed the gallery, the hallways, and the courthouse steps in an effort to catch a glimpse of the so-called atom spies in what some observers called the "trial of the century." Judge Kaufman conducted the VOIR DIRE and impaneled a jury in less than two days. Irving Saypol was the chief prosecuting attorney and was assisted by ROY COHN and James Kilsheimer. Julius Rosenberg was represented by Emanuel Bloch, while Emanuel's father, Alexander Bloch, represented Ethel.

The Prosecution's Case The first witness against the Rosenbergs was Max Elitcher, a thirty-two-year-old electrical engineer employed by the Naval Bureau of Ordnance during the 1940s. Elitcher testified that in June 1944 Julius asked him to assist the Soviet Union by providing classified information about naval equipment. Over the next several years, Elitcher said, Julius made other references to his central role in a Soviet espionage ring with members scattered across the United States. Nonetheless, Elitcher maintained that he never disclosed any confidential information to the Rosenbergs.

Elitcher also provided the only testimony against Sobell. Elitcher told the jurors that on several occasions Sobell attempted to entice him to commit espionage on behalf of the Soviet Union. Elitcher recalled one instance when he accompanied Sobell on a drive to Knickerbocker Village where the defendant delivered a can of film to Julius Rosenberg. Although Elitcher was unable to tell the court what, if anything, was inside the can, he did testify that Sobell described the contents as "too valuable to be destroyed and too dangerous to keep around."

David Greenglass, the twenty-nine-year-old brother of Ethel Rosenberg, was the prosecution's second witness. Greenglass, a member of the American Communist party, had enlisted in the army as a machinist in 1943. In July 1944 he was assigned to the Manhattan Project, the top secret Allied program based in Los Alamos, New Mexico, for the development of the atomic bomb. As part of his job, Greenglass performed research on high explosives.

Greenglass testified that he learned about the nature of the Manhattan Project in November 1944 when his wife, Ruth, visited him in Albuquerque. Before leaving for New Mexico, Ruth was invited to the Rosenbergs' apartment in New York where Ethel disclosed that Julius had been sharing classified information with the Soviets. During the same visit, Julius informed Ruth that her husband was working on a project to develop an atomic bomb and proposed that David help the Soviets by stealing secrets from Los Alamos. Upon learning of Julius's invitation from Ruth, David testified that he agreed to engage in atomic espionage for the Soviet Union.

In January 1945 David went home to New York on furlough and met with the Rosenbergs. David testified that during one visit he provided Julius with a verbal description of the atomic bomb, explaining that the Los Alamos scientists were designing a high explosive lens mold. David accompanied this description with a packet of sketches outlining the mold. He also provided Julius with a list of the scientists working on the Manhattan Project and an overview of the Los Alamos facilities. Because some of the written material was illegible, David told the jury, Ethel typed his notes.

A few days later the Greenglasses ate dinner at the Rosenbergs where a plan was designed for David to exchange information in New Mexico with a courier who would be sent by Julius. To enable David to identify this courier,

Ethel Rosenberg was convicted of conspiring with her husband and brother to transmit classified information about the atomic bomb to the Soviet Union. Documents released many years later suggest that the FBI concocted the evidence against her.

Julius cut a Jell-O box into two irregularly shaped pieces, gave one piece to David, and said the other piece would be given to the courier.

The next summer Ruth rented an apartment in Albuquerque where David usually spent the weekends. During the first weekend in June, a man visited the Greenglass apartment, identifying himself as "Dave from Pittsburgh." The man told the Greenglasses that he was a courier sent by "Julius." After the courier produced the matching half of the Jell-O box, David gave him some additional sketches of the lens mold experiments.

In September 1945 David returned to New York on a second furlough. Meeting with Julius and Ethel at the Rosenbergs' apartment, David drew a cross section of the atomic bomb and described the implosion principle underlying it. David testified that Ethel again typed up the written material, correcting spelling and grammar where necessary. The prosecution asked David to draw a replica of the sketches that he had given to the Rosenbergs and the courier. The prosecution then called Walter Koski, a physical chemist, who testified that the sketches

were "reasonably accurate" and revealed much of what the government had been attempting to keep secret at Los Alamos.

Ruth Greenglass, who testified next, corroborated the central elements of her husband's testimony. Ruth testified that she had assisted David in procuring classified information from Los Alamos for the Rosenbergs. She also testified that the Rosenbergs had showed her a mahogany table that they had received from the Soviets as a token of their appreciation. A portion of the table was hollow, Ruth said, and a lamp had been inserted so that microfilm pictures could be taken.

As the FEDERAL BUREAU OF INVESTIGATION (FBI) was closing in on the Greenglasses and the Rosenbergs, Ruth told the jurors, Julius developed a plan for David and Ruth to elude law enforcement. The plan called for David and Ruth to travel to Mexico where a Soviet agent would be waiting with passports and cash. The agent would then escort the Greenglasses to Czechoslovakia or Russia. Although Julius gave the Greenglasses more than $4,000 to defect from the United States, Ruth testified that neither she nor David ever left the country.

The primary corroborating witness for the Greenglasses' testimony was Harry Gold, a forty-year-old chemist who testified that he had been spying for the Soviet Union since 1935 and had been working with Anatoli Yakovlev, a Soviet agent, for a number of years. Gold said that Yakovlev had sent him on a vital mission to New Mexico during the first weekend of June 1945.

On Saturday, June 2, Yakovlev instructed Gold to travel to Santa Fe where he would meet with Klaus Fuchs, a nuclear scientist from Great Britain who was working on the Manhattan Project. During their meeting Fuchs provided Gold with diagrams and written descriptions of the atomic bomb. On a previous occasion, Fuchs had given Gold a complete set of his notes from Los Alamos. In February 1950 Fuchs was captured by British intelligence and confessed to his role in the atomic espionage conspiracy. Fuchs, who received a fourteen-year sentence, identified Gold as the Soviet liaison he met in Santa Fe.

Gold also testified that the day after meeting with Fuchs, he traveled to Albuquerque where he was scheduled to meet a man Yakovlev described only as "Greenglass." Yakovlev had given Gold the matching half of the Jell-O box and told him to bring Greenglass greetings from "Julius." When Gold arrived at the Greenglass apartment, a man Gold now identified as David Greenglass gave him an envelope of drawings and other materials in exchange for $400.

Gold testified that he turned this envelope over to Yakovlev who immediately transmitted it to the Soviet Union. Gold said that Yakovlev subsequently thanked him for obtaining such "excellent" and "valuable" data. The prosecution introduced two exhibits to bolster Gold's testimony, a receipt indicating that Ruth Greenglass had deposited $400 into her account at the Albuquerque National Bank on June 4, 1945, and a registration card from the Albuquerque Hilton Hotel signed by Harry Gold on June 3, 1945.

The final witness for the prosecution was Elizabeth Bentley, a forty-four-year-old former Soviet spy who was known to the public as the "Red Spy Queen." Bentley bragged that as a top-ranking member of the Communist party in the United States, she was responsible for pilfering a wide variety of industrial, military, and political secrets. Bentley then became a double agent for the FBI and was assigned to infiltrate and expose domestic Communist espionage networks.

In addition to testifying at the Rosenbergs' trial, Bentley had testified in a number of cases involving the prosecution of her former comrades in the American Communist party. In each case Bentley's testimony verged on the theatrical. At the Rosenbergs' trial, she testified that she had received a number of late night espionage-related phone calls from a man who called himself "Julius." Bentley admitted that she never met this man, however, and could not identify his voice.

The Defense Whereas the prosecution's theory of the case seemed relatively straightforward, the defense strategy was enigmatic. The defendants' case was fraught with errors, ranging from minor to monumental. Most of these mistakes have been attributed to lead defense attorney Emanuel Bloch.

Bloch's first major mistake occurred during the DIRECT EXAMINATION of David Greenglass. When the prosecution sought to introduce one of the sketches Greenglass had drawn, Bloch made a MOTION, asking the court to impound the exhibit. When the prosecution attempted to question Greenglass about his notes that accompanied the sketches, Bloch asked the court to clear the press and spectators from the courtroom to prevent any further leaks of atomic secrets. The prosecution, who had been expecting Bloch to challenge Greenglass's qualifications to testify as an expert regarding the scien-

US GOVERNMENT
J-131

Julius Rosenberg, a member of the Communist party, was convicted of transmitting secret atomic information to the Soviets. Some believe he was an innocent victim of the Communist hysteria in U.S. politics in the 1950s.

tific significance of the sketches, happily concurred with Bloch's dual motions.

As it turns out, the prosecution had reason to be relieved. Several nuclear physicists vehemently disputed whether an ordinary machinist such as Greenglass possessed sufficient experience and educational background to testify or explain the complex principles behind the atomic bomb. In an effort to obtain executive CLEMENCY for the Rosenbergs in 1953, for example, Nobel Prize–winning physicist Harold Urey told President DWIGHT D. EISENHOWER that a "man of Greenglass's capacity is wholly incapable of transmitting the physics, chemistry, and mathematics of the bomb to anyone." Other physicists wondered why the Soviets would even want Greenglass's sketches since they already had received diagrams of the bomb from Fuchs, a nuclear scientist. Bloch never called any scientists to challenge Greenglass's testimony.

Historians have argued that by failing to challenge Greenglass's scientific expertise and by asking the court to impound his sketches, Bloch convinced the jury that it was about to hear the secret of the atomic bomb. At least one of the Rosenberg jurors agreed with this analysis, stating that it was not until Bloch asked the court to keep the Greenglass exhibits confidential that he had become impressed with the importance of the trial.

A second major mistake occurred when Bloch failed to cross-examine Gold. Gold was an admitted liar. During a previous legal proceeding, he told the court that as a result of his espionage activities he "had become so tangled up in a web of lies that it was easier to continue telling an occasional lie than to try and straighten out the whole hideous mess." When the IMPEACHMENT value of this prior TESTIMONY is coupled with the large number of glaring inconsistencies between Gold's testimony during the Rosenbergs' trial and his pretrial accounts of the same events, Bloch's decision against cross-examining Gold looms larger.

The Controversy Continues Why Bloch made these mistakes is a question that remains unanswered. Although some historians claim that he was simply a bumbling attorney, Bloch had defended a number of defendants accused of espionage and had developed a reputation as a competent litigator. Other historians have suggested that Bloch purposely botched the trial in an effort to make martyrs of the Rosenbergs as part of a larger socialist agenda. In any event Bloch later expressed regret for his mistakes, attributing them in part to the politically charged legal climate of the times.

Indeed, during the early 1950s, hysteria over COMMUNISM pervaded almost every aspect of life in the United States. As a result, criminal defendants who were associated with Communist influences often received less than impartial hearings from judges and jurors. This paranoid fear of Communism began to manifest itself shortly after World War II.

Several events contributed to the concern about Communism. In 1948 Greece, Turkey, and Czechoslovakia were under siege by Communists. China came under Communist control in the spring of 1949. On January 21, 1950, ALGER HISS, a former member of President FRANKLIN D. ROOSEVELT's administration, was convicted of PERJURY for statements he had made in response to espionage charges that had been lodged against him. A few weeks after the Hiss conviction, an obscure senator from Wisconsin named JOSEPH R. McCARTHY startled the nation by brandishing a list of 205 Communists that he asserted were employed by the federal government. In June 1950 the Korean War erupted and the Rosenbergs were arrested.

This series of events affected the FBI's investigation of the Rosenberg conspiracy. J. EDGAR HOOVER, the director of the FBI, had become concerned about public perception of his organization. Some officials had begun to question whether Hoover and the FBI were acting with sufficient vigilance to extinguish the internal Communist threat. With each new revelation about Communist spies in the U.S. government, Hoover took more severe measures to shore up what some perceived as national security breaches. The Rosenberg case was an example of the most extreme measures taken by the FBI.

Government files demonstrate that the FBI had expressed little interest in prosecuting Ethel Rosenberg until her husband refused to

A New York jury convicted Julius and Ethel Rosenberg of conspiracy to commit espionage and they were executed for these crimes in 1953.

UPI/CORBIS-BETTMANN

confess and implicate others in his spy ring. "There is no doubt," Hoover wrote to Attorney General J. HOWARD MCGRATH, that "it would be possible to proceed against other individuals" if "Julius Rosenberg would furnish details of his extensive espionage activities." "Proceeding against his wife," Hoover emphasized, "might serve as a lever in this matter." Shortly after this letter was written, Ethel was arrested and charged with the same crime as her husband.

When Julius obstinately refused to cooperate with the FBI, the government informed the defendants that the death penalty would be sought in the event of their conviction. The FBI never relented from its use of Ethel as a "lever" against Julius, ultimately executing Ethel for her role as an accessory to the crime committed by her husband and brother. Declassified documents show that the entire testimony relating to Ethel's role as a typist for her husband's espionage ring, which was the only evidence offered to implicate her in the conspiracy, was concocted by the FBI and the Greenglasses just eight days before the trial began.

Historians have raised other suspicions with regard to the FBI's investigation of the Rosenbergs. On May 22, 1950, Gold submitted an initial written confession to the FBI. The confession made a passing reference to Albuquerque but made no assertion that he had been sent by "Julius" to see a man named "Greenglass" from whom he had acquired secret information about the atomic bomb. Nor did the confession allude to irregularly shaped pieces of a Jell-O box or a Soviet agent named Yakovlev.

After a number of subsequent interviews with the FBI, some of which were conducted in the presence of David Greenglass, Gold said he was able to remember each of the missing details that he had earlier "forgotten." Walter and Miriam Schneir, authors of *Invitation to an Inquest*, have argued that these allegedly "forgotten" details were supplied to Gold by the FBI so that his story would corroborate the Greenglasses' testimony. The FBI has steadfastly maintained that it did nothing improper, unethical, or illegal to jog Gold's memory, and declassified government files from the case have offered no "smoking gun."

Many supporters of the Rosenbergs who have long suspected that the FBI manufactured evidence to strengthen its case do not deny that Julius was involved in some form of espionage for the Soviet Union. In 1995 the U.S. government released forty-nine decoded Soviet intelligence messages that it had intercepted during World War II. These messages offer proof that Julius, whose code name was "Liberal," was the ringleader of an espionage network of young U.S. Communists who provided the Soviets with documents relating to classified radar and aircraft information.

The intercepted messages imply that Julius may have been involved in efforts to obtain information from the Manhattan Project but reveal nothing specific. Nikita Khruschev, the former Soviet premier, noted in his memoirs, however, that the Rosenbergs "provided very significant help in accelerating the production of the atomic bomb." As the federal government declassifies and releases more documents from the Rosenberg files, a clearer picture of the Rosenberg espionage network will emerge. The most recently released files suggest that Ethel did not participate in her husband's espionage efforts due to her health.

In light of the murky questions that still surround the Rosenberg case, the jury's guilty VERDICT and the judge's death sentence remain a source of controversy. Supporters of the verdict and sentence point out that Justice WILLIAM O. DOUGLAS granted a temporary stay of the Rosenbergs' execution so that the Supreme Court could consider whether to hear the case on APPEAL. After reviewing the Rosenbergs' petitions to determine whether they presented any legal issues that were appropriate for appellate review, the Supreme Court denied CERTIORARI. Justice HUGO L. BLACK was the lone dissenter. On June 19, 1953, the day after their twenty-second wedding anniversary, the Rosenbergs were put to death in the electric chair.

See also COLD WAR; RED SCARE.

ROSS, JOHN   As the head of the largest branch of the Cherokee nation from 1828 to 1866, John Ross led the Cherokee through a period of profound cultural change. Under Ross's leadership, the Cherokee nation engaged in a historic and controversial legal battle to preserve their SOVEREIGNTY and underwent a disastrous forced march from Georgia to Oklahoma.

Ross was born in what is now Alabama on October 3, 1790. Although he was only one-eighth Cherokee by blood, Cherokee cultural identity in the early 1800s was as much a matter of upbringing and choice as genetics, and Ross was raised and considered himself a Cherokee.

In 1809 at age nineteen, Ross was sent, at the behest of both U.S. officials and Cherokee leaders, to confer with the western Cherokee, who had accepted payments from the United States in exchange for an agreement to relocate

BIOGRAPHY

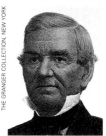

John Ross

THE GRANGER COLLECTION, NEW YORK

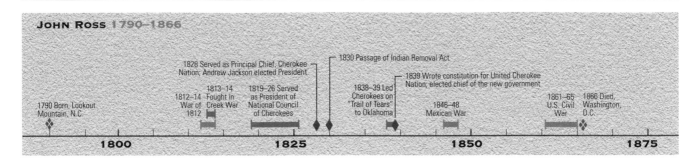

JOHN ROSS 1790–1866

1790 Born, Lookout Mountain, N.C.

1812

1812–14 War of 1812

1813–14 Fought in Creek War

1819–26 Served as President of National Council of Cherokees

1828 Served as Principal Chief, Cherokee Nation; Andrew Jackson elected President

1830 Passage of Indian Removal Act

1838–39 Led Cherokees on "Trail of Tears" to Oklahoma

1839 Wrote constitution for United Cherokee Nation; elected chief of the new government

1846–48 Mexican War

1861–65 U.S. Civil War

1866 Died, Washington, D.C.

1800   1825   1850   1875

to Oklahoma. Ross's quiet and reserved manner inspired confidence among both whites and Indians, and his skill at easing the tensions with the western Cherokee greatly increased his influence within the Cherokee nation.

Ross served as President of the National Council of the Cherokee from 1819 to 1826 and became principal chief of the eastern Cherokee in 1828. He thought the Cherokee could benefit from adopting certain aspects of European-American culture. Accordingly, with the help of two other Cherokee leaders, Major Ridge and Charles Hicks, Ross convinced many Cherokee to convert from an economy based on hunting and the fur trade to one of agriculture. Some Cherokee adopted the Southern tradition of slave-holding. By the 1830s many members of the Cherokee nation were among the wealthiest individuals in what is now north Georgia. Ross himself was a slaveholder with a two hundred–acre farm.

A well-educated man, Ross promoted literacy and education, advocating that all Cherokee utilize the achievement of Sequoia, the Cherokee who had created a written lexicography for the Cherokee language. Ross's efforts brought the Cherokee from near illiteracy to over 90 percent literacy in less than three years. Ross also supported the efforts of Christian Congregationalist missionaries who wished to set up schools in Cherokee territory. When it became apparent that the missionaries' primary objective was religious conversion rather than education, however, Ross informed them that they could stay only if they focused on education. The missionaries complied.

In addition to his emphasis on literacy and education, Ross encouraged the Cherokee to adopt a written system of laws, a bicameral legislative body, and a government with legislative, judicial, and executive branches. In 1827 the Cherokee nation adopted a republican constitution, written by Ross and modeled after the U.S. Constitution.

Under Ross's leadership the Cherokee eliminated the BLOOD FEUD as a primary means of settling criminal homicides. Under the customs

"IF IT HAS BEEN OUR MISFORTUNE TO SUFFER WRONGS FROM THE HANDS OF OUR WHITE BRETHREN, WE SHOULD NOT DESPAIR OF HAVING JUSTICE STILL EXTENDED BY THE UNITED STATES."

of the blood feud, when a person was killed, the victim's clan was obligated to kill a member of the murderer's clan. This often resulted in years of feuding between clans. Through Ross's influence the blood feud was replaced with a court system, trial by jury, and a written criminal code.

Despite their embrace of many aspects of U.S. society, Ross and his people wished to preserve Cherokee sovereignty—a goal the U.S. and Georgia governments would not accept. Beginning in 1828, Georgia passed a series of laws declaring the invalidity of Cherokee sovereignty. Meanwhile, the U.S. government, under President ANDREW JACKSON, was advocating removal of the Cherokee to the lands west of the Mississippi, even though treaties such as the Treaty of Hopewell (1785) recognized the Cherokee's sovereign right to their lands.

Ross refused to advocate violence as a means for the Cherokee to retain their land. Having grown up with warfare, ethnic violence, and GENOCIDE between various Indian tribes and the Cherokee and between European-Americans and the Cherokee, Ross had witnessed the destructive effects of violence on the Cherokee nation and had also seen the disastrous results of the armed struggles of other Indian tribes against the European-Americans. Putting his faith in the U.S. legal system, he believed that the U.S. Supreme Court would recognize the Cherokee's right to their land and sovereignty. In two historic cases, *Cherokee Nation v. Georgia*, 30 U.S. 1, 8 L. Ed. 25 (1831), and *Worcester v. Georgia*, 31 U.S. 515, 8 L. Ed. 483 (1832), Ross and the Cherokee fought for legal recognition of their sovereignty. The Cherokee lost in *Cherokee Nation*. Then, in a stunning reversal, the Supreme Court recognized Cherokee sovereignty in *Worcester* and ruled that the Georgia laws claiming JURISDICTION in Indian Territory were void. Both Georgia and Jackson refused to abide by the Court's decision, however. Instead, the U.S. government stepped up its efforts to relocate the Cherokee.

The Reverend John F. Schermerhorn, who was appointed by Jackson as commissioner in charge of convincing the Cherokee to leave Georgia, met with the Cherokee leaders and offered to pay them for ceding their lands. The Cherokee were split between the treaty party, led by Major Ridge, who were willing to accept the government's offer, and those like Ross, who were against the offer. When the ruling body of the Cherokee, led by Ross, refused to sign the agreement, Schermerhorn ordered Ross to be arrested.

On December 29, 1835, while Ross was being held without charge, Major Ridge and seventy-four others out of a tribe of seventeen thousand signed a treaty in what is now New Echota, Georgia, by which the Cherokee ceded all lands east of the Mississippi River in return for western lands and other considerations. All who signed received payment and land. In protest, Ross went to Washington carrying a petition with fifteen thousand signatures, 90 percent of all Cherokee. The treaty passed the U.S. Senate by one vote. David ("Davy") Crockett lost his seat in Congress for opposing Jackson's policy on Indian removal.

When Ross returned home, he found that the Georgia government had granted his property to a Georgian. In the summer of 1838, Jackson, who had refused to send U.S. troops to enforce the Supreme Court's *Worcester* decision, sent seven thousand soldiers to remove the Cherokee. Rather than leave their homeland, more than a thousand Cherokee fled to the Great Smoky Mountains, where their descendants still live.

During the winter of 1838–39, the remaining Cherokee were forced to march from Rattlesnake Springs, Tennessee, to Tahlequah, Oklahoma, in what became known as the "Trail of Tears." Four thousand Cherokee, including Ross's wife, Quatie, died on the march.

Once in Oklahoma, Ross was reelected principal chief. Major Ridge was killed the same day for his part in the signing of the Treaty of New Echota. In Tahlequah, land was set aside for schools, a newspaper, and a new Cherokee capital. During the Civil War, the Cherokee aligned themselves with the Confederacy, believing the U.S. government untrustworthy. They also ratified a declaration repudiating all treaties with the federal government, a move that led to bad relations with the U.S. government in the first months after the defeat of the Confederacy. In September 1865, however, Ross attended the Grand Council of Southern Indians at Fort Smith, where a new treaty between the Cherokee and the federal government was prepared. This treaty declared that it rejuvenated all prior, valid treaties between the Cherokee and the government. Despite his failing health, Ross accompanied the delegation to Washington, where the treaty was signed on July 19, 1866. Less than two weeks later, on August 1, 1866, Ross died in Washington, D.C.

CROSS-REFERENCES

Native American Rights; *Worcester v. Georgia*.

BIOGRAPHY

UPI/CORBIS-BETTMANN

Nellie Tayloe Ross

ROSS, NELLIE TAYLOE   On January 5, 1925, Nellie Tayloe Ross became the first female governor in U.S. history. Ross's election in Wyoming occurred less than five years after U.S. women were granted the right to vote by the NINETEENTH AMENDMENT to the U.S. Constitution. As governor, Ross was known as an exceptional administrator and a polished public speaker. Although she lost her bid for reelection, Ross's single term as Wyoming's top official led to other important state and federal positions.

Ross's date of birth is unclear. It is thought that she was born in 1876 in St. Joseph, Missouri. She married William Ross, an attorney, and in 1902 moved with him to Cheyenne, Wyoming. Ross's husband had political ambitions and was elected governor of Wyoming in 1922. In 1924 he died unexpectedly while in office. Ross was approached by the Democratic party to run for the remaining two years of her late husband's term. Although Wyoming was a Republican state, Ross won the election by eight thousand votes.

Ross's victory came on the same day that Miriam ("Ma") Ferguson was elected governor

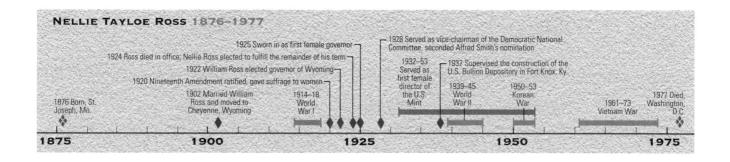

NELLIE TAYLOE ROSS 1876–1977

1928 Served as vice-chairman of the Democratic National Committee, seconded Alfred Smith's nomination

1925 Sworn in as first female governor

1924 Ross died in office; Nellie Ross elected to fulfill the remainder of his term

1922 William Ross elected governor of Wyoming

1920 Nineteenth Amendment ratified, gave suffrage to women

1932–53 Served as first female director of the U.S. Mint

1937 Supervised the construction of the U.S. Bullion Depository in Fort Knox, Ky.

1902 Married William Ross and moved to Cheyenne, Wyoming

1914–18 World War I

1939–45 World War II

1950–53 Korean War

1876 Born, St. Joseph, Mo.

1961–73 Vietnam War

1977 Died, Washington, D.C.

1875   1900   1925   1950   1975

of Texas. Because Ross was sworn into office two weeks before Ferguson, she is recognized as the first female governor in the United States.

As governor, Ross backed progressive public education measures. She also managed to reduce the state debt by more than $1 million. Ross supported Prohibition and opposed professional prizefighting, two unpopular positions that contributed to her defeat in the 1926 gubernatorial election. Her affiliation with the Democratic party was also a factor in her loss.

Ross later was elected to the Wyoming state legislature and remained active in Democratic politics at both the state and national level. In 1928 she was an influential supporter of unsuccessful Democratic presidential nominee Alfred E. Smith.

In 1932 Ross scored another first for women when she was appointed by President FRANKLIN D. ROOSEVELT to head the U.S. Mint. Ross became the Mint's first female director. She stayed there for twenty years, overseeing the Mint during the economic throes of the Great Depression and throughout a critical paper shortage during World War II.

Ross also supervised the construction in 1937 of the U.S. Bullion Depository in Fort Knox, Kentucky. She is honored on the cornerstone of the fortified building. Ross was also the first woman to have her likeness printed on a medal made by the Mint. In 1953 she retired as director after Republican DWIGHT D. EISENHOWER was elected president.

An early role model for women in government, Ross served both Wyoming and the United States with distinction. She died in Washington, D.C., in 1977, at the approximate age of 101.

ROSTKER v. GOLDBERG A U.S. Supreme Court decision, 453 U.S. 57, 101 S. Ct. 2646, 69 L. Ed. 2d 478 (1981), that upheld the constitutionality of a male-only draft registration law enacted by Congress in 1980. Emphasizing its traditional deference to Congress in the areas of military affairs and national defense, the Court refused by a vote of 6 to 3 to apply PRECEDENT that might have invalidated the law because of gender discrimination. Even the dissenters, however, did not challenge the right of Congress to exclude women from combat.

Rostker v. Goldberg actually began years before Congress enacted the Military Selective Service Act (MSSA) (50 App. U.S.C.A. § 451 et seq.) in 1980. In 1971, during the last part of the VIETNAM WAR, Robert Goldberg and several other men challenged the male-only draft policy, arguing that EQUAL PROTECTION of the

laws, as guaranteed by the FIFTH AMENDMENT, had been violated. When Congress discontinued military CONSCRIPTION in 1972, the lawsuit became inactive, but it was not dismissed. It was revived in 1980 when Congress, acting at the request of President JIMMY CARTER, revived the registration process. Carter was concerned about the Soviet Union's invasion of Afghanistan and believed that the government had to be ready to draft soldiers if the situation warranted it.

In his proposal to Congress, Carter asked for the authority to register both men and women. Congress refused to allocate funds to register women but did fund the registration of males. Carter signed MSSA, and on July 2, 1980, he ordered the registration of specified groups of young men pursuant to the authority conferred by Section 3 of the act. Registration was to commence on July 21, 1980.

At that point Goldberg's lawsuit took on new life and became a CLASS ACTION lawsuit. A three-judge panel in the U.S. District Court for the Eastern District of Pennsylvania held a hearing on the plaintiffs' claims against Bernard Rostker, director of the SELECTIVE SERVICE SYSTEM, the agency that administers military registration. The plaintiffs again asserted that the law violated equal protection. The panel agreed, declaring it unconstitutional three days before registration was to start. Rostker requested that the court's order be stayed (temporarily lifted) pending appeal. Justice WILLIAM J. BRENNAN, JR., granted the STAY, allowing registration to proceed.

In his majority opinion, Justice WILLIAM H. REHNQUIST rejected the idea that MSSA violated the Fifth Amendment in authorizing the president to require the registration of males and not females. Rehnquist noted that the statute involved national defense and military affairs, areas in which the Court traditionally had deferred to Congress. Under the Constitution, Congress has broad powers to raise and regulate armies and navies. More important, Rehnquist stated, the Court's "lack of competence" had to be considered when assessing legislation in this area.

Rehnquist concluded that Congress had not acted unthinkingly or reflexively in rejecting the registration of women. He pointed out that the question had received national attention and was the subject of public debate in and out of Congress. Congress heard testimony and collected evidence during the legislative process. All these actions persuaded the Court that the decision to exempt women from registration was not the accidental by-product of a traditional way of categorizing females.

The key issue for Congress in planning a future draft was the need for combat troops. Rehnquist noted that "women as a group, unlike men as a group, are not eligible for combat" under statute and established policy. These combat restrictions meant that Congress had a legitimate basis for concluding that women "would not be needed in the event of a draft." Therefore, there was no need to register women.

Turning to the issue of equal protection, Rehnquist ruled that because of the combat restrictions on women, men and women "are not similarly situated for purposes of a draft or registration for a draft." The law did not violate equal protection because the exemption of women from registration closely related to the congressional purpose of registration as a way to "develop a pool of potential combat troops." Rehnquist concluded by noting that the "Constitution requires that Congress treat similarly situated persons similarly, not that it engage in gestures of superficial equality."

Justices Brennan, BYRON R. WHITE, and THURGOOD MARSHALL dissented. In his dissent, Marshall lamented the majority's failure to apply the "heightened" scrutiny test announced in *Craig v. Boren*, 429 U.S. 190, 97 S. Ct. 451, 50 L. Ed. 2d 397 (1976). In that case the Court held that gender-based classifications "must serve important governmental objectives and must be substantially related to achievement of those objectives." The burden is on the party defending the classification to meet these requirements.

In Marshall's view, there was a difference between registration and conscription. He did not agree that exclusion of women from draft registration "substantially furthers the goal of preparing for a draft of combat troops," or that the registration of women "would substantially impede its efforts to prepare for such a draft." The majority had crafted a "hypothetical program for conscripting only men," where "conscripts are either assigned to those specific combat posts presently closed to women or must be available for rotation into such positions." He noted that only two-thirds of those persons conscripted in a future draft would serve in combat roles. There appeared to be no important or substantial government objective in not registering women for the draft.

Marshall, however, did not discuss the more fundamental issue of excluding women from combat. Both the majority and minority opinions assumed that it was legitimate to exclude women from the front lines. In other contexts, this type of gender-role classification has been ruled unconstitutional.

CROSS-REFERENCES
Armed Services; Sex Discrimination; Women's Rights.

ROTH v. UNITED STATES The U.S. Supreme Court, in *Roth v. United States* and *Alberts v. California*, 354 U.S. 476, 77 S. Ct. 1304, 1 L. Ed. 2d 1498 (1957), issued a landmark ruling on obscenity and its relation to the FIRST AMENDMENT. The Court held that obscenity was not a protected form of expression and could be restricted by the states. In addition, the Court announced a test for courts to use in evaluating whether material was OBSCENE.

The Court consolidated the appeals of Samuel Roth and David Alberts. Roth had been convicted of violating a federal statute (18 U.S.C.A. § 1461) that made it a crime to mail obscene advertising and reading materials. Alberts, a California mail-order seller, was convicted for keeping obscene books in violation of California law. Both the federal and state courts of appeal had upheld their respective convictions.

The issue before the Court was clear: Was obscenity entitled to protection under the First Amendment guarantees of freedom of speech and press? Until *Roth*, the Court had largely ignored the constitutionality of obscenity statutes, creating the assumption that obscenity was not protected speech. Consequently, obscenity convictions were routinely upheld by the lower courts.

Justice WILLIAM J. BRENNAN, JR., in his majority opinion, reviewed the history of freedom of expression and concluded that not every type of utterance was protected in the thirteen original colonies. LIBEL, BLASPHEMY, and PROFANITY were among the statutory crimes. In addition, that every state and the federal government had obscenity statutes showed that the First Amendment "was not intended to protect every utterance." Obscenity is denied protection because it is "utterly without redeeming social importance."

Having ruled that obscenity is not within the area of constitutionally protected speech or press, Brennan noted that sex in art and literature was not, by itself, obscene. Indeed, "sex, a great and mysterious motive force in human life" had interested "mankind through the ages; it is one of the vital problems of human interest and public concern." In the past, however, mere sexual content was enough to have a novel banned under the test courts used in assessing whether something was obscene.

For a legal definition of obscenity, U.S. courts looked to the English case of *Regina v. Hicklin*, L.R. 3 Q.B. 360 (1868). The *Hicklin* test was "whether the tendency of the matter charged as obscenity is to deprave and corrupt those whose minds are open to such immoral influences, and into whose hands a publication of this sort may fall." This test permitted prosecutors and judges to select objectionable words or passages without regard for the work as a whole and without respect to any artistic, literary, or scientific value the work might have.

Brennan rejected the *Hicklin* test as being "unconstitutionally restrictive of the freedoms of speech and press." It was essential that the work as a whole be evaluated before being declared obscene. Brennan endorsed the test used in both Roth's and Alberts's trials: "whether to the average person, applying contemporary community standards, the dominant theme of the material taken as a whole appeals to a prurient [lewd or lustful] interest." The new test was applicable to both state and federal government obscenity prosecutions.

The *Roth* test did not settle the question of what is obscenity, however. In fact, the Court was drawn into a long-term inquiry over virtually every element of the new obscenity test. The Court has never reached full agreement on what constitutes an appeal to "prurient interest." The phrase "redeeming social importance" has also failed to generate a consensus. Nor, in the years immediately following *Roth*, could the Court agree on whether "community" referred to the nation as a whole or to individual states or localities.

CROSS-REFERENCES
Freedom of Speech; Freedom of the Press; Pornography.

ROUSSEAU, JEAN JACQUES
Jean Jacques Rousseau achieved prominence as a philosopher and political theorist in eighteenth–century France. A talented musical composer and botanist, Rousseau's ideas on the nature of society made him an influential figure in Western thought. His belief that civilization had corrupted humankind was a central part of his philosophy. His work elevated the importance of the individual and personal liberty, providing support for U.S. revolutionary ideology.

Rousseau was born on June 28, 1712, in Geneva, Switzerland. By the age of sixteen, he had left home. In Savoy he met Baronne Louise De Warens, a wealthy woman who took Rousseau into her home and transformed him into a philosopher through a rigorous course of study. Rousseau also studied music during his time with De Warens. In 1742 he moved to Paris, where he became associated with Denis Diderot, a philosopher who was editor of the French *Encyclopédie*, a monumental work of scholarship about the arts and society. Diderot commissioned Rousseau to write articles about music for the work.

In 1750 Rousseau won a prize for his essay *Discourse on the Sciences and the Arts*. The essay announced one of Rousseau's life–long tenets: human beings are inherently good but have been corrupted by society and civilization. In 1752 he won fame as a composer for his opera *The Village Sage*. Despite the accolades, Rousseau abandoned his musical career, believing it was morally unworthy to work in the theater. Instead he pursued his investigation of society, writing *Discourse on the Origin of Inequality among Mankind* in 1752. He enlarged on his first work, criticizing civilization for its corrupting influence and praising the natural, or primitive, state as morally superior to the civilized state.

Rousseau left Paris in 1756 and secluded himself at Montmorency, so as to be closer to nature. He did not return to writing until 1761, when he wrote the romance *Julie, or the New Eloise*. The following year he wrote one of his most enduring and influential works, *The Social Contract*. The book opens with the famous sentence, "Man was born free, but he is everywhere in chains." Rousseau believed that society and government created a social contract when their goals were freedom and the benefit

BIOGRAPHY

CULVER PICTURES

Jean Jacques Rousseau

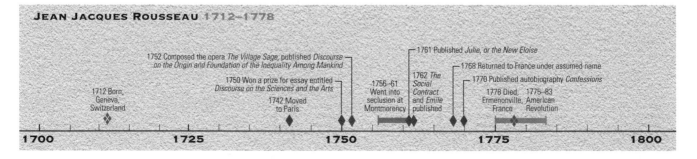

JEAN JACQUES ROUSSEAU 1712–1778

1752 Composed the opera *The Village Sage*; published *Discourse on the Origin and Foundation of the Inequality Among Mankind*

1750 Won a prize for essay entitled *Discourse on the Sciences and the Arts*

1712 Born, Geneva, Switzerland

1742 Moved to Paris

1756–61 Went into seclusion at Montmorency

1761 Published *Julie, or the New Eloise*

1762 *The Social Contract* and *Emile* published

1768 Returned to France under assumed name

1770 Published autobiography *Confessions*

1778 Died, Ermenonville, France

1775–83 American Revolution

1700   1725   1750   1775   1800

of the public. Government became the supreme ruler, but its existence depended on the will of the people. The social order was based on the general will, a shared belief in a common set of interests, which he believed was the natural choice of rational people. The general will was also a form of freedom, and the purpose of law was to combine the general will with the desires of the people.

Rousseau was convinced that laws could not be unjust if the general will of the people was followed. *The Social Contract* was suffused with the belief that freedom and civil liberty are essential to a just society. Society should not be ruled by elites but by the general will of all people. Rousseau, like the English philosopher JOHN LOCKE (1632–1704), provided justification for the idea of a liberal society based on popular will that would be embraced by the American colonists in the years leading up to the U.S. Revolution. The American colonists believed that the social contract with England had been broken. Rousseau's belief in the primacy of the individual, however, has proved to be an idea that found its greatest acceptance in the United States.

Rousseau wrote the novel *Émile* in 1762, which was a platform for his ideas on education. He believed that the purpose of education is not to impart new information but to bring out what is inherently within each person and to encourage the full development of the human being. Children should be allowed self–expression and the opportunity to develop their own views about the world, rather than to submit to repression and conformity. Rousseau's ideas were radical for the time but have proved enduring.

The political climate was hostile to Rousseau following the publication of *The Social Contract* and *Émile*. The French Catholic Church banned both books, and Rousseau was forced to begin a period in exile. Driven from Switzerland for his ideas, he eventually arrived in England, where he was befriended by the philosopher DAVID HUME. While in England he prepared a treatise on botany.

In 1768 he returned to France under an assumed name. In 1770 he completed his *Confessions*, an autobiography of relentless self–examination in which he documented the emotional and moral conflicts of his life. He died on July 2, 1778, in Ermenonville, France.

ROYALTY 📖 Compensation for the use of property, usually copyrighted works, patented inventions, or natural resources, expressed as a percentage of receipts from using the property or as a payment for each unit produced. 📖

When a person creates a book, song, play, or painting, the work is considered INTELLECTUAL PROPERTY. Similarly, when an inventor receives a patent on his invention, the inventor has intellectual PROPERTY RIGHTS in the thing created. Typically, authors, songwriters, composers, playwrights, and inventors do not have the financial ability to fully exploit the commercial use of their creations. They must turn to businesses that specialize in the marketing of intellectual property. When a business obtains the right to market the creation, the creator usually receives compensation in the form of a royalty.

A royalty agreement is part of the CONTRACT that the creator of the work negotiates with the business that seeks to exploit the creation. A royalty can be as simple as a fixed amount of money for each copy of a book or compact disc sold by the business. For example, a novelist agrees to let a publisher publish her new book. For granting the publisher the rights to the book, the novelist will receive $3 for each copy sold. If the novelist is a best-selling author, the publisher may agree to a higher royalty rate. Book and music publishers sometimes give an

Singers and songwriters may earn as compensation from the music publisher a royalty of a fixed dollar amount for each compact disc sold.

W. HILL/THE IMAGE WORKS

advance against royalties to an author or musician when the contract is signed. For example, the novelist might receive $5,000 as an advance against her royalties. In this case the publisher will keep the first $5,000 of the royalties to cover the cash advance. Typically, if the book failed to produce enough royalties to cover the advance, the publisher would write off the difference as a loss. However, a publisher might sue an author to recover an advance if the author never produces a publishable manuscript.

A playwright's royalty may be based on a percentage of the box office receipts from each performance of the play. An inventor's royalty might be an amount per unit sold or a percentage of the profits generated by the invention. In some cases it might be both. Because a royalty is one of the terms negotiated in a contract, the type and amount will depend on the bargaining power of the parties.

Under the law royalties are PERSONAL PROPERTY. When a person dies, the heirs receive the royalties. For example, when Elvis Presley died, his ESTATE went to his daughter Lisa Marie, who now collects the royalties from the music company that sells her father's recordings.

Royalty agreements are also used in the mineral and GAS industries. These agreements have much in common with the origin of the term. For many centuries in Great Britain, the Crown owned all the gold and silver mines. A private business could mine these "royal" metals only if it made a payment, a royalty, to the Crown.

When, for example, a petroleum company wants to drill for oil on a person's land, the company negotiates a royalty agreement with the owner of the MINERAL RIGHTS. If the company strikes oil, the owner of the mineral rights will receive a royalty based on a percentage of the barrels pumped out of the wells. The owner may receive the royalty in kind (the actual oil) or in value (the dollar amount agreed to in the contract), based on the total production from the property.

The schedule for royalty payments is specified in the contract. Quarterly or annual payments are typical. The royalty owner has the right to make an independent accounting of the business records to ensure that the figures upon which the royalty is based are accurate.

CROSS-REFERENCES

Copyright; Entertainment Law; Literary Property; Mine and Mineral Law; Music Publishing; Patents; Publishing Law.

BIOGRAPHY

RUBENSTEIN, WILLIAM BRUCE William Bruce Rubenstein is a lawyer, law professor, and author who is recognized as a leading national expert on sexual orientation and the law. For eight years Rubenstein was an attorney with and director of the Lesbian and Gay Rights Project of the AMERICAN CIVIL LIBERTIES UNION (ACLU).

Rubenstein was born on September 3, 1960, in Pittsburgh, Pennsylvania. He graduated from Yale University in 1982 and earned a law degree from Harvard University in 1986. Rubenstein then served as a law clerk to a federal district court judge. He was admitted to the Pennsylvania bar in 1986 and the District of Columbia bar in 1988.

In 1987 Rubenstein joined the national office of the ACLU's Lesbian and Gay Rights Project, which has its headquarters in New York City. The national office intervenes in legal disputes involving discrimination against gays and lesbians, acts as a PUBLIC POLICY advocate for GAY AND LESBIAN RIGHTS, and provides education for lesbians, gay men, and people with HIV and AIDS. The national office also works with local Lesbian and Gay Rights Project chapters on pending litigation and legislation.

Rubenstein is a noted legal scholar on sexual orientation issues. He has published *Rubenstein's Cases and Materials on Sexual Orientation and the Law* (2d. ed. 1996), which is used in many U.S. law schools. In addition, he is the author of *Lesbians, Gay Men, and the Law* (1993). Rubenstein has taught courses on lesbian and gay law

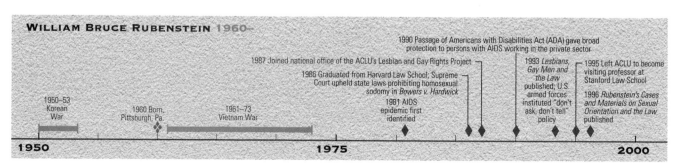

WILLIAM BRUCE RUBENSTEIN 1960–

1990 Passage of Americans with Disabilities Act (ADA) gave broad protection to persons with AIDS working in the private sector

1987 Joined national office of the ACLU's Lesbian and Gay Rights Project

1986 Graduated from Harvard Law School; Supreme Court upheld state laws prohibiting homosexual sodomy in *Bowers v. Hardwick*

1993 *Lesbians, Gay Men and the Law* published; U.S. armed forces instituted "don't ask, don't tell" policy

1995 Left ACLU to become visiting professor at Stanford Law School

1996 *Rubenstein's Cases and Materials on Sexual Orientation and the Law* published

1950–53 Korean War

1960 Born, Pittsburgh, Pa.

1961–73 Vietnam War

1981 AIDS epidemic first identified

1950   1975   2000

at Harvard and Yale Law Schools. He left the ACLU in 1995 and accepted a position as visiting professor at Stanford University Law School.

RUBRIC OF A STATUTE 📖 The title of a statute indicating the objective of the legislation and providing a means of interpreting the body of the act. 📖

RUBY, JACK Jack Ruby was a Dallas, Texas nightclub owner who shot and killed Lee Harvey Oswald, the accused assassin of President JOHN F. KENNEDY, two days after Kennedy's ASSASSINATION in Dallas. Millions of people watched on national television as Ruby shot Oswald while the Dallas police were attempting to move Oswald from the police station to another location. Questions about how Ruby was able to gain access to the police station and why he killed Oswald have never been fully answered. These questions, as well as the silencing of Oswald himself, are among the reasons why some persons believe that Oswald was part of a CONSPIRACY to kill Kennedy.

Ruby was born Jack Rubenstein on March 25, 1911, in Chicago, Illinois. He quit school after sixth grade and lived a life on the streets during adolescence. He was known for his explosive temper and willingness to fight. In the early 1930s he lived in California but soon moved back to Chicago. He tried short-lived careers as a salesman, union organizer, and boxer. In 1943 he was drafted into the Army Air Force and served until 1946. In 1947 Ruby moved to Dallas to help his sister manage a nightclub she owned. He served as manager and unofficial bouncer of the club and soon became acquainted with members of the Dallas police force. He later moved to the Carousel Club and, anxious to be accepted, befriended many police officers by giving them free drinks and hospitality. The police regarded Ruby as a harmless figure who enjoyed the aura of law enforcement. Those in the criminal world considered Ruby an informer, who told the police everything he knew about criminal activity.

On November 22, 1963, President Kennedy was shot and killed in Dallas. Ruby was distraught at the news of the assassination and headed for the Dallas police headquarters. A well-known face at the police station, he was allowed into headquarters on November 23. On Sunday, November 24, Oswald was scheduled to be transferred to the county jail around 10:00 A.M., but a series of events delayed his move until 11:00 A.M. Ruby, who had parked his car one block away from the police station around that time, walked down the rampway to the basement garage of the police station. The guard at the basement entrance had momentarily left his post to stop traffic so that the police convoy with Oswald could leave the building. Ruby walked into the garage, which was filled with police officers, reporters, and camera crews. As Oswald appeared, flanked by police detectives, Ruby approached him with a .38-caliber gun and fatally shot him. Ruby was immediately arrested.

As Ruby prepared for his murder trial, his attorney, Tom Howard, prepared a defense based on the theory that the killing was a crime of passion committed without malice or premeditation by an unstable man. If this defense had been successful, Ruby would have received a maximum of five years in prison under Texas law. Before trial, however, Ruby's family discharged Howard and retained Melvin M. Belli, a well-known and controversial San Francisco attorney. Belli elected to present a defense of

In 1964 a Texas jury convicted Jack Ruby (center) of killing Lee Harvey Oswald, the man accused of assassinating President John F. Kennedy.

UPI/CORBIS-BETTMANN

total insanity in the hope Ruby would be acquitted. Belli asserted that Ruby had experienced an epileptic seizure and had shot Oswald while under the influence of this impairment.

The case against Ruby was substantial. After the shooting, Ruby had given statements to the police, one of which suggested premeditation. Medical authorities did not support Belli's medical diagnosis of Ruby. On March 16, 1964, a jury convicted Ruby of premeditated murder, and he was sentenced to death.

Ruby's conviction was reversed by the Texas Court of Criminal Appeals in October 1966, but he died in prison of a blood clot, complicated by cancer, on January 3, 1967.

Many questions surrounding Ruby's motives and actions remain unanswered. The Kennedy assassination and the Oswald shooting were investigated by a presidential commission headed by Chief Justice EARL WARREN. The Warren Report, issued in 1964, concluded that the bullets that killed Kennedy had been fired by Oswald's rifle and that there was no evidence that either Oswald or Ruby was part of any conspiracy, domestic or international, to assassinate the president.

Many people were unpersuaded by the Warren Report's conclusion that Oswald acted alone. Since 1964 numerous books and theories have asserted that the Kennedy assassination was the result of a conspiracy. One theory proposed that ORGANIZED CRIME had killed Kennedy and that Ruby had underworld connections. In 1979 a committee of the U.S. House of Representatives reexamined the evidence from 1963 and concluded that there had probably been two gunmen and that a conspiracy was likely. This committee noted that in the weeks preceding the assassination Ruby had made several phone calls to persons associated with organized crime. Other commentators have discounted the phone calls, as they were made before Kennedy's trip to Dallas and the route his motorcade would take were announced.

RULE To command or require pursuant to a principle of the court, as to rule the SHERIFF to serve the SUMMONS.

To settle or decide a point of law at a trial or hearing.

An established standard, guide, or regulation governing conduct, procedure, or action.

The word *rule* has a wide range of meanings in the law, as in ordinary English. As a verb, it most commonly refers to the action of a court of law in settling a legal question. When a court rules, the decision is called a *ruling*. As a noun,

rule generally refers to either settled principles of substantive law or procedural regulations used by courts to administer justice.

One of the most basic concepts in the Anglo-American legal tradition is called the *rule of law*. The RULE OF LAW refers to a set of rules and procedures governing human and institutional behavior that are autonomous and possess their own logic. These rules are fundamental to society and provide the guides for all other rules that regulate behavior. The rule of law argues for the legitimacy of the legal system by claiming that all persons will be judged by a neutral and impartial authority and that no one will receive special treatment. The concept of DUE PROCESS OF LAW is an important component of the rule of law.

Courts and legislatures produce substantive law in all areas of human behavior and social arrangement. Over time certain guiding principles emerge that rise to the level of a rule. When this happens, it usually means that the courts have firmly established a standard for assessing an issue. The source of a rule may be a previous set of court decisions or a legislative act that clearly sets out how the law is to be interpreted. Substantive rules help guide attorneys in giving advice to clients. For example, the RULE AGAINST PERPETUITIES governs the way in which property may be given. Knowing this rule, a lawyer can draft a legal document that will not violate the rule.

Courts of law have many procedural rules that determine how the judicial system will handle disputes. Courts have the authority, either by legislative act or by their own inherent power, to promulgate (issue) rules of procedure. State and federal courts have rules of criminal and civil procedure that set out in great detail the requirements of every party to a criminal or civil proceeding. Rules of evidence provide guidelines for what a court may properly allow into evidence at a trial.

Courts promulgate rules of professional conduct that govern the ethical behavior of attorneys. Other rules specify how many hours of continuing legal education an attorney must attend to remain in good standing. Courts also issue rules on technology. For example, the highest court in a JURISDICTION usually decides whether television cameras will be allowed in a courtroom and issues a rule to that effect.

There are also rules of interpretation that guide courts in making their rulings. For example, the PLAIN-MEANING RULE is a general principle of statutory interpretation. If the meaning of the words in a writing (such as a statute, contract, or will) is clear, other evidence is inadmissible to change the meaning. The interpretation of criminal statutes is guided by the *rule of lenity*. A court will decline to interpret a criminal law so as to increase the penalty, unless it has clear evidence of legislative intent to do otherwise.

Since the 1930s the growth in the number of government administrative agencies with rule-making authority has led to thousands of rules and regulations. The *Federal Register* is an official U.S. government publication that regularly prints proposed and final rules and regulations of government agencies. The INTERNAL REVENUE SERVICE, for example, issues administrative rulings that interpret the INTERNAL REVENUE CODE.

RULE AGAINST ACCUMULATIONS

📖 A principle that prohibits adding income or interest earned by a TRUST back into the PRINCIPAL of the fund beyond the time allowed by the RULE AGAINST PERPETUITIES. 📖

See also RULE AGAINST PERPETUITIES.

RULE AGAINST PERPETUITIES 📖 Under the COMMON LAW, the principle that no interest in PROPERTY is valid unless it vests not later than twenty-one years, plus the period of gestation, after some life or lives in being which exist at the time of the creation of the interest. 📖

The courts developed the rule during the seventeenth century in order to restrict a person's power to control perpetually the ownership and possession of his or her property after death and to ensure the transferability of property. The rule includes the period of gestation to cover cases of posthumous birth.

Vesting A property interest vests when it is given to a person in being (someone who is currently living) and is not subject to a CONDITION precedent. For example, if Donald Smith transfers his REAL PROPERTY to his son Howard for life and then to Howard's children who are alive at the time of Howard's death, the children's interest is not VESTED. Their interest is subject to the condition precedent that they survive their father Howard. If Donald transfers his property to his son Howard for life, and then to Howard's children Ann and Richard, the children's interest is vested. Although the children's right to possess and enjoy the property might be delayed for many years, the rule does not relate to the time when property vests in actual possession but only when the property vests in interest. The interest that the children possess is known as a future interest.

Under the rule, a future interest must vest within a certain period of time. This period is

The Rule Against Perpetuities, adopted from English common law, restricts the power of a person to control perpetually the ownership and possession of property after death. The courts upheld a will that named as measuring lives all the lineal descendants of Queen Victoria who were alive at the time of the testator's death.

limited to the duration of a life or lives in being (the "measuring lives") at the time the interest in the property is transferred, plus twenty-one years.

The period of the rule can be extended by one or more gestation periods. For purposes of the rule against perpetuities, a person is in being at the time of conception if he or she is born thereafter. Therefore the measuring life, or lives, might be the life of a person who has been conceived at the time the instrument takes effect but who is born afterward. For example, a TESTATOR—one who makes a WILL—leaves property "to the descendants of Jones who are living twenty-one years after the death of my last surviving child." Six months after his death, the testator's wife gives birth to their only child. This child is the measuring life, and the descendants of Jones who are alive twenty-one years after the death of the testator's child will take the property.

The period of gestation can also occur at the end of the measuring life or lives. A person conceived before but born after the death of a measuring life is considered to be in being for purposes of the rule. For example, a testator leaves his ESTATE to his grandchildren who attain the age of twenty-one. The testator's only child, William, is born six months after the testator's death. William himself has only one child, Pamela, who is born six months after

William's death. The will provisions that leave the property to Pamela are valid, and she will inherit her grandfather's estate when she reaches twenty-one.

The twenty-one year period must be added on after the deaths of the persons or person who are used as the measuring lives.

The measuring lives, or life, are usually persons who are named in the instrument creating the future interest, such as a will or a TRUST. Frequently the person whose life is used as the measuring life also has a preceding interest in the property, such as a person who is given LIFE ESTATE. A large number of persons can be used as measuring lives, as long as the date of the last survivor's death can be learned without too much difficulty. For example, a BEQUEST by a testator who used as measuring lives all of Queen Victoria's LINEAL descendants living at the time of the testator's death was upheld as valid. On the date of the testator's death, 120 of the queen's lineal descendants were alive.

If the interest will not vest until after the expiration of the life or lives in being plus twenty-one years, or there is a *possibility* that the interest might not vest until after the expiration of such time, the transfer is VOID and fails completely. The following fact pattern is an example of a situation that would violate the rule. George Bennet owns a farm, and his son Glen and Glen's wife, Susan, live on the farm and help George manage it. Glen and Susan are childless, but George wants grandchildren. To encourage them to have children, George promises that he will give Glen a life estate in the farm and leave the REMAINDER to George's grandchildren. He executes a will devising the farm to Glen for life and then to Glen's children when they reach the age of twenty-five. George's will creates the future interest, which takes effect at the time of his death. Glen's is the measuring life—the life in being at the time the interest is created. Since it is possible for the vesting to occur more than twenty-one years after the deaths of Glen and Susan, the devise of the future interest to the grandchildren is void. For instance, one year after George's death, Susan has a baby girl. Two years later, she has twin boys. Six months after the birth of the twin boys, both Susan and Glen are killed in an automobile accident. The interest in the farm will not vest in the three children within twenty-one years after their parent's deaths.

Wait and See Statutes Under the COMMON-LAW rule, if there is a possibility that the future interest will not vest until after the expiration of the life or lives in being, plus twenty-one years, the interest is void. The determination is made at the time the future interest is created. In order to avoid the harshness of this rule, some states have enacted statutes providing that the validity of the interest is to be decided at the time the interest actually does vest, rather than at the time it is created. Under these statutes the courts "wait and see" if the interest does in fact vest within the period of the rule. If it does vest within the period of the life or lives in being plus twenty-one years, then the interest is valid. Under other more limited "wait and see" statutes, a decision is made at the time of the death of the life tenant or tenants. These statutes are also called second look statutes.

See also LIFE IN BEING; SECOND LOOK DOCTRINE.

RULE IN SHELLEY'S CASE An English common-law doctrine that provided that a CONVEYANCE that attempts to give a person a LIFE ESTATE, with a REMAINDER to that person's HEIRS, will instead give both the life estate and the remainder to the person, thus giving that person the land in FEE SIMPLE absolute (full ownership without restriction).

Although *Wolfe v. Shelley*, 1 Co. Rep. 93b, 76 Eng. Rep. 206 (C.P.), generally known as *Shelley's Case*, took place in 1581, the rule that made it famous had already been in existence for approximately 150 years. The rule was enacted to close a tax loophole that allowed people to circumvent an inheritance tax, known as a *relief*. Any person who received property by means of inheritance was required to pay the relief to the feudal lord. Attempting to save their clients money, scriveners (drafters of written instruments such as deeds and wills) came up with a plan to allow a person who would otherwise have been an heir to receive property by means of a conveyance rather than by direct inheritance. The judges quickly saw through this attempt to circumvent the tax law and adopted the rule to close the loophole. As stated in *Shelley's Case*, the rule held that "when the ancestor by any gift or conveyance takes an estate of freehold, and in the same gift or conveyance an estate is limited either mediately or immediately to his heirs in fee or in tail, that always in such cases, 'the heirs' are words of limitation of estate, and not words of purchase" (statement of defendant's counsel, probably SIR EDWARD COKE).

The effect of the rule was to frustrate the intent of an owner of REAL PROPERTY who transferred her ESTATE to another by GIFT or conveyance and, by the same instrument, gave a remainder to the heirs of the transferee. In that circumstance the rule would ignore the intention of the owner and give the transferee the estate in fee as opposed to a life estate. For example, in the conveyance "Owner of Blackacre conveys it to X for life, remainder to X's heirs," X would not just get a life estate as the owner desired; instead, due to the rule, X would receive both the life estate and the remainder (intended for X's heirs) in fee simple absolute as the rule worked a merger of the life estate and the remainder. Consequently, the rule effectively changed the conveyance to "Owner to X and his heirs."

Even after the relief tax was abolished in 1660 by the Statute of Tenures (12 Ar. 2, ch. 24) scriveners were careful to draft documents so as to avoid application of the rule, which still survived even though the reason for its existence had disappeared. In 1770 William Murray, Lord Mansfield, the chief justice of the Court of King's Bench declared that the rule was "a strange law" and eradicated it (*Perrin v. Blake*, 1 F. Hargrave, Collectanea Juridica 283 [K.B.]). Lord Mansfield was an innovative jurist and experienced great frustration with the feudal peculiarities that existed in English land law. Unlike many of his fellow jurists, he was deeply concerned with giving legal meaning to the intention of TESTATORS and owners of property. As a result of these dynamics, the Court of Exchequer Chamber reversed Lord Mansfield's decision in *Perrin* and reinstated the Rule in Shelley's Case in 1772, holding that the rule "was a rule of law, not a rule of construction; that is, it was explicitly recognized to be applicable regardless of intention." Consequently, this ancient rule lived on until the growing desire to give effect to the owner's intention could be stifled no longer, and Great Britain decisively and finally abolished the rule in the Law of Property Act in 1925 (15 & 16 Geo. 5, ch. 20, § 131). Today, only a handful of states in the United States continue to give effect to the rule; the vast majority prefer to give effect to the intention behind the words used to transfer property.

See also FEUDALISM; MANSFIELD, WILLIAM MURRAY, FIRST EARL OF.

RULE OF LAW ▢ Rule according to law; rule under law; or rule according to a higher law. ▢

The rule of law is an ambiguous term that can mean different things in different contexts. In one context the term means rule according to law. No individual can be ordered by the government to pay civil damages or suffer criminal punishment except in strict accordance with well-established and clearly defined laws and procedures. In a second context the term means rule under law. No branch of government is above the law, and no public official may act arbitrarily or unilaterally outside the law. In a third context the term means rule according to a higher law. No written law may be enforced by the government unless it conforms with certain unwritten, universal principles of fairness, morality, and justice that transcend human legal systems.

Rule according to Law The rule of law requires the government to exercise its power in accordance with well-established and clearly written rules, regulations, and legal principles. A distinction is sometimes drawn between power, will, and force on the one hand, and law on the other. When a government official acts pursuant to an express provision of a written law, he acts within the rule of law. But when a government official acts without the imprimatur of any law, she does so by the sheer force of her will and power.

Under the rule of law, no person may be prosecuted for an act that is not punishable by law. When the government seeks to punish someone for an offense that was not deemed criminal at the time it was committed, the rule of law is violated because the government exceeds its legal authority to punish. The rule of law requires that government impose LIABILITY only insofar as the law will allow. Government exceeds its authority when a person is held to answer for an act that was legally permissible at the outset but was retroactively made illegal. This principle is reflected by the prohibition against EX POST FACTO LAWS in the U.S. Constitution.

For similar reasons, the rule of law is abridged when the government attempts to punish someone for violating a vague or poorly worded law. Ill-defined laws confer too much discretion upon government officials who are charged with the responsibility of prosecuting individuals for criminal wrongdoing. The more prosecutorial decisions are based on the personal discretion of a government official, the less they are based on law.

For example, the Due Process Clause of the Fifth and Fourteenth Amendments requires that statutory provisions be sufficiently definite to prevent arbitrary or discriminatory enforcement by a prosecutor. Government officials must not be given unfettered discretion to prosecute individuals for violating a law that is so vague or of such broad applicability that even-handed administration is not possible. Thus, a Florida law that prohibited vagrancy was held VOID FOR VAGUENESS because it was so generally worded that it encouraged erratic prosecutions and made possible the punishment of normally innocuous behavior (*Papachristou v. City of Jacksonville*, 405 U.S. 156, 92 S. Ct. 839, 31 L. Ed. 2d 110 [1972]).

Well-established and clearly defined laws allow individuals, businesses, and other entities to govern their behavior accordingly (*United States v. E.C. Investments, Inc.*, 77 F. 3d 327 [9th Cir. 1996]). Before the government may impose civil or criminal liability, a law must be written with sufficient precision and clarity that a person of ordinary intelligence will know that certain conduct is forbidden. When a court is asked to shut down a paint factory that is emitting pollutants at an illegal rate, for example, the rule of law requires the government to demonstrate that the factory owner failed to operate the business in accordance with publicly known environmental standards.

Rule under Law The rule of law also requires the government to exercise its authority under the law. This requirement is sometimes explained with the phrase "no one is above the law." During the seventeenth century, however, the English monarch was vested with absolute SOVEREIGNTY, including the prerogative to disregard laws passed by the House of Commons and ignore rulings made by the House of Lords. In the eighteenth century, absolute sovereignty was transferred from the British monarchy to Parliament, an event that was not lost on the colonists who precipitated the American Revolution and created the U.S. Constitution.

Under the Constitution, no single branch of government in the United States is given unlimited power. The authority granted to one branch of government is limited by the authority granted to the coordinate branches and by the BILL OF RIGHTS, federal statutory provisions, and historical practice. The power of any single branch of government is similarly restrained at the state level.

During his second term, President RICHARD M. NIXON tried to place the EXECUTIVE BRANCH of the federal government beyond the reach of legal PROCESS. When served with a SUBPOENA ordering him to produce a series of tapes that linked him to the WATERGATE conspiracy and cover-up, Nixon refused to comply, asserting that the confidentiality of these tapes was protected from disclosure by an absolute and unqualified EXECUTIVE PRIVILEGE. In *United States v. Nixon*, 418 U.S. 683, 94 S. Ct. 3090, 41 L. Ed. 2d 1039 (1974), the Supreme Court disagreed, compelling the president to hand over the tapes because the Constitution forbids any branch of government from unilaterally thwarting the legitimate ends of a criminal investigation.

The rule of law requiring government to exercise its authority under the law justified the Supreme Court's decision ordering President Richard M. Nixon to comply with a subpoena and turn over tapes of White House conversations to a congressional impeachment probe.

Members of the state and federal JUDICIARY face a slightly different problem when it comes to the rule of law. Each day judges are asked to interpret and apply legal principles that defy clear exposition. Terms like "due process," "reasonable care," and "undue influence" are not self-defining. Nor do judges always agree about how these terms should be defined, interpreted, or applied. When judges issue controversial decisions, they are often accused of deciding cases in accordance with their own personal beliefs, be they political, religious, or philosophical, rather than in accordance with the law.

Scholars have spent centuries examining this issue. Some believe that because the law is written in such indefinite and ambiguous terms, all judicial decisions will inevitably reflect the personal predilections of the presiding judge. Other scholars assert that most laws can be interpreted in a neutral, objective, and apolitical fashion even though all judges may not agree on the appropriate interpretation. In either case the rule of law is better served when judges keep an open mind to alternative readings of constitutional, statutory, and common-law principles. Otherwise, courts run the risk of prejudging certain cases in light of their own personal philosophy.

Rule according to Higher Law A conundrum is presented when the government acts in strict accordance with well-established and clearly defined legal rules and still produces a result that many observers consider unfair or unjust. Before the Civil War, for example, African Americans were systematically deprived of their freedom by carefully written codes that prescribed the rules and regulations between master and slave. Even though these slave codes were often detailed, unambiguous, and made known to the public, government enforcement of them produced unsavory results.

Do such repugnant laws comport with the rule of law? The answer to this question depends on when and where it is asked. In some countries the political leaders assert that the rule of law has no substantive content. These leaders argue that a government may deprive its citizens of fundamental liberties so long as it does so pursuant to a duly enacted law. At the NUREMBERG TRIALS, the political, military, and industrial leaders of Nazi Germany unsuccessfully advanced this argument as a defense to Allied charges that they had committed abominable crimes against European Jews and other minorities during World War II.

In other countries the political leaders assert that all written laws must conform with universal principles of morality, fairness, and justice. These leaders argue that as a necessary corollary to the axiom that "no one is above the law," the rule of law requires that the government treat all persons equally under the law. Yet the right to equal treatment is eviscerated when the government categorically denies a minimal level of respect, dignity, and autonomy to a single class of individuals. These unwritten principles of equality, autonomy, dignity, and respect are said to transcend ordinary written laws that are enacted by government. Sometimes known as NATURAL LAW or higher law theory, such unwritten and universal principles were invoked by the Allied powers during the Nuremberg trials to overcome the defense asserted by the Nazi leaders.

The rule of law is a concept as old as Western civilization itself. In classical Greece ARISTOTLE wrote that "law should be the final sovereign; and personal rule, whether it be exercised by a single person or a body of persons, should be sovereign in only those matters which law is unable, owing to the difficulty of framing general rules for all contingencies." In ancient Rome the CORPUS JURIS CIVILIS established a complex body of procedural and substantive rules, reflecting a strong commitment to the belief that law, not the arbitrary will of an emperor, is the appropriate vehicle for dispute resolution. In 1215 MAGNA CHARTA reined in the corrupt and whimsical rule of King John by declaring that government should not proceed except in accordance with the law of the land.

During the thirteenth century, Thomas Aquinas argued that the rule of law represents the natural order of God as ascertained through divine inspiration and human reason. In the seventeenth century, the English jurist SIR EDWARD COKE asserted that the "king ought to be under no man, but under God and the law." With regard to the legislative power in England, Coke said that "when an act of Parliament is against common right and reason, or repugnant, or impossible to be performed, the common law will control it, and adjudge such act to be void." In the United States, ALEXANDER HAMILTON applied the rule of law to the judiciary when he argued in *The Federalist*, no. 78, that judges "have neither Force nor Will, but merely judgment."

Despite its ancient history, the rule of law is not celebrated in all quarters. The English philosopher JEREMY BENTHAM described the rule of law as "nonsense on stilts." The twentieth century has seen its share of political leaders who have oppressed disfavored persons or groups without warning or reason, governing as

LIBRARY OF CONGRESS

English jurist Sir Edward Coke advanced a rule of law under which the king of England had to answer not to other men, but to the law and God.

if no such thing as the rule of law existed. For many people around the world, the rule of law is essential to freedom.

CROSS-REFERENCES
Discretion in Decision Making; Due Process of Law; Judicial Review; Jurisprudence; Legal Realism; Moral Law.

RULE OF 78 📖 A method of computing refunds of unearned finance charges on early payment of a loan so that the refund is proportional to the monthly unpaid balance. 📖

The figure *78* is the sum of the digits of one to twelve—that is, the number of months in a one-year INSTALLMENT contract.

RULES OF DECISION ACT 📖 A federal statute (28 U.S.C.A. § 1652 [1948]) that provides that where the Constitution, treaties, or acts of Congress are inapplicable, the law of the state in which the federal court is sitting should apply to CIVIL ACTIONS. 📖

The Rules of Decision Act, first enacted in 1789, is designed to discourage forum-shopping and to avoid the unfair administration of laws in cases heard by FEDERAL COURTS because of the DIVERSITY OF CITIZENSHIP of the parties. The landmark decision in *Erie Railroad Co. v. Tompkins*, 304 U.S. 64, 58 S. Ct. 817, 82 L. Ed. 1188 (1938), interpreted the Rules of Decision Act to include not only state statutes, but also controlling judicial decisions or state COMMON LAW as constituting the laws of the state. *Erie* overruled the case of *Swift v. Tyson*, 41 U.S. (16 Pet.) 1, 10 L. Ed. 865 (1842), which construed the Rules of Decision Act as not requiring federal courts to apply state common law in diversity cases.

See also ERIE RAILROAD V. TOMPKINS; SWIFT V. TYSON.

RULES OF WAR 📖 A body of customs, practices, usages, conventions, protocols, treaties, laws, and other norms that govern the commencement, conduct, and termination of hostilities between belligerent states or parties. 📖

Frequently violated and sometimes ridiculed, the rules of war have evolved over centuries. They distinguish nations whose armed forces respect some minimal standard of human decency from terrorists, marauders, and other outlaws who use illegal and unrestricted methods of warfare to achieve political, economic, or military objectives.

Origins and Development   The modern rules of war trace their origins to the chivalric practices of medieval Europe. Feudal knights were bound by the law of chivalry, a customary code of conduct that could be enforced in local courts throughout western Europe by a military commander of any nation. Premised on notions of justice and fairness, the law of chivalry gave birth to the distinction between soldier and civilian and the idea that women, children, and older persons should be shielded from the bloody fields of combat. The Roman Catholic Church also influenced the development of these rules, differentiating between just and unjust wars and denouncing certain weapons as odious to God.

CODIFICATION of the rules of warfare began in the nineteenth century. In 1862 President ABRAHAM LINCOLN commissioned Francis Lieber to draft a code of regulations summarizing the laws and usages of war. A year later, Lieber submitted a draft that the EXECUTIVE BRANCH promulgated as General Orders No. 1, entitled Instructions for the Government of Armies of the United States in the Field. Known as the Lieber code, this systematic articulation of the rules of war remained the official pronouncement of the U.S. Army for more than a half a century. It addressed the concept of military necessity, detailed the rights of prisoners, noncombatants, and spies, and discussed the use of poisons, unnecessary violence, and cruelty.

In 1864 the codification movement took on an international flavor when twelve nations signed a Convention for the Amelioration of the Condition of the Wounded in Armies in the Field, 129 Consol. T.S. 361, the first of a series of Red Cross initiatives for this purpose. In 1899 the United States, Mexico, Japan, Persia (now Iran), Siam (now Thailand), and nineteen other nations, including all of the major European powers, signed a Convention with Respect to the Laws and Customs of War, 187 Consol.

T.S. 429, an initiative that followed the broad outlines of the Lieber code and also addressed the relationship between an occupying power and noncombatant civilian inhabitants. In 1914 the Lieber code was replaced by an army manual entitled *The Law of Land Warfare*, which is still in force today.

Codification of the international rules governing land, sea, and air warfare accelerated following the conclusions of the two World Wars, the KOREAN WAR, the VIETNAM WAR, and the many other hostilities that have taken place during the twentieth century. In addition to building upon the principles previously established, this period witnessed the creation of several new concepts, including certain categories of war crimes, such as crimes against peace and crimes against humanity.

Crimes against peace are committed by persons who plan or wage aggressive wars. Crimes against humanity are committed by persons who knowingly participate in the deportation, enslavement, persecution, or programmatic extermination of certain segments of society during times of war. Soldiers, military leaders, political officials, members of the judiciary, industrialists, and civilians are all subject to prosecution for violating any of these rules of war.

Leaders and officials who wage aggressive war, disregard the territorial or political independence of another state, or violate the express terms of a peace settlement may be prosecuted as war criminals under the United Nations Charter. They may also be prosecuted under the Nuremberg principles, derived from the NUREMBERG TRIALS after World War II in which the Allied powers tried twenty-four leading Nazis for an assortment of war crimes, including crimes against peace and crimes against humanity. The Allies later prosecuted more than a hundred German civilians, including industrialists, doctors, and judges, who were enlisted by the Nazis to further their system of terror.

War, Terrorism, and Subversion The rules of war do not apply to every act of hostility against an established government. Openly declared wars between sovereign states clearly implicate the rules of war. When the belligerents do not issue formal declarations of war, the legal status of a military conflict becomes murky. Isolated acts of TERRORISM or subversion, however, neither constitute acts of war nor create a state of war. Such acts are normally punishable under the criminal laws of the country in which they are perpetrated.

Wider internal disturbances within the territorial borders of a country are more difficult to classify. When such disturbances begin, the ruling government is apt to classify them as RIOTS or rebellions, while those who cause the disturbances are likely to classify them as acts of CIVIL WAR. INTERNATIONAL LAW provides no definitive classification for such hostilities. But subversive groups that acquire sustained control over substantial territory and win measurable domestic support are more likely to receive the benefit of the rules governing warfare than are small bands of insurgents whose seditious efforts are stifled and repelled.

Even when a state of war indisputably exists, the rules of war do not apply to all combatants. Regular land, air, and naval forces are typically governed by the rules of warfare. Irregular armed forces, such as guerrillas and other insurgents, are governed by these rules only when they carry their weapons openly, wear a recognizable emblem, conduct their operations in accordance with the laws of war, and are commanded by a superior who is responsible for subordinates.

The point of these rules is not only to distinguish combatants from noncombatants but to distinguish conventional soldiers from hired assassins, spies, and mercenaries who circumvent the customs of war in order to accomplish an end that could not be achieved by regular armed forces. Because assassins, spies, and mercenaries do not play by the rules of war, their captors need not either. Similarly, combatants who attempt to flout the rules of war by disguising themselves in civilian clothing or enemy uniforms may be treated as ordinary criminals, though most other methods of deceit are considered permissible tactics of warfare.

Prisoners of War The difference between an ordinary criminal and a prisoner of war is important. An ordinary criminal may be detained, prosecuted, and punished in accordance with the domestic criminal laws of the country in which the crime is committed. A conventional soldier who is captured by the enemy must be humanely treated in accordance with the international rules of war. Under these rules prisoners of war are required to give their captors only enough information for identification, such as name, rank, serial number, and date of birth. Captors may not torture prisoners to extract information from them nor subject prisoners to punishment without first complying with specific legal procedures.

Under the rules of war, prisoners of war may not be punished for wrongs committed by the armed forces to which they belong, and medical and scientific experiments upon prisoners are forbidden. Captors must provide prisoners with sufficient food and beverages to maintain good health, and adequate standards of clothing, housing, sanitation, and hygiene are prescribed. To encourage accountability, captors are required to disclose the names of prisoners to the belligerent for which they were fighting when captured.

Although prisoners of war may be compelled to work while in captivity, they cannot be forced to contribute directly to the captor's war effort, and they must receive pay for their work on a scale commensurate with their rank. Prisoners are not permitted to harm their captors under the rules of war, but they may attempt to escape. Prisoners of war are entitled to full freedom of RELIGION, and DISCRIMINATION based on race, color, or ethnicity is prohibited. Given the breadth of these rights, prisoners of war often enjoy greater protection under the rules of war than they would under the domestic laws of their captor.

In certain cases being granted the status of prisoner of war can mean the difference between life and death. Summary execution of prisoners is expressly proscribed, as are orders to "take no prisoners" on the battlefield, which is tantamount to an order for their execution. The rules of war place other limitations on the use of CAPITAL PUNISHMENT and affirmatively require captors to provide sick and wounded prisoners with medical care. Violations of these rules, though not uncommon in the heat of battle, are deterred by the threat of reprisal. Prisoner exchanges, which benefit both sides, also provide belligerents with incentive for reciprocal compliance with these rules.

Soldiers and Civilians The difference between soldier and civilian is another important distinction under the rules of war. War is fought by trained soldiers armed with guns, tanks, and an assortment of other strategic weapons that they are authorized to use for tactical advantage, both offensive and defensive. The object of war is to thoroughly defeat an enemy by destroying its armed forces, which may be accomplished in an infinite number of ways, including killing and attrition. It is anticipated that much blood will be shed during a war, regardless of its length.

Civilians, by and large, are neither trained in combat nor armed, and they are not authorized to kill except in self-defense. However, civilians do have families to feed, mortgages to pay, and jobs to perform, obligations that are not suspended during times of war. Hence, the rules of war attempt to insulate civilians from many of the inconveniences, distractions, tragedies, and horrors of war.

War provides combatants with no IMMUNITY from ordinary criminal laws against RAPE and plunder, even when such transgressions are committed pursuant to an order given by a superior. Crimes committed against civilians because of their race, religion, and national origin, including GENOCIDE, are considered war crimes. Like prisoners of war, civilians may not be punished for wrongs committed by their government or military forces, and they may not be held as HOSTAGES under any circumstances.

Civilians may lose their protected status in certain circumstances. When insurgents or guerrillas live among the civilian population, soldiers may take measures to ferret out the enemy, including the use of interrogations, searches, and curfews. Although the individual liberty of civilians can be temporarily curtailed in such situations, it cannot be permanently eliminated. Protracted internment of entire villages or groups of civilians is not allowed. Civilian supporters who carry weapons or grenades forfeit their protected status, however, and may be detained as prisoners of war or saboteurs. If soldiers seek to destroy an entire village that is known to be an enemy stronghold, civilians must normally be informed of the action ahead of time and permitted to evacuate.

Military practice differs as to whether children, older persons, and pregnant women should be allowed egress from a besieged area. At the same time, it is common practice to permit clergy and medical personnel ingress to besieged locales. Once a besieged area has been overtaken, the military is considered an occupying power with the responsibility to administer the laws for the preservation of public order and public safety. Supplies of food and hospital services must be ensured.

Military Occupation Although an occupying power may exercise dominion over a conquered nation and acquires actual authority to administer the law, complete SOVEREIGNTY is not transferred until a TREATY or other settlement has been reached. An occupying power is not bound by the constitution or laws of the territory occupied, but it is prohibited from altering them except in cases of military necessity. Inhabitants owe no duty of allegiance to an occupying power during a state of MARTIAL LAW.

Occupation is an important aim of warfare, enabling a belligerent to exploit an enemy's resources and deny them to a foe. The occupying power may seize any governmental property that is necessary for military operations but may not sell public land or buildings. Municipalities and institutions dedicated to religion, charity, education, arts, and sciences are exempt from seizure. The status of public officials, including members of the judiciary, cannot be changed by the occupying power, although officials can be removed for misconduct or asked to retire. Any system of public education must be allowed to continue.

Taxes may be collected from local residents, but the basic tax structure should remain intact. The occupying power is not permitted to destroy private property, except in cases of military necessity, and must fairly compensate individuals from whom it confiscates personal belongings. The occupying power may require private residents to house its troops, but the troops must honor familial rights, religious practices, and other customs in the community. In response to MILITARY OCCUPATION, allies of the conquered nation may freeze its ASSETS or establish a naval BLOCKADE around the occupied territory.

Aerial Warfare Protection of civilian populations is also a primary concern of the rules governing aerial warfare. Indiscriminate bombing of undefended cities or other areas densely inhabited by civilians is considered a serious war crime. Aerial bombardment of private property that is unrelated to military operations, such as private homes, commercial establishments, philanthropic institutions, historical landmarks, and educational facilities, is also forbidden. Aerial assaults on hospitals, public or private, are banned as well.

The incidental destruction of private property during an aerial attack may not violate the rules of war, however, if the attack is carried out for military purposes. These include the interdiction of military communication and transportation, the enervation of military forces and installations, and the destruction of factories manufacturing arms or military supplies. Nonetheless, the bombing of such targets may be illegal if it endangers high concentrations of civilians, and the stated military objective is unclear or unimportant.

Rules regarding aerial warfare are frequently violated. During World War II, both the Axis and the Allied powers engaged in bombing attacks that inflicted high casualties directly on civilian populations. In the Battle of Britain, the German Luftwaffe bombed certain English cities to weaken the residents' will to resist. The Allies bombed Dresden and Hamburg in Germany and Tokyo, Yokohama, Hiroshima, and Nagasaki in Japan without discriminating between military and noncombatant targets. Since World War II, improved fighter planes and anti-aircraft defenses have made surgical aerial assaults more difficult.

Aircraft must be identified by external markings to allow belligerents to distinguish military from civilian aerial units. Additionally, such markings allow neutral countries to identify their own aircraft and permit the peaceful entry of aerial medical units onto a battlefield. Regardless of the nature of an aerial unit, belligerents are prohibited from firing on persons parachuting from a disabled aircraft, unless they are paratroopers engaged in an ESPIONAGE mission. Distinguishing paratroopers from other parachutists is left to the discretion of individual pilots and gunners.

Naval Warfare The rules governing naval warfare also leave much discretion to the participants. Although belligerent warships may attack and sink an enemy warship encountered on the high seas, they may neither sink nor attack an enemy merchant ship unless it refuses to obey a signal to stop and submit to inspection. Conversely, belligerent merchant ships are not obliged to stop or submit to inspection but may attempt to escape or act in self-defense. However, the line separating an act of self-defense from an offensive maneuver is subject to some debate. In 1916 a British merchant ship captain was court-martialed for ramming a German U-boat, despite the captain's claim that his vessel was acting in self-defense.

When an enemy warship has been captured, it becomes the property of the captor and may be sunk or brought into port. If an enemy merchant ship is captured, it must be taken into port for adjudication regarding the ownership of the vessel and its cargo pursuant to international law. In either case the passengers and crew of a captured ship may not be harmed. Captured members of enemy naval forces are entitled to treatment as prisoners of war. Shipwrecked belligerents are also entitled to humane treatment under the rules of war and may not be abandoned or refused quarter. Many of the same rules governing surface warships have been applied to submarine warfare as well.

Weapons All military forces, land, air, and sea, are restricted as to the type of weapons and explosives they may employ. Military forces may not use arms, projectiles, or other materials calculated to cause unnecessary suffering, such as weapons that leave fragments of glass and plastic in the body. The UNITED NATIONS has condemned thermal nuclear weapons because of their propensity to inflict unnecessary suffering and their inability to discriminate between combatants and noncombatants, or military and nonmilitary targets.

The use of poisons, poisoned weapons, and poisonous gases by any branch of the armed forces is flatly prohibited, as is the use of bacteriological materials and devices that spread disease. However, incendiary weapons, such as napalm, and chemical herbicides, such as Agent Orange, have been employed by military tacticians when enemy forces conceal themselves in a jungle or forest. Several countries have objected to the use of chemical and incendiary weapons even for such limited purposes.

Neutral Countries All military forces are similarly bound by the rules of war with regard to neutral countries. By definition a neutral country is not a party to a military conflict between belligerent states. Unless bound by a treaty, governments are not required to remain neutral in a war, but they are presumed to be neutral unless they manifest adherence to one side or the other by word or act. Neutral countries must neither help nor harm a belligerent state, nor allow a belligerent to make use of their territory or resources for military purposes. Instead, neutral states must assume a position of strict impartiality.

Neutral territory is considered an asylum for prisoners of war, who become free upon reaching neutral ground. Belligerent troops may enter neutral territory to avoid capture but may be rejected or disarmed by the host country. Belligerent aircraft are not permitted to enter neutral airspace, and if they land, the host country may intern them. Belligerent warships may be granted asylum when they are in distress or in need of repairs. If belligerents abuse this privilege, however, asylum may be revoked, and their forces may be ordered to leave.

Lawful and Unlawful Wars The only type of war recognized by the United Nations as lawful is one fought in self-defense. The rules of warfare are not suspended, however, or otherwise rendered inapplicable merely because the grounds for fighting a particular war are unlawful. In an illegal war both the aggressor and other belligerents must still comport their behavior with the international customs, practices, and conventions of war. At the same time, some authority suggests that one belligerent may disregard certain rules of war in reprisal for its enemy's disregard of the same rules. Such reprisals have a tendency to spiral downward, however, with each act of retaliation straying further from the lawful norms of warfare.

Enforcement It is sometimes observed that the phrase *rules of war* constitutes an oxymoron because the business of war is treachery and chaos while rules and regulations seek to impose order and structure. No permanent and impartial international body has been created to administer the rules of war. Although the United Nations has acted with multinational support in the Korean and Gulf Wars, and the INTERNATIONAL COURT OF JUSTICE has adjudicated claims against democratic and totalitarian regimes alike, neither body exercises sovereignty over individual member states in any meaningful sense, and powerful countries generally wield more influence over these bodies than do weaker countries.

In most instances it is left to the victorious powers to enforce the rules of war. Following World War II, for example, the Allies prosecuted the Axis powers in Europe and the South Pacific despite the claims of the vanquished that such proceedings amounted to little more than victor's justice, or revenge. These claims were not entirely hollow, in that the Allies had committed a variety of war crimes themselves. During the course of the war, for example, the United States interned more than a hundred thousand Americans of Japanese descent simply because of their ancestry; the British bombed civilian populations in Germany; and the Russians massacred Polish soldiers in the Katyn Forest.

Thus, the current system of international law remains imperfect. Nonetheless, international law attempts to embody the rudiments of human decency, rudiments that are reflected by the customs, practices, and rules of war.

CROSS-REFERENCES

Armed Services; Arms Control and Disarmament; Court-Martial; Hirohito; Hitler, Adolf; Human Rights; Japanese American Evacuation Cases; Just War; *Korematsu v. United States*; Military Government; Military Law; Militia; Neutrality; Prize Law; Tokyo Trials; Uniform Code of Military Justice.

RULING 📖 A judicial or administrative interpretation of a provision of a statute, order, regulation, or ordinance. The judicial determination of matters before the court such as the admissibility of EVIDENCE or the granting of a MOTION, which is an application for an order. 📖

RUN 📖 To have legal validity in a prescribed territory; as in, the WRIT (a court order) *runs* throughout the county. To have applicability or legal effect during a prescribed period of time; as in, the STATUTE OF LIMITATIONS has *run* against the claim. To follow or accompany; to be attached to another thing in pursuing a prescribed course or direction; as in, the COVENANT (a written promise or restriction) *runs* with the land. 📖

RUNNING WITH THE LAND 📖 Passing with a transfer of the property. A provision in a

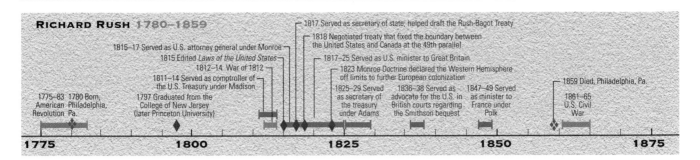

RICHARD RUSH 1780–1859

1775–83 American Revolution

1780 Born, Philadelphia, Pa.

1797 Graduated from the College of New Jersey (later Princeton University)

1811–14 Served as comptroller of the U.S. Treasury under Madison

1812–14 War of 1812

1815 Edited *Laws of the United States*

1815–17 Served as U.S. attorney general under Monroe

1817 Served as secretary of state; helped draft the Rush-Bagot Treaty

1818 Negotiated treaty that fixed the boundary between the United States and Canada at the 49th parallel

1817–25 Served as U.S. minister to Great Britain

1823 Monroe Doctrine declared the Western Hemisphere off limits to further European colonization

1825–29 Served as secretary of the treasury under Adams

1836–38 Served as advocate for the U.S. in British courts regarding the Smithson bequest

1847–49 Served as minister to France under Polk

1859 Died, Philadelphia, Pa.

1861–65 U.S. Civil War

1775   1800   1825   1850   1875

DEED by which the person to whom the land is transferred agrees to maintain a fence is an example of a COVENANT that runs with the land. 📖

A covenant, a written promise or restriction on the use of land, is said to run with the land when either the obligation to perform it or the right to take advantage of it passes to the one to whom the land is transferred.

RUSH, RICHARD Richard Rush served as U.S. attorney general from 1814 to 1817. Although he was recognized as an able lawyer, Rush's greatest contributions came in the field of diplomacy. He negotiated treaties that demilitarized the Great Lakes and set the northernmost boundaries between the United States and Canada. He also played a part in the establishment of the Smithsonian Institution.

Rush was born on August 29, 1780, in Philadelphia, Pennsylvania. His father was Dr. Benjamin Rush, a signer of the DECLARATION OF INDEPENDENCE and one of the towering intellectual figures of his day. Rush entered Princeton University in 1793 at the age of thirteen and graduated in 1797. He went on to study law and was admitted to the Pennsylvania bar in 1800. In 1811 he became Pennsylvania attorney general but left that position when President JAMES MADISON appointed him comptroller of the U.S. Treasury.

In 1814, after declining the office of secretary of the treasury, Rush was appointed attorney general under President JAMES MONROE. At age thirty-four, he is the youngest attorney general in U.S. history. His major contribution was to edit the *Laws of the United States* (1815), a CODIFICATION of all federal statutes enacted between 1789 and 1815. For a short time in 1817, Rush performed the duties of the secretary of state and was instrumental in the drafting of the Rush-Bagot Treaty between the United States and Great Britain, which restricted the use of naval forces on the Great Lakes.

Late in 1817 Rush resigned as attorney general to serve as the U.S. minister to Britain. He remained in this position until 1825. While in London he negotiated the 1818 agreement be-

BIOGRAPHY

Richard Rush

BIOGRAPHY

John Rutledge

tween the two countries that fixed the forty-ninth parallel as the boundary between Canada and the United States, from the Lake of the Woods in northern Minnesota to the Rocky Mountains. Rush also participated in discussions with British foreign minister George Canning concerning South America. These discussions led to the announcement of the MONROE DOCTRINE of 1823, which declared that the Western Hemisphere was closed to further European colonization and that any European intervention would be regarded as a threat to the security of the United States.

President JOHN QUINCY ADAMS recalled Rush in 1825 to serve as his secretary of the treasury. In 1828 he was Adams's unsuccessful vice presidential running mate. In the 1830s, Rush published *A Residence at the Court of London* (1833) and returned to England, where he served as an official agent of the United States. In this capacity he received the bequest by which James Smithson founded the Smithsonian Institution in Washington, D.C. Rush became involved with the planning of the Smithsonian and served on its board of regents.

In 1847 President JAMES POLK appointed Rush minister to France. He served for two years before retiring from public service and devoting himself to his writing. Rush died on July 30, 1859, in Philadelphia.

RUTLEDGE, JOHN Few justices of the U.S. Supreme Court combined outstanding achievement with mishap and tragedy to the extent of John Rutledge. Rutledge's career spanned three decades of public service during the early years of the nation. From 1761 until the 1780s, he enjoyed success as a lawyer, politician, Revolutionary War leader, and judge in South Carolina. His prominence at the Constitutional Convention—and his role in opposing British rule—brought him national fame and made him a favorite of President GEORGE WASHINGTON. Washington appointed him to the Supreme Court twice, first in 1789 and again in 1795.

Born in September 1739 to a prominent family in Charleston, South Carolina, Rutledge was groomed for success. His wealthy physician

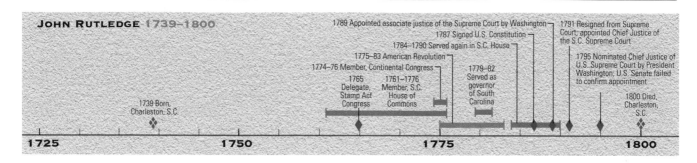

JOHN RUTLEDGE 1739–1800

1789 Appointed associate justice of the Supreme Court by Washington
1787 Signed U.S. Constitution
1784–1790 Served again in S.C. House
1775–83 American Revolution
1774–76 Member, Continental Congress
1765 Delegate, Stamp Act Congress
1761–1776 Member, S.C. House of Commons
1779–82 Served as governor of South Carolina
1739 Born, Charleston, S.C.
1791 Resigned from Supreme Court; appointed Chief Justice of the S.C. Supreme Court
1795 Nominated Chief Justice of U.S. Supreme Court by President Washington; U.S. Senate failed to confirm appointment
1800 Died, Charleston, S.C.

1725   1750   1775   1800

father died when he was eleven, and thereafter his uncle, Andrew Rutledge, guided Rutledge's education. Andrew Rutledge, a lawyer and speaker of the South Carolina Commons House of Assembly, saw to it that his nephew was prepared for a legal and political career: the teenager was sent to England to study law at the Middle Temple, one of the INNS OF COURT, and in 1760 he was admitted to the English bar. At the age of twenty-one, Rutledge returned home, instantly won a seat in the state Assembly, and began a successful legal practice. Within a few years, Rutledge and two other lawyers were handling the affairs of South Carolina's wealthiest businessmen.

Rutledge's rise in politics was aided by his involvement in the growing revolutionary movement. In 1765 he attended the emergency conference held in New York City to discuss the colonists' anger at Britain's imposition of the Stamp Tax. Rutledge wrote an official declaration to the British House of Lords opposing the tax. When the Revolutionary War came, he led the defense of South Carolina. Rutledge's performance in the war cemented his growing national reputation, and a string of successes followed.

In 1775 Rutledge helped write the constitution for South Carolina, and a year later, he was elected president of its new state assembly. He was elected governor in 1779. From 1782 to 1784, he served in the U.S. Congress under the ARTICLES OF CONFEDERATION and then as chief judge of a court of chancery in South Carolina. He was one of the authors of the U.S. Constitution at the Constitutional Convention in Philadelphia in 1787.

At the national level, President Washington was Rutledge's chief political sponsor. He offered Rutledge a federal judgeship and appointment as minister to the Netherlands, which he declined. He accepted when Washington named him to the Supreme Court in 1789 (though not, as Rutledge had hoped, as its chief justice). The Court heard no cases during its first two years, but Rutledge traveled great distances to fulfill his duties as a judge on the southern circuit. The position did not suit him,

"SO LONG AS WE MAY HAVE AN INDEPENDENT JUDICIARY, THE GREAT INTERESTS OF THE PEOPLE WILL BE SAFE."

BIOGRAPHY

Wiley Blount Rutledge, Jr.

however. Bored and upset that he was merely an associate justice, he quit the Court in 1791 and returned to South Carolina, where he became chief justice of the Court of Common Pleas.

By June 1795 Rutledge was ready to return to the Supreme Court. JOHN JAY, the chief justice, was resigning, and Rutledge wrote to Washington suggesting that he should have the position. The president agreed and promptly nominated him. Over the next six months, while awaiting Senate approval of his nomination, Rutledge, as acting chief justice, heard his only two cases and wrote his only opinion: *Talbot v. Jansen*, 3 U.S. 133, 1 L. Ed. 540 (1795), an unimportant decision concerning goods captured at sea.

In the interim Rutledge undid his career. At a meeting in Charleston in July 1795, he spoke out wildly against Jay's Treaty, a controversial postwar agreement between the United States and Britain. The treaty was highly unpopular across the nation, but Rutledge went too far, denouncing it as "prostitution" and declaring that the president should die rather than sign it. Indeed, since the death of his wife in 1792, Rutledge had been depressed, and reports of insanity had begun to spread. His supporters—Washington among them—disbelieved the rumors, but Rutledge's enemies seized on them and blocked his confirmation in the Senate in December 1795. Upon hearing the news, he jumped off a wharf into Charleston Bay. Although two passing slaves foiled his suicide attempt, Rutledge's public career was over. Seldom seen again, he died five years later, on June 21, 1800.

RUTLEDGE, WILEY BLOUNT, JR. A stalwart defender of civil liberties, Associate Justice Wiley B. Rutledge, Jr., sat on the U.S. Supreme Court for six years during the transitional NEW DEAL era. Rutledge was a distinguished law professor and dean who became a judge through his support of President FRANKLIN D. ROOSEVELT. In 1939 Roosevelt named him to the U.S. Court of Appeals for the District of Columbia, and four years later to the Supreme Court. From 1943 until his death in 1949, Rutledge championed the rights of minorities and unpopular groups.

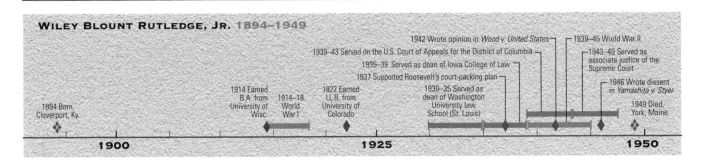

WILEY BLOUNT RUTLEDGE, JR. 1894–1949

1894 Born, Cloverport, Ky.
1914 Earned B.A. from University of Wisc.
1914–18 World War I
1922 Earned LL.B. from University of Colorado
1930–35 Served as dean of Washington University law School (St. Louis)
1935–39 Served as dean of Iowa College of Law
1937 Supported Roosevelt's court-packing plan
1939–43 Served on the U.S. Court of Appeals for the District of Columbia
1942 Wrote opinion in *Wood v. United States*
1939–45 World War II
1943–49 Served as associate justice of the Supreme Court
1946 Wrote dissent in *Yamashita v. Styer*
1949 Died, York, Maine

1900   1925   1950

Born in Cloverport, Kentucky, on July 20, 1894, Rutledge was the son of a fundamentalist Baptist minister. His father, Wiley, Sr., rode the backwaters of Kentucky preaching hellfire and brimstone, often with his son in tow. By his teens, however, Rutledge had left for the University of Wisconsin where he immersed himself in debate, classical literature, and ancient languages, earning a B.A. in 1914.

In his twenties, tuberculosis and financial trouble forced Rutledge to postpone the legal education he desired. Between 1915 and 1920, he supported himself and his wife, Annabel Person, by teaching high school in Indiana, New Mexico, and finally in Colorado, where he enrolled in a full-time law program at the state university. By 1922 he had earned his law degree, and immediately accepted a job with a Boulder firm. But he left practice two years later in order to embark on a fifteen-year long career as a law professor. He taught at three universities, promoted modern teaching methods, and ultimately served as dean at Washington University (1930–1935) and the Iowa College of Law (1935–1939). It was during these later years, while engaging in debate over local and national issues, that he developed a reputation as a champion of the underdog.

Rutledge was an ardent supporter of President Roosevelt's New Deal, a series of legislative reforms designed to pull the nation out of economic depression. Yet the U.S. Supreme Court struck down one after another of the president's programs. Roosevelt then announced his controversial plan to reorganize the federal judicial system—the so-called court-packing plan that would have filled even the Supreme Court with pro-Roosevelt justices. Rutledge backed it. In 1939 the president appointed him to the U.S. Court of Appeals for the District of Columbia, and in 1943 he appointed Rutledge to the Supreme Court.

Rutledge consistently upheld the rights of the individual, including the rights to a JURY trial, to practice RELIGION freely, to be free from unreasonable SEARCHES AND SEIZURES, and not to suffer cruel and unusual punishment. In his concurring opinion in *Schneiderman v. United*

"PRECEDENT IS NOT ALL CONTROLLING IN LAW. THERE MUST BE ROOM FOR GROWTH, SINCE EVERY PRECEDENT HAS AN ORIGIN."

States, 320 U.S. 118, 63 S. Ct. 1333, 87 L. Ed. 1796 (1943), he voted to restore citizenship to an immigrant who, twelve years after his naturalization, had been targeted for DEPORTATION by the Justice Department because of membership in the Communist Party. In *Yamashita v. Styer*, 327 U.S. 1, 66 S. Ct. 340, 90 L. Ed. 499 (1946), Rutledge dissented from the denial of HABEAS CORPUS relief to Japanese general Yamashita Tomoyuki, who had been sentenced to death for war crimes on the basis of hearsay evidence.

Rutledge regularly joined the opinions of Justices HUGO L. BLACK, FRANK MURPHY, and WILLIAM O. DOUGLAS. He worked exhaustively, and, in the opinion of some of his brethren on the Court, too much. He died on September 10, 1949, in York, Maine, at the age of 54.

RYLANDS v. FLETCHER *Rylands v. Fletcher* was the 1868 English case (L.R. 3 H.L. 330) that was the progenitor of the doctrine of STRICT LIABILITY for abnormally dangerous conditions and activities.

The defendants, mill owners in the coal mining area of Lancashire, had constructed a reservoir on their land. The water broke through the filled-in shaft of an abandoned coal mine and flooded connecting passageways into the plaintiff's active mine nearby. In 1865, the trial court found that the defendants were ignorant of the abandoned mine shaft and free of NEGLIGENCE and decided the case in favor of the defendants.

In 1866, on appeal by the plaintiffs, the Exchequer Chamber decided to REVERSE the lower court and imposed strict liability on the defendants, but the case did not readily fit within the existing TORT theories. No TRESPASS had occurred since the premises of plaintiff and defendants did not adjoin; therefore, the flooding was not direct, nor was it a NUISANCE, since there was nothing offensive to the senses and the damage was not continuous or recurring. Justice Colin Blackburn, comparing the situation to trespasses involving cattle and dangerous animals, declared: "The true rule of law is, that the person who for his own purposes brings on his lands and collects and keeps there anything likely to do mischief if it escapes, must keep it in at his peril, and, if he does not do so, is prima facie answerable for all the damage which is the natural consequence of its escape." This language, frequently quoted, is often erroneously regarded as the "rule" of the case.

In 1868 the defendants appealed to the House of Lords, which decided to AFFIRM the ruling of the Exchequer Chamber, but Lord Cairns sharply limited Justice Blackburn's broad statement. Lord Cairns ruled that the principle applied only to a "nonnatural" use of the defendant's land, as distinguished from "any purpose for which it might in the ordinary course of the enjoyment of land be used." Thereby he shifted the emphasis from the mere tendency of all water to escape to the abnormal and inappropriate character of the defendant's reservoir in coal mining country. Strict liability exists for harm resulting from the miscarriage of lawful activity that, considering its place and manner, is unusual, extraordinary, or inappropriate. As a result, water collected in household pipes or a stock watering tank or a cistern is a natural use, but water collected in large tanks in dangerous proximity to the plaintiff's land is not.

The same activity might be appropriate or normal in one location but not in another; therefore, the primary basis of liability is the creation of an extraordinary RISK. A water reservoir is an inappropriate use of land in a coal mining area, but not in an arid state. Blasting creates unusual and unacceptable risks in the midst of a large city, but not in remote rural areas. If the activity, such as crop dusting, is appropriate to the area, strict liability exists only if the activity is conducted in an unusual or abnormal way.

Until 1947, the English courts had liberally applied the doctrine enunciated in this case. Whereas the rule was originally stated in terms of an "escape" of that which caused the harm, subsequent cases imposed no such requirement. The rule was also extended to cover personal injuries as well as property damage. In a 1947 case, however, the House of Lords refused to impose strict liability in favor of a government inspector injured in an explosion at the defendant's munitions plant on the ground that there had been no escape of a dangerous substance from the defendant's land. Two of the judges thought that the rule did not apply to personal injuries.

At first, U.S. courts generally did not apply the *Rylands* doctrine. Curiously, a number of cases spurning the "rule" rejected it in the broad form stated by Justice Blackburn, ignoring or overlooking the fact that the final formulation by Lord Cairns was narrower. Much of the earlier hostility to the rule was probably due to the strength of the fault ethic and to a desire to protect emerging industries. At present, a majority of U.S. JURISDICTIONS accept the rule, in name or in fact. In comparison, however, to the English decisions, U.S. cases have been slightly less liberal in applying the rule.

Even where *Rylands v. Fletcher* is expressly rejected or narrowly applied, the same result can be reached by actions for absolute nuisance or trespass.

The case of Rylands v. Fletcher *first promulgated the doctrine of strict liability for abnormally dangerous conditions and activities on the land, such as a coal mining operation.*

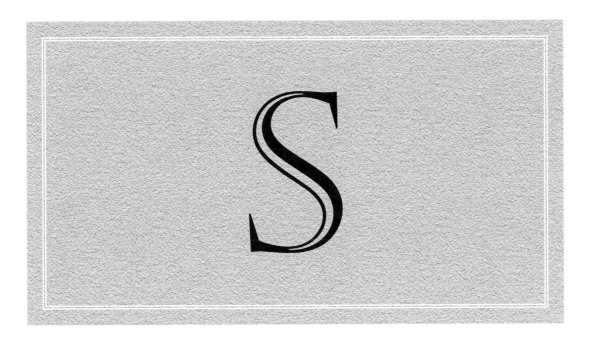

SABOTAGE The willful destruction or impairment of, or defective production of, WAR material or national defense material, or harm to war premises or war utilities. During a labor dispute, the willful and MALICIOUS destruction of an employer's property or interference with his normal operations.

The objective of sabotage is to halt all production, rather than to destroy or imperil human life. The original act of sabotage is thought to have occurred not long after the introduction of machinery when someone slipped a workman's wooden shoe, called a *sabot*, into a loom in order to stop production. Sabotage is a CRIME.

SACCO (NICOLA) AND VANZETTI (BARTOLOMEO) Two young Italian immigrants who were tried for MURDER in 1921 in Massachusetts. Their trial has proved to be one of the most controversial trials in U.S. history. For some observers, the trial was a way to bring two criminals to justice. For others, however, the two men were innocent of the crime but were found guilty because they were immigrants and political radicals. Defenders of Sacco and Vanzetti waged a fierce legal and public relations battle to save their lives, but the men were executed in 1927.

On April 15, 1920, in South Braintree, Massachusetts, a paymaster and a security guard for a shoe company were delivering a $15,000 payroll for the business. Two men in an automobile fatally shot the two men, stole the money, and fled. Eventually, the police focused on Sacco and Vanzetti as their prime suspects.

The men appeared to be unlikely armed robbers. They had arrived in the United States in 1908. Sacco found work as a shoemaker, and

Vanzetti became a fish vendor. Politically they were anarchists who opposed all governments. Their opposition to World War I led them to emigrate to Mexico to avoid military conscription. They returned to the United States in 1920 and settled in Massachusetts.

The police took Sacco and Vanzetti into custody primarily on the basis of two pieces of EVIDENCE. Sacco owned a pistol of the type used in the murders, and the men were arrested at a garage attempting to reclaim a repaired automobile that had been seen in the vicinity of the South Braintree crime scene. Sacco and Vanzetti knew very little English and gave confusing and false answers during their interrogation, which diminished their credibility.

Sacco and Vanzetti were indicted on September 11, 1920, for the murders and the robbery. The trial began on May 31, 1921, before Judge Webster Thayer. The defendants were represented by Fred Moore, who had been hired on their behalf by the recently formed AMERICAN CIVIL LIBERTIES UNION.

Eyewitness TESTIMONY at the trial was contradictory. A few WITNESSES gave detailed descriptions of Sacco and Vanzetti, but on CROSS-EXAMINATION many of the details proved inaccurate. Several defense witnesses testified that Sacco had been in Boston at the time of the murders.

Prosecutor Frederick G. Katzman used the unreliable answers that the defendants had given during their initial interrogation to impugn their credibility. He also made irrelevant remarks about the defendants' unpopular political beliefs and their lack of patriotism. Judge Thayer allowed these remarks to pass. Some

UPI/CORBIS-BETTMANN

Sacco and Vanzetti in 1923. Many legal observers believed then, as now, that the men should have been granted a new trial after their conviction in 1921.

trial observers noted that Thayer was hostile to the defense and that he may have been biased in favor of the prosecution.

Moore argued that the defendants' poor English was at the root of the false information they provided and that they were innocent men thrown into an incomprehensible situation.

The jury convicted Sacco and Vanzetti of the murders and the robbery on July 14, 1921. The convictions drew cries of outrage from socialists, radicals, and prominent intellectuals in the United States and Europe. Investigators were hired to look for new evidence that would prove that Sacco and Vanzetti were innocent.

Over the next six years, Sacco and Vanzetti's lawyers presented many MOTIONS to Judge Thayer, asking that a new trial be granted so that new evidence could be introduced. Investigators claimed to have uncovered evidence that would refute damaging testimony of several prosecution witnesses. At that time Massachusetts law gave the trial judge the final power to reopen a case on the basis of new evidence. Thayer adamantly refused to order a new trial.

In 1925 Celestine Madeiros, a convicted murderer awaiting execution, confessed to being a member of a gang that had committed the South Braintree crimes. He absolved Sacco and Vanzetti of any involvement. Thayer refused to recognize the statement as adequate evidence to

justify a new trial. The Supreme Judicial Court of Massachusetts agreed to review the case but affirmed the VERDICT (*Commonwealth v. Sacco and Vanzetti*, 255 Mass. 369, 151 N.E. 839 [1926]).

FELIX FRANKFURTER, a Harvard law professor and future member of the U.S. Supreme Court, believed that the trial had been a travesty of justice and labored on the many posttrial motions. He and others used the press to make their claim that Sacco and Vanzetti were victims of political and ethnic bias.

On April 9, 1927, Sacco and Vanzetti received the death sentence. This set off a storm of protest, with mass meetings throughout the United States. Massachusetts Governor Alvin T. Fuller appointed an independent advisory committee composed of two university presidents and a former judge to review the trial and its aftermath. On August 3 the governor announced that he would follow the panel's recommendation and not grant Sacco and Vanzetti CLEMENCY.

More protests erupted in many cities, and bombs were set off in New York and Philadelphia. On August 23, 1927, Sacco and Vanzetti, still maintaining their innocence, were executed in the electric chair.

The guilt or innocence of Sacco and Vanzetti continues to be debated. Most commentators agree, however, that the defendants should have been granted a new trial because the first one was tainted with political and ethnic prejudice that made a fair proceeding impossible.

See also ANARCHISM.

SAID 📖 Mentioned earlier. 📖

This term is frequently used in CONTRACTS and other legal documents, with the same force as *aforesaid*.

SAILORS 📖 Persons who navigate ships or assist in the conduct, maintenance, or service of ships. 📖

Sailors have historically received special treatment under the law because of the nature of their work. Sailing a vessel through treacherous waters, often for long distances, is an isolated and dangerous undertaking. Although most countries have developed comprehensive policing methods on land, the international community has not been able to muster the resources necessary to police the entire expanse of every body of water. Thus, except when moving along coasts or on rivers, ships are essentially cut off from the rest of the world as they sail from port to port.

The unique problems sailors face have often aroused judicial concern. In 1823, for example, while serving as a circuit court justice, Supreme Court justice JOSEPH STORY wrote in *Harden v. Gordon*, 11 F. Cas. 480 (Cir. Ct. D. Maine 1823) that sailors are

> liable to sudden sickness from change of climate, exposure to perils, and exhausting labour. They are generally poor and friendless, and acquire habits of gross indulgence, carelessness, and improvidence. If some provision be not made for them in sickness at the expense of the ship, they must often in foreign ports suffer the accumulated evils of disease, and poverty, and sometimes perish from the want of suitable nourishment.

Although sailors still face unusual challenges and dangers, their situation now is far less desperate than that described by Story in 1823. Merchant marines (professional sailors), at least in the United States, are well-paid professionals; they are represented by unions and receive the same employment benefits as other organized professionals.

Sailors sign employment CONTRACTS for specific voyages. The contract may be made with the ship itself in the ship's capacity as a corporate entity, or it may be made directly with the master of the ship. In any contract, a sailor is entitled to sail in a staunch and watertight ship that is properly equipped and handled by a competent crew. The employer must supply wholesome food during the voyage, and any sailor who becomes sick is entitled to maintenance and cure. *Maintenance and cure* is the duty of an employer to provide medical services to a sailor until the sailor recovers or the voyage ends. If a sailor requires immediate medical attention, the master of the ship may be required to change its course to find the closest hospital. A sailor's right to maintenance and cure is not limited to illnesses or injuries suffered while at sea; employers are similarly required to provide maintenance and cure for illnesses or injuries that occur during shore leave.

Courts have developed the right to maintenance and cure in deference to the sailor's difficult and unique employment situation. Fear of MUTINY is one reason for providing maintenance and cure. As Story observed in *Harden*, if sailors' earnings were taken away for illnesses or injuries suffered while at sea, "the great motives for good behaviour might be ordinarily taken away."

Congress passed the Merchant Marine Act of 1920 (46 App. U.S.C.A. § 688 [1997]) to provide sailors with a remedy in federal court for employment-related injuries. The act, also known as the JONES ACT, specifically grants to a "seaman" the right to recover from an employer for the NEGLIGENCE of the employer or the unseaworthiness of the vessel. The act authorizes a trial by jury, and it also gives relatives of sailors a right to recover DAMAGES for a sailor's death.

Because Congress failed to define the term *seaman* in the Jones Act, much of the litigation involving the act has been over who qualifies for the remedies it provides. Originally only persons engaged in the navigation of a ship qualified for coverage. In 1995, in *Chandris, Inc. v. Latsis*, 515 U.S. 347, 115 S. Ct. 2172, 132 L. Ed. 2d 314, the U.S. Supreme Court suggested that a shore-based engineer who takes occasional voyages may be deemed a sailor under the act. According to the Court, to qualify as a seaman under the Jones Act, the worker's duties must contribute to the accomplishment of a vessel's mission, and the worker must have a connection to a vessel or group of vessels in navigation. The connection must be substantial in both duration and nature. Thus a shore-based person who works on the ventilation system in a ship but does not sail on a ship does not qualify as a sailor, but a shore-based vessel engineer who takes occasional voyages may be deemed a seaman under the Jones Act.

See also ADMIRALTY AND MARITIME LAW; SOLDIERS' AND SAILORS' CIVIL RELIEF ACT.

ST. CLAIR, JAMES DRAPER

James Draper St. Clair is a distinguished attorney who attained national prominence in 1974 as special counsel to President RICHARD M. NIXON during the WATERGATE scandal. As special counsel, St. Clair defended Nixon before the U.S. House of Representatives Judiciary Committee during its IMPEACHMENT hearings against the president and argued before the U.S. Supreme Court that Nixon did not have to turn over his secretly recorded White House tapes to the Watergate special prosecutor.

St. Clair was born on April 14, 1920, in Akron, Ohio. He graduated from the University of Illinois in 1941 and served in the Navy during World War II. Following the war St. Clair attended Harvard Law School, graduating in 1947. He was admitted to the Massachusetts bar that year and began work at Hale and Dorr, the most prominent law firm in Boston. St. Clair remained with the firm during his entire legal career.

A skilled litigator, St. Clair assisted JOSEPH N. WELCH, a senior attorney with Hale and Dorr, at the Army-McCarthy hearings in 1954. These hearings marked a turning point in Senator JOSEPH R. MCCARTHY's four-year quest to expose supposed Communist subversion in the federal government. Welch, representing the Army, skillfully rebuffed McCarthy's charges during the televised hearings.

St. Clair returned to Washington, D.C., and political controversy in 1974, when Congress and a special criminal prosecutor moved aggressively to obtain information on Nixon's role in the Watergate scandal. By early 1973 the botched 1972 burglary of the Democratic National Committee's offices in the Watergate building complex in Washington had been linked to members of Nixon's campaign and White House staff. The revelation in the summer of 1973 that Nixon had secretly recorded all conversations in the Oval Office led to demands by special prosecutor ARCHIBALD COX that Nixon surrender the tapes. Nixon refused, firing Cox. Cox's replacement, LEON JAWORSKI, renewed the demand.

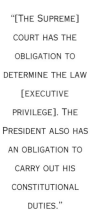

"[THE SUPREME] COURT HAS THE OBLIGATION TO DETERMINE THE LAW [EXECUTIVE PRIVILEGE]. THE PRESIDENT ALSO HAS AN OBLIGATION TO CARRY OUT HIS CONSTITUTIONAL DUTIES."

Nixon then hired St. Clair to argue against disclosure of the tapes and to prevent the House of Representatives from voting impeachment charges against the president. In the Judiciary Committee proceedings, St. Clair was permitted to hear the evidence, question witnesses, and present a defense. He argued that Nixon could be impeached only on hard proof that the president had committed serious criminal acts. Most committee members believed that a president might also be impeached for wrongdoing that was not strictly criminal. In July 1974, the committee approved impeachment resolutions that charged Nixon with assisting in the Watergate cover-up, abusing his powers, and failing to honor committee subpoenas for the White House tapes.

As to the question of producing evidence, St. Clair argued that the doctrine of EXECUTIVE PRIVILEGE gave Nixon the right to withhold the tapes. In *United States v. Nixon*, 418 U.S. 683, 94 S. Ct. 3090, 41 L. Ed. 2d 1039 (1974), the Supreme Court agreed with St. Clair that executive privilege was a legitimate shield for the EXECUTIVE BRANCH but held that the doctrine could not prevent the disclosure of materials needed for a criminal prosecution.

Shortly after the Supreme Court decision, St. Clair learned that one of the sixty-four tapes in question included a conversation between Nixon and his chief of staff, H. R. (Harry Robbins) Haldeman, in which Nixon sought to stop the Federal Bureau of Investigation from investigating the Watergate burglary. The conversation, which took place a few days after the 1972 burglary, was the so-called smoking gun that proved Nixon had obstructed justice. St. Clair insisted that Nixon publish the tape. After its disclosure, Nixon's political support vanished. He resigned on August 9, 1974, rather than face certain impeachment and removal from office.

Following the Nixon debacle, St. Clair returned to Boston and his litigation practice. He lectured at Harvard Law School for twenty-five years and has remained active in many civic and philanthropic organizations.

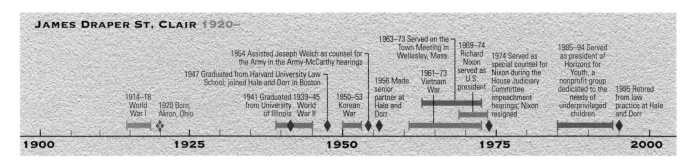

JAMES DRAPER ST. CLAIR 1920–

1914–18 World War I

1920 Born, Akron, Ohio

1941 Graduated from University of Illinois

1939–45 World War II

1947 Graduated from Harvard University Law School; joined Hale and Dorr in Boston

1950–53 Korean War

1954 Assisted Joseph Welch as counsel for the Army in the Army-McCarthy hearings

1956 Made senior partner at Hale and Dorr

1961–73 Vietnam War

1963–73 Served on the Town Meeting in Wellesley, Mass.

1969–74 Richard Nixon served as U.S. president

1974 Served as special counsel for Nixon during the House Judiciary Committee impeachment hearings; Nixon resigned

1985–94 Served as president of Horizons for Youth, a nonprofit group dedicated to the needs of underprivileged children

1995 Retired from law practice at Hale and Dorr

1900   1925   1950   1975   2000

See also UNITED STATES V. NIXON.

SALEM WITCH TRIALS In 1692 the community of Salem, Massachusetts, was engulfed in a series of witchcraft afflictions, accusations, trials, and executions. During the course of the year, more than a dozen persons claimed to be afflicted by spells of black magic and sorcery that had been allegedly cast by men and women who had enlisted the supernatural powers of the devil. Most of the persons claiming to be afflicted were teenage girls.

Those persecuted for allegedly practicing witchcraft included Salem residents who deviated in some way from Puritan religious, cultural, or economic norms. Other victims of the witch craze were nothing more than enemies of the largest family in Salem. A few victims were simply weak and sickly people who were in the wrong place at the wrong time. The legal institutions offered little protection for those accused of witchcraft because the primitive Massachusetts judicial system was still governed by superstitious rules of evidence permitting testimony about malevolent apparitions and broomsticks capable of flight. Although some ordinary Salem residents doubted the credibility of the witchcraft accusations, it was not until they were joined by authorities from Boston that the witch-hunt came to a close.

The outbreak of witchcraft hysteria took place in Salem Village, a small community a few miles inland from Salem Town. Salem Village was not an autonomous entity and lacked a government of its own until 1752 when it achieved independence and became known as Danvers. Salem Village was almost exclusively agrarian, cut off from the ports and tributaries that made Salem Town more mercantile and international in character. Although both communities were predominantly Puritan, during the seventeenth century Salem Town acquired an increasingly secular appearance through the growth of its fur, fish, and timber industries.

The Salem witch craze was largely fueled by personal differences between two families, the Putnams and the Porters. John Putnam, Sr. (1579–1662) was the patriarch of the largest family in Salem. He had three sons, Thomas Putnam, Sr. (1615–86), Nathaniel Putnam (1619–1700), and John Putnam, Jr. (1627–1710). John Porter, Sr. (1595–1676) was the patriarch of the richest family in Salem. He had four sons, John Porter, Jr. (1618–84), Joseph Porter (1638–1714), Benjamin Porter (1639–1723), Israel Porter (1644–1706), and a daughter, Sarah Porter (1649–1725).

The Putnams were a family of farmers who followed the simple and austere lifestyle of traditional Puritans. Although the Porters derived much of their wealth from agricultural operations as well, they were also entrepreneurs, developing commercial interests in Salem Town, throughout New England, and in the Caribbean. The Porters' diversified business interests allowed them to increase their family's wealth while the Putnam family wealth stagnated.

This interfamily rivalry began in 1672 when a dam and sawmill run by the Porters flooded the Putnam farms, resulting in a lawsuit brought by John Putnam, Sr. A few years later the Putnams petitioned the town in an effort to obtain political independence for the village, and the Porters opposed them. The arrival of Reverend Samuel Parris in 1689 intensified the Putnam-Porter conflict.

Twenty-six villagers, eleven of whom were Putnams, voted to give Parris a parsonage, a barn, and two acres of land. Some villagers thought that these gifts were too generous. In October 1691 a faction of Parris-Putnam supporters was ousted from the village committee and replaced by individuals who were openly hostile to the reverend, including Daniel Andrew, the son-in-law of John Porter, Sr.; Joseph Hutchinson, one of the sawmill operators responsible for flooding the Putnams' farms; Francis Nurse, a village farmer who had been involved in a bitter boundary dispute with Nathaniel Putnam; and Joseph Porter. The new committee quickly voted down a tax levy that would have raised revenue to pay the salary of Reverend Parris.

It is no coincidence, then, that the witchcraft afflictions and accusations originated in the Parris household. In February 1692 the reverend returned home from his congregation one evening to discover his nine-year-old daughter, Elizabeth Parris, her eleven-year-old cousin, Abigail Williams, and their twelve-year-old friend, Ann Putnam, Jr. (the daughter of Thomas Putnam, Jr., and Ann Putnam, Sr.) gathered around the kitchen table with the Parris family slave, Tituba, who was helping the girls experiment in fortune telling. Realizing that they had been caught attempting to conjure up evil spirits, the girls soon became afflicted by strange fits that temporarily deprived them of their ability to hear, speak, and see. During these episodes of sensory deprivation, the girls suffered from violent convulsions that twisted their bodies into what observers called impossible positions.

When the girls regained control of their senses, they complained of being bitten, pinched, kicked, and tormented by apparitions that would visit them in the night. These ghostly visions, the afflicted girls said, pricked their necks and backs and contorted their arms and legs like pretzels. Witnesses reported seeing the girls extend their tongues to extraordinary lengths. After examining the afflicted girls, Dr. William Griggs, the village physician, pronounced them under an evil hand.

Nearly two hundred people were accused of practicing witchcraft in Salem during the summer of 1692. Twenty accused witches were executed, fifteen women and five men. Nineteen were hung following conviction, and one was pressed to death for refusing to enter a plea. Four prisoners, three women and a man, died in jail. The trials began in June and continued for four months, the final executions taking place on September 22. In October the governor of Massachusetts, William Phipps, dissolved the tribunal that had been established to preside over the witchcraft prosecutions. The following spring the governor ordered the release of all the accused witches who remained incarcerated upon payment of their fines.

The persons accused of witchcraft ranged from a four-year-old girl, Dorcas Good, to an octogenarian farmer, Giles Cory. The accused also included an angry, muttering beggar, Sarah Good, who rarely attended church, and an ailing village matriarch, Rebecca Nurse, who was respected for her goodness and piety. Yet

the witchcraft accusations were far from random. Historians have identified a pattern of accusations that strongly suggests that the afflicted girls singled out social deviants, outcasts, outsiders, merchants, tradesman, and others who threatened traditional Puritan values.

For example, Sarah Osborne, one of the first persons accused of witchcraft in Salem, had earlier scandalized the village by having premarital sexual relations with an indentured servant from Ireland. Another accused witch, Martha Cory, had given birth to an illegitimate mulatto child. Tituba, an Indian slave from Barbados, relished her reputation as a sorcerer in black magic until she landed in jail after being accused of witchcraft. Bridget Bishop, the owner of a small Salem tavern known for its disorderliness, and Abigail Hobbs, a village rebel who was neither a church member nor a churchgoer, were two assertive and independent women whose scornful attitude toward Puritan social order was silenced by their arrests for practicing witchcraft.

Like Bridget Bishop, John and Elizabeth Proctor were tavern keepers on Ipswich Road, the thoroughfare separating Salem Town from Salem Village. The tavern was frequented only by persons from outside Salem Village, and its loud, debauched patrons were a source of concern for residents of the village. John Proctor was one of the first Salem residents to openly

This 1853 depiction of the Salem witch trials of 1692 may not be melodramatic. Courtrooms were often filled with hysterical witnesses and rowdy onlookers.

criticize the witch craze, maintaining that the afflicted girls were shamming. The day after he questioned their credibility, the afflicted girls implicated his wife in the witch conspiracy. Other Salem residents who were bold enough to express skepticism about the sincerity of the accusations made by the afflicted girls, including George Jacobs, Dorcas Hoar, Sarah Cloyce, and Susannah Martin, soon found themselves ensnared by the malignant web of witchcraft allegations.

The largest common denominator among the accused witches was the source of the complaints against them. Eight members of the Putnam family were involved in the prosecution of approximately fifty witches. Thomas Putnam, Jr., signed ten legal complaints against the defendants and provided TESTIMONY against twenty-four accused witches. His wife, Ann Putnam, Sr., was the most prominent citizen among those who were purportedly afflicted by witchcraft, and his daughter, Ann Putnam, Jr., was the most prolific accuser, providing testimony against forty-eight accused witches. Members of the Porter family attempted to mobilize the village against the witch trials but were stymied when nineteen of their allies found themselves facing witchcraft ALLEGATIONS.

Daniel Andrew, Phillip English, Francis Nurse, and George Burroughs were representative of the group of defendants accused of witchcraft by the Putnam family. Andrew was born and raised in Watertown, Massachusetts. In 1669 he moved to Salem where he married Sarah Porter, daughter of Putnam family rival John Porter, Sr. Through an inheritance, Andrew and his wife received a large parcel of land, helping them become the fourth wealthiest couple in Salem Village. Andrew was also one of the Salem residents selected to replace the Putnam-Parris faction on the village committee. Along with his village committee colleagues Francis Nurse and Phillip English, Andrew was accused of practicing witchcraft by the Putnam clan. None of the three were executed.

The legal environment in Salem offered defendants few protections against fabricated allegations of witchcraft. Similar to modern legal procedure, criminal proceedings were instituted upon the filing of a formal COMPLAINT by a party allegedly injured by witchcraft. Such complaints usually prompted the issuance of an ARREST WARRANT by a local MAGISTRATE who then conducted a preliminary examination in public to determine whether there was sufficient EVIDENCE to hold the ACCUSED in CUSTODY pending GRAND JURY deliberations. If the grand jury chose to indict a particular accused witch, the defendant was then tried by the Court of Oyer and Terminer, an emergency tribunal established by gubernatorial proclamation to resolve the burgeoning crisis. The law applied by the court was an English statute passed in 1604 during the reign of James I and carried with it the death penalty. The law prohibited "conjuration, witchcraft, and dealing with evil and wicked spirits" (Hill 1995). The INDICTMENT against the accused closely mirrored the language of the English law, charging the defendants with having "killed, destroyed, wasted, consumed, pined, and lamed" certain individuals by witchcraft.

During both the preliminary examinations and the ensuing trials, the accused witches were presumed guilty. The presiding judges and magistrates frequently asked leading questions designed to elicit answers that would disclose whom the defendants had bewitched and how, instead of more neutral and impartial questions aimed at ascertaining whether they had actually bewitched anyone at all. Although juries were impaneled to determine guilt and innocence, in at least one instance the court directed the jurors to reconsider an unpopular VERDICT they had rendered. After further deliberations, the jury reversed itself, declaring a previously acquitted defendant guilty. No accused witches were afforded the right to legal counsel, and only those defendants who confessed were saved from the gallows upon conviction.

The afflicted girls were normally present during the courtroom proceedings. When an accused witch entered the courtroom, the afflicted girls invariably collapsed into traumatic fits of hysteria that only ceased when the accused began to confess. In contrast to the dignified courtroom decorum demanded by most U.S. judges today, the Salem witches were confronted by belligerent magistrates, rabid witnesses, and apoplectic spectators in the gallery. One defendant was struck in the head with a shoe thrown by an onlooker.

The evidence offered to incriminate the defendants typically reflected the medieval superstitions of the Puritan community. Nine witches were convicted on the strength of spectral evidence alone, meaning that the only connection between the accused and the afflicted girls was testimony that an alleged victim had been visited during the night by a ghostly figure who resembled the defendant. Other defendants were convicted based on evidence that they could not properly recite the Lord's Prayer, owned mysterious dolls and puppets, or suffered from a reputation for witchcraft in the community. Jurors were told that unusual protuberant growths proverbially represented signs of a witch's nipple through which the defendant had ostensibly consummated intimate relations with the devil or lesser demons.

The Salem witch trials ground to a halt when the esteemed Reverend Increase Mather from Harvard University questioned the reliability of spectral evidence. The witch trials had been based on the premise that the devil could not assume the shape of a particular person without her consent. Mather turned this premise on its head, arguing that a deceitfully evil creature like the devil could assume the likeness of even the most unwilling and innocent person. Mather proclaimed that it is better for ten suspected witches to escape, than for one innocent person to be condemned.

SALES LAW 📖 The law relating to the TRANS-FER of ownership of PROPERTY from one person to another for VALUE, which is codified in article 2 of the UNIFORM COMMERCIAL CODE (UCC), a body of law governing MERCANTILE transactions adopted in whole or in part by the states. 📖

The sale of a good, or an item of value, is a transaction designed to benefit both buyer and seller. However, sales transactions can be complex, and they do not always proceed smoothly. Problems can arise at several phases of a sale, and at least one of the parties may suffer a loss. In recognition of these realities and of the basic importance of orderly commerce to society, legislatures and courts create laws governing sales of goods.

The most comprehensive set of laws on sales is the Uniform Commercial Code (UCC). The UCC is a collection of model laws on an assortment of commercial activities. The UCC itself does not have legal effect; it was written by the lawyers, judges, and professors in the American Law Institute and the National Conference of Commissioners on Uniform State Laws. All states have adopted the UCC in whole or in part by enacting the model laws contained in its eleven articles. See also MODEL ACTS.

Article 2 of the UCC deals with the sale of GOODS. All states with the exception of Louisiana have enacted at least some of the model laws in article 2. Laws on the sale of REAL ESTATE and the sale of services are different from laws on the sale of goods, and they are excluded from article 2. A service contract may be covered by the provisions in article 2 insofar as it involves the transfer of goods, and courts may use article 2 as a reference for interpreting laws on the sale of services. Some contracts are a blend of the sale of goods and the sale of services and may be covered by article 2. For example, the service of food by a restaurant may be considered, for some purposes, a contract for a sale of goods (U.C.C. § 2-314).

Article 2 covers sales by both private individuals and merchants. Merchants are persons engaged in the business of buying or selling goods. A small number of provisions apply only to merchants, but otherwise the provisions cover all sales.

Contract Formation A CONTRACT for the sale of goods can be made in any manner that shows agreement between the buyer and seller. A contract may be made in writing, orally, or through any other conduct by both parties that acknowledges the existence of a contract.

To form a contract, one of the parties must make an OFFER, the other party must accept the offer, and CONSIDERATION, or something of value, must be exchanged. An offer may be revoked without any loss to the offeror if the REVOCATION is made before the other party accepts the offer and gives consideration. However, an offer may not be revoked for up to ninety days if it is (1) accompanied by an assurance that the offer will be kept open; (2) made by a merchant; and (3) in writing signed by the offering merchant (U.C.C. § 2-205).

If a party accepts an offer but in the process of accepting changes MATERIAL terms of the offer, the ACCEPTANCE may be considered a COUNTEROFFER. A counteroffer eliminates the first offer, and no contract is formed until the original offeror accepts the counteroffer and consideration is exchanged. In contracts between merchants, additional or different terms by the offeree become part of the contract unless (1) the offer expressly limited acceptance to the terms of the offer; (2) the new terms materially alter the contract; or (3) the offeror objects within a REASONABLE time.

Many basic principles of contract law also apply to the sale of goods. The STATUTE OF FRAUDS requires that an agreement to sell goods at $500 or more must be in writing or it cannot be enforced in court. The writing must be signed by the party to be charged, it must contain language indicating that a contract has been made, and it must identify the parties to the contract and the quantity of goods sold. There are a few exceptions to the Statute of Frauds.

A sales contract that is UNCONSCIONABLE may be struck down in whole or in part by a court. A sale is unconscionable if a person in a superior bargaining position dictates terms that are grossly unfair to the other party. A court will determine whether a sale is unconscionable by examining the circumstances at the time the

The haggling that takes place on a car dealer's lot is, strictly speaking, an exchange of offers and counteroffers.

contract was made. Courts rarely find unconscionability in sales between merchants because merchants generally are more sophisticated in sales negotiations than are non-merchants.

Parties to a sale sometimes do not include all the terms of the sale at the time the agreement is made. Such omissions will not destroy the agreement if the parties intend to add terms at a later date. If the parties wish to modify an existing sales contract, the modifications should be in writing if they increase the value of the sale to $500 or more.

Issues Arising Prior to Performance

PERFORMANCE is the fulfillment of a PROMISE in the contract. Many issues can arise in a sales contract after the contract is made and before a party's performance is required.

Sometimes performance may be made impracticable. If the goods are completely destroyed before the RISK of loss has passed to the buyer, and the goods have not been destroyed through the FAULT of either party, the seller may be excused from performing. Risk of loss is responsibility for any damage or destruction of goods; the parties may decide in the contract when the risk of loss of the goods passes from the seller to the buyer. If the goods are only partially destroyed or have deteriorated, the buyer may demand to inspect the goods and either VOID the contract or accept the goods with a reduction in the contract price.

A seller may avoid performing only if the destroyed goods were specifically identified when the sale was made. For instance, if the sale is of a lamp handpicked by the buyer, the destruction of that particular lamp would excuse the seller's performance, and the seller would not be liable to the buyer for the loss. However, if the contract is simply for a lamp of a specific description, the seller could tender any lamp that meets the description, and the buyer would not be excused from performing.

There are two situations in which a party must make a substituted performance in case the agreed method of performance becomes impracticable. First, when the goods cannot be transported by the agreed-upon method of transportation, the seller must use available transportation that is a commercially reasonable substitute. Second, if an agreed-upon method of payment fails, the buyer must use a commercially reasonable substitute method of payment if one is available. If a party fails to substitute transportation or payment, she could be liable to the other party for losses resulting from the failure.

In some cases the purpose of a sale may be frustrated by circumstances beyond the control of both buyer and seller. For example, assume that a party agrees to buy one thousand T-shirts in anticipation of a local rock concert. If the concert is cancelled after the sales contract is made, the buyer may escape the contract under the doctrine of FRUSTRATION of purpose.

At times it may appear to a party that the other party will be unable to perform by the expected date. For example, assume that a party agrees to sell goods on CREDIT. If the buyer becomes financially insolvent before the goods are delivered, the seller may demand cash before delivering the goods. If the goods are in transit, the seller may instruct the carrier to withhold delivery of the goods. A party is considered insolvent if she cannot pay DEBTS as they come due, has ceased to pay debts, or has LIABILITIES that exceed ASSETS.

If a party has reasonable grounds to feel insecure about the other party's ability to perform, the insecure party may demand assurances before performing. For example, a seller may be insecure if a buyer falls behind in payments, or a buyer may feel insecure if a seller delivers defective goods to another party and those goods are of a kind similar to those expected by the buyer. In such cases the concerned party may demand assurances such as an advance payment or some other affirmative action, and if the other party does not provide any assurance, the concerned party may withhold performance. Alternatively, if the other party gives the assurance, the concerned party must follow through on his obligations. Precisely what constitutes an effective assurance is a question of fact that depends on the nature of the goods, the size of the contract, the length of time until performance, and similar considerations. In any case a concerned party may not make commercially unreasonable demands on a party prior to performance and then withhold performance if the other party does not meet the demands.

If a party unequivocally declares an unwillingness to perform prior to the time of performance, the other party may consider the declaration an anticipatory breach of the sales contract. An anticipatory breach operates in the same way as an actual breach and gives the non-breaching party the right to sue for losses resulting from the breach. A refusal to give assurances after a demand for assurances may be considered an anticipatory breach. A party may retract a repudiation if the retraction is made before the aggrieved party cancels the contract.

Seller's Obligations Generally, the seller's primary obligations are to transfer ownership of the goods and deliver the goods. A seller may agree with the buyer to perform other obligations. For instance, a seller may agree to package or label the goods in a certain way or service the goods for a specific period of time.

A seller should convey the TITLE to the goods free from any security interest or other LIEN or CLAIM, unless the buyer was aware at the time of the sale that other persons had a claim to the goods. If the sales contract does not specify a time of DELIVERY, the seller should deliver the goods within a reasonable time after the contract is made. Delivery should occur in one shipment unless the parties agree otherwise. If the sales agreement does not indicate where the goods are to be turned over, the delivery of the goods should occur at the seller's place of business. The TENDER of the goods should be at a reasonable hour of the day, and the buyer should have the ability to take the goods away.

If the goods are in the possession of a third party, or BAILEE, at the time of the sale, the seller must arrange matters with the bailee so that the buyer may take possession. If the goods are to be transported, there are two ways to handle delivery. The buyer and seller may agree to a shipment contract, in which case the seller must arrange for the transportation. In a shipment contract, the seller's duties for delivery are complete as soon as the goods are delivered to the carrier. With a destination contract, the seller's obligation to deliver does not end until the goods are delivered to the buyer or at a selected location.

Warranties In the context of the sale of goods, a WARRANTY is concerned with identifying the kind and quality of the goods that are tendered by the seller. The two basic types of warranties are EXPRESS warranties and implied warranties.

An express warranty is any representation or affirmation about the goods made by the seller's words or conduct. For example, the description of the goods in the sales contract constitutes an express warranty that the goods will conform to the description.

Implied warranties are warranties that are imposed on sellers by law. A warranty of merchantability is implied in every sales contract. This warranty is a promise that the goods pass without objection in the trade, are adequately packaged, conform to any promises or affirmations of fact on the container, and are fit for the ordinary purposes for which such goods are used. The IMPLIED WARRANTY of merchantability also includes a promise that multiple goods will be of even kind and quality.

Another implied warranty recognized by courts is the warranty of fitness for a particular purpose. This warranty requires that goods be fit for an identifiable, particular purpose. It is effective only if the seller has reason to know of any particular purpose for which the goods are required and also knows that the buyer is relying on the seller's expertise to select suitable goods.

Some sellers attempt to disavow any responsibility for the quality of their merchandise. Sellers may not disclaim the warranty of merchantability unless they use the word "merchantability" in the DISCLAIMER, which may be oral or written. If written, the disclaimer clause or term must be conspicuous. The implied warranty of fitness for a particular purpose may be disclaimed in writing, but it cannot be disclaimed orally. In some states, statutes or court decisions prohibit the disclaimer of warranties in consumer sales.

If a seller fails to tender goods, the buyer may choose one of three remedies. First, the buyer may seek DAMAGES from the seller. Damages are the total financial losses resulting from the failure to tender. Generally, damages for non-delivery consist of the market price of the goods minus the sale price. Market price is figured by determining the market price at the time the buyer learned of the breach at the place the tender was to have been made.

Second, the buyer may cover, or purchase

similar goods elsewhere, and then recover for losses resulting from the purchase. If the purchase price of replacement goods is greater than the original sale price, the buyer may recover the difference from the seller. The buyer must cover in GOOD FAITH, without delay, and on reasonable terms. When a seller is unable to perform a sale as agreed, the buyer should try to minimize her damages by covering the loss. If an aggrieved buyer fails to make reasonable efforts to cover, a court may reduce any damage award to account for the failure.

Third, a buyer may force the seller to perform by taking the seller to court and obtaining an ORDER for SPECIFIC PERFORMANCE or maintaining an ACTION for REPLEVIN. An action for specific performance may be ordered if the goods are unique and in other proper circumstances. Goods may be considered unique if the buyer is unable to find the goods elsewhere. An action for replevin is a method of recovering goods that is similar to specific performance. Replevin is allowed where the goods are specifically identified in the contract and the buyer is unable to cover the goods after a reasonable effort, or the circumstances indicate that the buyer will be unable to cover. If a buyer has paid only part of the sale price and the seller becomes financially insolvent within ten days of the first payment and is unable to tender the goods, the buyer may pay any remaining balance and sue to obtain the goods. This would give the buyer the goods and prevent the seller from using the goods to pay other debts.

If the buyer elects to collect damages after covering or damages for non-delivery, the buyer may collect additional damages called INCIDENTAL damages and CONSEQUENTIAL DAMAGES. Incidental damages are those resulting from the seller's breach. These include expenses incurred

Consumers rely on the implied warranty of merchantability when purchasing articles such as clothing; the implied promise of "even kind and quality" means one size 42 jacket will fit like another of the same manufacture.

in inspection, receipt, transportation, care, and custody of goods rightfully rejected; any commercially reasonable charges or expenses incurred in covering; and any other reasonable expense incident to a delay in tender of the goods or other breach on the part of the seller. Consequential damages include any loss that results from requirements of which the seller is aware at the time of contracting and that could not have been prevented by cover or other method, and foreseeable and avoidable injuries to persons or property resulting from a breach of warranty.

In some cases the buyer and seller may agree in the sales contract to LIQUIDATED DAMAGES. Generally, a liquidated damages clause is placed into a sales contract to fix damages at a certain amount in case a party is unable to perform. A court may strike down a liquidated damages clause if it does not bear a reasonable relationship to actual damages or anticipated damages.

If a seller tenders nonconforming goods, or goods that do not meet the specifications in the sales contract, the tender constitutes a breach of the contract. In such a situation, the buyer may either accept or reject the goods. Any recovery by the buyer will depend on whether the buyer accepts or rejects the goods.

A buyer has the right to inspect goods before accepting them. If the goods are nonconforming, the buyer may accept the goods and recover from the seller the difference between the value of the goods as warranted and their actual value with the defects.

A buyer may elect to reject nonconforming goods. To reject goods, the buyer must take some positive action to give the seller notice of the rejection. If the seller can CURE the problem, the buyer should tell the seller why he is rejecting the goods or risk a reduction in damages. In transactions between merchants, a buyer should specify the problem to the seller if the seller makes a written request for a full and final written statement of all defects on which the buyer bases the rejection.

A seller has the right to cure nonconforming goods if he gives notice to the buyer and if conforming goods can be delivered before the last date for delivery under the sales contract. In any case a buyer may agree to extend the time for delivery of conforming goods. In some cases a buyer may have no choice. Under section 2-508(2) of the UCC, if a seller sends nonconforming goods that he reasonably believed would be acceptable, the seller has additional time to deliver conforming goods if he gives notice of such intent to the buyer.

If a buyer rejects goods, the buyer may not exercise any ownership over the goods. The buyer must hold the goods for a reasonable time and permit the seller to remove them or await instructions from the seller. If the seller issues instructions to the buyer, the buyer should follow any reasonable requests. For example, if the goods are perishable and the seller has no local AGENT, the buyer should attempt to sell the goods for the account of the seller. The buyer then could recover the difference between the amount that the buyer could have made with the goods and the amount that the buyer actually received.

If the buyer rejects nonconforming, nonperishable goods and the seller has no agent near the buyer, the buyer should follow instructions from the seller. If the seller issues no instructions, the buyer may either store the goods for the seller's account, reship the goods to the seller, or sell the goods for the seller's account. An aggrieved buyer may then recover any losses incurred in storing, shipping, or reselling the goods.

If a buyer rejects nonconforming goods and cannot sell them, the buyer may hold the goods for the seller and recover the difference between the market price of the goods as warranted and the value of the goods as delivered. A buyer also may ask for specific performance. If the seller is unable to provide the goods as requested, the buyer may recover any money already paid toward the sale plus any consequential or incidental damages resulting from the breach.

Buyer's Obligations A buyer's basic obligations are to accept the goods and pay the sale price. If the goods are nonconforming, the buyer may reject the goods. If the goods conform to the specifications of the sales contract and the buyer wrongfully rejects them, the seller may choose one of four options, or a blend of two or more options.

First, the seller may sue for damages. The amount of damages for a wrongful rejection would be the sale price minus the market price of the goods, measured at the time and place of the tender. Second, the seller may sue for the price of the goods, but only if the goods cannot be resold in the seller's ordinary course of business, or if circumstances indicate that resale efforts will be fruitless. Third, the seller could cancel the contract, putting an end to shipments and reserving the right to sue for damages or collect unpaid balances. Fourth, the seller could resell the goods to a third party and recover the difference between the sale price

and the resale price plus any incidental damages.

The resale of wrongfully rejected goods presents a few special problems. Under section 2-706 of the UCC, the sale may be either public or private. A private sale is made personally by the seller, whereas a public sale is made with public notice and carried out by a SHERIFF or at a publicly held AUCTION. In either case the sale must be commercially reasonable in method, manner, time, place, and terms. Furthermore, the seller must notify new buyers that the goods are being resold under a breached contract to disclose the potential for legal conflict.

A seller who resells wrongfully rejected goods must inform the original buyer of the resale. If wrongfully rejected goods are perishable, the seller need not give notice to the buyer of the time and place of the resale. If the resale of wrongfully rejected goods is at a public sale, only goods identified in the contract may be sold, and the sale must be made at a usual place for public sale, provided such a site is reasonably available. If the goods are not in view of bidders at a public sale, the public notice of the sale must state the place where the goods are located, and the seller must give bidders an opportunity to inspect the goods. If the seller resells the goods for a price higher than the price in the original sales contract and the extra profit covers costs incident to the resale, the seller has no damages, and the original buyer is not liable to the seller for the wrongful rejection.

In sales where the buyer pays a deposit and then wrongfully rejects the goods, the seller may keep the goods and the deposit. However, a seller is not entitled to a deposit that far

When competition for sales increases, merchants offer attractive payment options, such as generous credit terms, to entice customers.

exceeds her actual or expected damages. Under section 2-718 of the UCC, a buyer is entitled to restitution of any amount by which the sum of the payments already made exceeds either (1) the amount of any reasonable liquidated damages clause, or (2) 20 percent of the value of the total performance for which the buyer is obligated under the contract, or $500, whichever amount is smaller.

When a buyer accepts a seller's tender of conforming goods, the buyer is obligated to pay the sale price contained in the contract for sale. In some cases the parties may fail to agree to a price or choose to leave the price terms open. Under section 2-305 of the UCC, if a price term is left open, the price should be set in good faith at a reasonable market price at the time of delivery. If the parties intend that there is to be no contract unless a price is agreed to or fixed by a particular market indicator and the parties ultimately are unable to agree to a price term, there is no contract. In such a case the buyer must return any goods received, and the seller must return any money paid by the buyer.

Generally, a buyer has the right to pay in any manner observed in the business unless the seller demands a particular form of payment. Unless the parties agree otherwise, payment should be made when the goods are delivered to the buyer. A buyer does not have the right to inspect the goods if they are delivered cash on delivery or on similar terms, or if the contract provides for payment before inspection.

Installment Contracts   INSTALLMENT contracts have a few of their own special rules. An installment contract is a contract that calls for periodic performances over a length of time. The parties may agree to make payments in any way, but if the sale price can be divided, the buyer usually makes payments on installment contracts upon each delivery of goods.

Buyers in installment sales do not have the same full rights of rejection as buyers in other sales. If a seller tenders an installment of nonconforming goods, the buyer may reject the installment only if it substantially impairs the value of that installment and cannot be cured. Under section 2-612 of the UCC, if the nonconformity is not substantial and can be cured by the seller, the buyer must accept a nonconforming installment and sue for damages.

The tender of one nonconforming installment in an installment contract for sale does not always constitute a total breach of the entire installment contract. Generally, a nonbreaching party to an installment contract may cancel the contract only when a breach or cumulative breaches substantially impair the value of the entire contract.

CROSS-REFERENCES
Carriers; Consumer Protection; Freight; Merchantable; Product Liability; Shipping Law.

SALES TAX 📖 A state or local-level tax on the retail sale of specified property or services. It is a percentage of the cost of such. Generally, the purchaser pays the tax but the seller collects it as an AGENT for the government. Various taxing JURISDICTIONS allow exemptions for purchases of specified items, including certain foods, services, and manufacturing equipment. If the purchaser and seller are in different states, a USE TAX usually applies. 📖

SALVAGE 📖 The portion of GOODS or PROPERTY that has been saved or remains after some type of CASUALTY, such as a fire. 📖

The term *salvage* is defined more specifically depending on the industry referring to it. In business, salvage is any property that is no longer useful but has scrap value. An example of business salvage is obsolete equipment. In INSURANCE, salvage is the portion of property that the insurance company takes after paying the claim for the loss. The insurance company may deduct the salvage value from the amount of the claim paid and leave the property with the insured. In admiralty or maritime law, salvage is the compensation allowed to persons who voluntarily save a ship or its cargo from impending danger. In addition to compensation, maritime salvage may be property that is recovered from vessels that were shipwrecked, derelict, or recaptured. Salvage as a legal concept typically concerns maritime salvage.

To establish a valid salvage claim under maritime law, the claimant must prove the following: the salvage was needed because of a marine peril; the claimant's service was rendered voluntarily and not because of an existing DUTY or CONTRACT; and the claimant's service contributed to the success of the salvage in whole or in part.

The element of PERIL is an important, yet misunderstood, element. The maritime interpretation of peril is broad and liberal. IMMINENT and absolute danger is not a requirement for maritime peril. If the property is in danger, or stranded "so that it [is] subject to the potential danger of damage or destruction," then peril exists (*McNabb v. O. S. Bowfin*, 565 F. Supp. 22 [W.D. Wash. 1983]). Also, the degree of peril does not determine whether the salvor will be entitled to a salvage award, but it will be considered in determining the amount of the award. According to the admiralty law of the

United States, a stranded vessel that may be exposed to wind, weather, and waves is considered to be in a position where it may be destroyed and is therefore in peril.

A wide variety of services can support a claim for a salvage award. For example, a claim for salvage has been granted where the salvor provided assistance in putting out a fire when the fire was not under immediate control. A salvage service claim may even succeed where the salvor assisted in putting out a nearby fire that had the potential to endanger the vessel.

Voluntarily towing a drifting vessel to safety has also supported a claim for salvage award, even where the drifting vessel was not in danger of immediate or absolute harm and apprehension of danger was minimal. Along the same lines, towing a stranded vessel has also constituted salvage service. In the towing situation, courts have held that although there is no apprehension of immediate harm or danger, a stranded vessel is subject to high winds and other severe weather, placing the vessel in peril.

Courts have also upheld a salvage service claim when the crew, master, or officers were incapacitated, and when the vessel was exposed to a hazard of the sea as a result of its master's uncertainty.

In all situations of salvage service, the service must be entirely voluntary. The salvor cannot have provided the service pursuant to any type of contract or agreement or other existing duty. When the U.S. Navy or Coast Guard provided the salvage service, the issue as to whether those services were in fact voluntary has arisen.

When the Navy performs the salvage service, courts have held that, because salvage is not one of the functions of the Navy, any assistance provided by the Navy is voluntary, regardless of whether the Navy is in the area where the salvaged vessel is in peril. Federal law now provides that "the Secretary of Navy may settle any claim by the United States for salvage services rendered by the Department of Navy and may receive payment of any such claim" (10 U.S.C.A. § 7363 [1996]).

Similar claims by the Coast Guard have had different outcomes. According to statute, the Coast Guard may "perform any and all acts necessary to rescue and aid persons and protect and save property" (14 U.S.C.A. § 88 [1996]). Most courts and commentators have interpreted this language as creating a legal duty. Therefore, under this interpretation the government would not have a right to a salvage award for services rendered by the Coast Guard. The Fifth Circuit Court of Appeals declined to follow this interpretation in the case of *United States v. American Oil*, 417 F.2d 164 (1969). In its decision, the court held that the Coast Guard did not have a preexisting duty to perform salvage services and that the statutory language defining the Coast Guard's duties was permissive. Although the Fifth Circuit Court of Appeals may allow the United States to recover salvage awards for services rendered by the Coast Guard, other courts have declined to follow this interpretation, leaving the right of the government to recover salvage awards for services rendered by the Coast Guard still under debate.

The salvage service rendered must also have been successful, either in whole or in part. Furthermore, the salvor must have contributed to the success. The salvor, however, does not have a right to force his or her services on a distressed vessel. The doctrine of rejection applies when the master of a distressed vessel directly and unequivocally rejects the salvor's services. In that situation, the salvor does not have a right to a salvage award.

In determining the amount of the salvage award, the court will go beyond the value of the services. In 1869 the U.S. Supreme Court, in *The Blackwall*, 77 U.S. (10 Wall.) 1, 19 L. Ed. 870, set forth the following criteria in determining the amount of the award: (1) the labor expended by the salvors in rendering the salvage service; (2) the promptitude, skill, and energy displayed in rendering the service and saving the property; (3) the value of the property employed by the salvors in rendering the service and the danger to which such property was exposed; (4) the risk incurred by the salvors in securing the property from the impending peril; (5) the value of the property saved; and (6) the degree of danger from which the property was rescued.

When a salvage award is granted, all of the parties who participated in the salvage service will share in the award based on their participation. In addition, the owner, master, and crew of the salvaged vessel are entitled to share in the award. If the salvaged property is damaged as a result of the salvage effort, the owner may claim that the salvor was negligent. If the court finds that the salvor did not adhere to a standard of reasonable care, the salvage award will be reduced depending on the degree of NEGLIGENCE.

An action for salvage is generally an IN REM action. This means that the suit is brought against the property saved, such as the ship or its cargo. In the event that the property is no longer within the JURISDICTION or has been destroyed, an IN PERSONAM action may be brought to recover the salvage award. These salvage actions fall under the jurisdiction of the admiralty courts.

Anyone with a direct pecuniary interest in the property salved, such as the owner, may be liable for the salvage award. In addition, anyone who may be liable for the property, for instance a BAILEE, may also be liable for the salvage award. The persons liable for the salvage award are not necessarily the individuals who requested the salvage services.

In the event that the salvage claim involves a shipwreck, the court has "qualified jurisdiction" when the wreck site is exclusively within the waters of the contiguous zone of the United States. In addition, U.S. admiralty courts have asserted jurisdiction of wrecks in international waters when certain pieces of the wreck were brought into the jurisdiction of the court. This is based on the "first salvor rule," which protects the first salvor from losing the "trove" once it has started salving the wreck to other parties who may intervene and attempt to take over the salvage operations. Most countries recognize the right of the first salvor and will uphold a LIEN issued by another jurisdiction according to this rule.

According to the agreement, the convention was to become effective one year after fifteen states had expressed their consent to be bound by it. In 1996 the agreement became binding, or entered into force, upon 22 countries.

See also ADMIRALTY AND MARITIME LAW.

SANCTION 📖 To assent, concur, confirm, approve, or ratify. The part of a law that is designed to secure enforcement by imposing a penalty for violation of the law or offering a reward for its observance. A punitive act taken by one nation against another nation that has violated a TREATY or INTERNATIONAL LAW. 📖

Sanction is a broad term with different meanings in different contexts. *Sanction* can be used to describe tacit or explicit approval. Used in this sense, the term usually is used in assigning LIABILITY to a party who was not actively involved in wrongdoing but who did nothing to prevent it. For example, if the upper-level managers of a business knew that their employees were using unfair employment practices and did nothing to stop them, it may be said that the managers sanctioned the unfair practices.

The term *sanction* also can describe disagreement and condemnation. In CRIMINAL LAW, a sanction is the punishment for a criminal offense. The criminal sanction for a criminal

defendant varies according to the crime and includes such measures as death, INCARCERATION, PROBATION, community service, and monetary FINES.

In CIVIL LAW, a sanction is that part of a law that assigns a penalty for violation of the law's provisions. The most common civil sanction is a monetary fine, but other types of sanctions exist. Depending on the case, a sanction may be the suspension or revocation of a business, professional, or hobby LICENSE, or a court ORDER commanding a person to do or refrain from doing something. A sanction may even be tailored to the case at hand. For instance, under rule 37 of the Federal Rules of Civil Procedure, if a party refuses to obey a DISCOVERY order, or an order to relinquish requested EVIDENCE, the court may order that the evidence sought be automatically construed in favor of the requesting party, refuse to allow the disobedient party to make claims or defenses related to the evidence, STAY or postpone the case until the discovery order is obeyed, dismiss the ACTION or render JUDGMENT for the requesting party, declare the disobedient party in CONTEMPT of court, or make any other order that is just under the circumstances.

In civil litigation, sanctions are slightly different from remedies. A REMEDY is the RELIEF accorded to a victorious litigant. The remedy may be money DAMAGES, an order that forbids or commands the opposing party or parties to do or refrain from doing a certain act or acts, or some other result favorable to the victorious litigant. Remedies are not always intended to punish a person, while sanctions are always punitive. Nevertheless, remedies and sanctions are similar in that they refer to a loss that a civil litigant must bear if she is found liable for a civil wrong.

In some cases a party may have to remedy another party's loss as well as suffer criminal and civil sanctions, all for the same act. For example, if an attorney is professionally negligent in his handling of a client's case and steals funds from the client's trust account, the attorney may face a MALPRACTICE civil suit from the aggrieved client in which the client asks for money as a remedy for the malpractice. The attorney also may suffer sanctions from the professional conduct committee of the state BAR ASSOCIATION and criminal sanctions from a prosecution for the theft.

The contempt-of-court offense provides a flexible form of sanction. Contempt-of-court sanctions may be either civil or criminal. The court may order a party to pay a fine or suffer some setback in the case (civil contempt), or it may order that the party be placed in jail (criminal contempt). The basic difference between the two is that criminal contempt is an act of disrespect toward the court, whereas civil contempt acts tend to be less offensive transgressions, such as the unintentional failure to comply with discovery orders or to perform other acts ordered by the court.

A common form of sanction is the ADMINISTRATIVE AGENCY sanction against a corporation. CORPORATIONS must follow various rules passed by federal, state, and local administrative agencies authorized by lawmaking bodies to regulate specific topics of government concern. If a business does not obey agency rules that apply to it, it may face sanctions levied by the administrative agency responsible for enforcing the rules. For example, federal and state environmental protection agencies are authorized by statute to levy fines against businesses that violate environmental laws and regulations.

An international sanction is a special form of sanction taken by one country against another. International sanctions are measures that are designed to bring a delinquent or renegade state into compliance with expected rules of conduct. International sanctions may be either non-forceful or military. Military sanctions can range from cutting off access to limited strikes to full-scale war. Non-forceful international sanctions include diplomatic measures such as the withdrawal of an ambassador, the severing of diplomatic relations, or the filing of a protest with the UNITED NATIONS; financial sanctions such as denying aid or cutting off access to financial institutions; and economic sanctions such as partial or total trade EMBARGOES. The U.N. Security Council has the authority to impose economic and military sanctions on nations that pose a threat to peace.

SANFORD, EDWARD TERRY An important influence on the development of civil liberties, Edward Terry Sanford served on the U.S. Supreme Court from 1923 to 1930. Sanford was a native of Tennessee with a cosmopolitan education, and before serving on the

BIOGRAPHY

PORTRAIT BY EBEN F. COMINS, COLLECTION OF THE SUPREME COURT OF THE UNITED STATES

Edward Terry Sanford

Court, he had a private law practice, served in the Justice Department, and was a federal district judge in his home state for fourteen years. While on the Court, Sanford's views were largely moderate, and in his lifetime, he was overshadowed by his highly visible contemporaries. Nonetheless, Sanford's opinions on civil liberties helped advance the guarantees of the BILL OF RIGHTS: in two major opinions delivered in the 1920s, he laid the groundwork for modern Supreme Court decisions that restrict the power of states to limit FIRST AMENDMENT rights to FREEDOM OF SPEECH.

Sanford was born in Knoxville, Tennessee, on July 23, 1865, the son of a lumber and construction millionaire. He earned four degrees from the University of Tennessee and Harvard, and studied languages in France and Germany. At Harvard Law School, he distinguished himself as the editor of the *Harvard Law Review* and graduated magna cum laude. He began practicing law in Tennessee in the 1890s. He then lectured in law at the University of Tennessee from 1898 to 1906 before moving to Washington, D.C., for his first federal job.

Sanford's federal law career began in prosecution and rapidly took him to the federal bench. He joined the Justice Department in 1906 as a special assistant prosecutor, and a year later he was made an assistant attorney general. By 1908 Sanford returned to Tennessee as a federal district judge, a position he held until 1923. His specialties were BANKRUPTCY and EQUITY cases. On the bench he developed a reputation for open-mindedness, fairness, and leniency, at times reversing his own decisions. He was highly driven and nervously energetic, and would pace and chain-smoke in his chambers while considering his busy docket.

In 1923 Sanford's nomination to the Supreme Court came at the behest of his friends, Chief Justice WILLIAM HOWARD TAFT and Attorney General Harry M. Daugherty. The two men convinced President WARREN G. HARDING of Sanford's breadth of education and varied experience, which included service on the LEAGUE OF NATIONS. The nomination succeeded

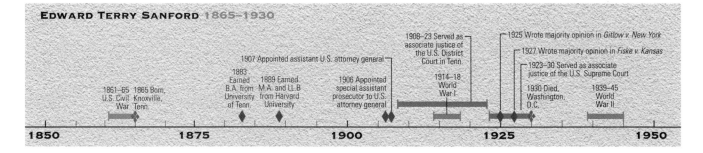

EDWARD TERRY SANFORD 1865–1930

1861–65 U.S. Civil War

1865 Born, Knoxville, Tenn.

1883 Earned B.A. from University of Tenn.

1889 Earned M.A. and LL.B from Harvard University

1906 Appointed special assistant prosecutor to U.S. attorney general

1907 Appointed assistant U.S. attorney general

1908–23 Served as associate justice of the U.S. District Court in Tenn.

1914–18 World War I

1923–30 Served as associate justice of the U.S. Supreme Court

1925 Wrote majority opinion in *Gitlow v. New York*

1927 Wrote majority opinion in *Fiske v. Kansas*

1930 Died, Washington, D.C.

1939–45 World War II

1850　1875　1900　1925　1950

easily in the Senate, and Sanford sat on the Court for seven years until his death in 1930. He wrote 130 opinions, many of them addressing issues related to government, business, and especially bankruptcy.

Although neglected by history because of the accomplishments of his celebrated contemporaries, Sanford made a major contribution in the area of civil liberties. In particular, he helped develop the so-called INCORPORATION DOCTRINE—the Supreme Court's view that the Bill of Rights applies not only to the federal government but also, in large part, to the states. During much of the nineteenth century, states conferred fewer rights upon their citizens than those extended by the federal Bill of Rights, even after ratification of the FOURTEENTH AMENDMENT. With the intervention of the Supreme Court, this began to change at the turn of the century. In the mid-1920s, Sanford helped effect the change in two important cases concerning freedom of speech.

The first case dealt with a state's power to control the press. In *Gitlow v. New York*, 268 U.S. 652, 45 S. Ct. 625, 69 L. Ed. 1138 (1925), the Court considered New York's conviction of a leftist author under the state's anarchy law of 1902. The broader question for the Court was, Should the First Amendment be extended to the states? Sanford's opinion upheld the conviction because, in the Court's view, states should be free to prosecute citizens who advocate violent overthrow of government. But on the broader question of the Bill of Rights, Sanford wrote that the First Amendment applied to the states through the Fourteenth Amendment. *Gitlow* served as the foundation for subsequent cases in which the Court would strike down state laws that violated the First Amendment. In 1927 the Court upheld a defense based on the doctrine enunciated in *Gitlow* in *Fiske v. Kansas*, 274 U.S. 380, 47 S. Ct. 655, 71 L. Ed. 1108. In his opinion, Sanford underscored that states must guarantee First Amendment rights.

Throughout his tenure on the Court, Sanford voted consistently with Chief Justice Taft. Sanford died at age sixty-four on March 8, 1930—the same day that Taft died.

See also GITLOW V. NEW YORK.

SAN FRANCISCO VIGILANCE COMMITTEES OF 1851 AND 1856 Self-appointed law enforcement committees that were organized to maintain order in San Francisco, California, during the mid-nineteenth century.

As a result of the Treaty of Guadalupe Hidalgo in 1848, which concluded the Mexican War, the United States acquired a vast territory in the Southwest including California and New Mexico. After gold was discovered at Sutter's Mill in 1848, thousands of gold hunters flocked into northern California. Many of the gold rush towns where the immigrants settled had been little more than villages before the gold rush and lacked the municipal institutions that were needed to cope with the rapidly expanding populations. As government and law enforcement became increasingly disorganized and chaotic, vigilance committees were formed in many towns. The San Francisco Vigilance Committees of 1851 and 1856 provide two of the most famous examples of vigilante activity.

Before gold was discovered in 1848, the population of San Francisco had been around 800 persons. By 1851, nearly 25,000 gold seekers had arrived, most of whom settled in or near the city. Crime quickly became a problem. In 1856, a Sacramento newspaper claimed that there had been 1400 murders in San Francisco in the previous six years and that only three murderers had been hanged.

In 1851, a group of citizens, including a large number of businesspersons, under the leadership of Sam Brannan, formed the first San Francisco Vigilance Committee. The city government had failed to curb gangs of outlaws known as the "Regulators" or "Hounds," who preyed upon the inhabitants of the city and were suspected of having set a series of fires that had destroyed much of the city. The committee promptly sought out several of the alleged outlaws and sentenced them to death, deportation, or whipping.

In 1856, after a county supervisor named James P. Casey killed newspaper editor James King, the committee came back into existence under the leadership of William T. Coleman to combat lawlessness among the general population and corruption and mismanagement in the city government. The committee began by trying and executing Casey and Charles Cora, a notorious criminal. Next the committee barricaded the streets in an area where the crime rate was high and captured and punished all the criminals it could find within the barricades.

In the meantime, other citizens including a number of city officials and attorneys had formed the "Law and Order" faction to oppose the vigilantes. DAVID SMITH TERRY, a justice of the California Supreme Court, tried to prevent one of the vigilantes from arresting a certain Reuben Maloney on the ground that the committee had no legal authority to conduct arrests. A fight ensued in which Terry stabbed Sterling A. Hopkins, the vigilante. Although Terry was imprisoned for a few weeks, the vigilantes' attempt to put him on trial failed, and the

"WE MAY AND DO ASSUME THAT THE FREEDOM OF SPEECH AND OF THE PRESS . . . ARE AMONG THE FUNDAMENTAL PERSONAL RIGHTS AND LIBERTIES PROTECTED . . . FROM IMPAIRMENT BY THE STATES."

committee disbanded a short time later. By that time, it had lost most of its supporters and its power had waned.

Although the committees declared that the safety of the public was their purpose, the committees ignored the principles of government on all levels. Their trials did not follow standard procedures, but used only a skeletal version of established legal practices.

SANGER, MARGARET HIGGINS A feminist and founder of the Planned Parenthood Federation of America, Margaret Higgins Sanger battled the government and the Roman Catholic Church to establish the legitimacy of BIRTH CONTROL.

Sanger was born September 14, 1879, in Corning, New York, to Michael Higgins, an Irish stonecutter, and Annie Purcell Higgins, the daughter of an Irish day laborer. Sanger's mother, who had five more children and suffered chronic tuberculosis, died at the age of fifty in 1899. Sanger blamed her death on the strain of bearing eleven children.

Following her mother's death, Sanger began nursing training at White Plains Hospital. She often accompanied doctors to patients' homes to deliver babies, and she frequently had to deliver children herself. Many of the new mothers asked Sanger what they could do to prevent another pregnancy. She, in turn, asked the doctors, but they gave her no information and took little interest in the women's dilemma.

While completing her nursing training, Sanger met William Sanger, an architect, whom she married in 1902. He was a German Jew and a socialist who was active in the radical causes of the day.

By 1912, the Sangers and their three children had moved to Greenwich Village, where the couple became involved in politics and the arts, and entertained some of the most radical intellectuals of the time. Sanger became deeply involved with the Socialist party. While recruiting for the organization, she visited many working-class families with six and seven children that were forced to make their home in two- and three-room tenements. She found that

Margaret Higgins Sanger

the women lived in dread of having more children and the resulting increase in poverty, and she concluded that women needed the right to control their own bodies.

She soon began speaking publicly on the problems of family life, connecting the size of the family with the economic problems of the working class. Her speeches became so popular that she was asked to turn them into a series of articles for the *Call*, a New York socialist newspaper. In her twelve-week series, entitled "What Every Woman Should Know," Sanger explained puberty, the reproductive organs, and sexually transmitted diseases. After the paper printed an article about gonorrhea, the authorities threatened that if it published a planned article on syphilis, its mailing permit would be canceled under the Comstock Act of 1873, a strict CENSORSHIP law that barred the mailing of "obscene" material. The law was named for Anthony Comstock, a special agent of the post office with authority to open the mail and determine whether materials were OBSCENE.

Along with her speaking and writing, Sanger returned to nursing in New York and spent much of her time assisting with home births and living with the families for several weeks afterward. She observed that the women had repeated pregnancies and were obsessed with methods of preventing conception. They sought illegal and cheap ABORTIONS, which often caused injury or death, and tried dangerous cures of their own, such as drinking turpentine and inserting instruments into the uterus. After one woman died following her second self-induced abortion, Sanger was distraught and walked the streets for hours before returning home. That night, Sanger decided to devote her life to educating women about their bodies and methods of contraception.

Sanger began her work by scouring libraries for information on preventing conception. After months of reading and research, she was convinced that no practical information existed in the United States, and she traveled to France with her family. In Paris, Sanger found that

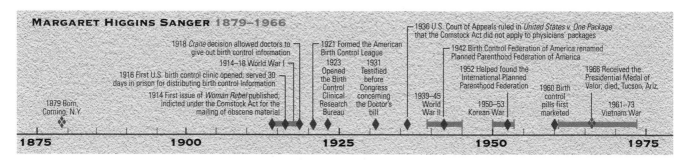

French women were well versed in contraceptive methods. She talked to druggists, midwives, doctors, and working women, and noted formulas for suppositories and douches, which she planned to write up as a pamphlet for U.S. women.

Returning home to New York, she began publishing a monthly magazine called the *Woman Rebel.* She deliberately decided to use the publication to engage in a frank discussion of women's liberation from the fear and reality of unplanned pregnancies, knowing that she would soon run afoul of Anthony Comstock. Sanger realized that the new movement needed a name, and after much discussion, she and a group of supporters agreed to call it birth control.

In April 1914, four weeks after the first issue of the *Woman Rebel* was published, the post office notified Sanger that the magazine was unmailable under the Comstock Act. While she skirmished with Comstock over her magazine, Sanger worked on her pamphlet on contraceptive techniques, called *Family Limitation,* in which she described the practical knowledge she had gathered in Europe. Sanger visited twenty-two printers in one week, trying to find someone who would produce the pamphlet. Finally, one hundred thousand copies were printed, addressed, and stored in San Francisco, Chicago, and Pittsburgh, to be mailed on her prearranged signal, when she thought she would be safe from Comstock's interference.

In August 1914, Sanger was indicted on charges of violating the Comstock Act. When it became clear that the judge hearing her case was biased against her, she fled to Europe to gain time to prepare her case properly. She sailed from Canada under a false name and without a passport. From the ship, where she was safely outside U.S. legal JURISDICTION, Sanger sent telegrams containing the prearranged code word that indicated it was time to send out her pamphlet on contraception. After landing in Liverpool, she traveled on to London, where news of the *Woman Rebel* had made her a celebrity in radical circles. She later moved to Holland, which had the lowest infant death rate in the world and where all mothers were taught about contraception. There, Sanger learned how to examine women and advise them on which of the fifteen available birth control devices were appropriate. As a result of her experience in Europe, she learned the necessity of the medical community's involvement in the birth control movement and the importance of keeping thorough records and conducting follow-up studies.

In October 1915, Sanger sailed home. She contacted the district attorney about her case, and a hearing was scheduled for the following January. But in November 1915, the Sangers' daughter, Peggy, died of pneumonia, and Sanger sank into a severe depression. She insisted on going ahead with her trial, however, and received an outpouring of support from people across the country who had heard of her loss. Eventually, the charges were dismissed on the grounds that they were two years old and that Sanger had not made a practice of publishing obscene articles. Although this dismissal prevented the Comstock Act from being challenged in the courts, the publicity surrounding Sanger's case made the entire country aware of the birth control movement.

Sanger next notified her supporters of her intent to establish free clinics throughout the country, at which women could receive instruction in birth control. Sanger rented a storefront tenement in the Brownsville section of Brooklyn, where many newly arrived immigrants lived. The three women printed five thousand circulars in English, Yiddish, and Italian, advertising the clinic and offering contraceptive information for ten cents, and posted them around the neighborhood. The posters read, "Mothers! Can you afford to have a large family? Do you want any more children? If not, why do you have them?"

In October 1916, Sanger, along with her sister Ethel Byrne, who was a nurse, and another supporter, Fania Mindell, opened the first birth control clinic in the United States. After only nine days, over four hundred women had come to the clinic for assistance. Among them was an undercover policewoman, who arrested Sanger, Byrne, and Mindell and confiscated all the patient records, pamphlets, and contraceptives. The women were charged with disseminating birth control information and maintaining a public nuisance. Byrne was found guilty and sentenced to thirty days in jail, where she nearly died from a hunger strike before the governor pardoned her. Mindell was found guilty of selling copies of "What Every Woman Should Know" and fined fifty dollars. Sanger was convicted and sentenced to thirty days in the workhouse, where she gave lectures on birth control to the other inmates and taught them to read and write.

After her release, Sanger decided to focus on changing the laws on contraception and educating women about birth control techniques. Her conviction for running the birth control clinic had been upheld by the New York Supreme Court in *People v. Sanger,* 179 App. Div. 939,

"A FREE RACE CANNOT BE BORN OF SLAVE MOTHERS."

166 N.Y.S. 1107 (1917), and she appealed to the state's high court, the New York Court of Appeals. In January 1918, in an opinion that became known as the *Crane* decision after the authoring judge, Frederick Crane, the appellate court upheld the lower court (*Sanger*, 222 N.Y. 192, 118 N.E. 637). But the court interpreted the criminal laws broadly, holding that doctors could give out birth control information to any married person to protect his or her health. This meant that clinics could operate freely and that they would be under the supervision of medical personnel, where Sanger thought they belonged.

By 1920, over twenty-five birth control leagues were operating, and Mindell's conviction for distributing literature about contraception was reversed, which meant that pamphlets and books could more easily be distributed. In 1921, Sanger formed the American Birth Control League. The Catholic Church came to lead the opposition to Sanger's efforts, and she continued to battle the church throughout her life.

Sanger attacked the Comstock law, establishing the National Committee for Federal Legislation for Birth Control, headquartered in Washington, D.C., to gather support for federal legislation dubbed the Doctor's Bill. By 1931, hundreds of medical, political, religious, and labor organizations supported the bill. When Sanger appeared before a subcommittee of the Senate Judicial Committee in February 1931, she testified that based on statistics for the period since the Comstock Act took effect in 1873, one-and-a-half million women had died during pregnancy and childbirth; seven hundred thousand illegal abortions had been performed each year; and fifteen million children had died during their first year because of poverty or their mother's poor health. But the proposed legislation was vehemently opposed by the Catholic Church, the Patriotic Society, the Purity League, and other groups, and was defeated.

After further attempts to pass the legislation were unsuccessful, Sanger decided to turn to the courts. In 1933 she had had a new type of pessary (vaginal suppository) sent to Dr. Hannah Stone, in New York, and the package had been seized under the Comstock Act. Stone filed charges. After a trial, the court ruled that the doctor was entitled to the package (*United States v. One Package*, 13 F. Supp. 334 [S.D.N.Y. 1936]). The government appealed to the U.S. Court of Appeals for the Second Circuit, which upheld the lower court, ruling that the aim of the Comstock law was not to "prevent the importation, sale, or carriage by mail of things

which might intelligently be employed by conscientious and competent physicians for the purpose of saving life or promoting the well being of their patients" (*One Package*, 86 F.2d 737 [2d Cir. 1936]). In 1937 the American Medical Association adopted the position that all doctors should receive information about the legal dispensation of contraceptives and that new contraceptive techniques should be studied.

In 1939 the Birth Control Clinical Research Bureau and the Birth Control League merged into the Birth Control Federation of America, which was renamed the Planned Parenthood Federation of America in 1942. Sanger continued her work, initiating birth control programs in rural clinics. Here, she decided that the relatively expensive and difficult-to-use diaphragm was impractical and that women needed a birth control pill or injection. In the 1950s, she supported the work of Dr. Gregory Pincus, whose research eventually produced the birth control pill.

In 1966 at the age of eighty-two, Sanger received the Presidential Medal of Valor from LYNDON B. JOHNSON. Later that year, she died in Tucson, Arizona.

See also GRISWOLD V. CONNECTICUT; WOMEN'S RIGHTS.

SANITY 📖 Reasonable understanding; sound mind; possessing mental faculties that are capable of distinguishing right from wrong so as to bear legal responsibility for one's actions. 📖

SANTA CLARA COUNTY v. SOUTHERN PACIFIC RAILROAD COMPANY

An 1886 Supreme Court decision, *Santa Clara County v. Southern Pacific Railroad Company*, 118 U.S. 394, 6 S. Ct. 1132, 30 L. Ed. 118, is often cited for the principle that the term *person* as used in the Equal Protection Clause of the FOURTEENTH AMENDMENT applies to CORPORATIONS as well as to natural persons.

The Southern Pacific Railroad Company refused to pay a tax assessed by the California Board of Equalization upon its franchise, roadways, roadbeds, fences, and rolling stock. The county brought an ACTION in state court against the railroad to recover the delinquent taxes. The railroad had the action removed to the federal district court. The court agreed with the defendant that the ASSESSMENT of the tax was VOID because the board had no JURISDICTION to act. It also ruled that the defendant had been denied EQUAL PROTECTION of the law because the assessment of the property was made at full monetary value without the discount that was given to individual property owners for outstanding MORTGAGES on their property. The county filed a WRIT of error to the federal court, and the U.S. Supreme Court heard the case.

The Court agreed with the railroad that the state board had no jurisdiction to assess the tax. The assessment of taxes by the board on fences belonging to the railroad was deemed void because the board was authorized by the state constitution to assess only "the franchise, roadway roadbed, rails, and rolling stock." The Court rejected the argument that the fences constituted part of the roadway for purposes of taxation. The constitution required a separate assessment for "land, and improvements thereon" and a state statute expressly included the term *fence* within the categories of improvements. The state board acting through the county sought to have the plaintiff liable for a single sum, incorporating taxes assessed upon various types of property, including property that the board had no power to assess. The Court declared that since part of the assessment was illegal, it could not support an action for the county to recover the entire tax; therefore, it affirmed the judgment for the defendants.

The Court did not explicitly discuss the Fourteenth Amendment in its opinion, basing its decision on the invalidity of the assessment. In its statement of the facts of the case, it did, however, set out the Fourteenth Amendment claims of the railroad. The California constitution denied "railroads and other quasi public corporations" equal protection of laws as guaranteed by the Fourteenth Amendment to the Constitution because the board did not reduce the value of property for assessment purposes by the amount of any outstanding mortgage debts on it, as it did for property owned by natural persons or other corporations. Although the Supreme Court did not specifically rule on the constitutionality of the treatment of the railroad by the state, the case of *County of Santa Clara v. Southern Pacific Railroad Company* is cited to support the principle that both corporations and natural persons are entitled to equal protection of laws pursuant to the Fourteenth Amendment to the Constitution.

SARGENT, JOHN See *WEAL 1998 Supplement.*

SATISFACTION 📖 The DISCHARGE of an obligation by paying a party what is due—as on a MORTGAGE, LIEN, or CONTRACT—or by paying what is awarded to a person by the JUDGMENT of a court or otherwise. An entry made on the record, by which a party in whose favor a judgment was rendered declares that she has been satisfied and paid.

The fulfillment of a GIFT by WILL, whereby the TESTATOR—one who dies leaving a will— makes an INTER VIVOS gift, one which is made while the testator is alive to take effect while the testator is living, to the beneficiary with the intent that it be in lieu of the gift by will. In EQUITY, something given either in whole or in part as a substitute or equivalent for something else. 📖

SAVE 📖 To except, reserve, or exempt; as where a statute *saves* VESTED—fixed—rights. To toll, or suspend the running or operation of; as, to *save* the STATUTE OF LIMITATIONS. 📖

SAVING CLAUSE 📖 In a STATUTE, an exception of a special item out of the general things mentioned in the statute. A restriction in a repealing act, which is intended to save rights, while proceedings are pending, from the obliteration that would result from an unrestricted repeal. The provision in a statute, sometimes referred to as the severability clause, that rescues the balance of the statute from a declaration of unconstitutionality if one or more parts are invalidated. 📖

With respect to existing rights, a saving clause enables the repealed law to continue in force.

All acts of limitation, whether applicable to civil causes and proceedings, or to the prosecution of offenses, or for the recovery of penalties or forfeitures, embraced in the Revised Statutes and covered by the repeal contained therein, shall not be affected thereby, but suits, proceedings, or prosecutions, whether civil or criminal, for causes arising, or acts done or committed prior to said repeal, may be commenced and prosecuted within the same time as if said repeal had not been made. July 30, 1947, c. 388, § 1, 61 Stat. 633.

An example of a saving clause

SAVINGS AND LOAN ASSOCIATION

📖 A financial institution owned by and operated for the benefit of those using its services. The savings and loan association's primary purpose is making loans to its members, usually for the purchase of REAL ESTATE or homes. 📖

The savings and loan industry was first established in the 1830s as a BUILDING AND LOAN ASSOCIATION. The first savings and loan association was the Oxford Provident Building Society in Frankfort, Pennsylvania. As a building and loan association, Oxford Provident received regular weekly payments from each member and then lent the money to individuals until each member could build or purchase his own home. Building and loan associations were financial intermediaries, which acted as a conduit for the flow of investment funds between savers and borrowers.

Savings and loan associations may be state or federally chartered. When formed under state law, savings and loan associations are generally incorporated and must follow the state's requirements for incorporation, such as providing ARTICLES OF INCORPORATION and BYLAWS. Although it depends on the applicable state's law, the articles of incorporation usually must set forth the organizational structure of the association and define the rights of its members and the relationship between the association and its stockholders. A savings and loan association may not convert from a state CORPORATION to a federal corporation without the consent of the state and compliance with state laws. A savings and loan association may also be federally chartered. Federal savings and loan associations are regulated by the OFFICE OF THRIFT SUPERVISION.

Members of a savings and loan association are stockholders of the corporation. The members must have the capacity to enter into a valid CONTRACT, and as stockholders they are entitled to participate in management and share in the profits. Members have the same LIABILITY as stockholders of other corporations, which means that they are liable only for the amount of their stock interest and are not personally liable for the association's NEGLIGENCE or DEBTS.

OFFICERS and DIRECTORS control the operation of the savings and loan association. The officers and directors have the duty to organize and operate the institution in accordance with state and federal laws and regulations and with the same degree of diligence, care, and skill that an ordinary prudent person would exercise under similar circumstances. The officers and directors are under the COMMON-LAW duty to exercise due care as well as the duty of loyalty. Officers and directors may be held liable for breaches of these common-law duties, for losses that result from violations of state and federal laws and regulations, or even for losses that result from a violation of the corporation's bylaws.

The responsibilities of the officers and directors of a savings and loan association are generally the same as the responsibilities of officers and directors of other corporations. They must select competent individuals to administer the institution's affairs, establish operating policies and internal controls, monitor the institution's operations, and review examination and audit reports. Furthermore, they also have the power to assess losses incurred and to decide how the institution will recover those losses.

Prior to the 1930s, savings and loan associations flourished. However, during the Great Depression the savings and loan industry suffered. More than 1,700 institutions failed, and because depositor's insurance did not exist, customers lost all of the money they had deposited into the failed institutions. Congress responded to this crisis by passing several banking acts. The Federal Home Loan Bank Act of 1932, 12 U.S.C.A. § 1421 et seq., authorized the government to regulate and control the financial services industry. The legislation created the Federal Home Loan Bank Board (FHLBB) to oversee the operations of savings and loan institutions. The Banking Act of 1933, 48 Stat. 162, created the FEDERAL DEPOSIT INSURANCE CORPORATION (FDIC) to promote stability and restore and maintain confidence in the nation's banking system. In 1934 Congress passed the National Housing Act, 12 U.S.C.A. § 1701 et seq., which created the National Housing Administration (NHA) and the Federal Savings and Loan Insurance Corporation (FSLIC). The NHA was created to protect MORTGAGE lenders by insuring full repayment, and the FSLIC was created to insure each depositor's account up to $5,000.

The banking reform in the 1930s restored depositors' faith in the savings and loan industry, and it was once again stable and prosperous. However, in the 1970s the industry began to feel the impact of competition and increased interest rates; investors were choosing to invest in money markets rather than in savings and loan associations. To boost the savings and loan industry, Congress began deregulating it. Three types of deregulation took place during this time.

The first major form of deregulation was the enactment of the Depository Institutions Deregulation and Monetary Control Act of 1980 (94 Stat. 132). The purpose of this legislation was to allow investors higher rates of return, thus making the savings and loan associations more competitive with the money markets. The industry was also allowed to offer money-market options and provide a broader range of services to its customers.

The second major form of deregulation was the enactment of the Garn-St. Germain Depository Institutions Act of 1982 (96 Stat. 1469). This act allowed savings and loan associations to diversify and invest in other types of loans besides home construction and purchase loans, including commercial loans, state and municipal SECURITIES, and unsecured real estate loans.

The third form of deregulation decreased the amount of regulatory supervision. This deregulation was not actually an "official" deregulation; instead it was the effect of a change in required accounting procedures. The Generally Accepted Accounting Principles were changed to Regulatory Accounting Procedures, which allowed savings and loan associations to include speculative forms of capital and exclude certain liabilities, thus making the thrifts appear to be in solid financial positions. This resulted in more deregulation.

In the 1980s the savings and loan industry collapsed. By the late 1980s at least one-third of the savings and loan associations were on the brink of INSOLVENCY. Eight factors were primarily responsible for the collapse: a rigid institutional design, high and volatile interest rates, deterioration of asset quality, federal and state deregulation, FRAUDULENT practices, increased competition in the financial services industry, tax law changes, and moral hazard (the risk that their owners would allow them to fail to collect the insurance).

In an effort to restore confidence in the thrift industry, Congress enacted the Financial Institutions Reform, Recovery, and Enforcement Act of 1989 (FIRREA) (103 Stat. 183). The purpose of FIRREA, as set forth in section 101 of the bill, was to promote a safe and stable system of affordable housing finance; improve supervision; establish a general oversight by the TREASURY DEPARTMENT over the director of the Office of Thrift Supervision; establish an independent insurance agency to provide deposit insurance for savers; place the Federal Deposit Insurance System on sound financial footing; create the Resolution Trust Corporation; provide the necessary private and public financing to resolve failed institutions in an expeditious manner; and improve supervision, enhance enforcement powers, and increase criminal and civil penalties for crimes of FRAUD against financial institutions and their depositors.

FIRREA increased the enforcement powers of the federal banking regulators and conferred a wide array of administrative sanctions. FIRREA also granted federal bank regulators the power to hold liable "institution-affiliated parties" who engage in unsound practices that harm the insured depository institution. The institution-affiliated parties include directors, officers, employees, agents, and any other persons, including attorneys, appraisers, and accountants, participating in the institution's affairs. FIRREA also allows federal regulators to seize the institution early, before it is "hopelessly insolvent" and too expensive for federal insurance funds to cover.

Criminal penalties were also increased in 1990 by the Crime Control Act, 104 Stat. 4789,

which included the Comprehensive Thrift and Bank Fraud Prosecution and Taxpayer Recovery Act of 1990 (104 Stat. 4859). This act increased the criminal penalties "attaching" to crimes related to financial institutions.

FIRREA created the Office of Thrift Supervision (OTS) and the Resolution Trust Corporation (RTC). FIRREA eliminated the FHLBB and created the OTS to take its place. The RTC was created solely to manage and dispose of the ASSETS of thrifts that failed between 1989 and August 1992. In addition, the FSLIC was eliminated, and the FDIC, which oversaw the banking industry, began dealing with the troubled thrifts.

The RTC was in existence for six years, closing its doors on December 31, 1996. During its existence, it merged or closed 747 thrifts and sold $465 billion in assets, including 120,000 pieces of property. The direct cost of resolving the failed thrifts amounted to $90 billion; however, when indirect costs such as the interest on government spending for the rescue are included, the cost of the bailout is estimated to be $480.9 billion.

The need for savings and loan associations has declined considerably. In 1980 savings and loan associations originated 40 percent of residential mortgage loans, mortgage banks originated 29 percent, commercial banks originated 22 percent, and other lenders originated 8 percent of home mortgage loans. However, by 1994 savings and loan association mortgage loans had dropped to 18 percent of all home mortgage loans, whereas the percentage of mortgage bank loans had increased to 52 percent, and the percentage of commercial bank loans had increased to 26 percent.

See also BANKS AND BANKING.

SAXBE, WILLIAM BART William Bart Saxbe, a quotable lawyer, politician, and United States senator from Ohio, served as U.S. attorney general under President RICHARD M. NIXON. He also served as ambassador to India under President GERALD R. FORD.

Saxbe was born on June 24, 1916, in the farming community of Mechanicsburg, Ohio, to Bart Rockwell Saxbe, a religious and plain-spoken community leader who made his living as a cattle buyer, and Faye Henry Carey Saxbe, a political free spirit who counted PATRICK HENRY among her ancestors. Saxbe's education seemed to be influenced by his parents' example; when he entered Ohio State University in 1936, he chose political science as his major field of study. He received a bachelor of arts degree in 1940. In the fall of that year, he married Ardath Louise ("Dolly") Kleinhans. They eventually had three children:

BIOGRAPHY

William Bart Saxbe

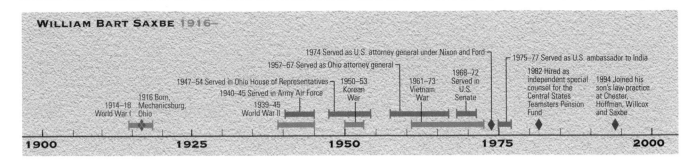

WILLIAM BART SAXBE 1916–

1974 Served as U.S. attorney general under Nixon and Ford
1957–67 Served as Ohio attorney general
1975–77 Served as U.S. ambassador to India
1947–54 Served in Ohio House of Representatives
1950–53 Korean War
1968–72 Served in U.S. Senate
1982 Hired as independent special counsel for the Central States Teamsters Pension Fund
1994 Joined his son's law practice at Chester, Hoffman, Willcox and Saxbe
1940–45 Served in Army Air Force
1961–73 Vietnam War
1916 Born, Mechanicsburg, Ohio
1914–18 World War I
1939–45 World War II

1900   1925   1950   1975   2000

William Bart, Jr., Juliet Louise, and Charles Rockwell.

While attending college, Saxbe was a member of the Ohio National Guard. After college he enlisted in the Army Air Force, serving from 1940 to 1945. Saxbe was called to serve again during the Korean conflict in the 1950s; he was discharged from the reserve with the rank of colonel in 1963.

Immediately after World War II, Saxbe returned to Ohio with the intention of furthering his education. He gave serious thought to pursuing a career in the ministry of the Episcopal Church, but his long-standing interest in political and community service prevailed. Saxbe entered law school at Ohio State University in 1945 and, simultaneously, launched a campaign to serve in the Ohio House of Representatives. He was elected and served four terms from 1947 to 1954. Saxbe completed his law degree at the end of his second term. He served as House majority leader in 1951 and 1952, and as speaker of the House in 1953 and 1954.

Saxbe left the Ohio legislature at the conclusion of his fourth term. He returned to Mechanicsburg where he raised cattle on the family farm. He also partnered with two longtime friends to establish the Columbus, Ohio, law firm of Saxbe, Boyd, and Prine. He practiced law for two years before reentering the political arena in 1956. In 1957 he ran as the Republican candidate for state attorney general. Over the next decade, he served four terms as Ohio's attorney general. As attorney general Saxbe proved to be a tough and capable crime fighter. He believed that CAPITAL PUNISHMENT was a strong deterrent and that stiff prison sentences should be imposed for gun-related crimes.

Although conservative in his views on crime and money, Saxbe described himself as "liberal on the rights of people." In 1968 Saxbe took his unique mix of fiscal conservatism and social responsibility to the electorate. He ran as the Republican candidate for a U.S. Senate seat, and he won a close election over liberal Democrat John J. Gilligan. His stand against the Pentagon's deployment of antiballistic missiles

"I FEEL VERY STRONGLY THAT THE JUSTICE DEPARTMENT IS THE VERY HEART AND SOUL OF OUR COUNTRY, BECAUSE GOVERNMENT WITHOUT LAW IS TYRANNY."

during the VIETNAM WAR surprised many of those who thought his campaign promises were just rhetoric. Gilligan was quoted as saying, "If I had known he was going to be like this, I would have voted for him myself." Saxbe's voting record on most major issues showed that he moved gradually to the right during his four years in the U.S. Senate.

Saxbe was quickly disenchanted with life as a senator. He thought many of his senate colleagues were sadly out of touch with the electorate. He alienated most of Washington when he said, "The first six months I kept wondering how I got [here]. After that, I started wondering how all of them did."

In addition to his disdain for the insulated lives of Washington politicians, Saxbe was frustrated with the pace of legislation on Capitol Hill. To address the problem, Saxbe joined forces with Senator Alan M. Cranston to develop a two-track system of moving legislation through the Senate. The system allowed less controversial bills to pass through the legislative process quickly, while more volatile measures were held for debate and discussion. When other efforts to improve the process stalled, Saxbe removed himself from the Senate entirely by taking part in travel junkets. Saxbe's plea for aid to East Bengal and for discontinuation of aid to Pakistan was a direct result of his findings on a junket; he considered this action to be among his greatest achievements in the Senate.

Saxbe's frustration with Washington was not limited to the Senate. (In 1968 Saxbe had defied protocol by challenging Nixon's Vietnam policy during a social gathering at the White House for freshman senators.) In response, the president's staff kept Saxbe out of the Oval Office and away from Nixon for almost two years after that disastrous first meeting with the chief executive.

Saxbe's growing contempt for the White House staff reached a new height in 1971 when he referred to Nixon aides H. R. Haldeman and John D. Ehrlichman as "a couple of Nazis" and again in 1972 when he commented on Nixon's professed innocence in the WATERGATE scandals, saying that the chief executive sounded "like the fellow who played the piano in a brothel for twenty years, and insisted that he didn't know what was going on upstairs." (The Watergate scandals began with a break-in at the Democratic National Committee headquarters—located in the Watergate Office Towers—and eventually toppled the Nixon administration.)

In September 1973 Saxbe announced that he would not seek reelection to the Senate. Just a month later, Nixon asked him to accept an appointment as attorney general of the United States to replace ELLIOT RICHARDSON. Richardson, Nixon's third attorney general, had resigned rather than obey an executive order to fire Watergate prosecutor ARCHIBALD COX. Saxbe was reluctant to accept the nomination. But he knew that the administration wanted to avoid a long confirmation battle and that his past criticism of the president would make him a credible candidate with both Nixon supporters and detractors.

After a two-hour discussion with Nixon, in which the president denied any knowledge or involvement in the Watergate scandals, Saxbe accepted the nomination. He took office in January 1974. His goal was to restore the Justice Department's credibility with the U.S. public and to keep the public informed of the department's activities.

Saxbe initiated weekly news conferences at the beginning of his term but curtailed them quickly when he found that his offhand comments generated more interest than his substantive efforts. Among Saxbe's more printable gaffs were his reference to PATTY HEARST as a common criminal and his observation that Jewish intellectuals of the 1950s were enamored with the Communist party.

As attorney general, Saxbe supported legislation limiting access to criminal records of arrested and convicted persons, and he continued to favor capital punishment and tough sentences for gun-related crimes. He conducted an investigation into the FBI's counterintelligence program—Cointelpro—and condemned the program for its harassment of left-wing groups,

black leaders, and campus radicals. He also presided over two of the biggest ANTITRUST cases in history against IBM and AT&T.

After Nixon's resignation Saxbe continued to serve as attorney general in the Ford administration. He resigned in December 1974 to accept an appointment as U.S. ambassador to India.

For the next twenty years, Saxbe practiced law in Florida, Ohio, and Washington, D.C., and he remained active in Republican party politics. In March 1994 he announced that he would join the Columbus, Ohio, law firm of Chester, Hoffman, Willcox, and Saxbe where his son was a partner.

Saxbe is often called upon to speak about the turmoil of the Watergate years and his experience in the final days of the Nixon administration. On the eve of Nixon's funeral in April 1994, Saxbe acknowledged that he had never made an attempt to see Nixon after his resignation because the former president had lied to him about his involvement in the Watergate scandals.

SCAB A pejorative term used colloquially in reference to a nonunion worker who takes the place of a union employee on STRIKE or who works for wages and other conditions that are inferior to those guaranteed to a union member by virtue of the union contract.

See also LABOR UNION.

SCALIA, ANTONIN In 1986 Antonin Scalia was appointed to the U.S. Supreme Court by President RONALD REAGAN, becoming the first American of Italian descent to serve as an associate justice. Known for his conservative judicial philosophy and narrow reading of the Constitution, Scalia has repeatedly urged his colleagues on the Supreme Court to overturn *Roe v. Wade*, 410 U.S. 113, 93 S. Ct. 705, 35 L. Ed. 2d 147 (1973), the decision recognizing a woman's right to terminate her pregnancy under certain circumstances.

Scalia was born March 11, 1936, in Trenton, New Jersey. Before he began grade school, Scalia and his family moved to Elmhurst, New York, where he spent much of his boyhood.

BIOGRAPHY

PHOTOGRAPHER, JOSEPH D. LAVENBURG. COLLECTION OF THE SUPREME COURT OF THE UNITED STATES.

Antonin Scalia

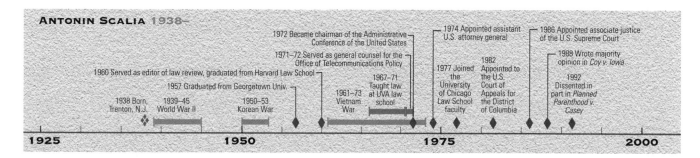

ANTONIN SCALIA 1938–

1960 Served as editor of law review, graduated from Harvard Law School

1957 Graduated from Georgetown Univ.

1938 Born, Trenton, N.J.   1939–45 World War II   1950–53 Korean War

1961–73 Vietnam War

1967–71 Taught law at UVA law school

1971–72 Served as general counsel for the Office of Telecommunications Policy

1972 Became chairman of the Administrative Conference of the United States

1977 Joined the University of Chicago Law School faculty

1982 Appointed to the U.S. Court of Appeals for the District of Columbia

1974 Appointed assistant U.S. attorney general

1986 Appointed associate justice of the U.S. Supreme Court

1988 Wrote majority opinion in *Coy v. Iowa*

1992 Dissented in part in *Planned Parenthood v. Casey*

1925   1950   1975   2000

Scalia is the only child of Eugene Scalia, an Italian immigrant who taught romance languages at Brooklyn College for thirty years, and Catherine Scalia, a first-generation Italian American who taught elementary school.

In 1953 Antonin Scalia graduated first in his class at St. Francis Xavier High School, a Jesuit military academy in Manhattan. Four years later Scalia was valedictorian at Georgetown University, receiving a bachelor's degree in history. In the spring of 1960 Scalia graduated magna cum laude from Harvard Law School where he served as an editor for the *Harvard Law Review*. Known to his friends as Nino, Scalia was known to many of his classmates as an eager and able debater.

Upon graduation from law school, Scalia accepted a position as an associate attorney with a large firm in Cleveland, Ohio, where he practiced law until 1967 when he resigned to teach at the University of Virginia School of Law. In 1970 Scalia joined the Nixon Administration to serve as general counsel for the Office of Telecommunications Policy. Under President GERALD R. FORD, Scalia served as assistant attorney general for the Department of Justice where he worked a number of subjects, including the information-gathering activities of the Central Intelligence Agency and Federal Bureau of Investigation.

In 1977 Scalia left public office to become a visiting scholar at the American Enterprise Institute, a conservative think tank in Washington, D.C. During this same year Scalia also returned to academia, accepting a position as law professor at the University of Chicago where he developed a reputation as an expert in administrative law. In 1982 President Reagan appointed Scalia to the U.S. Court of Appeals for the District of Columbia, considered by many lawyers to be the second most powerful court in the country.

When Chief Justice WARREN BURGER retired in 1986, President Reagan elevated sitting Justice WILLIAM REHNQUIST to the chair of chief justice and nominated Scalia to fill the vacancy of associate justice. Confirmed by a vote of 98–0 in the Senate, Scalia became the first Roman Catholic appointed to the Supreme Court since WILLIAM J. BRENNAN, Jr., in 1957.

Scalia's tenure on the Supreme Court has been marked by a JURISPRUDENCE of ORIGINAL INTENT. Proponents of original intent, also called originalists, believe that the Constitution must be interpreted in light of how it was understood at the time it was framed and ratified. According to Scalia, originalism has two virtues: preserving the separation of powers in a democratic society, and curbing judicial discretion.

The Constitution delegates specific enumerated powers to the three branches of the federal government. The legislative branch is given the power to make law under Article I; the EXECUTIVE BRANCH is given the power to enforce the law under Article II; and the JUDICIARY is given the power to interpret and apply the law under Article III. Democracy is enhanced, originalists state, when the lawmaking power is exercised by the federal legislature because, unlike federal judges who are appointed by the president and given life tenure on the bench, members of Congress are held accountable to the electorate at the ballot box.

This SEPARATION OF POWERS is blurred, Scalia argues, when unelected federal judges decide cases in accordance with their own personal preferences, which may be contrary to those expressed by the framers and ratifiers. In such instances, Scalia asserts, federal judges usurp the legislative function by making new law that effectively replaces the popular understanding of the Constitution at its time of adoption. The only way to curb this type of judicial discretion and preserve the separation of powers, Scalia concludes, is by requiring federal judges to interpret and apply the Constitution in light of its original meaning. This meaning can be illuminated, Scalia says, by paying careful attention to the express language of the Constitution and the debates surrounding the framing and ratification of particular provisions.

Scalia's interpretation and application of the EIGHTH AMENDMENT best exemplifies his judicial philosophy. The Eighth Amendment prohibits CRUEL AND UNUSUAL PUNISHMENT. Courts that evaluate a claim under the Cruel and Unusual Punishments Clause, Scalia argues, must determine whether a particular punishment was allowed in 1791 when the Eighth Amendment was framed and ratified. Courts must not take into account, Scalia emphasizes, notions of the evolving standards of human decency. For example, Scalia contends that CAPITAL PUNISHMENT was clearly contemplated by the framers and ratifiers of the federal Constitution. The Fifth Amendment explicitly references capital crimes, Scalia observes, and capital punishment was prevalent in the United States when the Constitution was adopted. Whether states presently support or oppose capital punishment plays only a negligible role in Scalia's analysis.

Scalia's interpretation of the DUE PROCESS Clause of the Fifth and Fourteenth Amendments provides another example of his judicial philosophy. According to Scalia, the Due Pro-

> "JUDGES IN A REAL SENSE 'MAKE' LAW . . . [T]HEY MAKE IT AS JUDGES MAKE IT, WHICH IS TO SAY AS THOUGH THEY WERE 'FINDING' IT— DISCERNING WHAT THE LAW IS, RATHER THAN DECREEING WHAT IT IS TODAY CHANGED TO, OR WHAT IT WILL TOMORROW BE."

cess Clause was originally understood to offer only procedural protection, such as the right to a fair hearing before an impartial judge and an unbiased jury. Nowhere in the text of the Constitution, Scalia notes, is there any hint that the Due Process Clause offers substantive protection. It is not surprising then that Scalia has dissented from Supreme Court decisions that have relied on the Due Process Clause in protecting the substantive right of women to terminate their pregnancies under certain circumstances (*Planned Parenthood v. Casey*, 505 U.S. 833, 112 S. Ct. 2791, 120 L. Ed. 2d 674 [1992]). No such right, Scalia has commented, can be found in the express language of any constitutional provision.

Scalia has surprised some observers by his literal reading of the SIXTH AMENDMENT, which guarantees the right of criminal defendants to be "confronted with witnesses against them." In *Coy v. Iowa*, 487 U.S. 1012, 108 S. Ct. 2798, 101 L. Ed. 2d 857 (1988), Scalia, writing for the Court, said that the Sixth Amendment requires a face-to-face confrontation and this was denied when a large screen was placed between a defendant charged with child molestation and the child who accused him. The Sixth Amendment, Scalia concluded, intended for courts to preserve the adversarial nature of the criminal justice system by protecting the rights guaranteed by the Confrontation Clause over governmental objections that face-to-face CROSS-EXAMINATION may be emotionally traumatic for some victims.

Whether Scalia is writing about the Sixth Amendment, the Eighth Amendment, or some other Constitutional provision, his judicial opinions are regarded by some as among the most well written in the history of the Supreme Court. The clarity, precision, and incisiveness with which he writes is frequently praised. However, some of Scalia's opinions take on an acerbic quality. Often relegated to the role of dissenting justice, Scalia is not above hurling invectives at his colleagues on the Court, sometimes criticizing their opinions as silly and preposterous.

SCHECHTER POULTRY CORP. v. UNITED STATES   *A.L.A. Schechter Poultry Corp. v. United States*, 295 U.S. 495, 55 S. Ct. 837, 79 L. Ed. 1570 (1935), is one of the most famous cases from the Great Depression era. The case tested the legality of certain methods used by Congress and President FRANKLIN D. ROOSEVELT to combat the devastating economic effects of the Depression. After the U.S. Supreme Court declared the methods unconstitutional, Roosevelt publicly scolded the

Court and later used the decision as one justification for a controversial plan to stock the Court with justices more receptive of Roosevelt's programs.

At the heart of the *Schechter* case was legislation passed by Congress in 1933. The NATIONAL INDUSTRIAL RECOVERY ACT (NIRA) (48 Stat. 195) was passed in response to the unemployment and poverty that swept the nation in the early 1930s and provided for the establishment of local codes for fair competition in industry. The codes were written by private trade and industrial groups. If the president approved the codes, they became law. Businesses were required to display a Blue Eagle insignia from the NATIONAL RECOVERY ADMINISTRATION to signify their compliance with the codes. Typical local codes set MINIMUM WAGES and maximum hours for workers and gave workers the right to organize into unions and engage in COLLECTIVE BARGAINING with management. Codes also prescribed fair trade practices, and many codes set minimum prices for the sale of goods.

The Schechter Poultry Corporation, owned and operated by Joseph, Martin, Alex, and Aaron Schechter, was in the business of selling chickens at wholesale. The corporation purchased some of the poultry from outside the state of New York. It bought the poultry at markets and railroad terminals in New York City and sold the poultry to retailers in the city and surrounding environs. In April 1934 President Roosevelt approved the code of fair competition for the live poultry industry of the New York City metropolitan area (Live Poultry Code). In July 1934 the Schechters were arrested and indicted on sixty counts of violating the Live Poultry Code. The INDICTMENT included charges that Schechter Poultry had failed to observe the minimum wage and maximum hour provisions applicable to workers and that it had violated a provision of the Live Poultry Code prohibiting the sale of unfit chickens. The case became popularly known as the *Sick Chicken* case.

The Schechters pleaded not guilty to the charges. At trial, the Schechters were convicted on eighteen counts of violating the Live Poultry Code and two counts of conspiring to violate the Live Poultry Code. An appeals court affirmed their convictions, but the U.S. Supreme Court agreed to hear their APPEAL.

The Schechters presented several arguments challenging the Live Poultry Code. According to the Schechters, the code system of the NIRA was an unconstitutional abdication of the legislative power vested in Congress by Article I,

Section 1, of the U.S. Constitution. The Schechters argued further that their intrastate wholesale business was not subject to congressional authority under the COMMERCE CLAUSE of Article I, Section 8, Clause 3, of the Constitution and that the procedures for enforcing the NIRA codes violated the Due Process Clause of the FIFTH AMENDMENT.

In support of the Live Poultry Code, the federal government argued that the code was necessary for the good of the nation. According to the government, the Live Poultry Code ensured the free flow of chickens in interstate commerce. This kept chicken prices low and helped ease, however slightly, the financial burden on the general public. The government also argued that it was within the power of Congress to enact the NIRA regulatory scheme that gave rise to the Live Poultry Code because codes such as the Live Poultry Code applied only to businesses engaged in interstate commerce.

The Court unanimously disagreed with the federal government. Under the Commerce Clause, Congress had the power to regulate commerce between the states, not intrastate commerce. The power to enact legislation on intrastate commerce was reserved to the states under the TENTH AMENDMENT to the Constitution. According to the Court, the business conducted by the Schechters was decidedly intrastate. Their business was licensed in New York, they bought their poultry in New York, and they sold it to retailers in New York. Because it was intended to reach intrastate businesses like Schechter Poultry, the Live Poultry Code regulated intrastate commerce, and it was therefore an unconstitutional exercise of congressional power. The Court reversed the Schechters' convictions and declared the Live Poultry Code unconstitutional.

The *Schechter* decision was decided around the same time as other, similar Supreme Court decisions striking down federal attempts to address the economic crises of the Depression. However, the *Schechter* decision was a particularly troublesome setback for the Roosevelt administration. The NIRA was the centerpiece of Roosevelt's plan to stabilize the national economy (the NEW DEAL), and the government's loss in the *Sick Chicken* case marked the end of the NIRA and its fair trade codes. Less than one week after the *Schechter* decision was announced, Roosevelt publicly condemned the Court. Roosevelt declared that the Court's "horse-and-buggy definition of interstate commerce" was an obstacle to national health.

Roosevelt's remarks were controversial because they appeared to cross the line that separated the powers of the EXECUTIVE BRANCH from those of the judicial branch. Nevertheless, they sparked a national debate on the definition of interstate commerce, the role of the U.S. Supreme Court, and the limits of federal power. Several citizens and federal legislators began to propose laws and constitutional amendments in an effort to change the makeup of the Supreme Court. At first, Roosevelt refused to back any of the plans, preferring instead to wait and see if the Court would reconsider its stand and reverse the *Schechter* holding. After the Supreme Court delivered another series of opinions in 1936 that nullified New Deal legislation, Roosevelt began to push for legislation that would modify the makeup of the Court. In 1937 the Supreme Court began to issue decisions upholding New Deal legislation. Congress never enacted Roosevelt's so-called court-packing plan.

CROSS-REFERENCES

Butler, Pierce; Federalism; Hughes, Charles Evans; McReynolds, James Clark; Roberts, Owen Josephus; Stone, Harlan Fiske; Sutherland, George; Van Devanter, Willis.

SCHENCK v. UNITED STATES *Schenck v. United States*, 249 U.S. 47, 39 S. Ct. 247, 63 L. Ed. 470 (1919), is a seminal case in constitutional law, representing the first time that the U.S. Supreme Court heard a FIRST AMENDMENT challenge to a federal law on free speech grounds. In upholding the constitutionality of the Espionage Act of 1917 (40 Stat. 217), the Supreme Court articulated the CLEAR AND PRESENT DANGER doctrine, a test that still influences the manner in which state and federal courts decide free speech issues. This doctrine pioneered new territory by drawing a line that separates protected speech, such as the public criticism of government and its policies, from unprotected speech, such as the advocacy of illegal action.

On December 20, 1917, Charles Schenck was convicted in federal district court for violating the Espionage Act, which prohibited individuals from obstructing military recruiting, hindering enlistment, or promoting insubordination among the armed forces of the United States. Schenck, who was the general secretary of the Socialist party in the United States, had been indicted for mailing antidraft leaflets to more than fifteen thousand men in Philadelphia. The leaflets equated the draft with slavery, characterized conscripts as criminals, and urged opposition to American involvement in World War I.

Schenck appealed his conviction to the Supreme Court, which agreed to hear the case. Attorneys for Schenck challenged the constitutionality of the Espionage Act on First Amendment grounds. FREEDOM OF SPEECH, Schenck's attorneys argued, guarantees the liberty of all Americans to voice their opinions about even the most sensitive political issues, as long as their speech does not incite immediate illegal action. Attorneys for the federal government argued that freedom of speech does not include the freedom to undermine the SELECTIVE SERVICE SYSTEM by casting aspersions upon the draft.

In a 9–0 decision, the Supreme Court affirmed Schenck's conviction. Justice OLIVER WENDELL HOLMES, JR., delivered the opinion. Holmes observed that the constitutionality of all speech depends on the circumstances in which it is spoken. No reasonable interpretation of the First Amendment, Holmes said, protects utterances that have the effect of force. For example, Holmes opined that the Freedom of Speech Clause would not protect a man who falsely shouts fire in a crowded theater.

"The question in every case," Holmes wrote, "is whether the words are used in such circumstances and are of such a nature as to create a clear and present danger that they will bring about the substantive evils that Congress has a right to prevent." Holmes conceded that during peacetime Schenck's vituperative leaflets might have received constitutional protection. However, Holmes said, during times of war no American has the right to speak or publish with the intent of obstructing the conscription process when such speech has a tendency to incite others to this unlawful purpose.

The Supreme Court's decision in *Schenck* established two fundamental principles of constitutional law. First, *Schenck* established that the First Amendment is not absolute. Under certain circumstances, the rights protected by the Freedom of Speech Clause must give way to important countervailing interests. Preserving the integrity of the military draft during wartime and protecting theater patrons from the perils of pandemonium are two examples of countervailing interests that will override First Amendment rights.

Second, *Schenck* established the standard by which subversive and seditious political speech would be measured under the First Amendment for the next fifty years. Before the government may punish someone who has published scurril-

ous political material, the Court in *Schenck* said, it must demonstrate that the material was published with the intent or tendency to precipitate illegal activity and that it created a clear and present danger that such activity would result.

Schenck did not settle every aspect of free speech jurisprudence. It left unresolved a number of crucial questions and created ambiguities that could only be clarified through the judicial decision-making process. It was unclear after *Schenck*, for example, how immediate or probable a particular danger must be before it becomes clear and present. If *Schenck* permitted the government to regulate speech that has an unlawful tendency, some observers feared, Congress could ban speech that carried with it any harmful tendency without regard to the intent of the speaker or the likely effect of the speech on the audience.

In 1969 the Supreme Court articulated the modern clear-and-present-danger doctrine in *Brandenburg v. Ohio*, 395 U.S. 444, 89 S. Ct. 1827, 23 L. Ed. 2d 430, stating that the government may not forbid or punish subversive speech except where it advocates or directs imminent lawless action and is likely to incite or produce such action.

Under *Brandenburg*, courts must consider the intention of the speaker or writer, as well as her ability to persuade and arouse others when evaluating the danger presented by particular speech. Courts must also consider the susceptibility of an audience to a particular form of expression, including the likelihood that certain members of the audience will be aroused to illegal action. Despite the reformulation of the clear-and-present-danger test, *Schenck* retains constitutional vitality in cases concerning the Freedom of Speech Clause, having been cited in more than one hundred state and federal judicial opinions in the 1980s and 1990s.

CROSS-REFERENCES

Communism; *Dennis v. United States*; Smith Act.

BIOGRAPHY

Phyllis Stewart Schlafly

SCHLAFLY, PHYLLIS STEWART The demise of the EQUAL RIGHTS AMENDMENT (ERA) on June 30, 1982, can be attributed in large part to Phyllis Stewart Schlafly. During the 1970s, Schlafly was the United States' most visible opponent of the ERA, a CONSTITUTIONAL AMENDMENT that she predicted would undermine the traditional family and actually diminish the rights of U.S. women.

The ERA stated, "Equality of rights under the law shall not be denied or abridged by the United States or by any State on account of sex." After passing Congress, the amendment

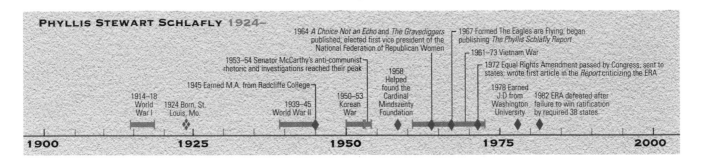

PHYLLIS STEWART SCHLAFLY 1924–

1964 *A Choice Not an Echo* and *The Gravediggers* published; elected first vice president of the National Federation of Republican Women

1967 Formed The Eagles are Flying; began publishing *The Phyllis Schlafly Report*

1953–54 Senator McCarthy's anti-communist rhetoric and investigations reached their peak

1961–73 Vietnam War

1972 Equal Rights Amendment passed by Congress; sent to states; wrote first article in the *Report* criticizing the ERA

1958 Helped found the Cardinal Mindszenty Foundation

1945 Earned M.A. from Radcliffe College

1978 Earned J.D from Washington University

1914–18 World War I

1924 Born, St. Louis, Mo.

1939–45 World War II

1950–53 Korean War

1982 ERA defeated after failure to win ratification by required 38 states

1900   1925   1950   1975   2000

was sent to the fifty states on March 22, 1972, for ratification. To become law, the amendment needed to be passed by thirty-eight states within seven years. By 1973, thirty states had already ratified the ERA. However, as momentum for Schlafly's anti-ERA campaign grew, the ratification process slowed. Only four states approved the ERA in 1974 and 1975, and it became unlikely that pro-ERA forces could persuade four more states to ratify it. In 1977, Indiana became the last state to ratify the amendment. Despite a congressional reprieve in July 1978 that extended the ratification deadline to June 30, 1982, the ERA failed.

Schlafly was born August 15, 1924, in St. Louis, to Odile Dodge Stewart and John Bruce Stewart. She excelled academically at her parochial school, Academy of the Sacred Heart. After graduating as class valedictorian in 1941, she enrolled at Maryville College of the Sacred Heart. As a junior, she transferred to Washington University, in St. Louis, where she graduated Phi Beta Kappa in 1944. After receiving a scholarship, Schlafly earned a master's degree in political science from Radcliffe College in 1945. In 1978 she returned to Washington University and earned a law degree.

For about a year after receiving her master's degree, Schlafly worked in Washington, D.C., as a researcher for several members of Congress. Returning to St. Louis in 1946, she became an aide and campaign worker for a Republican representative and then a librarian and researcher for a bank.

In 1949 she married Fred Schlafly, also a lawyer. After moving to Alton, Illinois, Schlafly and her husband became involved in anti-Communist activities. Schlafly was a researcher for Senator JOSEPH R. MCCARTHY during the 1950s and helped found the Cardinal Mindszenty Foundation, an organization opposed to COMMUNISM.

Schlafly supported Republican BARRY M. GOLDWATER's presidential campaign in 1964. Her first book, *A Choice Not an Echo*, was written in 1964 specifically for the Goldwater

"VIRTUOUS WOMEN ARE SELDOM ACCOSTED BY UNWELCOME SEXUAL PROPOSITIONS . . . OBSCENE TALK OR PROFANE LANGUAGE."

campaign. In 1964 Schlafly published *The Gravediggers*, a book accusing key figures in the administration of President LYNDON B. JOHNSON with deliberately undermining the United States' military strength and leaving the country vulnerable to Communist aggression. Schlafly is the author of several other books on political topics.

While raising six children, Schlafly kept her hand in community activities and Republican politics. Schlafly's interest in public policy and government affairs prompted her to run for Congress three times: once in 1952 as the GOP candidate from the Twenty-fourth District of Illinois, once in 1960 as a write-in candidate, and once in 1970 as the endorsed candidate of Chicago insurance mogul W. Clement Stone. All three campaigns were unsuccessful.

Schlafly had more luck in her successful 1964 bid to be elected the first vice president of the National Federation of Republican Women. Her victory came at a time when Goldwater Republicans dominated the party. Usually, the first vice president of the federation automatically advanced to president, but in 1967, Schlafly was opposed by a more moderate candidate who ultimately defeated her. In the wake of her loss, Schlafly formed a separatist group called The Eagles Are Flying. Bolstered by a core of conservative supporters, she began publishing the *Phyllis Schlafly Report*, a newsletter assessing current political issues and candidates. In a 1972 issue of the *Report*, Schlafly wrote the first of many articles criticizing the ERA. As her personal opposition to the amendment grew, Schlafly formed StopERA and the Eagle Forum, organizations supported by conservative U.S. citizens, fundamental religious groups, and factions of the John Birch Society.

Schlafly argued that ratification of the ERA would lead to compulsory military service for all mothers, unisex toilets in public places, automatic fifty percent financial responsibility for all wives, and homosexual marriages.

Since the defeat of the ERA, Schlafly has remained active with the Eagle Forum and other conservative causes, including the anti-abortion movement.

See also REPUBLICAN PARTY; WOMEN'S RIGHTS.

SCHLESINGER, RUDOLF B. Legal scholar, author, and professor, Rudolf B. Schlesinger achieved fame for his groundbreaking work in the study of international legal systems. Schlesinger was known as the dean of comparative law, a discipline that examines the differences and similarities among the legal systems of nations. His arrival in the field during the early 1950s helped to give it both greater legitimacy and popularity in legal academia. *Comparative Law: Cases-Texts-Materials* (1950), written while Schlesinger taught at Cornell University, became a staple of law school curricula that entered its fifth edition in the late 1990s. He also wrote important studies of civil procedure and international business transactions and directed a ten-year international research project on contracts.

Born in Munich, Germany, in 1909, Schlesinger fled Nazism before World War II to live in the United States. He already had earned his degree in law from the University of Munich in 1933. He developed a background in finance while working in a Munich bank where he helped German Jews transfer their assets out of the country in order to escape persecution. In 1938, with the Nazi party gaining strength, Schlesinger emigrated and promptly enrolled at Columbia Law School, earning his degree in 1942. He briefly practiced financial law, was a professor at Cornell from 1948 to 1975, and upon retirement from Cornell joined the faculty of the Hastings College of Law at the University of California.

Schlesinger had an enormous impact on U.S. and European legal studies. Foremost was his pioneering 1950 book on comparative law, which ultimately influenced two generations of readers. In 1955, working on behalf of the New York Law Revision Commission, he examined the important question of whether to codify commercial law. His study, *Problems of Codification of Commercial Law* (1955), anticipated the

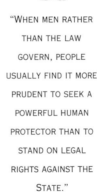

"WHEN MEN RATHER THAN THE LAW GOVERN, PEOPLE USUALLY FIND IT MORE PRUDENT TO SEEK A POWERFUL HUMAN PROTECTOR THAN TO STAND ON LEGAL RIGHTS AGAINST THE STATE."

subsequent development of the UNIFORM COMMERCIAL CODE. In 1995 the *American Journal of Comparative Law* published a tribute to Schlesinger that praised the brilliance of his "heroic work" and noted that its influence went beyond U.S. law: "Today's serious efforts to find and develop a unitary European private law is, consciously or unconsciously, a continuation of Schlesinger's effort."

Schlesinger and his wife, Ruth Hirschland Schlesinger, both died on November 10, 1996, in San Francisco.

SCHOOL DESEGREGATION The attempt to end the practice of separating children of different races into distinct public schools.

Beginning with the landmark Supreme Court case of *Brown v. Board of Education*, 347 U.S. 483, 74 S. Ct. 686, 98 L. Ed. 873 (1954), the United States' legal system has sought to address the problem of racial segregation, or separation, in public schools. In *Brown*, a unanimous Supreme Court found that segregating children of different races in distinct schools violates the Equal Protection Clause of the FOURTEENTH AMENDMENT, which guarantees that "[n]o state shall . . . deny to any person . . . the equal protection of the laws" (§ 1). In writing the Court's opinion, Chief Justice EARL WARREN stressed the crucial role education plays in socializing children, and he maintained that racial segregation "generates a feeling of inferiority" in children that will limit their opportunities in life. A related decision, *Brown v. Board of Education*, 349 U.S. 294, 75 S. Ct. 753, 99 L. Ed. 1083 (1955), (*Brown II*), empowered lower courts to supervise desegregation in local school districts and held that desegregation must proceed "with all deliberate speed."

A number of Supreme Court decisions in the decades since *Brown* have further defined the constitutional claims regarding desegregation first set forth in *Brown*. In many cases, these decisions have resulted in court-imposed desegregation plans, sometimes involving controversial provisions for busing students to schools outside of their immediate neighborhood. De-

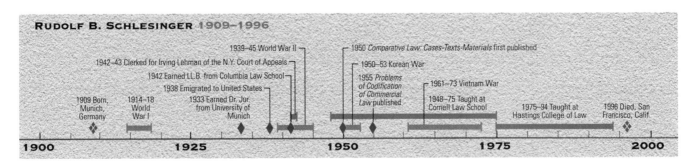

RUDOLF B. SCHLESINGER 1909–1996

1909 Born, Munich, Germany

1914–18 World War I

1933 Earned Dr. Jur. from University of Munich

1938 Emigrated to United States

1942 Earned LL.B. from Columbia Law School

1942–43 Clerked for Irving Lehman of the N.Y. Court of Appeals

1939–45 World War II

1950 *Comparative Law: Cases-Texts-Materials* first published

1950–53 Korean War

1955 *Problems of Codification of Commercial Law* published

1948–75 Taught at Cornell Law School

1961–73 Vietnam War

1975–94 Taught at Hastings College of Law

1996 Died, San Francisco, Calif.

1900   1925   1950   1975   2000

spite such judicial actions, desegregation in the United States has achieved mixed success. Although many more children attend school with children of other races now than in 1954, in numerous cities, racial segregation in education remains as high as ever. Faced with the challenges of shifting populations, segregated housing patterns, impatient courts, and the stubborn persistence of racism, comprehensive school desegregation—long a hoped-for remedy to past discrimination against African Americans—remains an elusive goal.

1954–1970: School Desegregation after Brown *Brown* and *Brown II* inspired a great deal of hope that the races would soon be joined in public schools and that the United States would take a giant step toward healing the racial animosities of its past. THURGOOD MARSHALL, an African American who led the NATIONAL ASSOCIATION FOR THE ADVANCEMENT OF COLORED PEOPLE's Legal Defense Fund in its challenge to school segregation in *Brown* and later became a justice of the Supreme Court, predicted that after *Brown*, schools would be completely desegregated within six months.

Marshall's statement proved to be wildly optimistic. By 1964, ten years after *Brown*, a Department of Health, Education, and Welfare (HEW) study indicated that only 2.4 percent of African Americans in the South were attending largely white schools. Such statistics indicated that *Brown* had led to only token INTEGRATION. By the mid-1960s, many observers felt that the Supreme Court, and the United States as a whole, had lost an opportunity to more quickly

create a desegregated society. DE FACTO segregation (segregation in fact or actuality)—as opposed to DE JURE segregation (segregation by law)—remained a stubborn reality, and racism remained its leading cause. Whites who did not want their children attending school with children of another race found many ways to avoid desegregation, from gerrymandering school boundaries (adjusting school boundaries to their advantage) to manipulating school transportation and construction policies. And in a phenomenon dubbed white flight, many transferred their children to private schools or simply moved to suburbs where few, if any, nonwhites lived.

Congress joined the Supreme Court in its efforts to assist desegregation, by passing the CIVIL RIGHTS ACT of 1964 (28 U.S.C.A. § 1447, 42 U.S.C.A. §§ 1971, 1975a to 1975d, 2000a to 2000h-6). Among its many features, the act authorized HEW to create specific guidelines with which to measure the progress of school desegregation. In 1966, for example, these guidelines called for specific levels of integration: 16 to 18 percent of African American children in all school districts must be attending predominantly white schools. The act also allowed HEW to cut off federal funding to school districts that did not meet integration guidelines. However, this punishment proved difficult to use as a means of enforcement.

In the mid-1960s, a judge on the Fifth Circuit Court of Appeals, JOHN MINOR WISDOM, issued a number of influential opinions that strengthened the cause of racial integration of

Little Rock, Arkansas, 1957. Little Rock Central High School is opened to students of all races for the first time. When the Arkansas National Guard refused to let nine black students enter the school, the U.S. Army was summoned to ensure the students' safety.

MICHAEL NEWMAN/PHOTOEDIT

schools. Wisdom's rulings established that it was not enough simply to end segregation; instead, school districts must actively implement desegregation. In one of these cases, *United States v. Jefferson Board of Education*, 372 F.2d 836 (5th Cir. 1966), he wrote, "[T]he only adequate redress for a previously overt system-wide policy of segregation directed against Negroes as a collective entity is a system-wide policy of integration." Wisdom's ruling also detailed measures that the school district must take toward the goal of integration, including deciding how children were to be informed of the schools available to them for attendance, where new schools must be constructed, where transportation routes must run, and how faculty and staff were to be hired and assigned.

In 1968, the Supreme Court again addressed the issue of school desegregation, in *Green v. County School Board*, 391 U.S. 430, 88 S. Ct. 1689, 20 L. Ed. 2d 716, which dealt with the schools of New Kent County, a rural area in eastern Virginia. In its opinion, the Court acknowledged that the integration guidelines set forth in *Brown II* had not produced adequate results. School districts such as those of New Kent County—where in 1967, 85 percent of black children still attended an all-black school—had avoided meaningful integration. It was not enough, the Court argued, to simply end segregation and allow a "freedom-of-choice" plan—by which African American children supposedly had the freedom to attend predominantly white schools—to be the only means of combining the races in an educational setting. In comments during Court hearings on the case, Chief Justice Warren noted that though the "fence" of outright segregation had been taken down, socially constructed "booby traps" still prevented most children from attending integrated schools.

Green also introduced two concepts—dual school systems and unitary school systems—that remain a part of the school desegregation debate. A dual school system is a segregated school system. In other words, it consists of separate segments—one black, the other white—existing side by side but with widely different educational conditions and outcomes. The Court in *Green* identified six indicators of a dual system: racial separation of students, faculty, staff, transportation, extracurricular activities, and facilities. A unitary school system, on the other hand, is racially integrated at every level. In a later ruling, *Alexander v. Holmes County Board of Education*, 396 U.S. 19, 90 S. Ct. 29, 24 L. Ed. 2d 19 (1969), the Court described a unitary system as one "within which no per-

son is to be effectively excluded from any school because of race or color."

Even more important, in its opinion in *Green*, the Court held that New Kent County would be expected to immediately begin remedying the lasting effects of segregation. "The burden on a school board today," the Court said, "is to come forward with a plan that promises realistically to work, and promises realistically to work *now*" (*Green*). Thus, the Court abandoned its previous position that school desegregation must proceed "with all deliberate speed" in favor of a call for immediate and prompt action.

The Court also held that the Fourteenth Amendment required action to remedy past racial discrimination—or what has come to be called AFFIRMATIVE ACTION. It found an "affirmative duty to take whatever steps might be necessary to convert to a unitary system in which racial discrimination would be eliminated root and branch" (*Green*). Moreover, school boards would have to provide meaningful statistical evidence that their school district was moving toward the goal of integration.

In a footnote to its opinion, the Court advanced suggestions for achieving school desegregation, including combining all children in a particular age range, white and black, into the same building.

Green and subsequent judicial decisions through 1970 caused a remarkable change in school desegregation. By 1971, HEW statistics indicated that the South had become the most racially integrated region in the United States. HEW estimated that 44 percent of African American students attended majority white schools in the South, as opposed to 28 percent in the North and West. In many communities, however, these changes resulted in white flight. In Mississippi, for example, white public school enrollment dropped between 25 and 100 percent in the thirty school districts with the highest black enrollment.

The 1970s: Swann and Busing In *Swann v. Charlotte-Mecklenburg Board of Education*, 402 U.S. 1, 91 S. Ct. 1267, 28 L. Ed. 2d 554 (1971), the focus of school desegregation shifted from largely rural school districts to urban ones, a change of scene that offered new challenges to desegregation. In the rural South before the *Brown* decision, blacks and whites lived largely in the same communities or areas, and requiring that their children attend the same neighborhood schools could resolve segregation. In urban settings, however, blacks and whites lived in different neighborhoods, so combining the two races in the same schools

THE BUSING DEBATE

Busing is a plan for promoting school desegregation, by which minority students are transported to largely white schools and white students are brought to largely minority schools. It is intended to safeguard the civil rights of students and to provide equal opportunity in public education. Busing is also an example of affirmative action—that is, the attempt to undo or compensate for the effects of past discrimination. Such action is sometimes called compensatory justice.

Busing was first enacted as part of school desegregation programs in response to federal court decisions establishing that racial segregation of public schools violates the Equal Protection Clause of the Fourteenth Amendment to the Constitution. In *Green v. County School Board*, 391 U.S. 430, 88 S. Ct. 1689, 20 L. Ed. 2d 716 (1968), and *Swann v. Charlotte-Mecklenburg Board of Education*, 402 U.S. 1, 91 S. Ct. 1267, 28 L. Ed. 2d 554 (1971), the Supreme Court established that federal courts could require school districts to implement busing programs as a means of achieving racial integration of public schools.

However, busing was nothing new in U.S. education. Even before these decisions, nearly 40 percent of the nation's schoolchildren were bused to school. And before 1954, when the Court declared racial segregation in public schools unconstitutional in *Brown v. Board of Education*, 347 U.S. 483, 74 S. Ct. 686, 98 L. Ed. 873, children were often bused to segregated schools that were beyond walking distance from their homes.

With the Supreme Court decisions in *Green* and *Swann*, busing became one of the most controversial topics in U.S. law and politics, particularly in the 1970s. Although the zeal for busing as a

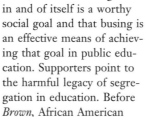

IN FOCUS

remedy for past racial injustice had waned greatly by the 1990s, busing remained a feature—if many times a limited one—of most school desegregation programs and continued to inspire heated debate.

Those who are in favor of busing claim, as did the Supreme Court in *Green* and *Swann*, that racial integration in and of itself is a worthy social goal and that busing is an effective means of achieving that goal in public education. Supporters point to the harmful legacy of segregation in education. Before *Brown*, African American children were schooled in separate facilities that were usually inferior to the facilities used by whites, despite official claims that they were equal. Such segregation often kept African Americans at a disadvantage in relation to whites. It instilled feelings of inferiority in African American children and seriously diminished their educational achievement and opportunities.

Supporters of busing also often claim that de facto (actual) segregation exists even decades after the civil rights movement and the striking down of racial segregation laws, which occurred in the 1960s. A largely white, wealthy upper class and a largely minority, poor underclass, they argue, are transported, employed, housed, and educated in different settings. Often wealthy people live in the suburbs, and the poor live in the cities. Growing up in their separate neighborhoods, children from higher socioeconomic levels thus have many advantages that poorer children do not: more space at home, better nutrition and health care, greater cultural and intellectual stimulation, and friends and acquaintances with higher social status providing better job and career prospects. Some even compare the isolation

of impoverished minorities in the United States' inner cities with that of impoverished blacks under South Africa's former apartheid system.

Advocates of desegregation through busing assert that these existing inequalities must not become greater and that desegregation in education will go a long way toward ending them and creating a more just society. They also point out that U.S. education has historically worked to ensure a society in which class hierarchy is minimized and social mobility—both upward and downward—is maximized. Busing, they argue, will therefore help avoid the creation of a permanent underclass in the United States.

Supporters of busing also maintain that it is an affordable way to achieve school desegregation. While admitting that the initial start-up costs of a busing program can be large, they point to statistics that indicate the operating costs of compulsory busing are generally less than five percent of a school district's entire budget.

Those who oppose busing make a variety of different points against it, although they do not necessarily oppose integration itself. Opponents claim that busing serves as a distraction from more important educational goals such as quality of instruction. Busing, they hold, too easily becomes a case of form over substance, in which the form of racial integration of education becomes of greater value than the substance of what is actually taught in schools. Critics of busing would rather focus on the environment in a school and in its classrooms than on achieving a particular number of each race in a school. Justice Lewis F. Powell, Jr., echoed these sentiments in an opinion to a school desegregation case, *Keyes v. Denver School District*, 413 U.S. 189, 93 S. Ct. 2686, 37 L. Ed. 2d 548 (1973). In *Keyes*, he wrote that in an era of declining student achievement, it is wrong to turn the attention of communities "from the paramount goal of quality in education to a perennially divisive debate over who is to be transported where."

Critics also claim that busing causes white flight—where whites move their children from integrated public schools to private and suburban schools that are largely white—and an even greater disparity between white and black, rich and poor. According to this scenario, busing only exacerbates the current situation, making public schools and cities even more the exclusive province of the poor.

Some noted experts on the issue of busing have concluded that although they favor a society that is racially integrated, the social costs of busing and the resulting white flight are too high. Others have sought a middle ground on the issue by arguing that judges should choose carefully the districts in which they decide to implement busing. For example, they claim that white flight is more likely to occur in communities and schools where whites form a small minority, and that as a result, busing has higher social costs in such districts.

Another prominent complaint in antibusing opinion is that court-ordered busing programs represent an abuse of judicial power. According to this view, busing is an example of undesirable judicial activism. The large-scale social changes caused by transporting thousands of children many miles each day should be imposed only by an elected body of representatives such as a state legislature or Congress. Moreover, adherents of this view argue that supervising school desegregation programs only bogs down the courts and takes time away from other pressing legal matters.

Critics of busing also point out that many times, the same court that requires busing does not provide guidance as to funding it, thereby creating financial headaches for school districts. Related to this issue is the claim that bus-

ing is too costly, especially when school districts are forced to purchase new buses in order to start a busing program. In financially strapped school districts, spending on busing sometimes takes away funding for other educational priorities.

Some of those who oppose busing favor racial desegregation but do not view busing as a good way to achieve that goal. Instead, they support a gradualist approach to social reform. According to the gradualist view, it will take generations to achieve the goal of racial desegregation in education and in society as a whole. Busing only interferes with the overall goal of integration, because of the sudden and disruptive changes—including white flight—that it imposes on society.

Others oppose busing on the ground that neighborhood schools are the best way to educate children. In this camp are both those in favor of racial integration in education and those against it. Neighborhood schools, it is argued, allow parents to have a greater influence on their child's education by making it easier, for example, to visit the school and speak with a teacher. Such schools also give children a sense of identity and instill pride in their community. Busing children to a school across town, they argue, will not inspire pride in their school. Advocates of neighborhood schools also point to statistics that indicate that bused students are more alienated from their school and thus experience greater problems, including poorer academic performance and increased delinquency.

An even more fundamental question related to busing is whether racial integration is in itself a valuable goal for public schools. Those who take opposite sides on this question marshal different sociological evidence. In the 1950s and 1960s the Supreme Court was influenced by the "contact" theory of racial integration. According to this theory, the better one knew those of another race, the more one would get

along with them. Sociologists reasoned, therefore, that integrated schools would increase understanding between the races and lower racial tensions.

In the same years, many studies claimed to show that racial integration would boost the self-esteem, academic achievement, and ultimately opportunities and choices of members of minorities. For example, a well-known report issued by sociologist James S. Coleman in 1966, *Equality of Educational Opportunity*, concluded that minority children improve their academic performance when they attend classes where middle-class white pupils are the majority. Coleman's report also claimed that the most important indicator of the academic performance of minority and lower-class students is the educational level of their classmates. The report was seized upon by many as a reason to institute court-imposed busing plans for school districts.

By the 1970s and later, other sociologists challenged the liberal theories that school desegregation would lead to greater racial harmony and improved academic performance by African Americans. Coleman, too, became more skeptical about busing and argued that voluntary programs were more effective than government-imposed plans in achieving school desegregation. Others went so far as to claim that integration only increases hostility and tensions between the races. African American students who are bused, they argued, experience a decline in their educational achievement in school. Some studies have in fact shown that students who are bused grow more rather than less hostile toward the other race or races. In addition, some studies have indicated that in many schools where the desired percentages of races have been achieved through busing, students interact largely with those of their own race and thus segregation *within* the school prevents true desegregation.

meant transporting children, usually by bus, to institutions that were often far from their homes.

In *Swann*, the Court took the final step toward making busing a part of school desegregation plans, by giving the lower courts power to impose it as a means for achieving integration. *Swann* involved the Charlotte-Mecklenburg School District, in North Carolina, a district in which African Americans made up 29 percent of the student body. After the Supreme Court's decision in *Green*, a federal district judge ruled that the school district had not achieved adequate levels of integration: 14,000 of the 24,000 African American students still attended schools that were all black, and most of the 24,000 did not have any white teachers. The judge called for the adoption of a desegregation plan that involved busing 13,300 additional children at an initial start-up cost of over $1 million.

The Supreme Court upheld the district court's plans. Just as in *Brown II*, it gave school authorities and district judges primary responsibility for school desegregation. This time, however, the Court provided more guidance. To create desegregated schools, it encouraged faculty reassignment; the redrawing of school attendance zones; and an optional, publicly funded transfer program for minority students. Most important, the Court recommended mandatory busing to achieve desegregation. It did note that busing could be excessive when it involved especially great distances. It also hinted at an end to court-imposed desegregation plans, saying, "Neither school authorities nor district courts are constitutionally required to make year-by-year adjustments of the racial composition of student bodies" (*Brown II*). In Court decisions decades later, these words would be cited in support of ending court-supervised school desegregation programs.

As a result of *Swann*, throughout the 1970s, courts ordered busing to achieve desegregation in many city school districts, including Boston, Cleveland, Indianapolis, and Los Angeles. However, *Swann* was one of the last desegregation opinions in which all nine justices were in complete agreement. The Court's unanimity on the issue of school desegregation, which had been the rule in every decision since *Brown*, broke down in the next major case, *Milliken v. Bradley*, 418 U.S. 717, 94 S. Ct. 3112, 41 L. Ed. 2d 1069 (1974).

Milliken shifted the scene of school desegregation from the South to the North—specifically, to Detroit. In *Milliken*, the Supreme Court addressed the issue of whether courts could bus suburban pupils to desegregate inner-city schools. The case dealt with federal district judge Stephen Roth's decision to join the Detroit School District with fifty-three of the city's eighty-five outlying suburbs in a desegregation decree. The proposed plan would have created a metropolitan school district with 780,000 students, of which 310,000 would be bused daily to achieve desegregation goals. The shocked white community, much like others in the South, and its elected representatives denounced the plan.

Detroit reflected the situation of many U.S. cities. Although African Americans made up only 23 percent of the city's population in 1970, they constituted 61 percent of its school-age population. Whites were underrepresented in the inner-city public schools for various reasons. Young white married couples, who constituted the demographic group most likely to have school-age children, were also the most likely to move to the suburbs. The whites who did live in the cities tended to be older people, singles, and childless couples. Urban whites who did have school-age children often sent them to private schools.

Such a situation caused Judge Roth to ask the question, "How do you desegregate a black city, or a black school system?" (*Milliken*). Busing within city limits alone would still leave many schools 75 to 90 percent black. The only solution was one that took into consideration the entire metropolitan area of Detroit by joining the city school district with the surrounding suburban school districts.

In support of this position, Judge Roth argued that a variety of causes had led to the concentration of blacks in ghettos. Governments, he wrote in his opinion, "at all levels, federal, state and local, have combined, with . . . private organizations, such as loaning institutions and real estate associations and brokerage firms, to establish . . . residential segregation throughout the Detroit metropolitan area" (*Bradley*). Residential segregation had resulted from a whole variety of types of discrimination that caused African Americans and members of other minorities to live in segregated neighborhoods and, as a result, attend segregated schools. Thus, Roth framed his metropolitan school desegregation plan as a remedy for past discriminatory conduct.

Judge Roth's plan promised to promote class as well as racial interaction, complicating still further the issue of desegregation. Mixing of the different classes of U.S. society became as much a goal of desegregation decrees as did mixing of different races. Such a plan, its proponents argued, might also remedy the funding inequities between different school districts and even end white flight.

In 1974, by a vote of 5–4, the Supreme Court ruled in *Milliken* that Judge Roth had wrongly included the suburbs with the city in his desegregation decree. The district court's plan, the Court held, could only be justified if de jure segregation existed in outlying suburbs; remedies to past discriminatory conduct must be limited to Detroit, since it was the only district that had such policies. Disagreeing with Roth, the Court also held that state housing practices were not relevant to the case. Writing the Court's opinion, Chief Justice WARREN E. BURGER argued for local control of school districts, over court control: "No single tradition in public education is more deeply rooted than local control over the operation of schools; local autonomy has long been thought essential both to the maintenance of community concern and support for public schools and to the quality of the educational process."

Many saw the *Milliken* decision as the first Supreme Court defeat for the cause of school desegregation. Some, including Justice Marshall, the first African American to sit on the Court, interpreted *Milliken* as an abandonment of the cause of racial justice. "Today's holding, . . ." Marshall wrote in his dissenting opinion, "is more a reflection of a perceived public mood that we have gone far enough in enforcing the Constitution's guarantee of equal justice than it is the product of neutral principles of law." Supporters of the decision, on the other hand, pointed to the myriad potential problems a plan like Roth's might impose, including greater bureaucratic red tape, more white flight, and even greater racial tensions.

The 1980s and After In the 1980s, the attitude of the public and of the courts toward activist school desegregation programs—and toward other forms of affirmative action, for that matter—became more skeptical and sometimes even hostile. Courts began to require that busing, for example, be used as a remedy only in school districts where there had been "deliberate" or "intentional" segregation. A large busing program that had been begun in Los Angeles in 1978 was ended in 1981 through a statewide referendum that banned compulsory busing except in districts where there had been deliberate segregation. By the late 1980s and 1990s, the Supreme Court, now having the influence of more conservative justices appointed by Republican presidents RONALD REAGAN and GEORGE BUSH, established that court-ordered desegregation decrees, including

Percentage of Blacks in White Majority Schools

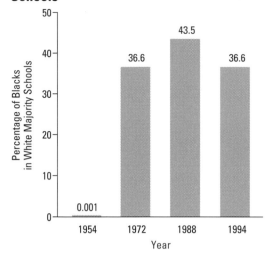

Source: U.S. Department of Education

busing plans, could end short of specific statistical goals of integration when everything "practicable" had been done to eliminate the vestiges of past discrimination.

Two court decisions in the early 1990s— *Board of Education v. Dowell*, 498 U.S. 237, 111 S. Ct. 630, 112 L. Ed. 2d 715 (1991), which dealt with the Oklahoma City School District, and *Freeman v. Pitts*, 503 U.S. 467, 112 S. Ct. 1430, 118 L. Ed. 2d 108 (1992), which covered the schools of DeKalb County, Georgia— addressed the manner in which court supervi-

Percentage of Students by Race and Ethnicity Who Attended a U.S. Public School with More Than 50% Minority Enrollment in 1991

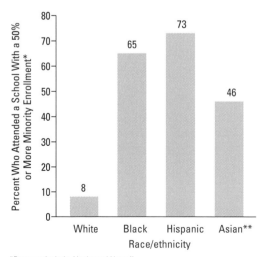

*Does not include Alaska and Hawaii.
**Percent of Asians would be higher if Hawaii were included.

Source: U.S. Department of Education.

AP/WIDE WORLD PHOTOS

Despite the courts'—and the public's—more conservative approach to school desegregation from the 1980s onward, increasing numbers of minority children in many communities are making for more racially diverse classrooms.

sion of school districts and their desegregation programs may end. In *Freeman*, the Court identified three factors that may be used in such determinations: (1) whether the school system has complied with the desegregation decree's provisions, (2) whether continued judicial control is necessary or practicable to achieve compliance with any aspect of the decree, and (3) whether the school system has demonstrated to the once-disfavored race its GOOD FAITH commitment to the whole of the decree. Ultimately, the school system must be held to have engaged in a good faith effort to comply with any judicially supervised desegregation program, and to have eliminated to the extent practicable any vestiges of discrimination. *Freeman* also established that courts may end desegregation decrees in incremental stages, gradually returning administrative functions and decisions to local authorities.

In another case—*Missouri v. Jenkins*, 515 U.S. 70, 115 S. Ct. 2038, 132 L. Ed. 2d 63 (1995), which dealt with the Kansas City (Missouri) School District—the Court stopped just short of ending judicial supervision of desegregation programs. However, the decision did strike down two requirements imposed by a district court on the state of Missouri, declaring them outside that court's authority. Those two requirements would have attempted to improve the "desegregative attractiveness"—in this case, the ability to attract white students from the suburban school districts—of the school district by requiring the state to fund salary increases for all staff in the school district, as well as "quality education" programs, including magnet schools. Such "interdistrict" remedies, the Court held, are beyond the scope of the district court. The Court, citing *Milliken*, disagreed with the contention that white flight justifies an

interdistrict remedy to segregation. The Court also rejected student test scores as evidence for determining whether a school district has adequately responded to judicial desegregation decrees.

Those who support these decisions see them as returning to local authorities their proper control over their schools. They also see these decisions as guiding the courts back to a more proper and limited social role. The courts, they argue, should not be engaged in programs of "social engineering." Others, both black and white, have simply abandoned desegregation as a goal and instead focus on improving neighborhood schools, even when those schools remain largely segregated.

Critics of these decisions have seen them as a step backward for the CIVIL RIGHTS of minorities in the United States. Such decisions, they argue, merely perpetuate racism by returning school districts to those who often do not share the goal of creating racially integrated public schools. Others have argued that the changing pattern in the judicial response to desegregation has been caused by the legal system's exhaustion and impatience in the face of complex and protracted desegregation plans. Accustomed to seeing more rapid results, district courts, according to this argument, have been eager to return the control of school districts to local authorities.

Others have argued that the Supreme Court decisions on school desegregation have ignored the effect of discriminatory housing patterns. They maintain that without a change in segregated housing patterns, desegregation, whether in schools or in the larger society, cannot be achieved. They claim that by ignoring housing as an issue, the Supreme Court enabled white America to escape its responsibilities in creating the urban ghetto.

Still others argue that school desegregation can yet be achieved through the court system, maintaining that social change of the kind required for true desegregation will take many years. In the mid-1990s, organizations such as the AMERICAN CIVIL LIBERTIES UNION began to focus on making the case for school desegregation on the state rather than federal level. Some state constitutions, they pointed out, contain language more conducive to their cause. Connecticut's constitution, for example, declares that no person "shall . . . be subjected to segregation" (Conn. Const. art. 1, § 20), and Minnesota's requires that all students be given an adequate education.

School desegregation has not been the panacea that it was claimed to be in the heady days of *Brown*. Though significant success in integration has been achieved, there is little evidence that comprehensive school desegregation will come any time soon, and some fear that there may be no adequate answer to the question of how to desegregate schools in a way that is fair to all races.

CROSS-REFERENCES

Brown v. Board of Education of Topeka, Kansas; Civil Rights Movement; Equal Protection; Schools and School Districts.

SCHOOL PRAYER See ENGEL V. VITALE; RELIGION.

SCHOOLS AND SCHOOL DISTRICTS

School districts are quasi-municipal CORPORATIONS created and organized by state legislatures and charged with the administration of public schools within the state. A quasi-municipal corporation is a political body created for the sole purpose of performing one public function. States divide up their school systems into districts because localized administration and policy making are more efficient and more responsive to community needs than one state-level bureaucracy.

A school district encompasses a specific geographical area with defined boundaries. In most areas, the head of the school district is called the superintendent. Each school district contains at least one school. Typically, a school district includes primary schools, also called grade schools, middle or junior high schools, and high schools. A school district's boundaries may be the same as the boundaries of a city. Multiple school districts may exist within larger cities, and in rural areas, a school district may encompass several towns.

Each state has numerous laws pertaining to public schools and school districts, but state statutes do not cover every educational concern. State legislatures delegate many aspects of public education to school districts. School districts have the power to fashion curricula and make rules and regulations that apply to the schools, school employees, and students within the district. School districts also have power over such matters as arranging for the construction and maintenance of educational buildings and facilities in the district. School districts may, in turn, delegate some of their powers to individual schools.

State and federal revenues pay for only about half of all educational costs. The rest of the burden for construction, maintenance, and improvement of school facilities, salaries, and other educational costs is borne by local government. Most states give school districts the power to levy local taxes for educational purposes. This taxing power is limited by the state legislature. If a school district wants to raise taxes beyond what the legislature allows, it may seek approval from the voters in the district in a REFERENDUM or proposition vote.

Most state legislatures require that school districts be governed by a school board, board of education, or similar body. School boards govern the school district's actions and can also take action on their own. School boards appoint superintendents, review important decisions made by the district's administrators, and fashion educational policies for the district. Most school boards are comprised of several members elected by voters who live within the boundaries of the district. In some states, school board members may be appointed by a state or local governing body or a designated government official.

School boards hold regular meetings that are open to the public. A school board must give NOTICE to the public prior to the meeting. Notice generally is given through mailings or by publishing the time and place of the meeting in local newspapers. School board meetings give the public an opportunity to express opinions on educational policy.

State statutes set forth minimum qualifications for public school teachers. Most states require full-time teachers to have a four-year degree from a college or university and to have completed a student teaching program. States may add other prerequisites, such as physical

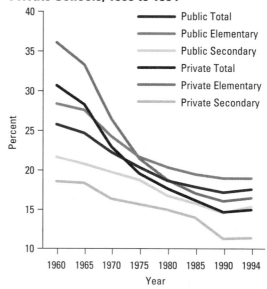

Pupil-Teacher Ratios for Public and Private Schools, 1960 to 1994

Source: U.S. National Center for Education Statistics, *Digest of Education Statistics.*

PRIVATE SCHOOL VOUCHERS: CHURCH V. STATE

The specifics of school tuition voucher systems vary from program to program, but generally such systems offer parents of schoolchildren a tax-funded voucher that is redeemable at the educational institution of their choice. The vouchers are issued yearly or at some other regular interval, and they pay for a certain amount of tuition fees each year at nonpublic and alternative charter schools. The most controversial programs allow parents to use the publicly funded vouchers to pay tuition at a sectarian, or religious, school.

Private school vouchers implicate at least two provisions in the U.S. Constitution: the Establishment and Free Exercise of Religion Clauses in the First Amendment. According to the U.S. Supreme Court, the Establishment Clause prohibits the federal government and the states from setting up a religious place of worship, passing laws that aid religion, and giving preference to one religion or forcing belief or disbelief in any religion (*Everson v. Board of Education*, 330 U.S. 1, 67 S. Ct. 504, 91 L. Ed. 711 [1947]). Private school vouchers have been challenged under the Establishment Clause because they involve a form of governmental support that may be used for religious-oriented activities.

Critics of private school vouchers charge that taxpayer support for religious schools is a blatant and patent violation of the Establishment Clause. Critics also note that because vouchers do not cover the entire amount of tuition at a private school, the option of private school remains out of reach of the lowest-income students. Opponents of private school vouchers further claim that vouchers rob public schools of funds because funding is based in part on student enrollment. Finally, critics maintain that vouchers implicate other constitutional provisions, such as the Equal Protection Clause of the Fourteenth Amendment, because they provide taxpayer funds to institutions that may discriminate on the basis of race,

religion, disability, or socioeconomic status.

Supporters of private school vouchers argue that voucher systems are actually protected by the First Amendment. According to advocates, the First Amendment, with its guarantee of the free exercise of religion, protects vouchers because they give devoutly religious parents the same rights as less devout parents: public funding for the education of their children. In this view educational systems without private school vouchers violate the First Amendment by discouraging religion and placing devout parents at a disadvantage. Supporters contend that vouchers merely provide some balance of rights between devoutly religious parents and less devout or nonreligious parents.

Other supporters of private school vouchers focus on the aspect of choice. Whereas public schools are increasingly perceived as inadequate and dangerous, private schools are viewed by many as offering safe, high-quality education. In response to these perceptions, legislators have offered private school vouchers as a means of escape from public schools. Supporters of private school vouchers assert that they offer potential benefits for impoverished children. Under some proposals private school vouchers would give a limited number of low-income families another choice for their children's schooling.

Proponents of private school vouchers cite such intellectual stalwarts as John Stuart Mill, Thomas Paine, and Adam Smith as early advocates of school vouchers. Mill, Paine, and Smith did in fact argue that the fairest and most efficient way to fund public education would be to give parents money that they could spend on tuition at a school of their choice. Detractors counter that these views received no attention until 1955, the year after the Supreme Court outlawed racial segregation in public schools in *Brown v. Board of Education of Topeka*, 347 U.S. 483, 74 S. Ct. 686, 98 L. Ed. 873 (1954). Ac-

cording to many voucher opponents, the real driving force behind private school vouchers is an effort to facilitate the flight of white persons from city schools that have large nonwhite student populations.

Proposals for private school voucher systems have been rejected by courts and defeated at the polls, but voucher advocates have been unrelenting. In 1993, California voters voted two-to-one against legislation that would have created a voucher system, and voucher advocates in that state failed to place a voucher initiative on the ballot in the November 1996 elections. Undeterred, the California Assembly passed a bill in 1996 that would provide state-funded vouchers to students in the worst-performing public schools in the state. In 1997 an Ohio court overturned on First Amendment grounds a Cleveland program that permitted private school vouchers, but that decision was appealed to the Ohio Supreme Court (*Simmons-Harris v. Goff*, 1997 WL 217583 [Ohio App. 10 Dist.]). In Milwaukee, Wisconsin, a state court enjoined a city voucher program. When an action was brought in the Wisconsin Supreme Court to resolve the issue, the justices split over the constitutionality of the program and sent the case back to the lower court undecided (*State ex rel. Thomson v. Jackson*, 546 N.W. 2d 140 [1996]). In some states voucher supporters are finding ways around the rejections. In Texas the state legislature refused to enact a school voucher program, but the city of Houston's Independent School District proposed to contract with private schools to ease overcrowding in its public school system, and this measure was unopposed by the Texas Education Agency.

Despite the setbacks school voucher programs continue to find support among legislators, governors, and state and local education officials. School voucher programs have been proposed in Congress for the District of Columbia and in at least two dozen states, as well as the Commonwealth of Puerto Rico.

and psychological examinations and drug tests. Upon completing all the prerequisites, a teacher may obtain the license or permit necessary to teach in a particular state.

States require public school teachers to complete a probationary period before they receive tenure. In the context of employment, TENURE is a status that carries with it certain rights and protections, the most important of which is the protection from summary dismissal. A teacher who has gained tenure status may not be terminated from a teaching position without the benefit of a lengthy procedure. The termination process may include a detailed account of reasons for the termination, an opportunity for the teacher to correct any problems, a hearing with school district administrators, review and judgment by school district administrators, and, finally, a meeting with the school board, which votes on whether the teacher should be dismissed. Teachers who have not attained tenure have no recourse for a firing. In any case, a public school teacher can only be terminated for cause, or some substantial, articulable reason.

A teaching LICENSE may be revoked if the teacher engages in conduct that demonstrates unfitness to teach. The prohibited conduct varies with different states, school districts, and school boards. A criminal conviction that involves MORAL TURPITUDE, such as a conviction for THEFT, dishonesty, or sexual assault, generally is a valid ground for the revocation of a teaching license.

Schools and school districts have a great deal of control over public school students. Rules and regulations can vary from school to school and range from restrictions on appearance and hair length to prohibitions on electronic transmission devices, or beepers. Schools may not implement unreasonable rules, however. Before a student can be suspended from school for a lengthy time period, the school must give the student notice of the intent to suspend and an opportunity to be heard by school officials. Students may not be forced to pray in school or to pledge allegiance to the U.S. FLAG. Teachers may inflict CORPORAL PUNISHMENT to control, train, or educate a student but may use only such force as is necessary for those purposes. The amount of force that is permissible varies according to the situation, with careful consideration given to the student's age and maturity. A teacher may use more force on an older, physically mature high school student than on a younger, less mature student. Despite the general acceptance by the courts of some measure of corporal punishment, the threat of litigation

Enrollment in Public and Private Schools, 1993–1994

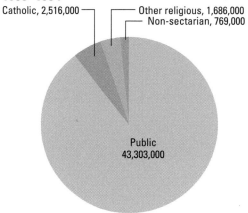

Source: U.S. National Center for Education Statistics, *Digest of Education Statistics.*

makes corporal punishment a potentially risky endeavor.

A school board has power only over the public schools within its school district. Private schools must comply with generally applicable federal, state, and local laws, but they are privately owned and operated and are not obligated to follow the rules and regulations of the school district in which they are located. Private schools are not governed by the U.S. Constitution and state constitutions in the same way that public schools are. Constitutions are designed mainly to protect persons from the actions of government. Public schools are funded by governments and so must answer to constitutions, but private schools are not funded by public monies, so their actions are not deemed governmental in nature.

Public school districts have little involvement with private schools for another reason: the Establishment Clause of the First Amendment. Under the Establishment Clause, Congress may not make any laws respecting the establishment of, or prohibiting the free exercise of, RELIGION. The Establishment Clause has been made applicable to the states by the U.S. Supreme Court, which has interpreted the clause to mean that public schools should be free of religious influences. This does not mean that public schools can have no connection with private schools. In many school districts, public schools share buses and textbooks with private schools, and these arrangements have not been declared unconstitutional.

Excessive entanglement with religion, however, may run afoul of the Establishment Clause. Many states have set up programs that challenge the limits of the Establishment

Charter Schools: The Educational Petri Dish

Most families think that they have only three choices for the education of their school-age children: a sectarian school or other form of private school that charges tuition, a free public school, or home schooling. In many states there is a fourth option: a charter school. Charter schools do not have a religious agenda and are free of cost, but they differ from the typical public school. Although charter schools are governed by the public school district in which they are located, they are free of many of the constraints imposed on other public schools in the district.

Charter schools are created to be innovative and experimental in nature and to serve as models for future changes in ordinary public schools. The classes offered by charter schools may differ in substance from classes in public schools, and the teachers may use new, alternative approaches to education. Charter schools represent an opportunity to experience a form of experimental, alternative schooling that was previously open only to students who could afford alternative private schools or who could be educated at home. Parents also like charter schools because they have a say in the school's administration.

Charter schools usually are run by a board comprised of the teachers in the school and a few of the students' parents. The board makes its own decisions on-site. Unlike other public schools, a charter school does not have to seek approval from the school district or school board before it can take action. To teach English literature, for example, the teachers at a charter school might discard the traditional texts prescribed for other public schools and assign only contemporary poetry. They might even decide that their students should study poetry by attending open poetry readings or by setting up their own regular poetry readings.

The first charter school legislation was passed in Minnesota in 1991 (Minn. Stat. Ann. §§ 120.064, 124.248 [West 1996]). Since 1991 approximately half of the states have enacted some form of charter school legislation. The details vary, but the programs share the basic goal of creating a limited number of schools where teachers may experiment with a variety of learning techniques. The schools have a high degree of independence, but they are all results oriented. Thus, each school must show a state or local governmental education agency that its students are making satisfactory progress. A state may, for example, require that students in charter schools pass a yearly achievement test to prove that they are receiving a well-rounded education.

By virtue of their experimental nature, charter schools are highly individualistic. Some schools focus on a particular area of study, such as computers, the environment, the arts, or aeronautics. A school that emphasizes computers, for instance, will have a large number of personal computers and many teachers who specialize in computer education. Other schools are designed for certain types of students, such as teenage students who have dropped out before earning their high school degree.

Clause. VOUCHER programs are a recent example of education-related legislative experimentation with the Establishment Clause. Under a voucher program, the state provides taxpayer money to parents and guardians of public school students to be used to send the students to religious or private schools. The Supreme Court has yet to rule on the constitutionality of voucher programs, but any decision in the volatile area of the separation of church and state will likely not be the last word on the topic. In 1997, in *Agostini v. Felton*, __U.S.__ , 117 S. Ct. 1997, 138 L. Ed. 2d 391, the Supreme Court reversed its decisions in *Aguilar v. Felton*, 473 U.S. 402, 105 S. Ct. 3232, 87 L. Ed. 2d 290 (1985) and *School District of the City of Grand Rapids v. Ball*, 473 U.S. 373, 105 S. Ct. 3216, 87 L. Ed. 2d 267 (1985), and held that a public school teacher may teach disadvantaged students in a private school classroom if the legislation authorizing such activity contains safeguards that prevent the teacher from advancing religion.

School districts do not have power over sectarian private schools, but they do have authority over home schools. Home schooling is a form of education provided by parents or guardians.

Schools and school districts continually adapt their policies, rules, and regulations to keep pace with societal changes and to meet the needs of students and the community. Curricula, grades, attendance requirements, and age standards vary from district to district and even from school to school.

CROSS-REFERENCES

Abington School District v. Schempp; Brown v. Board of Education of Topeka, Kansas; Civil Rights; Education Law; *Engel v. Vitale;* In Loco Parentis; Integration; School Desegregation.

SCIENTER 📖 [*Latin, Knowingly.*] Guilty knowledge that is sufficient to charge a person with the consequences of his or her acts. 📖

The term *scienter* refers to a state of mind often required to hold a person legally accountable for her acts. The term often is used interchangeably with MENS REA, which describes criminal INTENT, but *scienter* has a broader application because it also describes knowledge required to assign LIABILITY in many civil cases.

Scienter denotes a level of intent on the part of the defendant. In *Ernst and Ernst v. Hochfelder*, 425 U.S. 185, 96 S. Ct. 1375, 47 L. Ed. 2d 668 (1976), the U.S. Supreme Court described *scienter* as "a mental state embracing intent to deceive, manipulate, or defraud." The definition in *Ernst* was fashioned in the context of a financial dispute, but it illustrates the sort of guilty knowledge that constitutes *scienter*.

Scienter is relevant to the PLEADINGS in a case. Plaintiffs and PROSECUTORS alike must include in their pleadings ALLEGATIONS that the defendant acted with some knowledge of wrongdoing or guilt. If a legislative body passes a law that has punitive sanctions or harsh civil sanctions, it normally includes a provision stating that a person must act willfully, knowingly, intentionally, or recklessly, or it provides similar *scienter* requirement. Legislative bodies do not, however, always refer to *scienter* in statutes.

In the *Ernst* case, the investors in a brokerage firm brought suit against an accounting firm after the principal investor committed suicide and left a note revealing that the brokerage firm was a scam. The investors brought suit for DAMAGES against the brokerage firm's accounting firm under sections 10(b) and 10b-5 of the Securities Exchange Act of 1934 (15 U.S.C.A. § 78a et seq.), which makes it unlawful for any person to engage in various financial transgressions, such as employing any device, scheme, or artifice to DEFRAUD, or engaging in any act, practice, or course of business that operates as a fraud or deceit upon any person in connection with the purchase or sale of any security.

Significantly, the Securities Exchange Act does not mention any standard for intent. The courts had to decide whether a party could make a claim under the act against a person without alleging that the person acted intentionally, knowingly, or willfully.

The investors in *Ernst* did not allege that the accounting firm had an intent to defraud the investors. Rather, they alleged only that the accounting firm had been negligent in its accounting and that the NEGLIGENCE constituted a violation of the Securities Exchange Act. The Supreme Court ruled that an allegation of negligent conduct alone is insufficient to prove a violation of the Securities Exchange Act. According to the Court, the language in the act reflected a congressional intent to require plaintiffs to prove *scienter* on the part of the defendant to establish a claim under the act.

Most courts hold that reckless conduct may also constitute *scienter*. The definition of *reckless* includes conduct that reasonable persons know is unsafe or illegal. Thus, even if a defendant did not have actual knowledge that his behavior was criminal, *scienter* may be implied by his reckless actions.

In some cases the level of *scienter* required to find a defendant liable or culpable may fluctuate. In *Metge v. Baehler*, 762 F.2d 621 (1985), a group of investors brought suit against a bank, alleging that the bank had aided and abetted a securities fraud operation. To establish a defendant's liability for aiding and abetting a securities FRAUD transaction, the plaintiff must prove that there was a securities law violation, that the defendant knew about the violation, and that the defendant substantially assisted in the violation. In sending the case back to the trial court, the U.S. Court of Appeals for the Eighth Circuit stated that in a case alleging aiding and abetting, more *scienter* is required if the plaintiff has little proof that the defendant substantially assisted in the violation. The court noted that the bank seemed blameworthy only because it failed to act on possible suspicions of impropriety and that the bank had no duty to notify the plaintiffs about the actions of others. In such a case, the court advised that "an alleged aider-abettor should be found liable only if scienter of the high 'conscious intent' variety can be proved. Where some special duty of disclosure exists, then liability should be possible with a lesser degree of scienter." See also AID AND ABET.

In some cases or claims, a plaintiff need not prove that the defendant acted with any *scienter*. These cases or claims are based on STRICT LIABILITY statutes, which impose criminal and civil liability without regard to the mental state of the defendant. For example, a statute that prohibits the sale of cigarettes to minors may authorize punishment for such a sale even if the seller attempted to verify the buyer's age and believed that the buyer was not a MINOR. Courts have held that a legislative body may not authorize severe punishment for strict liability crimes because severe punishment is generally reserved for intentional misconduct, reckless conduct, or grossly negligent conduct.

In *United States v. Wulff*, 758 F.2d 1121 (1985), the U.S. Court of Appeals for the Sixth Circuit declared that the FELONY provision of the MIGRATORY BIRD TREATY Act, 16 U.S.C.A. § 703 et seq., was unconstitutional because it made the sale of part of a migratory bird a felony without proof of *scienter*. According to the court, eliminating the element of criminal intent in a criminal prosecution violates the Due Process Clause of the FIFTH AMENDMENT to the U.S. Constitution unless the penalty is relatively small and the conviction does not gravely besmirch the reputation of the defendant. The penalty in the act authorized two years in prison and a $2,000 fine, and the court considered that punishment too onerous to levy against a person who had acted without any *scienter*.

SCIENTIFIC EVIDENCE 📖 EVIDENCE presented in court that is produced from scientific tests or studies. 📖

Scientific evidence is evidence culled from a scientific procedure that helps the trier of fact understand evidence or determine facts at issue in a judicial proceeding. Under rule 702 of the Federal Rules of Evidence and similar state court rules of evidence, "a witness qualified as an expert by knowledge, skill, experience, training, or education" may testify and offer opinions in court if "scientific, technical, or other specialized knowledge will assist the trier of fact to understand the evidence or to determine a fact in issue." Article VII of the Federal Rules of Evidence contains other rules on expert TESTIMONY and scientific evidence. All states have rules on expert testimony and scientific evidence that are similar to the rules in article VII.

Expert testimony on scientific evidence is different from ordinary testimony from laypersons. A lay WITNESS may TESTIFY to INFERENCES and give opinions only if they are rationally based upon her perceptions of the subject of the testimony. Experts, by contrast, may give opinions and testify about possible inferences based in part on information obtained from secondhand sources and not from observation of the object of the testimony. For example, a layperson would not be allowed to take the witness stand and offer an opinion on a plaintiff's injury unless he had witnessed relevant information regarding the injury. However, a doctor who is certified as a specialist in the particular injury could take the stand and offer opinions on the injury based not only on an examination of the plaintiff but also on secondhand information that is normally relied on by experts in that particular field of medical study.

One of the most important issues that arises in expert testimony is which scientific procedures a court should accept as evidence. Many scientific procedures are not seriously in dispute and are accepted by courts with little or no inquisition into their validity. Examples include fingerprint tests for purposes of identification, blood tests, breathalyzer tests for ALCOHOL consumption, and ballistics tests of bullets and their impact areas. These scientific procedures are so widely accepted that a court may take JUDICIAL NOTICE of the procedure's validity. Judicial notice means that the parties in the case do not have to present evidence to the court to establish the validity of the scientific procedure. In some instances legislatures have specifically authorized the use of scientific tests, such as breathalyzer tests for suspected drunk drivers.

Whether they are judicially noticed or legislatively mandated, scientific tests that are universally accepted must be presented by a qualified expert. A person is established as a qualified expert before the court through questioning by the attorney who is using the witness as an expert. The attorney asks a series of questions to establish that the witness has adequate education and training to testify as an expert—a process called laying a foundation for the witness. Once the court is convinced that the witness is an expert on the procedure or subject matter that will be presented as evidence, the witness gives an expert opinion to the exact procedures that were used or the factual circumstances that arose in the case at hand. For example, assume that a person sues a doctor for medical malpractice, arguing that the defendant failed to set a broken bone properly. If the plaintiff offers a bone specialist as an expert witness on the issues surrounding the care he received from the defendant, the expert witness must testify to her credentials and give details about the plaintiff's treatment.

Some scientific tests and examinations that are not universally accepted are nevertheless generally considered reliable. Some examples include neutron activation analysis to determine the identity of goods, voiceprints to determine a person's identity, and genetic testing, or DNA analysis. These types of scientific procedures may be accepted in the medical communities, but they are not so established that they may be judicially noticed as automatically valid sources of scientific evidence. They may be admitted as evidence, but only after an expert witness has testified to the validity of the test. In determining whether to admit scientific evidence from procedures that are not universally accepted, a court must ask whether the test is reliable. A technique's reliability depends on a number of factors, including whether the technique can be or has been tested, whether it has been subjected to peer review, whether the test procedures have been published, whether the test has a margin of error and, if so, at what rate, and whether the technique, as applied, conformed to existing standards for the test (*Daubert v. Merrell Dow Pharmaceuticals, Inc.*, 509 U.S. 579, 113 S. Ct. 2786, 125 L. Ed. 2d 469 [1993]).

In some instances courts are reluctant to admit certain scientific evidence because the procedures yield results that are not considered sufficiently reliable to be used as evidence. Such procedures include POLYGRAPH and chemical tests that have been created to determine whether a person is telling the truth. If all parties agree that testimony derived from such procedures shall be admissible, however, a court is free to allow the evidence to be introduced.

In any case, regardless of the level of acceptance of a particular scientific procedure, the scientific evidence presented must be relevant to the issue at hand. Furthermore, the scientific evidence must have been obtained in a manner that is consistent with the way such evidence is normally obtained. For instance, assume that a physicist intends to testify to the speed of the defendant's vehicle in a personal injury case stemming from a car accident. If the physicist used different methods from those used by other physicists in determining a vehicle's speed, the court may refuse to allow the physicist to testify as to the vehicle's speed.

An expert witness giving testimony on scientific evidence may offer opinions on issues related to that evidence. An expert witness may also give an opinion on the ultimate issue in the case. Under rule 704 of the Federal Rules of Evidence, however, an expert witness testifying with respect to the mental state or condition of a criminal defendant may not state "an opinion or inference as to whether the defendant did or did not have the mental state or condition constituting an element of the crime charged or of a defense thereto." This rule, which is applied by courts only in criminal cases, was approved by the U.S. Congress in 1984, largely in response to the outcome of the criminal prosecution of John Hinckley, who attempted to assassinate President RONALD REAGAN in 1981. Hinckley was charged with attempted ASSASSINATION, ASSAULT on a federal officer, and use of a firearm in the commission of a federal offense, but was found not guilty by reason of insanity after the jury heard testimony from a psychiatrist who declared that Hinckley could not be found guilty because he lacked the knowing mental state required for a conviction on the charges.

The weight given to scientific evidence may vary according to the particular test that yielded the evidence. One party's expert testimony may be convincing, but it may not be dispositive of the case because the other party may have experts from the same field who have studied the same evidence and come to different conclusions. Experts have become indispensable to the vast majority of litigated cases, and many cases, civil and criminal alike, come down to a battle between experts. One notable exception to this trend is the PATERNITY case, where blood test results or DNA test results can establish the ultimate issue in the case. This is true, however, only if the parties in the paternity case agree that the particular tests will be conclusive and if the tests show that the individual named as the father could not be a parent of the child in question. If the tests show that the individual named as the father could be the parent, the test results will not dispose of the case, and the parties will have to present further evidence.

Courts have the discretion to appoint an expert witness to testify to scientific evidence. Under rule 706 of the Federal Rules of Evidence and similar state court rules of evidence, a court may appoint an expert to present evidence on a particular topic and order compensation for the expert's time and effort. Typically, in a civil case, the parties must apportion the costs as the court directs. In just compensation cases under the Fifth Amendment and in criminal cases, the court orders payment for the expert out of government funds.

CROSS-REFERENCES

DNA Evidence; Fingerprints; Forensic Science; Insanity Defense; Paternity Suit.

SCINTILLA   A glimmer; a spark; the slightest particle or trace.

"Scintilla of evidence" is a metaphorical expression describing a very insignificant or trifling item of EVIDENCE. The COMMON-LAW rule provides that if there is any evidence at all in a case, even a mere scintilla, that tends to support a material issue, the case cannot be taken from the jury but must be left to its decision.

SCIRE FACIAS   [*Latin, Made known.*] A judicial WRIT requiring a defendant to appear in court and prove why an existing JUDGMENT should not be executed against him or her.

In the law, scire facias is a judicial writ that is brought in a case that has already been before a court. *Writ* is the old English term for a judicial order. Some states still use the term. A scire facias writ commands the person against whom it is brought to appear before the court and show why the record should not be resolved in favor of the party who brought the writ.

The scire facias writ originated in England, and its use was adopted by the American colonists. In eighteenth-century England, the writ was used to repeal letters patent. Letters patent were letters written by the king or queen that granted inventors exclusive PATENT rights over their inventions. Any person who thought a patent was invalid based on false information or the existence of a prior invention could ask the royal Court of CHANCERY to request the presence of the patent holder to justify the patent. If there was a genuine dispute about the validity of the patent, the patent holder could request a trial before a JURY in the Court of KING'S BENCH. The jury resolved any issues of fact, and then the case was sent back to the Chancery. The CHANCELLOR made the final judgment on whether to revoke the patent.

The scire facias writ did not survive in patent law. Under modern law, only a person with a CASE OR CONTROVERSY with respect to a particular patent may challenge the patent. Also, a claim of patent invalidity is not tried before a royal court but a federal patent court. However, the issue of patent validity may be tried before a jury, much like the old scire facias writ.

In modern practice, the writ of scire facias is used in the enforcement and collection of judgments. When a plaintiff in a civil case obtains a money judgment against a defendant, the court order to pay the judgment may expire after a certain number of years if the judgment remains unpaid. State and federal laws allow the plaintiff to make a MOTION to the court before the time period expires to continue the effect of the court's order. If the plaintiff fails to make such a motion, she may file a writ of scire facias to revive the judgment. The defendant would then have to appear before the court and explain why the judgment should not be revived. If the defendant has already paid the plaintiff, or if the defendant has EVIDENCE that he owes the plaintiff nothing, the defendant may present evidence and shift the burden of proof to the plaintiff.

If the defendant is unable to defend his failure to pay the judgment, the court will order EXECUTION of the judgment. The court may order the defendant to submit to a financial status examination, to sell property to satisfy the judgment, or to take other measures to satisfy the judgment.

The writ of scire facias has been abolished on the federal level and in most states. Plaintiffs may revive an expired or dormant judgment by filing a civil claim in a court of GENERAL JURISDICTION and asking for revival of the judgment. The courts that have eliminated the writ have found its complex procedures unsuited to the needs of modern society.

In some jurisdictions that still permit a scire facias writ, the writ has fallen into disuse. In Connecticut, for example, the judicially created creditor's bill has supplanted the writ. This bill creates an equitable remedy for a person who cannot enforce a judgment in a court of law. A court provides an equitable remedy based not on legal authority but on principles of fairness.

States that maintain the scire facias writ require it to be filed within a certain time after expiration of the judgment. In Texas, for example, the Civil Practice and Remedies Code specifies that a scire facias writ may be brought no later than two years after the date that the judgment became dormant (Tex. Civ. Prac. & Rem. Code Ann. § 31.002 [West 1995]).

The term *scire facias* also is used in the law to describe a particular form of judicial FORECLOSURE of a MORTGAGE. After a mortgagor of property DEFAULTS on payment obligations, the mortgagee may obtain a writ of scire facias, which is an order commanding the RESPONDENT to appear and explain why the mortgaged property should not be sold to satisfy the mortgage debt.

SCOPE OF EMPLOYMENT Activities of an employee that are in furtherance of duties that are owed to an employer and where the employer is, or could be, exercising some control, directly or indirectly, over the activities of the employee.

Under the doctrine of RESPONDEAT SUPERIOR, a PRINCIPAL is liable for the TORTS, civil wrongs, of an AGENT committed within the ambit of the agent's occupation.

The scope of employment includes all acts reasonably necessary or incident to the performance of work, including matters of personal convenience and comfort that do not conflict with specific instructions.

SCOPES, JOHN T. The criminal prosecution of John T. Scopes was an attack by citizens of Dayton, Tennessee, on a Tennessee statute that banned the teaching of evolution in public schools. The Butler Act, passed in early 1925 by the Tennessee General Assembly, punished public school teachers who taught "that man has descended from a lower order of animals" or any theory "that denies the story of the Divine Creation of man as taught in the Bible."

Some citizens of Dayton decided to challenge the statute. On the last day of school in May 1925, they congregated in Robinson's Drug Store and devised a plan to use a willing teacher to challenge the constitutionality of the statute. According to the plan, a teacher would admit to teaching evolution and volunteer to face criminal charges under the statute. One person in the assemblage suggested John T. Scopes, a popular substitute teacher who had taught science and coached athletics at the high school for the past year.

Scopes agreed and within days, he was accused of criminal teachings. Scopes was arrested, indicted, and released pending trial in the town of Dayton. He faced no jail time. If convicted of the offense, Scopes would have had to pay a fine of at least $100 but no more than $500.

News of the case touched off a national debate on creationism, evolution, and public school teaching. Vendors, preachers, journalists, and gawkers descended on the town of Dayton during the months of June and July. The case also attracted legal celebrities. General A. T. Stewart was joined by a host of special counsel for the prosecution, including WILLIAM JENNINGS BRYAN. Bryan, age sixty-five, was a skilled speaker, veteran lawyer, and former presidential candidate. A Dayton newspaper asked the eminent litigator Clarence Seward Darrow, age sixty-eight, to defend Scopes. Darrow, an ardent opponent of religious fundamentalism, agreed to defend Scopes free of charge. Darrow was assisted by Dudley Field Malone and Arthur Garfield Hays of the AMERICAN CIVIL LIBERTIES UNION.

Trial began on July 10 in the midst of a blistering heat wave, but the intense heat did not deter spectators. The courtroom was so crowded that the last part of the trial was held outside in the courthouse yard to accommodate the large viewing audience.

Much of the trial was consumed by arguments on evidence and orations delivered by Bryan, Darrow, or Hays. Some of these orations were directed not toward the judge and jury but toward the gallery, which responded with jeers, cheers, and catcalls. Because Scopes did not deny that he had taught evolution, his lawyers sought to sway the jury into nullifying the statute by acquitting him in spite of the evidence. Darrow, Malone, and Hays attempted to win over the jury by attacking creationism and confirming the theory of evolution.

The most significant evidence offered by the defense did not make it into the record. Darrow placed Bryan on the witness stand and questioned him on the merits of evolution and creationism. The most memorable moments of the trial consisted of the debate between the two men. However, the examination of Bryan had little impact on the jury's decision because the jury was not present to hear it. After Bryan stepped down from the witness stand, the defense rested. The Tennessee jury found Scopes guilty.

Raulston instructed the jury that it could leave the punishment to the court. The jury did not set the fine, so Raulston set it at $100. Scopes appealed the verdict to the Tennessee Supreme Court, arguing that the statute was unconstitutional because it violated the separation of church and state under the FIRST AMENDMENT to the U.S. Constitution. Unfortunately, his local counsel, John R. Neal, failed to file a bill of exceptions within thirty days after the trial. Without such a bill, Scopes's arguments on APPEAL were limited to the actual trial transcript.

The Tennessee Supreme Court did not decide whether the statute was constitutional. It held merely that the fine was invalid under the state constitution (*Scopes v. State*, 154 Tenn. 105, 289 S.W. 363 [1927]). Under article VI, section 6, of the Tennessee Constitution, a judge could not fine anyone more than $50. In the opinion, written by Chief Justice Grafton Green, the court urged the state to dismiss the case against Scopes, noting that Scopes was no longer in the employ of the state and declaring, "We see nothing to be gained by prolonging the life of this bizarre case."

Bryan died shortly after the trial. Darrow litigated several more high profile cases and Scopes returned to his teaching career. Scopes never had to pay the fine levied by Raulston. When asked later in life whether he had any regrets about the case, Scopes said, "... my

John T. Scopes challenged a Tennessee state law that prohibited public school teachers from teaching evolution.

decision would be the same as it was in 1925. I would go home and think about it. I would sleep on it. And the next day I would do it again."

Scopes received a measure of vindication shortly before his death in 1970. In 1968 the U.S. Supreme Court declared unconstitutional statutes that forbid the teaching of evolution (*Epperson v. Arkansas*, 393 U.S. 97, 89 S. Ct. 266, 21 L. Ed. 2d 228). Since the *Epperson* case, advocates of creationism have been hard pressed to find public schools willing to teach scientific creationism. In a gradual reversal of fortune, scientific creationists have been unable to obtain equal time for the teaching of creationism in public schools. In 1987 a splintered Supreme Court ruled that a Louisiana statute that mandated equal time for the teaching of creationism violated the First Amendment because it served no identified secular purpose and had the primary purpose of promoting a particular religious belief (*Edwards v. Aguillard*, 482 U.S. 578, 107 S. Ct. 2573, 96 L. Ed. 2d 510).

CROSS-REFERENCES

Darrow; Clarence; Religion; Schools and School Districts.

SCORCHED-EARTH PLAN 📖 A slang expression for a defensive tactic used by an unwilling corporate takeover target to make itself less attractive to a buyer. 📖

Scorched-earth tactics include selling off assets or entering into long-term contractual commitments. A difficulty with such maneuvers is that they tend to be irreversible and may permanently harm the company. As a result, they tend to be used as a last resort in a takeover struggle.

See also MERGERS AND ACQUISITIONS.

S CORPORATION 📖 A type of CORPORATION that is taxed under subchapter S of the INTERNAL REVENUE CODE (26 U.S.C.A. § 1 et seq.). 📖

An S corporation differs from a regular corporation in that it is not a separate taxable entity under the Internal Revenue Code. This means that the S corporation does not pay taxes on its net income. The net profits or losses of the corporation pass through to its owners.

An S corporation must conform to a state's laws that specify how a corporation must be formed. At minimum, ARTICLES OF INCORPORATION must be filed with the secretary of state. An S corporation must also file a special form with federal and state tax authorities that notifies them of the election of the subchapter S status.

A corporation may be granted S status if it does not own any subsidiaries, has only one class of stock, and has no more than seventy-five shareholders, all of whom must be U.S. citizens or U.S. residents. A corporation may elect S status when it is incorporated or later in its corporate life. Likewise, a corporation may elect to drop its S status at any time.

An S corporation status is attractive to smaller, family-owned corporations that want to avoid double taxation: a tax on corporate income and a second tax on amounts distributed to shareholders. This status may also make financial sense if a new corporation is likely to have an operating loss in its first year. The losses from the business can be passed through to the individual shareholder's tax return and be used to offset income from other sources.

An S corporation also avoids audit issues that surround regularly taxed corporations, such as unreasonable compensation to office-shareholders. Finally, S status may avoid problems raised by corporate accounting rules and the corporate alternative minimum tax. These problems are eliminated because the income is taxed to the shareholders.

An S corporation can deduct the cost of employee benefits as a business expense. However, shareholders who own more than two percent of the stock are not considered employees for income tax purposes and their benefits may not be deducted. Tax advantages can be achieved in some cases because income can be shifted to other family members by making them employees or shareholders (or both) of the corporation.

Appreciation of the business also can be shifted to other family members as a way to minimize death taxes when an owner dies. When an S corporation is sold, the taxable gain on the business may be less than if it had been operated as a regular corporation.

SCOTTSBORO CASES See POWELL V. ALABAMA.

SEA See LAW OF THE SEA.

SEABED ARMS CONTROL TREATY OF 1971 📖 An agreement for the denuclearization of the seabed, the ocean floor, and the subsoil of the seabed. 📖

The Seabed Arms Control Treaty of 1971 may be regarded as a nuclear nonproliferation treaty since it limits or prevents the spread of nuclear devices to the seabed areas.

See also ARMS CONTROL AND DISARMAMENT.

SEAL 📖 To close records by any type of fastening that must be broken before access can be obtained. An impression upon wax, wafer, or some other substance capable of being impressed. 📖

The use of seals began at a time when writing was not common, but when every person of means possessed a coat-of-arms or other

Seals once had a practical importance, often being used as a signature or imprimatur. (The seal of Louis IX of France is shown here.) Today, many government offices have seals associated with them, though these are mainly decorative now.

distinctive device. Great significance was attached to the use of seals as a means of distinguishing persons. With the spread of education, the SIGNATURE on an instrument became more important than the seal, and seals lost their former dignity and importance.

Modern judicial decisions minimize or eliminate the distinctions between sealed and unsealed instruments, and most statutes have abolished the use of seals. Other statutes abolishing the use of private seals do not make sealed instruments unlawful, but merely render the seals ineffective. In JURISDICTIONS that still recognize the use of seals, the seal can assume the form of a wax impression, an impression made on paper, or a gummed sticker attached to the document. The letters *L.S.*, an abbreviation for the Latin phrase *locus sigilli*, meaning "the place of the seal," can also be used in place of a material seal, as can the word *seal* or a statement to the effect that the document is to take effect as a sealed instrument.

Seals are currently used for authenticating documents, such as birth and marriage records and DEEDS to REAL PROPERTY. They are also used to authenticate signatures witnessed by a NOTARY PUBLIC and in formalizing corporate documents.

In regard to CONTRACTS, at COMMON LAW a promise under seal was enforceable without the necessity of legal CONSIDERATION—something of value—either because the seal was a substitute for consideration or because the existence of consideration was conclusively presumed. Although most states have abolished seals, some states have provided by statute that a seal raises a PRESUMPTION of consideration. Article 2 of the UNIFORM COMMERCIAL CODE (UCC)—a body of law adopted by the states to govern commercial transactions—has eliminated the seal as consideration in commercial SALES to which the act is applicable. At one time, the STATUTE OF LIMITATIONS—the prescribed period during which legal proceedings must be instituted—was longer for an action brought on a contract under seal than for one not under seal.

SEALE, BOBBY See *WEAL 1998 Supplement.*

SEALED VERDICT ◫ A decision reached by the JURY when the court is not in session, which is placed in a closed envelope by the jurors, who then separate. ◫

A sealed verdict is opened and read when the court reconvenes, and it has the same effect as if it had been returned in open court before the jury separated. However, the court holds that a sealed verdict is merely an agreement reached by the jurors and does not become final until it is read into the record and the jurors are discharged.

SEAL OF THE UNITED STATES ◫ The official die or signet, which has a raised emblem and is used by federal officials on documents of importance. ◫

The United States seal is sometimes officially known as the great seal. The secretary of state has custody and charge of the official seal and makes out, records, and affixes the seal to all civil commissions for officers of the United States, who are appointed by the PRESIDENT alone, or by the president with the advice and consent of the Senate. In order for the seal to be affixed to any commission or other instrument, the president must sign or specially warrant the commission. When the seal is affixed to an appointment, such appointment is made and the commission is valid.

Each state also has an official seal, which is carefully described by law and serves functions on the state level of government that are similar to those of the seal of the United States on the federal level.

SEARCH AND SEIZURE ◫ In INTERNATIONAL LAW, the right of ships of war, as regulated by treaties, to examine a merchant vessel during war in order to determine whether the ship or its cargo is liable to seizure.

A hunt by law enforcement officials for property or communications believed to be evidence of crime, and the act of taking possession of this property. ◫

Search and seizure is a necessary exercise in the ongoing pursuit of criminals. Searches and seizures are used to produce EVIDENCE for the prosecution of alleged criminals. Under federal, state, and local laws, a police officer may search people and places when the officer has PROBABLE CAUSE to suspect criminal activity. This means that the officer must possess sufficient trustworthy facts to believe that a crime has been committed. In some cases, an officer may need only a REASONABLE suspicion of criminal activity to conduct a limited search. *Reasonable suspicion* means that the officer has sufficient knowledge to believe that criminal activity is at hand. This level of knowledge is less than that of probable cause, so reasonable suspicion is usually used to justify a brief frisk in a public area. To possess either probable cause or reasonable suspicion, an officer must be able to cite specific articulable facts to warrant the intrusion. Items related to suspected criminal activity found in a search may be taken, or seized, by the officer.

Under the FOURTH AMENDMENT, *seizure* also refers to the taking, or arrest, of persons. An arrest occurs when a police officer takes a person against his or her will for questioning or criminal prosecution. To make an arrest, an officer must have probable cause.

A WARRANT is not generally required for an arrest, except for an arrest in the home. A seizure may be less than an arrest, such as an investigatory stop. Investigatory stops are used by police to briefly detain, frisk, and question persons in public. This is permissible where an officer has reasonable suspicion to believe that a person has committed or is committing a crime.

Search and seizure law generally refers to the search of persons and places and the SEIZURE of evidence by law enforcement officials. It does not refer to searches carried out by private parties. Evidence of a crime acquired by a private party and given unsolicited to a police officer may be used in a criminal trial. Many searches conducted by private parties—such as drug tests by employers—can be intrusive, but the law provides limited protection from these intrusions.

The police have the power to search and seize, but individuals are protected against arbitrary, unreasonable police intrusions. Freedom from unrestricted search warrants was critical to American colonists. Under England's rule, many searches were unlimited in scope and conducted without justification. Customs officials could enter the homes of colonists at will to search for violations of customs and trade laws, and suspicionless searches were carried out against outspoken political activists.

Searches in the colonies came to represent governmental oppression.

To guard against arbitrary police intrusions, the newly formed United States in 1791 ratified the U.S. Constitution's Fourth Amendment, which states,

> The right of the people to be secure in their persons, houses, papers, and effects, against unreasonable searches and seizures, shall not be violated, and no Warrants shall issue, but upon probable cause, supported by Oath or affirmation, and particularly describing the place to be searched, and the persons or things to be seized.

Like much of the Constitution, the Fourth Amendment left ample room for interpretation. Over the years the U.S. Supreme Court has held it to mean that unreasonable searches are prohibited, and that any search conducted by or at the direction of law enforcement personnel without a warrant is unreasonable unless it falls within an established exception.

A SEARCH WARRANT is a judicially approved document that authorizes law enforcement officials to search a particular place. To obtain a search warrant, a police officer must provide an account of information supporting probable cause to believe that evidence of a crime will be found in a particular place or places. The officer must also make a list of the particular places to be searched and the items sought. Finally, the

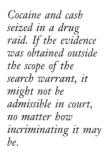

Cocaine and cash seized in a drug raid. If the evidence was obtained outside the scope of the search warrant, it might not be admissible in court, no matter how incriminating it may be.

MARK RICHARDS/PHOTOEDIT

officer must swear to the truthfulness of the information. The officer presents the information in an AFFIDAVIT to a MAGISTRATE or judge, who determines whether to approve the warrant.

An officer may search only the places where items identified in the search warrant may be found. For example, if the only item sought is a snowmobile, the officer may not rummage through desk drawers. Only the items listed in the warrant may be seized, unless other evidence of illegal activity is in plain view. Judges or magistrates may approve a variety of types of searches. The removal of blood from a person's body, a search of body cavities, and even surgery may be approved for the gathering of evidence. ELECTRONIC SURVEILLANCE and phone records may also be used to gather evidence upon the issuance of a warrant.

A warrant is not required for a search incident to a lawful arrest, the seizure of items in plain view, a border search, a search effected in open fields, a vehicle search, an inventory search of an impounded vehicle, and any search necessitated by exigent circumstances. It is also not required for a STOP AND FRISK, a limited search for weapons based on a reasonable suspicion that the subject has committed or is committing a crime. A police officer may also conduct a warrantless search if the subject consents.

In theory, the Fourth Amendment protects a person's right to PRIVACY. Thus, search warrants are required only for items or qualities in which a person has a reasonable expectation of privacy. A person has no reasonable expectation of privacy in things like bank records, vehicle location and vehicle paint, garbage left for collection, handwriting, the smell of luggage, and land visible from a public place; the police may therefore inspect such things without acquiring a warrant.

Administrative agencies may conduct warrantless searches of highly regulated industries, such as strip mining and food service. Federal and state statutes authorize warrantless, random drug testing of persons in sensitive positions, such as air traffic controllers, drug interdiction officers, railroad employees, and customs officials.

The U.S. Supreme Court has approved warrantless, suspicionless searches at roadside sobriety checkpoints. These searches must be carried out in some neutral, articulable way, such as by stopping every fifth car. Warrantless searches of public housing projects have been ruled unconstitutional. Similar searches continue as legislators and police officers test the boundaries of the Fourth Amendment.

A. LICHTENSTEIN/THE IMAGE WORKS

Warrant exceptions have been carved out by courts because requiring a warrant in certain situations would unnecessarily hamper law enforcement. For example, it makes little sense to require an officer to obtain a search warrant to seize CONTRABAND that is in plain view. However, if the officer has gained unwarranted access to the plain view—for example, by entering a home without permission or a warrant—he may not thereafter seize the contraband.

The law of search and seizure is often more theoretical than practical. In practice, police officers generally seize evidence of illegal activity and leave the parsing of their actions to prosecutors, criminal defense attorneys, and, ultimately, the court. When a judge deems a search unreasonable, she frequently applies the EXCLUSIONARY RULE.

For the entire nineteenth century, a Fourth Amendment violation had little consequence. Evidence seized by law enforcement from a warrantless or otherwise unreasonable search was ADMISSIBLE at trial if the judge found it reliable. This made the Fourth Amendment essentially meaningless to criminal defendants.

In 1914, the U.S. Supreme Court devised a way to enforce the Fourth Amendment. In *Weeks v. United States*, 232 U.S. 383, 34 S. Ct. 341, 58 L. Ed. 652 (1914), a federal agent conducted a warrantless search for evidence of gambling at the home of Fremont Weeks. The evidence seized in the search was used at trial, and Weeks was convicted. On appeal, the Supreme Court held that the Fourth Amendment barred the use of evidence secured through a warrantless search and seizure. Weeks's conviction was reversed, and thus was born the exclusionary rule.

The warrant requirement and the exclusionary rule are the only judicial checks on law

The Constitution protects individuals and their homes against arbitrary, unreasonable police intrusions. If these officers are operating without a warrant, their actions might be illegal.

enforcement's power to search and seize. The exclusionary rule is a judicially created remedy used to deter police misconduct in obtaining evidence. Under the exclusionary rule, a judge may exclude incriminating evidence from a criminal trial if there was police misconduct in obtaining the evidence. Without the evidence, the prosecutor may lose the case or drop the charges for lack of proof. This rule provides some substantive protection against illegal search and seizure.

The exclusionary rule was constitutionally required only in federal court until *Mapp v. Ohio*, 367 U.S. 643, 81 S. Ct. 1684, 6 L. Ed. 2d 1081 (1961). In *Mapp*, the Court held that the exclusionary rule applied to state criminal proceedings through the Due Process Clause of the Fourteenth Amendment. Before the *Mapp* ruling, not all states excluded evidence obtained in violation of the Fourth Amendment. After *Mapp*, a defendant's claim of unreasonable search and seizure became commonplace in criminal prosecutions.

The application of the exclusionary rule has been significantly limited by a GOOD FAITH exception created by the Supreme Court in *United States v. Leon*, 468 U.S. 897, 104 S. Ct. 3405, 82 L. Ed. 2d 677 (1984). Under the good faith exception, evidence obtained in violation of a person's Fourth Amendment rights will not be excluded from trial if the law enforcement officer, though mistaken, acts reasonably. For example, if an officer reasonably conducts a search relying on information that is later proved to be false, any evidence seized in the search will not be excluded if the officer acted in good faith, with a reasonable reliance on the information. The Supreme Court has carved out this exception to the exclusionary rule because, according to a majority of the court, the rule was designed to deter police misconduct, and excluding evidence when the police did not misbehave would not deter police misconduct.

A companion to the exclusionary rule is the FRUIT OF THE POISONOUS TREE doctrine, established by the Supreme Court in *Nardone v. United States*, 308 U.S. 338, 60 S. Ct. 266, 84 L. Ed. 307 (1939). Under this doctrine, a court may exclude from trial any evidence derived from the results of an illegal search. For example, assume that an illegal search has garnered evidence of illegal explosives. This evidence is then used to obtain a warrant to search the suspect's home. The exclusionary rule excludes the evidence initially used to obtain the search warrant, and the fruit of the poisonous tree doctrine excludes any evidence obtained in a search of the home.

A criminal defendant's claim of unreasonable search and seizure is usually heard in a suppression hearing before the presiding judge. This hearing is conducted before trial to determine what evidence will be suppressed, or excluded, from trial.

CROSS-REFERENCES

Alcohol; Automobiles; Clark, Tom C.; Criminal Law; Criminal Procedure; Drugs and Narcotics; Due Process of Law; *Mapp v. Ohio*; *Olmstead v. United States*; Plain View Doctrine; *Terry v. Ohio*; Warren Court; Wiretapping.

SEARCH WARRANT ▥ A court order authorizing the examination of a place for the purpose of discovering CONTRABAND, stolen property, or EVIDENCE of guilt to be used in the prosecution of a criminal action. ▥

A search warrant is a judicial document that authorizes police officers to search a person or place to obtain evidence for presentation in criminal prosecutions. Police officers obtain search warrants by submitting AFFIDAVITS and other evidence to a judge or MAGISTRATE to establish PROBABLE CAUSE to believe that a search will yield evidence related to a crime. If satisfied that the officers have established probable cause, the judge or magistrate will issue the warrant.

The FOURTH AMENDMENT to the U.S. Constitution states that persons have a right to be free from unreasonable searches and seizures and that "no Warrants shall issue, but upon probable cause, supported by Oath or affirmation, and particularly describing the place to be searched, and the persons or things to be seized." State constitutions contain similar provisions.

The U.S. Supreme Court has not interpreted the Fourth Amendment to mean that police must always obtain a search warrant before conducting a search. Rather, the Supreme Court holds that a search warrant is required for a search unless it fits into a recognized exception.

The exceptions to the search warrant requirement are numerous. One common exception is the search of a person incident to a lawful arrest. The Supreme Court held in *Chimel v. California*, 395 U.S. 752, 89 S. Ct. 2034, 23 L. Ed. 2d 685 (1969), that an officer may search the arrestee as well as those areas in the arrestee's immediate physical surroundings that may be deemed to be under the arrestee's control. Other exceptions to the warrant requirement include situations where an officer is in HOT PURSUIT of a person, where an emergency exists, and where the item to be searched is

A sample affidavit
for search warrant

UNITED STATES DISTRICT COURT
FOR THE
EASTERN DISTRICT OF KENTUCKY

Commissioner's Docket No. 2
Case No. 166
UNITED STATES OF AMERICA
vs.
Green Brick Constructed Building W/Green Shingled
Roof Known As 413 E. 17th Street, Covington, Kentucky
and Occupied by Southern Scientific Co.
AFFIDAVIT FOR SEARCH
WARRANT

Eastern District of Kentucky
Filed Apr. 17, 1968
Davis T. McGarvey, Clerk
U.S. District Court

Before Robert Cetrulo [Commissioner], Covington, Kentucky.

The undersigned being duly sworn deposes and says:

That he has reason to believe that on the premises known as 413 E. 17th Street, Coving-ton, Kentucky, in the Eastern District of Kentucky, there is now being concealed certain property, namely hallucinogenic drugs, to wit: Diethyltryptamine and Dimethyltryptamine, commonly known as DET and DMT; and certain paraphernalia and chemical precursors utilized in the illicit manufacture of said drugs, which are the means and instrumentalities used to commit offenses in violation of 21 U.S.C. § 331 (q) (1) and (3) and which are also subject to seizure and condemnation under 21 U.S.C. § 334(a) (2).

And that the facts tending to establish the foregoing grounds for issuance of a Search Warrant are as follows:

(SEE ATTACHED, WHICH IS MADE A PART OF THIS AFFIDAVIT)

/s/ Chantland Wysor, Agent, Bureau
of Drug Abuse Control

Sworn to before me and subscribed in my presence, March 31, 1968.

/s/ Robert C. Cetrulo, U.S. Commissioner

During the first part of March, 1968 the Chicago Field Office of the Bureau of Drug Abuse Control received information from the New York Field Office, Bureau of Drug Abuse Con-trol, reporting that a firm using the name of AA, 100 N. LaSalle Street, Chicago, Illinois, allegely (*sic*) a Cosmetic Firm, had ordered a large quantity of chemical precursors which are known to be used in the illicit manufacture of hallucinogenic drugs, within the meaning of the Drug Abuse Control Amendments of 1965.

Investigation then revealed the following as regards AA: Responsible person in this al-leged firm is Thomas R. Anderson and it was later determined that this individual's true identity may possibly be C. M. and that the name A. is fictitious. Investigation shows that the address listed for this firm is an answering service which has been contracted to accept all telephone calls, correspondence and parcels. Persons associated with AA who transact business with the answering service are C. M. and R. T. Investigation revealed that Moore is a resident of Columbus, Ohio and Terry is a resident of Chicago, Illinois. During the month of March 1968, the answering service received parcels containing chemical precursors for utilization in the manufacture of hallucinogenic drugs, to be held for C. M. Inquiry with the U.S. Food and Drug Administration revealed that this firm is not of record with that Agency as a legitimate cosmetic firm.

A sample affidavit
for search warrant
(continued)

Further investigation determined that arrangements had been made for C. M. to travel from Columbus, Ohio, to Chicago, Illinois, on March 29, 1968, to pick up the chemical precursors, which were being held for AA. Surveillance determined that M. did arrive in Chicago on March 29, 1968, and that on March 30, 1968, the subject did pick up the chemical precursors. Continuous surveillance on subject M. by Agents of the Bureau of Drug Abuse Control determined that the subject did leave Chicago on March 30, 1968, with the chemical precursors in his vehicle and delivered the items to Southern Scientific Company, 413 E. 17th Street, Covington, Kentucky, on that same date. After remaining inside 413 E. 17th Street for a short period of time subject M. left the rear of the building, walked to an alleyway behind the building and placed a cardboard container on the ground. Examination of that container revealed that it was empty and had labeled thereon "American Indole," which is a common precursor utilized in the illicit manufacturing of hallucinogens.

Surveillance determined that subject M. and an individual tentatively identified as J. S., and an unknown person, were inside Southern Scientific Company from 7:30 PM to 11:30 PM, on March 30, 1968; this being a Saturday and if the firm is legitimate these are not normal working-business hours. Surveillance again determined that the same three subjects went to the building on Sunday, March 31, 1968, at approximately 11:00 AM.

Indications that persons at Southern Scientific Company are engaged in the illegal manufacture of Hallucinogenic Drugs are: Unusual manner utilized in ordering, receiving and ultimate delivery of chemical precursors, which is a known Modus Operandi used by individuals engaged in the illicit manufacture of hallucinogenic drugs; the unusual activity at the building not during normal working-business hours; it is known that the chemical precursors in question are utilized in the illicit manufacture of Diethyltryptamine (DET) and Dimethyltryptamine (DMT), which are hallucinogenic drugs within the meaning of the Drug Abuse Control Amendments of 1965; it is a known factor that either is utilized in the illicit manufacture of DET and DMT; and during surveillance of said location on Sunday, March 31, 1968, surveillance Agents could smell strong odors coming from the building in question which is believed to be ether. In addition it is known that the chemical precursors obtained are not common in the manufacture of cosmetics.

/s/ Chantland Wysor, Agent Bureau
of Drug Abuse Control

Sworn to before me, and subscribed in my presence this 31st day of March, 1968.

/s/ Robert C. Cetrulo, Commissioner

mobile, such as an automobile. Similarly searches at public way checkpoints, airports, and international borders may be conducted without first obtaining a search warrant.

To obtain a search warrant, an officer must personally appear before, or speak directly with, a judge or magistrate. The officer must present information that establishes probable cause to believe that a search would yield evidence related to a crime. Probable cause exists when an officer has either personal knowledge or trustworthy HEARSAY from an informant or WITNESS. The officer must fill out an affidavit stating with particularity the person to be seized and searched, the area to be searched, and the objects sought. The warrant need not specify the manner in which the search will be executed.

The officer must sign the affidavit containing the supporting information establishing the grounds for the warrant. By signing the affidavit, the officer swears that the statements in the affidavit are true to the best of his or her knowledge. A police officer who lies when obtaining a warrant may be held personally liable to the searched person. According to the Supreme Court's ruling in *Anderson v. Creighton*, 483 U.S. 635, 107 S. Ct. 3034, 97 L. Ed. 2d 523 (1987), however, a police officer is not personally liable for a wrongful search if a reasonable officer could have believed that the warrantless search would be lawful in light of clearly established law and the information the officer possessed at the time.

See also AUTOMOBILE SEARCHES; SEARCH AND SEIZURE.

SEASONABLE Within a reasonable time; timely.

The term *seasonable* is usually used in connection with the performance of contractual obligations that must be completed "seasonably." The facts and circumstances of each case define a reasonable period of time.

SEAT BELTS A restraining device used to secure passengers in motorized vehicles.

Congress first passed seat-belt legislation in 1966. Under Section 402 of 23 U.S.C.A. (1997), a portion of federal HIGHWAY funds may be withheld from states if they do not have an approved highway safety program to reduce the number and severity of traffic accidents. One of the measures a state must include in its highway safety program is a provision that encourages drivers and passengers to use seat belts. Most states have passed and continue to maintain legislation requiring drivers and front-seat passengers in motorized vehicles to wear seat belts.

In states that require the use of seat belts by all drivers and front-seat passengers, the failure to use a seat belt is a violation that carries a small fine. In most of these states, police officers do not stop persons in vehicles for failing to use a seat belt. In West Virginia, for example, Section 17C-15-49 of West Virginia Code states, "Enforcement . . . shall be accomplished only as a secondary action when a driver of a passenger vehicle has been detained for probable cause of violating another section of this code." In other words, once a vehicle is stopped for any other infraction, the driver may be ticketed if the driver or a front-seat passenger is not belted. The fine for violating a mandatory seat-belt law usually is minimal; in West Virginia, the fine is $25.

Seat-belt requirements in states without mandatory seat-belt laws are less comprehensive. In New Hampshire, for example, motor vehicle passengers under the age of twelve must wear a seat belt, but adults have no such mandate (N.H. Rev. Stat. Ann. § 265: 107-a [1995]). The New Hampshire Department of Safety administers programs that increase public awareness of the importance of seat belts, and roadside signs placed throughout the state remind drivers that buckling up is mandatory for children and sound advice for all persons.

The failure of a driver or front-seat passenger to wear a seat belt can have consequences in PERSONAL INJURY lawsuits. Under court decisions

Seat Belts
1996 National Occupant Protection Use Survey

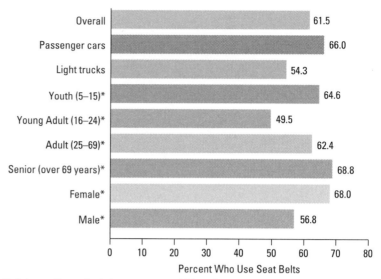

*Includes overall usage, i.e., both passenger cars and light trucks

Source: National Highway Traffic Safety Administration, National Center for Statistics and Analysis, *1996 National Occupant Protection Use Survey.*

and statutes in some states, the plaintiff's failure to wear a seat belt can decrease his or her recovery for injuries in a car accident. In other states, cases and statutes hold that the failure to wear a seat belt may not be used in court as a mitigating factor in figuring the plaintiff's DAMAGES.

In states that limit the recovery of unbelted plaintiffs, courts employ various methods to mitigate damages. Under the causation approach, a plaintiff may not recover damages for injuries caused by the failure to wear a seat belt. Some states require that the plaintiff prove that the accident injuries would have occurred even if the plaintiff had worn a seat belt. Other states hold that the defendant must prove that the plaintiff's injuries would not have occurred had the plaintiff worn a seat belt. Identifying and apportioning the various factors contributing to the plaintiff's injuries is a difficult task. Personal injury cases involving unbelted plaintiffs in these states rely heavily on medical expert TESTIMONY.

Under the plaintiff misconduct approach, the court examines whether the plaintiff was at FAULT in failing to wear a seat belt. If the plaintiff should have been wearing a seat belt under the state seat-belt laws, the failure to wear the belt may mitigate the plaintiff's damages or completely bar any recovery.

See also AUTOMOBILES; MITIGATION OF DAMAGES.

SEC An abbreviation for the SECURITIES AND EXCHANGE COMMISSION.

SECESSION 📖 The act of withdrawing from membership in a group. 📖

Secession occurs when persons in a country or state declare their independence from the ruling government. When a dissatisfied group secedes, it creates its own form of government in place of the former ruling government. Secessions are serious maneuvers that lead to, or arise from, military conflict.

A secession can affect international relationships as well as the civil peace of the nation from which a group secedes. Most countries consider secession by a town, city, province, or other body to be a criminal offense that warrants retaliation using force. Because the primary mission of most governments is to maximize the comfort and wealth of its citizens, nations jealously guard the land and wealth that they have amassed. In rare cases a government may recognize the independence of a seceding state. This recognition may occur when other countries support the independence of the seceding state. However, for most countries, the involuntary loss of land and wealth is unthinkable.

Most countries have laws that punish persons who secede or attempt to secede. The United States has no specific law on secession, but the federal government and state governments maintain laws that punish SEDITION and other forms of INSURRECTION against the government. On the federal level, for example, chapter 115 of title 18 of the U.S. Code Annotated identifies TREASON, rebellion, or insurrection, seditious CONSPIRACY, and advocation of the overthrow of the government as criminal offenses punishable by several years of imprisonment and thousands of dollars in fines. These are the types of crimes that can be charged against persons who attempt to secede from the United States.

The Civil War was the result of the single most ambitious secession in the history of the United States. In February 1861 South Carolina seceded from the Union, and Virginia, North Carolina, Georgia, Florida, Alabama, Mississippi, Texas, Arkansas, and Tennessee followed suit shortly thereafter. These states seceded because they objected to attempts by the federal government to abolish the enslavement of black people. The mass secession led to four years of civil war and the death of hundreds of thousands of people. The seceding states established their own government called the Confederate States of America and fought the U.S. military forces with their own army. When the Confederate forces were defeated in April 1865, the seceding states rejoined the United States.

See also U.S. CIVIL WAR.

SECOND AMENDMENT　　The Second Amendment to the U.S. Constitution reads:

> A well regulated Militia, being necessary to the security of a free State, the right of the people to keep and bear Arms, shall not be infringed.

The subject matter and unusual phrasing of this amendment have led to much controversy and analysis, especially in the last half of the twentieth century. Nevertheless, the meaning and scope of the amendment have long been decided by the Supreme Court.

Firearms played an important part in the colonization of America. In the seventeenth and eighteenth centuries, European colonists relied heavily on firearms to take land away from Native Americans and repel attacks by Native Americans and Europeans. Around the time of the Revolutionary War, male citizens were required to own firearms for fighting against the British forces. Firearms were also used in hunting.

In June 1776, one month before the signing of the DECLARATION OF INDEPENDENCE, Virginia became the first colony to adopt a state constitution. In this document, the state of Virginia pronounced that "a well regulated Militia, composed of the body of the people, trained to arms, is the proper, natural, and safe defence of a free State." After the colonies declared their independence from England, other states began to include the right to bear arms in their constitution. Pennsylvania, for example, declared that

> the people have a right to bear arms for the defence of themselves and the state; and as standing armies in the time of peace are dangerous to liberty, they ought not to be kept up; And that the military should be kept under strict subordination to, and governed by, the civil power.

The wording of clauses about bearing arms in late-eighteenth-century state constitutions varied. Some states asserted that bearing arms was a "right" of the people, whereas others called it a "duty" of every able-bodied man in the defense of society.

Pennsylvania was not alone in its express discouragement of a standing (professional) army. Many of the Framers of the U.S. Constitution rejected standing armies, preferring instead the model of a citizen army, equipped with weapons and prepared for defense. According to Framers such as Elbridge Gerry, of Massachusetts, and GEORGE MASON, of Virginia, a standing army was susceptible to tyrannical use by a power-hungry government.

At the first session of Congress in March 1789, the Second Amendment was submitted as a counterweight to the federal powers of Congress and the president. According to constitutional theorists, the Framers who feared a central government extracted the amendment as a compromise from those in favor of centralized authority over the states. The Revolutionary War had, after all, been fought in large part by a citizen army against the standing armies of England.

The precise wording of the amendment was changed two times before the U.S. Senate finally cast it in its present form. As with many of the amendments, the exact wording proved critical to its interpretation.

In 1791 a majority of states ratified the BILL OF RIGHTS, which included the Second Amendment. In its final form, the amendment presented a challenge to interpreters. It was the only amendment with an opening clause that appeared to state its purpose. The amendment even had defective punctuation; the comma before *shall* seemed grammatically unnecessary.

Legal scholars do not agree about this comma. Some have argued that it was intentional, and that it was intended to make *militia* the subject of the sentence. According to these theorists, the operative words of the amendment are "[a] well regulated Militia . . . shall not be infringed." Others have argued that the comma was a mistake, and that the operative words of the sentence are "the right of the people to . . . bear arms . . . shall not be infringed." Under this reading, the first part of the sentence is the rationale for the absolute, personal right of the people to own firearms. Indeed, the historical backdrop—highlighted by a general disdain for professional armies—would seem to support this theory.

Some observers argue further that the Second Amendment grants the right of INSURRECTION. According to these theorists, the Second Amendment was designed to allow citizens to rebel against the government. THOMAS JEFFERSON is quoted as saying that "a little rebellion every now and then is a good thing."

The Supreme Court makes the ultimate determination of the Constitution's meaning, and it has defined the amendment as simply granting to the states the right to maintain a MILITIA separate from federally controlled militias. This interpretation first came in *United States v. Cruikshank*, 92 U.S. 542, 23 L. Ed. 588 (1875). In *Cruikshank*, approximately one hundred persons were tried jointly in a Louisiana federal

court with felonies in connection with an April 13, 1873, assault on two African American men. One of the criminal counts charged that the mob intended to hinder the right of the two men to bear arms. The defendants were convicted by a jury, but the circuit court arrested the judgment, effectively overturning the verdict. In affirming that decision, the Supreme Court declared that "the second amendment means no more than that [the right to bear arms] shall not be infringed by Congress, and has no other effect than to restrict the powers of the national government."

In *Presser v. Illinois*, 116 U.S. 252, 6 S. Ct. 580, 29 L. Ed. 615 (1886), Herman Presser was charged in Illinois state court with parading and drilling an unauthorized militia in the streets of Chicago in December 1879, in violation of certain sections of the Illinois Military Code. One of the sections in question prohibited the organization, drilling, operation, and parading of militias other than U.S. troops or the regular organized volunteer militia of the state. Presser was tried by the judge, convicted, and ordered to pay a fine of $10.

On appeal to the U.S. Supreme Court, Presser argued, in part, that the charges violated his Second Amendment right to bear arms. The Court disagreed and upheld Presser's conviction. The Court cited *Cruikshank* for the proposition that the Second Amendment means only that the federal government may not infringe on the right of states to form their own militias. This meant that the Illinois state law forbidding citizen militias was not uncon-

Ten Most Popular Handguns Manufactured in the United States, 1973 to 1993

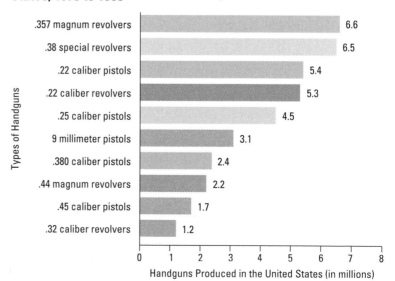

Source: Bureau of Alcohol, Tobacco and Firearms, *ATF Facts*.

PRIVATE MILITIAS

Private militias are armed military groups that are composed of private citizens and not recognized by federal or state governments. Private militias have been formed by individuals in America since the colonial period. In fact, the Revolutionary War against England was fought in part by armies comprising not professional soldiers but ordinary male citizens.

Approximately half the states maintain laws regulating private militias. Generally, these laws prohibit the parading and exercising of armed private militias in public, but do not forbid the formation of private militias. In Wyoming, however, state law forbids the very formation of private militias. Under section 19-1-106 of the Wyoming Statutes, "[n]o body of men other than the regularly organized national guard or the troops of the United States shall associate themselves together as a military company or organization, or parade in public with arms without license of the governor." The Wyoming law also prohibits the public funding of private militias. Anyone convicted of violating the provisions of the law is subject to a fine of not more than $1,000, imprisonment of six months, or both, for each offense.

In states that do not outlaw them, private militias are limited only by the criminal laws applicable to all of society. Thus, if an armed private militia seeks to parade and exercise in a public area, its members will be subject to arrest on a variety of laws, including disturbing-the-peace, firearms, or even riot statutes.

Many private militias are driven by the insurrection theory of the Second Amendment. Under this view, the Sec-

ond Amendment grants an unconditional right to bear arms for self-defense and for rebellion against a tyrannical government—when a government turns oppressive, private citizens have a duty to "insurrect," or take up arms against it.

The U.S. Supreme Court has issued a qualified rejection of the insurrection theory. According to the Court in *Dennis v. United States*, 341 U.S. 494, 71 S. Ct. 857, 95 L. Ed. 1137 (1951), "[W]hatever theoretical merit there may be to the argument that there is a 'right' to rebellion against dictatorial governments is without force where the existing structure of the government provides for peaceful and orderly change." Scholars have interpreted this to mean that as long as the government provides for free elections and trials by jury, private citizens have no right to take up arms against the government.

Some people have disagreed with the Supreme Court's definition of tyranny. Many of these people label the state and federal governments as tyrannical based on issues such as taxes and government regulations. Others cite government-sponsored racial and ethnic integration as driving forces in their campaign against the federal and state governments. Many of these critics have formed private militias designed to resist perceived government oppression.

Some private militias have formed their own government. The legal problems of these private militias are generally unrelated to military activities. Instead, any criminal charges usually arise from activities associated with their political beliefs. The Freemen of Montana

is one such militia. This group denied the legitimacy of the federal government and created its own township called Justus. The Freemen established its own court system, posted bounties for the arrest of police officers and judges, and held seminars on how to challenge laws its members viewed as beyond the scope of the Constitution. According to neighbors, the group also established its own common-law court system and built its own jail for the imprisonment of trespassers and government workers, or "public hirelings."

In the 1990s, the Freemen came to the attention of federal prosecutors after members of the group allegedly wrote worthless checks and money orders to pay taxes and to defraud banks and credit card companies. One Freeman had also allegedly threatened a federal judge, and some had allegedly refused to pay taxes for at least a decade.

In March 1996, law enforcement officials obtained warrants for the arrest of many of the Freemen. However, remembering the violence that occurred when officials attempted to serve arrest warrants on another armed group in Waco, Texas, in 1993, law enforcement authorities did not invade the Freemen's 960-acre ranch in Jordan, Montana. Although the Freemen constituted an armed challenge to all government authority, its beliefs and its military activities were not illegal, and most of its members were charged with nonviolent crimes, such as fraud and related conspiracy. Two men were also charged with threatening public officials. In addition, several Freemen faced charges of criminal syndicalism, which is the advocacy of violence for political goals.

See also *Dennis v. United States*.

IN FOCUS

---

stitutional. However, in its opinion, the Court in *Presser* delivered a reading of the Second Amendment that seemed to suggest an absolute right of persons to bear arms: "It is undoubtedly true that all citizens capable of bearing arms constitute the reserved military force or reserve militia of the United States," and "states

cannot . . . prohibit the people from keeping and bearing arms."

Despite this generous language, the Court refused to incorporate the Second Amendment into the Fourteenth Amendment. Under the first section of the FOURTEENTH AMENDMENT, passed in 1868, states may not abridge the

PRIVILEGES AND IMMUNITIES of citizens of the United States. The privileges and immunities of citizens are listed in the Bill of Rights, of which the Second Amendment is part. Presser had argued that states may not, by virtue of the Fourteenth Amendment, abridge the right to bear arms. The Court refused to accept the argument that the right to bear arms is a personal right of the people. According to the Court, "The right to drill or parade with arms, without, and independent of, an act of congress or law of the state authorizing the same, is not an attribute of national citizenship."

The *Presser* opinion is best understood in its historical context. The Northern states and the federal government had just fought the Civil War against Southern militias unauthorized by the federal government. After this ordeal, the Supreme Court was in no mood to accept an expansive right to bear arms. At the same time, the Court was sensitive to the subject of federal encroachment on STATES' RIGHTS.

Several decades later, the Supreme Court ignored the contradictory language in *Presser* and cemented a limited reading of the Second Amendment. In *United States v. Miller*, 307 U.S. 174, 59 S. Ct. 816, 83 L. Ed. 1206 (1939), defendants Jack Miller and Frank Layton were charged in federal court with unlawful transportation of firearms in violation of certain sections of the National Firearms Act of June 26, 1934 (ch. 757, 48 Stat. 1236–1240 [26 U.S.C.A. § 1132 et seq.]). Specifically, Miller and Layton had transported shotguns with barrels less than eighteen inches long, without the registration required under the act.

The district court dismissed the INDICTMENT, holding that the act violated the Second Amendment. The United States appealed. The Supreme Court reversed the decision and sent the case back to the trial court. The Supreme Court stated that the Second Amendment was fashioned "to assure the continuation and render possible the effectiveness of . . . militia forces."

The *Miller* opinion confirmed the restrictive language of *Presser* and solidified a narrow reading of the Second Amendment. According to the Court in *Miller*, the Second Amendment does not guarantee the right to own a firearm unless the possession or use of the firearm has "a reasonable relationship to the preservation or efficiency of a well regulated militia."

The legislative measures that inspire most Second Amendment discussions are GUN CONTROL laws. Since the mid–nineteenth century, state legislatures have been passing laws that infringe a perceived right to bear arms. Con-

Gun Ownership in 1993

Statistics are for the fifty states and the District of Columbia. Represents respondents indicating there is a gun in the home or garage. Based on sample of noninstitutionalized English-speaking persons 18 years old and over.

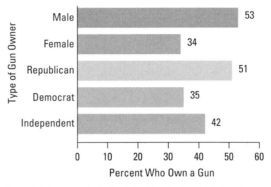

Source: U.S. Bureau of Justice Statistics, *Sourcebook of Criminal Justice Statistics.*

gress has also asserted the power to regulate firearms. No law regulating firearms has ever been struck down by the Supreme Court as a violation of the Second Amendment.

Historically, the academic community has largely ignored the Second Amendment. However, gun control laws have turned many laypersons into scholars of the Second Amendment's history. The arguments for a broader interpretation are many and varied. Most center on the original intent of the Framers. Some emphasize that the Second Amendment should be interpreted to grant an unconditional personal right to bear arms for defensive and sporting purposes. Others adhere to an insurrection theory, under which the Second Amendment not only grants the personal right to bear arms, it gives citizens the right to rebel against a government perceived as tyrannical.

In response to these arguments, supporters of the prevailing Second Amendment interpretation maintain that any right to bear arms should be secondary to concerns for public safety. They also point out that other provisions in the Constitution grant power to Congress to quell insurrections, thus contradicting the insurrection theory. Lastly, they argue that the Constitution should be interpreted in accordance with a changing society, and that the destructive capability of semiautomatic and automatic firearms was not envisioned by the Framers.

In response to the last argument, critics maintain that because such firearms exist, it should be legal to use them against violent criminals who are themselves wielding such weapons.

SECONDARY AUTHORITY 📖 Sources of information that describe or interpret the law, such as legal treatises, LAW REVIEW articles, and other scholarly legal writings, cited by lawyers to persuade a court to reach a particular decision in a case, but which the court is not obligated to follow. 📖

Secondary authority is information cited by lawyers in arguments and used by courts in reaching decisions. Secondary authority is distinct from primary authority. The sources of PRIMARY AUTHORITY are written laws passed by legislative bodies, prior judicial decisions, government administrative regulations, and court rules. Courts are obliged to decide cases by following the dictates of primary authority, and lawyers must make arguments based on the primary authority that is applicable to the case.

Neither lawyers nor courts are required to use secondary authority, but both may do so to buttress arguments based on primary authority. Among the most commonly cited sources of secondary authority are the RESTATEMENTS OF LAW, written by the authors, scholars, and legal professionals that make up the American Law Institute. The restatements contain suggested laws and rules on a wide assortment of legal topics ranging from contracts to torts to conflicts of laws.

Law reviews and other scholarly works are other commonly cited sources of secondary authority. Law reviews are articles about legal topics published by law schools and other legal organizations and written by law professors, law students, and other academics. Other groups publish legal literature that may be cited by lawyers and courts. The *American Law Reports* provide case synopses of recent legal developments with a focus on court decisions, and continuing legal education programs conducted by and for attorneys produce literature that may be used by lawyers and judges.

Legal encyclopedia articles and legal dictionaries are less commonly cited in court although the U.S. Supreme Court has, on occasion, used *Black's Law Dictionary* to support its definition of a legal word or phrase.

SECONDARY BOYCOTT 📖 A group's refusal to work for, purchase from, or handle the products of a business with which the group has no dispute. 📖

A secondary boycott is an attempt to influence the actions of one business by exerting pressure on another business. For example, assume that a group has a complaint against the Acme Company. Assume further that the Widget Company is the major supplier to the Acme Company. If the complaining group informs the Widget Company that it will persuade the public to stop doing business with the company unless it stops doing business with Acme Company, such a boycott of the Widget Company would be a SECONDARY boycott. The intended effect of such a boycott would be to influence the actions of Acme Company by organizing against its major supplier.

Labor unions are the most common practitioners of secondary boycotts. Typically a LABOR UNION involved in a dispute with an employer will arrange a secondary boycott if less drastic measures to reach a satisfactory accord with the employer have been ineffective. Secondary boycotts have two main forms: a secondary consumer boycott, in which the union appeals to consumers to withhold patronage of a business, and a secondary employee boycott, in which the union dissuades employees from working for a particular business.

Generally a secondary boycott is considered an UNFAIR LABOR PRACTICE when it is organized by a labor union. Congress first acted to prohibit secondary boycotts in the LABOR-MANAGEMENT RELATIONS ACT of 1947 (29 U.S.C.A. § 141 et seq.), also called the Taft-Hartley Act. The Taft-Hartley Act was a set of amendments to the NATIONAL LABOR RELATIONS ACT, also known as the Wagner Act of 1935 (29 U.S.C.A. § 151 et seq.). Congress limits the right of labor unions to conduct secondary boycotts because such activity is considered basically unfair and because it can have a devastating effect on intrastate and interstate commerce and the general state of the economy.

On the federal level, the right of a labor union to arrange a secondary boycott is limited by section 8(b)(4) of the National Labor Relations Act. Under the act, no labor union may threaten, coerce, or restrain any person engaged in commerce in order to force that person to cease doing business with any other person (29 U.S.C.A. § 158(b)(4)(ii)(B)). Secondary boycotts may be enjoined, or stopped, by order of a federal court, and an aggrieved business may file suit in court against the party initiating the secondary boycott to recover any monetary DAMAGES that resulted. If the federal act somehow does not cover the actions of a labor union in a particular case, an aggrieved business may seek relief under state laws.

The statutory limitation on the right of labor unions to instigate a secondary boycott is an exception to the guarantee of free speech contained in the FIRST AMENDMENT to the U.S. Constitution. But in balancing free speech rights against the rights of secondary employers and the right of Congress to manage interstate commerce, Congress has carved out an important exception to the ban on secondary boycotts by labor unions. Under this section of the act, a labor union may induce a secondary boycott if the information dispensed by the labor union is truthful, does not cause a work stoppage, and has the purpose of informing the general public that the secondary neutral employer distributes a product that is produced by the primary employer. This exception is called the publicity exception to the ban on secondary boycotts by labor unions.

The publicity proviso does not cover PICKETING. Picketing is a physical presence at a business to publicize a labor dispute, influence customers and employees, or show a union's desire to represent employees. The U.S. Supreme Court has held that Congress may prohibit a union from picketing against a secondary employer if the picketing would predictably result in financial ruin for the picketed secondary employer (*National Labor Relations Board v. Retail Store Employees, Local 1001 [Safeco]*, 447 U.S. 607, 100 S. Ct. 2372, 65 L. Ed. 2d 377 [1980]). The Supreme Court also has ruled that the publicity exception does not apply to the distribution of handbills that encourage a boycott of a shopping mall department store if the dispute is with the company constructing the department store and the boycott includes cotenants of the shopping mall who had no relationship with the construction company (*Edward J. DeBartolo Corp. v. National Labor Relations Board*, 463 U.S. 147, 103 S. Ct. 2926, 77 L. Ed. 2d 535 [1983]). In 1988 the High Court held that section 158(b)(4)(ii)(B) of 29 U.S.C.A. did not prohibit the peaceful distribution of handbills at a shopping mall urging consumers not to shop at the mall until the mall's owner promised that all mall construction would be done by contractors paying fair wages (*Edward J. DeBartolo Corp. v. Florida Gulf Coast Building and Construction Trades Council*, 485 U.S. 568, 108 S. Ct. 1392, 99 L. Ed. 2d 645 [1988]). According to the Court, such activity did not constitute threats, coercion, or restraint and therefore did not fall within the prohibition of the National Labor Relations Act.

See also LABOR LAW; STRIKE.

SECONDARY EVIDENCE ▣ A reproduction of, or substitute for, an original DOCUMENT or item of proof that is offered to establish a particular issue in a legal ACTION. ▣

Secondary evidence is EVIDENCE that has been reproduced from an original document or substituted for an original item. For example, a photocopy of a document or photograph would be considered secondary evidence. Another ex-

ample would be an exact replica of an engine part that was contained in a motor vehicle. If the engine part is not the very same engine part that was inside the motor vehicle involved in the case, it is considered secondary evidence.

Courts prefer original, or primary, evidence. They try to avoid using secondary evidence wherever possible. This approach is called the BEST EVIDENCE rule. Nevertheless, a court may allow a party to introduce secondary evidence in a number of situations. Under rule 1003 of the Federal Rules of Evidence, a duplicate is ADMISSIBLE unless a genuine question is raised as to its authenticity or unless it would be unfair to admit the duplicate in place of the original piece of evidence.

After hearing arguments by the parties, the court decides whether to admit secondary evidence after determining whether the evidence is in fact authentic or whether it would be unfair to admit the duplicate. However, when a party questions whether an asserted writing ever existed, or whether a writing, recording, or photograph is the original, the trier of fact makes the ultimate determination. The trier of fact is the judge if it is a BENCH TRIAL; in a jury trial, the trier of fact is the jury.

Rule 1004 of the Federal Rules of Evidence lists specific exceptions to the best evidence rule. Under rule 1004, secondary evidence of a writing, recording, or photograph is admissible if (1) all originals are lost or destroyed, unless they were lost or destroyed in BAD FAITH by the party seeking to introduce the secondary evidence; (2) no original can be obtained by judicial process or procedure; (3) the party's opponent in the case has possession of the original and does not produce it after being given sufficient notice that the evidence would be subject to examination at a court hearing; or (4) the original evidence is not closely related to a controlling issue in the case.

See also PRIMARY EVIDENCE.

SECONDARY MEANING ▣ A doctrine of TRADEMARK law that provides that protection is afforded to the user of an otherwise unprotectable mark when the mark, through advertising or other exposure, has come to signify that an item is produced or sponsored by that user. ▣

Under trademark law a mark associated with a marketed product generally cannot receive full trademark protection unless it is distinctive. Trademark protection gives the holder of a mark the exclusive right to use that mark in connection with a product.

Full trademark protection is given when the U.S. PATENT AND TRADEMARK OFFICE places the mark on the principal register of trademarks.

Suggestive, arbitrary, and fanciful marks distinguish a product from other products, so they automatically qualify for the principal register. Descriptive and generic marks ordinarily do not qualify for the principal register. A person may not, for example, claim the right to the word "fine" in connection with a product because the word is merely descriptive. A descriptive or generic mark may, however, be placed on the supplemental register, which gives the holder of the mark a certain measure of trademark protection. If the mark acquires a secondary meaning after five years of continuous, exclusive use on the market, the mark may be placed on the principal register (15 U.S.C.A. § 1052(f)).

A descriptive or generic mark attains a secondary meaning if the producer so effectively markets the product with the mark that consumers come to immediately associate the mark with only that producer of that particular kind of goods. To illustrate, assume that an apple grower markets red apples under the term "Acme." Because the term is generic, it would not qualify for full trademark protection at first. If, however, customers immediately recognize Acme apples as the apples produced by that grower, after five years the producer may prevent all others from using the mark "Acme" in connection with red apples.

Under 15 U.S.C.A. § 1052(a)–(d), (f), immoral or scandalous marks, national symbols, and names of living figures cannot acquire trademark protection, even through secondary meaning. Surnames generally are not given trademark protection, but a surname may qualify for protection if it acquires a secondary meaning (*Ex parte Rivera Watch Corp.*, 106 U.S.P.Q. 145, 1955 WL 6450 [Com'r 1955]).

SECOND LOOK DOCTRINE In the law of future interests, a rule that provides that even though the validity of interests created by the exercise of a power of appointment is ordinarily measured from the date the power is created, not from its exercise, the facts existing on the date of its exercise can be considered in order to determine if the RULE AGAINST PERPETUITIES has been violated.

At COMMON LAW, the rule against perpetuities prescribed that no interest in property is valid unless it vests, if at all, not later than twenty-one years plus the period of gestation after some life or lives in being at the time of the creation of the interest. A property interest vests when it is given to a person in being and is not subject to a condition precedent (the occurrence of a designated event). This rule restricts a person's power to control the ownership and possession of her property after her death and ensures the transferability of property.

The second look doctrine has been applied to mitigate the harsh effect of the rule against perpetuities on a power of appointment—authority granted by one person by DEED or WILL to another, the DONEE, to select a person or persons who are to receive PROPERTY.

For example, B was the life income BENEFICIARY (one who profits from the act of another) of a TRUST and the donee of a special power over the succeeding REMAINDER—the property that passes to another after the expiration of an intervening income interest. His father, F, who predeceased him, established the trust in his will. B exercised his power through his own will, directing that the income be paid after his death to his children for the life of the survivor and that, upon the death of his last surviving child, the CORPUS—the main body or principal of a trust—be paid to his grandchildren. At F's death, B had two children, X and Y. No other children were born to B, and at his death, X and Y are still alive.

B's appointment is valid. The perpetuity period is measured from F's death. If only the facts existing at F's death could be considered, however, B's appointment would partly fail because of the possibility that he might have another child after F's death who would have children more than twenty-one years after the deaths of B, X, and Y. In considering the validity of B's appointment, however, not just the facts existing when the perpetuity period commences to run on B's appointment are considered. The facts existing at B's death can be taken into account under the second look doctrine, which thereby saves B's appointment. At B's death, it is known that no additional children were born to him after F's death. Thus B's last surviving child will be either X or Y, both of whom were "in being" at F's death and, therefore, constitute the measuring lives.

The second look doctrine is a departure from the fundamental principle that only the facts in existence when the perpetuity period commences to run can be taken into account in determining validity. Until the appointment is made, the appointed interests cannot be litigated. No useful purpose, therefore, is served by invalidating appointed interests because of what might happen after the power is created, but which at the time of exercise can no longer happen.

In some JURISDICTIONS, this doctrine has been extended to gifts-in-default, which involve the expiration of the power, such as when the donee releases the power or dies without having exercised it.

For example, B was the life income beneficiary of a trust and the donee of a power over the succeeding remainder interest. In DEFAULT of appointment (that is, B fails to name anyone to receive the property after he dies), the income after B's death was to be paid to his children for the life of the survivor, and on the death of B's last surviving child, the corpus was to be paid to B's grandchildren. B's father, F, who predeceased him, created the trust in his will. At F's death, B had two children, X and Y. B died without having additional children and without exercising his power. B was survived by X and Y.

F's death marks the commencement of the running of the perpetuity period as to the gift-in-default. Nevertheless if a second look at the facts existing at B's death is permissible, the gift-in-default is valid. The measuring lives are X and Y. If no second look is permissible, the remainder interest in favor of B's grandchildren is invalid. As of F's death, there was a possibility that B might have a child after F's death, that such a child might have survived B, and that such child might have had a child, B's grandchild, more than twenty-one years after the death of the survivor of B, X, and Y.

A default clause creates property interests no different from other property interests except that they are subject to divestment upon the exercise of the power. If B had not been granted a power of appointment in the above example, the interests created by the default clause would clearly be judged on the basis of the facts existing when F died. No second look as of B's death would be permissible, unless the jurisdiction had adopted the WAIT AND SEE DOCTRINE. Until the power of appointment expires, it cannot be known whether the gift-in-default of appointment is to control the disposition of the property or whether it is to be superseded by some appointment that the donee makes. Therefore no possible delay in adjudging the validity of the remainder is entitled in examining facts that exist at the date the power expires unexercised.

Jurisdictions that do not apply the doctrine to gifts-in-default maintain that its application to appointments is justified because the appointed interests are unknown, and, consequently, it is impossible to adjudicate their validity until the appointment is made, not because it is unlikely that anyone would want to adjudicate their validity until that time. The interests created by a default clause, unlike appointed interests, are known, and their validity can be litigated before the expiration of the power. These jurisdictions reason that the ra-tionale for taking a second look in the case of appointed interests does not apply to interests created in the default clause.

See also ESTATE; LIFE IN BEING; VESTED.

SECRETARY GENERAL See UNITED NATIONS.

SECRETARY OF STATE   Holding one of the ranking positions in the president's CABINET, the secretary of state is the president's principal foreign policy adviser. In this pivotal role, the secretary undertakes the overall direction, coordination, and supervision of relations between the United States and foreign nations. The position is fourth in line of presidential succession. Like other cabinet members who implement the president's policies, the secretary heads a federal department: the Department of State. As its director, the secretary oversees a vast network of U.S. offices and agencies, conducts negotiations with foreign governments, and often travels in the role of chief U.S. representative abroad. In 1997 President BILL CLINTON named Madeleine K. Albright as the first female secretary of state.

The position of secretary of state developed shortly after the founding of the nation in the late eighteenth century. In 1781 Congress created the Department of Foreign Affairs but abolished it and replaced it with the Department of State in 1789. Lawmakers designated the secretary of state as head of the State Department with two principal responsibilities: to assist the president in foreign policy matters and to be the chief representative of the United States abroad. Nomination of the secretary was left to the president, but the appointment was made contingent upon the approval of the U.S.

Madeleine Albright, as secretary of state, is President Bill Clinton's chief foreign policy adviser. She directs relations between the United States and foreign countries.

Senate. The first secretary of state, THOMAS JEFFERSON, served under President GEORGE WASHINGTON from 1790 to 1793.

Since the end of World War II, the U.S. foreign policy apparatus has greatly expanded, and its principal body is the State Department. The United States maintains diplomatic relations with some 180 countries worldwide as well as ties to many international organizations, and most of this diplomatic business flows through the State Department. The secretary is aided by a deputy secretary and five undersecretaries who serve as key advisers in political affairs; economic, business, and agricultural affairs; arms control and international security affairs; management; and global affairs. Additionally, the secretary has general responsibility for the U.S. INFORMATION AGENCY, the Arms Control and Disarmament Agency, and the Agency for International Development.

The secretary is very important. Under the U.S. Constitution, the president has most of the power to set foreign policy; some of this power is shared by the U.S. Senate, which approves treaties as well as diplomatic and consular appointments. In practical terms the secretary of state generally becomes the architect of U.S. foreign policy by implementing the president's objectives. Not all foreign policy advice is given by the secretary, however. In 1947 the creation of the NATIONAL SECURITY COUNCIL provided the president with an additional advisory board (National Security Act of 1947, 50 U.S.C.A. §§ 401–412 [1982]).

Some secretaries have exerted enormous influence on U.S. policy—largely as a reflection of the president under whom they served. HENRY KISSINGER, who served as secretary of state from 1973 to 1976 under Presidents RICHARD M. NIXON and GERALD R. FORD, had a leading role in shaping the nation's participation in nuclear arms treaties and in the Vietnam War. By contrast, Secretary of State George Schultz found his influence eclipsed by that of the National Security Council during the IRAN-CONTRA scandal that rocked the presidency of RONALD REAGAN in the mid-1980s.

CROSS-REFERENCES

Ambassadors and Consuls; Arms Control and Disarmament; International Law; State Department.

SECTION ◻ The distinct and numbered subdivisions in legal codes, statutes, and textbooks. In the law of REAL PROPERTY, a parcel of land equal in area to one square mile, or 640 acres. ◻
SECTION 1983 Section 1983 of title 42 of the U.S. Code is part of the Civil Rights Act of 1871. This provision was formerly enacted as

part of the KU KLUX KLAN ACT of 1871 and was originally designed to combat post–Civil War racial violence in the Southern states. Reenacted as part of the Civil Rights Act, section 1983 is today the primary means of enforcing all constitutional rights.

Section 1983 provides:

> Every person who, under color of any statute, ordinance, regulation, custom, or usage, of any State or Territory or the District of Columbia, subjects, or causes to be subjected, any citizen of the United States or other person within the jurisdiction thereof to the deprivation of any rights, privileges, or immunities secured by the Constitution and laws, shall be liable to the party injured in an action at law, suit in equity, or other proper proceeding for redress.

On March 23, 1871, President ULYSSES S. GRANT sent an urgent message to Congress calling for national legislation that could combat the alarming increase in racial unrest and violence in the South. Congress reacted swiftly to this request, proposing a BILL just five days later. The primary objective of the bill was to provide a means for individuals and states to enforce, in the federal or state courts, the provisions of the FOURTEENTH AMENDMENT. The proposed bill created heated debate lasting several weeks but was eventually passed on April 20, 1871.

During the first ninety years of the act, few causes of action were brought due to the narrow and restrictive way that the U.S. Supreme Court interpreted the act. For example, the phrase "person . . . [acting] under color of any statute" was not interpreted to include those wrongdoers who happened to be state or municipal officials acting within the scope of their employment but not in accordance with the state or municipal laws. Those officials were successfully able to argue that they were not acting under color of statute and therefore their actions did not fall under the mandates of section 1983. In addition, courts narrowly construed the definition of "rights, privileges, or immunities." See also SCOPE OF EMPLOYMENT.

But the Supreme Court decisions in *Monroe v. Pape*, 365 U.S. 167, 81 S. Ct. 473, 5 L. Ed. 2d 492 (1961), and *Monell v. Department of Social Services*, 436 U.S. 658, 98 S. Ct. 2018, 56 L. Ed. 2d 611 (1978), finally recognized the full scope of Congress's original intent in enacting section 1983. The Supreme Court began accepting an expansive definition of rights, privileges, or immunities and held that the act does cover the actions of state and municipal officials, even if they had no authority under state statute to act as they did in violating someone's federal rights.

Jurisdiction   Federal courts are authorized to hear cases brought under section 1983 pursuant to two statutory provisions: 28 U.S.C.A. § 1343(3) (1948) and 28 U.S.C.A. § 1331 (1948). The former statute permits federal district courts to hear cases involving the deprivation of CIVIL RIGHTS, and the latter statute permits federal courts to hear all cases involving a FEDERAL QUESTION or issue. Cases brought under section 1983 may therefore be heard in FEDERAL COURTS by application of both jurisdictional statutes.

State courts may also properly hear section 1983 cases pursuant to the SUPREMACY CLAUSE of Article VI of the U.S. Constitution. The Supremacy Clause mandates that states must provide hospitable FORUMS for federal claims and the vindication of federal rights. This point was solidified in the Supreme Court decision of *Felder v. Casey*, 487 U.S. 131, 108 S. Ct. 2302, 101 L. Ed. 2d 123 (1988). The *Felder* case involved an individual who was arrested in Wisconsin and later brought suit in state court against the police officers and city for violations of his federal rights. The state court dismissed the claim because the plaintiff failed to properly comply with a state procedural law. But the Supreme Court overturned the state decision, holding that the Wisconsin statute could not bar the individual's federal claim.

To bring an ACTION under section 1983, the plaintiff does not have to begin in state court. However, if the plaintiff chooses to bring suit in state court, the defendant has the right to remove the case to federal court.

Elements of a Section 1983 Claim
To prevail in a claim under section 1983, the plaintiff must prove two critical issues: a person subjected the plaintiff to conduct that occurred under color of state law, and this conduct deprived the plaintiff of rights, privileges, or immunities guaranteed under federal law or the U.S. Constitution.

A state is not a "person" under section 1983, but a city is a person under the law (*Will v. Michigan Department of State Police*, 491 U.S. 58, 109 S. Ct. 2304, 105 L. Ed. 2d 45 [1989]). Similarly, state officials sued in their official capacities are not deemed persons under section 1983, but if sued in their personal capacities, they are considered to be persons. Thus if a plaintiff wants to bring a section 1983 claim against a state official, she or he must name the defendants in their personal capacity and not in

their professional capacity. Like a state, a TERRITORY, such as the territory of Guam, is not considered to be a person for the purposes of section 1983.

The Supreme Court has broadly construed the provision "under color of any statute" to include virtually any state action including the exercise of power of one "possessed by virtue of state law and made possible only because the wrongdoer is clothed with the authority of state law" (*United States v. Classic*, 313 U.S. 299, 61 S. Ct. 1031, 85 L. Ed. 1368 [1941]). Thus, the wrongdoer's employment by the government may indicate state action, although it does not conclusively prove it. Even if the wrongdoer did not act pursuant to a state statute, the plaintiff may still show that the defendant acted pursuant to a "custom or usage" that had the force of law in the state. In *Adickes v. S. H. Kress & Co.*, 398 U.S. 144, 90 S. Ct. 1598, 26 L. Ed. 2d 142 (1970), the plaintiff was able to prove that she was refused service in a restaurant due to her race because of a state-enforced custom of racial segregation, even though no state statute promoted racial segregation in restaurants.

A successful section 1983 claim also requires a showing of the deprivation of a constitutional or federal statutory "right." This showing is required because section 1983 creates a REMEDY when rights are violated but does not create any rights itself. It is not enough to show a violation of a federal law because all federal laws do not necessarily create federal rights. A violation of the FOURTH AMENDMENT's guarantee against unreasonable searches and seizures or a violation of the COMMERCE CLAUSE are examples of federal constitutional rights that may be deprived. Deprivation of federal statutory rights is also actionable when it can be shown that the statute creates a federal right. To show that a federal statute creates a federal right, the plaintiff must demonstrate that the federal law was designed and clearly intended to benefit the plaintiff, resulting in the creation of a federal right. For example, the Supreme Court held that a person's ENTITLEMENT to WELFARE benefits under the federal SOCIAL SECURITY ACT is a federal right stemming from a federal statute that can be protected by section 1983 (*Maine v. Thiboutot*, 448 U.S. 1, 100 S. Ct. 2502, 65 L. Ed. 2d 555 [1980]).

If the plaintiff can demonstrate that a federal law granted her a federal right that was then violated, the defendant can defeat the plaintiff's claim by demonstrating that Congress specifically foreclosed a remedy under section 1983 for the type of injury that the plaintiff is pleading. The Supreme Court has held that the defendant must prove that a section 1983 action would be inconsistent with the cautious and precise scheme of remedies provided by Congress. For example, if a federal law specifically provides for a means to privately enforce that law, or if the statute does not create "rights" within the meaning of section 1983, the defendant may prevail in showing that Congress did not intend a section 1983 remedy to apply in that circumstance. It is the defendant's burden to demonstrate congressional intent to prevent a remedy under section 1983.

Absolute and Qualified Immunities

Although section 1983 does not specifically provide for absolute IMMUNITY for any parties, the Supreme Court has deemed that some officials are immune. The Supreme Court reached this conclusion by applying the COMMON-LAW principles of tort immunity that existed in the United States at the time section 1983 was enacted, assuming that Congress had intended those common-law immunities to apply without having to specifically so provide in the statute. State and regional legislators are absolutely immune, as long as they are engaged in traditional legislative functions. Although the Supreme Court has not had the opportunity to extend this rule to municipal legislators, lower courts have done so (*Reed v. Village of Shorewood*, 704 F.2d 943 [7th Cir. 1983]).

Judges have also been held to be absolutely immune from section 1983 actions, as long as they are performing adjudicative functions (*Pierson v. Ray*, 386 U.S. 547, 87 S. Ct. 1213, 18 L. Ed. 2d 288 [1967]; *Stump v. Sparkman*, 435 U.S. 349, 98 S. Ct. 1099, 55 L. Ed. 2d 331 [1978]). Judges are considered to be performing their adjudicative functions as long as they had JURISDICTION over the subject matter at the time they acted and the action was a judicial act. A minority of lower courts have extended this absolute JUDICIAL IMMUNITY to QUASI-JUDICIAL agencies, such as parole boards, when they have performed functions similar to those of judges (*Johnson v. Wells*, 566 F.2d 1016 [5th Cir. 1978]). Absolute judicial immunity has also been extended in some cases to those judicial employees who act under the direction of the judge, such as a law clerk, COURT ADMINISTRATOR, PARALEGAL, or court REPORTER (*Lockhart v. Hoenstine*, 411 F.2d 455 [3d Cir. 1969]).

State prosecuting attorneys who are acting within the scope of their duty in presenting the state's case are also absolutely immune from suits for DAMAGES under section 1983 claims but are not absolutely immune from suits seeking prospective relief (*Imbler v. Pachtman*, 424 U.S. 409, 96 S. Ct. 984, 47 L. Ed. 2d 128 [1976]). Other state officials who act in a prosecutorial role are similarly immune. The Supreme Court differentiated PUBLIC DEFENDERS, however, in *Polk County v. Dodson*, 454 U.S. 312, 102 S. Ct. 445, 70 L. Ed. 2d 509 (1981), holding that they do not act under color of state law when performing their duties and therefore are not in need of immunity because their conduct is not covered by section 1983.

WITNESSES who testify in court are absolutely immune from section 1983 actions for damages, even if the claim arises out of the witness's perjured TESTIMONY (*Briscoe v. LaHue*, 460 U.S. 325, 103 S. Ct. 1108, 75 L. Ed. 2d 96 [1983]).

The Supreme Court has also recognized a qualified immunity defense to section 1983 actions in certain circumstances. Most state and local officials and employees, who do not enjoy absolute immunity, are entitled to qualified immunity. Thus, a prosecuting attorney who enjoys absolute immunity in performing her prosecutorial functions may also enjoy a qualified immunity in hiring and firing subordinates. The Supreme Court has held that school board members, state mental institution administrators, law enforcement officers, prison officials, and state and local executives have qualified immunity (*Wood v. Strickland*, 420 U.S. 308, 95 S. Ct. 992, 43 L. Ed. 2d 214 [1975]; *O'Connor v. Donaldson*, 422 U.S. 563, 95 S. Ct. 2486, 45 L. Ed. 2d 396 [1975]; *Pierson v. Ray*, 386 U.S. 547, 87 S. Ct. 1213, 18 L. Ed. 2d 288 [1967]; *Procunier v. Navarette*, 434 U.S. 555, 98 S. Ct. 855, 55 L. Ed. 2d 24 [1978]; *Scheuer v. Rhodes*, 416 U.S. 232, 94 S. Ct. 1683, 40 L. Ed. 2d 90 [1974]). Most federal circuit courts have deemed that parole board members and prison disciplinary committee members have qualified immunity (*Fowler v. Cross*, 635 F.2d 476 [5th Cir. 1981]; *Thompson v. Burke*, 556 F.2d 231 [3d Cir. 1977]). Lower courts have extended the defense of qualified immunity to a number of other officials, such as city managers, county health administrators, and state Department of Veterans' Affairs trust officers.

If the defendant can raise the defense of absolute or qualified immunity, then it is his duty to plead it (*Gomez v. Toledo*, 446 U.S. 635, 100 S. Ct. 1920, 64 L. Ed. 2d 572 [1980]).

Remedies

The Supreme Court has held that section 1983 creates "a species of tort liability" (*Imbler v. Pachtman*, 424 U.S. 409, 96 S. Ct. 984, 47 L. Ed. 2d 128 [1976]). Thus, the Supreme Court has held that, as in TORT LAW, a section 1983 plaintiff is entitled to receive only

NOMINAL DAMAGES, not to exceed one dollar, unless she or he can prove actual damages (*Carey v. Piphus*, 435 U.S. 247, 98 S. Ct. 1042, 55 L. Ed. 2d 252 [1978]). The jury is not entitled to place a monetary value on the constitutional rights of which the plaintiff was deprived (*Memphis Community School District v. Stachura*, 477 U.S. 299, 106 S. Ct. 2537, 91 L. Ed. 2d 249 [1986]). Plaintiffs bear the burden, therefore, of presenting EVIDENCE of all expenses incurred, such as medical or psychiatric expenses, lost wages, and any damages due to pain and suffering, emotional distress, or damage to reputation. The plaintiff is also under a burden to mitigate his damages, and the award of damages may be reduced to the extent that the plaintiff failed to do so. See also MITIGATION OF DAMAGES.

A section 1983 plaintiff is also required to prove that a federal right was violated and, similar to tort law, that the alleged violation was a proximate or legal cause of the damages that the plaintiff suffered (*Arnold v. IBM Corp.*, 637 F.2d 1350 [9th Cir. 1981]). See also PROXIMATE CAUSE.

The Supreme Court has also held that, similar to tort law, PUNITIVE DAMAGES are available under section 1983 (*Smith v. Wade*, 461 U.S. 30, 103 S. Ct. 1625, 75 L. Ed. 2d 632 [1983]). A plaintiff is entitled to punitive damages if the jury finds that the defendant's conduct was reckless or callously indifferent to the federally protected rights of others, or if the defendant was motivated by an evil intent. The jury has the duty to assess the amount of punitive damages. Because the purpose of punitive damages is to punish the wrongdoer, such damages may be awarded even if the plaintiff cannot show actual damages (*Basista v. Weir*, 340 F.2d 74 [3d Cir. 1965]). As in tort law, the judge has the right to overturn a jury VERDICT if the jury awards what the judge considers to be excessive punitive damages.

Courts also have broad power to grant equitable relief to plaintiffs in section 1983 actions. Equitable remedies that courts have provided in the past include SCHOOL DESEGREGATION, restructuring of state mental health facilities, and restructuring of PRISONS (*United States v. City of Yonkers*, 96 F. 3d 600 [2nd Cir. 1996]; *Wyatt v. Stickney*, 344 F. Supp. 373 [M.D. Ala. 1972]; *Hutto v. Finney*, 437 U.S. 678, 98 S. Ct. 2565, 57 L. Ed. 2d 522 [1978]). When the court does provide equitable relief, it usually also provides ongoing evaluation and supervision of the enforcement of its orders.

The Civil Rights Attorney's Fee Awards Act of 1976 (42 U.S.C.A. § 1988[b]) allows for the award of reasonable attorneys' fees to the prevailing party in cases brought under various federal civil rights laws, including section 1983. This provision applies whether or not COMPENSATORY DAMAGES were awarded. This provision also applies whether the plaintiff or the defendant prevails. However, if the defendant is the prevailing party, attorneys' fees have been held to be appropriate only where the lawsuit was "vexatious, frivolous, or brought to harass or embarrass the defendant" (*Hensley v. Eckerhart*, 461 U.S. 424, 103 S. Ct. 1933, 76 L. Ed. 2d 40 [1983]). In addition, section 1988 does not require that the attorneys' fees awarded be in proportion to the amount of damages recovered (*City of Riverside v. Rivera*, 477 U.S. 561, 106 S. Ct. 2686, 91 L. Ed. 2d 466 [1986]).

Rule 68 of the Federal Rules of Civil Procedure can lead to the adjustment of the amount of damages awarded by a jury in a section 1983 case. Enacted to encourage parties to settle their matters out of court, rule 68 provides that if the plaintiff rejected a SETTLEMENT offer made by the defendant before trial that is better than the award the plaintiff ultimately received in the trial, the defendant is not liable for plaintiff's attorneys' fees incurred after the time the defendant made the settlement offer (*Marek v. Chesny*, 473 U.S. 1, 105 S. Ct. 3012, 87 L. Ed. 2d 1 [1985]). Under rule 68, section 1983 plaintiffs need to carefully consider any settlement offers made by the defendants.

Bars to Relief Section 1983 does not provide a specific STATUTE OF LIMITATIONS, which is a time limit in which a claim must be brought after the alleged violation occurred. But 42 U.S.C.A. § 1988 (1976) states that where the federal law does not provide a statute of limitations, state law shall apply. In determining which state statute of limitations to apply in a section 1983 case, the Supreme Court has held that in the interests of national uniformity and predictability, all section 1983 claims shall be treated as tort claims for the recovery of PERSONAL INJURIES (*Wilson v. Garcia*, 471 U.S. 261, 105 S. Ct. 1938, 85 L. Ed. 2d 254 [1985]). If the state has various statutes of limitations for different intentional torts, the Supreme Court mandates that the state's general or residual personal injury statute of limitations should apply (*Owens v. Okure*, 488 U.S. 235, 109 S. Ct. 573, 102 L. Ed. 2d 594 [1989]).

The Supreme Court has also held that state tolling statutes, which provide a plaintiff with an additional period of time in which to bring a lawsuit equal to the period of time in which the plaintiff was legally disabled, apply to section 1983 cases (*Board of Regents v. Tomanio*, 446 U.S. 478, 100 S. Ct. 1790, 64 L. Ed. 2d 440 [1980]).

Under section 1983, the statute of limitations does not begin to run until the CAUSE OF ACTION accrues. The cause of action accrues when "the plaintiff knows or has reason to know of the injury which is the basis of the action" (*Cox v. Stanton*, 529 F.2d 47 [4th Cir. 1975]). However, in EMPLOYMENT LAW cases, the Supreme Court has held that the cause of action accrues when the discriminatory act occurs (*Delaware State College v. Ricks*, 449 U.S. 250, 101 S. Ct. 498, 66 L. Ed. 2d 431 [1980]). Thus, if an employee is being terminated for reasons that violate section 1983, the statute of limitations begins on the day that the employee learns of the termination, not when the termination actually begins (*Chardon v. Fernandez*, 454 U.S. 6, 102 S. Ct. 28, 70 L. Ed. 2d 6 [1981]).

The legal rules of RES JUDICATA (claim preclusion) and COLLATERAL ESTOPPEL (issue preclusion) apply to section 1983 claims. This means that federal courts must give state court JUDGMENTS the same preclusive effect that the law of the state in which the judgment was rendered would give. Plaintiffs need to be careful to raise all potential federal claims in cases brought in STATE COURT because they will not be allowed to bring those claims later in federal court after the state court has rendered a decision on the issues before it.

A plaintiff may waive his or her right to sue under section 1983, but such a waiver may be deemed unenforceable if "the interest in its enforcement is outweighed in the circumstances by a public policy harmed by enforcement of the agreement" (*Town of Newton v. Rumery*, 480 U.S. 386, 107 S. Ct. 1187, 94 L. Ed. 2d 405 [1987]).

See also COLOR OF OFFICE.

SECURE 📖 To assure the payment of a DEBT or the performance of an obligation; to provide SECURITY. 📖

A DEBTOR "secures" a CREDITOR by giving him or her a LIEN, MORTGAGE, or other security to be used in case the debtor fails to make payment.

SECURED CREDITOR 📖 One who holds some special monetary assurance of payment of a DEBT owed to him or her, such as a MORTGAGE, COLLATERAL, or LIEN. 📖

SECURED TRANSACTIONS 📖 Business dealings that grant a CREDITOR a right in PROPERTY owned or held by a DEBTOR to assure the payment of a DEBT or the performance of some obligation. 📖

A secured transaction is a transaction that is founded on a SECURITY agreement. A security agreement is a provision in a business transaction in which the OBLIGOR, or debtor, in the AGREEMENT gives to the creditor the right to own property owned or held by the debtor. This property, called COLLATERAL, is then held by either the debtor or the secured party to ensure against loss in the event the debtor cannot fulfill the obligations under the transaction.

The purchase of a car through financing is an example of a secured transaction. The car dealership or some other lender pays for the vehicle in return for a promise from the buyer to repay the loan with interest. The buyer receives the vehicle, but the lender retains the TITLE to the car as security against the risk that the buyer will be unable to make the loan payments. If the buyer DEFAULTS on the payments, the lender, called the secured party, may repossess the car to recover losses from the default.

If the same transaction was unsecured, the buyer would receive the title to and possession of the car, and the lender would receive only the buyer's PROMISE to repay the loan. If the buyer defaulted on the payments, the lender could sue the buyer, but the simple remedy of taking the property would not be available.

A security interest may be transferred, or assigned, to a third party. The party receiving the ASSIGNMENT becomes the secured party, and the original secured party no longer holds a claim to the collateral.

The law of secured transactions varies little from state to state because most states have adopted Article 9, the secured transactions portion of the UNIFORM COMMERCIAL CODE (UCC). The UCC is a set of model laws written by lawyers, professors, and other legal professionals in the American Law Institute.

Common Forms of Secured Transactions   Secured transactions come in many forms, but three types are most common for consumers: pledges, chattel mortgages, and conditional sales. A PLEDGE is the DELIVERY of goods to the secured party as security for a debt or the performance of an act. For example, assume that one person has borrowed $500 from another. Assume further that the debtor gives a piece of expensive jewelry to the creditor. If the jewelry is to be returned to the debtor after the debt is repaid, and if the creditor has the right to take full ownership of the jewelry if the debtor does not pay the debt, the arrangement is called a pledge.

A CHATTEL MORTGAGE is like a pledge, but in a chattel mortgage transaction, the debtor is allowed to retain possession of the property that is put up as collateral. If the debtor fails to repay the debt, the creditor may take ownership of the property.

A third type of secured transaction, the conditional sale, uses a purchase money security interest. A purchase money security interest arises when a creditor lends money to a borrower, who uses the money to purchase a particular item. To secure repayment of the loan, the creditor receives a LIEN on, or claim to, the purchased item. The lien gives the creditor a claim to the property that may be asserted if the borrower does not repay the loan.

Common Forms of Collateral Any property accepted as security by a creditor can serve as collateral, but generally collateral falls into one of five categories: consumer goods, equipment, farm products, inventory, and property on paper. Consumer goods are items used primarily for personal, family, or household purposes. Equipment consists of items of value used in business or governmental operations. Farm products are items such as CROPS, livestock, or supplies used or produced in a farming operation. INVENTORY consists of goods held for sale or LEASE or furnished under CONTRACTS of service, raw materials, works in process, materials used or consumed in a business, and goods held for sale or lease or furnished under contracts of service.

Paper collateral consists of a writing that serves as EVIDENCE of a debtor's rights in PERSONAL PROPERTY. STOCKS and BONDS are examples of paper collateral. Another common form of paper collateral is chattel paper. CHATTEL PAPER is a writing that indicates that the holder is owed money and has a security interest in valuable goods associated with the debt. For example, assume that a car dealership has sold a car on financing to a buyer and has retained the title as security. The dealership may then use the security agreement with the buyer as collateral for a loan of its own from the bank.

The Formalities To be valid, a secured transaction must contain an EXPRESS agreement between the debtor and the secured party. The agreement must be in writing, must be signed by both parties, must describe the collateral, and must contain language indicating a grant of a security interest to the creditor. Furthermore, something of value must be given by one party to the other party. This can be a binding commitment to extend CREDIT, the satisfaction of an already existing claim, the delivery and

ACCEPTANCE of goods under a contract, or any other exchange of value sufficient to create a contract. Once these formalities have been completed, the security associated with the principal agreement is said to attach. ATTACHMENT simply means that the security side of the agreement is complete and legally enforceable.

To completely secure a secured transaction, or PERFECT the security, the secured party should file a financing statement with the local public records office, secretary of state, or other appropriate government body. Perfecting the security makes the secured party's claim official, puts the rest of the world on notice as to the creditor's rights in the property, and gives the creditor the right to take advantage of special remedies in the event the debtor does not repay the loan. A financing statement is a document that fully describes the secured transaction. The written document that created the agreement may serve as a financing statement, but the law on financing statements varies from state to state. A state may require the secured party to file a financing statement in addition to a copy of the agreement.

In most states financing statements are effective only for a limited duration, such as five years. A SECURED CREDITOR may extend the length of perfection by filing a continuation statement before the designated time period has expired. If a secured creditor fails to continue the perfection, the security is not lost, but other creditors may claim the property. The secured creditor may file another financing statement, but this would require another signature from the debtor.

Amendments may be made to a financing statement. A secured party may file a statement of release on some of the collateral once the debtor has made payments equal in value to the value of the released collateral. If the amendment adds collateral, the security for the new collateral is effective from the date of the amendment, and not the date of the filing of the original financing statement.

One exception to the filing rule is where the secured party has possession of the collateral. In this situation the creditor's security is complete once the parties have agreed to the primary transaction. Another exception is the purchase money security interest in consumer goods other than building fixtures and motor vehicles. The filing of a purchase money security interest for such consumer goods is optional. If a secured party to a conditional sale does not record or file the agreement, however, he may lose the security if the buyer sells the goods to a third party.

Failure to perfect the security may have drastic consequences for the secured party who does not possess the collateral, although such failure does not automatically mean that the security will be lost. If, however, another party later stakes a claim to the collateral and files the proper papers, the secured party may lose her claim to the property because claims that have been properly recorded or filed have priority. Thus a secured party is wise to file a financing statement and other required documents to perfect the security and protect against claims by other creditors of the debtor.

Article 9 of the UCC is primarily concerned with protecting the secured party's right to the collateral. Many sections of Article 9 delineate who has the first right to a debtor's property if multiple claims arise. Precisely who has the first right to the debtor's property depends on a number of factors, including whether the security was perfected, who the other claimant is, and the time that the claims arose.

If a security interest has not been perfected, the secured party's claim to the collateral property may be subordinate to any number of creditors. A person who has a lien on the property takes before the secured party, as does a person who has received a court order for attachment of the property. If a person buys the collateral from the debtor and did not know of the security interest, the secured party loses the property if the security was not perfected. This is true only if the buyer purchases the property in the ordinary course of business from a person who is in the business of selling goods of that particular kind. A pawnbroker, for example, is not such a seller because a pawnbroker will sell almost anything if the profit is worth the time and trouble.

The identity of the buyer may influence the outcome of a dispute between a buyer of secured goods and the secured party. Generally, a merchant, or a buyer who purchases property for a business, is held to a higher standard than a person who buys an item for personal use. Merchants are more familiar with markets than are ordinary consumers, and they may be expected to know that a seller was insolvent and that the goods being sold were subject to claims from other parties. In any case, if any buyer knows that another party has a security interest in the property at the time the buyer made the purchase, the secured party retains the first claim to the property and may keep the property out of that buyer's possession until the debt

associated with the secured property is fully paid.

If two parties have a security interest in the same property, the party who filed first takes first. If the competing security interests are both unperfected, the party who was first to attach the property as collateral has priority.

Other creditors of a debtor may have the first claim on secured property. The federal government has priority in some instances for collection of federal tax liens. Most states have artisan's lien statutes, which give servicers of property the right to hold the property in their possession as security for payment of the service bill. If the bill remains unpaid, the servicer has priority even over a secured party who has perfected her interest. Once a servicer or repairperson is paid for his services, he must release the goods to either their owner or the party with the security interest in the goods.

If the debtor to a secured party defaults, the secured party who has failed to perfect the security interest may lose first claim to the secured property to a RECEIVER or an assignee for the benefit of creditors. A receiver is a party who is appointed by the BANKRUPTCY court to manage the finances of the debtor for the benefit of the debtor's creditors. An assignee for the benefit of creditors is a person chosen by the debtor to manage all or substantially all of the debtor's property and to distribute it to creditors. A secured party who has perfected the security interest has priority over an assignee or a receiver, but even a secured party who has perfected may not receive all of the debt owed under a security agreement by a bankrupt debtor. Federal bankruptcy laws are designed to distribute the assets of an insolvent debtor in a fair and ratable manner among all of the debtor's creditors.

Satisfaction of the Secured Debt
Once a secured debt is repaid in full, the secured party must, upon written request by the debtor, send a TERMINATION statement to the debtor and file a termination statement with all offices that hold the financing statement. A termination statement serves as evidence that the debt has been paid in full. If the debtor makes a written request for the termination statement, the creditor must send the statement within ten days of the date of the request. Even if the debtor does not so request, the secured party must send a termination statement to offices that hold the financing statement within thirty days of the satisfaction of the debt.

Default If a debtor defaults on his obligations under a secured transaction, the secured party may foreclose on the security interest. Fore-closure can be accomplished in different ways. The secured party may calculate the amount of the debt owed and sue the debtor without taking possession of the property. Alternatively, unless the parties have agreed otherwise, the secured party may take possession of the collateral property and either keep it or sell it. In either case, if the value received by the secured party does not fully satisfy the debt, the secured party may sue the debtor for the deficiency.

In most states a secured party may take possession of the collateral without judicial involvement if this can be accomplished without a BREACH OF THE PEACE. For example, the secured party may repossess a vehicle if it is parked outdoors. If, however, the agent of the secured party must break into a garage to repossess the vehicle, such action would be a breach of the peace because it would require breaking and entering, a criminal offense.

If a consumer has defaulted on a secured transaction but has paid 60 percent or more on the debt, most states prohibit a secured party from taking the security and keeping the windfall. In such cases the secured party may either sue in court for the money outstanding or take the property and return part of the money. In other situations a secured party may be entitled to any excess value or income that results from the debtor's default.

The retention of collateral by a secured party after the debtor's default is called STRICT FORE-CLOSURE. If a secured party decides to keep collateral in satisfaction of a debt, the secured party must send written notice to the debtor. In transactions involving collateral other than consumer goods, a secured party may be obliged to send notice of the strict foreclosure to any other parties who have security in the collateral property. If a party objects to the strict foreclosure, the secured party must sell or otherwise dispose of the collateral. If no other party objects to the strict foreclosure, the secured party may keep the collateral.

A secured party who sells or leases collateral after a debtor defaults may charge the debtor for reasonable expenses incurred in the sale or lease. This can include attorneys' fees and court costs. The money made from a sale of collateral rarely satisfies a debt because such sales do not bring favorable prices. If there is a surplus of money after the collateral is sold, all expenses are accounted for, and the sale or lease is applied to the debt, other parties holding a security interest in the collateral must be paid with the surplus money.

Unless the parties have agreed otherwise, a debtor who is in possession of the collateral and who has defaulted on the obligations in a secured transaction has the right to redeem the collateral before the secured party takes action. To avoid FORECLOSURE of the security interest by the secured party, the debtor may pay the unpaid balance of the debt secured by the collateral, as well as any reasonable expenses incurred by the secured party in taking, holding, and preparing the foreclosure. This does not mean the debtor must pay the entire amount of the debt; rather, the debtor must make those payments that are in default. Some security agreements have an ACCELERATION CLAUSE that makes all payments due immediately upon default, but a court may hold that such a clause should not be enforced if the debtor has brought the payments up to date before the secured party has acted on the delinquency. A secured party who violates default provisions may be liable to the debtor for losses resulting from that conduct.

See also CONSUMER CREDIT; SALES LAW.

SECURITIES Evidence of a corporation's debts or property.

Types of securities include NOTES, STOCKS, treasury stocks, BONDS, DEBENTURES, certificates of interest or participation in profit-sharing agreements, collateral-trust certificates, preorganization certificates or subscriptions, transferable shares, investment contracts, VOTING-TRUST certificates, CERTIFICATES OF DEPOSIT for a security, and a fractional undivided interest in gas, oil, or other MINERAL RIGHTS. Under certain circumstances, interests in oil- and gas-drilling programs, interests in partnerships, real estate condominiums and cooperatives, and farm animals and land also have been found to be securities. Certain types of notes, such as a note secured by a home MORTGAGE or a note secured by ACCOUNTS RECEIVABLE or other business ASSETS, are not securities.

Securities are documents that merely represent an interest or a right in something else; they are not consumed or used in the same way as traditional consumer goods. Government regulation of consumer goods attempts to protect consumers from dangerous articles, misleading advertising, or illegal pricing practices. Securities laws, on the other hand, attempt to ensure that investors have an informed, accurate idea of the type of interest they are purchasing and its value.

Both federal and state laws regulate securities. Before 1929 companies could issue stock at will. Bogus corporations sold worthless stock;

other companies issued and sold large amounts of stock without considering the effect of unlimited issues on shareholders' interests, the value of the stock, and ultimately the U.S. economy. Federal securities law consists of a handful of laws passed between 1933 and 1940, as well as legislation enacted in 1970. The federal laws stem from Congress's power to regulate interstate commerce. Therefore the laws are generally limited to transactions involving transportation or communication using interstate commerce or the mail. Federal laws are generally administered by the SECURITIES AND EXCHANGE COMMISSION (SEC), established by the Securities Exchange Act of 1934 (15 U.S.C.A. § 78a et seq.). Securities regulation focuses mainly on the market for COMMON STOCKS.

Securities are traded on markets. Some, but not all, markets have a physical location. The essence of a securities market is its formal or informal communications systems whereby buyers and sellers make their interests known and execute transactions. These trading markets are susceptible to manipulative and deceptive practices, such as manipulation of prices or "insider trading," that is, gaining an advantage on the basis of nonpublic information. To prevent such FRAUDULENT practices, all securities laws contain general antifraud provisions.

Exchange markets, of which the New York Stock Exchange is the largest, have traditionally operated in a rigid manner by carefully delineating the numbers and qualifications of members and the specific functions members may perform. Conversely, over-the-counter markets (OTC) are less structured and typically do not have a physical location.

Based upon dollar volume, the bond market is the largest. Bonds are the debt instruments issued by federal, state, and local government, as well as CORPORATIONS. The bond market attracts mainly professional and institutional investors, rather than the general public. In addition, many of these obligations are exempt from direct regulatory provisions of the federal securities laws and consequently usually receive little attention from SEC regulators. However, in the mid-1980s, a debacle occurred in the JUNK BOND market, which included INSIDER trading charges. (Junk bonds are highly risky bonds with a high yield.) The scandal, which involved the investment firm of Drexel Burnham Lambert Inc. and trader Michael R. Milken, attracted much attention and a flurry of SEC enforcement activity.

Securities Act of 1933 The first significant federal securities law was the Securities Act of 1933 (15 U.S.C.A. § 77a et seq.), passed in the wake of the great stock market crash of 1929. This law is essentially a disclosure statute. Although the 1933 Act applies by its terms to any sale by any person of any security, it contains a number of exemptions. The most important exemption involves securities sold in certain kinds of transactions, including transactions by someone other than an issuer, underwriter, or dealer. In essence, this provision effectively exempts almost all secondary trading, which involves securities bought and sold after their original issue. Certain small offerings are also exempt.

Although the objective of the 1933 Act's registration requirements is to enable a prospective purchaser to make a reasoned decision based on reliable information, this goal is not always easy to accomplish. For example, an issuer may be reluctant to divulge real weaknesses in an operation and so may try to obfuscate some of the problems while complying in theory with the law. In addition, complex financial information can be extremely difficult to explain in terms understandable to the average investor.

Disclosure is accomplished by the registration of security offerings. In general, the law provides that no security may be offered or sold to the public unless it is registered with the SEC. Registration does not imply that the SEC approves of the issue but is intended to aid the public in making informed and educated decisions about purchasing a security. The law delineates the procedures for registration and specifies the type of information that must be disclosed.

The registration statement has two parts: information that eventually forms the PROSPECTUS, and "Part II" information, which does not need to be furnished to purchasers but is available for public inspection within the SEC's files. Full disclosure includes management's aims and goals; the number of shares the company is selling; what the issuer intends to do with the money; the company's tax status; contingent plans if problems arise; legal standing, such as pending lawsuits; income and expenses; and inherent RISKS of the enterprise.

A registration statement is automatically effective twenty days after filing, and the issuer may then sell the registered securities to the public. Nevertheless, if a statement on its face appears incomplete or inaccurate, the SEC may refuse to allow the statement to become effective. A misstatement or omission of a material fact may result in the registration's suspension. Although the SEC rarely exercises these powers, it does not simply give cursory approval to registration statements. The agency frequently issues "letters of comment," also known as "deficiency letters," after reviewing registration documents. The SEC uses this method to require or suggest changes or request additional information. Most issuers are willing to cooperate because the SEC has the authority to permit a registration statement to become effective less than twenty days after filing. The SEC will usually accelerate the twenty-day waiting period for a cooperative issuer.

For many years an issuer was entitled only to register securities that would be offered for sale immediately. Since 1982, under certain circumstances an issuer has been permitted to register securities for a quick sale at a date up to two years in the future. This process, known as shelf registration, enables companies that frequently offer debt securities to act quickly when interest rates are favorable.

The 1933 Act prohibits offers to sell or to buy before a registration is filed. The SEC takes a broad view of what constitutes an offer. For example, the SEC takes the position that excessive or unusual publicity by the issuer about a business or the prospects of a particular industry may arouse such public interest that the publicity appears to be part of the selling effort.

OFFERS but not sales are permitted, subject to certain restrictions, after a registration statement has been filed but before it is effective. Oral offers are not restricted. Written information may be disseminated to potential investors during the waiting period via a specially designed preliminary prospectus. Offers and sales may be made to anyone after the registration statement becomes effective. A copy of the final prospectus must usually be issued to the purchaser.

The 1933 Act provides for civil LIABILITY for DAMAGES arising from misstatements or omissions in the registration statement, or for offers made in violation of the law. In addition, the law provides for civil liability for misstatements or omissions in any offer or sale of securities, whether or not the security is registered. Finally, the general antifraud provision in the law makes it unlawful to engage in fraudulent or deceitful practices in connection with any offer or sale of securities, whether or not they are registered.

In general, any person who acquires an equity whose registration statement, at the time it became effective, contained an "untrue statement of a material fact or omitted to state a material fact" may sue to recover the difference between the price paid for the security (but not more than the public offering price) and the

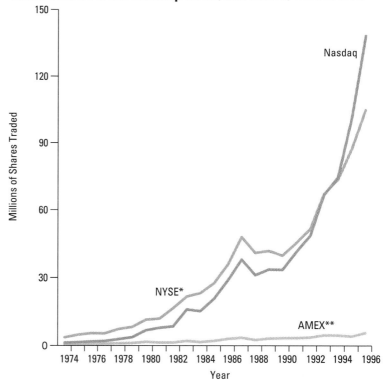

Share Volume of the Nasdaq, NYSE, and AMEX, 1974 to 1996

*New York Stock Exchange
**American Stock Exchange
Source: National Association of Securities Dealers, Inc.

price for which it was disposed or (if it is still owned) its value at the time of the lawsuit. A purchaser must show only that the registration statement contained a MATERIAL misstatement or omission and that she lost money. In many circumstances the purchaser need not show that she relied on the misstatement or omission or that a prospectus was even received. The SEC defines "material" as information an average prudent investor would reasonably need to know before purchasing the security.

Securities Exchange Act of 1934
The Securities Exchange Act of 1934 addresses many areas of securities law. Issuers, subject to certain exemptions, must register with the SEC if they have a security traded on a national exchange. This requirement should not be confused with the registration of an offering under the 1933 Act; the two laws are distinct. Securities registered under the 1933 Act for a public offering may also have to be registered under the 1934 Act.

To provide the public with adequate information about companies with publicly traded stocks, issuers of securities registered under the 1934 Act must file various reports with the SEC. Since 1964 this disclosure requirement has applied not only to companies with securities listed on national securities exchanges but also to companies with more than five hundred shareholders and more than $5,000,000 in assets. False or misleading statements in any documents required under the 1934 Act may result in liability to persons who buy or sell securities in reliance on these statements.

Under the 1934 Act, the SEC may revoke or suspend the registration of a security if after notice and opportunity for hearing it determines that the issuer has violated the 1934 Act or any rules or regulations promulgated thereunder. Moreover, the 1934 Act authorizes the SEC to suspend trading in any security for not more than ten days, or, with the approval of the president, to suspend trading in all securities for not more than ninety days, or to take other measures to address a major market disturbance.

Proxy Solicitation The 1934 Act also regulates PROXY solicitation, which is information that must be given to a corporation's shareholders as a prerequisite to soliciting votes. Prior to every shareholder meeting, a registered company must provide each stockholder with a proxy statement containing certain specified material, along with a form of proxy on which the security holder may indicate approval or disapproval of each proposal expected to be presented at the meeting. For securities registered in the names of brokers, banks, or other nominees, a company must inquire into the beneficial ownership of the securities and furnish sufficient copies of the proxy statement for distribution to all the beneficial owners.

Copies of the proxy statement and form of proxy must be filed with the SEC when they are first mailed to security holders. Under certain circumstances preliminary copies must be filed ten days before mailing. Although a proxy statement does not become "effective" in the same way as a statement registered under the 1933 Act, the SEC may comment on and require changes in the proxy statement before mailing. Proxies for an annual meeting calling for election of DIRECTORS must include a report containing financial statements covering the previous two fiscal years. Special rules apply when a contest for election or removal of directors is scheduled.

A security holder owning at least $1,000, or one percent, of a corporation's securities may present a proposal for action via the proxy statement. Upon a shareholder's timely notice to the corporation, a statement of explanation is included with the proxy statement. Security holders will have an opportunity to vote on the proposal on the proxy form. The device is unpopular with management, but shareholders have used this provision to change or challenge management compensation, the conduct of annual meetings, shareholder voting rights, and issues involving discrimination and pollution in company operations.

A company that distributes a misleading proxy statement to its shareholders may incur liability to any person who purchases or sells its securities based on the misleading statement. The U.S. Supreme Court has held that an omitted fact is material if a "substantial likelihood" exists that a reasonable shareholder would consider the information important in deciding how to vote. Mere NEGLIGENCE is sufficient to permit recovery; no evil motive or reckless disregard need be shown. Oftentimes, an appropriate remedy might be a PRELIMINARY INJUNCTION requiring circulation of corrected materials; it may not be feasible to RESCIND a tainted transaction after voting. Courts have, however, sometimes ordered a new election of directors, but such action must be in the best interests of all shareholders.

Takeover Bids and Tender Offers Since the 1960s, increasing numbers of TAKEOVER bids and TENDER OFFERS have resulted in bitter contests between the aggressor and the target of the bid. A corporate or individual aggressor might attempt to acquire controlling stock in a publicly held corporation in a number of ways: by buying it outright for cash, by issuing its own securities in exchange, or by a combination of both methods. Stock may be acquired in private transactions, by purchases through brokers in the open market, or by making a public offer to shareholders to tender their shares either for a fixed cash price or for a package of securities from the corporation making the offer.

Takeover bids that involve a public offer for securities of the aggressor company in exchange for shares of the targeted company require that the securities be registered under the 1933 Act and that a prospectus be delivered to solicited shareholders. For many years, however, cash tender offers had no SEC filing requirements. The Williams Act of 1968, 15 U.S.C.A. §§ 78l, 78m, 78n, amended many sections of the 1934 Act to address problems with tender offers. Although most litigation under the Williams Act is between contending parties, courts generally focus on whether the relief sought serves to protect public stockholders.

Pursuant to the Williams Act, any person or group who takes ownership of more than five percent of any class of specific registered securities must file a statement within ten days with the issuer of the securities, as well as with the SEC. Required information includes the background of the person or group; the source of funds used and the purpose of the acquisition; the number of shares owned; and any relevant contracts, arrangements, or understandings. The issue of whether an acquisition has taken place, thereby triggering the filing requirement, has been the subject of litigation. Courts have disagreed on this issue when confronted with a group of shareholders who in the aggregate own more than five percent and who agree to act together for the purpose of affecting control of the company but who do not act to acquire any more shares.

Restrictions also apply to persons making a tender offer that would result in ownership of more than five percent of a class of registered securities. Such a person must first file with the SEC and furnish to each offeree a statement similar to that required of a person who has obtained more than five percent of registered stock. A tender offer must be held open for twenty days; a change in the terms holds an offer open at least ten more days. In addition, the offer must be made to all holders of the class of securities sought, and a uniform price must be paid to all tendering shareholders. A shareholder may withdraw tendered shares at any time while the tender offer remains open. Moreover, if the person making the offer seeks fewer than all outstanding shares and the response is oversubscribed, shares will be taken up on a PRO RATA basis.

The 1934 Act also requires every person who directly or indirectly owns more than 10 percent of a class of registered equity securities, and every officer and director of every company with a class of equity securities registered under that section, to file a report with the SEC at the time he acquires the status, and at the end of any month in which he acquires or disposes of these securities. This provision is designed to prevent "short-swing" profits, earned when an individual with inside information engages in short-term trading.

Antifraud Provisions One impetus for enactment of the 1934 Act was the damage caused by "pools," which were a device used to run up the prices of securities on an exchange. The pool would engage in a series of well-timed transactions, designed solely to manipulate the market price of a security. Once prices were high, the members of the pool unloaded their holdings just before the price dropped. The 1934 Act contains specific provisions prohibit-

ing a variety of manipulative activities with respect to exchange-listed securities. It also contains a catchall section giving the SEC the power to promulgate rules to prohibit any "manipulative or deceptive device or contrivance" with respect to any security. Although isolated instances of manipulation still exist, the provisions manage to prevent widespread problems.

Section 10(b) of the 1934 Act contains a broadly worded provision permitting the SEC to promulgate rules and regulations to protect the public and investors by prohibiting manipulative or deceptive devices or contrivances via the mails or other means of interstate commerce. The SEC has promulgated a rule, known as rule 10b-5, that has been invoked in countless SEC proceedings. The rule states:

> It shall be unlawful for any person, directly or indirectly, by use of any means or instrumentality of interstate commerce, or of the mails, or of any facility of any national securities exchange, (1) to employ any device, scheme, or artifice to defraud, (2) to make any untrue statement of a material fact or to omit to state a material fact necessary in order to make the statements made, in light of circumstances under which they were made, not misleading, or (3) to engage in any act, practice, or course of business which operates or would operate as a fraud or deceit upon any person, in connection with the purchase or sale of any security.

In the 1960s and early 1970s, the courts broadly interpreted rule 10b-5. For example, the rule was applied to impose liability for negligent misrepresentations and for breach of FIDUCIARY duty by corporate management and to hold directors, lawyers, accountants, and underwriters liable for their failure to prevent wrongdoing by others. Beginning in 1975, the U.S. Supreme Court sharply curtailed this broad reading. Doubt exists as to the continued viability of the decisions in some of the prior cases. Nevertheless, although rule 10b-5 does not address civil liability for a violation, since 1946 courts have recognized an implied private right of action in rule 10b-5 cases, and the Supreme Court has acknowledged this implied right (*Superintendent v. Bankers Life*, 404 U.S. 6, 30 L. Ed. 2d 128, 92 S. Ct. 165 [1971]).

Rule 10b-5 applies to any purchase or sale, by any person, of any security. There are no exemptions: it applies to registered or unregistered securities, publicly held or closely held companies, and any kind of entity that issues securities, including federal, state, and local government securities.

Clauses 1 and 3 of rule 10b-5 use the terms *fraud* and *deceit*. FRAUD or DECEIT must occur "in connection with" a purchase or sale but need not relate to the terms of the transaction. For example, in *Superintendent v. Bankers Life*, the U.S. Supreme Court found a violation of rule 10b-5 where a group obtained control of an insurance company, then sold certain securities and misappropriated the proceeds for their own benefit. In another case a publicly held corporation made misstatements in a press release. Even though the company was not engaged at that time in buying or selling its own shares, a U.S. court of appeals ruled that the statements were made "in connection with" purchases and sales being made by shareholders on the open market.

Insider Trading Rule 10b-5 protects against insider trading, which is a purchase or sale by a person or persons with access to information not available to those with whom they deal or to traders generally. Originally, the prohibition against insider trading dealt with purchases by corporations or their officers without disclosure of material, favorable corporate information. Beginning in the early 1960s, the SEC broadened the scope of the rule. The rule now operates as a general prohibition against any trading on inside information in anonymous stock exchange transactions, in addition to traditional face-to-face proceedings. For example, in *In re Cady, Roberts & Co.*, 40 S.E.C. 907 (1961), a partner in a brokerage firm learned from the director of a corporation that it intended to cut its DIVIDEND. Before the news was generally disseminated, the broker placed orders to sell the stock of some of his customers. In another case officers and employees of an oil company made large purchases of company stock after learning that exploratory drilling on some company property looked extremely promising (*SEC v. Texas Gulf Sulphur*, 401 F. 2d 833 [2d Cir. 1968]). In these cases the persons who made the transactions, or persons who passed information to those individuals, were found to have violated rule 10b-5.

However, not every instance of financial unfairness rises to the level of fraudulent activity under rule 10b-5. In *Chiarella v. United States*, 445 U.S. 222, 100 S. Ct. 1108, 63 L. Ed. 2d 348 (1980), Vincent F. Chiarella, an employee of a financial printing firm, worked on some documents relating to contemplated tender offers. He ascertained the identity of the targeted companies, purchased stock in those companies, and then sold the stock at a profit once the tender offers were announced. The Supreme Court overturned Chiarella's criminal conviction for violating rule 10b-5, ruling that an allegation of fraud cannot be supported absent a duty to speak and that duty must arise from a relationship of "trust and confidence between the parties to a transaction." However, following *Chiarella*, criminal convictions of lawyers, printers, stockbrokers, and others have been upheld by courts that have ruled that these employees traded on confidential information that was "misappropriated" from their employers, an issue that was not raised in *Chiarella*. Moreover, courts have also ruled that the person who passes inside information to another person who then uses it for a transaction is as CULPABLE as the person who uses it for his or her own account.

The test for materiality in a rule 10b-5 insider information case is whether the information is the kind that might affect the judgment of reasonable investors, both of a conservative and speculative bent. Furthermore, an insider may not act the moment a company makes a public announcement but must wait until the news could reasonably have been disseminated.

The Insider Trading Sanctions Act of 1984 (Pub. L. No. 98-376, 98 Stat. 1264) and the Insider Trading and Security Fraud Enforcement Act of 1988 (15 U.S.C.A. §§ 78u-1, 806-4a, and 78t-1) amended the 1934 Act to permit the SEC to seek a civil penalty of three times the amount of profit gained from the illegal transaction or the loss avoided by it. The penalty may be imposed on the actual violator, as well as on the person who "controlled" the violator—generally the employing firm. A whistle-blower may receive up to 10 percent of any civil liability penalty recovered by the SEC. The maximum criminal penalties were increased from $100,000 to $1 million for individuals and from $500,000 to $2.5 million for business or legal entities.

Regulation of the Securities Business Only dealers or brokers who are registered with the SEC pursuant to the 1934 Act may engage in business (other than individuals who deal only in exempted securities or handle only intrastate business). Firms act in three principal capacities: broker, dealer, and investment adviser. A BROKER is an AGENT who handles the public's orders to buy and sell securities for a commission. A dealer is a person in the securities business who buys and sells securities for her or his own account, and an investment adviser is paid to advise others on investing in, purchasing, or selling securities. Investment advisers are regulated under the Investment Advisers Act of 1940 (15 U.S.C.A. § 80b et seq.). This law provides for registration similar to that in the 1934 Act for brokers and dealers, but its coverage is generally not as comprehensive. Certain fee arrangements are prohibited, and adverse personal interests in a transaction must be disclosed. Moreover, the SEC may define and prohibit certain fraudulent and deceptive practices.

The SEC has the power to revoke or suspend registration or impose a censure if the broker-dealer has violated federal securities laws or committed other specified misdeeds. Similar provisions apply to municipal securities dealers and investment advisers.

Problems may arise in a number of ways. For example, a broker-dealer may recommend or trade in securities without adequate information about the issuer. "Churning" is another problem. CHURNING occurs when a broker-dealer creates a market in a security by making repeated purchase from and resale to individual retail customers at steadily increasing prices. This conduct violates securities antifraud provisions if the broker-dealer does not fully disclose to customers the nature of the market. Churning also occurs when a broker causes a customer's account to experience an excessive number of transactions solely to generate repeated commissions. Fraudulent "scalping" occurs when an investment adviser publicly recommends the purchase of securities without disclosing that the adviser purchases such securities before making the recommendation and then sells them at a profit when the price rises after word of the recommendation spreads.

In 1990 Congress enacted the Penny Stock Reform Act (15 U.S.C.A. § 78q-2), which gives the SEC authority to regulate the widespread incidence of high-pressure sales tactics in the peddling of low-priced speculative stocks to unsophisticated investors. Dealers in penny stocks must provide customers with disclosure documents discussing the risk of such investments, the customer's rights in the event of fraud or abuse, and compensation received by the broker-dealer and the salesperson handling the transaction.

Securities Investor Protection Corporation The Securities Investor Protection Act of 1970 (15 U.S.C.A. § 78aaa et seq.) created the Securities Investor Protection Corporation (SIPC) to supervise the liquidation of securities firms suffering from financial difficulties and to arrange for the payment of custom-

ers' claims through its trust fund in the event of a broker-dealer's BANKRUPTCY. SIPC is a government-sponsored, private, nonprofit corporation. It relies on the SEC and self-regulatory organizations to refer brokers or dealers having financial difficulties. In addition, SIPC has authority to borrow money (through the SEC) if its trust fund from which it pays claims is insufficient. SIPC guarantees repayment of money and securities up to $100,000 in cash equity and up to $500,000 overall per customer.

Self-Regulatory Organizations Although the SEC plays a major role in regulating the securities industry, regulation responsibilities also exist for self-regulatory organizations. These organizations are private associations to which Congress has delegated the authority to devise and enforce rules for the conduct of an association's members. Before 1934 stock exchanges had regulated themselves for well over a century. The 1934 Act required every national security exchange to register with the SEC. An exchange cannot be registered unless the SEC determines that its rules are designed to prevent fraud and manipulative acts and practices and that the exchange provides appropriate discipline for its members.

Congress extended federal registration to non-exchange, or OTC, markets in 1938 and authorized the establishment of national securities associations and their registration with the SEC. Only one association, the National Association of Securities Dealers, had been established as of the mid 1990s.

In 1975 Congress expanded and consolidated the SEC's authority over all self-regulatory organizations. The SEC must give prior approval for any exchange rule changes, and it has review power over exchange disciplinary actions.

Investment Companies Under the Investment Company Act of 1940 (15 U.S.C.A. § 80a et seq.), investment companies must register with the SEC unless they qualify for a specific exception. Investment companies are companies engaged primarily in the business of investing, reinvesting, or trading in securities. They may also be companies with more than 40 percent of their assets consisting of "investment securities" (securities other than securities of majority owned subsidiaries and government securities). Investment companies include "open-end companies," commonly known as MUTUAL FUNDS. The SEC regulatory responsibilities under this act encompass sales load, management contracts, the composition of BOARDS OF DIRECTORS, capital structure of investment companies, approval of adviser contracts, and changes in investment policy. In addition, a 1970 amendment imposed restrictions on management compensation and sales charges.

Every investment company must register with the SEC. Registration includes a statement of the company's investment policy. Moreover, an investment company must file ANNUAL REPORTS with the SEC and maintain certain accounts and records. Strict procedures safeguard against looting of investment company assets. Officers and employees with access to the company's cash and securities must be bonded, and LARCENY or EMBEZZLEMENT from an investment company is a federal crime. In addition, the Investment Company Act of 1940 imposes substantive restrictions on the activities of registered investment companies and persons connected with them and provides for a variety of SEC and private sanctions.

State Regulation State securities laws are commonly known as BLUE SKY LAWS because of an early judicial opinion that described the purpose of the laws as preventing "speculative schemes which have no more basis than so many feet of blue sky" (*Hall v. Geiger-Jones,* 242 U.S. 539, 372 S. Ct. 217, 61 L. Ed. 480 [1917]). A Uniform Securities Act has been partially or substantially adopted by a majority of states, but much diversity among state securities laws still exists. Typical provisions include prohibitions against fraud in the sale of securities, registration requirements for brokers and dealers, registration requirements for securities to be sold within the state, and sanctions and civil liability under certain circumstances. In addition to complying with the registration requirements of the 1933 Act, a nationwide distribution of a new issue requires compliance with state blue sky provisions as well.

A majority of states have laws regulating takeovers of companies incorporated or doing business within the state. Although the courts have invalidated some of these statutes, these laws tend to aid in preserving the status quo of management.

CROSS-REFERENCES

Mergers and Acquisitions; Risk Arbitrage; Stock Market; Stockholder's Derivative Suit.

SECURITIES AND EXCHANGE COMMISSION

The Securities and Exchange Commission (SEC) is the federal agency primarily responsible for administering and enforcing federal SECURITIES laws. The SEC strives to protect investors by ensuring that the securities markets are honest and fair. When necessary, the SEC enforces securities laws through a variety of means, including FINES, referral for criminal prosecution, revocation or suspension of LICENSES, and INJUNCTIONS.

Headquartered in Washington, D.C., the Commission itself is comprised of five members appointed by the president; one position expires each year. No more than three members may be from one political party. With more than nine hundred employees, the agency has five regional and six district offices throughout the country and enjoys a generally favorable reputation.

Securities Laws Before the October 29, 1929, STOCK MARKET crash on Wall Street, a company could issue STOCK without disclosing its financial status. Many bogus or severely undercapitalized CORPORATIONS sold stock, eventually leading to the disastrous plunge in the market and an ensuing panic. From the havoc wreaked by the crash came the first major piece of federal securities legislation, the Securities Act of 1933 (15 U.S.C.A. § 77a et seq.). The act regulates the primary, or new issue, market. The following year, Congress provided for the creation of the Securities and Exchange Commission when it enacted far-reaching securities legislation in the Securities Exchange Act of 1934 (15 U.S.C.A. § 78a et seq.). These two laws, along with the Trust Indenture Act of 1939 (15a U.S.C.A. §§ 77aaa–77bbbb), the Investment Company Act of 1940 (15 U.S.C.A. §§ 80-1–80a-64), the Investment Advisers Act of 1940 (15 U.S.C.A. §§ 80b-1–80b-21), and the Public Utility Holding Company Act of 1935 (15 U.S.C.A. §§ 79a–79z-6) make up the bulk of federal securities laws under the JURISDICTION of the SEC.

In addition to federal statutory authority, the SEC has broad rule-making authority. It has used this power to fashion procedural and technical rules, define terms used in the laws, and make substantive rules implementing the laws. The SEC also devises forms that must be used to fulfill various requirements in the statutes and rules. Moreover, the SEC engages in a significant amount of informal lawmaking through the distribution of SEC releases containing its opinions on questions of current concern. These releases are disseminated to the press, companies and firms registered with the SEC, and other interested persons. In addition to these general public statements of policy, the SEC also responds to individual private inquiries.

Securities Act of 1933 The Securities Act of 1933 regulates the PUBLIC OFFERING of new issues. All public offerings of securities in interstate commerce or through the mails must be registered with the SEC before they can be offered and sold, subject to exemptions for specifically enumerated types of securities, such as government securities, nonpublic offerings, offerings below a certain dollar amount, and intrastate offerings. The registration provisions apply to issuers of securities or others acting on their behalf. Issuers must file a registration statement with the SEC containing financial and other pertinent data about the issuer and the securities that are being offered. The Securities Act of 1933 also prohibits FRAUDULENT or deceptive practices in the offer or sale of securities, whether or not the securities are required to be registered.

A major part of the SEC's work is to review the registration documents required by the 1933 Act and determine when registration is required. Registration with the SEC is intended to allow potential investors to make an informed evaluation regarding the worth of securities. Registration does not mean that the commission approves of the issue or that the disclosures in the registration are accurate, nor does it insure an investor against loss in the purchase.

Registration requires extensive disclosure on behalf of a corporation. For example, full disclosure includes management's aims and goals; the number of shares the company is selling; what the issuer intends to do with the money; the company's tax status; contingent plans if problems arise; legal standing, such as pending lawsuits; income and expenses; and inherent risks of the enterprise. Registration consists of two parts: a PROSPECTUS, which must be furnished to every purchaser of the security, and other information and attachments that need not be furnished to purchasers but are available in SEC files for public inspection. A registration statement is generally effective twenty days after filing, but the SEC has the power to delay or suspend the effectiveness of the registration statement. When a disclosure or registration statement becomes effective, it is called a prospectus and is used to solicit orders for the security.

Securities Exchange Act of 1934 The Securities Exchange Act of 1934 transferred responsibility for administration of the 1933 Act from the Federal Trade Commission to the newly created SEC. The 1934 Act also provided for federal regulation of trading in already issued and outstanding securities. Other provisions include disclosure requirements for publicly held corporations; prohibitions on various manipulative or deceptive devices or contrivances; SEC registration and regulation of BROKERS and dealers; and registration, oversight, and regulation of national securities exchanges, associations, clearing agencies, transfer agents, and securities information processors.

The SEC has broad oversight responsibilities for the self-regulatory organizations within the securities industry. For approximately 140 years prior to 1934, stock exchanges regulated their own members. Self-regulation is still an important component of the industry, but now the SEC provides additional regulation, including authority to review disciplinary actions taken by a self-regulatory organization. The 1934 Act also established the Municipal Securities Rulemaking Board and conferred oversight power upon the commission. The Municipal Securities Rulemaking Board formulates rules for the municipal securities industry. The commission has the authority to approve or disapprove most proposed rules of the board.

The 1934 Act seeks to provide the public with adequate information about companies with publicly traded securities. Subject to certain exemptions, disclosure requirements apply not only to companies with securities listed on national securities exchanges but to all companies with more than five hundred shareholders and more than $5,000,000 in assets. Companies must file detailed statements with the SEC when first registering under the 1934 Act and must provide periodic reports as prescribed by the commission.

Under the 1934 Act, the SEC also regulates the solicitation of proxies. Proxies are voting solicitations allowing stockholders to participate in the annual or special meetings of shareholders without actually attending the meeting; the PROXY empowers someone else to vote on behalf of the shareholder. Detailed SEC regulations delineate the form of proxies and the information that must be furnished to stockholders. A registered company must furnish each shareholder, before every stockholder meeting, a proxy statement and a proxy form on which she can indicate approval or disapproval of each proposal expected to be introduced at the meeting. Companies must file with the commission copies of the proxy statement and the proxy form. The SEC may comment on the proxy statement and insist on changes before it is mailed to security holders.

The Williams Act of 1968 (Pub. L. No. 90-439, 82 Stat. 454) amended the 1934 Act to address recurring problems arising in tender offers and corporate takeovers. A TENDER offer is a formal request that stockholders sell their shares in response to a large purchase bid; the buyer reserves the right to accept all, none, or a certain number of shares tendered for sale. A TAKEOVER occurs when a corporation assumes control of another corporation through an acquisition or merger. Pursuant to the law as amended, any person or group that takes ownership of more than five percent of any class of specific registered securities must file a statement within ten days with the issuer of the security and with the SEC. This statement provides the background of the purchaser, the source of funds used in the purchase, the purpose of the purchase, the number of shares owned, and any relevant contracts, arrangements, or understandings. In addition, no person may make a tender offer unless he has first filed with the SEC and provided certain specific information to each offeree. A tender offer must remain open for a minimum of twenty days and at least ten days after any change in the terms of the offer.

The Securities Act of 1934 also requires any person who beneficially owns, whether directly or indirectly, more than 10 percent of a class of certain registered securities and every officer or director of every company with specific registered securities to report to the SEC. Reports must be filed at the time the status is acquired and at the end of any month in which such a person acquires or disposes of any equity securities of that company. This provision is designed to discourage short-term trading by preventing corporate insiders from unfairly using nonpublic information.

Investment Company Act of 1940 Pursuant to the Investment Company Act of 1940, investment companies must register with the SEC. Investment companies are companies engaged primarily in the business of investing, reinvesting, or trading in securities. They may also be companies with more than 40 percent of their ASSETS consisting of investment securities, that is, securities other than those of majority-owned subsidiaries and government securities. Among other types of companies, this act covers "open-end companies," commonly known as MUTUAL FUNDS. The SEC regulatory responsibilities under this act encompass sales load, management contracts, the composition of BOARDS OF DIRECTORS, capital structure of investment companies, approval of adviser contracts, and changes in investment policy. In addition, a 1970 amendment imposed restrictions on man-agement compensation and sales charges.

The act prohibits various transactions by investment companies, unless the commission has first made a determination that the transaction is fair. Moreover, the act permits the SEC to bring a court ACTION to ENJOIN the execution of mergers and other reorganization plans of investment companies if the plans are unfair to security holders. The SEC also has the power to impose sanctions pursuant to administrative proceedings for violation of this act and may file suit to enjoin the acts of management officials involving breaches of FIDUCIARY duties or personal misconduct and may bar such officials from office.

Investment Advisers Act of 1940 This act provides for SEC regulation and registration of investment advisers. The act is comparable to provisions of the 1934 Act with respect to broker-dealers but is not as comprehensive. Generally speaking, an investment adviser is a person who engages in the business of advising others with respect to securities and does so for compensation. Certain fee arrangements are prohibited; adverse personal interests in a transaction must be disclosed. Moreover, the SEC may define and prohibit certain fraudulent and deceptive practices.

Other Securities Laws The Trust Indenture Act of 1939 applies to public issues of DEBT securities in excess of a certain amount. This law prescribes requirements to ensure the independence of INDENTURE trustees. It also requires the exclusion of certain types of exculpatory clauses and the inclusion of certain protective clauses in indentures. In addition, the Public Utility Holding Company Act of 1935 (15 U.S.C.A. §§ 79a–79z-6) was enacted to correct abuses in the financing and operation of electric and gas public utility HOLDING COMPANIES; the SEC's functions under these provisions were substantially completed by the 1950s.

SEC Enforcement Authority The commission enforces the myriad laws and regulations under its jurisdiction in a number of ways. The SEC may seek a court injunction against acts and practices that deceive investors or otherwise violate securities laws; suspend or revoke the registration of brokers, dealers, investment companies, and advisers who have violated securities laws; refer persons to the Department of Justice for criminal prosecution in situations involving criminal FRAUD or other willful violation of securities laws; and bar attorneys, accountants, and other professionals from practicing before the commission.

SECURITY 179

The SEC may conduct investigations to determine whether a violation of federal securities laws has occurred. The SEC has the power to SUBPOENA witnesses, administer OATHS, and compel the production of records anywhere in the United States. Generally, the SEC initially conducts an informal inquiry, including interviewing WITNESSES. This stage does not usually involve sworn statements or compulsory TESTIMONY. If it appears that a violation has occurred, SEC staff members request an order from the commission delineating the scope of a formal inquiry.

Witnesses may be subpoenaed in a formal investigation. A witness compelled to TESTIFY or produce evidence is entitled to see a copy of the order of investigation and be accompanied, represented, and advised by counsel. A witness also has the absolute right to inspect the transcript of her testimony. Typically the same privileges one could assert in a judicial proceeding, such as the FOURTH AMENDMENT to the U.S. Constitution's prohibition against unreasonable SEARCHES AND SEIZURES and the FIFTH AMENDMENT's privilege against SELF-INCRIMINATION, apply in an SEC investigation. Proceedings are usually conducted privately to protect all parties involved, but the commission may publish information regarding violations uncovered in the investigation. In a private investigation, a targeted person has no right to appear to rebut charges. In a public investigation, however, a person must be afforded a reasonable opportunity to cross-examine witnesses and to produce rebuttal testimony or evidence, if the record contains implications of wrongdoing.

When an SEC investigation unearths EVIDENCE of wrongdoing, the commission may order an administrative HEARING to determine responsibility for the violation and impose sanctions. Administrative proceedings are only brought against a person or firm registered with the SEC, or with respect to a security registered with the commission. Offers of SETTLEMENT are common. In these cases the commission often insists upon publishing its findings regarding violations.

An administrative hearing is held before an administrative law judge, who is actually an independent SEC employee. The hearing is similar to that of a nonjury trial and may be either public or private. After the hearing the judge makes an initial written decision containing findings of fact and CONCLUSIONS OF LAW. If either party requests, or if the commission itself

chooses, the commission may review the decision. The SEC must review cases involving a suspension, denial, or revocation of registration. The commission may request oral argument, will study BRIEFS, and may modify the decision, including increasing the sanctions imposed. Possible sanctions in administrative proceedings include censure, limitations on the registrant's activities, or revocation of registration. In 1990 the SEC's powers were expanded to include the authority to impose civil penalties of up to $500,000, to order disgorgement of profits, and to issue CEASE AND DESIST ORDERS against persons violating or about to violate securities laws, whether or not the persons are registered with the SEC.

The U.S. Court of Appeals for the District of Columbia or another applicable circuit court of appeals has jurisdiction to review most final orders from an SEC administrative proceeding. Certain actions by the commission are not reviewable.

The SEC may request an injunction from a federal district court if future securities law violations are likely or if a person poses a continuing menace to the public. An injunction may include a provision that any future violation of law constitutes CONTEMPT of court.

The SEC may request further relief, such as turning over profits or making an offer to rescind the profits gained from an INSIDER trading transaction. In cases of pervasive corporate mismanagement, the SEC may obtain appointment of a RECEIVER or of independent DIRECTORS and special counsel to pursue claims on behalf of the corporation.

Willful violations may be punished by fines and imprisonment. The SEC refers such cases to the Department of Justice for criminal prosecution. Willfulness means only that the defendant intended the act, not that he knew that it was a violation of securities laws.

CROSS-REFERENCES
Administrative Law and Procedure; Bonds; Mergers and Acquisitions.

SECURITY Protection; assurance; indemnification.

The term *security* is usually applied to a deposit, LIEN, or MORTGAGE voluntarily given by a DEBTOR to a CREDITOR to guarantee payment of a DEBT. Security furnishes the creditor with a resource to be sold or possessed in case of the debtor's failure to meet his or her financial obligation. In addition, a person who becomes a SURETY for another is sometimes referred to as a "security."

A sample security agreement

_____ Date

Name   No. and Street   City   County   State

(hereinafter called "Debtor") hereby grants to _____

Name

No. and Street   City   County   State

(hereinafter called "Secured Party") a security interest in the following property (hereinafter called the "Collateral"): _____

_____

to secure payment and performance of obligations identified or set out as follows (hereinafter called the "Obligations"): _____

_____

Default in payment or performance of any of the Obligations or default under any agreement evidencing any of the Obligations is a default under this agreement. Upon such default Secured Party may declare all Obligations immediately due and payable and shall have the remedies of a secured party under the _____ Uniform Commercial Code.

Signed in (duplicate) triplicate.

_____   _____
Debtor   Secured Party
By _____   By _____

SECURITY COUNCIL See UNITED NATIONS.

SECURITY DEPOSIT 📖 Money aside from the payment of rent that a LANDLORD requires a TENANT to pay to be kept separately in a fund for use should the tenant cause damage to the premises or otherwise violate terms of the LEASE. 📖

A security deposit is usually in the amount of one or two months' rent. It usually must be paid at the time that the landlord and tenant sign the lease. The landlord must place the funds in an ESCROW account and give the tenant any interest generated by such funds. Upon the termination of the lease, the landlord must return the security deposit to the tenant if no violations of the lease occurred. He or she may keep the security deposit or portion thereof for the amount of any damages, which can be proven, pursuant to the terms of the lease.

See also LANDLORD AND TENANT.

SEDITION 📖 A revolt or an incitement to revolt against established authority, usually in the form of TREASON or DEFAMATION against government. 📖

Sedition is the crime of revolting or inciting revolt against government. However, because of the broad protection of free speech under the FIRST AMENDMENT, prosecutions for sedition are rare. Nevertheless, sedition remains a crime in the United States under 18 U.S.C.A. § 2384 (1948), a federal statute that punishes seditious CONSPIRACY, and 18 U.S.C.A. § 2385 (1948), which outlaws advocating the overthrow of the federal government by force. Generally, a person may be punished for sedition only when he or she makes statements that create a CLEAR AND PRESENT DANGER to rights that the government may lawfully protect (_Schenck v. United States_, 249 U.S. 47, 39 S. Ct. 247, 63 L. Ed. 470 [1919]).

The crime of seditious conspiracy is committed when two or more persons in any state or U.S. territory conspire to levy war against the U.S. government. A person commits the crime of advocating the violent overthrow of the federal government when she willfully advocates or teaches the overthrow of the government by force, publishes material that advocates the overthrow of the government by force, or organizes persons to overthrow the government by force. A person found guilty of seditious conspiracy or advocating the overthrow of the government may be fined and sentenced to up to twenty years in prison. States also maintain laws that punish similar advocacy and conspiracy against the state government.

Governments have made sedition illegal since time immemorial. The precise acts that constitute sedition have varied. In the United States, Congress in the late eighteenth century believed that government should be protected from "false, scandalous and malicious" criticisms. Toward this end, Congress passed the Sedition Act of 1798, which authorized the criminal prosecution of persons who wrote or spoke falsehoods about the government, Congress, the president, or the vice president. The act was to expire with the term of President JOHN ADAMS.

The Sedition Act failed miserably. THOMAS JEFFERSON opposed the act, and after he was narrowly elected president in 1800, public opposition to the act grew. The act expired in 1801, but not before it was used by President Adams to prosecute numerous public supporters of Jefferson, his challenger in the presidential election of 1800. One writer, Matthew Lyon, a congressman from Vermont, was found guilty of seditious libel for stating, in part, that he would not be the "humble advocate" of the Adams administration when he saw "every consideration of the public welfare swallowed up in a continual grasp for power, in an unbounded thirst for ridiculous pomp, foolish adulation, and selfish avarice" (*Lyon's Case*, 15 F. Cas. 1183 [D. Vermont 1798] [No. 8646]). Vermont voters reelected Lyon while he was in jail. Jefferson, after winning the election and assuming office, pardoned all persons convicted under the act.

In the 1820s and 1830s, as the movement to abolish SLAVERY grew in size and force in the South, Southern states began to enact seditious libel laws. Most of these laws were used to prosecute persons critical of slavery, and they were abolished after the Civil War. The federal government was no less defensive; Congress enacted seditious conspiracy laws before the Civil War aimed at persons advocating SECESSION from the United States. These laws were the precursors to the present-day federal seditious conspiracy statute.

In the late nineteenth century, Congress and states began to enact new limits on speech, most notably statutes prohibiting OBSCENITY. At the outset of World War I, Congress passed legislation designed to suppress antiwar speech. The Espionage Act of 1917 (ch. 30, tit. 1, § 3, 40 Stat. 219), as amended by ch. 75, § 1, 40 Stat 553, put a number of pacificists into prison. Socialist leader Eugene V. Debs was convicted for making an antiwar speech in Canton, Ohio (*Debs v. United States*, 249 U.S. 211, 39 S. Ct. 252, 63 L. Ed. 566 [1919]). Charles T. Schenck and Elizabeth Baer were convicted for circulating to military recruits a leaflet that advocated

opposition to the draft and suggested that the draft violated the Thirteenth Amendment's ban on INVOLUNTARY SERVITUDE (*Schenck v. United States*, 249 U.S. 47, 39 S. Ct. 247, 63 L. Ed. 470 [1919]).

The U.S. Supreme Court did little to protect the right to criticize the government until after 1927. That year, Justice LOUIS D. BRANDEIS wrote an influential concurring opinion in *Whitney v. California*, 274 U.S. 357, 47 S. Ct. 641, 71 L. Ed. 1095 (1927), that was to guide First Amendment JURISPRUDENCE for years to come. In *Whitney* the High Court upheld the convictions of political activists for violation of federal anti-syndicalism laws, or laws that prohibit the teaching of crime. In his concurring opinion, Brandeis maintained that even if a person advocates violation of the law, "it is not a justification for denying free speech where the advocacy falls short of incitement and there is nothing to indicate that the advocacy would be immediately acted on." Beginning in the 1930s, the Court became more protective of political free speech rights.

Through the 1970s the High Court became more rigorous in its examination of statutes and prosecutions targeting sedition. The High Court has protected the speech of racial supremacists and separatists, labor organizers, advocates of racial integration, and opponents of the draft for the war in Vietnam. However, it has refused to declare unconstitutional all sedition statutes and prosecutions. In 1940, to silence radicals and quell Nazi or communist subversion during the burgeoning Second World War, Congress enacted the SMITH ACT (18 U.S.C.A. §§ 2385, 2387), which outlawed sedition and seditious conspiracy. The Supreme Court upheld the constitutionality of the act in *Dennis v. United States*, 341 U.S. 494, 71 S. Ct. 857, 95 L. Ed. 1137 (1951).

Sedition prosecutions are extremely rare, but they do occur. Shortly after the 1993 bombing of the World Trade Center in New York City, the federal government prosecuted Sheik Omar Abdel Rahman, a blind Egyptian cleric living in New Jersey, and nine codefendants on charges of seditious conspiracy. Rahman and the other defendants were convicted of violating the seditious conspiracy statute by engaging in an extensive plot to wage a war of TERRORISM against the United States. With the exception of Rahman, they all were arrested while mixing explosives in a garage in Queens, New York, on June 24, 1993.

The defendants committed no overt acts of war, but all were found to have taken substantial steps toward carrying out a plot to levy war against the United States. The government did not have sufficient evidence that Rahman participated in the actual plotting against the government or any other activities to prepare for terrorism. He was instead prosecuted for providing religious encouragement to his coconspirators. Rahman argued that he only performed the function of a cleric and advised followers about the rules of Islam. He and the others were convicted, and on January 17, 1996, Rahman was sentenced to life imprisonment by Judge Michael Mukasey.

CROSS-REFERENCES

Cold War; Communism; *Dennis v. United States;* Freedom of Speech; *Schenck v. United States;* Socialism.

SEDUCTION 📖 The act by which a man entices a woman to have unlawful sexual relations with him by means of persuasions, solicitations, promises, or bribes without the use of physical force or violence. 📖

At COMMON LAW, a woman did not ordinarily have the right to sue on her own behalf; the right to sue for seduction belonged to a father who could bring an action against a man who had sexual relations with his daughter. A woman who was seduced by a marriage promise could sue for breach of promise, and if she became sexually involved with a man due to force or DURESS, she might be able to sue for RAPE or ASSAULT. Regardless of whether the woman was a legal adult or an INFANT, seduction was considered to be an injury to her father.

Seduction suits are rarely brought in modern times and have been eliminated by some states, primarily because they publicize the victim's humiliation.

See also BREACH OF MARRIAGE PROMISE.

SEGREGATION 📖 The act or process of separating a race, class, or ethnic group from a society's general population. 📖

Segregation in the United States has been practiced, for the most part, on African Americans. Segregation by law, or DE JURE segregation, of African Americans was developed by state legislatures and local lawmaking bodies in southern states shortly after the Civil War. DE FACTO segregation, or inadvertent segregation, continues to exist in varying degrees in both northern and southern states.

De facto segregation arises from social and economic factors and cannot be traced to official government action. For example, ZONING laws that forbid multifamily housing can have the effect of excluding all but the wealthiest persons from a particular community.

De jure segregation was instituted in the southern states in the late nineteenth and early twentieth centuries. The state legislatures in the southern states accomplished de jure segregation by creating separate facilities, services, and areas for African Americans. Blacks were separated from the rest of society in virtually every facility, service, and circumstance, including schools, public drinking fountains, public lavatories, restaurants, theaters, hotels and motels, welfare services, hospitals, cemeteries, residences, military facilities, and all modes of transportation.

The quality of these facilities and services was invariably inferior to the facilities and services used by the rest of the communities. Laws in many states also prohibited MISCEGENATION, or marriage between racially mixed couples. If an African American failed to observe segregation and used facilities reserved for white persons, she could be arrested and prosecuted.

In 1896 the U.S. Supreme Court gave explicit approval to segregation in *Plessy v. Ferguson,* 163 U.S. 537, 16 S. Ct. 1138, 41 L. Ed. 256 (1896). The High Court declared in *Plessy* that segregation did not violate the Equal Protection Clause of the U.S. Constitution's FOURTEENTH AMENDMENT if the separate facilities and services for African Americans were equal to the facilities and services for white persons. This SEPARATE-BUT-EQUAL doctrine survived until 1954.

That year, in *Brown v. Board of Education,* 347 U.S. 483, 74 S. Ct. 686, 98 L. Ed. 873 (1954), the Court reversed the *Plessy* decision. In *Brown,* the Court ruled that state-sponsored segregation did violate the guarantee of EQUAL PROTECTION under the laws provided to all citizens in the Fourteenth Amendment. The *Brown* case concerned only the segregation of schools, but the Court's rationale was used throughout the 1950s to strike down all the remaining state and local segregation laws.

In the 1960s Congress took steps to curtail segregation in private life. The CIVIL RIGHTS ACT OF 1964 (42 U.S.C.A. § 2000a et seq.) forbade segregation in all privately owned public facilities subject to any form of federal control under the Interstate Commerce Clause in Article I, Section 8, Clause 3, of the U.S. Constitution. Facilities covered by the act included restaurants, hotels, retail stores, and recreational facilities. States began to follow suit by passing laws that prohibited DISCRIMINATION in housing and employment. In 1968 the Supreme Court ruled that a seller or lessor of property could not refuse to sell or rent to a person based on that person's race or color

(*Jones v. Alfred H. Mayer Co.*, 392 U.S. 409, 88 S. Ct. 2186, 20 L. Ed. 2d 1189 [1968]).

In 1971 the Court held in *Swann v. Charlotte-Mecklenburg Board of Education*, 402 U.S. 1, 91 S. Ct. 1267, 28 L. Ed. 2d 554 (1971), that busing schoolchildren to different schools was an acceptable means of combating de facto segregation in schools. However, subsequent court decisions have rejected the forced integration of predominantly white suburban school districts with largely black urban districts, and public education remains effectively segregated in many areas of the United States.

CROSS-REFERENCES

Brown v. Board of Education of Topeka, Kansas; Civil Rights; Integration; Jim Crow Laws; *Plessy v. Ferguson;* School Desegregation.

SEISIN See LIVERY OF SEISIN.

SEIZURE 📖 Forcible possession; a grasping, snatching, or putting in possession. 📖

In CRIMINAL LAW, a seizure is the forcible taking of property by a government law enforcement official from a person who is suspected of violating, or is known to have violated, the law. A SEARCH WARRANT usually must be presented to the person before his property is seized, unless the circumstances of the seizure justify a warrantless SEARCH AND SEIZURE. For example, the police may seize a pistol in the coat pocket of a person arrested during a robbery without presenting a warrant because the search and seizure is incident to a lawful arrest. Certain federal and state laws provide for the seizure of particular property that was used in the commission of a crime or that is illegal to possess, such as explosives used in violation of federal law or illegal narcotics.

In the law of civil practice, the term refers to the act performed by an officer of the law under court order when she takes into CUSTODY the property of a person against whom a court has rendered a JUDGMENT to pay a certain amount of money to another. The property is seized so that it can be sold under the authority of the court to satisfy the judgment. Property can also

John Selden

"IGNORANCE OF THE LAW EXCUSES NO MAN; NOT ALL MEN KNOW THE LAW, BUT BECAUSE IT IS AN EXCUSE EVERY MAN WILL PLEAD, AND NO MAN CAN TELL HOW TO CONFUTE HIM."

be seized if a substantial likelihood exists that a defendant is concealing or removing property from the JURISDICTION of the court so that in the event a judgment is rendered against her, the property cannot be used to pay the judgment. By attaching or seizing a defendant's property, the court prevents her from perpetrating a FRAUD on the courts.

SELDEN, JOHN John Selden was a brilliant lawyer, author, politician, legal analyst, and historian in seventeenth-century England. John Milton, the famed poet and a contemporary of Selden, called Selden "the chief of learned men reputed in this Land."

Selden was born in Salvington, Sussex, England, on December 15, 1584. After attending Oxford University and the INNS OF COURT, Selden began to practice law in 1612. He published a number of works about English legal history before he was admitted to the bar, and he continued to write while practicing law. His most important works included *DeDiis Syria*, a treatise published in 1617 that established his reputation as of one Europe's leading authorities on Asian law, and *History of Tithes*, a masterpiece of research on the history of English law published in 1618.

In *History of Tithes*, Selden argued that the clergy had a legal but not a divine right to tithes, or 10 percent of a person's income. Selden also claimed that tithes were not ordained by God's law. This conclusion was controversial because it implicitly denied the DIVINE RIGHT OF KINGS, or the notion that kings and queens were descended from rulers appointed by God. The divine right of kings supported the rule that kings could not forfeit their right to the throne through misconduct, but *History of Tithes* put this rule in doubt.

Three years after the publication of *History of Tithes*, Selden became embroiled in another controversy when he helped Parliament draft the House of Commons Protestation, a complaint to the Crown about the rights and privileges of the House of Commons. Selden professed the belief that Parliament did not owe its

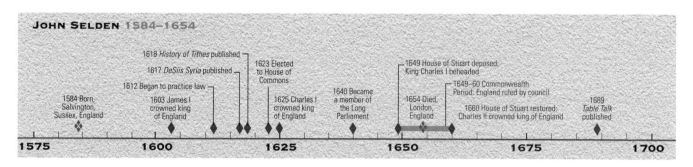

JOHN SELDEN 1584–1654

1618 *History of Tithes* published

1617 *DeSiis Syria* published

1623 Elected to House of Commons

1649 House of Stuart deposed; King Charles I beheaded

1612 Began to practice law

1649–60 Commonwealth Period; England ruled by council

1584 Born, Salvington, Sussex, England

1603 James I crowned king of England

1625 Charles I crowned king of England

1640 Became a member of the Long Parliament

1654 Died, London, England

1660 House of Stuart restored; Charles II crowned king of England

1689 *Table Talk* published

1575   1600   1625   1650   1675   1700

powers to the Crown and that the independence of Parliament was rooted in the lawful and traditional heritage of the English people. This belief, argued Selden, was supported by early records that showed that parliamentary government was an ancient Anglo-Saxon custom. King James I imprisoned Selden in the Tower of London for five weeks for these treasonous statements.

In 1623 Selden was elected to the House of Commons. He promptly earned a reputation for candor and conviction in his support of religious and civil freedoms. He also became known for his opposition to the taxation of cargo by its weight. Selden was so persuasive that the House of Commons passed a resolution prohibiting the tax. The resolution did not win the approval of King Charles I, and Selden was sent to the Tower of London for another brief stay.

Selden continued to publish works that used historical analysis to explain or correct England's order of affairs. Along with predecessor SIR EDWARD COKE (1552–1634) and protégé Sir Matthew Hale (1609–76), Selden helped provide an intellectual basis for the early seventeenth-century parliamentary revolution against the power of the Crown. In 1640 Selden became a member of the Long Parliament, a special parliament created in that year by Charles I, who had governed without a parliament for eleven years. Ironically, Selden spent his later years keeping the rolls and records for the Tower of London.

Selden's most famous work was published after his death. This was *Table Talk*, a survey of Selden's witty conversations with famous friends such as poet Ben Jonson. Published in 1689, *Table Talk* presented a more relaxed, colorful image of Selden that was not apparent in his scholarly works. Selden's emphasis on the importance of history lives on through the Selden Society, a group that promotes the study of English legal history.

Selden died in London in 1654.

SELDEN SOCIETY An association of legal historians that publishes scholarly works on the legal history of England.

The Selden Society was founded in 1886 by English legal professionals and scholars, including the renowned historian FREDERIC WILLIAM MAITLAND. Named for the revered seventeenth-century legal historian JOHN SELDEN, the Selden Society exists to encourage the study and advance the knowledge of the history of English law. Selden Society members include legal historians, lawyers, and law librarians, primarily from English-speaking countries.

The principal activity of the Selden Society is the publication of an annual series on the history of English law. This series is of considerable value to courts in countries with legal systems that have borrowed heavily from the English legal system. The Selden Society also publishes books about various legal topics and holds lectures and symposiums about historical topics of legal significance.

SELECTIVE PROSECUTION Criminal prosecution based on an unjustifiable standard such as race, religion, or other arbitrary classification.

Selective prosecution is the enforcement or prosecution of criminal laws against a particular class of persons and the simultaneous failure to administer criminal laws against others outside the targeted class. The U.S. Supreme Court has held that selective prosecution exists where the enforcement or prosecution of a CRIMINAL LAW is "directed so exclusively against a particular class of persons . . . with a mind so unequal and oppressive" that the administration of the criminal law amounts to a practical denial of equal protection of the law (*United States v. Armstrong*, __U.S.__, 116 S. Ct. 1480, 134 L. Ed. 2d 687 [1996], quoting *Yick Wo v. Hopkins*, 118 U.S. 356, 6 S. Ct. 1064, 30 L. Ed. 220 [1886]). Specifically, police and PROSECUTORS may not base the decision to arrest a person for, or charge a person with, a criminal offense based on "an unjustifiable standard such as race, religion, or other arbitrary classification" (*United States v. Armstrong*, quoting *Oyler v. Boles*, 368 U.S. 448, 82 S. Ct. 501, 7 L. Ed. 2d 446 [1962]).

Selective prosecution is a violation of the constitutional guarantee of EQUAL PROTECTION for all persons under the law. On the federal level, the requirement of equal protection is contained in the Due Process Clause of the FIFTH AMENDMENT to the U.S. Constitution. The Equal Protection Clause of the FOURTEENTH AMENDMENT extends the prohibition on selective prosecution to the states. The equal protection doctrine requires that persons in similar circumstances must receive similar treatment under the law.

Selective prosecution cases are notoriously difficult to prove. Courts presume that prosecutors have not violated equal protection requirements, and claimants bear the burden of proving otherwise. A person claiming selective prosecution must show that the prosecutorial policy had a discriminatory effect and that it was motivated by a discriminatory purpose. To demonstrate a discriminatory effect, a claimant must show that similarly situated individuals of a different class were not prosecuted. For example, a person claiming selective prosecution of white Protestants must produce evidence that shows that white Protestants were prosecuted for a particular crime and that persons outside this group could have been prosecuted but were not.

The prohibition of selective prosecution may be used to invalidate a law. In *Yick Wo v. Hopkins*, the U.S. Supreme Court struck down a San Francisco ordinance that prohibited the operation of laundries in wooden buildings. San Francisco authorities had used the ordinance to prevent Chinese from operating a laundry business in a wooden building. Yet the same authorities had granted permission to eighty individuals who were not Chinese to operate laundries in wooden buildings. Because the city enforced the ordinance only against Chinese-owned laundries, the Court ordered that Yick Wo, who had been imprisoned for violating the ordinance, be set free.

See also CRIMINAL PROCEDURE.

SELECTIVE SERVICE SYSTEM   The Selective Service System is responsible for supplying the armed forces of the United States with people should a national emergency occur. It is an independent agency of the federal government's EXECUTIVE BRANCH.

The agency was established in its first form in 1917 and is authorized by the Military Selective Service Act (50 U.S.C.A. app. 451–471a). This act, as amended, requires male citizens of the United States, and all other male persons who are in the United States and who are between the ages of eighteen and a half and twenty-six, to register for possible military service. It exempts active members of the armed forces, personnel of foreign embassies and consulates, and nonimmigrant ALIENS.

All registrants between the ages of eighteen and a half and twenty-six, except those who are deferred, are liable for training and service in the armed forces should Congress decide to conscript registrants. Those who have received a deferral are liable for training and service until age thirty-five. Aliens are not liable for training and service until they have remained in the United States for more than one year. In the event of the CONSCRIPTION of registrants into the armed forces, CONSCIENTIOUS OBJECTORS are required to do civilian work in place of conscription.

In 1980 President JIMMY CARTER issued a proclamation (Proclamation 4771, July 2, 1980) requiring all males who were born after January 1, 1960, and who have attained age eighteen, to register with the Selective Service.

Registration is conducted at U.S. post offices and at U.S. embassies and consulates outside the United States. The Selective Service maintains several field offices in addition to its headquarters in Arlington, Virginia.

See also ARMED SERVICES; SOLOMON AMENDMENT.

SELECTMAN OR SELECTWOMAN 📖 A municipal officer elected by a town in the New England states. 📖

A selectman possesses executive authority and is usually empowered to transact the general public business of the town. The "first selectman" usually holds a position equivalent to the position held by a mayor.

SELF-DEALING 📖   The conduct of a TRUSTEE, an ATTORNEY, or other FIDUCIARY that consists of taking advantage of his or her position in a transaction and acting for his or her own interests rather than for the interests of the beneficiaries of the TRUST or the interests of his or her clients. 📖

Self-dealing is wrongful conduct by a fiduciary. A fiduciary is a person who has duties of GOOD FAITH, trust, special confidence, and candor toward another person. Examples of fiduciary relationships include attorneys and their clients, doctors and their patients, investment bankers and their clients, trustees and trust beneficiaries, and corporate DIRECTORS and stockholders. Fiduciaries have expert knowledge and skill, and they are paid to apply that knowledge and skill for the benefit of another party. Under the law, a fiduciary relationship imposes certain duties on fiduciaries because a fiduciary is in a special position of control over an important aspect of another person's life.

One important duty of a fiduciary is to act in the best interests of the benefited party. When a fiduciary engages in self-dealing, she breaches this duty by acting in her own interests instead of the interests of the represented party. For example, self-dealing occurs when a trustee uses money from the trust account to make a loan to a business in which he has a substantial personal interest. A fiduciary may make such a transaction with the prior permission of the trust BENEFICIARY, but if the trustee does not obtain permission, the beneficiary can void the transaction and sue the fiduciary for any monetary losses that result.

The laws pertaining to self-dealing are found mainly in CASE LAW, judicial opinions, and some statutes. Case law authorizes the recovery of monetary damages from the self-dealing fiduciary.

One of the most notable statutes relating to self-dealing is 26 U.S.C.A. § 4941 (1969), which allows the INTERNAL REVENUE SERVICE to impose a five percent excise tax on each act of self-dealing by a disqualified person with a private, nonprofit foundation. Disqualified persons include substantial contributors to the foundation, foundation managers, owners of more than 20 percent of the foundation's interest, and members of the family of disqualified persons. If the self-dealing act is not timely corrected, the IRS may impose on the self-dealer an additional 200 percent excise tax on the amount of the transaction.

See also ATTORNEY MISCONDUCT.

SELF-DEFENSE 📖 The protection of one's person or property against some INJURY attempted by another. 📖

Self-defense is a DEFENSE to certain criminal charges as well as to some civil claims. Under both CRIMINAL LAW and TORT LAW, self-defense is commonly asserted in cases of HOMICIDE, ASSAULT AND BATTERY, and other crimes involving the attempted use of violence against an individual. Statutory and CASE LAW governing self-defense is generally the same in tort and criminal law.

A person claiming self-defense must prove at trial that the self-defense was justified. Generally a person may use REASONABLE force when it appears reasonably necessary to prevent an impending injury. A person using force in self-defense should use only so much force as is required to repel the attack. Nondeadly force can be used to repel either a nondeadly attack or a deadly attack. DEADLY FORCE may be used to fend off an attacker who is using deadly force but may not be used to repel an attacker who is not using deadly force.

In some cases, before using force that is likely to cause death or serious bodily harm to the aggressor, a person who is under attack should attempt to retreat or escape, but only if an exit is reasonably possible. Courts have held, however, that a person is not required to flee from his own home, the fenced ground surrounding the home, his place of business, or his AUTOMOBILE.

A person who is the initial aggressor in a physical encounter may be able to claim self-defense if the tables turn in the course of the fight. Generally a person who was the aggressor may use nondeadly force if the victim resumes fighting after the original fight ended. If the original aggressor attacked with nondeadly force and was met with deadly force in return, the aggressor may respond with deadly force.

Courts and tribunals have historically accepted self-defense as a defense to a legal action. As a matter of PUBLIC POLICY, the physical force or violence associated with self-defense is considered an acceptable response to aggression.

The same values that underpin self-defense support the defense of PROPERTY. Generally a person has greater latitude in using physical

Self-Defense or Unjustified Shooting?

On December 22, 1984, at approximately 1:00 P.M., Troy Canty, Darryl Cabey, James Ramseur, and Barry Allen boarded an express subway train in the Bronx borough of New York City. The young black men sat in the rear section of their car. A short time later, Bernhard Goetz boarded the same car and took a seat near the youths. Goetz, a white computer technician, had been mugged some two years earlier.

Canty and Allen approached Goetz, and Canty said "Give me five dollars." Goetz responded by standing up and firing at the youths with a handgun. Goetz fired four shots before pausing. He then walked up to Cabey and reportedly said, "You seem to be all right, here's another," whereupon he fired his fifth and final bullet into Cabey's spinal cord. Goetz had shot two of the youths in the back.

Ramseur and Cabey each had a screwdriver, which they said they used to break into coin boxes and video machines.

Goetz fled the scene and traveled north to New Hampshire. On December 31, 1984, he turned himself in to police in Concord, New Hampshire. Goetz was returned to New York where he was indicted on a charge of criminal possession of a weapon. The state fought for a second grand jury, and Goetz was eventually indicted a second time on charges of attempted murder, assault, criminal possession of a weapon, and reckless endangerment. At trial Goetz argued that he had acted in self-defense, and a jury convicted him only of illegal gun possession. Ultimately Goetz was sentenced to one year in jail and fined $5,000.

Goetz's shooting of Darryl Cabey left Cabey with brain damage and paralyzed from the chest down. Cabey sued Goetz, and in April 1996, a Bronx jury found Goetz liable for Cabey's injuries and awarded Cabey $43 million.

force in the defense of her dwelling than in the defense of other property. In most JURISDICTIONS deadly force is justified if a person unlawfully enters onto property and the property owner reasonably believes that the trespasser is about to commit a FELONY or do harm to a person on the premises. Deadly force may also be justified to prevent a BURGLARY if the property owner reasonably believes the burglar intends to kill or seriously injure a person on the premises. However, a person may not, for example, rig a door handle so that any person who enters the dwelling is automatically shot by a gun. (*Katko v. Briney*, 183 N.W.2d 657 [Iowa 1971]).

Use of deadly force is never justified to protect PERSONAL PROPERTY other than a dwelling. For example, a person would not be justified in shooting a person who is taking an automobile, no matter how expensive. Reasonable nondeadly force may be used to protect such personal property.

A person may use force to defend a third person from attack. If the defender is mistaken, however, and the third party does not need assistance, most jurisdictions hold that the defender may be held liable in civil court for injuries inflicted on the supposed attacker. In criminal cases a defendant would be relieved of LIABILITY if she proved she had made a reasonable mistake.

A defendant who successfully invokes self-defense may be found not guilty or not liable. If the defendant's self-defense was imperfect, the self-defense may only reduce the defendant's liability. Imperfect self-defense is self-defense that was arguably necessary but somehow unreasonable. For example, if a person had a GOOD FAITH belief that deadly force was necessary to repel an attack, but that belief was unreasonable, the defendant would have a claim of imperfect self-defense. In some jurisdictions, the successful invocation of such a defense reduces a MURDER charge to MANSLAUGHTER. Most jurisdictions do not recognize imperfect self-defense.

SELF-DETERMINATION The political right of the majority to the exercise of power within the boundaries of a generally accepted political unit, area, or territory.

The principle of self-determination is mentioned in the UNITED NATIONS Charter and has often been stressed in resolutions passed by the UN General Assembly. The concept is most often used in connection with the right of colonies to independence. It does not relate to attempts at independence by groups, such as the French Canadians or the Nagas of India, who do not possess their own sovereign states.

SELF-EXECUTING Anything (e.g., a document or legislation) that is effective immediately without the need of intervening court action, ANCILLARY legislation, or other type of implementing action.

A constitutional provision is self-executing when it can be given effect without the aid of legislation, and there is nothing to indicate that legislation is intended to make it operative. For example, a constitutional provision that any municipality by vote of four-sevenths of its qualified electors may issue and sell revenue bonds in order to pay for the cost of purchasing a municipally owned public utility is *self-executing* and effective without a legislative enactment.

Constitutional provisions are not self-executing if they merely set forth a line of policy or principles without supplying the means by which they are to be effectuated, or if the language of the constitution is directed to the legislature. As a result, a constitutional provision that the legislature shall direct by law in what manner and in what court suits may be brought against the state is not self-executing.

Just as with constitutional provisions, statutes and court JUDGMENTS can be self-executing.

SELF-EXECUTING TREATY A compact between two nations that is effective immediately without the need for ANCILLARY legislation.

A TREATY is ordinarily considered self-executing if it provides adequate rules by which given rights may be enjoyed or imposed duties may be enforced. Conversely it is generally not self-executing when it merely indicates principles without providing rules giving them the force of law.

SELF-HELP Redressing or preventing wrongs by one's own action without recourse to legal proceedings.

Self-help is a term in the law that describes corrective or preventive measures taken by a private citizen. Common examples of self-help include action taken by LANDLORDS against TENANTS, such as EVICTION and removal of property from the premises, and REPOSSESSION of leased or mortgaged goods, such as automobiles, watercraft, and expensive equipment. Persons may use self-help remedies only where they are permitted by law. State and local laws permit self-help in commercial transactions, tort and NUISANCE situations, and LANDLORD AND TENANT relationships.

Self-help is permissible where it is allowed by law and can be accomplished without committing a BREACH OF THE PEACE. A breach of the peace refers to violence or threats of violence. For example, if a person buys a ship financed by a MORTGAGE, the mortgage company may repossess the ship if the buyer fails to make the mortgage payments. If the buyer is present when the ship is being taken away and the buyer objects to the repossession, the mortgage company breaches the peace if it can repossess the ship only through violence or the threat of violence. In such a case, the mortgage company would be forced to file suit in court to repossess the ship. Repossessors attempt to circumvent objections by distracting or deceiving the defaulting party during the repossession.

A majority of states have banned self-help by landlords in the eviction of delinquent tenants. These legislatures have determined that the interests of the landlord in operating a profitable business must be balanced against a tenant's need for shelter. In place of the self-help remedy, states have devised expedited judicial proceedings for evictions. These proceedings make it possible for a landlord to evict a tenant without unacceptable delays while giving the tenant an opportunity to present to a court arguments against eviction.

In states that give landlords the right of self-help, landlords may evict a tenant on their own only if they can do so in a peaceful manner. The precise definition of *peaceful* varies from state to state. In some states any entry by a landlord that does not involve violence or a breach of the peace is acceptable. In other states any entry that is conducted without the tenant's consent is illegal.

In any case, if a landlord evicts a tenant through self-help, the eviction must be performed reasonably. For example, a landlord may not nail plywood across the entrance to a tenant's second-story apartment while the tenant is inside and then remove the steps leading up to the apartment. One landlord who performed such self-help faced criminal penalties after the trapped tenant and her two-year-old daughter needed the help of the local fire department to escape the apartment. A landlord who violates laws on self-help may face criminal charges and a civil suit for DAMAGES filed by the tenant.

One new form of self-help that poses interesting problems is self-help by providers of computer software. Businesses in the United States that use computers have become dependent on computer software. Sometimes when disputes have arisen between the buyer of software and the software provider, software providers have disabled the buyer's software from a remote location. In one case a software supplier called Logisticon entered into a contract with Revlon Group to provide it with computer software. After a dispute arose between the two parties, Logisticon accessed Revlon's software system and disabled it, causing Revlon to suffer $20 million in product delivery delays. Revlon brought suit against Logisticon, alleging that Logisticon had violated the contract and that it had misappropriated Revlon's TRADE SECRETS. The two parties settled the suit out of court, and the terms of the SETTLEMENT remain undisclosed.

Self-help measures are controversial because they amount to taking the law into one's own hands. Opponents of self-help laws argue that they encourage unethical and sometimes illegal practices by CREDITORS and that they diminish public respect for the law. Proponents counter that self-help, if performed peaceably, is a valuable feature of the justice system because it gives creditors an opportunity to alleviate losses and keeps small, simple disputes from glutting the court system.

See also SECURED TRANSACTIONS.

SELF-INCRIMINATION   Giving TESTIMONY in a trial or other legal proceeding that could subject one to criminal prosecution.

The right against self-incrimination forbids the government from compelling any person to give testimonial EVIDENCE that would likely INCRIMINATE him during a subsequent criminal case. This right enables a defendant to refuse to TESTIFY at a criminal trial and "privileges him not to answer official questions put to him in any other proceeding, civil or criminal, formal or informal, where the answers might incriminate him in future criminal proceedings" (*Lefkowitz v. Turley*, 414 U.S. 70, 94 S. Ct. 316, 38 L. Ed. 2d 274 [1973]).

CONFESSIONS, admissions, and other statements taken from a defendant in violation of this right are inadmissible against him during a criminal prosecution. Convictions based on statements taken in violation of the right against self-incrimination normally are overturned on APPEAL, unless there is enough ADMISSIBLE evidence to support the VERDICT. The right of self-incrimination may only be asserted by persons and does not protect artificial entities such as CORPORATIONS (*Doe v. United States*, 487 U.S. 201, 108 S. Ct. 2341, 101 L. Ed. 2d 184 [1988]).

This testimonial privilege derives from the FIFTH AMENDMENT to the U.S. Constitution. Most state constitutions recognize a similar testimonial privilege. However, the term *self-incrimination* is not actually used in the Fifth Amendment. It provides that "[n]o person . . . shall be compelled in any criminal case to be a witness against himself."

Although the language of the Fifth Amendment suggests that the right against self-incrimination applies only during criminal cases, the Supreme Court has ruled that it may be asserted during civil, administrative, and legislative proceedings as well. The right applies during nearly every phase of legal proceedings, including GRAND JURY hearings, preliminary investigations, pretrial MOTIONS, DISCOVERY, and the trials themselves. However, the right may not be asserted after conviction when the verdict is final because the constitutional protection against DOUBLE JEOPARDY protects defendants from a second prosecution for the same offense. Nor may the privilege be asserted when an individual has been granted IMMUNITY from prosecution to testify about certain conduct that would otherwise be subject to criminal punishment.

At the same time, the right against self-incrimination is also narrower than the Fifth Amendment suggests. The Fifth Amendment allows the government to force a person to be a WITNESS against herself when the subject matter of the testimony is not likely to incriminate her at a future criminal proceeding. Testimony that would be relevant to a civil suit, for example, is not protected by the right against self-incrimination if it does not relate to something that is criminally inculpatory. By the same token, testimony that only subjects a witness to embarrassment, disgrace, or opprobrium is not protected by the Fifth Amendment.

The right against self-incrimination is sometimes referred to as the right to remain silent. The Self-Incrimination Clause affords defendants the right not to answer particular questions during a criminal trial or to refuse to take the witness stand altogether. When the accused declines to testify during a criminal trial, the government may not comment to the jury about her silence. However, the prosecution may assert during CLOSING ARGUMENT that its case is "unrefuted" or "uncontradicted" when the defendant refuses to testify (*Lockett v. Ohio*, 438 U.S. 586, 98 S. Ct. 2954, 57 L. Ed. 2d 973 [1978]). However, before the jurors retire for deliberations, the court must instruct them that the defendant's silence is not evidence of guilt and that no adverse inferences may be drawn from the failure to testify.

In *Miranda v. Arizona*, 384 U.S. 436, 86 S. Ct. 1602, 16 L. Ed. 2d 694 (1966), the Supreme Court extended the right to remain silent to pretrial CUSTODIAL INTERROGATIONS. The Court said that before a suspect is questioned, the police must apprise him of his right to remain silent and that if he gives up this right, any

statements may be used against him in a subsequent criminal prosecution. Under *Miranda*, suspects also have a Fifth Amendment right to consult with an attorney before they submit to questioning. *Miranda* applies to any situation in which a person is both held in "custody" by the police, which means that he is not free to leave, and is being "interrogated," which means he is being asked questions that are designed to elicit an incriminating response. A person need not be arrested or formally charged for *Miranda* to apply.

In *Miranda* the Supreme Court examined a number of police manuals outlining a variety of psychological ploys and stratagems that they employed to overcome the resistance of defiant and stubborn defendants. Such interrogation practices, the Court said, harken back to the litany of coercive techniques used by the English government during the seventeenth century.

The Founding Fathers drafted the Fifth Amendment to forestall the use of torture and other means of COERCION to secure confessions. The founders believed that coerced confessions not only violate the rights of the individual being interrogated but also render the confession untrustworthy. Once a confession has been coerced, it becomes difficult for a judge or jury to distinguish between those defendants who confess because they are guilty and those who confess because they are too weak to withstand the coercion.

Defendants may waive their Fifth Amendment right to remain silent. However, the government must demonstrate to the satisfaction of the court that any such waiver was freely and intelligently made. The Supreme Court ruled that a confession that was obtained after the

A defendant in a criminal action cannot be compelled to testify against himself, nor can his silence be offered as evidence of guilt.

suspect had been informed that his wife was about to be brought in for questioning was not the product of a free and rational choice (*Rogers v. Richmond*, 365 U.S. 534, 81 S. Ct. 735, 5 L. Ed. 2d 760 [1961]). It also held that a statement was not freely and intelligently made when a defendant confessed after being given a drug that had the properties of a truth serum (*Townsend v. Sain*, 372 U.S. 293, 83 S. Ct. 745, 9 L. Ed. 2d 770 [1963]).

The right against self-incrimination is not absolute. A person may not refuse to file an INCOME TAX return on Fifth Amendment grounds or fail to report a hit-and-run accident. The government may compel defendants to provide FINGERPRINTS, voice exemplars, and writing samples without violating the right against self-incrimination because such evidence is used for the purposes of identification and is not testimonial in nature (*United States v. Flanagan*, 34 F.3d 949 [10th Cir. 1994]). Despite the dubious grounds for the distinction between testimonial and non-testimonial evidence, courts have permitted the use of videotaped field sobriety tests over Fifth Amendment objections.

CROSS-REFERENCES

Alcohol; Criminal Law; Criminal Procedure; Exclusionary Rule; Lineup; *Miranda v. Arizona*.

SENATE 📖 The upper chamber, or smaller branch, of the U.S. Congress. The upper chamber of the LEGISLATURE of most of the states. 📖

The U.S. Constitution reserves for the Senate special powers not available to the other branch of Congress, the HOUSE OF REPRESENTATIVES. These powers include the trial of all IMPEACHMENTS of federal officials; the ratification, by a two-thirds vote, of all TREATIES obtained by the president of the United States; and approval or rejection of all presidential appointments to the federal JUDICIARY, ambassadorships, CABINET positions, and other significant EXECUTIVE BRANCH posts.

The Senate, with terms of six years for its members—as opposed to two years for members of the House of Representatives—and a tradition of unlimited debate, has long prided itself as the more deliberate of the two branches of Congress. Under its rules a senator may speak on an issue indefinitely, which is known as the FILIBUSTER. Sixty senators present and voting may pass a motion of CLOTURE to stop debate.

Members Under Article II, Section 3, of the Constitution, the Senate is made up of two members from each state, each of whom has one vote. Unlike the House of Representatives, in which the entire chamber is up for election every two years, only one-third of the senators are up for reelection every two years.

The Constitution requires that a senator be at least thirty years of age and a U.S. citizen for a minimum of nine years. A senator must make her legal residence in the state that she represents.

The Constitution originally provided for the election of senators by state legislatures. However, the SEVENTEENTH AMENDMENT to the Constitution, adopted in 1913, mandated the election of senators by popular vote. The Senate may punish members for disorderly behavior. With the concurrence of two-thirds of the senators, it can expel a member.

When a vacancy occurs in the representation of any state in the Senate, the governor of that state issues a WRIT of election to fill the vacancy. The state legislature, however, can empower the governor to make a temporary appointment until the people fill the vacancy through an election.

The VICE PRESIDENT of the United States is president of the Senate but has no vote unless the senators are equally divided on a question. His vote breaks the tie.

Committees The Senate uses a committee system to evaluate, draft, and amend legislation before it is submitted to the full chamber. During the 104th Congress (1995–97), the Senate had sixteen standing, or permanent, committees: Agriculture, Nutrition, and Forestry; Appropriations; Armed Services; Banking, Housing, and Urban Affairs; Budget; Commerce, Science, and Transportation; Energy and Natural Resources; Environment and Public Works; Finance; Foreign Relations; Governmental Affairs; Judiciary; Labor and Human Resources; Rules and Administration; Small Business; and Veterans' Affairs. The committees have an average of six to seven subcommittees. Senators typically belong to three committees and eight subcommittees. The Senate also has joint committees with the House, special committees, and investigative committees.

Officers The vice president acts as the president of the Senate. In the vice president's absence, that position is filled by the president pro tempore, who is usually the most senior senator of the majority party. The majority leader has significant powers in the appointment of majority senators to committees. Political parties also elect majority and minority leaders to lead their efforts in the Senate. They are assisted by an assistant floor leader (whip) and a party secretary.

Other Senate officers include the secretary, who oversees Senate finances and official Senate

A Day in the Life of the Senate

As the bells ring in the halls of the Capitol and its office buildings, the U.S. Senate starts the day's session. The presiding officer of the Senate, sometimes the vice president but usually the president pro tempore, accompanies the Senate chaplain to the rostrum to lead the chamber in an opening prayer.

After short speeches by the majority and minority leaders, the Senate begins the "morning hour"—a session that generally lasts two hours. During this time senators introduce bills, resolutions, and committee reports and speak briefly on subjects of concern. Bills are referred to approrpiate committees at this time.

Following the morning hour, the Senate may take up executive or legislative business. If in executive session, the Senate considers treaties or nominations that the president has submitted for Senate approval. Before 1929 executive sessions were conducted behind closed doors. Since then, however, the public and the press have been allowed to observe these sessions.

Most of the Senate's time, however, is spent in legislative session. This time is used to debate and vote on bills. Bills with unanimous consent are enacted by a simple voice vote without debate, whereas more controversial bills may be debated at length and may undergo roll call votes. Some bills may not come up for a vote at all.

During debate of a bill, assistant floor leaders, or whips, from each party usually occupy the seats of the majority and minority leaders, located in the front row, center aisle, of the Senate chamber. They enforce established time limits, if any, for debate on specific bills. Frequently, only a few senators are on the Senate floor, while the majority are attending committee meetings or working in their offices. From their offices, senators may apprise themselves of Senate proceedings either through "hot lines" to the Senate floor or live television coverage on the Cable-Satellite Public Affairs Network (C-SPAN), which began broadcasting Senate sessions in 1986.

A Senate legislative day may end in either adjournment or recess. If the Senate adjourns, a legislative day is officially over. If it merely recesses, however, the legislative day resumes on the following calendar day. In the case of a recess, the Senate may forego the rituals of the morning hour on the next calendar day. This is frequently done to save time during busy legislative sessions.

Sometimes, when there is a filibuster or heavy legislative load, the Senate does not stop at the end of the day but continues through the night. During these night sessions, a lantern at the top of the Capitol dome remains lit. The public has access to Senate galleries at all times that the Senate is in session, day or night.

---

pronouncements related to impeachment proceedings and treaty ratification, and the sergeant at arms, who serves as the law enforcement and protocol officer and organizes ceremonial functions.

See also CONGRESS OF THE UNITED STATES; CONSTITUTION OF THE UNITED STATES.

SENIOR CITIZENS 📖 Elderly persons, usually more than sixty or sixty-five years of age. 📖

People in the United States who are more than sixty years of age are commonly referred to as *senior citizens* or *seniors*. These terms refer to people whose stage in life is generally called old age, though there is no precise way to identify the final stage of a normal life span. People are said to be senior citizens when they reach the age of sixty or sixty-five because those are the ages at which most people retire from the workforce.

U.S. law and society recognize the special needs of senior citizens. The most important aid to senior citizens is the SOCIAL SECURITY program. More than twenty-five million Americans receive old-age benefits each month under federal OLD-AGE, SURVIVORS, and DISABILITY INSURANCE, and those payments amount to almost $20 billion a year. Senior citizens who are age sixty-five or older qualify for a full benefit payment by having been employed for the mandatory minimum amount of time and by having made contributions to Social Security. A person may retire at age sixty-two and receive less than full benefits. There is no financial need requirement to be satisfied.

Because of enormous financial pressures on the Social Security program, changes have been made that will push the retirement age higher in the coming decades. Persons born before 1950 can retire at age sixty-five with full benefits based on the average income during working years. Those born between 1950 and 1960 can retire at age sixty-six with full benefits. For those born in 1960 or later, full benefits will be awarded for retirement at age sixty-seven.

Senior citizens are also protected by the MEDICARE program. This program provides ba-

SENIOR CITIZENS: SCAMMING THE ELDERLY

Senior citizens are often the victims of street crimes, such as robbery and assault. But they are more often the target of trained con artists who use a variety of techniques to trick senior citizens into giving them money for their fraudulent schemes. Whether it is a promise of a lucrative investment, a free vacation, or a great deal on home repair, senior citizens too often succumb to a variety of scams.

It is estimated that U.S. consumers lose up to $60 billion annually to consumer fraud. An estimated 50 percent of phone scam victims are over the age of sixty-five. Convicted con artists report that senior citizens are more trusting than younger persons. Some commentators attribute this to the fact that today's senior citizens grew up and matured in a society that was less threatening. Nevertheless, a study by the American Association of Retired Persons indicates that the stereotypical victim—a lonely, forgetful, gullible senior—bears little resemblance to the persons who are scammed. Victims are relatively affluent, educated, well-informed, and connected with their communities. Most, however, are not aware that con artists use the telephone to accomplish their fraudulent schemes. They believe that the person on the other end of the phone line is honest and hardworking.

Legitimate telemarketing is big business, generating nearly $460 billion a year in sales. It is estimated that about $40 billion a year is lost to fraudulent telemarketers. The dishonest telemarketers are fly-by-night operators working out of leased space with banks of telephones staffed by trained con artists. Once they steal enough money in a location, they quickly pack up and move to another city, leaving their victims with little chance to reclaim their money.

A common scam involves bogus prize announcements. A senior will receive a phone call and be told that he has won the grand prize in a contest. The senior is told to either buy a product or pay shipping and taxes ranging from $200 to $24,000. When the prize arrives, it turns out to be cheap junk, worth a small fraction of the amount the senior has paid.

Con artists also use junk mail for their fraudulent contest solicitations. One of the scams that is most financially ruinous to a senior, whether it is done by phone or mail, is a "contest" set up in stages. The solicitations announce that the senior is in a select group eligible for a grand prize but that she must send in an entry fee to participate. Once the fee, ranging from $5 to $20, is paid, the process is repeated over and over, as the contest promoters make more solicitations to the senior. Each time the senior "advances" from one stage to another, she must pay a new entry fee. Some seniors have lost tens of thousands of dollars by spending $5 to $20 at a time.

Another phone scam is based on convincing the victim that an extremely profitable business opportunity is available, but only for a limited time. With the promise of becoming millionaires, some seniors have sent thousands of dollars to con artists who give little, if anything, in return.

Fewer than 10 percent of people cheated out of their money report the fraud to authorities. Some seniors are embarrassed or ashamed to report the crime, fearing that they will look foolish for their gullible behavior. Some con artists even keep con games going by threatening to expose seniors to their family and friends.

Another scam plays on the anger and shame of seniors who have been duped by fraudulent telemarketers. A caller offers to help the senior recover the money the senior had paid to other dishonest companies in hopes of receiving a prize. The caller asks the senior to pay a fee ranging from $200 to $800 for this service. The services typically turn out to be worthless.

The "bank examiner" scam has been perpetrated on senior citizens for generations. An elderly person, usually living alone, gets a call from a con artist posing as a bank examiner. The senior is told that the examiner is investigating a bank teller suspected of embezzling money by falsifying withdrawal receipts. The teller gives each customer the amount asked for and steals a small amount with each transaction. The con artist asks the senior to withdraw $5,000 from his savings account and give it to a detective waiting outside the bank. The money, the senior is told, will be used as evidence and returned with a reward. Once the senior hands over the money, he usually never hears from the con artist. Some scams, however, involve a second call and a plea for another $5,000 withdrawal.

Fraudulent home repair services are a bane to all consumers, but seniors are often the victims. A large organized crime group, known by law enforcement agencies as the Travelers, move from town to town. They go into a neighborhood and tell homeowners that they have finished a home repair job nearby and are willing to fix their houses with leftover materials at an extremely low price. These scam artists demand their money up front. Whether it is painting the exterior of a house, fixing a leaky roof, or sealing a driveway, these con artists do little or no work and are quickly out of town before the homeowners realize they have been tricked.

Because of the growing population of senior citizens, law enforcement agencies have sought to educate seniors about telephone fraud and other common scams. Pamphlets distributed to senior citizens and community programs tell seniors to hang up the phone if they are pressured to part with their money and to toss the "you've won a prize" mailing in the wastebasket.

How to Avoid Being Defrauded

Local law enforcement agencies, state attorneys general, the federal Consumer Protection Agency, and groups such as the American Association of Retired Persons provide information to senior citizens on how to avoid being defrauded. These organizations advise the following:

- Watch out if a caller promises prizes for buying products such as vitamins, beauty and health aids, or office supplies. These products are sold at outrageously inflated prices, costing a buyer $500 to $2,000 for items with a value of less than $100.
- Never give a caller your credit card number or checking account number.
- Be especially cautious if a caller reaches you when you are feeling lonely. The person may call day after day until you feel that the caller is a friend, not a stranger trying to sell you something.
- If you think a caller is dishonest, hang up the phone. If a caller is trying to cheat you, it is not rude to hang up.
- Never act in haste. If a caller is pressuring you to make a quick decision, consult with friends and family or your state or local consumer protection office before taking a financial risk.
- Always remember that if you really win a prize, you will get it absolutely free, with no fee required.
- Beware if you have been cheated by con artists. They sell information to other con artists, who are likely to call.
- Remember, con artists are liars. They will say anything to get your money.
- If it sounds too good to be true, it usually is not true. Be skeptical of offers that promise rewards greatly out of proportion to your investment.

sic health care benefits to recipients of Social Security and is funded through the Social Security Trust Fund. Medicare is divided into a hospital insurance program and a supplementary medical insurance program. The hospital insurance plan covers reasonable and medically necessary treatment in a hospital or skilled nursing home, meals, regular nursing care services, and the cost of necessary special care. Medicare also pays for home health services and hospice care for terminally ill patients.

Medicare's supplementary medical insurance program is financed by monthly insurance premiums paid by people who sign up for coverage, combined with money contributed by the federal government. The government contributes the major portion of the cost of the program, which is funded out of general tax revenues. Persons who enroll pay a regular monthly PREMIUM and also a small annual DEDUCTIBLE fee for any medical costs incurred during the year above the amount funded by the government. Once the deductible has been paid, Medicare pays 80 percent of any medical bills.

Some warm-weather states such as Arizona and Florida have senior citizen retirement communities. These planned communities allow only senior citizens to buy or rent housing. Many seniors feel more independent and secure in a retirement community than in an ordinary neighborhood. Legal provisions in a retirement community's development plan are incorporated into the DEEDS of all property owners, prohibiting, for example, children from residing in the community. In this way, the special nature of the neighborhood is preserved.

However, not all senior citizens wish to retire from the workforce. Amendments to the federal Age Discrimination in Employment Act of 1967 (ADEA) (29 U.S.C.A. § 621 et seq.) have eliminated the age of mandatory retirement for most employees and have made the act applicable to more workers. The ADEA itself prohibits employers from discriminating on the basis of age.

Senior citizens also are concerned about crime. Because of their physical vulnerability and personal isolation, they are robbed more often than are the members of other age groups. Seniors are also the most likely group in society to be swindled. The American Association of Retired Persons and state and local governments seek to educate senior citizens about mail and telemarketing schemes that DEFRAUD thousands of seniors each year.

CROSS-REFERENCES

Age Discrimination; Consumer Protection; Death and Dying; Elder Law; Health Care Law; Health Insurance; Pension.

SENIOR INTEREST 📖 A right that takes effect prior to others or has preference over others. 📖

For example, a first MORTGAGE is an interest that is senior to a second mortgage and all subsequent mortgages.

SENIORITY 📖 Precedence or preference in position over others similarly situated. As used, for example, with reference to job seniority, the worker with the most years of service is first promoted within a range of jobs subject to seniority, and is the last laid off, proceeding so on down the line to the youngest in point of service. The term may also refer to the priority of a LIEN or ENCUMBRANCE. 📖

A person who holds a lien or has an encumbrance against the property of another, so that her claim must be satisfied before any others, has seniority or priority.

An employee has seniority if he is among those with the most years of service at the place of employment. Such seniority entitles the employee to compete for promotion to jobs for which junior (less senior) employees would be ineligible or would receive less consideration. Traditionally, it also gives him the status of being among the last to lose his job in case of lay-offs.

In the 1984 case of *Firefighters Local Union No. 1784 v. Stotts*, 467 U.S. 561, 104 S. Ct. 2576, 81 L. Ed. 2d 483, the Supreme Court upheld the validity of a seniority system that protected the jobs of white firefighters with seniority at the expense of recently hired black firefighters. The fire department in Memphis, Tennessee, implemented the traditional seniority principle of "last hired, first fired." In 1981 three white firefighters who otherwise would have kept their jobs under the system were laid off for a month while minority firefighters with less seniority continued working. This change in the seniority system resulted from an INJUNCTION to enforce consent decrees that resolved equal employment opportunity cases in Memphis. The lower court fashioned the decrees to remedy the past discriminatory practices of the fire department in its hiring and promotion of minorities. The district court concluded that the seniority system was not a bona fide one under section 706(g) of Title VII of the CIVIL RIGHTS ACT of 1964 since lay-offs made pursuant to it would have a racially discriminatory effect. The court, therefore, directed the modification of the system to increase and maintain the percentage of black firefighters. The court of appeals affirmed the revision of the seniority system but disagreed with the holding that the system was not bona fide.

On CERTIORARI, the Supreme Court decided that the district court exceeded its authority in issuing the injunction that ultimately led to the lay-off of the senior white firefighters. The injunction was not a proper remedy. There was no finding that any of the black employees protected by the revised system had been a direct victim of DISCRIMINATION, a requirement imposed by the Court in *International Brotherhood of Teamsters v. United States*, 431 U.S. 324, 97 S. Ct. 1843, 52 L. Ed. 2d 396 (1977). The Court, however, did not decide whether the consent decree was valid or whether the Memphis Fire Department could, on its own, protect the jobs of black firefighters at the expense of their white colleagues who had more seniority.

CROSS-REFERENCES

Affirmative Action; Civil Rights; Employment Law; Equal Protection; Labor Law.

SENTENCING 📖 The postconviction stage of the criminal justice process, in which the defendant is brought before the court for the imposition of a penalty. 📖

If a defendant is convicted in a criminal prosecution, the event that follows the VERDICT is called sentencing. A sentence is the penalty ordered by the court. Generally, the primary goals of sentencing are punishment, deterrence, incapacitation, and rehabilitation. In some states, juries may be entitled to pronounce sentence, but in most states, and in federal court, sentencing is performed by a judge.

For serious crimes, sentencing is usually pronounced at a sentencing hearing, where the PROSECUTOR and the defendant present their arguments regarding the penalty. For violations and other minor charges, sentencing is either predetermined or pronounced immediately after conviction.

Sentencing in the United States has undergone several dramatic transformations. In the eighteenth century, the sentencing of criminal defendants was left to juries. If a defendant was convicted, the JURY decided the facts that would affect sentencing, and a predetermined sentence was imposed based on those findings. In the late eighteenth century, legislatures began to prescribe imprisonment as punishment, replacing such punishments as public whipping and confinement in stocks.

Beginning in the late nineteenth century, legislatures began to pass statutes that left sentencing to the discretion of judges. This movement toward INDETERMINATE sentencing allowed judges to order a sentence tailored to the needs of both the defendant and society. Under sentencing statutes, a sentence could be any combination of PROBATION, FINES, RESTITUTION (repayment to victims), imprisonment, and community service. Judges were allowed to consider a wide range of EVIDENCE in fashioning a sentence, including mitigating factors (circumstances that reduced the defendant's culpability).

Percent of Felons Sentenced to Prison and Length of Sentence Imposed by State and Federal Courts in 1994

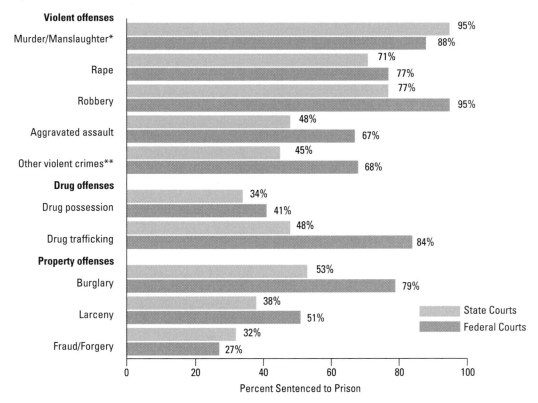

Violent offenses

Offense	State Courts	Federal Courts
Murder/Manslaughter*	95%	88%
Rape	71%	77%
Robbery	77%	95%
Aggravated assault	48%	67%
Other violent crimes**	45%	68%

Drug offenses

Offense	State Courts	Federal Courts
Drug possession	34%	41%
Drug trafficking	48%	84%

Property offenses

Offense	State Courts	Federal Courts
Burglary	53%	79%
Larceny	38%	51%
Fraud/Forgery	32%	27%

Percent Sentenced to Prison

State Courts
Federal Courts

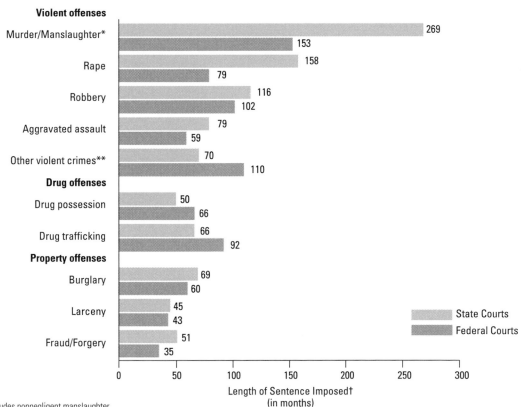

Violent offenses

Offense	State Courts	Federal Courts
Murder/Manslaughter*	269	153
Rape	158	79
Robbery	116	102
Aggravated assault	79	59
Other violent crimes**	70	110

Drug offenses

Offense	State Courts	Federal Courts
Drug possession	50	66
Drug trafficking	66	92

Property offenses

Offense	State Courts	Federal Courts
Burglary	69	60
Larceny	45	43
Fraud/Forgery	51	35

Length of Sentence Imposed†
(in months)

State Courts
Federal Courts

* Includes nonnegligent manslaughter.
** Includes offenses such as negligent manslaughter, sexual assault and kidnapping.
†Includes persons receiving a combination of sentences. Only the prison portion of the sentence is listed.

Source: U.S. Department of Justice, Office of Justice Programs,"Felony Sentences in the United States, 1994." Prepared by Patrick A. Langan and Jodi M. Brown. July 1997.

In the 1950s, Congress passed a spate of federal legislation requiring that judges impose mandatory minimum sentences for drug offenses. These laws directed that defendants must serve a minimum number of years in prison upon conviction for certain offenses, and prevented judges from reducing sentences in consideration of mitigating factors. In the 1960s, these laws came under attack for failing to deter drug crimes. Moreover, prosecutors were reluctant to prosecute mandatory minimum cases because they were considered unjustly severe.

By the late 1970s, indeterminate sentencing had fallen into disfavor. Many perceived that crime rates were soaring, and a powerful lobby emerged demanding sentencing reform. These critics argued for longer prison sentences, and they also pushed for uniformity in sentencing, noting that discretionary sentencing produced widely various sentences for the same crime.

Several states' legislatures enacted sentencing guidelines in the 1970s and early 1980s. These guidelines increased punishment for criminal offenses and limited judicial discretion in sentencing by identifying the punishment required upon conviction for a particular offense. Under many of the new sentencing statutes, PAROLE for prison inmates was either abolished or restricted to certain offenses. Conservatives hailed this "truth-in-sentencing" framework as a victory over liberal judges. Liberals endorsed sentencing reform because it purported to eliminate the possibility of racial disparity in sentencing.

Following the lead of these state legislatures, Congress passed the Sentencing Reform Act of 1984 (SRA) (Pub. L. No. 98-473, 98 Stat. 1987 [1984] [codified in 18 U.S.C.A. §§ 3551–3556 (1988 & Supp. V 1993)]). The SRA abolished parole for federal prisoners and reduced the amount of time off granted for good behavior.

The SRA also established the U.S. Sentencing Commission (USSC) and directed it to create a new sentencing system (28 U.S.C.A. §§ 991(b), 994(a)(1)–(2) [1988]). Between 1984 and 1987, the USSC crafted the Federal Sentencing Guidelines. Since Congress did not object to the guidelines, they became effective on November 1, 1987 (28 U.S.C.A. § 994 [1988 & Supp. V 1993]).

The Federal Sentencing Guidelines shift the focus in sentencing from the offender to the offense. The guidelines categorize offenses and identify the sentence required upon conviction. Judges are allowed to increase or decrease sentences, or depart from the guidelines, but only if they have a very good explanation and clearly

Stephen Jones, defense attorney for Timothy McVeigh, reacts after the jury sentenced his client to death for the 1995 Oklahoma City bombing.

AP/WIDE WORLD PHOTOS

state the reasons on the record.

Upward departures, or increases in sentences, are easy to achieve under section 1B1.2 of the sentencing guidelines. This section allows the sentencing judge to consider all "relevant conduct," including the circumstances surrounding the conviction, offenses that were committed at the same time as the charged offense but were not charged, prior convictions, and acts for which the defendant was previously tried but acquitted.

In limited circumstances, judges may decrease a sentence. For example, a judge may downwardly depart if the defendant accepts responsibility for the crime, or committed the crime to avoid a more serious offense. Prosecutors often challenge decreased sentences on APPEAL, and they usually win because the guidelines call for adherence in all but exceptional cases.

Prosecutors receive tremendous discretion in the sentencing process, and they have virtually taken over the sentencing process in federal court. Under the guidelines, prosecutors can easily increase or decrease a sentence by tinkering with the number of counts either in the initial charge or pursuant to a plea agreement. For example, a prosecutor may not use evidence of certain conduct in pursuing a criminal charge. However, upon conviction or a guilty plea, the prosecutor can, in the sentencing hearing, introduce that evidence to increase the defendant's sentence. At this point, if the prosecutor is able to prove by a PREPONDERANCE OF THE EVIDENCE that the defendant committed the acts, the court is obliged to increase the defendant's sentence.

Furthermore, state police officers and prosecutors can make secret decisions about what cases to refer to federal prosecutors. State prosecutors can thus pressure defendants to enter a guilty plea in state court to avoid federal sentencing. The decision of whether to move the court for a downward departure in exchange for substantial assistance to law enforcement is also left to the prosecutor.

At first, many federal judges refused to recognize the Federal Sentencing Guidelines. In *Mistretta v. United States*, 488 U.S. 361, 109 S. Ct. 647, 102 L. Ed. 2d 714 (1989), the U.S. Supreme Court held that the guidelines did not violate the SEPARATION-OF-POWERS doctrine and were not an excessive delegation of legislative power. Since the *Mistretta* decision, federal courts have abandoned the indeterminate approach to sentencing and have used the sentencing guidelines to determine criminal sentences.

As part of the Comprehensive Crime Control Act of 1984 (Pub. L. No. 98-473, Title II, October 12, 1984, 98 Stat. 1976 to 2193), Congress passed legislation requiring mandatory minimum sentences for drug and firearm offenses (Pub. L. No. 98-473, §§ 503(a), 1005(a), 98 Stat. 2069, 2138 [1984] [amending 21 U.S.C.A. § 860 (formerly § 845a), 18 U.S.C.A. § 924(c)]). In 1986, as public fears of drug abuse increased, Congress enacted the Anti–Drug Abuse Act of 1986 (Pub. L. No. 99-570, 100 Stat. 3207 [1986]). This act created mandatory minimum sentences for drug trafficking and distribution, using the quantity of the drug involved to determine the minimum terms of imprisonment. In 1988, Congress broadened the mandatory minimums to cover conspiracy in certain drug offenses (Anti–Drug Abuse Act of 1988 [Pub. L. No. 100-690, § 6470(a), 102 Stat. 4377 (21 U.S.C.A. §§ 846, 963 [1988])]).

The 1988 act also established a minimum sentence for simple possession of crack cocaine. Under 21 U.S.C.A. § 844(a) (1988 & Supp. II 1990 & Supp. III 1991), a first-time offender caught with five grams of a mixture or substance containing a "cocaine base" must be sentenced to no less than five years in prison. In contrast, a person must possess at least five hundred grams of powder cocaine to receive a five-year sentence (21 U.S.C.A. §§ 841(b)(1)(B)(ii)–(iii) [1982 & Supp. V 1987]).

In 1994, Congress moved to limit the applicability of mandatory minimums to low-level, nonviolent drug offenders. Under 18 U.S.C.A. § 3553(f), a judge may use the guidelines instead of the statutory minimum sentence if (1) the defendant does not have a criminal history of more than one point (one minor conviction, such as a petit MISDEMEANOR); (2) the defendant did not use violence or credible threats or a firearm in the offense, and did not coerce another to do so; (3) the offense did not result in death or serious bodily injury; (4) the defendant was not an organizer of others in the offense, and was not engaged in a continuing criminal enterprise (such as a racketeering scheme or the functioning of a street gang); and (5) by the time of the sentencing hearing, the defendant has informed the prosecutor of all the facts surrounding the case, including facts regarding offenses related to the case.

Also in 1994, Congress exercised its power over sentencing by passing the Violent Crime Control and Law Enforcement Act of 1994 (Pub. L. No. 103-322, September 13, 1994, 108 Stat. 1796). Under provisions of this act, violent

SENTENCING GUIDELINES: FAIR OR UNFAIR?

Sentencing guideline systems for determining criminal sentences have dramatically changed the way punishment is meted out in U.S. courtrooms. Twenty-two states and the federal government use sentencing guidelines, which require a judge to calculate a criminal sentence using a mathematical formula. Points are assigned based on the defendant's offenses, prior criminal record, and other factors. A total is calculated, and the sentence is computed. A judge has very little room to depart from the sentence mandated by the guidelines.

There has been controversy over the fairness and the legitimacy of using sentencing guidelines, with the most criticism directed at the U.S. Sentencing Guidelines. The criticism comes mostly from defense attorneys and judges, who argue that the guidelines give prosecutors too much power in the criminal justice system and give too little discretion to judges to shape a sentence to fit the individual defendant. Defenders of sentencing guidelines contend that they are a vast improvement over the way sentencing has traditionally been done, eliminating "judge shopping" and the arbitrary and disparate sentencing practices that come with unbridled judicial discretion.

Congress authorized the U.S. Sentencing Guidelines in 1984. The U.S. Sentencing Guidelines Commission, a seven-member panel appointed by the president and confirmed by the Senate, issued the first set of guidelines in 1987. The guidelines have been constantly changed, mostly by the commission, but also by congressional legislation. In addition, Congress has exercised its veto power over amendments proposed by the commission. By 1996 the federal guidelines had grown to an 850-page manual, containing complex formulas for computing different types of sentences.

Proponents of federal sentencing guidelines believe that they reduce sentencing disparity and guarantee harsher punishment for federal felons, many of whom are convicted for selling illegal narcotics. Before the guidelines were created, the proponents argue, defendants tried to avoid judges who handed out tough sentences and to find one who would be lenient. Thus, in one court a bank robber would get an eighteen-year sentence, while in another a robber convicted of the same crime would receive only five years in prison. In addition, there was evidence to suggest that minorities received the harshest treatment. Sentencing guidelines have, therefore, reduced the arbitrary dispensation of punishment.

IN FOCUS

Proponents also contend that because the guidelines provide predictable sentences, they serve as a deterrent to crime. Criminals know the formula of past conviction plus new conviction equals a certain criminal sentence. Criminals no longer can play the angles in the criminal justice system to their advantage but must face a definite punishment.

Defenders of the guidelines also believe that the reduction of judicial discretion reduces the stress suffered by federal trial judges. No longer do judges have to wrestle with their emotions in devising an appropriate sentence. The guidelines provide an efficient means of delivering a criminal sentence that conforms to public policy goals set out by Congress and the guidelines commission.

Critics of the federal guidelines contend that while the idea of uniform criminal sentences may seem attractive, in practice the guidelines have created another arbitrary system of sentencing. A major criticism is the shift in power from the judge to the federal prosecutor. Because the criminal charge will trigger, upon conviction, a particular sentence in the guidelines, a prosecutor's charging decision is the most important one in the case. A prosecutor can determine whether a defendant's time in prison is short or long by manipulating the charges and a case's extenuating circumstances.

Critics argue that prosecutorial discretion has replaced judicial discretion, allowing defendants who hire defense counsel knowledgeable in the workings of the guidelines to negotiate plea agreements that reduce the charges and accompanying jail time. Defendants with less effective counsel receive longer sentences. Critics point to the disparate sentences received by defendants involved in the same crime. Therefore, it is clear that prosecutors can manipulate the charges, with judges powerless to change the sentencing outcome.

Critics, especially federal judges, decry the loss of discretion to shape a criminal sentence that is appropriate to the individual. The federal guidelines impose mathematical formulas, reducing a human being to the number of points on a sentencing grid worksheet. Judges are forced to ignore the particular circumstances of the case and the individual and hand out the sentence dictated by the guidelines. Those judges who depart from the guidelines and give more lenient or more severe sentences invariably invite appellate review of their decisions.

Another criticism is that the guidelines reflect political concerns more than penological ones. Critics charge that Congress, in its zeal to be regarded as tough on crime, has imposed severe penalties that are out of proportion to the nature of some of the offenses. In addition, Congress has vetoed some sentencing commission revisions to the guidelines that it has regarded as politically unacceptable.

Critics also object to the growing complexity of the guidelines, analogizing the various provisions to the Internal Revenue Code. The sentencing commission's continuous revisions, contend critics, have undermined the stability of the guidelines and lessened the goals of predictability and uniformity.

offenders convicted of their third FELONY must be sentenced to life imprisonment (Pub. L. No. 103-322, §§ 70001–70002, 108 Stat. 1796, 1982–1985 [1984] [codified as amended at 18 U.S.C.A. §§ 3559, 3582(c)(1)(A) (1988)]). Many states have also passed so-called three-strikes-and-you're-out laws.

Mandatory minimums are not the same as the Federal Sentencing Guidelines. Mandatory minimum sentences remove all discretion from the sentencing judge, whereas the guidelines allow for some leeway. In *United States v. Mad-kour*, 930 F.2d 234 (2d Cir. 1991), Michael P. Madkour, a recent graduate of the University of Vermont with no criminal record, received a mandatory minimum sentence of five years in federal prison for possessing more than one hundred marijuana plants with an intent to manufacture marijuana. Under the guidelines, the prison sentence would have been fifteen to twenty-one months.

The most common punishments identified in state statutes are community service, probation, fines, restitution, and imprisonment. In the 1990s, some southeastern states authorized sentences of hard labor on chain gangs. Many states have also reinstated the death penalty. Death penalty sentences are usually delivered by a jury, not a judge, and only after a hearing.

Criminal defendants are sentenced at a sentencing HEARING. In the hearing, the judge may consider all relevant evidence, TESTIMONY, and a presentence report from a probation or court services officer. The rules of evidence do not apply in presentencing hearings, so HEARSAY and other fallible evidence may be introduced.

In both federal and state courts, the sentencing hearing is preceded by a PRESENTENCE INVESTIGATION and report. These are conducted by a court services or probation officer, who then submits the report to all parties to the prosecution. At the hearing, the prosecutor and defendant are entitled to argue against the recommendations for sentencing made in the presentence report.

In many states, courts still possess the authority to craft sentences within the bounds of sentencing statutes. In these states, criminal statutes contain a sentencing provision that identifies minimum and maximum punishments for specific crimes. For example, in Georgia, a person convicted of hunting alligators without a license "shall be punished by a fine of not less than $500.00 and, in the discretion of the sentencing court, imprisonment for not more than 12 months" (Ga. Code Ann. § 27-3-19). This means that the judge *must* order a fine of at least $500, and *may* also order imprisonment of up to twelve months.

Juvenile court judges possess tremendous discretion in sentencing. In 1995, Judge Wayne Creech, of the Berkeley County Family Court, in South Carolina, ordered fifteen-year-old Tonya Kline to be physically tied, twenty-four hours a day, to her mother, Deborah Harter. This order was imposed on Kline and Harter after Kline was charged with truancy, shoplifting, and housebreaking. Under the tethering conditions, Kline and Harter were allowed to separate only to go to the bathroom and to shower.

CROSS-REFERENCES

Capital Punishment; Corporal Punishment; Criminal Law; Criminal Procedure; Cruel and Unusual Punishment; Drugs and Narcotics; Eighth Amendment; Incarceration; Juvenile Law; Mitigating Circumstances; Plea Bargaining; Prison.

SEPARATE BUT EQUAL

The doctrine first enunciated by the U.S. Supreme Court in *Plessy v. Ferguson*, 163 U.S. 537, 16 S. Ct. 1138, 41 L. Ed. 256 (1896), to the effect that establishing different facilities for blacks and whites was valid under the Equal Protection Clause of the FOURTEENTH AMENDMENT as long as they were equal.

The theory of separate but equal was used to justify segregated public facilities for blacks and whites until in *Brown v. Board of Education of Topeka, Kansas*, 347 U.S. 483, 74 S. Ct. 686, 98 L. Ed. 873 (1954), the Supreme Court recognized that "separate but equal" schools were "inherently unequal." The principle of "separate but equal" was further rejected by the CIVIL RIGHTS ACTS (42 U.S.C.A. § 2000a et seq.) and in subsequent cases, which ruled that racially segregated public facilities, housing, and accommodations violated the constitutional guarantee of EQUAL PROTECTION of laws.

CROSS-REFERENCES

Brown v. Board of Education of Topeka, Kansas; Civil Rights; Integration; *Plessy v. Ferguson*.

SEPARATE MAINTENANCE

Money paid by one married person to the other for support if they are no longer living as husband and wife. Commonly it is referred to as separate support and follows from a court order.

See ALIMONY.

SEPARATION

A termination of COHABITATION of husband and wife either by mutual agreement or, in the case of *judicial separation*, under the decree of a court.

See also DIVORCE.

A sample
separation
agreement

This Agreement entered into this _____ day of _____ , 19_____ , by and between _____ , hereinafter referred to as the wife, and _____ , hereinafter referred to as the husband;

WITNESSETH:

Whereas the parties hereto were married by a Minister authorized to solemnize marriages in the State of _____ on [*Date*] at _____ , _____ , and lived together thereafter as husband and wife; and

Whereas there were born of this marriage the following children:

_____ , born _____ , now age 8
_____ , born _____ , now age 6

and

Whereas certain serious differences have arisen between the parties hereto as a consequence of which they are no longer living together as husband and wife, and it is contemplated that the wife will forthwith file an action for absolute divorce in the Circuit Court for the County of _____ , _____ ; and

Whereas both parties are desirous of definitely and for all times settling and determining all property and money matters between them, and all matters of custody, visitation, support, and education of the minor children and all matters of dower, inheritance, alimony, maintenance, allowance for attorney fees, costs, and expenses which have arisen or might arise out of the marriage relation between said parties and as a result of any action for divorce; and

Whereas each of the parties is fully informed and advised of the property and estate of the other, and of his or her respective rights and liabilities against and to the other and to all the property and estate of the other.

Now, therefore, in consideration of their mutual promises, the parties hereto agree as follows:

Right to Live Separately

1. The parties may and shall continue to live apart for the rest of their lives. Each shall be free from interference, direct or indirect, by the other as fully as though unmarried. Each may, for his or her separate benefit, engage in any employment, business, or profession as he or she may choose. Neither of the parties shall molest or interfere with the other, nor shall either attempt to compel the other to cohabit or dwell with him or her by any means whatsoever.

Custody, Domicile and Visitation of Children

2. The wife shall have the legal and physical custody, care, control, and education of the minor children of the parties, to wit:

_____ , born _____ , now age 8
_____ , born _____ , now age 6

subject to the husband's liberal and reasonable rights of visitation.

3. It is recognized by the parties that in view of the tender years of their children, to wit:

_____ , born _____ , now age 8
_____ , born _____ , now age 6

that it is important for the children to be in the near vicinity of their father, _____ , and their paternal grandparents, aunts, uncles, nieces, and nephews, where they have resided since birth. It is agreed by the parties hereto that the minor children of the parties shall not be removed from this community for at least five (5) years from the date of this Agreement, it being expressly understood that the custody provisions as herein provided have been made in recognition of the fact that such children will reside in this area for at least that period of time. The parties recognize that in view of their respective ages, that it is impossible to agree that each party will remain in the State of _____ for an indefinite period of time and until the children reach the age of eighteen (18) years respectively. Therefore, after the expiration of said five (5) year period, the wife may apply to the Court for permission to remove the children from this State, the parties agreeing that the removal of such children from the State shall be personally and closely scrutinized by the Court for the purpose of ascertaining whether such a change would clearly be in the best interests of such children in view of all of the facts and circumstances then existing. The continued residence of the children in this community as above provided is subject to the condition that the husband continues to remain in this community and in close proximity to the minor children of the parties.

Support for Children

4. The husband shall pay to the wife for the support and maintenance of the two (2) minor children of the parties, the sum of _____ and 00/100 [$_____] Dollars per month per child (a total of _____ and 00/100 [$_____] Dollars in two [2] equal payments of _____ and 00/100 [$_____] Dollars on the first and fifteenth of each month), commencing [Date], until each child reaches the age of eighteen (18) years or graduates from high school.

5. The child support provisions as herein provided have been arrived at in contemplation of the overall settlement of all financial matters between the parties as set forth herein. Accordingly, upon the termination of the payments to the wife as set forth in Paragraph 11K, either because of the passage of time or the wife's remarriage, such fact shall not in and of itself be sufficient basis for modification of the aforesaid child support. Such settlement also contemplates that the husband's income shall increase in the future and that such increase shall not be a sufficient basis to seek modification of the child's support until such time as the husband's adjusted gross income is _____ 00/100 ($_____) Dollars per year or more.

6. The husband shall maintain in full force and effect medical and hospital insurance for each of the minor children of the parties until each child reaches the age of eighteen (18) years or graduates from high school, whichever occurs last. To the extent that the aforesaid insurance does not cover the cost thereof or is not maintained in full force and effect during the aforesaid period, the husband shall pay all medical, dental, hospital, optometric, orthodontic, and prescription drug expenses necessarily incurred in their behalf.

7. The husband shall name each child as primary beneficiary of _____ and 00/100 ($_____) Dollars of life insurance until each child reaches the age of eighteen (18) years or graduates from high school, whichever shall last occur.

8. It is agreed and understood between the parties hereto that the husband may claim the children of the parties hereto as dependency exemptions on his Federal, State and Local Income Tax Returns, commencing with the year 19_____ and thereafter.

Alimony

9. Neither of the parties hereto shall pay to the other nor be entitled to receive from the other temporary or permanent alimony.

Insurance

10. Except as hereinabove provided, any interest which either of the parties hereto may now have or may heretofore have had in any of the life insurance contracts or policies of the other party shall, effective on the date of execution of this Agreement, be and the same hereby is extinguished and the parties hereto shall in the future hold all such insurance free and clear of any right or interest which the other party now has or may heretofore have had therein or thereto by virtue of being the beneficiary, the contingent beneficiary or otherwise.

Property Settlement and Provision in Lieu of Dower

11. By way of property settlement, the parties agree as follows:

A. The wife shall become and be the sole and separate owner of the marital home located at _____ , subject to the existing mortgage in favor of Standard Federal Savings & Loan Association, which she shall assume and pay along with the taxes, insurance and all other obligations that shall become due on the premises, and shall hold the husband harmless thereon. Further, the husband shall hereafter have a lien against the aforesaid marital home in the amount of _____ and 00/100 ($_____) Dollars, which sum the wife agrees to pay to the husband upon the wife's remarriage, the sale of the marital home, or the youngest child reaching the age of eighteen (18) years, whichever shall first occur; provided, however, that in the event the wife shall, prior to [Date], sell the home and

[continued on page 202]

coincident therewith, purchase another residence in her sole name, the husband agrees to assist her in any reasonable manner to obtain a mortgage therefor, including cosigning the same. In the event the husband shall cosign such note and mortgage as provided in the preceding sentence, the wife does hereby hold him harmless from any liability in connection therewith.

B. The wife shall become and be the sole and separate owner of all household furniture, furnishings, appurtenances, household goods and appliances, and all other items of personal property located in or about the marital home at _____ , except for selected items which shall become and be the sole and separate property of the husband and which have been agreed upon between the parties hereto.

C. The wife shall become and be the sole and separate owner of the 1973 Wombat automobile which she presently drives, subject to the existing lien which she will assume and pay and hold the husband harmless thereon.

D. The wife shall become and be the sole and separate owner of the checking account at XYZ National Bank over which she presently has control.

E. The husband shall assist the wife in obtaining Blue Cross reimbursement for medical bills incurred by her until entry of the Judgment of Divorce.

F. The husband shall retain any and all interest which he has in _____ and the undistributed interest in his ABRA Plan, free and clear of any claim or interest of the wife.

[Additional material omitted for purpose of illustration.]

Mutual Releases

12. Except as otherwise herein expressly provided, the parties shall and do hereby mutually remise, release, and forever discharge each other from any and all actions, suits, debts, claims, demands, and obligations whatsoever both in law and in equity which either of them ever had, now has or may hereafter have against the other, upon or by reason of any matter, cause or thing up to the date of the execution of this Agreement.

Residence of Parties

13. Both husband and wife acknowledge that they are bona fide residents of and domiciled in the State of _____ at the time of the execution of this Agreement.

Modification, Waiver or Breach

14. No modification or waiver of any of the terms hereof shall be valid unless in writing and signed by both the parties. No waiver of any breach hereof or default hereunder shall be deemed a waiver of any subsequent breach or default of the same or similar nature.

In the Event of Divorce

15. In the event of a divorce between the parties, this Agreement shall be offered in evidence in such action, and if acceptable to the Court, shall be incorporated by reference in the Judgment that may be granted herein. Notwithstanding such incorporation, this Agreement shall not be merged in the Judgment but shall survive the same and shall be binding and conclusive on the parties for all time.

Implementing Agreement

16. Each party shall, at any time and from time to time hereafter take any and all steps and execute, acknowledge and deliver to the other party any and all further instruments and assurances that the other party may reasonably require for the purpose of giving full force and effect to the provisions of this Agreement.

Independent Advice of Counsel

17. The parties respectively acknowledge that each has had independent legal advice by counsel of his or her own selection; that each fully understands the facts and has been fully informed as to his or her legal rights and obligations; and that having had such advice, and with such knowledge, each of them is signing the Agreement freely and voluntarily.

A sample
separation
agreement
(continued)

Counsel Fees

18. Each of the parties shall be responsible for any legal fees or expenses incurred by him or her in connection with the negotiation of this Agreement and any ensuing action for divorce.

Governing Law

19. This Agreement shall be governed by the laws of the State of _____ .

Entire Agreement

20. This Agreement constitutes the entire understanding of the parties. It supersedes any and all prior agreements between them. There are no representations or warranties other than those expressly herein set forth.

In witness whereof, the parties have executed this Agreement this day and year set forth above.

Witness to the Signature of

_____   _____

Witness to the Signature of

_____   _____

ADDENDUM FOR DEFINITIONAL PURPOSES TO SEPARATION
AGREEMENT BETWEEN _____ and _____ ,
DATED THE _____ DAY OF _____ , 19_____

Cohabitation shall be deemed to be that continuous conduct between a man and a woman as is traditionally associated with the marriage relationship but shall not necessarily require continuous occupancy of a dwelling together. For purposes of this definition, the wife's relationship with an unrelated male while away from her principal residence and the children, or while the children are in the custody of the father, shall not be taken in account.

_____

_____

SEPARATION OF POWERS

The division of state and federal government into three independent branches.

The first three articles of the U.S. Constitution call for the powers of the federal government to be divided among three separate branches: the legislative, the executive, and the judiciary branch. Under the separation of powers, each branch is independent, has a separate function, and may not usurp the functions of another branch. However, the branches are interrelated. They cooperate with one another and also prevent one another from attempting to assume too much power. This relationship is described as one of checks and balances, where the functions of one branch serve to contain and modify the power of another. Through this elaborate system of safeguards, the Framers of the Constitution sought to protect the nation against tyranny.

Under the separation of powers, each branch of government has a specific function. The legislative branch—the Congress—makes the laws. The EXECUTIVE BRANCH—the president—implements the laws. The JUDICIARY—the court system—interprets the laws and decides legal controversies. The system of federal TAXATION provides a good example of each branch at work. Congress passes legislation regarding taxes. The president is responsible for appointing a director of the INTERNAL REVENUE SERVICE to carry out the law through the collection of taxes. The courts rule on cases concerning the application of the tax laws.

Under the system of checks and balances, each branch acts as a restraint on the powers of the other two. The president can either sign the LEGISLATION of Congress, making it law, or VETO it. The Congress, through the Senate, has the power of advise and consent on presidential appointments and can therefore reject an appointee. The courts, given the sole power to interpret the Constitution and the laws, can uphold or overturn acts of the legislature or rule on actions by the president. Most judges are appointed, and therefore Congress and the president can affect the judiciary. Thus at no time does all authority rest with a single branch of government. Instead, power is measured, apportioned, and restrained among the three government branches. The states also follow the three-part model of government, through state governors, state legislatures, and the state court systems.

Our system of government in the United States is largely credited to JAMES MADISON and is sometimes called the Madisonian model. Madison set forth his belief in the need for balanced government power in *The Federalist*, No. 51. However, the concept of separation of powers did not originate with Madison. It is often attributed to the French philosopher BARON MONTESQUIEU, who described it in 1748. At the Constitutional Convention of 1787, Madison played a leading role in persuading the majority of the Framers to incorporate the concept into the Constitution.

CROSS-REFERENCES

Congress of the United States; Constitution of the United States; Judicial Review; President of the United States; Presidential Powers; Supreme Court of the United States.

SEQUESTRATION ◫ In the context of trials, the isolation of a JURY from the public, or the separation of WITNESSES to ensure the integrity of TESTIMONY. In other legal contexts the seizure of PROPERTY or the freezing of ASSETS by court order. ◫

In jury trials, judges sometimes choose to sequester the jurors, or place them beyond public reach. Usually the jurors are moved into a hotel, kept under close supervision twenty-four hours a day, denied access to outside media such as television and newspapers, and allowed only limited contact with their families.

Although unpopular with jurors, sequestration has two broad purposes. The first is to avoid the accidental tainting of the jury, and the second is to prevent others from intentionally tampering with the jurors by bribe or threat. Trial publicity, public sentiment, interested parties, and the maneuverings and machinations of lawyers outside the courtroom can all taint the jurors' objectivity and deny the defendant a fair trial. Judges are free to sequester the jury whenever they believe any of these factors may affect the trial's outcome.

Jury sequestration is rare. Typically ordered in sensational, high-profile criminal cases, sequestration begins immediately after the jury is seated and lasts until the jury has delivered its verdict. It is unusual for juries to be sequestered longer than a few days or a week. Occasionally, however, jurors are sequestered for weeks. The 1995 trial of former football star O. J. (Orenthal James) SIMPSON for murder was highly unusual: the Simpson jury was sequestered for eight and a half months—half as long as the period Simpson was imprisoned while under arrest and on trial. The experience provoked protest from the jurors and calls for legal reform.

The sequestration of witnesses differs from that of jurors. Whereas jurors are kept away from the public, witnesses typically are ordered not to attend the trial—or follow accounts of it—until they are to testify. This judicial order is intended to assure that the witnesses will TESTIFY concerning their own knowledge of the case without being influenced by testimony of prior witnesses. Witness sequestration also seeks to strengthen the role of CROSS-EXAMINATION in developing facts.

Other definitions of sequestration relate to property. In CIVIL LAW, *sequester* has three distinct meanings. First, it means to renounce or disclaim, as when a widow appears in court and disclaims any interest in the estate of her deceased husband; the widow is said to sequester. Second, it means to take something that is the subject of a controversy out of the possession of the contending parties and deposit it in the hands of a third person; this neutral party is called a sequestor. Third and most commonly, sequestration in civil law denotes the act of seizing property by court order.

In litigation and EQUITY practice, sequestration also refers to court-ordered confiscation of property. When one party sues another over an unpaid DEBT, the plaintiff may secure a WRIT of ATTACHMENT. As another form of sequestration, this legal order temporarily seizes the alleged debtor's property in order to secure the debt or claim in the event that the plaintiff is successful. In equity practice—an antiquated system of justice that is now incorporated into civil justice—courts seize a defendant's property until the defendant purges herself of a charge of CONTEMPT.

In INTERNATIONAL LAW, the term *sequestration* signifies confiscation. Typically, it means the appropriation of private property to public use. Following a war, sequestration means the seizure of the property of the private citizens of a hostile power, as when a belligerent nation sequesters debts due from its own subjects to the enemy.

SERIATIM [*Latin, Severally; separately; individually; one by one.*]

SERJEANT AT LAW In English legal history, an elite order of attorneys who had the exclusive privilege of arguing before the Court of COMMON PLEAS and also supplied the judges for both Common Pleas and the Court of the KING'S BENCH.

For six centuries starting in the 1300s, the serjeants at law ranked above all other attorneys in the kingdom. Only twelve hundred men were ever promoted to the dignity of serjeant, the last dying in 1921. Although the serjeants have never had an exact counterpart in the United States, the order has had a lasting impact on U.S. law: it has been cited as a reason for regarding U.S. attorneys as OFFICERS OF THE COURT and specifically for requiring court-appointed attorneys to subsidize the legal representation of clients who cannot afford private attorneys.

The serjeants at law originated in the Court of Common Pleas, one of the four superior courts at Westminster, in the fourteenth century. They had an antecedent in the thirteenth-century legal practitioners known as *countors*, a term from the French meaning storytellers. Countors helped formulate the plaintiff's counts, or CAUSES OF ACTION, and the preparatory work called *counting*. In the fourteenth century their role evolved and became a profession. The countors became *servientes ad legem*, or serjeants at law.

The serjeants were an exalted order. Paid by the Crown and admitted to practice before a single court, they belonged to a closed society that had significant power. Only serjeants could argue in the Court of Common Pleas, and their ranks provided the only candidates for judges of the Common Pleas and the King's Bench. By the fifteenth century, regard for the serjeants was so high that no practitioner in the legal profession was considered their equal.

Serjeants came from the elite of the legal profession. The chief justice of the Common Pleas prepared a list of seven or eight of the best lawyers who had at least sixteen years' experience, and the CHANCELLOR selected the new inductees. At their induction, an elaborate ceremony, they swore to serve the king's people. The serjeants' costume also distinguished them from other English attorneys. They wore a long, loose garment called a tabard, a hood, and a close-fitting white headdress called a coif. Eventually, from this costume, the serjeants became known as the ORDER OF THE COIF. The influence of the serjeants declined in the eighteenth century, and by the nineteenth century, their monopoly on the Court of Common Pleas had ended. After the reorganization of the English justice system with the JUDICATURE ACTS of 1875, no more serjeants were created.

In U.S. law, the legacy of the serjeants derives from their role as officers of the court. The position was similar to holding public office and, as such, carried duties: the serjeants could be commanded to serve indigent clients. In the twentieth century, U.S. FEDERAL COURTS turned to this tradition for justification in viewing attorneys as officers of the court who also could be appointed to serve the needy. A significant example is the opinion in *United States v. Dillon*, 346 F.2d 633 (9th Cir. 1965), where the Ninth Circuit Court of Appeals required a court-appointed attorney to subsidize the costs of vacating the conviction of an indigent client. In citing "an ancient and established tradition" for this practice, the court looked in part to the English tradition of the serjeants at law.

SERVICE Any duty or labor performed for another person.

The delivery of a legal document that notifies the recipient of the commencement of a legal ACTION or proceeding in which he or she is involved.

The term *service* has various meanings, depending upon the context of the word.

Under feudal law, tenants had a duty to render service to their lords in exchange for use of the land. The service required could take many forms: monetary payments, farm products, loyalty, attendance upon the lord as an armed horseman, carrying the king's banner, providing a sword or a lance, or plowing or other farm labor done for the king. See also FEUDALISM.

In CONTRACT law, service refers to an act or deed, rather than property. It is a duty or labor done by a laborer under the direction and control of the one for whom the service is performed. The term implies that the recipient of the service selects and compensates the laborer. It is the occupation, condition, or status of being a servant and often describes every kind of employment relationship. In addition, *service* may be used to denote employment for the government, as in the terms *civil service, military service* or *the armed service*, or *public service*.

In the area of domestic relations, the term refers to the uncompensated work, guidance, and upkeep an injured or deceased family member previously provided for the family; the injury or death of the provider of these services means that the work will have to be obtained from another source and at a price. In this context the term traditionally was restricted to the "services" of a wife under the theory that the husband's duty was to provide support and the wife's duty was to provide service. After injury to his wife, a husband could bring an action on his own behalf against the responsible party for compensation of the loss of her aid, assistance, comfort, and society. The modern view holds that a wife may also sue for the loss of assistance and society of her husband.

Service also means the delivery of a WRIT, SUMMONS and COMPLAINT, criminal summons, or other NOTICE or ORDER by an authorized server upon another. Proper service thereby provides official notification that a legal action or proceeding against an individual has been commenced. See also SERVICE OF PROCESS.

SERVICE MARK 📖 A TRADEMARK that is used in connection with services. 📖

Businesses use service marks to identify their services and distinguish them from other services provided in the same field. Service marks consist of letters, words, symbols, and other devices that help inform consumers about the origin or source of a particular service. Roto-Rooter is an example of a service mark used by a familiar plumbing company. Trademarks, by contrast, are used to distinguish competing products, not services. Whereas trademarks are normally affixed to goods by means of a tag or label, service marks are generally displayed through advertising and promotion.

Service marks identify the providers of services, such as the corporations whose customers can acquire cash from this automated teller machine.

Service marks are regulated by the law of UNFAIR COMPETITION. At the federal level, service mark infringement is governed by the Lanham Trademark Act of 1946 (15 U.S.C.A. § 1051 et. seq.). At the state level, service mark infringement is governed by analogous INTELLECTUAL PROPERTY statutes that have been enacted in many JURISDICTIONS. In some states service mark infringement may give rise to a CAUSE OF ACTION under the COMMON LAW. Because service marks are a particular type of trademark, the substantive and procedural rules governing both types of marks are fundamentally the same.

The rights to a service mark may be acquired in two ways. First, a business can register the mark with the government. Most service marks are eligible for registration with the U.S. PATENT AND TRADEMARK OFFICE. Several state governments have separate registration requirements. Once a service mark has been registered, the law typically affords protection to the first mark filed with the government. Second, a business may acquire rights to a service mark through public use. However, a mark must be held out to the public regularly and continuously before it will receive legal protection. Sporadic or irregular use of a service mark will not insulate it from infringement.

To receive protection, a service mark must also be unique, unusual, or distinctive. Common, ordinary, and generic marks rarely qualify for protection. For example, a professional association of physicians could never acquire exclusive rights to register a service mark under the name "Health Care Services." Such a mark does little to distinguish the services provided by the business and tells consumers nothing about the health care practitioners involved. The law would give full legal protection to these same doctors, however, if they applied for a mark under the name "Snap and Jerk Chiropractic Services."

Once a business has established a vested right in a service mark, the law forbids other businesses from advertising their services with deceptively similar marks. Service mark infringement occurs when a particular mark is easily confused with other marks already established in the same trade and geographic market. Greater latitude is given when businesses that share similar marks are in unrelated fields or offer services in different consumer markets. For example, a court would be more inclined to allow two businesses to share the same mark when one business provides pest control services in urban areas, while the other provides film developing services in rural areas.

SERVICETILL

Two remedies are available for service mark infringement: injunctive relief (court orders restraining defendants from infringing on a plaintiff's service mark), and money DAMAGES (compensation for any losses suffered by an injured business). Both remedies are normally available whether a claim for infringement is pursued under state or federal law. However, the LANHAM ACT allows an injured business to recover significantly greater damages for infringement of a federally registered mark than it could recover under comparable state legislation.

Service marks protect the GOOD WILL and reputation earned by businesses that have invested time, energy, and money in bringing quality services to the public. Service marks also encourage competition by requiring businesses to associate their marks with the quality of services they offer. In this way service marks function as a barometer of quality upon which consumers may rely when making decisions to purchase. However, service marks are often infringed, and consumers grow leery when inferior services are passed off as a competitor's through use of a deceptively similar mark. Thus legal protection of service marks can save consumers from making improvident expenditures for services of dubious or unknown origin.

See also CONSUMER PROTECTION.

SERVICEMEN'S READJUSTMENT ACT OF 1944 See GI BILL.

SERVICE OF PROCESS Delivery of a WRIT, SUMMONS, or other legal papers to the person required to respond to them.

PROCESS is the general term for the legal document by which a lawsuit is started and the court asserts its JURISDICTION over the parties and the controversy. In modern U.S. law, process is usually a summons. A summons is a paper that tells a DEFENDANT that he is being sued in a specific court that the PLAINTIFF believes has jurisdiction. Served with the summons is a COMPLAINT that contains the plaintiff's ALLEGATIONS of wrongdoing by the defendant and the legal remedy sought by the plaintiff. The summons also informs the defendant that he has a specified number of days under law to respond to the summons and complaint. If the defendant does not respond, the plaintiff may seek a DEFAULT JUDGMENT from the court, granting the plaintiff the legal relief specified in the complaint.

Rules of CIVIL PROCEDURE and CRIMINAL PROCEDURE determine the proper form of legal process and how it should be served. The rules vary among federal and state courts, but they are meant to give the defendant notice of the proceedings and to command him to either respond to the allegations or to appear at a specified time and answer the claim or criminal charge. The concept of NOTICE is critical to the integrity of legal proceedings. Due process forbids legal action against a person unless the person has been given notice and an opportunity to be heard.

Process must be properly served on all parties in an action. Anyone who is not served is not bound by the decision in the case. A person who believes that proper service has not taken place may generally challenge the service without actually making a formal appearance in the case.

Whether service was proper is usually determined at a pretrial hearing. A defendant must request a SPECIAL APPEARANCE before the court. A special appearance is made for the limited purpose of challenging the sufficiency of the service of process or the PERSONAL JURISDICTION of the court. No other issues may be raised without the proceeding becoming a general appearance. The court must then determine whether it has jurisdiction over the defendant.

Methods of Service Three basic methods are used for service of process: (1) actual, or personal, service, (2) substituted service, and (3) service by publication. Although each method is legally acceptable, PERSONAL SERVICE is preferred because it is the most effective way of providing notice and it is difficult for the defendant to attack its legality.

Personal service means in-hand delivery of the papers to the proper person. Traditionally personal service was the only method of service allowed by law because it was best suited to give the defendant notice of the proceedings.

SUBSTITUTED SERVICE is any method used instead of personal service. Forms of substituted service vary among different jurisdictions, but all are intended to offer a good chance that the defendant actually will find out about the proceedings. If a defendant is not at home, many states permit service by leaving the summons and complaint with any person at the defendant's home who is old enough to understand the responsibility of accepting service. Some states permit service by affixing the summons and complaint to the entrance of the defendant's home or place of business and then mailing a copy of the papers to that individual at her last known address. This method is often called "nail and mail" service. A number of states allow service simply by mailing the papers to the defendant's actual address; generally registered mail is required. States also consider service valid if the defendant's property is attached, or legally seized, within the state and the papers are then mailed to her.

Under the laws of some states, substituted service may be used only after diligent efforts to effect personal service have failed. Some forms of substituted service may have to be tried before others can be used. Other states permit substituted service at any time or after a single attempt to find the defendant and serve the papers personally.

A third method of service is publication of a notice in a newspaper. Publication is also called constructive service because the court construes it to be effective whether the defendant actually reads the notice or not. Generally service by publication is allowed only by leave of the court, which usually grants permission only when the plaintiff can show that no other method of service can be effected. Usually the legal notice must be published in at least one newspaper of general circulation where the defendant is likely to be found or where the court is located or in both places. Ordinarily the notice must be published on more than one occasion, such as once a week for three weeks. This form of service is deemed complete, or effective, a certain time after the first publication, such as thirty days, if the required subsequent publications are in fact made.

In truth, courts realize that defendants rarely read notices published in newspapers, but the effort must be made when the defendant cannot be found and served in any other way. Plaintiffs prefer not to use publication because it is expensive and a court might later find that the defendant could have been served personally.

Where Process May Be Served Legal papers may have to be served within the geographical reach of the jurisdiction, or authority, of the court. If the service itself is the basis for the court's jurisdiction over the defendant, then the service usually must be made within the state. For lower-level courts, service may have to be made within the county where the court is located. Trial courts of GENERAL JURISDICTION usually permit service anywhere within the state. Service of process for an action in a federal district court may be made anywhere within the state where the court sits or, for some parties, anyplace in the United States that is not more than one hundred miles from the courthouse.

A variety of statutes permit state courts to exercise authority over persons not physically present within the state. These are called LONG-ARM STATUTES. They specify factors, other than the defendant's physical presence within the state, that provide sufficient justification for the court to exercise jurisdiction over the defendant, such as doing business within the state or having an automobile accident within the state. When one of these factors exists, the prospective defendant can be served with legal process outside the state because the service itself is not the basis of the court's jurisdiction.

Substituted or CONSTRUCTIVE methods of service may be used on a defendant who comes within the long-arm jurisdiction of the state. For example, many states permit a plaintiff to serve an out-of-state resident who was involved in a traffic accident in the state by serving legal process on the attorney general of the defendant's state and then sending copies to the defendant at her residence. The statute makes the attorney general the agent for the service of process on out-of-state drivers. Such a statute is based on the theory that a nonresident driver has consented to this method of service by using the highways and facilities within the state.

Who Must Be Served Service of process is effective only if the right person is served. When the defendant can be described but not named, service by publication can be made with a fictional name like Richard Roe. Where the defendant is not a natural person but a CORPORATION, statutes generally provide for effective service on a managing agent, a director, an officer, or anyone designated an AGENT in the corporation's application for a CHARTER or a LICENSE to do business within the state.

If the person to be sued is a child or a person incapable of managing her own legal affairs, service may be made on a parent, GUARDIAN, or someone else entrusted with the defendant's care or affairs. The plaintiff may ask the court to designate a proper person when there is doubt. An ESTATE can be sued by service of process on an executor or administrator. The plaintiff may ask the court to appoint such a person if none has yet been named.

When more than one person is being sued, each of them must be served. For example, a PARTNERSHIP can be sued by service of process on each partner.

When Papers Can Be Served The proper time for service of process depends on the law of the jurisdiction. Service must be made within the time that the STATUTE OF LIMITATIONS allows for starting that particular kind of action because it is service that starts the lawsuit.

Many states have long prohibited personal or substituted service on Sunday. Service is also prohibited on legal holidays in some states.

Process Servers Every jurisdiction specifies who may serve process. Many states take a simple approach and allow service by any person over the age of eighteen who is not a party to the suit. Under federal law service of anything other than a summons, complaint, or SUBPOENA must be made by a U.S. MARSHAL, a deputy marshal, or someone else appointed by the court. Some states also follow this procedure and designate that such qualified service shall be by a SHERIFF or similar PEACE OFFICER.

A professional PROCESS SERVER may be hired where service does not have to be made by an officer, but this is not necessary. In some jurisdictions anyone who serves more than a specified small number of summonses a year must be licensed. Laws generally provide for fines or imprisonment of a process server who fails to obtain a required license, but a court will not dismiss cases started with service by an unlicensed process server.

For the most part, courts have allowed process servers to use any means necessary to serve papers on reluctant defendants as long as no law is broken. For example, a process server can knock on the defendant's door and state that he has a package for the defendant. If the defendant opens the door, the resulting service of process is valid.

A defendant cannot avoid the service of process by refusing to accept delivery of the papers. Many cases have upheld service where the process server dropped the papers at the defendant's feet, hit the defendant in the chest with them, or even laid them on the defendant's car when she refused to get out or open the door.

Invalid Service The tricks of serving process papers can, however, reach a point that the courts will not tolerate because they subvert the purpose of service or threaten to disrupt the administration of justice. The most intolerable abuse is called sewer service. It is not really service at all but is so named on the theory that the server tossed the papers into the sewer and did not attempt to deliver them to the proper party. Sewer service is a FRAUD on the court, and an attorney who knowingly participates in such a scheme can be disbarred.

Anyone who serves process must file an AFFIDAVIT of service with the court, giving details of the delivery of the papers. If the facts in an affidavit of service falsely assert that the papers were delivered, the person who swears to them can be prosecuted for the crime of PERJURY. In addition, the plaintiff's action will not have commenced. If the statute of limitations has expired by the time the true facts of the im-

proper service are disclosed, the action is completely barred and the plaintiff has lost the right to sue.

Service is also invalid if the defendant has been enticed into the jurisdiction by fraud. Courts have ruled that luring a potential defendant into the state in order to serve him with process when no other grounds exist to assert jurisdiction over him in that state violates the individual's right to DUE PROCESS OF LAW. Service of process by fraud is null and void.

Immunity from Service of Process Courts typically grant IMMUNITY from process to anyone who comes within reach of the authority of the court only because she is required to participate in judicial proceedings. The purpose of this immunity is to encourage the active participation by witnesses and parties that helps ensure fair trials. If a WITNESS was discouraged from coming into a state because of the risk of being sued in that state, justice would not be served.

Immunity also protects nonresident attorneys, parties, and witnesses from being served with process in unrelated actions while attending, or traveling to, criminal or civil trials within a state. This immunity has been extended to protect out-of-state parties who enter a state not for trial but to settle a controversy out of court. Diplomatic personnel, AMBASSADORS, and consuls who are in the United States on official business are also immune from process.

SERVITUDE The state of a person who is subjected, voluntarily or involuntarily, to another person as a servant. A charge or burden resting upon one ESTATE for the benefit or advantage of another.

Involuntary servitude, which may be in the form of SLAVERY, PEONAGE, or compulsory labor for DEBTS, is prohibited by the THIRTEENTH AMENDMENT to the U.S. Constitution. Article I, Section 9, of the original Constitution had given Congress the power to restrict the slave trade by the year 1808, which it did, but slavery itself was not prohibited until the Thirteenth Amendment was enacted in 1865. The slave trade had begun in the American colonies in the seventeenth century and involved the forcible taking and transport of Africans and others to sell as slaves. The Thirteenth Amendment's prohibition against slavery encompasses situations where an individual is compelled by force, coercion, or imprisonment, and against his will, to labor for another, whether he is paid or not.

The term *servitude* is also used in PROPERTY LAW. In this context, servitude is used with the term *easement*, a right of some benefit or beneficial use out of, in, or over the land of another. Although the terms *servitude* and *easement* are sometimes used as synonyms, the two concepts differ. A servitude relates to the servient estate or the burdened land, whereas an EASEMENT refers to the dominant estate, which is the land benefited by the right. Not all servitudes are easements because they are not all attached to other land as APPURTENANCES (an appurtenance is an appendage or that which belongs to something else).

All servitudes affecting lands are classified as either personal or real. Personal servitudes are established for the benefit of a particular person and terminate upon the death of that individual. A common example of a personal servitude is the use of a house. Real servitudes, also called landed servitudes, benefit the owner of one estate through some use of a neighboring estate.

At CIVIL LAW, real servitudes are divided into two types: rural and urban. Rural servitudes are established for the benefit of a landed estate; examples include a RIGHT OF WAY over a servient tenement and a right of access to a spring, sandpit, or coal mine. Urban servitudes are established for the benefit of one building over another; some examples are a right of support, a right to a view, and a right to light. Despite the name *urban servitude*, the buildings do not have to be in a city.

Servitudes are also classified as positive and negative. A positive servitude requires the owner of the servient estate to permit something to be done on her property by another. A negative servitude does not bind the servient owner in this manner but merely restrains her from using the property in a manner that would impair the easement enjoyed by the owner of the dominant estate.

SESSION 📖 The sitting of a court, legislature, council, or commission for the transaction of its proper business. 📖

A session can be the period of time within any one day during which the body is assembled and engaged in business. In a more extended sense, the session can be the whole space of time from the first assembling of the body to its adjournment.

A *joint session* is the convening of the two houses of a legislative body to sit and act together as one body, instead of separately in their respective houses.

As applied to a court, the word *session* is not strictly synonymous with the word *term*. The session of a court is the time during which it actually sits each day for the transaction of judicial business. A TERM of a court is the period fixed by law—usually amounting to many days or weeks—during which it is open for judicial business and during which it can hold sessions from day to day. The two words are, however, frequently used interchangeably.

SET ASIDE 📖 To cancel, annul, or revoke a JUDGMENT or order. 📖

SETBACK 📖 A distance from a curb, PROPERTY line, or structure within which building is prohibited. 📖

Setbacks are building restrictions imposed on property owners. Local governments create setbacks through ORDINANCES and building codes, usually for reasons of PUBLIC POLICY such as safety, PRIVACY, and environmental protection. Setbacks prevent landowners from crowding the property of others, allow for the safe placement of pipelines, and help to preserve wetlands. Setbacks form BOUNDARIES by establishing an exact distance from a fixed point, such as a property line or an adjacent structure, within which building is prohibited. Generally, prospective buyers learn that land is subject to setback provisions when they are considering purchasing it. This information is important to future development plans, because setbacks remain in effect until changed by law or special action of a local government.

Setbacks can significantly affect a property owner's right to develop land or to modify existing structures on the land. For this reason they can influence property values; severe restrictions on land can decrease its value. Violating setback provisions can lead to legal action against a property owner, and penalties can include fines as well as an order to remove noncompliant structures. Property owners whose desire to build is stymied by setbacks have few remedies. They can petition their local government by applying for a VARIANCE—a special permission to depart from the requirements of ZONING ordinances—but variances are generally granted only in cases of extreme hardship. Litigation over setbacks is common.

See also LAND-USE CONTROL.

SET DOWN 📖 To list a case in a court calendar or DOCKET for trial or hearing during a particular term. 📖

SET-OFF 📖 A demand made by the DEFENDANT against the PLAINTIFF that is based on some transaction or occurrence other than the one that gave the plaintiff grounds to sue. 📖

The set-off is available to defendants in civil lawsuits. Generally, CIVIL ACTIONS are brought by plaintiffs seeking an award of DAMAGES for injuries caused by the defendant. In customary practice the plaintiff files the suit and the defendant answers it. The defendant may assert a *counterclaim* against the plaintiff based on an event or transaction other than the event or transaction that forms the basis of the plaintiff's suit. A set-off is a COUNTERCLAIM with the particular goal of defeating or diminishing the amount the defendant will have to pay if the plaintiff's suit succeeds.

The set-off has two distinctive features. It must be based on an entirely different CLAIM from that of the plaintiff, and it must be a valid legal claim that the defendant could bring as a separate suit. For example, a stereo store sues a customer for $700 due in outstanding payments on a CD player. However, the customer's car was damaged in the store's parking lot when the store's delivery van backed into it, and the repairs cost $500. As the defendant, the customer has the right to assert a counterclaim for damages to the car; if the customer is successful, the set-off reduces the amount owed to the plaintiff store so that the defendant owes the plaintiff only $200.

The remedy of *recoupment* is similar in effect to a set-off but differs from it in several respects. Whereas a set-off is based on a different claim, RECOUPMENT is a COMMON-LAW remedy based specifically on the CONTRACT between the plaintiff and defendant that gave rise to the suit. It allows defendants to claim damages against the plaintiff under two conditions: where the plaintiff has not complied with some contractual obligation or where the plaintiff has violated some duty that the law imposed in the making or PERFORMANCE of the contract. Recoupment usually occurs in cases where the plaintiff has performed only a portion of the contract and sues for compensation for the partial performance. For example, the defendant in the stereo store's action might demand recoupment for the store's failure to service the stereo under its WARRANTY.

Like all counterclaims, set-off and recoupment seek to achieve justice by balancing the plaintiff's and the defendant's rights. They are designed to prevent a plaintiff from recovering complete damages from a defendant who has suffered injury or damages caused by the plaintiff. They can also save time and money. By combining the entire controversy within one action, recoupment and set-off prevent the courts from being inundated with multiple lawsuits.

SETTLE 📖 To agree, to approve, to arrange, to ascertain, to LIQUIDATE, or to reach an agreement. 📖

Parties are said to settle an account when they examine its items and ascertain and agree upon the balance due from one to the other. When the person who owes money pays the balance, he or she is also said to settle it. A TRUST is settled when its terms are established and it goes into effect.

The term *settle up* is a colloquial rather than legal phrase that is applied to the final collection, adjustment, and distribution of the estate of a DECEDENT, a bankrupt, or an insolvent corporation. It includes the processes of collecting the property, paying the debts and charges, and remitting the balance to those entitled to receive it.

SETTLEMENT 📖 The act of adjusting or determining the dealings or disputes between persons without pursuing the matter through a trial. 📖

In civil lawsuits, settlement is an alternative to pursuing litigation through trial. Typically, it occurs when the defendant agrees to some or all of the plaintiff's claims and decides not to fight the matter in court. Usually, a settlement requires the defendant to pay the plaintiff some monetary amount. Popularly called *settling out of court*, a settlement agreement ends the litigation. Settlement is a popular option for several reasons, but a large number of cases are settled simply because defendants want to avoid the high cost of litigation. Settlement may occur before or during the early stages of a trial. In fact, simple settlements regularly take place before a lawsuit is even filed. In complex litigation, especially CLASS ACTION suits or cases involving multiple defendants, a settlement requires court approval.

Civil lawsuits originate when a claimant decides that another party has caused him or her injury and files suit. The plaintiff seeks to recover DAMAGES from the defendant. The defendant's attorney will evaluate the plaintiff's claim. If the plaintiff has a strong case and the attorney believes defendant is likely to lose, the attorney may recommend that the defendant settle the case. By settling, the defendant avoids the financial cost of litigating the case. Trials are often extremely expensive because of the amount of time required by attorneys, and even alternatives to trials, such as MEDIATION and ARBITRATION, can be costly. In deciding whether to settle a claim, attorneys act as intermediaries. The parties to the suit must decide whether to offer, accept, or decline a settlement.

The cost of litigation is only one factor that encourages settlement. Both plaintiffs and defendants are often motivated to settle for other reasons. For one thing litigation is frequently unpleasant. The process of DISCOVERY—in which both sides solicit information from each other—can cause embarrassment because considerable personal and financial information must be released. Litigation can also have a harmful impact on the public reputation of the parties. Employers, for example, sometimes settle SEXUAL HARASSMENT claims in order to avoid unwanted media exposure or damage to employee morale.

Like litigation itself, settlement is a process. Generally, the easiest time to settle a dispute is before litigation begins, but many opportunities for settlement present themselves. As litigation advances toward trial, attorneys for both sides communicate with each other and with the court and gauge the relative strength of their cases. If either of the parties believes he is unlikely to prevail, he is likely to offer a settlement to the other party.

Litigation ends when a settlement is reached. The plaintiff typically agrees to forgo any future litigation against the defendant, and the defendant agrees to pay the plaintiff some monetary amount. Additionally, settlements can require the defendant to change a policy or stop some form of behavior.

Often, the exact terms of settlements are not disclosed publicly, particularly in high-profile cases where the defendant is seeking to protect a public reputation. In high-profile cases, settlements are often followed by a public statement by the defendant. It is not unusual for a large company to settle with a plaintiff for an undisclosed amount and then to issue a statement saying that the company did nothing wrong.

In some forms of litigation, settlement is more complex. In class actions, for example, attorneys represent a large group of plaintiffs, known as the class, who typically seek damages from a company or organization. Courts review the terms of a class action settlement for fairness. Complexities also arise in cases involving multiple defendants. In particular, when only some of the defendants agree to settle, the court must determine the share of LIABILITY that accrues to those defendants who choose to pursue litigation.

SETTLEMENT STATEMENT A breakdown of costs involved in a REAL ESTATE sale.

Before real estate is sold, federal law requires both the buyer and seller to provide a settlement statement. This official document lists all the costs involved in the sale. A settlement statement is typically prepared by either a lender or a third party known as an escrow agent, who must follow the regulations set forth in the Real Estate Settlement Procedures Act of 1974 (RESPA) (12 U.S.C.A. § 2601 et seq.).

RESPA is a CONSUMER PROTECTION law enforced by the federal Department of Housing and Urban Development (HUD).

Historically, the secondary costs in real estate transactions have been expensive. These costs include broker's fees and appraiser's fees, some of which are required by lenders in real estate deals. Buyers and sellers have not always known the full extent of these costs in advance. Responding to the maze of hidden costs during the early 1970s, both the secretary of HUD and the administrator of Veterans' Affairs petitioned Congress on behalf of reform that would reduce the likelihood of unpleasant surprises for consumers.

RESPA set forth four goals. First, it attempted to improve advance disclosure of settlement costs to home buyers and sellers. Second, it sought to eliminate corruption in the form of KICKBACKS or referral fees that unfairly inflate settlement costs. Third, it aimed to reduce the amounts home buyers are required to deposit in an ESCROW account—in this case, a bank account established to ensure the payment of real estate taxes and insurance. Finally, Congress wished to modernize an outmoded system of local record keeping of land TITLE information.

Besides a full accounting of sale costs, RESPA requires lenders to keep settlement statement records for five years or until they dispose of the loan. It provides no civil penalties for lenders who fail to properly disclose information. However, section 8, which includes anticorruption measures, sets forth criminal and civil penalties for illegal referral fees: it is designed to keep intermediaries in the deal from cheating consumers by piling up costs.

In the 1990s the scope of RESPA expanded. Initially RESPA had only covered home purchase loans, but it grew to include refinances and subordinate LIEN loans with the enactment of the Housing and Community Development Act of 1992 (Pub. L. No. 102-550, 106 Stat. 3672). These changes took effect in 1994 after HUD amended its rules (24 C.F.R. pt. 3500). As a result, lenders providing equity or second MORTGAGE loans, home improvement financing, and mobile home financing came under the regulation of RESPA.

The expansion of RESPA brought complaints from the finance industry about the burden of excess regulation. Yet with the signing of the Housing and Community Development Act by the usually antiregulatory President GEORGE BUSH, Washington signaled its approval of the benefits for consumers in regulating costs in real estate transactions.

A.		B. Type of Loan		
U.S. Department of Housing and Urban Development		1. ☐ FHA 2. ☐ FmHA 3. ☐ CONV. UNINS. 4. ☐ VA 5. ☐ CONV. INS.		
SETTLEMENT STATEMENT		6. File Number:		7. Loan Number:
		8. Mortgage Insurance Case Number:		

C. NOTE: *This form is furnished to give you a statement of actual settlement costs. Amounts paid to and by the settlement agent are shown. Items marked "(p.o.c.)" were paid outside the closing; they are shown here for informational purposes and are not included in the totals.*

D. NAME OF BORROWER:	E. NAME OF SELLER:	F. NAME OF LENDER:
G. PROPERTY LOCATION:	H. SETTLEMENT AGENT:	I. SETTLEMENT DATE:
	PLACE OF SETTLEMENT:	

J. SUMMARY OF BORROWER'S TRANSACTION		K. SUMMARY OF SELLER'S TRANSACTION	
100. GROSS AMOUNT DUE FROM BORROWER:		*400. GROSS AMOUNT DUE TO SELLER:*	
101. Contract sales price		401. Contract sales price	
102. Personal property		402. Personal property	
103. Settlement charges to borrower (*line 1400*)		403.	
104.		404.	
105.		405.	
Adjustments for items paid by seller in advance		*Adjustments for items paid by seller in advance*	
106. City/town taxes to		406. City/town taxes to	
107. County taxes to		407. County taxes to	
108. Assessments to		408. Assessments to	
109.		409.	
110.		410.	
111.		411.	
112.		412.	
120. GROSS AMOUNT DUE *FROM BORROWER*		*420. GROSS AMOUNT DUE* *TO SELLER*	
200. AMOUNTS PAID BY OR IN BEHALF OF BORROWER:		*500. REDUCTIONS IN AMOUNT DUE TO SELLER:*	
201. Deposit or earnest money		501. Excess deposit (*see instructions*)	
202. Principal amount of new loan(s)		502. Settlement charges to seller (*line 1400*)	
203. Existing loan(s) taken subject to		503. Existing loan(s) taken subject to	
204.		504. Payoff of first mortgage loan	
205.		505. Payoff of second mortgage loan	
206.		506.	
207.		507.	
208.		508.	
209.		509.	
Adjustments for items unpaid by seller		*Adjustments for items unpaid by seller*	
210. City/town taxes to		510. City/town taxes to	
211. County taxes to		511. County taxes to	
212. Assessments to		512. Assessments to	
213.		513.	
214.		514.	
215.		515.	
216.		516.	
217.		517.	
218.		518.	
219.		519.	
220. TOTAL PAID BY/FOR *BORROWER*		*520. TOTAL REDUCTION AMOUNT* *DUE SELLER*	
300. CASH AT SETTLEMENT FROM/TO BORROWER		*600. CASH AT SETTLEMENT TO/FROM SELLER*	
301. Gross amount due from borrower (*line 120*)		601. Gross amount due to seller (*line 420*)	
302. Less amounts paid by/for borrower (*line 220*)	( )	602. Less reductions in amount due seller (*line 520*)	( )
303. CASH (☐ FROM) (☐ TO) BORROWER		*603. CASH (☐ TO) (☐ FROM) SELLER*	

[*continued on page 214*]

A sample settlement statement

L. SETTLEMENT CHARGES	PAID FROM BORROWER'S FUNDS AT SETTLEMENT	PAID FROM SELLER'S FUNDS AT SETTLEMENT
700. TOTAL SALES/BROKER'S COMMISSION based on price $ @ %=		
Division of Commission (line 700) as follows:		
701. $ to		
702. $ to		
703. Commission paid at Settlement		
704.		
800. ITEMS PAYABLE IN CONNECTION WITH LOAN		
801. Loan Origination Fee %		
802. Loan Discount %		
803. Appraisal Fee to		
804. Credit Report to		
805. Lender's Inspection Fee		
806. Mortgage Insurance Application Fee to		
807. Assumption Fee		
808.		
809.		
810.		
811.		
900. ITEMS REQUIRED BY LENDER TO BE PAID IN ADVANCE		
901. Interest from to @ $ /day		
902. Mortgage Insurance Premium for months to		
903. Hazard Insurance Premium for years to		
904. years to		
905.		
1000. RESERVES DEPOSITED WITH LENDER		
1001. Hazard Insurance months @ $ per month		
1002. Mortgage Insurance months @ $ per month		
1003. City property taxes months @ $ per month		
1004. County property taxes months @ $ per month		
1005. Annual assessments months @ $ per month		
1006. months @ $ per month		
1007. months @ $ per month		
1008. months @ $ per month		
1100. TITLE CHARGES		
1101. Settlement or closing fee to		
1102. Abstract or title search to		
1103. Title examination to		
1104. Title insurance binder to		
1105. Document preparation to		
1106. Notary fees to		
1107. Attorney's fees to		
includes above item numbers:		
1108. Title insurance to		
includes above item numbers:		
1109. Lender's coverage $		
1110. Owner's coverage $		
1111.		
1112.		
1113.		
1200. GOVERNMENT RECORDING AND TRANSFER CHARGES		
1201. Recording fees: Deed $; Mortgage $; Releases $		
1202. City/county tax/stamps: Deed $; Mortgage $		
1203. State tax/stamps: Deed $; Mortgage $		
1204.		
1205.		
1300. ADDITIONAL SETTLEMENT CHARGES		
1301. Survey to		
1302. Post inspection to		
1303.		
1304.		
1305.		
1400. TOTAL SETTLEMENT CHARGES (enter on lines 103, Section J and 502, Section K)		

A sample settlement statement (continued)

SETTLOR 📖 One who establishes a TRUST—a right of PROPERTY, real or personal—held and administered by a TRUSTEE for the benefit of another. 📖

SEVEN BISHOPS' TRIAL A turning point in the history of English law, the Seven Bishops' Trial, 12 Howell's State Trials 183 (1688), involved issues of church and state, the authority of the monarchy, and the power of the judiciary. In 1688 King James II brought the proceeding against seven prominent bishops of the Church of England. For defying a controversial order of the king, the prelates were accused of seditious libel, a grave offense that constituted rebellion against the Crown. Their successful defense against the charge helped to encourage the opposition to the king that culminated six months later in the so-called Glorious Revolution of 1688. The king fled, and subsequently England had a new monarchy and a new Bill of Rights. The bishops' challenge to authority and the subsequent expression of popular political will were important precedents that helped to inspire later revolutionaries among the American colonists.

The trial took place against a backdrop of anti-Catholicism. The English Parliament had restricted the rights of Catholics to hold public office and engage in other activities. James II was a devout Catholic, however, and believed that it was his duty to protect the rights of English Catholics. Accordingly, on April 4, 1687, he issued the First Declaration of Indulgence, which suspended the restrictions and led directly to Catholics holding public offices. A year later, on April 27, 1688, James repeated his first order and went further: to better inform the citizenry, he commanded the Anglican clergy to read his Second Declaration of Indulgence in their churches.

The king's order was universally unpopular. Seven senior prelates took action. Led by William Sancroft, the archbishop of Canterbury, they sent the king a petition professing their loyalty to him but also indicating their refusal to read the declaration in church. The petition enraged James, especially since the ostensibly private statement was published throughout the kingdom. Viewing the bishops' petition as an act of rebellion, he began the process of prosecuting them for seditious libel. In such a case, the accused were required to post a payment called a RECOGNIZANCE or else await trial in prison. This the bishops refused to do, claiming that as members of the House of Lords, they were exempt from paying recognizances. The bishops' claim may have been a bit audacious in that the exemption probably did not extend to such serious offenses. In any event James promptly jailed the bishops in the Tower of London.

At trial both sides argued over the issue of SEDITION. The Crown maintained that the bishops should have taken their grievances to the king's courts or appealed to Parliament for action. Their failure to do so amounted to an attempt to incite popular hostility against the king. Lawyers for the bishops argued that they had simply exercised the same rights available to all English subjects. Anyone, they asserted, was free to petition the king when legal rights were infringed. Four judges presided at the trial. In giving their opinion on the law to the jury, they divided equally over whether the bishops had committed seditious libel. Boldly, the jury ruled against the Crown.

The acquittal of the bishops had immediate and lasting implications. The verdict of not guilty was received with great popular acclaim and contributed to exactly what the king had feared—rebellion. During James's dispute with the bishops, his second wife had given birth to a son. Hitherto James's heir apparent had been Mary, his Protestant daughter from his first marriage, who was married to William of Orange, the ruler of the Netherlands. Now the birth of a son aroused fear that James would be succeeded by a Catholic. Accordingly, a coalition of nobles, encouraged by the popular response to the bishops' acquittal, invited the Protestant William of Orange and Mary to assume the throne. The so-called Glorious Revolution of 1688 saw King James II flee to France, while William and his wife Mary became king and queen. Their appointment by Parliament underscored that institution's supremacy as the maker of law in England; in a short time, the nation had not only new sovereigns but also a new Bill of Rights.

The significance of the Seven Bishops' Trial reached beyond England. Historically, it marked one of the first major decisions against an executive branch of government. A jury had nullified what it considered an unjust law. Thus, historians see the case as marking the emancipation of the judiciary from executive control. This lesson was not lost on the American colonists. They viewed the case as an exercise of popular political will against a tyrannical monarch; as such, it inspired early American republicans (and ultimately revolutionaries) who believed in the decentralization of power.

SEVENTEENTH AMENDMENT The Seventeenth Amendment to the U.S. Constitution reads:

The Senate of the United States shall be composed of two Senators from each State, elected by the people thereof for six years; and each Senator shall have one vote. The electors in each State shall have the qualifications requisite for electors of the most numerous branch of the State legislatures.

When vacancies happen in the representation of any State in the Senate, the executive authority of such State shall issue writs of election to fill such vacancies: Provided, That the legislature of any State may empower the executive thereof to make temporary appointments until the people fill the vacancies by election as the legislature may direct.

This amendment shall not be so construed as to affect the election or term of any Senator chosen before it becomes valid as part of the Constitution.

The Seventeenth Amendment, which was ratified in 1913, provided for the direct election of U.S. senators by citizens. Until 1913 state legislatures had elected U.S. senators. Ratification of the amendment followed decades of insistence that the power to elect senators should be placed in the hands of ordinary voters. This successful struggle marked a major victory for *progressivism*—the early twentieth-century political movement dedicated to pushing government at all levels toward reform. In addition to serving the longer-range goals of the reformers, the campaign on behalf of the amendment sought to end delays and what was widely perceived as corruption in the election of senators by state legislatures.

From 1787 until 1913, the U.S. Constitution specified that state legislatures would elect U.S. senators. Article 1, Section 3, reads:

> The Senate of the United States shall be composed of two Senators from each State, chosen by the Legislature thereof, for six Years; and each Senator shall have one Vote.

In giving the elective power to the states, the framers of the Constitution hoped to protect state independence. The framers were suspicious of majority rule and sought to restrain what they regarded as the potentially destructive forces of democracy. Thus, while providing for direct election to the HOUSE OF REPRESENTATIVES, they countered this expression of the people's will by allowing legislatures to select members of the SENATE. At the Constitutional Convention, the proposal for state election of senators aroused no controversy. Only one proposal for senatorial election by popular vote was

offered, and it was soundly defeated. The states were receptive and did not protest when the Constitution was sent to them for ratification. Nor, over the next decades, did the system incur more than occasional criticism.

By the late nineteenth century, however, political opinion was changing in favor of a more fully participatory democracy. Starting in the 1880s, the concentration of elective power in the hands of state legislatures provoked criticism. The critics complained that the legislatures were dominated by party bosses who prevented citizen participation and thwarted popular political action. The critics also pointed to practical and ethical problems: lengthy deadlocks, which sometimes resulted when legislatures could not agree upon a candidate, and alleged BRIBERY. Progressivism, the reform movement that sought to address social inequities by broadening government power, helped to bring about this change in outlook. Under the pressure of the Progressive movement and the popular belief that citizens were capable of choosing their own senators, the states began to bend. By the turn of the century, several states were holding popular elections that served as advisories to the legislatures in selecting senators.

Over the next decade, increasing calls for change reached Congress, where the resistance to change was considerable. Federal lawmakers argued that direct election would strip states of their independence and SOVEREIGNTY. The pressure continued to increase, however, until by 1910, thirty-one state legislatures had requested that Congress hold a constitutional convention to propose an amendment. The next year Congress buckled and passed the amendment; within two years, the amendment had been ratified by the states. It read, in relevant part:

> The Senate of the United States shall be composed of two Senators from each State, elected by the people thereof, for six years; and each Senator shall have one vote.

Only ten states opposed ratification.

Ratification of the Seventeenth Amendment introduced significant changes to Congress. When states elected senators, they exercised the power of *instruction*—they could direct their senators to vote a certain way on important matters. The Seventeenth Amendment formally ended this power, for now senators were beholden to the voters. Historians and legal scholars continue to debate the other effects of the amendment. Some view it as a grave surrender of state sovereignty; others see it as a benign or even positive outgrowth of popular will. Direct election has seemingly contributed to the decline in the power of party bosses, but its impact upon the actual practice of Senate business has been negligible.

See also CONGRESS OF THE UNITED STATES.

SEVENTH AMENDMENT   The Seventh Amendment to the U.S. Constitution reads:

> In suits at common law, where the value in controversy shall exceed twenty dollars, the right of trial by jury shall be preserved, and no fact tried by a jury, shall be otherwise re-examined in any court of the United States, than according to the rules of the common law.

The Seventh Amendment to the U.S. Constitution guarantees the right to a JURY trial in most civil suits that are heard in FEDERAL COURT. However, before the Seventh Amendment right to a jury trial attaches, a lawsuit must satisfy four threshold requirements. First, it must assert a CLAIM that would have triggered the right to a jury trial under the English COMMON LAW of 1791 when the Seventh Amendment was ratified. If a lawsuit asserts a claim that is sufficiently analogous to an eighteenth-century English common-law claim, a litigant may still invoke the Seventh Amendment right to a jury trial even though the claim was not expressly recognized in 1791 (*Markman v. Westview Instruments,* __U.S.__, 116 S. Ct. 1384, 134 L. Ed. 2d 577 [1996]). Claims brought under a federal statute that confer a right to trial by jury also implicate the Seventh Amendment (*Chauffeurs, Teamsters and Helpers, Local No. 391 v. Terry,* 494 U.S. 558, 110 S. Ct. 1339, 108 L. Ed. 2d 519 [1990]).

Second, a lawsuit must be brought in federal court before a litigant may invoke the Seventh Amendment right to a jury trial. This right is one of the few liberties enumerated in the BILL OF RIGHTS that has not been made applicable to the states through the doctrine of selective incorporation (*Minneapolis & St. Louis Railroad v. Bombolis,* 241 U.S. 211, 36 S. Ct. 595, 60 L. Ed. 961 [1916]). The Seventh Amendment does not apply in state court even when a litigant is enforcing a right created by federal law. However, most state constitutions similarly afford the right to trial by jury in civil cases. See also INCORPORATION DOCTRINE.

Third, a lawsuit must assert a claim for more than $20. Because nearly all lawsuits are filed to recover much larger sums, this provision of the Seventh Amendment is virtually always met.

Fourth, a lawsuit must assert a claim that is essentially legal in nature before the Seventh Amendment applies. There is no right to a jury trial in CIVIL ACTIONS involving claims that are essentially equitable in nature (*Tull v. United States,* 481 U.S. 412, 107 S. Ct. 1831, 95 L. Ed. 2d 365 [1987]). Lawsuits that seek INJUNCTIONS, SPECIFIC PERFORMANCE, and other types of nonmonetary remedies are traditionally treated as equitable claims. Lawsuits that seek money DAMAGES, conversely, are traditionally treated as legal claims. However, these traditional categories of LAW and EQUITY are not always neatly separated.

If the monetary RELIEF sought is only "incidental" to an equitable claim for an injunction, the right to a jury trial will be denied (*Stewart v. KHD Deutz of America,* 75 F.3d 1522 [11th Cir. 1996]). Even if a lawsuit is couched in terms of a legal claim for monetary relief, a court will

The Seventh Amendment provides for the right to a jury trial for controversies with a value exceeding twenty dollars.

deny a litigant's request for a jury trial if an essentially equitable claim is being asserted. Lawsuits seeking RESTITUTION, though representing claims for monetary reimbursement, have been treated as equitable claims for the purposes of the Seventh Amendment (*Provident Life and Accident Insurance v. Williams*, 858 F. Supp. 907 [W.D. Ark. 1994]). On the other hand, an employee's action for back pay under title VII of the CIVIL RIGHTS ACT OF 1964 (42 U.S.C.A. § 2000e et seq.) represents a legal claim despite the fact that the statute characterizes the remedy as equitable (*Local No. 391 v. Terry*).

When a lawsuit involves mixed questions of law and equity, litigants may present the legal questions to a jury under the Seventh Amendment, while leaving the equitable questions for judicial resolution (*Snider v. Consolidation Coal Co.*, 973 F.2d 555 [7th Cir. 1992]). For example, an ACTION to recover attorneys' fees pursuant to a written agreement normally would be decided by a jury in accordance with the common law of CONTRACTS. However, in a subsequent proceeding to determine the amount of attorneys' fees owed, equitable principles of accounting would normally be applied by a judge alone (*McGuire v. Russell Miller, Inc.*, 1 F.3d 1306 [2nd Cir. 1993]). Any factual determinations made by the jury in the first proceeding would be binding on the judge during the second proceeding (*Lebow v. American Trans Air*, 86 F.3d 661 [7th Cir. 1996]).

Some types of lawsuits present issues that are neither wholly legal nor entirely equitable. In many such cases, the Seventh Amendment offers no protection. For example, there is no right to trial by jury for lawsuits that involve issues of maritime law or admiralty rights (*Parsons v. Bedford*, 28 U.S. [3 Pet.] 433, 7 L. Ed. 732 [1830]). Nor is the Seventh Amendment implicated in proceedings that relate to the naturalization (*Luria v. United States*, 231 U.S. 9, 34 S. Ct. 10, 58 L. Ed. 101 [1913]) or DEPORTATION (*Gee Wah Lee v. United States*, 25 F.2d 107 [5th Cir. 1928], *cert. denied*, 277 U.S. 608, 48 S. Ct. 603, 72 L. Ed. 1013 [1928]) of ALIENS. Litigants also have no Seventh Amendment right to trial by jury in lawsuits brought against the federal government (*Lehman v. Nakshian*, 453 U.S. 156, 101 S. Ct. 2698, 69 L. Ed. 2d 548 [1981]).

The underlying rationale of the Seventh Amendment was to preserve the historic line separating the province of the jury from that of the judge in civil cases. Although the line separating QUESTIONS OF LAW from QUESTIONS OF FACT is often blurred, the basic functions of judges and juries are clear. Judges are charged with the responsibility of resolving issues concerning the admissibility of evidence and instructing jurors regarding the pertinent laws governing the case. Judges are also permitted to comment on the evidence, highlight important issues, and otherwise express their opinions in open court as long as each factual question is ultimately submitted to the jury. However, a judge may not interject her personal opinions or observations to such an extent that they impair a litigant's right to a fair trial (*Rivas v. Brattesani*, 94 F.3d 802 [2nd Cir. 1996]).

Juries perform three main functions. First, jurors are charged with the responsibility of listening to the evidence, ascertaining the relevant facts, and drawing reasonable inferences that are necessary to reach a verdict. Second, jurors are required to heed the instructions read by the court and apply the governing legal principles to the facts of the case. Third, jurors are obliged to determine the legal consequences of the litigants' behavior through the process of group deliberation and then publicly announce their verdict.

The Seventh Amendment expressly forbids federal judges to "re-examin[e]" any "fact tried by a jury" except as allowed by the common law. This provision has been interpreted to mean that no court, trial or APPELLATE, may overturn a jury verdict that is reasonably supported by the evidence (*Taylor v. Curry*, 17 F.3d 1434 [4th Cir. 1994]). A jury must be allowed to hear a lawsuit from start to finish unless it presents a legal claim that is completely lacking an evidentiary basis (*Gregory v. Missouri Pacific Railroad*, 32 F.3d 160 [5th Cir. 1994]).

Together with the Due Process Clause of the FIFTH AMENDMENT, the Seventh Amendment guarantees civil litigants the right to an IMPARTIAL jury (*McCoy v. Goldston*, 652 F.2d 654 [6th Cir. 1981]). A juror's impartiality may be compromised by communications with sources outside the courtroom, such as friends, relatives, and members of the media. The presence of even one partial, biased, or prejudiced juror creates a presumption that the Seventh Amendment has been violated (*Haley v. Blue Ridge Transfer Co.*, 802 F.2d 1532 [4th Cir. 1986]). A litigant seeking to overcome this presumption bears a heavy burden to establish the harmlessness of an unauthorized jury communication. In *Haley*, for example, the Supreme Court overturned a verdict against the defendant because jurors had communicated with an outside source who attempted to persuade them to side with the plaintiff.

Although every juror must be impartial, there is no Seventh Amendment right to a jury of twelve persons. In *Colgrove v. Battin*, 413

U.S. 149, 93 S. Ct. 2448, 37 L. Ed. 2d 522 (1973), the Supreme Court ruled that the quality of the deliberation process is not impaired when the size of a jury is reduced from twelve to six members. The Court cited one study suggesting that smaller juries promote more robust deliberations. Regardless of a jury's size, the Seventh Amendment requires unanimity among jurors who hear civil cases in federal court (*Murray v. Laborers Union Local No. 324*, 55 F.3d 1445 [9th Cir. 1995]). By contrast, the SIXTH AMENDMENT to the Constitution does not require juror unanimity in criminal trials, except in death penalty cases.

SEVERABLE 📖 That which is capable of being separated from other things to which it is joined and maintaining nonetheless a complete and independent existence. 📖

The term *severable* is used to describe a CONTRACT that can be divided and apportioned into two or more parts that are not necessarily dependent upon each other. For example, a seller accepted a buyer's order for sixty dozen hats and caps of different sizes and colors. He shipped all but five dozen to the buyer, who then refused to accept the order. The seller brought an action against the buyer for breach of contract. There was no evidence to show that the contract called for delivery of the whole order at one time. The court held that the buyer could not escape LIABILITY because the seller had failed to ship five dozen hats and caps, since the order calling for hats and caps of different patterns, sizes, and colors constituted a "severable contract."

The term *severable* is also used in connection with statutes. A severable statute is one that after an invalid portion of it has been stricken remains self-sustaining and capable of separate enforcement without regard to the stricken provisions.

SEVERAL 📖 Separate; individual; independent. 📖

In this sense, the word *several* is distinguished from JOINT. When applied to a number of persons, the expression *severally liable* usually implies that each person is liable alone.

See also JOINT AND SEVERAL LIABILITY.

SEVERALTY OWNERSHIP 📖 Sole proprietorship of PROPERTY; individual dominion. 📖

SEVERANCE 📖 The act of dividing, or the state of being divided. 📖

The term *severance* has unique meanings in different branches of the law. Courts use the term in both civil and criminal litigation in two ways: first, when dividing a lawsuit into two or more parts, and second, when deciding to try multiple defendants' cases separately. In addition, severance also describes several ACTIONS relevant to PROPERTY and EMPLOYMENT LAW.

In civil suits severance refers to the division of a trial into two or more parts. Plaintiffs in civil suits base their cases on a CAUSE OF ACTION— facts that give the plaintiff the right to sue. For reasons of judicial economy, the court may order the lawsuit divided into two or more independent causes of action. This type of severance occurs only when each distinct cause of action could be tried as if it were the only claim in controversy. As a result of severance, the court renders a separate, final, and enforceable JUDGMENT on each cause. A second type of severance occurs in cases involving multiple defendants. The court may sever one or more defendants from the trial and try their cases separately.

Severance works somewhat differently in federal criminal trials. When these cases involve the INDICTMENT of more than one defendant, usually only one trial is held. This process is called JOINDER. Rule 8 of the Federal Rules of Criminal Procedure permits the joinder of the indictments of two or more defendants if they are alleged to have participated in the same act or transaction. For policy reasons courts prefer using joinder to holding separate trials because it saves time and money. However, joinder can create potential prejudices against a defendant, resulting in greater likelihood of conviction, and thus a defense attorney will often ask the court to sever his client's case. Less often, the prosecution requests severance because it believes joinder will prejudice its case. Severance results in a defendant being tried separately on one or all of the pending charges.

Severance is not automatic. Federal rule 14 allows judges broad discretion in deciding whether to grant severance. To be successful, a defense MOTION for severance must show that concerns for the defendant's right to a fair trial outweigh the goals of joinder. Concerns for judicial economy and efficiency make trial courts reluctant to grant severance, and rarely do APPELLATE COURTS overturn a lower court decision to refuse severance. One of the most successful grounds for seeking severance arises when a defendant wishes not to TESTIFY on all counts in a trial but chooses to claim her FIFTH AMENDMENT privilege on one or more counts.

In property and employment law severance is used in several different contexts. First, it applies to JOINT TENANCY, a form of shared ownership of REAL PROPERTY. Joint tenancy requires each tenant to share in the four unities of time, title, interest, and possession. When any of these unities no longer applies to any or all of the joint tenants, the joint tenancy is said to be severed, and the tenancy is terminated. Second, in regard to real property, severance is the cutting and removal of anything that is attached to the land, such as standing timber or CROPS. Third, severance is used when the government exercises its power to take private property for public use through the right of EMINENT DOMAIN. If only part of the property is taken and the value of the remaining property depreciates because of the government's proposed use of the taken share, the owner is entitled to compensation called severance damage. Fourth, severance pay is an amount of money paid to employees upon the termination of their employment. It is usually based on the employee's salary and duration of employment.

SEX DISCRIMINATION 📖 Discrimination on the basis of gender. 📖

Women have historically been subjected to legal discrimination based on their gender. Some of this discrimination has been based on cultural stereotypes that cast women primarily in the roles of wives and mothers. In a patriarchal (male-dominated) U.S. society, women have been viewed as the "weaker sex," who needed protection from the rough-and-tumble world outside their homes. Such beliefs were used as justifications for preventing women from voting, holding public office, and working outside the home. In a culture that portrayed

The Springfield, Massachusetts, police force took a step likely to combat sex discrimination, at least in its own ranks, when Paula Meara became the city's first female police chief.

wives as appendages of their husbands, women have often been invisible to the law.

The ability of women to use the law to fight sex discrimination in employment, education, domestic relations, and other spheres is a recent development. With the passage of title VII of the CIVIL RIGHTS ACT OF 1964 (42 U.S.C.A. § 2000e et seq.), discrimination in employment based on sex became illegal. In the 1970s and 1980s, the U.S. Supreme Court began to wrestle with the implications of sex discrimination in many contexts, often with conflicting or ambiguous results. Employers and social institutions have sought to justify discriminatory treatment for women on the basis of long-held traditions. In some cases the Court has agreed, while in others the justifications have been dismissed as cultural stereotypes that have no basis in fact.

Historical Background   To reshape gender roles, women have had to overcome centuries of tradition, much of which originated in medieval England. After the Norman Conquest in 1066, the legal status of a married woman was fixed by COMMON LAW. The identity of the wife was merged into that of the husband; he was a legal person but she was not. Upon MARRIAGE, he received all her PERSONAL PROPERTY and managed all property that she owned. In return, the husband was obliged to support his wife and children.

This legal definition of marriage persisted in the United States until the middle of the nineteenth century, when states enacted married women's property acts. These acts conferred legal status upon wives and permitted them to own and transfer property in their own right, to sue and be sued, and to enter into CONTRACTS. Although these acts were significant advances, they dealt only with property a woman inherited. The husband, by placing TITLE in his name, could control most of the ASSETS acquired during marriage, thereby forcing his wife to rely on his bounty.

The passage of the married women's property acts resulted from the efforts of feminist reformers, including LUCY STONE, ELIZABETH CADY STANTON, and SUSAN B. ANTHONY. The feminist political movement began in the nineteenth century with the call for female suffrage. At a convention in Seneca Falls, New York, in 1848, a group of women and men drafted and approved the Declaration of Sentiments. This declaration, which was modeled on the language and structure of the Declaration of Independence, was a bill of rights for women, including the right to vote. Anthony, Stanton, and Stone were persistent critics of male society's refusal to grant women political and social equality. Not until the NINETEENTH AMENDMENT to the U.S. Constitution was ratified in 1920, however, did women have VOTING RIGHTS in the United States.

The U.S. Supreme Court confronted the issue of sex discrimination in *Bradwell v. Illinois*, 83 U.S. 130, 21 L. Ed. 442 (1872). MYRA BRADWELL sought to practice law in Illinois, but the Illinois Supreme Court refused to admit her to the bar because she was a woman. Bradwell appealed to the U.S. Supreme Court, arguing that the refusal to grant her a LICENSE violated the PRIVILEGES AND IMMUNITIES Clause of the FOURTEENTH AMENDMENT. By an 8–1 vote, the Court rejected Bradwell's argument. Though the majority opinion was on the argument that the Privileges and Immunities Clause applied only to matters involving U.S. citizenship and not state citizenship, a concurring opinion written by Justice JOSEPH P. BRADLEY and signed by two other justices revealed the cultural stereotypes that lay behind the legal analysis. Observing that there is "a wide difference in the respective sphere and destinies of man and woman," Bradley went on to write that the "natural and proper timidity and delicacy which belongs to the female sex evidently unfits it for many of the occupations of civil life." For Bradley, the "paramount destiny and mission of woman are to fulfill the noble and benign offices of wife and mother. This is the law of the Creator."

By the late nineteenth century, mass immigration from Europe to the industrialized cities of the United States had resulted in many immigrant women seeking work in factories. Though the Supreme Court was hostile to state laws that sought to regulate working conditions, the Court was more hospitable to laws aimed at protecting women in the workplace. The idea that women were the weaker sex and needed special treatment constituted discrimination based on sex, but the Court willingly embraced the concept. The landmark case in this regard was *Muller v. Oregon*, 208 U.S. 412, 28 S. Ct. 324, 52 L. Ed. 551 (1908). The Court upheld an Oregon law that prohibited the employment of women for more than ten hours a day, in large part because of the brief submitted in support of the law by LOUIS D. BRANDEIS. The brief contained information about the possible injurious effects of long work hours on women's health and morals, as well as on the health and welfare of their children, including their unborn children. Brandeis emphasized the differences between women and men. The Court unanimously agreed, noting that "woman's physical structure and the performance of maternal functions place her at a disadvantage in the struggle for subsistence."

World War II played a decisive role in changing the social status of women. Large numbers of women left the home and entered the industrial workplace when men joined the armed services. Many women performed jobs that were previously thought to be beyond their physical and mental abilities. Though these women were unceremoniously fired after the war to free up jobs for returning servicemen, many of society's assumptions about women had been shaken.

By the 1970s women had begun to compete with men for managerial and professional positions. Nevertheless, sex discrimination in employment and other areas of U.S. society remained a troubling issue. Congress, state legislatures, and the courts began to address the legality of this type of discrimination.

Sex Discrimination Laws The first significant piece of federal legislation that dealt with sex discrimination was the Equal Pay Act (EPA) of 1963 (29 U.S.C.A. § 206(d)), which amended the FAIR LABOR STANDARDS ACT of 1938 (29 U.S.C.A. §§ 201–219) by prohibiting discrimination in the form of different compensation for jobs requiring equal skill, effort, and responsibility.

The inclusion of a prohibition against gender-based discrimination in title VII of the Civil Rights Act of 1964 was a landmark achievement, though the provision was added by opponents of the comprehensive act in a last-minute attempt to prevent its passage. Title VII defines sex discrimination in employment as including failure or refusal to hire, discrimination in discharge, classification of employees or applicants so as to deprive individuals of employment opportunities, discrimination in apprenticeship and on-the-job training programs, retaliation for opposition to an unlawful employment practice, and sexually stereotyped advertisements relating to employment (42 U.S.C.A. §§ 2000e-2(a) & (d), 2000e-3(a) & (b)).

The Pregnancy Discrimination Act (PDA) of 1978 (42 U.S.C.A. § 2000e(k)) was the congressional response to the ruling of the Supreme Court in *General Electric Co. v. Gilbert*, 429 U.S. 125, 97 S. Ct. 401, 50 L. Ed. 2d 343 (1976), that an employer's refusal to grant pregnancy disability benefits under an otherwise all-inclusive short-term disability INSURANCE program did not violate title VII. The PDA prohibits discrimination against employees on the basis of pregnancy and childbirth with respect to employment and benefits.

Sex Discrimination and Title VII: An Unusual Political Alliance

The legislative battle to pass the Civil Rights Act of 1964 (42 U.S.C.A. § 2000e et seq.) required the leadership of President Lyndon B. Johnson and the bipartisan support of legislators from outside the South. The original draft of title VII of the act, which prohibits employment discrimination, limited its scope to discrimination based on race, color, religion, and national origin. Sex was not included as a "protected class" because supporters of the bill feared such a provision might kill the act itself.

In February 1964 Representative Howard W. Smith, a powerful Democrat from Virginia, offered an amendment to include sex as a protected class. Supporters of the bill were suspicious of Smith's motives, as he had, for three decades, consistently opposed civil rights laws prohibiting racial discrimi-

nation. Many suspected that he was including sex discrimination in title VII in an attempt to break the bipartisan consensus for the entire bill.

Smith, however, claimed he had no ulterior motive. Since the 1940s he had formed a loose alliance with the National Woman's party (NWP), a feminist organization headed by Alice Paul. Since 1945 Smith had been a sponsor of the Equal Rights Amendment, which Paul had originally drafted in 1923. Smith said he had introduced the amendment to title VII at the request of Paul and the NWP.

Sponsors of the bill urged that the amendment be defeated, but female representatives, such as Martha W. Griffiths of Michigan, led a bipartisan effort to adopt the amendment. The amendment was passed by a vote of 164 to 133, with most southern Democrats voting for it. The Senate then adopted the House language. If Smith and the other southerners thought the amendment would scuttle the bill, they were mistaken. The law was enacted on July 2, 1964, with Smith and other southern Democrats voting against the entire bill. Nevertheless, Smith had proved an unlikely hero for women's rights.

Other legislation aimed at eradicating sex-based discrimination was also passed during this era. The Equal Credit Opportunity Act (15 U.S.C.A. § 1691) prohibits discrimination on the basis of sex or marital status in the extension of CREDIT. Title IX of the Education Amendments of 1972 (20 U.S.C.A. §§ 1681–1686) prohibits educational institutions receiving federal financial assistance from engaging in sex discrimination, including the exclusion of individuals from noncontact team sports on the basis of sex. (In 1982 the Supreme Court extended this prohibition to sex-stereotyped admissions and employment practices of schools.)

The Equal Rights Amendment The boldest attempt to outlaw sex discrimination was Congress's passage in 1972 of a CONSTITUTIONAL AMENDMENT, popularly known as the EQUAL RIGHTS AMENDMENT (ERA). The ERA, which had originally been introduced in Congress in 1928, stated that "Equality of rights under the law shall not be denied or abridged by the United States or by any State on account of sex." It gave Congress the authority to enforce this provision by appropriate legislation.

The ERA, like all constitutional amendments, had to be ratified by at least three-fourths of the states to become part of the Constitution. At first the amendment was met with enthusiasm and little controversy in the state legislatures. By 1976 the ERA had been

ratified by thirty-five of the needed thirty-eight states. In the late 1970s, however, conservative groups mounted strong opposition in those states that had yet to ratify. Opponents contended that the ERA would lead to women in combat, unisex bathrooms, and the overturning of legitimate sex-based classifications. Although Congress extended the period for RATIFICATION until 1982, the ERA ultimately failed to win approval from the required thirty-eight states.

Judicial Review of Sex-Based Discrimination With the defeat of the ERA, constitutional interpretation in the area of sex discrimination has been largely based on the Fourteenth Amendment. In 1971, in *Reed v. Reed*, 404 U.S. 71, 92 S. Ct. 251, 30 L. Ed. 2d 225, the Supreme Court extended the application of the Equal Protection Clause of the Fourteenth Amendment to gender-based discrimination in striking down an Idaho law that preferred men to women as PROBATE administrators.

In *Reed* the Court appeared to be moving toward making sex a "suspect classification" under the Fourteenth Amendment. The suspect classification doctrine holds that laws classifying people according to race, ethnicity, and religion are inherently suspect and are subject to the STRICT SCRUTINY test of JUDICIAL REVIEW. Strict scrutiny forces the state to provide a COMPELLING STATE INTEREST for the challenged law and demonstrate that the law has been narrowly tailored to achieve its purpose. Although strict scrutiny is not a precise test, it is far more stringent than the traditional RATIONAL BASIS TEST, which requires only that the government offer a REASONABLE ground for the legislation. Therefore, making sex a suspect classification would have dramatically improved the chances that sex-based laws would be struck down.

The Supreme Court, however, has declined to make sex a suspect classification. Nevertheless, it has invalidated a number of sex-based policies under a "heightened scrutiny" or "intermediate scrutiny" test. In *Craig v. Boren*, 429 U.S. 190, 97 S. Ct. 451, 50 L. Ed. 2d 397 (1976), the Court articulated its intermediate standard of review for sex-based policies. According to this test, "classifications by gender must serve important governmental objectives and must be substantially related to the achievement of those objectives." Presumably, this test is stricter than the rational basis test but less strict than the compelling state interest test.

In *Craig* the Court struck down an Oklahoma law that outlawed the sale of beer containing less than 3.2 percent alcohol to females under the age of eighteen and males under the age of twenty-one. Oklahoma argued that the law was a public safety measure and purported to show that men between eighteen and twenty-one were more likely to be arrested for drunk driving than were women in the same age bracket. The Court rejected this argument, holding that the state had failed to demonstrate a substantial relationship between its sexually discriminatory policy and its admittedly important interest in traffic safety.

In *Orr v. Orr*, 440 U.S. 268, 99 S. Ct. 1102, 59 L. Ed. 2d 306 (1979), the Court reviewed an Alabama law that required divorced men, under certain circumstances, to make ALIMONY payments to their ex-wives but exempted women in the same circumstances from paying alimony to their ex-husbands. The state argued that this policy was designed to compensate women for economic discrimination produced by the institution of marriage. Though the Court accepted that such compensation was an important state interest, it concluded that the law was not substantially related to the achievement of this objective. Justice WILLIAM J. BRENNAN, JR., in his majority opinion, pointed out that wives who were not dependent on their husbands benefited from the disparate treatment.

In other cases, however, the Court has upheld gender-based policies. In one of its most controversial decisions, *Rostker v. Goldberg*, 453 U.S. 57, 101 S. Ct. 2646, 69 L. Ed. 2d 478 (1981), the Court upheld the constitutionality of a male-only draft registration law, the Military Selective Service Act (MSSA) of 1980 (50 U.S.C.A. App. § 451 et seq.). In his majority opinion, Justice WILLIAM REHNQUIST rejected the idea that the MSSA violated the FIFTH AMENDMENT by authorizing the president to require the registration of males and not females. Rehnquist noted that the statute involved national defense and military affairs, an area that the Court had accorded the greatest deference. He concluded that Congress had not acted unthinkingly or reflexively in rejecting the registration of women. He pointed out that the question had received national attention and was the subject of public debate in and out of Congress.

Rehnquist noted that "women as a group, unlike men as a group, are not eligible for combat" under statute and established policy. These combat restrictions meant that Congress had a legitimate basis for concluding that women "would not be needed in the event of a draft." Therefore, there was no need to register women. The law did not violate EQUAL PROTECTION because the exemption of women from registration was closely related to the congressional purpose of registration as a way to "develop a pool of potential combat troops." In upholding the draft law, the Court avoided applying the intermediate scrutiny test.

Sex Discrimination by Educational Institutions Numerous state-operated or publicly operated or supported educational institutions have limited enrollment to one sex. The Supreme Court first addressed whether such limitations on enrollment constituted sex discrimination in *Mississippi University for Women v. Hogan*, 458 U.S. 718, 102 S. Ct. 3331, 73 L. Ed. 2d 1090 (1982). The Court voted 5 to 4 to require the Mississippi University for Women to admit a male student to its nursing school. In defending its refusal to admit Joe Hogan, the school argued that having a school solely for women compensated for sex discrimination in the past and that the presence of men would detract from the performance of female students.

Writing for the majority, Justice SANDRA DAY O'CONNOR rejected both of the school's arguments. O'Connor rejected the "compensation" argument as contrived since the school had made no showing that women had historically lacked opportunities in the field of nursing. As for the concern that the presence of men would hurt the performance of female students, O'Connor pointed out that the school had been willing to admit Hogan to classes on a non-credit basis. In the Court's view, the principal effect of the female-only nursing program was to "perpetuate the stereotyped view of nursing as an exclusively woman's job."

In 1996 the Supreme Court again addressed the issue of educational sex discrimination in the highly publicized case of *United States v. Virginia*, ___U.S. ___ , 116 S. Ct. 2264, 135 L. Ed. 2d 735. The Court ruled that the Virginia Military Institute (VMI), a publicly funded military college, must give up its all-male enrollment policy and admit women. The all-male policy violated the Equal Protection Clause of the Fourteenth Amendment.

The lower federal courts had upheld VMI's admission policy, basing their decision on the need to preserve the "VMI experience," a physically and emotionally demanding military regimen that has remained the same since the early nineteenth century. Co-education would prevent both men and women from undergoing the "VMI experience" and would distract the male cadets. During the litigation the state of Virginia proposed the establishment of a parallel program for women, called the Virginia Women's Institute for Leadership (VWIL), with VMI remaining an all-male institution.

The Supreme Court rejected the arguments advanced by the courts below. Justice RUTH BADER GINSBURG, writing for the majority, stated that "Neither the goal of producing citizen-soldiers nor VMI's implementing methodology is inherently unsuitable to women." Ginsburg rejected Virginia's contention that single-sex education yields such important educational benefits that it justified the exclusion of women from VMI. The generalizations about the dif-

Compensation of Men's and Women's Athletic Team Coaches in the NCAA, 1996

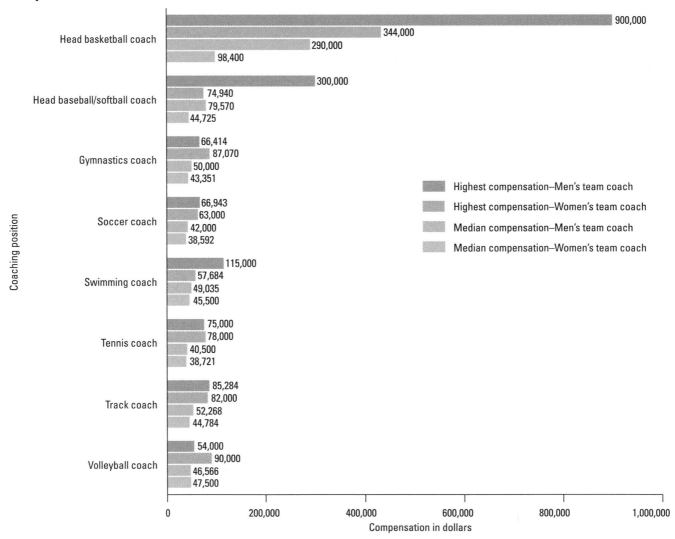

Source: R. Vivian Acosta & Linda Jean Carpenter, "Women in Intercollegiate Sport: A Longitudinal Study—Nineteen Year Update, 1977 to 1996."

ferences between men and women that the state offered to justify the exclusion of women were suspect. According to Ginsburg, the generalizations were too broad and stereotypical, with the result that predictions about the downgrading of VMI's stature if women were admitted were no more than self-fulfilling prophecies. The categorical exclusion of women from VMI denied equal protection to women.

The Court was also unimpressed with the creation of the VWIL as a remedy for the constitutional violation of equal protection. Justice Ginsburg noted numerous deficiencies, pointing out that VWIL afforded women no opportunity to "experience the rigorous military training for which VMI is famed."

Sex Discrimination to Protect Fetal Health In the 1980s female employees in certain industries complained that they were barred from certain jobs because the employer believed the jobs exposed women to health hazards that could affect their ability to reproduce and could also affect the health of a fetus. The Supreme Court, in *UAW v. Johnson Controls*, 499 U.S. 187, 111 S. Ct. 1196, 113 L. Ed. 2d 158 (1991), ruled that a female employee cannot be excluded from jobs that expose her to health risks that might harm a fetus she carries. The Court found that the exclusion of the women violated title VII of the Civil Rights Act of 1964 because the company policy applied only to fertile women, not fertile men. The Court noted that the policy singled out women on the basis of gender and childbearing capacity rather than on the basis of fertility alone. If a job presented potential dangers to the worker or the worker's fetus, it was up to the worker to decide whether to accept the position.

Gender Bias in the Courts Beginning in the 1980s, many state court systems have established task forces to investigate the existence of gender bias in the courts. The reports of these task forces have documented sex discrimination, with its victims more often women than men. The task forces have found that much gender-biased behavior is unconscious and that the manifestations of bias, although often subtle, are deeply ingrained in state judicial systems. For example, the studies have noted the existence of stereotypes concerning victims of DOMESTIC VIOLENCE and sexual assault; many judges believe that women who are beaten by a spouse or raped have provoked the attack. These studies also have shown that judges do not always treat men and women equally in the courtroom. For example, judges may identify women appearing before them by their first name but use professional titles or

Total Expenses of Men's and Women's Athletic Programs in NCAA Division I-A

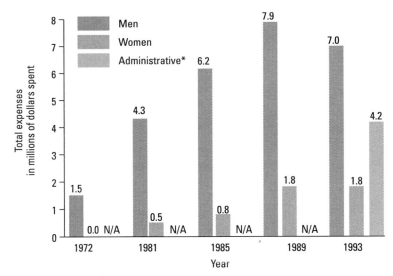

*Non-gender specific items were reported as Administrative expenses

Source: Dr. Christine H.B. Grant, "Title IX and Gender Equity," Presentation given at the 1995 NACWWA Fall Forum, Cedar Rapids, IA.

"Mister" when addressing men. In response to these findings, states have set up judicial educational programs on the dangers of gender-based stereotypes and have modified judges' and lawyers' codes of conduct to explicitly prohibit gender-biased behavior. These task forces have also recommended that more women be appointed to the bench.

CROSS-REFERENCES

Armed Services; Dworkin, Andrea; Employment Law; Feminist Jurisprudence; Fetal Rights; Friedan, Betty; Husband and Wife; Ireland, Patricia; Millett, Katherine Murray; Schlafly, Phyllis; Sexual Harassment; Women's Rights.

SEX OFFENSES 📖 A class of sexual conduct prohibited by the law. 📖

Since the 1970s this area of the law has undergone significant changes and reforms. Although the commission of sex offenses is not new, public awareness and concern regarding sex offenses have grown, resulting in the implementation of new rules of evidence and procedure, new police methods and techniques, and new approaches to the investigation and prosecution of sex offenses.

Forcible Sex Offenses Forcible RAPE and SODOMY are sexual offenses that have been widely recognized since the beginning of American common law. Rape was defined as an act of forcible sexual intercourse with a female other than the perpetrator's wife. Modern legislation in the United States has expanded that definition to include the act of forcible sexual intercourse with any person, even the spouse of the actor. The offense of rape combines the crime of ASSAULT (fear of imminent bodily harm) with the elements of FORNICATION (sexual intercourse between two unmarried persons) or ADULTERY (sexual intercourse with someone other than the actor's spouse).

Sodomy is defined as anal intercourse but is often used in the law as a generic classification including BESTIALITY (sexual intercourse with an animal) and FELLATIO and CUNNILINGUS (two forms of oral sex). These forms of sexual conduct were outlawed because widely accepted religious beliefs and moral principles dictate that they are unnatural forms of sexual activity, often called "crimes against nature." Forcible rape and sodomy are generally perceived as similarly grave offenses.

Most state criminal statutes require some physical penetration in order to consummate the crime of rape or sodomy, but many statutes have a low threshold for demonstrating penetration, calling only for a showing of "some penetration, however slight." Completion of the sex act as evidenced by orgasm, ejaculation, or achievement of sexual gratification, however, is not required to prove a rape or sodomy case.

Most forcible sex offense statutes do require some forcible compulsion to submit and earnest resistance. However, courts will consider the circumstances of the attack, including the characteristics of the perpetrator and the victim, the presence of a weapon, threats of harm, and the assault itself, in assessing the victim's resistance. Statutes do not require victims to resist if to do so would be futile or dangerous.

Although modern statutes have eliminated the marital rape exception, a dozen states still have some form of restrictions in the prosecution of the crime of marital rape. For example, some states will only prosecute marital rape claims if the couple is legally separated or have filed for DIVORCE. However, due to legal criticism and growing public awareness of spousal abuse, the trend in the United States is toward the elimination of all exceptions to the prosecution of these crimes.

In the 1990s the public became more aware of issues involving violence in the home among family members. Many studies showed that women are far more likely to be victims of violence at the hand of a husband or boyfriend than by a stranger. Victims of DOMESTIC VIOLENCE or rape are believed to be reluctant to report these crimes for fear of continued or retaliatory violence. In response to these issues,

Congress enacted the Violent Crime Control and Law Enforcement Act of 1994 (42 U.S.C.A. § 3796dd et seq.). One part of that act is the section entitled the Safe Homes for Women Act of 1994 (18 U.S.C.A. § 2261 et seq.). This section created new federal crimes and penalties for domestic violence.

Non-Forcible Sex Offenses   Non-forcible sex offenses include sexual conduct with individuals that the law assumes are not capable of giving CONSENT to sexual acts. Because of this legal principle, it is said that in non-forcible sex offense cases, lack of consent by the victim may be a MATTER OF LAW. In other words, statutes will assume that underage, physically helpless, and mentally incompetent victims are incapable of giving consent to sexual acts and will not consider consent as a valid defense to the crime.

The age at which criminal statutes acknowledge that an individual is capable of consenting to sexual acts varies by state. Most JURISDICTIONS have special statutes for sex offenses committed with an underage victim, usually termed STATUTORY RAPE laws. In some states non-forcible sexual acts with an underage individual are considered as serious as forcible sexual acts. In other states forcible sexual acts are deemed more serious and are punished more severely. Where the offense is committed forcibly with an underage individual, the more serious statute and punishments will apply. It does not matter if the perpetrator reasonably believed that the victim was of the AGE OF CONSENT because MISTAKE OF FACT is no defense in a statutory rape case.

The law also considers physically helpless and mentally disabled victims to be incapable of giving consent to sexual acts. Physically helpless individuals include those who are unconscious, paralyzed, restrained, or otherwise incapable of resisting the sexual acts. Mentally disabled victims may include those who are permanently mentally disabled or those who are drugged and in a temporary state of mental disability. Some state statutes even include involuntarily intoxicated individuals in the category of temporarily mentally disabled victims. Although mistake of fact is no defense for sexual offenses with a minor, it is a defense for a physically helpless or mentally disabled adult victim if the perpetrator can show that he reasonably believed that the victim was not physically helpless or mentally disabled.

Fornication and Adultery   Fornication (sexual intercourse between two unmarried persons) and adultery (sexual intercourse with someone other than one's spouse) are non-forcible sex offenses that have been recognized since early American COMMON LAW. These acts are still unlawful under most state statutes. Fornication, however, has been eliminated as a criminal offense in some jurisdictions as a result of a more liberal view of the role of public law in mandating moral principles. However, neither fornication nor adultery is prosecuted with much regularity. The requirements of penetration that must be proved in other sexual offenses involving sexual intercourse also must be proved for fornication and adultery.

Consensual Sodomy Consensual sodomy statutes outlaw the act of sodomy even when it is consensual, meaning that it is accomplished without the use of force. The view supporting these statutes, which still exist in some states, is that sodomy is an unnatural act, and when the act is consensual, all participants are guilty of wrongdoing. However, since the 1980s some state courts have overturned consensual sodomy laws, calling them unconstitutional prohibitions of sexual conduct between two consenting adults.

The Supreme Court addressed the issue of the constitutionality of consensual sodomy laws in *Bowers v. Hardwick*, 478 U.S. 186, 106 S. Ct. 2841, 92 L. Ed. 2d 140 (1986). In *Bowers* two consenting men were found engaged in sodomy in a private home in a state that had an anti-sodomy law. The Supreme Court found no basis in the Constitution supporting the argument that homosexuals have a fundamental right to engage in sodomy. The issue of heterosexual sodomy was not addressed.

Bigamy BIGAMY, another non-forcible sex offense, is the crime of marrying a second spouse while the MARRIAGE to the first spouse is still valid and existing. Bigamy PER SE consists simply of a person's attempt to marry another person while already married. Bigamy per se does not require a showing of living together as husband and wife or of sexual intercourse. Most statutes state that the person must know of the continued validity of the first marriage to be guilty of bigamy. Thus if a woman reasonably believed that her husband was dead, which would have ended their marriage, she could marry another man without violating bigamy statutes. See also MORMON CHURCH; POLYGAMY.

Indecent Exposure Indecent exposure, also called public LEWDNESS, is the intentional exposure of one's genitals to unwilling viewers for one's sexual gratification. This crime is generally classified as a MISDEMEANOR (a less serious crime).

Obscenity and Pornography OBSCENITY and PORNOGRAPHY are non-forcible sex offenses that have proven very difficult for the legislatures and courts to define. In *Miller v. California*, 413 U.S. 15, 93 S. Ct. 2607, 37 L. Ed. 2d 419 (1973), the Supreme Court held that material is pornographic or OBSCENE if the average person, applying contemporary community standards, would find that the work taken as a whole appeals to the prurient interest, that it depicts sexual conduct in a patently offensive way, and that taken as a whole, it lacks serious literary, artistic, political, or scientific value. The Supreme Court has also held that obscenity and child pornography are not protected by the FIRST AMENDMENT.

With the advent of new technology, the law has changed to address and encompass more methods of disseminating obscene and pornographic materials. For example, current laws forbid obscenity and pornography transmitted via TELEVISION and CABLE TELEVISION programs, telephone services, and the INTERNET.

The Internet in particular is one of the fastest-growing media for the transmission of information. Because the Internet is easily accessible to children as well as adults, many leaders advocate the restriction of obscene or pornographic material via the Internet. In 1996 Congress passed the Communications Decency Act (47 U.S.C.A. §§ 230, 560, 561), which made it a felony to place indecent or patently offensive material on the Internet that is accessible to children. However, this act came under fire almost immediately as violating the First Amendment. In 1997, the Supreme Court in *Reno v. American Civil Liberties Union*, __U.S.__, 117 S. Ct. 2329, 138 L. Ed. 2d 874, struck down the indecent and patently offensive provisions of the act as unconstitutional. See also TELECOMMUNICATIONS.

Other Sex-related Offenses Another sex-related offense is INCEST (sexual intercourse with a close relative). Generally, laws against incest forbid sexual intercourse with those close relatives that the law forbids one from marrying.

PROSTITUTION is another offense in and of itself, but that crime is often intermingled with other sex offenses, such as statutory rape or adultery where the prostitute or the john (the customer) is underage or married to someone else, respectively. Another criminal offense commonly charged in conjunction with other sex offenses is the offense of impairing the morals of a MINOR. Prosecutions for that offense are generally pursued when the evidence is insufficient to support a statutory or forcible rape or sodomy charge.

Child Sexual Assault Child sexual assault, long considered to be one of the most horrific of sexual offenses, presents many difficult issues to courts and legislatures. One controversial issue is the balancing of the defendant's right to confront an accuser versus the need to protect child WITNESSES from undue trauma in facing their abusers. The Supreme Court has considered this issue in several cases. In *Coy v. Iowa*, 487 U.S. 1012, 108 S. Ct. 2798, 101 L. Ed. 2d 857 (1988), the Court held that it is a violation of the right of CONFRONTATION to allow a child victim to TESTIFY in court separated from the defendant by a screen. But in *Maryland v. Craig*, 497 U.S. 836, 110 S. Ct. 3157, 111 L. Ed. 2d 666 (1990), the Court upheld the use of a one-way closed-circuit television to receive the out-of-court TESTIMONY of a child witness. In *Craig* the Court held that the defendant does not have an absolute right to confront his accuser face-to-face, especially where it is necessary to protect a child victim from trauma.

States have addressed this problem by enacting statutes allowing various means of effectuating constitutionally mandated confrontation without requiring the child witness to be physically present. More than half of the states permit one-way barriers or closed-circuit television to protect the child witness. Even more states allow the child's testimony to be videotaped outside the courtroom as long as the defendant is allowed to be in the room when the videotape of the testimony is shown.

Every state, and the District of Columbia, Puerto Rico, and the Virgin Islands have mandatory reporting statutes that require certain individuals who work with children to report all suspected cases of CHILD ABUSE or neglect. The general definition of child abuse is any non-accidental injury or pattern of injuries, including sexual molestation, to a child under the age of eighteen. The individuals who must report these cases include doctors, teachers, social workers, child care providers, and psychologists. In some states priests, ministers, coroners, and attorneys are included. Individuals who report suspected abuse or neglect, even if their suspicions turn out to be false, are protected by IMMUNITY against legal action as long as they acted in GOOD FAITH. Reporters may also ask to be kept anonymous when making such ALLEGATIONS.

Prosecution of Sex Offenses The prosecution of sex offenses differs in many respects from the prosecution of other crimes. The experience of the victim is very different from that of the victims of other crimes, the reaction of the police may be different, and sex offense prosecutions present many difficult issues. The Uniform Crime Reports and other national studies indicate that rape is the most underreported crime. Because of the victims' emotional trauma and the widespread bias in the legal system, whether perceived or real, many rape victims do not want to report the crime because they do not want to undergo the ordeal of testifying at the criminal trial.

Well-trained police officers are taught about the difficulties presented in sex offense investigations and prosecutions, including their own susceptibility to societal biases toward sex offenses. Some police departments have specially trained sex offense detectives, including female officers, who may reduce the amount of trauma victims undergo in reliving and recounting their injuries.

Investigators' biases may be manifested in several ways. They may disbelieve or doubt the victim, which may discourage the victim from cooperating with police investigations. In child sex offense cases, defendants often have argued that the police officers or prosecuting attorneys coerced or powerfully suggested certain facts until the child victim adopted them as real.

Prosecution of Non-Forcible Sex Offenses Some non-forcible sex offenses have been called victimless crimes, because the victim has been difficult to identify. For example, in the case of prostitution, it is argued that neither the prostitute nor the customer are victims because they each willingly enter into the agreement. However, some argue that society itself is the victim of such crimes. Others argue that the prostitute is in fact the victim, even though she willing commits the act, and that statutes should protect the individual from herself.

Society's responsibility to protect individuals from themselves is the rationale accepted for non-forcible sex offenses involving minors. These statutes simply assume that minors are not able to make sound judgments for themselves. Similar theories support statutes prohibiting sexual conduct with mentally impaired individuals.

For other non-forcible sex offenses such as adultery or bigamy, statutes are based on the premise that society strives to protect families and their stability. However, such justifications are not as easily applied to the sex offenses of fornication and consensual sodomy.

Prosecuting attorneys have some discretion to choose which non-forcible sex offenses to prosecute. Where the constitutionality of a statute is at issue, such as statutes forbidding consensual sodomy, prosecutors generally choose not to enforce those statutes through prosecution. Adultery and fornication are other non-forcible sex offenses that are rarely prosecuted.

Private individuals who are not the victims of the particular sex offense, whether forcible or non-forcible, do not have a legal right of action against the offender. Prosecuting attorneys carry out the public function of pursuing criminal complaints against sex offenders on behalf of the people of the state.

Constitutionality Issues Many statutes making sexual conduct criminal have been attacked as unconstitutional. The most common claims made are that the statutes are too VAGUE, violate personal rights to PRIVACY, or violate the Equal Protection Clause.

The Supreme Court considered the argument that statutes violating sodomy are unconstitutionally vague in *Rose v. Locke*, 423 U.S. 48, 96 S. Ct. 243, 46 L. Ed. 2d 185 (1975). The *Rose* case involved a state statute that forbade "crimes against nature," and the defendants argued that the terms of the statute were imprecise and vague. The Supreme Court held that the statute did not violate the Constitution because even though the language may have been imprecise, it was still possible to determine the meaning of the statute so as to provide sufficient warning to people who may be affected by it. Courts have held that "crimes against nature" include sodomy, fellatio, and cunnilingus.

Statutes forbidding obscene language or conduct have also been challenged on the ground that they are vague under the argument that it is not clear what is considered obscene. State legislatures have attempted to define or describe the term *obscene*, but this often results in the use of other arguably vague terms such as *lewd*, *lascivious*, and *wanton*.

Sex offense statutes have also been challenged on the ground that they violate an individual's right to privacy. There have been mixed results on those claims. The Supreme Court addressed this argument in the 1986 case of *Bowers v. Hardwick*, involving consensual sodomy. But the Supreme Court held that there is no federal privacy right to engage in same-sex acts. Many state courts have since issued similar rulings (*State v. Neal*, 500 So. 2d 374 [La. 1987]; *Miller v. State*, 636 So. 2d 391 [Miss. 1994]; *State v. Walsh*, 713 S.W.2d 508 [Mo. 1986]; *State v. Santos*, 122 R.I. 799, 413 A.2d 58 [R.I. 1980]).

Sex offenses have also been challenged on the ground that they violate EQUAL PROTECTION guarantees under the Constitution. Most courts have followed the Supreme Court's decision in

Michael M. v. Superior Court, 450 U.S. 464, 101 S. Ct. 1200, 67 L. Ed. 2d 437 (1981), in holding that gender-based classifications as applied to state statutory rape laws are constitutionally valid. The *Michael M.* case involved a state statutory rape law that prohibited sexual intercourse with a woman who is under eighteen years old and who is not the perpetrator's wife. The defendant was a seventeen-year-old boy who had sexual intercourse with a sixteen-year-old girl. The defendant argued that the statute violated the Equal Protection Clause of both the federal and state constitutions. The Supreme Court held that the "obviously discriminatory classification" was justified by the important state interest in protecting women who, unlike men, can become pregnant and suffer the harmful and inescapable consequences of pregnancy. It has also been held that non-statutory rape laws do not violate the Equal Protection Clause (*State v. Kelley*, 111 Ariz. 181, 526 P.2d 720 [1974], *cert. denied*, 420 U.S. 935, 95 S. Ct. 1143, 43 L. Ed. 2d 411 [1975]; *Wilson v. State*, 288 So. 2d 480 [Fla. 1974]; *State v. Rivera*, 62 Haw. 120, 612 P.2d 526 [1980]; *State v. Lorenze*, 592 S.W.2d 523 [Mo. Ct. App. 1979]; *Griffin v. Warden*, 277 S.C. 288, 286 S.E.2d 145 (1982), *cert. denied*, 459 U.S. 942, 103 S. Ct. 255, 74 L. Ed. 2d 199 [1982]).

Evidentiary Issues A modern and revolutionary means of identifying criminal defendants in sex offense cases is the use of DNA evidence, often called DNA fingerprinting. Most of the cells of the body and bodily fluids contain a copy of the individual's DNA. Because every person has unique DNA (with the exception of identical twins), it can be used as reliably as a fingerprint in identifying someone. The Florida District Court of Appeals, in *Andrews v. State*, 533 So. 2d 841 (1988), *review denied*, 542 So. 2d 1332 (1989), was the first APPELLATE COURT in the country to uphold the admissibility of DNA evidence in a criminal case. The *Andrews* case involved DNA testing of semen left at the crime scene that matched the DNA of the defendant. The court permitted the admission of the DNA evidence on the ground that it was considered scientifically reliable.

Most states now permit such EVIDENCE to eliminate an individual from the list of criminal suspects. However, it remains controversial whether DNA evidence should be used as a basis for convicting an individual of a crime. Critics argue that DNA testing is not yet reliable enough for that purpose.

DNA testing has also been used to examine evidence from crime scenes gathered years before DNA testing was available. These tests have been successful in many post-conviction proceedings to show that the individual convicted and incarcerated was not the actual offender. Thus, DNA evidence has secured the release of many innocent people.

DNA evidence has been successfully challenged based on the laboratory's methods of running or performing the DNA tests. Human error can render unreliable results and make the basis for a challenge to such evidence in any trial. These attacks generally affect the weight of the evidence but usually do not make the evidence inadmissible.

Rape Shield Laws Rape SHIELD LAWS are state statutes that restrict the admission of a rape victim's sexual history into evidence in rape trials. British and American common law routinely admitted evidence of a rape complainant's past sexual history. It was believed that this evidence could bear adversely on the complainant's credibility as a witness. In addition, courts adhered to the belief that if a woman had consented to sexual activities in the past, it was an indication that she was more likely to have consented to the sexual acts alleged.

Rape law reform gathered momentum in the 1970s and resulted in the enactment of rape shield laws in every jurisdiction in the United States in little more than a decade. Some states enacted special laws and other states amended their existing evidentiary rules to greatly restrict evidence of a rape victim's sexual history. However, there are several general exceptions in which such evidence is deemed relevant and thus ADMISSIBLE.

If the prosecution raises the issue of the complainant's physical condition, by arguing that the defendant was the source of pregnancy, sexually transmitted disease, or semen found on the complainant, the defendant may bring up the complainant's sexual history to show that another man was the actual source. Defendants may also introduce such evidence to show the complainant's MODUS OPERANDI (method of operating), most commonly used to demonstrate that the complainant regularly exchanged sexual favors for money, in other words, that she was known as a prostitute. Another exception to most rape shield laws is using past sexual history of the complainant's sexual relations with the defendant to show that if she consented in the past, she was more likely to have consented on the occasion in which she alleges rape. Some states also permit evidence of prior sexual history to show that the defendant was informed of something that led him to believe that the complainant would readily consent to sex,

thereby negating the defendant's MENS REA (criminal intent) necessary to convict him. Past sexual history can also be introduced like any other evidence where it contradicts the witness's previous testimony, showing that the witness has been untruthful when testifying under oath. Evidence that a complainant has previously fabricated sexual assault charges is also generally admissible to IMPEACH the complainant's credibility as a witness. Finally, past sexual history may be admitted into evidence to show the complainant's MOTIVE to testify falsely—where the complainant may be trying to explain a pregnancy or hide the fact that she had sex with a boyfriend, for example.

HIV and AIDS Like other areas of law, sex offense law has been affected by the growing health concerns related to the HIV and AIDS epidemic.

In 1990 Congress passed the Ryan White Comprehensive AIDS Resource Emergency Act (42 U.S.C.A. § 300ff et seq.), which requires states to prosecute people who knowingly or intentionally expose others to the virus through sexual contact, blood or tissue donations, or sharing of hypodermic needles, in order for the states to be eligible for federal grant money.

Some states have used traditional criminal statutes to prosecute such offenders, by charging them with attempted MURDER or assault. For example, in *State v. Haines*, 545 N.E.2d 834 (Ind. Ct. App. 1989), the defendant was convicted of attempted murder for biting, scratching, spitting, and throwing blood on others with the intent to infect them with his HIV condition. In *Zule v. State*, 802 S.W.2d 28 (Tex. Ct. App. 1990), the court upheld the conviction of aggravated sexual assault and transmission of HIV where the defendant, who knew that he was HIV positive, engaged in sodomy with a fifteen-year-old boy who, two years later, tested positive for HIV.

Approximately half of the states have specific statutes that address the crime of knowingly transmitting HIV through sexual and other conduct. For a defendant to know that he is HIV positive is enough to establish INTENT under these statutes. Many of these statutes forbid "intimate contact" or conduct reasonably likely to result in the transmission of "bodily fluids." These statutes have withstood constitutionality challenges that they are vague (*People v. Russell*, 158 Ill. 2d 23, 630 N.E.2d 794 [1994], *cert. denied*, *Lunsford v. Illinois*, 513 U.S. 828, 115 S. Ct. 97, 130 L. Ed. 2d 47 [1994]; *People v. Dempsey*, 242 Ill. App. 3d 568, 610 N.E.2d 208 [1993]). Consent is generally a defense to these crimes; however, lack of medical evidence supporting a likelihood of transmission or a lack of actual transmission of the disease is not a defense.

Another new legal development that has arisen over the public concern about HIV and AIDS is mandatory AIDS testing of accused and convicted sexual offenders. This issue presents a delicate balance of the concerns of sexual assault victims with the FOURTH AMENDMENT rights of accused or convicted sex offenders.

Approximately seventeen states have enacted laws requiring individuals accused of certain crimes to be tested for AIDS. At least eight states require such testing only after conviction. Other states permit testing if the alleged victim can demonstrate a compelling need to have the test results. Congress passed the Crime Control Act of 1990 (42 U.S.C.A. § 3756 et seq.), which requires HIV testing of certain sex offenders when requested by a second victim of sexual assault.

These laws have been challenged in the courts on the grounds that they violate privacy rights, Fourth Amendment rights against unreasonable searches, and the PRESUMPTION OF INNOCENCE of criminal defendants. Most courts have rejected such claims based on the Supreme Court's decision in *Schmerber v. California*, 384 U.S. 757, 86 S. Ct. 1826, 16 L. Ed. 2d 908 (1966), that a routine blood ALCOHOL test is not a substantial intrusion into one's bodily integrity. Reasoning by analogy, most courts have held that a blood test for AIDS, where necessary to further an important government interest in the health and safety of the victim, is constitutional.

Sexual Psychopath Legislation A minority of states have statutes designed to address sentencing and rehabilitation problems created by dangerous sex offenders and sexual psychopaths. These statutes are designed to protect public safety by removing habitual sex offenders from society for extended periods of time.

Criminal defendants treated differently from others based on their classification as sexual psychopaths have challenged these laws, arguing that they violate equal protection, but the laws have withstood such challenges (*Minnesota ex rel. Pearson v. Probate Court*, 309 U.S. 270, 60 S. Ct. 523, 84 L. Ed. 744 [1940]).

These statutes require that the court must specifically find that the sex offender suffers from mental illness that leads to sexually deviant behavior, and that the behavior is likely to continue in the future, in order to classify the offender as a sexual psychopath. These statutes also permit the state to retain custody of the sexual psychopath, or sexually dangerous person, until she is cured of the mental illness. In effect, this allows the state to impose an indeterminate, and often lifetime, sentence.

Sex Offender Registration and Community Notification Because of growing public concern since the 1980s over RECIDIVISM (repeated offenses) among sexual offenders, the majority of the states have enacted sex offender registration acts. In 1994 Congress passed legislation that required states to enact such laws in order to receive certain federal funding (42 U.S.C.A. § 14071).

Although these laws vary in scope and effect, they share the common goal of protecting the public by requiring repeat sex offenders to register their names and addresses with local law enforcement officials. Some statutes allow the public to have access to this information. Other statutes, commonly called community notification laws, mandate that all residents in a certain geographic area be notified before a convicted sex offender moves into their neighborhood.

Although there have been numerous constitutional challenges to sex offender registration acts, most courts have found no constitutional violations. Specific attacks that have been unsuccessfully made include the arguments that the statutes constitute CRUEL AND UNUSUAL PUNISHMENT, they are EX POST FACTO LAWS (laws that retroactively punish behavior), they are BILLS OF ATTAINDER (acts of the legislature to impose punishment without a court trial), they constitute DOUBLE JEOPARDY (multiple prosecutions for the same offense), or they violate the offender's right to privacy.

CROSS-REFERENCES

Acquired Immune Deficiency Syndrome; Criminal Law; Criminal Procedure; DNA Evidence; Family Law; Gay and Lesbian Rights; Husband and Wife; Sexual Abuse; Victims of Crime.

SEXUAL ABUSE 📖 Illegal sex acts performed against a MINOR by a parent, GUARDIAN, relative, or acquaintance. 📖

Sexual abuse is a general term for any type of sexual activity inflicted on a child by someone with whom the child is acquainted. It is considered an especially heinous crime because the abuser occupies a position of trust. Until the 1970s the prevalence of sexual abuse had been seriously underestimated. Growing awareness of the problem led legislatures to enact reporting requirements, which mandate that any professional person (doctor, nurse, teacher, social worker) who knows or has reason to believe that a child is being abused report this information to the local welfare agency or law enforcement department. Statistics vary widely about the level of sexual abuse, but most researchers agree that it occurs at a higher rate than previously believed. Experts on the subject estimate that more than 130,000 children a year are sexually abused in the United States.

Perpetrators of sexual abuse are prosecuted under state CRIMINAL LAW statutes that have been toughened for sexual assaults on minors. The prosecution of reported sexual abuse has required children to TESTIFY in court about the abuse. Children are often unwilling to testify against the abuser, who may be a family member and may exert control over the victim. To relieve these pressures, courts have allowed the use of closed-circuit television to protect the child witness from the trauma of testifying in court before the defendant, expanded the HEARSAY evidence exception to allow TESTIMONY about what the child said if the child lacks a motive to lie or if the child uses sexual terminology unexpected of a child, and made rules that suspended the STATUTE OF LIMITATIONS until the abusive conduct is discovered.

During the 1980s a rash of sexual abuse cases involving day care centers drew national attention. The McMartin preschool case in Manhattan Beach, California, which began in 1984, accused a group of day care employees of sexual abuse and bizarre rituals of animal sacrifice. Though none of the defendants was ever convicted, similar ALLEGATIONS around the United States resulted in 113 convictions.

A difference of opinion exists within the legal and medical communities over the truthfulness of child WITNESS testimony in sexual abuse cases. Prosecutors and some health professionals argue that children do not lie. Defense attorneys and social researchers contend that faulty interviewing by parents, psychologists, and law enforcement can lead children to make up stories. LEADING QUESTIONS and demands that a child reveal abuse can pressure the child into making false statements in order to please the questioner.

The debate over child witnesses has led many law enforcement agencies to develop standard investigatory protocols that seek to prevent contamination of the child's testimony. Interviews are routinely videotaped to document the interview process.

Apart from criminal remedies, in the 1980s CHILD ABUSE victims gained the ability to sue their abusers for DAMAGES. Before that time, civil remedies were available only for child victims who filed claims soon after attaining the AGE OF MAJORITY. State courts and legislatures accepted the concept of repressed memory, in which traumatic episodes are repressed by the victim for many years. In more than twenty-three states, adults who "recover" their memories of childhood sexual abuse, either spontaneously or through psychiatric and psychological counseling, may now bring a civil lawsuit against the perpetrator. These states have rewritten their laws to start the statute of limitations from the time the victim knows or has reason to know that sexual abuse occurred.

During the 1980s and 1990s, many lawsuits were filed using these new laws. Adults successfully sued a number of Roman Catholic priests for sexual abuse that the victims had endured many years before. Health professionals argued that the victims needed the lawsuits as much for therapeutic as legal reasons. Confronting the abuser and holding the abuser accountable for the actions is a significant step for the victim, who often feels shame, guilt, and responsibility for the abuse.

However, a controversy has arisen over the validity of recovered memories. The dispute centers on memories that are coaxed or brought forth through the efforts of therapists. Some experts in law and mental health question the veracity of these memories and challenge their use as the evidentiary basis for lawsuits over conduct that allegedly occurred years, and sometimes decades, in the past. They contend that these are "implanted memories," brought about by hypnosis, truth serums, and therapists' suggestive remarks. They are also troubled that therapists may be allowed to testify as expert witnesses, when there is no SCIENTIFIC EVIDENCE to support their theories regarding recovered memories.

A 1994 California lawsuit by Gary Ramona was the first case in the United States where an alleged abuser won a large damages award against the therapist who had treated his child. Ramona's daughter Holly had filed suit, accusing her father of sexually molesting her when she was a child. As a result of the lawsuit and the charges, Ramona's wife divorced him and he lost his high-paying job. He argued that Holly's recollections were the result of the psychiatrist's giving her the hypnotic drug sodium amytal and then eliciting from her confabulations, or false but coherent memories spliced together from true events, that convinced Holly that she had been abused by her father. The jury agreed with the father, awarding him $500,000. The jury concluded that the recovered memories were unreliable and that the methods used to elicit them were improper.

See also CHILDREN'S RIGHTS; INFANTS.

CHILD TESTIMONY IN DAY CARE CENTER SEXUAL ABUSE CASES

Between 1983 and 1991, a series of cases involving allegations of sexual abuse by day care center workers drew national attention. During this period, investigations of suspected sexual abuse of preschool children by their teachers took place in more than one hundred U.S. cities. Many persons were convicted of crimes, but others were either acquitted or had their convictions overturned on appeal. The key issue in these cases was whether the children involved had told the truth or whether their testimony had been tainted by the way they were interviewed by parents, social workers, and psychologists. Though this type of multiple victim, multiple offender sexual abuse charge has disappeared, the issue of the credibility of children discussing sexual matters and sexual abuse remains a charged issue.

IN FOCUS

The most famous case involved the McMartin preschool in Manhattan Beach, California. In 1984 authorities charged Virginia McMartin, age seventy-six, her daughter Peggy McMartin Buckey, her grandson Raymond Buckey, a granddaughter, and three female teachers with sexually abusing 120 children. The children reported violent rituals where rabbits were mutilated and the children were forced to touch corpses. Eventually prosecutors dropped charges for lack of evidence against everyone except Peggy Buckey and her son Raymond. They went on trial in 1987.

In January 1990, after the longest (two-and-a-half years) and most expensive ($15 million) criminal trial in U.S. history, Peggy and Raymond Buckey were acquitted on fifty-two counts of child molestation. The jury deadlocked on twelve counts of molestation against Raymond Buckey and on one count of conspiracy against both defendants. The charge against Peggy Buckey was dismissed, but Raymond was retried on

eight of the thirteen counts. In July 1990 his second trial ended in a mistrial, and the case was finally dismissed.

The McMartin preschool case revealed troubling questions about the way the investigation had been conducted and how evidence had been obtained from young children. The initial allegation of abuse was made by a mother later diagnosed as paranoid schizophrenic. She accused Raymond Buckey of molesting her son. The police investigated and declined to file charges because of lack of evidence. The Manhattan police chief then sent a letter to the two hundred parents of past or present McMartin preschool students and alleged that Buckey may have molested their children. Parents were urged to question their children about any sexual abuse.

The letter caused a panic. Hundreds of children were given medical exams and interviewed by a group of psychologists at a counseling center. During these interviews, children were asked leading and suggestive questions and were rewarded for giving the "right" answers. Children reported bizarre events, including being taken into subterranean passages at the school where animal sacrifices were performed. No passages nor any traces of animal sacrifices were found at the school. Several children reported that they were taken on airplanes and molested.

At trial the jurors had difficulty distinguishing between fact and fantasy in the children's accounts. The prosecution argued that children seldom lie about abuse but that they are often reluctant to disclose what has happened to them. Therefore, the prosecution said, a therapist interviewing a child will often use suggestive questioning, prompting, and manipulation to encourage the child to disclose the truth about sexual abuse. As for the bizarre tales,

they were simply the children's way of dealing with what had happened to them. The jurors did not accept these explanations, expressing concern that the children's testimony had been influenced by adults. The videotapes of the interviews showed therapists asking leading questions and the children appearing to try to provide answers that would please the interviewers.

Prosecutors and many therapists contend that children rarely lie about sexual abuse and that the implanting of false memories through leading and suggestive questions is unlikely. They worry that refusing to believe children's testimony victimizes the children a second time and sends a message that society does not want to hear about sexual abuse.

Others are more skeptical. About twenty studies have shown that suggestive questioning about events that never happened can contaminate young children's memories with fantasies. When police, social workers, therapists, and prosecutors conduct multiple interviews, details they provide in their questions and statements are likely to find their way into the statements of children. Children will use their imagination and confabulate stories that are richly detailed but are a mix of fact and fantasy. This is not to say that children are not to be believed. Children rarely lie when they spontaneously disclose abuse on their own or when a person seeks the complete story with the least probing or leading yes-no questions.

The McMartin preschool outcome has forced investigators to learn better ways of asking children questions. Many interviewers are trained to gain a child's trust, evaluate the child's ability to remember and give details of past events, and let the child tell what happened in her own words. Interviews are generally videotaped to allow both the prosecution and the defense to evaluate the investigator's methods.

SEXUAL HARASSMENT 📖 Unwelcome sexual advances, requests for sexual favors, and other verbal or physical conduct of a sexual nature that tends to create a hostile or offensive work environment. 📖

Sexual harassment is a form of SEX DISCRIMINATION that occurs in the workplace. Persons who are the victims of sexual harassment may sue under Title VII of the CIVIL RIGHTS ACT of 1964 (42 U.S.C.A. § 2000e et seq.), which prohibits sex discrimination in the workplace.

The federal courts did not recognize sexual harassment as a form of sex discrimination until the 1970s, because the problem originally was perceived as isolated incidents of flirtation in the workplace. Employers are now aware that they can be sued by the victims of workplace sexual harassment. The accusations of sexual harassment made by ANITA F. HILL against Supreme Court Justice CLARENCE THOMAS during his 1991 confirmation hearings also raised societal consciousness about this issue.

Courts and employers generally use the definition of sexual harassment contained in the guidelines of the U.S. EQUAL EMPLOYMENT OPPORTUNITY COMMISSION (EEOC). This language has also formed the basis for most state laws prohibiting sexual harassment. The guidelines say:

> Unwelcome sexual advances, requests for sexual favors, and other verbal or physical conduct of a sexual nature constitute sexual harassment when
> (1) submission to such conduct is made either explicitly or implicitly a term or condition of an individual's employment.
> (2) submission to or rejection of such conduct by an individual is used as the basis for employment decisions affecting such individuals, or
> (3) such conduct has the purpose or effect of unreasonably interfering with an individual's work performance or creating an intimidating, hostile, or offensive working environment. (29 C.F.R. § 1604.11 [1980])

A key part of the definition is the use of the word *unwelcome*. Unwelcome or uninvited conduct or communication of a sexual nature is prohibited; welcome or invited actions or words are not unlawful. Sexual or romantic interaction between consenting people at work may be offensive to observers or may violate company policy, but it is not sexual harassment.

The courts have generally concluded that a victim need not say or do a particular thing to indicate unwelcomeness. Instead, a court will review all of the circumstances to determine whether it was reasonably clear to the harasser that the conduct was unwelcome. The courts have recognized that victims may be afraid to express their discomfort if the harasser is their boss or is physically intimidating. Victims may be coerced into going along with sexual talk or activities because they believe they will be punished or fired if they protest. Consent can be given to a relationship and then withdrawn when the relationship ends. Once it is withdrawn, continued romantic or sexual words or actions are not protected by the past relationship and may be sexual harassment.

The law prohibits unwelcome "sexual" conduct and words or actions "of a sexual nature." Some conduct, such as hugging, may be sexual or nonsexual and must be evaluated in context. Sexual harassment may be physical, such as kissing, hugging, pinching, patting, grabbing, blocking the victim's path, leering or staring, or standing very close to the victim. It may also be verbal, which may be oral or written and could include requests or demands for dates or sex, sexual jokes, comments about the victim's body or clothing, whistles, catcalls, or comments or questions about the victim's or harasser's social life or sexual life. Sexual harassment may also be visual, such as cartoons, pictures, or objects of a sexual nature.

The laws against sexual harassment are violated when "submission to such conduct is made either explicitly or implicitly a term or condition of . . . employment." This language refers to what is sometimes called quid pro quo sexual harassment, in which a victim's hire, job security, pay, receipt of benefits, or status depends on her or his response to a superior's sexual overtures, comments, or actions. The quid pro quo may be direct, as when a superior explicitly demands sexual favors and threatens firing if the demands are not met, or it may be indirect, as when a superior suggests that employment success depends on "personality" or "friendship" rather than competence.

Sexual harassment also occurs when sexual conduct or communication "unreasonably interfer[es] with an individual's work performance." Tangible loss of pay, benefits, or the job itself is not required for sexual harassment to be claimed and proven. Generally, occurrences must be significant or repeated or both for substantial interference to be established.

Unreasonable interference can occur between coworkers of equal status as well as between superiors and subordinates. The employer of the coworker may be legally liable for

Same-sex Sexual Harassment

Sexual harassment in the workplace is usually associated with a heterosexual employee making unwelcome sexual advances to another heterosexual employee of the opposite gender. There are also cases where a homosexual employee harasses an employee of the same sex. But can a heterosexual employee sexually harass another heterosexual employee of the same gender?

The Supreme Judicial Court of Massachusetts, in *Melnychenko v. 84 Lumber Company,* 424 Mass. 285, 676 N.E.2d 45 (1997), concluded that same-sex sexual harassment is prohibited under state law regardless of the sexual orientation of the parties.

Leonid Melnychenko and two other employees at a Massachusetts lumberyard were subjected to humiliating verbal and physical conduct by Richard Raab and two other employees. Raab loudly demanded sexual favors from the men, exposed himself, and simulated sexual acts. Eventually the three employees quit their jobs with the lumber company and sued, claiming that sexual harassment was the reason for their departure.

At trial, the judge concluded that Raab's actions were not "true romantic overtures to the plaintiffs, and that they were not inspired by lust or sexual desire." Raab, who was "physically violent and sadistic," sought to "degrade and humiliate" the men.

The judge and the Supreme Judicial Court agreed that Raab's behavior constituted sexual harassment because it interfered with the three plaintiffs' work performance by creating an intimidating, hostile, humiliating, and sexually offensive work environment. Raab's sexual orientation did not excuse the conduct. The unwelcome sexual advances and requests for sexual favors were more than lewd horseplay and raunchy talk. They constituted sexual harassment.

---

such harassment if the employer knows or should know about it and fails to take timely and appropriate responsive action.

The most far-reaching part of the EEOC definition is that dealing with a hostile or offensive working environment. The U.S. Supreme Court upheld the concept of a hostile work environment as ACTIONABLE under the 1964 Civil Rights Act in *Meritor Savings Bank v. Vinson,* 477 U.S. 57, 106 S. Ct. 2399, 91 L. Ed. 49 (1986). The Court rejected a narrow reading of the statute, under which an employer could not be held liable for sexual harassment unless the employee's salary and promotions were affected by the actions.

In the *Vinson* case, plaintiff Mechelle Vinson, an employee of Meritor Savings Bank, claimed that her male supervisor, Sidney Taylor, had sexually harassed her. Taylor made repeated demands for sexual favors, and the pair engaged in sexual relations at least forty times. Vinson testified that she engaged in sexual relations because she feared losing her job if she refused. The harassment stopped after Vinson began a steady relationship with a boyfriend. One year later, Taylor fired Vinson for excessive use of medical leave. Although the bank had a procedure for reporting harassment, Vinson had not used it because it required her to report the alleged offenses to her supervisor—Taylor.

Justice WILLIAM H. REHNQUIST, writing for the Court, established several basic principles for analyzing hostile environment cases. First, for sexual harassment to be actionable, it must be severe enough to change the conditions of the victim's employment and create an abusive working environment. Here, Rehnquist implied that isolated occurrences of harassment (such as the telling of a dirty joke or the display of a sexually explicit photograph) would not constitute a hostile work environment.

Second, Rehnquist made clear that there is a difference between voluntary behavior and welcome behavior. Noting that Vinson and Taylor's sexual relations were voluntary, Rehnquist rejected the conclusion that Vinson's willingness constituted a defense to sexual harassment. The critical issue was whether the sexual advances were welcome. If sexual advances are unwelcome, the inequality of power between a supervisor and subordinate strongly suggests that the employee engages in sexual relations out of fear.

Third, Rehnquist held that courts must view the totality of the circumstances when deciding the issue of welcomeness. In *Vinson,* however, the Court did not address the question of whose perspective should be used in determining whether certain behavior so substantially changes the work environment that it becomes abusive: should the standard be that of a reasonable man, a REASONABLE WOMAN, or a REASONABLE PERSON?

In *Robinson v. Jacksonville Shipyards,* 760 F.

CLARENCE THOMAS AND ANITA HILL HEARINGS

The issue of sexual harassment drew national attention during the 1991 Senate hearings on the confirmation of Clarence Thomas to the U.S. Supreme Court. Anita F. Hill, a professor at the University of Oklahoma Law Center, accused Thomas of sexually harassing her when she worked for him at the U.S. Department of Education and the Equal Employment Opportunity Commission (EEOC) between 1981 and 1983. The public disclosure of the allegations resulted in nationally televised hearings before the Senate Judiciary Committee.

The hearings, which drew a large national viewing audience, raised questions about Thomas's behavior, Hill's credibility, and the nature of sexual harassment in the workplace. The demeanor of the twelve white male members of the Senate Judiciary Committee and the questions they asked Hill raised the ire of many women's groups, who saw in the senators' behavior an unwillingness to acknowledge the dynamics of sexual harassment.

Thomas, then a judge on the U.S. Court of Appeals for the District of Columbia, had been nominated by President George Bush to fill the seat vacated by Justice Thurgood Marshall. Thomas's opponents, including many Democrats and interest groups, tried to block his nomination because they didn't want Thomas, an outspoken conservative African American, replacing Marshall, an African American and one of the few remaining liberals on the Court. After questioning Thomas at length, the Judiciary Committee deadlocked 7–7 on whether to recommend the nominee to the full Senate and then sent the nomination to the floor without a recommendation. Nevertheless, it appeared that Thomas would win confirmation by a comfortable, though not necessarily large, margin.

Then on October 6, 1991, Anita Hill publicly accused Thomas of sexual harassment. The charges rocked the Senate. Hill had been contacted earlier by Senate staff members, and she told

IN FOCUS

them of her allegations. The Judiciary Committee asked the Federal Bureau of Investigation (FBI) to talk to Hill and Thomas about the allegations. The FBI produced a report that was inconclusive, being largely a matter of "he said, she said." The allegations would probably never have come to public attention except that Hill's statement was leaked to National Public Radio (NPR). Once NPR broke the story, Thomas's confirmation was thrown into doubt. In response, the Judiciary Committee announced that Thomas and Hill would be given a chance to testify before the committee.

The Hill-Thomas hearings took place on a weekend from October 11 to 13. Hill testified that after she had refused to date Thomas, he had initiated a number of sexually oriented conversations, some of which alluded to pornographic films. She provided vivid details about these conversations, but her credibility was questioned by Thomas supporters, who suggested, among other things, that Hill might have fantasized the conversations. Republican Senator

Supp. 1486 (M.D. Fla. 1991), federal district judge Howell Melton applied the reasonable woman test to determine if the work environment was abusive to women. He held that a reasonable woman, exposed to the pictures of nude or partially nude women that were posted in the workplace, and to the sexually demeaning remarks and jokes by male workers, would find that the work environment at the shipyards was abusive. The totality of the circumstances would lead a reasonable woman to these conclusions.

The Ninth Circuit Court of Appeals echoed this reasoning in *Ellison v. Brady*, 924 F.2d 872 (1991). In *Ellison*, the court rejected the reasonable person standard in favor of the reasonable woman standard. The court believed that using the reasonable person standard would risk enforcing the prevailing level of discrimination because that standard would be male biased.

Even with the acceptance of the reasonable woman standard by the courts, the diversity of outcomes in harassment claims created confu-

sion as to what constitutes harassment. In *Harris v. Forklift Systems*, 510 U.S. 17, 114 S. Ct. 367, 126 L. Ed. 295 (1993), the Supreme Court attempted to clarify this issue. Teresa Harris had filed a discrimination claim based on the behavior of the company president, Charles Hardy. Hardy had insulted Harris and other women with demeaning references to their gender and with unwanted sexual innuendo.

The district court ruled that although Hardy's comments were sufficiently offensive to cause discomfort for a reasonable woman, they did not rise to the level of interfering with that woman's work performance. The court also held that Harris had not been injured by the comments.

The Supreme Court overruled the lower court, holding that courts must not focus their inquiry on concrete psychological harm, which is not required by title VII of the Civil Rights Act. To maintain such a requirement would force employees to submit to discriminatory behavior until they were completely broken by

Arlen Specter of Pennsylvania interrogated Hill as if she were a criminal suspect and suggested that she might be charged with perjury. Other senators wondered why she had followed Thomas from the Department of Education to the EEOC if he had sexually harassed her. She replied that the harassment seemingly had ended and that she was uncertain about the future of her job at Education.

Thomas forcefully denied all of Hill's allegations and portrayed himself as the victim of a racist attack. According to him, Hill's allegations were "charges that play into racist, bigoted stereotypes." He reminded the committee that historically, when African American men were lynched, they were almost always accused of sexual misconduct, and he characterized the hearings as a "high-tech lynching."

Thomas's impassioned defense proved to be effective. It not only disarmed his Democratic opponents on the committee, who in the opinion of many commentators failed to question Thomas effectively, but it also won him sympathy throughout the country. A *New York Times*/CBS News poll taken after the hearing (October 28, 1991) found that 58 percent of the respon-

dents believed Thomas and only 24 percent believed Hill.

The committee also heard from witnesses who said that Hill had discussed the harassment with them during the time she worked for Thomas. Thomas's supporters produced several men as character references, one of whom alleged that Hill's statements were a product of romantic fantasy. Several women who would have testified that Thomas exhibited similar behavior with them either declined to testify after seeing the committee's grilling of Hill or were not called by the committee.

Thomas was confirmed two days after the hearings, on a vote of 52–48, the narrowest margin for a Supreme Court justice since 1888.

Thomas's confirmation did not end the controversy. Some commentators characterized the hearings as a perversion of the process and suggested that Hill's charges should have been aired in closed committee hearings. Others criticized Hill as a pawn of liberal and feminist interest groups that sought to derail Thomas's nomination by any means. Some critics also accused Hill of being an active participant in the move to defeat Thomas; they claimed that she was a Democrat who pretended to be a Re-

publican so as to appear politically impartial.

Hill's defenders were outraged by the committee's treatment of her. They described her plight as typical of women who bring sexual harassment claims. Unless the woman has third-party testimony backing up her charges, the "he said, she said" scenario always favors the man. The senators' questioning of Hill's motivations was also evidence of how men fail to understand sexual harassment. Many of the senators saw her as either a liar, a publicity seeker, or an emotionally disturbed woman who fantasized the alleged incidents. In response, T-shirts appeared that stated "I believe Anita Hill." There was also concern that Hill's treatment might discourage women from reporting sexual harassment. The Thomas-Hill hearings were a watershed event in the discussion of sexual harassment. Various authors have written books that examine Hill and Thomas and the allegations. Not surprisingly, these books reach widely divergent conclusions about the participants and the outcome.

it. So long as the workplace environment would reasonably be perceived as hostile or abusive, it did not need also to be psychologically injurious.

Thus, the plaintiff in a hostile work environment case must show that sexually harassing behavior is more than occasional, but need not document an abusive environment that causes actual psychological injury. The courts recognize that a hostile work environment will detract from employees' job performance, discourage employees from remaining in their position, and keep employees from advancing in their career. Title VII's guiding rule of workplace equality requires that employers prevent a hostile work environment.

Many employers, realizing the potential LIABILITY arising from hostile work environment complaints, have sought to prevent the occurrence of sexual harassment. A first step is determining if a problem exists. Some companies conduct informal surveys of their employees concerning sexual harassment. In addition, employers often inspect the workplace for objec-

tionable material, such as photographs of nude people or insensitive or explicit jokes with sexual connotations.

Employers typically include a policy against sexual harassment in personnel policies or employee handbooks. These policies use the EEOC definition of prohibited conduct as a guideline. The prohibited conduct must be stated in an understandable way.

A complaint procedure should also be part of the policy. Employers should recognize that a prompt and thorough investigation of a complaint, followed by appropriate disciplinary action, is the wisest course. These procedures also should specify to whom a victim of harassment can complain if the victim's supervisor is the alleged harasser.

Companies also routinely train supervisors to recognize sexual harassment. Finally, some employers provide sexual harassment training for all their employees as a way of trying to improve workplace culture and behavior.

See also EMPLOYMENT LAW; WOMEN'S RIGHTS.

SHAM 📖 False; without substance. 📖

A sham PLEADING is one that is good in form but is so clearly false in fact that it does not raise any genuine issue.

SHAPIRO, ROBERT LESLIE Robert Leslie Shapiro is a prominent West Coast defense lawyer. Shapiro entered private practice in 1972 after a brief stint as a prosecutor. Within a decade, he was representing film stars, producers, professional athletes, and other celebrities. Shapiro is known for his calm, tactful manner in negotiations and for building relationships with law enforcement agencies and the press. In 1994 he turned these abilities to the defense of O. J. (ORENTHAL JAMES) SIMPSON in a case followed closely throughout the nation.

Shapiro was born on September 2, 1942, in Plainfield, New Jersey. While still a child, he moved to California with his family. He later studied finance at the University of California, Los Angeles, and then law at Loyola Law School. After earning his law degree in 1968, he joined the Los Angeles County District Attorney's Office as an assistant district attorney. That same office also served as a stepping-stone for another noted West Coast attorney— JOHNNIE L. COCHRAN, JR., who later became Shapiro's colleague on the Simpson defense team. In 1972 Shapiro left the public sector for private practice.

Shapiro's first well-known case was his defense of Linda Lovelace, an adult film star charged with a cocaine offense in 1975. Shapiro got the charges dismissed. Famous figures in sports and entertainment began to call on Shapiro. He represented television comedian Johnny Carson, New York Mets outfielder Vince Coleman, film producer Robert Evans, and Christian Brando, son of actor Marlon Brando. Shapiro also won an acquittal for his friend, attorney F. (FRANCIS) LEE BAILEY, who was charged with drunk driving.

After two decades of success, Shapiro published some of his insights for other lawyers. In February 1993 he wrote an essay called "Using the Media to Your Advantage," which was published by the National Association of Criminal

Robert Leslie Shapiro

"PUT SIMPLY, A DEFENSE ATTORNEY'S JOB IS TO SEE TO IT THAT THE MAN OR WOMAN WHO STANDS UNDER . . . SCRUTINY DOES NOT STAND ALONE."

Defense Lawyers. The essay's message is that big cases are tried as much in the media as in court, and usually to the prosecution's advantage. Prosecutors know how to play to reporters, and defense attorneys usually do not. Shapiro contends that media headlines proclaiming an arrest destroy the presumption of innocence and instead create an assumption of guilt. Shapiro believes that combating the public mindset that "if the press said it, it must be true," is the defense attorney's most challenging task. He advises defense lawyers to get to know reporters, to look into the camera, and to speak in sound bites, so that the defense's position also finds its way into news reports.

Shapiro's most prominent case was the trial of former football star O. J. Simpson for the 1994 murders of his ex-wife, Nicole Brown Simpson, and her friend, Ronald Lyle Goldman. One of Shapiro's first moves in the case was to arrange for Simpson's surrender to Los Angeles police, something he had done for other clients. Instead of surrendering as arranged, however, Simpson fled, leaving a suicide note; shortly thereafter, he led police on a slow speed chase along Los Angeles highways. Massive publicity followed, putting the case and Shapiro under virtually ceaseless scrutiny.

Shapiro worked to ensure that the defense's perspective would be part of the media's coverage of the case. He also assembled a powerful team of lawyers and scientific experts to prepare for trial. Shapiro's team of experts, though widely praised, may have been as big a challenge as the media, for the many well-known attorneys did not always agree on strategy or on who should play what role. Serious disagreements arose within the team, including one between Shapiro and Bailey, whom Shapiro accused of trying to undermine his reputation. Though Shapiro handled most of the early trial work, it was Cochran who assumed the lead role toward the end of the trial, delivering the most widely quoted defense remarks in closing arguments.

Simpson was ultimately acquitted of murder, and the team Shapiro had assembled disbanded.

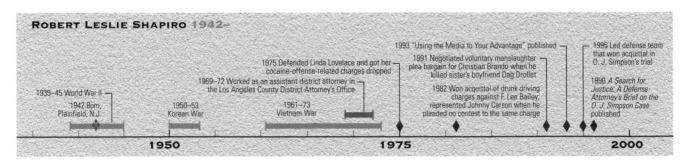

ROBERT LESLIE SHAPIRO 1942–

1939–45 World War II

1942 Born, Plainfield, N.J.

1950–53 Korean War

1961–73 Vietnam War

1969–72 Worked as an assistant district attorney in the Los Angeles County District Attorney's Office

1975 Defended Linda Lovelace and got her cocaine-offense-related charges dropped

1982 Won acquittal of drunk driving charges against F. Lee Bailey; represented Johnny Carson when he pleaded no contest to the same charge

1991 Negotiated voluntary manslaughter plea bargain for Christian Brando when he killed sister's boyfriend Dag Drollet

1993 "Using the Media to Your Advantage" published

1995 Led defense team that won acquittal in O. J. Simpson's trial

1996 *A Search for Justice: A Defense Attorney's Brief on the O. J. Simpson Case* published

1950   1975   2000

By the trial's conclusion, Shapiro had gained nationwide fame for his part in one of the most widely followed cases in U.S. history. He continues to practice law in Los Angeles.

See also CLARK, MARCIA.

SHARE 📖 A portion or part of something that may be divided into components, such as a sum of money. A unit of stock that represents ownership in a CORPORATION. 📖

SHAW, LEMUEL   Lemuel Shaw served as chief justice of the Supreme Judicial Court of Massachusetts from 1830 to 1860. Shaw was a judicial pioneer. His long career as a judge coincided with a crucial period in the development of the United States, and his personal, idiosyncratic opinions fashioned legal doctrines that accommodated the tumultuous changes of the time. It is likely that no other state judge in the nineteenth century wielded the same influence as Shaw in the areas of commercial and constitutional law. This influence was not merely on law in his state: Shaw's ideas and precedents were adopted nationally. Many decades after his death in 1861, Shaw's ideas still affected EMPLOYMENT LAW and CIVIL RIGHTS cases.

Born on January 9, 1781, in West Barnstable, Massachusetts, Shaw was the second son of the Reverend Oaks Shaw, who taught his son English, the classics, and the Bible. In 1800 Shaw graduated from Harvard University with high distinction. A brief writing career led to studying law with a Boston lawyer, and in 1804 Shaw was admitted to the bar in both New Hampshire and Massachusetts. Over the next two decades, he practiced some law while immersing himself in his home state's politics. He was by turns a justice of the peace, an ardent Federalist organizer, a delegate to the Massachusetts Constitutional Convention of 1820, and a state senator in 1821 and 1822.

Shaw's decision to devote himself fully to legal practice marked the turning point in his career. From 1823 on, he devoted himself to the practice of commercial law. The nation was in the process of transforming itself from an agrarian society into a modern urban industrial one. Alert to the changes underway, Shaw became

BIOGRAPHY

Lemuel Shaw

"[WHILE] THE MAINTENANCE OF SEPARATE SCHOOLS TENDS TO DEEPEN AND PERPETUATE THE ODIOUS DISTINCTION OF CASTE, . . . PREJUDICE, IF IT EXISTS, IS NOT CREATED BY LAW, AND PROBABLY CANNOT BE CHANGED BY LAW."

wealthy and prominent as a lawyer to growing industrial concerns. In 1830, on the basis of this reputation, Governor LEVI LINCOLN offered Shaw the office of chief justice of the Supreme Judicial Court of Massachusetts. Shaw took the offer despite the sacrifice of a lucrative career and the prospect of long absences from his family.

Shaw's opinions broke from precedent. In *Farwell v. Boston and Worcester Rail Road*, 45 Mass. (4 Met.) 49 (1842), he denied recovery of DAMAGES to a railroad worker whose hand was lost due to the NEGLIGENCE of another worker. The injured worker had sued the employer. Shaw's concern was to limit the LIABILITY of employers, and he accomplished this by importing from English COMMON LAW the so-called FELLOW-SERVANT RULE. This rule protected employers from being sued in such cases on the theory that workers know that they take risks and that their salaries are compensation enough. By introducing to U.S. law this doctrine, which became widely popular, Shaw hoped to benefit the commonwealth with unhindered industrial growth. His decision helped frustrate injured workers' claims for more than a half century, until the advent of WORKERS' COMPENSATION laws in the early twentieth century eviscerated the doctrine in most JURISDICTIONS.

Yet Shaw was not against labor. In his best-known and most praised decision, Shaw cleared the way for labor unions to operate freely in Massachusetts. *Commonwealth v. Hunt*, 45 Mass. (4 Met.) 111 (1842), freed the state's unions from the prevailing judicial application of the law of criminal CONSPIRACY to labor actions. In the twentieth century, the opinion has been hailed as the foremost nineteenth-century ruling on LABOR UNIONS because it removed from them the stigma of criminality.

Shaw's views on civil rights were among his most controversial. He was praised by abolitionists and condemned by southern slave states for his opinion in *Commonwealth v. Aves*, 35 Mass. (18 Pick.) 193 (1836). *Aves* held that a slave brought voluntarily into the state became

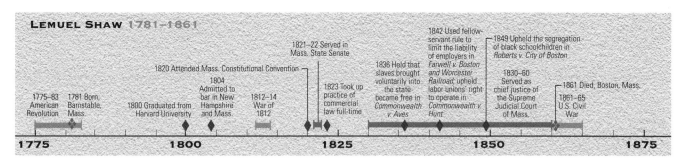

free and could not be required by his or her master to leave to return to SLAVERY. But subsequently, Shaw always denied writs of HABEAS CORPUS to free fugitive slaves. In 1849 he upheld the segregation of black schoolchildren in *Roberts v. City of Boston*, 59 Mass. (5 Cush.) 198. As the first in a line of state and federal cases that supported school segregation, Shaw's opinion in *Roberts* was cited by the Supreme Court in 1896 when it upheld a Louisiana law requiring the separation of races in railroad cars in the infamous case of *Plessy v. Ferguson*, 163 U.S. 537, 16 S. Ct. 1138, 41 L. Ed. 256.

Shaw's thirty years on the Massachusetts bench ended with his retirement in 1860. He died in Boston on March 30, 1861.

SHAW v. HUNT In 1996 the U.S. Supreme Court dealt a severe blow to states' attempts to create election districts containing a majority of minority voters to ensure minority representation. In *Shaw v. Hunt*, __U.S. __, 116 S. Ct. 1894, 135 L. Ed. 2d 207, the Court ruled that the redrawing of a North Carolina congressional district into a "bizarre-looking" shape to include a majority of African Americans could not be justified by the VOTING RIGHTS ACT OF 1965 (42 U.S.C.A. § 1973c), because it violated the Equal Protection Clause of the FOURTEENTH AMENDMENT to the U.S. Constitution.

The case arose out of two disputed congressional election districts created by the North Carolina legislature following the 1990 census. North Carolina increased its congressional delegation from eleven to twelve seats in the House of Representatives. In 1991 the state legislature reapportioned the election districts and included one black-majority district. The Justice Department, which under the Voting Rights Act must "preclear" redistricting plans, rejected it. The department found that one black-majority district was insufficient in a state where 22 percent of the population is black.

In 1992 the North Carolina legislature prepared a new plan that created two black-majority districts, the First and the Twelfth. In November 1992 Eva Clayton and Mel Watt were elected from these districts, the first blacks to represent North Carolina since 1901. However, the Republican party and five white voters challenged the two election districts in federal court. The white plaintiffs argued that the two districts amounted to unlawful racial gerrymandering.

The Twelfth District was worm-shaped, stretching 160 miles from Gastonia to Durham, hugging the thin line of Interstate 85. The district was so narrow at one point that drivers in the northbound lane of the interstate were in the district while drivers in the southbound lane were in another district. Of the ten counties through which the district passed, five were cut into three different districts, with some towns divided. The First District was hook-shaped, with fingerlike extensions. It had been compared to a "Rorschach ink-blot test" and a "bug splattered on a windshield."

A three-judge panel reviewed the claims of the plaintiffs and dismissed the case. The court ruled that the plaintiffs had failed to state an EQUAL PROTECTION claim because favoring minority voters was not discriminatory in the constitutional sense and the plan did not lead to proportional underrepresentation of white voters statewide (808 F. Supp. 461 [E.D.N.C. 1992]).

An APPEAL followed to the U.S. Supreme Court (*Shaw v. Reno*, 509 U.S. 630, 113 S. Ct. 2816, 125 L. Ed. 2d 511 [1993]), which laid the groundwork for the Court's 1996 decision. On a 5–4 vote, the Supreme Court reversed the three-judge panel and reinstated the lawsuit, ruling that the plaintiffs did have a CAUSE OF ACTION under the Fourteenth Amendment's Equal Protection Clause. Justice SANDRA DAY O'CONNOR, in her majority opinion, noted the long history of court cases involving efforts by southern states to restrict voting rights for black Americans. In *Gomillion v. Lightfoot*, 364 U.S. 339, 81 S. Ct. 125, 5 L. Ed. 2d 110 (1960), the state of Alabama redefined the boundaries of the city of Tuskegee "from a square to an uncouth twenty-eight-sided figure" to exclude black voters from the city limits. The passage of the Voting Rights Act of 1965 had a dramatic effect on these kinds of practices. By the early 1970s, voter registration had significantly improved for black voters. But black voters were frustrated in their efforts to elect their candidates because of multimember or at-large districts, which diluted their votes and enabled the white majority to elect its candidates. In 1982 section 2 of the Voting Rights Act was amended to prohibit legislation that results in the dilution of a minority's voting strength, regardless of the legislature's intent.

It was against this background that O'Connor shaped her analysis. Reviewing the two districts in dispute, she found it "unsettling how closely the North Carolina plan resembles the most egregious racial gerrymandering of the past." O'Connor agreed that prior cases had never made race-conscious redistricting "impermissible in all circumstances," yet agreed with the plaintiffs that the redistricting was "so extremely irregular on its face that it rationally can be viewed only as an effort to segregate races for purposes of voting, without regard for traditional districting principles and without sufficiently compelling justification."

Under a constitutional challenge regarding the Equal Protection Clause, legislation that involves racial classification requires a court to use the STRICT SCRUTINY standard of review. A law will be upheld under strict scrutiny if it is supported by a COMPELLING STATE INTEREST and is narrowly drawn to achieve that interest in the least restrictive manner possible. O'Connor agreed that district lines "obviously drawn for the purpose of separating voters by race" required application of the strict scrutiny standard.

In examining the districts, O'Connor held that race-based districts will be considered suspect if they disregard traditional districting principles "such as compactness, contiguity, and respect for political subdivisions." These "objective" criteria are required because in reapportionment, "appearances do matter." O'Connor stated that a reapportionment plan that draws in persons of one race from widely separated geographic and political boundaries and "who may have little in common with one another but the color of their skin, bears an uncomfortable resemblance to political apartheid." This type of redistricting reinforces "impermissible racial stereotypes" and may "exacerbate the very patterns of racial bloc voting that majority-minority districting is sometimes said to counteract."

O'Connor also characterized the redistricting plan as "pernicious," sending a message to voters that elected officials are to represent members of their voting group and not their entire constituency. For these reasons, the majority concluded that a reapportionment statute may be challenged when the plaintiffs claim that the plan is an "effort to separate voters into different districts on the basis of race, and that the separation lacks sufficient justification."

The Court remanded the case to the lower court, directing it to apply the standards articulated in the opinion to its analysis of the congressional districts. The lower-court panel ruled that the redistricting plan was narrowly tailored to serve compelling state interests and did not violate equal protection (861 F. Supp. 408 [E.D.N.C. 1994]). The plaintiffs again appealed.

In *Shaw v. Hunt*, the Court again split 5–4, with Chief Justice WILLIAM H. REHNQUIST writing the majority opinion that struck the redistricting plan. Compared with the first Court opinion, the decision was relatively brief and to the point. Rehnquist applied the strict scrutiny

test because race was the predominant consideration in drawing the district lines. Therefore, North Carolina had to prove that its scheme was narrowly tailored to serve a compelling state interest. This burden, the majority concluded, it did not meet.

Rehnquist found the three "compelling interests" asserted by North Carolina to be lacking in merit. In addition, none were narrowly tailored. North Carolina had claimed that it had an interest in eradicating the effects of past DISCRIMINATION, but the lower court had found that this interest did not precipitate the use of race in the redistricting plan. As Rehnquist noted, to prove a "compelling interest," North Carolina had to show that the alleged objective was the legislature's "actual purpose" for the redistricting plan. Therefore, the state could not assert this interest after the fact.

North Carolina also asserted a compelling interest in complying with section 5 of the Voting Rights Act, arguing that it was the state's duty to follow the mandates of the Justice Department in the preclearance process and create two rather than one black-majority districts. Rehnquist rejected this interest because the Court disagreed with the Justice Department that section 5 requires maximizing the number of black-majority districts wherever possible. Under the legislature's original plan, it had only proposed one black-majority district. Rehnquist concluded that this maximization policy was not grounded in section 5 and therefore no compelling interest was at stake.

Rehnquist also saw no merit in the state's argument that under section 2 of the Voting Rights Act it had a compelling interest to create a second black-majority district. North Carolina contended that failure to do so would have brought a charge under section 2 that it was diluting minority voting strength by confining most African Americans to one district. Rehnquist found this contention misplaced because a potential section 2 violation could only be lodged if the minority group was "geographically compact." In this case the original one-district plan was anything but compact.

CROSS-REFERENCES
Apportionment; Elections; Gerrymander; Voting.

SHAYS'S REBELLION A revolt by desperate Massachusetts farmers in 1786, Shays's Rebellion arose from the economic hardship that followed the War of Independence. Named for its reluctant leader, Daniel Shays, the rebellion sought to win help from the state legislature for bankrupt and dispossessed farmers. More than a thousand rebels blocked courts, skirmished with state MILITIA, and were ultimately defeated, and many of them were captured. But the rebellion bore fruit. Acknowledging widespread suffering, the state granted relief to DEBTORS. More significantly, the rebellion had a strong influence on the future course of federal government. Because the federal government had been powerless under the ARTICLES OF CONFEDERATION to intervene, the Framers created a more powerful national government in the U.S. Constitution.

Three years after peace with Great Britain, the states were buffeted by inflation, devalued currency, and mounting DEBT. Among the hardest hit was Massachusetts. Stagnant trade and rampant unemployment had devastated farmers who, unable to sell their produce, had their property seized by courts in order to pay off debts and overdue taxes. Hundreds of farmers were dispossessed; dozens of them were jailed. The conditions for revolt were ripe, stoked by rumors that the state's wealthy merchants were plotting to seize farm lands for themselves and turn the farmers into peasants.

The rebellion that followed came in two stages. The first steps were taken in the summer and fall of 1786. In five counties, mobs of farmers stopped the courts from sitting. Their goal was to stop the trials of debtors until elections could be held. They hoped that a new legislature would follow the example of other states by providing legal relief for them. This action provoked the state's governor, James Bowdoin, into sending out the state militia. Reluctantly, Daniel Shays, a destitute thirty-nine-year-old former captain in the Continental Army, was pressed into leadership of the insurgents. Shays sought to prevent the court from sitting in Springfield, and on September 26, he defied the state militia with his own force of five hundred men. The men prevailed at first, forcing the court to adjourn. But with the capture of another rebel leader in November, the rebellion collapsed.

By December the rebels had regrouped for another stand. Because they feared that this time the state was going to indict them on charges of TREASON, they marched on the federal arsenal in Springfield on January 25, 1784, planning to continue on to the courthouse. Shays had some eleven hundred men under his command. But the militia there, under the command of Major General William Shepherd, easily held them off: four people died before a single cannon volley dispersed Shays's men, who were pursued and arrested. Despite scattered resistance, the rebellion was crushed by February 4.

However, by popularizing the plight of debtors, the defeated rebels succeeded in their goals. Massachusetts elected a new legislature that quickly acceded to several demands of Shays's followers, chiefly by enacting relief measures. Moreover, although fourteen of the rebel leaders were convicted and sentenced to death, they all received PARDONS or short prison sentences. Within a year's time, the state was prosperous again and enmities had cooled.

The most lasting and significant impact came at the federal level. In light of the events in Massachusetts, it was clear to the congress of the Confederation that it lacked the legal power to send aid to the states in a time of crisis. Only six years earlier, the thirteen original states had drawn up their governing document, the Articles of Confederation. Now the congress invited the states to send delegates to a convention in Philadelphia in May 1787 to revise the Articles. This plan was quickly dropped in favor of much broader action—the drafting of a new constitution that would establish a more powerful national government. In part due to the weaknesses exposed by Shays's Rebellion, many delegates at the Constitutional Convention gave support to greater federal power, ultimately embodied in the Constitution.

See also CONSTITUTION OF THE UNITED STATES.

SHELLEY'S CASE See RULE IN SHELLEY'S CASE.

SHELTER A general term used in statutes that relates to the provision of food, clothing, and housing for specified individuals; a home with a proper environment that affords protection from the weather.

SHEPARDIZING A term used in the legal profession to describe the process of using a CITATOR to discover the history of a case or statute to determine whether it is still good law.

The expression is derived from the act of using *Shepard's Citations*. An individual checking a CITATION by shepardizing a case will be able to find out various information, such as how often the opinion has been followed in later cases and whether a particular case has been overruled or modified.

See also SHEPARD'S CITATIONS.

SHEPARD'S® CITATIONS A set of volumes published primarily for use by judges when they are in the process of writing judicial decisions and by lawyers when they are preparing BRIEFS, or memoranda of law, that contain a record of the status of cases or statutes.

Shepard's Citations provide a judicial history of cases and statutes, make note of new cases, and indicate whether the law in a particular case has been followed, modified, or overruled in subsequent cases. They are organized into columns of CITATIONS, and various abbreviations indicate whether a case has been overruled, superseded, or cited in the dissenting opinion of a later case.

The term *shepardizing* is derived from the act of using Shepard's citators.

SHEPPARD, SAMUEL H. In 1953 a sensational MURDER trial laid the groundwork for a significant U.S. Supreme Court ruling on the rights of criminal defendants to a fair trial. This was the Sheppard murder trial—the conviction of Dr. Samuel H. Sheppard, a prominent Cleveland osteopath, on charges of murdering his pregnant wife, Marilyn Sheppard. Sheppard was sentenced to life in prison, where he remained before his APPEAL reached the Supreme Court in 1966. The Court ordered a new trial, which led to Sheppard's eventual ACQUITTAL. *Sheppard v. Maxwell*, 384 U.S. 333, 86 S. Ct. 1507, 16 L. Ed. 2d 600, became the leading case on PRETRIAL PUBLICITY, shaping how judges have since treated the difficult problem of guaranteeing a defendant a fair trial in the face of media attention.

One evening in July 1953, Mrs. Sheppard, age thirty-one, was bludgeoned to death in the bedroom of the couple's impressive Lake Erie home. According to Sheppard, he had been sleeping on a downstairs couch when he heard his wife's screams. He ran to her aid and saw a bushy-haired man at her bedside, and then was knocked unconscious. He awoke to find her slain, ran downstairs and confronted the trespasser again, and was knocked out a second time. After awakening on the beach outside the house, he immediately telephoned the mayor of Cleveland, his friend, and related the story.

Both prosecutors and the media seized on Sheppard as the murderer. Even before his arrest three weeks later, police interrogated Sheppard at the coroner's INQUEST without his lawyer present. They wanted to know about his sex life, in and outside of his marriage. Fed such tidbits by police both before and during the trial, Cleveland newspapers sensationalized the case until it became notorious nationwide.

At the trial in the fall of 1954, PROSECUTORS had no clear-cut motive to explain why Sheppard had allegedly killed his wife. The best they could offer was the intimation that he had been having an affair with a former laboratory technician. Following a chaotic trial, in which the media had telephones, special tables, opportunities to photograph the jurors, and even interviews with the judge on the courthouse steps,

the jury returned a guilty VERDICT. Sheppard received a life sentence.

From 1954 to 1966, Sheppard fought his way through appeals. He argued that pretrial publicity had destroyed his chance of a fair trial by prejudicing jurors. His appeals failed until 1964, when U.S. District Court Judge Carl A. Weinman ruled in his favor (*Sheppard v. Maxwell*, 231 F. Supp. 37 [S.D. Ohio]). Without addressing Sheppard's innocence or guilt, Weinman held that he had been denied DUE PROCESS because negative reporting by the Cleveland press had adversely affected the jurors' verdict. But a year later, the U.S. Court of Appeals in Cincinnati overruled Judge Weinman (*Sheppard v. Maxwell*, 346 F.2d 707 [6th Cir. 1965]). The appeals court said that qualified jurors are able to make thoughtful rulings in the face of publicity.

But the U.S. Supreme Court ruled that Sheppard's trial had been prejudiced by pretrial publicity. So virulent had been the negative publicity that PREJUDICE could safely be presumed, the Court held. It blamed the trial judge for not minimizing the effect of the publicity, which it likened to a circus atmosphere. The decision heightened consideration of criminal defendants' SIXTH AMENDMENT right to due pro-

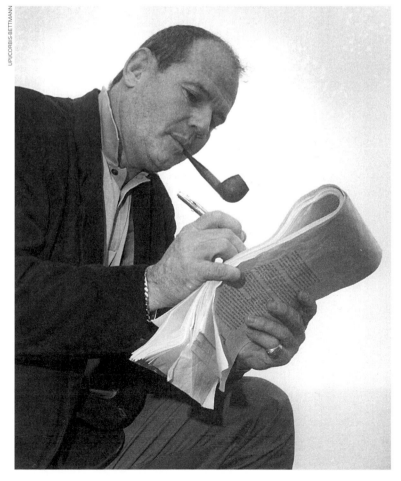

Physician Sam Sheppard spent over a decade in prison for the murder of his wife before he was acquitted in a second trial ordered by the Supreme Court.

UPI/CORBIS-BETTMANN

cess. Significantly, the Court did not seek to curtail the FREEDOM OF THE PRESS to report on trials. Instead, the Court said that in a case where a defendant's rights are threatened by pretrial publicity, the trial judge must protect the defendant. This, it said, could be accomplished by taking such measures as isolating the jury through a process called SEQUESTRATION, where jury members are shielded from contact with the outside world during the course of a trial.

Although the Supreme Court did not rule on Sheppard's guilt or innocence, it reversed his conviction and ordered a new trial. In November 1966, thirteen years after his conviction, he stood trial again. This time, represented by the high-profile attorney F. LEE BAILEY, Sheppard was acquitted. He lived only another four years, dying on April 7, 1970, at the age of forty-six.

In February 1997 DNA tests of evidence from the crime scene proved that a third person was present at the time of the murder. The tests were made in conjunction with a lawsuit against the state of Ohio for wrongful imprisonment, filed by Sheppard's son, Sam Reese Sheppard, on behalf of his father. They included an analysis of a blood sample from Richard Eberling, who had been hired to wash windows at the Sheppard home. The tests could not rule out Eberling as the third person at the murder scene; however, they also could not prove that he was that person.

Eberling is serving life in prison for the murder of an elderly woman. During an arrest of Eberling for theft in 1959, police discovered a ring that belonged to Marilyn Sheppard. Eberling has said that he had nothing to do with the Sheppard murder.

See also DNA EVIDENCE; FIRST AMENDMENT.

SHERIFF ▥ Usually the chief PEACE OFFICER of a COUNTY. ▥

The modern office of sheriff in the United States descends from a one-thousand-year-old English tradition: a "shire-reeve" (shire-keeper) is the oldest appointment of the English crown. Because county governments were typically the first established units of government in newly settled American territories, sheriffs were among the first elected public officials in an area and thus developed a leading role in local law enforcement.

A dichotomy frequently exists today between a sheriff's JURISDICTION and the jurisdiction of a local police department. A metropolitan area may encompass an entire county or more; police departments and sheriffs will often maintain concurrent jurisdiction in the overlapping area. A sheriff may assume that a local police department will do its duty in enforcing the law, but the primary obligation rests with the sheriff and requires him to act when evidence of neglect of that duty exists.

Some state constitutions specifically provide for the office of sheriff, and state legislatures frequently establish conditions of office. Sheriffs are typically chosen in a county election. To serve as sheriff, an individual must usually meet certain requirements: residence within the jurisdiction, no criminal record, U.S. citizenship, and compliance with provisions guarding against nepotism. Sometimes officeholders must also satisfy certain age, physical, and educational requirements. A sheriff typically takes an OATH and posts a BOND upon taking office to ensure the faithful performance of the duties of the office. Compensation typically consists of commissions or fees for particular services performed, a fixed salary, or a combination of fees and salary.

State statutes or state constitutions regulate many duties of a sheriff and emphasize preserving the peace and enforcing criminal laws. Sheriffs arrest and commit to jail felons and other lawbreakers, including pretrial detainees and sentenced prisoners. They transport prisoners to state penal facilities and mental patients to state commitment facilities. In addition, a sheriff is usually responsible for the custody and care of the county courthouse and the JAIL, attends upon courts of record in serving process, and often has the power to summon jurors. As an OFFICER OF THE COURT, a sheriff is subject to a court's orders and direction. Sheriffs also have the power to serve PROCESS, including SUMMONS, mesne (intermediate) process, and final process.

State statutes define a sheriff's role in serving process. Generally a sheriff is the proper officer to EXECUTE all WRITS returnable to court, unless another person is appointed. A sheriff must execute process without attempting to determine its validity. A court will not direct or advise a sheriff as to the manner of executing process, but she has a duty to effect service promptly, respectfully, and without unnecessary violence. A sheriff must exercise due diligence but need not expend all possible efforts in effecting service. See also SERVICE OF PROCESS.

As part of the traditional COMMON-LAW duties passed down from the English, sheriffs retain the power to summon the aid of a posse, or POSSE COMITATUS, as it is sometimes called. Ideally, a posse furnishes immediate, able-bodied assistance to a sheriff in need. For example, a sheriff may summon bystanders to assist in recapturing an escaped prisoner. These persons are neither officers nor private citizens. They are generally clothed with the same protection of the law as the sheriff and have full authority to provide the sheriff with any necessary assistance.

Sheriffs also levy writs of ATTACHMENT, that is, the seizure of a DEBTOR'S property pursuant to a court order. The sheriff must safeguard seized goods from damage or loss, but he does not absolutely ensure their safety. Generally, property that is lost, destroyed, or damaged by something other than a sheriff's neglect will not result in LIABILITY for the sheriff. After seizure, the goods are sold at a sheriff's auction to satisfy CREDITORS' claims. A sheriff decides the time, manner, and place of a JUDICIAL SALE, collects purchase monies, and distributes the proceeds pursuant to court instructions. A sheriff may not purchase property at a sheriff's sale.

In general, a sheriff may be liable in DAMAGES to any person injured as a consequence of a breach of duty connected with the office. A sheriff may not exceed the authority given by law: a sheriff who uses legal authority for illegal conduct is liable as if she had acted without process of law. Some instances where liability may be imposed include a negligent failure to seize sufficient available property that would reasonably be expected to satisfy a DEBT, a failure to execute process delivered for EXECUTION, a LEVY upon the wrong party, or an excessive levy. Liability is in a personal capacity, not in an official capacity. Limited IMMUNITY usually protects a sheriff from liability for acts performed in conjunction with official duties but will not shield her from liability caused by overstepping the authority of the office.

A sheriff typically has broad discretion in appointing, removing, and setting conditions of employment for deputies. A DEPUTY is said to be clothed with the power and authority of the sheriff with respect to the sheriff's ministerial duties. For example, a deputy may act for the sheriff in the service and return of process, in making an execution or other judicial sale (including the APPRAISAL of the property as a prerequisite to such sale), in executing a DEED to a

purchaser, in serving an execution for taxes, and in serving a GARNISHMENT summons.

A deputy's acts, breaches, or misconduct committed in the performance of official duties may result in liability on the sheriff's behalf. For example, in the absence of statutory authority to the contrary, a sheriff could be held liable for a deputy's reckless or wanton acts during an arrest, NEGLIGENCE in caring for and protecting prisoners, or failure to serve process or return a writ.

A sheriff may be removed from office for a variety of reasons, including habitual intoxication or intoxication on the job; misconduct in office, such as misuse of public funds or property; refusal to enforce the law; mistreatment of prisoners; neglect of duty; nepotism; or conviction of a crime.

SHERIFF'S DEED 📖 A document giving ownership rights in property to a buyer at a sheriff's sale (a sale held by a SHERIFF to pay a court JUDGMENT against the owner of the property). A DEED given at a sheriff's sale in FORECLOSURE of a MORTGAGE. The giving of said deed begins a statutory redemption period. 📖

SHERMAN, JOHN John Sherman was an attorney who devoted most of his professional life to public service. He served in the U.S. House of Representatives, the U.S. Senate, and the cabinets of Presidents RUTHERFORD B. HAYES and WILLIAM MCKINLEY. An unsuccessful candidate for president, Sherman is best known for sponsoring the SHERMAN ANTI-TRUST ACT of 1890 (15 U.S.C.A. § 1 et seq.), the landmark federal legislation that sought to prevent industrial monopolies.

Sherman was born on May 10, 1823, in Lancaster, Pennsylvania. His father was a judge and his older brother, William Tecumseh Sherman, became a renowned Union general during the Civil War. Sherman was admitted to the Ohio bar in 1844 and established a successful law practice in Mansfield, Ohio. Soon, however, his interests turned to politics.

Elected to the U.S. House of Representatives as a Republican in 1854, Sherman soon gained a reputation as an expert on government

BIOGRAPHY

LIBRARY OF CONGRESS

John Sherman

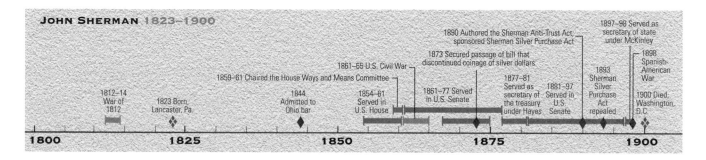

JOHN SHERMAN 1823–1900

1812–14 War of 1812

1823 Born, Lancaster, Pa

1844 Admitted to Ohio bar

1854–61 Served in U.S. House

1859–61 Chaired the House Ways and Means Committee

1861–65 U.S. Civil War

1861–77 Served in U.S. Senate

1873 Secured passage of bill that discontinued coinage of silver dollars

1877–81 Served as secretary of the treasury under Hayes

1881–97 Served in U.S. Senate

1890 Authored the Sherman Anti-Trust Act; sponsored Sherman Silver Purchase Act

1893 Sherman Silver Purchase Act repealed

1897–98 Served as secretary of state under McKinley

1898 Spanish-American War

1900 Died; Washington, D.C.

1800   1825   1850   1875   1900

finance. He served as chair of the House Ways and Means Committee, the chief budgetary body, from 1859 to 1861. Sherman was then elected to the Senate, where he served from 1861 to 1877. From 1867 to 1877, he chaired the Senate Finance Committee.

During the 1870s Sherman's fiscal policies drew national attention. As a senator, he helped establish a national banking system, but he aroused the wrath of farmers in 1873 when he secured the passage of a bill that discontinued the coinage of silver dollars. As secretary of the treasury during the Hayes administration (1877–1881), he placed the United States on the gold standard. Ultimately, however, he was forced to compromise and support legislation that restored the silver dollar as legal tender.

Although Sherman was a conservative, he was a master of political compromise, always willing to grant small concessions to his opponents. This skill, however, proved fatal to his higher political ambitions. He lost the Republican presidential nomination in 1880, 1884, and 1888.

Sherman was reelected to the Senate in 1880, serving until 1897. During the late 1880s, public concern mounted about the increasing concentration of economic power in monopolistic businesses. Sherman's 1888 presidential bid had focused on this problem, and in 1890 he became the author of the antitrust act that bears his name. The Sherman Anti-Trust Act deliberately contained general language that required the Supreme Court to define its scope. Though not always an effective tool, the act remains a central part of federal antitrust enforcement.

Sherman continued to be a force in government currency policy. In 1890 he sponsored the Sherman Silver Purchase Act (28 Stat. 4), which required the federal government to increase its purchase of silver by 50 percent. The act was designed as a subsidy for silver miners, but was repealed in 1893 in the aftermath of a financial panic.

President McKinley appointed Sherman secretary of state in 1897, but Sherman soon realized that leaving the Senate had been a mistake. An opponent of U.S. imperial ambi-

tions, he resigned on April 25, 1898, the day Congress declared war against Spain. Two years later, on October 22, 1900, Sherman died in Washington, D.C.

See also ANTITRUST LAW; MONOPOLY.

SHERMAN, ROGER Roger Sherman was a colonial and U.S. politician and judge who played a critical role at the Constitutional Convention of 1787, devising a plan for legislative representation that was accepted by large and small states. His actions at the convention in Philadelphia came near the end of a distinguished life in public service.

Sherman was born on April 19, 1721, in Newton, Massachusetts. He was admitted to the Massachusetts bar in 1754 and later served as a justice of the peace. In 1761 Sherman moved to New Haven, Connecticut, where he established a business as a merchant. From 1764 to 1785 he served in the Connecticut legislature and was a superior court judge from 1766 to 1788. During these years Sherman became recognized as a national political leader. Though conservative, he was an early supporter of American independence from Great Britain.

Sherman's belief in independence led him to serve as a delegate to the Continental Congress from 1774 to 1784. He was instrumental in the creation of the DECLARATION OF INDEPENDENCE in 1776 and signed the declaration. He also helped draft the ARTICLES OF CONFEDERATION.

After America won its independence, Sherman devoted himself to Connecticut politics, serving as the first mayor of New Haven from 1784 to 1793. He also helped revise Connecticut statutes, eliminating material related to the state's former colonial status.

In 1787 Sherman was a member of the Constitutional Convention in Philadelphia. He recognized that the Articles of Confederation had not provided a stable and secure method of national government. The convention, however, was soon divided over the issue of legislative representation. The small states feared a federal Congress apportioned by population, in which a few large states would control most of the seats. Therefore, WILLIAM PATERSON of New

BIOGRAPHY

Roger Sherman

"[THE EXECUTIVE BRANCH] IS NOTHING MORE THAN AN INSTITUTION FOR CARRYING THE WILL OF THE LEGISLATURE INTO EFFECT."

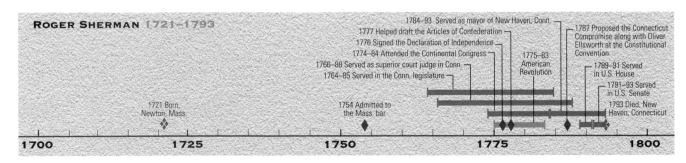

ROGER SHERMAN 1721–1793

1784–93 Served as mayor of New Haven, Conn.
1777 Helped draft the Articles of Confederation
1776 Signed the Declaration of Independence
1774–84 Attended the Continental Congress
1766–88 Served as superior court judge in Conn.
1764–85 Served in the Conn. legislature
1775–83 American Revolution
1787 Proposed the Connecticut Compromise along with Oliver Ellsworth at the Constitutional Convention
1789–91 Served in U.S. House
1791–93 Served in U.S. Senate
1793 Died, New Haven, Connecticut

1721 Born, Newton, Mass.
1754 Admitted to the Mass. bar

1700   1725   1750   1775   1800

Jersey proposed a plan that provided for equal representation in Congress. EDMUND RANDOLPH of Virginia, speaking for the interests of the large states, proposed a plan for a BICAMERAL legislature, with representation in both houses based on population or wealth.

Neither side would yield on the issue of representation. Sherman, along with OLIVER ELLSWORTH, proposed the Connecticut Compromise, or Great Compromise. This plan created a bicameral legislature, with proportional representation in the lower house and equal representation in the upper house. All revenue measures would originate in the lower house. The compromise was accepted, and the convention soon approved the Constitution.

Sherman served in the U.S. House of Representatives from 1789 to 1791 and in the U.S. Senate from 1791 to 1793. He strongly supported the establishment of a national bank and the enactment of a TARIFF.

Sherman died on July 23, 1793, in New Haven, Connecticut.

See also CONGRESS OF THE UNITED STATES; CONSTITUTION OF THE UNITED STATES.

SHERMAN ANTI-TRUST ACT The Sherman Anti-Trust Act of 1890 (15 U.S.C.A. § 1 et seq.), the first and most significant of the U.S. antitrust laws, was signed into law by President BENJAMIN HARRISON and is named after its primary supporter, Ohio Senator JOHN SHERMAN.

The prevailing economic theory supporting antitrust laws in the United States is that the public is best served by free competition in trade and industry. When businesses fairly compete for the consumer's dollar, the quality of products and services increases while the prices decrease. However, many businesses would rather dictate the price, quantity, and quality of the goods that they produce, without having to compete for consumers. Some businesses have tried to eliminate competition through illegal means, such as fixing prices and assigning exclusive territories to different competitors within an industry. Antitrust laws seek to eliminate such illegal behavior and promote free and fair marketplace competition.

The COMMON LAW traditionally has favored competition, finding AGREEMENTS and CONTRACTS that restrain trade to be illegal and unenforceable. During the 1800s several states enacted antitrust statutes, but by the late 1800s these statutes proved ineffective in stopping the rapidly growing and powerful trusts, because many forms of restraint on commercial competition extended across state lines. The trusts were corporate HOLDING COMPANIES that, by 1888, had consolidated a very large share of U.S. manufacturing and mining industries into nationwide monopolies. These monopolies were popularly called "trusts" because the original legal form of their organization had been as business trusts. But changes in state business laws in the 1800s allowed them to act as holding companies, leading to the combinations. The trusts found that through consolidation they could charge monopoly prices and thus make excessive profits and large financial gains. Access to greater political power at state and national levels led to further economic benefits for the trusts, such as TARIFFS or discriminatory RAILROAD rates or rebates. The most notorious of the trusts were the Sugar Trust, the Whisky Trust, the Cordage Trust, the Beef Trust, the Tobacco Trust, John D. Rockefeller's Oil Trust (Standard Oil of New Jersey), and J. P. Morgan's Steel Trust (U.S. Steel Corporation).

Consumers, workers, farmers, and other suppliers were directly hurt monetarily as a result of the monopolizations, and they demanded legislative action. Even more important, perhaps, was that the trusts fanned into renewed flame a traditional U.S. fear and hatred of unchecked power, whether political or economic, and particularly of monopolies that ended or threatened equality of opportunity to aspiring business venturers. The public's intense demands for legislative action in the late 1800s prompted Congress to pass the Sherman Act, followed by several other antitrust acts. The CLAYTON ACT of 1914 (15 U.S.C.A. § 12 et seq.), the Federal Trade Commission Act of 1914 (15 U.S.C.A. § 41 et seq.), and the ROBINSON-PATMAN ACT of 1936 (15 U.S.C.A. §§ 13a, 13b, 21a) are also significant antitrust laws that, together with the Sherman Act, prohibit anticompetitive practices and prevent unreasonable concentrations of economic power that stifle or weaken competition.

The Sherman Act made agreements "in restraint of trade" and "monopolization" illegal, subject to civil remedies and criminal penalties. Courts can issue INJUNCTIONS to stop violations of the act, also subjecting the violator to treble (triple) damages by anyone injured by the violation. Private parties can bring ACTIONS seeking TREBLE DAMAGES, and the U.S. Department of Justice and the Federal Trade Commission (FTC) have the duty to institute actions for other violations of the antitrust laws. The purpose of the act was to make competition the rule in U.S. trade and commerce and to outlaw conduct that might lead to monopoly, but its general language provided virtually no standards. Congress enacted the Sherman Act pursuant to its constitutional power to regulate commerce, and this was only the second occasion in the one hundred years of the existence of the nation in which Congress relied on that power. Because Congress was somewhat uncertain of the reach of that legislative power, it framed the law in broad common-law concepts that lacked details. This in effect passed the problem along to the EXECUTIVE BRANCH to determine how to enforce the law and also to the judicial branch to determine how to interpret the law. Still, the act was a far-reaching legislative departure from the predominant laissez-faire philosophy of the era.

Initial enforcement of the Sherman Act was halting, set back in part by the decision of the Supreme Court in *United States v. E. C. Knight Co.*, 156 U.S. 1, 15 S. Ct. 249, 39 L. Ed. 325 (1895), that manufacturing was not interstate commerce. This problem was soon circumvented, and President THEODORE ROOSEVELT promoted the antitrust cause, calling himself a "trustbuster." A number of major cases were successfully brought in the first decade of the century, largely terminating the trusts and basically transforming the face of U.S. industrial organization. During the 1920s, enforcement efforts were more modest, and during much of the 1930s, the national recovery program of the NEW DEAL encouraged industrial collaboration rather than competition. During the late 1930s, an intensive enforcement of the antitrust laws was undertaken. Since World War II, antitrust enforcement has become increasingly institutionalized in the Antitrust Division of the Justice Department and in a more professional Federal Trade Commission. Justice Department enforcement activities against CARTELS are particularly vigorous, and criminal sanctions are increasingly sought. The number of private treble damage suits, often in CLASS ACTIONS, has grown rapidly in recent years. In 1992 the Justice Department expanded its enforcement policy to cover foreign company conduct that harms U.S. exports.

Restraint of Trade Section one of the Sherman Act provides that "[e]very contract, combination in the form of trust or otherwise, or conspiracy, in restraint of trade or commerce among the several states, or with foreign nations is hereby declared to be illegal." The broad language of this section has been slowly defined and narrowed through judicial decisions.

The courts have interpreted the act to forbid only unreasonable restraints of trade. The Supreme Court promulgated this flexible rule, called the rule of reason, in *Standard Oil Co. of New Jersey v. United States*, 221 U.S. 1, 31 S. Ct.

502, 55 L. Ed. 619 (1911). Under the rule of reason, the courts will look to a number of factors in deciding whether the particular RESTRAINT OF TRADE unreasonably restricts competition. Specifically, the court considers the makeup of the relevant industry, the defendants' positions within that industry, the ability of the defendants' competitors to respond to the challenged practice, and the defendants' purpose in adopting the restraint. This analysis forces courts to consider the pro-competitive effects of the restraint as well as its anticompetitive effects.

The Supreme Court has also declared certain categories of restraints to be illegal PER SE: that is, they are conclusively presumed to be unreasonable and therefore illegal. For those types of restraints, the court does not have to go any further in its analysis than to recognize the type of restraint, and the plaintiff does not have to show anything other than that the restraint occurred.

Restraints of trade can be classified as horizontal or vertical. A horizontal agreement is one involving direct competitors at the same level in a particular industry, and a vertical agreement involves participants who are not direct competitors because they are at different levels. Thus, a horizontal agreement can be among manufacturers or retailers or wholesalers, but it does not involve participants from across the different groups. A vertical agreement involves participants from one or more of the groups—for example, a manufacturer, a wholesaler, and a retailer. These distinctions become difficult to make in certain fact situations, but they can be significant in determining whether to apply a per se rule of illegality or the rule of reason. For example, horizontal market allocations are per se illegal, but vertical market allocations are subject to the rule-of-reason test.

Concerted Action Section one of the Sherman Act prohibits concerted action, which requires more than a unilateral act by a person or business alone. The Supreme Court has stated that an organization may deal or refuse to deal with whomever it wants, as long as that organization is acting independently. But if a manufacturer and certain retailers agree that a manufacturer will only provide products to those retailers and not others, that is a concerted action that may violate the Sherman Act. A company and its employees are considered an individual entity for the purposes of this act. Likewise, a parent company and its wholly owned SUBSIDIARIES are considered an individual entity.

Evidence of a concerted action may be shown by an express or written agreement, or it may be inferred from CIRCUMSTANTIAL EVIDENCE. Conscious parallelism (similar patterns of conduct among competitors) is not sufficient in and of itself to imply a CONSPIRACY. The courts have held that conspiracy requires an additional element such as complex actions that would benefit each competitor only if all of them acted in the same way.

JOINT VENTURES, which are a form of business association among competitors designed to further a business purpose, such as sharing cost or reducing redundancy, are generally scrutinized under the rule of reason. But courts first look at the reason that the joint venture was established to determine whether its purpose was to fix prices or engage in some other unlawful activity. Congress passed the National Cooperative Research Act of 1984 (15 U.S.C.A. §§ 4301-06) to permit and encourage competitors to engage in joint ventures that promote research and development of new technologies. The rule of reason will apply to those types of joint ventures.

Price Fixing The agreement to inhibit price competition by raising, depressing, fixing, or stabilizing prices is the most serious example of a per se violation under the Sherman Act. Under the act, it is immaterial whether the fixed prices are set at a maximum price, a minimum price, the actual cost, or the fair market price. It is also immaterial under the law whether the fixed price is REASONABLE.

All horizontal and vertical PRICE-FIXING agreements are illegal per se. Horizontal price-fixing agreements include agreements among sellers to establish maximum or minimum prices on certain goods or services. This can also include competitors' changing their prices simultaneously in some circumstances. Also significant is the fact that horizontal price-fixing agreements may be direct or indirect and still be illegal. Thus, a promotion or discount that is tied closely to price cannot be raised, depressed, fixed, or stabilized, without a Sherman Act violation. Vertical price-fixing agreements include situations where a wholesaler mandates the minimum or maximum price at which retailers may sell certain products.

Market Allocations Market allocations are situations where competitors agree to not compete with each other in specific markets, by dividing up geographic areas, types of products, or types of customers. Market allocations are another form of price fixing. All horizontal market allocations are illegal per se. If there are only two computer manufacturers in the country and they enter into a market allocation agreement whereby manufacturer A will only sell to retailers east of the Mississippi and manufacturer B will only sell to retailers west of the Mississippi, they have created monopolies for themselves, a violation of the Sherman Act. Likewise, it is an illegal agreement that manufacturer A will only sell to retailers C and D and manufacturer B will only sell to retailers E and F.

Territorial and customer vertical market allocations are not per se illegal but are judged by the rule of reason. In 1985 the Department of Justice announced that it would not challenge any restraints by a company that has less than 10 percent of the relevant market or whose vertical price index, a measure of the relevant market share, indicates that COLLUSION and exclusion are not possible for that company in that market.

Boycotts A BOYCOTT, or a concerted refusal to deal, occurs when two or more companies agree not to deal with a third party. These agreements may be clearly anticompetitive and may violate the Sherman Act because they can result in the elimination of competition or the reduction in the number of participants entering the market to compete with existing participants. Boycotts that are created by groups with market power and that are designed to eliminate a competitor or to force that competitor to agree to a group standard are per se illegal. Boycotts that are more cooperative in nature, designed to increase economic efficiency or make markets more competitive, are subject to the rule of reason. Generally, most courts have found that horizontal boycotts, but not vertical boycotts, are per se illegal.

Tying Arrangements When a seller conditions the sale of one product on the purchase of another product, the seller has set up a TYING ARRANGEMENT, which calls for close legal scrutiny. This situation generally occurs with related products, such as a printer and paper. In that example, the seller only sells a certain printer (the tying product) to consumers if they agree to buy all their printer paper (the tied product) from that seller.

Tying arrangements are closely scrutinized because they exploit market power in one product to expand market power in another product. The result of tying arrangements is to reduce the choices for the buyer and exclude competitors. Such arrangements are per se illegal if the seller has considerable economic power in the tying product and affects a substantial amount of interstate commerce in the tied product. If the seller does not have economic power in the tying product market, the tying arrangement is judged by the rule of reason. A seller is considered to have economic power if it occupies a dominant position in the market, its product is advantaged over other competing products as a result of the tying, or a substantial number of consumers has accepted the tying arrangement (evidencing the seller's economic power in the market).

Monopolies Section two of the Sherman Act prohibits monopolies, attempts to monopolize, or conspiracies to monopolize. A MONOPOLY is a form of market structure where only one or very few companies dominate the total sales of a particular product or service. Economic theories show that monopolists will use their power to restrict production of goods and raise prices. The public suffers under a monopolistic market because it does not have the quantity of goods or the low prices that a competitive market could offer.

Although the language of the Sherman Act forbids all monopolies, the courts have held that the act only applies to those monopolies attained through abused or unfair power. Monopolies that have been created through efficient, competitive behavior are not illegal under the Sherman Act, as long as honest methods have been employed. In determining whether a particular situation that involves more than one company is a monopoly, the courts must determine whether the presence of monopoly power exists in the market. Monopoly power is defined as the ability to control price or to exclude competitors from the marketplace. The courts look to several criteria in determining market power but primarily focus on market share (the company's fractional share of the total relevant product and geographic market). A market share greater than 75 percent indicates monopoly power, a share less than 50 percent does not, and shares between 50 and 75 percent are inconclusive in and of themselves.

In focusing on market shares, courts will include not only products that are exactly the same but also those that may be substituted for the company's product based on price, quality, and adaptability for other purposes. For example, an oat-based, round-shaped breakfast cereal may be considered a substitutable product for a rice-based, square-shaped breakfast cereal, or possibly even a granola breakfast bar.

In addition to the product market, the geographic market is also important in determining market share. The relevant geographic market, the territory in which the firm sells its products or services, may be national, regional, or local in nature. Geographic market may be limited by transportation costs, the types of product or service, and the location of competitors.

Once sufficient monopoly power has been proved, the Sherman Act requires a showing that the company in question engaged in unfair conduct. The courts have differing opinions as to what constitutes unfair conduct. Some courts require the company to prove that it acquired its monopoly power passively or that the power was thrust upon them. Other courts consider it an unfair power if the monopoly power is used in conjunction with conduct designed to exclude competitors. Still other courts find an unfair power if the monopoly power is combined with some predatory practice, such as pricing below marginal costs.

Attempts to Monopolize Section two of the Sherman Act also prohibits attempts to monopolize. As with other behavior prohibited under the Sherman Act, courts have had a difficult time developing a standard that distinguishes unlawful attempts to monopolize from normal competitive behavior. The standard that the courts have developed requires a showing of specific intent to monopolize along with a dangerous probability of success. However, the courts have no uniform definition for the terms *intent* or *success*. Cases suggest that the more market power a company has acquired, the less flagrant its attempt to monopolize must be.

Conspiracies to Monopolize Conspiracies to monopolize are unlawful under section two of the Sherman Act. This offense is rarely charged alone, because a conspiracy to monopolize is also a COMBINATION IN RESTRAINT OF TRADE, which violates section one of the Sherman Act.

In accordance with traditional conspiracy law, conspirators to monopolize are liable for the acts of each coconspirator, even their superiors and employees, if they are aware of and participate in the overall mission of the conspiracy. Conspirators who join in the conspiracy after it has already started are liable for every act during the course of the conspiracy, even those events that occurred before they joined.

CROSS-REFERENCES

Antitrust Law; Mergers and Acquisitions; Unfair Competition; Vertical Merger.

SHERMAN COMPROMISE The Philadelphia Convention convened in 1787 to discuss the establishment of a new federal government to replace the unsatisfactory system that existed under the ARTICLES OF CONFEDERATION.

Representatives from twelve of the thirteen

states attended the meeting; Rhode Island feared changes in the existing monetary system and refused to send delegates. One of the most pressing issues was the formation of a legislative body that would fairly represent the interests of the states.

ROGER SHERMAN of Connecticut proposed a plan known as the Sherman Compromise, or Connecticut Compromise. Sherman advocated a bicameral legislature with the two houses of Congress composed of members from all the states; the number of delegates to the House of Representatives would be determined by the population of each state, but each state would be equally represented in the Senate. The plan was accepted and is the basis for the congressional representation of today.

See also CONSTITUTION OF THE UNITED STATES.

SHIELD LAWS Statutes affording a privilege to journalists not to disclose in legal proceedings confidential information or sources of information obtained in their professional capacities.

Statutes that restrict or prohibit the use of certain EVIDENCE in sexual offense cases, such as evidence regarding the lack of chastity of the victim.

Journalist Shield Laws   Journalist shield laws, which afford news reporters the privilege to protect their sources, are controversial because the privilege must be balanced against a variety of competing government interests such as the right of the government to apprehend criminals and to prevent the impairment of GRAND JURY investigations. Still, most states have enacted such laws, based on the FIRST AMENDMENT guarantee of FREEDOM OF THE PRESS. However, there is no federal journalist shield law because the U.S. Supreme Court has refused to interpret the First Amendment as mandating a news reporter's privilege.

There is a long history behind the current state statutes that provide a privilege for journalists to protect the sources of their information. BENJAMIN FRANKLIN's older brother James was jailed for refusing to reveal the source of a story he published in his newspaper. The first reported case, however, was not until 1848 when a reporter was jailed for CONTEMPT of the Senate for refusing to disclose who had given him a copy of the secret proposed treaty to end the Mexican-American War (*Ex Parte Nugent*, 18 F. Cas. 471 [Cir. Ct. D.C.]). Similar conflicts between a reporter's desire to keep sources confidential and the demands of the courts or legislatures for disclosure continued throughout the nineteenth century. During the early 1900s,

journalists repeatedly were brought to the witness stand to reveal their sources in the growing number of news stories about labor unrest and municipal corruption.

These early conflicts led to the advancement of several legal theories that justified the reporter's refusal to disclose. For example, reporters maintained that they were acting pursuant to a journalistic code of ethics, that their employers would not let them reveal their sources, that they were relying on the privilege against SELF-INCRIMINATION, and that the forced disclosure of sources amounted to the taking of proprietary information. However, the courts did not widely accept any of these theories because the COMMON LAW did not recognize reporters' privilege.

Legislatures were more receptive to the journalists' plight, and the states began to enact privilege statutes, albeit slowly. In 1898 Maryland became the first state to enact such a privilege, and thirty-three years later, New Jersey was the second state to do so. By 1973 half of the states had followed suit. Legislatures enacted their statutes under various theories, such as the claim that the public interest in the free flow of information is useless without a journalist's right of access to information and that journalists must rely on confidential informants to gain access to information. Legislatures also accepted the argument that journalists are entitled to privilege rights in their professions, similar to those of doctors, lawyers, or clergy. Critics point out that the professional privilege of doctors, lawyers, or clergy belongs to the client, not the professional (it is the client's right to assert the privilege and withhold information), and that journalists are not in a service business like the other professionals who are afforded privileges. See also PRIVILEGED COMMUNICATION.

The states that did enact journalist shield laws generally enacted them in a hasty manner, resulting in many different types of laws that often did not provide the protection sought. For these reasons, journalists began to rely instead on the theory that the First Amendment freedom of the press supports the journalist privilege.

In the late 1960s, with the trial of the CHICAGO EIGHT, a group of antiwar activists, the reporters' privilege entered a new era of heightened public awareness and controversy. A large number of press SUBPOENAS was issued in that case, perhaps as a result of the growing adversarial stance taken by journalists who, during the VIETNAM WAR, had become increasingly skeptical of government officials. In 1972 in *Branzburg v. Hayes*, 408 U.S. 665, 92 S. Ct. 2646, 33 L. Ed. 2d 626, the U.S. Supreme Court held that news reporters do not have a right under the First Amendment to refuse to appear or TESTIFY before a grand jury. The Court stated that the burden on news-gathering in not allowing reporters' privilege was not sufficient to override the compelling PUBLIC INTEREST in law enforcement and effective grand jury proceedings. Lower courts that interpreted this decision did so narrowly—by limiting its scope to investigations before grand juries, for example. Other courts limited the effect of the *Branzburg* decision in other ways.

Following the Supreme Court decision, Congress in 1975 passed an evidentiary rule that has been interpreted to allow reporters to enjoy a qualified privilege against revealing their sources. That rule, Federal Rule of Evidence 501, simply upholds the applicable state law in federal cases where state law is to be applied. Legislative history behind the enactment of Federal Rule of Evidence 501 indicates that Congress intended it to provide qualified reporters' privilege. Still, a number of problems arise concerning the scope and application of this privilege.

One such dilemma is determining to whom the privilege applies. Unlike other privileged professionals, journalists are not licensed or certified in any manner that would make it easy to tell who can rely on the rule. Many state statutes attempt to define a newsperson as one who communicates via newspaper, is employed by a newspaper, or whose communication is classified as "news." The question then arises of whether books, magazine articles, or pamphlets are encompassed in the definition of a newspaper. Some of the broader state statutes do cover these media. Although as recently as 1949 no state statute protected TELEVISION or radio broadcasts, most of the statutes today do protect them, although some limit protection to "news" programs. Some courts have held that documentary films are included in the scope of the privilege protection.

Another question is how the term *news* is defined. The statutes seldom define this term, and some commentators are not convinced that an adequate definition can be devised. Presumably poetry or works of fiction are not news, but it is a more difficult question when considering sensationalism or gossip. Some legal scholars advocate avoiding consideration of the supposed worth of the communication and making the privilege available to those who generally acquire information for public dissemination.

Another important issue that arises under state statutes that protect only the journalist's sources is whether a "source" can only be a human informant or whether it can include a book, document, tape recording, or photograph. These and many other issues have led to varying court decisions based on the particular state statute and facts before the court.

Rape Shield Laws   In the context of criminal SEX OFFENSES, rape shield laws forbid certain evidence in the trial that is believed to be prejudicial and harassing. These statutes are called rape shield laws because they first originated in the context of RAPE cases.

Under the common law in England and the United States up until the 1970s, evidence of a rape victim's past sexual conduct was broadly admissible and accepted in every rape case. It was believed that if a rape victim consented to sex in the past, she was more likely to have consented to the sexual acts that she claimed amounted to rape. This evidence was also admitted under the theory that a woman's past sexual history could be important in assessing her credibility as a WITNESS. The common-law rules discouraged women from complaining of the offenses for fear they would be embarrassed and humiliated at trial.

Great efforts at reforming these rules gained momentum in the 1970s. These efforts were very successful, and within little over a decade every JURISDICTION in the United States had reformed its laws to prohibit those two broad uses of a woman's past sexual history. Special evidentiary rules were enacted on the state and federal level to protect the PRIVACY of the victim, encourage rape victims to report offenses and participate in the prosecution of offenses, and prevent distracting and highly prejudicial inquiries into such matters at trial.

Typical rape shield laws provide that in a prosecution for rape, attempted rape, or CONSPIRACY to commit rape, reputation or opinion evidence of the alleged victim's prior sexual conduct is not ADMISSIBLE. Evidence of specific instances of the victim's prior sexual conduct is also inadmissible except in the following circumstances: (1) the evidence regards the sexual conduct between the victim and the defendant and is introduced to show CONSENT; (2) the evidence is introduced to prove an alternate source or origin of semen, disease, or pregnancy; (3) the evidence regards the immediate surrounding circumstances of the alleged crime; or (4) the evidence of previously chaste character is necessary to the successful prosecution of the particular criminal charge. The procedure involved in introducing evidence covered by rape shield laws is also fairly typical. Generally the defendant must make a MOTION supported by an offer of proof in which the defendant details what evidence he wishes to introduce and why. The court will generally require that a HEARING be held out of the presence of the jury to review the motion and hear arguments in support of and against the motion. If the court finds some of the evidence admissible pursuant to one of the exceptions under the applicable laws, an order must be issued stating the scope of the evidence that may be admitted.

Rape shield laws have expanded to include other evidence that legislatures deem prejudicial, such as clothing of the victim that the defendant tries to introduce to show that the victim consented to or asked for the sexual contact. Those state statutes that do restrict the admissibility of clothing, however, make exceptions where it is introduced to show a struggle (or lack thereof) or proof of the presence (or absence) of bodily fluid such as semen or blood. Rape shield laws have also been expanded in most states to protect victims of all different sexual offenses, regardless of the victim's age or sex.

Defendants have challenged the constitutionality of rape shield laws on many occasions, generally arguing that the laws violate their right to DUE PROCESS and their right to confront their accuser. However, the constitutionality of these laws has consistently been upheld. Specifically, courts have held that the state's interest in protecting sexual assault victims from harassment and humiliation at trial, as well as the highly prejudicial effect such evidence may have on a jury, outweighs the rights of the defendant that may be implicated.

SHIFTING THE BURDEN OF PROOF

The process of transferring the obligation to affirmatively prove a fact in controversy or an issue brought during a lawsuit from one party in a legal controversy to the other party.

When the individual upon whom the burden of proof initially rested has brought evidence that tends to prove a particular fact or issue, the other party then takes on the duty to rebut such fact or issue through the use of defensive or contradictory EVIDENCE.

SHIPPING LAW

The area of maritime law that is concerned with ships and the individuals employed in or around them, as well as the shipment of goods by merchant vessels.

U.S. shipping law is a complex body of customs, legislation, international treaties, and court decisions dealing with the rights and responsibilities of ownership and operation of vessels that travel on the high seas. Much of the commercial law surrounding transportation of GOODS by ship involves contractual agreements between the shipowner and the party wishing to ship the goods. However, these agreements generally are based on long-standing customs and business practices peculiar to the shipping industry.

Registration and Ownership A sovereign nation has the authority to regulate all vessels that fly its flag on the high seas. Congress, accordingly, is empowered to enact legislation controlling domestic merchant ships that sail the high seas. Title 46 of the United States Code Annotated, entitled Shipping, contains most of the pertinent federal laws regarding U.S. shipping.

All the ships in the U.S. merchant fleet are registered in the United States and completely staffed by U.S. citizens. Because of the higher labor costs associated with employing U.S. personnel, many ships are registered in other countries to avoid this labor requirement.

Ships can be owned by either one person or co-owners. Because of the enormous cost of merchant vessels, the majority are held by more than one owner. A BILL OF SALE is the ordinary evidence of TITLE to, and ownership of, a vessel. Between co-owners, the right to control and use the vessel is generally reserved for the majority interest. In the event that co-owners absolutely cannot come to an agreement on how to use the vessel, one or more of them may obtain a court DECREE for sale of it. In general,

The use of ships for the movement of goods between nations continues to rise with the growth of international trade, bringing new issues and developments in the area of shipping law.

STEVE WELSH/LIAISON INTERNATIONAL

however, a part owner shares in the profits and expenses from use of the ship in proportion to her interest.

Agents The owners of merchant vessels are bound by the acts of their agents and must pay for all services, supplies, and repairs that they order. A ship's husband is the general AGENT of the owner for affairs conducted in the home port of the vessel. Generally known as the managing owner, he determines that the ship is prepared for navigation and commercial use. In the absence of express authority, a ship's husband usually is powerless to bind the co-owners for money borrowed on the account of the vessel. He is entitled to be reimbursed for services rendered and to be paid for expenditures incurred.

Shipping Contracts The great majority of CONTRACTS governing the transportation of goods by ships are made either by bills of lading or charter parties. The term *charter party* is a corruption of the Latin *carta partita*, or "divided charter." It is used to describe three types of contracts dealing with the use of ships owned or controlled by others. Under a demise charter, the shipowner gives possession of the vessel to the charterer, who engages the ship's master and crew, arranges for repairs and supplies, takes on the cargo, and acts much like the owner during the term of the charter.

A more common arrangement is the time charter. In this arrangement, the shipowner employs the master and crew, and the charterer only acquires the right, within contractual limits, to direct the movements of the ship and decide what cargoes are to be transported during the charter period. Under both demise and time charters, the charterer pays "charter hire" for the use of the ship at a specified daily or monthly rate.

The third type is the voyage charter, which is a contract of affreightment, or carriage. Essentially, a voyage charter is a contract to rent all or part of the cargo space of a merchant vessel on one voyage or a series of voyages. When a charterer contracts for only a portion of the cargo space, the governing contract is called a space charter. Under a voyage charter, it is customary for the master or her agent to issue a BILL OF LADING to the shipper, who is usually the charterer. However, the voyage charter remains the governing contract.

A bill of lading is an acknowledgment, by the master or owner, that serves as confirmation of the receipt of the goods specified to be taken aboard the vessel. Each charterer is entitled to receive a bill of lading from the shipowner or an agent of the owner. In ordinary transactions, a

Twenty Largest Merchant Fleets in the World in 1993
Vessels of 1,000 gross tons and over. As of January 1 of the following year.

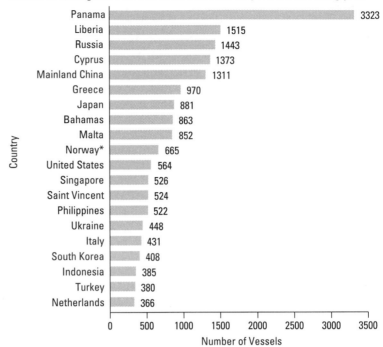

*International Shipping Registry which is an open registry under which the ship flies the flag of the specified nation but is exempt from certain taxation and other regulations.

Source: U.S. Maritime Administration, *Merchant Fleets of the World,* summary report, annual.

bill of lading, signed by the master, is binding upon the owner of a vessel. It can circumvent disputes that might otherwise arise over whether goods were ever received and their condition when placed upon the vessel.

Ocean bills of lading are usually in order form, calling for DELIVERY of the order to the shipper or some other designated party. This type of bill of lading may be negotiated similarly to a CHECK, DRAFT, or NEGOTIABLE INSTRUMENT, which means that a BONA FIDE purchaser of the bill of lading takes it free and clear of any defects not appearing on its face. A bona fide purchaser is one who has purchased PROPERTY for VALUE without any notice of any defects in the TITLE of the seller. Therefore, if cargo is externally damaged on shipment but the damage is not recorded on the bill of lading, the carrier will be barred from establishing that the cargo was damaged before it came into the carrier's CUSTODY. Once a bill of lading issued under a voyage charter is negotiated to a bona fide purchaser, it becomes the governing contract between the carrier and the holder of the bill.

When a ship strands or collides with another vessel, cargo loss or damage may occur. If the damage was caused by a sea peril or an error in navigation, the carrier will not be liable if the goods were being carried under a statutory or contractual provision based on the 1923 Brussels Convention on Limitation on Liability. If, however, the damage was caused by the carrier's failure to exercise due diligence to make the ship seaworthy and to ensure that it was properly staffed, equipped, and supplied, the carrier will be held responsible.

Under the Carriage of Goods by Sea Act (46 U.S.C.A. § 1300 et seq. [1936]), a "clause paramount" must be included in any bill of lading involving a contract for transportation of goods by sea from U.S. ports in foreign trade. This clause states that the bill of lading is subject to the act, which governs the rights, obligations, and liabilities of the issuer to the holder of the bill of lading in regard to the loss or damage of goods.

Maritime Liens When a ship is charged with a maritime TORT, or when services have been rendered to it to facilitate its use in navigation and the shipowner has not paid for the services, a MARITIME LIEN can be placed on the ship. A maritime lien is a special PROPERTY RIGHT in a ship given to a CREDITOR by law as security for a DEBT or CLAIM. The ship may be sold and the debt paid out of the proceeds.

The Maritime Lien Act (46 U.S.C.A. §§ 971–975 [1920]) provides that an ACTION can be brought IN REM, against the vessel, cargo, or FREIGHT itself. Under the act, the ship is personified to the extent that it may sometimes be held responsible under circumstances in which the shipowner would not be liable. For example, where a state law requires that a local PILOT guide the ship in and out of the harbor, the pilot's NEGLIGENCE is not imputed to the shipowner. In rem proceedings allow the ship itself to be charged with the pilot's fault and make it subject to a maritime lien enforceable in court.

In an in rem proceeding, the vessel, cargo, or freight can be arrested and kept in the custody of the court unless the owner posts a BOND or some other security. Usually the owner posts security to avoid an arrest, and the property is never taken into custody. Where the owner fails to post security and the plaintiff is awarded a JUDGMENT against the vessel, the court will order that the property be sold or the freight released to satisfy the judgment.

Marine Insurance Marine INSURANCE plays an important role in the shipping industry and in shipping law. Most shipowners carry hull insurance on their ships and protect themselves against claims by third parties by purchasing "protection and indemnity" insurance. Cargo is usually insured against the perils of the sea, which are defined as natural accidents peculiar to the sea. For example, storms, waves, and all types of actions caused by wind and water are classified as perils of the sea. If a shipowner or cargo owner wishes to be protected against losses incurred from WAR, the owner must purchase separate war-risk insurance or pay an additional PREMIUM to include war RISK in the basic policy.

Salvage In shipping law, SALVAGE is the compensation allowed to persons who voluntarily assist in saving a vessel or its cargo from impending or actual PERIL from the sea. Generally salvage is limited to vessels and their cargoes, or to property lost in the sea or other NAVIGABLE WATERS, that have been subsequently found and rescued. Except for salvage performed under contract, the rescuer, known as the salvor, must act voluntarily without being under any legal duty to do so. As long as the owner or the owner's agent remains on the ship, unwanted offers of salvage may be refused. Typical acts of salvage include releasing ships that have run aground or on reefs, raising sunken ships or their cargo, or putting out fires.

The salvor has a maritime lien on the salvaged property, in an amount determined by a court based on the facts and circumstances of the case. The salvor may retain the property until the claim is satisfied or until security to meet an award is given. The owner may elect to pay salvage money to the salvor or to not reclaim the property.

Shipping law requires shipowners to provide a safe environment for workers who load and unload cargo.

ALLEN MCINNIS/LIAISON INTERNATIONAL

General Average Under the law of general average, if cargo is jettisoned in a successful effort to refloat a grounded vessel, the owners of the vessel and the cargo saved are required to absorb a proportionate share of the loss to compensate the owner of the cargo that has been singled out for sacrifice. All participants in the maritime venture contribute to offset the losses incurred. The law of general average became an early form of marine insurance.

The York-Antwerp Rules of General Average establish the rights and obligations of the parties when cargo must be jettisoned from a ship. These uniform rules on the law of general average are included in private shipping agreements and depend on voluntary acceptance by the maritime community. The rules are incorporated by reference into most bills of lading, contracts of affreightment, and marine insurance policies.

The rules provide for the shipowner to recover the costs of repair, loading and unloading cargo, and maintaining the crew, if these expenses are necessary for the safe completion of the voyage. Claims are generally made against the insurer of the cargo and the shipowner's insurance underwriters.

Personal Tort Liability Until 1920, U.S. seapersons who were injured or killed as a result of negligence by a shipowner, master, or a fellow seaperson had a difficult time obtaining compensation through a tort action. Shipowners often defeated such actions by claiming contributory negligence on the injured seaperson's part. In addition, under federal law the seaperson did not have a right to a jury trial.

Congress enacted the JONES ACT of 1920 (46 U.S.C.A. § 688) to correct these problems. It granted the seaperson a right to a jury trial and abolished the contributory negligence defense. Under the act, an injured seaperson or a PERSONAL REPRESENTATIVE in the event of the seaperson's death can sue the shipowner if the injury or death occurred in the course of the seaperson's employment on, or in connection with, a vessel.

In addition, Congress granted rights to those persons who work near ships in the Longshoremen's and Harbor Workers' Compensation Act of 1927 (33 U.S.C.A. §§ 901–910). This act established a federal system to compensate maritime workers for work-related injuries.

CROSS-REFERENCES

Admiralty and Maritime Law; Carriers; Collision; Common Carrier.

BIOGRAPHY

George Shiras, Jr.

"... TO DECLARE UNLAWFUL RESIDENCE WITHIN THE COUNTRY TO BE AN INFAMOUS CRIME, PUNISHABLE BY DEPRIVATION OF LIBERTY AND PROPERTY ... [WITHOUT] A JUDICIAL TRIAL ... IS NOT CONSISTENT WITH THE THEORY OF OUR GOVERNMENT."

SHIRAS, GEORGE, JR. George Shiras, Jr., served on the U.S. Supreme Court as an associate justice from 1892 to 1903. Plucked by political necessity at the age of sixty from his highly successful law practice, Shiras, who had never been a judge or politician, brought a lawyerly, pragmatic perspective to the Court. He wrote some opinions in favor of civil liberties, occasionally blocked the Court's full embrace of laissez-faire economics, and became notorious as the justice whose vote in 1895 torpedoed the new federal INCOME TAX. This last decision, for which Shiras was incorrectly blamed, ultimately led to the ratification of the SIXTEENTH AMENDMENT in 1913.

Shiras was born in Pittsburgh, Pennsylvania, on January 26, 1832, to a wealthy brewing family. He attended Yale Law School in 1853. Two years later he completed his training at a law office in Allegheny County, Pennsylvania, before starting a legal practice with his brother. The practice specialized in representing the railroads and other big industries during the boom era of Pittsburgh. So successful was Shiras that, by the late 1880s, he was earning the then-phenomenal income of $75,000 annually. He developed no national reputation, steering clear of partisan politics even when the state legislature nominated him for a senate seat. Independent in nature, he sometimes represented interests opposed to his business clients.

In 1892 President BENJAMIN HARRISON nominated Shiras to fill the vacancy on the Supreme Court left by the death of Justice JOSEPH P. BRADLEY. Like Bradley, Shiras was a Pennsylva-

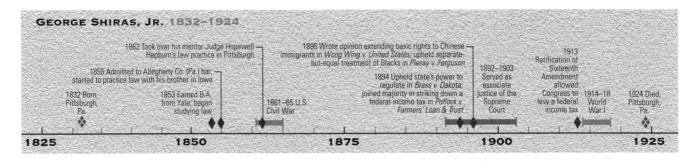

GEORGE SHIRAS, JR. 1832–1924

1832 Born, Pittsburgh, Pa.

1853 Earned B.A. from Yale; began studying law

1855 Admitted to Allegheny Co. (Pa.) bar; started to practice law with his brother in Iowa

1862 Took over his mentor Judge Hopewell Hepburn's law practice in Pittsburgh

1861–65 U.S. Civil War

1894 Upheld state's power to regulate in *Brass v. Dakota*; joined majority in striking down a federal income tax in *Pollock v. Farmers' Loan & Trust*

1896 Wrote opinion extending basic rights to Chinese immigrants in *Wong Wing v. United States*; upheld separate-but-equal treatment of Blacks in *Plessy v. Ferguson*

1892–1903 Served as associate justice of the Supreme Court

1913 Ratification of Sixteenth Amendment allowed Congress to levy a federal income tax

1914–18 World War I

1924 Died, Pittsburgh, Pa.

1825　1850　1875　1900　1925

nia Republican, and convention dictated that Bradley's replacement be of similar political and geographic origin. Thus for political reasons Shiras was a good choice, even though he had no judicial or political experience. Strong opposition to the nomination came from the president's enemies. But support from powerful, private figures, including Andrew Carnegie, was ultimately persuasive.

When Shiras joined the Court, the chief issue of the day was regulation of business. The Court was conservative, believing in the hands-off policy of laissez-faire economics. Shiras usually joined his fellow justices in voting to restrict antitrust and labor legislation. But he occasionally stood apart, as in *Brass v. North Dakota*, 153 U.S. 391, 14 S. Ct. 857, 38 L. Ed. 757 (1894), where he upheld state power to regulate. Moreover, he was committed to civil liberties. In *Wong Wing v. United States*, 163 U.S. 228, 16 S. Ct. 977, 41 L. Ed. 140 (1896), he wrote a landmark opinion extending basic rights to Chinese immigrants; it held that Congress had unconstitutionally allowed federal authorities to summarily sentence illegal Chinese aliens to twelve months of hard labor without INDICTMENT or a JURY trial.

In his lifetime, Shiras became notorious for having cast the swing vote to kill the first peacetime federal income tax. The tax, passed in 1894, was a popular response to the growing disparity in income levels caused by industrial growth. The case was *Pollock v. Farmers' Loan & Trust*, 158 U.S. 601, 15 S. Ct. 912, 39 L. Ed. 1108, decided in three parts in 1895. The final vote, on May 20, was 5–4 against. Critics vilified Shiras for apparently changing his mind from an earlier vote. For nearly three decades, his reputation suffered until, after his death, it was persuasively argued that another justice had provided the swing vote. *Pollock* led directly to the ratification of the Sixteenth Amendment in 1913, allowing Congress to levy a federal income tax.

Shiras stepped down from the Court in 1903 at age seventy. He died on August 2, 1924, in Pittsburgh.

See also POLLOCK V. FARMERS' LOAN & TRUST CO.

SHOCK-THE-CONSCIENCE TEST A determination of whether a state agent's actions fall outside the standards of civilized decency.

The U.S. Supreme Court established the "shock-the-conscience test" in *Rochin v. California*, 342 U.S. 165, 72 S. Ct. 205, 96 L. Ed. 183 (1952). Based on the Fourteenth Amendment's prohibition against states depriving any person of "life, liberty, or property without due process of law," the test prohibits conduct by state agents that falls outside the standards of civilized decency. Little used since the 1960s, the test has been criticized for permitting judges to assert their subjective views on what constitutes "shocking."

The *Rochin* decision was made during an era when the Supreme Court still adhered to the precedent that the Bill of Rights applied only to actions by the federal government. Thus, all the rights afforded federal criminal defendants in the Fourth, Fifth, and Sixth amendments were not available to state criminal defendants. This reading made the Due Process Clause of the Fourteenth Amendment difficult to apply to state actions.

The Supreme Court, in *Twining v. New Jersey*, 211 U.S. 78, 29 S. Ct. 14, 53 L. Ed. 97 (1908), concluded that some of the rights contained in the Bill of Rights "are of such a nature that they are included [with]in the conception of due process of law" and are applicable to the states. But succeeding generations of justices had difficulty defining a test that would reveal which rights were important enough to apply to state and local government. In 1937 the Court considered whether a right was "of the very essence of a scheme of ordered liberty" or "implicit in the concept of ordered liberty" (*Palko v. Connecticut*, 302 U.S. 319, 58 S. Ct. 149, 82 L. Ed. 288). Only those rights that were found "fundamental" or "implicit in the concept of ordered liberty" were made applicable to prevent state action.

In *Rochin* three state law enforcement officers, acting on information that Antonio Rochin was selling narcotics, illegally entered Rochin's room. When the officers noticed two capsules on a bedside table, Rochin grabbed the capsules and put them in his mouth. The three officers then wrestled with Rochin and sought to open his mouth so they could extract the pills. When this failed, the officers handcuffed Rochin and took him to a hospital, where at their direction a doctor forced an emetic solution through a tube into Rochin's stomach. The solution induced vomiting, and in the vomited matter the deputies found two morphine capsules. Rochin was convicted of narcotics possession. The conviction was based solely on the morphine capsules, which Rochin had vainly sought to have suppressed as evidence.

Justice Felix Frankfurter, writing for the Court, held that such conduct by state agents, although not specifically prohibited by explicit language in the Constitution, "shocks the conscience" in that it offends "those canons of decency and fairness which express the notions of justice of English-speaking peoples." Due process of law requires the state to observe those principles that are "so rooted in the traditions and conscience of our people as to be ranked as fundamental."

The Court reasoned that to permit the use of such capsules as evidence under the circumstances would "afford brutality the cloak of law." The officers' conduct "shocks the conscience," offending even those with "hardened sensibilities. They are methods too close to the rack and screw to permit of constitutional differentiation." Therefore, the Court reversed Rochin's conviction because the stomach pumping violated the Due Process Clause.

Since *Rochin*, the Supreme Court has made most of the rights enumerated in the first eight amendments also applicable to state action by selectively incorporating them, one by one, into the scope of the Fourteenth Amendment's Due Process Clause. Justices Hugo L. Black and William O. Douglas, who, in their concurring opinions in *Rochin*, had argued for incorporation of the Fourth Amendment, were instrumental in diminishing the importance of the shock-the-conscience test. They believed that the test was too general and that its vagueness allowed judges to apply their subjective judgment as to what was shocking and what offended the Due Process Clause.

Nevertheless, *Rochin* remains important because it stands for the proposition that the Due Process Clause provides a protection for persons separate from, and independent of, the Bill of Rights provisions that have now been applied to the states.

SHOP-BOOK RULE 📖 A doctrine that allows the admission into EVIDENCE of books that consist of original entries made in the normal course of a business, which are introduced to the court from proper custody upon general authentication. 📖

In the law of evidence, the shop-book rule is one of several exceptions to the rule against HEARSAY.

SHOPLIFTING 📖 Theft of merchandise from a store or business establishment. 📖

Although the crime of shoplifting may be prosecuted under general LARCENY statutes, most JURISDICTIONS have established a specific category for shoplifting. Statutes vary widely, but generally the elements of shoplifting are (1) willfully taking POSSESSION of or concealing unpurchased GOODS that are offered for sale (2) with the intention of converting the merchandise to the taker's personal use without paying the purchase price. Possession or concealment of goods typically encompasses actions both on and outside the premises.

Concealment is generally understood in terms of common usage. Therefore, covering an object to keep it from sight constitutes concealment, as would other methods of hiding an object from a shop owner. A shopper's actions and demeanor in the store, her lack of money to pay for merchandise, and the placement of an object out of a retailer's direct view are all examples of CIRCUMSTANTIAL EVIDENCE that may establish INTENT.

Shoplifting costs businesses billions of dollars every year. To enable store owners to recoup some of their losses, most states have enacted civil recovery or civil demand statutes. These laws enable retailers to seek restitution from shoplifters. Criminal prosecution is not a prerequisite to a civil demand request. Typically, a representative of or attorney for a victimized business demands a statutorily set compensation in a letter to the offender. If an offender does not respond favorably to the civil demand letter, the retailer may bring an ACTION in SMALL CLAIMS COURT or another appropriate FORUM.

To forestall any ALLEGATIONS of COERCION, many companies initiate civil recovery proceedings only after the shoplifter has been released from the store's CUSTODY. It is a criminal offense to threaten prosecution if a civil demand is not paid. Moreover, if a store accuses a customer of shoplifting and the individual is acquitted or if a store makes an erroneous detention, the store may face claims of FALSE IMPRISONMENT, EXTORTION, DEFAMATION, or intentional or negligent infliction of emotional distress.

SHOP STEWARD 📖 A labor union official elected to represent members in a plant or particular department. The shop steward's duties include collection of dues, recruitment of new members, and initial negotiations for settlement of grievances. 📖

See also LABOR UNION.

SHORT CAUSE 📖 A legal matter that will not take up a significant amount of the time of the court and may be entered on the list of short causes upon application of one of the parties, where it will be dealt with more expediently than it would be in its regular order. 📖

The time permitted for a short cause, which is also known as a short calendar, varies from one court to another.

SHORT SALE 📖 A method of gaining profit from an anticipated decline in the price of a STOCK. 📖

An individual who sells short sells either stock or securities that he or she does not own and that are not immediately ready for delivery.

Generally the seller borrows the shares needed to cover the sale from a BROKER and then delivers these shares to the buyer. The seller deposits an amount that is equal to the value of the borrowed shares with the broker. This amount stays on deposit with the broker until the stock is returned. The seller must ultimately return the same number of shares of the same stock to the broker, and the transaction is not fully executed until the stock is returned. The broker lending the stock is entitled to all the benefits he or she would have received if the stock had not been lent. When a DIVIDEND is paid, then the seller-borrower is required to pay the broker-lender an amount equal to the dividend.

SHOW CAUSE 📖 An order by a court that requires a party to appear and to provide reasons why a particular thing should not be performed or allowed and mandates such party to meet the prima facie case set forth in the COMPLAINT or AFFIDAVIT of the applicant. 📖

A show cause order mandates that an individual or CORPORATION make a court appearance to explain why the court should not take a proposed action. In the event that such individual or corporation does not appear or provide adequate reasons why the court should take no action, action will be taken by the court.

SHOW CAUSE ORDER 📖 A court order, made upon the motion of an applicant, that requires a party to appear and provide reasons why the court should not perform or not allow a particular action and mandates this party to meet the prima facie case set forth in the complaint or affidavit of the applicant. 📖

A show cause order, also called an order to show cause, mandates that an individual or corporation make a court appearance to explain why the court should not take a proposed action. A court issues this type of order upon the application of a party requesting specific relief and providing the court with an affidavit or declaration (a sworn or affirmed statement alleging certain facts). A show cause order is generally used in contempt actions, cases involving injunctive relief, and situations where time is of the essence.

A show cause order can be viewed as an accelerated motion. A motion is an application to the court for an order that seeks answers to questions that are collateral to the main object of the action. For example, in a civil lawsuit the plaintiff generally requests from the defendant documents pertinent to the case. If the defendant refuses to provide the documents or does not make a timely response to the request, the plaintiff may file a motion with the court asking that it issue an order to compel the defendant to produce the documents.

A show cause order is similar to a motion but it can produce a court order on the requested relief much more quickly than a motion can. For example, after a motion is served on the opposing party, that party has a certain number of days under the jurisdiction's rules of civil procedure to prepare a response. A show cause order is submitted to a judge, who reads the applicant's papers and decides the deadline for the responding party's submission of papers. The judge may order an opposing party to

A sample show cause order

> [*Title of Court and Cause*]
>
> Upon the annexed affidavit of _____ , verified the _____ day of _____ , 19_____ , and _____ [*enumerate other moving papers*], and on all the proceedings heretofore had herein, let the plaintiff [*or* "defendant" *or as the case may be*] show cause, if any he has, before the undersigned, one of the judges of the District Court of the _____ District of _____ , at his chambers in the _____ building in the city of _____ [*or* "at a term of this court to be held at the courthouse in _____ , on the _____ day of _____ , 19_____"], at _____ o'clock in the forenoon [*or* "afternoon"] of that day, or as soon thereafter as counsel can be heard, why a rule or order should not be made and entered permitting _____ to _____ [*or as the case may be*].
>
> [In the meantime, and until the hearing and determination of this order to show cause, let all proceedings on the part of _____ , his attorneys and agents, for _____ , be stayed.]
>
> Service of this order and the papers on which it is granted on _____ on or before the _____ day of _____ , 19_____ , shall be deemed sufficient.
>
> Dated _____ , 19_____ .
>
> _____
> District Judge

appear "forthwith" in urgent cases. The judge may hear arguments on the matter at some place other than the courthouse, if necessary, and may allow papers to be served on opposing parties by a method not ordinarily permitted.

A judge may include in the show cause order a temporary restraining order or stay that maintains the status quo as long as the matter is pending before the court. At the hearing on the show cause order, if the responding party fails to rebut the prima facie case (evidence sufficient to establish a fact if uncontradicted) made by the applicant, the court will grant the relief sought by the applicant.

SHOW-UP 📖 The live presentation of a criminal suspect to a victim or WITNESS of a crime. 📖

A show-up usually occurs immediately or shortly after a crime has occurred. If law enforcement personnel see a person who they suspect is the perpetrator of a very recent crime, the officers may apprehend the suspect and bring him back to the scene of the crime and show him to witnesses, or the officers may take the suspect to a police station and bring the witnesses to the station. This method of identification of a criminal suspect is a legitimate tool of law enforcement and is encumbered by few judicial restraints.

The U.S. Supreme Court has ruled that an unnecessarily suggestive identification procedure is a violation of DUE PROCESS (*Stovall v. Denno*, 388 U.S. 293, 87 S. Ct. 1967, 18 L. Ed. 2d 1199 [1967]). EVIDENCE from such an identification should be excluded from a trial of the suspect. A show-up is inherently suggestive because police generally do not present to a witness a person who they believe is innocent of wrongdoing. Nevertheless, show-ups do not violate due process if they are conducted near the scene of the crime and shortly after the crime was committed.

Show-ups are a valuable and practical tool in apprehending criminals. If a witness affirmatively identifies a suspect as the perpetrator of a crime, police can detain the suspect without delay to serve the interests of public safety. If a witness fails to identify the subject of a show-up as the perpetrator, the show-up will result in the quick release of the innocent suspect and allow police to redirect their efforts.

A show-up should be conducted shortly after a crime has been committed. If police do not apprehend a suspect until the next day, or several days or weeks afterward, they will have time to conduct a traditional, in-person LINEUP. One exception is when a traditional lineup is impractical. For example, if the sole witness to a crime is bedridden and approaching death, police may bring the suspect to the victim even if the crime occurred several days before the show-up (*Stovall*).

A show-up should not be performed for a witness unless the witness has displayed an ability to make a clear identification of the perpetrator of the crime. A show-up for a witness who cannot cite any identifying characteristics of the perpetrator may be unnecessarily suggestive and may be excluded from a subsequent trial of the suspect.

Because a show-up generally involves detention of a criminal suspect, police must have a REASONABLE suspicion that the suspect committed a crime before subjecting the suspect to a show-up. This is a low level of certainty and need only be supported by enough articulable facts to lead a reasonable officer to believe that the suspect may have committed a crime.

See also CRIMINAL LAW; CRIMINAL PROCEDURE.

SIC 📖 *Latin, In such manner; so; thus.* 📖

A misspelled or incorrect word in a quotation followed by "[sic]" indicates that the error appeared in the original source.

SICK CHICKEN CASE See SCHECHTER POULTRY CORP. V. UNITED STATES.

SIGHT DRAFT 📖 A COMMERCIAL PAPER that is payable upon presentment. 📖

When a DRAFT or BILL OF EXCHANGE is payable at sight, money may be immediately collected

A sample sight draft

$_____   [*City, State*] _____ , 19_____
At sight (*or* on presentation; *or* on demand) pay to the order of _____ (*or* to bearer) _____ dollars at _____ .

To _____   _____
    Name of Drawee   Signature of Drawer

upon presentment to the DRAWEE named in the instrument.

SIGNATURE 📖 A mark or sign made by an individual on an INSTRUMENT or document to signify knowledge, approval, acceptance, or obligation. 📖

The term *signature* is generally understood to mean the signing of a written document with one's own hand. However, it is not critical that a signature actually be written by hand for it to be legally valid. It may, for example, be type-written, engraved, or stamped. A signature consists of the act of writing one's name, coupled with the intention of authenticating the instrument or document signed. The purpose of a signature is to authenticate a writing, or provide notice of its source, and to bind the individual signing the writing by the provisions contained in the document.

Because a signature can obligate a party to terms of a CONTRACT or verify that the person intended to make a last WILL and testament, the law has developed rules that govern what constitutes a legally valid signature. The INTERNET and other forms of telecommunication have created the desire to transact legally binding agreements electronically. Some states are beginning to pass laws that recognize the validity of "digital signatures."

Requisites and Validity When an instrument must be signed, it is ordinarily adequate if the signature is made in any commonly used manner. Variations between the signature and the name appearing in the body of the instrument do not automatically invalidate the instrument.

In the absence of a statutory prohibition, an individual can use any character, symbol, figure, or designation he wishes to adopt as a signature, and if he uses it as a substitute for his name, he is bound by it. For example, if a contract refers to "William Jones" but Jones signs his name "Bill Jones," the contract is still enforceable against him. An individual can also use a fictitious name or the name of a business firm. A signature might also be adequate to validate an instrument even if it is virtually illegible. The entire name does not have to be written, and the inclusion of a middle name is not significant.

An individual satisfies the signing requirement when someone who has been duly authorized to sign for him does so. In the event a statute mandates an instrument be signed in person, the signature must be made in the signer's own hand or at his request and in his presence by another individual.

In a situation where an individual intends to sign as a WITNESS but instead inadvertently signs the instrument in the place where the principal is to sign, the fact that she should have signed as a witness can be shown. Conversely when a signer intends to sign as a principal but instead signs in the place for a witness, that fact can also be shown.

Abbreviations, Initials, or Mark In situations that do not require a more complete signature, an instrument can be properly signed when the initial letter or letters of the given name or names are used together with the surname (J. Doe), when only the full surname is used (Doe), when only the given name is used (John), or even when only the initials are used (J. D.).

A mark is ordinarily a cross or *X* made in substitution for the signature of an individual who is unable to write. In the absence of contrary statutory provision, a mark can be used by an individual who knows how to write but is unable to do so because of a physical illness or disability. A mark has the same binding effect upon the individual making it as does a signature. In some statutes a signature is defined as including a mark made by an individual who is infirm or illiterate.

Generally the name of the person who makes her mark can be written by anyone, and the mark is not necessarily invalidated because the individual writing the name accompanying the mark misspells the name or because the words stating that the symbol is intended as a mark are omitted. In the absence of a statute that requires a name to accompany the mark, the validity of the mark as a signature is not affected by the fact that a name does not accompany it.

When a mark is used as a signature, it can be put wherever the signature can appear. When there is a requirement that the name must accompany the mark, the fact that the mark and the name are not in immediate proximity does not invalidate the mark.

Certain statutes mandate that a witness must ATTEST to a signature made by a mark. Under such statutes, if the mark is not properly witnessed, the instrument is not signed and is legally ineffective. These laws were enacted to prevent FRAUD, because it is difficult, if not impossible, to later determine if the alleged signer actually made the mark.

Hand of Party or Another A signature can be written by the hand of the purported signer, either through the signer's unaided efforts or with the aid of another individual who guides the signer's pen or pencil. In cases when the maker's hand is guided or steadied, the signature is the maker's act, not the act of the assisting individual.

A signature can generally be made by one individual for another in her presence and at her direction, or with her assent, unless prohibited by statute. A signature that is made in this manner is valid, and the individual writing the name is regarded merely as an instrument through which the party whose signature is written exercises personal discretion and acts for herself.

Method Ordinarily a signature can be affixed in a number of different ways. It can be hand written, printed, stamped, typewritten, engraved, or photographed. This allows, for example, a business to issue its payroll checks with the signature of its financial officer stamped rather than handwritten.

Digital Signatures The computer and telecommunications have changed how work is done and how it is exchanged. Both business and the legal system have begun to explore ways of using the Internet and other forms of electronic communication to transact work. Court systems cannot permit the electronic filing of legal documents, however, unless the documents have been authenticated as coming from the sender. Similarly, businesses will not enter into contracts using the Internet or electronic mail unless they can authenticate that the other contracting party actually made the agreement. Computers and digital scanners can reproduce handwritten signatures, but they are susceptible to FORGERY.

A proposed solution is the legal recognition of "digital signatures." By 1997 five states had enacted laws that recognize the validity of digital signatures and thus bind parties to agreements or documents signed electronically.

A digital signature is based on cryptography, which uses mathematical formulas, or algorithms, to scramble messages. Using encryption and decryption software, the sender can scramble the message and the recipient can unscramble it. To affix a digital signature to an electronic document, a signer must obtain electronic "keys." The keys are assigned in pairs: a private key and a public key.

A person creates his keys using a software program. The digital signature is affixed to the electronic document using the private key. The "signer" types in a password, similar to a personal identification number for an automatic teller machine. The private key then generates a long string of numbers and letters that represent the digital signature, or public key. The recipient of the message runs a software program using this public key to authenticate that the document was signed by the private key and

that the document has not been altered during transmission.

It is mathematically infeasible for a person to derive another person's private key. The only way to compromise a digital signature is to give another person access to the signature software and the password to the private key.

See also AUTHENTICATION.

SIMPLE 📖 Unmixed; not aggravated or compounded. 📖

A simple ASSAULT, for example, is one that is not accompanied by any circumstances of AGGRAVATION, such as assault with a deadly weapon.

Simple interest is a fixed amount paid in exchange for a sum of money lent. The interest generated on the amount borrowed does not itself earn interest, unlike interest earned where parties agree to COMPOUND INTEREST.

SIMPSON, O. J. The criminal and civil trials of Orenthal James ("O. J.") Simpson, a former football star, actor, and television personality, regarding the MURDERS of his former wife, Nicole Brown Simpson, and Ronald Goldman, a local restaurant waiter, were two of the most controversial and highly publicized proceedings in U.S. legal history. The lengthy criminal trial, which ended in Simpson's ACQUITTAL for the two murders in October 1995, was nationally televised. In the civil trial, in which the ESTATES of the two murder victims sued Simpson for DAMAGES for the victims' WRONGFUL DEATHS, a JURY in February 1997 awarded the HEIRS of the victims a total of $33.5 million. In both proceedings, but especially in the criminal trial, the issue of race played a dominant role. Simpson, an African American, was portrayed by his attorneys as another victim of the racist beliefs and behavior of members of the Los Angeles Police Department (LAPD).

In the early hours of June 13, 1994, the bodies of Nicole Brown Simpson and Ronald Goldman were found lying in a pool of blood outside Nicole Simpson's Brentwood, California, condominium. Both victims had been brutally stabbed to death on the evening of June 12, but there were no eyewitnesses. After the slayings, Nicole Simpson's dog was found wandering around the upscale neighborhood with bloody paws.

Simpson voluntarily gave an interview to LAPD detectives the day after the murder. Five days after the murders, LAPD charged Simpson with the deaths, citing a trail of EVIDENCE they said linked the celebrity to the crime scene, including a bloody glove found outside the condominium that allegedly matched one found

APWIDE WORLD PHOTOS

The criminal trial of former football star and actor O. J. Simpson was among the most highly publicized trials in U.S. history. Simpson was acquitted of murder, but found guilty of wrongful death in a later, civil trial.

at Simpson's estate. On the day Simpson was to surrender to police, he and a friend, Al C. Cowlings, disappeared. Simpson left behind a note professing his love for Nicole, claiming his innocence, and implying that he would commit suicide. Police traced calls from Simpson's cellular phone, locating him in a vehicle traveling on a Los Angeles freeway. The ensuing slow-speed chase, which was nationally televised from helicopter cameras, ended back at Simpson's Brentwood home, where he was arrested.

Simpson's criminal trial began on January 25, 1995. He had assembled a team of lawyers that included ROBERT L. SHAPIRO, JOHNNIE L. COCHRAN, Jr., a leading Los Angeles defense attorney, F. LEE BAILEY, a nationally known criminal defense attorney, ALAN M. DERSHOWITZ, a Harvard law professor, Gerald F. Uelman, the dean of Stanford University Law School, and Barry Scheck and Peter J. Neufeld, New York attorneys skilled in handling DNA evidence. The group of PROSECUTORS from the Los Angeles county attorney's office was led by MARCIA R. CLARK and Christopher A. Darden. Presiding at the trial was Superior Court Judge Lance A. Ito.

In its OPENING STATEMENTS the prosecution argued that Simpson's history of DOMESTIC VIOLENCE against Nicole Brown Simpson showed a link to her murder. His pattern of abuse and his need to control his former wife culminated, according to Clark, in her murder, "the final and ultimate act of control." Goldman was

murdered, continued Clark, because he got in the way, arriving at the Brentwood condominium to return a pair of misplaced eyeglasses at the same time that Simpson was attacking Nicole Brown Simpson.

The defense team, which Cochran dominated, asserted that the LAPD fabricated the physical evidence and that Simpson had been on his way to a golf outing in Chicago when the crimes were committed.

The prosecution presented the TESTIMONY of neighbors in the vicinity of the murder scene and of a limousine driver who arrived early at Simpson's home that night to establish that Simpson had time to commit the murders and return home shortly after the driver arrived. It also introduced the "bloody glove" found behind Simpson's guest house, a glove that matched one found at the crime scene. The prosecution called DNA experts to testify that blood found at the crime scene matched Simpson's blood and that blood from both of the victims was found in Simpson's vehicle and on socks found in his bedroom. In addition, a bloody shoe print found at the crime scene appeared to match an expensive brand of shoes that Simpson had owned, but which could not be found.

The defense team aggressively challenged almost every prosecution WITNESS but leveled its harshest attacks on the credibility of the LAPD. Scheck attacked the way the blood and fiber evidence was collected and suggested that the police had used blood from a sample given by the defendant to concoct false evidence. Scheck and Neufeld also challenged the credibility of the prosecution's DNA experts, subjecting the jury to weeks of highly technical discussion of DNA analysis.

The defense also argued that the police had rushed to judgment that Simpson was the prime suspect. Cochran and Bailey cross-examined the police officers who had gone to Simpson's home early on the morning after the murders. These officers had not sought a SEARCH WARRANT but went into the residence based on the belief that Simpson himself might have been the target of the murderer. The defense challenged this justification and attempted to show that one of the officers, Mark Fuhrman, was a racist who planted the bloody glove that morning. Events in the trial confirmed that Fuhrman had lied under oath when he said he had not said the word "nigger" in the past ten years. As the prosecution case proceeded, the defense used every opportunity to demonstrate to the predominantly African American jury that the police had engaged in a CONSPIRACY to frame Simpson.

The dramatic point of the trial was the prosecution's request that Simpson try on the bloody gloves. Simpson, wearing thin plastic gloves, strained to pull on the leather gloves and announced that they were too small and did not fit. This proved to be a damaging incident for the prosecution. In his closing argument, Cochran repeatedly stated, "If the gloves don't fit, you must acquit."

In October 1995, after 266 days of trial, the jury found Simpson not guilty of the murders. Cochran, in his CLOSING ARGUMENT, had implored the jury to acquit Simpson and send a message to the LAPD and white America that African Americans should not be the victims of a racist police and justice system. According to opinion polls, his argument sounded a strong chord in African Americans, because a majority of them believed that Simpson was innocent. Polls also showed that, in contrast, most whites believed that Simpson was guilty.

Despite the acquittal, Simpson had to defend himself in a civil lawsuit filed by the parents of Nicole Brown Simpson and Ronald Goldman. In contrast to the criminal trial, the civil case was not televised, thereby reducing the intensity of the press coverage. In addition, the plaintiffs had the opportunity to DEPOSE many witnesses before trial, including Simpson, who did not testify at the criminal trial.

The plaintiffs' lead attorney, Daniel M. Petrocelli, fiercely examined Simpson at the deposition and again at the trial, pointing out the inconsistencies in his various accounts. Petrocelli mocked Simpson's contention that he had never beaten Nicole Brown Simpson, despite police reports, photographs, and testimony of other witnesses. The most crucial piece of evidence became the bloody shoe print at the crime scene. At his DEPOSITION Simpson said he had never owned a pair of the "ugly-assed shoes" that had made the shoe print. Simpson repeated this claim at trial, but Petrocelli produced thirty-one photographs of Simpson at public events showing that he had indeed worn the exact model of shoes prior to the murders. Finally Petrocelli argued that Simpson committed the murders because he could not control his temper: when Nicole Brown Simpson rejected him for good in the spring of 1994, he erupted in the same uncontrollable rage that had caused him to lash out at her in the past, only this time he used a knife.

In February 1997 the jury awarded the plaintiffs $8.5 million in COMPENSATORY DAMAGES and $25 million in PUNITIVE DAMAGES. The jury awarded the punitive damages based on an expert's testimony that Simpson could earn $25 million over the rest of his life by trading on his notoriety with book deals, movie contracts, speaking tours, and memorabilia sales. The jury did not want Simpson to profit from the crimes. Superior Court Judge Hiroshi Fujisaki, who had conducted the trial, upheld the DAMAGES award. Simpson announced that he planned to APPEAL the case.

The plaintiffs obtained a court order permitting the seizure of many of Simpson's assets to pay the multimillion-dollar judgment. Simpson, who had regained custody of his two children that he had with Nicole Brown Simpson, claimed he was near financial INSOLVENCY. Nevertheless, the plaintiffs' attorneys returned to court numerous times in 1997 seeking disclosure of Simpson's ASSETS, contending that he was attempting to hide them.

See also CAMERAS IN COURT; DNA EVIDENCE.

SIMULTANEOUS DEATH 📖 Loss of life by two or more individuals concurrently or pursuant to circumstances that render it impossible to ascertain who predeceased whom. 📖

The issue of who died first frequently arises in cases determining the INHERITANCE of property from spouses who die simultaneously. Generally the answer must be derived from all the surrounding circumstances. At COMMON LAW, the law would not intervene and make the assumption that one individual or another had died first but would await proof, no matter how slight that might be. Since this created a problem when no satisfactory proof existed, various states enacted statutes allowing judges to presume that one individual survived another under certain circumstances.

Because those state statutes that created presumptions proved inadequate, a majority of the states enacted the Uniform Simultaneous Death Act. Although some slight variations exist from one state to another, the law essentially provides that property will be inherited or distributed as if each person had outlived the other. This prevents the property from passing into the estate of a second person who is already de-

Tragic accidents such as this multivehicle pileup often lead to the death of both spouses, triggering simultaneous death provisions in the spouses' wills.

AP/WIDE WORLD PHOTOS

ceased only to be distributed immediately from that estate, a wasteful procedure that precipitates additional legal proceedings, costs, and estate taxes.

The Simultaneous Death Act cannot be applied if evidence exists that one individual outlived the other. The act only applies when it cannot be determined who died first. Ordinarily the persons involved need not have died in a COMMON DISASTER but might have died in different places and under different circumstances, and it still might be impossible to prove that one survived the other.

See also DEATH AND DYING; ESTATE AND GIFT TAXES.

SINE DIE [*Latin, Without day.*] Without day; without assigning a day for a further meeting or hearing.

A legislative body adjourns sine die when it adjourns without appointing a day on which to appear or assemble again.

SINE QUA NON [*Latin, Without which not.*] A description of a requisite or condition that is indispensable.

In the law of TORTS, a causal connection exists between a particular act and an injury when the injury would not have arisen but for the act. This is known as the BUT FOR RULE or *sine qua non* rule.

SINGLE NAME PAPER A type of COMMERCIAL PAPER, such as a CHECK or PROMISSORY NOTE that has only one original signer or more than one maker signing for the exact same purpose.

A single name paper is distinguishable from a *suretyship* where, for a certain sum, one individual cosigns to support another individual's DEBT.

SINGLE NAME PARTNERSHIP A business arrangement whereby two or more individuals, the partners, unite their skill, capital, and work in exchange for a proportional alloca-

A sample form for a single or fictitious name partnership or business

FICTITIOUS BUSINESS NAME STATEMENT

The following person (persons) is (are) doing business as*.............................

....................................at** ....

*** ....

....

....

....

This business is conducted by **** ....

Signed ....

Statement filed with the County Clerk of .... County on ....

NOTICE—THIS FICTITIOUS NAME STATEMENT EXPIRES ON DECEMBER 31, 19___ . A NEW FICTITIOUS BUSINESS NAME STATEMENT MUST BE FILED PRIOR TO DECEMBER 31, 19___ .

The statement shall contain the following information set forth in the manner indicated in the form:

(1) Where the asterisk (*) appears in the form, insert the fictitious business name or names. Only those businesses operated at the same address may be listed on one statement.

(2) Where the two asterisks (**) appear in the form: If the registrant has a place of business in this state, insert the street address of his principal place of business in this state. If the registrant has no place of business in this state, insert the street address of his principal place of business outside this state.

(3) Where the three asterisks (***) appear in the form: If the registrant is an individual, insert his full name and residence address. If the registrant is a partnership or other association of persons, insert the full name and residence address of each general partner. If the registrant is a corporation, insert the name of the corporation as set out in its articles of incorporation and the state of incorporation.

(4) Where the four asterisks (****) appear in the form insert whichever of the following best describes the nature of the business: (i) "an individual," (ii) "a general partnership," (iii) "a limited partnership," (iv) "an unincorporated association other than a partnership," (v) "a corporation," (vi) "a business trust * * *," (vii) "copartners," (viii) "husband and wife," (ix) "joint venture," or (x) "other—please specify."

tion of the profits and losses incurred but who engage in business under one name rather than the names of all the partners. 📖

Although technically not a legal term, the phrase *single name partnership* describes the situation when a traditional PARTNERSHIP arrangement deviates from the custom of using the surnames of all its partners (except for silent partners) to conduct its activities. The partners select one name, whether it be the name of one partner, an acronym of their names, or a fictitious name. This assumed name must be set out under the provision for the name in the partnership agreement. A single name partnership is also known as an assumed or fictitious name partnership.

Almost all states require by statute that such a partnership file an assumed or fictitious name certificate with the secretary of state or other appropriate official. In addition to the assumed name, the certificate sets out the full names and addresses of the individuals doing business under that name. Some JURISDICTIONS also mandate that a notice to file the certificate appear under the legal notice column in designated newspapers.

The registration requirement is designed to provide the public with information about the persons with whom they choose to do business or extend credit.

Failure to file an assumed or fictitious name partnership agreement might constitute a MISDEMEANOR under state penal laws, resulting in a fine upon conviction.

SINGLE PROPRIETORSHIP See SOLE PROPRIETORSHIP.

SIT 📖 To hold court or perform an act that is judicial in nature; to hold a session, such as of a COURT, GRAND JURY, or legislative body. 📖

SITUS 📖 [*Latin, Situation; location.*] The place where a particular event occurs. 📖

For example, the situs of a CRIME is the place where it was committed; the situs of a TRUST is the location where the TRUSTEE performs his or her duties of managing the trust.

SIXTEENTH AMENDMENT The Sixteenth Amendment to the U.S. Constitution reads:

> The Congress shall have power to lay and collect taxes on incomes, from whatever source derived, without apportionment among the several States, and without regard to any census or enumeration.

Congress passed the Sixteenth Amendment to the U.S. Constitution in 1909, and the states ratified it in 1913. The ratification of the amendment overturned an 1895 U.S. Supreme Court decision that had ruled a two percent federal flat tax on incomes over $4,000 unconstitutional (*Pollock v. Farmer's Loan & Trust Co.*, 157 U.S. 429, 15 S. Ct. 673, 39 L. Ed. 759). Article I of the Constitution states that "direct taxes shall be apportioned among the several states . . . according to their respective numbers." By a 5–4 vote, the Court in *Pollock* held that the new INCOME TAX was a DIRECT TAX insofar as it was based on incomes derived from land and, as such, had to be apportioned among the states. Because the law did not provide for APPORTIONMENT, it was unconstitutional.

The decision was unpopular and took the public by surprise because a federal income tax levied during the Civil War had not been struck down. Critics contended that the conservative majority on the *Pollock* Court was seeking to protect the economic elite. Industrialization had led to the creation of enormous corporate profits and personal fortunes, which could not be taxed to help pay for escalating federal government services. The Democratic party made the enactment of a CONSTITUTIONAL AMENDMENT a plank in its platform beginning in 1896.

The language of the Sixteenth Amendment addressed the issue in *Pollock* concerning apportionment, repealing the limitation imposed by article I. Soon after the amendment was ratified, Congress established a new personal income tax with rates ranging from one to seven percent on income in excess of $3,000 for a single individual.

See also POLLOCK V. FARMER'S LOAN & TRUST CO.

SIXTH AMENDMENT The Sixth Amendment to the U.S. Constitution reads:

> In all criminal prosecutions, the accused shall enjoy the right to a speedy and public trial, by an impartial jury of the State and district wherein the crime shall have been committed, which district shall have been previously ascertained by law, and to be informed of the nature and cause of the accusation; to be confronted with the witnesses against him; to have compulsory process for obtaining witnesses in his favor, and to have the Assistance of Counsel for his defense.

The Sixth Amendment to the U.S. Constitution affords criminal defendants seven discrete personal liberties: (1) the right to a SPEEDY TRIAL, (2) the right to a public TRIAL, (3) the right to an impartial JURY, (4) the right to be informed of pending charges, (5) the right to confront and cross-examine adverse WITNESSES, (6) the right to compel favorable witnesses to TESTIFY at trial through the SUBPOENA power of the judiciary, and (7) the right to legal counsel. Ratified in 1791, the Sixth Amendment originally applied only to criminal actions brought by the federal government.

Over the last century all of the protections guaranteed by the Sixth Amendment have been made applicable to the state governments through the doctrine of selective incorporation. Under this doctrine, the Due Process and Equal Protection Clauses of the FOURTEENTH AMENDMENT require each state to recognize certain fundamental liberties that are enumerated in the BILL OF RIGHTS because such liberties are deemed essential to the concepts of freedom and equality. Together with the SUPREMACY CLAUSE of Article VI, the Fourteenth Amendment prohibits any state from providing less protection for a right conferred by the Sixth Amendment than is provided under the federal Constitution. See also INCORPORATION DOCTRINE.

Speedy Trial The right to a speedy trial traces its roots to twelfth-century England when the Assize of Clarendon declared that justice must be provided to robbers, murderers, and thieves "speedily enough." (See also CLARENDON, CONSTITUTIONS OF.) The Speedy Trial Clause was designed by the Founding Fathers to prevent defendants from languishing in JAIL for an indefinite period before trial, to minimize the time in which a defendant's life is disrupted and burdened by the anxiety and scrutiny accompanying public criminal proceedings, and to reduce the chances that a prolonged delay before trial will impair the ability of the accused to prepare a defense. The longer the commencement of a trial is postponed, courts have observed, the more likely it is that witnesses will disappear, EVIDENCE will be lost or destroyed, and memories will fade.

A person's right to a speedy trial arises only after the government has arrested, indicted, or otherwise formally accused the person of a crime. Before the point of formal accusation, the government is under no Sixth Amendment obligation to discover, investigate, accuse, or PROSECUTE a particular defendant within a certain amount of time. The Speedy Trial Clause is not implicated in posttrial criminal proceedings such as PROBATION and PAROLE hearings. Nor may a person raise a speedy trial claim after the government has dropped criminal charges, even if the government refiles those charges at a much later date. However, the government must comply with the fairness requirements of the Due Process Clause during each juncture of a criminal proceeding.

The Supreme Court has declined to draw a bright line separating permissible pretrial delays from delays that are impermissibly excessive. Instead, the Court has developed a BALANCING test in which length of delay is just one factor considered when evaluating the MERITS of a speedy trial claim. The other three factors a court must consider are the reason for delay, the severity of PREJUDICE or injury suffered by the defendant from delay, and the stage during the criminal proceedings in which the defendant asserted the right to a speedy trial. Defendants who fail to assert this right early in a criminal proceeding, or who acquiesce in the face of protracted pretrial delays, typically lose their speedy trial claims.

Defendants whose own actions lengthen the pretrial phase normally forfeit their rights under the Speedy Trial Clause as well. For example, defendants who frivolously inundate a court with pretrial MOTIONS are treated as having waived their rights to a speedy trial (*United States v. Lindsey*, 47 F.3d 440 [D.C. Cir. 1995]). In such situations defendants are not allowed to benefit from their own misconduct. On the other hand, delays that are attributable to the government, such as delays due to prosecutorial NEGLIGENCE in misplacing a defendant's file, will violate the Speedy Trial Clause (*United States v. Shell*, 974 F.2d 1035 [9th Cir. 1992]).

A delay of at least one year in bringing a defendant to trial following arrest will trigger a PRESUMPTION that the Sixth Amendment has been violated, with the level of judicial scrutiny increasing in direct proportion to the length of delay (*United States v. Gutierrez*, 891 F. Supp. 97 [E.D.N.Y. 1995]). The government may overcome this presumption by offering a "plausible reason" for the delay (*United States v. Thomas*, 55 F.3d 144 [4th Cir. 1995]). Courts generally will condone longer delays when the prosecution has requested additional time to prepare for a complex or difficult case. When prosecutors have offered only implausible reasons for delay, courts have traditionally dismissed the indictment, overturned the conviction, or vacated the sentence, depending on the remedy requested by the defendant.

Public Trial The right to a public trial is another ancient liberty Americans have inherited from Anglo-Saxon jurisprudence. In the seventeenth century, when the English Court of OYER AND TERMINER attempted to exclude members of the public from a criminal proceeding that the Crown had deemed to be sensitive, defendant John Lilburn successfully argued that immemorial usage and British COMMON LAW entitled him to a trial in open court where spectators are admitted. The Founding Fathers believed that public criminal proceedings would operate as a check against malevolent prosecutions, corrupt or malleable judges, and perjurious witnesses. The public nature of criminal proceedings also aids the fact-finding mission of the judiciary by encouraging citizens to come forward with relevant information, inculpatory or exculpatory.

Under the Public Trial Clause, friends and relatives of a defendant must be initially permitted to attend trial. However, the right to a public trial is not absolute, and parents, spouses, and children will be excluded if they disrupt the proceedings (*Cosentino v. Kelly*, 926 F. Supp. 391 [S.D.N.Y. 1996]). Toddlers and infants, ranging from one month to two years in age, may be summarily excluded from a courtroom consistent with the Sixth Amendment, even if the judge fails to articulate a reason for doing so (*United States v. Short*, 36 M.J. 802 [A.C.M.R. 1993]). Children in this age group are too young to understand legal proceedings, are easily agitated, and present a substantial risk of hindering a trial with distractions.

The Sixth Amendment right to a public trial is personal to the defendant and may not be asserted by the media or the public in general. However, both the public and media have a qualified FIRST AMENDMENT right to attend criminal proceedings. The First Amendment does not accommodate everyone who wants to attend a particular proceeding. Nor does the First Amendment require courts to televise any given legal proceeding. Oral arguments before the Supreme Court, for example, have never been televised. See also CAMERAS IN COURT; COURTROOM TELEVISION NETWORK.

Courtrooms are areas of finite space and limited seating in which judges diligently attempt to maintain decorum. In cases that generate tremendous public interest, courts sometimes create lottery systems that randomly assign citizens a seat in the courtroom for each day of trial. A separate lottery may be established for the purpose of determining which members of the media are permitted access to the courtroom on a given day, although local and national newspapers and television stations may be given a permanent courtroom seat. Members of the media and public who are excluded from attending trial on a given day are sometimes provided admission to an audio room where they can listen to the proceedings.

In rare cases criminal proceedings will be closed to all members of the media and public. However, a compelling reason must be offered before a court will follow this course. For example, when the First Amendment rights of the media to attend a criminal trial collide with a defendant's Sixth Amendment right to a fair trial, the defendant's Sixth Amendment right takes precedence, and the legal proceeding may be closed (*In re Globe Newspaper*, 729 F.2d 47 [1st Cir. 1984]). See also FREEDOM OF THE PRESS.

Criminal proceedings also have been conducted in private when the complaining witness is a child who is young and immature and is being asked to testify about an emotionally charged issue such as SEXUAL ABUSE (*Fayerweather v. Moran*, 749 F. Supp. 43 [D.R.I. 1990]). If the court determines that only one stage of a legal proceeding will be jeopardized by the presence of the public or the media, then only that stage should be conducted in private (*Waller v. Georgia*, 467 U.S. 39, 104 S. Ct. 2210, 81 L. Ed. 2d 31 [1984]). For example, if a witness is expected to testify about classified government information or confidential TRADE SECRETS, the court may clear the courtroom for the duration of such testimony, but no longer.

The right to a public trial extends to pretrial proceedings that are integral to the trial phase, such as jury selection and evidentiary HEARINGS (*Rovinsky v. McKaskle*, 722 F.2d 197 [5th Cir. 1984]). Despite the strong constitutional preference for public criminal trials, both COURTS-MARTIAL and juvenile delinquency hearings typically are held in a closed session, even when they involve criminal wrongdoing. In all other proceedings, the defendant may waive his right to a public trial, in which case the entire criminal proceeding can be conducted in private. See also JUVENILE LAW.

Right to Trial by an Impartial Jury In both England and the American colonies, the British Crown retained the prerogative to interfere with jury deliberations and overturn VERDICTS that embarrassed, harmed, or otherwise challenged the authority of the royal government. Finding such interference unjust, the Founding Fathers created a constitutional right to trial by an impartial jury. This Sixth Amendment right, which can be traced back to the MAGNA CHARTA in 1215, does not apply to juvenile delinquency proceedings (*McKeiver v. Pennsylvania*, 403 U.S. 528, 91 S. Ct. 1976, 29 L. Ed. 2d 647 [1971]), or to petty criminal offenses, which consist of crimes punishable by imprisonment of six months or less (*Baldwin v. New York*, 399 U.S. 66, 90 S. Ct. 1886, 26 L. Ed. 2d 437 [1970]).

The Sixth Amendment entitles defendants to a jury pool that represents a fair cross section of the community. From the jury pool, also known as a venire, a panel of jurors is selected to hear the case through a process called VOIR DIRE. During voir dire the presiding judge, the prosecution, and attorneys for the defense are allowed to ask members of the jury pool a variety of questions intended to reveal any latent biases, prejudices, or other influences that might affect their impartiality. The jurors who are ultimately impaneled for trial need not represent a cross section of the community as long as each juror maintains impartiality throughout the proceedings. The presence of even one biased juror is not permitted under the Sixth Amendment (*United States v. Aguon*, 813 F.2d 1413 [9th Cir. 1987]).

A juror's impartiality may be compromised by sources outside the courtroom, such as the media. Jurors may not consider newspaper, television, and radio coverage before or during trial when evaluating the guilt or innocence of the defendant. Before trial, judges will take special care to filter out those jurors whose neutrality has been compromised by extensive media coverage. During trial, judges will instruct jurors to avoid exposing themselves to such extraneous sources. Exposure to information about the trial from an extraneous source, whether it is the media, a friend, or a family member, creates a presumption of prejudice to the defendant that can only be overcome by persuasive evidence that the juror can still render an impartial verdict (*United States v. Rowley*, 975 F.2d 1357 [8th Cir. 1992]). Failure to overcome this presumption will result in the reversal of any conviction. See also PRETRIAL PUBLICITY; SEQUESTRATION.

The Sixth Amendment requires a trial judge to inquire as to the possible racial biases of prospective jurors when defendants request such an inquiry and there are substantial indications that racial prejudice could play a decisive role in the outcome of the case (*United States v. Kyles*, 40 F.3d 519 [2d Cir. 1994]). But an all-white jury does not by itself infringe on a black defendant's right to an impartial jury despite her contention that white jurors are incapable of acting impartially due to their perceived ignorance of inner-city life and its problems (*United States v. Nururdin*, 8 F.3d 1187 [7th Cir. 1993]). However, if a white juror is biased by an indelible prejudice against a black defendant, she will be stricken from the jury panel or venire. See also PEREMPTORY CHALLENGE.

For similar reasons, jurors are not permitted to begin deliberations until all of the evidence has been offered, the attorneys have made their CLOSING ARGUMENTS, and the judge has read the instructions. FEDERAL COURTS have found that premature deliberations are more likely to occur after the prosecution has concluded its case in chief and before the defense has begun its presentation (*United States v. Bertoli*, 40 F.3d 1384 [3d Cir. 1994]). Federal courts have also determined that once a juror has expressed a view, he is more likely to view the evidence in a light most favorable to that initial opinion. If premature deliberations were constitutionally permitted, then, the government would obtain an unfair advantage over defendants because many jurors would enter the final deliberations with a prosecutorial slant (*United States v. Resko*, 3 F.3d 684 [3d Cir. 1993]).

Although a jury must be impartial, there is no Sixth Amendment right to a jury of twelve persons. In *Williams v. Florida*, 399 U.S. 78, 90 S. Ct. 1893, 26 L. Ed. 2d 446 (1970), the Supreme Court ruled that a jury of at least six persons is "large enough to promote group deliberation, free from outside attempts at intimidation, and to provide a fair possibility for obtaining a cross-section of the community." Conversely, the Court has declared that a jury of only five members is unconstitutionally small (*Ballew v. Georgia*, 435 U.S. 223, 98 S. Ct. 1029, 55 L. Ed. 2d 234 [1978]).

Similarly, there is no Sixth Amendment right to a unanimous jury (*Apodaca v. Oregon*, 406 U.S. 404, 92 S. Ct. 1628, 32 L. Ed. 2d 184 [1972]). The "essential feature of a jury lies in the interposition between the accused and the accuser of the common sense judgment of a group of laymen," the Supreme Court said in *Apodaca*. "A requirement of unanimity," the Court continued, "does not materially contribute to the exercise of that judgment." If a defendant is tried by a six-person jury, however, the verdict must be unanimous (*Burch v. Louisiana*, 441 U.S. 130, 99 S. Ct. 1623, 60 L. Ed. 2d 96 [1979]).

Notice of Pending Criminal Charges
The Sixth Amendment guarantees defendants the right to be informed of the nature and cause of the ACCUSATION against them. Courts have interpreted this provision to have two elements. First, defendants must receive notice of any criminal accusations that the government has lodged against them through an INDICTMENT, INFORMATION, COMPLAINT, or other formal charge. Second, defendants may not be tried, convicted, or sentenced for a crime that materially varies from the crime set forth in the formal charge. If a defendant suffers prejudice or injury, such as a conviction, from a MATERIAL variance between the formal charge and the PROOF offered at trial, the court will vacate the verdict and sentence.

The Sixth Amendment NOTICE requirement reflects the efforts of the Founding Fathers to constitutionalize the common-law concept of fundamental fairness that pervaded civil and criminal proceedings in England and the American colonies. Receiving notice of pending criminal charges in advance of trial permits defendants to prepare a defense in accordance with the specific nature of the accusation. Defendants who are incarcerated by totalitarian governments are frequently not apprised of pending charges until the trial begins. By requiring substantial conformity between the criminal charges and the incriminating proof at trial, the Sixth Amendment eliminates any confusion as to the basis of a particular verdict, thereby decreasing the chances that a defendant will be tried later for the same offense in violation of DOUBLE JEOPARDY.

Many appeals have focused on the issue of what constitutes a material variance. In *Stirone v. United States*, 361 U.S. 212, 80 S. Ct. 270, 4 L. Ed. 2d 252 (1960), the Supreme Court found a material variance between an indictment charging the defendant with illegal importing activities and trial evidence showing that the defendant had engaged in illegal exporting activities. In *United States v. Ford*, 88 F.3d 1350 (4th Cir. 1996), the U.S. Court of Appeals for the Fourth Circuit found a material variance between an indictment charging the defendant with a single CONSPIRACY and trial proof demonstrating the existence of multiple conspiracies.

However, no material variance was found between an indictment that charged a defendant with committing a crime in Little Rock, Arkansas, and trial evidence showing that the crime was actually committed in North Little Rock, because both cities were within the JURISDICTION of the court hearing the case (*Moore v. United States*, 337 F.2d 350 [8th Cir. 1964]). Nor was a material variance found in a check FORGERY case where the indictment listed the middle name of the defendant and the forged instrument included only a middle initial (*Helms v. United States*, 310 F.2d 236 [5th Cir. 1962]).

Confrontation of Adverse Witnesses The Sixth Amendment guarantees defendants the right to be confronted by witnesses who offer testimony or evidence against them. The Confrontation Clause has two prongs. The first prong assures defendants the right to be present during all critical stages of trial, allowing them to hear the evidence offered by the prosecution, consult with their attorneys, and otherwise participate in their defense. However, the Sixth Amendment permits courts to remove defendants who are disorderly, disrespectful, and abusive (*Illinois v. Allen*, 397 U.S. 337, 90 S. Ct. 1057, 25 L. Ed. 2d 353 [1970]). If an unruly defendant insists on remaining in the courtroom, the Sixth Amendment authorizes courts to take appropriate measures to restrain him. In some instances, courts have shackled and gagged stubbornly recalcitrant defendants in the presence of the jury (*Stewart v. Corbin*, 850 F.2d 492 [9th Cir. 1988]). In other instances defiant defendants have been removed from court and forced to watch the remainder of trial from their prison cell through closed-circuit television.

The second prong of the Confrontation Clause guarantees defendants the right to face adverse witnesses in person and subject them to CROSS-EXAMINATION. Through cross-examination defendants may test the credibility and reliability of witnesses by probing their recollection and exposing any underlying prejudices, biases, or motives to distort the truth or lie. CONFRONTATION and cross-examination are vital components of the U.S. adversarial system.

Although defendants are usually given wide latitude in exercising their rights under the Confrontation Clause, courts retain broad discretion to impose reasonable restrictions on particular avenues of cross-examination. Defendants may be forbidden from delving into areas that are irrelevant, collateral, confusing, repetitive, or prejudicial. Nor may defendants pursue a line of questioning solely for the purpose of harassment. For example, courts have prohibited defendants from cross-examining alleged RAPE victims about their sexual history because such questioning is frequently demeaning and is unlikely to illicit answers that bear more than a remote relationship to the issue of consent (*Bell v. Harrison*, 670 F.2d 656 [6th Cir. 1982]). See also SHIELD LAWS.

In exceptional circumstances defendants may be prevented from confronting their accusers face-to-face. If a judge determines that a fragile child would be traumatized by testifying in front of a defendant, the Sixth Amendment authorizes the court to videotape the child's testimony outside the presence of the defendant and later replay the tape during trial (*Spigarolo v. Meachum*, 934 F.2d 19 [2d Cir. 1991]). However, counsel for both the prosecution and defense must be present during the videotaped testimony. If neither the defendant nor her attorney are permitted the opportunity to confront a witness, even if the witness is a small child whose welfare might be harmed by rigorous cross-examination, the Sixth Amendment has been violated (*Tennessee v. Deuter*, 839 S.W.2d 391 [Tenn. 1992]). See also SEXUAL ABUSE.

Occasionally defendants are denied the opportunity to confront and cross-examine their accusers under the controversial rules of HEARSAY evidence. Hearsay is a written or verbal statement made out of court by one person that is later repeated in court by another person who heard or read the statement. Because such out-of-court statements are not typically made under OATH or subject to cross-examination, the law treats them as untrustworthy when introduced into evidence by a person other than the original declarant. When hearsay statements are offered for their truth, they generally are deemed INADMISSIBLE by state and federal law.

However, certain hearsay statements, such as DYING DECLARATIONS, excited utterances, and officially kept records, are deemed admissible when made under reliable circumstances. Dying declarations are considered reliable when made by persons who have been informed of their impending death because such persons are supposedly more inclined to tell the truth. Excited utterances are considered reliable when made spontaneously and without time for premeditation. Business and public records are considered reliable when kept in the ordinary and official course of corporate or government activities. The prosecution may introduce all four types of evidence, as well as other "firmly rooted" exceptions to the hearsay rule, without violating the Sixth Amendment even though the defendant is not afforded the opportunity to confront or cross-examine the out-of-court declarant (*United States v. Jackson*, 88 F.3d 845 [10th Cir. 1996]).

Compulsory Process for Favorable Witnesses As a corollary to the right of confrontation, the Sixth Amendment guarantees defendants the right to use the COMPULSORY PROCESS of the JUDICIARY to subpoena witnesses who may provide exculpatory testimony or have other information favorable to the defense. The Sixth Amendment guarantees this right even if an indigent defendant cannot afford to pay the expenses that accompany the use of judicial resources to subpoena a witness (*United States v. Webster*, 750 F.2d 307 [5th Cir. 1984]). Courts may not take actions to undermine the testimony of a witness subpoenaed by the defense. For example, a trial judge who discourages a witness from testifying by issuing unnecessarily stern warnings against PERJURY has violated the precepts of the Sixth Amendment (*Webb v. Texas*, 409 U.S. 95, 93 S. Ct. 351, 34 L. Ed. 2d 330 [1972]).

A statute that makes particular persons incompetent to testify on behalf of a defendant is similarly unconstitutional. At issue in *Washington v. Texas*, 388 U.S. 14, 87 S. Ct. 1920, 18 L. Ed. 2d 1019 (1967), was a state statute prohibiting ACCOMPLICES from testifying for one another. Overturning the statute as a violation of the Sixth Amendment Compulsory Process Clause, the Supreme Court said that the defendant was denied the right to subpoena favorable witnesses "because the state arbitrarily denied him the right to put on the stand a witness who was physically present and mentally capable of testifying to events that he had personally observed and whose testimony was relevant and material to the defense."

Under certain circumstances the prosecution may be required to assist the defendant in locating potential witnesses. In *Roviaro v. United States*, 353 U.S. 53, 77 S. Ct. 623, 1 L. Ed. 2d 639 (1957), the defendant was charged with the illegal sale of heroin to "John Doe." When the prosecution refused to disclose the identity of John Doe, the Supreme Court concluded that the Sixth Amendment had been abridged because the disclosure of Doe's identity may have produced "testimony that was highly relevant and . . . helpful to the defense."

Defendants also have a Sixth Amendment right to testify on their own behalf. Before the American Revolution, defendants were not permitted to take the witness stand in Great Britain and in many of the colonies. The common law presumed all defendants incompetent to give reliable or credible testimony on their own behalf because of their vested interest in the outcome of the trial. Each defendant, regardless of his innocence or guilt, was declared incapable of offering truthful testimony when his life, liberty, or property were at stake. The Sixth Amendment laid this common-law rule to rest in the United States. The amendment permits, but does not require, a defendant to testify on his own behalf.

Right to Counsel Because of the law's complexity and the often substantial deprivations a criminal conviction can produce, the Sixth Amendment provides criminal defendants a right to counsel. A defendant's Sixth Amendment RIGHT TO COUNSEL attaches when the government initiates adversarial criminal proceedings, whether by way of formal charge, PRELIMINARY HEARING, indictment, information, or arraignment (*United States v. Larkin*, 978 F.2d 964 [7th Cir. 1992]). Unlike the right to a speedy trial, this Sixth Amendment right does not arise at the moment of arrest unless the government has already filed formal charges (*Kirby v. Illinois*, 406 U.S. 682, 92 S. Ct. 1877, 32 L. Ed. 2d 411 [1972]). However, defendants may assert a FIFTH AMENDMENT right to consult with an attorney during CUSTODIAL INTERROGATION by the police, even though no formal charges have been brought and no arrest has been made (*Miranda v. Arizona*, 384 U.S. 436, 86 S. Ct. 1602, 16 L. Ed. 2d 694 [1966]). See also MIRANDA V. ARIZONA.

Defendants do not enjoy a Sixth Amendment right to be represented by counsel during every phase of litigation that follows the initiation of formal adversarial proceedings by the state. Instead, defendants may only assert this right during "critical stages" of the proceedings (*Maine v. Moulton*, 474 U.S. 159, 106 S. Ct. 477, 88 L. Ed. 2d 481 [1985]). A critical stage of prosecution includes every instance in which the advice of counsel is necessary to ensure a defendant's right to a fair trial or in which the absence of counsel might impair the preparation or presentation of a defense (*United States v. Hidalgo*, 7 F.3d 1566 [11th Cir. 1993]).

Obviously the trial is a critical stage in any criminal proceeding, as is jury selection, sentencing, and nearly every effort by the government to elicit information from the accused, including interrogation. However, courts are divided on the issue of whether the state may perform a consensual search of a defendant's premises without the advice or presence of counsel. At the same time, courts generally agree that pretrial hearings involving issues related to BAIL, the suppression of evidence, or the viability of the prosecution's case all qualify as critical stages of criminal proceedings (*Smith v. Lockhart*, 923 F.2d 1314 [8th Cir. 1991]). The Supreme Court has ruled that the denial of counsel during a critical stage amounts to an unconstitutional deprivation of a fair trial, warranting the reversal of conviction (*United States v. Cronic*, 466 U.S. 648, 104 S. Ct. 2039, 80 L. Ed. 2d 657 [1984]).

Courts also generally agree on a number of instances that do not constitute critical stages. For example, pretrial scientific analysis of FINGERPRINTS, blood samples, clothing, hair, handwriting, and voice samples have all been ruled to be noncritical stages (*United States v. Wade*, 388 U.S. 218, 87 S. Ct. 1926, 18 L. Ed. 2d 1149 [1967]). Nor is a PROBABLE CAUSE hearing sufficiently critical to trigger the right to counsel (*Gerstein v. Pugh*, 420 U.S. 103, 95 S. Ct. 854, 43 L. Ed. 2d 54 [1975]). Each of these noncritical stages has been described as a preliminary facet of criminal prosecution that is largely unassociated with the more adversarial phases invoking the right to counsel.

If a defendant cannot afford to hire an attorney, the Sixth Amendment requires that the trial judge appoint one on her behalf (*Gideon v. Wainwright*, 372 U.S. 335, 83 S. Ct. 792, 9 L. Ed. 2d 799 [1963]). In instances where an indigent defendant has some financial resources, she may be required to reimburse the government for a portion of the fees paid to the court-appointed lawyer. The Sixth Amendment right of indigent criminal defendants to receive a court-appointed lawyer applies to every case involving a FELONY offense and to all other cases in which the defendant is actually incarcerated for any length of time, regardless of whether the crime is categorized as a MISDEMEANOR or PETTY OFFENSE (*Argersinger v. Hamlin*, 407 U.S. 25, 92 S. Ct. 2006, 32 L. Ed. 2d 530 [1972]). See also GIDEON V. WAINWRIGHT.

However, if an indigent defendant is prosecuted for a non-felony offense punishable by a potential jail or PRISON sentence, the Sixth Amendment is not violated if he is denied a court-appointed attorney as long as no penalty of INCARCERATION is actually imposed (*Scott v. Illinois*, 440 U.S. 367, 99 S. Ct. 1158, 59 L. Ed. 2d 383 [1979]). In other words, an indigent defendant has no Sixth Amendment right to a court-appointed lawyer in a non-felony case when the only punishment he receives is a FINE, the FORFEITURE of property, or some other penalty not involving incarceration. Thus, in a forfeiture proceeding where the government seized almost $300,000 from an arrested drug smuggler, the Sixth Amendment right to counsel was not infringed when the court denied the smuggler's request for a court-appointed attorney because no jail or prison sentence was ultimately imposed (*United States v. $292,888.04 in U.S. Currency*, 54 F.3d 564 [9th Cir. 1995]).

Nor is the Sixth Amendment right to counsel infringed when an indigent defendant is denied a court-appointed lawyer of her choice (*Ford v. Israel*, 701 F.2d 689 [7th Cir. 1983]). The selection of counsel to represent an indigent defendant is within the discretion of the trial court. The attorney selected need not be a great litigator, a savvy negotiator, or the best attorney available. Rather, the court-appointed lawyer must be a member in good standing of the bar who gives the client his complete and undivided loyalty, as well as a zealous and GOOD FAITH defense (*United States v. Cariola*, 323 F.2d 180 [3rd Cir. 1963]). The quality of representation need not be perfect but only effective and competent enough to assure the defendant DUE PROCESS OF LAW (*Pineda v. Bailey*, 340 F.2d 162 [5th Cir. 1965]). If the attorney representing a defendant is incompetent, whether the attorney has been appointed by the court or privately retained, the Sixth Amendment right to the effective assistance of counsel has been violated.

The court can replace any attorney, publicly appointed or privately retained, if that is in the best interests of the defendant. A court will normally replace an attorney who has a conflict of interest that prevents her from faithfully discharging her obligation of loyalty to the client. Courts also retain the prerogative to deny a defendant's request to substitute attorneys if the request comes too late in the proceedings, is made solely to delay the trial, or is not for a good reason. However, if a defendant demonstrates a good reason for the substitution of attorneys, such as the complete breakdown in communication between lawyer and client, the court must honor the request for substitution unless a compelling reason exists for denying it. The efficient administration of justice is one reason that has been deemed sufficiently compelling to deny such requests (*United States v. D'Amore*, 56 F.3d 1202 [9th Cir. 1995]).

Finally, all defendants have a Sixth Amendment right to decline the representation of counsel and proceed on their own behalf. Defendants who represent themselves are said to be proceeding PRO SE. However, defendants who wish to represent themselves must first make a knowing and intelligent WAIVER of the Sixth Amendment right to counsel before a court will allow them to do so. Courts must ensure that the defendant appreciates the disadvantages of appearing *pro se* and understands the consequences. The defendant must be informed that the presentation of a defense in a criminal case is not a simple matter of telling a story but requires skills in examining a witness, knowledge of the rules of evidence and procedure, and persuasive oratory abilities.

See also CRIMINAL LAW; CRIMINAL PROCEDURE.

S.J.D. 📖 An abbreviation for doctor of judicial science, a degree awarded to highly qualified individuals who have successfully completed a prescribed course of legal doctorate study after having earned J.D. and LL.M. degrees. 📖

S.J.D. is more commonly abbreviated J.S.D.

SLANDER See LIBEL AND SLANDER.

SLATING 📖 The procedure by which law enforcement officials record on the BLOTTER information about an individual's arrest and charges, together with identification and facts about his or her background. 📖

The term *slating* is used synonymously with BOOKING.

SLAUGHTER-HOUSE CASES The U.S. Supreme Court ruling in the *Slaughter-House* cases, 83 U.S. (16 Wall.) 36, 21 L. Ed. 394 (1873), was the first Court decision to interpret the FOURTEENTH AMENDMENT, which had been ratified in 1870. In a controversial decision, the Court, on a 5–4 vote, interpreted the Privileges and Immunities Clause of the amendment as protecting only rights of national citizenship from the actions of the state government. This restrictive reading robbed the Privileges and Immunities Clause of any constitutional significance.

The case involved three lawsuits filed by Louisiana meat-packing companies, challenging a Louisiana state law that allowed one meat company the exclusive right to slaughter livestock in New Orleans. Other packing companies were required to pay a fee for using the slaughterhouses. The state justified this monopoly as a way to prevent health risks to people who lived near slaughterhouses, at a time when there was no refrigeration and no way to control insects. The company that was awarded the MONOPOLY and accompanying financial windfall was politically connected to state legislators, inviting charges of corruption.

The three companies filed suit, claiming that the law violated the Privileges and Immunities Clause of the Fourteenth Amendment. They argued that this clause protected the right to labor freely. The Louisiana law restricted their freedom to butcher meat. Their challenge was unsuccessful in state court, after which they appealed to the U.S. Supreme Court.

The Supreme Court affirmed the state court. Justice SAMUEL F. MILLER, writing for the majority, ruled that the Privileges and Immunities Clause had limited effect because it only reached PRIVILEGES AND IMMUNITIES guaranteed by U.S. citizenship, not state citizenship. The clause was meant only to prohibit a state from restricting the rights of noncitizens within its borders if it did not similarly limit the rights of its CITIZENS. Miller noted that because the action challenged privileges of state citizenship, the Privileges and Immunities Clause did not apply.

Some of the rights of national citizenship enumerated by Miller included the right to travel from state to state, the right to vote for federal officeholders, the right to petition Congress to redress grievances, and the right to use the WRIT of HABEAS CORPUS. Any restriction on these national rights of citizenship by a state would be unconstitutional under the Privileges and Immunities Clause. In the case of the meat packers, however, the Court concluded that no national citizenship right was at stake.

Miller also expressed concern that an expansive reading of the Privileges and Immunities Clause would shift too much power to the FEDERAL COURTS and Congress. In his view the Fourteenth Amendment was designed to grant former slaves legal equality, not to grant expanded rights to the general population. The concept of FEDERALISM, which grants the states a large measure of power and autonomy, played a role in the majority's decision. The Court reasoned that Congress and the states could not have contemplated the expansion of federal power as argued by the meat packers.

The four dissenting justices thought otherwise, believing that the Fourteenth Amendment was intended to do more than just protect the newly freed slaves. Justice STEPHEN J. FIELD, in a dissent joined by the other justices, maintained that "[t]he privileges and immunities designated are those which of right belong to the citizens of all free governments." He saw the clause as a powerful tool to keep state government out of the affairs of business and the economy.

The Privileges and Immunities Clause no longer had any constitutional impact. The Supreme Court came to rely on the Due Process and Equal Protection Clauses of the Fourteenth Amendment to protect persons from unconstitutional actions by state government.

See also DUE PROCESS OF LAW; EQUAL PROTECTION.

SLAVERY 📖 A civil relationship in which one person has absolute power over the life, fortune, and liberty of another. 📖

History At some point in history, slavery has plagued nearly every part of the world. From ancient Greece to the modern Americas, innumerable governments have sanctioned the complete control of certain persons for the benefit of other persons, usually under the guise of social, mercantile, and technological progress.

The United States' legacy of slavery began in the early seventeenth century. However, the stage for U.S. slavery was set as early as the fourteenth century, when the rich nations of Spain and Portugal began to capture Africans for enslavement in Europe. When Spain, Portugal, and other European countries conquered and laid claim to the New World of the Caribbean and West Indies in the late sixteenth century, they brought along the practice of slavery. Eventually, slavery expanded to the north, to colonial America.

The first Africans in colonial America were brought to Jamestown by a Dutch ship in 1619. These twenty Africans were indentured servants, which meant that they were to work for a certain period of time in exchange for transportation and room and board. They were assigned land after their service and were considered free Negroes. Nonetheless, their settlement was involuntary.

The status of Africans in colonial America underwent a rapid evolution after 1619. One early judicial decision signaled the change in European attitudes toward Africans. In 1640, three Virginia servants—two Europeans and one African—escaped from their masters. Upon recapture, a Virginia court ordered the European servants to serve their master for one more year, and the African servant to serve his master, or his master's ASSIGNS, for the rest of his life.

As early as 1641, colonial Massachusetts recognized slavery as a legal institution, announcing in its Body of Liberties that "[t]here shall never be any bond slaverie . . . unless it be lawful Captives taken in just warres, and such strangers as willingly sell themselves or are sold to us." Twenty years later, just two generations after the arrival of the first Africans in colonial America, the first statute recognizing African slavery was passed in Virginia.

In the mid-1600s, Virginia colonists began to take note of the phenomenal agricultural production occurring in the Caribbean and West Indies. The extreme labor demands and savage punishments of European colonists there had depleted the population of productive Amerindian slaves, but those same colonists were continuing to prosper. By purchasing masses of able-bodied pubescent and adult Africans, the colonists avoided waiting for a slave population to increase by native birth, and in the scramble for quick, easy, and substantial profits in the New World, this gave them an edge. Virginia colonists, eager to achieve the same prosperity, endeavored to sanction African slavery.

In 1661, Virginia colonists enacted a law that legitimized African slavery and provided that the status of an African child would be determined by the status of its mother. If the mother of a child was a slave, then her child was doomed to slavery. In the following years, colonial Virginia passed more laws that severely restricted the rights of African slaves and expanded the rights of owners of African slaves. Each of the original colonies eventually followed Virginia's lead by enacting similar laws that promoted or recognized the enslavement of Africans.

Two women attend a 1916 convention of former slaves, held in Washington, D.C.

Most of the first African slaves were captured in Africa by the Dutch or by fellow Africans. They were then manacled and delivered in crowded, brutal conditions across the Atlantic Ocean by the Dutch West India Company, an organization formed in Holland for the sole purpose of trafficking in slaves. English companies such as the East India Company and the Royal African Company also contributed to the seventeenth-century American slave trade. Although untold numbers of Africans died en route, the profitable slave trade so increased the African slave population in America that by the late 1600s, European colonists were already beginning to anticipate insurrections and slave revolts. By 1750, populations of displaced Africans would range from an estimated 550 in New Hampshire to over 101,000 in Virginia.

From the beginning, African slaves resisted their servitude by running away, fighting back, poisoning food, and plotting revolts. The first Europeans to openly denounce slavery and work for its abolition were Quakers, or members of the Society of Friends, who were concentrated in Pennsylvania. As early as 1688, the Quakers publicly declared that slavery was at odds with Christianity. Along with other European abolitionists, they actively worked to help African slaves escape their owners.

The legal treatment of African slaves varied slightly from colony to colony according to the area's economic structure. Northern colonies such as Massachusetts, Connecticut, and Rhode Island relied on the export of various local commodities such as fish, liquor, and dairy products, so their involvement with African slavery was in large part limited to slave trading. Nonetheless, the New England colonies sanctioned the use of slave labor, and they enacted codes that prevented African slaves from exercising such basic rights as FREEDOM OF ASSOCIATION and movement. Though generally regarded as less harsh than those of such southern colonies as Virginia and the Carolinas, the New England slave codes nevertheless legalized the enslavement of Africans.

The middle colonies—New York, Pennsylvania, Delaware, and New Jersey—also had codes that promoted the slave industry and deprived African slaves of most basic rights. Laws were often tailored especially for African slaves. In New York, for example, any slave found forty miles north of Albany was presumed to be escaping to Canada and could be executed upon the oath of two witnesses. In New York City, slaves could not appear on the street after dark without a lighted lantern. From 1700 to 1740, growth of the African slave population in New York outdistanced growth of the European population and gave the city the largest slave population in the region. Many of the slaves here provided domestic service to wealthy families. Except in New York, slavery in the middle colonies was not widespread, because the commercial economies and small-scale agriculture practiced by the Germans, Swedes, and Danes in this region did not require it. Further, many settlers in the rural areas of the middle colonies were morally opposed to slavery. Neither of these conditions prevailed in the southern colonies.

Georgia was originally established as a slavery-free English colony in 1733, but the prohibition against slavery was repealed in 1750 after repeated entreaties from European settlers. The economies of colonial Virginia, Maryland, and North and South Carolina centered on large-scale agricultural production. The vast majority of the South's colonial agrarians profited at first from the sale of tobacco, rice, and indigo. These products were planted, cultivated, and harvested exclusively by African slaves on vast farms known as plantations. Plantation production relied on manual labor and required tremendous numbers of workers to be successful, and thus the southern colonies found their needs met by the widespread enslavement of Africans.

Because of the importance of slavery to the plantation-based economies, slave codes in the southern colonies were made quite elaborate. For example, South Carolina prevented slave owners from working their slaves for more than fifteen hours a day in spring and summer, and more than fourteen hours a day in fall and winter. Slave owners were also warned against undue cruelty to slaves. At the same time, Europeans were not allowed to teach African slaves to read or write; freedom of movement was severely restricted for slaves; liquor could not be sold to slaves; and whippings, mutilations, and other forms of punishment for slaves were explicitly authorized by law.

The laws regarding slaves reflected the terrorism and paternalism of slavery. A slave had a nebulous right to self-defense, but a slave owner was allowed to restrain and punish a slave with impunity. A slave owner could not beat a slave publicly, but a slave could not avoid punishment for a crime committed at an owner's command. A free Negro could not voluntarily submit to slavery for a price, and Europeans were not allowed to subject a free African to slavery by treating one as a slave for any length of time. However, every African was presumed to be a slave until she or he could prove otherwise. This PRESUMPTION was abolished in the northern states shortly after the United States won its independence from England, but it remained unchanged in the southern states until the end of the Civil War.

Not all Africans were slaves. Some free Africans had bought their freedom, some were the descendants of Jamestown's first free African servants, some had escaped their owner, and some had been freed, or manumitted, by their owner. A slave owner could not free a slave if doing so left the slave unable to pay his or her debts. Some statutes allowed a slave owner to free only slaves who could work and support themselves, and other statutes required a slave owner to provide continuing financial support to freed slaves.

In some areas in the South, manumission of a slave was illegal, but the law did not prevent a slave owner from sending or taking slaves to another state to set them free. In states where manumission was legal, an owner could free a slave by executing a DEED declaring the slave's liberty. Generally, the deed had to be filed in a county clerk's office or authorized or proved in court. Some states allowed for the manumission of slaves in the slave owner's WILL. A GIFT of land to a slave by a slave owner was often held to be a manumission of the slave, since only a free individual could own land. A manumitted slave was entitled to work for wages and to own land and PERSONAL PROPERTY through acquisition or inheritance.

After the United States won the War of Independence, Vermont, Pennsylvania, New Hampshire, Connecticut, Rhode Island, New York, and New Jersey all passed legislation that gradually abolished slavery. These northern states, inspired mostly by the revolutionary, liberal philosophies of the period, began advocating expanding notions of freedom that were being rejected in Delaware, Maryland, Virginia, the Carolinas, and Georgia.

In May 1787, delegations from each of the thirteen colonies began to meet in Philadelphia to devise a federal constitution. The Constitutional Convention was to begin on May 14, but few representatives had arrived by then, and it was postponed. On May 25, seven states were represented, and the convention began. Delegates from the various colonies continued to arrive through June, with the last ones coming from New Hampshire on July 22, four days before the convention was adjourned. Slavery was just one topic on a very long agenda.

The ABOLITION of the United States' enslavement of Africans was not seriously entertained at the convention. Virginia's GEORGE MASON and many delegates from the northern states argued against any recognition of slavery in the Constitution, but the overriding concern at the convention was to unify the states under a system of government that left substantial control of social and political questions to the individual states. It seemed clear to the majority of the representatives that a country founded on individual freedoms could not participate in slave trading, but it was equally clear that if the widespread enslavement of Africans by the southern states were prohibited by the new federal government, there would be no United States.

North Carolina, South Carolina, and Georgia insisted that a state's right to import slaves be left untouched. Delegates from other states argued for the abolition of slavery, and still other delegates wanted no hint of the practice included in the Constitution. A committee comprising one delegate from each state was dispatched to settle the issue. The committee returned with a constitutional clause, couched in the negative, that made slave trade vulnerable to prohibition after the year 1800. The strange set of bedfellows produced by this issue—New Jersey, Pennsylvania, Delaware, and Virginia were against the clause—illustrated the variety of considerations at play.

After further debate and modification by the entire convention, the Slave Trade Clause was inserted into Section 9 of Article I: "The Migration or Importation of such Persons as any of the States now existing shall think proper to admit, shall not be prohibited by the Congress prior to the Year one thousand eight hundred and eight." Attached to this language was another clause that allowed for the imposition of a tax or duty on such importation, not to exceed $10 for "each Person" (read, "each Slave").

The one other opaque reference to slavery in the Constitution was the so-called Three-fifths Compromise. In Article I, Section 2, the Framers wrote that the population of a state, for purposes of determining taxation and representation in the HOUSE OF REPRESENTATIVES, would be measured by counting the "Number of free Persons, including those bound to Service for a Term of Years, and excluding Indians not taxed, three fifths of all other Persons." This language struggled mightily to avoid the mention of African slavery, but was understood as allowing the southern states to count each slave as three-fifths of a person in a government CENSUS.

This method of population measurement, three-fifths, was actually developed by Congress in 1783, during debate over state representation in the federal government. The northern states opposed the inclusion of African slaves in the determination of population, because the southern states contained thousands of African slaves who played no part in the political process. The southern states argued that a state's African slave population reflected its true power and wealth, which should in turn be reflected in its federal representation. The northern states eventually compromised with the southern states to allow five African slaves to equal three free men for purposes of population determinations and federal representation.

At the Constitutional Convention, standing alone, the three-fifths proviso did not immediately satisfy the majority of states. Opposition to the measure was not organized: no single cause unified the dissatisfied states, and no split occurred between slave states and free states. Opposition also was not based on the morality of counting slaves as less than full citizens: very little wrangling took place over this concern, and an amendment to count slaves as whole persons was rejected by a vote of 8–2. Eventually, the three-fifths ratio was adopted for the Constitution, but only after direct taxation of the states was also tied to state population. Thus, the only compromise regarding the recognition of African slaves grew from struggles over money and political power, not a concern over morality. A showdown between the slave states and the free states over African slavery never occurred. Although the United States was to cease the purchase and sale of slaves, the practice of slavery in the southern states survived the Constitutional Convention.

While all this politicking was taking place, the land in the southern states was fast becoming infertile. Farmers and plantation owners realized they needed to diversify their crops to save the soil. Shortly after the Constitution was ratified in 1789, the southern states sought the development of a cotton gin in order to convert agricultural production from rice, tobacco, and indigo to cotton. The cotton gin, which mechanically extracted cotton seeds, was eventually designed by Eli Whitney and Phineas Miller in 1792. The production of cotton did not require large start-up funds, and with the cotton gin for seed removal, African slaves had more time for cultivation. This all added up to large profits for southern plantation owners. With the help of New England slave traders, they imported African slaves by the tens of thousands in the years following the Constitutional Convention. Nevertheless, in March 1807, Congress passed a law prohibiting the importation of African slaves. Effective January 1, 1808, in fulfillment of the suggestion contained in Article I, Section 2, of the Constitution, the U.S. slave trade officially ended. But a state's right to sanction slavery did not.

In the early 1800s, the United States was expanding, and the question of slavery began to consume the country. In 1819, leaders in the U.S. House of Representatives proposed a bill that would allow the Missouri Territory to enter the Union as a slave state. Although northern

Amistad: Mutiny on a Slave Ship

African slaves occasionally revolted against their masters, and the result was usually severe punishment for the slaves. The mutiny of fifty-four slaves on the Spanish ship *Amistad* in 1839 proved an exception, however, as the U.S. Supreme Court granted the slaves their freedom and allowed them to return to Africa.

The fifty-four Africans were kidnapped in West Africa, near modern-day Sierra Leone, and illegally sold into the Spanish slave trade. They were transported to Cuba, fraudulently classified as native Cuban slaves, and sold to two Spaniards. The slaves were then loaded on the schooner *Amistad,* which set sail for Haiti.

Three days into the journey, the slaves mutinied. Led by Sengbe Pieh, known to the Spanish crew as Cinque, the slaves unshackled themselves, killed the captain and the cook, and forced all but two of the crew to leave the ship. The Africans demanded to be returned to their homeland, but the crew tricked them and sailed toward the United States. In August 1839 the ship was towed into Montauk Point, Long Island, in New York.

Cinque and the others were charged with murder and piracy. A group of abolitionists formed the Amistad Committee, which organized a legal defense that sought the slaves' freedom. President Martin Van Buren, pressed by Spain to return the slaves without trial, hoped the court would find the slaves guilty and order them returned to Cuba. The federal circuit court dismissed the murder and piracy charges because the acts had occurred outside the jurisdiction of the United States. It referred the case to the federal district court for trial to determine if the slaves must be returned to Cuba.

At the trial the slaves argued that there was no legal basis for returning them to Cuba because the importation of slaves from Africa was illegal under Spanish law. The district court agreed, ruling that the Africans were free and should be transported home. Van Buren ordered an immediate appeal to the Supreme Court.

Former president John Quincy Adams represented the slaves before the Supreme Court, making an impassioned argument for their freedom. The Court, in *The Amistad,* 40 U.S. 518 (15 Pet. 518), 10 L. Ed. 826, affirmed the district court and agreed that the Africans were free persons. By the end of 1841, thirty-five of the *Amistad* survivors had sailed for Sierra Leone; the rest remained in the United States.

---

legislators outnumbered southern legislators at the time, House Speaker HENRY CLAY, of Kentucky, arranged an accord between enough congress members to pass a version of the bill that admitted Missouri as a slave state. In exchange for legal slavery in Missouri, the southern legislators agreed to limit the northern boundaries of slavery to the same latitude as the southern boundary of Missouri. Thus were the terms of the MISSOURI COMPROMISE of 1820, which became a watershed in the United States' experience with slavery.

In its constitution, Missouri declared it would not allow slaves to be emancipated without their owner's consent. Furthermore, free African Americans were not allowed to enter the state. Antislavery congress members objected to the latter clause on the ground that it violated the federal Constitution's mandate that "the Citizens of each State shall be entitled to all Privileges and Immunities of Citizens in the several States" (art. IV, § 2). African Americans had, after all, gained citizenship in the northern states.

Again Clay maneuvered votes in Congress. Missouri agreed not to discriminate against citizens from other states, but did so in a resolution that was abstract and unclear and left unsettled the question of precisely who was a citizen of the several states. In 1821, Missouri's constitution was approved, and Missouri was officially a slave state.

Once Missouri was admitted to the Union as a slave state, Maine was admitted as a free state; the Senate had refused to accept Maine until the House altered its position on Missouri. As a result, in 1821, the Union consisted of twelve free states, twelve slaves states, and a deepening divide between the two.

European settlements pressed westward. After the United States acquired the Southwest by force in the Mexican War, it again faced the question of slavery. In 1850, Congress altered the geographic limits on slavery established by the Missouri Compromise. California was admitted as a free state, but the Utah and New Mexico Territories were opened to slavery. The KANSAS-NEBRASKA ACT of 1854 further eroded the dictates of the Missouri Compromise by admitting slavery in those territories.

One particular case brought by a slave came to a head in the 1850s and caught the attention of the Republican presidential candidate for the 1860 election, former Illinois congressman ABRAHAM LINCOLN. In *Dred Scott v. Sandford*, 60 U.S. (19 How.) 393, 15 L. Ed. 691 (1857), Dred Scott sued the widow of his deceased owner in Missouri state court, asking for his freedom. The dispute began in 1834 and ended with an 1857 Supreme Court decision confirming Scott's slave status. The decision galvanized abolitionists in the north and Lincoln railed against the decision in his campaign for the presidency. The decision also strengthened the resolve of pro-slavery forces in the South. As the struggle for power between slavers and emancipators intensified, the geographic lines proscribing slavery, drawn and redrawn, were fast becoming battle lines.

In 1860, Republican Abraham Lincoln won the presidency on an anti-slavery platform, and like-minded Republicans gained a majority in Congress. In February 1861, with the abolition of slavery imminent, South Carolina seceded from the Union, and Virginia, North Carolina, South Carolina, Georgia, Florida, Alabama, Mississippi, Texas, Arkansas, and Tennessee soon followed suit. Before Lincoln's inauguration in March, the Confederacy was in place. On April 12, the Confederates attacked South Carolina's Fort Sumter, and the United States' internal war over the issue of slavery had begun.

Many early American colonists had believed they were justified in enslaving Africans because Africans were not Christians. After the American Revolution, as the country became polarized over the issue of slavery, slavery supporters in the South worked to clear the southern states of anti-slavery leaders and their forces. One abolitionist, for example, was beaten, tarred and feathered, set afire, doused in water, and whipped. As late as the 1820s, more than one hundred abolitionist groups operated in the slave states, but by the 1840s, virtually none were left. Slavers in the southern states also began to cultivate more ambitious rationales for African slavery. Slavery supporters cited essays written by the ancient Greek philosopher ARISTOTLE that declared that slavery was the natural order of things.

Aristotle had claimed that slaves were slaves because they had allowed themselves to become enslaved. This was just and right, his theory continued, because if those with strong bodies (Africans, to U.S. slavers) performed the labor, those with upright bodies (European colonists and their descendants) would have the time and energy for technological and economic advancement. U.S. slavery enthusiasts expanded on the theories of Aristotle and other philoso-phers to explain that it was the Africans' lot in life to be slaves because it was inherent in their nature to be servile and hardworking. Other southern slavers forwent any philosophies of slavery and simply enjoyed the luxuries realized through the enslavement of Africans.

Throughout the Civil War, President Lincoln and the U.S. Congress were busy passing federal legislation on the subject of slavery. On August 6, 1861, Congress passed the Confiscation Act, which allowed the United States to lay claim to any property used in INSURRECTION against it. Under this act, slaves who served in the Confederate army were to be set free upon capture by Union forces. In June 1862, Lincoln signed a bill passed by Congress that abolished slavery in all territories owned by the federal government. On January 1, 1863, Lincoln issued the EMANCIPATION PROCLAMATION, which declared that all slaves in the United States were free persons and that they were to remain free persons.

In April 1865, the Confederate army surrendered to the Union forces. This touched off a flurry of constitutional amendments. The THIRTEENTH AMENDMENT, which abolished slavery, was ratified by Congress on December 6, 1865. The FOURTEENTH AMENDMENT, ratified July 9, 1868, was designed to, in part, establish former slaves as full citizens and ensure that no African American would be deprived of any of the PRIVILEGES AND IMMUNITIES that come with citizenship. The Fourteenth Amendment also deleted the offensive three-fifths ratio from the measurement of populations in Section 2 of Article I, and declared that any debts relating to the loss or EMANCIPATION of slaves were illegal and void. The FIFTEENTH AMENDMENT, ratified February 3, 1870, gave male African Americans and male former slaves the right to vote.

African slavery in the United States has continued to haunt the country long after its abolition. In the North, segregation of African Americans from the European populations has been a reality, if not sanctioned by law. Beginning in the 1880s, many southern states enacted Black Codes, or JIM CROW LAWS, which restricted the freedom of movement and expression of African Americans and enforced their segregation from the rest of society.

Contemporary Slavery Notions of slavery in the United States have expanded to include any situation in which one person controls the life, liberty, and fortune of another person. All forms of slavery are now widely recognized as inherently immoral and thoroughly evil. Slavery still occurs in various forms, but when it does, accused offenders are aggressively prosecuted. Federal statutes punish by fine or imprisonment the enticement of persons into slavery (18 U.S.C.A. § 1583), and the holding to or selling of persons into INVOL-UNTARY SERVITUDE (§ 1584). In addition, whosoever builds a ship for slave carriage, serves on a ship carrying slaves, or owns a slave-carrying ship will be fined or imprisoned under 18 U.S.C.A. §§ 1582, 1586, and 1587, respectively.

The statute 18 U.S.C.A. § 1581 prohibits PEONAGE, which is involuntary servitude for the payment of a debt. Labor camps are perhaps the most common violators of the law against peonage. The operators of some labor camps keep victims for work in fields through impoverished conditions, threats, acts of violence, and ALCO-HOL consumption. Offenders often provide rudimentary shelter to migrant workers and demand work in return, which can constitute involuntary servitude. An individual can also be convicted of sale into involuntary servitude for delivering victims under false pretenses to such labor camps.

CROSS-REFERENCES

Celia, a Slave; Civil Rights; Civil Rights Acts; Constitution of the United States; Douglass, Frederick; *Dred Scott v. Sandford*; Fugitive Slave Act of 1850; Indenture; Ku Klux Klan; Ku Klux Klan Act; *Prigg v. Pennsylvania*; Republican Party; States' Rights; Taney, Roger Brooke.

SLIP DECISION 📖 A copy of a judgment by the U.S. Supreme Court or other tribunal that is printed and distributed almost immediately subsequent to the time that it is handed down by the court. 📖

SLIP LAW 📖 A copy of a BILL that is passed by a state legislature and endorsed by the governor, or passed by Congress and signed by the president, and is printed and distributed almost immediately. 📖

An example of a slip law

Public Law 97-297
97th Congress
October 12, 1982

An Act

To amend title 18, United States Code, to provide a criminal penalty for threats against former Presidents, major Presidential candidates, and certain other persons protected by the Secret Service, and for other purposes.

Be it enacted by the Senate and House of Representatives of the United States of America in Congress assembled, That (a) chapter 41 of title 18, United States Code, is amended by adding at the end the following new section:

"**§ 879. Threats against former Presidents and certain other persons protected by the Secret Service**

"(a) Whoever knowingly and willfully threatens to kill, kidnap, or inflict bodily harm upon—

"(1) a former President or a member of the immediate family of a former President;

"(2) a member of the immediate family of the President, the President-elect, the Vice President, or the Vice President elect; or

"(3) a major candidate for the office of President or Vice President, or the spouse of such candidate;

who is protected by the Secret Service as provided by law, shall be fined not more than $1,000 or imprisoned not more than three years, or both.

"(b) As used in this section—

"(1) the term 'immediate family' means—

"(A) with respect to subsection (a)(1) of this section, the wife of a former President during his lifetime, the widow of a former President until her death or remarriage, and minor children of a former President until they reach sixteen years of age; and

"(B) with respect to subsection (a)(2) of this section, a person to whom the President, President-elect, Vice President, or Vice President elect—

"(i) is related by blood, marriage, or adoption; or

"(ii) stands in loco parentis;

"(2) the term 'major candidate for the office of President or Vice President' means a candidate referred to in the first section of the joint resolution entitled 'Joint resolution to authorize the United States Secret Service to furnish protection to major Presidential or Vice Presidential candidates', approved June 6, 1968 (18 U.S.C. 3056 note); and

(continued on next page)

An example of a
slip law
(continued)

"(3) the terms 'President-elect' and 'Vice President elect' have the meanings given those terms in section 871(b) of this title."

(b) The table of sections for chapter 41 of title 18, United States Code, is amended by adding at the end the following new item:

SEC. 2. Section 871(a) of title 18, United States Code, is amended by inserting after "to take the life of" the following: ", to kidnap,".

SEC. 3. The sentence beginning "Subject to the direction" in section 3056(a) of title 18, United States Code, is amended—

(1) by striking out "and 871 of this title" and inserting in lieu thereof "871, and 879 of this title"; and

(2) by striking out ", joint-stock land banks and Federal land bank associations are concerned, of sections 218, 221" and inserting in lieu thereof "and Federal land bank associations are concerned, of sections 213, 216".

SEC. 4. (a) Section 1013 of title 18, United States Code, is amended by striking out ", or by any joint-stock land bank or banks".

(b) Section 1014 of such title is amended by striking out "a joint-stock land bank,".

(c) Section 1907 of such title is amended by striking out ", Federal land bank, or joint-stock land bank" and inserting in lieu thereof "or Federal land bank".

Approved October 12, 1982.

SMALL BUSINESS 📖 A type of enterprise that is independently owned and operated, has few employees, does a small amount of business, and is not predominant in its area of operation. 📖

See also SOLE PROPRIETORSHIP.

SMALL BUSINESS ADMINISTRATION

The Small Business Administration (SBA) is a federal agency that seeks to aid, counsel, assist, and protect the interests of small business. The SBA ensures that small business concerns receive a fair portion of federal government purchases, CONTRACTS, and subcontracts, as well as of the sales of government property. The agency is best known for its loans to small business concerns, state and local development companies, and the victims of floods or other catastrophes.

The SBA was created by the Small Business Act of 1953 (67 Stat. 232 [15 U.S.C.A. § 631 et seq.]) and derives its present authority from this act and the Small Business Investment Act of 1958 (15 U.S.C.A. § 661).

Financial Assistance The SBA provides guaranteed loans to small businesses to help them finance plant construction, conversion, or expansion and acquire equipment, facilities, machinery, supplies, or materials. It also provides them with working capital. Since 1976 farms have been considered to be small business concerns.

The SBA also provides loan guarantees to finance residential or commercial construction. The administration may finance small firms that manufacture, sell, install, service, or develop specific energy measures. In an effort to reach more businesses, the SBA provides loans and grants to private, nonprofit organizations that, in turn, make small loans and provide technical assistance to small businesses.

Through its Surety Bond Guarantee Program, the SBA helps to make the contract bonding process accessible to small and emerging contractors who find bonding unavailable. A BOND is posted as a guarantee that the contracted work will be performed. If the work is not performed, the money pledged in the bond will be used to cover the contractor's default. The SBA program guarantees to reimburse the issuer of the bond up to 90 percent of losses incurred under bid, payment, or performance bonds issued to small contractors on contracts valued up to $1.25 million.

Disaster Assistance The SBA lends money to help the victims of floods, riots, or other catastrophes repair or replace most disaster-damaged property. Direct loans with subsidized interest rates are made to assist individuals, homeowners, businesses, and small agricultural cooperatives without credit elsewhere that have sustained substantial economic injury resulting from natural disasters.

Investment Assistance The administration LICENSES, regulates, and provides financial assistance to small business investment companies and section 301(d) licensees (formerly minority enterprise small business investment companies). The sole function of these investment companies is to provide venture capital in the form of equity financing, long-term loan funds, and management services to small business concerns.

Government Contracting The SBA works closely with the purchasing agencies of the federal government and with the leading U.S. contractors in developing policies and procedures that will increase the number of contracts awarded to small businesses.

The administration has a number of services that help small firms obtain and fulfill government contracts. It sets aside suitable government purchases for competitive award to small business concerns and provides an appeal procedure for a low-bidding small firm whose ability to perform a contract is questioned by the contracting officer. The SBA maintains close ties with prime contractors and refers qualified small firms to them. In addition, it works with federal agencies in setting goals for procuring prime contracts and subcontracts for small businesses, especially those owned by women and members of disadvantaged groups.

Business Initiatives The SBA is recognized for its longtime effort to provide education, counseling, and information to small business owners and prospective owners. It has increasingly relied on forging partnerships with nongovernment groups to deliver business education and training programs at low cost. For example, the Service Corps of Retired Executives (SCORE) provides one-on-one counseling free of charge.

The Business Information Center (BIC) program is an innovative approach to providing a one-stop location for information, education, and training. Components of BIC include the latest computer hardware and software, an extensive small business reference library, and a collection of current management videotapes.

The SBA also produces many pamphlets and publications about a variety of business and management topics. It has also established SBA Online, a toll-free electronic bulletin board for small businesses.

Minority Enterprise Development Sections 7(j) and 8(a) of the Small Business Act provide for the Minority Enterprise Development Program, designed to promote business ownership by socially and economically disadvantaged persons. Participation is available to small businesses that are at least 51 percent unconditionally owned, controlled, and managed by one or more individuals determined by the SBA to be socially and economically disadvantaged. Program participants receive a wide variety of services, including management and technical assistance, loans, and federal contracts.

Advocacy The Office of Advocacy serves as a leading advocate within PUBLIC POLICY councils for the more than twenty-two million small businesses in the United States. The office, which is headed by the chief counsel for advocacy, lobbies Congress, the executive branch, and state agencies concerning the interests and needs of small business. The office also is a leading source of information about the state of small business and the issues that affect small business success and growth.

Women's Business Ownership The Office of Women's Business Ownership (OWBO) provides assistance to the increasing number of women business owners and acts as their advocate in the public and private sector. It is the only office in the federal government specifically targeted to women business owners, assisting them through technical, financial, and management information and business training, skills counseling, and research.

The OWBO has established fifty-four training centers in twenty-eight states and the District of Columbia, which provide community-based training for women at every stage of their entrepreneurial careers. In addition, the office created the Women's Network for Entrepreneurial Training, a one-year mentoring program linking experienced entrepreneurs with women whose businesses are poised for growth. This program is designed to help women avoid the common mistakes of new business owners.

Small Business Development Centers Small Business Development Centers provide counseling and training to existing and prospective small business owners. The 950 centers operate in every state, as well as in Puerto Rico, the U.S. Virgin Islands, and Guam. Each center is a partner with state government in economic development activities to support and assist small businesses.

Administration The SBA has its headquarters in Washington, D.C. It maintains ten regional offices and has field offices in most major U.S. cities.

SMALL CLAIMS COURT A SPECIAL COURT, sometimes called CONCILIATION court, that provides expeditious, informal, and inexpensive adjudication of small claims.

Every state has established a small claims or conciliation court to resolve legal disputes involving an amount of money that is less than a set dollar amount. At one time, $1,000 was the limit. However, many courts have raised the limit to $3,000, and a few will hear disputes involving amounts of up to $5,000 or more. Small claims courts and the rules that govern them emphasize informality and timely resolution of disputes. Most parties represent themselves in small claims court, in part because the facts of the dispute are simple but also because it makes little economic sense to pay attorneys' fees.

The first small claims court was created in Cleveland in 1913. Within a few years every state had such a court of limited JURISDICTION. Small claims courts are attractive for consumers who want to collect a small DEBT or recover DAMAGES for a faulty product or for shoddy service. However, small claims courts are used heavily by businesses and PUBLIC UTILITIES that want to collect payments from customers for unpaid bills. In a single court session, a department store, utility company, or hospital may obtain JUDGMENTS against a long list of DEBTORS, making the process very economical.

To bring an ACTION in small claims court, a person must complete a form that is available from the local COURT ADMINISTRATOR. The person must provide the correct names and addresses of all defendants, make a simple statement of the dispute, and state a CLAIM for the amount of money involved. As PLAINTIFF in the action, the person must pay a small filing fee, usually less than $100, to the court administrator. If the plaintiff is successful in the lawsuit, he can recover the filing fee from the DEFENDANT, together with any money awarded.

A copy of the plaintiff's statement must be properly served upon the defendant or the action will be dismissed. In some states a deputy SHERIFF or a PROCESS SERVER must personally serve a small claims court SUMMONS and COMPLAINT for a small fee. In many states, however, service can be accomplished by mailing a copy of the complaint to the defendant. In these jurisdictions it is essential to have an accurate name and address for the defendant.

When the defendant is a CORPORATION, a plaintiff can check with the office of the secretary of state or corporate registration department to obtain the correct address because a corporation must register the name and address where it can be served with legal process. No restriction ordinarily exists on the type of individual or business that can be sued in small claims court, but a defendant must live, work, or have an office within the area served by the court.

Once the defendant is served with the statement, she will be on NOTICE that a HEARING has been scheduled on the matter. A defendant may file a COUNTERCLAIM growing out of the same dispute against the plaintiff. For example, a plaintiff sues a landscape contractor for planting diseased and dying trees. The plaintiff asks for money to pay to have the trees removed and for a refund of money already paid to the contractor. The contractor could file a counterclaim, disputing the plaintiff's ALLEGATIONS and demanding payment still owed by the plaintiff.

Hearings may be conducted by a judge or by a judicial officer who is not a judge but is usually an attorney. Some sessions of small claims court may be held in the evening so that people need not miss work to attend court. Generally there is no jury, and the judge or judicial officer will make a decision at the end of the presentation of the EVIDENCE.

The informality of small claims court extends to courtroom procedure. The rules of CIVIL PROCEDURE and evidence, which in other courts must be rigorously followed, are generally relaxed in small claims court. Nevertheless, HEARSAY testimony (where one WITNESS attempts to tell what another person said) is not admitted. Most small claims courts also will not allow AFFIDAVITS or notarized statements into evidence because the other side cannot cross-examine the witness. Therefore, a party must bring witnesses to TESTIFY to events that they have observed.

Once the court makes a decision, the losing party has a period of time to file an APPEAL. The appealing party must pay a filing fee to initiate the new review, which in most states results in a new trial before a court of GENERAL JURISDICTION. The new trial will be conducted with more formality.

If the losing party does not appeal the case, judgment will be entered for the winning party. Once judgment is entered, the losing party can voluntarily pay the amount awarded. If the losing party refuses to pay, the party holding the judgment can take steps to make the judgment collectible. A court can enter an order authorizing the sheriff to serve a WRIT of EXECUTION on the losing party. This writ permits the sheriff to seize and sell ASSETS to pay the judgment.

Though small claims court is an attractive option for many persons, it is not designed to handle complicated litigation or areas of the law that deal with human relationships. Thus, small claims courts do not hear DIVORCE, CHILD SUPPORT, or other FAMILY LAW cases.

SMART MONEY Vindictive, punitive, or exemplary DAMAGES given by way of punishment and example, in cases of gross misconduct of a defendant.

SMITH, ROBERT Robert Smith was a lawyer and statesman who served as attorney general of the United States under President THOMAS JEFFERSON and as secretary of state under President JAMES MADISON.

BIOGRAPHY

CULVER PICTURES

Robert Smith

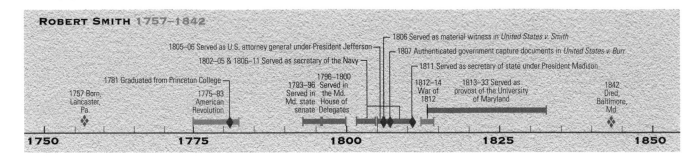

1805–06 Served as U.S. attorney general under President Jefferson

1806 Served as material witness in *United States v. Smith*

1807 Authenticated government capture documents in *United States v. Burr*

1802–05 & 1806–11 Served as secretary of the Navy

1811 Served as secretary of state under President Madison

1781 Graduated from Princeton College

1796–1800
1793–96 Served in
Served in the Md.
Md. state House of
senate Delegates

1757 Born,
Lancaster,
Pa.

1775–83
American
Revolution

1812–14
War of
1812

1813–33 Served as
provost of the University
of Maryland

1842
Died,
Baltimore,
Md.

1750   1775   1800   1825   1850

Smith's father, John Smith, a native of Strabane, Ireland, immigrated to the American colonies in the 1740s. By 1759, he was living in Baltimore and had established himself as a merchant and shipping agent. In 1766, he financed the building of Baltimore's first market house and the development of the city's first residential neighborhood. He was an advocate of independence for the American colonies and active in politics and the military.

Smith was born in November 1757 in Lancaster, Pennsylvania. He came of age at the height of the American Revolution and, like his father and his brother, Samuel Smith, volunteered to serve. He distinguished himself at the Battle of Brandywine, but his experience convinced him that he was not suited to a military career.

After the war, Smith attended Princeton College. He graduated in 1781 and went on to study law. Following his admission to the bar, he established a practice in Baltimore, and looked after family business interests while his father served the first of two terms in the Maryland state senate.

By 1793, Smith had followed his father into the political arena. He served in the Maryland state senate from 1793 to 1796 and in the Maryland House of Delegates from 1796 to 1800. While in the house of delegates, he served a concurrent term on Baltimore's city council.

In 1801, Smith was appointed secretary of the Navy when his brother stepped down from that post following an APPROPRIATIONS dispute with Congress. Up to that time, military appropriations had not been monitored or controlled as closely as other government expenditures— and President Jefferson and members of his cabinet had become increasingly concerned about moneys drawn from the Treasury by the Secretaries of War and the Navy. When the cabinet curtailed lump-sum payments and demanded an itemized accounting of how funds were spent, Smith's brother considered the demands to be a personal attack, and he resigned. Smith, who had a far better understanding of

business and accounting practices, was less inclined to view the increased scrutiny as an attack on his character.

Most historians record that Smith served as secretary of the Navy from January 1802 to March 1805, but there are indications that he continued to act as secretary during his appointment as attorney general of the United States from March 1805 to the end of the year. Though his was an official appointment as attorney general, he argued no cases before the U.S. Supreme Court and wrote no opinions.

There are reasons to believe that Smith's cabinet service as secretary of the Navy and official duties as attorney general were curtailed for personal as well as political reasons. By 1805, his family had been involved in a number of incidents that caused embarrassment in Washington, D.C. One celebrated event covered by Washington papers was a party given by Smith and his wife for a niece who married Napoléon Bonaparte's brother. Elizabeth Patterson Bonaparte scandalized Washington with her transparent ball gown, and offended the British ambassador with her suggestive dancing.

In January 1806, Smith was asked by the president to consider an appointment as chancellor of Maryland and chief judge of the District of Baltimore. (*Chancellor* is the name given to the presiding judge of a court of chancery.) Smith declined the opportunity and remained in Washington.

By July 1806, Smith was once again acting as the secretary of the Navy. In *United States v. Smith*, 27 F. Cas. 1192 (D.N.Y. July 15, 1806), he was called to testify in this capacity as a material witness in a New York trial. And in *United States v. Burr*, 25 F. Cas. 55 (D. Va. Aug. 31, 1807), Smith, as secretary of the Navy, was asked to verify the authenticity of government documents ordering AARON BURR'S capture.

Smith was named secretary of state on March 6, 1811, by President Madison. He served until November 25, when Madison called for his resignation. Madison intimates regarded Smith as an "ornamental" secretary of state because Madison, who had been secretary of state in the Jefferson administration, continued to discharge the duties of his previous office while serving as president. Before calling for Smith's resignation, Madison attempted to ease him out of office by offering him an embassy post in Russia. Smith declined the offer and decided to return to Baltimore.

In 1813, Smith was appointed provost of the University of Maryland. For the next twenty years, he devoted his time to building the university's prestige and securing its financial future.

Smith died in Baltimore on November 26, 1842.

SMITH, WILLIAM FRENCH

William French Smith served as U.S. attorney general from 1981 to 1985. A longtime friend and confidant of President RONALD REAGAN, Smith helped formulate the conservative policies that came to be identified with the Reagan administration.

Smith was born on August 26, 1917, in Wilton, New Hampshire. He graduated from the University of California at Los Angeles in 1939 and from the Harvard Law School in 1942. From 1942 to 1946, Smith served in the U.S. Navy Reserve, reaching the rank of lieutenant.

In 1946 Smith joined the Los Angeles law firm of Gibson, Dunn, and Crutcher, one of the largest and most prominent corporate firms in California. He specialized in labor law, eventually becoming a senior partner and head of the firm's labor department. He enjoyed a reputation as a tough but flexible negotiator. He served as a director of the Legal Aid Foundation of Los Angeles from 1963 to 1972.

During the 1960s Smith became active in conservative Republican party politics. During Arizona Senator BARRY M. GOLDWATER's 1964 presidential campaign, Smith met Ronald Reagan, who was working for Goldwater. Smith was impressed by Reagan's views and his political potential and was a member of a small group of southern California business leaders who

BIOGRAPHY

UPI/CORBIS-BETTMANN

William French Smith

"WE HAVE LOST CONTROL OF OUR BORDERS. WE HAVE PURSUED UNREALISTIC POLICIES. WE HAVE FAILED TO ENFORCE OUR LAWS EFFECTIVELY."

urged Reagan to run for governor in 1966. After Reagan was elected governor, Smith became his personal adviser. In 1968 Reagan appointed him to the University of California Board of Regents. Smith later served three terms as chairman of the board.

Smith remained a close adviser to Reagan after he left the governorship and began his quest for the presidency. When Reagan was elected president in 1980, one of his first appointments was the naming of Smith as his attorney general.

During Smith's tenure the Justice Department shifted its position on a number of issues, including ABORTION, CIVIL RIGHTS, and ANTITRUST LAWS. Adhering to his conservative political views, Smith urged the U.S. Supreme Court to reassess its rulings in earlier abortion cases and to accord greater deference to states that wished to restrict abortions. The Justice Department also placed less emphasis on AFFIRMATIVE ACTION as a means of addressing past racial discrimination and on mandatory busing as a means of creating integrated public school systems. Although Smith maintained that he vigorously enforced civil rights laws, his critics argued that the department filed fewer cases in the areas of housing and educational discrimination than it did under previous administrations.

In creating antitrust policy, Smith contended that bigness in business is not necessarily bad and that the government should be concerned only with grossly anticompetitive behavior. He was instrumental in developing a more tolerant policy toward mergers. This shift in the federal government's antitrust position has been credited with contributing to the wave of MERGERS AND ACQUISITIONS that occurred during the 1980s.

Smith also pursued a strong anticrime initiative, increasing the resources used to fight the distribution and sale of illegal narcotics by 100 percent. He also successfully lobbied for the passage of the Comprehensive Crime Control Act of 1984 (Pub. L. No. 98-473, 98 Stat. 1838), a sweeping measure that included revised federal rules on BAIL and the establishment of a

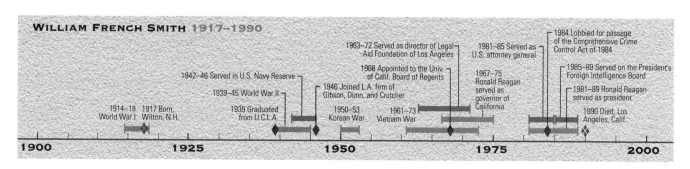

WILLIAM FRENCH SMITH 1917–1990

1914–18 World War I
1917 Born, Wilton, N.H.
1939 Graduated from U.C.L.A.
1939–45 World War II
1942–46 Served in U.S. Navy Reserve
1946 Joined L.A. firm of Gibson, Dunn, and Crutcher
1950–53 Korean War
1961–73 Vietnam War
1963–72 Served as director of Legal-Aid Foundation of Los Angeles
1967–75 Ronald Reagan served as governor of California
1968 Appointed to the Univ. of Calif. Board of Regents
1981–85 Served as U.S. attorney general
1981–89 Ronald Reagan served as president
1984 Lobbied for passage of the Comprehensive Crime Control Act of 1984
1985–89 Served on the President's Foreign Intelligence Board
1990 Died, Los Angeles, Calif.

1900   1925   1950   1975   2000

commission to create new federal SENTENCING guidelines.

In January 1984 Smith announced his resignation, saying that he wished to work on President Reagan's reelection campaign and to return to private life. He did not leave office, however, until February 1985. This delay was caused by the difficulties that his eventual successor, EDWIN MEESE III, encountered in obtaining Senate confirmation.

Smith died on October 29, 1990, in Los Angeles.

SMITH ACT 📖 An antisedition enactment (54 Stat. 670) by Congress in 1940 that proscribed, among other things, the ADVOCACY of the forcible or violent overthrow of the government. 📖

The Smith Act in 1940 became the analogue of the New York Criminal Anarchy Act sustained in *Gitlow v. New York*, 268 U.S. 652, 45 S. Ct. 625, 69 L. Ed. 1138 (1925). New York had passed that law in 1902, shortly after the ASSASSINATION of President WILLIAM McKINLEY. Between the occupation of Czechoslovakia and the Ribbentrop-Molotov pact of 1939, the House of Representatives drafted the Smith Act because of a fear that there might be a repetition of the anarchist agitation that had occurred in 1900 or the antipathy toward alien radicalism that had surfaced in 1919. Congress was also worried about Nazi or Communist subversion after war broke out in Europe.

Under a 1956 amendment to the Smith Act, if two or more persons conspire to commit any offense described in the statute, each is subject to a maximum fine of $20,000 or a maximum term of imprisonment of twenty years, or both, and is ineligible for employment by the United States or its agencies for five years after convic-

Defendants Claudia Jones, Elizabeth Gurley Flynn, Pettis Perry, and Betty Gannett left a federal courthouse during a break in their trial under the Smith Act. Jones and Gannett were members of the Communist party, Perry was a member of the Farm Commission, and Jones was an officer of the Women's Commission.

tion. The Smith Act, as enacted in 1940, contained a CONSPIRACY provision, but effective September 1, 1948, the Smith Act was repealed and substantially reenacted as part of the 1948 recodification, minus the conspiracy provision. On June 25, 1948, the Federal general conspiracy statute was passed, effective September 1, 1948, which contained the same provisions as the deleted conspiracy section of the original Smith Act except that the showing of overt acts was required and the maximum penalty became five years' imprisonment instead of ten (18 U.S.C.A. § 2385). The general conspiracy statute became operative, with respect to conspiracies to violate the Smith Act, substantially in the same manner and to the same extent as previously.

The conspiracy provisions of the Smith Act and its provisions defining the substantive offenses have been upheld. An intent to cause the overthrow of the government by force and violence is an essential element of the offenses. The advocacy of peaceful change in U.S. social, economic, or political institutions, irrespective of how fundamental or expansive or drastic such proposals might be, is not forbidden.

A conspiracy can exist even though the activities of the defendants do not culminate in an attempt to overthrow the government by force and violence. A conspiracy to advocate overthrow of the government by force or violence, as distinguished from the advocacy itself, can be constitutionally restrained even though it consists of mere preparation because the existence of the conspiracy creates the peril.

An agreement to advocate forcible overthrow of the government is not an unlawful conspiracy under the Smith Act if the agreement does not call for advocacy of action; the act covers only advocacy of action for the overthrow of the government by force and violence rather than advocacy or teaching of theoretical concepts. Those to whom the advocacy is directed must be urged to do something, immediately or in the future, rather than merely to believe in a doctrine. A Smith Act conspiracy requires an agreement to teach people to engage in TANGIBLE action toward the violent overthrow of the existing government as soon as possible.

An individual defendant cannot be convicted of willful adherence to a Smith Act conspiracy unless something said by the defendant or communicated to another person manifests her understanding that, beyond supporting the idea and objective of violent overthrow of the existing government, particular action to that end is to be advocated. Advocacy of immediate action is not necessary; advocacy of action at a crucial time in the future when the time for action would seem ripe and success would seem achievable is sufficient. There must be a plan to use language reasonably calculated to incite the audience to employ violence against the government. The use of lawful speech, an agreement to share abstract revolutionary doctrine, and an agreement to use force against the government in the future do not constitute a conspiracy to use illegal language. Cooperative action on the part of a number of persons comprising a political party having as its goal the overthrow of the government by force and violence violates the conspiracy provision.

The "membership clause" of the Smith Act has also been the subject of controversy. Although the Smith Act does not proscribe mere membership in an organization that advocates the forcible overthrow of the government as a theoretical matter, it does cover active members who, with a culpable knowledge and intent, engage in significant action to achieve this objective or commit themselves to undertake such action. Present advocacy of future action for violent overthrow violates the Smith Act, but an expression of sympathy with the purported illegal conduct is not within the ambit of the statute. Guilt cannot be imputed to a person solely on the basis of his associations.

CROSS-REFERENCES

Anarchism; Communism; *Dennis v. United States*; *Gitlow v. New York*; Red Scare.

SMUGGLING 📖 The criminal offense of bringing into, or removing from, a country items that are prohibited or upon which customs or excise duties have not been paid. 📖

Smuggling is the secret movement of goods across national borders to avoid CUSTOMS DUTIES or import or export restrictions. It typically occurs when either the customs duties are high enough to allow a smuggler to make a large profit on the clandestine goods or when there is a strong demand for prohibited goods, such as narcotics or weapons. The United States polices smuggling through various federal agencies, including the U.S. Customs Service, the U.S. Border Patrol, the U.S. Coast Guard, and the Drug Enforcement Administration.

Federal law prohibits the importation of a number of items that are injurious to public health or welfare, including diseased plants or animals, OBSCENE films and magazines, and illegal narcotics. Importation of certain items is prohibited for economic or political purposes. For example, the United States bans trade with Cuba, which means that Cuban cigars may not

be legally imported. This restriction inevitably results in the smuggling of Cuban cigars into the United States. Federal law also bans the export of military weapons or items related to the national defense without an export permit.

In addition, federal law prohibits the importation of goods on which required customs or excise duties have not been paid. Such duties are fixed by federal law to raise revenue and to influence commerce.

Travelers at international borders can properly be stopped by customs agents, required to identify themselves, and asked to submit to a search. To combat smuggling, customs agents have the authority to search an individual and his baggage or any packages or containers sent into the country. Within the United States, police cannot conduct searches unless they have a warrant, probable cause to suspect unlawful activity, or the consent of the individual being searched. Such requirements do not apply to border searches. Customs agents have a right to search anyone at a border for no reason at all, although they ordinarily only conduct extensive and thorough searches of individuals who arouse suspicion. Law enforcement agencies have developed "drug courier profiles" that help customs agents identify and question individuals who are likely carriers of narcotics.

Smugglers use two methods to move goods. One is to move cargoes undetected across borders. Smugglers move illegal narcotics from Mexico into remote areas of the Southwest United States using airplanes, trucks, and human "mules." These "mules" walk across an isolated region of the Mexico-U.S. border with backpacks full of illegal narcotics.

The other method is one of concealment. For example, a smuggler may hide illegal narcotics in unlikely places on ships or cars, in baggage or cargo, or on a person. Some drug couriers swallow containers of narcotics to avoid detection of the drugs if searched.

In the event that a traveler possesses anything that he did not declare to customs inspectors, or any prohibited items, he can be compelled to pay the required duties, plus penalties, and he can also be arrested. Customs agents can seize the illegal goods.

Federal law imposes harsh sanctions for the offense of smuggling. An individual can be convicted merely for having illegal goods in her possession if she fails to adequately explain their presence. Anyone who is guilty of knowingly smuggling any goods that are prohibited by law or that should have come through customs, or who receives, buys, sells, transports, or aids in the commission of one of these acts can be charged with a FELONY and can also be assessed civil penalties. The merchandise itself, as well as any vessel or vehicle used to transport it, can be forfeited to the United States under forfeiture proceedings.

See also DRUGS AND NARCOTICS; SEARCH AND SEIZURE.

SOCIALISM

An economic and social theory that seeks to maximize wealth and opportunity for all people through public ownership and control of industries and social services.

The general goal of socialism is to maximize wealth and opportunity, or to minimize human suffering, through public control of industry and social services. Socialism is an alternative to capitalism, where the means and profits of production are privately held. Socialism became a strong international movement in the early nineteenth century as the Industrial Revolution brought great changes to production methods and capacities and led to a decline in working conditions. Socialist writers and agitators in the United States helped fuel the labor movement but were often branded as radicals and jailed under a variety of laws punishing attempts to overthrow the government. Although government programs such as SOCIAL SECURITY and WELFARE incorporate some socialist tenets, socialism has never posed a serious challenge to capitalism in the United States.

One of the early forms of socialism was the communitarian movement, popularized by the brothers George and Frederick Evans, who came to New York from England in 1820. Communitarianism, which was based on the ideals of the French theorists JEAN-JACQUES ROUSSEAU and François-Noël Babeuf, involved the pursuit of utopian living in small cooperative communities. Cooperative living gained greater popularity under the utopian socialists, such as the Welsh industrialist Robert Owen and the French philosopher Charles Fourier. Owen's followers established a self-sufficient utopian community in New Harmony, Indiana, in 1825 and Fourier's followers did the same in the 1830s and 1840s on the east coast. Both of these efforts failed, however.

In 1848 the German philosophers KARL MARX and Friedrich Engels introduced scientific socialism with their extremely influential work, the *Communist Manifesto*. Scientific socialism became the definitive ideology of a second, more powerful phase of socialism. Scientific socialism applied the dialectic method of the German philosopher GEORG HEGEL to the political and social spheres. Using discussion and

reasoning as a form of intellectual investigation, Marx and Engels identified a historical progression in human society from SLAVERY to FEUDALISM and finally to capitalism. Under capitalism—defined as a global system based on technology transcending national boundaries—society was divided into two components: the bourgeoisie, who owned the methods of production, and the proletariat, the laborers who operated the production facilities to produce goods. Marx and Engels predicted the disappearance of the middle class and ultimately a REVOLUTION as the vast proletariat wrested the methods of production from the control of the small bourgeoisie elite. This revolution would usher in an era when resources were owned by the people as a whole and markets were subject to cooperative administration.

The *Communist Manifesto* made less of an impact in the United States than in Europe, in part because the nation's attention was focused on the issue of slavery and the growing division between the North and South. When these tensions escalated into the Civil War, a great increase in industrialization led to the emergence of socialist labor organizations. At the same time, political refugees from Europe contributed socialist theories to labor and political movements. In 1866 socialists who had been heavily influenced by German immigrants helped create the National Labor Union. Their efforts led to an 1868 statute (15 Stat. 77) establishing the eight-hour day for federal government workers; however, it went ignored and unenforced. The National Labor Union disappeared a few years after the death of its founder, William Sylvis, in 1869, but the ties between labor and socialism remained.

As socialists across Europe and the United States debated and extrapolated on Marx's initial definitions and their application under widely varying conditions, socialism gradually divided into three major philosophies: revisionism, ANARCHISM, and bolshevism. Revisionist socialism promoted gradual reform, compromise, and nonviolence. Initially, "reform" meant the nationalization of state and local public works and large-scale industries. Dedicated to democratic ideals, revisionists believed they could achieve civilized progress and higher consciousness through economic justice and complete equality.

Anarchic socialism, best exemplified by the Russian Mikhail Bakunin (1814–1876), sought the abolition of both property and the state. Under anarchic socialism society would be composed of small collectives of producers, distributors, and consumers. Anarchism reflected the desire of the dispossessed to eliminate bourgeois institutions altogether. Like its contemporary syndicalism in France, anarchic socialism sought the immediate implementation of the dictatorship of the proletariat. Anarchic socialism and its derivations failed to attract a mass following, but its doctrines of disrespect for political institutions and immediate action found a home in the INDUSTRIAL WORKERS OF THE WORLD.

Bolshevism advocated the use of a select revolutionary cadre to seize control of the state. Bolshevists asserted that this cadre was needed to raise the consciousness of the proletariat and move toward a socialist future through absolute dictatorship. Their preferred method of redistributing wealth and resources was authoritarian collectivism, commonly known as COMMUNISM. Under authoritarian collectivism the state would own and distribute all goods and services. In envisioning this role for the state, the Bolshevists rejected both classical and theoretical socialism. Their only tie to classical socialism, besides the rhetorical one, was their view of the state as having a role in ameliorating the suffering brought about by industrial capitalism.

The Knights of Labor, which was formed in 1871 in Philadelphia, became the first truly national and broadly inclusive union in the United States. Revisionists worked within this union and other labor and third-party groups, often in leadership roles, to achieve definable goals that would culminate in a socialist state. Preaching reform, education, and cooperation, the union grew in numbers until 1886. In May of that year, during a STRIKE sanctioned by the Knights against the McCormick Harvester plant in Chicago, an unknown person threw a bomb into the ranks of police sent to disperse a public gathering organized by anarchist socialists. The HAYMARKET RIOT, as it became known, set the stage for the first RED SCARE in U.S. history. Eight anarchist leaders were charged with MURDER on the basis of speech defined as CONSPIRACY. The use of a judge-selected jury and his instructions to them led to the conviction of the anarchists, four of whom were sentenced to death and hanged. The U.S. Supreme Court could find no principle of federal law to review the case.

The reaction that followed the riot signaled the end of anarchism as a force in U.S. politics. It was also the end of the first phase of inclusive, or industrial unionism, as opposed to TRADE UNIONS. Under the pressure of economic downturns, factionalization, and the stigma of being affiliated with anarchists, the Knights of Labor declined into a negligible force.

In 1887 revisionists created the Socialist Labor party. Beset with internal strife over policy, its refutation of trade unionism led to its demise. Only the reemergence of the theory of "one big union" brought socialism back as a force in U.S. politics. Eugene V. Debs (1855–1926) became a national figure at this time, having previously proved his abilities as a leader and orator as head of the American Railway Union (ARU). The SHERMAN ANTI-TRUST ACT of 1890, ostensibly passed to curb the accelerating trend of monopolization, was used to stop the ARU's strike against the Pullman Palace Car Company in 1895. When the ARU ignored the INJUNCTION granted under authority of the act, Debs was sentenced to six months in prison for CONTEMPT of court. On appeal the sentence was upheld by the U.S. Supreme Court in *In re Debs*, 158 U.S. 564, 15 S. Ct. 900, 39 L. Ed. 1092 (1895). Throughout the 1880s and 1890s, the revisionists attempted to unionize various companies but suffered a series of defeats, as at Andrew Carnegie's Homestead Steel in 1892, where private armies and the Pennsylvania state MILITIA were used to break up the strike. Such defeats ultimately led the revisionists to join with Progressives and Populists to form the Social Democratic party in 1905.

In the early twentieth century, socialists worked with members of the Progressive movement in calling for changes to currency and taxation, an eight-hour day, an end to adulteration of food, more attention to product safety, improved working conditions, urban sanitation, and relief for the poor and homeless. Congress took notice of these demands and passed various laws granting the government the authority to regulate industry. As an electoral force, socialism peaked in 1912, when Debs garnered six percent of the popular vote.

The Supreme Court, however, was slow to recognize workers' rights and government regulation of industry. The Court repeatedly struck down state laws restricting the hours women and children could work on the ground that the laws violated the doctrine of liberty of contract. In 1910, the Court forced Standard Oil to divest itself of some of its operations; the decision was the first real antitrust victory, although it was limited in scope. *Standard Oil v. United States*, 221 U.S. 1, 31 S. Ct. 502. Not until *Muller v. Oregon* (208 U.S. 412, 28 S. Ct. 324, 52 L. Ed. 551) in 1908 did the Court recognize a limited legislative right to protect health and morals.

During World War I (1914–1918) socialism faced new setbacks. In the United States, the Espionage Act of 1917 (codified in scattered sections of 22 and 50 U.S.C.A.) was used to prevent socialist literature from being sent through the mail. The Industrial Workers of the World, which had been formed in 1905 and represented the legacy of direct action advocated by the earlier anarchists, was one of the main targets of the wartime hysteria. The "Wobblies," as they were called, and their leaders, WILLIAM D. ("Big Bill") HAYWOOD and Mary Harris Jones, were effectively silenced during this period. Debs was jailed again, this time for interfering with military recruitment in violation of the Espionage Act of 1917. Again the Supreme Court upheld the conviction (*Debs v. United States*, 249 U.S. 211, 39 S. Ct. 252, 63 L. Ed. 566 [1919]). Many other socialists were imprisoned for antiwar activities.

After World War I democratic socialists came into power, alone or as part of coalition governments, in Germany, France, Great Britain, and Sweden. They all faced the problem of how to make socialist principles viable within a capitalist system. Only in Sweden, and only after a lengthy conflict, were labor and capital able to cooperate to establish a socialist system without abandoning socialism's philosophic foundation.

In the United States, socialists faced another wave of repression during the strikes that erupted after the war. The Russian Revolution of 1917 had aroused new fears of Bolshevism, which led to greater intolerance. Under the auspices of the Justice Department, Attorney General A. MITCHELL PALMER conducted raids against individuals and organizations considered a threat to U.S. institutions. The nationwide arrest of dissidents ultimately prompted the Supreme Court to reconsider federal protection of individual rights. Justices OLIVER WENDELL HOLMES, Jr., and LOUIS D. BRANDEIS argued for greater protection of the right to voice unpopular ideas.

The Great Depression marked another turning point for socialism. Overproduction, underconsumption, and speculation led to an implosion of markets, a result predicted by Marx. One response was powerful centralized governments in the form of totalitarian regimes such as those of ADOLF HITLER in Germany and JOSEPH STALIN in the Soviet Union. Socialism was revived by the British economist John Maynard Keynes who advocated that the government stimulate consumption and investment during economic downturns. Previously used only on a limited scale, deficit financing, as it came to be called, was now used by socialists in Europe and liberals in the United States to revive capitalism. Many countries still use Keynesian economics to provide a bridge between capitalism and socialism.

As the Depression deepened from 1929 to 1933, U.S. socialism attracted more adherents, but its influence was still relatively slight. In the 1932 presidential elections, Socialist party candidate Norman M. Thomas won only 267,000 votes. Increasingly made up of middle-class intellectuals, socialists became isolated from the needs and demands of workers. Socialism's greatest achievement during this period was President FRANKLIN D. ROOSEVELT's NEW DEAL program, which expanded government services to help the poor and stimulate economic growth. The Supreme Court, however, struck down much of the New Deal legislation, most notably, the NATIONAL INDUSTRIAL RECOVERY ACT (48 Stat. 195) in 1935 (*A.L.A. Schechter Poultry Corp. v. United States*, 295 U.S. 495, 55 S. Ct. 837, 79 L. Ed. 1570). Only when Roosevelt threatened to enlarge the Court to include justices with his perspective did the Court begin to uphold New Deal legislation.

The WAGNER ACT, also known as National Labor Relations Act of 1935 (29 U.S.C.A. § 151 et seq.), the first recognition of labor's right to organize, was the culmination of eighty years of socialist-labor efforts. Ironically, however, the socialists' message lost its urgency with the broadening of workers' rights and regulatory reform. With the coming of the COLD WAR, politicians and the public began to equate socialism with Communism. People with socialist backgrounds, who had been part of the Roosevelt administration, were denied employment, fired, and blacklisted during the late 1940s and 1950s. In 1951, in *Dennis v. United States* (341 U.S. 494, 71 S. Ct. 857, 95 L. Ed. 1137), the Supreme Court upheld the SMITH ACT (18 U.S.C.A. § 2385), which had been passed in 1940. The decision established the legality of anti-subversive legislation under the theory that a vast underground horde of Communists and "fellow travelers" was working for the violent overthrow of the government. Senator JOSEPH R. MCCARTHY of Wisconsin proclaimed that Communists had infiltrated U.S. politics on a broad scale. Meanwhile the House Un-American Activities Committee tried suspects in the popular media, destroying numerous careers in the arts, entertainment, and politics. Only when McCarthy charged that the Army had been infiltrated by Communists and then failed to prove his allegations did his power decline.

By the time the CIVIL RIGHTS ACT of 1964 (42 U.S.C.A. § 2000a et seq.) was passed in the aftermath of President JOHN F. KENNEDY'S ASSAS-SINATION, socialist precepts had again become acceptable topics of conversation. The remedies politicians and scholars proposed for urban blight, poverty, and inequitable distribution of wealth drew heavily on the traditional socialist tenet that the state should play a role in alleviating suffering and directing society toward desirable ends. The socialist perspective on the treatment of third-world nations in the transnational capitalist system also influenced protests against the VIETNAM WAR.

Socialists, such as Debs, have argued that the legal system under capitalism serves only to protect the status quo, that is, the control of the wealthy over the means of production. Capitalists make a similar criticism of law under socialism, arguing that socialist regimes use law as a means of implementing policy. Widespread abuse of the law under either system can lead to revolution. The collapse of the iron curtain in the late 1980s and early 1990s brought an end to Communism's biggest regime and led to the renaming of many "socialist" states. Yet the vast disparities in resources that exist between wealthy and poor nations and between individuals keep the state control of industry and resources in practice, or under consideration, in many of the world's countries.

CROSS-REFERENCES

Dennis v. United States; Jurisprudence; Kunstler, William Moses; Labor Law; Labor Union.

SOCIAL SECURITY   The Social Security Program was created by the SOCIAL SECURITY ACT OF 1935 (42 U.S.C.A. § 301 et seq.) to provide OLD AGE, SURVIVORS, AND DISABILITY INSURANCE benefits to the workers of the United States and their families. The program, which is administered by the SOCIAL SECURITY ADMINISTRATION (SSA), an independent federal agency, was expanded in 1965 to include HEALTH INSURANCE benefits under the MEDICARE program and to assist the states in establishing UNEMPLOYMENT COMPENSATION programs. Unlike WELFARE, which is financial assistance given to persons who qualify on the basis of need, Social Security benefits are paid to an individual or his family on the basis of that person's employment record and prior contributions to the system.

History   As a general term, *social security* refers to any plan designed to protect society from the instability that is caused by individual catastrophes, such as unemployment or the death of a wage earner. It is impossible to predict which families will have to endure these burdens in a given year, but disaster can be expected to strike a certain number of house-holds each year. A government-sponsored plan of social insurance spreads the risk among all members of society so that no single family is completely ruined by an interruption of, or end to, incoming wages.

Germany was the first industrial nation to adopt a program of social security. In the 1880s Chancellor Otto von Bismarck instituted a plan of compulsory sickness and old age insurance to protect wage earners and their dependents. Over the next thirty years, other European and Latin American countries created similar plans with various features to benefit different categories of workers.

In the United States, the federal government accepted the responsibility of providing pensions to disabled veterans of the Revolutionary War. Pensions were later paid to disabled and elderly veterans of the Civil War. The first federal old age pension bill was not introduced until 1909, however. To fill this void, many workers joined together to form BENEFICIAL ASSOCIATIONS, which offered funeral, sickness, and old age benefit insurance. The federal government encouraged people to set aside money for future emergencies with a popular postal savings plan. People who could not manage were helped, if at all, by private charity because it was generally believed that those who wanted to help themselves would.

Congress enacted the Social Security Act of 1935 as part of the economic and social reforms that made up President FRANKLIN D. ROOSEVELT'S NEW DEAL. The act provided for the payment of monthly benefits to qualified wage earners who were at least sixty-five years old or payment of a lump-sum death benefit to the estate of a wage earner who died before reaching age sixty-five.

In 1939 Congress created a separate benefit for secondary beneficiaries—the dependent spouses, children, widows, widowers, and parents of wage earners—to soften the economic hardship created when they lost a wage earner's support. Such beneficiaries are entitled to benefits because the wage earner made contributions to the plan. Beneficiaries can receive their payments directly upon the retirement or death of the worker.

Social Security originally protected only workers in industry and commerce. It excluded many classes of workers because collecting their contributions was considered too expensive or inconvenient. Congress exempted household workers, farmers, and workers in family businesses, for example, because it believed that they were unlikely to maintain adequate employment records. In the 1950s, however, Con-

The First Payments of Social Security

After the enactment of the Social Security Act of 1935 (42 U.S.C.A. § 301 et seq.) and the creation of the Social Security Administration (SSA), the federal government had a short time to establish the program before beginning to pay benefits. Monthly benefits were to begin in 1940. The period from 1937 to 1940 was to be used both to build up the trust funds and to provide a minimum period for participation for persons to qualify for monthly benefits.

From 1937 until 1940, however, Social Security paid benefits in the form of a single, lump-sum payment. The purpose of these one-time payments was to provide some compensation to people who contributed to the program but would not participate long enough to be vested for monthly benefits.

The first applicant for a lump-sum benefit was Ernest Ackerman, a Cleveland motorman who retired one day after the Social Security Program began. During his one day of participation in the program, five cents was withheld from Ackerman's pay for Social Security, and upon retiring, he received a lump-sum payment of seventeen cents.

Payments of monthly benefits began in January 1940. On January 31, 1940, the first monthly retirement check was issued to Ida May Fuller of Ludlow, Vermont, in the amount of $22.54. Fuller died in January 1975 at the age of one hundred. During her thirty-five years as a beneficiary, she received more than $20,000 in benefits.

gress extended Social Security protection to most self-employed individuals, most state and local government employees, household and farm workers, members of the armed forces, and members of the clergy. Federal employees, who previously had their own retirement and benefit system, were given Social Security coverage in 1983.

Old Age, Survivors, and Disability Insurance Federal Old Age, Survivors, and Disability Insurance (OASDI) benefits are monthly payments made to retired people, to families whose wage earner has died, and to workers who are unemployed because of sickness or accident. Workers qualify for such protection by having been employed for the mandatory minimum amount of time and by having made contributions to Social Security. There is no financial need requirement to be satisfied. Once a worker qualifies for protection, his family is also entitled to protection. The entire program is geared toward helping families as a matter of social policy.

Two large funds of money are held in trust to pay benefits earned by people under OASDI: the Old Age and Survivors Trust Fund and the Disability Insurance Trust Fund. As workers and employers make payroll contributions to these funds, money is paid out in benefits to people currently qualified to receive monthly checks.

The OASDI program is funded by payroll taxes levied on employees and their employers and on the self-employed. The tax is imposed upon the employee's TAXABLE INCOME, up to a maximum taxable amount, with the employer contributing an equal amount. The self-employed person contributes twice the amount levied on an employee. In 1996 the rate was 6.2 percent, levied on earned income up to a maximum of $62,887.

Old Age Benefits A person becomes eligible for Social Security old age benefits by working a minimum number of calendar quarters. The number of quarters required for full insurance increases with the worker's age. Forty quarters is the maximum requirement. The individual is credited for income up to the maximum amount of money covered by Social Security for those years. This amount is adjusted to reflect the impact of inflation on normal earnings and ensure that a worker who pays increasing Social Security contributions during her work life will receive retirement benefits that keep pace with inflation.

Persons born before 1950 can retire at age sixty-five with full benefits based on their average income during their working years. For those born between 1950 and 1960, the retirement age for full benefits has increased to age sixty-six. Persons born in 1960 or later will not receive full retirement benefits until age sixty-seven. Any person, however, may retire at age sixty-two and receive less than full benefits. At age sixty-five, a worker's spouse who has not contributed to Social Security receives 50 percent of the amount paid to the worker.

Since 1975 Social Security benefits have increased annually to offset the corrosive effects of inflation on fixed incomes. These increases, known as cost of living allowances (COLAs), are based on the annual increase in consumer prices. Allowing benefits to increase automatically ended the need for special acts of Congress, but it has also steadily increased the cost of the Social Security Program.

A person who continues to work past the retirement age may lose some benefits because Social Security is designed to replace lost earnings. If earnings from employment do not exceed the amount specified by law, the person receives the full benefits. If earnings are greater than that amount, one dollar of benefit is withheld for every two dollars in wages earned above the exempt amount. Once a person reaches age seventy, however, he does not have to report earnings to the SSA, and the benefit is not reduced.

Survivors' Benefits Survivors' benefits are paid to family members when a worker dies. Survivors can receive benefits if the deceased worker was employed and contributed to Social Security long enough for someone her age to qualify for Social Security.

Both mothers and fathers earn protection for their families by working and contributing to Social Security. If a wage earner dies, his unmarried children are entitled to receive benefits. If the child of a wage earner becomes permanently disabled before age twenty-two, she can continue to receive survivors' benefits at any age unless she becomes self-supporting or marries.

Survivors' benefits can also go to a surviving spouse when the worker dies. A surviving spouse who retires can begin collecting survivors' benefits as early as age sixty. If a worker

Old-Age and Survivors Insurance Trust Fund, 1940–1995

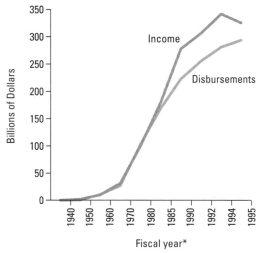

*Fiscal years after 1976 consist of the 12 months ending on Sept. 30 of each year. Fiscal years prior to 1977 consisted of the 12 months ending on June 30 of each year.

Source: Social Security Administration, U.S. Department of Health and Human Services.

dies leaving a divorced spouse who was married to the worker for at least ten years, the ex-spouse can receive survivors' benefits at age sixty if she retires. In addition to monthly checks, the worker's widow or widower, or if there is none, another eligible person, may receive a lump-sum payment of $255 on the worker's death.

Disability Benefits In the 1970s, the SSA became responsible for a new program, Supplemental Security Income (SSI). The original 1935 Social Security Act had included programs for needy aged and blind individuals, and in 1950 programs for needy disabled individuals were added. These three programs were known as the "adult categories" and were administered by state and local governments with partial federal funding. Over the years the state programs became more complex and inconsistent until as many as 1,350 administrative agencies were involved and payments varied more than 300 percent from state to state. In 1969 President RICHARD M. NIXON identified a need to reform these and related welfare programs. In 1972 Congress federalized the "adult categories" by creating the SSI program and assigned responsibility for it to the SSA.

A person who becomes unable to work and expects to be disabled for at least twelve months or who will probably die from the condition can receive SSI payments before reaching retirement age. A worker is eligible for disability benefits if she has worked enough years under Social Security prior to the onset of the disability. The amount of work credit needed depends on the worker's age at the time of the DISABILITY. That time can be as little as one and one-half years of work in the three years before the onset of the disability for a worker under twenty-four years of age, but it is never more than a total of ten years.

A waiting period of five months after the onset of the disability is imposed before SSI payments begin. A disabled worker who fails to apply for benefits when eligible can sometimes collect back payments. No more than twelve months of back payments may be collected, however. Even if the worker recovers from a disability that lasted more than twelve months, she can apply for back benefits within fourteen months of recovery. If a worker dies after a long period of disability without having applied for SSI, her family may apply for disability benefits within three months of the date of the worker's death. The family members are also eligible for survivors' benefits.

A disability is any physical or mental condition that prevents the worker from doing substantial work. Examples of disabilities that meet the Social Security criteria include brain damage, heart disease, kidney failure, severe arthritis, and serious mental illness.

The SSA uses a sequential evaluation process to decide whether a person's disability is serious enough to justify the awarding of benefits. If the impairment is so severe that it significantly affects "basic work activity," the worker's medical data are compared with a set of guidelines known as the Listing of Impairments. A claimant found to suffer from a condition in this listing will receive benefits. If the condition is less severe, the SSA determines whether the impairment prevents the worker from doing his former work. If not, the application will be denied. If so, the SSA proceeds to the final step, determining whether the impairment prevents the applicant from doing other work available in the economy.

At this point, the SSA uses a series of medical-vocational guidelines that consider the applicant's residual functional capacity as well as his age, education, and experience. The guidelines look at three types of work: one type is for persons whose residual physical capacity enables them to perform only "sedentary" work on a sustained basis, another for those able to do "light" work, and a third for those able to do "medium" work.

If the SSA determines that an applicant can perform one of these types of work, benefits will be denied. A claimant may APPEAL this decision and ask for a HEARING in which to present further EVIDENCE, including personal TESTIMONY. If the recommendation of the ad-

ministrative law judge conducting the hearing is adverse, the claimant may appeal to the SSA's Appeals Council. If the claimant loses his appeal, he may file a CIVIL ACTION in federal district court seeking review of the agency's adverse determination.

Persons who meet the OASDI disability eligibility requirements may receive three types of benefits: monthly cash payments, vocational rehabilitation, and medical insurance. Provided proper application has been made, cash payments begin with the sixth month of disability. The amount of the monthly payment depends upon the amount of earnings on which the worker has paid Social Security taxes and the number of his eligible dependents. The maximum for a family is usually roughly equal to the amount to which the disabled worker is entitled as an individual plus allowances for two dependents.

Vocational rehabilitation services are provided through a joint federal-state program. A person receiving cash payments for disability may continue to receive them for a limited time after beginning to work at or near the end of a program of vocational rehabilitation. Called the "trial work period," this period may last as long as nine months.

Medical services are available through the Medicare Program (a federally sponsored program of hospital and medical insurance). A recipient of OASDI disability benefits begins to participate in Medicare twenty-five months after the onset of disability.

In 1980 Congress made many changes in the disability program. Most of these changes focused on various work incentive provisions for both Social Security and SSI disability benefits. The SSA was directed to review current disability beneficiaries periodically to certify their continuing eligibility. This produced a massive workload for the SSA and one that was highly controversial, as persons with apparently legitimate disabilities were removed from SSI. By 1983 the reviews had been halted.

The Contract with America Advancement Act of 1996 (Pub. L. No. 104-121) changed the basic philosophy of the disability program. New applicants for Social Security or SSI disability benefits are no longer eligible for benefits if drug addiction or alcoholism is a material factor in their disability. Unless they can qualify on some other medical basis, they cannot receive disability benefits. Individuals in this category already receiving benefits had their benefits terminated as of January 1, 1997.

The Personal Responsibility and Work Opportunity Reconciliation Act of 1996 (Pub. L. No. 104-193), which concerns welfare reform,

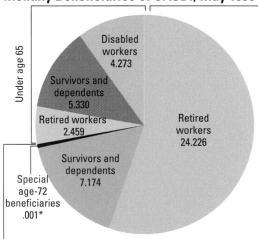

Monthly Beneficiaries of OASDI, May 1996

Under age 65

Disabled workers
4.273

Survivors and dependents
5.330

Retired workers
2.459

Retired workers
24.226

Special age-72 beneficiaries
.001*

Survivors and dependents
7.174

Aged 65 and over

*Percent of pie comes to .0023, which rounded to tenths (.1) is zero (0).

Source: Social Security Administration, U.S. Department of Health and Human Services.

THE FUTURE OF SOCIAL SECURITY

The payment of Old-Age, Survivors, and Disability Insurance (OASDI) benefits has been a cornerstone of U.S. social welfare policy since the establishment of Social Security in 1935. The long-term financial stability of OASDI has been a constant concern. Concerns about Social Security in the twenty-first century have mounted as policy makers have assessed the impact of the retirement of the baby boom generation. Many younger people have raised the issue of "generation equity." They express doubt that Social Security benefits will be available when they retire, and anger that they will be forced to pay, through payroll taxes, for the baby boomers' retirement benefits.

Reform of the Social Security system has always been a political hot potato. Retirees and those approaching retirement zealously protect their benefits, while employers and employees oppose higher payroll taxes to fund OASDI. Past changes in Social Security have required bipartisan support, which has only come in the face of an impending crisis. The 1982–83 National Commission on Social Security Reform successfully secured from Congress the short-term financing of OASDI, largely because the Social Security trust fund faced imminent exhaustion.

The increased payroll taxes for Social Security created a surplus, with planners estimating that the income from the trust fund will exceed expenses each year until 2020. The trust fund balances will then start to decline as investments are cashed in to meet the payments coming due. Although it is estimated that 75 percent of the costs would continue to be met from current payroll and income taxes, in the absence of any changes, full benefits could not be paid beginning in 2030.

Faced with this looming problem, the Social Security Administration's Advisory Council looked at various long-term financing options for OASDI. In its 1996 report, the council could not reach consensus on a specific long-term plan, but it did suggest several types of

financing that represent a marked departure from previous efforts to fund Social Security.

The council noted that past efforts have generally featured cutting benefits and raising tax rates on a "pay-as-you-go" basis. The council agreed that this approach must be changed and offered three ways of restoring financial solvency.

One approach, called Maintenance of Benefits (MB), calls for an increase in income taxes on OASDI benefits, a redirection of some revenue from other trust funds, and, most importantly, the adoption of a plan allowing the federal government to invest a portion of the trust fund assets directly in common stocks. Rates of returns on stocks have historically exceeded those on federal government bonds, where all Social Security funds are now invested. If the returns were to continue, the MB plan would maintain Social Security benefits for all income groups of workers and reassure younger workers that they will get their money's worth when they retire.

A second approach, labeled the Individual Accounts (IA) plan, would create individual accounts that would work alongside Social Security. The IA plan would increase the income taxation of benefits, accelerate the scheduled increase in retirement age, reduce the growth of future benefits to middle- and upper-income workers, and increase employees' mandatory contributions to Social Security by 1.6 percent. This increase would be allocated to individual investment accounts held by the government and controlled by the worker, but with a limited set of investment options available. It is estimated that the combined income from both funds would yield essentially the same benefits as promised under the current system for all groups.

A third approach, labeled the Personal Security Accounts (PSA) plan, would create larger, fully funded individual accounts that would replace a portion of Social Security. Under this

plan, five percent of an individual's current payroll tax would be invested in his PSA, which he then could use to invest in a range of financial instruments. The rest of his payroll tax would be used to fund a modified OASDI program. It would provide a flat dollar amount (the equivalent of $410 monthly in 1996), in addition to the proceeds of the individual's PSA. This approach would also change the taxation of benefits and move eligibility for early retirement benefits from age sixty-two to sixty-five. The combination of the flat benefit payment and the income from the PSA would exceed, on average, the benefits promised under the current system.

These three proposals all seek to generate more advance funding of Social Security's long-term obligations. They would also result in a higher level of national saving for retirement. The IA and PSA plans represent a significant shift, privatizing a portion of Social Security. Nonetheless, these plans reject the more radical idea of ending universal, compulsory Social Security contributions and allowing individuals to invest as much or as little in Social Security plans and private retirement plans as they choose. The council agreed that a compulsory Social Security system is necessary. A voluntary plan would allow, in the words of the council, "the improvident to escape their share of paying for their own future retirement needs—leaving the community as a whole to pay for them through some safety net program like SSI [Supplemental Security Income]."

Most policy makers acknowledge the need to change the funding of Social Security as soon as possible. The council noted that delaying any changes for another ten years would require a 25 percent reduction in benefits to rebalance the system without tax increases. In 1997, however, Congress and President Bill Clinton avoided making any hard choices when they negotiated a balanced budget agreement. Instead, they agreed to appoint another commission to study the problem.

terminated SSI eligibility for most noncitizens. Previously, lawfully admitted ALIENS could receive SSI if they met the other requirements. All existing noncitizen beneficiaries were to be removed from the rolls unless they met one of the exceptions in the law.

Medicare The Medicare Program provides basic health care benefits to recipients of Social Security and is funded through the Social Security Trust Fund. President HARRY S. TRUMAN first proposed a medical care program for the aged in the late 1940s, but it was not enacted until 1965, when Medicare was established as one of President LYNDON B. JOHNSON's Great Society programs (42 U.S.C.A. § 1395 et seq.).

The Medicare Program is administered by the HEALTH CARE FINANCING ADMINISTRATION (HCFA). The federal government enters into contracts with private insurance companies for the processing of Medicare claims. To qualify for Medicare payments for their services, health care providers must meet state and local licensing laws and standards set by the HCFA.

Medicare is divided into a hospital insurance program and a supplementary medical insurance program. The Medicare hospital insurance plan is funded through Social Security payroll taxes. It covers reasonable and medically necessary treatment in a hospital or skilled nursing home, meals, regular nursing care services, and the cost of necessary special care.

Medicare's supplementary medical insurance program is financed by a combination of monthly insurance PREMIUMS paid by people who sign up for coverage and money contributed by the federal government. The government contributes the major portion of the cost of the program, which is funded out of general tax revenues. Persons who enroll pay a small annual deductible fee for any medical costs incurred above that amount during the year and also a regular monthly premium. Once the deductible has been paid, Medicare pays 80 percent of any bills incurred for physicians' and surgeons' services, diagnostic and laboratory tests, and other services, but does not pay for routine physical checkups, drugs and medicines, eyeglasses, hearing aids, dentures, and orthopedic shoes. Doctors are not required to accept Medicare patients, but almost all do.

Medicare's hospital insurance is financed by a payroll tax of 2.9 percent, divided equally between employers and employees. The money is placed in a trust fund and invested in U.S. Treasury securities. The fund accumulated a surplus during the 1980s and early 1990s, but according to projections, it will run out of money by 2002 as outlays rise more rapidly than future payroll tax revenues.

The Future of Social Security From its modest beginnings, Social Security has grown to become an essential facet of modern life. In 1940 slightly more than 222,000 people received monthly Social Security benefits; in 1997 more than 42 million people received such benefits. One in seven individuals receives a Social Security benefit, and more than 90 percent of all workers are covered by Social Security. The SSI program has nearly doubled in size since its inception in 1974.

By the 1980s the Social Security Program faced a serious long-term financing crisis. President RONALD REAGAN appointed a blue-ribbon panel, known as the Greenspan Commission, to study the issues and recommend legislative changes. The final bill, signed into law in 1983 (Pub. L. 98-21, 97 Stat. 65), made numerous changes in the Social Security and Medicare Programs; these changes included taxing Social Security benefits, extending Social Security coverage to federal employees, and increasing the retirement age in the next century. By the 1990s, however, concerns were again raised about the long-term financial viability of Social Security and Medicare. Various ideas and plans to ensure the financial stability of these programs were put forward, but no political consensus as to what changes should be made had emerged by 1997.

CROSS-REFERENCES

Disabled Persons; Elder Law; Health Care Law; Senior Citizens.

SOCIAL SECURITY ACT OF 1935

📖 Legislation (42 U.S.C.A. § 301 et seq.) designed to assist in the maintenance of the financial well-being of eligible persons, enacted in 1935 as part of President FRANKLIN D. ROOSEVELT's New Deal. 📖

In the United States, SOCIAL SECURITY did not exist on the federal level until the passage of the Social Security Act of 1935. This statute provided for a federal program of old-age retirement benefits and a joint federal-state venture of UNEMPLOYMENT COMPENSATION. In addition, it dispensed federal funds to aid the development at the state level of such programs as vocational rehabilitation, public health services, and child welfare services, along with assistance to the elderly and the handicapped. The act instituted a system of mandatory old-age insurance, issuing benefits in proportion to the previous earnings of persons over sixty-five and establishing a reserve fund financed through the imposition of payroll taxes on employers and employees. The original levy was 1 percent, but the rate has increased over the years. Only employees in industrial and commercial occupations were eligible for protection under the Social Security Act of 1935, but numerous important amendments have expanded the categories of coverage.

See also MEDICARE; NEW DEAL.

SOCRATIC METHOD See LANGDELL, CHRISTOPHER COLUMBUS.

SODOMY 📖 Anal or oral intercourse between human beings, or any sexual relations between a human being and an animal, the act of which may be punishable as a criminal offense. 📖

The word *sodomy* has acquired different meanings over time. Under the COMMON LAW, sodomy consisted of anal intercourse. Traditionally courts and statutes have referred to it as a "crime against nature" or as copulation "against the order of nature." In the United States, the term eventually encompassed oral sex as well as anal sex. The crime of sodomy was classified as a FELONY.

Because homosexual activity involves anal and oral sex, gay men were the primary target of sodomy laws. Culturally and historically, homosexual activity has been seen as unnatural or perverse. The term *sodomy* refers to the homosexual activities of men in the story of the city of Sodom in the Bible. The destruction of Sodom and Gomorrah because of their residents' immorality became a central part of Western attitudes toward forms of nonprocreative sexual activity and same-sex relations.

Beginning with Illinois in 1961, state legislatures have reexamined their sodomy statutes. Twenty-seven states have repealed these laws, usually as a part of a general revision of the criminal code and with the recognition that heterosexuals engage in oral and anal sex. The remaining twenty-three states have various criminal provisions. Some totally prohibit sodomy, whereas others exempt married (heterosexual) couples from the law. In general, however, sodomy laws are rarely enforced because sexual acts occur primarily in private.

State sodomy laws are not unconstitutional. In *Bowers v. Hardwick*, 478 U.S. 186, 106 S. Ct. 2841, 92 L. Ed. 2d 140 (1986), the U.S. Supreme Court upheld the Georgia sodomy statute. Michael Hardwick was arrested and charged with sodomy for engaging in oral sex with a consenting male adult in his home. A police officer was let into Hardwick's home to serve a warrant and saw the sexual act. Although the state prosecutor declined to prosecute the case, Hardwick brought suit in federal court asking that the statute be declared unconstitutional.

On a 5–4 vote, the Court upheld the law. Writing for the majority, Justice BYRON R. WHITE rejected the argument that previous decisions such as the Court's rulings on ABORTION and contraception had created a right of PRIVACY that extended to homosexual sodomy. Instead, the Court drew a sharp distinction between the previous cases, which involved "family, marriage, or procreation," and homosexual activity.

The Court also rejected the argument that there is a fundamental right to engage in homosexual activity. Prohibitions against sodomy were in the laws of most states since the nation's founding. To the argument that homosexual activity should be protected when it occurs in the privacy of a home, White said that "otherwise illegal conduct is not always immunized whenever it occurs in the home." Because the claim in the case involved only homosexual sodomy, the Court expressed no opinion about the constitutionality of the statute as applied to acts of heterosexual sodomy.

See also GAY AND LESBIAN RIGHTS; SEX OFFENSES.

SOFTWARE Software instructs a computer what to do. (The computer's physical components are called hardware.) *Computer software* is the general term for a variety of procedures and routines that harness the computational power of a computer to produce, for example, a general operating system that coordinates the basic workings of the computer or specific applications that produce a database, a financial spreadsheet, a written document, or a game. Computer programmers use different types of programming languages to create the intricate sets of instructions that make computing possible.

Until the personal computer revolution began in the 1980s, software was written mainly for business, government, and the military, which employed large mainframe computers as hardware. With the introduction of personal computers, which have rapidly increased in power and performance, software has emerged as an important commercial product that can be marketed to individuals and small business as well as big business and the government.

Software is, under the law, INTELLECTUAL PROPERTY and therefore entitled to protection from persons who seek to exploit it illegally. Software can be protected through the use of trade secrets, COPYRIGHT, PATENTS, and TRADEMARKS.

Trade secret protection may apply to unpublished works and the basic software instructions called source code. Typically trade secrets will be effective if a company develops software and wishes to prevent others from finding out about it. A person who works on developing the software will be required to sign a nondisclosure agreement, which is a CONTRACT that obligates the person signing it to keep the project a secret.

Once software is developed and is ready to be sold, it can be copyrighted. Copyright protects the expression of an idea, not the idea itself. For example, a person could not copyright the idea of a computer database management system but could copyright the structure and content of a database software program that expresses the idea of a database system.

Court decisions appear to have limited copyright protection for some features of software. In *Apple Computer v. Microsoft Corporation*, 35 F.3d 1435 (9th Cir. 1994), the court held that Apple Computer could not copyright the graphical user interface (GUI) it had developed for its Macintosh computer. Microsoft Corporation's Windows software program contained a GUI nearly identical to Apple's. The court stated that Microsoft and other software developers were free to copy the "functional" elements of Apple's GUI because there are only a limited number of ways that the basic GUI can be expressed differently.

In *Lotus Development Corp. v. Borland International*, 49 F.3d 807 (1st Cir. 1995), Lotus alleged that Borland had copied the hierarchical menu system of the Lotus 1-2-3 spreadsheet program, which contained 469 commands, in its Quattro spreadsheet program. The court of appeals ruled that Borland had not infringed on Lotus's copyright because the menu command hierarchy was a "method of operation," which is not copyrightable under federal copyright law (17 U.S.C.A. § 102(b)).

Patent law supplies another avenue of protection for software companies. A patent protects the idea itself. It is often an unattractive option, however, because it takes a significant amount of time, usually two years, and money to obtain a patent from the U.S. PATENT AND TRADEMARK OFFICE. The patent process is complicated and technical, with the applicant required to prove to the Patent and Trademark Office that a patent is deserved. Because the shelf life of a software program is often short, seeking a patent for the program is often impractical.

Trademark law protects the name of the software, not the software itself. Protecting a name from being used by others can be more valuable than other forms of protection.

When software is leased or sold, the purchaser usually must agree to accept a software LICENSE. When a business negotiates with a software company, it will sign a license agreement that details how the software is to be used and limits its distribution. A software license is an effective tool in preventing piracy.

When consumers buy software from a software company or through a third-party business, they find in the packaging a software license. The license is typically on the sealed envelope that contains the software media, which itself is sealed in plastic wrapping. These "shrink-wrap licenses" describe contractual conditions regarding the purchaser's use of the software. The opening of the shrink-wrap, according to the license, constitutes ACCEPTANCE of all of the terms contained in the license agreement.

The purchaser is informed that the software is licensed and not sold to the purchaser. By retaining TITLE to the software, the computer software company seeks to impose conditions upon the purchaser, or licensee, that are not otherwise permissible under federal copyright law. The principal terms of the shrink-wrap license include prohibiting the unauthorized copying and renting of the software, prohibiting reverse engineering (figuring out how the software works) and modifications of the software, limiting the use of the software to one computer, disclaiming warranties, and limiting liabilities.

Estimated North American PC Software Sales for 1990 to 1996

Measured at retail in millions of U.S. dollars. Includes sales to all of North America: both the United States and Canada.

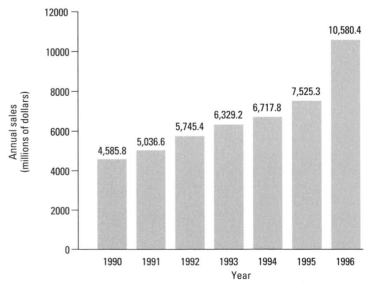

Source: Software Publishers Association, Washington, DC, *SPA Software Sales Report*, News Release, annual.

Estimated North American PC Software Sales for 1996

Measured at retail in millions of U.S. dollars. Includes sales to all of North America: both the United States and Canada.

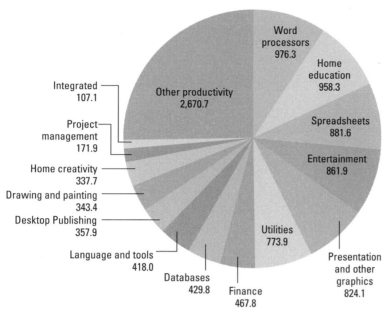

Source: Software Publishers Association, Washington, DC, *SPA Software Sales Report,* News Release, 1997.

The enforceability of shrink-wrap licenses has been challenged in the courts. The prevailing view is that when mass-market prepackaged software is sold, the transaction is a sale of goods and not a true license agreement. The key issue is whether the license document is part of an enforceable contract. Defenders of shrink-wrap licenses argue that the purchaser agrees to the conditions of the license after breaking the packaging seal and therefore contract law must uphold the written terms of the contract. Opponents argue that the sequence of events in the typical software purchase transaction is skewed. The purchaser is not aware of the license agreement until after the sale is consummated. The purchaser's acceptance of the license agreement is inferred when he or she opens the package or uses the software. However, the purchaser does not sign the license agreement. She may not even read the terms of the license agreement and, in any case, does not expressly agree to them.

In *Step-Saver Data Systems v. Wyse Technology,* 939 F.2d 91 (1991), the Third Circuit Court of Appeals held that the shrink-wrap license did not become part of the contract and therefore was not a valid modification to a previously existing contractual relationship for the sale of prepackaged computer software. The court concluded that, under the UNIFORM COMMERCIAL CODE § 2-207, a contract had existed prior to the opening of the package, the license contained new terms that materially altered the contract, and the purchaser did not expressly accept these terms. Because of these conclusions, the license agreement was invalid and unenforceable.

Software developers have legitimate concerns about software piracy. Counterfeiting is an international problem that results in the sale of millions of dollars of pirated software. The Software Publisher's Association (SPA) and the Business Software Alliance (BSA) are major organizations that combat software piracy. The SPA is the leading international trade association for the personal computer software industry. Both SPA and BSA have collected millions of dollars worldwide from companies that have used pirated software. Most companies using pirated software are reported by former employees.

CROSS-REFERENCES

Computer-Assisted Legal Research; Computer Crime; E-mail; Internet; Sales Law.

SOLDIERS' AND SAILORS' CIVIL RELIEF ACT

A federal statute (50 App. U.S.C.A. § 501 et seq.) created to ensure that individuals in the ARMED SERVICES are totally informed of legal proceedings against them and have sufficient time and opportunity to appear and defend their rights.

Congress passed the first Soldiers' and Sailors' Civil Relief Act in 1918. This act was designed to protect the CIVIL RIGHTS and legal interests of the armed forces in World War I and ensure that they would not be distracted by legal obligations at home. The act did not prevent persons from suing servicemembers. Rather, it allowed a court to stay civil proceedings against them. The act authorized a court to suspend legal ACTIONS against a member of the armed forces during his time of service if the court determined that he was unable to defend himself in court because of active duty.

Congress passed a revised version of the act in 1940. The major difference between it and the original was that the 1940 act authorized courts to postpone proceedings against a servicemember beyond the time of active duty and until she was capable of protecting her interests. The 1940 act had three objectives concerning servicemembers: to suspend civil judicial actions until they could appear in court, to provide them peace of mind during their fighting in World War II, and to give them time to return home after service to protect their endangered interests. Congress has amended the act several times since 1940, usually to keep courts from interpreting the act too narrowly against servicemembers.

The act provides a servicemember with three types of RELIEF from judicial proceedings. She may request a STAY of proceedings, a reopening of a DEFAULT JUDGMENT, or a stay of EXECUTION against a JUDGMENT. To obtain any relief, a court first must find that the servicemember's ability to defend the case was affected by her service.

A servicemember may postpone proceedings during service or within sixty days after service. A servicemember or acquaintance of a servicemember may apply for a stay of proceedings with the court, or the court may decide on its own to issue a stay. If a stay is issued, the case remains postponed until the court determines that the servicemember's ability to defend against the suit is no longer affected by his military service.

If a servicemember fails to obtain a stay of the proceedings and the trial court issues a default judgment, the servicemember may reopen the case. To reopen a default judgment, a servicemember must apply with the trial court while still on active duty or within ninety days of discharge. Congress has allowed servicemembers to reopen only those default judgments that were rendered during the servicemember's term of service or within thirty days after discharge. Reopening a default judgment gives a servicemember an opportunity to present her defense to the lawsuit.

If a servicemember is unable to obtain a stay or reopen a default judgment, he may stay the execution of the judgment. This does not eliminate the default judgment; rather, it gives the servicemember time to appeal the judgment and prevents authorities from taking the property of the servicemember in satisfaction of the judgment during the APPEAL process.

SOLE PROPRIETORSHIP 📖 A form of business in which one person owns all the ASSETS of the business, in contrast to a PARTNERSHIP or a CORPORATION. 📖

A person who does business for himself is engaged in the operation of a sole proprietorship. Anyone who does business without formally creating a business organization is a sole proprietor. Many small businesses operate as sole proprietorships. Professionals, consultants, and other service businesses that require minimum amounts of capital often operate this way.

A sole proprietorship is not a separate legal entity, like a partnership or a corporation. No legal formalities are necessary to create a sole proprietorship, other than appropriate licensing

Sole proprietors, such as this grocer, typically enjoy a more intimate relationship with their business than shareholders in larger business concerns.

to conduct business and registration of a business name if it differs from that of the sole proprietor. Because a sole proprietorship is not a separate legal entity, it is not itself a taxable entity. The sole proprietor must report income and expenses from the business on Schedule C of her or his personal federal INCOME TAX return.

A major concern for persons organizing a business enterprise is limiting the extent to which their personal assets, unrelated to the business itself, are subject to claims of business CREDITORS. A sole proprietorship gives the least protection because the personal LIABILITY of the sole proprietor is generally unlimited. Both the business assets and the personal assets of the sole proprietor are subject to claims of the sole proprietorship's creditors. In addition, existing liabilities of the sole proprietor will not be extinguished upon the dissolution or sale of the sole proprietorship.

Unlike the managers of a corporation or a partnership, a sole proprietor has total flexibility in managing and controlling the business. The organizational expenses and level of formality in a sole proprietorship are minimal as compared with those of other business organizations. However, because a sole proprietorship is not a separate legal entity, it terminates when the sole proprietor becomes disabled, retires, or dies. As a result, a sole proprietorship lacks business continuity and does not have a perpetual existence as does a corporation.

For working capital, a sole proprietorship is generally limited to the individual funds of the sole proprietor, along with any loans from outsiders willing to provide extra capital. During her lifetime, a sole proprietor can sell or give away any asset because the business is not legally separate from the sole proprietor. At the death of the sole proprietor, the business is usually dissolved. The proprietor's ESTATE, however, can sell the assets or continue the business.

See also S CORPORATION.

SOLICITATION 📖 Urgent request, plea, or entreaty; enticing, asking. The criminal offense of urging someone to commit an unlawful act. 📖

The term *solicitation* is used in a variety of legal contexts. A person who asks someone to commit an illegal act has committed the criminal act of solicitation. An employee who agrees in an employment CONTRACT not to solicit business after leaving her employer and then mails a letter to customers asking for business may be sued by the former employer for violating the non-solicitation clause of the contract. The letter constitutes a solicitation. However, if the person had placed a newspaper advertisement, this would not have been a solicitation because a solicitation must be addressed to a particular individual.

Many solicitations in everyday life appear to be legal. For example, a telemarketer who tries to sell a legitimate product by calling potential customers is making a solicitation. It may or may not be legal, however, depending on the laws of the states where the telemarketer and the caller reside. If either of the states requires that telemarketers register with the state government, then the legality of the solicitation will depend on whether the telemarketer met this registration requirement. Failure to register may make the telemarketing company liable for civil fines or criminal penalties.

Solicitation laws and regulations govern specific types of organizations and economic activities. For example, charitable organizations must register with state agencies before legally soliciting money. The federal SECURITIES AND EXCHANGE COMMISSION has rigid rules concerning the solicitation of shareholders for votes involving changes in corporate structure or leadership.

Criminal solicitation commonly involves crimes such as PROSTITUTION and drug dealing, though politicians have been convicted for solicitation of a bribe. The crime of solicitation is completed if one person intentionally entices, advises, incites, orders, or otherwise encourages another to commit a crime. The crime solicited need not actually be committed for solicitation to occur.

When law enforcement agencies seek to curtail prostitution, they use decoy operations. A person who offers to perform a sex act with an undercover officer for money can be arrested for solicitation of prostitution. Police decoys are also used to nab customers. When a person looking to pay for sex approaches a decoy officer and makes, by words or gestures, this request, the person can be arrested for solicitation of prostitution. Similar operations are used to reduce the sale of narcotics.

SOLICITOR 📖 A type of practicing lawyer in England who handles primarily office work.

The title of the chief law officer of a government body or department, such as a city, town, or MUNICIPAL CORPORATION. 📖

England has two types of practicing lawyers: solicitors and BARRISTERS. Unlike the United States, where a lawyer is allowed to handle office and trial work, England has developed a division of labor for lawyers. Solicitors generally handle office work, whereas barristers plead cases in court. However, there is some overlap. Solicitors may appear as legal counsel in the lower courts, and barristers often prepare trial BRIEFS and other written documents. Barristers depend on solicitors to provide them with trial work because they are not allowed to accept work on their own.

The distinction between solicitors and barristers was originally based on their roles in the English court system. Solicitors were lawyers who were admitted to practice in EQUITY courts, whereas barristers were lawyers who practiced in COMMON-LAW courts. The modern English judicial system has abolished this distinction. Barristers may appear in legal and equitable court proceedings, and solicitors handle out-of-court lawyering.

The role of the solicitor is similar to that of a lawyer in the United States who does not appear in court. The solicitor meets prospective clients, hears the client's problems, gives legal advice, drafts letters and documents, negotiates on the client's behalf, and prepares the client's case for trial. When a court appearance appears inevitable, the solicitor retains a barrister on the client's behalf. The solicitor instructs the barrister on how the client wishes to proceed in court.

There are more solicitors than barristers because most legal work is done outside the courtroom. Solicitors are required to take a law school course, but they must serve an apprenticeship with a practicing solicitor for five years (three years for a college graduate) before becoming fully accredited.

The regulation and administration of solicitors is managed by the Law Society, a voluntary group incorporated by Parliament. The Law Society is similar to U.S. BAR ASSOCIATIONS, setting standards of professional conduct, disciplining solicitors for ethical violations, and maintaining a client compensation fund to repay losses that result from dishonesty by solicitors.

In the United States, the term *solicitor* generally has not been applied to attorneys. Some towns and cities in the Northeast have called their chief law enforcement officer a solicitor, rather than a chief of police.

Also, the officer in the Justice Department who represents the government in cases before the U.S. Supreme Court is called the solicitor general.

SOLICITOR GENERAL An officer of the U.S. Department of Justice who represents the U.S. government in cases before the U.S. Supreme Court.

The solicitor general is charged with representing the EXECUTIVE BRANCH of the U.S. government in cases before the U.S. Supreme Court. This means that the solicitor and the solicitor's staff are the chief courtroom lawyers for the government, preparing legal BRIEFS and making oral arguments in the Supreme Court. The solicitor general also decides which cases the United States should APPEAL from adverse lower-court decisions.

Congress established the office of solicitor general in 1870 as part of the legislation creating the Department of Justice. Although early solicitors occasionally handled federal trials, for the most part the solicitor general has concentrated on appeals to the Supreme Court. In this role the solicitor has come to serve the interests of both the executive branch and the Supreme Court.

The federal government litigates thousands of cases each year. When a government agency loses in the federal district court and the federal court of appeals, it usually seeks to file a petition for a WRIT of CERTIORARI to the Supreme Court. The Court uses this writ procedure as a tool for discretionary review. The solicitor general reviews these agency requests and typically will reject most of them. This screening function reduces the workload of the Supreme Court in processing petitions, and it enhances the credibility of the solicitor general when he or she requests certiorari. The Court grants review in approximately 80 percent of the certiorari petitions filed by the solicitor general, compared with only 3 percent filed by other attorneys.

The solicitor general occasionally files AMICUS CURIAE (friend of the court) briefs in cases where the U.S. government is not a party but important government interests are at stake. Sometimes the Court itself will request that the solicitor file a brief where the government is not a party. The Court also allows the solicitor general to participate in oral arguments as an amicus.

Four former solicitors general later served on the Supreme Court: WILLIAM HOWARD TAFT, STANLEY F. REED, ROBERT H. JACKSON, and THURGOOD MARSHALL.

SOLID WASTES, HAZARDOUS SUBSTANCES, AND TOXIC POLLUTANTS

Millions of homes and residential neighborhoods contain hidden killers such as lead, mercury, and cyanide. These harmful substances can cause cancer, neurological damage, and even death. They can also hurt various aspects of the environment, including the wilderness, wildlife, and aquatic life.

In many instances, these harmful substances cause environmental and residential damage by migrating through the soil from nearby landfills. Both state and federal governments regulate landfills and the pollutants deposited there. Federal regulation comes in the form of legislation; state regulation comes through state and local legislation as well as COMMON-LAW principles.

Legislation

Solid Wastes Solid waste is useless, unwanted, and discarded material lacking sufficient liquid content to be free-flowing. More than 10 billion tons of solid waste is generated each year in the United States, most of it from agricultural activities. This waste is primarily produced by farm animals, slaughterhouses, and crop harvesting. The mining industry is another

Materials Generated in Municipal Solid Waste in 1995

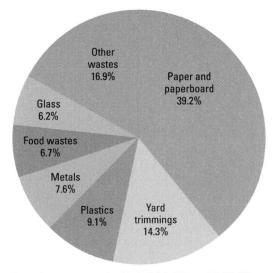

The total waste amount produced in the U.S. in 1995 was 205,050,000 tons.

Source: U.S. Environmental Protection Agency, *Characterization of Municipal Solid Waste in the United States, 1996 Update,* June 1997.

major producer of solid waste, generating over 2 billion tons a year. Its solid waste comes from the extraction, beneficiation (preparation for smelting), and processing of ores and minerals. But residential and commercial wastes are probably more familiar to the average person. These include everything from plastic bottles, aluminum cans, and rubber tires to yard trimmings, food wastes, and discarded appliances.

Solid waste management, which involves the storage, collection, transportation, processing, recovery, and disposal of solid waste, has been a daunting task. The United States spends more than $6 billion a year on it, most of which goes to collection and transportation. Most solid waste is transported to dumps and landfills; the rest is incinerated. In 1970, when Congress began studying solid waste, as many as 90 percent of the dumps and 75 percent of the municipal incinerators were considered inadequate, and were major polluters of air, land, and water.

Disposal sites pose two chronic problems for communities. First, they are an aesthetic nuisance, or an "eyesore." The federal Highway Beautification Act of 1965 (23 U.S.C.A. § 131 et seq.) aimed at this problem with some success. The second, more vexatious problem is created by disease-carrying agents that transmit bacteria from landfills to nearby human populations. Such agents include water, wind, soil, birds, insects, and rodents.

In the late 1980s and early 1990s, state and federal attention turned to productive uses for landfills, such as resource recovery. Resource recovery, sometimes called reclamation or salvage, is the process by which energy and other resources are extracted from solid waste for recycling or reuse. Aluminum cans and plastic bottles are two forms of solid waste that can be both recycled and reused. Energy extracted from solid waste has been used to generate steam, ELECTRICITY, and fuel.

Federal regulation of solid waste is governed by the Resource Conservation and Recovery Act (RCRA), 42 U.S.C.A. § 690 et seq., sometimes called the Solid Waste Disposal Act. When enacting the RCRA, Congress stated that "land is too valuable a national resource to be needlessly polluted by discarded materials, [yet] most solid wastes are disposed of on land in open dumps and sanitary landfills." At the same time, Congress determined that millions of tons of solid waste were being buried each year that could have been treated and salvaged. Better technology must be developed, Congress concluded, to recover useful resources from solid wastes.

The RCRA defines solid waste as garbage, refuse, and sludge generated by treatment plants and air pollution control facilities. Other discarded materials, such as semisolid and some liquid materials, are also included within the RCRA's broad definition of solid waste. Excluded from this definition are solid and dissolved materials from domestic sewage and irrigation systems, both of which are regulated at the state and local levels.

Under the RCRA, the administrator of the ENVIRONMENTAL PROTECTION AGENCY (EPA) is required to publish guidelines for the collection, storage, transportation, treatment, and disposal of solid waste. During the first several years after the RCRA's enactment, particularly during President RONALD REAGAN's administration, the EPA was slow to enact any guidelines whatsoever. In 1987, four environmental groups sued the EPA in an effort to compel the agency to fulfill its responsibilities under the RCRA. After that case was settled, the EPA began promulgating a number of guidelines concerning solid waste management, three of which govern the management of paper products, oil lubricants, and retread tires.

Paper is the largest single component, by both weight and volume, of municipal solid waste. More than 50 million tons of such waste are discarded each year, primarily in solid waste landfills. Oil lubricants are also discarded in massive amounts. Of the more than 1.2 billion gallons of oil generated each year, 30 percent is discharged into sewers and land. The numbers of discarded tires is equally staggering. Over 4 billion tires have been dumped into landfills and stockpiles around the country, and that

These metal tanks reinforced with concrete were built in Richland, Washington, for the storage of nuclear waste.

number grows by 200 million each year. Because tires do not biodegrade, they provide enduring shelter for many rodents and insects, both carriers of disease.

The guidelines drafted by the EPA were designed to diminish the magnitude of these problems by encouraging technological innovation, recycling, and reuse. In particular, the guidelines require that such waste be treated through new or available technology so that valuable resources can be identified and separated from materials that are truly waste. These guidelines may be enforced by the state or federal governments, as well as by private individuals through so-called citizen suits. Criminal and civil penalties are imposed on offenders who fail to comply with the guidelines. Violators may also face additional penalties imposed by state and local governments that have enacted solid waste regulations of their own.

Hazardous Substances and Toxic Pollutants The alarming dangers posed by hazardous substances and toxic pollutants were brought to the fore in Niagara Falls, New York, where the infamous Love Canal incident took place. The canal was originally excavated in the 1890s as part of an unsuccessful scheme to divert the Niagara River for hydroelectric power. Between 1942 and 1953, Hooker Chemical Corporation filled the canal with drums containing 21,800 tons of hazardous and toxic chemicals. Later, Hooker sold the dump site to the Niagara Falls School Board for $1, with a DEED containing a provision that relieved the chemical company of LIABILITY for any harm resulting from hazardous and toxic materials deposited at the canal.

A school was built near the site, and a residential neighborhood grew up surrounding the canal. But as the drums holding the chemicals gradually corroded, their contents migrated from the canal through the neighboring residential soil. In the late 1970s, following several years of heavy rainfall, the presence of the chemicals became more apparent as sludge seeped into basements and emitted toxic fumes. Numerous lawsuits soon followed.

Regulation of hazardous and toxic materials is marked by its nomenclature. Hazardous substances are defined by federal law as "solid wastes" that "cause, or significantly contribute to an increase in mortality or illness" or "pose a substantial present or potential hazard to human health or the environment when improperly treated, stored, transported or disposed" (42 U.S.C.A. § 6903). Toxic pollutants, a subset of hazardous substances, include pollutants that "after discharge and upon exposure, ingestion or inhalation . . . [by] any organism" will "cause death, disease, behavioral abnormalities, cancer, genetic mutations, physiological malfunctions, . . . or physical deformations in such organisms or their offspring" (33 U.S.C.A. §1362).

Because toxic pollutants are a subset of hazardous materials, a pollutant may be hazardous without being toxic, but not vice versa. The EPA has published a list of pollutants it deems toxic, including arsenic, asbestos, benzene, cyanide, DDT, lead, mercury, nickel, and silver. Pollutants not included on this list, such as acetic acid, ammonia, and cobalt, may still be considered hazardous if they pose a substantial threat to human health or the environment.

Myriad federal and state regulations govern the management of hazardous and toxic materials. The manufacturing of hazardous chemicals is governed at the federal level by the Toxic Substance Control Act (TSCA), 42 U.S.C.A. § 9604. The purpose of the TSCA is to identify potentially harmful substances before they are manufactured and placed in the market, in order to protect the public from any "unreasonable risk." Pursuant to the TSCA, the EPA has adopted rules requiring manufacturers to test chemicals that "enter the environment in substantial quantities" or present a likelihood of "substantial human exposure." The TSCA also requires manufacturers to give the EPA notice

Generation and Recovery of Municipal Waste in the United States, 1960 to 1995

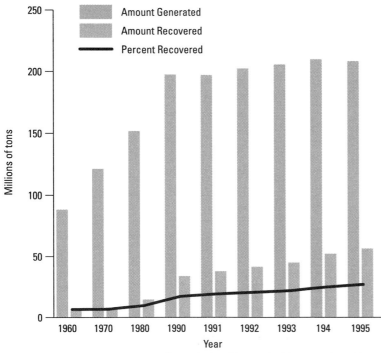

Source: U.S. Environmental Protection Agency, *Characterization of Municipal Solid Waste in the United States, 1996 Update,* June 1997.

ninety days before they begin manufacturing any new chemicals.

Facilities that transport, store, and dispose of hazardous and toxic substances, also called TSDs, are governed by the RCRA. The RCRA provides "cradle-to-grave" regulation of toxic and hazardous substances based partly on their persistence, degradability, corrosiveness, and flammability. TSDs must obtain a permit under the RCRA before they are allowed to manage toxic or hazardous materials. To obtain a permit, the applicant must demonstrate the ability to manage such materials in compliance with stringent standards. One of these standards requires TSDs to take corrective action immediately after any improper release of toxic chemicals.

The RCRA makes landfills the last alternative for the disposal of hazardous and toxic materials. Before land disposal is permitted under the RCRA, TSDs must comply with treatment standards that mandate the use of certain technology to minimize the harmfulness of particular substances. When land disposal is authorized, new landfills must use double liners and groundwater monitoring systems unless the EPA finds that an alternative design or practice would be equally effective in preventing hazardous and toxic materials from migrating through the soil. The EPA has broad powers under the RCRA to inspect TSDs for violations.

The Comprehensive Environmental Response, Compensation, and Liability Act (CERCLA), 42 U.S.C.A. § 9622, is the third major piece of federal legislation governing hazardous and toxic materials. Congress established CERCLA in 1980 to deal with thousands of inactive and abandoned hazardous waste sites in the United States. CERCLA directs the EPA to identify sites at which hazardous or toxic substances may have been released, and ascertain the parties potentially responsible for cleaning up these sites. Potentially responsible parties (PRPs) include the owners and operators of sites where hazardous material has been discharged, as well as the dischargers themselves.

CERCLA imposes JOINT AND SEVERAL LIABILITY on responsible parties—which means that once liability is established among a group of owners, operators, and dischargers, any one of them could be held liable for the entire cost of cleanup. Although responsible parties can seek reimbursement from each other, the wealthiest defendants are usually stuck with the CERCLA cleanup bills.

Some responsible parties escape liability because they cannot be identified or located. Oth-

ers have become insolvent or bankrupt. In such situations, CERCLA's Superfund provisions are triggered. The Superfund creates a multi-billion-dollar hazardous substance trust fund for cleaning up seriously contaminated sites in which the responsible parties avoid liability. Revenue for the Superfund is raised through federal appropriation and taxes paid by some TSDs.

The sale and distribution of pesticides is governed at the national level by a separate piece of legislation known as the Federal Insecticide, Fungicide, and Rodenticide Act (FIFRA), 7 U.S.C.A. § 136 et seq. Under FIFRA, no pesticide may be introduced into the stream of commerce without approval by the administrator of the EPA. A pesticide will not be approved if the administrator finds it is likely to "cause unreasonable adverse effects on the environment." The reasonableness of an adverse environmental effect is measured by taking into account the economic, social, and environmental costs and benefits of the pesticide.

Common Law In addition to the remedies provided under federal and state legislation for injuries caused by solid waste, hazardous substances, and toxic pollutants, common-law principles of NUISANCE, TRESPASS, and NEGLIGENCE provide alternative avenues of recourse against landfill owners. The common-law doctrine of nuisance gives injured landowners a cause of action when "substantial" injuries result from an "unreasonable" use of a particular landfill. The gravity of the injury and the reasonableness of the use are measured by a cost-benefit analysis in which the utility and appropriateness of the landfill's activities are balanced against the value of the landowner's interests.

Under the common law of trespass, landowners can recover for *any* unlawful interference with their rights or interests. Trespass requires proof that the landfill owner intentionally or knowingly interfered with the landowner's rights or interests. Mere accidental or inadvertent interferences will not suffice.

Landowners suffering injuries from accidents and inadvertence can turn to the common law of negligence, which allows recovery for injuries caused by a landfill owner's failure to act with reasonable care.

CROSS-REFERENCES

Air Pollution; Environmental Law; Land-Use Control; Pollution; Water Pollution.

SOLOMON AMENDMENT Federal legislation, 50 U.S.C.A. App. § 462(f), that denies male college students between the ages of 18 and 26 who fail to register for the military DRAFT (under the Selective Service Act, 50 U.S.C.A. App. § 451 et seq.) eligibility to receive financial aid provided by the Basic Educational Opportunity Grant Program.

Registration for the draft, which had been suspended on July 1, 1973, resumed in 1980. To compel compliance with the registration requirement, Congress enacted the Solomon Amendment, sponsored by New York Representative Gerald B. H. Solomon. The amendment provides that applicants for financial aid under the Basic Educational Opportunity Grant Program certify that they have satisfied the registration requirement relating to the draft. In 1984 the Supreme Court upheld the constitutionality of the Solomon Amendment in the case of *Selective Service System v. Minnesota Public Interest Research Group*, 468 U.S. 841, 104 S. Ct. 3348, 82 L. Ed. 2d 632. See also ARMED SERVICES; SELECTIVE SERVICE SYSTEM.

SOLVENCY The ability of an individual to pay his or her debts as they mature in the normal and ordinary course of business, or the financial condition of owning property of sufficient value to discharge all of one's debts.

See also INSOLVENCY.

SON OF SAM LAWS Laws that enable a state to use the proceeds a criminal earns from recounting his or her crime in a book, movie, television show, or other depiction. The laws are named after David Berkowitz, a New York serial killer who left a note signed "Son of Sam" at the scene of one of his crimes.

Since 1977 forty-two states and the federal government have enacted various types of Son of Sam laws that take any proceeds a criminal earns for selling the story of his crime and give them to the victims of the crime or to a victims' compensation fund. Since a 1991 U.S. Supreme Court ruling struck down the New York law as unconstitutional, states have sought ways to modify their laws to avoid similar decisions. Despite the apparent virtue of denying criminals the ability to profit from their crimes, serious FIRST AMENDMENT issues have been raised about Son of Sam laws.

The New York legislature enacted the first Son of Sam law (N.Y. Exec. Law § 632-a) in 1977 after it learned that David Berkowitz was planning to sell his story of serial killing. The statute affected an accused or convicted person who contracted to speak or write about her crime. It required the person contracting with the criminal to turn over the criminal's proceeds to the state's Crime Victims Compensation Board, which established an ESCROW account for the benefit of the crime's victims and publicized the existence of the account. To obtain funds, a victim had to bring a CIVIL ACTION and obtain a JUDGMENT against the criminal within three years (originally five years) of the establishment of the account. At the end of this time period, the criminal received any funds in the account upon showing that no actions were pending against her.

Forty-one other states adopted similar laws, and the federal government established such a process in the Victims of Crime Act of 1984 (18 U.S.C.A. §§ 3681–3682). In a few states, victims may apply directly to a victims' compensation program rather than sue the criminal directly. Some states seek to prevent criminals from ever profiting from their crimes by retaining any money remaining in the escrow account at the end of the statutory period. Under the federal statute, a court directs the disposition of the remaining funds and may require that part or all of the money be turned over to the Federal Crime Victims Fund.

The constitutionality of the New York Son of Sam law was challenged in *Simon and Schuster, Inc. v. New York Victims Crime Board*, 502 U.S. 105, 112 S. Ct. 501, 116 L. Ed. 2d 476 (1991). This case involved profits from the book *Wiseguy: A Life in a Mafia Family*, a nonfiction work about ORGANIZED CRIME in New York City, published by Simon and Schuster. Nicholas Pileggi wrote the book with the paid cooperation of Henry Hill, a career criminal who agreed in 1980 to testify against organized crime figures. The book told Hill's life story from 1955, when he first became involved with crime, until 1980.

Simon and Schuster argued that the law was based on the content of a publication and therefore violated the First Amendment. The Court agreed. Writing for a unanimous Court, Justice SANDRA DAY O'CONNOR struck down the law, concluding, "A statute is presumptively inconsistent with the First Amendment if it imposes a financial burden on speakers because of the content of their speech."

The Son of Sam law singled out income derived from expressive activity and was directed only at works having a specified content. Because of the financial disincentive to publication that the act created, and its differential treatment among authors, the Court applied the strictest form of review to the New York law. The Court acknowledged that the state had a compelling interest in compensating victims from the fruits of crime but concluded that the law was not narrowly tailored to achieve that interest. The New York law was over-inclusive, applying to works on any subject as long as the work expressed the author's thoughts or recollections about the crime, however tangentially or incidentally. If the author admitted to committing the crime, it did not matter whether she was ever actually accused or convicted. Under this standard, works by St. Augustine, HENRY DAVID THOREAU, and MALCOLM X would be covered because their writings discussed crimes that they committed.

The *Simon and Schuster* decision has put the validity of all Son of Sam laws in doubt. New York quickly amended its law to apply to any economic benefit to the criminal derived from the crime, not just the proceeds from the sale of the offender's story. This redefinition was intended to eliminate the unconstitutional regulation of expressive activity and reconceptualize the law as a regulation of economic proceeds from crime.

The Supreme Court did not strike down all Son of Sam laws as unconstitutional, yet states have followed New York in modifying their statutes to designate that all profits of the offender be subject to ATTACHMENT, not just those derived from selling his crime story. It remains unclear, however, whether these other laws will withstand a First Amendment challenge.

CROSS-REFERENCES
Freedom of Speech; Publishing Law; Victims of Crime.

SONOSKY, MARVIN J.   Marvin J. Sonosky's legal work on behalf of Native Americans resulted in victories in Congress and the courts. Sonosky championed Indian causes during his long career as an attorney, representing several tribes. His single greatest accomplishment was winning the *Black Hills* case, a twenty-four-year legal odyssey in which the Sioux nation asserted its claim to sacred ground taken by the federal government a century earlier.

Born on February 20, 1909, in Duluth, Minnesota, Sonosky completed his undergraduate and law studies at the University of Minnesota and was admitted to the state bar in 1932. He practiced briefly in Duluth before moving to Washington, D.C., in 1937 to join the Depart-

BIOGRAPHY

ment of Justice. He spent more than a decade as a special assistant to the attorney general in the Justice Department's Lands Division.

In 1951 Sonosky returned to private practice with a focus on Indian law. Over the next three decades, he would successfully represent the Assiniboin, Shoshone, and Sioux tribes in a number of cases involving land claims against the federal government. His work went beyond trial practice; his clients were often stymied by discriminatory federal laws, especially in the area of court JURISDICTION, and Sonosky's efforts helped to remove barriers that prevented their full use of the FEDERAL COURTS.

Sonosky played a leading role in the effort by the Sioux to reclaim the Black Hills of South Dakota. The case had a long history: the Sioux had temporarily ceded TITLE to the land to the federal government in 1876 under controversial circumstances. They began attempting to reclaim the land in the 1920s, but legal mismanagement stalled their claim until the late 1950s, when the Sioux turned to Sonosky and his colleague Arthur Lazarus.

Sonosky and Lazarus spent twenty-four years fighting the case in various courts, Congress, and even the White House. Legislative reform was necessary for their victory, and they helped change the Indian Claims Commission Act of 1946 (Ch. 959, § 1, Pub. L. No. 79-726 [omitted from 25 U.S.C.A. § 70 on termination of the commission on September 30, 1978, pursuant to Pub. L. No. 94-465, sec. 2, 90 Stat. 1990 (1976)]) as well as bring about passage of the Indian Civil Rights Act of 1968 (Pub. L. No. 90-284, tit. II, 82 Stat. 77 [codified at 25 U.S.C.A. §§ 1301–1303 (1988)]).

Their success was mixed. In 1980 the U.S. Supreme Court affirmed a JUDGMENT for the Sioux in the amount of $105 million (*Sioux Nation v. United States*, 602 F.2d 1157 [Ct. Cl. 1979], aff'd., 448 U.S. 371, 100 S. Ct. 2716, 65 L. Ed. 2d 844 [1980]). Although the amount represented the largest judgment ever won by Native Americans against the federal government, the Sioux refused it, preferring return of the land to a monetary award. The attorneys,

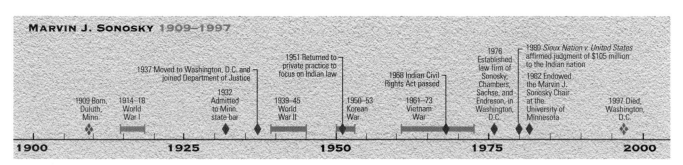

MARVIN J. SONOSKY 1909–1997

1909 Born, Duluth, Minn.

1914–18 World War I

1932 Admitted to Minn. state bar

1937 Moved to Washington, D.C. and joined Department of Justice

1939–45 World War II

1950–53 Korean War

1951 Returned to private practice to focus on Indian law

1961–73 Vietnam War

1968 Indian Civil Rights Act passed

1976 Established law firm of Sonosky, Chambers, Sachse, and Endreson, in Washington, D.C.

1980 *Sioux Nation v. United States* affirmed judgment of $105 million to the Indian nation

1982 Endowed the Marvin J. Sonosky Chair at the University of Minnesota

1997 Died, Washington, D.C.

1900   1925   1950   1975   2000

who had accepted the case on a contingency fee basis, received a $10 million legal fee from the federal Court of Claims.

In 1976 Sonosky established the firm of Sonosky, Chambers, Sachse, and Endreson in Washington, D.C. As one of the leading firms specializing in Indian law, its work includes lobbying, general tribal practice, mineral and natural resources issues, and representation of tribes before federal agencies. In 1982 Sonosky endowed the Marvin J. Sonosky Chair at the University of Minnesota. He remained in active practice at his firm until his death on July 16, 1997, in Washington, D.C.

See also NATIVE AMERICAN RIGHTS.

SONY CORP. OF AMERICA v. UNIVERSAL CITY STUDIOS

In *Sony Corp. of America v. Universal City Studios*, 464 U.S. 417, 104 S. Ct. 774, 78 L. Ed. 2d 574 (1984), also known as the *Betamax* case, the U.S. Supreme Court determined that Sony, a manufacturer of videocassette recorders (VCRs) did not infringe on copyrights owned by Universal City Studios and Walt Disney Productions by manufacturing and marketing Betamax VCRs. (The Court's opinion uses the terms *videotape recorders* and *VTRs* in referring to VCRs.) Universal and Disney, which owned copyrights on many popular TELEVISION programs in the late 1970s, sued Sony after Sony introduced its Betamax VCR in 1976. Universal and Disney claimed that the Copyright Revision Act (17 U.S.C.A. § 101 et seq. [1976]) did not permit home viewers to record their television programs without their permission. The studios argued that Sony contributed to the COPYRIGHT infringement by enabling and encouraging Betamax owners to record the copyrighted television programs.

The Supreme Court, in a 5–4 vote, determined that Sony did not infringe on the studios' copyrights by manufacturing and marketing Betamax VCRs. The decision, which analyzed difficult questions of copyright law, turned on two important legal concepts. First, the Court held that home recording of copyrighted television programs is a "fair use" of the copyrighted material and, thus, does not violate the Copyright Act. The Court's discussion of the "fair use doctrine" makes the *Betamax* case a landmark decision in copyright law. The Court also held that Sony was not liable for "contributory infringement" of the studios' copyrights. In other words, Sony was not liable to Universal and Disney for supplying television viewers with the means to record copyrighted television programs.

In 1976 Sony introduced the Betamax videocassette recorder. The Betamax was the first compact, affordable VCR available to consumers. Sony encouraged potential Betamax buyers to engage in "time-shift viewing" by recording television programs and viewing them later. Universal and Disney believed that the unauthorized recording of television programs by home viewers infringed on the copyrights they held on those programs. The studios filed suit in federal district court against Sony, Sony's U.S. SUBSIDIARY, Sony's advertising agency, four retailers of Betamax VCRs, and one individual Betamax owner.

The district court ruled against Universal and Disney, finding an implied exemption for home video recording in the 1976 Copyright Revision Act (*Universal City Studios, Inc. v. Sony Corp. of America*, 480 F. Supp. 429 [C.D. Calif. 1979]). The district court also held that Sony was not a contributory infringer of the studios' copyrights because it did not know that home video recording was an infringement when it manufactured and sold the VCRs. Most importantly, the district court held that home video recording was a fair use of the copyrighted television programs. Universal and Disney believed that the district court was the first court to hold that copying copyrighted material for mere entertainment or convenience could be a fair use, and they immediately appealed.

The Ninth Circuit Court of Appeals reversed the district court, holding that private home videotaping infringed on the studios' copyrights (*Universal City Studios, Inc. v. Sony Corp. of America*, 659 F. 2d 963 [1981]). The appeals court also determined that Sony was liable to the studios for contributory infringement because it knew that Betamax VCRs would be used to reproduce copyrighted programs. The Supreme Court agreed to hear Sony's appeal.

On January 17, 1984, the Supreme Court announced its decision reversing the Ninth Circuit court, holding that Sony had not infringed on copyrights held by Universal and Disney by manufacturing and marketing Betamax VCRs. The Court was sharply divided, and both Justice JOHN PAUL STEVENS, who wrote for the majority, and Justice HARRY A. BLACKMUN, who wrote for the dissent, issued lengthy opinions. As noted earlier, the *Betamax* case focused on two main issues: (1) whether home recording of copyrighted television programs constitutes a "fair use" of the copyrighted material, and (2) whether Sony committed "contributory infringement" by selling VCRs, thereby enabling VCR owners to copy the copyrighted television programs.

Article I of the U.S. Constitution grants Congress the power to pass laws to protect the works of "Authors and Inventors" from copying by others. Pursuant to this power, Congress created copyrights and PATENTS. To encourage creativity, Congress gave copyright holders the exclusive right to their creative works. The courts, however, have permitted reproduction of copyrighted works without the copyright holder's permission for a "fair use"; the copyright owner does not possess the exclusive right to a fair use. For example, a teacher may reproduce limited portions of a copyrighted book for the purpose of teaching without the permission of the author. This concept is referred to as the "fair use doctrine," which was codified by Congress in the Copyright Revision Act of 1976 (17 U.S.C.A. § 107). The *Betamax* decision is one of the most important cases interpreting this doctrine.

In determining that home recording of copyrighted television programs was a fair use under the copyright laws, the Supreme Court focused on the noncommercial nature of home recording. The Court stated that noncommercial use of copyrighted material is presumptively fair. The majority of the Court agreed with the district court that home recording of copyrighted television programs simply does not harm the owners of the copyrights. The Court noted that television programs are broadcast free of charge and that Betamax VCRs enable viewers to watch programs they might otherwise miss. The Court also pointed out that copyright owners besides Universal and Disney had testified at trial that they did not object to the home recording of their television programs. Based on all of these factors, the Court held that home recording of copyrighted television programs constitutes a fair use of the copyrighted material.

Clearly, Sony was not itself infringing on the copyrights owned by Universal and Disney, regardless of whether home recording of television programs could be considered a fair use. Thus, the studios argued instead that Sony was liable for *contributory* infringement of their copyrights. The studios' theory was that Sony supplied the means for the copyright infringement and actively encouraged infringement through advertising. The Supreme Court rejected the studios' argument. The Court agreed that contributory infringement of a copyright could occur in certain circumstances; however, manufacturing and marketing the Betamax

could not constitute contributory infringement because the Betamax was capable of a number of uses that did not infringe on any copyrights. As examples of non-infringing uses, the Court noted that many copyright owners did not object to having their television programs recorded. Also, the Betamax could be used to play rented or purchased tapes of copyrighted programs, thereby compensating the copyright holders for the right to view their works.

Justices Blackmun, THURGOOD MARSHALL, LEWIS F. POWELL, JR., and WILLIAM H. REHNQUIST dissented in an opinion by Blackmun. First, the dissent found that home recording of copyrighted television programs was not a fair use of the copyrighted material. Blackmun stated that "when a user reproduces an entire work and uses it for its original purpose, with no added benefit to the public, the doctrine of fair use usually does not apply." Although the majority found no harm in allowing VCR owners to record copyrighted television programs, the dissent claimed that these recordings could harm the owners of the copyrights. The dissent pointed out, for example, that persons who tape television programs for later viewing are much more likely to skip through the commercials that ultimately pay for the television program, thereby potentially reducing advertising revenue. Also, the television ratings system, on which advertising prices are based, is unable to account for taped programs. The dissent further believed that Sony could be liable to the studios for contributory infringement of their copyrights, stating that "if virtually all of the product's use . . . is to infringe, contributory liability may be imposed." The dissent would have remanded the case to determine whether the Betamax VCRs were used primarily for infringing or non-infringing uses.

See also BROADCASTING; INTELLECTUAL PROPERTY.

SOUTER, DAVID HACKETT

David Hackett Souter was appointed to the U.S. Supreme Court on July 25, 1990, by President GEORGE BUSH. Chosen by the Bush administration because of his conservative judicial style, Souter has proven to be a moderate justice whose personality and temperament have enabled him to build a centrist coalition that has garnered support from the Court's ideological extremes.

Souter was born on September 17, 1939, in Melrose, Massachusetts, six miles north of Boston. The only son of Joseph Souter, a bank manager, and Helen Souter, a gift store clerk, the future associate justice is remembered by his childhood friends as an intense, intelligent, and family-oriented person who was endowed

BIOGRAPHY

PHOTOGRAPHER: JOSEPH H. BAILEY. COLLECTION OF THE SUPREME COURT OF THE UNITED STATES.

David Hackett Souter

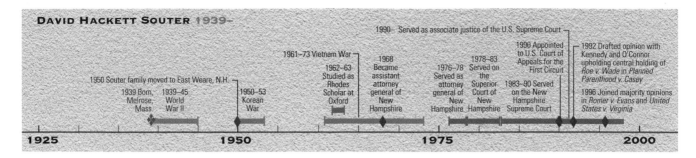

DAVID HACKETT SOUTER 1939–

1939 Born, Melrose, Mass.

1939–45 World War II

1950 Souter family moved to East Weare, N.H.

1950–53 Korean War

1961–73 Vietnam War

1962–63 Studied as Rhodes Scholar at Oxford

1968 Became assistant attorney general of New Hampshire

1976–78 Served as attorney general of New Hampshire

1978–83 Served on the Superior Court of New Hampshire

1983–90 Served on the New Hampshire Supreme Court

1990 Appointed to U.S. Court of Appeals for the First Circuit

1990– Served as associate justice of the U.S. Supreme Court

1992 Drafted opinion with Kennedy and O'Connor upholding central holding of *Roe v. Wade* in *Planned Parenthood v. Casey*

1996 Joined majority opinions in *Romer v. Evans* and *United States v. Virginia*

1925   1950   1975   2000

with a sharp wit, but no athletic ability. At age eleven Souter and his parents moved to a ten-acre farm in the rural community of East Weare, New Hampshire.

In 1957 Souter graduated second in a class of two hundred at Concord High School where his classmates named him as being the most literary, most sophisticated, and most likely to succeed. During high school Souter was named president of the National Honor Society and coeditor of the yearbook. According to legend, the only time Souter got into trouble as a teenager was when he stayed past closing time at the local historical society.

After high school Souter attended Harvard University. Graduating magna cum laude with a philosophy major in 1961, Souter was inducted into Harvard's prestigious chapter of Phi Beta Kappa, considered by many to be the nation's highest undergraduate academic award. Souter wrote his senior thesis on Supreme Court Justice OLIVER WENDELL HOLMES, JR., which helped him earn a Rhodes Scholarship to study at Oxford University, where he received a bachelor's degree in jurisprudence in 1963.

Upon returning to the United States, Souter entered Harvard Law School, quickly developing a reputation as a serious student and an independent thinker. However, Souter was not prone to debate issues with his peers, or volunteer in class. Although Souter was a solid law student, he graduated without academic honors and was not chosen for a place on the *Harvard Law Review*, Harvard's esteemed legal journal, which was a highly coveted position among the students.

In 1966 Souter joined Orr and Reno, a leading New Hampshire firm that handled corporate, probate, tax, and family law cases. Not feeling sufficiently challenged or stimulated by private practice, Souter went to work for the New Hampshire attorney general, ascending from assistant attorney general in 1968 to deputy attorney general in 1971 to attorney general in 1976. Souter did very little prosecuting during his tenure with the attorney general's office, directly handling only nine cases in ten years.

"... IN THE FIELD OF STATE CONSTITUTIONAL LAW ... IF WE PLACE TOO MUCH RELIANCE ON FEDERAL PRECEDENT WE WILL RENDER THE STATE RULES A MERE ROW OF SHADOWS; IF WE PLACE TOO LITTLE, WE WILL RENDER STATE PRACTICE INCOHERENT."

In 1978 Souter was appointed to the bench as a superior court judge in New Hampshire. Attorneys who appeared before Souter described him as an even-handed trial judge with a penchant for detail. Five years later Souter was elevated to the New Hampshire Supreme Court, where he authored more than two hundred opinions and established himself as an assertive judge who often questioned lawyers during oral arguments.

In February 1990 President Bush appointed Souter to the U.S. Court of Appeals for the First Circuit. Five months later, before Souter had written his first opinion as a federal judge, Bush appointed Souter to the U.S. Supreme Court. Subsequently confirmed by a vote of 90–9 in the Senate, Souter became the 105th jurist to serve on the nation's highest court.

Souter has disappointed those in the Bush administration who hoped he would provide the decisive fifth vote for the conservative wing of the Court, comprised of Chief Justice WILLIAM H. REHNQUIST and Associate Justices ANTONIN SCALIA, CLARENCE THOMAS, and SANDRA DAY O'CONNOR. Instead, Souter has proven to be a temperate justice, with a mainstream judicial philosophy. He has taken some positions that have upset conservatives, and other positions that have upset liberals.

Souter offended liberals when he voted to uphold federal regulations that prohibited doctors from providing ABORTION counseling at federally funded clinics, despite objections that such regulations violated the FIRST AMENDMENT (*Rust v. Sullivan*, 500 U.S. 173, 111 S. Ct. 1759, 114 L. Ed. 2d 233 [1991]). Some liberals were again dismayed when Souter voted to affirm a state ban on nude dancing in *Barnes v. Glen Theatre*, 501 U.S. 560, 111 S. Ct. 2456, 115 L. Ed. 2d 504 (1991), even though four dissenting justices said the ban violated freedom of expression. Souter also regularly votes in favor of CAPITAL PUNISHMENT.

On the other hand, many conservatives were distraught by Souter's concurring opinion in *Lee v. Weisman*, 505 U.S. 577, 112 S. Ct. 2649, 120 L. Ed. 2d 467 (1992), which relied on the Establishment Clause of the First Amendment to declare unconstitutional a nonsectarian prayer delivered by a clergyman at a public high school graduation ceremony. In *Romer v. Evans*, ___U.S. , 116 S. Ct. 1620, 134 L. Ed. 2d 855 (1996), Souter joined the Court's majority opinion that relied on the Equal Protection Clause of the FOURTEENTH AMENDMENT to strike down a Colorado constitutional provision prohibiting all legislative, executive, and judicial action designed to protect homosexuals from discrimination. Many conservatives were also upset when Souter voted to invalidate the male-only admissions policy at the University of Virginia Military Institute because it discriminated against women who sought entrance to the school's citizen-soldier program (*United States v. Virginia*, ___U.S.___ , 116 S. Ct. 2264, 135 L. Ed. 2d 735 [1996]).

Observers have increasingly recognized Souter as the intellectual leader of the emerging moderate core of the Supreme Court. In a number of important decisions, Souter has allied himself with Justices ANTHONY M. KENNEDY and O'Connor to forge an influential coalition that has been joined by members of the Court's ideological extremes. In this regard Souter has played a critical role in building a consensus of judicial philosophy among the Supreme Court justices.

In *Planned Parenthood v. Casey*, 505 U.S. 833, 112 S. Ct. 2791, 120 L. Ed. 2d 674 (1992), for example, the state of Pennsylvania asked the Supreme Court to overturn *Roe v. Wade*, 410 U.S. 113, 93 S. Ct. 705, 35 L. Ed. 2d 147 (1973), the decision guaranteeing women the right to terminate their pregnancies under certain circumstances. After oral arguments, five justices—Rehnquist, Scalia, O'Connor, Kennedy, and BYRON R. WHITE—expressed serious reservations about the holding in *Roe*. Based on these reservations, Rehnquist was prepared to draft a majority opinion that would have gutted virtually every tenet in the 1973 precedent.

Before Rehnquist finished writing the opinion, however, Souter, O'Connor, and Kennedy met outside the presence of the other justices to discuss the case. Following this meeting, the three justices presented a joint opinion that affirmed the central holding of *Roe*. Neither the state nor federal governments, the joint opinion in *Casey* stressed, may pass laws that place an "undue burden" on a woman's right to have an abortion. Souter, O'Connor, and Kennedy drew support from the traditionally liberal JOHN PAUL STEVENS and HARRY A. BLACKMUN, who concurred in principle with the joint opinion, and from the traditionally conservative Rehnquist, who concurred in judgment.

Souter continues to occupy a pivotal seat on the Supreme Court, using his polite and friendly personality, his patient and contemplative temperament, and his diligent work ethic to earn respect and win support across the ideological spectrum.

SOUTHEAST ASIA TREATY ORGANIZATION   The Southeast Asia Treaty Organization (SEATO) was an alliance organized pursuant to the Southeast Asia Defense Treaty to oppose the growing communist influence in Southeast Asia. The United States, the United Kingdom, France, Australia, New Zealand, Thailand, the Philippines, and Pakistan signed the treaty and accompanying Pacific Charter in Manila on September 8, 1954. The TREATY became operative in February 1955 and bound the signatories to mutual aid to resist armed attack or subversion; an armed attack on one signatory was interpreted as a danger to all.

Headquartered in Bangkok, SEATO relied on the military forces of member nations rather than commanding its own standing forces, as did the NORTH ATLANTIC TREATY ORGANIZATION. In its first few years of operation, SEATO's effectiveness was not tested, but at the beginning of the 1960s, conflicts in South Vietnam and Laos challenged the strength of the alliance and ultimately found it lacking. France withdrew from military cooperation in SEATO in 1967, and Great Britain refused active military cooperation in the Vietnam conflict. Moreover, a 1960s dispute between Pakistan and India further undermined the efficacy of the alliance: Pakistan drew closer to communist China, while the United States provided aid to India.

In 1972 Pakistan completely withdrew from the alliance; in 1974 France suspended its membership payments. In September 1975 the signatories decided to phase out the operations, and SEATO was formally dissolved on June 30, 1977. The collective defense treaty remains in effect, however.

SOUTHERN CHRISTIAN LEADERSHIP CONFERENCE   As a principal organization of the CIVIL RIGHTS MOVEMENT, the Southern Christian Leadership Conference (SCLC) championed the use of nonviolent direct action to end legal and social DISCRIMINATION against African Americans. Identified strongly with its original leader, the Reverend MARTIN LUTHER KING, JR., the SCLC organized and sponsored many protest marches and demonstrations during the late 1950s and the 1960s. Although the group's influence declined after King's assassination in 1968, the SCLC continues to work for the betterment of the lives of African Americans.

The SCLC emerged in the wake of a successful BOYCOTT of buses in Montgomery, Alabama, by the city's black citizens in 1955, which

The Southern Christian Leadership Conference practiced acts of non-violent protest, such as this sit-in at a whites-only lunch counter at Katz drugstore in Oklahoma City.

had led to a December 1956 Supreme Court ruling upholding the desegregation of those buses (*Gayle v. Browder,* 352 U.S. 903, 77 S. Ct. 145, 1 L. Ed. 2d 114). Prodded by African American social activist Bayard Rustin, who hoped to carry the Montgomery victory to the rest of the South, King and other clerics formed the Southern Negro Leaders Conference, forerunner of the SCLC, during a meeting in Atlanta in January 1957. King—who had gained national renown through his role as head of the Montgomery Improvement Association, the organizer of the bus boycott—was a natural choice to lead the group. Other early SCLC leaders included the Reverends Ralph D. Abernathy and Fred Shuttlesworth. Later in 1957, the group changed its name to the Southern Christian Leadership Conference.

The SCLC hoped to initiate Gandhian, nonviolent direct action throughout the South. It hoped that such action would secure racial desegregation, VOTING RIGHTS, and other gains for African Americans. Through this approach, the SCLC sought to take the CIVIL RIGHTS cause out of the courtroom and into the community, hoping to negotiate directly with whites for social change. As one of its first actions, the group led the 1957 Prayer Pilgrimage to Washington, D.C., which drew an estimated twenty-five thousand people. In 1959, it organized a youth march on Washington, D.C., that attracted forty thousand people.

Despite these successful marches, the SCLC was hampered by disorganization during its early years. It experienced difficulty in meeting many of its major goals during the late 1950s, particularly in voter registration. It charted a new course in the early 1960s, when it recruited leaders such as the Reverends Wyatt T. Walker and Andrew J. Young. Between 1960 and 1964, the number of full-time SCLC staff members grew from five to sixty, and the organization's effect on the civil rights movement reached its zenith.

The SCLC's growth allowed it to coordinate historic demonstrations that played a vital role in the civil rights movement. In April 1963, the SCLC led protests and boycotts in Birmingham, Alabama, that prompted violent police repression. Television viewers around the United States were shocked at the violence they saw directed at the clearly peaceful demonstrators. The SCLC won the sympathy of the nation again in a difficult 1965 civil rights campaign in Selma, Alabama, which also drew a violent response from whites. These protests are widely credited with hastening the passage of the CIVIL RIGHTS ACT of 1964 (42 U.S.C.A. § 2000a et seq.) and the Voting Rights Act of 1965 (42 U.S.C.A. § 1973 et seq.), laws that granted African Americans many of the gains they had been seeking.

By the mid-1960s, other African Americans began to question whether nonviolent direct action could achieve significant changes for their communities. More radical civil rights groups, notably the STUDENT NONVIOLENT COORDINATING COMMITTEE and the Congress of Racial Equality, publicly renounced the nonviolent approach of the SCLC. They pointed to the poverty and DE FACTO (actual) segregation experienced by African Americans in the northern cities, and argued that the SCLC's tactics were ineffective in the urban ghetto.

King and the SCLC were sensitive to such criticism, and increasingly began to focus their attention on the North. By 1967, the SCLC launched several new operations there: the Chicago Freedom Movement, Operation Breadbasket, and the Poor People's Campaign. It brought in young, new leaders, including a divinity student named JESSE JACKSON, to lead these efforts.

The SCLC suffered a staggering setback when King was assassinated in April 1968. The group had always been closely identified with the charismatic preacher, and his death cost it the vital leadership, publicity, and fund-raising he had provided. Abernathy became president of the organization. By 1972, the staff had declined to twenty and leaders such as Young and Jackson had moved on to other pursuits.

Joseph E. Lowery succeeded Abernathy as president of the SCLC in 1977. The Atlanta-based group has continued to work for the improvement of the lives of African Americans through leadership training and citizen education. It has also created campaigns to battle drug abuse and crime.

CROSS-REFERENCES

Integration; Jim Crow Laws; National Association for the Advancement of Colored People; Parks, Rosa Louise McCauley.

SOVEREIGN IMMUNITY ◻ The legal protection that prevents a sovereign state or person from being sued without consent. ◻

Sovereign immunity is a judicial doctrine that prevents the government or its political subdivisions, departments, and agencies from being sued without its consent. The doctrine stems from the ancient English principle that the monarch could do no wrong.

Suits against the United States In early American history, the courts supported the traditional view that the United States could not be sued without congressional authorization (*Chisholm v. Georgia*, 2 U.S. [2 Dall.] 419, 478, 1 L. Ed. 440 [1793]; *Cohens v. Virginia*, 19 U.S. [6 Wheat.] 264, 412, 5 L. Ed. 257 [1821]). This immunity applied to suits filed by states as well as individuals (*Kansas v. United States*, 204 U.S. 331, 27 S. Ct. 388, 51 L. Ed. 510 [1906]). Thus, for many years, those who had contract and tort claims against the government had no legal recourse except through the difficult, inconvenient, and often tardy means of convincing Congress to pass a special bill awarding compensation to the injured party on a case by case basis.

The federal government first began to waive its sovereign immunity in areas of law other than torts. In 1855 Congress established the U.S. Court of Claims, a special court created to hear cases against the United States involving CONTRACTS based upon the Constitution, federal statutes, and federal regulations. In 1887 Congress passed the TUCKER ACT (28 U.S.C.A. §§ 1346 (a) (2), 1491) to authorize federal district courts to hear contractual claims not exceeding $10,000 against the United States. Other special courts were later created for particular types of nontort claims against the federal government. The U.S. Board of General Appraisers was created in 1890 and was replaced in 1926 by the U.S. Customs Court, and the U.S. Court of Customs Appeals was created in 1909 and then replaced in 1926 by the U.S. Court of Customs and Patent Appeals. These courts handled complaints about duties levied on imports. The Board of Tax Appeals, created in 1924 to handle internal revenue complaints, was replaced in 1942 by the TAX COURT of the United States.

Not until 1946, however, did Congress address the issue of LIABILITY for torts committed by the government's agencies, officers, or employees. Until 1946 civil servants could be individually liable for torts, but they were protected by sovereign immunity from liability for tortious acts committed while carrying out their official duties. The courts were not always consistent in making that distinction, however.

Finally, in 1946 Congress passed the Tort Claims Act (28 U.S.C.A. §§ 1346(b), 2671–2678), which authorized U.S. district courts to hold the United States liable for torts committed by its agencies, officers, and employees just as the courts would hold individual defendants liable under similar circumstances. This general WAIVER of immunity had a number of exceptions, however, including the torts of BATTERY, FALSE IMPRISONMENT, FALSE ARREST, MALICIOUS PROSECUTION, ABUSE OF PROCESS, LIBEL, SLANDER, MISREPRESENTATION, DECEIT, interference with contractual rights, tort in the fiscal operations of the Treasury, tort in the regulation of the monetary system, and tort in combatant activities of the armed forces in wartime.

By 1953 the U.S. Supreme Court had drawn distinctions under the Tort Claims Act between tortious acts committed by the government at the planning or policy-making stage and those committed at the operational level. In *Dalehite v. United States*, 346 U.S. 15, 73 S. Ct. 956, 97 L. Ed. 1427 (1953), the Supreme Court held that the Tort Claims Act did not waive sovereign immunity as to tortious acts committed at the planning stage; immunity applied only to torts committed at the operational stage.

Congress also waived sovereign immunity in cases seeking injunctive or other nonmonetary relief against the United States in a 1976 amendment to the Administrative Procedure Act (5 U.S.C.A. §§ 702–703).

Suits against the States The doctrine of sovereign immunity applies to state governments within their own states, but it was not initially clear whether states had immunity as to suits involving other states or citizens of other states. In the 1793 case of *Chisholm v. Georgia*, the U.S. Supreme Court permitted a North Carolina citizen to sue Georgia for property that Georgia had seized during the American Revolution. The states' strong disapproval of the Court's decision in *Chisholm* led to the prompt adoption of the ELEVENTH AMENDMENT to the U.S. Constitution in 1795. The Eleventh Amendment specifically grants immunity to the states as to lawsuits by citizens of other states, foreign countries, or citizens of foreign countries in the federal courts. This limitation was judicially extended to include suits by a state's own citizens in *Hans v. Louisiana*, 134 U.S. 1, 10 S. Ct. 504, 33 L. Ed. 842 (1890).

The U.S. Supreme Court still has JURISDICTION to hear suits by one state against another. In addition, the courts have construed the Eleventh Amendment as permitting APPELLATE proceedings in cases originally instituted by a state if the defendant asserted rights under the U.S. Constitution, statutes, or treaties (*Cohens v. Virginia*), or in cases against state officials alleged to have violated such rights (*Osborn v. Bank of the United States*, 22 U.S. [9 Wheat.] 738, 6 L. Ed. 204 [1824]). The latter category has resulted in extensive litigation in FEDERAL COURTS against state and local officers alleged to have violated the Civil Rights Act of 1871 (42 U.S.C.A. § 1983). Claims brought under the act are not subject to sovereign immunity.

In state court actions, immunity continues to be allowed in the absence of consent to be sued. Depending on the type of case, however, different levels of immunity may apply. Absolute immunity is generally allowed for judges and quasi-judicial officers, such as prosecuting attorneys and parole board members. For executive officers, immunity is a function of the amount of discretion they possess to make decisions and the circumstances in which they act (*Scheuer v. Rhodes*, 416 U.S. 232, 94 S. Ct. 1683, 40 L. Ed. 2d 90 [1974]). But immunity has been denied to officials acting in excess of statutory authority (*Greene v. Louisville and Interurban Railroad Co.*, 244 U.S. 499, 37 S. Ct. 673, 61 L. Ed. 1280 [1917]) or under an unconstitutional statute (*Ex parte Young*, 209 U.S. 123, 28 S. Ct. 441, 52 L. Ed. 714 [1908]). Immunity has been allowed when state property is involved or the state is an essential party for granting relief (*Cunningham v. Macon and Brunswick Railroad Co.*, 109 U.S. 446, 3 S. Ct. 292, 27 L. Ed. 992 [1883]).

Until a Supreme Court decision in 1979, it was generally assumed, and decided by a court in at least one case (*Paulus v. South Dakota*, 52 N.D. 84, 201 N.W. 867 [1924]), that a state's immunity must be recognized not only in its own courts, but also in the courts of other states throughout the country. The U.S. Supreme Court addressed the issue in *Nevada v. Hall*, 440 U.S. 410, 99 S. Ct. 1182, 59 L. Ed. 2d 416 (1979). That case involved an employee of the University of Nevada who was driving in California on official business and injured a California resident in an automobile accident. The Supreme Court held that the COMMON-LAW doctrine of sovereign immunity had not passed to the states when the United States was created and therefore it is up to the states to decide whether to recognize and respect the immunity of other states. Thus, the Supreme Court held in *Hall* that California could properly refuse to respect Nevada's sovereign immunity in the California courts.

Like the federal government, the states often relied on PRIVATE LAWS to provide relief to specific individuals who would otherwise be unable to sue due to sovereign immunity doctrines. Recognizing that this was an inefficient and nonuniform way to provide relief from immunity doctrines, the states began to waive all or parts of their immunity from lawsuits. Many states created administrative bodies with limited capacity to settle claims against the state. Several states authorized suits against municipal corporations, counties, and school districts whose officers or employees injured individuals while performing proprietary, but not government, services. The distinction between proprietary and government services proved impossible to apply uniformly. Under modern law government services are widely considered to include police services, fire department services, and public education. Depending on the state involved, streets, sidewalks, bridges, parks, recreational facilities, electricity suppliers, gas suppliers, and airport functions can be considered either government or proprietary services.

Most states now have waived their immunity in various degrees at both the state and local government levels. Generally, state supreme courts first abolished immunity via judicial decisions; later, legislative measures were enacted at the state and local level to accept liability for torts committed by civil servants in the performance of government functions. The law still varies by state and locality, however.

Suits against Foreign Governments
Until the twentieth century, mutual respect for the independence, legal equality, and dignity of all nations was thought to entitle each nation to a broad immunity from the judicial process of

other states. This immunity was extended to heads of state, in both their personal and official capacities, and to foreign property. In the 1812 case of *The Schooner Exchange v. M'Faddon*, 11 U.S. (7 Cranch.) 116, 3 L. Ed. 287, a ship privately owned by a U.S. citizen was seized in French waters by Napoleon's government and converted into a French warship. When the ship entered the port of Philadelphia, the original owner sought to regain title, but the Supreme Court respected the confiscation of the ship because it occurred in accordance with French law in French waters.

With the emergence of socialist and Communist countries after World War I, the traditional rules of SOVEREIGNTY placed the private companies of free enterprise nations at a competitive disadvantage compared to state-owned companies from socialist and Communist countries, which would plead immunity from lawsuits. European and U.S. businesses that engaged in transactions with such companies began to insist that all contracts waive the sovereign immunity of the state companies. This situation led courts to reconsider the broad immunity and adopt instead a doctrine of restrictive immunity that excluded commercial activity and property.

Western European countries began waiving immunity for state commercial enterprises through bilateral or multilateral treaties. In 1952 the U.S. Department of State decided that, in considering future requests for immunity, it would follow the shift from absolute immunity to restrictive immunity. In 1976 Congress passed the Foreign Sovereign Immunities Act (28 U.S.C.A. § 1601 et seq.) to provide foreign nations with immunity from the jurisdiction of U.S. federal and state courts in certain circumstances. This act, which strives to conform to INTERNATIONAL LAW, prohibits sovereign immunity with regard to commercial activities of foreign states or their agencies or with regard to property taken by a foreign sovereign in violation of international law. Customary international law has continued to move toward a restrictive doctrine.

CROSS-REFERENCES

Federal Tort Claims Act; Feres Doctrine; Immunity; Judicial Immunity; Section 1983; Tort Law.

SOVEREIGNTY

The supreme, absolute, and uncontrollable power by which an independent state is governed and from which all specific political powers are derived; the intentional independence of a state, combined with the right and power of regulating its internal affairs without foreign interference.

Sovereignty is the power of a state to do everything necessary to govern itself, such as making, executing, and applying laws; imposing and collecting taxes; making war and peace; and forming treaties or engaging in commerce with foreign nations.

The individual states of the United States do not possess the powers of external sovereignty, such as the right to deport undesirable persons, but each does have certain attributes of internal sovereignty, such as the power to regulate the acquisition and transfer of property within its borders. The sovereignty of a state is determined with reference to the U.S. Constitution, which is the supreme law of the land.

SPANISH-AMERICAN WAR

The Spanish-American War of 1898 was brief, lasting only a few months. It resulted in a U.S. victory that not only ended Spain's colonial rule in the Western Hemisphere but also marked the emergence of the United States as a world power, as it acquired Puerto Rico, the Philippines, and Guam. THEODORE ROOSEVELT's military exploits in Cuba catapulted him onto the national stage and led to the vice presidency and, ultimately, the presidency.

The conflict had its origins in Spain's determined effort in the 1890s to destroy the Cuban independence movement. As the brutality of the Spanish authorities was graphically reported in U.S. newspapers, especially Joseph Pulitzer's *New York World* and William Randolph Hearst's *New York Journal*, the U.S. public began to support an independent Cuba.

In 1897 Spain proposed to resolve the conflict by granting partial autonomy to the Cubans, but the Cuban leaders continued to call for complete independence. In December 1897, the U.S. battleship *Maine* was sent to Havana to protect U.S. citizens and property. On the evening of February 15, 1898, the ship was sunk by a tremendous explosion, the cause of which was never determined. U.S. outrage at the loss of 266 sailors and the sensationalism of the New York press led to cries of "Remember the *Maine*" and demands that the United States intervene militarily in Cuba.

President WILLIAM McKINLEY, who had originally opposed intervention, approved an April 20 congressional resolution calling for immediate Spanish withdrawal from Cuba. This resolution precipitated a Spanish declaration of war against the United States on April 24. Congress immediately reciprocated and declared war on Spain on April 25, stating that the United States sought Cuban independence but not a foreign empire.

The war itself was brief due to the inferiority

of the Spanish forces. On May 1, 1898, the Spanish fleet in Manila Bay in the Philippines was destroyed by the U.S. Navy under the command of Commodore George Dewey. On July 3, U.S. troops began a battle for the city of Santiago, Cuba. Roosevelt and his First Volunteer Cavalry, the "Rough Riders," led the charge up San Juan Hill; he emerged as one of the war's great heroes. With the sinking of the Spanish fleet off the coast of Cuba on July 3 and the capture of Santiago on July 17, the war was effectively over.

An armistice was signed on August 12, ending hostilities and directing that a peace conference be held in Paris by October. The parties signed the Treaty of Paris on December 12, 1898. Cuba was granted independence, and Spain agreed to pay the Cuban debt, which was estimated at $400 million. Spain gave the United States possession of the Philippines and also ceded Puerto Rico and Guam to the United States. Many members of the U.S. Senate opposed the treaty, however. They were concerned that the possession of the Philippines had made the United States an imperial power, claiming colonies just like European nations. This status as an imperial power, they argued, was contrary to traditional U.S. foreign policy, which was to refrain from external entanglements. The Treaty of Paris was ratified by only one vote on February 6, 1899.

SPECIAL APPEARANCE 📖 The act of presenting oneself in a court and thereby submitting to the court's JURISDICTION, but only for a specific purpose and not for all the purposes for which a lawsuit is brought. 📖

A party makes a special appearance before a state court for the sole purpose of objecting to the court's jurisdiction over that party. If the party makes a GENERAL APPEARANCE to respond to the lawsuit, instead of a special appearance, then COMMON LAW dictates that the party thereby WAIVES any objection to the court's jurisdiction over her. A party may object to the court's jurisdiction for a number of reasons, such as when SERVICE OF PROCESS was insufficient or defective, there is a VARIANCE between the COMPLAINT and the SUMMONS, or the lawsuit was brought in the wrong court. When a party wants to make a jurisdictional objection, she has the right to appear for the special purpose of making that objection, but according to common law, the party must clearly and specifically state to the court that she is specially appearing.

Rule 12(b) of the Federal Rules of Civil Procedure has abolished the distinction between general and special appearances for FED-ERAL COURTS. Therefore, parties can raise a jurisdictional objection along with other defenses in a responsive pleading in federal court. However, if a party wishes to make the jurisdictional objection initially without having to prepare a full responsive pleading, the federal courts will permit that party to do so if he specially appears.

Some states have followed the Federal Rules of Civil Procedure and have eliminated for state court matters the distinction between general and special appearances. Many states still acknowledge the distinction, however, and some specifically provide for the distinction by statute.

SPECIAL ASSESSMENT 📖 A REAL PROPERTY tax proportionately levied on homeowners and landowners to cover the costs of improvements that will be for the benefit of all upon whom it is imposed. 📖

For example, a special assessment might be made to pay for sidewalks or sewer connections.

SPECIAL COURTS 📖 Bodies within the judicial branch of government that are organized to administer justice and generally address only one area of law or have specifically defined powers. 📖

The best-known courts are courts of GENERAL JURISDICTION, which have unlimited trial jurisdiction, both civil and criminal, within their jurisdictional area. At the federal level, these are called DISTRICT COURTS. At the state level, these courts have many different titles, including district court, trial court, county court, circuit court, municipal court, and superior court. APPELLATE courts of general jurisdiction review the decisions of inferior courts and are typically called either courts of appeal or supreme courts.

The bulk of U.S. courts, however, are special courts, which include all courts of limited and specialized jurisdiction that are not courts of general jurisdiction or appellate courts. A special court generally addresses only one or a few areas of law or has only specifically defined powers.

Special courts in the United States developed out of the English custom of handling different kinds of cases by establishing many different special courts. Many of the special courts established in the United States during colonial times and shortly after the Constitution was adopted have been abolished, but new special courts continue to be created, especially at the state and local level. Special courts now handle the vast majority of all cases brought in the United States. The majority of all cases brought in any particular state jurisdiction go to special courts.

Special courts exist for both civil and criminal disputes. Cases tried in special, limited-jurisdiction criminal courts, such as traffic court or misdemeanor court, may be reheard in a general-jurisdiction trial court without an appeal upon the request of the parties.

Special courts do not include the many administrative law courts that exist at both the federal and state government level; administrative courts are considered part of the EXECUTIVE BRANCH, rather than the judicial branch. However, a general-jurisdiction court that hears only specific kinds of cases, such as a landlord-tenant branch of a general-jurisdiction trial court, is usually considered a special court.

Special courts differ from general-jurisdiction courts in several other respects besides having a more limited jurisdiction. Cases are more likely to be disposed of without trial in special courts, and if there is a TRIAL or HEARING, it is usually heard more rapidly than in a court of general jurisdiction. Special courts usually do not follow the same procedural rules that general-jurisdiction courts follow; often special courts proceed without the benefit or expense of attorneys or even law-trained judges.

The judges who serve in special courts are as varied as the special courts themselves. Most special court judges obtain their positions through election, rather than through the merit selection system common in general-jurisdiction courts. In addition, the majority of special court judges are not lawyers. In *North v. Russell*, 427 U.S. 328, 96 S. Ct. 2709, 49 L. Ed. 2d 534 (1976), the U.S. Supreme Court upheld the use of nonlawyer judges in special courts as constitutional as long as a trial DE NOVO (a new trial) in a court of general jurisdiction with a lawyer-judge is given upon the request of the parties.

State and Local Special Courts The states and localities have created many special courts. Juvenile courts are special courts that have jurisdiction over delinquent, dependent, and neglected children. Juvenile courts have special rules to protect the privacy of the juveniles before them, such as requiring that only the initials and not the full names of juveniles be used in court paperwork so that their identities are not revealed to the public. Juvenile court proceedings are closed to the public, and generally the records are sealed.

Probate courts are special courts of limited jurisdiction that generally have powers over the PROBATE of WILLS and the administration of ESTATES. In some states probate courts are empowered to appoint GUARDIANS or approve the ADOPTION of MINORS.

SMALL-CLAIMS COURTS, called conciliation courts in some states, provide expeditious, informal, and inexpensive adjudication of small claims. The jurisdiction of small-claims courts is usually limited to the collection of small DEBTS and accounts. In most states parties are allowed to represent themselves in small-claims court, and some states prohibit lawyers from representing the parties.

Many states have also established family courts that typically have jurisdiction over several types of cases, including CHILD ABUSE and neglect proceedings, child and spousal support proceedings, PATERNITY determinations, CHILD CUSTODY proceedings, juvenile delinquency proceedings, and marital dissolutions. Some states still have justice's courts, inferior tribunals of limited jurisdiction presided over by JUSTICES OF THE PEACE. These courts are the primary legacy of the special courts of colonial times. Most states, however, have abolished justice's courts and transferred their powers and duties to courts of general jurisdiction.

Massachusetts is unique in that it has a land court with exclusive jurisdiction over all applications for registration of TITLE to land within the commonwealth, WRITS of entry and various petitions for clearing title to REAL ESTATE, petitions for determining the validity and extent of municipal ZONING ordinances and regulations, and all proceedings for FORECLOSURE. Some cities have established mayor's courts in which the mayor sits with the powers of a police judge or MAGISTRATE with respect to offenses committed within the city, such as traffic or ORDINANCE violations. In other states these courts are called police courts and are not presided over by the mayor. Several states have established tax courts that have jurisdiction to hear appeals in all tax cases and have the power to modify or change any valuation, assessment, classification, tax, or final order.

Federal Special Courts Congress has also established several special courts to adjudicate federal matters. Admiralty courts are federal district courts that have jurisdiction over admiralty and maritime actions pursuant to federal statute (28 U.S.C.A. § 1333). Bankruptcy courts are federal courts that are concerned exclusively with the administration of BANKRUPTCY proceedings; they were also created pursuant to federal statute (28 U.S.C.A. § 1334). The U.S. TAX COURT tries and adjudicates controversies involving deficiencies or overpayments in income, estate, and gift taxes. U.S. magistrates try MISDEMEANOR cases and conduct preliminary proceedings in civil and criminal proceedings.

The Court of Veterans Appeals is a federal court created in 1988 to review decisions of the Board of Veterans' Appeals, which hears cases involving benefit programs for veterans and their dependents. Cases appealed from the Court of Veterans Appeals are heard by the U.S. court of appeals for the applicable federal circuit.

The U.S. Claims Court was created in 1982 to replace the former COURT OF CLAIMS. Its powers are mandated by federal statute (28 U.S.C.A. § 1491 et seq.). The Claims Court has jurisdiction to render money JUDGMENTS upon any claim against the United States based on the Constitution, a federal statute, or a federal regulation; any claim based on an express or implied CONTRACT with the United States; or any claim for liquidated or unliquidated damages in cases not sounding in tort (not involving torts).

The Court of International Trade has jurisdiction over any CIVIL ACTION against the United States arising from federal laws governing import transactions. It also has jurisdiction to review determinations as to the eligibility of workers, firms, and communities for adjustment assistance under the Trade Act of 1974 (19 U.S.C.A. §2101 et seq.). Insular courts are special courts created by Congress with jurisdiction over insular possessions (island territories) of the United States, such as Puerto Rico.

Military courts are courts convened pursuant to the CODE OF MILITARY JUSTICE (10 U.S.C.A. § 801 et seq.); they include courts-martial, courts of military review, the Military Court of Inquiry, and the U.S. Court of Appeals for the Armed Forces. These courts are designed to deal exclusively with issues arising under MILITARY LAW, which governs the armed forces. Courts-martial are ad hoc military courts, convened under authority of the UNIFORM CODE OF MILITARY JUSTICE (10 U.S.C.A. § 801 et seq.) to try and punish violations of military law committed by persons subject to that law. The courts of military review are intermediate appellate criminal courts, established by the Military Justice Act of 1968 (10 U.S.C.A. § 866) to review COURT-MARTIAL convictions of members of their respective ARMED SERVICES in which the punishment imposed extends to death, dismissal or punitive discharge, or confinement for one year or more. The U.S. Court of Appeals for the Armed Forces (USCAAF), formerly known as the Court of Military Appeals, which was created by Congress in 1950 (10 U.S.C.A. § 867), functions as the primary civilian appellate tribunal responsible for reviewing court-martial convictions of all the services. Cases heard by the Courts of Military Review may be appealed

to the USCAAF; any appeals from that court are heard by the U.S. Supreme Court. The Military Court of Inquiry is a court of special and limited jurisdiction, convened to investigate specific matters and advise whether further proceedings should be pursued.

A Court for the Trial of Impeachments is a tribunal empowered to try any officer of government or other person brought to its bar by the process of IMPEACHMENT. At the national level, the Senate is the Court for the Trial of Impeachments of federal officers, and in most states the upper house of the legislature is the Court for the Trial of Impeachments of state officers.

CROSS-REFERENCES

Court; Courts; Federal Courts; Jurisdiction; Juvenile Law; Military Law; State Courts.

SPECIALIZATION 📖 A career option pursued by some attorneys that entails the acquisition of detailed knowledge of, and proficiency in, a particular area of law. 📖

As the law in the United States becomes increasingly complex and covers a greater number of subjects, more and more attorneys are narrowing their practice to a limited field or fields. Even small-town general practitioners limit the range of matters they handle to some degree, if only out of practical necessity. Although specialization has become commonplace, the formal recognition and regulation of specialties are still controversial issues in the legal profession.

In the 1950s the Special Committee on Specialization and Specialized Legal Education of the AMERICAN BAR ASSOCIATION (ABA) considered whether it should identify, recognize, and regulate legal specialists. In 1969 the ABA decided not to promulgate a national plan to regulate legal specialization until some initial specialization plans could be studied at the state level. In 1971 California became the first state to adopt a pilot specialization program. Florida adopted a designation plan in 1976, and Texas adopted a full certification plan in 1980. Several other states followed suit in the 1980s.

In the late 1970s, the ABA adopted several ethical and disciplinary rules that addressed some of the issues presented by attorney specialization. Disciplinary rule 2-102(5) restricted the headings that attorneys could list themselves under in telephone books or other directories. Disciplinary rule 2-102(6) allowed lawyers to list the areas of law in which they practiced but did not allow them to state that they specialized in those fields. Disciplinary rule 2-105 prohibited lawyers from holding themselves out as specialists in certain areas of law, except for patent and trademark lawyers in states that authorized and approved of those fields of specialization. Ethical consideration 2-14 also suggested that with the exception of admiralty, trademark, and patent lawyers, lawyers should not represent to the public that they are specialists with special training or ability.

Also in the late 1970s, the ABA House of Delegates adopted a resolution that recommended that several elements be included in any state specialization program. The ABA Standing Committee on Specialization began assisting states in defining and identifying specialty fields and in establishing basic regulatory guidelines.

In 1979 the ABA adopted the Model Plan of Specialization, which incorporated the earlier principles and guidelines developed by the Standing Committee on Specialization. The ABA reached a compromise between two popular types of specialization plans that had developed in the states: designation and certification plans. Designation plans established basic requisites for specialist recognition, such as a minimum number of years in practice and a minimum number of continuing legal education classes, but did not review the expertise of the applicants through an examination. Under the designation plans, lawyers had to apply to designate themselves as specialists in a certain field, and that application had to be approved by the state. However, the standards were not very stringent. In contrast, certification plans required a prior review of the applicant's credentials, such as through a written examination, and also required certain minimum standards. Most certifying mechanisms required that applicants be licensed to practice law, be substantially involved in a particular area of law (such as devoting 25 percent of their practice to their specialty), and be involved in continuing legal education and peer review.

By 1990 thirteen states had formal plans for the recognition and regulation of legal specialties. That number continues to grow, as states adopt designation or certification plans or some variation of the two. The growth of state specialization plans was boosted considerably after the U.S. Supreme Court's decision in *Bates v. State Bar of Arizona*, 433 U.S. 350, 97 S. Ct. 2691, 53 L. Ed. 2d 810 (1977), in which the Court held that states cannot prevent lawyers from advertising. Court decisions since *Bates* have held that states may regulate attorney advertising to protect the public from false, misleading, or deceptive advertising. Many state specialization plans, therefore, were developed to regulate how lawyers portrayed themselves and their practice areas to the public through advertising and other communications.

Until the 1980s, it was not uncommon for a lawyer to advertise that his practice was limited to certain areas of law, but it was commonly believed that if a lawyer advertised himself as a specialist in a certain field, he implied a degree of special competence. Courts considered state regulation of specialty designations to be justified to protect the public from misleading or deceptive advertising.

In 1983 the ABA adopted the Model Rules of Professional Conduct, some of which addressed the issues presented by attorney specialization. Model rule 7.4, for example, provided that a lawyer could not state or imply that she was a specialist in any area except admiralty, patent, or trademark law unless she was specially certified or recognized under a formal state specialization plan. By that time attorneys were being certified by several national organizations, such as the National Board of Trial Advocacy (NBTA), which certified trial specialists. Because these organizations were not formal state plans, the issue arose as to whether attorneys certified by such organizations could call themselves specialists. The courts addressed this issue by suggesting that states either screen the certifying organizations or require them to issue disclaimers indicating that they were not authorized by the state.

Most of the states that have enacted some formal recognition plan have adopted certification rather than designation plans. These plans recognize a number of specialty areas, including civil trial practice, criminal trial practice, family law, tax law, and real estate law. The ABA has drafted model standards for specialization in several other areas as well; these standards include the administrative procedures necessary to implement the plans.

Despite the growing trend toward lawyer specialization, there is widespread opposition to formal specialization plans. Many lawyers feel that the state's interest in regulating claims of expertise is not as important as the individual's FIRST AMENDMENT right to advertise. Other lawyers, especially general practitioners, feel that the formal recognition of specialization detracts from the presumption that any lawyer licensed to practice law is competent to handle any legal problem. They also fear that formal specialization programs will lead to a class system, with general practitioners or nonspecialists relegated to a second-class status. Attorneys who practice in rural or isolated areas make the practical objection that due to their locations, they do not have access to enough continuing legal education opportunities to qualify as specialists.

Attorneys who support specialization plans argue that the plans lead to more competent lawyers by requiring specialists to attend many continuing legal education courses and to provide evidence of their expertise before being recognized as specialists. Some also argue that specialization plans lead to improved delivery of legal services to the public by providing more accurate information about lawyers and their specialties.

As lawyers advertise in increasing numbers, they are also finding more formats in which to advertise such as telephone books, radio, television, newspapers, journals, magazines, the Internet, direct mail, and billboards. Although advertising makes it easier for the public to find a lawyer and learn more about that lawyer, it can lead to misrepresentation or misunderstanding. Thus, in dealing with the issue of legal specialization, the legal profession is striving to reach a compromise between the need to protect the public from false or misleading advertisement and the First Amendment right of lawyers to advertise with minimal state regulation.

CROSS-REFERENCES

Attorney; Continuing Legal Education; Ethics; Legal Advertising.

SPECIAL PROSECUTOR See INDEPENDENT COUNSEL.

SPECIAL TERM In court practice in some JURISDICTIONS, a branch of the court system held by a single judge for hearing and deciding MOTIONS and equitable ACTIONS in the FIRST INSTANCE.

This type of term is called special to distinguish it from a GENERAL TERM, which is ordinarily held by three judges sitting EN BANC to hear APPEALS or to hear and determine cases brought during the regular session of the court.

SPECIALTY A CONTRACT under SEAL.

A specialty is a written document that has been sealed and delivered and is given as SECURITY for the payment of a specifically indicated DEBT. The term *specialty debt* is used in reference to a debt that is acknowledged to be due by an instrument under seal.

SPECIAL WARRANTY DEED A written instrument that conveys REAL PROPERTY in which the GRANTOR (original owner) only COVENANTS to warrant and defend the TITLE against CLAIMS and demands by him or her and all persons claiming by, through, and under him or her.

In the special warranty DEED, the grantor warrants that neither he nor anyone claiming under him has ENCUMBERED the property and that he will defend the title against defects arising under and through him, but no others.

A GENERAL WARRANTY DEED, in contrast, warrants and defends the title against all claims whatsoever by anyone. In some JURISDICTIONS the special warranty deed is called a QUITCLAIM DEED, but in other jurisdictions they are different types of instruments.

SPECIFIC INTENT The mental purpose, aim, or design to accomplish a specific harm or result by acting in a manner prohibited by law.

The term *specific intent* is commonly used in criminal and tort law to designate a special state of mind that is required, along with a physical act, to constitute certain crimes or torts. Specific intent is usually interpreted to mean intentionally or knowingly. Common-law LARCENY, for example, requires both the physical act of taking and carrying away the property of another and the mental element of INTENT to steal the property. Similarly, common-law BURGLARY requires breaking and entering into the dwelling of another with an intent to commit a FELONY therein. These crimes and others that require a specific-intent element are called *specific-intent crimes* and are distinguished from *general-intent crimes*. GENERAL-INTENT crimes require only a showing that the defendant intended to do the act prohibited by law, not that the defendant intended the precise harm or the precise result that occurred.

Courts have defined specific intent as the subjective desire or knowledge that the prohibited result will occur (*People v. Owens*, 131 Mich. App. 76, 345 N.W.2d 904 [1983]). Intent and MOTIVE are commonly confused, but they are distinct principles and differentiated in the law. Motive is the cause or reason that prompts a person to act or fail to act. Intent refers only to the state of mind with which the act is done or omitted. Because intent is a state of mind, it can rarely be proved with DIRECT EVIDENCE and ordinarily must be inferred from the facts of the case. Evidence of intent is always ADMISSIBLE to prove a specific-intent crime, but evidence of motive is only admissible if it tends to help prove or negate the element of intent.

Courts generally allow a wide range of direct and CIRCUMSTANTIAL EVIDENCE to be introduced at trial in order to prove the difficult element of criminal or tortious intent. In addition, the doctrine of presumed intent may be helpful in proving specific intent because it holds individuals accountable for all the NATURAL AND PROBABLE CONSEQUENCES of their acts.

A defendant may TESTIFY at trial as to his intent. Whether the defendant intended to break the law does not matter, however; rather, the issue is whether he intended to do that which is unlawful. For example, a defendant may maintain that he took money without permission in order to buy food for his hungry children and that he intended to repay the money. In such a case, the defendant's intent to repay the money does not negate the fact that he intentionally took money that did not belong to him without permission. In addition, it does not matter that he planned to feed his children with the money, because that is his motive in acting, not his intent.

An individual will be guilty or liable for a crime or tort if she had the intent to commit the crime or tort, even though the intended injury occurred in an unexpected way. For example, suppose that an assassin tries to shoot a person but misses and hits an automobile gasoline tank. If the tank explodes and kills the intended victim, the assassin is still guilty of MURDER even though the victim's death did not occur in the manner intended.

A defendant still possessed the element of intent even though his intended act could not possibly have succeeded as planned. Suppose, for example, that a burglar intended to break into a house and steal an original painting. Once he broke in, however, he discovered that the painting had been removed or that it was just a print and not an original painting at all. The burglar still had the necessary intent for burglary.

Because specific intent is an essential element in proving many torts and crimes, defendants often argue that they did not possess the specific intent required and therefore are not guilty or liable for the crime or tort committed. In fact, most JURISDICTIONS recognize by statute or case law certain defenses to the formation of specific intent. For example, a defendant may argue that at the time a crime was committed she was intoxicated and that her mental impairment kept her from formulating the specific intent to commit the crime. Voluntary intoxication is not a defense to the commission of general-intent crimes, but in many jurisdictions it is a defense to specific-intent crimes. In other jurisdictions voluntary intoxication is never a defense to the commission of a crime. Most jurisdictions permit the defense of involuntary intoxication even if they do not recognize voluntary intoxication. Courts generally permit expert witness testimony on the issue of whether the defendant had the ability to form specific intent.

See also CRIMINAL LAW; TORT LAW.

SPECIFIC LEGACY 📖 A GIFT by WILL of designated PERSONAL PROPERTY. 📖

A specific legacy is revoked if the TESTATOR—the maker of the will—no longer owned the property at the time of his or her death or the property no longer existed. In some JURISDICTIONS, a court will continue a provision for a specific legacy as one for a DEMONSTRATIVE LEGACY if it is clear that the testator intended the heir to receive the gift in any event.

SPECIFIC PERFORMANCE 📖 An extraordinary equitable REMEDY that compels a PARTY to execute a contract according to the precise terms agreed upon or to execute it substantially so that, under the circumstances, justice will be done between the parties. 📖

Specific performance grants the plaintiff what he actually bargained for in the contract rather than DAMAGES (pecuniary compensation for loss or injury incurred through the unlawful conduct of another) for not receiving it; thus specific performance is an equitable rather than legal remedy. By compelling the parties to perform exactly what they had agreed to perform, more complete and perfect justice is achieved than by awarding damages for a breach of contract.

Specific performance can be granted only by a court in the exercise of its EQUITY powers, subsequent to a determination of whether a valid contract that can be enforced exists and an evaluation of the RELIEF sought. As a general rule, specific performance is applied in breach of contract ACTIONS where monetary damages are inadequate, primarily where the contract involves land or a unique CHATTEL (personal property). Damages for the breach of a contract for the sale of ordinary PERSONAL PROPERTY are, in most cases, readily ascertainable and recoverable so that specific performance will not be granted.

An important advantage to this remedy is that, since it is an order of an equity court, it is supported by the enforcement power of that court. If the defendant refuses to obey that order, she can be cited for criminal CONTEMPT and even imprisoned. The defendant can also be cited for civil contempt for continuing to refuse to obey the order and can be incarcerated until she agrees to obey it. In such a situation, it is said that "she has the keys to freedom in her pocket," which signifies that the defendant can release herself by complying with the court order. These enforcement powers are one of the principal reasons why plaintiffs seek specific performance of CONTRACTS.

Right to Specific Performance
Specific performance is ordered only on equitable grounds in view of all the conditions surrounding the particular case. The determining factor is whether, in equity and good con-

science, the court should specifically enforce the contract because the legal remedy of monetary damages would inadequately compensate the plaintiff for the loss.

Valid Contract The remedy of specific performance presupposes the existence of a valid contract between the parties to the controversy. The terms of the contract must be definite and certain. This is extremely significant because equity cannot be expected to enforce either an invalid contract or one that is so vague in its terms that equity cannot determine exactly what it must order each party to perform. It would be unjust for a court to compel the performance of a contract according to ambiguous terms interpreted by the court, since the court might erroneously order what the parties never intended or contemplated.

Plaintiff's Conduct A plaintiff seeking specific performance of a contract must have contracted in GOOD FAITH. If the plaintiff has acted fraudulently or has taken unfair advantage of superior bargaining power in drafting extremely harsh contract terms with respect to the defendant, the plaintiff has thereby contravened the doctrine of clean hands. Under that doctrine, the court will deny relief to a party who has acted unjustly in regard to a transaction for which that party is seeking the assistance of the court.

A classic example of the clean hands doctrine involved Charles Flowers, an outstanding college football player who was drafted by the New York Giants and Los Angeles Chargers. In November 1959, he signed to play football with the Giants. According to the college rules, however, any player who signed a contract to play for a professional team was ineligible for further intercollegiate games. Because Flowers wanted to play in the Sugar Bowl on January 1, 1960, he and the Giants agreed to keep his signing of the contract confidential, deceiving his college, the opposing team, and the football public in general. One of the terms of the contract provided that it was binding only when approved by the commissioner of football. Part of the plan was that the contract would not be submitted for approval until after January 1. Flowers subsequently attempted to withdraw from the contract, but the Giants promptly filed it with the commissioner, who approved it on December 15. Public announcement was withheld until after January 1.

On December 29, Flowers negotiated a better contract with the Chargers and signed it after the Sugar Bowl game. He notified the Giants on December 29 that he was withdrawing from his contract with them and returned his uncashed bonus checks. The Giants sought

University of Mississippi football star Charles Flowers examines court papers filed after he tried to back out of a contract with the New York Giants. The Giants sued for specific performance of the contract.

specific performance of their contract with Flowers. The court denied relief because the Giants did not come into equity with clean hands (*New York Football Giants, Inc. v. Los Angeles Chargers Football Club, Inc.*, 291 F.2d 471 [5th Cir. 1961]).

Equitable relief will be denied to anyone who has acted unjustly or with BAD FAITH in the matter in which she seeks relief, irrespective of any impropriety in the behavior of the defendant. The misconduct does not necessarily have to be of such nature as to be punishable as a crime or to justify any legal proceedings. Any intentional act concerning the CAUSE OF ACTION that violates the standards of fairness and justice is sufficient to prohibit the granting of equitable relief. The Giants club accepted from Flowers what it claimed to be a binding contract, but it agreed that it would represent to the public that there was no contract in order to deceive others who had a material interest in the matter. If there had been a straightforward execution of the contract, followed by its filing with the commissioner, none of these legal problems would have existed. The Giants created the situation by their devious conduct and, therefore, had no right to obtain relief from a court of equity. The court refused to specifically enforce the contract.

At all times, a plaintiff must be willing to "do equity," which means that the plaintiff must fulfill whatever equitable obligations the court imposes upon her in order to do what is just and fair to the defendant. A person will be granted specific performance only if that person has done, has offered to do, or is ready and willing to do all acts that were required of her to execute the contract according to its terms.

Inadequate Legal Remedy Specific performance will be denied where money would adequately compensate the plaintiff for the loss. The court determines whether money would be adequate after examining the subject matter of the contract itself. If it is land, money is inadequate because land is traditionally viewed as being unique, in that no two parcels of land are exactly alike. An award of damages will not enable the plaintiff to acquire the same parcel of land anywhere else.

If the contract involves the sale of ordinary chattels—such as furniture, appliances, or machinery—rather than land, the general measure of damages for breach of contract is the difference between the market price and the contract price. Damages are adequate since the item could be easily repurchased on the open market and the buyer would be compensated for the amount he was compelled to spend in excess of the original contract price. The UNIFORM COMMERCIAL CODE (UCC) (a body of law adopted by the states that governs commercial transactions) permits specific performance for the breach of a SALES contract for GOODS under limited circumstances.

Specific performance will be granted where the contract involves a unique chattel; the court determines whether a chattel is unique. A rare stamp collection is a unique chattel for purposes of specific performance, whereas stock listed on the New York or American Stock Exchange is not unique. Antiques, heirlooms, or one-of-a-kind items are considered unique because money cannot replace their value to the plaintiff. The claim that an object has sentimental value to the plaintiff is not, in and of itself, sufficient to justify specific performance. When the sentiment or personal desire for the object is based upon facts and circumstances that endow the item with a special value so that it becomes a family heirloom, specific performance will be granted.

Damages are inadequate if the estimate is difficult to make, such as in a REQUIREMENTS CONTRACT—a written agreement whereby one party assents to purchase from the other all the merchandise of a designated type that he might require for his business. The same principle applies where the chattel is scarce and cannot be readily repurchased on the open market even though it is not unique. Where the same contract combines unique and ordinary items, the entire contract will be specifically enforced.

As a general rule, breaches of personal service contracts are compensated at law by damages unless the services are unique. In such a case, the contract usually contains a NEGATIVE COVENANT that prohibits a person from practicing her profession or performing those unique services for anyone else within a certain distance from a former employer for a specified period of time. The employer would seek to specifically enforce this negative covenant against the person who violates it. These provisions, sometimes called covenants not to compete, are enforced only if they are REASONABLE in scope; otherwise monetary damages are awarded. A court will never specifically enforce an employment contract by ordering an employee to work for an employer because the THIRTEENTH AMENDMENT to the Constitution prohibits SLAVERY.

INSOLVENCY of the defendant, which prevents the plaintiff from collecting damages, does not determine whether specific performance will be granted. The court ascertains only whether an adequate legal remedy exists, not whether the defendant has the financial resources to pay the JUDGMENT.

Supervision of Performance As a general rule, equity will not order acts that it cannot supervise. In many instances, specific performance is denied where courts would be unduly burdened with the task of supervising the performance. Supervision is a particular problem in building or repair contracts because the court lacks the technical expertise, means, or agencies to learn exactly what tasks the contractor is performing or whether she is performing them properly.

There are, however, certain exceptions to this rule. If the plans for the building are clearly defined, or if there has been sufficient partial performance so that supervision of the remainder is not difficult, the court might grant specific performance for its completion. An attempt to enforce a building repair contract is more problematic for the court. It must initially determine what repairs are to be made and the time within which they are to be performed; then it must decide whether there has been substantial performance and, if not, whether the defendant had any excuse. Usually an adequate remedy at law exists in the form of damages that represent the excess of the construction cost paid over the original contract price. Where damages are inadequate, however, the court can order specific performance.

Defenses A contract that is unenforceable because it has not complied with the STATUTE OF FRAUDS (an old English law, adopted in the

United States, that requires certain contracts to be in writing) cannot be enforced through specific performance.

LACHES is an equitable DEFENSE (matter asserted to diminish a plaintiff's cause of action or to defeat recovery) that prevents the enforcement of a contract by specific performance. Laches is an unreasonable delay in asserting a right with the result that its enforcement would cause injury, prejudice, or disadvantage to others. Laches is applied only where enforcement of a right will cause injustice.

The doctrine of clean hands is a defense in an action for specific performance. As explained in the discussion of the case of Charles Flowers, cited above, a court will deny specific performance if the plaintiff has acted in BAD FAITH or fraudulently in the same transaction for which he is seeking relief.

A contract might not be specifically enforced if, as a result of superior bargaining power, the plaintiff takes unfair advantage of the defendant who is in a debilitated position. This situation transpires when the CONSIDERATION (the inducement to enter into a contract) is so inadequate as to "shock the conscience," or when "sharp dealings" are involved, such as where the defendant is ill. Failure to disclose material facts to the defendant that, if revealed, would have prevented a contract from being made is a ground to deny specific performance.

MISTAKES and misrepresentations in the terms of a contract might constitute a defense against specific performance. If such mistakes are sufficient to justify RESCISSION of a contract, they are sufficient to prevent the enforcement of the contract. A court will enforce only a contract with definite and certain terms.

SPECULATIVE DAMAGES 📖 Alleged injuries or losses that are uncertain or contingent and cannot be used as a basis of recovery for TORT or CONTRACT actions. 📖

An individual cannot be compensated for mere speculative probability of future loss unless he can prove that such negative consequences can reasonably be expected to occur. The amount of DAMAGES sought in a lawsuit need not be established with absolute certainty provided they are anticipated with reasonable certainty. Where the plaintiff cannot establish with reasonable certainty that any injury resulted from the act of omission complained of, he might be entitled to recover NOMINAL DAMAGES. Mere uncertainty concerning the measure or extent of damages does not preclude their recovery in either tort or contract cases.

When an individual seeks to recover COMPENSATORY DAMAGES, she must establish EVIDENCE of their nature and extent as well as some data from which they can be calculated. No extensive recovery can be founded upon guesswork alone. Recovery must be backed with evidence that justifies an inference that the damage award is a fair and reasonable form of compensation for the injury incurred. In addition, when compensatory damages can be proved with approximate accuracy and determined with some degree of certainty, it is essential that they be so proved. If evidence of damage from various causes exists, but no evidence is available as to the portion of damage that the defendant caused, the proof is too uncertain to allow the jury to award damages against the defendant.

SPEECH, FREEDOM OF See FREEDOM OF SPEECH.

SPEECH OR DEBATE CLAUSE Article I, Section 6, Clause 1, of the U.S. Constitution states in part, "for any Speech or Debate in either House, [senators and representatives] shall not be questioned in any other place." The purpose of the clause is to prevent the arrest and prosecution of unpopular legislators based on their political views.

The U.S. Supreme Court has gradually defined and redefined the Speech or Debate Clause in several cases over the years. The first case concerning the Speech and Debate Clause was *Kilbourn v. Thompson*, 103 U.S. (13 Otto) 168, 26 L. Ed. 377 (1880). The Court has interpreted the Speech or Debate Clause to mean that members of Congress and their aides are immune from prosecution for their "legislative acts." This does not mean that members of Congress and their aides may not be prosecuted. Rather, evidence of LEGISLATIVE ACTS may not be used in a prosecution against a member of Congress or a congressional aide.

The main controversy surrounding the Speech or Debate Clause concerns the scope of the phrase "legislative acts." The phrase obviously encompasses speeches and debates on the floor of the SENATE or the HOUSE OF REPRESENTATIVES. According to the Supreme Court, voting, preparing committee reports, and conducting committee hearings also are legislative acts, but republishing legislative materials for distribution to constituents and accepting a bribe to influence a vote are not.

Legislators and their aides have invoked the Speech or Debate Clause with varying results. In May 1994 former Illinois congressman Daniel Rostenkowski was indicted for allegedly devising schemes to DEFRAUD the federal government of money and Rostenkowski's fair and honest services. Rostenkowski argued in part that he could not be prosecuted for misappropriating a Clerk Hire Allowance by using it to pay employees for personal services rather than for official work because the allowance was connected with hiring a clerk, which is a legislative activity. In *United States v. Rostenkowski*, 59 F.3d 1291 (D.C. Cir. 1995), the U.S. Court of Appeals for the District of Columbia rejected this argument, noting that the INDICTMENT had not charged that the persons who performed the personal services had any relationship whatsoever to the legislative process.

In contrast, the clerk of the House of Representatives and other House personnel have been shielded from an employment DISCRIMINATION suit by the Speech or Debate Clause. In *Browning v. Clerk, U.S. House of Representatives*, 789 F.2d 923 (D.C. Cir. 1986), the U.S. Court of Appeals for the District of Columbia Circuit held that the clerk and other House personnel did not have to answer to charges of employment discrimination brought by an official House reporter because the employee's duties were directly related to the legislative process.

See also CONGRESS OF THE UNITED STATES.

SPEECH PLUS A form of expression in which behavior is used by itself or in coordination with written or spoken words to convey an idea or message.

Speech plus, which is known as SYMBOLIC SPEECH, involves the communication of ideas through the combination of language and action—such as the burning of a draft card while stating opposition to the military—as opposed to PURE SPEECH, which involves the use of written or oral words alone. Like any other mode of expression, speech plus may be entitled to protection from interference by the government pursuant to the guarantee of the FIRST AMENDMENT to the Constitution, depending upon the nature of the expression, the circumstances in which it is expressed, and the danger it poses to society. Speech plus is often called *speech plus conduct*.

See also FREEDOM OF SPEECH.

SPEED, JAMES James Speed served as U.S. attorney general under President ABRAHAM LINCOLN.

"PEACE IS THE NORMAL CONDITION OF A COUNTRY, AND WAR ABNORMAL, NEITHER BEING WITHOUT LAW, BUT EACH HAVING LAWS APPROPRIATE TO THE CONDITION OF SOCIETY."

BIOGRAPHY

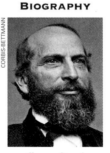

James Speed

Speed was born March 11, 1812, in Jefferson County, Kentucky. He was the son of Kentucky pioneers John Speed and Lucy Gilmer Fry Speed and counted among his ancestors a Revolutionary War hero (Captain James Speed) and an English historian (John Speed). Speed attended local schools and then St. Joseph's College, Bardstown, Kentucky. After graduating from St. Joseph's in 1828, he was employed for several years as a clerk in the local circuit and county courts. Finding he had an interest in the law, in 1831, he enrolled at Transylvania University, in Lexington, Kentucky, for further study.

In 1833 he moved to Louisville, Kentucky, and opened a law office. He was also offered—and accepted—a teaching position at Louisville University. While living in Louisville, Speed met and married Jane Cochran, the daughter of a local wholesale merchant. With her encouragement, he ran for a seat in the state legislature and was elected in 1841. However, his antislavery opinions proved to be unpopular with many of his constituents, and he left the legislature after one term to resume teaching.

Speed entered politics again in 1847. He was elected to the state legislature as the Emancipation candidate, then lost his seat in 1849 to a pro-SLAVERY rival. Speed's early political fortunes in his home state were closely tied to Kentucky's internal pre–Civil War struggle over slavery. As a border state, it experienced frequent shifts in the balance of power and popular opinion, between antislavery and pro-slavery forces.

In the years between his 1849 defeat and the beginning of the Civil War, Speed held a chair in the law department at the University of Louisville. There, he developed a reputation as a man of integrity and ability—even among those who disagreed with his antislavery views. When President Lincoln needed help to hold Kentucky in the Union at the outbreak of the war, he called on Speed.

Lincoln and Speed had met as young men and maintained a close friendship throughout the years. Speed's younger brother, Joshua Fry Speed, was also a confidant of Lincoln's and acted as the president's emissary with the

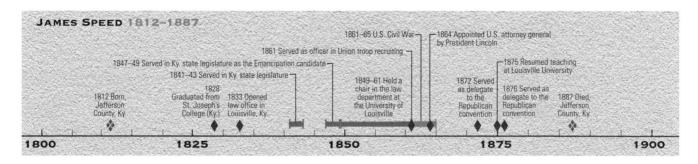

JAMES SPEED 1812–1887

1812 Born, Jefferson County, Ky.
1828 Graduated from St. Joseph's College (Ky.)
1833 Opened law office in Louisville, Ky.
1841–43 Served in Ky. state legislature
1847–49 Served in Ky. state legislature as the Emancipation candidate
1849–61 Held a chair in the law department at the University of Louisville
1861 Served as officer in Union troop recruiting
1861–65 U.S. Civil War
1864 Appointed U.S. attorney general by President Lincoln
1872 Served as delegate to the Republican convention
1875 Resumed teaching at Louisville University
1876 Served as delegate to the Republican convention
1887 Died, Jefferson County, Ky.

1800 1825 1850 1875 1900

Southern states on a number of occasions before and during the war. Kentucky's refusal to join the Confederacy can be largely attributed to the efforts of the Speed brothers.

When the Civil War began, Speed honored President Lincoln's request to recruit Union troops from Kentucky. He acted as the mustering officer in 1861 for the first call for Kentucky volunteers. Throughout the war, Speed worked tirelessly for the Union cause. In 1864 he was rewarded for his loyalty when Lincoln named him U.S. attorney general.

At the close of the war, Speed initially held a moderate view of how the Union should deal with the secessionists. But the ASSASSINATION of President Lincoln caused him to develop a less forgiving stance, a tougher, Radical Republican position. After the assassination, Speed maintained that "the rebel officers who surrendered to General Grant have no homes within the loyal states and have no right to come to places which were their homes prior to going into rebellion." And in an 1865 opinion, Speed concluded that in killing Lincoln, John Wilkes Booth had acted as a public enemy on behalf of the Confederacy. He recommended that Booth and his accomplices be tried for their offenses by a military tribunal rather than a civil court.

Speed resigned his cabinet post in 1866 when he found himself opposed to the policies of President ANDREW JOHNSON. Afterward, he toured the United States speaking about his friendship and professional association with the late president Lincoln.

Speed resumed his teaching duties at Louisville University in 1875. He continued to play a role in state and national politics, acting as a delegate to the Republican conventions of 1872 and 1876. His last public appearance was on May 4, 1887, when he delivered to the Loyal League of Cincinnati a speech on his association with Lincoln and his lifelong efforts to preserve the Union. Speed died at his home in Jefferson County, Kentucky, on June 25, 1887.

SPEEDY TRIAL The SIXTH AMENDMENT to the U.S. Constitution guarantees all persons accused of criminal wrongdoing the right to a speedy trial. Although this right is derived from the federal Constitution, it has been made applicable to state criminal proceedings through the U.S. Supreme Court's interpretation of the Due Process and Equal Protection Clauses of the FOURTEENTH AMENDMENT. See also INCORPORATION DOCTRINE.

The right to a speedy trial is an ancient liberty. During the reign of HENRY II (1154–1189), the English Crown promulgated the Assize of Clarendon, a legal code comprised of twenty-two articles, one of which promised speedy justice to all litigants. In 1215 the MAGNA CHARTA prohibited the king from delaying justice to any person in the realm. Several of the charters of the American colonies protected the right to a speedy trial, as did most of the constitutions of the original thirteen states.

The Founding Fathers intended the Speedy Trial Clause to serve two purposes. First, they sought to prevent defendants from languishing in JAIL for an indefinite period before trial. Pretrial INCARCERATION is a deprivation of liberty no less serious than post-conviction imprisonment. In some cases pretrial incarceration may be more serious because public scrutiny is often heightened, employment is commonly interrupted, financial resources are diminished, family relations are strained, and innocent persons are forced to suffer prolonged injury to reputation.

Second, the Founding Fathers sought to ensure a defendant's right to a fair trial. The longer the commencement of trial is postponed, the more likely it is that WITNESSES will disappear, memories will fade, and EVIDENCE will be lost or destroyed. Of course, both the prosecution and the defense are threatened by these dangers, but only the defendant's life, liberty, and property are at stake in a criminal proceeding.

The right to a speedy trial does not apply to every stage of a criminal case. It arises only after a person has been arrested, indicted, or otherwise formally accused of a crime by the government. Before the point of formal accusation, the government is under no Sixth Amendment obligation to investigate, accuse, or PROSECUTE a defendant within a specific amount of time.

Nor does the Speedy Trial Clause apply to post-trial criminal proceedings, such as PROBATION and PAROLE hearings. If the government drops criminal charges during the middle of a case, the Speedy Trial Clause does not apply unless the government later refiles the charges, at which point the length of delay is measured only from the time of refiling. However, the fairness requirements of the Due Process Clause apply during each juncture of a criminal case, and an unreasonably excessive delay can be challenged under this constitutional provision even if the delay occurs before formal accusation or after conviction.

The U.S. Supreme Court has declined to draw a bright line separating permissible pretrial delays from delays that are impermissibly excessive. Instead, the Court has developed a BALANCING test in which the length of delay is just one factor to be considered when evaluating the merits of a speedy trial claim. The other factors to be considered by a court include the reason for the delay, the severity of PREJUDICE suffered by the defendant from the delay, and the stage during the criminal proceedings at which the defendant asserted the right to a speedy trial.

A delay of at least one year in bringing a defendant to trial following arrest will trigger a PRESUMPTION that the Sixth Amendment has been violated, with the level of judicial scrutiny increasing in direct proportion to the length of delay. A longer delay may be deemed constitutional, however, and a shorter delay may be deemed unconstitutional, depending on the circumstances.

Longer delays will be permitted to accommodate the schedules of important witnesses, and to allow the prosecution to prepare for a complex case. Longer delays will also be tolerated when a defendant is dilatory in asserting the right to a speedy trial. In general, defendants must assert their Sixth Amendment right in a timely MOTION before the trial court. If the defendant fails to assert the right in this manner, or acquiesces in the face of protracted pretrial delays, she may not raise the issue for the first time on APPEAL, unless the defendant's failure to raise the issue earlier was due to her attorney's NEGLIGENCE. Defendants who delay prosecution by inundating the trial court with frivolous pretrial motions are also treated as having forfeited their rights to a speedy trial. The law does not allow defendants to profit from their own wrong under these circumstances.

Delays shorter than a year will be ruled unconstitutional if the reason for delay offered by the prosecution is unpersuasive or inappropriate. Delays attributable to prosecutorial misconduct, such as the deliberate attempt by the government to delay a proceeding and hamper the defense, will run afoul of the Speedy Trial Clause. Prosecutorial negligence, such as misplacing a defendant's file or losing incriminating evidence, is also considered an inappropriate reason for delay. Additionally, delays shorter than a year will be deemed unconstitutional when the delay has severely limited an accused's opportunity to defend himself. For example, the death of an alibi witness who would have been available for a timely trial is considered PRIMA FACIE evidence of prejudice under the Speedy Trial Clause.

Despite the strictures of the Speedy Trial Clause, criminal justice has not always moved swiftly in the United States. During the 1970s FEDERAL COURTS had backlogs of thousands of cases on their DOCKETS. Lengthy pretrial delays clogged local jails at great expense to taxpayers.

Increasing numbers of defendants were jumping BAIL while free during extended pretrial release. In 1974 Congress enacted the Speedy Trial Act (18 U.S.C.A. § 3161 et seq.) to ameliorate the situation.

Unlike the balancing test created by the Supreme Court to evaluate a claim under the Speedy Trial Clause, the Speedy Trial Act establishes specific time limits between various stages of federal criminal proceedings. The act requires federal authorities to file an INFORMATION or INDICTMENT within thirty days of a defendant's arrest. A PROSECUTOR who knows that an accused is incarcerated at the time of indictment must take immediate steps to initiate prosecution. If a defendant enters a plea of not guilty, trial must commence within seventy days from the filing of the information or indictment, or seventy days from the accused's first appearance in court, whichever is later.

Certain types of delays are exempted from the act's time limitations. For example, the act exempts delays caused by the absence of the defendant, the unavailability of an essential witness, or the conduct of a codefendant. Delays resulting from a defendant's involvement in other legal proceedings are typically exempted as well. Additionally, the act gives courts discretion to grant the prosecution a CONTINUANCE in the interests of justice. Courts are also given discretion to dismiss charges when a defendant suffers prejudice from a pretrial delay that is of a kind not exempted under the act.

Many state jurisdictions have passed legislation similar to the Speedy Trial Act. Like the federal act, most state legislation permits courts to provide prosecutors with additional time upon a showing of exceptional circumstances. Most state laws also authorize courts to dismiss charges that have not been brought within a reasonable amount of time following arrest or indictment. Thus, defendants faced with an unreasonable pretrial delay have a number of constitutional and statutory provisions that may provide them with effective relief.

CROSS-REFERENCES

Criminal Law; Criminal Procedure; Due Process of Law.

SPENDING POWER 📖 The power of LEGISLATURES to tax and spend. 📖

Spending power is conferred to state and federal legislatures through their constitution. JUDICIAL REVIEW of legislative spending varies from state to state, but the law of federal spending informs courts in all states.

The power of the U.S. Congress to tax and spend for the GENERAL WELFARE is granted under

Article I, Section 8, Clause 1, of the U.S. Constitution: "The Congress shall have Power To lay and collect Taxes, Duties, Imposts and Excises, to pay the Debts and provide for the common Defence and general Welfare of the United States." This clause is known as the Spending Power Clause or the General Welfare Clause. The Spending Power Clause does not grant to Congress the power to pass all laws for the general welfare; that is a power reserved to the states under the TENTH AMENDMENT. Rather, it gives Congress the power to control federal taxation and spending.

Before 1913, federal spending was relatively minuscule and was generally reserved for military support in time of war. Federal revenues were generated through TARIFFS on imports, excise taxes on certain activities and professions, and state and local property taxes. In 1913, the States ratified the SIXTEENTH AMENDMENT to the Constitution, which guaranteed to Congress the power to lay and collect income taxes on individuals. The federal INCOME TAX, hailed for its uniformity and fairness, paved the way for a massive expansion in the scope of the federal government.

Federal spending increased dramatically in the 1930s. Congress created new federal agencies and spending programs to manage the economic effects of the Great Depression, and the U.S. Supreme Court was forced to decide a spate of challenges to federal spending programs. See also NEW DEAL.

In 1936 the Court construed the Spending Power Clause as giving Congress broad power to spend for the general welfare, while ruling that the spending program in question was invalid (*United States v. Butler*, 297 U.S. 1, 56 S. Ct. 312, 80 L. Ed. 477). The *Butler* decision established a permissive view of the Spending

Power Clause: Congress was not limited to spending money to carry out the direct grants of legislative power found elsewhere in the Constitution; rather, it could tax and spend for what it determined to be the general welfare of the country.

The U.S. Supreme Court has identified a few factors that limit congressional spending power. One of these is derived from the Spending Power Clause: the spending power must be exercised in pursuit of the general welfare. However, Congress has broad discretion to determine the general welfare, and no court has ever invalidated a federal spending program on the ground that it did not promote the general welfare of the country.

Congressional spending power receives serious scrutiny when Congress seeks to withhold federal funds from states that refuse to enact laws consistent with federal mandates. Incident to the Spending Power Clause, Congress may condition a state's receipt of federal revenues on the fulfillment of certain criteria. For example, assume Congress wants all schoolteachers to obtain a master's degree. The Constitution does not grant Congress the power to pass a law to that effect. However, Congress may appropriate federal money that states can obtain if they enact legislation requiring a master's degree.

When Congress allocates conditional funding, it must do so unambiguously, so that states and other affected parties are adequately advised of their choices and are aware of the consequences of noncompliance. Conditional federal spending must relate to a national interest, as opposed to state, local, or individual interests. Finally, conditional spending may be invalidated if it is excessively coercive. For example, withholding of an excessively high percentage of federal funds may be invalidated by a court.

According to many constitutional scholars, conditional federal spending is a violation of state SOVEREIGNTY over matters reserved to the states. Without a meaningful check on conditional federal spending, Congress can withhold federal benefits from states under the Spending Power Clause on any rational condition it desires. This has the effect of creating one central government, a system that was repugnant to the Framers of the Constitution when not properly balanced with the rights of state governments. Indeed, THOMAS JEFFERSON predicted that the Spending Power Clause would reduce the Constitution "to a single phrase, that of instituting a Congress, with power to do . . . whatever evil they pleased." Proponents of conditional federal funding argue that it does not force states

State and federal governments have the power to impose taxes and spend money for the public benefit, such as for this federal highway.

TONY FREEMAN/PHOTOEDIT

to change their laws, and that states are free to forgo the receipt of some federal funds in order to retain their autonomy.

Nevertheless, conditional federal spending has been used in a number of settings to persuade states to change their laws. Congress uses HIGHWAY funds in a variety of statutes to encourage changes in environment-related laws. It also enacts spending schemes favorable to minority small-business owners, to combat the effects of racial discrimination.

In *South Dakota v. Dole*, 483 U.S. 203, 107 S. Ct. 2793, 97 L. Ed. 2d 171 (1987), the U.S. Supreme Court reviewed a federal statute authorizing the U.S. secretary of transportation to withhold a percentage of federal highway funds from states that refused to raise the legal drinking age to twenty-one. According to the Court, the federal government's interest in a uniform drinking age related to highway safety because, in part, young persons in states with higher drinking ages were driving to border states with lower drinking ages. The conditional spending was upheld because it had a federal purpose (improving interstate highway safety) and the condition (establishing a uniform legal drinking age) was related to the spending purpose.

Some constitutional provisions expressly prohibit certain federal spending. Under the FIRST AMENDMENT, Congress may not spend federal money in the aid of religion. Under Article II, Section 1, Clause 7, Congress may not increase or decrease the salary of a president during her or his term. Under the FOURTEENTH AMENDMENT, Congress may not spend money on "any debt or obligation incurred in aid of insurrection or rebellion against the United States."

Congressional spending limits also may be found in the Constitution. If, for example, Congress allocates federal funding for libraries on the condition that all libraries ban certain literature, the spending scheme may run afoul of the First Amendment guarantee of free speech.

In *Adarand Constructors v. Peña*, 515 U.S. 200, 115 S. Ct. 2097, 132 L. Ed. 2d 158 (1995), the U.S. Supreme Court reviewed a federal spending program designed to provide federal highway construction contracts to disadvantaged business enterprises. Under the Surface Transportation and Uniform Relocation Assistance Act of 1987 (STURAA) (Pub. L. No. 100-17, 101 Stat. 132), Congress appropriated certain funds to the Department of Transportation. The DOT was obliged to spend not less than 10 percent of those funds on businesses certified as "owned and operated by socially

and economically disadvantaged individuals" (§ 106(c)(1)). These individuals were defined by STURAA as members of racial minorities and women.

Despite submitting the lowest bid for a subcontract to build guardrails for the Central Federal Lands Highway Division (part of the DOT), Adarand Constructors lost the contract to a business certified as disadvantaged. Adarand brought suit against Frederico F. Peña, secretary of transportation, arguing that the spending scheme violated the EQUAL PROTECTION component of the FIFTH AMENDMENT Due Process Clause. The district court granted SUMMARY judgment to the secretary, and the court of appeals affirmed, but the Supreme Court vacated the judgment. According to the Court, federal spending based on racial classifications should be subject to STRICT SCRUTINY to determine whether the means employed by the spending scheme were narrowly tailored to achieve a compelling federal interest. This decision overruled PRECEDENT, and signaled a greater willingness of the Court to examine the way in which Congress and states exercise their spending power.

CROSS-REFERENCES

Congress of the United States; Federal Budget; Federalism.

SPENDTHRIFT 📖 One who spends money profusely and improvidently, thereby wasting his or her ESTATE. 📖

Under various statutes, a spendthrift is a person who wastes or reduces her estate through excessive drinking, gambling, idleness, or debauchery in a manner that exposes that individual or her family to indigence or suffering or who exposes the government to expense for the support of that person or her family.

When authorized by law, a GUARDIAN can manage a spendthrift's property. The purpose of the guardianship is to protect the WARD and her property from her wasteful habits. Statutes that provide for the guardianship of spendthrifts are based on the right of the government to protect the property of its citizens for the benefit of themselves and their families and the community.

See also SPENDTHRIFT TRUST.

SPENDTHRIFT TRUST 📖 An arrangement whereby one person sets aside property for the benefit of another in which, either because of a direction of the SETTLOR (one who creates a trust) or because of statute, the BENEFICIARY (one who profits from the act of another) is unable to transfer his or her right to future payments of income or capital, and his or her creditors are unable to subject the beneficiary's interest to the payment of his or her DEBTS. 📖

Spendthrift trusts are usually established with the object of providing a fund for the maintenance of another person, known as the SPENDTHRIFT, while also protecting the trust against the beneficiary's imprudence, extravagance, and inability to manage financial affairs. For example, a settlor establishes a spendthrift trust for his son, a compulsive gambler, who spends money injudiciously with no concern for the future. Under the terms of the $400,000 trust, which is to be administered by the family's lawyer, the son is to receive $15,000 a year. Any words that indicate the settlor's intention to impose a direct restraint on the transferability of the beneficiary's interest can be used to create a spendthrift trust.

Such TRUSTS do not limit the rights of the spendthrift's creditors to the property after it is received by the beneficiary from the TRUSTEE (one appointed or required by law to execute a trust). The creditors cannot compel the trustee to pay them directly. This means that any of the spendthrift's creditors can seek to have the money the spendthrift has already received applied to satisfy their claims. A creditor's claims to future payments under the trust, however, are restrained. The spendthrift's creditors cannot reach the $15,000 that he is to be paid in a subsequent year until it is actually paid out to him. If such a person could dispose of his right to receive income from the trust, his incompetence or carelessness might lead him to anticipate his income and transfer to monetary lenders and creditors the right to receive future income as it became due. By restricting the spendthrift so that he can do nothing with the income until it is paid into his hands by the trustee, he is more likely to be protected, at least to some extent, against impoverishment.

A spendthrift trust can continue for the life of the beneficiary or be limited to a period of years.

A settlor cannot create a spendthrift trust for herself. If the settlor attempts to do so, the trust is valid but the spendthrift clause is legally ineffective as to the present and future creditors of the property owner. To allow otherwise would be to provide unscrupulous people with the opportunity to shelter their property before engaging in speculative business enterprises and to mislead creditors into believing that the settlor still owned the property because she appeared to be receiving its income, thereby fraudulently deceiving creditors who might rely on the former financial property of the debtor.

In some states, under the doctrine of "surplus income," creditors can reach any trust income that exceeds what is necessary to support and educate the beneficiary. The court hears EVIDENCE as to the amount necessary to support the beneficiary in the manner to which he has been accustomed. Any excess of trust income over the sum will be awarded to the CREDITOR and paid directly to her by the trustee. A few states have enacted statutes fixing the percentage of trust income that is exempt from creditor's claims that have been legally determined in a court ACTION.

Certain classes are permitted to reach the beneficiary's interest in a spendthrift trust on the ground of PUBLIC POLICY in many states. These include persons whom the beneficiary is legally bound to support, such as a spouse and children; persons who render necessary personal services to the beneficiary, such as a physician; and persons whose services preserve the beneficiary's interest in the trust. TORT claims against the beneficiary as well as claims by a state or the United States, such as for INCOME TAX, are not subject to spendthrift provisions.

In some states, when a beneficiary and spouse are divorced and the spouse has been awarded ALIMONY, the trustee of the trust cannot be compelled to pay the full amount of alimony until the court that has JURISDICTION over the administration of the trust deems it to be fair.

The majority of states authorize spendthrift trusts; those that do not will VOID such provisions so that the beneficiary can transfer his or her rights and the creditors can attach the right to future income.

SPIN-OFF 📖 The situation that arises when a parent CORPORATION organizes a subsidiary corporation, to which it transfers a portion of its ASSETS in exchange for all of the subsidiary's CAPITAL STOCK, which is subsequently transferred to the parent corporation's shareholders. 📖

When a spin-off occurs, the shareholders of the parent corporation are not required to surrender any of their parent corporation stock in exchange for the subsidiary's stock.

In the event that the distribution of stock to the parent corporation's shareholders amounts to a DIVIDEND, the distribution can be taxed pursuant to provisions of INCOME TAX statutes.

SPLIT DECISION 📖 A decision by an APPELLATE COURT that is not unanimous. 📖

When the members of an appellate court cannot reach full agreement, a split decision occurs. A split decision is distinct from a unanimous decision in which all the judges join in agreement. In a split decision, the will of the majority of the judges is binding, and one member of the majority delivers the opinion of the court itself. One or more members of the minority can also write a dissent, which is a critical explanation of the minority's reasons for not joining in the majority decision. A court that reaches a split decision is called a divided court. Split decisions cannot occur at the trial level because there only one judge presides. Instead, split decisions occur in state and federal appellate courts, including state supreme courts and the U.S. Supreme Court. Split decisions also occur in regulatory boards, government commissions, and juries (where a split decision can result in a hung or deadlocked jury).

Although split decisions carry the same legal authority as unanimous decisions, they have a problematic place in U.S. JURISPRUDENCE. Most important, they can reflect significant disagreement among the members of a court: for example, the judges may not fully agree on a constitutional question, the application of PRECEDENTS in CASE LAW, or the interpretation of a statute. Occasionally, a split decision indicates sharp divisions over an issue that has not yet been settled in the law. In appealing such a case to a higher court, APPELLEES often note that the lower court has rendered a split decision in order to impress upon the higher court that the decision in question is less than wholly convincing. A split decision may be seen as less stable than a unanimous one, allowing more room for a change in the law as society and the court's composition change.

Split decisions by the U.S. Supreme Court attract special attention, particularly when the vote is 5–4. At such times, and especially in the face of controversial cases that are accompanied by sharply worded DISSENTS, the Court is described as "deeply divided." Not surprisingly, since the Court is the final arbiter of U.S. law, a split decision is often seen as an indication of the justices' divergent legal and political ideologies. Legal scholars and reporters, who traditionally assess the justices' political leanings, frequently pay special attention to split decisions when analyzing the Court's decisions for a given term.

Some commentators have argued that a deeply divided Supreme Court fails in its duty to provide guidance to lower courts and also loses legitimacy in the eyes of the public. Justice FELIX FRANKFURTER feared such a possibility in 1955, when the Court was preparing to consider the question of MISCEGENATION laws which prohibited interracial marriage. Frankfurter urged the Court not to hear the case because he feared that a split decision would plunge the Court into "the vortex of the present disquietude . . . [and] embarrass the carrying-out of the Court's decree." Nevertheless, unanimous agreement by the Court is not the rule. Many of the twentieth century's most controversial cases have produced split decisions, including the decisions to uphold AFFIRMATIVE ACTION (*Regents of the University of California v. Bakke*, 438 U.S. 265, 98 S. Ct. 2733, 57 L. Ed. 2d 750 [1978]) and to uphold a woman's right to an ABORTION (*Roe v. Wade*, 410 U.S. 113, 93 S. Ct. 705, 35 L. Ed. 2d 147 [1973]).

See also COURT OPINION.

SPLIT-OFF The process whereby a parent CORPORATION organizes a subsidiary corporation to which it transfers part of its ASSETS in exchange for all of the subsidiary's CAPITAL STOCK, which is subsequently transferred to the shareholders of the parent corporation in exchange for a portion of their parent stock.

A split-off differs from a SPIN-OFF in that the shareholders in a split-off must relinquish their shares of stock in the parent corporation in order to receive shares of the subsidiary corporation whereas the shareholders in a spin-off need not do so.

SPLIT-UP An arrangement whereby a parent CORPORATION transfers all of its ASSETS to two or more corporations and then winds up its affairs.

When a split-up occurs, the shareholders of the parent corporation surrender the total amount of their stock in exchange for stock in the transferee corporation.

SPOLIATION Any erasure, interlineation, or other alteration made to COMMERCIAL PAPER, such as a CHECK or PROMISSORY NOTE, by an individual who is not acting pursuant to the consent of the parties who have an interest in such instrument.

A spoliator of EVIDENCE in a legal ACTION is an individual who neglects to produce evidence that is in her possession or control. In such a situation, any inferences that might be drawn against the party are permitted, and the withholding of the evidence is attributed to the person's presumed knowledge that it would have served to operate against her.

SPORKIN, STANLEY As an attorney, regulator, and outspoken federal judge, Stanley Sporkin has often embraced controversy in his thirty years of federal service. Sporkin first earned national recognition in the 1970s for his criminal investigations into corporate misbehavior as the director of enforcement at the SECURITIES AND EXCHANGE COMMISSION (SEC). From 1981 to 1986, he was general counsel of the CENTRAL INTELLIGENCE AGENCY (CIA). In

BIOGRAPHY

APWIDE WORLD PHOTOS

Stanley Sporkin

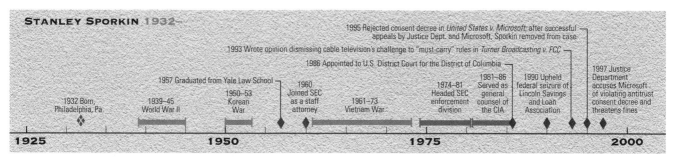

1986 President RONALD REAGAN appointed him to the U.S. District Court for the District of Columbia. Throughout the 1980s and 1990s, Sporkin attracted widespread comment for his passionate and idiosyncratic rulings on major cases involving business regulation and ANTITRUST. Frequently, he found himself in conflict with the U.S. Court of Appeals for the District of Columbia, which often overruled him. A writer and speechmaker, Sporkin is widely known in law circles for his reformist views on legal ethics, SENTENCING guidelines, and the federal judiciary.

Sporkin was born in Philadelphia, Pennsylvania, in 1932. He earned his law degree from Yale University in 1957, and worked in private practice before joining the SEC as a staff attorney in 1960. The SEC, which was created in the 1930s to oversee the SECURITIES laws that protect shareholders, had a quiet, even moribund reputation. This began to change in 1972, when an enforcement division was added. When Sporkin took charge of enforcement in 1974, the division vigorously pursued criminal cases against U.S. CORPORATIONS. In particular, Sporkin prosecuted a series of cases involving the use of corporate funds for political contributions that had come to the surface during the WATERGATE scandal; his investigations uncovered illegal domestic and foreign expenditures. Critics thought he had gone too far and exceeded the SEC's JURISDICTION. Nevertheless, his eight-year tenure survived federal oversight review and helped set the stage for even tougher compliance practices in later years.

After Sporkin had served five years as general counsel to the CIA, Reagan appointed him to the U.S. District Court for the District of Columbia, which hears major federal cases involving regulation. Here he has showed the same zeal he displayed at the SEC. In upholding the federal seizure of the Lincoln Savings and Loan Association in 1990, he criticized the attorneys and accountants for the savings and loan with a widely quoted comment on their failure to blow the whistle on violations: "Where were the professionals . . . while these clearly improper transactions were being consummated?" In 1993, as part of a three-judge panel, he wrote the opinion dismissing the

"PLAINTIFFS HAVE COME BEFORE THIS COURT, NOT BECAUSE THEIR FREEDOM OF SPEECH IS SERIOUSLY THREATENED, BUT BECAUSE THEIR PROFITS ARE; TO DRESS UP THEIR COMPLAINT IN FIRST AMENDMENT GARB DEMEANS THE PRINCIPLES FOR WHICH THE FIRST AMENDMENT STANDS AND THE PROTECTION IT WAS DESIGNED TO AFFORD."

FIRST AMENDMENT challenge of CABLE TELEVISION companies to the constitutionality of federal rules requiring that they carry broadcast stations (*Turner Broadcasting v. FCC*, 819 F. Supp. 32 [D.D.C. 1993]).

Sporkin's most controversial decision came in 1995 in one of the most widely followed antitrust cases of the decade. Following a four-year investigation, the Department of Justice had entered an agreement with computer software giant Microsoft, Inc., to reform licensing practices that the department said were monopolistic. Under provisions in the Tunney Act (15 U.S.C.A. § 16(e) [1988]), Sporkin had the authority to review the consent decree to determine if it was in the PUBLIC INTEREST. In addition to criticizing Microsoft during the hearings, he took the rare step of allowing its competitors to file friend-of-the-court (AMICUS CURIAE) briefs anonymously so as to protect them from retaliation by Microsoft. Ultimately, Sporkin rejected the consent decree as being insufficient and ordered the Justice Department to expand its investigation. (*United States v. Microsoft Corp.*, 159 F.R.D. 318 [D.D.C. 1995]).

In a surprising move, both the Justice Department and Microsoft filed separate appeals. Not only did both parties win, but Sporkin was removed from the case by the U.S. Court of Appeals for the District of Columbia Circuit for apparent bias; the court then remanded the case to another judge with orders to approve the consent decree (*United States v. Microsoft Corp.*, 56 F.3d 1448 [D.C. Cir. 1995]).

In addition to his uncompromising work as a lawyer and judge, Sporkin has distinguished himself as a legal critic. He has written on the need for separate codes of ethical conduct for various disciplines within the law, urged the adoption of multimedia presentations of evidence in courtrooms, and argued against what he sees as unfairness in the federal sentencing guidelines for drug offenses.

SPORTS LAW The laws, regulations, and judicial decisions that govern sports and athletes.

Sports law is an amalgam of laws that apply to athletes and the sports they play. It is not a singular legal topic with generally applicable principles. Sports law touches on a variety of matters, including contract, tort, agency, antitrust, constitutional, labor, trademark, sex discrimination, criminal, and tax issues. Some laws depend on the status of the athlete, some laws differ according to the sport, and some laws vary for other reasons.

Amateur Athletes A common misconception about amateurs and professionals is that professionals are paid to play sports whereas amateur athletes are not. Amateur athletes often receive some compensation for their efforts. In ancient Greece, for example, victorious athletes in the Olympics were handsomely rewarded for their efforts. Today many college athletes receive academic scholarships for playing on a college team. Remuneration for amateur athletes is even promoted with federal legislation. The Amateur Sports Act of 1978 (36 U.S.C.A. § 391) created the Athletic Congress, a national governing body for amateur athletes, which administers a trust fund that allows amateur athletes to receive funds and sponsorship payments without losing their amateur status.

The most basic difference between amateur athletic events and professional events lies in their rewards for participation. Amateur events, by definition, do not reward victors with a prize of great value. Professional events, by contrast, reward participants and victors with money or other prizes. An accomplished athlete may choose to compete as an amateur if her sport does not have a thriving professional organization. Some athletes can make a living in amateur sports because victories in high-profile amateur events can lead to advertising deals and other business opportunities.

Amateur sports can be divided into two categories: restricted and unrestricted competition. Restricted competition includes elementary school, high school, and college athletics. Sports on these levels are controlled by athletic conferences, associations, and leagues connected to high schools and colleges. Athletes in restricted competition must be eligible to play. Eligibility is determined by conferences, associations, and leagues formed by the schools.

Unrestricted competition is open to all amateur athletes, with some qualifications. The Olympics is an example of unrestricted competition. Although only a select few amateur athletes are chosen to represent the United States, any person may seek entry into this elite group by entering recognized contests in the years before the Olympiad and qualifying for tryouts.

Whether an athlete is eligible to compete in amateur events depends on the rules of the governing conference, league, or association. Many events formerly reserved for amateurs,

such as the Olympics, were opened to professionals in the 1980s and 1990s. Gymnasts, figure skaters, soccer players, track stars, and other athletes once concerned with maintaining amateur status now may enjoy the fruits of professional competitions without losing access to prestigious amateur events. Often difficult eligibility issues for amateur athletes do not concern professional status. Qualification requirements for particular events and rules prohibiting drug use are among the more challenging roadblocks.

Eligibility requirements for amateur athletes are many and varied. Generally, amateur athletes do not have an absolute right to participate in sports events. In analyzing whether an athlete is eligible to participate, a court must first decide whether the individual has a RIGHT to play, as opposed to a mere PRIVILEGE to play. Privileges can be revoked by the grantor of the privilege. If the individual has a right to participate, the court examines the individual's relationship with the institution denying access. If the institution is private, the dispute generally is decided according to contract or tort principles. If the institution is a public school or university, or any other publicly funded organization, courts change their analysis.

When public funds are involved, the institution is deemed a state actor, and the institution's action is subject to the Due Process and Equal Protection Clauses of the FOURTEENTH AMENDMENT. DUE PROCESS usually consists of

GAMMA LIAISON

Sports stars, such as skater Nancy Kerrigan, often retain lawyers specializing in sports law to help them negotiate and comply with performance and advertising contracts.

notice to the person affected by the state action and an opportunity for the aggrieved person to argue against the action. Courts also strike down vague, overbroad, and overly restrictive regulations by state institutions on due process grounds.

The Fourteenth Amendment's EQUAL PROTECTION Clause, as interpreted by courts, requires that similarly situated persons receive equal treatment under the law. If a classification touches on a fundamental right, such as freedom of religion or the right to marry, or if it is based on a suspect criterion, such as race or national origin, a court will strictly scrutinize the classification to see whether it promotes a compelling interest of the institution. Because participation of amateurs in sports is not a fundamental right, ordinarily the exclusion of amateurs from participation is not subjected to STRICT SCRUTINY.

If a regulation of amateur sports does not infringe on a fundamental right or burden a suspect class, courts determine whether the regulation bears a rational relationship to a legitimate state interest. This is a lower level of inquiry than strict scrutiny, but it does not give public institutions the unlimited freedom to act unreasonably in the absence of fundamental rights or suspect class concerns. In 1981 the Texas Supreme Court struck down the state high school athletic association's non-transfer rule, which declared all non-seniors ineligible for varsity football and basketball competition for one year following their transfer to a new school. The purpose of the act was to discourage the recruiting of student athletes. According to the court, the rule was over-inclusive because it presumed that a student athlete who had switched schools had been recruited and did not give the student the opportunity to rebut the presumption (*Sullivan v. University Interscholastic League*, 616 S.W.2d 170 [1981]). See also RATIONAL BASIS TEST.

The rights of student athletes can be infringed by reasonable measures that are implemented for sound PUBLIC POLICY reasons. Eligibility criteria can vary from school to school, and even from sport to sport. No pass-no play rules, or rules that keep flunking students off school teams, are permissible in light of the government's overriding interest in educating children. Schools may artificially control the number of student athletes, allowing students to be cut from popular sports to keep athlete-to-coach ratios at manageable levels.

Schools may enact other limitations, such as rules limiting the number of sports a student can play at one time and rules authorizing students to be suspended or expelled from athletics for consuming alcohol or using other drugs. Discovery of student-athlete drug use was made easier under a 1995 U.S. Supreme Court decision. In *Vernonia School District 47J v. Acton*, 515 U.S. 646, 115 S. Ct. 2386, 132 L. Ed. 2d 564 (1995), the Court held that random drug testing of student athletes does not violate the constitutional right to be free from unreasonable SEARCHES AND SEIZURES.

The National Collegiate Athletic Association (NCAA) is the most important administrative body governing sports on the college level. Many colleges and universities are members of the NCAA, and they give the association the authority to exercise control over their student-athletes, coaches, and other athletic operatives. The NCAA, headquartered in Shawnee, Kansas, arranges for television and radio contracts and performs other functions to promote the well-being of college sports.

The NCAA exerts a tremendous amount of control over its members. Under NCAA rules, college athletes must meet and maintain a certain grade-point average before playing, may not hire an agent while playing for a college, and may not participate in an annual professional draft of college athletes without losing their eligibility. The NCAA may discipline coaches and scouts for violating restrictions on the recruiting of high school athletes. Athletes may be suspended or banned from a team for drug use or even for ALCOHOL consumption. Each team has its own set of rules that complement the NCAA rules.

Most courts hold that participation in intercollegiate athletics is not a constitutionally pro-

Volleyball player Meg Fitzgerald attended the University of North Carolina on a scholarship made possible by Title IX's ban on sex discrimination by schools receiving federal funds.

APWIDE WORLD PHOTOS

tected interest. However, one federal district court has recognized a student athlete's limited property interest in college athletics. In *Hall v. University of Minnesota*, 530 F. Supp. 104 (1982), University of Minnesota basketball guard Mark Hall, who had a satisfactory grade-point average, was kept off the basketball team when he failed to earn enough credits for a particular academic program. Hall appealed the decision, arguing that his application to a different college within the university had been rejected in BAD FAITH and without due process. U.S. District Court Judge Miles W. Lord held that Hall had a sufficient property interest in playing basketball because the competition would affect his ability to be drafted by a professional team, and Lord ordered the school to let Hall play.

College athletic scholarships are unusual agreements that can pose problems for schools, athletes, and courts. A typical athletic scholarship requires the athlete to maintain certain grade levels and to perform as an athlete for the school in exchange for tuition, books, and other educational expenses. Most courts treat scholarships as CONTRACTS, with OBLIGATIONS and rights assigned to both parties. One party may be liable to the other if a breach of the contract occurs. For instance, a college may revoke the scholarship of an athlete who fails to maintain good grades or violates any other condition of the scholarship. A school, for its part, may violate its obligations by failing to provide an education to a student athlete. At least one court has held that a school violates its duties under an athletic scholarship if it fails to provide a student athlete meaningful access to its academic curriculum (*Ross v. Creighton University*, 957 F.2d 410 [7th Cir. 1992]).

The revenues produced by some college sports have made college athletics a multi-million-dollar entertainment industry. Although student-athletes are an integral part of the entertainment, most contemporary courts do not view them as employees of their schools. Thus, a school is not liable under WORKERS' COMPENSATION statutes to a student-athlete if the student-athlete is injured in an accident related to the student's sport. For tax purposes, most courts examine the scholarship agreements of most students to determine whether they bargained for the scholarship money. If the students bargained for the scholarship money in return for services, the money can be taxed. Under INTERNAL REVENUE SERVICE regulations and revenue rulings, scholarship funds for student-athletes are exempt from federal tax if the college does not require the student to participate in a particular sport, requires no particular activity

in lieu of participation, and does not cancel the scholarship if the student cannot participate. Funds for such athletic scholarships may be taxed if they exceed the expenses for tuition, fees, room, board, and necessary supplies. As of 1996, the Internal Revenue Service had never challenged the tax-exempt status of student-athletes on scholarship.

Sex Discrimination Women and girls have long been excluded from many sports. In the 1970s Congress passed title IX of the 1972 Education Amendments (20 U.S.C.A. §§ 1681–1688 [1994]) to ban SEX DISCRIMINATION in publicly funded educational programs. After a round of litigation, followed by legislative amendments, a presidential veto, and a congressional override of the veto, title IX was modified to give women and girls equal access to sports programs in schools that receive any measure of federal funding.

Under title IX schools must provide athletic opportunities to females that are proportionate to those provided to males. Courts do not require that complete equality occur overnight. Most courts engage in a three-pronged analysis to determine whether a school is fulfilling its obligations. First, the court examines whether athletic participation opportunities are provided to each sex in numbers substantially proportionate to their enrollment. If a school does not provide substantially proportionate participation opportunities, the court then determines whether the school can demonstrate a history of expanding the athletic programs for the underrepresented sex. If the school cannot so demonstrate, the court then asks whether the interests and abilities of the underrepresented sex have been accommodated by the school. If the court finds that the school has not accommodated student-athletes of the underrepresented sex, it may rule that the school is in violation of title IX and order the school to take affirmative steps toward more equal treatment between the sexes.

Traditionally, courts have differentiated between contact and noncontact sports in determining a female's right to participation. A school may refrain from offering a contact sport for females if the reasoning is not based on an archaic, paternalistic, overbroad view of women. Courts are hesitant to mandate the creation of new teams, but most have no problem ordering that qualified females be allowed to play on exclusively male teams.

Sex-based classifications by publicly funded entities are subject to equal protection claims. Courts review such claims under an intermediate standard of review. Specifically, a sex-based classification must serve an important govern-

1919 Black Sox Scandal

The 1919 Black Sox scandal is the most famous example of athletes conspiring with gamblers to fix the outcome of a sporting event. Eight members of the Chicago White Sox were charged with taking bribes to lose the 1919 World Series to the Cincinnati Reds. The most prominent player charged was "Shoeless" Joe Jackson, the star outfielder for the White Sox. It was alleged that the players received $70,000 to $100,000 for losing the World Series five games to three.

During the World Series, a number of sportswriters suspected that White Sox players were throwing the games. The writers published their charges after the series ended, but by the beginning of the 1920 baseball season, it appeared nothing would come of the allegations. However, a federal grand jury, presided by Judge Kenesaw Mountain Landis, was impaneled in September 1920. Within days, four of the players, including Jackson, admitted that they had taken bribes to lose games in the 1919 series. The eight players were indicted.

The team suspended the players, and they went on trial in the summer of 1921. They were acquitted on insufficient evidence, under suspicious circumstances. Key pieces of evidence were missing from the grand jury files, including the players' confessions. No gamblers were ever brought to trial for bribery, though it was alleged that New York racketeer Arnold Rothstein was behind the plan to fix the World Series.

Major league baseball had named Landis commissioner of baseball in 1921, in an attempt to restore the integrity of the game. The day after the eight White Sox players were acquitted, Landis banned them from baseball for life.

See also Landis, Kenesaw Mountain.

---

ment interest and must be substantially related to the achievement of that interest. High school girls in Arkansas used the Equal Protection Clause of the Fourteenth Amendment to abolish a school rule that limited the girls' basketball games to half-court play. In *Dodson v. Arkansas Activities Association*, 468 F. Supp. 394 (1979), a federal district court in Arkansas ruled that the half-court rule deprived the girls of their equal protection rights because it was based solely on tradition and not on any supportable sex-based reason.

Professional Athletes Professional athletes are paid for their services. Professional sports organizations use a tremendous number of relationships and a similarly high number of agreements and contracts to support their industries. The parties involved include team owners, promoters, athletes, agents, lawyers, accountants, advertisers, builders, carriers, journalists, media outlets, politicians, courts, and the governing body of the particular sport.

For the professional athlete, the most immediate concern is the employment contract. The contract between the athlete and the employer determines the rights and duties of both parties. These contracts are bargained agreements, and the bargaining power of the respective parties is reflected in the terms. Unproven or average athletes generally obtain contracts for a salary and benefits that are less than those received by athletes of proven skill. Most professional leagues that have a players' union negotiate with management or promoters to draft a standard player's contract. A standard player's contract is a document that establishes basic rights and privileges for the athletes. Owners, managers, and promoters may violate agreements with unions if they tender contracts that offer fewer rights and privileges than are contained in the standard player's contract.

Because their sport enjoyed widespread popularity before any other sport, BASEBALL players led other professional athletes in the reform of laws on professional sports contracts. The earliest and most infamous of the contract issues addressed by baseball players was the reserve clause. This clause, placed into contracts by the owners of professional baseball teams, prevented a player from playing for another team for at least one year following the expiration of his contract. Owners of teams could trade or sell players to other teams, but players had no say in where they would play. The intent of the clause was to keep players on the same team to build the team's identity and increase fan loyalty. Players objected to the clause because it restricted their right to freely market their skills and their right to choose where they would live and play baseball.

The reserve clause was used in the first professional baseball league, the National League, in the late nineteenth century, and it survived until 1975. For years, the Supreme Court and other federal courts held that professional baseball was not subject to ANTITRUST LAWS because the game held a special place in American society. Antitrust laws prevent businesses from engaging in acts that restrain free trade if the commercial activity affects interstate commerce. Applying antitrust laws to professional baseball would have made it illegal for owners of professional baseball teams to restrain trade with the reserve clause. Players challenged the clause but lost in court.

In 1966 the Major League Baseball Players Association (MLBPA) hired Marvin Miller as its first executive director. Miller was instrumental in winning concessions from the owners of the major league teams. In 1970, after threats of strikes and hours of COLLECTIVE BARGAINING, the Major League Baseball Players Relations Committee, representing the major league teams, agreed with the MLBPA to the neutral ARBITRATION of their disputes. Arbitration is a process whereby two disputing parties agree to have their dispute settled by a third party.

The players' movement for market freedom suffered a temporary setback when St. Louis Cardinals star center fielder Curt Flood challenged baseball's antitrust exemption and lost. Flood was traded in 1969 to the Philadelphia Phillies when he was at the peak of his career. Flood refused to play for the Phillies, and he sat out the entire 1970 season. That year, Flood filed suit in federal court against Bowie Kuhn, then the commissioner of Major League Baseball. Flood argued that the actions of major league baseball club owners violated the federal antitrust laws, CIVIL RIGHTS laws, laws prohibiting PEONAGE, and laws on SLAVERY, including the THIRTEENTH AMENDMENT to the Constitution. The Supreme Court disagreed, holding that major league baseball maintained a special exemption from antitrust laws under Supreme Court precedent and that any changes in the law should come from Congress. Major league baseball remains the only professional sport to which courts have not applied antitrust laws.

In 1974 pitchers Andy Messersmith of the Los Angeles Dodgers and Dave McNally of the Baltimore Orioles played the entire season without new contracts. Both pitchers were paid their previous year's salary (Messersmith received a slight raise), but both had refused to sign their contracts. At the end of the season they declared that they were free agents because the reserve clause in the last contract they had signed lasted for only one year. The club owners argued that the clause could be renewed unilaterally (by one party, here, the owners), year after year. Messersmith and McNally brought their cases to a panel of arbitrators, and the panel held that the reserve clause was actually an OPTION clause: it gave the teams an additional option year to sign a player to a new contract. Without a new contract, the player was a free agent and could market his service to other professional teams.

After almost a century of attempts to shake the reserve clause through the court system, major league baseball players finally gained their freedom through collective bargaining and arbitration. The decision was upheld on APPEAL, and baseball players instantly gained bargaining power. In 1976 the players relations committee agreed to remove the reserve clause from standard contracts and install a system of free agency that gave free-agent status after six years of service to players who did not otherwise qualify through the option clause. By 1994 the average salary for major league baseball players was $1.2 million, compared to an average salary of $19,000 in 1967.

Baseball players now are free to negotiate contracts with any number of clauses. A player may sign a contract that guarantees a salary for a certain number of years, negotiate clauses that limit the club's right to trade the player, and enjoy the benefits of incentive clauses, or clauses in the contract that grant extra compensation in the event the player achieves certain goals. A last vestige of the reserve clause remains in some contracts as the option clause. This clause states that in the event the player and the team cannot come to terms on a new contract upon the expiration of a contract, the club may retain the player for another year at a percentage of his previous year's salary, usually

Major League Baseball Players' Average Salaries, 1967 to 1997

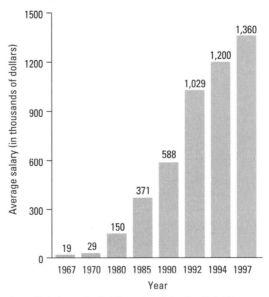

Source: Major League Baseball Players Association, New York, NY.

COME BACK, SHANE: THE MOVEMENT OF PROFESSIONAL SPORTS TEAMS

One of the most controversial issues in modern professional sports is the mobility of professional sports franchises. Teams in the four major sports leagues—the National Basketball Association (NBA), Major League Baseball (MLB), the National Hockey League (NHL), and the National Football League (NFL)—have long been capable of moving their franchises from one city to another, with the requisite approval of the other teams in the league. Nevertheless, the practice did not become common until relatively recently. The incidence of franchise movement became a plague in the 1990s, as owners of sports franchises sought to offset rising player salaries and maximize the values of their teams.

Many people perceive professional sports teams as beneficial for the local economy and essential to an area's civic identity. Professional sports teams have been credited with providing jobs and injecting millions of dollars into local economies. The presence of a professional sports franchise from one of the four major sports is often regarded a prerequisite to becoming a "big league" city or state. As Wisconsin state representative Marlin Schneider joked in 1995, "Without the Milwaukee Brewers, Bucks, and Packers, [Wisconsin] ain't nothing but another Nebraska." With so much money and status on the line, professional sports teams have be-

come highly sought after, and their movements from city to city have led to public outrage, lawsuits, and legislative proposals.

The owners of professional sports teams have been able to obtain generous deals from city and state officials by threatening to move their franchises. If the owners do not receive the support they seek, they move their team to a more accommodating city. Typical benefits include the use of sports facilities at below-market rents and taxpayer funding for the construction and maintenance of new facilities. Most of the funding comes from the team's home state, but some funding comes from the federal government.

At times, owners have moved their teams even after receiving what they demanded. Harris County, Texas, incurred $67.5 million in bond indebtedness in 1987 to finance stadium improvements to keep the Houston Oilers football team from moving to Jacksonville, Florida. After the 1997 season, the Oilers will be playing in Nashville, Tennessee, and Harris County, without the Oilers, will still be paying off its bonds.

Owners have been able to achieve their powerful bargaining positions largely through the judicial construction of antitrust laws. Courts have given each major league the power to restrain trade by limiting the number of franchises within the league. At the same

time, courts have limited the ability of the leagues to prevent team relocations by finding that such restrictions are unreasonable restraints of trade. For example, a federal court found that the NFL rule requiring the approval of three-fourths of the teams in the league before a team could move was an unreasonable restraint of trade (*Los Angeles Memorial Coliseum Commission v. NFL*, 726 F.2d 1381 [9th Cir. 1984]).

The judicial holdings have emboldened the owners of professional sports teams. The owners' willingness to move their teams has led to frenzied bidding wars between cities and the relocation of many franchises.

The owners' laissez-faire attitude has been roundly criticized by fans, but owners have simply followed their best business instincts. Owning a professional sports team is a risky, speculative endeavor, and owners must act to protect their interests and maximize the values of their franchises. Owners are split on the issue of franchise relocation. Most owners understand that much of the value of their franchises depends on fan loyalty and that loyalty decreases as teams move. At the same time, the antitrust decisions have created a seller's market for owners, allowing them to seek the best deal possible. If another city is more willing to provide support for a team, there is little reason for the owner to stay put.

The most important bargaining chip for many owners is the team's stadium

ninety percent. Players with bargaining power do not sign contracts with such option clauses.

Another product of Miller's collective bargaining for the MLBPA was arbitration of salary disputes. The MLBPA was concerned about a perceived tendency of club owners to collude against demanding players. Specifically, players who played out their options were finding that no teams were interested in hiring them for their FAIR MARKET VALUE. In 1976, the year after the Messersmith-McNally case, the MLBPA and the club owners agreed that any player with at least two years of experience who was ineli-

gible for free agency could renegotiate his salary through a neutral arbitrator.

The spirit of cooperation over salaries was short lived. In 1986 the MLBPA alleged that the club owners had colluded against free agents by agreeing amongst themselves to offer relatively low salaries to free agents. The MLBPA filed a grievance in 1986, and in 1988 an arbitration panel ordered the teams to pay more than $10 million to 139 players who had been harmed by the COLLUSION. In 1988 another arbitration panel found that the club owners had continued to collude over the 1987 and or arena. Typically, owners lease a stadium or arena for a certain number of years. When the lease is up, or sometimes before it has expired, an owner may demand public funding for a new stadium or improvements to the old stadium. If the city or state does not ante up for a new stadium or improvements, the owner threatens to move the team. Sometimes the community reluctantly foots the bill. When this happens, persons who object to the public financing of an essentially private business may attempt to stop the funding through the judiciary, but they usually fail. Most courts hold that the use of public funds to build or improve sports stadiums is a legal expenditure for a legitimate public purpose. Sometimes a community refuses to bow to an owner's demands and the team leaves. Other times the city or state attempts to prevent the relocation of a team by taking legal action.

The city of Baltimore, Maryland, tried to keep its NFL team, the Colts, through the exercise of eminent domain. Eminent domain is the power of a government to take private property for public use, with compensation to the party deprived of the property. In early 1984 the Baltimore Colts were having difficulty obtaining a satisfactory lease for Baltimore's Memorial Stadium. Owner Robert Irsay began to receive solicitations from the city of Indianapolis, Indiana, for the Colts to play in the city's Hoosier Dome. In February 1984 the Maryland Senate entertained a bill that would give the city of Baltimore the authority to condemn and take over professional sports franchises, but it postponed a vote on the bill.

On February 28, 1984, the U.S. Court of Appeals for the Ninth Circuit announced its decision in the *Los Angeles Memorial Coliseum* case, which affirmed the right of Oakland Raiders' owner Al Davis to move the team to Los Angeles. The NFL told Irsay in a private meeting that, in light of the decision in the Raiders' case, it would not oppose any move by the Colts. Irsay continued to negotiate for a financial package that would keep the Colts in Baltimore until he learned that the Maryland Senate had passed the eminent domain legislation.

Irsay decided to move the Colts to Indianapolis immediately. That day, vice president and general manager Michael Chernoff arranged for a moving company to come to the Colts' training facility and load the team equipment into vans. The Colts left Baltimore, their home city for thirty years, during the night of March 28–29, 1984.

On March 30, 1984, the Maryland Senate passed an emergency bill that gave the city of Baltimore the power of eminent domain over the team. The city immediately passed an ordinance that authorized the condemnation and then filed a petition in court, seeking to acquire the Colts by eminent domain and to prevent the team from doing anything to further the movement of the franchise, but it was too late. A federal court eventually held in December 1985 that Baltimore did not have the power of eminent domain over the Colts because it had not attempted to compensate the franchise and because the franchise had relocated to another state (*Indianapolis Colts v. Mayor of Baltimore*, 741 F.2d 954 [7th Cir. 1984], cert. denied, 470 U.S. 1052, 105 S. Ct. 1753, 84 L. Ed. 2d 817 [1985]).

Sports fans in Baltimore grew even more beleaguered after the Colts' departure. Their last remaining major professional sports team, the Baltimore Orioles, threatened to move if it did not get a new stadium. In 1990 the state of Maryland was forced to spend millions in taxpayer funds to build a new stadium to keep the Orioles. In 1996 Baltimore regained an NFL franchise at the expense of Cleveland, which lost its beloved Browns after fifty years in part because Baltimore offered the Browns free rent at a new football stadium. The city of Baltimore enjoyed the new Baltimore Ravens' inaugural season in 1996 as dedicated Browns fans suffered through the same nightmare that Colts fans endured in 1984.

Lawmakers on the federal, state, and local levels have proposed legislation that would help communities hang on to their professional sports teams. In 1995 and 1996, several legislators in the U.S. Congress proposed laws that would allow leagues to make their own rules restricting the movement of franchises. For all the activity, no legislation changing the application of antitrust laws to professional sports teams has been passed.

See also Antitrust Law; Eminent Domain; Franchise; Restraint of Trade.

1988 seasons to keep player salaries low or keep players out of the game, and in 1990 the owners were forced to pay players more than $100 million in lost salaries. The arbitration process now is applied to a number of disputes between players and management, including disputes about fines, suspensions, and other punitive measures taken by a club or by the league.

Labor issues are another chief concern of professional athletes. In major sporting leagues, players' unions and management enter into collective bargaining agreements that establish standards and cover the basic rights and duties of all major league players and club owners. Collective bargaining agreements address such issues as club discipline, injury grievances, noninjury grievances, discipline by the commissioner of Major League Baseball, standard player's contract, college drafts, option clauses, terminations of contracts, base salaries, access to personnel files, medical rights, retirement and insurance benefits, and the duration of the existing COLLECTIVE BARGAINING AGREEMENT.

Collective bargaining agreements last only for specified periods of time, so occasionally they need to be renewed. If the players are collectively unable to come to an agreement with the club owners, players may go on strike to gain what they feel they deserve or prevent the owners from enforcing detrimental regulations, such as a salary cap on the amount a club can spend on its payroll. The 1994–95 professional hockey season was shortened by a players' strike. The MLBPA also conducted a strike that began on August 12, 1994, lasted through the end of the 1994 season, and ended in March 1995. The players conducted the strike to thwart a proposed salary cap, and it ended without a new collective bargaining agreement or a final resolution of the salary cap issue.

The four most popular team sports in the United States—baseball, football, basketball, and hockey—have created leagues that exercise monopolistic powers. Owners of the professional teams in Major League Baseball, the National Football League (NFL), the National Basketball Association, and the National Hockey League have been able to keep the number of FRANCHISES lower than they would be in a free market. This artificially created scarcity gives owners of these teams leverage to force fans and taxpayers in cities across the country to provide billions of dollars in subsidies or risk losing professional sports entertainment. The scarcity also ensures a high level of talent in the league, making the creation of new leagues difficult.

Courts and legislators have been successful in removing some elements of antitrust activity, such as limits on the freedom of movement of players. One court has held that the National Football League violated antitrust laws by unreasonably restricting the right of owners to move their franchises (*Los Angeles Memorial Coliseum Commission v. National Football League*, 726 F.2d 1381 [9th Cir. 1984]). However, by and large, courts and legislators have been unable or unwilling to strike down or repeal other monopolistic activities. Legislators have even taken steps to give certain leagues special privileges. Under federal law the NFL may enter into agreements with television networks to pool and sell a unitary video package (15 U.S.C.A. § 1291 [1966]). Another federal law allows blackouts of nonlocal NFL games televised into home territories when the home team is playing and blackouts of home games in the home team's territory (15 U.S.C.A. § 1292 [1966]).

A professional sport is a complex business for the average athlete, and many athletes require the services of an AGENT. Agents negotiate personal service contracts with teams or individual promoters, and they manage the personal affairs of their clients. Agents may handle such concerns as taxes, financial planning, money management, investments, income tax preparation, incorporation, estate planning, endorsements, medical treatment, counseling, development of a career after sports, insurance, and legal matters. The agent is a FIDUCIARY of the client-athlete, which means that the agent has a responsibility to act with the utmost care and GOOD FAITH and to act in the athlete's best interests. Agents must avoid activities that conflict with the interests of the client-athlete, and they must inform the athlete of any circumstances that might affect the athlete's rights or interests. Many states require that agents obtain a license and post a security BOND before they may work in the state.

Torts in Sports Many sports pose serious dangers to participants. Generally, a person who suffers a sports-related INJURY may recover for medical expenses and other losses if the injury was caused by the NEGLIGENCE of another party. Injuries and DAMAGES resulting from intentional torts, such as BATTERY or ASSAULT, likewise are recoverable.

Courts generally decide suits involving injuries to athletes, spectators, and other parties involved in sports according to basic TORT LAWS. If a party owes a DUTY of CARE toward another party and that duty is breached, the party owing the duty is liable for any injuries suffered by the party to whom the duty is owed that result from the breach. The level of care that must be exercised depends on the situation: dangerous situations require a high degree of care, whereas less dangerous situations require less care. Expectations may also play a part. For example, a spectator who is hit by a foul ball while sitting in the stands at a baseball game cannot recover for injuries because most fans know that stray balls in the stands are an inescapable by-product of baseball. However, a patron who is standing in the interior walkway of a stadium concourse may recover for injuries resulting from a foul ball. A spectator in the unfamiliar environs of a stadium is not aware of the dangers and thus is owed a greater duty of care by the baseball organization.

Athletes may recover for injuries resulting from another party's negligence or intentional acts. Athletes in contact sports consent to some physical contact, but courts do not find that participants consent to contact that goes outside the bounds of the game. This is true for professional sports as well as amateur sports.

In some cases schools may be held liable for injuries to athletes. If an employee of the school, such as a coach, teacher, or referee, fails to properly supervise a student and the student suffers an injury as a result of the failure to supervise, the school may be held liable for its employee's negligence. Generally, coaches, teachers, and referees must exercise reasonable care to prevent foreseeable injuries.

Defendants in sports-related PERSONAL INJURY suits may possess any number of defenses. One of the most successful of these defenses is that the party assumed the RISK of being injured by playing in or watching the sporting event. Defendants also may argue that the plaintiff was negligent and therefore should recover only a portion of his damages or nothing at all. For example, a plaintiff may have ignored warnings or signed a document that waived the defendant's LIABILITY for any injury suffered by the plaintiff. Finally, public institutions may argue that they are immune from suit under the doctrine of sovereign IMMUNITY, a judicial doctrine that prohibits suits against government entities unless such suits have been explicitly authorized by the government. Legislators have made many public institutions open to lawsuits, and in cases where a public institution still enjoys immunity, courts often find ways to circumvent immunity and attach liability.

CROSS-REFERENCES
Drugs and Narcotics; Employment Law; Entertainment Law; Monopoly.

SPOT ZONING 📖 The granting to a particular parcel of land a classification concerning its use that differs from the classification of other land in the immediate area. 📖

Spot zoning is invalid because it amounts to an arbitrary, capricious, and unreasonable treatment of a limited area within a particular district and is, therefore, a deviation from the comprehensive plan.

See also LAND-USE CONTROL; ZONING.

SPOUSAL ABUSE See DOMESTIC VIOLENCE.

SQUATTER 📖 An individual who settles on the land of another person without any legal authority to do so, or without acquiring a LEGAL TITLE. 📖

In the past, the term *squatter* specifically applied to an individual who settled on public land. Currently it is used interchangeably with *intruder* and *trespasser.*

SS 📖 An abbreviation used in the portion of an AFFIDAVIT, PLEADING, or record known as the statement of VENUE. 📖

The abbreviation is read as "to wit" and is intended to be a contraction of the Latin term *scilicet.*

STALE CHECK 📖 A document that is a promise to pay money that is held for too long

a period of time before being presented for payment. 📖

A CHECK is considered to be stale when it is outstanding for a period of six months or more. A bank is not obligated to pay a stale check.

See also COMMERCIAL PAPER.

STALIN, JOSEPH Joseph Stalin was the leader of the Soviet Union and the Communist party from 1929 to 1953. He used ruthless methods to consolidate his power and ruled the Soviet Union by terror. His actions shaped the relationship between the United States and the Soviet Union, leading to the COLD WAR after World War II.

Stalin was born Iosif Vissarionovich Dzhugashvili on December 21, 1879, in Gori, now in the Republic of Georgia. He adopted the name Stalin, meaning "man of steel," in 1910. The son of peasants, his academic prowess led to a scholarship at a theological seminary. While studying for the priesthood, he began reading the works of KARL MARX. He soon left the seminary and joined the Social-Democratic party in 1899. His revolutionary activities led to his arrest and exile to Siberia seven times between 1902 and 1913. He escaped six times.

He aligned himself with the Bolshevik faction of the party, which was under the leadership of VLADIMIR ILYICH LENIN. Lenin named Stalin to the Bolshevik's Central Committee in 1912 and in 1913 named him editor of the party newspaper, *Pravda.* He spent from 1913 until

Joseph Stalin expanded the influence of the Soviet Union following World War II by refusing to withdraw Soviet forces from much of Germany and Eastern Europe.

GAMMA

early 1917 in Siberian exile, returning to St. Petersburg to aid the Bolsheviks in overthrowing first the monarchy and then the provisional government. The November 1917 Bolshevik REVOLUTION put Lenin in charge. Stalin became a top aid to Lenin and helped the regime in winning a civil war against those who opposed the Bolsheviks.

In the early 1920s, Stalin began plotting to gain power. Before Lenin died in 1924, he expressed misgivings about Stalin's use of power. Nevertheless, Stalin joined in a three-man leadership group, called a troika, to govern the Soviet Union after Lenin's death. He quickly pushed aside all his rivals, including Leon Trotsky, and became the supreme ruler by 1929.

During the 1930s Stalin collectivized all private farms in the Soviet Union and in the process sent a million farmers into exile. He embarked on a process of "russification," which put minority nationalities under strict control of the national government. In 1939, in concert with the Nazi government of ADOLF HITLER, Stalin invaded eastern Poland. In 1940 he conquered the Baltic countries of Estonia, Latvia, and Lithuania.

Stalin also encouraged the growth of COMMUNISM throughout the world. The Communist party of the United States grew rapidly during the Great Depression of the 1930s, in the process raising questions whether the party was a mere tool of Stalin and the international Communist movement. As a result of concerns about Communist subversion, Congress enacted the SMITH ACT (54 Stat. 670) in 1940. The legislation required ALIENS to register and be fingerprinted by the federal government. More importantly, the act made it illegal not only to conspire to overthrow the government but to advocate or conspire to advocate its overthrow. The U.S. Supreme Court upheld the constitutionality of the act in *Dennis v. United States*, 341 U.S. 494, 71 S. Ct. 857, 95 L. Ed. 1137 (1951).

Stalin's 1939 nonaggression pact with Hitler proved futile: Hitler invaded the Soviet Union in 1941. Stalin then aligned the Soviet Union with the United States and Great Britain in World War II. When the war in Europe ended in 1945, the Soviet Army occupied Eastern Europe and a large part of Germany. Stalin ignored agreements between the Allies and proceeded to impose Communist rule on these occupied countries.

The United States and Great Britain perceived Stalin's actions as attempts to force Communism on the world. In the late 1940s, the Soviet Union was captioned by the United States as the Red Menace, seeking to subvert democracy and capitalism. Stalin pushed the United States to the brink of a third world war when he ordered the blockade of Berlin in 1948 and 1949.

Fears about Communism were further stirred by the arrest of JULIUS AND ETHEL ROSENBERG in 1950 for providing the Soviet Union with secrets about the atomic bomb. To many people, the Rosenbergs were tools of Stalin and the Communist CONSPIRACY. Other people, however, saw them as victims of political hysteria. The Rosenbergs were executed in 1953, yet several generations of historians have argued over their guilt or innocence.

Stalin's hard-line policies were met in kind by the West. In 1949 the United States created the NORTH ATLANTIC TREATY ORGANIZATION, which committed U.S. forces to the defense of Europe. The outbreak of the KOREAN WAR in 1950, which was started by Communists in North Korea, led to the deployment of U.S. troops to stave off Communist aggression. Stalin's determination to expand Soviet power and influence created the climate for the Cold War. The United States practiced a policy of containment, with the goal of preventing the spread of Communism.

In his later years, Stalin literally rewrote the Soviet history books, turning himself into a heroic, godlike figure. Those who opposed him were exiled to Siberian labor camps or executed. Always suspicious of those around him, in 1953 he prepared to purge more party leaders. His plans were cut short, however, when he suffered a brain hemorrhage and died on March 5, 1953, in Moscow.

Stalin's methods were replicated by later Soviet leaders. The demise of European Communist regimes in the 1980s and the collapse of the Soviet Union in the 1990s signaled an end to Stalinism.

See also DENNIS V. UNITED STATES; RED SCARE.

STALKING 📖 Criminal activity consisting of the repeated following and harassing of another person. 📖

Stalking is a distinctive form of criminal activity composed of a series of actions that taken individually might constitute legal behavior. For example, sending flowers, writing love notes, and waiting for someone outside her place of work are actions that, on their own, are not criminal. When these actions are coupled with an intent to instill fear or injury, however, they may constitute a pattern of behavior that is illegal. Though anti-stalking laws are gender neutral, most stalkers are men and most victims are women.

Stalking first attracted widespread public concern when a young actress named Rebecca Shaeffer, who was living in California, was shot to death by an obsessed fan who had stalked her for two years. The case drew extensive media coverage and revealed how widespread a problem stalking was to both celebrity and noncelebrity victims. Until the enactment of anti-stalking laws, police had little power to arrest someone who behaved in a threatening but legal way. Even when the suspect had followed his victim, sent her hate mail, or behaved in a threatening manner, the police were without legal recourse. Law enforcement could not take action until the suspect himself first acted on his threats and assaulted or injured the victim.

In general, stalking victims are women from all walks of life, and most are trying to end a relationship with a man, often one who has been abusive. The persons involved may be married or divorced or may have been sexual partners. In other cases the stalker and the victim may know one another casually or be associated in an informal or formal way. For example, they may have had one or two dates or talked briefly but were not sexual partners, or they may be coworkers or former coworkers. In a small number of situations, the stalker and the victim do not know one another. Cases involving celebrities and other public figures usually fall into this category.

Advocates of battered women have estimated that up to 80 percent of stalking cases occur in a domestic context, though there is little data on how many stalkers and victims are former intimates, how many murdered women were stalked beforehand, or how many stalking incidents overlap with DOMESTIC VIOLENCE. Estimates of the number of stalkers in the United States vary from 20,000 to 200,000.

Research also indicates that teenagers are subjected to stalking and that they have difficulty extricating themselves from such situations. Stalkers may include a high school classmate or an older man with whom a teenager has developed a relationship. When a teenage stalker is involved, the victim may have difficulty convincing law enforcement and school officials that the behavior is more than adolescent "boys will be boys" conduct.

The motivations for stalking are many. They include the desire for contact and control, obsession, jealousy, and anger and stem from the real or imagined relationship between the victim and the stalker. The stalker may feel intense attraction or extreme hatred. Many stalkers stop their activity when confronted by police intervention, but many do not. The more trouble-some stalker may exhibit a personality disorder, such as obsessive-compulsive behavior, which leads him to devote an inordinate amount of time to writing notes and letters to the intended target, tracking the victim's movements, or traveling in an attempt to achieve an encounter.

The potentially dangerous consequences and the terrifying helplessness victims experienced led to calls for legislation criminalizing stalking. California enacted the first anti-stalking law in 1990, and by 1996 forty-nine states and the District of Columbia had passed legislation that addresses the problem of stalking. Initially these laws varied widely, containing provisions that made the laws virtually unenforceable due to ambiguities and the dual requirements to show specific criminal intent and a credible threat. Many states have amended these stalking statutes to broaden definitions, refine wording, stiffen penalties, and emphasize the suspect's pattern of activity.

In most states, to charge and convict a defendant of stalking, several elements must be proved BEYOND A REASONABLE DOUBT. These elements include a course of conduct or behavior, the presence of threats, and the criminal INTENT to cause fear in the victim.

A course of conduct is a series of acts that, viewed collectively, present a pattern of behavior. Some states stipulate the requisite number of acts, with several requiring the stalker to commit two or more acts. States designate as stalking a variety of acts, ranging from specifically defined actions, such as nonconsensual communication or lying in wait, to more general types of action, such as harassment.

Most states require that the stalker pose a threat or act in a way that causes a REASONABLE PERSON to feel fearful. The threat does not have to be written or verbal to instill fear. For example, a stalker can convey a threat by sending the victim black roses, forming his hand into a gun and pointing it at her, or delivering a dead animal to her doorstep.

To be convicted of stalking in most states, the stalker must display a criminal intent to cause fear in the victim. Various statutes require the conduct of the stalker to be "willful," "purposeful," "intentional," or "knowing." Many states do not require proof that the defendant intended to cause fear as long as he intended to commit the act that resulted in fear. In these states, if the victim is reasonably frightened by the alleged perpetrator's conduct, the intent element of the crime has been met.

Defendants have challenged the constitutionality of anti-stalking statutes in more than twenty states. They have alleged that the laws

How To Stop a Stalker

Although antistalking laws give police and prosecutors the tools to arrest and charge stalkers with serious criminal offenses, victims of stalking have an important role to play in making these laws work. Law enforcement officials, domestic violence counselors, and mental health professionals offer the following advice to victims on how to stop a stalker:

- *Know the law.* Because antistalking laws are new, some police officers may not know how the laws work. A stalking victim should visit the public library or a county law library and obtain a copy of the state's antistalking law. Victims should show the police the law when filing the stalking complaint and ask whether they should first seek a protective order against the stalker. In some states a violation of a protective order converts a stalking charge from a misdemeanor to a felony.
- *Cooperate with prosecutors.* Many stalking victims refuse to prosecute the stalker, thereby leaving themselves vulnerable to continued threats and violence. Some victims fear that prosecution will provoke worse behavior from the perpetrator. Nevertheless, victims should use the legal system and break any bond that may exist between themselves and the stalker.
- *Protect yourself.* Persons who are stalked should take steps to protect themselves and those around them. Neighbors and coworkers should be informed about the stalker, be given a photograph of the suspect, and be instructed on what to do if the stalker is sighted. Security officers at the victim's workplace should be provided with this information. Caller ID, which identifies telephone callers, should be installed on the victim's telephone. If the stalker makes repeated phone calls, the victim should ask the police to set up a phone tap.
- *Collect evidence.* A stalking victim should collect and preserve evidence that can be used to prosecute and convict the stalker. Police suggest that the victim keep a diary of stalking and other crimes committed by the perpetrator. It is also a good idea to photograph property destroyed by the stalker and any injuries inflicted by the stalker. The victim should keep all letters or notes written by the stalker and all answering machine tapes that contain messages from the perpetrator.

are so VAGUE as to violate DUE PROCESS OF LAW or are so broad that they infringe upon constitutionally protected speech or activity. Generally the courts have rejected these arguments and have upheld the anti-stalking laws.

Once a stalker is arrested, the prosecutor will ask the court to impose strict pretrial release conditions requiring the defendant to stay away from the victim. Violation of these conditions can lead to the revocation of BAIL and enhanced penalties at SENTENCING.

Before a stalker is arrested, a victim may obtain a civil protection, or restraining, order that directs the defendant not to contact or come within the vicinity of the victim. If the defendant violates the protection order, a court may hold him in contempt, impose fines, or incarcerate him, depending on state law. In some states a stalking penalty is enhanced if the stalker violates a PROTECTIVE ORDER.

Protective orders can serve as the first formal means of intervening in a stalking situation. The order puts the stalker on notice that his behavior is unwanted and that if his behavior continues, police can take more severe action. However, enforcement of a protection order has proved difficult, leaving the victim with not much more than a legal document to try to restrain a violent stalker.

Many states have both MISDEMEANOR and FELONY classifications for stalking. Misdemeanors generally carry a JAIL sentence of up to one year. Felony sentences range from three to five years, with the ability to enhance the penalty if one or more elements are present. For example, if the defendant brandished a gun, violated a protective order, committed a previous stalking offense, or directed his conduct toward a child, the sentence may be increased. In some states repeat offenses can result in INCARCERATION for as long as ten years.

Despite the nationwide awareness of stalking and the response of the criminal justice system, many women do not report these crimes to police. Failure to report stalking may be based on the private nature of the events and the belief that no purpose would be served by reporting the crime. Police departments and prosecutors have been criticized for continuing to minimize the seriousness of stalking and failing to provide adequate protection for victims. In addition, critics have claimed that courts are too lenient in sentencing stalkers.

See also VICTIMS OF CRIME.

STAMP ACT 📖 English act of 1765 requiring that revenue stamps be affixed to all official documents in the American colonies. 📖

In 1765 the British Parliament, under the leadership of Prime Minister George Grenville, passed the Stamp Act, the first DIRECT TAX on the American colonies. The revenue measure was intended to help pay the debt incurred by the British in fighting the French and Indian War (1756–63) and to pay for the continuing defense of the colonies. Unexpectedly and to Parliament's great surprise, the Stamp Act ignited colonial opposition and outrage, leading to the first concerted effort by the colonists to resist Parliament and British authority. Though the act was repealed the following year, the events surrounding the tax protest became the first steps towards revolution and independence from England.

By the mid-eighteenth century, the economies of the American colonies had matured. The colonies chafed under the rules of British mercantilism, which sought to exploit the colonies as a source of raw materials and a market for the mother country. During the French and Indian War, the colonies asserted their economic independence by trading with the enemy, flagrantly defying customs laws, and evading trade regulations. These actions convinced the British government to bring the colonies into proper subordination and to use them as a source of revenue.

The colonists had become accustomed to a limited degree of British regulation of trade. The Navigation Acts of 1660, for example, stipulated that no goods or commodities could be imported into or exported out of any British colony except in British ships. Later legislation stipulated that rice, molasses, beaver skins, furs, and naval stores could be shipped only to England. Duties were also imposed on the shipment of certain articles, such as rum and spirits. However, the Stamp Act was the first direct tax, a tax on domestically produced and consumed items, that Parliament ever levied upon the colonists.

The Stamp Act was designed to raise almost one-third of the revenue to support the military establishment permanently stationed in the colonies at the end of the French and Indian War. The act placed a tax on newspapers, almanacs, pamphlets and broadsides, legal documents of all kinds, insurance policies, ship's papers, licenses, and even playing cards and dice. These documents and objects had to carry a tax stamp. The act was to be enforced by stamp agents, with penalties for violating the act to be imposed by vice-admiralty courts, which sat without juries.

Parliament passed the act without debate. Similar stamp acts had become an accepted part of raising revenues in England, leading parliamentary leaders to mistakenly believe that the measure would generate some grumbling but not defiance. The colonies thought otherwise, interpreting the Stamp Act as a deliberate attempt to undercut their commercial strength and independence. They were also concerned about the implicit assault on their rights to trial by jury, the unprecedented use of a direct tax as a means of raising imperial revenue, and the all-inclusive character of the law that applied to all thirteen colonies.

The colonists raised the issue of taxation without representation. Some colonists drew a distinction between the English regulation of trade, which was viewed as legal, and the English imposition of internal taxes on the colonies, which was perceived to be illegal. Theories and arguments against the Stamp Act were distributed from assembly to assembly in the form of "circulars." PATRICK HENRY introduced seven resolutions against the Stamp Act in the Virginia House of Burgesses, five of which were passed. All seven resolutions were reprinted in newspapers such as the *Virginia Resolves.* These and other pamphlets pressed Parliament to repeal the act.

In October 1765 nine of the thirteen colonies sent delegates to New York to attend the Stamp Act Congress. The congress issued a "Declaration of Rights and Grievances," declaring that English subjects in the colonies had the same "rights and liberties" as the king's subjects in England. The congress, noting that the colonies were not represented in Parliament, concluded that no taxes could be constitutionally imposed on them except by their own legislatures. Petitions embracing these resolutions were prepared for submission to the king, the House of Commons, and the House of Lords.

The Stamp Act also led to the formation of formal opposition groups in the colonies. The Sons of Liberty, which remained active until the American Revolution, grew directly out of the Stamp Act controversy. Often organized by men of wealth and standing in the community, Sons of Liberty groups were active in towns throughout the colonies, and their members often engaged in violent acts. In Boston, for example, an angry mob forced the stamp agent to resign.

Colonial merchants also organized an effective economic BOYCOTT, with merchants in New York, Boston, and Philadelphia entering into nonimportation agreements. The drop in trade was dramatic, leading to the BANKRUPTCY of some London merchants. In addition, businesses flouted the act by carrying on their trade without purchasing the required stamps.

The virulence of the opposition to the Stamp Act surprised the colonists as much as the British government. The costs of simply maintaining order in the colonies threatened to negate any economic advantages of the legislation. BENJAMIN FRANKLIN, as the colonial agent for Pennsylvania, testified before the House of Commons in early 1766 that any attempt to enforce the Stamp Act by the use of troops might bring on rebellion. His call for repeal was joined by a committee of English merchants, which cited the dire economic consequences the act was producing. When Grenville's government fell from power, the new prime minister, Marquis of Rockingham, moved quickly to resolve the issue. In February 1766 the repeal of the Stamp Act was approved by the House of Commons. The House of Lords, under pressure from the king, approved the repeal as well, which became effective in May 1766. Nevertheless, in the Declaratory Act of March 1766, Parliament ominously asserted that it had full authority to make laws that were legally binding on the colonies.

England's need for revenue and Parliament's conviction that it alone, in the empire, was sovereign did not end with the repeal of the Stamp Act. New and harsher laws were enacted in succeeding years, producing a predictable reaction from the colonies. The full significance of the Stamp Act crisis is that it served as the initial event unifying all the colonies in their resistance to parliamentary authority. The opponents to the act laid a theoretical foundation for later revolutionary thought in their elaboration of the doctrine of consent by the governed. The act led to the creation of enduring resistance groups, such as the Sons of Liberty, which were capable of springing into action at the least provocation. And it established precedents for later resistance, including the use of a congress, the issuance of circulars, the resort to legislative resolves, and the adoption of economic sanctions. Most importantly, the Stamp Act crisis made the colonists more aware of the identity of their interests, which would ultimately lead them to think of themselves as "Americans."

CROSS-REFERENCES

Continental Congress; Declaration of Independence; Paine, Thomas; Townshend Acts; War of Independence.

BIOGRAPHY

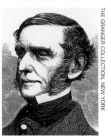

THE GRANGER COLLECTION, NEW YORK

Henry Stanbery

"THE CONSTITUTION IS . NOT SILENT. IT PROVIDES FOR INSURRECTION, WHETHER SMALL OR GREAT; . . . WHETHER IN ONE STATE OR MANY."

STAMP TAX ◫ A pecuniary charge imposed upon certain transactions. ◫

A stamp tax is, for example, levied when ownership of REAL PROPERTY is transferred. The tax is paid either by purchasing stamps that are then glued to the DEED or by the use of metering machines that imprint the stamps on the deed.

STANBERY, HENRY Henry Stanbery served as attorney general of the United States from 1866 to 1868 under President ANDREW JOHNSON.

Stanbery, the son of Jonas Stanbery, a physician, was born February 20, 1803, in New York. He moved with his family from New York to Zanesville, Ohio, in 1814. An excellent student, Stanbery required greater academic challenge than early Zanesville schools could provide. Recognizing his scholastic aptitude, his father made arrangements for him to attend Washington College, in Pennsylvania. He graduated in 1819 at the age of sixteen.

Stanbery studied law, and he was admitted to the bar in 1824 when he came of age. The same year, he entered into practice with Thomas Ewing, an attorney from Lancaster County, Ohio. They worked together for more than twenty years and handled a wide variety of cases.

Stanbery's growing prominence in the Ohio courts made him a natural candidate for public office. He dissolved his longtime partnership with Ewing in 1846 and moved to Columbus to serve as Ohio's first attorney general. He also served as a delegate to the convention that framed the Ohio state constitution in 1851. After the constitutional convention, Stanbery reestablished his private practice—first in Cincinnati (1853) and later in northern Kentucky (1857). He maintained an active law practice throughout the Civil War.

After the Civil War, Stanbery became embroiled in the conflict and controversy surrounding Johnson's presidency. Johnson supported the policies of reconstruction and reconciliation favored by the late president ABRAHAM LINCOLN, but his efforts were met with strong opposition from Radical Republicans in

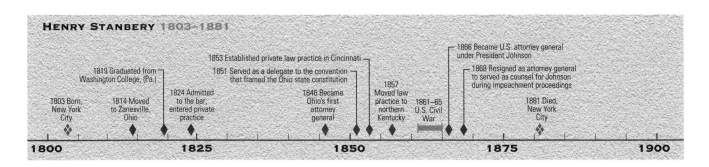

HENRY STANBERY 1803–1881

1803 Born, New York City

1814 Moved to Zanesville, Ohio

1819 Graduated from Washington College, (Pa.)

1824 Admitted to the bar; entered private practice

1846 Became Ohio's first attorney general

1851 Served as a delegate to the convention that framed the Ohio state constitution

1853 Established private law practice in Cincinnati

1857 Moved law practice to northern Kentucky

1861–65 U.S. Civil War

1866 Became U.S. attorney general under President Johnson

1868 Resigned as attorney general to served as counsel for Johnson during impeachment proceedings

1881 Died, New York City

1800   1825   1850   1875   1900

the Senate. Johnson's first attorney general, JAMES SPEED, resigned in 1866 when he could no longer support presidential initiatives.

Amid this turmoil, Stanbery was asked to step in, and accepted the post of attorney general. Almost immediately, he was nominated by Johnson to fill a U.S. Supreme Court vacancy left by the death of Justice JOHN CATRON. Most senators liked the new attorney general and recognized him to be an able lawyer, but Radical Republicans were determined to prevent the confirmation of *any* nominee put forth by Johnson. To ensure that Johnson would not be able to fill the vacancy, the Senate enacted legislation to reduce the number of High Court justices from ten to seven as vacancies occurred. Accordingly, the seat for which Stanbery had been considered in April 1866 was abolished, and his nomination was never considered.

Although sixty-three years old and in failing health, Stanbery served Johnson as a loyal and active attorney general. Prior to Stanbery's appointment, the president had vetoed early CIVIL RIGHTS legislation and was eager to restore full JURISDICTION to Southern state courts. As attorney general, Stanbery supported Johnson by refusing to encourage enforcement of the civil rights acts or providing any guidance to U.S. attorneys seeking to implement them.

When Johnson faced IMPEACHMENT by the Senate in March 1868, Stanbery resigned his office to serve as the president's counsel. So poor was Stanbery's physical health during Johnson's impeachment trial that he submitted most of his arguments in writing. Upon termination of the trial, Johnson sought to reappoint his friend and counsel as attorney general, but the Senate rejected Stanbery's reinstatement.

Stanbery remained in Washington, D.C., for the next few years and continued to participate in high-profile cases of the Reconstruction Era—including a number of cases that tested the constitutionality of the government's criminal prosecutions of the KU KLUX KLAN.

In the mid-1870s, Stanbery returned to Ohio and served a short term as president of the Cincinnati Bar Association. In retirement, he wrote occasionally on political and legal topics, but he devoted most of his time to the management of his vast property holdings. The year before his death, a newspaper account identified him as the largest property owner in Campbell County, Kentucky. Stanbery died in New York on June 26, 1881.

STAND ▥ The location in a courtroom where the parties and witnesses offer their testimony. To appear in court; to submit to the JURISDICTION of the court. ▥

To stand trial, for example, means to try, or be tried on, a particular issue in a particular court.

STANDARD DEDUCTION ▥ The name given to a fixed amount of money that may be subtracted from the ADJUSTED GROSS INCOME of a taxpayer who does not itemize certain living expenses for INCOME TAX purposes. ▥

STANDING ▥ The legally protectible stake or interest that an individual has in a dispute that entitles him to bring the controversy before the court to obtain judicial relief. ▥

Standing, sometimes referred to as standing to sue, is the name of the federal law doctrine that focuses on whether a prospective PLAINTIFF can show that some personal legal interest has been invaded by the DEFENDANT. It is not enough that a person is merely interested as a member of the general public in the resolution of the dispute. The person must have a personal stake in the outcome of the controversy.

The standing doctrine is derived from the U.S. Constitution's Article III provision that federal courts have the power to hear "cases" arising under federal law and "controversies" involving certain types of parties. In the most fundamental application of the philosophy of judicial restraint, the U.S. Supreme Court has interpreted this language to forbid the rendering of ADVISORY OPINIONS.

Once a federal court determines that a real CASE OR CONTROVERSY exists, it must then ascertain whether the parties to the litigation have standing. The Supreme Court has developed an elaborate body of principles defining the nature and scope of standing. Basically, a plaintiff must have suffered some direct or substantial injury or be likely to suffer such an injury if a particular wrong is not redressed. A defendant must be the party responsible for perpetrating the alleged legal wrong.

Most standing issues arise over the enforcement of an allegedly unconstitutional statute, ordinance, or policy. One may challenge a law or policy on constitutional grounds if he can show that enforcement of the law or implementation of the policy infringes on an individual constitutional right, such as FREEDOM OF SPEECH. For example, in *Tinker v. Des Moines Independent Community School District*, 393 U.S. 503, 89 S. Ct. 733, 21 L. Ed. 2d 731 (1969), high school officials in Des Moines, Iowa, had suspended students for wearing black armbands to school to protest U.S. involvement in the Vietnam War. There was no question that the parents of the students had standing to challenge the restrictions on the wearing of armbands. Mere ideological opposition to a particular government policy, such as the VIETNAM WAR, however, is not sufficient grounds to challenge that policy in court.

A significant economic injury or burden is sufficient to provide standing to sue, but in most situations a taxpayer does not have standing to challenge policies or programs that she is forced to support. In *Frothingham v. Mellon*, 288 F. 252 (C.A.D.C. 1923), the Supreme Court denied a federal taxpayer the right to challenge a federal program that she claimed violated the TENTH AMENDMENT, which reserves certain powers to the states. The Court said that a party must show some "direct injury as the result of the statute's enforcement, and not merely that he suffers in some indefinite way common with people generally."

Although the Supreme Court made a narrow exception to this prohibition on taxpayer suits in *Flast v. Cohen*, 392 U.S. 83, 88 S. Ct. 1942, 20 L. Ed. 2d 947 (1968), granting standing to a taxpayer to challenge federal spending that would benefit parochial schools, the Court has never gone beyond that. In fact, there is some doubt as to the vitality of the *Flast* decision. In 1974 the Court denied standing to a taxpayer who sought to challenge Congress's exempting the Central Intelligence Agency from the constitutional requirement under Article I, Section 9, Clause 7, that government expenditures be publicly reported (*United States v. Richardson*, 418 U.S. 166, 94 S. Ct. 2940, 41 L. Ed. 2d 678). Since *Richardson* the Court has continued to maintain the traditional barrier against taxpayer lawsuits.

The issue of standing has played a crucial role in CLASS ACTION lawsuits, especially those filed by environmental groups. In *Sierra Club v. Morton*, 405 U.S. 727, 92 S. Ct. 1361, 31 L. Ed. 2d 636 (1972), the Court denied standing to an environmental group that was challenging a decision by the secretary of the interior. The Court ruled that the Sierra Club had not demonstrated that its members would be substantially adversely affected by the secretary's decision. Later environmental class actions have

overcome the standing hurdle by including specific harms that group members would suffer, thus avoiding the Court's rule against generalized concerns.

The issue of standing is more than a technical aspect of the judicial process. A grant or denial of standing determines who may challenge government policies and what types of policies may be challenged. Those who believe that the FEDERAL COURTS should not increase their power generally believe standing should be used to limit access to the courts by persons or groups seeking to change PUBLIC POLICY. They believe the legislative branch should deal with these types of issues. Opponents of a strict standing test complain that plaintiffs never get a chance to prove their case in court. They believe that justice should not be denied by the application of judicially created doctrines such as standing.

See also JUDICIAL REVIEW.

STAND MUTE 📖 The state of affairs that arises when a defendant in a criminal action refuses to plead either guilty or not guilty. 📖

When a defendant stands mute, the court will generally order a not guilty PLEA to be entered.

STANFORD, AMASA LELAND Amasa Leland Stanford, known as Leland Stanford, along with partners Charles Crocker, Mark Hopkins, and Collis P. Huntington (the Big Four), founded the Central Pacific and Southern Pacific Rail Roads, and laid the tracks that would eventually link a nation. In the course of building the first transcontinental railroad, Stanford dominated California business, politics, and social life for almost fifty years.

Stanford was born on March 9, 1824, in Watervliet, New York. He was one of eight children born to Josiah Stanford and Elizabeth Phillips Stanford. His father was a prominent farmer and a prosperous merchant, who supplied building materials for the town's public works projects. Growing up, Stanford worked on the family farm and helped his father with local road and bridge construction. His boy-

BIOGRAPHY

LIBRARY OF CONGRESS

Amasa Leland Stanford

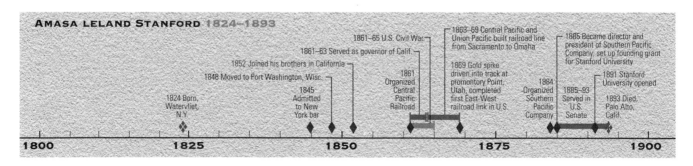

AMASA LELAND STANFORD 1824–1893

1824 Born, Watervliet, N.Y.

1845 Admitted to New York bar

1848 Moved to Port Washington, Wisc.

1852 Joined his brothers in California

1861 Organized Central Pacific Railroad

1861–63 Served as governor of Calif.

1861–65 U.S. Civil War

1863–69 Central Pacific and Union Pacific built railroad line from Sacramento to Omaha

1869 Gold spike driven into track at promontory Point, Utah, completed first East-West railroad link in U.S.

1884 Organized Southern Pacific Company

1885 Became director and president of Southern Pacific Company; set up founding grant for Stanford University

1885–93 Served in U.S. Senate

1891 Stanford University opened

1893 Died, Palo Alto, Calif.

1800   1825   1850   1875   1900

hood work on the local transportation infrastructure sparked an interest that would fuel his life's work.

Stanford's early education included attendance at the local public school and some home schooling. At eighteen, he enrolled at the Clinton Liberal Institute, in Clinton, New York. He completed his education at New York's Cazenovia Seminary. At twenty-one, he began clerking with the law firm of Wheaton, Doolittle, and Hadley, in Albany, New York. Three years later, in 1845, Stanford was admitted to the bar.

Like many young men of his era, Stanford saw tremendous opportunity for those who moved west. In 1848 he settled in Port Washington, Wisconsin, to establish a law practice. While Stanford was establishing his professional career in Wisconsin, several of his brothers headed to California, eager to apply their skills as merchants in its mining camps and growing towns.

In the spring of 1852, Stanford sent his wife, Jane Elizabeth Lathrop Stanford, to stay with her family in Albany, and he followed his brothers to the Pacific Coast. By all accounts, Stanford arrived in California with little or no money. His brothers provided him with a stock of miners' supplies and set him up as a merchant in a mining town. His business there was very successful. Popular with the miners and trained in the law, Stanford was often called upon to mediate claim disputes and other problems.

Convinced that his future was in California, Stanford persuaded his wife to join him there. In 1856 they established a home in Sacramento. Stanford continued to be involved with his brothers and their business interests, but he devoted most of his time—unsuccessfully—to politics.

He ran as a Republican candidate for state treasurer in 1857 and for governor in 1859. He was defeated in both races, but the campaigns made him a well-known political figure throughout the state. Finally, in 1861, when the outbreak of the Civil War split the state Democratic party, Stanford was successful in a bid for the governor's seat.

As the state's first Republican governor, he faced two immediate challenges: the possibility that California would split from the Union, and a serious flooding of the Sacramento River (which was so extensive that Stanford had to crawl out the window of his home and row himself to his inauguration). Stanford held California safely in the Union, and he coped with the damage caused by the flood. After providing for flood victims, and promoting mi-

nor administrative and legislative reforms, Stanford spent much of his time as governor pursuing his interest in RAILROADS as a growing industry.

Just before the Civil War, President ABRAHAM LINCOLN signed the PACIFIC RAILROAD ACT, authorizing the construction of a transcontinental railroad from Omaha to Sacramento. Despite the coming war, investors and entrepreneurs across the United States looked for ways to participate in, and profit from, the new venture.

Prior to his election as governor, Stanford and three other Sacramento merchants— Crocker, Hopkins, and Huntington—had financed railroad feasibility surveys and had organized the Central Pacific Rail Road Company on June 28, 1861. Stanford was named president.

During his two-year term as governor, Stanford committed a substantial amount of public money to the construction of the Central Pacific Rail Road. Any apprehensions Stanford may have had about mingling his official actions with his private interests were overshadowed by his conviction that a rail connection with the East would benefit all citizens of California.

When his term as governor expired, Stanford left government to construct his railroad. On January 8, 1863, workers from the Central Pacific Rail Road Company began laying track at Front and K Streets in Sacramento—one year before the Union Pacific started work in the East. Six years later, on May 10, 1869, Stanford drove a gold spike in the final section of track at Promontory Point, Utah. The Central Pacific Rail Road united the West with the rest of the country, and secured Stanford's place in railroad history.

After completion of the East-West link, Stanford continued to work with his partners. The four devoted their time to strengthening and expanding their railroad properties. In 1884, they organized the Southern Pacific Company as a HOLDING COMPANY. In 1885, the Southern Pacific Company leased the Southern Pacific Rail Road, the Central Pacific Rail Road, and other system properties, and became the dominant unit of the organization. Stanford served as president and director of the Central Pacific Rail Road Company from its inception until his death in 1893. He was director of the Southern Pacific Company from 1885 to 1893, and president from 1885 to 1890. He was director of the Southern Pacific Rail Road from 1889 to 1890.

Though no public accounting has ever been made of the profits Stanford and his partners drew from the construction of the Central

"A MAN WILL NEVER CONSTRUCT ANYTHING HE CANNOT IMAGINE."

Pacific and Southern Pacific Rail Roads, it is known that the enterprise made them all enormously wealthy. Stanford lived in grand style in Sacramento, and later in San Francisco. He also owned Palo Alto, a ranch in Tehama County, where he cultivated vineyards and bred racing stock. Stanford's horse-training methods were widely adopted, and his interest in how horses moved at high speeds prompted him to sponsor early experiments in motion picture photography.

Today, the Palo Alto ranch is the site of Stanford University, a memorial to Stanford's only child. Leland Stanford, Jr., died in 1884, at the age of fifteen, while touring in Italy. He had been his father's pride and joy. Stanford had placed him on an elaborate silver tray and presented him to guests at a party shortly after his birth in 1869. The tray can still be seen at the Leland Stanford House, in Sacramento.

Devastated by the death of his son and looking for a new challenge, Stanford allowed himself to be drafted by the Republican party as a candidate for the U.S. Senate. He was elected in 1885. It is generally conceded that Stanford was not suited to life as a senator. He was often absent and showed little enthusiasm for the work. His election also caused friction with his long-time business partners, who had supported another candidate. In spite of his poor performance—and poor health—he was reelected in 1891, and served until his death two years later.

The five-foot eleven-inch, 268-pound railroad giant succumbed to heart problems at his Palo Alto ranch on June 21, 1893. Upon his death, the bulk of his estate passed to his wife, who used it to support the university founded by Stanford and named for their son. Stanford is interred with his son and his wife in the family mausoleum on the Stanford University campus.

STANTON, EDWIN McMASTERS

Edwin McMasters Stanton served as U.S. attorney general from December 1860 to March 1861, at a time when the southern states were moving toward secession from the Union. He later served as secretary of war during the Civil War under President ABRAHAM LINCOLN and was a key figure in the events that led to the IMPEACHMENT of President ANDREW JOHNSON.

Stanton was born on December 19, 1814, in Steubenville, Ohio. He attended Kenyon College and studied law. He was admitted to the Ohio bar in 1836 and began his law practice in Cadiz, Ohio. From 1837 to 1839, Stanton was county prosecutor. In 1842 he was elected reporter of the decisions of the Ohio Supreme Court. In 1847 Stanton moved to Pittsburgh, Pennsylvania, where he established a successful law practice.

A skilled trial and appellate advocate, Stanton soon established a specialty in litigating federal law issues. In 1856 he relocated to Washington, D.C., where he argued several important cases before the U.S. Supreme Court. In 1858 he successfully defended the state of California in land fraud cases involving Mexican land acquired by the United States.

President JAMES BUCHANAN asked Stanton to serve as attorney general in late 1860, as Buchanan's term drew to a close. Southern politicians, worried that the next president, Abraham Lincoln, would implement antislavery measures, discussed secession from the Union. Stanton was a Democrat but he opposed slavery. He counseled Buchanan not to abandon Fort Sumter, a fortification in the harbor of Charleston, South Carolina, that was held by Union forces. Stanton also secretly advised Republican leaders of cabinet discussions involving secession.

In 1862 President Lincoln appointed Stanton secretary of war. During the remainder of the Civil War, Stanton proved to be an effective administrator, minimizing corruption and increasing the efficiency of the military by ensuring that the necessary supplies and troops were available. He continually argued for a more aggressive prosecution of the war, a position that provoked violent quarrels with military commanders.

After the ASSASSINATION of Lincoln in April 1865, Stanton played a leading role in the investigation and prosecution of the conspirators. Lincoln's successor, Andrew Johnson, retained Stanton as secretary of war, but they

BIOGRAPHY

LIBRARY OF CONGRESS

Edwin McMasters Stanton

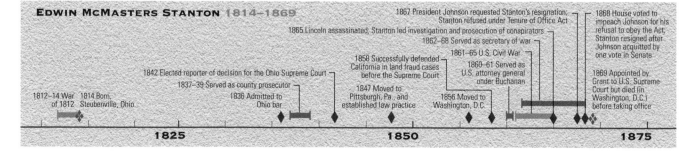

EDWIN McMASTERS STANTON 1814–1869

1812–14 War of 1812

1814 Born, Steubenville, Ohio

1836 Admitted to Ohio bar

1837–39 Served as county prosecutor

1842 Elected reporter of decision for the Ohio Supreme Court

1847 Moved to Pittsburgh, Pa., and established law practice

1856 Moved to Washington, D.C.

1858 Successfully defended California in land fraud cases before the Supreme Court

1860–61 Served as U.S. attorney general under Buchanan

1861–65 U.S. Civil War

1862–68 Served as secretary of war

1865 Lincoln assassinated; Stanton led investigation and prosecution of conspirators

1867 President Johnson requested Stanton's resignation; Stanton refused under Tenure of Office Act

1868 House voted to impeach Johnson for his refusal to obey the Act; Stanton resigned after Johnson acquitted by one vote in Senate

1869 Appointed by Grant to U.S. Supreme Court but died in Washington, D.C. before taking office

1825   1850   1875

soon clashed over Johnson's Reconstruction program for the South. Stanton sought stricter policies against the South and worked with the Radical Republicans in Congress, who were Johnson's bitterest enemies, to achieve his aims.

In 1867 Johnson asked Stanton to resign because of this betrayal, but Stanton refused. He defended his actions under the TENURE OF OFFICE ACT (14 Stat. 430), which prohibited the removal of any federal official without senatorial consent when the official's appointment had originally been approved by the Senate. The Radical Republicans had passed this act in 1867 over Johnson's VETO as a way of preventing the president from removing officials opposed to his Reconstruction policies.

Johnson ignored the Tenure of Office Act and appointed Lorenzo Thomas secretary of war. Johnson's action led to his impeachment by the House of Representatives, but thc Scnate acquitted him by one vote in 1868. After the acquittal Stanton finally resigned his cabinet post.

Stanton returned to private practice but his health was failing. In 1869 President ULYSSES S. GRANT appointed Stanton to the U.S. Supreme Court, but he died on December 24, 1869, in Washington, D.C., before he could assume the position.

STANTON, ELIZABETH CADY   The opening salvo in the battle for WOMEN'S RIGHTS was fired in 1848 by the grande dame of U.S. feminism, Elizabeth Cady Stanton. When Stanton and colleague Lucretia Mott organized the nation's first women's rights convention in 1848, in Seneca Falls, New York, they sought nothing less than a revolution. They pressed for equal education, better employment opportunities, and the vote for women—radical notions in the mid–nineteenth-century United States. For fifty years, Stanton was a key strategist and standard-bearer for the feminist movement. Along with fellow suffragist SUSAN B. ANTHONY and other activists, she helped elevate the legal, social, and political status of U.S. women.

Stanton was born November 12, 1815, in Johnstown, New York. She was the middle daughter of Daniel Cady and Margaret Living-

BIOGRAPHY

Elizabeth Cady Stanton

ston Cady, a prominent couple in Johnstown. Elizabeth was one of eleven children, but all five of her brothers and one sister died during childhood. In some ways, Stanton was raised by her parents as a substitute for those deceased brothers. Unlike most girls of her generation, Stanton participated in athletic activities and excelled in courses typically reserved for males, such as Latin, Greek, logic, philosophy, and economics. Stanton's father, a lawyer and a New York Supreme Court judge, even encouraged her to study law with him, although later he regretted his actions: as an adult, Stanton used her legal knowledge to craft well-reasoned arguments for women's rights, a cause he disliked.

After she graduated from Johnstown Academy in 1830 at age fifteen, Stanton's ambition was to attend New York's Union College. Her enrollment was impossible, however, because Union, like every other college in the entire nation, did not admit women as students. (Ohio's Oberlin College was the first U.S. college to accept female students, in 1834.) Instead of Union College, Stanton attended Troy Female Seminary, in Troy, New York. She graduated in 1833.

Stanton returned to Johnstown, where she divided her time between the pleasant diversions of upper-class life and the important social causes of the day. Despite her parents' objections, she married an abolitionist, Henry Brewster Stanton, in 1840. From the beginning of their marriage, Stanton insisted on being addressed in public by her full name. Throughout her long life, only her political enemies called her Mrs. Henry Stanton.

While attending an international antislavery conference in London with her new husband in 1840, Stanton met Mott, a Quaker activist involved in the nascent U.S. women's movement. Stanton and Mott became quick friends and allies. Both were outraged over the refusal of the male antislavery leaders to seat female delegates at the London conference. Back in the United States, the two corresponded and sometimes joined forces in abolitionist activi-

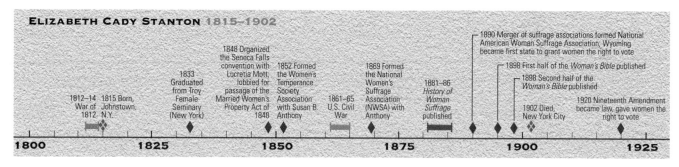

ELIZABETH CADY STANTON 1815–1902

- 1812–14 War of 1812
- 1815 Born, Johnstown, N.Y.
- 1833 Graduated from Troy Female Seminary (New York)
- 1848 Organized the Seneca Falls convention with Lucretia Mott; lobbied for passage of the Married Women's Property Act of 1848
- 1852 Formed the Women's Temperance Society Association with Susan B. Anthony
- 1861–65 U.S. Civil War
- 1869 Formed the National Women's Suffrage Association (NWSA) with Anthony
- 1881–86 *History of Woman Suffrage* published
- 1890 Merger of suffrage associations formed National American Woman Suffrage Association; Wyoming became first state to grant women the right to vote
- 1898 First half of the *Woman's Bible* published
- 1898 Second half of the *Woman's Bible* published
- 1902 Died, New York City
- 1920 Nineteenth Amendment became law, gave women the right to vote

1800   1825   1850   1875   1900   1925

ties. They also finalized plans for the nation's first women's rights convention.

In 1848, one hundred women and men gathered in Seneca Falls for the historic convention. The agenda included a speech by renowned African American abolitionist FREDERICK DOUGLASS, and a proposal to adopt Stanton's manifesto, the Declaration of Rights and Sentiments. The Seneca Falls declaration was inspired by the U.S. DECLARATION OF INDEPENDENCE. It boldly proclaimed that all men and women were equal and that women deserved greater protection under the law. The declaration called for the expansion of employment and educational opportunities for women, and the right for women to vote. After lengthy debate, it was adopted in its entirety by the convention.

The Seneca Falls convention was derided by the press—prompting Stanton to complain that its participants "were neither sour old maids, childless women, nor divorced wives as the newspapers declared them to be." Nevertheless, the convention succeeded in bringing women's issues to the political forefront.

After Seneca Falls, Stanton was an acknowledged leader of the U.S. women's movement. She soon joined forces with Anthony, the country's most prominent suffragist. For the next fifty years, Anthony was Stanton's staunchest feminist ally.

In addition to women's rights and abolition, Stanton was involved in temperance, the movement to ban the sale and consumption of ALCOHOL in the United States. Combining temperance with women's rights made sense to Stanton, both philosophically and practically. Drunken men destroyed the lives of powerless wives and children. Without laws to protect them, women who were married to chronic drinkers often faced physical abuse and financial ruin. The Married Women's Property Act of 1848 addressed this imbalance in legal power. Stanton helped win passage of the law by conducting an exhaustive petition drive throughout the state of New York.

Although Stanton supported temperance wholeheartedly, she was angered that the movement's male leaders were just as misguided as the abolitionists at the London antislavery conference. When Stanton attempted to participate in a Sons of Temperance meeting, she was summarily removed from the building. She and Anthony formed their own group, the Woman's State Temperance Society, in 1852.

The women's movement stalled around the time of the U.S. Civil War because many of its supporters focused exclusively on ABOLITION. As

president of the National Woman's Loyal League, Stanton helped gather four hundred thousand signatures on petitions in support of the THIRTEENTH AMENDMENT abolishing SLAVERY. After the war, Stanton and Anthony were bitterly disappointed when their abolitionist colleagues refused to support the inclusion of women in either the FOURTEENTH AMENDMENT, which granted African American males citizenship, or the FIFTEENTH AMENDMENT, which gave those males the right to vote. Stanton and Anthony formed the National Woman's Suffrage Association in 1869 with the sole purpose of winning the vote for women.

Because Stanton was busy with her family of seven children, she initially worked at her home on voting rights strategy while Anthony traveled the country delivering lectures. Later, this arrangement changed as Stanton became a sought-after speaker during the 1870s in the lyceum movement, a series of cultural and educational programs for adults.

As Stanton grew older, she became even more radical in her thinking. She shocked people with her pro-divorce, pro-labor, and antireligion opinions. In particular, her book *Woman's Bible*, published partially in 1895 and partially in 1898, drew fire because in it, Stanton lambasted what she viewed as the male bias of the Bible. When Stanton suggested that all organized religion oppressed women and should therefore be abolished, many felt she had gone too far. These unpopular opinions explain why some feminists disassociated themselves from Stanton and looked exclusively to Anthony for leadership.

Stanton also helped compile three of the six volumes of the less controversial *History of Woman Suffrage*, published from 1881 to 1886, with coauthor Matilda Joslyn Gage.

On Stanton's eightieth birthday, she was honored at a gala in New York City's Metropolitan Opera House. Looking back at her life, she told a crowd of six thousand people that she had been warned repeatedly against organizing the Seneca Falls convention. People told her it was a huge mistake because God had set the bounds of a woman's world and she should be satisfied with it. Stanton remarked that it was exactly this type of repressive attitude that led to her embrace of the women's movement.

Stanton died October 26, 1902, in New York City, at the age of eighty-six. Although she did not witness the passage of the NINETEENTH AMENDMENT, which gave nearly 25 million U.S. women the right to vote in 1920, she left her imprint on it.

See also TEMPERANCE MOVEMENT.

"THE BIBLE AND THE CHURCH HAVE BEEN THE GREATEST STUMBLING BLOCKS IN THE WAY OF WOMEN'S EMANCIPATION."

STAR CHAMBER 📖 An ancient high court of England, controlled by the monarch, which was abolished in 1641 by Parliament for abuses of power. 📖

The English court of Star Chamber was created by King Henry VII in 1487 and was named for a room with stars painted on the ceiling in the royal palace of Westminster where the court sat. The Star Chamber was an instrument of the monarch and consisted of royal councillors and two royal judges. The JURISDICTION of the court was based on the royal prerogative of administering justice in cases not remediable in the regular courts of law.

The Star Chamber originally assisted with some administrative matters, but by the 1530s it had become a pure court, relieving the king of the burden of hearing cases personally. It was a court of EQUITY, granting remedies unavailable in the COMMON-LAW COURTS. As such, the court was an informal body that dispensed with "due process" as it was then understood.

During Henry VII's reign (1485–1509), about half the cases involved REAL PROPERTY. During the sixteenth and early seventeenth centuries, the Star Chamber became a useful tool in dealing with cases involving members of the aristocracy who often defied the authority of the regular courts. It was during this period, moreover, that the court acquired criminal jurisdiction, hearing cases on issues concerning the security of the realm, such as SEDITION, criminal LIBEL, CONSPIRACY, and FORGERY. Later, FRAUD and the punishment of judges came within its jurisdiction.

The importance of the Star Chamber increased during the reigns of James I (1603–25) and Charles I (1625–49). Under Archbishop William Laud, the court became a tool of royal oppression, seeking out and punishing religious and political dissidents. In the 1630s Laud used the Star Chamber to persecute a group of Puritan leaders, most of whom came from the gentry, subjecting them to the pillory and CORPORAL PUNISHMENT. Though the Star Chamber could not mete out CAPITAL PUNISHMENT, it inflicted everything short of death upon those found guilty. During this time the court met in secret, extracting evidence by torturing witnesses and handing out punishments that included mutilation, life imprisonment, and enormous fines. It turned equity's traditionally broad discretion into a complete disregard for the law. The Star Chamber sometimes acted on mere rumors in order to suppress opposition to the king.

The Star Chamber's arbitrary use of power and the cruel punishments it inflicted produced a wave of reaction against it from Puritans, advocates of common-law courts, and others opposed to the reign of Charles I. In 1641 the Long Parliament abolished the court and made reparations to some of its victims.

The term *star chamber* has come to mean any lawless and oppressive tribunal, especially one that meets in secret. The constitutional concept of DUE PROCESS OF LAW is in part a reaction to the arbitrary use of judicial power displayed by the Star Chamber.

STARE DECISIS 📖 [*Latin, Let the decision stand.*] The policy of courts to abide by or adhere to principles established by decisions in earlier cases. 📖

In the United States and England, the COMMON LAW has traditionally adhered to the precedents of earlier cases as sources of law. This principle, known as stare decisis, distinguishes the common law from CIVIL-LAW systems, which give great weight to CODES of laws and the opinions of scholars explaining them. Under stare decisis, once a court has answered a question, the same question in other cases must elicit the same response from the same court or lower courts in that jurisdiction.

The principle of stare decisis was not always applied with uniform strictness. In medieval England, COMMON-LAW COURTS looked to earlier cases for guidance, but they could reject those they considered bad law. Courts also placed less than complete reliance on prior decisions because there was a lack of reliable written reports of cases. Official reports of cases heard in various courts began to appear in the United States in the early 1800s, but semiofficial reports were not produced in England until 1865. When published reports became available, lawyers and judges finally had direct access to cases and could more accurately interpret prior decisions.

For stare decisis to be effective, each JURISDICTION must have one highest court to declare what the law is in a precedent-setting case. The U.S. Supreme Court and the state supreme courts serve as precedential bodies, resolving conflicting interpretations of law or dealing with issues of FIRST IMPRESSION. Whatever these courts decide becomes judicial precedent.

In the United States, courts seek to follow precedent whenever possible, seeking to maintain stability and continuity in the law. Devotion to stare decisis is considered a mark of judicial restraint, limiting a judge's ability to determine the outcome of a case in a way that he or she might choose if it were a matter of first impression. Take, for example, the precedent set in *Roe v. Wade*, 410 U.S. 113, 93 S. Ct. 705, 35 L. Ed. 2d 147, the 1973 decision that defined a woman's right to choose ABORTION as a fundamental constitutional right. Despite the controversy engendered by the decision, and calls for its repudiation, a majority of the justices, including some conservatives who might have decided *Roe* differently, have invoked stare decisis in succeeding abortion cases.

Nevertheless, the principle of stare decisis has always been tempered with a conviction that prior decisions must comport with notions of good reason or they can be overruled by the highest court in the jurisdiction.

The U.S. Supreme Court rarely overturns one of its precedents, but when it does, the ruling usually signifies a new way of looking at an important legal issue. For example, in the landmark case *Brown v. Board of Education*, 347 U.S. 483, 74 S. Ct. 686, 98 L. Ed. 873 (1954), the Supreme Court repudiated the SEPARATE-BUT-EQUAL doctrine it endorsed in *Plessy v. Ferguson*, 163 U.S. 537, 16 S. Ct. 1138, 41 L. Ed. 256 (1896). The Court ignored stare decisis, renouncing a legal precedent that had legitimated racial segregation for almost sixty years.

See also CASE LAW; JUDICIAL REVIEW.

START TREATIES The Strategic Arms Reduction Talks (START) Treaties, START I (1991) and START II (1993), provided for large cuts in the nuclear arms possessed by the United States and the Soviet Union (later the Russian Federation). START I was the first arms control treaty to reduce, rather than merely limit, the strategic offensive nuclear arsenals of the United States and the Soviet Union, while START II required even deeper cuts in nuclear forces.

START I The Soviet Union and the United States began the START negotiations in 1982 following the disappointing results of the STRATEGIC ARMS LIMITATION TALKS (SALT), which had not led to significant reductions in the number of nuclear arms possessed by the superpowers. Nine years later, on July 31, 1991, presidents GEORGE BUSH of the United States and Mikhail Gorbachev of the Soviet Union signed the 700-page START Treaty (START I), formally designated as the Treaty Between the United States of America and the Union of Soviet Socialist Republics on the Reduction and Limitation of Strategic Offensive Arms.

START I provided for the reduction of U.S. nuclear capacity by roughly fifteen percent and Soviet capacity by twenty-five percent within seven years after ratification. The treaty contained a number of verification procedures, including on-site inspections with spot checks, monitoring of missile production plants, and the exchange of data tapes from missile tests.

Although START I reductions appeared formidable, critics noted that it simply returned both countries to the levels of nuclear arms that they possessed in 1982 when negotiations began. Both superpowers still maintained the capacity to destroy each other several times over. Others claimed that because START I allowed for the modernization and expansion of certain weapon categories by both parties, it would lead to a continuation of the arms race.

START II Changes in the political climate between the superpowers, particularly the dissolution of the Soviet Union in the summer of 1991, inspired further START negotiations. In September 1991, President Bush declared that the superpowers had an historic opportunity to negotiate significant reductions in nuclear weapons. He made a significant gesture towards this goal by calling U.S. long-range bombers off 24-hour alert and discontinuing development of the MX missile.

New Russian president Boris Yeltsin reciprocated Bush's conciliatory gestures when he announced on January 25, 1992, that Russia "no longer consider[ed] the United States our potential adversary" and declared that his country would no longer target U.S. cities with nuclear missiles. Four days later, President Bush announced further arms cuts in his State of the Union address, including cancellation of the B-2 bomber, the mobile Midgetman missile, and advanced cruise missiles. Yeltsin later responded with an even more ambitious proposal to reduce nuclear arsenals to 2,000 to 2,500 warheads each and to eliminate strategic nuclear weapons entirely by the year 2000. Although the latter goal proved too radical to implement, the former would be nearly achieved.

Yeltsin and Bush fulfilled their historic announcements in June 1992 by signing an accord, the Joint Understanding on the Elimination of MIRVed ICBMs (multiple warhead intercontinental ballistic missiles) and Further Reductions in Strategic Offensive Arms, that promised to reduce their combined nuclear arsenals from about fifteen thousand warheads to six or seven thousand by the year 2003. According to Bush, "With this agreement the nuclear nightmare recedes more and more for ourselves, for our children, and for our grandchildren."

The June 1992 accord led to the development of START II, formally called the Treaty Between the United States of America and the Russian Federation on the Further Reduction and Limitation of Strategic Offensive Arms. It was signed by Bush and Yeltsin on January 3, 1993. Under its provisions, the United States and Russia would each have between 3,000 and 3,500 warheads by 2003, an amount roughly two-thirds that of pre-START levels. Warheads on submarine-launched ballistic missiles would be limited to no more than 1,750 for each country. The treaty also required the elimination of all land-based heavy ICBMs and multiple warhead missiles. As a result, ICBMs may carry only one nuclear warhead, a development that many agreed would lead to improved strategic stability. START II goals may be reached by the earlier date of 2000 if the United States provides Russia with financial assistance in the dismantling of its nuclear arsenal.

In December 1994, President BILL CLINTON of the United States and the leaders of the nations of Belarus, Kazakhstan, Russia, and the Ukraine—the former Soviet republics still possessing nuclear arms—formally ratified the START I treaty into force, clearing the way for further consideration of START II by the U.S. Senate. On January 26, 1996, the U.S. Senate ratified the START II Treaty on a vote of eighty-seven to four.

START II incorporates the definitions, counting rules, and verification procedures of START I. Because START II builds upon START I, START I remains in effect. START I has a fifteen-year duration and can be extended for successive five-year periods by the parties.

See also ARMS CONTROL AND DISARMAMENT.

STATE 📖 As a noun, a people permanently occupying a fixed territory bound together by common habits and custom into one body politic exercising, through the medium of an organized government, independent SOVEREIGNTY and control over all persons and things within its boundaries, capable of making war and peace and of entering into international relations with other states. The section of territory occupied by one of the United States. The people of a state, in their collective capacity, considered as the party wronged by a criminal deed; the public; as in the title of a case, "The State v. A. B." The circumstances or condition of a being or thing at a given time.

As a verb, to express the particulars of a thing in writing or in words; to set down or set forth in detail; to aver, allege, or declare. To set down in gross; to mention in general terms, or by way of reference; to refer. 📖

STATE ACTION 📖 A requirement for CLAIMS that arise under the Due Process Clause of the FOURTEENTH AMENDMENT and CIVIL RIGHTS legislation, for which a private citizen seeks relief in the form of DAMAGES or REDRESS based on an improper intrusion by the government into his or her private life. 📖

The U.S. Supreme Court has established that the protections offered by the Fourteenth and Fifteenth Amendments to the U.S. Constitution apply only to actions authorized or sanctioned by state law. The "state-action" requirement means that private acts of racial discrimination cannot be addressed under these amendments or the federal civil rights laws authorized by the amendments.

The Fourteenth Amendment prohibits a state from denying any person DUE PROCESS OF LAW and the EQUAL PROTECTION of the law. The FIFTEENTH AMENDMENT prohibits a state from infringing on a person's right to vote. Both amendments were passed after the Civil War to guarantee these constitutional rights to newly freed slaves. During Reconstruction, Congress enacted many laws that it claimed were based on these amendments. Armed with this constitutional authority, Congress, in the CIVIL RIGHTS ACT of 1875, sought to prohibit racial discrimination by private parties in the provision of public accommodations, such as hotels, restaurants, theaters, and public transportation.

The Supreme Court struck down the 1875 act in the *Civil Rights* cases, 109 U.S. 3, 3 S. Ct. 18, 27 L. Ed. 835 (1883). It held that under the Fourteenth Amendment, "it is state action of a particular character that is prohibited. Individual invasion of individual rights is not the subject-matter of the amendment." The Court relied on language of the amendment that provides that "no state" shall engage in certain specified conduct.

This restrictive reading of the state-action requirement permitted racial discrimination to flourish in the South. For example, the Supreme Court upheld the "white primary," a device used to circumvent the Fifteenth Amendment, in *Grovey v. Townsend*, 295 U.S. 45, 55 S. Ct. 622, 79 L. Ed. 1292 (1935). The Court reasoned that because political parties were private organizations, their primary elections did not constitute state action.

The Supreme Court began to move away from a strict state-action requirement in the 1940s. In *Smith v. Allwright*, 321 U.S. 649, 64 S. Ct. 757, 88 L. Ed. 987 (1944), the Court struck down the white primary as violative of the Fifteenth Amendment, thus overruling *Grovey*. The Court now found that primary elections played an important part in the democratic process and must be considered as officially sanctioned by the state.

The Court extended this type of analysis in *Shelley v. Kraemer*, 334 U.S. 1, 68 S. Ct. 836, 92 L. Ed. 1161 (1948), ruling that racially discriminatory RESTRICTIVE COVENANTS affecting real estate were unenforceable in state courts, because any such enforcement would amount to state action in contravention of the Fourteenth Amendment. Groups of homeowners used restrictive covenants to prevent the sale or rental of their homes to African Americans, Jews, and other minorities. A restriction was included in their REAL ESTATE deeds forbidding such sale or rental. Until 1948 this form of private discrimination was thought to be legal because the state was not involved.

By the 1960s the Supreme Court was applying a more sophisticated analysis to determine if the state-action requirement had been met. In *Burton v. Wilmington Parking Authority*, 365 U.S. 715, 81 S. Ct. 856, 6 L. Ed. 2d 45 (1961), the Court found state action when a state agency leased property to a restaurant that refused to serve African Americans. It stated that state action in support of discrimination exists when there is a "close nexus" between the functions of the state and the private discrimination.

Nevertheless, the Court has not abandoned the state-action requirement. In *Moose Lodge v. Irvis*, 407 U.S. 163, 92 S. Ct. 1965, 32 L. Ed. 2d 627 (1972), a racially restrictive private club refused to serve the African American guest of a white member. The Court determined that the mere grant of a liquor LICENSE did not convert the private club's discriminatory policy into state action under the Fourteenth Amendment.

See also CIVIL RIGHTS CASES: INTEGRATION.

STATE COURTS 📖 Judicial tribunals established by each of the fifty states. 📖

Each of the fifty state COURT systems in the United States operates independently under the CONSTITUTION and the laws of the particular state. The character and names of the COURTS vary from state to state, but they have common structural elements.

State governments create state courts through the enactment of STATUTES or by constitutional provisions for the purpose of enforcing state law. Like the FEDERAL COURT system, the judicial branch of each state is an independent entity, often called "the third branch" of government (the other two being the executive and legislative branches). Though independent, state courts are dependent on the state legislatures for the appropriation of money to run the judicial system. Legislatures also authorize court systems to establish rules of procedure and sometimes direct the courts to investigate problems in the legal system.

Most states have a multilevel court structure, including a trial court, an intermediate court of appeals, and a supreme court. Only eight states have a two-tiered system consisting of a trial court and a supreme court. Apart from this general structure, the organization of state courts and their personnel are determined by the laws that created the court system and by the court's own rules.

State courts are designed to adjudicate civil and criminal cases. At the trial level, there are courts of limited and general JURISDICTION. Limited jurisdiction courts, sometimes called INFERIOR courts, handle minor civil cases, such as small claims or CONCILIATION matters, and lesser crimes that are classified as MISDEMEANORS. The persons who judge these cases may be part-time judges, and some states still allow persons not trained in the law to hear these cases. A JUSTICE OF THE PEACE falls within this category and handles typically minor matters such as traffic violations. Courts of GENERAL JURISDICTION, also known as superior courts, handle major civil matters and more serious crimes, called FELONIES.

Some states have a large number of trial courts. They can include small claims, municipal, county, and district courts. Since the 1980s, some states have simplified their systems, creating a unified trial court that hears all matters of limited and general jurisdiction.

Intermediate courts of appeal consider routine appeals brought by losing parties in the trial courts below. These are "error correcting" courts, which review the trial court proceedings to determine if the trial made ERRORS in procedure or law that resulted in an incorrect decision. If the court determines that an error was made (and it was not a HARMLESS ERROR), it reverses the decision and sends it back to the trial court for another proceeding. Intermediate courts of appeal are supposed to interpret the PRECEDENTS of the state's supreme court. However, in every state there are many areas of law in which its supreme court has not ruled, leav-

The New York Court of Appeals is the state's highest court. New York differs from most other states, which call their highest court the supreme court of the state.

STATE OF NEW YORK
COURT OF APPEALS

ing the APPELLATE COURTS free to make decisions on what the law should be. These courts process thousands of cases a year, and losing parties generally have a right to APPEAL to these courts, no matter how dubious the MERITS of the appeal.

The supreme court of a state fulfills a role similar to the U.S. Supreme Court. A state supreme court interprets the state constitution, the statutes enacted by the state legislature, and the body of state COMMON LAW. A supreme court is a precedential court: its rulings govern the interpretation of the law by the trial and appellate courts. A supreme court also administers the entire state court system, and the chief justice of the court is the spokesperson for the JUDICIARY. In New York and Maryland, the highest court is called the court of appeals. In New York, the trial court is called the supreme court. These and other names for courts are based on historical circumstances but do not alter the substance of the work these courts perform.

The supreme court also establishes rules of procedure for all state courts. These rules govern civil, criminal, and juvenile court procedure, as well as the admission of EVIDENCE. State supreme courts also promulgate CODES OF PROFESSIONAL RESPONSIBILITY for lawyers.

State courts have become highly organized systems. Beginning in the late 1960s, federal money helped states rethink how they deliver services. All states have a professional state COURT ADMINISTRATOR, who administers and supervises all facets of the state court system, in consultation with the trial, appellate, and supreme courts. Research and planning functions are now common, and state courts rely heavily on computers for record keeping and statistical analysis.

At the county level, court administrators, previously known as CLERKS of court, oversee the operations of the trial courts. Court clerks, officers, BAILIFFS, and other personnel are called upon to make the system work. Judges have court reporters, who record trial proceedings either stenographically or electronically, using audio or video recording devices.

State court judges, unlike federal judges, are not appointed for life. Most states require judges to stand for election every six to ten years. An election may be a contest between rival candidates, or it may be a "retention election," which asks the voters whether or not a judge should be retained.

STATE DEPARTMENT The Department of State is part of the EXECUTIVE BRANCH of government and is principally responsible for foreign affairs and foreign trade. It advises the president on the formulation and execution of foreign

U.S. Admiral Leighton Smith shows Assistant Secretary of State for Human Rights, John Shattuck, sites of suspected Serb atrocities in Bosnia.

policy. As chief executive, the president has overall responsibility for the foreign policy of the United States. The Department of State's primary objective in the conduct of foreign relations is to promote the long-range security and well-being of the United States. The department determines and analyzes the facts relating to U.S. overseas interests, makes recommendations on policy and future action, and takes the necessary steps to carry out established policy. In so doing, the department engages in continuous consultations with the Congress, other U.S. departments and agencies, and foreign governments; negotiates treaties and agreements with foreign nations; speaks for the United States in the UNITED NATIONS and in more than fifty major international organizations in which the United States participates; and represents the United States at more than eight hundred international conferences annually.

The Department of State, the senior executive department of the U.S. government, was established by an act of July 27, 1789, as the Department of Foreign Affairs and was renamed Department of State by an act of September 15, 1789.

Office of the Secretary

Secretary of State The secretary of state, the principal foreign policy adviser to the president, is responsible for the overall direction, coordination, and supervision of U.S. foreign relations and for the interdepartmental activities of the U.S. government overseas. The secretary is the first-ranking member of the cabinet, is a member of the NATIONAL SECURITY COUNCIL, and is in charge of the operations of the department, including the Foreign Service. The office of the secretary includes the offices of the deputy secretary, under secretaries, assistant secretaries, counselor, legal adviser, and inspector general.

Economic and Agricultural Affairs The under secretary for economic and agricultural affairs is principal adviser to the secretary and deputy secretary on the formulation and conduct of foreign economic policy. Specific areas for which the under secretary is responsible include international trade, agriculture, energy, finance, transportation, and relations with developing countries.

International Security Affairs The under secretary for international security affairs is responsible for ensuring the integration of all elements of the Foreign Assistance Program as an effective instrument of U.S. foreign policy and serves as chair of the Arms Transfer Management Group. Other areas of responsibility include international scientific and technological issues, communications and information policy, and technology transfers.

Regional Bureaus Six geographic bureaus, each directed by an assistant secretary, are responsible for U.S. foreign affairs activities throughout the world. These bureaus are organized by region as the bureaus of African Affairs, European and Canadian Affairs, East Asian and Pacific Affairs, Inter-American Affairs, Near Eastern Affairs, and South Asian Affairs. The regional assistant secretaries also serve as chairs of Interdepartmental Groups in the National Security Council system. These groups discuss and decide issues that can be settled at the assistant secretary level, including those arising out of the implementation of National Security Council decisions. They prepare policy papers for consideration by the council and contingency papers on potential crisis areas for council review.

Functional Areas

Diplomatic Security The Bureau of Diplomatic Security, established under the Omnibus Diplomatic Security and Antiterrorism Act of 1986, as amended (22 U.S.C.A. § 4803 et seq.), provides a secure environment for conducting U.S. diplomacy and promoting U.S. interests worldwide. The assistant secretary of state for diplomatic security is responsible for security and protective operations abroad and in the United States, counterterrorism planning and coordination, security technology development, foreign government security training, and personnel training.

The Security Awareness Staff directs the development and execution of bureauwide security and information awareness policies and programs, press and media relations, and public awareness. The Security Awareness Program

provides information on diplomatic security concerns and is a focal point for responding to public inquiries and maintaining media relations on diplomatic security issues and events. The Training Support Division provides publications and training videotapes on diplomatic security concerns.

The Private Sector Liaison Staff maintains daily contact with and actively supports the U.S. private sector by disseminating timely, unclassified security information concerning the safety of U.S. private-sector personnel, facilities, and operations abroad. The staff operates the Electronic Bulletin Board, a computerized, unclassified security information database accessible to U.S. private-sector enterprises. It also provides direct consultation services to the private sector concerning security threats abroad.

The Overseas Security Advisory Council promotes cooperation on security-related issues between U.S. private-sector interests worldwide and the Department of State, as provided in 22 U.S.C.A. § 2656 and the Federal Advisory Committee Act, as amended (5 U.S.C.A. app.). The council serves as a continuing liaison and provides for operational security cooperation between department security functions and the private sector. The council also provides for regular and timely exchange of information between the private sector and the department concerning developments in protective security. Additionally, it recommends methods and provides material for coordinating security planning and implementation of security programs.

Economic and Business Affairs The Bureau of Economic and Business Affairs has overall responsibility for formulating and implementing policy regarding foreign economic matters, including resource and food policy, international energy issues, trade, economic sanctions, international finance and development, and aviation and maritime affairs.

Intelligence and Research The Bureau of Intelligence and Research coordinates programs of intelligence, analysis, and research for the department and other federal agencies and produces intelligence studies and current intelligence analyses essential to the determination and execution of foreign policy. Through its Office of Research, the bureau maintains liaisons with cultural and educational institutions and oversees contract research and conferences on foreign affairs subjects.

International Communications and Information Policy The Bureau of International Communications and Information Policy is the principal adviser to the secretary of state on

State Department

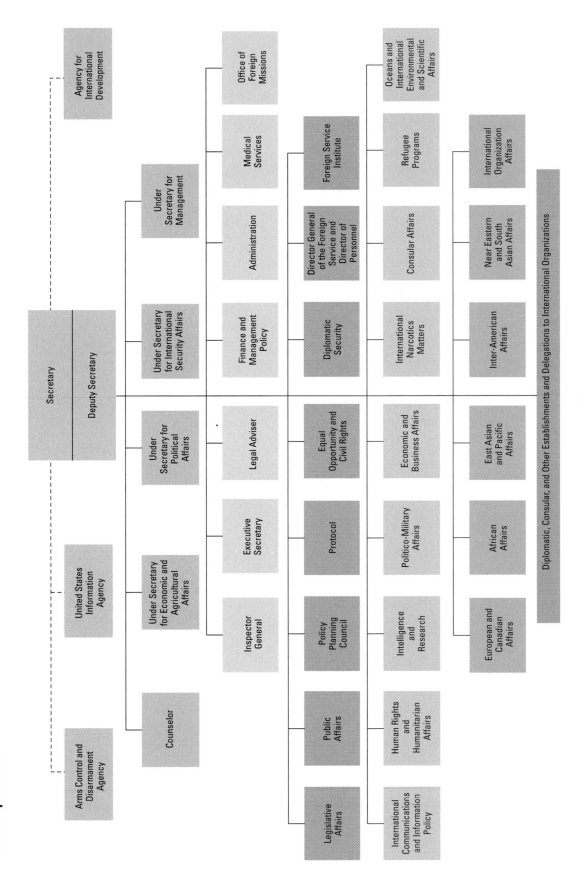

Secretary

Deputy Secretary

Arms Control and Disarmament Agency

United States Information Agency

Agency for International Development

Counselor

Under Secretary for Economic and Agricultural Affairs

Under Secretary for Political Affairs

Under Secretary for International Security Affairs

Under Secretary for Management

Inspector General

Executive Secretary

Legal Adviser

Finance and Management Policy

Administration

Medical Services

Office of Foreign Missions

Policy Planning Council

Protocol

Equal Opportunity and Civil Rights

Director General of the Foreign Service and Director of Personnel

Diplomatic Security

Foreign Service Institute

Public Affairs

Human Rights and Humanitarian Affairs

Intelligence and Research

Politico-Military Affairs

Economic and Business Affairs

International Narcotics Matters

Consular Affairs

Refugee Programs

Oceans and International Environmental and Scientific Affairs

Legislative Affairs

International Communications and Information Policy

European and Canadian Affairs

African Affairs

East Asian and Pacific Affairs

Inter-American Affairs

Near Eastern and South Asian Affairs

International Organization Affairs

Diplomatic, Consular, and Other Establishments and Delegations to International Organizations

The State Department's *Country Reports on Human Rights Practices*

One of the U.S. State Department's most important tasks is to submit to Congress annual reports on the state of human rights in countries throughout the world. The *Country Reports on Human Rights Practices,* as the book containing these reports is titled, contains extensive and detailed information that allows Congress and the State Department to make better decisions regarding U.S. policy toward foreign nations.

The State Department has submitted country reports to Congress each year since 1977. In the first year, the reports covered 82 countries, and by 1995 that number had grown to 194.

U.S. embassy staff members in each country write the preliminary report about the country. They obtain information from government and military officials, journalists, academics, and human rights activists. Embassy staff members often put themselves at great risk in collecting human rights information in countries with extensive rights violations. State Department staff members then edit the reports. They attempt to gather still more evidence from international human rights groups, international bodies such as the United Nations, and other sources.

The country reports are prefaced by an overview of human rights developments around the world, written by the assistant secretary of the Democracy, Human Rights, and Labor Division of the State Department. This overview summarizes the international human rights situation, identifies those nations with serious rights violations, and comments on the state of democracy around the world.

Each report begins with basic information regarding the government and economy of a nation, followed by detailed information on the status of human rights in the country.

The 1995 report about Brazil serves as an example of the extensive detail in the country reports. The Brazil report chronicles significant human rights abuses in that country, including killings by police and military death squads, the murder of street children in Rio de Janeiro, and numerous instances of torture. The report also describes the social, political, and legal factors in Brazil that contribute to human rights violations. These include overloaded courts and prisons, corruption of public officials and police, widespread poverty, and ineffective investigation into police and military brutality.

Each report also analyzes the human rights situation for women, racial and ethnic minorities, and workers in the country. The report about Brazil indicates a high incidence of physical abuse of women, while noting that the country has increased the number of special police stations assigned the task of preventing crimes against women. Serious violations against the rights of indigenous peoples are also recorded, including atrocities committed by the military and private parties during land disputes. On the subject of workers' rights, the Brazil report details unsafe working conditions, use of child labor in sugar and charcoal production, and use of forced labor in mining and agriculture.

See also Genocide; Human Rights.

international TELECOMMUNICATIONS policy issues affecting U.S. foreign policy and national security. The bureau acts as a coordinator with other U.S. government agencies and the private sector in the formulation and implementation of international policies relating to a wide range of rapidly evolving communications and information technologies. The bureau promotes U.S. telecommunications interests bilaterally and multilaterally.

International Narcotics and Law Enforcement Affairs The Bureau of International Narcotics and Law Enforcement Affairs is responsible for developing, coordinating, and implementing international narcotics control assistance activities of the Department of State as authorized under sections 481 and 482 of the Foreign Assistance Act of 1961, as amended (22 U.S.C.A. §§ 2291, 2292). It is the principal point of contact with and provides advice on international narcotics control matters for the Office of Management and Budget, the National Security Council, and the White House Office of National Drug Control Policy in ensuring implementation of U.S. policy in international narcotics matters. The bureau provides guidance on narcotics control matters to chiefs of missions and directs narcotics control coordinators at posts abroad. It also communicates or authorizes communication as appropriate with foreign governments on drug control matters including negotiating, concluding, and terminating agreements relating to international narcotics control programs.

International Organization Affairs The Bureau of International Organization Affairs provides guidance and support for U.S. participation in international organizations and conferences. It leads in the development, coordination, and implementation of U.S. multilateral policy. The bureau formulates and implements U.S. policy toward international organizations, with particular emphasis on those organizations that make up the United Nations system.

Legal Advisor The legal advisor advises the secretary and, through the secretary, the president, on all matters of INTERNATIONAL LAW arising in the conduct of U.S. foreign relations. The legal advisor also provides general legal advice and services to the secretary and other officials of the department on matters with which the department and overseas posts are concerned.

Consular Affairs The Bureau of Consular Affairs, under the direction of the assistant secretary, is responsible for the administration and enforcement of the provisions of the immigration and nationality laws, insofar as they concern the department and the Foreign Service, for the issuance of PASSPORTS and visas and related services, and for the protection and welfare of U.S. citizens and interests abroad.

Approximately 5 million passports are issued each year by the Passport Office of the bureau, which has agencies in Boston, Chicago, Honolulu, Houston, Los Angeles, Miami, New Orleans, New York, Philadelphia, San Francisco, Seattle, Stamford, and Washington, D.C.

Political-Military Affairs The Bureau of Political-Military Affairs provides guidance and coordinates policy formulation on national security issues, including nonproliferation of weapons of mass destruction and missile technology, nuclear and conventional arms control, defense relations and security assistance, and export controls. It acts as the department's primary liaison with the Department of Defense. The bureau also participates in all major arms control, nonproliferation, and other security-related negotiations.

The bureau's major activities are designed to further U.S. national security objectives by stabilizing regional military balances through negotiations and security assistance, negotiating reductions in global inventories of weapons of mass destruction and curbing their proliferation, maintaining global access for U.S. military forces, inhibiting adversaries' access to militarily significant technologies, and promoting responsible U.S. defense trade.

Protocol The Chief of Protocol is the principal adviser to the U.S. government, the president, the vice president, and the secretary of state on matters of diplomatic procedure governed by law or international custom and practice. The office is responsible for visits of foreign chiefs of state, heads of government, and other high officials to the United States, opera-

tion of the president's guest house, Blair House, and conduct of official ceremonial functions and public events. It also is charged with the accreditation of more than 100,000 embassy, consular, international organization, and other foreign government personnel and members of their families throughout the United States. In addition, the office determines entitlement to diplomatic or consular immunity.

Foreign Service Foreign relations are conducted principally by the U.S. Foreign Service. In 1996 representatives at 164 embassies, 12 missions, 1 U.S. liaison office, 1 U.S. interests section, 66 consulates general, 14 consulates, 3 branch offices, and 45 consular agencies throughout the world reported to the State Department on the foreign developments that have a bearing on the welfare and security of the United States. These trained representatives provide the president and the secretary of state with much of the raw material from which foreign policy is made and with the recommendations that help shape it.

Ambassadors are the personal representatives of the president and report to the president through the secretary of state. Ambassadors have full responsibility for implementation of U.S. foreign policy by any and all U.S. government personnel within their country of assignment, except those under military commands. Their responsibilities include negotiating agreements between the United States and the host country, explaining and disseminating official U.S. policy, and maintaining cordial relations with that country's government and people.

CROSS-REFERENCES

Ambassadors and Consuls; Arms Control and Disarmament; Treaty.

STATE INTEREST A broad term for any matter of public concern that is addressed by a government in law or policy.

State legislatures pass laws to address matters of PUBLIC INTEREST and concern. A law that sets speed limits on public highways expresses an interest in protecting public safety. A statute that requires high school students to pass competency examinations before being allowed to graduate advances the state's interest in having an educated citizenry.

Although the state may have a legitimate interest in public safety, public health, or an array of other issues, a law that advances a state interest may also intrude on important constitutional rights. The U.S. Supreme Court has devised standards of review that govern how a state interest will be constitutionally evaluated.

When a law affects a constitutionally protected interest, the law must meet the RATIONAL BASIS TEST. This test requires that the law be rationally related to a legitimate state interest. For example, a state law that prohibits a person from selling INSURANCE without a LICENSE deprives people of their right to make CONTRACTS freely. Yet the law will be upheld because it is a rational means of advancing the state interest in protecting persons from fraudulent or unscrupulous insurance agents. Most laws that are challenged on this basis are upheld, as there is usually some type of REASONABLE relation between the state interest and the way the law seeks to advance that interest.

When a law or policy affects a fundamental constitutional right, such as the right to vote or the right to privacy, the STRICT SCRUTINY test will be applied. This test requires the state to advance a COMPELLING STATE INTEREST to justify the law or policy. Strict scrutiny places a heavy burden on the state. For example, in *Roe v. Wade*, 410 U.S. 113, 93 S. Ct. 705, 35 L. Ed. 2d 147 (1973), the state interest in protecting unborn children was not compelling enough to overcome a woman's right to PRIVACY. When the state interest is not sufficiently compelling, the law is struck down as unconstitutional.

See also PUBLIC POLICY.

STATE LOTTERY 📖 A game of chance operated by a state government. 📖

Generally a lottery offers a person the chance to win a PRIZE in exchange for something of lesser value. Most lotteries offer a large cash prize, and the chance to win the cash prize is typically available for one dollar. Because the number of people playing the game usually exceeds the number of dollars paid out, the lottery ensures a profit for the sponsoring state.

Lotteries can come in a variety of forms, but there are three basic versions: instant lotteries, general lotteries, and lotto. Instant lotteries offer immediate prizes and consist of such games as scratch-off tickets and pull tabs. A general lottery is a drawing with a payout based on a percentage of the amount in the aggregate wagering pot; because all numbers bet for the particular game are included in the drawing, a winner is guaranteed. Lotto is similar to a general lottery in that the winning number is chosen in a drawing. However, the winning number in a lotto game is chosen by a computer, and the computer may not pick a number or sequence of numbers that is held by a player. If no player has a number that matches the number chosen by the computer, the cash prize rolls over into the next game's drawing. Lotto usually generates more money than other lot-

Go West, Young Lottery Player

Lotteries are ancient games, long predating the founding of the United States. Their popularity in Europe, and especially in England, helps explain why the first lotteries were held in the American colonies in 1612. The colonies were under the command of the British Crown, which did not permit them to levy taxes. But the British did authorize the Virginia Company of London to hold games for its benefit—at least until the scheme backfired. The lotteries drained the Crown's pockets and helped the upstart colonies, and within a decade, the colonists' own domestic lotteries had replaced them. A century later, the colonists held lotteries to raise funds for the Revolutionary War.

During the eighteenth and nineteenth centuries, lotteries played an important role in building the new nation. Its banking and taxation systems were still in their infancy, necessitating ways to raise capital quickly for public projects. Lotteries helped build everything from roads to jails, hospitals, and industries and provided needed funds for hundreds of schools and colleges. Famous American leaders like Thomas Jefferson and Benjamin Franklin saw great usefulness in them: Jefferson wanted to hold a lottery to retire his debts, and Franklin to buy cannons for Philadelphia. Lotteries expanded in the 1800s, prompting Congress in 1812 to authorize them in the District of Columbia. By midcentury, eastern states alone raised over $66 million annually, and lotteries were starting up in the West.

Despite their significance to early U.S. history, lotteries fell out of favor in the late 1800s. Corruption, moral uneasiness, and the rise of bond sales and standardized taxation proved their downfall. Only Louisiana, with a notorious lottery known as The Serpent, still held a state-run game at the end of the century. Congress put a stop to it with the Anti-Lottery Act of 1890 (Act of September 19, 1890, ch. 908, 26 Stat. 465), a federal ban on the use of the mails for conducting lotteries that effectively ended the games for the next seventy years.

New Hampshire swept in the modern era of state-sponsored lotteries in 1964. In 1974 Congress relaxed regulations for the benefit of the growing number of states holding the games (Pub. L. No. 93-583, 88 Stat. 1916 [1975]; H.R. Rep. No. 1517, 93d Cong., 2d Sess. [1974]).

STATES GAMBLE ON GAMBLING

As the ultimate high-odds game, a lottery produces very few winners. Since the rush to legalize government lotteries began in the 1970s, states have capitalized tremendously on the game's drastic odds. Thirty-five states and the District of Columbia reaped over $20 billion in 1995, and nearly every state is expected to cash in by the year 2000. Supporters tout the game as an easy revenue-raiser and a painless alternative to higher taxes. Opponents attack it as dishonest, unseemly, and undependable. They argue that the social and administrative costs do not actually skirt taxation but instead put the state in the role of con artist.

The case for lotteries is largely about funding state government. Lotteries are frequently touted as an alternative to raising taxes. Seldom is there much enthusiasm for cutting back on cherished state programs and services, even as federal subsidies to states shrink. Better, say lottery supporters, to offer citizens a choice: play or pay. Unlike paying mandatory income, property, or sales tax, buying lottery tickets is a personal decision. Funding government by lottery is quite different from funding it by taxation: under taxation, states can depend on a set amount of revenue each year from a captive base of taxpayers; under a lottery, revenue projections assume that enough tickets will be sold so that those who choose not to play are free to do so.

Besides casting lotteries as an alternative to taxes, supporters put forth other arguments in favor of lotteries, from the public's love to gamble to the desire to siphon money away from illegal gambling to simply keeping up with the Joneses, or other states, who draw residents and dollars across state boundaries.

Legal gambling in the U.S. takes in approximately $300 billion, an average of $1000 per person, per year. The Federal Bureau of Investigation estimates that illegal gambling brings in as much as another $100 billion annually.

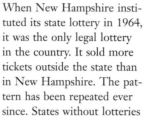

IN FOCUS

Supporters argue that both of these figures support the benefit of lotteries—to respond to the public's demand for gambling, and to diminish the profits of illegal gambling.

The public demand for gambling is so great, say supporters, that states who do not offer lotteries lose potential revenues to neighboring states that do.

When New Hampshire instituted its state lottery in 1964, it was the only legal lottery in the country. It sold more tickets outside the state than in New Hampshire. The pattern has been repeated ever since. States without lotteries see gambling money disappear into neighboring states, which fund their programs with it, necessitating a local lottery as a defensive mechanism.

Critics of lotteries attack the notion of lotteries substituting for taxation. Operating the games can require relatively high administrative overhead. In the early 1990s, the national average was six percent of revenues, and the highest rate was 29 percent in Montana. Costs result chiefly from the need to advertise constantly. Fickle players can always stray into competing states for tickets, satisfy gambling urges at casinos, or lose interest. For this reason, lottery revenues are far less dependable than tax revenues, and states can easily find themselves spending more and earning less than projected.

Some states have learned this lesson the hard way. Maryland, for example, faced a budget crisis in the early 1990s after heavily promoting a lottery game called El Gordo, anticipating $8 million to $10 million in revenues. When players failed to buy enough tickets, the state's profit after expenses was only $73,626. California experienced another kind of problem in fiscal year 1991–92, as drooping lottery sales forced it to exceed the 16 percent limit on administrative expenses specified by law. The shortfall led to a dispute over what to do with the interest earned on the State Lottery Fund, and reformers had to act to ensure that it would be used as in-

tended. They passed Chapter 1236, which requires that all interest be used to benefit public education.

Such problems lead critics to another complaint: states exaggerate the benefits of lotteries. In education, lottery proceeds may provide little help. The Educational Research Service (ERS), a think tank, has argued that lotteries are actually insignificant. Because lottery revenues are occasionally substituted for regular funding, ERS maintains, this unstable source of revenue yields no more for schools than they would have received otherwise, with an additional drawback—taxpayers, reassured that ticket sales are footing the bill, balk at the idea of raising taxes when shortfalls occur. Critics also scoff at claims about lotteries hurting illegal gambling. Most studies have found only inconclusive evidence that they have any effect at all on crime syndicates, and law enforcement agencies report that illegal gambling remains as healthy as it was before states reenacted lotteries.

Two popular moral arguments are advanced against lotteries. The first attacks the notion of voluntary taxation. Far from being the boon that the word *voluntary* suggests, critics say, the lottery is a form of regressive taxation that hurts those least able to afford it. (Taxes are considered regressive when they put a disproportionate burden on different taxpayers; a sales tax, which everyone pays at the same rate regardless of their personal wealth, is one example.) The evidence shows that the poor and working classes play lotteries the most. Some people say that preying on the illusory hopes of the poor is an unseemly way to avoid taxing the more affluent.

The second moral objection is to the hidden social costs. Throughout history, opponents of gambling have long held their position because players run a proven risk of addiction. In general, governments legislate against and spend money warning citizens about high-risk behaviors. But in the case of today's lotteries, they do the reverse: lottery advertising encourages playing often,

(continued on next page)

STATES GAMBLE ON GAMBLING
(CONTINUED)

and games are frequently redesigned to bring players back for more. No state blatantly tells its citizens to spend more than they should; yet no state stops anyone from going overboard, and it is doubtful that any could do so. The scope of the problem of compulsive lottery playing is difficult to measure, but commonly cited estimates in the 1990s said lottery players accounted for nine percent of all compulsive gamblers nationwide. A few states, such as New Jersey, have run hotlines for addicts. Others have considered doing so. A spate of crimes associated with compulsive lottery playing—from embezzlement to bank holdups—captured newspaper headlines in the mid-1990s, and prompted further hand-wringing by state officials, but little action.

Although the debate will continue, state lotteries are unlikely to go away anytime soon. Their sheer profitability makes them alluring to legislators who would rather not propose higher taxes, and the chance of winning big keeps players hooked. In all likelihood, the success of most states ensures that the rest will eventually join the bandwagon. Critics continue to fault lawmakers for relying on high-risk gambling, conning hapless players, plowing huge sums back into the games, and ignoring the resulting social costs. Yet, unlike arguments against lotteries a century ago, these complaints have mostly fallen on deaf ears, and lotteries have been skillfully transformed in the public eye from a vice into a form of entertainment. Jackpots, as every lottery player knows, speak louder than words.

teries. A player must match a long sequence of numbers, and this raises the odds against the players, which in turn makes it more likely that the cash prize will increase. Most of the other forms of lotteries are spin-offs of these three basic forms.

More than thirty states have state-run lotteries. These lotteries are administered by state agents and agencies, such as a director of the state lottery and a state lottery board. State legislatures create lotteries and lottery agencies in statutes. These statutes specify details of the game, such as the length of time a winner has to claim a prize after the relevant drawing, the documentation a winner must present to claim a prize, the manner of payment of the prize, and procedures in case a prize is won by a corporation or other legal entity.

State statutes also specify just how the money generated by the lotteries will be used. Many states direct that the profits should go into the state's general revenue fund, whereas other states earmark the profits for a particular endeavor, such as public school education, care of senior citizens, or economic development.

States must be careful to observe the dictates of the statute that creates the lottery or lotteries. Other kinds of GAMING that are not strictly limited to chance are not allowed under state lottery statutes. Indeed, most states make gambling a criminal offense and provide exceptions only for state lotteries and gaming by Native American tribes. A state may not, for example, sponsor a game that involves wagering against a house, such as a dice game, blackjack, or shell games. In *Western Telcon, Inc. v. California State Lottery*, 13 Cal. 4th 475, 917 P.2d 651, 53 Cal. Rptr. 2d 812 (1996), the Supreme Court of California ruled that a keno game offered by the California State Lottery (CSL) was not authorized under proposition 37, the 1984 initiative measure that created the state lottery. In keno, players try to match between one and ten numbers to a set of twenty numbers that are selected at random. Players pay a nominal fee for the opportunity to receive a large payoff. Keno, according to the court, did not meet the statutory definition of lottery because it was a game that persons played against the CSL, which, as banker, bet against each participant that the participant would not correctly guess the numbers to be drawn. This kind of game did not offer a prize by chance. Instead, the CSL could win all the bets and never have to pay a prize, or it could lose all the bets and pay a prize to each participant. This kind of gaming was too similar to a banking game, and the court noted that "the voters, in Proposition 37, did not establish a state gambling house, but a state lottery."

State lotteries often are planned to augment or even supplant other sources of state revenues, such as taxes. Whether they can actually achieve this objective depends on the lotteries' ability to attract players.

STATEMENT OF AFFAIRS ▣ A document that must be filed in BANKRUPTCY, which sets forth answers to questions concerning the debtor's past and present financial situation. ▣

The term *statement of affairs* is also used to describe a type of BALANCE SHEET that shows immediate LIQUIDATION amounts, as opposed to acquisition or original costs, and is generally prepared when INSOLVENCY or bankruptcy is about to take effect.

STATE'S EVIDENCE 📖 A colloquial term for TESTIMONY given by an ACCOMPLICE or joint participant in the commission of a crime, subject to an agreement that the person will be granted IMMUNITY from prosecution if she voluntarily, completely, and fairly discloses her own guilt as well as that of the other participants. 📖

State's evidence is slang for testimony given by criminal defendants to PROSECUTORS about other alleged criminals. A criminal defendant may agree to provide assistance to prosecutors in exchange for an agreement from the prosecutor that he will not be prosecuted. This agreement is commonly called turning state's evidence.

A criminal defendant who turns state's evidence may be offered a plea bargain or may have all criminal charges against him dismissed, depending on the nature of the case against the testifying defendant and the largesse of the prosecutor. A prosecutor may give a testifying defendant full immunity, which means the defendant cannot be charged with any crime related to the testimony he provides. A lesser form of immunity is called use immunity. Use immunity means that the prosecutor agrees only that she will not use any of the testimony given by the testifying defendant in any subsequent prosecution of that defendant.

Turning state's evidence plays an important role in the criminal justice system, in large part because the system is overwhelmed by criminal prosecutions. To ease the caseload, prosecutors regularly exercise their power to offer to drop or decrease charges in exchange for a plea of guilty. Another by-product of the backlog of cases is that prosecutors are most concerned with successfully prosecuting the most dangerous criminals. For these reasons, prosecutors commonly ask petty criminal defendants who have access to other alleged criminals to obtain EVIDENCE from the criminals.

For instance, assume that a person who has been arrested for possession of marijuana is willing to work with law enforcement to obtain inculpatory evidence from the dealer of the marijuana. To do so, the defendant would return to the dealer after the arrest, purchase marijuana in a transaction monitored by law enforcement, and then give the marijuana to the authorities as evidence.

A prosecutor may drop charges against a petty criminal in exchange for substantial assistance to law enforcement authorities in the prosecution of more dangerous criminals. Alternatively, a prosecutor may offer a plea bargain and ask the court to impose a sentence that is less severe than the sentence normally imposed for the crime.

State and federal SENTENCING statutes govern the effect of providing substantial assistance. Courts usually follow the recommendations of the prosecutor, but they are not obliged to do so. On the federal level, for example, section 5K1.1 of the Federal Sentencing Guidelines states that a court may evaluate the significance and usefulness of the assistance rendered by the defendant, the truthfulness and reliability of the defendant, the nature of the defendant's assistance, and other factors in determining whether to impose a relatively light sentence.

CROSS-REFERENCES

Criminal Law; Criminal Procedure; Plea Bargaining.

STATES' RIGHTS 📖 A doctrine and strategy in which the rights of the individual states are protected by the U.S. Constitution from interference by the federal government. 📖

The history of the United States has been marked by conflict over the proper allocation of power between the states and the federal government. The federal system of government established by the U.S. Constitution recognized the SOVEREIGNTY of both the state governments and the federal government by giving them mutually exclusive powers as well as concurrent powers. In the first half of the nineteenth century, arguments over states' rights arose in the context of SLAVERY. From the 1870s to the 1930s, economic issues shaped the debate. In the 1950s racial segregation and the CIVIL RIGHTS MOVEMENT renewed the issue of state power. By the 1970s economic and political conservatives had begun to call for a reduction in the power and control of the federal government and for the redistribution of responsibilities to the states.

At the Constitutional Convention in 1787, the delegates represented state governments that had become autonomous centers of power. The Constitution avoided a precise definition of the locus of sovereignty, leaving people to infer that the new charter created a divided structure in which powers were allocated between the central government and the states in such a way that each would be supreme in certain areas.

Nevertheless, defenders of states' rights were concerned that a powerful, consolidated national government would run roughshod over the states. With ratification of the Constitution in doubt, the Framers promised to add protection for the states. Accordingly, the TENTH

AMENDMENT was added to the Constitution as part of the BILL OF RIGHTS. The amendment stipulates that "powers not delegated to the United States by the Constitution, nor prohibited by it to the States, are reserved to the States respectively, or to the people." This amendment became the constitutional foundation for those who wish to promote the rights and powers of the states vis-à-vis the federal government.

In the early years of the Republic, states' rights were vigorously protected. An early ruling by the U.S. Supreme Court challenging state control of PROPERTY RIGHTS, *Chisholm v. Georgia*, 2 U.S. (2 Dall.) 419, 1 L. Ed. 440 (1793), was promptly overruled by states' rights advocates with the passage of the ELEVENTH AMENDMENT, which limits the rights of persons to sue a state in FEDERAL COURT.

The passage by the Federalists of the Alien Enemies and Sedition Acts of 1798 (1 Stat. 570, 1 Stat. 596), which restricted a number of personal liberties, provoked an impassioned response from THOMAS JEFFERSON and JAMES MADISON. In proposing the Virginia and Kentucky Resolutions of 1798, Jefferson went so far as to argue that the "sovereign and independent states" had the right to "interpose" themselves between their citizens and improper national legislative actions and to "nullify" acts of Congress they deemed unconstitutional. This was the origin of the doctrines of nullification and interposition, later employed by New England states during the War of 1812 and by South Carolina in opposing federal TARIFF legislation in 1832.

From 1815 until the end of the Civil War in 1865, states' rights played a major role in the U.S. political process. The doctrine was most fully articulated in the writings of the South Carolina statesman and political theorist JOHN C. CALHOUN. Calhoun's theory included the right of states to dissolve their contractual relationship with the federal government rather than submit to policies they saw as destructive to their local self-interests. By linking states' rights to slavery, Calhoun later helped to turn the concept into a defensive mechanism for protecting the "peculiar institution." Calhoun himself sought to go further and impose upon the federal government, in its capacity as agent for the sovereign states, a positive responsibility for protecting slavery. Thus, Calhoun sought to transform states' rights into an aggressive instrument for the protection of regional interests.

Northern leaders were also prepared to manipulate the concept. As early as the 1820s, Northern legislatures enacted personal liberty laws as devices to block the enforcement of the federal fugitive slave law. Although such laws were struck down by the Supreme Court in *Prigg v. Pennsylvania*, 41 U.S. (16 Pet.) 539, 10 L. Ed. 1060 (1842), the enactment of the more stringent FUGITIVE SLAVE ACT of 1850 by Congress led to a wave of reenactments of personal liberty laws in the North and a general defiance of federal fugitive slave policy based upon states' rights arguments.

The defeat of the South in the Civil War ended the dispute. The Fourteenth and Fifteenth Amendments were aimed in part at preventing the states from denying certain basic rights to U.S. citizens. Although the Supreme Court substantially restricted the power of these amendments during the late nineteenth century, it did so only indirectly, relying on states' rights arguments to justify its actions. Behind a judicial philosophy that supported the decisions was laissez-faire capitalism. Thus, the

States' rights are not absolute. Federal civil rights laws and a broader application of the Equal Protection Clause by the Supreme Court ended the practice in certain states of segregating public accommodations by race.

Court would invoke the Tenth Amendment to strike down federal laws that were characterized as hostile to state interests and then use the Fourteenth Amendment to strike down state legislation that sought to regulate business, labor, and the economy.

This trend continued into the twentieth century. Until the 1930s the Court frequently used the Tenth Amendment as a device for striking down federal measures, from CHILD LABOR LAWS to major pieces of President FRANKLIN D. ROOSEVELT's NEW DEAL legislation. Hundreds of state regulatory statutes were also overturned. Only when the states sought to restrict unions or control dissenters did the Court sustain these efforts.

In the late 1930s, however, the Court shifted course and abandoned its hard-line position on federal power. The New Deal dramatically increased the size and power of the federal government. States' rights arguments against overextensive use of the COMMERCE CLAUSE or the power to tax for the GENERAL WELFARE fell in the face of pressing national economic needs. By the end of World War II, the federal government had become the dominant power in the federal system.

States' rights were revived in the late 1940s over the matter of race. In 1948 President HARRY S TRUMAN pushed for a more aggressive CIVIL RIGHTS policy. Southern "Dixiecrats" bolted the Democratic party and ran their own candidate, J. STROM THURMOND, on a "states' rights" platform calling for continued racial segregation and denouncing proposals for national action in behalf of civil rights. The Supreme Court's decision in *Brown v. Board of Education of Topeka, Kansas*, 347 U.S. 483, 74 S. Ct. 686, 98 L. Ed. 873 (1954), which ruled that racially segregated public schools were unconstitutional, met with Southern resistance. Segregationists turned again to interposition, developing programs of massive resistance to racial INTEGRATION in public education, public facilities, housing, and access to jobs.

Beginning in the 1960s, other states' rights proponents started stressing the need for local control of government. Opposition to federal WELFARE and subsidy programs was based on a concern that along with federal money would come federal control, which would be deleterious to the maintenance of local standards and inappropriate for unique local conditions.

By the mid-1970s, the Supreme Court and the body politic had become concerned about federal power. In *National League of Cities v. Usery*, 426 U.S. 833, 96 S. Ct. 2465, 49 L. Ed. 2d 245 (1976), the Court ruled that Congress had exceeded its power to regulate interstate commerce when it extended federal MINIMUM WAGE and overtime standards to state and local governments. Determination of state government employees' wages and hours is one of the "attributes of sovereignty attaching to every state government," attributes that "may not be impaired by Congress." Less than ten years later, however, the Court overruled *National League* in *Garcia v. San Antonio Metropolitan Transit Authority*, 469 U.S. 528, 105 S. Ct. 1005, 83 L. Ed. 2d 1016 (1985). Nevertheless, the 5–4 majority in *Garcia* and the Court's difficulty in articulating a coherent Tenth Amendment jurisprudence have left this area of states' rights muddled.

In the political arena, however, the conservative philosophy of President RONALD REAGAN reinvigorated the states' rights movement. The 1980s saw a major shift in how the federal government was perceived. For the Reagan administration and political conservatives, reducing the size and power of the federal government became a top priority.

Though the size of government did not shrink substantially during the 1980s, states were given more authority to experiment with policy and initiatives that had previously been directed from Washington. The 1994 congressional elections, which resulted in the first Republican-controlled House of Representatives since 1948, appeared to signal a major change in the electorate's views about state-federal relations. Although little of the Republicans' "CONTRACT WITH AMERICA" platform was enacted, many of its most ardent supporters enunciated states' rights arguments.

CROSS-REFERENCES

Brown v. Board of Education of Topeka, Kansas; Federalism; Fifteenth Amendment; Fourteenth Amendment; Kentucky Resolution; *Prigg v. Pennsylvania*.

STATUS 📖 The standing, state, or condition of an individual; the rights, obligations, capacities, and incapacities that assign an individual to a given class. 📖

For example, the term *status* is used in reference to the legal state of being an INFANT, a ward, or a prisoner, as well as in reference to a person's social standing in the community.

STATUS OFFENSE 📖 A type of CRIME that is not based upon prohibited action or inaction but rests on the fact that the offender has a certain personal condition or is of a specified character. 📖

VAGRANCY—the act of traveling from place to place with no visible means of support—is an example of a status offense.

STATUS QUO 📖 [*Latin, The existing state of things at any given date.*] *Status quo ante bellum* means the state of things before the war. The *status quo* to be preserved by a PRELIMINARY INJUNCTION is the last actual, peaceable, uncontested status which preceded the pending controversy. 📖

STATUTE 📖 An act of a LEGISLATURE that declares, proscribes, or commands something; a specific LAW, expressed in writing. 📖

A statute is a written law passed by a legislature on the state or federal level. Statutes set forth general propositions of law that courts apply to specific situations. A statute may forbid a certain act, direct a certain act, make a declaration, or set forth governmental mechanisms to aid society.

A statute begins as a BILL proposed or sponsored by a legislator. If the bill survives the legislative committee process and is approved by both houses of the legislature, the bill becomes law when it is signed by the executive officer (the president on the federal level or the governor on the state level). When a bill becomes law, the various provisions in the bill are called statutes. The term *statute* signifies the elevation of a bill from legislative proposal to law. State and federal statutes are compiled in statutory CODES that group the statutes by subject. These codes are published in book form and are available at law libraries.

Lawmaking powers are vested chiefly in elected officials in the legislative branch. The vesting of the chief lawmaking power in elected lawmakers is the foundation of a representative democracy. Aside from the federal and state constitutions, statutes passed by elected lawmakers are the first laws to consult in finding the law that applies to a case.

The power of statutes over other forms of laws is not complete, however. Under the U.S. Constitution and state constitutions, federal and state governments are comprised of a system of checks and balances among the legislative, executive, and judicial branches. As the system of checks and balances plays out, the executive and judicial branches have the opportunity to fashion laws within certain limits. The EXECUTIVE BRANCH may possess certain lawmaking powers under the federal or state constitutions, and the JUDICIARY has the power to review statutes to determine whether they are valid under those constitutions. When a court strikes down a statute, it in effect creates a law of its own that applies to the general public.

Laws created through judicial opinion stand in contradistinction to laws created in statutes. CASE LAW has the same legally binding effect as statutory law, but there are important distinctions between statutes and case law. Case law is written by judges, not by elected lawmakers, and it is written in response to a specific case before the court. A judicial opinion may be used as PRECEDENT for similar cases, however. This means that the judicial opinion in the case will guide the result in similar cases. In this sense a judicial opinion can constitute the law on certain issues within a particular JURISDICTION. Courts can establish law in this way when no statute exists to govern a case, or when the court interprets a statute.

For example, if an appeals court holds that witness TESTIMONY on memory recovered through therapy is not ADMISSIBLE at trial, that decision will become the rule for similar cases within the appeals court's jurisdiction. The decision will remain law until the court reverses itself or is reversed by a higher court, or until the state or federal legislature passes a statute that overrides the judicial decision. If the courts strike down a statute and the legislature passes a similar statute, the courts may have an opportunity to declare the new statute unconstitutional. This cycle can be repeated over and over if legislatures continually test the constitutional limits on their lawmaking powers.

Judicial opinions also provide legal authority in cases that are not covered by statute. Legislatures have not passed statutes that govern every conceivable dispute. Furthermore, the language contained in statutes does not cover every possible situation. Statutes may be written in broad terms, and judicial opinions must interpret the language of relevant statutes according to the facts of the case at hand. REGULATIONS passed by ADMINISTRATIVE AGENCIES also fill in statutory gaps, and courts occasionally are called on to interpret regulations as well as statutes.

Courts tend to follow a few general rules in determining the meaning or scope of a statute. If a statute does not provide satisfactory definitions of ambiguous terms, courts must interpret the words or phrases according to ordinary rules of grammar and dictionary definitions. If a word or phrase is technical or legal, it is interpreted within the context of the statute. For example, the term *interest* can refer to a monetary charge or ownership of property. If the term *interest* appears in the context of a statute on REAL ESTATE ownership, a court will construe the word to mean property ownership. Previous interpretations of similar statutes are also helpful in determining a statute's meaning.

Statutes are not static and irreversible. A statute may be changed or repealed by the lawmaking body that enacted it, or it may be overturned by a court. A statute may lapse, or terminate, under the terms of the statute itself or under legislative rules that automatically terminate statutes unless they are reapproved before a certain amount of time has passed.

Although most legal disputes are covered at least in part by statutes, tort and contract disputes are exceptions, in that they are largely governed by case law. Criminal law, patent law, tax law, property law, and bankruptcy law are among the areas of law that are covered first and foremost by statute.

CROSS-REFERENCES

Judicial Review; Legislation; Legislative History; Statutory Construction.

STATUTE OF FRAUDS 📖 A type of state
law, modeled after an old English law, that requires certain types of CONTRACTS to be in writing. 📖

U.S. law has adopted a 1677 English law, called the Statute of Frauds, which is a device employed as a defense in a breach of contract lawsuit. Every state has some type of statute of frauds; the law's purpose is to prevent the possibility of a nonexistent AGREEMENT between two parties being "proved" by PERJURY or FRAUD. This objective is accomplished by prescribing that particular contracts not be enforced unless a written note or memorandum of agreement exists that is signed by the persons bound by the contract's terms or their authorized representatives.

The statute of frauds is invoked by a defendant in a breach of contract action. If the defendant can establish that the contract he has failed to perform is legally unenforceable because it has not satisfied the requirement of the statute, then the defendant cannot be liable for its breach. For example, suppose that a plaintiff claims that a defendant agreed to pay her a commission for selling his building. If the defendant can demonstrate that no commission contract was signed, the statute of frauds will prevent the plaintiff from recovering the commission.

The English Statute of Frauds, which was enacted by Parliament in 1677, applied to only specific types of contracts. These included promises to a CREDITOR of another to pay that individual's DEBTS when they became due, a MARRIAGE contract or PROMISE to marry, other than the mutual promises of a man and woman to wed, a contract for the sale of REAL ESTATE, and a contract that cannot be performed within one year of its formation and has not been completely performed by one side.

States have expanded the application of the statute to other categories of contracts, such as a life INSURANCE contract that is not to be performed within the lifetime of the person making the promise. It also applies to a contract to BEQUEATH or DEVISE property by WILL and to a contract that authorizes an AGENT to sell REAL PROPERTY for a commission.

A strict application of the statute of frauds can produce an unjust result. A party, who in GOOD FAITH believes a contract exists and therefore spends time and money to perform the contract, would be unable to force the other party to perform because the agreement was not in writing. Therefore, courts often employ the term *part performance* to determine whether a plaintiff's conduct based on her belief that a contract exists justifies enforcement of the contract even though it has failed to comply with the statute of frauds. Part performance refers to acts performed by the plaintiff in reliance on the PERFORMANCE of the duties imposed on the defendant by the terms of the contract. The plaintiff's actions must be substantial in order to demonstrate that he actually has relied on the terms of the contract.

When the alleged contract involves real property, the acts of taking POSSESSION and making part payment—when performed in reliance upon an ORAL CONTRACT under circumstances that clearly show a buyer-seller relationship—are usually sufficient to remove a contract from the requirements of the statute of frauds. The oral contract, therefore, would be enforced. However, payment or possession alone generally will not suffice to overcome the statute of frauds.

Where services have been performed based upon a contract that is unenforceable because of the statute of frauds, the value of those services can nevertheless be recovered on the basis of *quantum meruit*, or the REASONABLE value of those services. If a person performs services in reliance on an oral promise that he will inherit certain property and that promise is not fulfilled, that individual can sue the decedent's estate on a QUANTUM MERUIT basis for the reasonable value of his services.

If a contract is unenforceable, a person can recover expenses incurred at the other party's request even though they pertain to the unenforceable contract. The recovery of expenses is not affected because the law implies a promise by the defendant to pay for expenses incurred at her request, and LIABILITY is not based upon breach of contract.

If one party has performed in reliance on an oral contract and will be irreparably harmed if the contract is not enforced, some courts apply the theory of equitable ESTOPPEL to prevent the statute of frauds from being employed as a defense. Equitable estoppel holds that if a person has so altered his position that justice demands the enforcement of the contract, the court will enforce the contract even though it fails to comply with the statute.

See also QUASI CONTRACT.

STATUTE OF LIMITATIONS 📖 A type of federal or state law that restricts the time within which LEGAL PROCEEDINGS may be brought. 📖

Statutes of limitations, which date back to early ROMAN LAW, are a fundamental part of European and U.S. law. These statutes, which apply to both civil and criminal actions, are designed to prevent fraudulent and stale claims from arising after all EVIDENCE has been lost or after the facts have become obscure through the passage of time or the defective memory, death, or disappearance of WITNESSES.

The statute of limitations is a DEFENSE that is ordinarily asserted by the defendant to defeat an ACTION brought against him after the appropriate time has elapsed. Therefore, the defendant must plead the defense before the court upon answering the plaintiff's complaint. If the defendant does not do so, he is regarded as having waived the defense and will not be permitted to use it in any subsequent proceedings.

Statutes of limitations are enacted by the legislature, which may either extend or reduce the time limits, subject to certain restrictions. A court cannot extend the time period unless the statute provides such authority. With respect to civil lawsuits, a statute must afford a REASONABLE period in which an action can be brought. A statute of limitations is unconstitutional if it immediately curtails an existing remedy or provides so little time that it deprives an individual of a reasonable opportunity to start her lawsuit. Depending upon the state statute, the parties themselves may either shorten or extend the prescribed time period by agreement, such as a provision in a contract.

Criminal Actions A majority of states have a statute of limitations for all crimes except MURDER. Once the statute has expired, the court lacks JURISDICTION to try or punish a defendant.

Criminal statutes of limitations apply to different crimes on the basis of their general classification as either FELONIES or MISDEMEANORS. Generally, the time limit starts to run on the date the offense was committed, not from the time the crime was discovered or the accused was identified. The running of the statute may be suspended for any period the accused is absent from the state or, in certain states, while any other INDICTMENT for the same crime is pending. This suspension occurs so that the state will be able to obtain a new indictment in the event the first one is declared invalid.

Civil Actions In determining which statute of limitations will control in a CIVIL ACTION, the type of CAUSE OF ACTION that the claim will be pursued under is critical. States establish different deadlines depending on whether the cause of action involves a CONTRACT, PERSONAL INJURY, LIBEL, FRAUD, or other CLAIM.

Once the cause of action is determined, the date of the injury must be fixed. A cause of action ordinarily arises when the party has a right to apply to the proper court for relief. Some states, for example, require a person to bring a lawsuit for breach of contract within six years from the date the contract was breached. The action cannot be started until the contract has actually been violated, even though serious disagreements between the parties might have occurred earlier. Conversely, the time limit within which to bring an action for fraud does not begin until the fraud has been discovered.

A court cannot force a defendant to use a statute of limitations defense, but it is usually in the person's best legal interests to do so. Nevertheless, defendants do sometimes waive the defense. The defense may be waived by an agreement of the parties to the controversy, provided that the agreement is supported by adequate consideration. For example, a debtor's agreement to waive the statute of limitations in exchange for a creditor's agreement not to sue is valuable CONSIDERATION that prevents the debtor from using the defense.

A defendant may be unable to use the limitations defense due to her agreement, conduct,

J. B. Stoner appealed his 1977 conviction for bombing a church in 1958, arguing that the long delay between the two events was unconstitutional. However, because murder has no statute of limitations, the conviction was upheld.

AP/WIDE WORLD PHOTOS

Recovered Memory: Stopping the Clock

Statutes of limitations are intended to encourage the resolution of legal claims within a reasonable amount of time. Courts and legislatures have had to reconsider the purpose of time limits in dealing with the controversial issue of "recovered memory" by child sexual abuse victims. For the most part, the clock has been stopped until a victim remembers the abuse.

In the 1980s some mental health therapists began exploring the nature of child sexual abuse. They contended that memories of childhood trauma are so disturbing that the child represses them. Many years later, while in therapy or by happenstance, the person remembers the traumatic events. Therapists built on this concept, working with patients to fully recover these memories.

Victims of child sexual abuse who sought to sue their abusers for damages faced a statute of limitations question: Had the time expired to file a civil lawsuit because the memory of abuse was not recovered until many years after the actual abuse? Courts that faced this issue for the first time sought ways to circumvent the time barrier. One method was to apply the "discovery rule" found in tort law. The discovery rule applies if the injury is one that is not readily perceptible as having an external source. Thus, a person who has serious mental health problems but does not know the cause will be allowed to toll (suspend the running of) the statute of limitations until he or she discovers that the injury was caused by the defendant's tortious conduct.

Legislatures have been urged to amend their statutes of limitations to permit recovered memory plaintiffs to sue their abusers. By 1996 twenty-one states had amended their laws. Typically these laws provide that the action must be filed within a certain number of years after the plaintiff either reaches the age of majority or knew or had reason to know that sexual abuse caused the injury. Because of these judicial and legislative changes, many lawsuits have been filed alleging child sexual abuse that occurred many years before, sometimes as long as twenty years ago.

See also Child Abuse; Sexual Abuse.

or representations. To be estopped, or prevented, from using this defense, a defendant need not have signed a written statement, unless required by statute. The defendant must, however, have done something that amounted to an affirmative inducement to the plaintiff to delay bringing the action. Statements that only attempt to discourage a person from bringing a suit or mere negotiations looking toward an amicable settlement will not estop a defendant from invoking the statute of limitations.

Tolling the Statute Statutes of limitations are designed to aid defendants. A plaintiff, however, can prevent the dismissal of his action for untimeliness by seeking to *toll* the statute. When the statute is tolled, the running of the time period is suspended until some event specified by law takes place. Tolling provisions benefit a plaintiff by extending the time within which he is permitted to bring suit.

Various events or circumstances will TOLL a statute of limitations. It is tolled when one of the parties is under a legal DISABILITY—the lack of legal CAPACITY to do an act—at the time the cause of action accrues. A child or a person with a mental illness is regarded as being incapable of initiating a legal action on her own behalf. Therefore, the time limit will be tolled until some fixed time after the disability has been removed. For example, once a child reaches the AGE OF MAJORITY, the counting of time will be resumed. A personal disability that postpones the operation of the statute against an individual may be asserted only by that individual. If a party is under more than one disability, the statute of limitations does not begin to run until all the disabilities are removed. Once the statute begins to run, it will not be suspended by the subsequent disability of any of the parties unless specified by statute.

The unexcused failure to start an action within the statutory period bars the action. Mere ignorance of the existence of a cause of action generally does not toll the statute of limitations, particularly when the facts could have been learned by inquiry or diligence. In cases where a cause of action has been fraudulently concealed, the statute of limitations is tolled until the action is, or could have been, discovered through the exercise of due diligence. Ordinarily, silence or failure to disclose the existence of a cause of action does not toll the statute. The absence of the plaintiff or defendant from the jurisdiction does not suspend the running of the statute of limitations, unless the statute so provides.

The statute of limitations for a DEBT or OBLIGATION may be tolled by either an unconditional promise to pay the debt or an acknowledgement of the debt. The time limitation on bringing a lawsuit to enforce payment of the debt is suspended until the time for payment established under the promise or acknowledgment has arrived. Upon that due date, the period of limitations will start again.

STATUTE OF USES ☶ An English law enacted in 1535 to end the practice of creating USES in REAL PROPERTY by changing the purely equitable TITLE of those entitled to a use into absolute ownership with the right of POSSESSION. ☶

The Statute of Uses was a radical statute forced through a recalcitrant English Parliament in 1535 by a willful King Henry VIII. Essentially, the statute eliminated a sleight of hand that had been fashioned by landholders to avoid paying royal fees associated with land. These royal fees, called feudal incidents, had been slipping away from the Crown for a century or so before the statute was passed.

Landholders in sixteenth-century England were supposed to hold their land at the will of a lord, who worked in the service of the king or queen. In exchange for the land, landholders were obliged to pay certain fees to the lord, who kept some and turned the rest over to the Crown. Many of the royal incidents associated with real property were exacted by the Crown when the landholder died. However, the Crown could collect incidents only if the legal title passed from the landholder to an HEIR.

In the fourteenth and fifteenth centuries, landholders had devised a way to both profit from their land and avoid feudal incidents. The landholders would place their property in the name of one person for the benefit of a third party. This third party, called the CESTUI QUE use, the beneficiary of the use, was either the original landholder or a person of the landholder's choosing. The arrangement created a form of land ownership, or ESTATE in land, called a use.

Soon courts began to recognize the right of a landholder, as feoffor, to give possession of his land to a peasant TENANT while giving legal title to a third party, or feoffee. They also enforced agreements between a feoffor and feoffee in which the feoffee held title to the land only for the benefit of the cestui que use.

Under the COMMON LAW, when legal title to land was held by more than one feoffee, partial title did not pass to the deceased feoffee's heirs upon the death of a feoffee. Instead, the deceased feoffee's portion of the title passed to the other feoffees. A landholder, as a feoffor, could give legal title to several feoffees and add a new feoffee to the legal title upon the death of any feoffee. Under this system, the death of a title-holding feoffee did not give rise to an INHERITANCE incident. Thus, a landholder could avoid feudal incidents while he himself or a person of his choosing continued to reap profits from the land.

By giving legal title to two or more feoffees, a feoffor also was able to avoid other royal incidents, such as marriage fees and other fees associated with the death of a landholder. If the property was held in other persons' names, a landholder could also avoid losing the property due to DEBT or FELONY conviction. By the end of the fifteenth century, almost all of the land in England was owned in use. Because most of the land was owned by a relatively small number of wealthy landowners, in most cases the actual title owners did not actually live on their parcels of land. Another consequence was that the Crown had lost substantial revenues due to the avoidance of the land-based feudal incidents.

King Henry VIII attempted to reclaim these lost revenues with the passage of the Statute of Uses. Under the act, the full title to land was automatically given to the person for whom the property was being used, the cestui que use. The act also reinstated the old feudal rule of PRIMOGENITURE, which held that land should go to the oldest son upon the death of the landowner.

Landholders strenuously objected to the statute. Over the next four years they conducted a Pilgrimage of Grace to London in an effort to convince the king and Parliament to eliminate primogeniture and reverse the abolition of the use estate.

The campaign caused Henry VIII to loosen the royal grip on land ownership. In 1540 Parliament passed the STATUTE OF WILLS, which abolished primogeniture and gave landholders the right to DEVISE their property to whomever they pleased in a written WILL and testament. However, Parliament did not abolish the Statute of Uses.

Immediately after the act was passed, landholders set about creating loopholes. The courts also were hostile to the legislation. They accommodated landholders by giving the statute a strict technical construction and by expanding other methods for landholders to put their property in the name of another person while keeping it for their own use or profit or for the use or profit of another person. In particular, the English courts expanded the concept of the TRUST to fill the void. A land trust is an arrangement whereby one person holds full title to property for the benefit of another person, who may direct the management and use of the property.

Courts focused on the difference between a trust and a use to achieve essentially the same result for landowners. In a trust the title owner plays some active role in connection with the use of the property. In contrast, with a bare use, the feoffee performed no work in connection with the property and served only as a strawperson. If a feoffee was performing duties in connection with the property, the land was not in use, courts reasoned, but in trust. Many of the rules on land trusts that developed in response to the Statute of Uses were adopted in the United States and continue in effect today.

In 1660 Parliament abolished all remaining feudal incidents associated with land in the Statute of Tenure. This obviated the need for a Statute of Uses because there no longer was any need to evade feudal incidents. The Statute of Uses was finally repealed by Parliament in 1925 by the Law of Property Act (12 & 13 Geo. 5, ch. 16, sec. 1(7)).

See also FEUDALISM.

STATUTE OF WILLS 📖 An early English law that provided that all individuals who owned land were permitted to leave or DEVISE two-thirds of their property to anyone by written WILL and testament, effective upon their death. 📖

The Statute of Wills (32 Hen. 8, c. 1) gave to landowners in England the right to dispose of land through a written will. Before the Statute of Wills was enacted by the English Parliament in 1540, landowners did not have the right to determine who would become the new owner of the land upon their death. The inheritance of land was dependent on whether the deceased landowner was survived by a competent relative or descendant. Generally, if a landowner died with no relatives, the land reverted into the possession of the Crown. This reversion was called ESCHEAT.

The Statute of Wills made it possible for a landholder to decide who would inherit the land upon his death. The statute was passed a mere four years after the STATUTE OF USES banned the practice of splitting the TITLE to land to avoid paying royal fees associated with the property. The Statute of Wills was seen as a policy retreat by King Henry VIII, who faced tremendous opposition from landowners seeking relief from royal control of land.

Some of the procedures created by the Statute of Wills remain effective in modern law. The statute required that wills be in writing, that they be signed by the person making the will, or TESTATOR, and that they be properly witnessed by other persons. If any of these requirements was not met, the will could not be enforced in court. These requirements exist today in state law and are intended to ensure that wills are not fabricated and that the testator's intent is fulfilled.

STATUTE OF YORK 📖 An English law enacted in 1318 that required the consent of Parliament in all legislative matters. 📖

The Statute of York was an important step toward the development of a constitutional monarchy in England. The law was enacted in the city of York in 1318, at a time when King Edward II was attempting to reassert his control over the kingdom.

Historians generally regard Edward II as an unqualified failure as king. Seven years before the Statute of York, the nobility had forced him to accept the Ordinances of 1311, which required baronial consent for foreign war, restricted the Crown's power to interfere with the judicial system, and required the king to obtain the advice and consent of the barons in Parliament for a long list of officials he wished to appoint.

Edward II regained political strength in 1318 and managed to have the Ordinances repealed. The Statute of York, however, specified that the "consent of the prelates, earls, and barons, and of the community of the realm" was required for legislation. Though some historians believe the statute restored baronial control over English government, many historians see the phrase "community of the realm" as signifying a shift of power to those outside the noble class. In addition, the powers of the king were constrained.

STATUTES AT LARGE 📖 An official compilation of the acts and resolutions of each session of Congress published by the Office of the Federal Register in the National Archives and Record Service. 📖

The Statutes at Large are divided into two parts: the first is composed of public acts and JOINT RESOLUTIONS; the second includes private acts and joint resolutions, CONCURRENT RESOLUTIONS, treaties, proposed and ratified AMENDMENTS to the Constitution, and presidential proclamations. Volumes from 1951 to the present are arranged by PUBLIC LAW number; older volumes are arranged by chapter number.

The *Statutes at Large* are considered the official publication of the law for citation purposes when titles of the United States Code have not been enacted as POSITIVE LAW.

STATUTORY 📖 Created, defined, or relating to a STATUTE; required by statute; conforming to a statute. 📖

A statutory PENALTY, for example, is punishment in the form of a fine, prison sentence, or both, that is imposed against an offender for committing some statutory violation.

STATUTORY CONSTRUCTION See CANONS OF CONSTRUCTION.

STATUTORY RAPE 📖 Sexual intercourse by an adult with a person below a statutorily designated age. 📖

The criminal offense of statutory rape is committed when an adult sexually penetrates a person who, under the law, is incapable of consenting to sex. MINORS and physically and mentally incapacitated persons are deemed incapable of consenting to sex under RAPE statutes in all states. These persons are considered deserving of special protection because they are especially vulnerable due to their youth or condition.

Most legislatures include statutory rape provisions in statutes that punish a number of different types of sexual assault. Statutory rape is different from other types of rape in that force and lack of consent are not necessary for conviction. A defendant may be convicted of statutory rape even if the complainant explicitly consented to the sexual contact and no force was used by the actor. By contrast, other rape generally occurs when a person overcomes another person by force and without the person's consent.

The actor's age is an important factor in statutory rape where the offense is based on the victim's age. Furthermore, a defendant may not argue that he was mistaken as to the minor's age or INCAPACITY. Most rape statutes specify that a rape occurs when the complainant is under a certain age and the perpetrator is over a certain age. In Minnesota, for example, criminal sexual conduct in the first degree is defined as sexual contact with a person under thirteen years of age by a person who is more than thirty-six months older than the victim. The offense also is committed if the complainant is between thirteen and sixteen years old and the actor is more than forty-eight months older than the complainant (Minn. Stat. Ann. § 609.342 [West 1996]).

See also CHILD ABUSE; SEXUAL ABUSE.

STATUTORY REDEMPTION 📖 The right granted by legislation to a mortgagor, one who PLEDGES property as SECURITY for a DEBT, as well as to certain others, to recover the mortgaged property after a FORECLOSURE sale. 📖

Statutory redemption is the right of a mortgagor to regain ownership of PROPERTY after foreclosure. A mortgagor is a person or party who borrows money from a mortgagee to purchase property. The arrangement between a mortgagor and mortgagee is called a MORTGAGE. Foreclosure is the termination of rights to property bought with a mortgage. Most foreclosures occur when the mortgagor fails to make mortgage payments to the mortgagee. After foreclosing a mortgage, the mortgagee may sell the property at a foreclosure sale. Statutory redemption gives a mortgagor a certain period of time, usually one year, to pay the amount that the property was sold for at the foreclosure sale. If the mortgagor pays all of the foreclosure sale price before the end of one year after the foreclosure sale, or within the statutory redemption period, the mortgagor can keep the property.

A mortgagor in a state that offers statutory redemption may stay on the premises after foreclosure during the statutory redemption period. If the mortgagor does not redeem the property by the end of the period, the purchaser at the foreclosure sale receives TITLE to, and POSSESSION of, the property.

In states that have redemption statutes, an individual mortgagor cannot waive a statutory redemption period. Many states that offer statutory redemption make a special exception for CORPORATIONS, which may waive the statutory redemption period if it is incompatible with the reorganization or dissolution of the corporation.

Approximately half of all states have passed statutes that allow mortgagors to redeem property after a mortgage foreclosure. The states that allow statutory redemption have done so to drive up foreclosure sale prices for the benefit of both the defaulting mortgagor and CREDITORS of the mortgagor who have obtained an interest in the property. Statutory redemption is designed to prevent extremely low sale prices by giving the mortgagor an opportunity to match the sale price. Some legal commentators have observed, however, that statutory redemption has failed to increase the amount of bids on foreclosed property because title to property that is subject to statutory redemption is so uncertain. Because the mortgagor could redeem the property within a year and creditors of the mortgagor could make claims to the property, potential buyers of foreclosed property adjust their bids to account for these hazards.

Statutory redemption is distinct from equitable redemption. Equitable redemption is the right of a defaulting mortgagor to reclaim property by paying all past due mortgage payments anytime prior to foreclosure. Statutory redemption, by contrast, begins at the point of foreclosure and requires that the defaulting mortgagor pay the full foreclosure sale price. Equitable redemption is a COMMON-LAW concept, which means it exists as law in the form of judicial opinions. All state courts have recognized a mortgagor's right to equitable redemption.

STAY The act of temporarily stopping a judicial proceeding through the ORDER of a court.

A stay is a suspension of a case or a suspension of a particular proceeding within a case. A judge may grant a stay on the MOTION of a party to the case or issue a stay SUA SPONTE, without the request of a party. Courts will grant a stay in a case when it is necessary to secure the rights of a party.

There are two main types of stays: a stay of EXECUTION and a stay of proceedings. A stay of execution postpones the enforcement of a JUDGMENT against a litigant who has lost a case, called the JUDGMENT DEBTOR. In other words, if a civil litigant wins money DAMAGES or some other form of RELIEF, he may not collect the damages or receive the relief if the court issues a stay. Under rule 62 of the Federal Rules of Civil Procedure, every civil judgment is stayed for ten days after it is rendered. An additional stay of execution lasts only for a limited period. It usually is granted when the judgment debtor appeals the case, but a court may grant a stay of execution in any case in which the court feels the stay is necessary to secure or protect the rights of the judgment debtor.

The term *stay of execution* may also refer to a halt in the execution of a death penalty. This kind of stay of execution normally is granted when a court decides to allow an additional appeal by a condemned prisoner. Such stays of execution may be granted by executives, such as governors or the president of the United States, or by appeals courts. See also CAPITAL PUNISHMENT.

A stay of proceedings is the stoppage of an entire case or a specific proceeding within a case. This type of stay is issued to postpone a case until a party complies with a court order or procedure. For example, if a party is required to deposit COLLATERAL with the court before a case begins, the court may order the proceedings stayed for a certain period of time or until the money or property is delivered to the court. If the party fails to deposit the collateral, the court may cite the party for CONTEMPT of court and impose a FINE or order INCARCERATION.

A court may stay a proceeding for a number of reasons. One common reason is that another ACTION is under way that may affect the case or the rights of the parties in the case. For instance, assume that a defendant faces lawsuits from the same plaintiffs in two separate cases involving closely related facts. One case is filed in federal court, and the other case is filed in state court. In this situation one of the courts may issue a stay in deference to the other court. The stay enables the defendant to concentrate on one case at a time.

The term *stay* may also be used to describe any number of legal measures taken by a legislature to provide temporary relief to debtors. For example, under section 362(a) of the Bankruptcy Code, a DEBTOR who files for BANKRUPTCY receives an automatic stay immediately upon filing a voluntary bankruptcy petition. Used in this sense, the term *stay* refers to the right of the debtor to keep CREDITORS at bay during the resolution of the bankruptcy case.

STEERING The process whereby builders, brokers, and rental property managers induce purchasers or lessees of REAL PROPERTY to buy land or rent premises in neighborhoods composed of persons of the same race.

Steering is an unlawful practice and includes any words or actions by a REAL ESTATE sales representative or BROKER that are intended to influence the choice of a prospective buyer or tenant. Steering violates federal fair housing provisions that proscribe DISCRIMINATION in the sale or rental of housing.

STEINEM, GLORIA Gloria Steinem is one of the most important feminist writers and organizers of the late twentieth century. Since the 1960s Steinem has been a political activist and organizer who has urged equal opportunity for women and the breaking down of gender roles. As a writer she has produced influential essays about the need for social and cultural change.

Steinem was born on March 25, 1934, in Toledo, Ohio. Her parents divorced when she was eleven years old. Steinem enrolled at Smith College in 1952 and graduated in 1956. She became a freelance journalist. After graduation she went to India to study at the universities of Delhi and Calcutta. It was there that she began publishing freelance articles in newspapers.

In 1960 she pursued a writing career, working for a political satire magazine in New York. Her breakthrough came in 1963 with the publication of her article "I Was a Playboy Bunny,"

BIOGRAPHY

Gloria Steinem

WILLIAM WALDRON/THE GAMMA LIAISON NETWORK

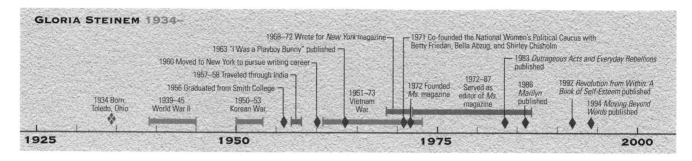

which retold her experiences working in the Manhattan Playboy Club. For the next few years, her articles appeared in many national women's magazines. She also wrote comedy scripts for a weekly political satire television show, *That Was the Week That Was.*

Her attention shifted to politics in 1968 when she began writing a column for *New York* magazine. During the late 1960s the "women's liberation movement" began and Steinem soon became a leading supporter of the movement. In 1971 she, along with BETTY N. FRIEDAN, Bella Abzug, and SHIRLEY A. CHISHOLM, founded the National Women's Political Caucus. The mission of the caucus was to identify and encourage women to run for political office.

In 1972 Steinem founded and served as editor of *Ms.* magazine. *Ms.* addressed feminist issues, including reproductive rights, employment discrimination, sexuality, and gender roles. The magazine presented Steinem with a platform to air her views about the contemporary social scene.

Since the 1970s Steinem has been a spokesperson for many feminist causes. She has sought to protect ABORTION rights, establish RAPE crisis centers, and guarantee work environments free from sexual discrimination. Steinem has distinguished between "erotica" and POR-NOGRAPHY, believing that nonviolent sexual material is acceptable but pornography should be banned. More radical feminists have criticized Steinem for this and other positions, arguing that she is content to mingle with the rich and powerful and to seek legal changes that falsely promise equal opportunity and fair treatment.

Despite these criticisms, Steinem has remained a popular public figure. A collection of her articles and essays, *Outrageous Acts and Everyday Rebellions,* was published in 1983. In 1986 she published *Marilyn,* a biography of film star Marilyn Monroe retold from a feminist perspective. In *Revolution from Within: A Book of Self-Esteem,* Steinem looked inward, discussing ways that women could empower themselves. In 1994 she wrote *Moving Beyond Words,* another work of social commentary.

"ECONOMIC SYSTEMS ARE NOT VALUE-FREE COLUMNS OF NUMBERS BASED ON RULES OF REASON, BUT WAYS OF EXPRESSING WHAT VARYING SOCIETIES BELIEVE IS IMPORTANT."

CROSS-REFERENCES

Dworkin, Andrea; Feminist Jurisprudence; Ireland, Patricia; MacKinnon, Catharine; Millett, Katherine Murray; Sex Discrimination; Women's Rights.

STENOGRAPHER   An individual who records court proceedings either in shorthand or through the use of a paper-punching device.

A court stenographer is an officer of the court and is generally considered to be a state or public official. Appointment of a court stenographer is largely governed by statute. A stenographer is ordinarily appointed by the court as an official act, which is a matter of public record. She is an official under the control of the court and is, therefore, generally subject to its direction. She is not under the dominion and control of the attorneys in a case. The term of office of a court stenographer is also regulated by statute in most cases.

The stenographer has the duty to attend court and to be present, or on call, throughout the entire trial, so that the court and the litigants can be protected by a complete record of the proceedings. The stenographer must take notes of what occurs before the court and transcribe and file the notes within the time permitted. The notes must comply with provisions requiring the stenographer to prepare and sign a certificate stating that the proceedings, evidence, and charges levied against the defendant were fully and accurately taken at the trial and that the TRANSCRIPT represents an accurate translation of the notes.

Some statutes provide that a judge who appoints the stenographer also has the power to remove him. Other statutes fix the term of office; in which case a stenographer cannot be removed at a judge's pleasure, even though the judge has the power to appoint him.

The compensation of a court stenographer may be in the form of an annual salary, a per diem allowance, or an allowance for work actually performed. In the absence of a statute fixing the fees, a duly appointed stenographer is entitled to be reasonably compensated. Some statutes require that a stenographer's fees must be paid by the parties.

STEVENS, JOHN PAUL A member of the U.S. Supreme Court since 1975, John Paul Stevens has developed a reputation as a judicial centrist on the High Court, although in recent years his voting has taken a more liberal turn.

Born on April 20, 1920, Stevens descended from Nicholas Stevens, who emigrated to America in 1659 after serving as a brigadier general in Oliver Cromwell's army. Stevens' father was a businessman and lawyer; he designed Chicago's Stevens Hotel and was its original managing director.

A political moderate during his college days at the University of Chicago, Stevens graduated Phi Beta Kappa in 1941. During World War II he served with the U.S. Navy and was awarded the Bronze Star. After the war he studied law at Northwestern University School of Law in Chicago, graduating first in his 1947 class.

Stevens began his legal career as a law clerk for U.S. Supreme Court Justice WILEY B. RUT-LEDGE. In 1948 he joined the Chicago firm of Poppenhausen, Johnston, Thompson, and Raymond, specializing in litigation and antitrust law. In 1951 he served as associate counsel on a study of monopoly power for a subcommittee of the Judiciary Committee of the House of Representatives. Upon returning to Chicago in 1952, Stevens founded the firm of Rothschild, Stevens, Barry, and Meyers. Along with his private practice, he taught antitrust law at the Northwestern University and the University of Chicago law schools throughout much of the 1950s. He also served for a time as a member of the U.S. attorney general's National Committee to Study Antitrust Laws.

In 1970 President RICHARD M. NIXON appointed Stevens as a judge of the U.S. Court of Appeals for the Seventh Circuit. He became known for his scholarly abilities and his carefully written, clear, and succinct opinions. His first opinion on the court of appeals was a dissent in a challenge to the summary incarceration of an antiwar activist who had disrupted a legislative session (*Groppi v. Leslie*, 436 F.2d 331 [1971]). Stevens viewed the incarceration as unconstitutional, and the following year

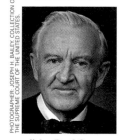

John Paul Stevens

PHOTOGRAPHER: JOSEPH H. BAILEY. COLLECTION OF THE SUPREME COURT OF THE UNITED STATES.

his minority view was vindicated by a unanimous Supreme Court (404 U.S. 496, 92 S. Ct. 582, 30 L. Ed. 2d 632).

The liberal Supreme Court justice WILLIAM O. DOUGLAS retired in 1975, providing President GERALD R. FORD his only opportunity to make a Supreme Court appointment. Stevens received high praise and active support from Ford's attorney general, EDWARD LEVI, and unqualified support from the AMERICAN BAR ASSO-CIATION. During the Senate confirmation hearing, Stevens remarked that he believed that litigants should know how judges viewed the arguments and that it was important to make a record to note diverse views for reference in later cases. Stevens was unanimously confirmed on December 17, 1975, and took his oath of office two days later.

Until Stevens became a justice, new justices were typically seen but not heard. Instead, they usually joined dissents or concurrences without offering their own opinions. Stevens did not fit that pattern. During the 1976–77 term, Stevens had seventeen separate majority concurrences and twenty-seven separate dissents, far more than any other justice.

From the start, Stevens evinced a concern that the legal system give particular care to ensure the rights of the underprivileged, including aliens, illegitimate children, and prisoners. However, Stevens cannot easily be classified as either a judicial liberal or a conservative. In a judicial context, a conservative judge generally will not decide issues that he or she believes are within the province of legislatures. Moreover, a conservative typically votes to enhance government power in a conflict between government interests and individual rights. A judicial liberal, on the other hand, tends to favor individual interests and will look beyond the bounds of a statute and past interpretations of the Constitution to decide social policy questions.

For example, although Stevens is generally perceived as being sympathetic to the rights of prisoners, his sympathy has not necessarily translated into leniency for criminal defendants. Stevens wrote the opinion in *United States v.*

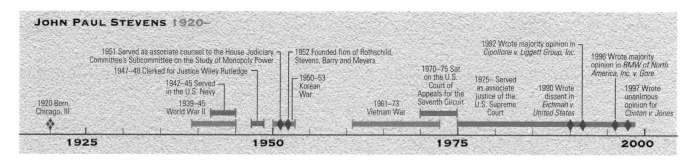

Ross, 456 U.S. 798, 102 S. Ct. 2157, 72 L. Ed. 2d 572 (1982), wherein the Court held that police may search compartments and containers within a vehicle even though the contents are not in plain view, as long as the search is based on PROBABLE CAUSE. Probable cause, the same standard needed to obtain a SEARCH WARRANT, is typically determined by a MAGISTRATE, but this case effectively gave that power to the police in searches of vehicle containers.

Stevens' nomination was opposed by some women's groups that claimed that he was unresponsive in several sexual discrimination cases while on the court of appeals. In 1981 he voted to uphold the all-male draft (*Rostker v. Goldberg*, 453 U.S. 57, 101 S. Ct. 2646, 69 L. Ed. 2d 478), and in another case he declined to consider the theory of COMPARABLE WORTH. On the other hand, he has typically voted to uphold *Roe v. Wade*, 410 U.S. 113, 93 S. Ct. 705, 35 L. Ed. 2d 147 (1973), and limit restrictions to a woman's right to ABORTION (*Planned Parenthood v. Casey*, 510 U.S. 1309, 114 S. Ct. 909, 127 L. Ed. 2d 352 [1994]); *Rust v. Sullivan*, 500 U.S. 173, 111 S. Ct. 1759, 114 L. Ed. 2d 233 [1991]). In the 1997 case of *Clinton v. Jones*, __U.S.__ , 117 S. Ct. 1636, 137 L. Ed. 2d 945, Stevens spoke for a unanimous Court in allowing a SEXUAL HARASSMENT lawsuit against President BILL CLINTON to . go forward. Stevens ruled that the Constitution does not afford a president temporary IMMUNITY, except in the most exceptional circumstances, for civil litigation arising from events that occurred before the president took office. The Court also held that Clinton was not entitled to a STAY of proceedings during his term in office.

One of Stevens' earliest opinions was *Young v. American Mini Theatres, Inc.*, 427 U.S. 50, 96 S. Ct. 2440, 49 L. Ed. 2d 310, (1976). He wrote for a plurality of the Court, upholding Detroit ZONING ordinances that prevented the concentration of "adult" establishments. The case was significant because the ORDINANCE in question did not require a finding that the establishment dealt in legally OBSCENE materials as a prerequisite to legal action. Before the ruling in *Young*, sexually oriented material that was not legally obscene appeared to be entitled to complete FIRST AMENDMENT protection. Stevens wrote that the material in question was so sexually explicit as to be entitled to less protection than other speech, stating that "few of us would march our sons and daughters off to war to preserve the citizen's right to see 'Specified Sexual Activities' exhibited in the theaters of our choice." He reasoned that the zoning restriction did not totally prohibit the availability of the material and was a reasonable action by the city to further its interest in preserving the quality of urban life. This ruling has been the basis for other restrictions that fall short of an outright prohibition of communication that is sexually explicit but not obscene.

Justice Stevens, along with Justices POTTER STEWART and LEWIS F. POWELL, JR., acted as a swing vote in a series of death penalty cases in the mid-1970s. The Court upheld death penalty statutes providing for discretion in imposition but overturned those calling for mandatory death sentences. Stevens voted against the death penalty in cases of RAPE and dissented from a 1989 decision permitting an execution for someone who committed a MURDER at age sixteen or seventeen.

In *Eichman v. United States*, 496 U.S. 310, 110 S. Ct. 2404, 110 L. Ed. 2d 287 (1990), the Supreme Court ruled that FLAG burning was a form of expression protected by the First Amendment and overturned a federal statute that attempted to protect flags. The majority ruled that the statute had to withstand the most exacting scrutiny and could not be upheld under the First Amendment. Stevens wrote a dissent joined by conservative Chief Justice WILLIAM H. REHNQUIST and two other justices, maintaining that the statute was consistent with the First Amendment.

Stevens wrote the opinion in *BMW of North America, Inc. v. Gore*, __U.S.__ , 116 S. Ct. 1589, 134 L. Ed. 2d 809 (1996), the first case in which the High Court overturned a jury's PUNITIVE DAMAGES award. A jury awarded an automobile owner $4 million (later reduced to $2 million) when the manufacturer failed to disclose a refinished paint job on a new BMW. Stevens called the award "grossly excessive" and set out criteria to determine the propriety of punitive damage awards. The four dissenting justices in the case argued that the ruling improperly intruded into states' prerogatives.

In 1992 Stevens wrote the opinion for *Cipollone v. Liggett Group, Inc.*, 505 U.S. 504, 112 S. Ct. 2608, 120 L. Ed. 2d 407 (1992), possibly exposing the TOBACCO industry to huge monetary awards by opening the door to increased litigation for smoking-related deaths. In a 7–2 decision, the Court ruled that cigarette manufacturers that lie about the dangers of smoking or otherwise misrepresent their products can be sued under state laws. At issue was whether federal law preempts state COMMON-LAW liability lawsuits; cigarette labeling is governed by federal law. The Court ruled that federal suits are the only avenue for pursuing failure-to-warn cases or claims of omissions in the manufacturer's advertising or promotions. However, litigants may sue in state court for claims of

"IT IS NOT OUR JOB TO APPLY LAWS THAT HAVE NOT YET BEEN WRITTEN."

breaches of express warranties, claims that cigarette advertisements are fraudulent, and claims that a company hid the dangers of smoking from state authorities or conspired to mislead smokers.

Stevens also authored *Wallace v. Jaffree,* 472 U.S. 38, 105 S. Ct. 2479, 86 L. Ed. 2d 29 (1985), holding that a state cannot provide a moment of silence at the beginning of the school day for the express purpose of facilitating meditation or prayer. The Court held that the Alabama statute in question could not pass constitutional scrutiny.

Justice Stevens was married in 1942 and has four children. He and his first wife divorced in 1979, and he subsequently remarried.

STEVENSON, ADLAI EWING Adlai Ewing Stevenson was a lawyer, statesman, and unsuccessful Democratic party candidate for the presidency in 1952 and 1956. An eloquent and witty speaker, Stevenson served as chief U.S. delegate to the UNITED NATIONS during the Kennedy administration.

Stevenson was born on February 5, 1900, in Los Angeles, California, and moved with his family to Bloomington, Illinois, in 1906. He graduated from Princeton University in 1922 and studied law at Northwestern University. He was admitted to the Illinois bar in 1926 and established a successful law practice in Chicago.

By the early 1930s Stevenson had set his sights on public service, following the course of his grandfather, Adlai E. Stevenson, who was vice president of the United States during the administration of President GROVER CLEVELAND (1893–1897). Stevenson joined the NEW DEAL administration of President FRANKLIN D. ROOSEVELT in 1933, serving as special legal adviser to the Agricultural Adjustment Administration. In 1934 he became general counsel for the Federal Alcohol Bureau.

Though Stevenson returned to his Chicago law practice in 1934, he remained an active civic leader. He headed the Chicago Bar Association's Civil Rights Committee and became the chair of the Chicago chapter of the Committee to Defend America by Aiding the Allies. This committee, composed of prominent business

BIOGRAPHY

Adlai Ewing Stevenson

"THE ESSENCE OF A REPUBLICAN GOVERNMENT IS NOT COMMAND. IT IS CONSENT."

and civic leaders, worked to overcome U.S. isolationist foreign policy and provide aid to Great Britain and France at the beginning of World War II.

Stevenson rejoined the Roosevelt administration in 1941 as special assistant to the secretary of the navy, and in 1943 he led a mission to Italy to establish a U.S. relief program. In 1945 Stevenson moved to the State Department, where he became a key participant in the establishment of the United Nations (U.N.). He was senior adviser to the U.S. delegation at the first meeting of the U.N. General Assembly in London in 1946 and was a U.S. delegate at meetings of the assembly in New York in 1946 and 1947.

In 1948 Stevenson returned to Illinois and ran as the Democratic candidate for governor. He was elected by the largest majority ever recorded in the state. He proved an effective chief executive, revitalizing the civil service, establishing a MERIT SYSTEM for the hiring of state police, improving the care of patients in state mental hospitals, and increasing state aid to public education.

When President HARRY S TRUMAN announced that he would not seek reelection in 1952, Democratic leaders urged Stevenson to seek the nomination. Although Stevenson declined to campaign for the nomination, the 1952 Democratic National Convention in Chicago drafted him as their presidential candidate. Stevenson ran a vigorous campaign but proved no match for the Republican candidate and popular war hero, General DWIGHT D. EISENHOWER. Eisenhower easily defeated Stevenson in 1952 and again in 1956.

Stevenson spent the 1950s practicing law in Chicago and serving as a spokesperson for the Democratic party. At the 1960 Democratic National Convention in Los Angeles, a small group of liberals again sought to draft Stevenson for president. The effort failed and Senator JOHN F. KENNEDY of Massachusetts was nominated.

Kennedy appointed Stevenson U.S. ambassador to the United Nations and gave him cabinet rank. Stevenson was deeply disappointed, however, believing he was the best-

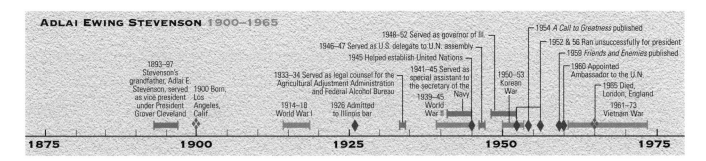

ADLAI EWING STEVENSON 1900–1965

1893–97 Stevenson's grandfather, Adlai E. Stevenson, served as vice president under President Grover Cleveland

1900 Born, Los Angeles, Calif.

1914–18 World War I

1926 Admitted to Illinois bar

1933–34 Served as legal counsel for the Agricultural Adjustment Administration and Federal Alcohol Bureau

1939–45 World War II

1941–45 Served as special assistant to the secretary of the Navy

1945 Helped establish United Nations

1946–47 Served as U.S. delegate to U.N. assembly

1948–52 Served as governor of Ill.

1950–53 Korean War

1954 *A Call to Greatness* published

1952 & 56 Ran unsuccessfully for president

1959 *Friends and Enemies* published

1960 Appointed Ambassador to the U.N.

1965 Died, London, England

1961–73 Vietnam War

1875   1900   1925   1950   1975

qualified person to serve as secretary of state. Despite his disappointment, Stevenson carried out his role at the United Nations with distinction. During the CUBAN MISSILE CRISIS of October 1962, Stevenson had a dramatic confrontation with the Soviet Union's delegate, telling the delegate he was prepared to wait "until Hell freezes over" for an answer to his question about Soviet missiles in Cuba.

Stevenson wrote two books, *A Call to Greatness* (1954) and *Friends and Enemies* (1959). He died on July 14, 1965, in London, England.

STEWART, POTTER As an associate justice from 1958 to 1981, Potter Stewart charted a middle course during a vigorous era on the U.S. Supreme Court. Before his appointment to the Court by President DWIGHT D. EISENHOWER, Stewart practiced law, served in local government in his native Cincinnati, Ohio, and sat on the Sixth Circuit Court of Appeals from 1954 to 1958. He joined the Supreme Court during a period when the Court was changing the social and political landscape by extending CIVIL RIGHTS and liberties under Chief Justice EARL WARREN, yet Stewart remained a moderate during his twenty-three-year tenure. Pragmatism, unpredictability, and plainspoken opinions were his hallmarks. His penchant for witty phrases made him highly quotable, but his inconsistent voting record left only an ambiguous mark on U.S. law. At age forty-three, he was among the youngest appointees to the Court and, at age sixty-six, also one of the youngest justices to retire from it.

Born in Jackson, Michigan, on January 23, 1915, Stewart came from old money and a family steeped in law and politics. Educated at University School, Hotchkiss, as well as at Yale, Cambridge, and Yale Law School, he earned his law degree from Yale in 1941. A stint on Wall Street followed. He served in the U.S. Navy during World War II and returned to Ohio after the war. After working for a large law firm in his home state, Stewart briefly followed his father's footsteps into politics. James Garfield Stewart had been mayor of Cincinnati and a justice of the Ohio Supreme Court. Potter Stewart served on the city council and as vice

BIOGRAPHY

Potter Stewart

"SWIFT JUSTICE DEMANDS MORE THAN JUST SWIFTNESS."

mayor, but he soon abandoned political life to build his own legal practice.

In 1954 President Eisenhower appointed Stewart to the federal bench. Stewart's high profile in the Ohio bar made him an attractive candidate for the Sixth Circuit Court of Appeals, where he served for the next four years. He was widely respected for his competence and efficiency as an appellate judge, and Eisenhower returned to him in 1958 when a seat opened on the Supreme Court. Although southern senators who disliked his embrace of SCHOOL DESEGREGATION offered scattered opposition to his appointment, the nomination easily succeeded.

On the Supreme Court, Stewart was a moderate justice. He was criticized for indecision, chiefly because he was often the unpredictable swing vote in cases that pitted the WARREN COURT'S activist and judicial restraint blocs against each other. Stewart, however, followed his instincts on the Court without obvious resort to ideology or doctrine. To the question of whether he was liberal or conservative, he replied, "I am a lawyer," explaining that the labels had little value for him in the political sphere and even less in law. Stewart's approach in his opinions is notable for its plain-edged pragmatism. He blasted a state's anti-contraception laws as "uncommonly silly" in *Griswold v. Connecticut* (381 U.S. 479, 85 S. Ct. 1678, 14 L. Ed. 2d [1965]), and in another case, he wrote of OBSCENITY, stating, "I know it when I see it" (*Jacobellis v. Ohio*, 378 U.S. 184, 84 S. Ct. 1676, 12 L. Ed. 2d 793 [1964]).

In the arena of civil rights and liberties, Stewart's moderate outlook clearly revealed itself. He sided with claimants in 52 percent of these cases. Among his most notable decisions in favor of civil liberties was *Jones v. Alfred H. Mayer Co.*, 392 U.S. 409, 88 S. Ct. 2186, 20 L. Ed. 2d 1189 (1968), in which the Warren Court upheld measures that protected African Americans against discrimination in housing. Stewart's pragmatism did not allow for subjectivity, however. Although he regarded Connecticut's ban on the use of contraceptives as silly, he found the law constitutional and dissented from

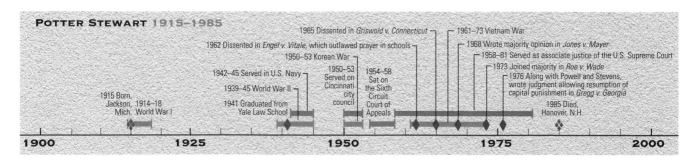

POTTER STEWART 1915–1985

1915 Born, Jackson, Mich. World War I 1914–18

1939–45 World War II
1941 Graduated from Yale Law School
1942–45 Served in U.S. Navy

1950–53 Served on Cincinnati city council
1950–53 Korean War

1954–58 Sat on the Sixth Circuit Court of Appeals

1962 Dissented in *Engel v. Vitale*, which outlawed prayer in schools
1965 Dissented in *Griswold v. Connecticut*

1961–73 Vietnam War
1968 Wrote majority opinion in *Jones v. Mayer*
1958–81 Served as associate justice of the U.S. Supreme Court
1973 Joined majority in *Roe v. Wade*
1976 Along with Powell and Stevens, wrote judgment allowing resumption of capital punishment in *Gregg v. Georgia*
1985 Died, Hanover, N.H.

1900   1925   1950   1975   2000

the majority in *Griswold v. Connecticut*. He maintained his moderate outlook in his later years on the Court. He agreed with the majority's expansion of a right to PRIVACY in the landmark ABORTION case, *Roe v. Wade*, 410 U.S. 113, 93 S. Ct. 705, 35 L. Ed. 2d 147 (1973), but he also attacked the Court's tendency to invalidate any state law it found unwise.

Stewart's legacy on the Court defies easy categorization. At best he is remembered for his pragmatism and at worst for leaving a less than cohesive body of opinions. He retired from the Court in 1981 and died in Hanover, New Hampshire, on December 7, 1985.

See also GRISWOLD V. CONNECTICUT; ROE V. WADE.

STIMSON, HENRY LEWIS Henry Lewis Stimson was a lawyer and a distinguished public servant, occupying key posts in the administrations of five presidents between 1911 and 1945. As secretary of state, he sought disarmament, while as secretary of war he advocated the use of the atomic bomb against Japan in World War II.

Stimson was born on September 21, 1867, in New York City. He earned a bachelor's degree from Yale in 1888, a master's degree from Harvard University in 1889, and a bachelor of laws degree from Harvard in 1890. He was admitted to the New York bar in 1891 and joined the law firm headed by Elihu Root, a prominent attorney and influential figure in the Republican party.

In 1906 President THEODORE ROOSEVELT appointed Stimson U.S. attorney for the southern district of New York. He left the post in 1909 to run as the Republican nominee for governor of New York. Although he lost the 1910 election, his stock continued to rise. President WILLIAM HOWARD TAFT named Stimson secretary of war in 1911, a position he held until the end of the Taft administration in 1913. He then returned to his New York law practice.

Stimson did not reenter public service until 1927, when President CALVIN COOLIDGE named him governor of the Philippine Islands. In 1929 President HERBERT HOOVER elevated Stimson to secretary of state, a position that put him on the world stage. As secretary, Stimson sought to

BIOGRAPHY

Henry Lewis Stimson

"THE BOMBS DROPPED ON HIROSHIMA AND NAGASAKI ENDED THE WAR. THEY ALSO MADE IT WHOLLY CLEAR THAT WE MUST NEVER HAVE ANOTHER WAR."

continue the policy of military disarmament, participating in the London Naval Conference of 1930.

Following the Japanese invasion of Manchuria in 1931, Stimson wrote a diplomatic note to both China and Japan, informing them that the United States would not recognize territorial or other changes made in violation of U.S. treaty rights. The "Stimson Doctrine" was invoked as the rationale for successive economic EMBARGOES against Japan during the 1930s.

With the election of President FRANKLIN D. ROOSEVELT, a Democrat, in 1932, Stimson returned to his law practice and private life. By the end of the 1930s, however, with the growing belligerence of Germany and Japan, Stimson emerged as an opponent of U.S. isolationist policies. When World War II began in 1939, Stimson became a leading member of the Committee to Defend America by Aiding the Allies, urging the U.S. government to provide aid to Great Britain and France.

President Roosevelt, who also sought to help the Allies, appointed Stimson secretary of war in 1940. By appointing a Republican to this key post, Roosevelt strengthened bipartisan support for his foreign policy. Stimson remained secretary of war during World War II and received praise for his quiet but firm administration of the war effort.

In 1945, acting as chief presidential adviser on atomic programs, Stimson directed the Manhattan Project, which resulted in the creation of the atomic bomb. He recommended to President HARRY S TRUMAN that atomic bombs be dropped on Japanese cities of military importance. Truman followed his advice, ordering the bombing of Hiroshima and Nagasaki that brought a swift end to World War II. Stimson defended his recommendation, arguing that the bombings ended the war quickly and therefore saved more lives than were lost.

Stimson left office in September 1945. He published his autobiography, *On Active Service in Peace and War*, in 1948. He died on October 20, 1950, in Huntington, New York.

STIPULATION An agreement between attorneys that concerns business before a court

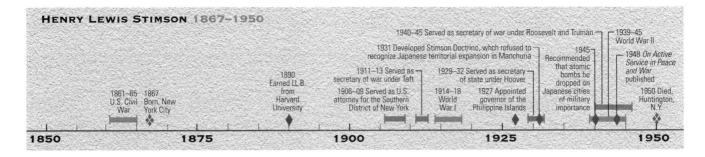

HENRY LEWIS STIMSON 1867–1950

1940–45 Served as secretary of war under Roosevelt and Truman

1939–45 World War II

1931 Developed Stimson Doctrine, which refused to recognize Japanese territorial expansion in Manchuria

1945 Recommended that atomic bombs be dropped on Japanese cities of military importance

1948 *On Active Service in Peace and War* published

1890 Earned LL.B. from Harvard University

1911–13 Served as secretary of war under Taft

1929–32 Served as secretary of state under Hoover

1861–65 U.S. Civil War

1867 Born, New York City

1906–09 Served as U.S. attorney for the Southern District of New York

1914–18 World War I

1927 Appointed governor of the Philippine Islands

1950 Died, Huntington, N.Y.

1850   1875   1900   1925   1950

An example of stipulations stated by counsel in open court

[Title of Court and Cause]

Mr. A _____ : Your Honor, I think we can state for the record the following stipulated matter—and Mr. X _____ can correct me if I'm wrong—that:

Mr. _____ , who is a boat captain and patrols the offshore waters of the State of _____ in the _____ limit, would testify that in the 19____ fishing season, the only season in which he has been employed with the Commission, which would be relevant to this proceeding, that he did not see the _____ fishing vessels operating in State of _____ waters for purposes of fishing.

We would have testimony from Mr. _____ , who is a fish spotter for _____ Corporation, who has been a fish spotter for _____ years with _____ Corporation and eight years previously with another company. He would testify that he is fully able to recognize the various boats of different companies and he has during the last three seasons seen no fishing by vessels owned by _____ or _____ . He would also testify that in years past, running back for _____ to _____ years, I believe he said, that there has been substantially little or no fishing by _____ or _____ .

Mr. _____ , also a fish spotter for _____ Corporation for _____ years, and _____ years previously with another company, would indicate that he has in the past three seasons seen _____ vessels only rarely in State of _____ waters engaged in fishing, but that in years past, perhaps _____ years past, _____ , did engage in some fishing of a substantial nature in State of _____ waters.

Judge _____ : Thank you, Mr. _____ .

Mr. X _____ .

Mr. X _____ : I would like to add to that, your Honor, that both Mr. _____ and Mr. _____ are employees of _____ Corporation, which is mentioned in the affidavits and briefs; that Mr. _____ , I believe would testify that the quantity of _____ fish available in State of _____ waters has dropped significantly in the last three or four years and is continuing to drop, and I believe he said that was true generally of the _____ Coast Fisheries, save for the _____ area, which this year experienced some increase. They would—

Judge _____ : Is that quantity, you said, quantity of fish?

Mr. X _____ : Quantity, yes, sir, of _____ fish.

I believe that they would also verify, for what it's worth, your Honor, that the men, the Captains and crews of the plaintiffs' boats, are largely residents of the State of _____ in the _____ area, and I believe that two of these gentlemen, Mr. _____ and Mr. _____ , formerly worked for the plaintiffs in the _____ fishery themselves.

May I have just one more moment?

Judge _____ : Yes.

Mr. X _____ : May it please the Court, we have one further stipulation, bearing on the same subject matter, which is that Mr. _____ , if asked, would testify that a full boatload of fish, average boat size, on today's market is worth about $ _____ and that even with the refrigerated equipment available on the boats today that _____ fish would begin to deteriorate, begin to spoil, after about a week.

Judge _____ : All right, sir.

Mr. A _____ , do you have any disagreement with that?

Mr. A _____ : We would agree that he would testify to that; yes, sir.

Judge _____ : All right.

Mr. A _____ : We would like, for the purposes of the information of the Court, to clarify that Mr. _____ , the defendant, is Chairman of the _____ , and that weighs upon his inability to be here, your Honor.

Judge _____ : There is no question that as much as $10,000 and more is involved in this case, is there?

Mr. X _____ : I don't think so, your Honor.

Mr. A _____ : No, sir.

This is with regard to the appropriateness of an injunctive relief. That's why we intended to introduce this evidence.

and is designed to simplify or shorten litigation and save costs. 📖

During the course of a civil lawsuit, criminal proceeding, or any other type of litigation, the opposing attorneys may come to an agreement about certain facts and issues. Such an agreement is called a stipulation. Courts look with favor on stipulations because they save time and simplify the matters that must be resolved. Stipulations are voluntary, however, and courts may not require litigants to stipulate with the other side. A valid stipulation is binding only on the parties who agree to it. Courts are usually bound by valid stipulations and are required to enforce them.

Parties may stipulate to any matter concerning the rights or obligations of the parties. The litigants cannot, however, stipulate as to the validity or constitutionality of a statute or as to what the law is, because such issues must be determined by the court.

Stipulations may cover a variety of matters. Parties are permitted to make stipulations to dismiss or discontinue an ACTION, to prescribe the issues to be tried, or to admit, exclude, or withdraw EVIDENCE. During a court proceeding, attorneys often stipulate to allow copies of papers to be admitted into evidence in lieu of originals or to agree to the qualifications of a WITNESS. The parties can also enter into agreements concerning the TESTIMONY an absent witness would give if he were present, and the stipulated facts can be used in evidence. Such evidentiary devices are used to simplify and expedite trials by dispensing with the need to prove uncontested factual issues.

Generally, parties to an action can stipulate as to an agreed statement of facts on which to submit their case to the court. Stipulations of this nature are encouraged by the courts. A number of other stipulations have been held to be valid, including those that relate to attorneys' fees and costs.

A stipulation does not need to be in a particular form, provided it is definite and certain. A number of statutes and court rules provide that stipulations reached out of court must be in writing to prevent FRAUDULENT claims of oral stipulation, circumvent disputes concerning the terms of the stipulation, and relieve the court of the burden of resolving such disputes. Though an oral stipulation in open court is binding, a stipulation made in the judge's chamber must be in writing.

STOCK 📖 A security issued by a CORPORATION that represents an ownership right in the ASSETS of the corporation and a right to a proportionate share of profits after payment of corporate liabilities and obligations. 📖

Shares of stock are reflected in written instruments known as stock certificates. Each share represents a standard unit of ownership in a corporation. Stock differs from consumer GOODS in that it is not used or consumed; it does not have any intrinsic value but merely represents a right in something else. Nevertheless, a stockholder is a real owner of a corporation's property, which is held in the name of the corporation for the benefit of all its stockholders. An owner of stock generally has the right to participate in the management of the corporation, usually through regularly scheduled stockholders' (or shareholders') meetings. Stocks differ from other securities such as NOTES and BONDS, which are corporate obligations that do not represent an ownership interest in the corporation.

The value of a share of stock depends upon the issuing corporation's value, profitability, and future prospects. The market price reflects what purchasers are willing to pay based on their evaluation of the company's prospects.

Two main categories of stock exist: common and preferred. An owner of COMMON STOCK is typically entitled to participate and vote at stockholders' meetings. In addition to common stock, some corporate BYLAWS or charters allow for the issuance of PREFERRED STOCK. If a corporation does not issue preferred stock, all of its stock is common stock, entitling all holders to an equal PRO RATA division of profits or net earnings, should the corporation choose to distribute the earnings as DIVIDENDS. Preferred stockholders are usually entitled to priority over holders of common stock should a corporation LIQUIDATE.

Preferred stocks receive priority over common stock with respect to the payment of dividends. Holders of preferred stock are entitled to receive dividends at a fixed annual rate before any dividend is paid to the holders of common stock. If the earnings to pay a dividend are more than sufficient to meet the fixed annual dividend for preferred stock, then the remainder of the earnings will be distributed to holders of common stock. If the corporate earnings are insufficient, common stockholders will not receive a dividend. In the alternative, a remainder may be distributed pro rata to both preferred and common classes of the stock. In such a case, the preferred stock is said to "participate" with the common stock.

A preferred stock dividend may be cumulative or noncumulative. In the case of cumulative preferred stock, an unpaid dividend becomes a charge upon the profits of the next and succeeding years. These accumulated and unpaid dividends must be paid to preferred stockholders before common stockholders receive any dividends. Noncumulative preferred stock means that a corporation's failure to earn or pay a dividend in any given year extinguishes the obligation, and no debit is made against the succeeding years' surpluses.

PAR value is the face or stated value of a share of stock. In the case of common stocks, par value usually does not correspond to the market value of a stock, and a stated par value is of little significance. Par is important with respect to preferred stock, however, because it often signifies the dollar value upon which dividends are figured. Stocks without an assigned stated value are called no par. Some states have eliminated the concept of par value.

Blue chip stocks are stocks traded on a securities exchange (listed stock) that have minimum risk due to the corporation's financial record. Listed stock means a company has filed an application and registration statement with both the SECURITIES AND EXCHANGE COMMISSION and a securities exchange. The registration statement contains detailed information about the company to aid the public in evaluating the stock's potential. Floating stock is stock on the open market not yet purchased by the public. Growth stock is stock purchased for its perceived potential to appreciate in value, rather than for its dividend income. PENNY STOCKS are highly speculative stocks that usually cost under a dollar per share.

See also SECURITIES; STOCK MARKET.

STOCK DIVIDEND 📖 A corporate distribution to shareholders declared out of profits, at the discretion of the directors of the CORPORATION, which is paid in the form of shares of stock, as opposed to money, and increases the number of shares. 📖

When a corporation declares a stock DIVIDEND, it adds undivided profits, which cannot be used to pay dividends, to the capital invested in the corporation, to reflect the additional shares it is issuing. The stockholder's increased number of shares represent the same proportion of the value of the company as the stockholder originally held (that is, the stockholder owns the same percentage of the corporation as prior to the declaration of the stock dividend); however, the cash value of an individual share is not reduced.

Shares issued as stock dividends are evidence that additional ASSETS have been added to the capital. The value of the shares of a corporation often, but not always, increases following a stock dividend. A stock dividend is actually a part of corporation bookkeeping.

A stock split is different from a stock dividend in that no adjustment is made to the capital; instead, the number of shares representing the capital increase. The cash value of an individual share, therefore, decreases in proportion to the size of the stock split.

STOCKHOLDER'S DERIVATIVE SUIT
📖 A legal action in which a shareholder of a CORPORATION sues in the name of the corporation to enforce or defend a legal right because the corporation itself refuses to sue. 📖

A stockholder's derivative suit is a type of litigation brought by one or more shareholders to remedy or prevent a wrong to the corporation. In a derivative suit, the plaintiff shareholders do not sue on a CAUSE OF ACTION belonging to themselves as individuals. Instead, they sue in a representative capacity on a cause of action that belongs to the corporation but that for some reason the corporation is unwilling to pursue. The real party in interest is the corporation, and the shareholders are suing on its behalf. Most often, the actions of the corporation's executives are at issue. For example, a shareholder could bring a derivative suit against an executive who allegedly used the corporation's assets for personal gain.

A derivative suit is different from a direct suit brought by a shareholder to enforce a claim based on the shareholder's ownership of shares. These direct suits involve contractual or statutory rights of the shareholders, the shares themselves, or rights relating to the ownership of shares. Such direct suits include actions to recover DIVIDENDS and to examine corporate books and records.

The principal justification for permitting derivative suits is that they provide a means for shareholders to enforce claims of the corporation against managing officers and DIRECTORS of the corporation. Officers and directors, who are in control of the corporation, are unlikely to authorize the corporation to bring suit against themselves. A derivative suit permits a shareholder to prosecute these claims in the name of the corporation. Other justifications for derivative litigation are that it prevents multiple lawsuits, ensures that all injured shareholders will benefit proportionally from the recovery, and protects CREDITORS and preferred shareholders against diversion of corporate ASSETS directly to shareholders.

In a derivative suit, the shareholder is the nominal PLAINTIFF, and the corporation is a nominal DEFENDANT, even though the corporation usually recovers if the shareholder prevails. Nevertheless, derivative litigation is essentially three-sided because the defendants include the persons who are alleged to have caused harm to the corporation or who have personally profited from corporate action. The claim of wrong-doing against these defendants is the central issue in a derivative suit, and the interest of the corporation is usually adverse to these defendants. Thus, individual defendants are usually represented by attorneys other than the attorneys for the corporation. The corporation may play different roles in a derivative suit. It may be an active party in the litigation, be entirely passive, or side with the individual defendants and argue that their conduct did not harm the corporation.

Generally, the plaintiff shareholder is not required to have a large financial stake in the litigation. As a result, the plaintiff's attorney is often the principal mover in filing a derivative suit; the attorney locates a possible derivative claim and then finds an eligible shareholder to serve as plaintiff. Consequently the attorney may have a much more direct and substantial financial interest in the case and its outcome than the plaintiff shareholder who is a purely nominal participant in the litigation. Because most derivative suits are taken on a CONTINGENT FEE basis, the plaintiff's attorney will receive compensation only on the successful prosecution of the suit or by its settlement. Such a recovery is justified on the theory that it encourages meritorious shareholder suits.

Most derivative suits are settled and do not go to trial and appeal. The lead attorney for the plaintiff usually determines whether a proposed settlement is acceptable. The fee to be paid to the lead attorney is usually negotiated as part of the overall settlement of a derivative suit. All aspects of the settlement are subject to judicial review and approval, however.

Derivative suits have proved controversial. Corporations complain that most litigation is brought at the behest of entrepreneurial attorneys who first find a potential violation and then find a shareholder qualified to maintain the derivative suit. Critics charge that the objective of these suits is to obtain a settlement with the principal defendants and the corporation that provides the attorney with a generous fee. In return for the attorney's fee, the plaintiff "goes away."

Derivative suits involve shareholder enforcement of corporate obligations, which may intrude on the traditional management powers of the BOARD OF DIRECTORS. Since the 1980s boards of directors have had considerable success in reasserting control over derivative litigation.

States have enacted laws that put a financial roadblock in the way of derivative actions. A minority of states require that the plaintiff make a DEMAND on the shareholders, which is very expensive, before a derivative suit is filed. The shareholder demand requirement may be excused if the plaintiff can show adequate reasons for not making the effort. Nineteen states require certain plaintiff shareholders in derivative suits to give the corporation security for reasonable expenses, including attorneys' fees, that the corporation or other defendants may incur in connection with the lawsuit. Despite these efforts to restrain derivative actions, they have not prevented the filing of doubtful claims by attorneys seeking a quick settlement.

Almost all states require the plaintiff to allege and prove that he first made a GOOD FAITH effort to obtain action by the corporation before filing a derivative suit. This good faith demand requirement is contained in state corporation laws and rules of court. A typical provision is rule 23.1 of the Federal Rules of Procedure, which states that the plaintiff's COMPLAINT must "allege with particularity the efforts, if any, made by the plaintiff to obtain the action he or she desires from the board of directors or comparable authority and the reasons for his or her failure to obtain the action or for not making the effort."

Plaintiffs have generally not made these demands, however, and have instead sought to convince the court that there were good reasons for not doing so. Much of this reluctance to make a demand can be traced to changes in the corporate law of Delaware in the 1980s. Delaware, which is the principal state of incorporation for publicly held corporations, empowers a corporation to appoint a litigation committee from its board of directors to review shareholder demands. If the litigation committee finds no merit in a demand, it can decide that the suit should not be pursued, and the court must accept the committee's decision and dismiss the case. The development of the litigation committee has expedited the disposition of many doubtful derivative claims and possibly some meritorious ones as well.

See also DERIVATIVE ACTION.

STOCK MARKET The various organized stock exchanges and over-the-counter markets.

The trading of SECURITIES such as STOCKS and BONDS is conducted in stock exchanges, which are grouped under the general term *stock market*. The stock market is an important institution for capitalist countries because it encourages investment in corporate securities, providing capital for new businesses and income for investors. In the 1990s large numbers of ordinary persons have come to own stock through PENSION funds, deferred employee savings plans, investment clubs, or MUTUAL FUNDS.

The New York Stock Exchange is the oldest (formed in 1792) and largest stock exchange in the United States, but other exchanges operate in many major U.S. cities. The activities of the stock market are closely monitored by the federal SECURITIES AND EXCHANGE COMMISSION to prevent the manipulation of stock prices and other activities that lessen investor confidence.

Stock exchanges are private organizations with a limited number of members. Stock brokerage houses generally cannot purchase seats on an exchange. Instead, a member of the firm holds a seat personally. In some cases several partners of a brokerage house will be members of an exchange. The price of a seat fluctuates depending on the state of the economy, but seats on the New York Stock Exchange have sold for more than $1 million.

Some exchange members are specialists in particular types of securities, while others act as agents for other brokers. A small number of brokers who pay an annual fee but are not members also have access to the trading floor.

A stock exchange is essentially a marketplace for stocks and bonds, with stockbrokers earning small commissions on each transaction they make. Stocks that are handled by one or more stock exchanges are called listed stocks. For a corporation's stock to be listed on an exchange, the company must meet certain exchange requirements. Each exchange has its own criteria and standards, but in general a company must show that it has sufficient capital and is in sound financial condition. Once a company is listed, trading in its stock will be suspended if the company's financial condition deteriorates to the point that it no longer meets the exchange's minimum requirements.

When a person wishes to purchase a stock, she places an order with a brokerage house. The BROKER gets a quotation or price and sends the order to the firm's representative on the floor of the stock exchange. The representative negotiates the sale and notifies the brokerage house. Transactions happen rapidly, and each one is recorded on a computer system and sent immediately to an electronic ticker that displays stock information on a screen. At one time this information was generally only available at stock brokerage houses, but the daily stock ticker is now available on television and through the Internet.

New York Stock Exchange transactions may be made in three ways. A cash transaction requires payment and delivery of the stock on the day of purchase. A regular transaction requires payment and delivery of the stock by noon on the third day following a full business day. Around 95 percent of stock is purchased under these terms. Finally, purchase can be made through a seller's OPTION contract, which requires payment and delivery of the stock within any specified time not exceeding sixty days, though seven days is the most common period.

All transactions not made in the stock exchanges take place in over-the-counter (OTC) trading. An OTC transaction is not an AUCTION

Trading of stocks on the stock market involves millions of shares per day and has a direct effect on the U.S. economy. As a result, the stock market is closely regulated by the federal government.

ALAN ODDIE/PHOTOEDIT

The 30 Companies That Make up the Dow Jones Industrial Average

(1) Allied Signal Inc.
(2) Aluminum Company of America (ALCOA)
(3) American Express Co.
(4) AT&T Corp.
(5) Boeing Co.
(6) Caterpillar Inc.
(7) Chevron Corp.
(8) Coca-Cola Co.
(9) DuPont Co.
(10) Eastman Kodak Co.
(11) Exxon Corp.
(12) General Electric Co.
(13) General Motors Corp.
(14) Goodyear Tire & Rubber Corp.
(15) Hewlett-Packard Co.
(16) IBM Corp.
(17) International Paper Co.
(18) J.P. Morgan & Co.
(19) Johnson & Johnson
(20) McDonald's Corp.
(21) Merck & Co.
(22) Minnesota Mining and Manufacturing Co. (3M)
(23) Philip Morris Co.
(24) Proctor & Gamble Co.
(25) Sears, Roebuck & Co.
(26) Travelers Property/Casualty
(27) Union Carbide Corp.
(28) United Technologies Corp.
(29) Wal-Mart Stores Inc.
(30) Walt Disney Co.

SOURCE: Dow Jones & Co.

on the stock exchange floor but a negotiation between a seller and a buyer. Most sales of bonds occur in OTC trading as do most new issues of securities. In the 1980s discount OTC brokerage firms appeared, offering lower commissions on stock transactions for investors who were willing to do more research on their own. By the 1990s these firms had proliferated.

Dealers in OTC trading are not confined just to large cities, as are stock exchanges, but can be found in many locations throughout the United States. In 1971 these firms were linked to an electronic communications system and became NASDAQ, the National Association of Securities Dealers Automated Quotations. By the 1990s NASDAQ had become the second largest U.S. stock market.

The health of the U.S. economy is typically measured by the stock market. When stock prices rise and there is a "bull market," U.S.

business is assumed to be doing well. When stock prices fall and there is a "bear market," this is usually an indication of a downturn in business and the economy.

See also COMMON STOCK; PREFERRED STOCK.

STOCK WARRANT A certificate issued by a CORPORATION that entitles the person holding it to buy a certain amount of stock in the corporation, usually at a specified time and price.

A stock warrant differs from a stock option only in that an OPTION is offered to employees and a warrant to the general public. A warrant gives the person holding it a right to subscribe to CAPITAL STOCK.

STOMACH PUMPING CASE See ROCHIN v. CALIFORNIA.

STONE, HARLAN FISKE Harlan Fiske Stone served as associate justice of the U.S. Supreme Court from 1925 to 1941 and as chief justice from 1941 to 1946. A believer in judicial restraint, he was also a defender of CIVIL RIGHTS and civil liberties. Stone was often a lone dissenter in the 1920s and 1930s when conservatives, who dominated the Court, struck down state and federal legislation that sought to regulate business and working conditions.

Stone was born on October 11, 1872, in Chesterfield, New Hampshire. He graduated from Amherst College in 1894 and Columbia Law School in 1898. Admitted to the New York bar the year of his graduation, Stone became a member of a prominent New York City law firm. He was also a part-time instructor at Columbia Law School from 1899 to 1902. In 1902 Stone left his law firm to become a professor of law at Columbia. From 1910 to 1923 he was dean of the law school. He resigned in 1924 to join Sullivan and Cromwell, the most prestigious law firm in New York City.

In 1924 President CALVIN COOLIDGE appointed Stone attorney general. The Department of Justice had been tarnished by the TEAPOT DOME scandal during the administration of Coolidge's predecessor, President WARREN G. HARDING. In addition, the Bureau of Investigation (BI), the forerunner of the Federal Bu-

BIOGRAPHY

PORTRAIT BY CHARLES J. FOX, COLLECTION OF THE SUPREME COURT OF THE UNITED STATES.

Harlan Fiske Stone

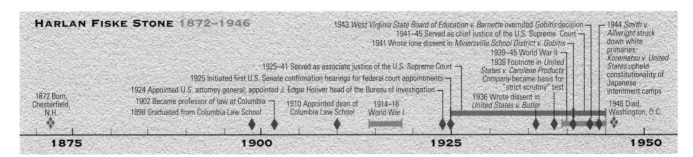

HARLAN FISKE STONE 1872-1946

1872 Born, Chesterfield, N.H.

1898 Graduated from Columbia Law School

1902 Became professor of law at Columbia

1910 Appointed dean of Columbia Law School

1914–18 World War I

1924 Appointed U.S. attorney general; appointed J. Edgar Hoover head of the Bureau of Investigation

1925 Initiated first U.S. Senate confirmation hearings for federal court appointments

1925–41 Served as associate justice of the U.S. Supreme Court

1936 Wrote dissent in *United States v. Butler*

1938 Footnote in *United States v. Carolene Products Company* became basis for "strict-scrutiny" test

1939–45 World War II

1941 Wrote lone dissent in *Minersville School District v. Gobitis*

1941–45 Served as chief justice of the U.S. Supreme Court

1943 *West Virginia State Board of Education v. Barnette* overruled *Gobitis* decision

1944 *Smith v. Allwright* struck down white primaries; *Korematsu v. United States* upheld constitutionality of Japanese internment camps

1946 Died, Washington, D.C.

1875   1900   1925   1950

reau of Investigation (FBI), had become a home to political cronyism and corruption. Stone appointed J. EDGAR HOOVER to head the BI and institute wide-ranging reforms. Stone's administration of the Department of Justice drew praise from Congress and President Coolidge.

Coolidge nominated Stone to the Supreme Court in 1925. Some senators were fearful that Stone's Wall Street connections would cause him to favor business interests. Responding to these concerns, Stone proposed that he appear before the Senate Judiciary Committee to answer questions. The committee accepted, thereby creating the now-traditional confirmation process used for federal court appointments. Stone was easily confirmed.

In the 1920s the Court was dominated by conservative justices who struck down many state and federal laws that sought to regulate labor, business, commerce, and working conditions. Stone dissented from these decisions, arguing that the Court should exercise judicial restraint and allow Congress and state legislatures to craft laws that address pressing social and economic problems.

With the election of President FRANKLIN D. ROOSEVELT in 1932, the Supreme Court's hostility to government regulation drew even greater attention as it declared unconstitutional a host of NEW DEAL economic reforms. Stone wrote a biting dissent in the case of *United States v. Butler*, 297 U.S. 1, 56 S. Ct. 312, 80 L. Ed. 477 (1936), which involved a processing tax paid by farmers to fund subsidies paid to eligible farmers under Roosevelt's Agricultural Adjustment Act. The act was declared unconstitutional because all farmers were taxed but only specific farmers received benefits. Stone argued that the subsidies were valid.

Although Stone was a Republican and President Roosevelt a Democrat, Roosevelt appointed Stone chief justice in 1941. Stone's tenure as chief justice was marked by bitter fighting among the justices, which has been blamed partly on Stone's inability to negotiate and build a consensus.

Stone's commitment to civil liberties was demonstrated in *Minersville School District v. Gobitis*, 310 U.S. 586, 60 S. Ct. 1010, 84 L. Ed. 1375 (1940). He was the lone dissenter when the Court upheld a state law that required Jehovah's Witnesses to salute the FLAG, even though this conflicted with their religious beliefs. Stone argued that the law infringed on the FIRST AMENDMENT right to the free exercise of RELIGION. Three years later his view was endorsed by the Court in *West Virginia State Board*

"THE LAW [SHOULD NOT BE SEEN AS] A HERMETICALLY SEALED COMPARTMENT OF SOCIAL SCIENCE, TO BE EXPLORED AND ITS PRINCIPLES FORMULATED WITHOUT REFERENCE TO THOSE SOCIAL AND ECONOMIC FORCES WHICH CALL LAW INTO EXISTENCE."

BIOGRAPHY

Lucy Stone

of Education v. Barnette, 319 U.S. 624, 63 S. Ct. 1178, 87 L. Ed. 1628 (1943), when it overruled *Gobitis*.

In the area of civil rights, Stone helped move the Court from tacit acceptance of the racially discriminatory status quo in the southern states to a more aggressive stance. In *United States v. Classic*, 313 U.S. 299, 61 S. Ct. 1031, 85 L. Ed. 1368 (1941), the Court ruled that the federal government could regulate party primaries to prevent election fraud that resulted in the failure to count African American votes. Three years later the Court struck down the white primary, which excluded African Americans from southern Democratic parties and Democratic primary elections (*Smith v. Allwright*, 321 U.S. 649, 64 S. Ct. 757, 88 L. Ed. 987 [1944]). Stone played a pivotal role in deciding these cases.

Stone contributed to modern constitutional analysis in a famous footnote to his opinion in *United States v. Carolene Products Company*, 304 U.S. 144, 58 S. Ct. 778, 82 L. Ed. 1234 (1938). Known as footnote four, it stated that "prejudice against discrete and insular minorities may be a special condition, which tends seriously to curtail the operation of those political processes ordinarily to be relied upon to protect minorities and which may call for a more searching judicial scrutiny." This footnote became the basis for the "strict scrutiny" test, which the Court applies to assess the constitutionality of legislation concerning the rights of racial minorities, religious sects, aliens, prisoners, and other "discrete and insular minorities." Under STRICT SCRUTINY the government must demonstrate more than just a rational basis for legislation. It must show a COMPELLING STATE INTEREST and prove that the legislation is narrowly tailored to meet that interest.

Stone's tenure, however, was not unblemished. In *Korematsu v. United States*, 323 U.S. 214, 65 S. Ct. 193, 89 L. Ed. 194 (1944), he upheld the forced relocation of Japanese Americans to detention camps during World War II. The decision was based on the wartime powers of the president to take emergency actions for national security reasons.

Stone died on April 22, 1946, in Washington, D.C.

CROSS-REFERENCES

Footnote Four; Japanese American Evacuation Cases; *Korematsu v. United States*.

STONE, LUCY Lucy Stone was one of the first leaders of the WOMEN'S RIGHTS movement in the United States. A noted lecturer and writer,

NATIONAL PORTRAIT GALLERY, SMITHSONIAN INSTITUTION, WASHINGTON, D.C.

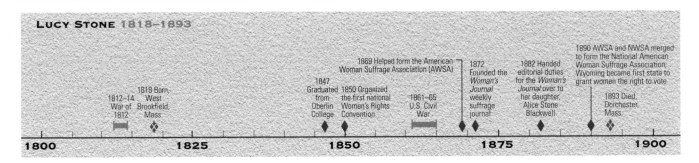

LUCY STONE 1818–1893

1812–14 War of 1812

1818 Born, West Brookfield, Mass.

1847 Graduated from Oberlin College

1850 Organized the first national Women's Rights Convention

1861–65 U.S. Civil War

1869 Helped form the American Woman Suffrage Association (AWSA)

1872 Founded the Woman's Journal weekly suffrage journal

1882 Handed editorial duties for the Woman's Journal over to her daughter, Alice Stone Blackwell

1890 AWSA and NWSA merged to form the National American Woman Suffrage Association; Wyoming became first state to grant women the right to vote

1893 Died, Dorchester, Mass.

1800   1825   1850   1875   1900

Stone spent most of her life working for women's SUFFRAGE. She is also believed to be the first married woman in the U.S. to keep her maiden name.

Stone was born on August 13, 1818, in West Brookfield, Massachusetts. Determined to attend college, she went to work as a teacher at the age of sixteen to earn money for the tuition. Nine years later she entered Oberlin College, the first coeducational college in the United States. While at Oberlin she formed the first women's college debating society. Stone was a fiery and forceful orator.

After graduating in 1847, Stone became a lecturer for the Massachusetts Anti-Slavery Society, one of the leading abolitionist organizations of its time. Stone became convinced that parallels existed between the positions of women and slaves. In her view both were expected to be passive, cooperative, and obedient. In addition, the legal status of both slaves and women was inferior to that of white men. Stone persuaded the society to allow her to spend part of her time speaking on the topic of women's rights. In 1850 she organized the first national Women's Rights Convention in Worcester, Massachusetts.

In 1855 Stone married Henry B. Blackwell, an Ohio merchant and abolitionist. The couple entered into the MARRIAGE "under protest"; at their wedding they read and signed a document explicitly protesting the legal rights that were given to a husband over his wife. They omitted the word "obey" from the marriage vows and promised to treat each other equally. Stone also announced that she would not take her husband's name and would be addressed instead as Mrs. Stone. This action drew national attention, and women who retained their maiden names were soon known as "Lucy Stoners."

After the Civil War Stone and Blackwell shifted their energies to women's suffrage. Although Stone was in agreement with ELIZABETH CADY STANTON and SUSAN B. ANTHONY on the goal of women's suffrage, she differed as to the best way to secure the vote for women. In 1869

"THE FLOUR-MERCHANT . . . AND THE POSTMAN CHARGE US NO LESS ON ACCOUNT OF OUR SEX, BUT WHEN WE ENDEAVOR TO EARN MONEY TO PAY ALL THESE, THEN, INDEED, WE FIND THE DIFFERENCE."

Stone helped form the American Woman Suffrage Association (AWSA). The AWSA worked for women's suffrage on a state by state basis, seeking amendments to state constitutions. Stanton and Anthony established a rival organization, the National Woman Suffrage Association (NWSA), that sought an amendment to the U.S. Constitution similar to the FIFTEENTH AMENDMENT that gave nonwhite men the right to vote. Whereas the AWSA concentrated on women's suffrage, the NWSA took a broader approach, lobbying for improvements in the legal status of women in areas such as FAMILY LAW as well as for suffrage.

Stone also helped found the Woman's Journal, a weekly suffrage journal, in 1872. She edited the journal for many years, eventually turning the task over to her daughter, Alice Stone Blackwell, in 1882. As editor, Stone focused on the AWSA's goal of suffrage.

In 1890 the AWSA and the NWSA merged into the National American Woman Suffrage Association (NAWSA). Stone became the chair of the executive committee, and Stanton served as the first president. In that same year, Wyoming became the first state to meet Stone's goal as it entered the Union with a constitution that gave women the right to vote.

Stone died on October 19, 1893, in Dorchester, Massachusetts.

See also NINETEENTH AMENDMENT.

STOP AND FRISK 📖 The situation where a police officer who is suspicious of an individual detains the person and runs his hands lightly over the suspect's outer garments to determine if the person is carrying a concealed weapon. 📖

One of the most controversial police procedures is the *stop and frisk* search. This type of limited search occurs when police confront a suspicious person in an effort to prevent a crime from taking place. The police frisk (pat down) the person for weapons and question the person.

A stop is different from an arrest. An arrest is a lengthy process in which the suspect is taken to the police station and booked, whereas a stop involves only a temporary interference with a person's liberty. If the officer uncovers further evidence during the frisk, the stop may lead to an actual arrest, but if no further EVIDENCE is found, the person will be released.

Unlike a full search, a frisk is generally limited to a patting down of the outer clothing. If the officer feels what seems to be a weapon, the officer may then reach inside the person's clothing. If no weapon is felt, the search may not intrude further than the outer clothing.

Though police had long followed the practice of stop and frisk, it was not until 1968 that the Supreme Court evaluated it under the FOURTH AMENDMENT's protection against unreasonable searches and seizures. Under Fourth Amendment CASE LAW, a constitutional SEARCH AND SEIZURE must be based on PROBABLE CAUSE. A stop and frisk was usually conducted on the basis of REASONABLE suspicion, a somewhat lower standard than probable cause.

In 1968 the Supreme Court addressed the issue in *Terry v. Ohio*, 392 U.S. 1, 88 S. Ct. 1868, 20 L. Ed. 2d 889. In *Terry* an experienced plainclothes officer observed three men acting suspiciously; they were walking back and forth on a street and peering into a particular store window. The officer concluded that the men were preparing to rob a nearby store and approached them. He identified himself as a police officer and asked for their names. Unsatisfied with their responses, he then subjected one of the men to a frisk, which produced a gun for which the suspect had no permit. In this case the officer did not have a WARRANT nor did he have probable cause. He did suspect that the men were "casing" the store and planning a ROBBERY. The defendants argued the search was unreasonable under the Fourth Amendment because it was not supported by probable cause.

The Supreme Court rejected the defendants' arguments. The Court noted that stops and frisks are considerably less intrusive than fullblown arrests and searches. It also observed that the interests in crime prevention and in police safety require that the police have some leeway to act before full probable cause has developed. The Fourth Amendment's reasonableness requirement is sufficiently flexible to permit an officer to investigate the situation.

The Court was also concerned that requiring probable cause for a frisk would put an officer in unwarranted danger during the investigation. The "sole justification" for a frisk, said the Court, is the "protection of the police officer and others nearby." Because of this narrow scope, a frisk must be "reasonably designed to discover guns, knives, clubs, or other hidden instruments for the assault of the police officer." As long as an officer has reasonable suspicion, a stop and frisk is constitutional under the Fourth Amendment.

After *Terry* this type of police encounter became known as a "*Terry* stop" or an "investigatory detention." Police may stop and question suspicious persons, pat them down for weapons, and even subject them to nonintrusive search procedures such as the use of metal detectors and drug-sniffing dogs. While a suspect is detained, a computer search can be performed to see if the suspect is wanted for crimes. If so, she may be arrested and searched incident to that arrest.

Investigatory detention became an important law enforcement technique in the 1980s as police sought to curtail the trafficking of illegal drugs. In *United States v. Sokolow*, 490 U.S. 1, 109 S. Ct. 1581, 104 L. Ed. 2d 1 (1989), the Supreme Court ruled that police have the power to detain, question, and investigate suspected drug couriers. The case involved a *Terry* stop at an international airport, where the defendant aroused suspicion by conforming to a controversial "drug courier profile" developed by the Drug Enforcement Agency (DEA). The Court said that the DEA profile gave the officer reasonable suspicion, "which is more than a mere hunch but less than probable cause."

The Supreme Court has become increasingly permissive regarding what constitutes reasonable suspicion. In *Alabama v. White*, 496 U.S. 325, 110 S. Ct. 2412, 110 L. Ed. 2d 301 (1990), the Court upheld a *Terry* stop of an

Police officers may stop and frisk criminal suspects to discover hidden weapons.

JOHN BOYKIN/THE PICTURE CUBE

———— Bank

———— [*City*], ———— [*State*]

Stop Payment Clerk Always request letter of confirmation and hold this memo until the confirmation is received.

Date Received ————————————
Time Received ————————————
Received By ————————————
If paid, check here ————————————
If unpaid, check here ————————————
Time received by bookkeepers ————————

MAKER	DATE	NUMBER	PAYEE	AMOUNT

A sample record of a telephoned stop payment request

automobile based solely on an anonymous tip that described a certain car that would be at a specific location. Police went to the site, found the vehicle, and detained the driver. The police then found marijuana and cocaine in the automobile. The Court observed that it was a "close case" but concluded that the tip and its corroboration were sufficiently reliable to justify the investigatory stop that ultimately led to the arrest of the driver and the seizure of the drugs.

CROSS-REFERENCES

Automobile Searches; Criminal Law; Drugs and Narcotics; *Terry v. Ohio.*

STOP ORDER ▣ A direction by a customer to a stock BROKER, directing the broker to wait until a stock reaches a particular price and then to complete the transaction by purchasing or selling shares of that stock. ▣

STOPPAGE IN TRANSIT ▣ The right of a seller to prevent the delivery of GOODS to a buyer after such goods have been delivered to a COMMON CARRIER for shipment. ▣

See also SALES LAW.

STOP PAYMENT ORDER ▣ Revocation of a CHECK; a notice made by a depositor to his or her bank directing the bank to refuse payment on a specific check drawn by the depositor. ▣

An individual who writes a check can revoke it unless it has been certified, accepted, or paid. If a bank pays a check after a timely stop payment order by the depositor, the bank is usually liable to the depositor for the amount paid.

STORY, JOSEPH Joseph Story served as associate justice of the U.S. Supreme Court from 1811 to 1845. One of the towering figures in U.S. legal history, Story shaped U.S. law both as a judge and as the author of a series of legal TREATISES. Some legal commentators believe Story's treatises were as influential in the development of nineteenth-century U.S. law as the works of the English jurists SIR WILLIAM BLACKSTONE and SIR EDWARD COKE had been earlier.

Story was born on September 18, 1779, in Marblehead, Massachusetts. He graduated from Harvard University in 1798 and read the law with Samuel Sewall. He established a practice

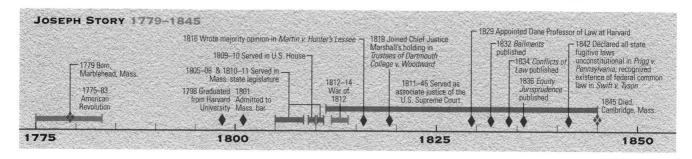

JOSEPH STORY 1779–1845

- 1779 Born, Marblehead, Mass.
- 1775–83 American Revolution
- 1798 Graduated from Harvard University
- 1801 Admitted to Mass. bar
- 1805–08 & 1810–11 Served in Mass. state legislature
- 1809–10 Served in U.S. House
- 1812–14 War of 1812
- 1816 Wrote majority opinion in *Martin v. Hunter's Lessee*
- 1811–45 Served as associate justice of the U.S. Supreme Court
- 1819 Joined Chief Justice Marshall's holding in *Trustees of Dartmouth College v. Woodward*
- 1829 Appointed Dane Professor of Law at Harvard
- 1832 *Bailments* published
- 1834 *Conflicts of Law* published
- 1836 *Equity Jurisprudence* published
- 1842 Declared all state fugitive laws unconstitutional in *Prigg v. Pennsylvania*; recognized existence of federal common law in *Swift v. Tyson*
- 1845 Died, Cambridge, Mass.

1775   1800   1825   1850

in Salem, Massachusetts, in 1801 and quickly developed an impressive professional career, becoming a DIRECTOR and eventually the president of the Merchant's Bank of Salem. He became a member of the Democratic party and was elected to the state legislature in 1805. He served part of a term in the U.S. House of Representatives from 1808 to 1809 and then returned to the state legislature in 1810. The following year he was elected speaker of the house.

In November 1811 President JAMES MADISON appointed Story, at the age of only thirty-two, to the U.S. Supreme Court. Madison hoped that Story would help move the Court in a more democratic direction, correcting the aristocratic tendencies of the federal bench, which had been dominated by the Federalists. In particular, Madison sought to check the influence of Chief Justice JOHN MARSHALL, whose nationalist philosophy led him to construe federal powers broadly. THOMAS JEFFERSON was opposed to the appointment, however, believing that Story did not subscribe to the Democratic party belief in according deference to state governments.

Jefferson proved to be correct as Story quickly revealed an inclination to accept most of Marshall's principles. In *Martin v. Hunter's Lessee*, 14 U.S. 304, 4 L. Ed. 97 (1816), the U.S. Supreme Court reviewed a decision by the Virginia Supreme Court declaring a section of the federal JUDICIARY ACT of 1789 unconstitutional. In his majority opinion, Story reversed the state supreme court and affirmed the Supreme Court's power to review the highest state courts in all civil cases involving the federal Constitution, statutes, and treaties. This decision was a key component of federal judicial power and antithetical to Jefferson's conception of state-federal relations.

In *Trustees of Dartmouth College v. Woodward*, 17 U.S. 518, 4 L. Ed. 629 (1819), Story joined in Chief Justice Marshall's holding that the grant of a corporate CHARTER was a CONTRACT with the state. As the state had not reserved a power of amendment, the charter grantees were immune from destructive state interference.

PORTRAIT BY GEORGE P. A. HEALY, COLLECTION OF THE SUPREME COURT OF THE UNITED STATES.

Joseph Story

"[THE LAW] IS A JEALOUS MISTRESS AND REQUIRES A LONG AND CONSTANT COURTSHIP. IT IS NOT TO BE WON BY TRIFLING FAVORS, BUT BY LAVISH HOMAGE."

Story noted that this corporate IMMUNITY should be extended only to private, not public, CORPORATIONS. In making this distinction, Story articulated for the first time that the public character of a corporation turned not on the services it performed but on the identity of the contributors of its capital. Thus, a corporation that was chartered to serve the public, such as a bank, would be considered a private corporation if it was owned by private individuals, and its charter could not be withdrawn or amended in the absence of a legislative reservation at the time of the original grant. This definition of private corporations by reference to their capitalization was critical to corporate development in the nineteenth century.

Story's most controversial decision came in *Prigg v. Pennsylvania*, 41 U.S. 539, 10 L. Ed. 1060 (1842), which involved the federal Fugitive Slave Act of 1793. Many northern states demonstrated their hostility to SLAVERY by enacting laws designed to frustrate southern slave owners who came north in search of runaway slaves. Slave owners were outraged at these laws and argued that the federal act gave them the right to reclaim their property without interference by state governments.

Story, writing for an 8–1 majority, declared unconstitutional all fugitive slave laws enacted by the states because the federal law provided the exclusive remedy for the return of runaway slaves. Story also ruled, however, that states were not compelled to enforce the federal fugitive slave provisions. It would be inconsistent and without legal basis, he reasoned, for the Court to declare the preeminence of federal law and then require state courts to help carry out that law.

Prigg was a crucial decision because it announced that slavery was a national issue that could not be disturbed by state action. It angered many opponents of slavery and hurt Story's reputation in the north. Some state judges took Story's opinion to heart and refused to participate in federal fugitive slave proceedings.

Story's other major contribution on the Court was the development of "federal common law," which was first articulated in the 1842 CIVIL PROCEDURE case of *Swift v. Tyson*, 41 U.S. 1, 10 L. Ed. 865. The controversy arose on a technical question involving the negotiability of a commercial BILL OF EXCHANGE. New York and other states were divided over whether the bill was negotiable. Under the federal Judiciary Act of 1789, the FEDERAL COURTS were instructed to follow state laws when deciding cases between parties from two different states.

Story, who believed the negotiability of such bills was crucial to the development of a national commercial community, declared that the decisions of the New York courts—based not on legislative statutes but on interpretations of the COMMON LAW—were not "laws" binding on federal judges. Common-law decisions were only "evidence" of the appropriate law. Story concluded that it was the duty of federal courts to examine evidence from all relevant state common-law jurisdictions before proclaiming the governing rule.

Story's opinion came to stand for the proposition that a general federal common law existed that federal courts were free to apply in virtually all common-law matters of private law. The idea of federal common law promoted national uniformity but also constituted a revolutionary expansion of federal JURISDICTION. The Supreme Court overruled this proposition in *Erie Railroad Co. v. Tompkins*, 304 U.S. 64, 58 S. Ct. 817, 82 L. Ed. 1188 (1938), declaring that federal courts must apply the law of the state, whether it is statutory or CASE LAW.

Story's influence went beyond his court decisions. In 1829 he was appointed to be the first Dane Professor of Law at Harvard. He remained in this position the rest of his life while simultaneously serving on the Supreme Court and acting as president of the Salem bank.

The endowment that Nathan Dane had given to Harvard Law School also paid for the publication of Story's many legal commentaries and treatises, which summarized and codified various areas of the law. Story's works included *Bailments* (1832), *Bills of Exchange* (1843), *Conflict of Laws* (1834), *Equity Jurisprudence*

(1836), *Equity Pleading* (1838), *Federal Constitution* (1833), and *Promissory Notes* (1845). They served as valuable reference works for lawyers, judges, and legislators and had a profound influence on the development of commercial law in particular. Alexis de Tocqueville, the French author of *Democracy in America* (1835–1840), a classic analysis of U.S. society and government, used Story's constitutional commentaries in writing his work.

Story died on September 10, 1845, in Cambridge, Massachusetts.

CROSS-REFERENCES

Erie Railroad Co. v. Tompkins; Fugitive Slave Act of 1850; Prigg v. Pennsylvania; Swift v. Tyson; Trustees of Dartmouth College v. Woodward.

BIOGRAPHY

Juanita Kidd Stout

STOUT, JUANITA KIDD Juanita Kidd Stout was the first African American woman to be elected judge in the United States. Before her election to the Pennsylvania bench, Stout worked in the Philadelphia district attorney's office. She later was appointed to the Pennsylvania Supreme Court, becoming the first African American woman to serve on that court.

Stout was born on March 7, 1919, in Wewoka, Oklahoma, the daughter of schoolteachers Henry Maynard Kidd and Mary Alice Kidd. She earned a bachelor's degree from the University of Iowa in 1939. At that time no accredited colleges in Oklahoma admitted African Americans. Between 1939 and 1942, Stout taught music in the high schools at Seminole and Sand Springs, Oklahoma. In 1942 she moved to Washington, D.C., and worked in a law office, which led to her decision to become a lawyer.

Stout graduated from the University of Indiana Law School in 1948. She taught at Florida A&M University in 1949 and Texas Southern University in 1950. In 1950 she became an administrative assistant to a federal appeals court judge in Philadelphia. She left this position in 1954 and went into private practice. In 1955 she joined the city's district attorney's office, serving as chief appellate attorney.

In September 1959 Governor David L.

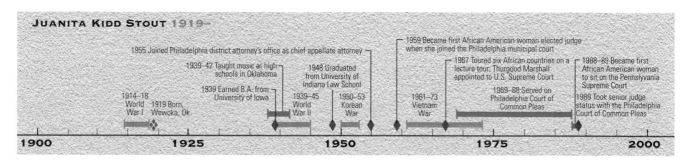

JUANITA KIDD STOUT 1919–

1955 Joined Philadelphia district attorney's office as chief appellate attorney

1959 Became first African American woman elected judge when she joined the Philadelphia municipal court

1939–42 Taught music at high schools in Oklahoma

1948 Graduated from University of Indiana Law School

1967 Toured six African countries on a lecture tour; Thurgood Marshall appointed to U.S. Supreme Court

1988–89 Became first African American woman to sit on the Pennsylvania Supreme Court

1939 Earned B.A. from University of Iowa

1969–88 Served on Philadelphia Court of Common Pleas

1989 Took senior judge status with the Philadelphia Court of Common Pleas

1914–18 World War I

1919 Born, Wewoka, Ok.

1939–45 World War II

1950–53 Korean War

1961–73 Vietnam War

1900　　　　1925　　　　1950　　　　1975　　　　2000

Lawrence appointed Stout a judge of the Philadelphia municipal court. Stout ran for a full term on the bench in November of that year and was elected, making her the first African American woman to be elected to a judgeship. In 1969 she was elected to the Philadelphia Court of Common Pleas and was reelected in 1979, both times receiving the highest number of votes of the Philadelphia Bar Association with respect to judicial qualifications.

During the 1960s Stout gained national recognition for her vigorous fight against crime and juvenile delinquency. She wrote numerous articles about race, crime, and justice and toured six African countries in 1967, lecturing at law schools, colleges, and high schools.

In 1988 Stout was appointed to the Pennsylvania Supreme Court. Her tenure was brief, however, because an age limit specified by the state constitution forced her to retire one year later at age seventy. Stout returned to the Philadelphia Court of Common Pleas to serve as a senior judge. She has continued to speak out on racial and gender bias in the courts.

STRADDLE ◫ In the STOCK and COMMODITY markets, a strategy in options CONTRACTS consisting of an equal number of PUT options and CALL options on the same underlying share, index, or commodity future. ◫

A straddle is a type of OPTION contract that gives the holder of the contract the option to either buy or sell or not buy or sell the SECURITIES or commodities specified in the contract. To understand how a straddle works, a basic understanding of options is required. An option is a type of contract used in the stock and commodity markets, in the leasing and sale of REAL ESTATE, and in other areas where one party wants to acquire the legal right to buy or sell something from another party within a fixed period of time.

In the stock and commodity markets, options come in two primary forms, known as "calls" and "puts." A call gives the holder the option to buy stock or a commodities FUTURES contract at a fixed price for a fixed period of time. A put gives the holder the option to sell stock or a commodities futures contract at a fixed price for a fixed period of time.

An option has four components: the underlying security, the type of option (put or call), the strike price, and the expiration date. Take, for example, a "National Widget November 100 call." National Widget stock is the underlying security, November is the expiration month of the option, 100 is the strike price (sometimes referred to as the exercise price), and the option is a call, giving the holder of the call the right,

not the OBLIGATION, to buy 100 shares of National Widget at a price of 100 (any number of shares can be involved, but usually options are sold for 100 shares or multiples of 100).

A straddle is the purchase of a call and a put with the same strike price, the same expiration date, and the same underlying security. For example, the purchase of a National Widgets November 95 call and the simultaneous purchase of a National Widgets November 95 put while the stock price is about 95 would be a straddle.

With highly volatile stocks or commodities that are likely to make big moves, investors may want to hedge because they do not know which way the investment will move. The use of a straddle allows the investor to spread the risk, preventing a total loss but also precluding the maximum profit that comes with a favorable put or call. The investor knows that either the put or the call option will not be exercised in a straddle, so a key factor in assessing potential profit is the cost of purchasing the put versus the cost of the call.

See also STOCK MARKET.

STRAIGHT-LINE DEPRECIATION ◫ A method employed to calculate the decline in the value of income-producing property for the purposes of federal taxation. ◫

Under this method, the annual DEPRECIATION deduction that is used to offset the annual income generated by the property is determined by dividing the cost of the property minus its expected SALVAGE value by the number of years of anticipated useful life.

STRANGER ◫ A third person; anyone who is not a PARTY to a particular legal ACTION or agreement. ◫

For example, all those who are not parties to a particular CONTRACT are considered strangers to the contract.

STRATEGIC ARMS LIMITATION TALKS (SALT I, SALT II)   See ARMS CONTROL AND DISARMAMENT.

STRATEGIC LAWSUITS AGAINST PUBLIC PARTICIPATION (SLAPPs) ◫ Retaliatory lawsuits intended to silence, intimidate, or punish those who have used public forums to speak, petition, or otherwise move for government action on an issue. ◫

The term *strategic lawsuits against public participation*, known by the acronym SLAPPs, applies to a variety of different types of lawsuits, including those claiming LIBEL, DEFAMATION, business interference, or CONSPIRACY. The term was coined by Professors George W. Pring and Penelope Canan of the University of Denver, who began to study this form of litigation in

1984. Pring and Canan define SLAPPs using four criteria: "[SLAPPs] (1) involve communications made to influence a government action or outcome, (2) which result in civil lawsuits (COMPLAINTS, COUNTERCLAIMS, or CROSS-CLAIMS), (3) filed against non-governmental individuals or groups (4) on a substantive issue of some public interest or social significance."

In a typical SLAPP, an individual or citizens' group—the "target" (using Pring and Canan's terminology), or defendant—is sued by the "filer," or plaintiff, for alleged wrongdoing simply because that individual or group has used constitutionally protected rights to persuade the government to take a particular course of action. SLAPPs have been directed against individuals and groups that have spoken in public forums on a wide variety of issues, particularly against REAL ESTATE development, the actions of public officials, environmental damage or POLLUTION, and unwanted land use. They have also been used against those who have worked publicly for the rights of consumers, workers, women, minorities, and others. SLAPP defendants have been sued for apparently lawful actions such as circulating a petition, writing to a local newspaper, speaking at a public meeting, reporting violations of the law, or participating in a peaceful demonstration.

For example, a Colorado environmental protection group opposed a commercial development and was eventually sued by the developer for $40 million. The lawsuit claimed that the environmental group was guilty of "conspiracy" and "abuse of process" (*Lockport Corporation v. Protect Our Mountain Environment*, No. 81CV973 [Dist. Ct., Jefferson County, Colo. 1981]). The suit dragged on for several years, cost the environmental group much time and money, and eventually resulted in its demise. Although the development did not go forward, many group members vowed that they would refrain from future community involvement out of fear of legal retribution.

Others who have been targeted by SLAPPs include a group of parents who voiced concern over unsafe school buses at a school board meeting, only to become defendants in a $680,000 suit for libel filed by the bus company, and neighbors who protested renewal of a bar's liquor license and were then faced with an $8 million libel suit initiated by the bar owner.

Judges dismiss the majority of SLAPPs as a violation of constitutional rights, generally on the grounds that the defendant's activities are protected by the Petition Clause of the FIRST AMENDMENT to the Constitution. That clause establishes "the right of the people . . . to petition the Government for a redress of grievances." However, in those cases where a SLAPP is not quickly dismissed, the expense of the litigation for SLAPP defendants, both in time and money, often serves as punishment itself and dissuades individuals from speaking out in the future. Individuals who have been hit with a SLAPP—or "SLAPPed"—often report a feeling of having been sued into silence and feel dissuaded from participating in public life again—quite often the very effect intended by the SLAPP filer. Although a SLAPP filer usually loses in court, he or she may achieve the goal of silencing future political opposition.

For these reasons, the legal system has widely viewed SLAPPs as an example of the use of law for the purpose of intimidation and as a threat to citizen involvement and public participation. SLAPPs, critics contend, attempt to privatize public debate and have a chilling effect on public speech and involvement.

SLAPPs date back to the earliest years of the United States, when citizens occasionally were sued for speaking out against corruption in government. Courts generally dismissed such lawsuits, however, and SLAPPs fell into general disuse until the 1960s and 1970s. During those decades a wave of political activism concerning many issues—from the environment to minority rights—sparked suits claiming defamation, libel, and business interference from affected parties, particularly corporations and business interests. By the 1980s and 1990s, many observers claimed that SLAPPs were seriously hampering participation in the U.S. political system.

Individuals and governments reacted to the growth of SLAPPs in a number of different ways. Targets of SLAPP cases sometimes have countersued—a process known as a "SLAPPback"—often making many of the same claims as the SLAPP filer: MALICIOUS PROSECUTION, ABUSE OF PROCESS, defamation, and business interference. Those who have filed SLAPPbacks generally have been successful in court and have won large cash settlements from juries. Advocates of SLAPPbacks say that they are a necessary deterrent to SLAPP filers.

Rulings of the U.S. Supreme Court have increasingly supported the rapid judicial review and dismissal of SLAPPs. Using standards developed in earlier cases (*Eastern Railroad Presidents' Conference v. Noerr Motor Freight, Inc.*, 365 U.S. 127, 81 S. Ct. 523, 5 L. Ed. 2d 464 [1961], and *United Mine Workers v. Pennington*, 381 U.S. 657, 85 S. Ct. 1585, 14 L. Ed. 2d 626 [1965]), the Court ruled in *City of Columbia v. Omni Outdoor Advertising Inc.*, 499 U.S. 365,

111 S. Ct. 1344, 113 L. Ed. 2d 382 (1991), that the First Amendment's Petition Clause protects "a concerted effort to influence public officials regardless of intent or purpose." The Court held that SLAPPs should be dismissed in all cases except those in which the target's activities are not genuinely directed at gaining favorable government action.

A number of states have passed laws intended to prevent SLAPPs and protect the right to participate in public activism. Washington became the first state to pass an anti-SLAPP law in 1989. By 1996 eight other states—California, Delaware, Massachusetts, Minnesota, Nebraska, Nevada, New York, and Rhode Island—had passed such laws. The Minnesota Citizens Participation Bill of 1994 (Minn. Stat. § 554.01-05), for example, protects public participation by requiring a court to dismiss a SLAPP unless the filer can prove that the target's activities were not directed toward producing government action. The law also shifts the burden of proof to the SLAPP filer and allows the SLAPP target to collect attorneys' fees, costs, and damages if the SLAPP is unsuccessful.

See also ENVIRONMENTAL LAW.

STRAW MAN 📖 An individual who acts as a front for others who actually incur the expense and obtain the profit of a transaction. 📖

In the terminology employed by REAL ESTATE dealers, a straw man is an individual who acts as a conduit for convenience in holding and transferring TITLE to the property involved. For example, such a person might act as an AGENT for another in order to take title to REAL PROPERTY and execute whatever documents and instruments the PRINCIPAL directs with respect to the transaction.

STREET RAILROAD 📖 A railway that is constructed upon a thoroughfare or HIGHWAY to aid in the transportation of people or property along the roadway. 📖

Street railroads run at moderate rates of speed and make frequent stops at particular points within a town or city. Subways and elevated railroads that are built above the surface of the roadway are two common examples of street railroads.

MUNICIPAL CORPORATIONS have the authority to regulate the operation of street railroads within their boundaries. This power is generally vested in a board of commission, which sets regulations for the protection of individuals and property. Common requirements mandate street railroads to (1) restrict the speed at which the cars operate; (2) provide the cars with reliable brakes; (3) furnish the cars with signal lights and sound devices; and (4) keep all tracks clear of ice and snow during periods of inclement weather.

Street railroads, such as this elevated transit line in New York City, provide an alternative to automobile or bus transportation. Like bus passengers, those aboard street railroads are free to read, work, or relax during their commute.

STRICT CONSTRUCTION 📖 A close or narrow reading and interpretation of a statute or written document. 📖

Judges are often called upon to make a CONSTRUCTION, or interpretation, of an unclear term in cases that involve a dispute over the term's legal significance. The COMMON-LAW tradition has produced various precepts, MAXIMS, and rules that guide judges in construing statutes or private written agreements such as CONTRACTS. Strict construction occurs when ambiguous language is given its exact and technical meaning, and no other equitable considerations or reasonable implications are made.

A judge may make a construction only if the language is ambiguous or unclear. If the language is plain and clear, a judge must apply the plain meaning of the language and cannot consider other EVIDENCE that would change the meaning. If, however, the judge finds that the words produce absurdity, ambiguity, or a literalness never intended, the plain meaning does not apply and a construction may be made.

In CRIMINAL LAW, strict construction must be applied to criminal statutes. This means that a criminal statute may not be enlarged by implication or intent beyond the fair meaning of the language used or the meaning that is reasonably justified by its terms. Criminal statutes, therefore, will not be held to encompass offenses and individuals other than those clearly described and provided for in their language. The strict construction of criminal statutes complements the rule of lenity, which holds that ambiguity in a criminal statute should be resolved in favor of the defendant.

Strict construction is the opposite of liberal construction, which permits a term to be reasonably and fairly evaluated so as to implement the object and purpose of the document. An ongoing debate in U.S. law concerns how judges should interpret the law. Advocates of strict construction believe judges must exercise restraint by refusing to expand the law through implication. Critics of strict construction contend that this approach does not always produce a just or reasonable result.

See also CANONS OF CONSTRUCTION; PLAIN-MEANING RULE.

STRICT FORECLOSURE 📖 A decree that orders the payment of a MORTGAGE of REAL PROPERTY. 📖

A strict foreclosure decree sets out the amount due under the mortgage, orders it to be paid within a particular time limit, and provides that if payment is not made, the mortgagor's right and EQUITY OF REDEMPTION are forever barred and foreclosed. If the mortgagor does not pay within the time designated, then TITLE to the property vests in the mortgagee without any sale thereof.

STRICT LIABILITY 📖 Absolute legal responsibility for an INJURY that can be imposed on the wrongdoer without proof of carelessness or FAULT. 📖

Strict liability, sometimes called absolute LIABILITY, is the legal responsibility for DAMAGES, or injury, even if the person found strictly liable was not at fault or negligent. Strict liability has been applied to certain activities in tort, such as holding an employer absolutely liable for the torts of her employees, but today it is most commonly associated with defectively manufactured products. In addition, for reasons of PUBLIC POLICY, certain activities may be conducted only if the person conducting them is willing to insure others against the harm that results from the RISKS the activities create.

In PRODUCT LIABILITY cases involving injuries caused by manufactured goods, strict liability has had a major impact on litigation since the 1960s. In 1963, in *Greenman v. Yuba Power Products*, 59 Cal. 2d 57, 377 P.2d 897, the California Supreme Court became the first court to adopt strict tort liability for defective products. Injured plaintiffs have to prove the product caused the harm but do not have to prove exactly how the manufacturer was careless. Purchasers of the product, as well as injured guests, bystanders, and others with no direct relationship with the product, may sue for damages caused by the product.

An injured party must prove that the item was defective, that the defect proximately caused the injury, and that the defect rendered the product unreasonably dangerous. A plaintiff may recover damages even if the seller has exercised all possible care in the preparation and sale of the product.

In TORT LAW strict liability has traditionally been applied for damages caused by animals. Because animals are not governed by a conscience and possess great capacity to do mischief if not restrained, those who keep animals have a duty to restrain them. In most JURISDICTIONS the general rule is that keepers of all animals, including domesticated ones, are strictly liable for damage resulting from the TRESPASS of their animals on the property of another. Owners of dogs and cats, however, are not liable for their pets' trespasses, unless the owners have been negligent or unless strict liability is imposed by statute or ordinance.

For purposes of liability for harm other than trespass, the law distinguishes between domesticated and wild animals. The keeper of domes-

GAMMA

The owner of this dog no doubt purchased its heavy collar with the understanding that it would restrain the dog. If the collar broke and the dog attacked someone, the collar's manufacturer might be liable under a strict liability claim.

ticated animals, which include dogs, cats, cattle, sheep, and horses, is strictly liable for the harm they cause only if the keeper had actual knowledge that the animal had the particular trait or propensity that caused the harm. The trait must be a potentially harmful one, and the harm must correspond to the knowledge. In the case of dogs, however, some jurisdictions have enacted statutes that impose absolute liability for dog bites without requiring knowledge of the dog's viciousness.

Keepers of species that are normally considered "wild" in that region are strictly liable for the harm these pets cause if they escape, whether or not the animal in question is known to be dangerous. Because such animals are known to revert to their natural tendencies, they are considered to be wild no matter how well trained or domesticated.

Strict liability for harm resulting from abnormally dangerous conditions and activities developed in the late nineteenth century. It will be imposed if the harm results from the miscarriage of an activity that, though lawful, is unusual, extraordinary, exceptional, or inappropriate in light of the place and manner in which the activity is conducted. Common hazardous activities that could result in strict liability include storing EXPLOSIVES or flammable liquids, blasting, accumulating sewage, and emitting toxic fumes. Although these activities may be hazardous, they may be appropriate or normal in one location but not another. For example, storing explosives in quantity will create an unusual and unacceptable risk in the midst of a large city but not in a remote rural area. If an explosion occurs in the remote area, strict li-

ability will be imposed only if the explosives were stored in an unusual or abnormal way.

CROSS-REFERENCES
Negligence; Proximate Cause; *Rylands v. Fletcher.*

STRICT SCRUTINY   A standard of JUDICIAL REVIEW for a challenged policy in which the court presumes the policy to be invalid unless the government can demonstrate a compelling interest to justify the policy.

The strict scrutiny standard of judicial review is based on the Equal Protection Clause of the FOURTEENTH AMENDMENT. FEDERAL COURTS use strict scrutiny to determine whether certain types of government policies are constitutional. The U.S. Supreme Court has applied this standard to laws or policies that impinge on a right explicitly protected by the U.S. Constitution, such as the right to vote. The Court has also identified certain rights that it deems to be fundamental rights, even though they are not enumerated in the Constitution.

The strict scrutiny standard is one of three employed by the courts in reviewing laws and government policies. The *rational basis test* is the lowest form of judicial scrutiny. It is used in cases where a plaintiff alleges that the legislature has made an arbitrary or irrational decision. When employed, the RATIONAL BASIS TEST usually results in a court upholding the constitutionality of the law, because the test gives great deference to the legislative branch. The *heightened scrutiny test* is used in cases involving matters of DISCRIMINATION based on sex. As articulated in *Craig v. Boren,* 429 U.S. 190, 97 S. Ct. 451, 50 L. Ed. 2d 397 (1976), "classifications by gender must serve *important* governmental objectives and must *be substantially related* to the achievement of those objectives."

Strict scrutiny is the most rigorous form of judicial review. The Supreme Court has identified the right to vote, the right to travel, and the right to PRIVACY as fundamental rights worthy of protection by strict scrutiny. In addition, laws and policies that discriminate on the basis of race are categorized as *suspect classifications* that are presumptively impermissible and subject to strict scrutiny.

Once a court determines that strict scrutiny must be applied, it is presumed that the law or policy is unconstitutional. The government has the burden of proving that its challenged policy is constitutional. To withstand strict scrutiny, the government must show that its policy is necessary to achieve a COMPELLING STATE INTEREST. If this is proved, the state must then demonstrate that the legislation is narrowly tailored to achieve the intended result.

BILL ARON/PHOTOEDIT

The case of *Roe v. Wade*, 410 U.S. 113, 93 S. Ct. 705, 35 L. Ed. 2d 147 (1973), which invalidated state laws that prohibited ABORTION, illustrates the application of strict scrutiny. The Court held that the right to privacy is a fundamental right and that this right "is broad enough to encompass a woman's decision whether or not to terminate her pregnancy." Based on these grounds, the Court applied strict scrutiny. The state of Texas sought to proscribe all abortions and claimed a compelling state interest in protecting unborn human life. Though the Court acknowledged that this was a legitimate interest, it held that the interest does not become compelling until that point in pregnancy when the fetus becomes "viable" (capable of "meaningful life outside the mother's womb"). The Court held that a state may prohibit abortion after the point of viability, except in cases where abortion is necessary to preserve the life or health of the mother, but the Texas law was not narrowly tailored to achieve this objective. Therefore, the state did not meet its burden of proof and the law was held unconstitutional.

Under the Supreme Court's strict scrutiny standard, most laws discriminating on the basis of race will be struck down. Public schools, which were segregated by race into the 1950s, must now include all races.

CROSS-REFERENCES

Civil Rights; Equal Protection; *Roe v. Wade;* Sex Discrimination; Voting Rights.

STRIKE 📖 A work stoppage; the concerted refusal of employees to perform work that their employer has assigned to them in order to force the employer to grant certain demanded concessions, such as increased wages or improved employment conditions. 📖

Since the 1930s U.S. employees have had the legal right to strike. A work stoppage is generally the last step in a labor-management dispute over wages and working conditions. Because employees are not paid when they go on strike

and employers lose productivity, both sides usually seek to avoid it. When negotiations have reached an impasse, however, a strike may be the only bargaining tool left for employees. A strike must be conducted in an orderly manner and cannot be used as a shield for violence or crime. Intimidation and coercion during the course of a strike are unlawful.

Employees can strike for economic reasons, for improvement of their working conditions, or for the mutual aid and protection of employees in another union. In addition, even if they do not have a union, employees can properly agree to stop working as a group; in that case they are entitled to all the protections that organized strikers are afforded.

LABOR UNIONS do not have the right to use a strike to interfere with management prerogatives or with policies that the employer is entitled to make that do not directly concern the employment relationship. Although a union can attempt to bargain for higher wages to be paid to employees who work unpopular hours, it cannot strike merely because members are dissatisfied with their hours of employment.

Federal Labor Law The development of labor unions in the nineteenth century was met by employer hostility. The concept of COLLECTIVE BARGAINING between employer and employee was viewed as antithetical to the right of individual workers and their employers to negotiate wages and working conditions—a concept known as liberty of contract. When unions did strike, they were left to deal with management without legal protections. Employers fired strikers and obtained INJUNCTIONS from courts that ordered unions to end the strike or risk CONTEMPT of court.

The unequal bargaining power of unions was remedied in the 1930s with the passage of two important federal labor laws. In 1932 Congress passed the NORRIS-LAGUARDIA ACT (29 U.S.C.A. § 101 et seq.), which severely limited the power of FEDERAL COURTS to issue injunctions in labor disputes. The act imposed strict procedural limitations and safeguards to prevent abuses by the courts. The NATIONAL LABOR RELATIONS ACT (Wagner Act) of 1935 (29 U.S.C.A. § 151 et seq.) clearly established the right of employees to form, join, or aid labor unions. The act authorized collective bargaining by unions and gave employees the right to participate in "concerted actions" to bargain collectively. The major concerted action was the right to strike.

Federal labor laws require a sixty-day waiting period before workers can strike to force termination or modification of an existing COLLECTIVE BARGAINING AGREEMENT. The terms of the agreement remain in full force and effect during this period, and any employee who strikes can be fired. The sixty-day "cooling-off period" begins when the union serves notice on the employer or when the existing contract ends. This provision does not affect the right of employees to strike in protest of some UNFAIR LABOR PRACTICE of their employer. It does help to prevent premature strikes, however.

Status Strikes can be divided into two basic types: economic and unfair labor practice. An economic strike seeks to obtain some type of economic benefit for the workers, such as improved wages and hours, or to force recognition of their union. An unfair labor practice strike is called to protest some act of the employer that the employees regard as unfair.

When employees strike, the employer may continue operating the business and can hire replacement workers. Upon settlement of an unfair labor practice strike, the strikers must be reinstated as soon as they offer unconditionally to return to work, even if the replacement workers must be fired.

In economic strikes, however, the employer is not required to take back the strikers immediately upon the settlement of the dispute. Economic strikers are still categorized as employees and are entitled to reinstatement in the event vacancies occur, but the employer does not have to reinstate any worker who has found substantially equivalent work elsewhere or who has given the employer a legitimate and substantial reason for not reinstating that worker.

The hiring of permanent replacement workers has become an important management weapon against economic strikes, giving the employer the ability to hire a nonunion workforce and to threaten the local union with destruction. U.S. labor unions have been unsuccessful in persuading Congress to amend the National Labor Relations Act to provide immediate job reinstatement to economic strikers.

An employee has no right to be paid while on strike, nor does the employee have a right to claim UNEMPLOYMENT COMPENSATION benefits, unless state law provides the benefit. Employees who refuse to cross a picket line on principle are treated in the same way as strikers, but those who are kept from their jobs through fear of violence are entitled to collect unemployment compensation.

Employees forfeit their right to maintain the employment relationship if their strike is illegal. Public employees are generally forbidden to strike. If they do, they risk dismissal. In 1981, for example, President RONALD REAGAN responded to an illegal strike by federal air traffic controllers by dismissing more than 10,000 employees.

Ordinarily, however, a strike is legal if employees are using it to exert economic pressure upon their employer in order to improve the conditions of their employment. A strike is unlawful if it is directed at someone other than the employer or if it is used for some other purpose. Federal law prohibits most BOYCOTTS or PICKETING directed at a party not involved in

The 1997 strike by workers for the United Parcel Service affected business activity around the world and overwhelmed the U.S. postal system, which had to handle millions of additional items of mail.

A Lexicon of Labor Strikes

Over the years different types of labor strikes have acquired distinctive labels. The following are the most common types of strikes, some of which are illegal:

- *Wildcat strike* A strike that is not authorized by the union that represents the employees. Although not illegal under law, wildcat strikes ordinarily constitute a violation of an existing collective bargaining agreement.
- *Walkout* An unannounced refusal to perform work. A walkout may be spontaneous or planned in advance and kept secret. If the employees' conduct is an irresponsible or indefensible method of accomplishing their goals, a walkout is illegal. In other situations courts may rule that the employees have a good reason to strike.
- *Slowdown* An intermittent work stoppage by employees who remain on the job. Slowdowns are illegal because they give the employees an unfair bargaining advantage by making it impossible for the employer to plan for production by the workforce. An employer may discharge an employee for a work slowdown.

- *Sitdown strike* A strike in which employees stop working and refuse to leave the employer's premises. Sitdown strikes helped unions organize workers in the automobile industry in the 1930s but are now rare. They are illegal under most circumstances.
- *Whipsaw strike* A work stoppage against a single member of a bargaining unit composed of several employers. Whipsaw strikes are legal and are used by unions to bring added pressure against the employer who experiences not only the strike but also competition from the employers who have not been struck. Employers may respond by locking out employees of all facilities that belong to members of the bargaining unit. Whipsaw strikes have commonly been used in the automobile industry.
- *Sympathy strike* A work stoppage designed to provide aid and comfort to a related union engaged in an employment dispute. Although sympathy strikes are not illegal, unions can relinquish the right to use this tactic in a collective bargaining agreement.
- *Jurisdictional strike* A strike that arises from a dispute over which labor union is entitled to represent the employees. Jurisdictional strikes are unlawful under federal labor laws because the argument is between unions and not between a union and the employer.

the primary dispute. These tactics are known as SECONDARY BOYCOTTS or secondary picketing, and they are strictly limited so that businesses that are innocent bystanders will not become victims in a labor dispute that they cannot resolve.

Unlawful Tactics Picketing can be regulated by statute because of the potential for violence inherent in this activity. Mass picketing is unlawful under federal law because large unruly crowds could be used for the purpose of intimidation. Employees are entitled to picket in small numbers outside the employer's facilities, but they cannot block entrances or demonstrate in front of an employer's home. Picketing is lawful when it is used to inform the public, the employer, or other workers about the dispute. However, it cannot be used to threaten people or to provoke violence.

A strike is generally lawful if it is peaceful, but workers forfeit the protection afforded by federal labor laws if they violate a law. A strike is never a legal excuse for violence, and acts of physical violence and damage to property will be viewed as criminal acts. Employers who use

violence against strikers are subject to the same penalties.

A union or an employer can be fined or adjudged guilty of an unfair labor practice and ordered to cease and desist when violent actions occur. An injunction from a state court can stop the strike or picketing. Because no labor disputes can proceed without minor problems, an isolated minor incident, such as name-calling or a shove, does not end the right to strike.

Union Members Labor unions can fine or expel members who cross picket lines, fail to honor a lawful strike, or indulge in violence during a strike. In addition, they can discipline members for conduct antagonistic to the union, such as spying for the employer or participating in an unauthorized strike. A union member is entitled to a written notice of specific charges against him and a full and fair hearing before he can be expelled.

Settlement Strikes are ordinarily settled by negotiation between the employer and the employees or the union that represents them. An employer who does not want to engage in negotiations can cease operations entirely.

However, an employer cannot avoid bargaining by relocating or by assigning the same work to another plant owned by the company. If the employer and employees bargain in GOOD FAITH, they generally settle their differences and sign a collective bargaining agreement.

See also LABOR LAW.

STRING CITATION

A series of references to cases that establish legal PRECEDENTS and to other authorities that appear one after another and are printed following a legal assertion or conclusion as supportive authority.

For example, in preparing a BRIEF, an attorney might set forth a particular assertion based upon the facts of the case and applicable law and immediately thereafter make a list of all the cases that lend support to it.

See also CITATION.

STRONG, WILLIAM

William Strong served as associate justice of the U.S. Supreme Court from 1870 to 1880. He is best remembered for his majority opinion in the controversial case of *Knox v. Lee*, 79 (12 Wall.) U.S. 457, 20 L. Ed. 287 (1871), commonly known as one of the *Legal Tender* cases.

Strong was born on May 6, 1808, in Somers, Connecticut. He graduated from Yale University in 1828 and received a master's degree from the same institution in 1831. He attended Yale Law School and was admitted to the Pennsylvania bar in 1832. He practiced law in Reading, Pennsylvania, for fifteen years.

In 1847 Strong entered politics with his election as a Democratic member of the U.S. House of Representatives. He left Congress in 1851 and reentered private practice. In 1857 Strong began a term as a justice of the Pennsylvania Supreme Court. He remained on the bench until 1868, when he resumed private law practice, this time in Philadelphia. During the Civil War, Strong changed his political affiliation from Democrat to Republican. This proved fortuitous, as President ULYSSES S. GRANT, a Republican, appointed Strong to the U.S. Supreme Court in 1870 to replace the retiring Justice ROBERT C. GRIER, a Pennsylvania Democrat.

BIOGRAPHY

William Strong

PORTRAIT BY ROBERT HINCKLEY COLLECTION OF THE SUPREME COURT OF THE UNITED STATES.

Strong's appointment and first year on the Court were marked by controversy concerning the *Legal Tender* cases. On the day he was nominated, the Court announced its decision in *Hepburn v. Griswold*, 75 U.S. 603, L. Ed. (1870), which dealt with the Legal Tender Act of 1862 (12 Stat. 345). The act, passed during the Civil War to finance the Union war effort, authorized the creation of paper money not redeemable in gold or silver. About $430 million of "greenbacks" were put into circulation, and this money by law had to be accepted for all taxes, debts, and other obligations, even those contracted before passage of the act.

The Court in *Hepburn* ruled, by a 4–3 vote, that Congress lacked the power to make the notes LEGAL TENDER because the law violated the FIFTH AMENDMENT's guarantee against deprivation of property without DUE PROCESS OF LAW. Grant's appointment of Strong and JOSEPH P. BRADLEY to the Supreme Court on the same day in 1870 was perceived as a court-packing scheme designed to overturn *Hepburn*.

This view proved correct. With Strong and Bradley on the bench, the Court agreed to reconsider the constitutionality of the Legal Tender Act. In 1871 Strong wrote the majority opinion in *Knox v. Lee* that reversed the *Hepburn* decision. This time the vote was 5–4 in favor of the act. Strong held that Congress had the authority to pass monetary acts such as the greenbacks law during a time of national emergency.

During the 1870s numerous CIVIL RIGHTS cases came before the Court. In *Blyew v. United States*, 80 U.S. (13 Wall.) 581, 20 L. Ed. 638 (1872), Strong ruled that the federal government could not prosecute a white man accused of murdering several African Americans under a civil rights law because the deceased victims were not persons "in existence" as required by the act, and because the interests of witnesses were not strong enough to give the federal government exclusive jurisdiction over the crime. The crime occurred in Kentucky where black witnesses were prohibited by law from testifying against whites. In *Strauder v. West Virginia*, 100 U.S. (10 Otto) 303, 25 L. Ed. 664

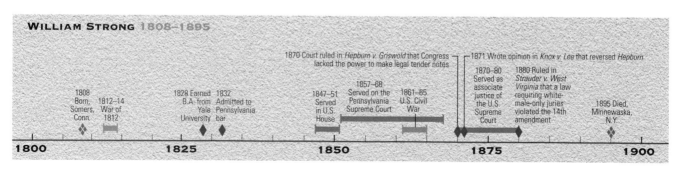

WILLIAM STRONG 1808–1895

1808 Born, Somers, Conn.

1812–14 War of 1812

1828 Earned B.A. from Yale University

1832 Admitted to Pennsylvania bar

1847–51 Served in U.S. House

1857–68 Served on the Pennsylvania Supreme Court

1861–85 U.S. Civil War

1870 Court ruled in *Hepburn v. Griswold* that Congress lacked the power to make legal tender notes

1870–80 Served as associate justice of the U.S. Supreme Court

1871 Wrote opinion in *Knox v. Lee* that reversed *Hepburn*

1880 Ruled in *Strauder v. West Virginia* that a law requiring white-male-only juries violated the 14th amendment

1895 Died, Minnewaska, N.Y.

1800   1825   1850   1875   1900

(1880), Strong ruled that a law that allowed only white males to serve as jurors violated the FOURTEENTH AMENDMENT's Equal Protection Clause.

Following his resignation from the Court in 1880, Strong devoted his time to many religious causes and organizations. He led the National Reform Association, which proposed a constitutional amendment that proclaimed Jesus Christ as the supreme authority. Though he disclaimed the idea of a national church, Strong believed Christian principles should govern many facets of U.S. society. Strong died on August 19, 1895, in Minnewaska, New York.

STRONG-ARM PROVISION 📖 The segment of the federal BANKRUPTCY law that grants the TRUSTEE the rights of the most secured CREDITOR, so that he or she is able to seize all of the DEBTOR's property for proper distribution. 📖

STROSSEN, NADINE M. Nadine M. Strossen is a lawyer and law professor who, in 1991, became the first woman president of the AMERICAN CIVIL LIBERTIES UNION (ACLU).

Born August 18, 1950, in Jersey City, New Jersey, Strossen moved with her family to Hopkins, Minnesota, at the age of eight. When she was growing up, she expected to pursue a traditional career, perhaps as a teacher. As an outstanding member of her high school debate team, she was impressed with her teammates' analytical skills and encouraged the boys among them to pursue a legal career. But she never imagined such a path for herself until, as a student at Radcliffe college, she became involved in debate and took an interest in feminist causes. These activities gave her the spark and confidence she needed to consider becoming a lawyer herself. After graduating from Radcliffe, she attended Harvard Law School, where she was editor of the law review, and graduated from Harvard magna cum laude in 1975.

After law school, Strossen was awarded a judicial clerkship at the Minnesota Supreme Court, then practiced law in several law firms. In 1984, she left private practice and began teaching at the School of Law of New York University. She joined the faculty at New York

BIOGRAPHY

Nadine M. Strossen

Law School in 1988, specializing in constitutional law, federal courts, and human rights. She has been a member of the ACLU since 1985, having served on the organization's executive committee and as its general counsel.

The ACLU has adopted controversial, unpopular positions on issues ranging from free speech and ABORTION rights to the rights of accused persons. Strossen has used steady, unrelenting persuasion, rather than confrontation, to educate others about the importance of safeguarding the individual liberties that are the heart of the U.S. Constitution.

In the late 1980s and into the 1990s, Strossen and the ACLU found themselves in an ironic and seemingly contradictory position when new ideas about multi-culturalism began to take root on college campuses. Proponents of these ideas, sometimes called "politically correct," or PC, seemed to espouse goals in common with the ACLU: protecting minority groups from discrimination, bias, hatred, or exclusion. However, in an effort to rid their institution of hatred and harassment, some academic groups adopted speech codes that banned the use of certain words or symbols they considered hateful, demeaning, violent, or merely inconsiderate. Strossen and the ACLU vehemently opposed these codes because they violate the FIRST AMENDMENT and discourage discussion of important but inflammatory subjects such as race and gender.

Strossen believes that the free and open exchange of ideas, even ideas that may be repugnant, is essential in a free society, and may actually defuse the hatred and bigotry that underlie racist or sexist expressions. However, Strossen maintains that laws imposing enhanced penalties for crimes motivated by bias or hatred differ from speech codes and are constitutional.

Similar to the controversy over speech codes is the debate over whether sexually explicit material can be constitutionally banned. During the 1980s, a group of feminists, led by ANDREA DWORKIN and CATHARINE A. MACKINNON, began a movement to outlaw all sexually explicit ma-

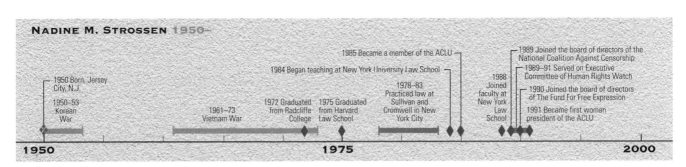

NADINE M. STROSSEN 1950–

- 1950 Born, Jersey City, N.J.
- 1950–53 Korean War
- 1961–73 Vietnam War
- 1972 Graduated from Radcliffe College
- 1975 Graduated from Harvard Law School
- 1978–83 Practiced law at Sullivan and Cromwell in New York City
- 1984 Began teaching at New York University Law School
- 1985 Became a member of the ACLU
- 1988 Joined faculty at New York Law School
- 1989 Joined the board of directors of the National Coalition Against Censorship
- 1989–91 Served on Executive Committee of Human Rights Watch
- 1990 Joined the board of directors of The Fund For Free Expression
- 1991 Became first woman president of the ACLU

1950   1975   2000

terials on the ground that they condone conduct that is violent, dangerous, and degrading to women. Strossen and the ACLU argue that such materials are speech rather than conduct, and that even if most U.S. citizens find them offensive, their publication and dissemination are protected by the Constitution.

Strossen contends that a prohibition on all sexually explicit material is a simplistic solution that only serves to drive the perpetrators underground. She says that CENSORSHIP does not solve the underlying problems of violence and discrimination and may ultimately be used as a means of oppressing the very groups it is intended to protect.

Strossen is committed to defending free speech whenever it is threatened, even if she disagrees with the individual or group being targeted. For example, she is opposed to Supreme Court decisions that limit the activities of antiabortion protesters, even though the ACLU has always defended a woman's right to reproductive freedom. Strossen believes that penalties imposed on antiabortion activists infringe on the activists' exercise of free speech.

In addition to working with the ACLU, Strossen has served on the boards of the Fund for Free Expression, the National Coalition against Censorship, the Coalition to Free Soviet Jews, Middle East Watch, Asia Watch, and Human Rights Watch.

See also HATE CRIME; PORNOGRAPHY.

STRUCK JURY 📖 A special JURY chosen in a manner whereby an appropriate official prepares a panel containing the names of forty-eight potential jurors and the parties strike off names until the number of jurors is reduced to twelve. 📖

STUDENT NON-VIOLENT COORDINATING COMMITTEE

As a focal point for student activism in the 1960s, the Student Non-violent Coordinating Committee (SNCC, popularly called Snick) spearheaded major initiatives in the CIVIL RIGHTS MOVEMENT. At the forefront of INTEGRATION efforts, SNCC volunteers gained early recognition for their lunch counter sit-ins at whites-only businesses, and later for their participation in historic demonstrations that helped pave the way for the passage of landmark federal civil rights legislation in 1964 and 1965. SNCC made significant gains in voter registration for blacks in the South, where it also ran schools and health clinics. Later adopting a more radical agenda, it ultimately became identified with the black power movement and distanced itself from traditional civil rights leaders, before disbanding in 1970.

SNCC grew out of the SOUTHERN CHRISTIAN LEADERSHIP CONFERENCE (SCLC), led by MARTIN LUTHER KING, JR. On Easter 1960, SCLC's executive director, ELLA J. BAKER, organized a meeting at Shaw University, in Raleigh, North Carolina, with the goal of increasing student participation in the civil rights movement. Already, students were taking action on their own: in February, they had staged a sit-in at a Woolworth store in Greensboro, North Carolina, refusing to leave the whites-only lunch counter. One hundred and forty students met with Baker and representatives of other civil rights organizations at the Easter conference, where SNCC was conceived and founded. SNCC soon set up offices in Atlanta. Among its earliest members were John Lewis, a divinity student; Marion S. Barry, Jr., a future mayor of Washington, D.C.; and Julian Bond, a future Georgia state senator and liberal activist leader.

In its statement of purpose, dated April 1960, SNCC embraced a philosophy of non-violence:

> We affirm the philosophical or religious ideal of non-violence as the foundation of our purpose, the presupposition of our faith, and the manner of our action. . . . By appealing to conscience and standing on the moral nature of human existence, non-violence nurtures the atmosphere in which reconciliation and justice become actual possibilities.

One method of non-violent protest adopted by SNCC was the sit-in. Used to integrate businesses in northern and border states as early as 1943, this tactic was a risky undertaking in the segregrated South of 1960. What SNCC met at lunch counter sit-ins was far from a spirit of reconciliation: whites taunted the demonstrators, poured ketchup and sugar on their heads, and sometimes hit them. SNCC volunteers persevered, and by late 1961, sit-ins had taken place in over one hundred southern communities.

The pressure brought by these actions soon increased as SNCC rallied white and black students to a number of causes. In 1961, it joined members of the Congress of Racial Equality (CORE) in a series of Freedom Rides—interstate bus trips through the South aimed at integrating bus terminals. Over the next three years, in states such as Georgia and Mississippi, SNCC began a grassroots campaign aimed at registering black voters. It also opened schools to teach illiterate farmers and established health clinics. In a 1964 project called Freedom Summer, it sent hundreds of

APWIDE WORLD PHOTOS

white and black volunteers, mostly northern, middle-class students, to Mississippi to test the newly passed CIVIL RIGHTS ACT of 1964 (42 U.S.C.A. § 2000a et seq.). Throughout these endeavors, volunteers were met with beatings and jailings, and three civil rights workers were slain in Mississippi during Freedom Summer.

By the mid 1960s, tensions had developed within the civil rights movement. Under King, SCLC stayed its course. Frustrated by the pace of civil rights gains and doubtful of traditional methods, SNCC and CORE became increasingly aggressive. In 1965, after the nation watched televised footage of black marchers being beaten in Selma, Alabama, SNCC decided to hold a second march, in which King chose to participate. More assaults and a murder followed. In their wake, President LYNDON B. JOHNSON appealed to the nation for stronger civil rights legislation. Consequently, the Selma marches hastened the passage of the Voting Rights Act of 1965 (42 U.S.C.A. § 1973 et seq.).

SNCC took a more radical course under the leadership of activist STOKELY CARMICHAEL. As a dramatically successful SNCC field organizer in Lowndes County, Mississippi, Carmichael had increased the number of registered black voters there from seventy to twenty-six hundred. He was elected chairman of SNCC in 1966, the year in which he coined the term *black power*. According to the organization's position paper, titled *The Basis of Black Power*, its message of political, economic, and legal liberation, rather than integration, for blacks marked a turning point in the civil rights movement: "In the beginning of the movement, we had fallen into a trap whereby we thought that our problems revolved around the right to eat at certain lunch counters or the right to vote, or to organize our

Police escorted nonviolent black and white protesters from a segregated beach in Biloxi, Mississippi, in 1963. Students carried out nonviolent protests through the Student Non-violent Coordinating Committee, which grew out of the Southern Leadership Conference led by Martin Luther King, Jr.

communities. We have seen, however, that the problem is much deeper." SNCC, which now called the NATIONAL ASSOCIATION FOR THE ADVANCEMENT OF COLORED PEOPLE reactionary and white U.S. citizens 180 million racists, was joined in espousing harsher views by CORE and the newly formed BLACK PANTHER PARTY for Self-Defense.

Along with the new rhetoric came new policies. SNCC purged white members from its ranks, declaring that they should work to rid their own communities of racism. When SNCC members began carrying guns, Carmichael's explanation drew a line between the old guard and the vanguard: "We are not King or SCLC. They don't do the kind of work we do nor do they live in the same areas we live in" (Johnson 1990, 71). The organization subsequently deepened this division by pulling out of the White House Conference on Civil Rights.

Toward the end of its existence, troubles tore SNCC apart. In 1966, clashes with the police in several cities began when eighty police officers raided SNCC's Philadelphia office, charging that dynamite was stored there. The FEDERAL BUREAU OF INVESTIGATION, which had been wiretapping SNCC since 1960, targeted the group in 1967 for a Counterintelligence Program effort aimed at disrupting it. Critics blamed Carmichael's inflammatory speeches for causing riots, and he left to join the Black Panthers. Amid growing militancy and an expanded vision that included antiwar protest, financial support began to dry up. SNCC disbanded in 1970 shortly after its last chairman, H. Rap Brown, went underground to avoid arrest.

SUA SPONTE 📖 [*Latin, Of his or her or its own will; voluntarily.*] 📖

For example, when a court takes action on its own MOTION, rather than at the request of one of the parties, it is acting *sua sponte*.

SUBCONTRACTOR 📖 One who takes a portion of a CONTRACT from the principal contractor or from another subcontractor. 📖

When an individual or a company is involved in a large-scale project, a contractor is often hired to see that the work is done. The contractor, however, rarely does all the work. The work that remains is performed by subcontractors, who are under contract to the contractor, who is usually designated the general or prime contractor. Subcontractors may, in turn, hire their own subcontractors to do part of the work that they have contracted to perform.

Building construction is a common example of how the contractor-subcontractor relationship works. The general contractor takes prime responsibility for seeing that the building is

RICK REINHARD/IMPACT VISUALS

General contractors who bid on large construction projects often hire subcontractors to carry out various phases of the job. This subcontractor is drilling holes to hang a ceiling.

constructed and signs a contract to do so. The cost of the contract is usually a fixed sum and may have been derived from a bid submitted by the contractor. Before offering the bid or before contract negotiations begin, the general contractor normally asks the subcontractors to estimate the price they will charge to do their part of the work. Thus, the general contractor will collect information from electricians, plumbers, dry wall installers, and a host of other subcontractors.

Once construction begins, the general contractor coordinates the construction schedule, making sure the subcontractors are at the building site when needed so that the project remains on schedule. The sequencing of construction and the supervision of the work that the subcontractors perform are key roles for the general contractor.

Subcontractors sign contracts with the general contractor that typically incorporate the agreement between the general contractor and the owner. A subcontractor who fails to complete work on time or whose work is not acceptable under the general contract may be required to pay DAMAGES if the project is delayed because of these problems.

A subcontractor's biggest concern is getting paid promptly for the work and materials provided to the project. The general contractor is under an obligation to pay the subcontractors any sums due them unless the contract states otherwise. Some contracts state that the subcontractors will not be paid until the general contractor is paid by the owner. If the owner refuses to pay the general contractor for work a subcontractor has performed, the subcontractor has the right to file a MECHANIC'S LIEN against the property for the cost of the unpaid work.

When changes are made to the project during construction, subcontractors expect to be paid for the time and materials expended on the change. Subcontractors must receive formal approval to make the change and have a cost attached to the change before doing the work. Otherwise, when they submit a compensation request, it may be denied either because too much time has passed or because the general contractor or the owner believes the work performed was within the scope of the original project.

SUBJECT MATTER JURISDICTION

The power of a court to hear and determine cases of the general class to which the proceedings in question belong.

For a court to have authority to adjudicate a dispute, it must have JURISDICTION over the parties and over the type of legal issues in dispute. The first type of jurisdiction is called PERSONAL JURISDICTION; the other is subject matter jurisdiction. Personal jurisdiction will be found if the persons involved in the litigation are present in the state or are legal residents of the state in which the lawsuit has been filed, or if the transaction in question has a substantial connection to the state.

Subject matter jurisdiction refers to the nature of the claim or controversy. The subject matter may be a criminal infringement, medical malpractice, or the probating of an estate. Subject matter jurisdiction is the power of a court to hear particular types of cases. In state court systems, statutes that create different courts generally set boundaries on their subject matter jurisdiction. One state court or another has subject matter jurisdiction of any controversy that can be heard in courts of that state. Some courts specialize in a particular area of the law, such as PROBATE law, FAMILY LAW, or JUVENILE LAW. A person who seeks custody of a child, for example, must go to a court that has authority in guardianship matters. A DIVORCE can be granted only in a court designated to hear matrimonial cases. A person charged with a FELONY cannot be tried in a criminal court authorized to hear only MISDEMEANOR cases.

In addition to the legal issue in dispute, the subject matter jurisdiction of a court may be determined by the monetary value of the dispute—the dollar AMOUNT IN CONTROVERSY. SMALL CLAIMS COURTS, also known as CONCILIATION courts, are limited by state statutes to small amounts of money in controversy, ranging from $1,000 to $5,000 depending upon the state. Therefore, if a plaintiff sues a defendant in small claims court for $50,000, the court will reject the lawsuit because it lacks subject matter jurisdiction based on the amount in controversy. The amount in controversy limitations are designed to regulate the flow of litigation in the various courts of the state, ensuring that complicated disputes over large sums of money will be heard in courts that have the time and resources to hear such cases.

The U.S. Constitution gives jurisdiction over some types of cases to FEDERAL COURTS only. Cases involving AMBASSADORS AND CONSULS or public ministers, admiralty and maritime cases, and cases in which the United States is a party must be heard in federal courts. Congress has also created subject matter jurisdiction by statute, mandating that antitrust suits, most SECURITIES lawsuits, BANKRUPTCY proceedings, and PATENT and COPYRIGHT cases be heard in federal courts.

The Constitution also allows federal district courts to hear cases involving any rights or obligations that arise from the Constitution or other federal law. This is called FEDERAL QUESTION jurisdiction. Federal courts also have diversity jurisdiction, which gives the courts authority to hear cases involving disputes among citizens of different states. If, however, the amount in controversy is less than $10,000, federal question and diversity jurisdiction will not apply, and the case must be brought in state court. Even if the $10,000 amount is satisfied, a plaintiff may start the lawsuit in state court. A defendant, however, may seek to have the case moved to the federal court in that state by filing a transfer request called a REMOVAL action.

A defendant who believes that a court lacks subject matter jurisdiction to hear the case may raise this issue before the trial court or in an APPEAL from the JUDGMENT. If a defect in subject matter jurisdiction is found, the judgment will usually be rendered void, having no legal force or binding effect.

SUBLETTING The leasing of part or all of the property held by a TENANT, as opposed to a LANDLORD, during a portion of his or her unexpired balance of the term of occupancy.

A landlord may prohibit a tenant from subletting the leased premises without the landlord's permission by including such a term in the LEASE. When subletting is permitted, the original tenant becomes, in effect, the landlord of the sublessee. The sublessee pays the rent to the tenant, not the landlord. The original tenant is not, however, relieved of his or her responsibilities under the original lease with the landlord.

A sublease is different from an assignment where a tenant assigns all of his or her rights under a lease to another. The assignee takes the place of the tenant and must deal with the landlord provided the landlord permits it. The original tenant is no longer responsible to the landlord who consents to the termination of their landlord-tenant relationship.

See also LANDLORD AND TENANT.

SUBMERGED LANDS Soil lying beneath water or on the oceanside of the tideland.

Minerals found in the soil of tidal and submerged lands belong to the state in its sovereign right. The federal government, however, has full control over all the natural resources discovered in the soil under the ocean floor beyond the three-mile belt extending from the ordinary low-water mark along the coast.

SUBMISSION OF CONTROVERSY A procedure by which the parties to a particular dispute place any matter of real controversy existing between them before a court for a final determination.

Some states have enacted laws that authorize parties in a legal dispute to bypass the normal procedures for resolving a civil lawsuit and use a process called submission of controversy. For a court to hear a case under a submission of controversy, the parties must agree to all the FACTS and present only QUESTIONS OF LAW for the court to resolve.

A submission of controversy dispenses with the need for the plaintiff to file a SUMMONS and COMPLAINT and the defendant to file an ANSWER. Instead, the parties must agree to a statement of facts, because the court does not take EVIDENCE in such a proceeding. The agreement to the facts must be absolute, without reservations, and unequivocal and must stipulate all of the facts necessary for a complete determination of the controversy. The parties must also describe a CAUSE OF ACTION, explain why the court has JURISDICTION over the parties, and propose what RELIEF is being sought from the court.

Once the facts of the controversy are agreed upon, the court cannot dispute them. It must hold a trial or hearing on the questions of law in dispute and then render a decision that determines how the law applies to the stipulated facts. The inability of the court to judge the facts as a JURY would distinguishes the submission of controversy from a trial without a jury.

The statutes that grant this right determine the type of controversies that can be submitted. Submission of controversy is not available in cases when the relief cannot be given or when the controversy involves a matter of PUBLIC POLICY. A submission can only be granted when the controversy affects the private rights of the parties.

Like any case presented to a court, the controversy must present a question of law, which must be real, and it must be one that can be followed by an effective JUDGMENT. The parties cannot submit abstract or MOOT questions for the purpose of obtaining the advice of the court. Nor will a court decide a question of law that does not arise from the facts in the case.

Submission of controversy is not used very often because of the difficulty in getting parties to agree to the facts of the case. Without such an agreement, this procedure cannot be used. Some states have repealed their statutes because the process has fallen into disfavor. ARBITRATION and MEDIATION are more commonly used to resolve disputes informally and without filing a lawsuit. Under both of these ALTERNATIVE DISPUTE RESOLUTION mechanisms, the parties may still present their version of the facts, but the process is informal and usually more timely than a submission of controversy.

SUBMIT 📖 To offer for determination; commit to the judgment or discretion of another individual or authority. 📖

To submit EVIDENCE means to present or introduce it. Similarly a political issue might be submitted to the voters' judgment.

SUB NOMINE 📖 [*Latin, Under the name; in the name of; under the title of.*] 📖

SUBORDINATION 📖 To put in an inferior class or order; to make subject to, or subservient.

A sample subordination agreement

Agreement, made the _____ day of _____ , nineteen hundred and _____ , between _____ , party of the first part, and _____ , party of the second part.

Witnesseth:

Whereas, the said party of the first part now owns and holds the following mortgage and the bond or note secured thereby: Mortgage dated the _____ day of _____ , 19_____ , made by _____ to _____ , in the principal sum of $_____ and recorded in the liber _____ of section _____ of Mortgages, page _____ in the office of the _____ of the _____ , covering premises hereinafter mentioned or a part thereof; and

Whereas, the present owner of the premises hereinafter mentioned is about to execute and deliver to said party of the second part, a mortgage to secure the principal sum of _____ dollars and interest, covering premises; [*description*] and more fully described in said mortgage; and

Whereas, said party of the second part has refused to accept said mortgage unless said mortgage held by the party of the first part be subordinated in the manner hereinafter mentioned;

Now therefore, in consideration of the premises and to induce said party of the second part to accept said mortgage _____ and also in consideration of one dollar paid to the party of the first part, the receipt whereof is hereby acknowledged, the said party of the first part hereby covenants and agrees with said party of the second part that said mortgage held by said party of the first part be and shall continue to be subject and subordinate in lien to the lien of said _____ mortgage for _____ dollars and interest about to be delivered to the party of the second part hereto, and to all advances heretofore made or which hereafter may be made thereon (including but not limited to all sums advanced for the purpose of paying brokerage commissions, consideration paid for making the loan, mortgage recording tax, documentary stamps, fee for examination of title, surveys, and any other disbursements and charges in connection therewith) to the extent of the last mentioned amount and interest, and all such advances may be made without notice to the party of the first part, and to any extensions, renewals and modifications thereof.

This agreement may not be changed or terminated orally. This agreement shall bind and enure to the benefit of the parties hereto, their respective heirs, personal representatives, successors and assigns. The word "party" shall be construed as if it read "parties" whenever the sense of this agreement so requires.

In Witness Whereof, the said party of the first part has duly executed this agreement the day and year first above written.

In presence of:

_____   _____

_____   _____

[*Acknowledgments*]

A legal status that refers to the establishment of priority between various existing LIENS or ENCUMBRANCES on the same parcel of PROPERTY. 📖

A *subordination agreement* is a CONTRACT whereby a CREDITOR agrees that the claims of specified senior creditors must be paid in full before any payment on a subordinate DEBT can be paid to the subordinate creditor.

A *subordination clause* in a MORTGAGE is a provision that gives a subsequent mortgage priority over one that has been executed at an earlier date.

SUBORNATION OF PERJURY 📖 The

criminal offense of procuring another to commit PERJURY, which is the crime of lying, in a material matter, while under OATH. 📖

It is a criminal offense to induce someone to commit perjury. In a majority of states, the offense is defined by statute.

Under federal criminal law (18 U.S.C.A. § 1622), five elements must be proved to convict a person of subornation of perjury. It first must be shown that the defendant made an agreement with a person to TESTIFY falsely. There must be proof that perjury has in fact been committed and that the statements of the perjurer were material. The prosecutor must also provide evidence that the perjurer made such statements willfully with knowledge of their falsity. Finally, there must be proof that the procurer had knowledge that the perjurer's statements were false.

When there is a criminal CONSPIRACY to suborn perjury, the conspirators may be prosecuted whether or not perjury has been committed. It is also quite common to join both subornation of perjury and OBSTRUCTION OF JUSTICE counts in a single INDICTMENT when they arise from the same activity.

The Federal Sentencing Guidelines recognize two types of circumstances that enhance the criminal sentence for subornation of perjury. An offense causing or threatening to cause physical injury to a person, or property damage, in order to suborn perjury is one circumstance. The other is when subornation of perjury resulted in substantial interference with the administration of justice, which includes a premature or improper termination of a FELONY investigation, an indictment, a VERDICT, or any judicial determination based on perjury, false TESTIMONY, or other false EVIDENCE, or the unnecessary expenditure of substantial government or court resources.

Under 18 U.S.C.A. § 1622, a person convicted of subornation of perjury may be fined $2,000 and sentenced to up to five years in prison.

SUBPOENA 📖 [*Latin, Under penalty.*] A

formal document that orders a named individual to appear before a duly authorized body at a fixed time to give TESTIMONY. 📖

A COURT, GRAND JURY, legislative body, or ADMINISTRATIVE AGENCY uses a subpoena to compel an individual to appear before it at a specified time to give testimony. An individual who receives a subpoena but fails to appear may be charged with CONTEMPT of court and subjected to civil or criminal penalties. In addition, a person who has been served with a subpoena and has failed to appear may be brought to the proceedings by a law enforcement officer who serves a second subpoena, called an instanter.

A subpoena must be served on the individual ordered to appear. In some states a law enforcement officer or PROCESS SERVER must personally serve it, whereas other states allow service by mail or with a telephone call. It is most often used to compel WITNESSES to appear at a civil or criminal trial. A trial attorney may receive an assurance from a person who says that she will appear in court on a certain day to TESTIFY, but if a subpoena is not issued and served on the witness, she is not legally required to appear.

It is up to the attorneys in a case to request subpoenas, which are routinely issued by the trial court administrator's office. The subpoena must give the name of the legal proceedings, the name of the person who is being ordered to appear, and the time and place of the court hearing.

Legislative investigating committees also issue subpoenas to compel recalcitrant witnesses to appear. Congressional investigations of political scandal, such as the WATERGATE scandals of the Nixon administration, the IRAN-CONTRA scandal of the Reagan administration, and the Whitewater scandal of the Clinton administration, rely on subpoenas to obtain testimony.

A subpoena that commands a person to bring certain EVIDENCE, usually documents or papers, is called a SUBPOENA DUCES TECUM, from the Latin "under penalty to bring with you." This type of subpoena is often used in a civil lawsuit where one party resists giving the other party documents through the DISCOVERY process. If a court is convinced that the document request is legitimate, it will order the production of documents using a subpoena duces tecum.

A party may resist a subpoena duces tecum by refusing to comply and requesting a court hearing. One of the most famous refusals of a subpoena was RICHARD M. NIXON's reluctance to turn over the tape recordings of his White House office conversations to the Watergate

A sample subpoena

UNITED STATES DISTRICT COURT

FOR THE

_____

Civil Action File No. _____ .

_____

vs.   }

_____

To: _____

You are hereby commanded to appear in the United States District Court for the
_____ District of _____ at _____ in the City of
_____ , on the _____ day of _____ , 19_____ , at
_____ o'clock _____ M. to testify on behalf of _____ in the above entitled
action.

_____ , 19_____ .

_____ ,   _____ ,
Attorney for _____ .   Clerk.

_____ .   By _____ ,
Address   Deputy Clerk.

[*Seal*]

SPECIAL PROSECUTOR. Nixon fought the subpoena all the way to the Supreme Court in *United States v. Nixon*, 418 U.S. 683, 94 S. Ct. 3090, 41 L. Ed. 2d 1039 (1974). The Court upheld the subpoena, leading Nixon to resign his office a short time later.

SUBPOENA DUCES TECUM The judicial process used to command the production before a court of papers, documents, or other TANGIBLE items of EVIDENCE.

A subpoena duces tecum is used to compel the production of documents that might be ADMISSIBLE before the court (*duces tecum* is Latin for *bring with you*). It cannot be used to require oral testimony and ordinarily cannot be used to compel a WITNESS to reiterate, paraphrase, or affirm the truth of the documents produced.

Although frequently employed to obtain discovery during litigation, a subpoena duces tecum may not be used for a "fishing expedition" to enable a party to gain access to massive amounts of documents as a means of gathering evidence. The SUBPOENA should be sufficiently definite so that a respondent can identify the documents sought without a protracted or extensive search. Moreover, a person ordinarily is required to produce only documents in her possession or under her control and supervision. A subpoena duces tecum may be used to compel the production of the papers and books of a business, however.

A subpoena duces tecum is not limited to parties to a lawsuit but may also be used for others who have relevant documents. In the absence of a valid excuse, an individual served with a subpoena duces tecum must produce the items sought, although a subordinate may comply instead. A subpoena duces tecum may be challenged by a MOTION to quash, modify, or vacate the subpoena or by a motion for a PROTECTIVE ORDER. The subpoena might not be permitted if alternative methods for obtaining the information sought are available. Determining whether a subpoena duces tecum should be enforced is a discretionary matter within the judgment of the court.

SUBROGATION The substitution of one person in the place of another with reference to a lawful CLAIM, demand, or right, so that he or she who is substituted succeeds to the rights of the other in relation to the DEBT or claim, and its rights, remedies, or securities.

There are two types of subrogation: *legal* and *conventional*. Legal subrogation arises by OPERA-

TION of law, whereas conventional subrogation is a result of a CONTRACT.

The purpose of subrogation is to compel the ultimate payment of a debt by the party who, in equity and good conscience, should pay it. This subrogation is an equitable device used to avoid injustice.

Legal subrogation takes place as a matter of EQUITY, with or without an agreement. The right of legal subrogation can be either modified or extinguished through a contractual agreement. It cannot be used to displace a contract agreed upon by the parties.

Conventional subrogation arises when one individual satisfies the debt of another as a result of a contractual agreement that provides that any claims or LIENS that exist as security for the debt be kept alive for the benefit of the party who pays the debt. It is necessary that the agreement be supported by CONSIDERATION; however, it does not have to be in writing and can be either express or implied.

The facts of each case determine the issue of whether or not subrogation is applicable. In general, the REMEDY is broad enough to include every instance in which one party, who is not a mere volunteer, pays a debt for which a second party is primarily liable and which, in equity and good conscience, should have been discharged by the second party. Subrogation is a highly favored remedy that the courts are inclined to extend and apply liberally.

The ordinary equity maxims are applicable to subrogation, which is not permitted when there is an adequate legal remedy. The plaintiff must come into court with clean hands, and the person who seeks equity must do equity. The remedy is not available when there are equal or superior equities in other individuals who are in opposition to the party seeking subrogation. The remedy is denied when the person seeking subrogation has interfered with the rights of others, committed FRAUD, or been negligent.

The right to subrogation accrues upon payment of the debt. The subrogee is generally entitled to all the creditor's rights, privileges, priorities, remedies, and judgments and is subject only to whatever limitations and conditions were binding on the creditor. He does not, however, have any more extensive rights than the CREDITOR.

SUBSCRIBE 📖 To write underneath; to put a signature at the end of a printed or written instrument. 📖

A *subscribing witness* is an individual who either sees the execution of a writing or hears its acknowledgment and signs his or her name as a WITNESS upon the request of the executor of the agreement.

In relation to the law of CORPORATIONS, a subscriber is one who has made an agreement to take a portion of the original issue of corporate stock.

SUBSCRIPTION 📖 The act of writing one's name under a written instrument; the affixing of one's signature to any document, whether for the purpose of authenticating or attesting it, of adopting its terms as one's own expressions, or of binding one's self by an engagement which it contains. A written CONTRACT by which one engages to take and pay for CAPITAL STOCK of a CORPORATION, or to contribute a sum of money for a designated purpose, either gratuitously, as in the case of subscribing to a charity, or in consideration of an equivalent to be rendered, as a subscription to a periodical, a forthcoming book, a series of entertainments, or the like. 📖

Subscriptions, such as those made to CHARITIES, are also known as PLEDGES and can be either oral or written.

State law determines the enforceability of oral and written subscriptions. Courts have regarded subscriptions that are not supported by some CONSIDERATION as mere OFFERS that become legally binding when accepted or when the recipient of the PROMISE has acted in reliance on the offers. The promise that forms the subscription need not be to pay money but might be for the performance of other acts, such as to convey land or provide labor for construction.

A subscription contract does not have to be in a particular form, or even in writing, provided the promisor clearly indicates an intention to have such an agreement or contract. Where a state law mandates a writing, the subscriber's name can be signed to the contract by the individual who solicits the contribution for the organization, if that person is authorized to do so by the subscriber.

The offered subscription must be accepted if it is to legally bind the subscriber. It is essential that acceptance occur within a reasonable time, since, as an offer, the subscription can be revoked any time prior to its acceptance. A subscription is also revocable upon notice given by the subscriber if a condition upon which it is based has not been performed. A subscriber may be prevented from claiming revocation in situations where it would be contrary to the interests of justice.

Where the subscriber dies or becomes insane prior to an acceptance of the subscription or the furnishing of consideration for it, the subscription lapses and is legally ineffective.

Courts, as a matter of policy, uphold subscriptions if any consideration can be found. In a situation where the recipient of the subscription has begun work or incurred LIABILITY in reliance upon it, such action constitutes a consideration. A benefit to the subscriber, although it is enjoyed by her in common with others or with the general public, is also deemed sufficient consideration for the promise.

The discovery of any false representations made intentionally for the purpose of deceiving an individual making a charitable subscription justifies the cancellation of the subscription. The FRAUD must bear a relation to the subject matter of the contract. If an individual is told that the subscription will go to finance the development of a recreation center for a student group when, in fact, it will be used to fund an arsenal for a group of political extremists, that individual is entitled to cancel the subscription. A subscription that has for its purpose the accomplishment of ends that are contrary to PUBLIC POLICY is invalid.

In situations where the terms of a subscription are vague or ambiguous, the court will interpret its meaning. Factors for evaluation include the subject matter of the agreement, the inducement that influenced the subscription, the circumstances under which it was made, and its language. The contractual rights against a subscriber may be assigned, unless the terms of the subscription expressly proscribe this. Any conditions required by a subscription contract must be satisfied before the contract will be enforced. The conditions of a subscription may include the time of performance or the requirement of a program of matching corporate grants. Where a subscription indicates that any material change in the plan or purpose for which the subscription was made cannot be done without the consent of the subscriber, the subscriber will be released from the obligation if such a change is made without consent.

In the event that an enterprise is abandoned prior to the time that its purpose, which was the basis of the subscription, is accomplished, the courts will not ordinarily enforce the subscription against the subscriber. There is an implied condition at law that an enterprise cannot be abandoned but must be in existence when payment is demanded. In order to relieve the subscriber from his duties, however, it is essential that there be a complete abandonment or frustration of the project. In cases where the project is partially completed, a cessation of work due to the shortage of funds precipitated by the failure of pledgors to pay the full amount of their pledges is not a complete abandonment relieving the subscriber from liability. This is also true when a project is temporarily suspended because of financial difficulties or because the purpose of the subscription is substantially accomplished, but the enterprise is subsequently stopped.

When the subscriber's liability has become fixed, based upon a fulfillment of all conditions, he must pay the subscription according to its terms. In cases where the promise is to pay as the work progresses, the work need not be completed before payment is due.

A subscription is a type of contract, and, therefore, the remedies for its breach are the same as those for breach of contract and include DAMAGES and SPECIFIC PERFORMANCE.

SUBSIDIARY   Auxiliary; aiding or supporting in an inferior capacity or position. In the law of CORPORATIONS, a corporation or company owned by another corporation that controls at least a majority of the shares.

A subsidiary corporation or company is one in which another, generally larger, corporation, known as the parent corporation, owns all or at least a majority of the shares. As the owner of the subsidiary, the parent corporation may control the activities of the subsidiary. This arrangement differs from a merger, in which a corporation purchases another company and dissolves the purchased company's organizational structure and identity.

Subsidiaries can be formed in different ways and for various reasons. A corporation can form a subsidiary either by purchasing a controlling interest in an existing company or by creating the company itself. When a corporation acquires an existing company, forming a subsidiary can be preferable to a merger because the parent corporation can acquire a controlling interest with a smaller investment than a merger would require. In addition, the approval of the stockholders of the acquired firm is not required as it would be in the case of a merger.

When a company is purchased, the parent corporation may determine that the acquired company's name recognition in the market merits making it a subsidiary rather than merging it with the parent. A subsidiary may also produce goods or services that are completely different from those produced by the parent corporation. In that case it would not make sense to merge the operations.

Corporations that operate in more than one country often find it useful or necessary to create subsidiaries. For example, a multinational corporation may create a subsidiary in a country to obtain favorable tax treatment, or a country may require multinational corporations to establish local subsidiaries in order to do business there.

Corporations also create subsidiaries for the specific purpose of limiting their LIABILITY in connection with a risky new business. The parent and subsidiary remain separate legal entities, and the obligations of one are separate from those of the other. Nevertheless, if a subsidiary becomes financially insecure, the parent corporation is often sued by CREDITORS. In some instances courts will hold the parent corporation liable, but generally the separation of corporate identities immunizes the parent corporation from financial responsibility for the subsidiary's liabilities.

One disadvantage of the parent-subsidiary relationship is the possibility of multiple taxation. Another is the duty of the parent corporation to promote the subsidiary's corporate interests, to act in its best interest, and to maintain a separate corporate identity. If the parent fails to meet these requirements, the courts will perceive the subsidiary as merely a business conduit for the parent, and the two corporations will be viewed as one entity for liability purposes.

See also MERGERS AND ACQUISITIONS; PARENT COMPANY.

SUB SILENTIO [*Latin, Under silence; without any notice being taken.*]

Passing a thing *sub silentio* may be EVIDENCE of consent.

SUBSTANCE Essence; the material or necessary component of something.

A matter of substance, as distinguished from a matter of form, with respect to PLEADINGS, AFFIDAVITS, INDICTMENTS, and other legal instruments, entails the essential sufficiency, validity, or merits of the instrument, as opposed to its method or style.

SUBSTANCE ABUSE AND MENTAL HEALTH SERVICES ADMINISTRATION

The Substance Abuse and Mental Health Services Administration (SAMHSA), an operating division of the Department of HEALTH AND HUMAN SERVICES (HHS), was established in 1992 by the Alcohol, Drug Abuse, and Mental Health Administration Reorganization Act (Pub. L. No. 102-321). SAMHSA provides national leadership in the prevention and treatment of addictive and mental disorders, through programs and services for individuals who suffer from these disorders.

Within SAMHSA are several major centers designated to carry out its purposes. The Center for Substance Abuse Prevention (CSAP) develops and implements federal policy for the prevention of ALCOHOL and drug abuse, and analyzes the effect of other federal, state, and local programs also designed to prevent such abuse. CSAP administers and operates grant programs for the prevention of alcohol and drug abuse among specific populations, such as high-risk youth and women with dependent children, and in particular settings, including schools and the workplace. CSAP also supports training for health professionals working in alcohol and drug abuse education and prevention.

The Center for Substance Abuse Treatment (CSAT) provides national leadership in developing and administering programs focusing on the treatment of substance abuse. CSAT works with states, local communities, and health care providers by providing financial assistance to improve and expand programs for treating substance abuse. CSAT, like CSAP, also focuses on specific populations by administering and evaluating grant programs like the Comprehensive Residential Drug Prevention and Treatment Program, which treats women who abuse substances, and their children, and helps to train health care providers working in substance abuse prevention.

The Center for Mental Health Services (CMHS) promotes, on the federal level, the prevention and treatment of mental disorders, by identifying national mental health goals and developing strategies to meet them. CMHS works to improve the quality of programs that serve both the individuals suffering from these disorders and their families. Like other component centers carrying out the goals of SAMHSA, CMHS administers grants and programs that help states and local governments provide mental health care and services. CMHS also works with the alcohol, drug abuse, and mental health institutes of the National Institutes of Health, the principal biomedical research agency of the federal government, in researching the effective delivery of mental health services.

The Office of Management, Planning, and Communications (OMPC) is responsible for the financial and administrative management of SAMHSA components, including their personnel management and computer support functions. OMPC also monitors and analyzes pending legislation affecting SAMHSA components and acts as a liaison between SAMHSA and congressional committees. In addition, OMPC oversees the public affairs activities of SAMHSA, including public relations and interaction with the media to facilitate coverage of SAM-

HSA programs and objectives. Finally, OMPC collects and compiles alcohol and drug abuse prevention and treatment literature and supports the CSAP National Clearinghouse for Alcohol and Drug Information. The clearinghouse then disseminates its materials to state and local governments, health care and drug treatment programs, health care professionals, and the general public.

See also DRUGS AND NARCOTICS.

ABBREVIATIONS

A.	Atlantic Reporter
A. 2d	Atlantic Reporter, Second Series
AAA	American Arbitration Association; Agricultural Adjustment Act of 1933
AAPRP	All African People's Revolutionary Party
ABA	American Bar Association; Architectural Barriers Act, 1968
ABM Treaty	Anti-Ballistic Missile Treaty of 1972; antiballistic missile
ABVP	Anti-Biased Violence Project
A/C	Account
A.C.	Appeal Cases
ACAA	Air Carrier Access Act
ACF	Administration for Children and Families
ACLU	American Civil Liberties Union
ACS	Agricultural Cooperative Service
Act'g Legal Adv.	Acting Legal Advisor
ACUS	Administrative Conference of the United States
ACYF	Administration on Children, Youth, and Families
A.D. 2d	Appellate Division, Second Series, N.Y.
ADA	Americans with Disabilities Act of 1990
ADAMHA	Alcohol, Drug Abuse, and Mental Health Administration
ADC	Aid to Dependent Children
ADD	Administration on Developmental Disabilities
ADEA	Age Discrimination in Employment Act of 1967
ADR	alternative dispute resolution
AEC	Atomic Energy Commission
AECB	Arms Export Control Board
A.E.R.	All England Law Reports
AFDC	Aid to Families with Dependent Children
aff'd per cur.	affirmed by the court
AFIS	automated fingerprint identification system
AFL	American Federation of Labor
AFL-CIO	American Federation of Labor and Congress of Industrial Organizations
AFRes	Air Force Reserve
AFSCME	American Federation of State, County, and Municipal Employees
AGRICOLA	Agricultural Online Access
AIA	Association of Insurance Attorneys
AID	artificial insemination using a third-party donor's sperm; Agency for International Development

AIDS	acquired immune deficiency syndrome
AIH	artificial insemination using the husband's sperm
AIM	American Indian Movement
AIUSA	Amnesty International, U.S.A. Affiliate
AJS	American Judicature Society
ALEC	American Legislative Exchange Council
ALF	Animal Liberation Front
ALI	American Law Institute
ALJ	administrative law judge
All E.R.	All England Law Reports
ALO	Agency Liaison
A.L.R.	American Law Reports
AMA	American Medical Association
Am. Dec.	American Decisions
amdt.	amendment
Amer. St. Papers, For. Rels.	American State Papers, Legislative and Executive Documents of the Congress of the U.S., Class I, Foreign Relations, 1832–1859
AMVETS	American Veterans (of World War II)
ANA	Administration for Native Americans
Ann. Dig.	Annual Digest of Public International Law Cases
ANZUS	Australia–New Zealand–United States Security Treaty Organization
AOA	Administration on Aging
APA	Administrative Procedure Act of 1946
APHIS	Animal and Plant Health Inspection Service
App. Div.	Appellate Division Reports, N.Y. Supreme Court
Arb. Trib., U.S.-British Convention of 1853	Arbitration Tribunal, Claim Convention of 1853, United States and Great Britain
ARS	Advanced Record System
Art.	article
ASCS	Agriculture Stabilization and Conservation Service
ASM	available seatmile
ASPCA	American Society for the Prevention of Cruelty to Animals
Asst. Att. Gen.	Assistant Attorney General
AT&T	American Telephone and Telegraph
ATFD	Alcohol, Tobacco and Firearms Division
ATLA	Association of Trial Lawyers of America
ATTD	Alcohol and Tobacco Tax Division
ATU	Alcohol Tax Unit
AZT	azidothymidine
BALSA	Black-American Law Student Association
BATF	Bureau of Alcohol, Tobacco and Firearms
BCCI	Bank of Credit and Commerce International
BEA	Bureau of Economic Analysis
Bell's Cr. C.	Bell's English Crown Cases
Bevans	United States Treaties, etc. *Treaties and Other International Agreements of the United States of America, 1776–1949* (compiled under the direction of Charles I. Bevans) (1968–76)
BFOQ	bona fide occupational qualification
BI	Bureau of Investigation
BIA	Bureau of Indian Affairs; Board of Immigration Appeals
BJS	Bureau of Justice Statistics
Black.	Black's United States Supreme Court Reports
Blatchf.	Blatchford's United States Circuit Court Reports
BLM	Bureau of Land Management
BLS	Bureau of Labor Statistics
BMD	ballistic missile defense
BOCA	Building Officials and Code Administrators International
BPP	Black Panther Party for Self-Defense

Brit. and For.	British and Foreign State Papers
Burr.	James Burrows, *Report of Cases Argued and Determined in the Court of King's Bench during the Time of Lord Mansfield* (1766–1780)
BVA	Board of Veterans Appeals
c.	Chapter
C³I	Command, Control, Communications, and Intelligence
C.A.	Court of Appeals
CAA	Clean Air Act
CAB	Civil Aeronautics Board
CAFE	corporate average fuel economy
Cal. 2d	California Reports, Second Series
Cal. 3d	California Reports, Third Series
CALR	computer-assisted legal research
Cal. Rptr.	California Reporter
CAP	Common Agricultural Policy
CATV	community antenna television
CBO	Congressional Budget Office
CCC	Commodity Credit Corporation
CCDBG	Child Care and Development Block Grant of 1990
C.C.D. Pa.	Circuit Court Decisions, Pennsylvania
C.C.D. Va.	Circuit Court Decisions, Virginia
CCEA	Cabinet Council on Economic Affairs
CCR	Center for Constitutional Rights
C.C.R.I.	Circuit Court, Rhode Island
CD	certificate of deposit
CDA	Communications Decency Act
CDBG	Community Development Block Grant Program
CDC	Centers for Disease Control and Prevention; Community Development Corporation
CDF	Children's Defense Fund
CDL	Citizens for Decency through Law
CD-ROM	compact disc read-only memory
CDS	Community Dispute Services
CDW	collision damage waiver
CENTO	Central Treaty Organization
CEQ	Council on Environmental Quality
CERCLA	Comprehensive Environmental Response, Compensation, and Liability Act of 1980
cert.	*certiorari*
CETA	Comprehensive Employment and Training Act
C & F	cost and freight
CFC	chlorofluorocarbon
CFE Treaty	Conventional Forces in Europe Treaty of 1990
C.F. & I.	Cost, freight, and insurance
CFNP	Community Food and Nutrition Program
C.F.R.	Code of Federal Regulations
CFTC	Commodity Futures Trading Commission
Ch.	Chancery Division, English Law Reports
CHAMPVA	Civilian Health and Medical Program at the Veterans Administration
CHEP	Cuban/Haitian Entrant Program
CHINS	children in need of supervision
CHIPS	child in need of protective services
Ch.N.Y.	Chancery Reports, New York
Chr. Rob.	Christopher Robinson, *Reports of Cases Argued and Determined in the High Court of Admiralty* (1801–1808)
CIA	Central Intelligence Agency
CID	Commercial Item Descriptions
C.I.F.	Cost, insurance, and freight
CINCNORAD	Commander in Chief, North American Air Defense Command
C.I.O.	Congress of Industrial Organizations

C.J.	chief justice
CJIS	Criminal Justice Information Services
C.J.S.	Corpus Juris Secundum
Claims Arb. under Spec. Conv., Nielsen's Rept.	Frederick Kenelm Nielsen, *American and British Claims Arbitration under the Special Agreement Concluded between the United States and Great Britain, August 18, 1910* (1926)
CLE	Center for Law and Education
CLEO	Council on Legal Education Opportunity
CLP	Communist Labor Party of America
CLS	Christian Legal Society; critical legal studies (movement), Critical Legal Studies (membership organization)
C.M.A.	Court of Military Appeals
CMEA	Council for Mutual Economic Assistance
CMHS	Center for Mental Health Services
C.M.R.	Court of Military Review
CNN	Cable News Network
CNO	Chief of Naval Operations
C.O.D.	cash on delivery
COGP	Commission on Government Procurement
COINTELPRO	Counterintelligence Program
Coke Rep.	Coke's English King's Bench Reports
COLA	cost-of-living adjustment
COMCEN	Federal Communications Center
Comp.	Compilation
Conn.	Connecticut Reports
CONTU	National Commission on New Technological Uses of Copyrighted Works
Conv.	Convention
Corbin	Arthur L. Corbin, *Corbin on Contracts: A Comprehensive Treatise on the Rules of Contract Law* (1950)
CORE	Congress of Racial Equality
Cox's Crim. Cases	Cox's Criminal Cases (England)
CPA	certified public accountant
CPB	Corporation for Public Broadcasting, the
CPI	Consumer Price Index
CPSC	Consumer Product Safety Commission
Cranch	Cranch's United States Supreme Court Reports
CRF	Constitutional Rights Foundation
CRS	Congressional Research Service; Community Relations Service
CRT	critical race theory
CSA	Community Services Administration
CSAP	Center for Substance Abuse Prevention
CSAT	Center for Substance Abuse Treatment
CSC	Civil Service Commission
CSCE	Conference on Security and Cooperation in Europe
CSG	Council of State Governments
CSO	Community Service Organization
CSP	Center for the Study of the Presidency
C-SPAN	Cable-Satellite Public Affairs Network
CSRS	Cooperative State Research Service
CSWPL	Center on Social Welfare Policy and Law
CTA	*cum testamento annexo* (with the will attached)
Ct. Ap. D.C.	Court of Appeals, District of Columbia
Ct. App. No. Ireland	Court of Appeals, Northern Ireland
Ct. Cl.	Court of Claims, United States
Ct. Crim. Apps.	Court of Criminal Appeals (England)
Ct. of Sess., Scot.	Court of Sessions, Scotland
CU	credit union

CUNY	City University of New York
Cush.	Cushing's Massachusetts Reports
CWA	Civil Works Administration; Clean Water Act
Dall.	Dallas' Pennsylvania and United States Reports
DAR	Daughter of the American Revolution
DARPA	Defense Advanced Research Projects Agency
DAVA	Defense Audiovisual Agency
D.C.	United States District Court
D.C. Del.	United States District Court, Delaware
D.C. Mass.	United States District Court, Massachusetts
D.C. Md.	United States District Court, Maryland
D.C.N.D.Cal.	United States District Court, Northern District, California
D.C.N.Y.	United States District Court, New York
D.C.Pa.	United States District Court, Pennsylvania
DCS	Deputy Chiefs of Staff
DCZ	District of the Canal Zone
DDT	dichlorodiphenyltrichloroethane
DEA	Drug Enforcement Administration
Decl. Lond.	Declaration of London, February 26, 1909
Dev. & B.	Devereux & Battle's North Carolina Reports
Dig. U.S. Practice in Intl. Law	Digest of U.S. Practice in International Law
Dist. Ct. D.C.	United States District Court, District of Columbia
D.L.R.	Dominion Law Reports (Canada)
DNA	deoxyribonucleic acid
DNase	deoxyribonuclease
DNC	Democratic National Committee
DOC	Department of Commerce
DOD	Department of Defense
Dodson	Dodson's Reports, English Admiralty Courts
DOE	Department of Energy
DOER	Department of Employee Relations
DOJ	Department of Justice
DOS	disk operating system
DOT	Department of Transportation
DPT	diphtheria, pertussis, and tetanus
DRI	Defense Research Institute
DSAA	Defense Security Assistance Agency
DUI	driving under the influence; driving under intoxication
DWI	driving while intoxicated
EAHCA	Education for All Handicapped Children Act of 1975
EBT	examination before trial
ECPA	Electronic Communications Privacy Act of 1986
ECSC	Treaty of the European Coal and Steel Community
EDA	Economic Development Administration
EDF	Environmental Defense Fund
E.D.N.Y.	Eastern District, New York
EDP	electronic data processing
E.D. Pa.	Eastern District, Pennsylvania
EDSC	Eastern District, South Carolina
E.D. Va.	Eastern District, Virginia
EEC	European Economic Community; European Economic Community Treaty
EEOC	Equal Employment Opportunity Commission
EFF	Electronic Frontier Foundation
EFT	electronic funds transfer
Eliz.	Queen Elizabeth (Great Britain)
Em. App.	Temporary Emergency Court of Appeals

ENE	early neutral evaluation
Eng. Rep.	English Reports
EOP	Executive Office of the President
EPA	Environmental Protection Agency; Equal Pay Act of 1963
ERA	Equal Rights Amendment
ERISA	Employee Retirement Income Security Act of 1974
ERS	Economic Research Service
ESF	emergency support function; Economic Support Fund
ESRD	End-Stage Renal Disease Program
ETA	Employment and Training Administration
ETS	environmental tobacco smoke
et seq.	*et sequentes* or *et sequentia*; "and the following"
EU	European Union
Euratom	European Atomic Energy Community
Eur. Ct. H.R.	European Court of Human Rights
Ex.	English Exchequer Reports, Welsby, Hurlstone & Gordon
Exch.	Exchequer Reports (Welsby, Hurlstone & Gordon)
Eximbank	Export-Import Bank of the United States
F.	Federal Reporter
F. 2d	Federal Reporter, Second Series
FAA	Federal Aviation Administration; Federal Arbitration Act
FAAA	Federal Alcohol Administration Act
FACE	Freedom of Access to Clinic Entrances Act of 1994
FACT	Feminist Anti-Censorship Task Force
FAO	Food and Agriculture Organization of the United Nations
FAR	Federal Acquisition Regulations
FAS	Foreign Agricultural Service
FBA	Federal Bar Association
FBI	Federal Bureau of Investigation
FCA	Farm Credit Administration
F. Cas.	Federal Cases
FCC	Federal Communications Commission
FCIA	Foreign Credit Insurance Association
FCIC	Federal Crop Insurance Corporation
FCRA	Fair Credit Reporting Act
FCU	Federal credit unions
FDA	Food and Drug Administration
FDIC	Federal Deposit Insurance Corporation
FDPC	Federal Data Processing Center
FEC	Federal Election Commission
Fed. Cas.	Federal Cases
FEMA	Federal Emergency Management Agency
FFB	Federal Financing Bank
FGIS	Federal Grain Inspection Service
FHA	Federal Housing Authority
FHWA	Federal Highway Administration
FIA	Federal Insurance Administration
FIC	Federal Information Centers; Federation of Insurance Counsel
FICA	Federal Insurance Contributions Act
FIFRA	Federal Insecticide, Fungicide, and Rodenticide Act
FIP	Forestry Incentives Program
FIRREA	Financial Institutions Reform, Recovery, and Enforcement Act
FISA	Foreign Intelligence Surveillance Act of 1978
FMCS	Federal Mediation and Conciliation Service
FmHA	Farmers Home Administration
FMLA	Family and Medical Leave Act of 1993
FNMA	Federal National Mortgage Association, "Fannie Mae"
F.O.B.	free on board

FOIA	Freedom of Information Act
FPC	Federal Power Commission
FPMR	Federal Property Management Regulations
FPRS	Federal Property Resources Service
FR	Federal Register
FRA	Federal Railroad Administration
FRB	Federal Reserve Board
FRC	Federal Radio Commission
F.R.D.	Federal Rules Decisions
FSA	Family Support Act
FSLIC	Federal Savings and Loan Insurance Corporation
FSQS	Food Safety and Quality Service
FSS	Federal Supply Service
F. Supp.	Federal Supplement
FTA	U.S.-Canada Free Trade Agreement, 1988
FTC	Federal Trade Commission
FTS	Federal Telecommunications System
FUTA	Federal Unemployment Tax Act
FWPCA	Federal Water Pollution Control Act of 1948
GAO	General Accounting Office; Governmental Affairs Office
GAOR	General Assembly Official Records, United Nations
GA Res.	General Assembly Resolution (United Nations)
GATT	General Agreement on Tariffs and Trade
Gen. Cls. Comm.	General Claims Commission, United States and Panama; General Claims Commission, United States and Mexico
Geo. II	King George II (Great Britain)
Geo. III	King George III (Great Britain)
GM	General Motors
GNMA	Government National Mortgage Association, "Ginnie Mae"
GNP	gross national product
GOP	Grand Old Party (Republican)
GOPAC	Grand Old Party Action Committee
GPA	Office of Governmental and Public Affairs
GPO	Government Printing Office
GRAS	generally recognized as safe
Gr. Br., Crim. Ct. App.	Great Britain, Court of Criminal Appeals
GRNL	Gay Rights National Lobby
GSA	General Services Administration
Hackworth	Green Haywood Hackworth, *Digest of International Law* (1940–44)
Hay and Marriott	Great Britain. High Court of Admiralty, *Decisions in the High Court of Admiralty during the Time of Sir George Hay and of Sir James Marriott, Late Judges of That Court* (1801)
HBO	Home Box Office
HCFA	Health Care Financing Administration
H.Ct.	High Court
HDS	Office of Human Development Services
Hen. & M.	Hening & Munford's Virginia Reports
HEW	Department of Health, Education, and Welfare
HHS	Department of Health and Human Services
Hill	Hill's New York Reports
HIRE	Help through Industry Retraining and Employment
HIV	human immunodeficiency virus
H.L.	House of Lords Cases (England)
H. Lords	House of Lords (England)
HNIS	Human Nutrition Information Service
Hong Kong L.R.	Hong Kong Law Reports
How.	Howard's United States Supreme Court Reports
How. St. Trials	Howell's English State Trials
HUAC	House Un-American Activities Committee

HUD	Department of Housing and Urban Development
Hudson, Internatl. Legis.	Manley O. Hudson, ed., *International Legislation: A Collection of the Texts of Multipartite International Instruments of General Interest Beginning with the Covenant of the League of Nations* (1931)
Hudson, World Court Reps.	Manley Ottmer Hudson, ed., *World Court Reports* (1934–)
Hun	Hun's New York Supreme Court Reports
Hunt's Rept.	Bert L. Hunt, *Report of the American and Panamanian General Claims Arbitration* (1934)
IAEA	International Atomic Energy Agency
IALL	International Association of Law Libraries
IBA	International Bar Association
IBM	International Business Machines
ICBM	intercontinental ballistic missile
ICC	Interstate Commerce Commission
ICJ	International Court of Justice
IDEA	Individuals with Disabilities Education Act, 1975
IEP	individualized educational program
IFC	International Finance Corporation
IGRA	Indian Gaming Regulatory Act, 1988
IJA	Institute of Judicial Administration
IJC	International Joint Commission
ILC	International Law Commission
ILD	International Labor Defense
Ill. Dec.	Illinois Decisions
ILO	International Labor Organization
IMF	International Monetary Fund
INA	Immigration and Nationality Act
IND	investigational new drug
INF Treaty	Intermediate-Range Nuclear Forces Treaty of 1987
INS	Immigration and Naturalization Service
INTELSAT	International Telecommunications Satellite Organization
Interpol	International Criminal Police Organization
Int'l. Law Reps.	International Law Reports
Intl. Legal Mats.	International Legal Materials
IPDC	International Program for the Development of Communication
IPO	Intellectual Property Owners
IPP	independent power producer
IQ	intelligence quotient
I.R.	Irish Reports
IRA	individual retirement account; Irish Republican Army
IRCA	Immigration Reform and Control Act of 1986
IRS	Internal Revenue Service
ISO	independent service organization
ISSN	International Standard Serial Numbers
ITA	International Trade Administration
ITI	Information Technology Integration
ITO	International Trade Organization
ITS	Information Technology Service
ITU	International Telecommunication Union
IUD	intrauterine device
IWC	International Whaling Commission
IWW	Industrial Workers of the World
JCS	Joint Chiefs of Staff
JDL	Jewish Defense League
JOBS	Jobs Opportunity and Basic Skills
John. Ch.	Johnson's New York Chancery Reports
Johns.	Johnson's Reports (New York)
JP	justice of the peace

K.B.	King's Bench Reports (England)
KGB	Komitet Gosudarstvennoi Bezopasnosti (the State Security Committee for countries in the former Soviet Union)
KKK	Ku Klux Klan
KMT	Kuomintang
LAPD	Los Angeles Police Department
LC	Library of Congress
LD50	lethal dose 50
LDEF	Legal Defense and Education Fund (NOW)
LDF	Legal Defense Fund, Legal Defense and Educational Fund of the NAACP
LEAA	Law Enforcement Assistance Administration
L.Ed.	Lawyers' Edition Supreme Court Reports
LMSA	Labor-Management Services Administration
LNTS	League of Nations Treaty Series
Lofft's Rep.	Lofft's English King's Bench Reports
L.R.	Law Reports (English)
LSAS	Law School Admission Service
LSAT	Law School Aptitude Test
LSC	Legal Services Corporation; Legal Services for Children
LSD	lysergic acid diethylamide
LSDAS	Law School Data Assembly Service
LTBT	Limited Test Ban Treaty
LTC	Long Term Care
MAD	mutual assured destruction
MADD	Mothers against Drunk Driving
MALDEF	Mexican American Legal Defense and Educational Fund
Malloy	William M. Malloy, ed., *Treaties, Conventions, International Acts, Protocols, and Agreements between the United States of America and Other Powers* (1910–38)
Martens	Georg Friedrich von Martens, ed., *Noveau recueil général de traités et autres act es relatifs aux rapports de droit international* (Series I, 20 vols. [1843–75]; Series II, 35 vols. [1876–1908]; Series III [1909–])
Mass.	Massachusetts Reports
MCH	Maternal and Child Health Bureau
Md. App.	Maryland, Appeal Cases
M.D. Ga.	Middle District, Georgia
Mercy	Movement Ensuring the Right to Choose for Yourself
Metc.	Metcalf's Massachusetts Reports
MFDP	Mississippi Freedom Democratic party
MGT	Management
MHSS	Military Health Services System
Miller	David Hunter Miller, ed., *Treaties and Other International Acts. of the United States of America* (1931–1948)
Minn.	Minnesota Reports
MINS	minors in need of supervision
MIRV	multiple independently targetable reentry vehicle
Misc.	Miscellaneous Reports, New York
Mixed Claims Comm., Report of Decs.	Mixed Claims Commission, United States and Germany, Report of Decisions
M.J.	Military Justice Reporter
MLAP	Migrant Legal Action Program
MLB	major league baseball
MLDP	Mississippi Loyalist Democratic party
Mo.	Missouri Reports
Mod.	Modern Reports, English King's Bench, etc.
Moore, Dig. Intl. Law	John Bassett Moore, *A Digest of International Law*, 8 vols. (1906)
Moore, Intl. Arbs.	John Bassett Moore, *History and Digest of the International Arbitrations to Which the United States Has Been a Party*, 6 vols. (1898)

Morison	William Maxwell Morison, *The Scots Revised Report: Morison's Dictionary of Decisions* (1908–09)
M.P.	member of Parliament
MPAA	Motion Picture Association of America
mpg	miles per gallon
MPRSA	Marine Protection, Research, and Sanctuaries Act of 1972
M.R.	Master of the Rolls
MS-DOS	Microsoft Disk Operating System
MSHA	Mine Safety and Health Administration
NAACP	National Association for the Advancement of Colored People
NAAQS	National Ambient Air Quality Standards
NABSW	National Association of Black Social Workers
NAFTA	North American Free Trade Agreement, 1993
NARAL	National Abortion Rights Action League
NARF	Native American Rights Fund
NARS	National Archives and Record Service
NASA	National Aeronautics and Space Administration
NASD	National Association of Securities Dealers
NATO	North Atlantic Treaty Organization
NAVINFO	Navy Information Offices
NAWSA	National American Woman's Suffrage Association
NBA	National Bar Association
NBC	National Broadcasting Company
NBLSA	National Black Law Student Association
NBS	National Bureau of Standards
NCA	Noise Control Act; National Command Authorities
NCAA	National Collegiate Athletic Association
NCAC	National Coalition against Censorship
NCCB	National Consumer Cooperative Bank
NCE	Northwest Community Exchange
NCJA	National Criminal Justice Association
NCLB	National Civil Liberties Bureau
NCP	national contingency plan
NCSC	National Center for State Courts
NCUA	National Credit Union Administration
NDA	new drug application
N.D. Ill.	Northern District, Illinois
NDU	National Defense University
N.D. Wash.	Northern District, Washington
N.E.	North Eastern Reporter
N.E. 2d	North Eastern Reporter, Second Series
NEA	National Endowment for the Arts
NEH	National Endowment for the Humanities
NEPA	National Environmental Protection Act; National Endowment Policy Act
NFIP	National Flood Insurance Program
NGTF	National Gay Task Force
NHRA	Nursing Home Reform Act, 1987
NHTSA	National Highway Traffic Safety Administration
Nielsen's Rept.	Frederick Kenelm Nielsen, *American and British Claims Arbitration under the Special Agreement Concluded between the United States and Great Britain, August 18, 1910* (1926)
NIEO	New International Economic Order
NIH	National Institutes of Health, the NIH
NIJ	National Institute of Justice
NIRA	National Industrial Recovery Act; National Industrial Recovery Administration
NIST	National Institute of Standards and Technology, the NIST
NTIA	National Telecommunications and Information Administration
N.J.	New Jersey Reports

N.J. Super.	New Jersey Superior Court Reports
NLRA	National Labor Relations Act
NLRB	National Labor Relations Board
No.	Number
NOAA	National Oceanic and Atmospheric Administration
NOW	National Organization for Women
NOW LDEF	National Organization for Women Legal Defense and Education Fund
NOW/PAC	National Organization for Women Political Action Committee
NPDES	National Pollutant Discharge Elimination System
NPL	national priorities list
NPR	National Public Radio
NPT	Non-Proliferation Treaty
NRA	National Rifle Association; National Recovery Act
NRC	Nuclear Regulatory Commission
NSC	National Security Council
NSCLC	National Senior Citizens Law Center
NSF	National Science Foundation
NSFNET	National Science Foundation Network
NTIA	National Telecommunications and Information Administration
NTID	National Technical Institute for the Deaf
NTIS	National Technical Information Service
NTS	Naval Telecommunications System
NTSB	National Transportation Safety Board
N.W.	North Western Reporter
N.W. 2d	North Western Reporter, Second Series
NWSA	National Woman Suffrage Association
N.Y.	New York Court of Appeals Reports
N.Y. 2d	New York Court of Appeals Reports, Second Series
N.Y.S.	New York Supplement Reporter
N.Y.S. 2d	New York Supplement Reporter, Second Series
NYSE	New York Stock Exchange
N.Y. Sup.	New York Supreme Court Reports
NYU	New York University
OAAU	Organization of Afro American Unity
OAP	Office of Administrative Procedure
OAS	Organization of American States
OASDI	Old-age, Survivors, and Disability Insurance Benefits
OASHDS	Office of the Assistant Secretary for Human Development Services
OCED	Office of Comprehensive Employment Development
OCHAMPUS	Office of Civilian Health and Medical Program of the Uniformed Services
OCSE	Office of Child Support Enforcement
OEA	Organización de los Estados Americanos
OFCCP	Office of Federal Contract Compliance Programs
OFPP	Office of Federal Procurement Policy
OICD	Office of International Cooperation and Development
OIG	Office of the Inspector General
OJARS	Office of Justice Assistance, Research, and Statistics
OMB	Office of Management and Budget
OMPC	Office of Management, Planning, and Communications
ONP	Office of National Programs
OPD	Office of Policy Development
OPEC	Organization of Petroleum Exporting Countries
OPIC	Overseas Private Investment Corporation
Ops. Atts. Gen.	Opinions of the Attorneys-General of the United States
Ops. Comms.	Opinions of the Commissioners
OPSP	Office of Product Standards Policy
O.R.	Ontario Reports
OR	Official Records

OSHA	Occupational Safety and Health Administration
OSHRC	Occupational Safety and Health Review Commission
OSM	Office of Surface Mining
OSS	Office of Strategic Services
OST	Office of the Secretary
OT	Office of Transportation
OTA	Office of Technology Assessment
OTC	over-the-counter
OUI	operating under the influence
OWBPA	Older Workers Benefit Protection Act
OWRT	Office of Water Research and Technology
P.	Pacific Reporter
P. 2d	Pacific Reporter, Second Series
PAC	political action committee
Pa. Oyer and Terminer	Pennsylvania Oyer and Terminer Reports
PATCO	Professional Air Traffic Controllers Organization
PBGC	Pension Benefit Guaranty Corporation
PBS	Public Broadcasting Service; Public Buildings Service
P.C.	Privy Council (English Law Reports); personal computer
PCIJ	Permanent Court of International Justice
	Series A—Judgments and Orders (1922–30)
	Series B—Advisory Opinions (1922–30)
	Series A/B—Judgments, Orders, and Advisory Opinions (1931–40)
	Series C—Pleadings, Oral Statements, and Documents relating to Judgments and Advisory Opinions (1923–42)
	Series D—Acts and Documents concerning the Organization of the World Court (1922–47)
	Series E—Annual Reports (1925–45)
PCP	phencyclidine (no need to spell out)
P.D.	Probate Division, English Law Reports (1876–1890)
PDA	Pregnancy Discrimination Act of 1978
PD & R	Policy Development and Research
Perm. Ct. of Arb.	Permanent Court of Arbitration
Pet.	Peters' United States Supreme Court Reports
PETA	People for the Ethical Treatment of Animals
PGM	Program
PHA	Public Housing Agency
Phila. Ct. of Oyer and Terminer	Philadelphia Court of Oyer and Terminer
PHS	Public Health Service
PIC	Private Industry Council
Pick.	Pickering's Massachusetts Reports
PIK	Payment in Kind
PINS	persons in need of supervision
PIRG	Public Interest Research Group
P.L.	Public Laws
PLAN	Pro-Life Action Network
PLI	Practicing Law Institute
PLO	Palestine Liberation Organization
PNET	Peaceful Nuclear Explosions Treaty
POW-MIA	prisoner of war–missing in action
Pratt	Frederic Thomas Pratt, *Law of Contraband of War, with a Selection of Cases from the Papers of the Right Honourable Sir George Lee* (1856)
Proc.	Proceedings
PRP	potentially responsible party
PSRO	Professional Standards Review Organization
PTO	Patents and Trademark Office
PURPA	Public Utilities Regulatory Policies Act

PUSH	People United to Serve Humanity
PWA	Public Works Administration
PWSA	Ports and Waterways Safety Act of 1972
Q.B.	Queen's Bench (England)
Ralston's Rept.	Jackson Harvey Ralston, ed., *Venezuelan Arbitrations of 1903* (1904)
RC	Regional Commissioner
RCRA	Resource Conservation and Recovery Act
RCWP	Rural Clean Water Program
RDA	Rural Development Administration
REA	Rural Electrification Administration
Rec. des Decs. des Trib. Arb. Mixtes	G. Gidel, ed., *Recueil des décisions des tribunaux arbitraux mixtes, institués par les traités de paix* (1922–30)
Redmond	Vol. 3 of Charles I. Bevans, *Treaties and Other International Agreements of the United States of America, 1776–1949* (compiled by C. F. Redmond) (1969)
RESPA	Real Estate Settlement Procedure Act of 1974
RFRA	Religious Freedom Restoration Act
RICO	Racketeer Influenced and Corrupt Organizations
RNC	Republican National Committee
Roscoe	Edward Stanley Roscoe, ed., *Reports of Prize Cases Determined in the High Court of Admiralty before the Lords Commissioners of Appeals in Prize Causes and before the Judicial Committee of the Privy Council from 1745 to 1859* (1905)
ROTC	Reserve Officers' Training Corps
RPP	Representative Payee Program
R.S.	Revised Statutes
RTC	Resolution Trust Company
Ryan White CARE Act	Ryan White Comprehensive AIDS Research Emergency Act of 1990
SAC	Strategic Air Command
SACB	Subversive Activities Control Board
SADD	Students against Drunk Driving
SAF	Student Activities Fund
SAIF	Savings Association Insurance Fund
SALT I	Strategic Arms Limitation Talks of 1969–72
SAMHSA	Substance Abuse and Mental Health Services Administration
Sandf.	Sandford's New York Superior Court Reports
S and L	savings and loan
SARA	Superfund Amendment and Reauthorization Act
Sawy.	Sawyer's United States Circuit Court Reports
SBA	Small Business Administration
SCLC	Southern Christian Leadership Conference
Scott's Repts.	James Brown Scott, ed., *The Hague Court Reports*, 2 vols. (1916–32)
SCS	Soil Conservation Service
SCSEP	Senior Community Service Employment Program
S.Ct.	Supreme Court Reporter
S.D. Cal.	Southern District, California
S.D. Fla.	Southern District, Florida
S.D. Ga.	Southern District, Georgia
SDI	Strategic Defense Initiative
S.D. Me.	Southern District, Maine
S.D.N.Y.	Southern District, New York
SDS	Students for a Democratic Society
S.E.	South Eastern Reporter
S.E. 2d	South Eastern Reporter, Second Series
SEA	Science and Education Administration
SEATO	Southeast Asia Treaty Organization
SEC	Securities and Exchange Commission
Sec.	Section
SEEK	Search for Elevation, Education and Knowledge
SEOO	State Economic Opportunity Office

SEP	simplified employee pension plan
Ser.	Series
Sess.	Session
SGLI	Servicemen's Group Life Insurance
SIP	state implementation plan
SLA	Symbionese Liberation Army
SLBM	submarine-launched ballistic missile
SNCC	Student Nonviolent Coordinating Committee
So.	Southern Reporter
So. 2d	Southern Reporter, Second Series
SPA	Software Publisher's Association
Spec. Sess.	Special Session
SRA	Sentencing Reform Act of 1984
SS	Schutzstaffel (German for Protection Echelon)
SSA	Social Security Administration
SSI	Supplemental Security Income
START I	Strategic Arms Reduction Treaty of 1991
START II	Strategic Arms Reduction Treaty of 1993
Stat.	United States Statutes at Large
STS	Space Transportation Systems
St. Tr.	State Trials, English
STURAA	Surface Transportation and Uniform Relocation Assistance Act of 1987
Sup. Ct. of Justice, Mexico	Supreme Court of Justice, Mexico
Supp.	Supplement
S.W.	South Western Reporter
S.W. 2d	South Western Reporter, Second Series
SWAPO	South-West Africa People's Organization
SWAT	Special Weapons and Tactics
SWP	Socialist Workers party
TDP	Trade and Development Program
Tex. Sup.	Texas Supreme Court Reports
THAAD	Theater High-Altitude Area Defense System
TIA	Trust Indenture Act of 1939
TIAS	Treaties and Other International Acts Series (United States)
TNT	trinitrotoluene
TOP	Targeted Outreach Program
TPUS	Transportation and Public Utilities Service
Tripartite Claims Comm., Decs. and Ops.	Tripartite Claims Commission (United States, Austria, and Hungary), Decisions and Opinions
TRI-TAC	Joint Tactical Communications
TRO	temporary restraining order
TS	Treaty Series, United States
TSCA	Toxic Substance Control Act
TSDs	transporters, storers, and disposers
TTBT	Threshold Test Ban Treaty
TVA	Tennessee Valley Authority
UAW	United Auto Workers; United Automobile, Aerospace, and Agricultural Implements Workers of America
U.C.C.	Uniform Commercial Code; Universal Copyright Convention
U.C.C.C.	Uniform Consumer Credit Code
UCCJA	Uniform Child Custody Jurisdiction Act
UCMJ	Uniform Code of Military Justice
UCPP	Urban Crime Prevention Program
UCS	United Counseling Service
UDC	United Daughters of the Confederacy
UFW	United Farm Workers
UHF	ultrahigh frequency
UIFSA	Uniform Interstate Family Support Act

UIS	Unemployment Insurance Service
UMDA	Uniform Marriage and Divorce Act
UMTA	Urban Mass Transportation Administration
UNCITRAL	United Nations Commission on International Trade Law
UNCTAD	United Nations Conference on Trade and Development
UN Doc.	United Nations Documents
UNDP	United Nations Development Program
UNEF	United Nations Emergency Force
UNESCO	United Nations Educational, Scientific, and Cultural Organization
UNICEF	United Nations Children's Fund
UNIDO	United Nations Industrial and Development Organization
Unif. L. Ann.	Uniform Laws Annotated
UN Repts. Intl. Arb. Awards	United Nations Reports of International Arbitral Awards
UNTS	United Nations Treaty Series
UPI	United Press International
URESA	Uniform Reciprocal Enforcement of Support Act
U.S.	United States Reports
USAF	United States Air Force
U.S. App. D.C.	United States Court of Appeals for the District of Columbia
U.S.C.	United States Code
U.S.C.A.	United States Code Annotated
U.S.C.C.A.N.	United States Code Congressional and Administrative News
USCMA	United States Court of Military Appeals
USDA	U.S. Department of Agriculture
USES	United States Employment Service
USFA	United States Fire Administration
USICA	International Communication Agency, United States
USSC	U.S. Sentencing Commission
U.S.S.R.	Union of Soviet Socialist Republics
UST	United States Treaties
USTS	United States Travel Service
v.	*versus*
VA	Veterans Administration, the VA
VGLI	Veterans Group Life Insurance
Vict.	Queen Victoria (Great Britain)
VIN	vehicle identification number
VISTA	Volunteers in Service to America
VJRA	Veterans Judicial Review Act of 1988
V.L.A.	Volunteer Lawyers for the Arts
VMI	Virginia Military Institute
VMLI	Veterans Mortgage Life Insurance
VOCAL	Victims of Child Abuse Laws
WAC	Women's Army Corps
Wall.	Wallace's United States Supreme Court Reports
Wash. 2d	Washington Reports, Second Series
WAVES	Women Accepted for Volunteer Service
WCTU	Women's Christian Temperance Union
W.D. Wash.	Western District, Washington
W.D. Wis.	Western District, Wisconsin
WEAL	West's Encyclopedia of American Law, Women's Equity Action League
Wend.	Wendell's New York Reports
WFSE	Washington Federation of State Employees
Wheat.	Wheaton's United States Supreme Court Reports
Wheel. Cr. Cases	Wheeler's New York Criminal Cases
Whiteman	Marjorie Millace Whiteman, *Digest of International Law*, 15 vols. (1963–73)
WHO	World Health Organization
WIC	Women, Infants, and Children program
Will. and Mar.	King William and Queen Mary (Great Britain)

WIN	WESTLAW Is Natural; Whip Inflation Now; Work Incentive Program
WIU	Workers' Industrial Union
W.L.R.	Weekly Law Reports, England
WPA	Works Progress Administration
WPPDA	Welfare and Pension Plans Disclosure Act
WWI	World War I
WWII	World War II
Yates Sel. Cas.	Yates' New York Select Cases

BIBLIOGRAPHY

REPUBLICAN PARTY

Boller, Paul F., Jr. 1996. *Presidential Campaigns.* New York: Oxford Univ. Press.

Moos, Malcolm. 1956. *The Republicans: A History of Their Party.* New York: Random House.

Wilson, James Q. 1992. *American Government.* Lexington, Mass.: D. C. Heath.

RES GESTAE

Moorehead, James Donald. 1995. "Compromising the Hearsay Rule: The Fallacy of Res Gestae Reliability." *Loyola of Los Angeles Law Review* 29 (November).

Morgan, Edmund M. 1922. "A Suggested Classification of Utterances Admissible as Res Gestae." *Yale Law Journal* 31.

Prater, Dennis D., and Virginia M. Klemme. 1996. "Res Gestae Raises Its Ugly Head." *Journal of the Kansas Bar Association* 65 (October).

RESIDENCY REQUIREMENTS

Stephens, Otis H., Jr., and John M. Scheb II. 1993. *American Constitutional Law.* St. Paul: West.

RESTITUTION

Shoben, Elaine W., and William Murray Tabb. 1989. *Remedies: Cases and Problems.* Westbury, N.Y.: Foundation Press.

Knapp, Charles L. 1987. *Problems in Contract Law: Cases and Materials.* Boston: Little, Brown.

RESTORATIVE JUSTICE

Claassen, Ron. 1997. "Restorative Justice I." Center for Peacemaking and Conflict Studies, Fresno Pacific College site. World Wide Web (May 16).

"Restorative Justice." 1997. Mennonite Central Committee site. World Wide Web (May 16).

"The Restorative Justice Project." 1997. The Restorative Justice Project site. World Wide Web (May 16).

RESTRAINING ORDER

American Law Institute–American Bar Association (ALI-ABA) 1996. *Obtaining a Preliminary Injunction and Temporary Restraining Order,* by James J. Brosna-

han. Course of study, August 14, 1996. SB24 ALI-ABA 247.

Peters, Donald M. 1995. "Temporary Restraining Orders and Preliminary Injunction." *Arizona Attorney,* 31 (April).

Walsh, Keirsten L. 1996. "Safe and Sound at Last? Federalized Anti-Stalking Legislation in the United States and Canada." *Dickinson Journal of International Law* 14 (winter).

REVOLUTION

Berman, Harold. 1983. *Law and Revolution: The Formation of the Western Legal Tradition.* Cambridge: Harvard Univ. Press.

Brinton, Crane. 1952. *The Anatomy of Revolution.* New York: Vintage Books.

Wood, Gordon. 1991. *The Radicalism of the American Revolution.* New York: Vintage Books.

REYNOLDS V. SIMS

Stephens, Otis H., Jr., and John M. Scheb II. 1993. *American Constitutional Law.* St. Paul: West.

RICHARDSON, ELLIOT LEE

U.S. Department of Justice. 1985. *Attorneys General of the United States, 1789–1985.* Washington, D.C.: U.S. Government Printing Office.

RIDER

"Understanding Congress." 1997. National Volunteer Free Council site. World Wide Web.

Borchard, Clark. Lyndale Insurance Company, Minneapolis. 1997. Interview, April 10.

RIGHT OF ELECTION

Derrick, John H. 1986. "Annotation: Construction, Application, and Effect of Statutes Which Deny or Qualify Surviving Spouse's Right to Elect against Deceased Spouse's Will." *American Law Reports* 48.

Practising Law Institute (PLI). 1994. *Recent Changes to the Right of Election Laws and Ethical Considerations,* by Arlene Harris. Commercial Law and Practice Course Handbook series, PLI Order no. d4-5252.

RIGHT OF SURVIVORSHIP

Ross, Bruce S., and Henry T. Moore, Jr. "Probate." Chap. 2 in *California Practice Guide*.

"Trust Decisions." 1992. *Banking Law Journal* 109 (July–August).

RIGHT TO COUNSEL

"CBA Ethics Committee Opinion." 1994. *Colorado Lawyer* 23.

Israel, Jerold H., Yale Kamisar, and Wayne R. LaFave. 1983. *Criminal Procedure and the Constitution: Leading Supreme Court Cases and Introductory Text*. St. Paul: West.

Winick, Bruce J. 1989. "Forfeiture of Attorneys' Fees under RICO and CCE and the Right to Counsel of Choice: The Constitutional Dilemma and How to Avoid It." *University of Miami Law Review* 43 (March).

RIGHT-TO-WORK LAWS

Stephens, Otis H., Jr., and John M. Scheb II. 1993. *American Constitutional Law*. St. Paul: West.

Sumner, David G. 1984. "Plumbers and Pipefitters: The Need to Reinterpret the Scope of Compulsory Unionism." *American University Law Review* 33.

RIPENESS

American Law Institute–American Bar Association (ALI-ABA). 1993. *The "Ripeness" Mess in the Federal Courts*, by Michael M. Berger. Course of study, September 30, 1993. C872 ALI-ABA 41.

———. 1996. *The Ripeness Mess: Part I—Getting into State Court*, by Michael M. Berger. Course of study, October 17, 1996. SB14 ALI-ABA 155.

RISK ARBITRAGE

Steckman, Laurence A. 1988. "Risk Arbitrage and Insider Trading—A Functional Analysis of the Fiduciary Concept under Rule 10b-5." *Touro Law Review* 5 (October).

ROBBERY

LaFave, Wayne R., and Austin W. Scott, Jr. 1986. *Substantive Criminal Law*. St. Paul: West.

ROBERTS, OWEN

Abraham, Henry. 1982. *Freedom and the Court*. New York: Oxford Univ. Press.

White, G. Edward. 1988. *The American Judicial Tradition*. New York: Oxford Univ. Press.

ROBERTS V. UNITED STATES JAYCEES

Stephens, Otis H., Jr., and John M. Scheb II. 1993. *American Constitutional Law*. St. Paul: West.

ROBINSON, SPOTTSWOOD WILLIAM, III

"Biographies: The United States Court of Appeals for the District of Columbia Circuit." 1996. *George Washington Law Review* 64.

Kluger, Richard. 1974. *Simple Justice*. New York: Knopf.

ROBINSON-PATMAN ACT

Briley, Michael M. 1996. "Price Discrimination under the Robinson-Patman Act." *University of Toledo Law Review* 27 (winter).

Calvani, Terry, and Gilde Breidenbach. 1991. "An Introduction to the Robinson-Patman Act and Its Enforcement by the Government." *Antitrust Law Journal* 59.

ROBINSON V. CALIFORNIA

Stephens, Otis H., Jr., and John M. Scheb II. 1993. *American Constitutional Law*. St. Paul: West.

ROCHIN V. CALIFORNIA

Stephens, Otis H., Jr., and John M. Scheb II. 1993. *American Constitutional Law*. St. Paul: West.

RODNEY, CAESAR AUGUSTUS

Hall, Kermit L. 1989. *The Magic Mirror: Law in American History*. New York: Oxford Univ. Press.

U.S. Department of Justice. 1985. *Attorneys General of the United States, 1789–1985*. Washington, D.C.: U.S. Government Printing Office.

ROE V. WADE

Butler, J. Douglas, and David F. Walbert, eds. 1986. *Abortion, Medicine, and the Law*. 3d ed. New York: Facts on File.

Drucker, Dan. 1990. *Abortion Decisions of the Supreme Court, 1973 through 1989: A Comprehensive Review with Historical Commentary*. Jefferson, N. C.: McFarland.

McCorvey, Norma. 1994. *I Am Roe: My Life*, Roe v. Wade, *and Freedom of Choice*. New York, HarperCollins.

Rubin, Eva R. 1987. *Abortion, Politics and the Courts:* Roe v. Wade *and Its Aftermath*. New York: Greenwood.

ROGERS, WILLIAM PIERCE

U.S. Department of Justice. 1985. *Attorneys General of the United States, 1789–1985*. Washington, D.C.: U.S. Government Printing Office.

ROOSEVELT, ELEANOR

Black, Allida M. 1996. *Casting Her Own Shadow: Eleanor Roosevelt and the Shaping of Postwar Liberalism*. New York: Columbia Univ. Press.

Hoff-Wilson, Joan, and Marjorie Lightman. 1984. *Without Precedent: The Life and Career of Eleanor Roosevelt*. Bloomington, Ind.: Indiana Univ. Press.

Lash, Joseph P. 1972. *Eleanor: The Years Alone*. New York: Norton.

ROOSEVELT, FRANKLIN DELANO

Stephens, Otis H., Jr., and John M. Scheb II. 1993. *American Constitutional Law*. St. Paul: West.

ROOSEVELT, THEODORE

Stephens, Otis H., Jr., and John M. Scheb II. 1993. *American Constitutional Law*. St. Paul: West.

ROSENBERG TRIAL

Christenson, Ron. 1991. *Political Trials in History: From Antiquity to the Present*. New Brunswick, N.J.: Transaction Press.

Jensen, Rita Henley. 1993. "Data Helps Rosenbergs Cheat Death." *National Law Journal* (August 23).

Nizer, Louis. 1973. *The Implosion Conspiracy*. Greenwich, Conn.: Fawcett Publications.

Radosh, Ronald and Joyce Milton. 1983. *The Rosenberg File: A Search for the Truth.* New York: Vintage Books.

Schneir, Walter, and Miriam Schneir. 1983. *Invitation to an Inquest.* New York: Pantheon Books.

ROSS, JOHN

Blair, Jack. 1995–96. "Demanding a Voice in Our Own Best Interest: A Call for a Delegate of the Cherokee Nation to the U.S. House of Representatives." *American Indian Law* 20.

Ehle, John. 1988. *Trail of Tears: The Rise and Fall of the Cherokee Nation.* New York: Anchor Press, Doubleday.

Norgren, Jill. 1996. *The Cherokee Cases: The Confrontation of Law and Politics.* Blue Ridge Summit, Pa.: McGraw-Hill.

ROSS, NELLIE TAYLOE

Sherr, Lynn, and Jurate Kazicka. 1994. *Susan B. Anthony Slept Here: A Guide to American Women's Landmarks.* New York: Times Books.

Weatherford, Doris. 1994. *American Women's History.* New York: Prentice-Hall.

ROSTKER V. GOLDBERG

Stephens, Otis H., Jr., and John M. Scheb II. 1993. *American Constitutional Law.* St. Paul: West.

ROTH V. UNITED STATES

Hall, Kermit L. 1989. *The Magic Mirror: Law in American History.* New York: Oxford Univ. Press.

Stephens, Otis H., Jr., and John M. Scheb II. 1993. *American Constitutional Law.* St. Paul: West.

RUBENSTEIN, WILLIAM BRUCE

American Civil Liberties Union site. 1997. World Wide Web (June 26).

RUBY, JACK

Posner, Gerald. 1993. *Case Closed: Lee Harvey Oswald and the Assassination of JFK.* New York: Random House.

RULE IN SHELLEY'S CASE

Orth, John. 1989. "Requiem for the Rule in Shelley's Case." *North Carolina Law Review* 67.

RULE OF LAW

Hamilton, Alexander, James Madison, and John Jay. 1787–88. *The Federalist Papers.* Reprint, edited by Gary Wills, New York: Bantam Books, 1988.

Scalia, Antonin. 1989. "The Rule of Law as a Law of Rules." *University of Chicago Law Review* 56.

Smith, Steven. 1995. "Nonsense and Natural Law." *Southern California Interdisciplinary Law Journal* 4.

Stoner, James. 1992. *Common Law and Liberal Theory.* Lawrence, Kan.: Univ. Press of Kansas.

RULES OF WAR

Green, L. C. 1996. "Enforcement of the Law in International and Non-international Conflicts." *Denver Journal of International Law and Policy* 24.

Jochnick, Chris, and Roger Normand. 1994. "The Legitimation of Violence: A Critical History of the Laws of War." *Harvard International Law Journal* 35.

Mitchell, Dennis. 1996. "All Is Not Fair in War: The Need for a Permanent War Crimes Tribunal." *Drake Law Review* 44.

Taylor, Telford. 1992. *The Anatomy of the Nuremberg Trials.* Toronto: Little, Brown.

Walzer, Michael. 1992. *Just and Unjust Wars: A Moral Argument with Historical Illustrations.* New York: Basic Books.

Winthrop, James. 1994. "The Laws of War." *Military Law Review* 146.

RUSH, RICHARD

U.S. Department of Justice. 1985. *Attorneys General of the United States, 1789–1985.* Washington, D.C.: U.S. Government Printing Office.

RUTLEDGE, JOHN

Friedman, Leon, and Fred L. Israel, eds. 1995. *The Justices of the United States Supreme Court, 1789–1969: Their Lives and Major Opinions.* New York: Chelsea House.

RUTLEDGE, WILEY B.

Friedman, Leon, and Fred L. Israel, eds. 1969. *The Justices of the United States Supreme Court, 1789–1969: Their Lives and Major Opinions.* New York: Chelsea House.

SAILORS

Alfieri, Mark. 1997. "*Guevara v. Maritime:* Caught in the Wake of *Miles v. Apex Marine Corp.*" *Houston Journal of International Law* 19 (winter).

Allbritton, Jack L., and David W. Robertson. 1995. "Seaman Status after *Chandris, Inc. v. Latsis.*" *University of San Francisco Maritime Law Journal* 8 (fall).

Madrid, Eileen R. 1992. "Seaman Status: The Supreme Court Overrules *Pizzitolo.*" *Louisiana Bar Journal* 39 (April).

ST. CLAIR, JAMES DRAPER

Hale and Dorr site, Boston. 1997. World Wide Web (June 24).

Stephens, Otis H., Jr., and John M. Scheb II. 1993. *American Constitutional Law.* St. Paul: West.

SALEM WITCH TRIALS

Boyer, Paul, and Stephen Nissenbaum. 1974. *Salem Possessed: The Social Origins of Witchcraft.* Cambridge: Harvard Univ. Press.

Christenson, Ron. 1991. *Political Trials in History: From Antiquity to Present.* New Brunswick: Transaction Press.

Hill, Frances. 1995. *A Delusion of Satan: The Full Story of the Salem Witch Trials.* New York: Doubleday.

Karlsen, Carol. 1989. *The Devil in the Shape of a Woman: Witchcraft in Colonial New England.* New York: Vintage Books.

Trever-Roper, H. R. 1967. *The European Witch-Craze of the Sixteenth and Seventeenth Centuries.* San Francisco: Harper Torchbooks.

Weisman, Richard. 1984. *Witchcraft, Magic and Religion in 17th Century Massachusetts.* Amherst, Mass.: Univ. of Massachusetts Press.

SALES LAW

"Sales." 1994. *SMH Bar Review.*

SALVAGE

Fry, John P. 1988. "The Treasure Below: Jurisdiction over Salving Operations in International Waters." *Columbia Law Review* 88.

Landrum, Bruce. 1989. "Salvage Claims for the Navy and Coast Guard: A Unified Approach." *Naval Law Review* 38.

Neilson, William L. 1992. "The 1989 International Convention of Salvage." *Connecticut Law Review* 24.

Rydstron, Jean F. 1976. "Nature and Extent of Peril Necessary to Support Claim for Marine Salvage." *American Law Reports Federal* 26.

SANFORD, EDWARD TERRY

Friedman, Leon, and Fred L. Israel, eds. 1995. *The Justices of the United States Supreme Court, 1789–1969: Their Lives and Major Opinions.* New York: Chelsea House.

SANGER, MARGARET HIGGINS

Chesler, Ellen. 1992. *Women of Valor: Margaret Sanger and the Birth Control Movement in America.* New York: Simon & Schuster.

Coigney, Virginia. 1969. *Margaret Sanger: Rebel with a Cause.* New York: Doubleday.

Topalian, Elyse. 1984. *Margaret Sanger.* New York: Watts.

SAVINGS AND LOAN ASSOCIATION

American Bar Association. 1995. "How a Good Idea Went Wrong: Deregulation and the Savings and Loan Crisis." *Administrative Law Review* 47.

American Bar Association. The Committee of Savings and Loan Associations Section of Corporation, Banking, and Business. 1973. *Handbook of Savings and Loan Law.* Chicago: American Bar Association.

Gorman, Christopher Tyson. 1994–95. "Liability of Directors and Officers under FIRREA: The Uncertain Standard of § 1821(K) and the Need for Congressional Reform." *Kentucky Law Journal* 83.

U.S. House. 1989. 101st Cong., 1st sess. H.R. 54 (I). *United States Code Congressional and Administrative News.*

SAXBE, WILLIAM BART

Moritz, Charles, et al., eds. 1974. *Current Biography Yearbook.* New York: Wilson.

SCALIA, ANTONIN

Frantz, Douglas. 1986. "Scalia Embodies President's Hope for Court's Future." *Chicago Tribune* (August 3).

Hasson, Judy. 1986. "Scalia Got Early Chance to Show His Legal Talents." *The Seattle Times* (August 5).

Morgan, Neil. 1996. *The San Diego Union-Tribune* (News Section) (June 2).

Scalia, Antonin. 1989. "Originalism: The Lesser Evil." *University of Cincinnati Law Review* 57.

SCHECHTER POULTRY CORP. V. UNITED STATES

Barrett, Edward L., Jr., William Cohen, and Jonathan D. Varat. 1989. *Constitutional Law: Cases and Materials.* 8th ed. Westbury, N.Y.: Foundation Press.

SCHENCK V. UNITED STATES

Rabban, David. 1983. "The Emergence of Modern First Amendment Doctrine." *University of Chicago Law Review* 50.

SCHLAFLY, PHYLLIS

Current Biography Yearbook. 1978. New York: Wilson.

SCHLESINGER, RUDOLF B.

Buxbaum, Richard M. 1995. "Rudolf B. Schlesinger—A Tribute." *American Journal of Comparative Law* 43 (summer).

Winship, Peter. 1996. "As the World Turns: Revisiting Rudolf Schlesinger's Study of the Uniform Commercial Code 'In the Light of Comparative Law.' " *Loyola of Los Angeles Law Review* 29 (April).

SCHOOL DESEGREGATION

Hansen, Chris. 1993. "Are the Courts Giving Up? Current Issues in School Desegregation." *Emory Law Journal* 42 (summer).

Keynes, Edward, with Randall K. Miller. 1989. *The Courts vs. Congress: Prayer, Busing, and Abortion.* Durham, N.C.: Duke Univ. Press.

Orfield, Gary, and David Thronson. 1993. "Dismantling Desegregation: Uncertain Gains, Unexpected Costs." *Emory Law Journal* 42 (summer).

Wilkinson, J. Harvie III. 1979. *From Brown to Bakke: The Supreme Court and School Integration, 1954–1978.* New York: Oxford Univ. Press.

SCHOOLS AND SCHOOL DISTRICTS

Allen, Bill, coordinator for charter schools, Minnesota Department of Children, Families, and Learning. 1997. Telephone interview, July 30.

Barrett, Amy, public relations coordinator, Commissioner's Office of Minneapolis Public Schools. 1997. Telephone interview, July 16.

Editors of *Court TV* and *The American Lawyer.* "Going to School." 1995. *Court TV Cradle-to-Grave Legal Survival Guide.* New York: The American Lawyer/ Little Brown.

Heubert, Jay P. 1997. "Schools without Rules? Charter Schools, Federal Disability Law, and the Paradoxes of Deregulation." *Harvard Civil Rights–Civil Liberties Law Review* 32 (summer).

Loeb, Harlan A., and Debbie N. Kaminer. 1996. "God, Money, and Schools: Voucher Programs Impugn the Separation of Church and State." *John Marshall Law Review* 30 (fall).

"School Reform—Charter Schools—Connecticut and South Carolina Pass Charter School Statutes." 1997. *Harvard Law Review Association* 110 (May).

Shomion, Larry, chief accountant, St. Paul School District #625. 1997. Telephone interview, July 16.

Valencia, Mark G. 1996. "Take Care of Me When I Am Dead: An Examination of American Church-State Development and the Future of American Religious Liberty." *Southern Methodist University Law Review* 49 (July–August).

Wallstrom, Carl, superintendent of schools, Lakeville School District #194. 1997. Telephone interview, July 17.

SCIENTER

Bard, Lawrence R. 1992. "A Distinct-responsibility Approach to Accountants' Primary Liability under Rule 10B-5." *George Washington Law Review* 61 (November).

SCIENTIFIC EVIDENCE

"Evidence." 1994. *SMH Bar Review.*

Faigman, David L., et al. 1997. *Modern Scientific Evidence: The Law and Science of Expert Testimony.* Vol. 1. St. Paul: West.

SCIRE FACIAS
Edward M. Reisner. Practising Law Institute (PLI). 1995. *Using Litigation Support Programs and Graphic Evidence Media in Patent Cases,* by Patents, Copyrights, Trademarks, and Literary Property Course Handbook series, PLI order no. G4-39.

SCOPES, JOHN T.
Paine, Donald F. 1996. "*State of Tennessee v. John Scopes* Revisited." *Tennessee Bar Journal* 32 (May–June).

Uelmen, Gerald F. 1996. "The Trial as a Circus: Inherit the Wind." *University of San Francisco Law Review* 30 (summer).

Williams, Sharon. 1988. "Establishment Clause: *Edwards v. Aguillard;* The United States Supreme Court Denies Equal Time for Scientific Creationism in the Public Schools—'Scopes-in-reverse?' " *University of Missouri at Kansas City Law Review* 56 (spring).

S CORPORATION
Esenau, Warren H., et al., eds. 1994. *Guide to Income Tax, 1995 Edition.* Yonkers, New York: Consumer Reports Books.

Internal Revenue Service. 1996. *Tax Information on S Corporations.* IRS Publication 589. Washington, D.C.

"S Corporation Fact Sheet." 1997. Northwestern Mutual Life Insurance Company site. World Wide Web (January 18).

SEARCH AND SEIZURE
Congressional Digest 1992 (April).

CQ Almanac. 1991. Washington, D.C.: Congressional Quarterly.

"Criminal Procedure." 1993. In *The Conviser Mini Review.* Orlando, Fla.: Harcourt Brace Jovonovich Legal & Professional Publications.

Hemphill, Geoffrey G. 1995. "The Administrative Search Doctrine: Isn't This Exactly What the Framers Were Trying to Avoid?" *Regent University Law Review* 5.

Savage, David G. 1992. *Turning Right: The Making of the Rehnquist Court.*

Scully, Leon. 1992. *National Review* (May 25).

SEAT BELTS
LeBel, Paul A. 1991. "Reducing the Recovery of Avoidable 'Seat-belt Damages': A Cure for the Defects of *Waterson v. General Motors Corporation.*" *Seton Hall Law Review* 22.

SECOND AMENDMENT
Dolan, Edward F., and Margaret M. Scariano. 1994. *Guns in the United States.* New York: Watts.

Dunlap, Charles J., Jr. 1995. "Revolt of the Masses: Armed Civilians and the Insurrectionary Theory of the Second Amendment." *Tennessee Law Review* 62.

Hook, Donald D. 1993. *Gun Control: The Continuing Debate.* Washington, D.C.: Second Amendment Foundation.

Reed Amar, Akhil. 1992. "The Bill of Rights and the Fourteenth Amendment." *Yale Law Journal* 101.

SECONDARY AUTHORITY
Kunz, Christina L., et al. 1992. *The Process of Legal Research: Successful Strategies.* 3d ed. Boston: Little, Brown.

SECONDARY BOYCOTT
Beard, Brian K. 1989. "Secondary Boycotts after *DeBartolo:* Has the Supreme Court Handed Unions a Powerful New Weapon?" *Iowa Law Review* 75 (October).

Brown, Steven L. 1989. "Nonpicketing Labor Publicity Not within the Secondary-boycott Prohibition of Section 8(B)(4) of the National Labor Relations Act: *Edward J. Debartolo Corporation v. Florida Gulf Coast Building and Construction Trades Council.*" *Boston College Law Review* 31 (December).

Goldman, Lee. 1983. "The First Amendment and Nonpicketing Labor Publicity under Section 8(b)(4)(ii)(B) of the National Labor Relations Act." *Vanderbilt Law Review* 36 (November).

SECONDARY EVIDENCE
Green, Eric D., and Charles R. Nesson. 1994. *Problems, Cases, and Materials on Evidence.* 2d ed. Boston: Little, Brown.

SECRETARY OF STATE
Fisher, Louis. 1988. "Review Essay: How to Avoid Iran-Contras." *California Law Review* 76 (July).

"Organization and Structure at State." U.S. State Department site. World Wide Web (December 12).

SECTION 1983
Rotunda, Ronald D., and John E. Nowak. 1992. *Treatise on Constitutional Law.* 2d ed. Vol. 3. St. Paul: West.

SECURED TRANSACTIONS
Dalton, Elizabeth. 1986. "The Consequences of Commercially Unreasonable Dispositions of Collateral: *Haggis Management, Inc. v. Turtle Management, Inc.*" *1986 Utah Law Review.*

SECURITIES
Dalton, John M., ed. 1993. *How the Stock Market Works.* 2d ed. New York: New York Institute of Finance.

United States Government Manual, 1996–1997. Washington, D.C.: U.S. Government Printing Office.

SECURITIES AND EXCHANGE COMMISSION
Dalton, John M., ed. 1993. *How the Stock Market Works.* 2d ed. New York: New York Institute of Finance.

United States Government Manual, 1996–1997. Washington, D.C.: U.S. Government Printing Office.

SEDITION
Curtis, Michael Kent. 1995. "Critics of 'Free Speech' and the Uses of the Past." *Constitutional Commentary* 12 (spring).

———. 1995. "The Curious History of Attempts to Suppress Antislavery Speech, Press, and Petition in 1835–37." *Northwestern University Law Review* 89 (spring).

Gibson, Michael T. 1986. "The Supreme Court and Freedom of Expression from 1791 to 1917." *Fordham Law Review* 55 (December).

Grinstein, Joseph. 1996. "Jihad and the Constitution: The First Amendment Implications of Combating Religiously Motivated Terrorism." *Yale Law Journal* 105 (March).

Weintraub, Leonard. 1987. "Crime of the Century: Use of the Mail Fraud Statute against Authors." *Boston University Law Review* 67 (May).

SELDEN, JOHN

Berman, Harold J. 1994. "The Origins of Historical Jurisprudence: Coke, Selden, Hale." *Yale Law Journal* 103 (May).

SELECTIVE SERVICE SYSTEM

United States Government Manual, 1995–1996. Washington, D.C.: U.S. Government Printing Office.

SELF-DEALING

Volkmer, Ronald R. 1992. "Breach of Fiduciary Duty for Self-Dealing." *Estate Planning* 19 (September–October).

SELF-DEFENSE

Ayyildiz, Elisabeth. 1995. "When Battered Woman's Syndrome Does Not Go Far Enough: The Battered Woman as Vigilante." *American University Journal of Gender and the Law* 4 (fall).

"Criminal Law." 1994. *SMH Bar Review.*

Gladwell, Malcolm. 1996. "Goetz Loses 43M Jury Verdict; Subway Vigilante's Victim Victorious in Bronx Trial." *Washington Post* (April 24).

Klansky, Nadine. 1988. "Bernhard Goetz, a 'Reasonable Man': A Look at New York's Justification Defense." *Brooklyn Law Review* 53 (winter).

Lee, Cynthia Kwei Yung. 1996. "Race and Self-Defense: Toward a Normative Conception of Reasonableness." *Minnesota Law Review* (December).

"Torts." 1994 *SMH Bar Review.*

SELF-HELP

Gerchick, Randy G. 1994. "No Easy Way Out: Making the Summary Eviction Process a Fairer and More Efficient Alternative to Landlord Self-Help." *UCLA Law Review* 41 (February).

Gitter, Henry. 1993. "Self-Help Remedies for Software Vendors." *Santa Clara Computer and High Technology Law Journal* 9 (November).

SELF-INCRIMINATION

LaFave, Wayne, & Jerold Israel. 1985. *Criminal Procedure: The Hornbook Series.* St. Paul: West.

SENATE

Bach, Stanley. 1996. "The Daily Order of Business." In *The Legislative Process on the Senate Floor: An Introduction.* Report 91-520 RCO. Washington, D.C.: Congressional Research Service, Library of Congress.

Hardeman, D. B. 1976. "Congress, United States." In *Dictionary of American History.* Vol. 2. Edited by Louise B. Ketz. New York: Schribner.

United States Government Manual, 1994–1995. Washington, D.C.: U.S. Government Printing Office.

SENIOR CITIZENS

American Association of Retired Persons site. 1997. World Wide Web (March 20).

Hang Up on Fraud. 1995. Office of Minnesota Attorney General Hubert H. Humphrey III.

SENTENCING

The Editors. 1995. "Forum: Parole and Sentencing Reform in Virginia." *Virginia Journal of Social Policy and the Law* 2.

Flaherty, Mary Pat, and Joan Biskupic. 1996. "Justice by the Numbers." Washington Post site. World Wide Web (October 6–10).

Kim, Stephanie J. 1995. "Sentencing and Cultural Differences: Banishment of the American Indian Robbers." *John Marshall Law Review* 29.

Oliss, Philip. 1995. "Mandatory Minimum Sentencing: Discretion, the Safety Valve, and the Sentencing Guidelines." *University of Cincinnati Law Review* 63.

Parson, Elizabeth A. 1994. "Shifting the Balance of Power: Prosecutorial Discretion under the Federal Sentencing Guidelines." *Valparaiso University Law Review* 29.

Wytsma, Laura A. 1995. "Punishment for 'Just Us'—A Constitutional Analysis of the Crack Cocaine Sentencing Statutes." *George Mason Law Review* 3.

SEQUESTRATION

Richtel, Murray. 1996. "The Simpson Trial: A Timid Judge and a Lawless Verdict." *University of Colorado Law Review* 67 (fall).

SERJEANT AT LAW

Zwart, David. 1990. "*Mallard v. United States District Court*: Relying on a Definition but Failing to Define the Rights of Court-Appointed Attorneys." *Nebraska Law Review* 69.

SERVICE MARK

Restatement (Third) of Unfair Competition, Section 9. 1995. New York: American Law Institute.

Sidoti, Christopher A. 1990. "Service Mark Protection." *New Jersey Lawyer* 28. (June).

SERVITUDE

Hirsch, Eric D., Jr., Joseph F. Kett, and James S. Trefil. 1988. *The Dictionary of Cultural Literacy.* Boston: Houghton Mifflin.

SETBACK

Practising Law Institute (PLI). 1993. *Highlights of Residential and Commercial Real Estate,* by Oscar H. Beasley. Real Estate Law and Practice Course Handbook series. Title Insurance 1993: Obtaining the Coverage You Want. PLI order no. N4-4581.

SETTLEMENT

Practising Law Institute (PLI). 1995. *Damages and Settlements in Sex Harassment Cases,* by Richard G. Moon. Litigation and Administrative Practice Course Handbook series: Litigation, PLI order no. H4-5213.

———. 1996. *Class Action Settlements,* by Roberta D. Liebenberg, Ralph G. Wellington, and Sherrie R. Savett. Corporate Law and Practice Course Handbook series: Financial Services Litigation, PLI order no. B4-7153.

———. 1996. *Settlement,* by Norma Polizzi. Litigation and Administrative Practice Course Handbook series: Litigation, PLI order no. H4-5247.

SETTLEMENT STATEMENT
Bernstein, Leonard A. 1994. "RESPA Storm Clouds." *Probate and Property* 8 (November–December).

SEVENTEENTH AMENDMENT
Bybee, Jay S. 1997. "Ulysses at the Mast: Democracy, Federalism, and the Sirens' Song of the Seventeenth Amendment." *Northwestern University Law Review* 91 (winter).
Zywicki, Todd J. 1994. "Senators and Special Interests: A Public Choice Analysis of the Seventeenth Amendment." *Oregon Law Review* 73 (winter).

SEVENTH AMENDMENT
Corwin, Edwin S. 1978. *The Constitution and What It Means Today.* Princeton, N.J.: Princeton Univ. Press.
Friedenthal, Jack H., Mary Kay Kane, and Arthur R. Miller. 1985. *Civil Procedure: Hornbook Series.* St. Paul: West.

SEVERANCE
Hein, Kevin P. 1993. "Joinder and Severance." *American Criminal Law Review* 30 (spring).

SEX DISCRIMINATION
Graham, Hugh Davis. 1990. *The Civil Rights Era.* New York: Oxford Univ. Press.
Hall, Kermit L. 1989. *The Magic Mirror: Law in American History.* New York: Oxford Univ. Press.
Stephens, Otis H., Jr., and John M. Scheb II. 1993. *American Constitutional Law.* St. Paul: West.

SEX OFFENSES
Morosco, B. Anthony. 1996. *The Prosecution and Defense of Sex Crimes.* New York: Bender.

SEXUAL ABUSE
Lazo, Joy. 1995. "True or False: Expert Testimony on Repressed Memory." *Loyola of Los Angeles Law Review* 28.
Mason, Mary Ann. 1995. "The Child Sex Abuse Syndrome." *Psychology, Public Policy, and Law* 1.

SEXUAL HARASSMENT
Christian Science Monitor site. 1997. World Wide Web (March 16).

SHEPPARD, SAMUEL H.
Flynn, Joseph F. 1993. "Prejudicial Publicity in Criminal Trials: Bringing *Sheppard v. Maxwell* into the Nineties." *New England Law Review* 27 (spring).

SHERMAN ANTI-TRUST ACT
Mann, Richard A., and Barry S. Roberts. 1995. *Essentials of Business Law.* 5th ed. St. Paul: West.

SHERIFF
Gullion, Steve. 1992. "Sheriffs in Search of a Role." *New Law Journal* 142 (August 14).

SHERMAN, JOHN
Hall, Kermit L. 1989. *The Magic Mirror: Law in American History.* New York: Oxford Univ. Press.
Stephens, Otis H., Jr., and John M. Scheb II. 1993. *American Constitutional Law.* St. Paul: West.

SHERMAN, ROGER
Stephens, Otis H., Jr., and John M. Scheb II. 1993. *American Constitutional Law.* St. Paul: West.

SHIELD LAWS
Mann, Richard A., and Barry S. Roberts. 1995. *Essentials of Business Law.* 5th ed. St. Paul: West.
Morosco, B. Anthony. 1996. *The Prosecution and Defense of Sex Crimes.* New York: Bender.
Torcia, Charles E. 1985. *Wharton's Criminal Evidence.* 14th ed. Vol. 1. New York: Lawyers Cooperative.
Wright, Charles Alan, and Kenneth W. Graham, Jr. 1980. *Federal Practice and Procedure.* Vol. 23. St. Paul: West.

SHIPPING LAW
Stephens, Otis H., Jr., and John M. Scheb II. 1993. *American Constitutional Law.* St. Paul: West.

SHIRAS, GEORGE, JR.
Friedman, Leon, and Fred L. Israel, eds. 1969. *The Justices of the United States Supreme Court, 1789–1969: Their Lives and Major Opinions.* New York: Chelsea House.

SHOCK THE CONSCIENCE TEST
Stephens, Otis H., Jr., and John M. Scheb II. 1993. *American Constitutional Law.* St. Paul: West.

SHOPLIFTING
Sennewald, Charles A., and John H. Christman. 1992. *Shoplifting.* Boston: Butterworth-Heinemann.

SHOW CAUSE ORDER
Mellinkoff, David. 1992. *Mellinkoff's Dictionary of American Legal Usage.* St. Paul: West.

SIGNATURE
Tinnes, Christy. 1997. "Digital Signatures Come to South Carolina: The Proposed Digital Signature Act of 1997." *South Carolina Law Review* 48.
Wims, Michael D. 1995. "Law and the Electronic Highway: Are Computer Signatures Legal?" *Criminal Justice* 10.

SIMPSON, O. J.
O. J. Simpson archive. 1997. CNN site. World Wide Web (April 17).
O. J. Simpson archive. 1997. *Los Angeles Times* site. World Wide Web (April 13).

SIXTEENTH AMENDMENT
Stephens, Otis H., Jr., and John M. Scheb II. 1993. *American Constitutional Law.* St. Paul: West.

SIXTH AMENDMENT
LaFave, Wayne R., and Jerold H. Israel. 1985. *Criminal Procedure.* Student ed. St. Paul: West.

SLAUGHTERHOUSE CASES
Stephens, Otis H., Jr., and John M. Scheb II. 1993. *American Constitutional Law.* St. Paul: West.

SLAVERY
Davis, David Brion. *Slavery and Human Progress.* David Brion Davis.

Farrand, Max. *The Framing of the Constitution of the United States*. New Haven, Conn.: Yale Univ. Press.

Franklin, John Hope, and Alfred A. Moss, Jr. *From Slavery To Freedom*. Blue Ridge Summit, Pa.: McGraw-Hill.

Hornsby, Alton, Jr. *Chronology of African-American History*. Detroit: Gale Research.

Phillips, William D., Jr. *Slavery from Roman Times to the Early Transatlantic Trade*. Minneapolis: Univ. Minnesota Press.

Sawyer, Roger. *Slavery in the Twentieth Century*. London: Routledge & Kegan Paul.

SMALL BUSINESS ADMINISTRATION

United States Government Manual, 1996–1997. Washington, D.C.: U.S. Government Printing Office.

SMALL CLAIMS COURT

"Small Claims Court." 1997. Court TV site. World Wide Web (March 21).

SMITH, ROBERT

Wilson, James Grant, and John Fiske, eds. *Appletons' Cyclopaedia of American Biography*. 1888–89. Vol. V. New York: D. Appleton. Reprint, Detroit: Gale Research, 1968.

SMITH, WILLIAM FRENCH

Justice Department. 1985. *Attorneys General of the United States, 1789–1985*. Washington, D.C. U.S. Government Printing Office.

SOCIALISM

Bernstein, Carl. 1989. *Loyalties: A Son's Memoir*. New York: Simon & Schuster.

Bornet, Vaughn D. 1983. *The Presidency of Lyndon B. Johnson*. Lawrence, Kan.: Univ. Press of Kansas.

Burns, James M. 1985. *The Workshop of Democracy*. New York: Random House.

Ely, Richard T. 1904. *The Labor Movement in America*. New York: Thomas Y. Crowell.

Fried, Albert, and Ronals Sanders, eds. 1992. *Socialist Thought*. New York: Columbia Univ. Press.

Haynes, Fred E. 1924. *Social Politics in the United States*. Boston: Houghton Mifflin.

Jezer, Marty. 1992. *Abbie Hoffman: American Rebel*. New Jersey: Rutgers Univ. Press.

Knappman, Edward W., ed. 1994. *Great American Trials*. New England Publishing Associates.

Kull, Andrew. 1992. *The Color-Blind Constitution*. Cambridge, Mass.: Harvard Univ. Press.

Nash, Gary B., and Julie R. Jeffrey, eds. 1986. *The American People*. New York: Harper & Row.

Schlesinger, Arthur M. 1934. *Political and Social Growth of the United States: 1852–1933*. New York: Macmillan.

Schwartz, Bernard. 1983. *Inside the Warren Court*. New York: Doubleday.

Weinstein, Allen, and R. Jackson Wilson. 1974. *Freedom and Crisis*. New York: Doubleday.

SOCIAL SECURITY

"A Brief History of Social Security." 1997. Social Security Administration site. World Wide Web (July 15).

"Medicare Reform" white paper. 1997. Twentieth Century Fund site. World Wide Web (January 5).

"Social Security—A Brief History." 1997. Social Security Administration site. World Wide Web (June 15).

SODOMY

Stephens, Otis H., Jr., and John M. Scheb II. 1993. *American Constitutional Law*. St. Paul: West.

Hall, Kermit L. 1989. *The Magic Mirror: Law in American History*. New York: Oxford Univ. Press.

SOFTWARE

Brochu, Jason. 1997. "Software Piracy." Marist College site. World Wide Web (January 22).

Rich, Lloyd L. 1997. "Shrink Wrap Licenses." Legal Information Association site. World Wide Web (January 22).

Zarrabian, Michael. 1997. "Copyright Protection for User Interfaces." Sheldon and Mak site, Pasadena, Cal. World Wide Web (January 22).

SOLDIERS' AND SAILORS' CIVIL RELIEF ACT

Day, Mary Kathleen. 1991. "Material Effect: Shifting the Burden of Proof for Greater Procedural Relief under the Soldiers' and Sailors' Civil Relief Act." *Tulsa Law Journal* 27 (fall).

SOLE PROPRIETORSHIP

Esenau, Warren H., et al., eds. 1994. *Guide to Income Tax, 1995 Edition*. Yonkers, New York: Consumer Reports Books.

Ritt, Roger M., and Michael J. Nathanson. 1995. *Choice of Business Entity*. Chicago: American Law Institute-American Bar Association Continuing Legal Education.

"Sole Proprietorship Fact Sheet." 1997. Northwestern Mutual Life Insurance Company site. World Wide Web (January 18). 1997.

SOLICITOR GENERAL

United States Government Manual, 1996–1997. Washington, D.C.: U.S. Government Printing Office.

SOLID WASTES, HAZARDOUS SUBSTANCES, AND TOXIC POLLUTANTS

Levine, Adelin Gordon. 1984. "*1984 Survey of Books Relating to the Law— Love Canal: Science, Politics, and People*." *Michigan Law Review* 82.

Lingo, Robert S. 1989. "Something New From Something Old: Federal Procurement of Recycled Products. *Air Force Law Review* 31.

Rogers, William H. Jr. 1977. *Environmental Law Hornbook*. St. Paul: West.

———. 1986. *Environmental Law: Air and Water Pollution*. St. Paul: West.

SON OF SAM LAWS

"Notoriety-for-profit/Son of Sam Legislation." 1997. National Victim Center site. World Wide Web (March 21).

SONOSKY, MARVIN J.

Review of *Black Hills White Justice: The Sioux Nation vs. the United States. 1775 to the Present*, by Edward Lazan. 1992. *Yale Law Journal* 101.

Zlock, Tracy N. 1996. "The Native American Tribe as a Client: An Ethical Analysis." *Georgetown Journal of Legal Ethics* 10 (fall).

SONY CORP. OF AMERICA V. UNIVERSAL CITY STUDIOS

Band, Jonathan, and Andrew J. McLaughlin. 1993. "The Marshall Papers: A Peek behind the Scenes at the Making of *Sony v. Universal*." *Columbia-VLA Journal of Law & the Arts* 17 (summer).

Burks, Margaret A. 1985. "*Sony Corporation of America v. Universal City Studios, Inc.*, 104 S. Ct. 774 (1984): Is Copyright Law in Need of Congressional Action?" *Northern Kentucky Law Review* 12.

SOUTER, DAVID HACKETT

Simon, James. 1995. *The Center Holds: The Power Struggle inside the Rehnquist Court*. New York: Simon & Schuster.

SOUTHEAST ASIA TREATY ORGANIZATION

Grenville, J. A. S., and Bernard Wasserstein. 1987. *The Major International Treaties since 1945*. London and New York: Methuen.

Kohn, George C. 1991. *Dictionary of Historical Documents*. New York and Oxford: Facts on File.

State Department. 1995. *Treaties in Force*. Publication 9433.

SOUTHERN CHRISTIAN LEADERSHIP CONFERENCE

Blumberg, Rhoda Lois. 1991. *Civil Rights: The 1960s Freedom Struggle*. Rev. ed. Boston: Twayne.

Fairclough, Adam. 1989. "The Southern Christian Leadership Conference and the Second Reconstruction, 1957–1973." In *We Shall Overcome*. Edited by David J. Garrow. Brooklyn: Carlson.

Ford, Linda G. 1992. "Southern Christian Leadership Conference." In *Encyclopedia of African-American Civil Rights*. Edited by Charles D. Lowery. San Diego: Greenwood Press.

Garrow, David J. 1986. *Bearing the Cross: Martin Luther King, Jr. and the Southern Christian Leadership Conference*. New York: Morrow.

"Southern Christian Leadership Conference." 1996. *Encyclopedia of Associations*. 31st ed. Edited by S. Jaszczak. Detroit: Gale Research.

SPECIAL COURTS

Wheeler, Russell R. 1987. "Courts of Limited and Specialized Jurisdiction." In *Encyclopedia of the American Judicial System*. Vol. 2. Edited by Robert J. Janosik. New York: Scribner's. •

SPECIALIZATION

American Bar Association Standing Committee on Specialization. 1983. *Handbook on Specialization*. Chicago: American Bar Association.

Rosen, Nathan Aaron. 1990. *Lawyer Specialization*. Chicago: American Bar Association.

SPECIFIC INTENT

Hanley, Julian R., and Wayne W. Schmidt. 1977. *Legal Aspects of Criminal Evidence*. Berkeley, Cal.: McCutchan.

Rob, Edith M. 1994. "A Question of 'Intent'—Intent and Motive Distinguished." *Army Lawyer*. Department of the Army pamphlet 27-50-261, August.

Torcia, Charles E. 1994. *Wharton's Criminal Law*. 15th ed. Vol. 2. New York: Clark Boardman Callaghan.

SPEECH OR DEBATE CLAUSE

Brodie, Katherine Deming. 1996. "The Scope of Legislative Immunity under the Speech or Debate Clause and the Rulemaking Clause." *George Washington Law Review* 64 (June–August).

SPEED, JAMES

Wilson, James Grant, and John Fiske, eds. 1888–89. *Appleton's Cyclopaedia of American Biography*. New York: D. Appleton.

Jacobs, Charles T. 1994. "Federal Officials Took Harsh Stance . . . ." *Washington Times* (Apr. 9).

SPEEDY TRIAL

Feldman, Steven D. 1996. "Twenty-fifth Annual Review of Criminal Procedure: Speedy Trial." *Georgetown Law Journal* 84.

Lafave, Wayne R., and Jerold H. Israel. 1985. *Criminal Procedure: The Hornbook Series*. St. Paul: West.

SPENDING POWER

Domenici, Pete V. 1994. "The Unamerican Spirit of the Federal Income Tax." *Harvard Journal on Legislation* 31.

Klein, William J. 1995. "Pressure or Compulsion? Federal Highway Fund Sanctions of the Clean Air Act Amendments of 1990." *Rutgers Law Journal* 26.

Rosentahl, Albert J. 1987. "Conditional Federal Spending and the Constitution." *Stanford Law Review* 39.

Segatol-Islami, Jahan. 1994. "Mr. Jefferson Must Be Smiling: How State Challenges to Immigration Policy May Prompt Re-Evaluation of Federalism as a Core Concept of Our Republic." *University of Miami Inter-American Law Review* 26.

SPLIT DECISION

Dickson, Del. 1994. "State Court Defiance and the Limits of Supreme Court Authority: *Williams v. Georgia* Revisited." *Yale Law Journal* 103 (April).

Wald, Patricia M. 1995. "The Rhetoric of Results and the Results of Rhetoric: Judicial Writings." *University of Chicago Law Review* 62 (fall).

SPORKIN, STANLEY

Garza, Deborah A. 1995. "The Court of Appeals Sets Strict Limits on Tunney Act Review: The Microsoft Consent Decree." *Antitrust* 10 (fall).

"SEC's Top Cops Go on Record." 1994. *National Law Journal* 16 (July 18).

"Where Lawyers?" 1991. *National Law Journal* 13 (April 8).

SPORTS LAW

Brake, Deborah, and Elizabeth Catlin. 1996. "The Path of Most Resistance: The Long Road toward Gender Equity in Intercollegiate Athletics." *Duke Journal of Gender Law and Policy* 3 (spring).

Cameron, Christopher D., and J. Michael Echevarria. 1995 "The Ploys of Summer: Antitrust, Industrial Distrust, and the Case against a Salary Cap for Major League Baseball." *Florida State University Law Review* 22 (spring).

Chalpin, Marc. 1996. "It Ain't Over 'til It's Over: The Century Long Conflict between the Owners and the Players in Major League Baseball." *Albany Law Review* 60.

Irwin, Richard L. 1991. "A Historical Review of Litigation in Baseball." *Marquette Sports Law Journal* 1 (spring).

Keller-Smith, Sara Lee, and Sherri A. Affrunti. 1996. "Going for the Gold: The Representation of Olympic Athletes." *Villanova Sports and Entertainment Law Journal* 3.

Mason, Daniel S., and Trevor Slack. 1997. "Appropriate Opportunism or Bad Business Practice? Stakeholder Theory, Ethics, and the Franchise Relocation Issue." *Marquette Sports Law Journal* 7 (spring).

Mitten, Matthew J., and Bruce W. Burton. 1987. "Professional Sports Franchise Relocations from Private Law and Public Law Perspectives: Balancing Marketplace Competition, League Autonomy, and the Need for a Level Playing Field." *Maryland Law Review* 56.

Piraino, Thomas A., Jr. 1996. "The Antitrust Rationale for the Expansion of Professional Sports Leagues." *Ohio State Law Journal* 57.

Willis, Stephen L. 1991. "A Critical Perspective of Baseball's Collusion Decisions." *Seton Hall Journal of Sport Law* 1.

Yankwitt, Russell M. 1996. "Buy Me Some Peanuts and Ownership: Major League Baseball and the Need for Employee Ownership." *Cornell Journal of Law and Public Policy* 5 (spring).

STALIN, JOSEPH

Hall, Kermit L. 1989. *The Magic Mirror: Law in American History.* New York: Oxford Univ. Press.

Stephens, Otis H., Jr., and John M. Scheb II. 1993. *American Constitutional Law.* St. Paul: West.

STALKING

U.S. Department of Justice, Office of Justice Programs, National Institute of Justice. 1996. *Domestic Violence, Stalking, and Antistalking Legislation. Annual Report to Congress, March 1996.* Department of Justice site. World Wide Web (March 28).

STANBERY, HENRY

Wilson, James Grant, and John Fiske, eds. 1988–89. *Appleton's Cyclopaedia of American Biography.* New York: D. Appleton.

Kaczorowski, Robert J. 1990. "The Common-Law Background of Nineteenth-Century Tort Law." *Ohio State Law Journal* 51.

Lawlor, John M. 1986. "Court Packing Revisited: A Proposal for Rationalizing the Timing of Appointments to the Supreme Court." *University of Pennsylvania Law Review* 134.

STANDING

Stephens, Otis H., Jr., and John M. Scheb II. 1993. *American Constitutional Law.* St. Paul: West.

STANTON, EDWARD MCMASTERS

Justice Department. 1985. *Attorneys General of the United States, 1789–1985.* Washington, D. C.: U. S. Government Printing Office.

STANTON, ELIZABETH CADY

Griffith, Elisabeth. 1984. *In Her Own Right: The Life of Elizabeth Cady Stanton.* New York: Oxford Univ. Press.

Stanton, Elizabeth Cady. 1898. *Eighty Years and More.* Boston: Northeastern Univ. Press.

STARE DECISIS

Stephens, Otis H., Jr., and John M. Scheb II. 1993. *American Constitutional Law.* St. Paul: West.

START TREATIES

Kegley, Charles W., Jr., and Eugene R. Wittkopf. 1993. *World Politics.* 4th ed. New York: St. Martin's Press.

Sohn, Louis B. 1994. "Start II Treaty." *The International Lawyer* 28 (summer).

"START II Chronology." 1996. U.S. Arms Control and Disarmament Agency site. World Wide Web.

STATE ACTION

Stephens, Otis H., Jr., and John M. Scheb II. 1993. *American Constitutional Law.* St. Paul: West.

STATE COURTS

Hall, Kermit L. 1989. *The Magic Mirror: Law in American History.* New York: Oxford Univ. Press.

Stephens, Otis H., Jr., and John M. Scheb II. 1993. *American Constitutional Law.* St. Paul: West.

STATE DEPARTMENT

State Department. 1996. *Country Reports on Human Rights Practices.* U.S. Department of State site. World Wide Web (August).

United States Government Manual, 1996–1997. Washington, D. C.: U. S. Government Printing Office.

STATE INTEREST

Stephens, Otis H., Jr., and John M. Scheb II. 1993. *American Constitutional Law.* St. Paul: West.

STATE LOTTERY

Crigler, John, John Wells King, and Amelia L. Brown. 1994. "Why Sparky Can't Bark - A Study of the Ban on Broadcast Advertisement for Lotteries." *Comm Law Conspectus* 2.

Eberle, Todd. 1994. "Education; California State Lottery—Revenue Allocations." *Pacific Law Journal* 26 (January).

Griffin, Linda S., and Richard V. Harrison. 1996. "Florida State Lottery Tax and Estate Planning Issues." *Florida Bar Journal* 70 (January).

Rychlack, Ronald J. 1992. "Lotteries, Revenues and Social Costs: A Historical Examination of State-Sponsored Gambling." *Boston College Law Review* 34.

Wyett, Todd A. 1991. "State Lotteries: Regressive Taxes in Disguise." *Tax Lawyer* 44 (Spring).

STATES' RIGHTS

Stephens, Otis H., Jr., and John M. Scheb II. 1993. *American Constitutional Law.* St. Paul: West.

STATUTE OF LIMITATIONS

Lazo, Joy. 1995. "True or False: Expert Testimony on Repressed Memory." *Loyola of Los Angeles Law Review* 28.

STATUTE OF USES

Baade, Hans W. 1994. "The Casus Omissus: A Pre-History of Statutory Analogy." *Syracuse Journal of International Law and Commerce* 20 (spring).

Haar, Charles M., and Lance Liebman. 1985. *Property and Law*. 2d ed. Boston and Toronto: Little, Brown.

Holmes, William J. 1995. "The Evolution of the Trust: A Creative Solution to Trustee Liability under CER-CLA." *Villanova Environmental Law Journal* 6.

Kurtz, Sheldon F., and Herbert Hovenkamp. 1987. *Cases and Materials on American Property Law*. St. Paul: West.

Reid, Charles J. 1995. "The Seventeenth-century Revolution in the English Land Law." *Cleveland State Law Review* 43.

STATUE OF WILLS

Kurtz, Sheldon F., and Herbert Hovenkamp. 1987. *Cases and Materials on American Property Law*. St. Paul: West.

STATUTORY REDEMPTION

Palace, Eric S. 1996. "In Re BFP: Just a Band-Aid?—Looking for a Stable Solution That Balances Creditors' and Debtors' Rights under Bankruptcy Code Section 548(A) (2)." *Annual Review of Banking Law* 15.

STAY

Louisell, David W., Geoffrey C. Hazard, Jr., and Colin C. Tait. 1989. *Pleading and Procedure: State and Federal; Cases and Materials*. 6th ed. Westbury, N.Y.: Foundation Press.

STEVENS, JOHN PAUL

Barnes, Catherine A. 1978. *Men of the Supreme Court: Profiles of the Justices*. New York: Facts on File.

Friedman, Leon, ed. 1978. *The Justices of the United States Supreme Court*. New York and London: Chelsea House.

Jost, Kenneth. 1996. *The Supreme Court Yearbook 1991–92*. Washington, D.C.: Congressional Quarterly.

———. 1996. *The Supreme Court Yearbook 1993–94*. Washington, D.C.: Congressional Quarterly.

———. 1996. *The Supreme Court Yearbook 1995–96*. Washington, D.C.: Congressional Quarterly.

The National Cyclopedia of American Biography. 1984. Clifton, N.J.: White.

Witt, Elder. 1996. *The Supreme Court A to Z*. Washington, D.C.: Congressional Quarterly.

STEWART, POTTER

Schwartz, Bernard. 1993. *A History of the Supreme Court*. New York: Oxford Univ. Press.

STONE, HARLAN FISKE

Stephens, Otis H., Jr., and John M. Scheb II. 1993. *American Constitutional Law*. St. Paul: West.

STONE, LUCY

Hall, Kermit L. 1989. *The Magic Mirror: Law in American History*. New York: Oxford Univ. Press.

STOP AND FRISK

Stephens, Otis H., Jr., and John M. Scheb II. 1993. *American Constitutional Law*. St. Paul: West.

STORY, JOSEPH

Stephens, Otis H., Jr., and John M. Scheb II. 1993. *American Constitutional Law*. St. Paul: West.

STRATEGIC LAWSUITS AGAINST PUBLIC PARTICIPATION

Hillberry, Rhonda. 1995. "Warning: Signing That Petition Could Get You Sued!" *Law and Politics* (July).

Pring, George W., and Penelope Canan. 1996. *SLAPPs: Getting Sued for Speaking Out*. Philadelphia: Temple Univ. Press.

STRICT SCRUTINY

Stephens, Otis H., Jr., and John M. Scheb II. 1993. *American Constitutional Law*. St. Paul: West.

STRIKE

Hall, Kermit L. 1989. *The Magic Mirror: Law in American History*. New York: Oxford Univ. Press.

STRONG, WILLIAM

Stephens, Otis H., Jr., and John M. Scheb II. 1993. *American Constitutional Law*. St. Paul: West.

STUDENT NONVIOLENT COORDINATING COMMITTEE

Harris, Janet. 1967. *The Long Freedom Road: The Civil Rights Story*. Blue Ridge Summit, Pa.: McGraw-Hill.

Johnson, Jacqueline. 1990. *Stokely Carmichael: The Story of Black Power*. Parsippany, N.J.: Silver Burdett Press.

Levy, Peter B. 1992. *Let Freedom Ring: A Documentary History of the Modern Civil Rights Movement*. New York: Praeger.

Student Nonviolent Coordinating Committee. *The Basis of Black Power*. Position paper. In The Sixties Project Primary Documents Collection. World Wide Web.

SUBJECT MATTER JURISDICTION

Stephens, Otis H., Jr., and John M. Scheb II. 1993. *American Constitutional Law*. St. Paul: West.

SUBORNATION OF PERJURY

Mellinkoff, David. 1992. *Mellinkoff's Dictionary of American Legal Usage*. St. Paul: West.

SUBPOENA

Mellinkoff, David. 1992. *Mellinkoff's Dictionary of American Legal Usage*. St. Paul: West.

Stephens, Otis H., Jr., and John M. Scheb II. 1993. *American Constitutional Law*. St. Paul: West.

SUBSTANCE ABUSE AND MENTAL HEALTH SERVICES

United States Government Manual, 1995–1996. Washington, D.C.: U.S. Government Printing Office.